Presidents of the United States

1789–1797	1. George Washington	
1797–1801	2. John Adams	Federa.
1801–1809	3. Thomas Jefferson	Democratic-Republican
1809–1817	4. James Madison	Democratic-Republican
1817–1825	5. James Monroe	Democratic-Republican
1825–1829	6. John Quincy Adams	Democratic-Republican
1829–1837	7. Andrew Jackson	Democratic
1837–1841	8. Martin Van Buren	Democratic
1841	9. William Henry Harrison	Whig
1841–1845	10. John Tyler	Whig
1845–1849	11. James K. Polk	Democratic
1849–1850	12. Zachary Taylor	Whig
1850–1853	13. Millard Fillmore	Whig
1853–1857	14. Franklin Pierce	Democratic
1857–1861	15. James Buchanan	Democratic
1861–1865	16. Abraham Lincoln	Republican/Union
1865–1869	17. Andrew Johnson	Union
1869–1877	18. Ulysses S. Grant	Republican
1877–1881	19. Rutherford B. Hayes	Republican
1881	20. James A. Garfield	Republican
1881–1885	21. Chester A. Arthur	Republican
1885–1889	22. Grover Cleveland	Democratic
1889–1893	23. Benjamin Harrison	Republican
1893–1897	24. Grover Cleveland	Democratic
1897–1901	25. William McKinley	Republican
1901–1909	26. Theodore Roosevelt	Republican
1909–1913	27. William Howard Taft	Republican
1913–1921	28. Woodrow Wilson	Democratic
1921–1923	29. Warren G. Harding	Republican
1923–1929	30. Calvin Coolidge	Republican
1929–1933	31. Herbert Hoover	Republican
1933–1945	32. Franklin Delano Roosevelt	Democratic
1945–1953	33. Harry S. Truman	Democratic
1953–1961	34. Dwight D. Eisenhower	Republican
1961–1963	35. John F. Kennedy	Democratic
1963–1969	36. Lyndon Johnson	Democratic
1969–1974	37. Richard M. Nixon	Republican
1974–1977	38. Gerald Ford	Republican
1977–1981	39. James E. Carter	Democratic
1981–1989	40. Ronald Reagan	Republican
1989–1993	41. George H. W. Bush	Republican
1993–2001	42. William J. Clinton	Democratic
2001–2009	43. George W. Bush	Republican
2009–	44. Barack Obama	Democratic

BVT Publishing

www.BVTPublishing.com

Publisher & Director of Business Development: Richard Schofield

Business Development Manager: Shannon Conley

Copy Editor: Anne Schofield

Designer & Typesetter: Tim Gerlach

Preproduction: Suzanne Schmidt

Proofreader: Tara Joffe

Front Cover Photo Credit: Shutterstock

Some ancillaries, including electronic and print components, may not be available to customers outside the United States.

Softcover ISBN: 978-1-62751-624-2
TEXTBOOK^Plus (Loose-Leaf Bundle) ISBN: 978-1-62751-627-3
Loose-Leaf ISBN: 978-1-62751-628-0
eBOOK^Plus ISBN: 978-1-62751-626-6

Introduction to

American Government

Eighth Edition

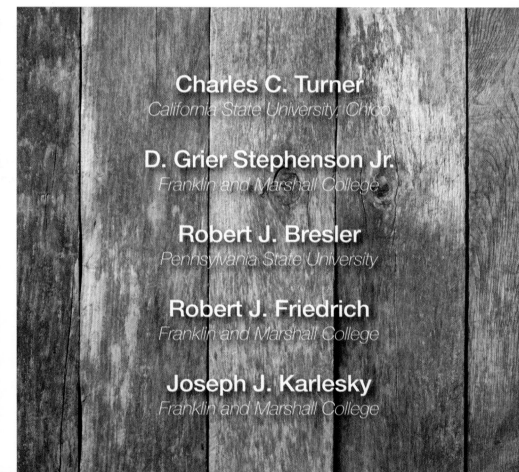

Charles C. Turner
California State University, Chico

D. Grier Stephenson Jr.
Franklin and Marshall College

Robert J. Bresler
Pennsylvania State University

Robert J. Friedrich
Franklin and Marshall College

Joseph J. Karlesky
Franklin and Marshall College

Brief Contents

Table of Contents

Chapter 02

Federalism: States in the Union   **42**

Chapter 03

Civil Liberties and Civil Rights   **72**

Chapter 04

Political Ideologies   **110**

Chapter 05

Public Opinion and Political Participation   **134**

Chapter 06

Politics and the Media   **166**

Chapter 07

Interest Groups and Political Parties   **200**

Chapter 08

Campaigns and Elections   **236**

Chapter 09

Congress   **272**

Chapter 10

The Presidency 302

Chapter 11

Bureaucracies   **338**

Chapter 12

The Supreme Court and American Judiciary — 370

Chapter 13

Government and Public Policy — 398

Chapter 14

Public Policy and Economics   **418**

Chapter 15

Domestic Policy   **446**

Chapter 16

Foreign Policy   476

Always vote for principle, though you may vote alone, and you may cherish the sweetest reflection that your vote is never lost.

John Quincy Adams

Preface

The need persists for widespread mastery of the political system John Quincy Adams once described as "the most complicated on the face of the globe." Adams was writing about two hundred years ago, and things certainly haven't gotten less complicated since then. In the early 2000s, we experienced a number of political complications, including three close and contentious presidential elections that geographically and ideologically divided our nation into "red" and "blue" states. We suffered a devastating terrorist attack on our own soil, plunging the nation into an open-ended and contentious "War on Terror." We went to war with Iraq for the second time in a dozen years. We saw the national economy reach great heights and disturbing lows, causing unemployment and recession in the private sector and a return of enormous deficit spending in the public sector. How do we make sense of all of these ups and downs of economics, ideology, and politics? We think the best approach is to take seriously our understanding of the political system in which all of these events take place. To that end, we offer today's students a comprehensive, readable, and balanced study of the context, structure, and process of American politics.

Economics, Ideology, and Politics

A distinguishing feature of this book is the explicit recognition that economics and ideology significantly influence American politics. No student or instructor in a course on American government is immune to the ideological and economic forces that help shape the perennial pursuit of power in a democracy. Nor is any class or instructor untouched by recurring problems ranging from budget deficits and health care to unemployment and the underclass. Economics and ideology, in one way or another, intersect nearly all of them.

This text highlights, in several ways, the importance of economics and ideology in the context of American government. The chapter on public policy and economics explores the relationship between politics and economics, as does a series of "Politics and Economics" boxes (described later) throughout the rest of the book. Students see how economic decisions have political consequences and how political decisions affect the economy. This is essential information in a day when economic topics frequently dominate electoral campaigns, television news, and conversation at the dinner table. However, the text assumes no prior knowledge of economics, and references to economic policy are free of confusing jargon.

Understanding differences among political beliefs is likewise essential at a time when the labels "liberal" and "conservative," "left" and "right" are hurled about. Such terms can be baffling, particularly because their meanings have not been consistent. Consequently, the text underscores the importance of political ideology—the ideas people have about what government should or should not do and what kind of government they should have. This emphasis is reflected in a series of "Politics and Ideas" boxes (described below) that appear throughout the text. The chapter on political ideologies is nearly unique among shorter volumes on American government because it draws a road map that guides students through intellectual debates, past and present, in American politics. Additionally, the chapter that deals with civil liberties and civil rights probes ideological distinctions among Americans concerning fundamental freedoms. Such an encompassing survey of the spectrum of political ideas encourages students both to comprehend and to tolerate points of view other than their own, enabling them to gain further insight into political differences that exist nationwide.

New to the Eighth Edition

American politics is a constantly changing montage of people and events, of facts and opinions. In order to keep up with our changing environment, and to make sure students have the most up-to-date information available, each new edition of *Introduction to American Government* undergoes a vigorous process of fact-checking and updating. In this edition, for example, readers will find revised weblinks and readings for further study; more critical thinking questions; and discussions of the latest events in American government—such as the 2014 elections, immigration reform, conflict with ISIS, racial tensions, and important Supreme Court decisions on same-sex marriage and on the First Amendment. In addition, each chapter contains important new material.

Pedagogical Features

This textbook is not a "theme" or point-of-view book. Aside from emphasizing the importance of politics and political involvement, the book embraces no single ideological perspective; it does not attempt to make readers Democrats or Republicans, liberals or conservatives. To ensure a single voice in this presentation, one author has served as general editor.

The goals are knowledge of, and critical thinking about, American politics and government. Accordingly, we have designed the book to encourage students to engage the material. Passive reading is not enough. Understanding so important and complex a subject necessitates active intellectual involvement.

To aid in learning, this textbook incorporates several serviceable pedagogical features.

Chapter Objectives

Each chapter begins with a brief overview of topics to be covered or a relevant story. Reading the information provided in the chapter objectives cues your critical thinking and analytical thought processes before you dig into the chapter itself.

e-Resources

Beyond the pages of this textbook lies a wealth of information about the American government concepts described here. Each chapter identifies online resources specific to the subject matter being presented. These resources offer you an opportunity to further explore topics from the text for an even more comprehensive experience.

Figures and Tables

Tables, graphs, and maps appear throughout the text to display both quantitative and conceptual data. Some illustrations present new data, while others summarize information covered in the body of the chapter.

Special Boxed Features

"Politics and Ideas"

These boxes appearing throughout the text explore ideological topics in depth. They demonstrate how ideological divisions generate different political consequences. The text includes the following Politics and Ideas boxes:

- Whose Constitution Is It?
- Race and (In)Justice: Ferguson, Missouri
- Millennials and Political Ideology
- Textbooks and Children's Ideas About American Politics
- Media Monopolies?
- Pluralism and Elitism
- Midterm Elections: Reflection and Change
- Two Ideologues Leave the House
- A "New Kind of War"—The Ongoing War on Terrorism

- A Six-Year Term for Presidents?
- Immigration Reform: Laws and Executive Orders
- The Road to a New Cabinet Department
- Political Ideologies and the Welfare State
- Contrasting Approaches to Foreign Policy: Idealism, Realism, and Isolationism

"Politics and Economics"

These boxes appearing throughout the text highlight special economics topics, illustrating the relationship between economics and politics. The text includes the following Politics and Economics boxes:

- Handling a Hurricane: Federalism and Disaster Relief
- Economic Status and Ideology
- Economic Status and Party Identification
- The President and Economic Policy Making
- Regulation and Cost-Benefit Analysis
- The Supreme Court and Economic Policy
- The Ideology of Economic Policy

"Contemporary Controversies"

These boxes are present in several chapters to illustrate how the subject matter covered in the chapter carries over into disputes that divide the nation. The text includes the following Contemporary Controversies boxes:

- America Attacked
- Changing State Constitutions
- How Much Affirmative Action?
- Public Opinion and Terrorism: American Government in the Eyes of the World
- Confidentiality of News Sources and Information
- Can Political News Be Both Entertaining and Informative?
- Turnout, Choice, and Economic Status
- Campaign and Electoral Reform: Comparative Perspective
- An Election Gone Wrong?
- Low Voter Turnout: A Comparative Perspective
- Congress Shows Several Members the Door
- Election 2008: A Presidential Election Breaks New Ground
- The Supreme Court and "Obamacare"
- Corporations and the Economy
- Nuclear Power and the Environment
- The U.S. vs. ISIS: A New Direction in the War on Terror?
- Can Presidents Take the Country to War on Their Own Authority?

Study Questions

Study questions conclude each of the special boxed features to encourage critical thinking and further inquiry.

End-of-Chapter Material

Each chapter concludes with a chapter review, a list of key terms, readings for further study, and a pop quiz.

- The chapter review contains, in numbered form, the main points presented in the chapter.

- Key terms, in boldface, are defined in the margins at the point at which they are introduced in the chapter.

- Readings for further study are widely available primary and secondary sources that students may consult in pursuing topics in the chapter.

- The pop quiz offers an opportunity to do a quick check of your knowledge retention. Similar to questions you might find on a test, these quiz questions can help you see if you are on the right track or if there are elements of a chapter's content you need to review further.

Instructor Supplements

A complete teaching package is available for instructors who adopt this book. This package includes an **online lab**, **instructor's manual**, **test bank**, **course management software**, and **PowerPoint™ slides**.

BVT*Lab*	An online lab is available for this textbook at www.BVTLab.com, as described in the BVT*Lab* section below.
Homework Grading System	Whether or not a class is being taught in the lab, instructors can take advantage of the BVT*Lab* Homework Grading System for all class assignments.
Instructor's Manual	A comprehensive manual provides chapter overviews, key terms and definitions, learning objectives, lecture suggestions, discussion questions, and in-class activities.
Test Bank	An extensive test bank is available to instructors in both hard copy and electronic form. Each chapter has 70 to 100 multiple choice questions, as well as 5 to 10 essay questions. Each question is referenced to the appropriate section of the text to make test creation quick and easy.
Course Management Software	BVT's course management software, Respondus, allows for the creation of tests and quizzes that can be downloaded directly into a wide variety of course management environments such as Blackboard, Web CT, Desire2Learn, ANGEL, E-Learning, eCollege, Canvas, Moodle, and others.
PowerPoint Slides	A set of PowerPoint slides includes about 40 to 50 slides per chapter, including a chapter overview, learning objectives, slides covering all key topics, key figures and charts, as well as summary and conclusion slides.

Student Resources

Student resources are available for this textbook at www.BVTLab.com. These resources are geared toward students needing additional assistance, as well as those seeking complete mastery of the content. The following resources are available:

Practice Quiz Questions	Students can work through hundreds of practice questions online. Questions are multiple choice or true/false format and are graded instantly for immediate feedback.
Flashcards	For each chapter, we offer a set of flashcards that reinforces the key terms and concepts from the textbook.
Chapter Summaries	A convenient and concise chapter summary is available as a study aid for each chapter.
Study Guide	A thorough and practical student study guide includes chapter overviews, key terms, learning objectives, multiple choice and true/false practice questions, as well as discussion questions. The study guide is available in both printed and online (printable) form.
PowerPoint Slides	All instructor PowerPoints are available for convenient lecture preparation and for students to view online for a study recap.

BVTLab and Student Study Center

BVT*Lab* includes an online classroom with grade book and chat room, a homework grading system, extensive test banks for quizzes and exams, and a host of student study resources.

Course Setup	BVT*Lab* has an easy-to-use, intuitive interface that allows instructors to quickly set up their courses and grade books and to replicate them from section to section and semester to semester.
Grade Book	Using an assigned passcode, students register themselves into the grade book; all homework, quizzes, and tests are automatically graded and recorded.
Chat Room	Instructors can post discussion threads to a class forum and then monitor and moderate student replies.
Student Study Center	All student resources for this textbook are available in BVT*Lab's* Student Study Center.
eBook	A downloadable eBook is available for both large-screen and small-screen devices. It includes searching, annotating, and highlighting features. A web-based eBook is also available within the lab for easy reference during online classes, homework, and study sessions.

Customization

BVT's Custom Publishing Division can help you modify this book's content to satisfy your specific instructional needs. The following are examples of customization:

- Rearrangement of chapters to follow the order of your syllabus
- Deletion of chapters not covered in your course
- Addition of paragraphs sections or chapters you or your colleagues have written for this course
- Editing of the existing content, down to the word level
- Customization of the accompanying student resources and online lab
- Addition of handouts, lecture notes, syllabus, etc.
- Incorporation of student worksheets into the textbook

All of these customizations will be professionally typeset to produce a seamless textbook of the highest quality, with an updated table of contents and index to reflect the customized content.

About the Authors

Charles C. Turner

Charles C. Turner is a professor of political science at California State University, Chico. His PhD is from Claremont Graduate University. He has taught at Chico State since 2000 and served as department chair from 2008 to 2014. He currently serves as president of the Chico chapter of the California Faculty Association. Turner's published research focuses on the political behavior of Congress and the Supreme Court, as well as on the scholarship of teaching and learning.

D. Grier Stephenson Jr.

Donald Grier Stephenson, Jr., is a Charles A. Dana Professor of Government at Franklin & Marshall College. He is general editor of ABC-CLIO's *America's Freedoms Series*, author of *Campaigns and the Court: The U.S. Supreme Court in Presidential Elections*, and co-author of *American Constitutional Law*, 15th edition.

Robert J. Bresler

Robert J. Bresler received his AB degree from Earlham College and his PhD from Princeton University. He has taught at the University of Wisconsin–Green Bay, the University of Delaware, and Penn State University–Harrisburg, where he completed a thirty-two-year career. During his time at Penn State, Professor Bresler served for some years as the director of the School of Public Affairs. He has been a visiting professor at the U.S. Army War College and the Franklin & Marshall College, and a Senior Fulbright Fellow at the National University of Singapore. He was the recipient of the James A. Jordan Award for Teaching Excellence and the Outstanding Civilian Award from the Department of the Army.

Professor Bresler is the National Affairs Editor of *USA Today: The Magazine of the American Scene*, where he writes a regular column on American politics. His recent books include *Us vs. Them: American Political and Cultural Conflict from WWII to Watergate* and *Freedom of Association: Civil Rights and Liberties Under the Law*. His articles have appeared in *Political Science Quarterly, Politics and Society, Bulletin of Atomic Scientists, Commonweal, Inquiry, the Nation, Intellect,* and *Telos*.

Robert J. Friedrich

Robert Friedrich is an associate professor in the Department of Government at Franklin & Marshall College, where he teaches courses in American government, public opinion and mass political behavior, political ideology, and research methods. His research interests are in electoral politics and electoral institutions, particularly the relationship between seats and votes in legislative elections, and in political values and ideology. He has reviewed manuscripts for the *American Political Science Review,* the *American Journal of Political Science,* and the *Journal of Politics,* for which he also served on the editorial board. Dr. Friedrich received his bachelor's degree from the University of Colorado and his master's and doctor of philosophy degrees from the University of Michigan.

Joseph J. Karlesky

Joseph J. Karlesky is the Honorable and Mrs. John C. Kunkel Professor of Government. He received his Bachelor's degree from La Salle College and his PhD in public law and government from Columbia University.

He is co-author of *The State of Academic Science: The Universities in the Nation's Research Effort* and co-author of *American Government,* an American government textbook. He has also authored the monograph, "Thinking About Environmental Policy."

He has been a guest scholar at the Brookings Institution in Washington, D.C., and has served as a consultant for the Commonwealth of Pennsylvania on home rule for municipalities and on academic science policy for the state of Montana. He has served as associate dean for academic affairs at Franklin & Marshall and as co-director of the University of Pennsylvania Master of Governmental Administration Program in Harrisburg.

His teaching and research interests focus on public policy, particularly the inter-relationships between public policy and science and technology and the consequences of these interrelationships for policies in energy and health. He is currently doing research on decision-making models and dry cask storage of spent nuclear fuel. He regularly teaches courses in American government, understanding public policy, public policy implementation, and a seminar on health policy.

Acknowledgments

The authors would like to express their appreciation to the many individuals who have offered helpful suggestions and criticisms for previous editions of this text. An introductory American government book can never hope to cover every important topic, but many generous reviewers have helped us make sure that not too many crucial issues were left unexplored.

We would also like to acknowledge the fine team at BVT Publishing that has made this book possible. We are especially grateful to Richard Schofield and Shannon Conley for managing this project and to Anne Schofield for her work as editor.

Finally, we would like to acknowledge our families, who have provided the inspiration and support necessary to see this project through to its completion. Specifically, we thank Jessica Bresler, Lin Carvell, and Jordan and Greg Rogoe; Rebecca, Philip, and Elizabeth Friedrich; Audrey, Christopher, and Matthew Karlesky; Ellen, Todd, and Claire Stephenson; and Meghan Turner and Wesley Ray.

Charles C. Turner
D. Grier Stephenson Jr.
Robert J. Bresler
Robert J. Friedrich
Joseph J. Karlesky

Introduction to

American
Government

Eighth Edition

(Shutterstock)

Introduction

This book is an introduction to American politics and government. Its objective is not to convince readers that a particular political position is "best." It does not celebrate the virtues of capitalism or socialism, the unfettered free market or a government-guided economy. Nor does this book argue that taxes are too high or too low, abortion is right or wrong, social welfare policies are too generous or too stingy, or government is too big or too small. This book is not designed to create more liberals or conservatives or capitalists or socialists. Its task is to examine the American political system and to stimulate informed critical thinking about politics and government.

The two fundamental goals of this book are (1) to explain why understanding politics and government is crucial to being an engaged citizen in our complex society, and (2) to clarify how the actions of politicians and the consequences of governmental decisions affect people's lives. The book highlights the importance of ideas and economic concerns in the resolution of political issues. Toward this end, every chapter contains one or more of the following special feature boxes: "Politics and Economics," "Politics and Ideas," and "Contemporary Controversies."

What Is Politics?

What exactly is politics? For many people the word evokes negative feelings. "It's just politics," people say when they don't like a decision that's been made or when a friend loses out on a promotion. The very mention of the word often conjures up a picture of a smooth-talking "wheeler-dealer" who uses cash to influence votes, or a corrupt officeholder who exploits his or her position for financial gain. However, politics is not all graft and kickbacks. Despite much of the current disillusionment with the political process, politics can be an honorable and noble profession. At its best, it is a moral activity reconciling social and economic differences and constructing a way of governing society without chaos, tyranny, or undue violence.[1]

The ancient Greek philosopher Aristotle once called politics the "master science." He did not mean that politics explained all the mysteries of human life and nature. Rather, Aristotle meant that politics provides the means by which a community of people with differing views and interests can strive for collective survival and advancement. The drama of the American Civil War illustrates the importance of politics as a means of resolving differences without resorting to violence. All societies inevitably have differences; the issue is how a society copes with those differences. In this sense, politics is better described as the "necessary science."

With over 300 million people, the American nation is diverse. Some people are white, and some are African American. Some Americans were born in other countries, and some have an American ancestry that dates back centuries. Some are religious fundamentalists and others liberal humanists. Some are young, paying Social Security taxes; and some are old, receiving Social Security benefits. Some earn high incomes, and others have little or no income at all. Some live in fashionable town houses or suburbs, and others live in blighted inner cities or on declining farms. Some make their living in high-tech industries, and others in traditional smokestack industries.

Politics is better described as a "necessary science," as its purpose is to allow for a community of people with differing views and interests to strive for collective survival and advancement. (iStock)

The point need not be belabored. America is a complex, multicultural society in which consensus is often difficult to achieve. Different groups want different things and have different values. Such differences are at the root of the political process. In its best-known and most straightforward definition, **politics** is the study of "who gets what, when, and how."[2] Put another way, politics is the process of peacefully reconciling social and economic differences.

Politics and Economics

Many of the conflicts that arise in a society—who has and who has not, who gives and who gets, who gains and who loses—are economic in their origins or their manifestations. Because money and material resources are limited and because human wants and demands are almost limitless, the need to make choices about spending money and using scarce resources becomes inevitable. Many government

politics

The process of peacefully reconciling social and economic differences

BVT *Lab*

Visit www.BVTLab.com to explore the student resources available for this chapter.

Introduction | 05

decisions are economic in nature because they affect the production, distribution, and consumption of wealth.

Even though our national government spends about $3.9 trillion annually, it still does not have enough capital to satisfy all the demands and expectations placed on it. Every year the president and Congress wrestle over the budget. Should we increase the funding for military operations or spend more on Medicare coverage? Not all programs can be funded to the complete satisfaction of their supporters, nor will all agree on who should provide the tax revenue to pay for these programs.

Politicians must make these choices under the pressure of people who clamor to advance their own interests. The elderly are likely to press for increases in Social Security, while the young are more likely to be interested in higher student aid grants and loans for college expenses. Steel and autoworkers may favor quotas on foreign imports. Farmers who depend on the export market may fear such quotas because foreign governments might retaliate against our agricultural products. Of course, not everyone takes predictable positions on every issue, nor is everyone motivated entirely by economic self-interest. Some of the wealthy are willing to pay higher taxes to help the poor, and some of the poor oppose higher social welfare spending. In general, when economic or occupational consequences are at stake, most people press for programs that serve their self-interests. Politicians must resolve the resulting conflicts.

In the face of scarcity, this task is difficult. Not all people will be satisfied; and few, if any, will be satisfied completely. Politics produces decisions that are almost guaranteed to be imperfect. Although the American system leaves most decisions about economics to the marketplace, it has never considered economic liberty an absolute right. Nor has America practiced any pure form of **capitalism**—an economic system based on private ownership of property and free economic competition among individuals and businesses. Minimum wage laws, child labor laws, and environmental regulations are a few examples of government restrictions on the functioning of the marketplace. From the beginning of the nation, government has provided certain infrastructural services (schools, roads, hospitals) in order for capitalism to flourish. Since President Franklin D. Roosevelt's New

Former President Franklin D. Roosevelt (Shutterstock)

Deal in the 1930s, the government has provided benefits for the elderly, the poor, and the unemployed. The American experience, particularly in the twenty-first century, has been witness to a strong central government that complements, coexists with, and regulates an economy largely in private hands. In the United States, economic and political powers have historically been divided; however, the line is always fluid and often hotly contested.

The genius of the American political experience comes from our ability, with the notable exception of the Civil War, to compromise claims and resolve differences without wrenching the system apart. As the country grows more complex and diverse, that challenge becomes more formidable.

capitalism

An economic system based on private ownership of property and free economic competition among individuals and businesses

Politics and Ideas

Money and its uses have a magnetic attraction. Even if the supply of money were infinite (which it clearly is not), conflict would still be present. Political systems are continually buffeted by debates over issues in which money and economic goods may be involved, but in which they do not play a central role. Such debates focus on the question of which political ideas and values should be reflected in a nation's laws and political institutions. In other words, many political disputes are ideological in origin. **Ideology** (used interchangeably in this book with the term *political ideas*) refers to the kind of government people think they should have. Ideology may also include ideas about the economic system. The prevailing political ideas have a lot to do with shaping the kind of life Americans enjoy, and ideological differences among Americans spark many political controversies.

Debates about LGBT rights are controversial. Here, protesters handcuff themselves to the fence outside the White House in Washington, D.C., during a protest for gay rights. The group demanded that President Obama keep his promise to repeal the Don't Ask, Don't Tell policy. This policy was repealed in December 2010. (AP World Wide Photo)

For example, should abortion be allowed or banned? What pro-choice groups see as the constitutional right of women to control their own bodies, pro-life groups see as the murder of innocents. Other examples of disputes over values include debates about LGBT* rights, the necessity and morality of capital punishment, the censorship of pornography and obscenity, and the teaching of evolution and sex education in public schools.

Opposition to the sums of money spent on public health insurance programs, therefore, comes not just from the people who are concerned about the costs but also from those who believe that mandating health coverage is an inappropriate role for the government. Likewise, others call for increased government aid to the homeless because they believe providing such aid is the humane thing to do.

No amount of money can bring people together on these issues, which involve fundamentally different views about what is right and just. In these matters, as in economic issues, politicians must get people to settle for less than their ideal in this imperfect world. Politicians are the brokers of the claims we make and the values we insist on. Politics becomes the art of reaching compromises when none seem possible.

Why Government?

ideology

A set of ideas concerning the proper political and economic system in which people should live

government

The political and administrative organization of a state, nation, or locality

People often use the words *politics* and *government* interchangeably. However politics is a process, and **government** is the set of organizations within which much of that process takes place.

---

* LGBT stands for lesbian, gay, bisexual, and transgender and is the most widely used term for describing this community.

Why government? What is its purpose? No better answer to these questions can be found than in the Preamble to the Constitution of the United States. In 1787, the framers summarized the answer in one sentence:

> We the People of the United States, in Order to form a more perfect Union, establish Justice, insure domestic Tranquility, provide for the common defense, promote the general Welfare, and secure the Blessings of Liberty to ourselves and our Posterity, do ordain and establish this Constitution for the United States of America.

"To Establish Justice, Insure Domestic Tranquility ... and Secure the Blessings of Liberty"

Government is essential to civilization. Restraint and decency among people are necessary prerequisites of a civilized society. To government falls the task of trying to ensure such behaviors. "Taxes," Justice Oliver Wendell Holmes (1902–1932)[*] wrote, "are what we pay for civilized society."[3] The English philosopher **Thomas Hobbes** wrote that in the absence of "the sovereign" or government, life among individuals would be "solitary, poor, nasty, brutish, and short."

Sovereign power is essential for protecting people from one another, by force if necessary. If people attempt to kill one another or steal from one another or assault one another, government must intervene. If it does not, civilization is simply not possible. People could not enjoy the fundamental pleasures of life—such as a walk in the park, a baseball game, a concert—if their physical well-being were constantly threatened by others whose violent acts went unhindered or unpunished. Although anarchists would disagree, government is essential to human liberty.

Yet government cannot by itself guarantee civil behavior. Civilization is a precious and fragile state of human existence that must be continually buttressed by the supporting values and beliefs of individuals in a society. Hobbes saw civilization as a thin veneer, beneath which surged a boiling caldron of human impulses.

Even in contemporary society the veneer is occasionally pierced. When civil tensions reach a breaking point, as they did during the chaotic aftermath

People could not enjoy certain pleasures of life—such as an outdoor music festival—if their physical well-being were constantly threatened by others whose violent acts went unhindered or unpunished. (Shutterstock)

of Hurricane Katrina in 2005, antisocial forms of behavior frequently emerge— vandalism, assault, or battery. These threats to civil behavior must be resisted, and it is government that does the resisting.

"To Provide for the Common Defense"

Government must also protect its citizens against threats from other societies or governments. National defense is among the most important and visible

Thomas Hobbes

Seventeenth-century English political philosopher who wrote about the basis of sovereignty residing in a social contract

---

[*] Throughout this book, dates in parentheses following the names of presidents and justices of the Supreme Court indicate their years in office.

functions of government. National security is essential to a society's preservation. The common defense has a long history, as any recounting of this nation's wars over the last two centuries will suggest. One of the principal concerns of the framers of the Constitution in 1787 was the creation of a stronger national government that could grapple more easily with the external threats and dangers of an uncertain world.

People may debate whether the government spends enough or too much on defense, but few will deny that the national government must be capable of defending the nation. Any organization or group calling itself a government that does not possess that capability may be a symbol or a wish—but it is not a government.

People may debate whether the government spends enough or too much on defense, but few will deny that the national government must be capable of defending the nation. (Wikimedia Commons)

"To Promote the General Welfare"

Government also exists to organize cooperative public efforts. Although some people believe in the adage "the government that governs least, governs best," few believe that government should do nothing. Throughout history government has subsidized railroads, constructed dams, protected the wilderness, provided for the needy, established schools, and built space shuttles. Such enterprises are **collective goods**, available for the benefit of all citizens whether or not they paid taxes to support them. These enterprises are generally too massive for private undertaking. They require a government that can tax and spend on a large scale.

The ideological debate over the size and scope of governmental enterprises has endured since the founding of our nation. Advocates of the **positive state** argue that government should play an active role in providing the goods, services, and conditions for a prosperous and equitable society. Adherents of the **minimalist state** argue that government is too inefficient and coercive and should be restricted to producing only goods that individuals themselves cannot provide.

collective goods

Something of value that, by its nature, can be made available only to everybody or not to anyone at all

positive state

A government that helps provide the goods, services, and conditions for a prosperous, equitable society

minimalist state

A government that restricts its activities to providing only goods that the free market cannot produce

democracy

A system of government based on majority rule, protection of minority and individual rights, and the equality of all citizens before the law

What Is Democracy?

It is a basic axiom of American society that a government cannot be accountable merely to itself. The legitimacy of government in America rests on the consent of the governed. The Preamble to the Constitution states, "We the people of the United States … do ordain and establish this Constitution." We live in a representative **democracy**, a system of government in which political authority is vested in the people. The underlying ideology of a representative democracy supposes that people are capable of controlling their own destiny, selecting their own leaders, and cooperating in creating a peaceful and wholesome society. Alexander Hamilton, a delegate from New York to the Constitutional Convention in 1787, thought the new American nation could answer "the important question whether societies … are really capable or not of establishing good government from reflection and choice, or whether they are forever destined to depend … on accident and force."[4]

Democratic Values and Goals

What makes a government democratic? Democracy requires a system of government based on four precepts:

1. *Majority rule* expressed in free, periodic elections

2. Full protection of *minority rights* against an irrational or tyrannical majority

3. Protection of *individual rights* to freedom of speech, press, religion, petition, and assembly

4. *Equality* before the law for all citizens, regardless of race, creed, color, gender, national origin, or other immutable characteristics

These four objectives can be reached in different ways. Governments can vary in form and still be labeled democratic. In the United States, the head of state and the head of government are combined in one president, elected by the people. In other lands these roles may be vested in two people.

These four objectives are also, to a degree, in conflict with one another. The achievement of one can entail limits on another. Minority rights limit the kinds of laws that majorities in Congress or in the state legislatures may pass. Being in control of government in the United States does not give unlimited power to a majority. If, for example, the Republicans lose an election to the Democrats, the latter have no authority to seize the property of the former or to say that Republicans no longer have the right to vote. Nor can members of a majority silence their critics (as much as they might like to) simply because they won an election.

Likewise, the command of equality before the law places limits on what a majority may do. Democratic governments may not design election laws so that some people have more votes than others, but the rule that everyone's vote counts equally does not guarantee everyone the same influence in public affairs. Citizens with money to contribute to the campaigns of certain candidates often have more influence than those who have less or who choose not to contribute. Equality before the law is often difficult to achieve in the face of economic inequality. For example, wealthier school districts often provide a better education than poorer districts. Educational opportunities relate to one's income potential and full development as an informed citizen.

Efforts to achieve equality may also involve restraints on individual liberty. Laws banning certain forms of racial and gender discrimination—thus ensuring equal treatment for employees in the workplace—decrease the liberty of employers to hire and fire whomever they please. In turn, the protection of certain liberties may result in economic inequalities. For example, the liberty to keep one's property and earnings (subject, of course, to taxation) may result in vast disparities in wealth and income.

So American-style democracy is not only, in Lincoln's immortal words, "government of the people, by the people, for the people." As we shall see in Chapter 1, American democracy also involves **constitutionalism**—the principle of limiting governmental power by a written charter. Our Constitution restricts the power of the state. It also establishes the basic idea that no official, no matter how high, is above the law. This point is reaffirmed on Inauguration Day each time a president promises to "preserve, protect, and defend the Constitution of the United States."

constitutionalism

The belief in limiting governmental power by a written charter

For a democracy to function effectively, the people and their leaders must be willing to accept compromise and the notion that no one group will get all it desires. They must also accept democratic values and goals such as majority rule and minority rights. For democracy to work, the public must support the process by which agreement is reached. As one political scientist described it, "The American way is by compromise in little bits, by persuasion, by much talk and little bitterness."[5]

Through the avenues of open debate and free elections, those who lose a political battle generally get another opportunity. Minority factions in a democracy are more likely to accept defeat today if they know the way is open for them to become a majority tomorrow.

Why Do Politics and Government Matter?

Although Americans have had political institutions since colonial days, the nature of government in the United States has undergone radical change. Today, government at all levels—state, local, and especially the national government—plays a much larger role in the life of the average citizen than it did 225 years ago during President Washington's administration, or even 150 years ago during President Lincoln's time.

Today, the national government pervades society, the economy, and the lives of its citizens. Its actions affect people all over the globe. Its $3.9 trillion budget creates work for over 2.7 million federal civilian employees. Governmental involvement is pervasive, regulating products from prescription drugs to toys. It insures banks, protects the air and drinking water, and warns against cigarette smoking.

With so broad a reach, the national government dwarfs every other organization in American society, including huge corporations like ExxonMobil and Walmart. Everyone who makes money must send some portion of it to the government in the form of taxes. In short, few people can get through a single day without being touched by the actions of the national government. These actions result from the process called politics. As the chapters that follow show, politics pervades American society, economy, and culture.

CHAPTER REVIEW

1. Politics is about the resolution of conflict in society. Conflicts frequently arise over resource allocation and value preferences. Politicians, at their best, find compromises between these issues when none seem available.

2. Government is essential to a civilized society. Its tasks are to ensure a peaceful society, to provide for the national defense, to secure basic freedoms, and to undertake cooperative enterprises for the general welfare.

3. American democracy provides for a government based on the consent of the governed, the protection of individual rights, and the equality of rights before the law. The Constitution, the basic charter of our government, preserves the principle of government under law.

4. In contemporary America, the tasks of government are extensive and varied. The national government spends about $3.9 trillion per year, and its activities pervade society. All Americans are directly affected by the policies and choices of government.

KEY TERMS

Readings for Further Study

Two classic discussions of politics can be found in Harold Lasswell, *Politics: Who Gets What, When, How* (Whitefish, MT: Literary Licensing, 2011), and Bernard Crick, *In Defense of Politics* (New York: Continuum International, 2001).

Much of the political theory underlying the American political system can be found in philosophical treatises such as *Leviathan* by Thomas Hobbes (New York: Cambridge University Press, 1996), *Two Treatises of Government* by John Locke (New York: Cambridge University Press, 1988), and *The Spirit of the Laws* by Montesquieu (New York: Cambridge University Press, 1989).

Richard Hofstadter's *The American Political Tradition* (New York: Vintage Books, 1989) remains a landmark study in American political history.

A searching examination of American politics in theory and practice can be found in Samuel P. Huntington, *Who Are We? The Challenges to America's National Identity* (New York: Simon and Shuster, 2005).

Notes

1. Bernard Crick, *In Defense of Politics* (New York: Continuum International, 2001), ch. 1.

2. Harold Lasswell, *Politics: Who Gets What, When, How* (Whitefish, MT: Literary Licensing, 2011).

3. *Campanio de Tobacos v. Collector*, 275 U.S. 87, 100 (1904).

4. *Federalist*, No. 1.

5. Frank Tannenbaum, "On Certain Characteristics of American Democracy," *Political Science Quarterly* 60 (1945): 350.

Chapter

01

The Constitution of the United States

In This Chapter

(Shutterstock)

Chapter Objectives

A nation's politics is given a special cast by the kind of government it has as well as by the values of its citizens. This country is no exception. The Constitution and the institutions that document summoned into being have shaped American politics mightily.

This chapter reviews the purposes of a constitution and traces the origins of our Constitution from the Revolutionary War and the first experiment with a national government under the Articles of Confederation to judicial review and the Supreme Court. Attention to the Philadelphia Convention of 1787 sheds light on what the framers of the Constitution wanted to avoid as well as what they wanted to achieve. Did they want to establish a democracy? What was the significance of dividing governmental authority among legislative, executive, and judicial branches? What is the unique relationship between the Supreme Court and the Constitution? How can a piece of parchment from the eighteenth century fit American needs in the twenty-first century?

Exploring such questions is essential to understanding American government today, particularly when one considers that the Constitution of the United States is the oldest written national charter still in force.

1.1 What Is a Constitution?

"What is a constitution?" asked Supreme Court Justice William Paterson (1793–1806) over two centuries ago. "It is," he answered, "the form of government, delineated by the mighty hand of the people, in which certain first principles of fundamental laws are established." Like Paterson and his contemporaries, most Americans embrace **constitutionalism**: the belief in limiting governmental power by a written charter. This makes a constitution a very special document.

1.1a Constitutionalism

Constitutionalism has long been important in American politics. Each of the fifty states has a constitution. In January 2013, President Barack Obama—like all his predecessors back to George Washington (1789–1797)—took an oath to "preserve, protect, and defend" the Constitution. Constitutionalism has also been contagious. Almost every country on earth has a constitution, but constitutions take different forms in different lands. Most, like the United States Constitution, are single documents, usually with amendments. A few, like the British Constitution, are made up of a series of documents and scattered major acts of Parliament (the British law-making body) that time and custom have endowed with paramount authority. The major difference between American-style constitutionalism and British-style constitutionalism is that the British Constitution can be changed by an act of Parliament. As described later in this chapter, the American Constitution can be formally altered only by an elaborate amendment procedure that includes the states—not Congress alone.

American style or British style, a constitution is more than a piece of paper. It is a living thing that embodies much more than mere words can convey—it embodies intangibles that enable it to work and to survive. Moreover, it provides clues to the political ideas that are dominant in a nation. The United States Constitution, for example, includes a cluster of values in its Preamble: "to form a more perfect *Union*, establish *Justice*, insure domestic *Tranquility*, provide for the common *defense*, promote the general *Welfare*, and secure the Blessings of *Liberty*."

1.1b Constitutional Functions

Constitutions matter because of what they do (or do not do) and what they are. First, a constitution *outlines the organization of government*. The outline may be long or short, detailed or sketchy, but it answers key questions about the design of a government. Are executive duties performed by a monarch, prime minister, president, or ruling committee? Who makes the laws? A constitution probably won't answer all of the structural questions about a political system, however. The American Constitution, for instance, makes no mention of political parties; yet a picture of American politics without them would be woefully incomplete. Thus, while knowledge about constitutions may be a good starting place for a student of politics, it is hardly the finishing point.

Second, a constitution *grants power*. Governments exist to do things; and under the idea of constitutionalism, governments need authority to act. For example, Article I of the Constitution (reprinted in the Appendix) contains a long list of topics on which Congress may legislate, from punishing counterfeiters and regulating commerce "among the several States" to declaring war.

Grants of power imply limits on power. This is the principle of constitutional government in America: Rulers are bound by the ruled to the terms of a written

constitutionalism

The belief in limiting governmental power by a written charter

charter. Thus, a constitution can also be a *mainstay of rights.* Constitutions commonly include a bill of rights or a declaration of personal freedoms that lists some of the things that governments may not do and proclaims certain liberties to be so valued that a society enshrines them in fundamental law.

Finally, a constitution may serve as a *symbol of the nation*—a repository of political values. When this happens, a constitution becomes more than the sum of its parts. More than a document that organizes, authorizes, and limits, it becomes an object of veneration.

(Shutterstock)

Americans have probably carried constitution veneration further than people of any other nation. Such emphasis on the Constitution has had an impact on the political system that can hardly be exaggerated. Frequently, people debate policy questions, not just in terms of whether something is good or bad, wise or foolish, but also whether it is *constitutional*. Debate may rage over the meaning of the Constitution, but contending forces accept the document as the fundamental law of the land. One group might argue that the Constitution bans state-sponsored prayer in public schools, for example, while another might argue just as vehemently that the Constitution permits it.

The Road to Nationhood

In order to reach a better understanding of how America developed such a relationship with its Constitution, it is important to first understand the origins of that document. American government does not begin with the Constitution. Prior to 1787, there were many years of British rule, followed by the turbulence of revolution and an experiment with national government under the Articles of Confederation.

1.2a The Declaration of Independence: The Idea of Consent

England first began developing **colonies** in North America in the early 1600s. By the mid-1700s, many British colonies had been established, thirteen of which were geographically contiguous along the eastern seaboard. While the colonies were profitable for Britain, there were also associated costs—such as defending British territory claims against Native American tribes and the claims of other European countries. At least thirteen years before the revolution, British leaders in London attempted to bring the American colonies under more direct control. Among other things, they wanted the colonists to pay a larger share of defense expenses and developed a series of tax and military policies to that end. These policies, however, ran head on into colonial self-interest, revolutionary ideas, and a feeling of a new identity—an American identity as opposed to a purely British one. A series of events between 1763 and 1776 encouraged organized resistance to British authority and culminated in independence. Politics and reasoned debate within the British Empire

colony

A territory under the direct control of a parent state

soon gave way to armed revolt against it. Near the end of this period, colonial political leaders—meeting as the Second Continental Congress—considered a resolution moved by Richard Henry Lee of Virginia on June 7, 1776: "Resolved, that these United Colonies are, and of right ought to be, free and independent states." A declaration embodying the spirit of Lee's resolution and largely reflecting Thomas Jefferson's handiwork soon emerged from committee. Twelve states (New York abstaining) accepted it on July 2, with approval by all thirteen coming on July 4.

At one level, the Declaration of Independence (reprinted in the Appendix) itemized and publicized the colonists' grievances against British rule, personified in King George III. The revolutionists felt obliged to justify what they had done. Reprinted in newspapers up and down the land, the document was one the revolutionists hoped might,

A depiction of the signing of the Declaration of Independence as seen on the back of a $2 bill. (iStock)

with luck, rally support at home and abroad to the cause of independence—especially for the military conflict underway. There was, after all, no unanimity within the colonies in 1776 on the wisdom of declaring independence. Loyalists were an active and hostile minority. Even among those who favored the break with England, some opposed fighting a war. Others were plainly indifferent.

In its goal of making the cause seem just and worth great sacrifice, the Declaration at another level said much about political thinking at the time. The authors of the Declaration were steeped in the thinking of English and Scottish natural rights philosophers, such as **John Locke**, who were trying to find a new source of legitimacy for political authority. Formerly, justification of authority stemmed from the belief that governments were ordained by God. Consequently, rulers governed on the basis of a covenant with the Deity, which implied limits to power, or on the basis of "divine right," which did not. If government were to have a secular basis, however, rulers could govern only by consent—not as an agent of God on earth but as an agent of the people.

American leaders were also aware of precedents for rebellion in British history. Tensions between the Crown and Parliament had climaxed in the Glorious Revolution of 1688, which secured the supremacy of Parliament over the monarchy. They knew also of the series of political battles, large and small, over the centuries that had won particular rights for English subjects. They were familiar with the writings of the seventeenth-century English jurist Sir Edward Coke (whose name rhymes with *look*), who maintained that even actions of Parliament had to conform to "common right and reason" as embodied in the law of the land. Ironically, Coke's ideas eventually took root in America but not in England.

The Declaration of Independence drew heavily on these traditions. At least four themes emerge from its text:

John Locke

English political philosopher whose ideas about political legitimacy influenced the American founders

1. *Humankind shares equality.* All persons possess certain rights by virtue of their humanity. The Declaration called them "unalienable rights" and mentioned three specifically: "Life, Liberty, and the Pursuit of Happiness." These rights were bestowed by the Creator and were "self-evident."

2. _Government is the creation and servant of the people._ It is an institution deliberately brought into being to protect the rights that all naturally possess. It maintains its authority by consent of the governed. When government is destructive of the rights it exists to protect, citizens have a duty to revolt when less drastic attempts at reform fail. Citizens would, then, replace a bad government with a good one.

3. _The rights that all intrinsically possess constitute a higher law binding government._ Constitutions, statutes, and policies must be in conformity with this higher law. That is, they must promote the ends that government was created to advance. Natural rights would become civil rights.

4. _Governments are bound by their own laws._ These laws must be in conformity with the higher law. No officer of government is above the law. To make this point, the authors of the Declaration detailed violations, by the king, of English law in a list that consumes more than half the text.

By eighteenth-century standards, the Declaration of Independence advanced objectives that were far removed from reality. Some newspapers of 1776 reprinted the Declaration alongside advertisements for slaves. Moreover, as a statement of American ideology, the Declaration's objectives remain unattained even today.

Tea Party supporters hold signs at a rally against the healthcare reform bill (Shutterstock)

1.2b   The Articles of Confederation: The Idea of Compact

Even if the Declaration of Independence proclaimed separation from England, it did little to knit the former colonies into a nation. Central political control disappeared in 1776. Something would now have to take its place for successful execution of the war and for development of the nation once liberty was won. Only eight days after the adoption of the Declaration of Independence, a committee of Congress chaired by John Dickinson placed before the entire body a plan of union. The **Articles of Confederation** became the first American national constitution. Meeting in York, Pennsylvania—a safe distance from the British who occupied Philadelphia—Congress approved Dickinson's Articles in amended form in November 1777 and referred them to the states for approval. All states, save one, gave assent by May 1779 (with Maryland holding out until March 1781 because of a land dispute).

The main provisions of the Articles of Confederation are summarized in Table 1.1. Several features distinguished the document. First, *the Articles preserved state autonomy.* The document read more like a treaty between nations than a device to link component states. Describing the compact as "a firm league of friendship," the Articles stated clearly that "each state retains its sovereignty, freedom and independence, and every power, jurisdiction and right which is not by this Confederation expressly delegated to the United States in Congress assembled." The word *confederation* accurately described the arrangement: It was a loose union of separate states.

Second, *the Articles guaranteed equal representation for the states.* Congress represented the states, not the people. While a state's delegation could range in size from two to seven, each state had only one vote. The delegates were to be appointed "in such

Articles of Confederation

This first plan of a national government for the thirteen American states was replaced by the Constitution; under the Articles, the states retained most political power

manner as the legislature of each state shall direct," and the states reserved the right to recall and replace their delegates at any time.

Third, *the Articles granted the central government only a few important powers.* The central government was given control over foreign affairs and military policy; however, it was denied taxing power completely, as well as the authority to regulate most trade.

table 1.1 | An Overview of the Articles of Confederation

The Articles of Confederation provided for the dominance of the states in the political system and granted only a few powers to Congress.

Article I:	Name of the confederacy: the United States of America
Article II:	Guaranteed the powers of the member states, except where the states expressly delegated powers to Congress
Article III:	Stated the purpose of the confederation: the defense and protection of the liberties and welfare of the states
Article IV:	Stated that, as they traveled from state to state, citizens of the several states were to enjoy the privileges each state accorded its own citizens and granted freedom of trade and travel between states
Article V:	Specified the processes of selection of delegates to Congress by state legislatures and of voting by states in Congress
Article VI:	Prohibited states from engaging in separate foreign and military policies or using duties to interfere with treaties; recognized that each state would maintain a militia and a naval force
Article VII:	Specified the appointment by state legislatures of all militia officers of or under the rank of colonel
Article VIII:	Specified that national expenses were to be paid by states to Congress, in proportion to the value of the land in each state; states retained sole power to tax citizens
Article IX:	Placed the sole power to make peace and war in Congress; restricted treaty-making power; designated Congress the "last resort" in all disputes between states; spelled out procedures for settling such disputes; gave the power to establish a postal system and to regulate the value of money issued by state and central governments to Congress; made provision for an executive committee of Congress, called a "Committee of the States," to manage the government; stipulated that most major pieces of legislation would require the affirmative vote of nine states
Article X:	Authorized the Committee of the States to act for Congress when Congress was not in session
Article XI:	Provided a provision for Canada to join the United States
Article XII:	Deemed debts previously incurred by Congress to be obligations of the government under the Articles of Confederation
Article XIII:	Specified the obligation of each state to abide by the provisions of the Articles of Confederation and all acts of Congress; provided for amendment by consent of the legislatures of every state

Revenues instead would be supplied by the states. If a state failed to make its proper payment, the Articles offered no remedy. Furthermore, most appropriations and laws of any significance required the affirmative vote of nine states.

Fourth, *the Articles provided for no separate executive branch and no national courts.* The rights of citizens lay in the hands of state courts. Congress was supposed to be the arbiter of last resort in disputes between states. Officers appointed by Congress performed the few executive duties permitted under the Articles.

Fifth, *the Articles made amendment almost impossible.* Changes in the terms of the Articles needed approval not only by Congress but also by the "legislatures of every state." For example, a single state could block any realignment of the balance the Articles struck between central direction and local autonomy. The states seemed destined to hold the dominant position for a long time to come.

1.3 The Making of the Constitution

Defects in the Articles of Confederation soon became apparent. Citizens who wanted change built their case on either of two deficiencies, and often on both. First was *an absence of sufficient power in the central government.* Absence of national taxation meant that Congress was hard pressed to carry out even the limited responsibilities it had, such as national defense. Absence of control over interstate commerce meant trade wars between the states, with some states prohibitively taxing imports from others. Congress could do little to promote a healthy economic environment. Absence of power to compel obedience by the states meant that foreign countries had no assurance that American states would comply with treaties to which the national government agreed.

Why did the founders call for a *constitutional convention?*

See for yourself by comparing the Constitution printed in the Appendix to this web version of the Articles of Confederation.

http://www.bvtlab.com/K67c8

The second deficiency often mentioned was *the presence of too much power in the hands of the state governments.* Local majorities, unchecked by national power, could infringe on an individual's property rights. Of particular concern were the "cheap money" parties that had been victorious in some of the states. The decade of the 1780s was generally one of economic depression. In the wake of the ravages of war and the loss of British markets, times were hard. In response, state legislatures suspended debts or provided for payment of debts in kind, not cash. Added to this was the circulation of different currencies issued by the states, even though the national government was supposed to have monetary power. Printing additional money drove down its value, aiding debtors and hurting creditors. The economic picture was unsettled at best—chaotic at worst.

1.3a Prelude to Philadelphia

A revolt of farmers led by Daniel Shays in Massachusetts in 1786–1787, known as **Shays' Rebellion,** was one of many events that heightened concerns about the Articles of Confederation. When farmers in the Berkshire Hills failed to get the debt relief they had demanded from the legislatures, they closed local courts and forced the

Shays' Rebellion

A revolt by farmers from Massachusetts in 1786–1787 over the lack of economic relief, which led many to believe that a stronger central government was necessary

table 1.2 | Comparing the Articles of Confederation and the U.S. Constitution

	Articles of Confederation	Constitution
Location of sovereign power	States	Federal government
Basis of representation	All states equally	Combination of state equality and population
Taxation power	States only	States and federal government
Trade regulation	States	Federal government
Approval of appropriations and other major legislation	Supermajority of states (9 of 13)	Simple majority of House and Congress, plus approval of president
Federal executive	None	President
Federal courts	None	U.S. Supreme Court and federal court system
Revision/amendment	Unanimous state approval	Three-quarters of states' approval

state supreme court at Springfield to adjourn before they were finally routed by a state military contingent of 4,400 men. Although it was a military failure, the rebellion demonstrated that the central government under the Articles was powerless to protect the nation from domestic violence. Other issues, such as the refusal of states to provide the national government with the funds it needed to pay debts, further emphasized the shortcomings of the Articles.

In September 1786, on the eve of Shays' Rebellion, delegates from five states attended the **Annapolis Convention** in Maryland to consider suggestions for improving commercial relations among the states. Alexander Hamilton was a delegate from New York. Along with Virginia's James Madison, Hamilton persuaded the gathering to adopt a resolution calling for a convention of all states to meet in Philadelphia the following May to "render the Constitution of the Federal Government adequate to the exigencies of the Union." In February 1787, Congress authorized the convention. All the states except Rhode Island selected delegates; those delegates, however, were limited to considering amendments to the Articles of Confederation.

Even though the Constitution soon replaced the Articles, the nation's first experiment with central government was not a complete failure. In June 1787, in one of its last actions, the Congress established by the Articles enacted the **Northwest Ordinance**. This statute provided for the government and future statehood of the lands west of Pennsylvania, laid the basis for a system of public education, and banned slavery in that territory.

1.3b The Philadelphia Convention

To appreciate fully what happened in Philadelphia in 1787, one must visualize America two centuries ago. Doing so may not be easy. Today our nation is a global power—economically, militarily, and politically—with a population exceeding 318 million people in fifty states, stretching from the Atlantic into the Pacific.

Annapolis Convention

The meeting of delegates from five states, held in Annapolis, Maryland, in 1786, to consider a common policy for trade among the American states; it resulted in a recommendation for a constitutional convention the following year

Northwest Ordinance

This major statute, enacted by Congress in 1787 under the Articles of Confederation, provided for the development and government of lands west of Pennsylvania

By contrast, the America of 1787 was a sparsely settled, weakly defended, and internationally isolated nation of thirteen coastal states with a combined population of under 4 million. Philadelphia boasted a population of 30,000, making it the largest city in the land. Virginia and Massachusetts were the most populous states, with 747,000 and 473,000 inhabitants, respectively. Rhode Island and Delaware were the smallest, with populations of only 68,000 and 59,000, respectively. Three other states had fewer than 200,000 inhabitants. The slave population, found mostly in the states from Maryland southward, numbered 670,000—or about 17 percent of the total population.

It was in this context that the Philadelphia Convention assembled. By modern standards, the convention was not a large body; the legislatures of twelve states had selected seventy-four delegates, and fifty-five eventually took their seats. Of these, fewer than a dozen did most of the work. Quality amply compensated for quantity, however. Probably no other American political gathering has matched the convention in talent and intellect.

Who were the framers? Twenty-nine were college graduates, and the remaining twenty-six included notables such as George Washington and Benjamin Franklin. The youngest delegate, Jonathan Dayton of New Jersey, was 26. Franklin, of Pennsylvania, was the oldest at 81. Thirty-four were lawyers; others were farmers and merchants. Some names were prominent by their absence. Thomas Jefferson was abroad. John Jay of New York was not chosen, even though he had been foreign affairs secretary for the Articles Congress. Patrick Henry of Virginia was chosen but declined because he "smelt a Rat." Richard Henry Lee, also of Virginia, and Samuel Adams of Massachusetts were likewise suspicious of what might happen and stayed away. Ten delegates were also members of the Articles Congress. Eight delegates had signed the Declaration of Independence, and the signatures of six appeared on the Articles of Confederation; but on balance, this was not a reassembling of the generation that had set the revolution in motion. Rather, the delegates came from a pool of men who were fast gaining a wealth of practical experience in the political life of the young nation. Most were also committed to making changes to the Articles of Confederation—otherwise they would not have sacrificed the time and effort to attend.

The appointed day for meeting was May 14, 1787, but the ten delegates who convened that day at the Pennsylvania statehouse (now called Independence Hall) could do nothing until more arrived. Not only did the convention need its quorum of states, but each state delegation also needed a quorum because voting would be by state. Finally, on May 25, the Philadelphia Convention began its work. From then until September 17 the delegates conferred almost without pause, formally at the statehouse and informally at the City and Indian Queen taverns, short walks away.

In one of their first actions, the delegates adopted a rule of secrecy. The delegates even closed the windows during the steamy Philadelphia summer to discourage eavesdroppers. Without secrecy, it is doubtful whether the group could have succeeded. With secrecy came the freedom to maneuver, explore, and compromise. Because no verbatim stenographic account was made at the time, knowledge of the proceedings has had to be re-created piece by piece over the years.[1] The official journal of the convention was not made public until 1818. James Madison's notes on the proceedings, which are the most extensive account of what occurred, were not published until 1840.

On May 29, the Virginia delegation, led by Governor Edmund Randolph, seized the high ground for the discussion to follow. His fifteen resolutions—largely Madison's handiwork—made it increasingly evident that replacement, not tinkering, awaited

BVT Lab

Improve your test scores. Practice quizzes are available at www.BVTLab.com.

21

The Constitution of the United States

Chapter 01

The historic Independence Hall in Philadelphia, Pennsylvania. (Shutterstock)

the Articles of Confederation. Called the **Virginia Plan** and depicted in Figure 1.1, the resolutions proposed a substantially stronger national government and a Congress based on numerical representation. This plan generated a counterproposal put forward by William Paterson of New Jersey. Known as the **New Jersey Plan** (see Figure 1.1), it called for only modest changes to the Articles of Confederation, keeping the state governments dominant. What divided the delegates most was the issue of representation, because legislative representation translates into power. Would some states and interests have more votes than others in Congress? In late June and early July, the convention was deadlocked between delegates who favored representation in proportion to a state's population and those who wanted to keep equality between the states. Without settling this matter, the convention could not proceed.

This division is sometimes seen as the less-populous states versus the more-populous ones (small against large). True, a state such as Delaware would lose voting strength in the national legislature if population became the basis for representation, but the divisions of opinion were not always based solely on state size. A majority of the New York delegation, for example, opposed numerical representation in either house because other states could lay claim to extensive western lands with the potential for significant population growth. Besides, the Virginia Plan meant a greatly reduced role *for states as states* in the Union. Local leaders viewed centralizing tendencies as a threat to their own influence, regardless of their state's population.

Credit for a breakthrough goes to Dr. William Samuel Johnson and Oliver Ellsworth, both delegates from Connecticut. Known as the **Great Compromise** or the Connecticut Compromise, their plan called for numerical representation in the lower house and equal state representation in the upper house. This compromise broke the deadlock, permitting the delegates to move along to other matters, and it forms the basis of congressional representation today: by population in the House of Representatives and by states in the Senate.

There were other compromises as well. The most notorious was the **three-fifths compromise**, which permitted slave states to count each slave as three-fifths of a person, thus enhancing these states' representation in the House while denying slaves—who were legally classified as property—the right to vote. Moreover, the Constitution let each state decide who could vote in national as well as state elections. As a result, a majority of Americans (women and all slaves) were denied basic rights of political participation for years to come. Property qualifications that existed in some states for a time barred the poorest white males from the polling places as well.

1.3c Ratification

The formal signing of the Constitution took place on September 17, 1787—109 days after the convention first met. Thirty-nine names appear on the document. Three delegates (Elbridge Gerry of Massachusetts and George Mason and Edmund

Virginia Plan

The first plan of union proposed at the Constitutional Convention in 1787; it called for a strong central government

New Jersey Plan

Introduced in the Constitutional Convention in opposition to the Virginia Plan, it emphasized the dominance of the states

Great Compromise

An agreement at the Constitutional Convention in 1787, arranged by the delegation from Connecticut, proposing to accept representation by population in the House and by states in the Senate; sometimes called the Connecticut Compromise

three-fifths compromise

A temporary resolution to the controversy over slavery, this agreement allowed slaveholding states to count each slave as three-fifths of a person for purposes of congressional representation

Figure 1.1 | The Virginia Plan, the New Jersey Plan, and the Constitution

In the form signed by the framers on September 17, 1787, the Constitution reflected some features of both the Virginia and New Jersey plans. Other features of the two plans were discarded during the summer's debates. The Great Compromise settled the issue of representation, drawing from both plans.

Virginia Plan

A two-house legislature, with numerical representation, where popularly elected lower house elects upper house

Broad but undefined legislative power, with absolute veto over laws passed by state legislatures and taxing power

Single executive elected by legislature for fixed term

National judiciary elected by the legislature

Council of Revision, composed of the executive and judiciary, to review laws passed by national legislature

New Jersey Plan

A one-house legislature, with equal state representation

Same legislative power as under Articles, plus power to levy some taxes and to regulate commerce

Plural executive, removable by legislature on petition from majority of state governors

Judiciary, appointed by executive, to hear appeals on violations of national laws in state courts

A "supremacy clause" similar to that found in Article VI of present Constitution

Constitution of 1787

A two-house legislature, with numerical representation in popularly elected House and equal state representation in state-selected Senate

Broad legislative power, including power to tax and to regulate commerce

Single executive, chosen by electoral college

National judiciary, appointed by president and confirmed by Senate

Supremacy clause; no Council of Revision

Randolph of Virginia) refused to sign. Others, such as New York's Robert Yates, had gone home early because the Constitution included too many changes.

Approval by the country was surely on the framers' minds. Just as the delegates had taken liberty with their instructions to revise the Articles of Confederation, they proposed to bypass the rule of legislative unanimity for amendment. Article VII of the Constitution stipulated, in revolutionary fashion, that the new government would go into effect when *conventions* in *nine* states gave their assent. On September 28, 1787, the Articles Congress resolved unanimously—though noncommittally—that the Constitution should be handed over to the state legislatures "to be submitted to a convention of Delegates chosen in each state by the people thereof." Ironically, approval by popularly elected conventions meant that ratification of the Constitution would be a more democratic process than adoption of either the Declaration of Independence or the Articles of Confederation.

Supporters of the proposed Constitution called themselves **Federalists** and dubbed the nonsupporters **Antifederalists**, thus scoring a tactical advantage by making it seem that opponents of ratification were against union altogether. Because ratification meant persuasion, both sides engaged in a great national debate in the months after the Philadelphia Convention adjourned. Not since the eve of the revolution had there

Federalists

A term for persons who advocated ratification of the Constitution in 1787 and 1788 and generally favored a strong central government; it was also the name of the dominant political party during the administrations of Presidents George Washington and John Adams

Antifederalists

In the first years of government under the Constitution, Antifederalists in Congress were persons who opposed ratification of the Constitution in 1787 and 1788 and opposed policies associated with a strong central government such as a national bank

John Jay, Alexander Hamilton, and James Madison wrote The Federalist, *a collection of eighty-five essays, as an authoritative commentary on the Constitution. (Wikimedia Commons)*

been such an outpouring of pamphlets and essays. Most prominent among the tracts was *The Federalist*, a collection of eighty-five essays written by Alexander Hamilton, John Jay, and James Madison under the pen name Publius, which originally appeared between October 27, 1787, and August 15, 1788, in New York state newspapers. One of the most important expositions of American political theory, *The Federalist* achieved early recognition as an authoritative commentary on the Constitution.

Who were the Antifederalists? Most were not opposed to all change in the government. Some fought ratification because the Constitution was to become the supreme law of the land in an illegal manner, replacing the Articles of Confederation in violation of the Articles' own amendment procedure. For many, the Constitution was unacceptable because it would severely weaken state governments, leading eventually to a loss of local authority. Other opponents believed that individual liberty could be preserved only in "small republics," or states. If states were subordinated in the new government, it was only a matter of time before liberty would be lost—especially since the Constitution contained no bill of rights. As the governments closest to the people, states offered the best chance for self-government and so would promote, Antifederalists thought, a virtuous citizenry. Conversely, a distant government endangered not just popular rule but also citizenship itself. Moreover, the Constitution seemed designed to promote a commercial empire. This prospect threatened the agrarian values many of the Antifederalists shared.

For a time, ratification by the requisite number of states was in doubt, causing John Quincy Adams to observe a half-century afterward that the Constitution "had been extorted from the grinding necessity of a reluctant nation."[2] Not until June 21, 1788, did the ninth state (New Hampshire) ratify. Practically, however, the new government could not have succeeded had the important states of Virginia and New York not signed on. These states ratified on June 25 and 26, respectively—the latter by the close vote of 30–27. Some states ratified only on the promise that a bill of rights would soon be added to the Constitution, which it was (see Chapter 3).

Meeting on September 13, 1788, the Articles Congress acknowledged ratification, set a date in February for electors to choose a president, and designated

Explore the classic defense of the U.S. Constitution by reading the searchable online version of the *Federalist Papers* at:

http://www.bvtlab.com/sA9cs

The Federalist

A series of eighty-five essays written by Alexander Hamilton, John Jay, and James Madison and published in New York newspapers in 1787 and 1788, urging ratification of the Constitution

"the first Wednesday in March next … for commencing proceedings under the said Constitution." The new House and Senate transacted their first business on April 2 and April 5, 1789, respectively, with George Washington's inauguration as president following on April 30. On September 24, Washington signed legislation creating the Supreme Court and setting February 1, 1790, as the day of its first session. Confirmation by the Senate of the first Supreme Court justices followed on September 26, 1789.

The Constitution is reprinted in the Appendix. The main provisions of the Constitution (without amendments) are summarized in Table 1.3. Amendments, including the Bill of Rights, are summarized in Table 1.4.

table 1.3 | An Overview of the Constitution of 1787

In the form in which it left the hands of the framers in 1787, the Constitution stressed the powers of the national government and did not include a bill of rights.

Article I:	Establishment of legislative departments; description of organizations; list of powers and restraints; election of legislators
Article II:	Establishment of executive department; powers, duties, restraints; election of the president and vice president
Article III:	Establishment of judicial departments; jurisdiction of Supreme Court and other courts established by Congress; definition of *treason;* appointment of judges
Article IV:	Relation of the states to the national government and to one another; guarantees of the states; provision for territories and statehood
Article V:	Amendment of the Constitution; assurance of equal representation of the states in the Senate
Article VI:	Guarantee of national debts; supremacy of the national constitution, laws, and treaties; obligation of national and state officials under the Constitution; no religious test for national office
Article VII:	Ratification of the Constitution

1.4 Features of the Constitution

Several features, implicit or explicit, in the document of 1787 (plus its Bill of Rights) suggest why the Constitution was important to the framers. More pertinent, these features help explain how the Constitution shapes American government today.

1.4a Republicanism, Divided Powers, and Federalism

The framers deliberately chose a **republican (or representative) government** with divided powers. They feared the excesses of democracy, or pure majority rule, that they had seen in the politics of their own states. At the same time, recalling the Declaration's insistence on "the consent of the governed," they knew that government

republican (or representative) government

A style of government in which people elect representatives to make decisions in their place

table 1.4 | Amendments to the Constitution by Subject

Since the Bill of Rights (Amendments 1–10) was added in 1791, only seventeen formal changes have been made to the Constitution. Most have occurred in periods of reform and have affected the manner in which officials are elected and the operation and powers of the national government.

Individual rights

I	(1791)	Free expression
II	(1791)	Bearing arms
III	(1791)	No quartering of troops
IV	(1791)	Searches, seizures, and warrants
V	(1791)	Criminal procedure and fair trial
VI	(1791)	Criminal procedure and fair trial
VII	(1791)	Jury trials in civil suits
VIII	(1791)	No cruel and unusual punishment
IX	(1791)	Recognition of rights not enumerated
XIII	(1865)	Abolition of slavery
XIV	(1868)	Restrictions on state interference with individual rights; equality under the law; also altered nation–state relations

Political process

XII	(1804)	Separate voting by electors for president and vice president
XV	(1870)	Removal of race as criterion for voting
XVII	(1913)	Popular election of U.S. senators
XIX	(1920)	Removal of gender as criterion for voting
XXIII	(1961)	Enfranchisement of District of Columbia in voting for president and vice president
XXIV	(1964)	Abolition of poll tax in federal elections
XXVI	(1971)	National voting age of eighteen in all elections

Nation–state relations

X	(1791)	Powers of the states
XI	(1798)	Restriction of jurisdiction of federal courts

Operation and powers of national government

XVI	(1913)	Income tax
XX	(1933)	Shift of start of presidential term from March to January; presidential succession
XXII	(1951)	Two-term presidency
XXV	(1967)	Presidential disability and replacement of vice president
XXVII	(1992)	Limitation on timing of change in congressional salaries

Miscellaneous

XVIII	(1919)	Prohibition of alcoholic beverages
XXI	(1933)	Repeal of Eighteenth Amendment

had to be generally responsive to the people if ratification were to occur and revolution to be avoided. So, the Constitution blended democratic and antidemocratic elements: popular election (voters, as qualified by their states, directly elected only the members of the House of Representatives); indirect popular election (state legislatures chose members of the Senate, while specially designated electors selected the president); and appointment (the president picked the national judiciary with the approval of the Senate).

In addition, the Constitution placed limits on what government can do. Implicit in the idea of a written constitution is that a government does not have unlimited power. As described later in this chapter, courts in the United States have assumed the role of deciding what those limits are and when they have been crossed. The Bill of Rights contains some of those restrictions; Sections 9 and 10 of Article I contain others.

The Constitution also diffused and dispersed power. Clearly concerned with the necessity of strengthening government, the framers divided power even as they added it. They were aware of an old dilemma: How

(Wikimedia Commons)

does one construct a government with sufficient strength without endangering the freedom of individuals? Madison put it this way in *Federalist* No. 51: "In framing a government … the greatest difficulty lies in this: you must first enable the government to control the governed; and in the next place oblige it to control itself." The solution, thought the framers, lay in design: dividing power both horizontally among the different parts of the national government and vertically between the national government and the states.

To be avoided at all costs was tyranny, which Madison defined as "the accumulation of all powers, legislative, executive, and judiciary, in the same hands, whether of one, a few, or many, and whether hereditary, self-appointed, or elective." This threat could take at least two forms: domination of the majority by a minority, or domination of a minority by the majority, with the latter running roughshod over the former in disregard of its rights. Ordinarily, the ballot box would give ample protection. The vote, after all, was the primary check on rulers. Madison, however, saw the "necessity of auxiliary precautions."

The division of responsibilities at the national level among the three branches of government (Congress, the president, and the Supreme Court) would help, but that would not be enough. What was to keep one branch from grabbing all of the power from the other two? Words on paper ("parchment barriers," Madison called them) would be inadequate—especially because experience had taught that the legislature might be too responsive to the popular will. The solution lay in juxtaposing power— "contriving the interior structure of the government, as that its several constituent parts may, by their mutual relations, be the means of keeping each other in their proper places." Rather than counting on noble motives to ward off tyranny, the Constitution assumed the existence of less noble motives. "Ambition," wrote Madison, "must be made to counteract ambition."

This is the constitutional arrangement commonly called **checks and balances**. Power is checked and balanced because the separate institutions of the national

checks and balances

The system of separate institutions sharing some powers that the Constitution mandates for the national government; its purpose is to keep power divided among the three branches: legislative, executive, and judicial

Figure 1.2 | The Constitutional System of Checks and Balances

The framers designed the Constitution not just to divide governmental function among three branches but also to create a tension among the branches by allowing each one influence over the other two. American constitutional government means not just a separation of powers but also separate institutions sharing certain powers. The objective was to safeguard liberty by preventing a concentration of power.

(Shutterstock)

President

Appoints all federal judges

Enforces court decisions

Proposes legislation

May veto legislation passed by Congress

Convenes Congress

Appoints many administrative officials

Serves as commander in chief of armed forces

Conducts foreign relations

Congress

(Each house may veto the other)

Has general law-making power

Appropriates all funds

Creates executive departments

Declares war

Approves certain executive appointments (Senate only)

Ratifies treaties (Senate only)

Removes president and federal judges by impeachment

Defines Supreme Court's appellate jurisdiction

Sets size of Supreme Court

Creates lower federal courts and their jurisdictions

Supreme Court

Lifetime appointment

No reduction in salary

May declare actions of president and subordinates unconstitutional

May declare acts of Congress unconstitutional

BVT Lab

Visit www.BVTLab.com to explore the student resources available for this chapter.

29 | The Constitution of the United States | Chapter 01

government—legislative, executive, and judicial—share some powers. As depicted in Figure 1.2, no one branch has exclusive dominion over its sphere of activity.

For example, a proposed law may pass both houses of Congress only to run headlong into a presidential veto, itself surmountable only by a two-thirds vote of each house. After scaling that obstacle, the law in question might well encounter a negative from the Supreme Court using its power of judicial review. Judicial review is not explicitly mentioned in the Constitution, but it soon joined the roster of Madison's "auxiliary precautions." Even the president's powers of appointment and treaty making require Senate cooperation; and although the president is designated commander in chief of the armed forces, Congress must declare war and appropriate money to finance the president's policies.

Securing liberty was also to be helped by federalism, the vertical division between national and state governments (explained in Chapter 2). The Constitution left the states with ample regulatory or police power—that is, control over the health, safety, and welfare of their citizens. As associate justice of the Supreme Court John Marshall Harlan II (1955–1971) argued many years later, "We are accustomed to speak of the Bill of Rights and the Fourteenth Amendment as the principal guarantees of personal liberty. Yet it would surely be shallow not to recognize that the structure of our political system accounts no less for the free society we have." Harlan echoed Alexander Hamilton's observation in *Federalist* No. 84 that the Constitution, even without amendments, "is itself, in every rational sense, and to every useful purpose, a Bill of Rights."

Coupled with divided power at the top, federalism was useful in guarding against majority tyranny. Some of the framers worried about "factions"—today we would call them tightly knit political parties or interest groups. The most productive source of factions, Madison acknowledged in *Federalist* No. 10, was economic inequality—rich versus poor, creditors versus debtors, and so forth. The Constitution was designed, in part, to limit the influence of factions. Minority factions could be outvoted. Majority factions would, with luck, exhaust themselves trying to fuse together what the Constitution had diffused. The Constitution would ultimately not prevent the majority from attaining its objectives, but the effort would have to be both long and hard. Short of this, the Constitution would work to insulate national policy from political fads that might capture majority sentiment in one or two states. The framers were especially concerned about movements like Shays' Rebellion that threatened the rights of political minorities.

Power was divided horizontally and vertically in order to check human ambition run amok. Measured by this standard, the Constitution has been largely successful, yet the scheme is by no means foolproof. The vaccination against tyranny has had some unpleasant side effects. First, the arrangements that held off the threats to the nation that Madison feared have sometimes made dealing with threats to individual liberty in the states more difficult. As Chapter 3 describes, even after the central government took a stand against continued racial and gender discrimination, fragmented powers and federalism hindered steps to alleviate existing wrongs. All checks, primary and auxiliary, failed to work for a long time. Second, the constitutional legacy of the framers has sometimes made the task of governing the nation (more than 225 years later) a difficult one. Separate national institutions and federalism have contributed to weak political parties, all of which combine to tax the skills of any leader (including the president) who calls for concerted action. Sometimes power has to be amassed, it seems, in spite of the Constitution. The advantage tends to lie with those who would delay, deflect, or derail. The framers institutionalized tension within the government.

America Attacked

On September 11, 2001, America changed. The most violent single foreign attack on American soil in history left nearly three thousand people dead and many more injured. Four domestic passenger planes took off from the East Coast to begin cross-country flights but were hijacked shortly after takeoff by terrorists wielding knives. The hijackers were believed to be connected to al Qaeda, an international terror organization headed by Osama bin Laden, a Saudi national being harbored in Afghanistan. Two of the planes crashed into New York's World Trade Center, completely destroying two of the tallest buildings in the world and an important symbol of global capitalism. Another plane crashed into the Pentagon, the nation's defense headquarters, and a fourth (possibly heading to Washington, D.C.) crashed in rural Pennsylvania. In one day the mood of the nation changed from one of security and confidence to one of grief, shock, fear, and anger.

Our government changed as well. Nearly every aspect of American government addressed in the pages of this textbook felt the shock of September 11. The Constitution's war-making powers were given new meaning when President George W. Bush (2001–2009) declared a "war on terrorism" that continues to this day. The emergency relief effort that followed the attacks raised federalism questions, as it required coordination of local, state, and national agencies (Chapter 2). The protection of civil rights and liberties became a concern as government officials weighed the trade-off between restricting freedom—through more invasive airport searches, for example—and providing Americans with a greater sense of security (Chapter 3). Political ideologies temporarily lost some significance when congressional leaders— liberal and conservative alike— passed nearly unanimous resolutions condemning the terrorist attacks and stating a need for armed response (Chapter 4). The public's response included heightened concern about terrorism that continues to this day. Ten years after the attack, 58 percent of respondents indicated that they believed Americans have permanently changed their way of life as a result of the 9/11 attacks. Many reported being less likely to fly on airplanes, go into skyscrapers, travel overseas, or attend large-scale events (Chapter 5). Media outlets responded by changing their programming to increase coverage of ongoing and developing acts of terror, as well as American responses (Chapter 6). Established interest groups, such as the American Red Cross, and newly created organizations, such as America's Fund for Afghan Children, collected millions of dollars from concerned Americans who wanted to show their support for victims and families (Chapter 7).

The institutions of American government responded to change as well. On November 6, 2001—fewer than two months after the attacks— New York City went to the polls and elected new mayor Michael Bloomberg.

Former president George W. Bush stands with a firefighter in front of the World Trade Center debris on Friday, September 14, 2001. (AP World Wide Photo)

Bloomberg replaced the retiring incumbent Rudolph Giuliani, who had earned acclaim for his leadership during the crisis. Congress responded to the terrorist attacks by drafting 123 pieces of emergency appropriation and anti-terrorism legislation in the first seven weeks following September 11; many of these bills and resolutions (including the Patriot Act) were quickly signed into law. The recently elected and relatively untested president, George W. Bush, had perhaps the toughest job of all—reassuring the nation while pursuing an internationally supported military response (Chapter 10). Part of the president's response involved expanding the bureaucracy; President Bush created the Department of Homeland Security and named Pennsylvania Governor Tom Ridge as its first head. The U.S. court system provided the setting for the trials of several individuals charged as accomplices or conspirators in terrorist activity (Chapter 12). The nation's budget, in a year that began with a strong economy, quickly found its surpluses turning to deficits as supplemental appropriations were approved to help pay for recovery and response efforts (Chapter 14). Finally, in the years following 9/11, America has reexamined its approach to both domestic and foreign policy (Chapters 15 and 16). Domestically, we have struggled to determine the most equitable way to run the new Transportation Security Administration. In foreign affairs, we have started to redesign our intelligence infrastructure and have rediscovered deep ideological rifts in preferred approaches to foreign policy—most notably regarding the wars in Iraq and Afghanistan.

Indeed, just as no American was left untouched by the events of September 11, no aspect of American government emerged unscathed either. How have these events affected you, and how have they affected your interactions with the American government? What further changes do you expect in the future?

SOURCE: The Gallup Organization, "One in Four Americans Say Lives Permanently Changed by 9/11," September 8, 2011, http://www.gallup.com/poll/149366/One-Four-Americans-Say-Lives-Permanently-Changed.aspx (June 26, 2012).

Yet on balance, the benefits of fragmented power have been worth the costs, as American constitutional government is now in its third century.

1.4b   A Single and Independent Executive

Although few doubted that the Philadelphia Convention would make provision for a legislature, controversy converged on issues such as representation and manner of selection for that legislature. What is perhaps astonishing about the Constitution is that it provided for a single *and* independently elected executive. Neither the Virginia Plan nor the New Jersey Plan offered both, as Figure 1.1 illustrates. After 1776, executive authority was understandably suspect; determining the kind of executive branch to implement in the new government was thus a topic of debate throughout the summer. State constitutions of the day typically enhanced legislative power and kept governors on a short leash. Some delegates to the Philadelphia Convention favored a plural executive or a single executive responsible to a council or to Congress.

The framers in Philadelphia finally reached a compromise about the selection of a president at the end of the convention. Their creation of the Electoral College, discussed in Chapter 8, meant that the delegates could avoid direct election by the people (a plan that allowed for too much democracy), election by Congress (a plan that would make the executive subservient to the legislature), and election by state legislatures (a plan that might make the executive a puppet of state governments). By allowing for selection of a single individual by specially chosen electors, the Constitution provided independence, strength, and eventually a popular base of power for the president.

1.4c   Adaptability

The Constitution today is a living charter that plays a significant role in government. Yet eighteenth-century men, with eighteenth-century educations, wrote the Constitution for an obscure and fragile eighteenth-century nation. Formal amendment of the document, a process that we will discuss shortly, has taken place only seventeen times since the ratification of the Bill of Rights in 1791. How, then, does a document written in a bygone era by a fledgling nation fit the needs of a world power in the twenty-first century? The answer is that the Constitution is adaptable. It is adaptable both because of particular characteristics built into it and because of the way the document has been regarded by successive generations.

The first factor in its adaptability is *brevity*. Including all twenty-seven amendments, the Constitution of the United States contains fewer than six thousand words, resulting in a shortage of detail and an absence of reference to many things the framers could conceivably have included. (By contrast, the constitutions of the fifty states today tend to be long and detailed; many are also short lived.) Tactically, brevity was wise in the face of the ratification debate—the less said, the less to arouse opposition. Later generations would have to flesh out the full potential of the document through interpretation and practice. For example, the "executive power" that Article II vests in the president is largely undefined.

Second, there is *elasticity* in the language of the Constitution. Some words and phrases do not have a precise meaning. Among Congress's powers listed in Section 8 of Article I is the regulation of foreign and interstate commerce. But what does "commerce" include? In the 1960s Congress prohibited racial discrimination in hotels, restaurants, and other places of public accommodation. Its authority? The power to regulate commerce.[3] Broadly speaking, to regulate commerce is to regulate the economic environment, particularly the buying and selling of goods and services. This meant a fairly narrow range of policies in the 1790s, but the **commerce clause** includes a much broader set of congressional policies today.

Following the list of Congress's powers is the **necessary and proper clause**, which authorizes Congress to pass "all Laws which shall be necessary and proper for carrying into Execution the foregoing Powers." Thus, an indefinite reservoir of implied powers was added to the scope of congressional authority. In different periods of American history this clause—often referred to as the "elastic clause"—has enabled government to meet new challenges and the needs of a changing nation. For instance, as explained in Chapter 2, the Supreme Court long ago relied on the elastic clause to uphold Congress's authority to charter a national bank. According to Chief Justice John Marshall (1801–1835), the Constitution was "intended to endure for ages to come, and consequently to be adapted to the various crises of human affairs."[4] Today, Congress uses that power to extend its reach into issues of public safety, environmental protection, and social welfare that were not contemplated by the very small national government of the late eighteenth century. That being said, the necessary and proper clause is not an infinite power—laws must be related to the prescribed authority, the legislature. When Congress attempts to stretch the elastic clause too far, the Supreme Court exercises its check of judicial review (described below) to rein in legislative overreaching.

Third, the Constitution exalts *procedure* over substance, containing far more about how policies are to be made than about what policies are to be chosen. The Constitution stresses means over ends. The result has been to avoid tying the Constitution, for long periods of time at least, to a certain way of life—whether agrarian, industrial, or technological—or to a certain economic doctrine.

1.4d Amendment of the Constitution

The framers knew that the Constitution must allow for change in its terms if it were to be an enduring force. The near impossibility of amending the Articles of Confederation,

commerce clause

Found in Article I, Section 8, of the Constitution, this clause gives Congress the authority to regulate the country's economic environment

necessary and proper clause

The "elastic clause" of Article I, Section 8, of the Constitution; this is the source of "implied powers" for the national government, as explained in *McCulloch v. Maryland* [17 U.S.(4 Wheaton) 316 (1819)]

after all, drove the framers to scrap the rule of unanimity that the Articles had required. Formal amendment is thus another means of ensuring adaptability.

Yet of the more than five thousand amendments that have been introduced in Congress, only twenty-seven amendments have been added to the document since 1789 (see Table 1.4). Article V of the Constitution mandates that only three-fourths of the states are needed to ratify an amendment to the Constitution. Compared with the Articles of Confederation, amending the Constitution is easier; however, it is still not an easy process. The national constitution is amended much less frequently than are state constitutions.

As shown in Figure 1.3, the Constitution specifies two different tracks for its own amendment: initiation by Congress and initiation by state legislatures. Only the first has been employed successfully. Since 1789 Congress has submitted thirty-three amendments to the states for ratification. Until 1992, all but seven had been approved. Of those to fail, the two most recent were the District of Columbia Amendment, which would have given the district voting representation in Congress, and the Equal Rights Amendment, which would have banned discrimination by government on the basis of gender.

On May 7, 1992, the Twenty-seventh Amendment—long known as the "lost amendment"—became part of the Constitution upon ratification by Michigan, the thirty-eighth state (two additional states ratified it later in May). The Twenty-seventh Amendment declares: "No law, varying the compensation for the services of the Senators and Representatives, shall take effect, until an election of Representatives shall have intervened."

Ironically, this newest amendment is actually one of the oldest. It was among the twelve amendments Congress submitted to the states in 1789. (Ten of this group of amendments became the Bill of Rights. Another, dealing with apportionment of the House of Representatives, was never ratified and is obsolete.) By December 1791, when the Bill of Rights amendments were ratified, only six states had approved the pay amendment. Only one additional state ratified it during all of the nineteenth century, but a drive to revive the amendment began in the late

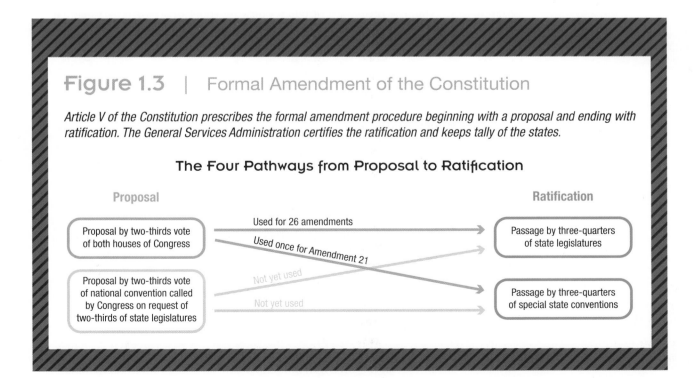

Figure 1.3 | Formal Amendment of the Constitution

Article V of the Constitution prescribes the formal amendment procedure beginning with a proposal and ending with ratification. The General Services Administration certifies the ratification and keeps tally of the states.

The Four Pathways from Proposal to Ratification

Proposal

Ratification

Proposal by two-thirds vote of both houses of Congress

Proposal by two-thirds vote of national convention called by Congress on request of two-thirds of state legislatures

Used for 26 amendments

Used once for Amendment 21

Not yet used

Not yet used

Passage by three-quarters of state legislatures

Passage by three-quarters of special state conventions

Prior to the amendment of the Constitution, not all citizens were guaranteed the right to vote. Today, anyone at least eighteen years of age, of any race, gender, or class, is free to vote. (Shutterstock)

1970s as many people became increasingly frustrated with Congress.

Today, Congress sets a time limit for ratification—usually seven years. An amendment that fails to obtain the required three-fourths approval by the specified date then "dies." No such limit applied to the early amendments. Critics say that accepting the lost amendment as part of the Constitution is a dangerous precedent because allowing the ratification process to be spread over so long a period of time does not guarantee a contemporary national consensus. Others reply that the amendment would not have been revived had there not been such support for setting the limits on congressional powers mandated by the amendment.[5]

The second track for amendment is the closest the Constitution comes to popular initiation of amendments. As depicted in Figure 1.3, the legislatures of two-thirds of the states first make application to Congress for an amendment. Congress then calls a convention, which in turn submits the amendment for ratification by the legislatures (or conventions) of three-fourths of the states. From time to time, people have attempted to amend the Constitution by campaigning for a second convention when Congress declined to propose the desired amendment in the usual way. Recently, efforts to obtain an amendment that would mandate a balanced budget for Congress proceeded along this second and untraveled track. By 1993, thirty-two states—two short of the required number—had petitioned Congress for a convention to propose such an amendment. This thrust from the states led the House of Representatives to pass a balanced-budget amendment on multiple occasions in the 1990s, most recently in March 1997. Had the proposal not fallen one vote short of a two-thirds majority in the Senate, the amendment would have been submitted to the states for ratification. Although some legislators continue to introduce a similar amendment from time to time, since 1997 bipartisan agreements to reduce spending have largely derailed the movement for the amendment. In this instance, Congress used track one of the amendment process to head off the drive along track two. The issue may again rise to the forefront of public debate, as evidenced by the fact that the Ohio legislature voted to petition Congress for this amendment in late 2013.

Grave doubts persist over the wisdom of summoning a second convention. Many questions understandably remain unanswered. *Must* Congress call a convention when two-thirds of the states request one? Would such a convention be limited to proposing the amendment sought by the petitioning states, or could a convention propose other changes in the Constitution? Would the delegates vote as individuals, or would they cast the vote of a state, as was done in 1787? The Constitution does not answer any of these questions.

Aside from formal amendment and judicial interpretation (which we will discuss next), the political system has also changed by custom. Even without changing the words in the Constitution, the public's expectations of governmental institutions continue to evolve. Democratic values, socioeconomic conditions, industrialization, urbanization, and technology have all influenced attitudes and practices. For example,

BVT Lab

Flashcards are available
for this chapter at
www.BVTLab.com.

35

The Constitution of the United States

Chapter 01

political parties—which developed early in our political history—are not mentioned in the Constitution. An even more obvious example of change by custom is the pledge of presidential electors to support their party's ticket, a practice the Constitution does not require. For a very long time members of the Electoral College have been expected to register the choice of the voters on election day, rather than to exercise an independent choice for president and vice president (voters would feel both anger and betrayal if the latter occurred).

1.5 Judicial Review Comes to the Supreme Court

Most changes to the Constitution since its inception have resulted not in adding or deleting words but in applying new meaning to existing words—a task that has largely fallen to the Supreme Court. Through its interpretative powers, the Supreme Court is rather like an ongoing constitutional convention. Thus, we must often look to court cases to interpret the meaning of various parts of the Constitution. Whether the framers intended the Court to occupy a place of such prominence in the political system is uncertain. For more about the Supreme Court and its power of judicial review, see Chapter 12.

1.5a *Marbury v. Madison*: The Case of the Undelivered Commissions

Following the presidential election of November 1800, the nation witnessed the modern world's first peaceful electoral transfer of political power from one party to another.[6] The "out group" of Democratic-Republicans led by Thomas Jefferson (1801–1809) captured the presidency and Congress, displacing the "in group" of Federalists led by President John Adams (1797–1801). Partisan tensions ran high.

In the wake of Adams's defeat, Oliver Ellsworth (1796–1800) resigned as the third chief justice of the U.S. Supreme Court. If Adams moved swiftly, he—and not Jefferson—would be able to make the new appointment. Adams offered the job to John Jay (1789–1795), who had been the first chief justice; Jay declined because he doubted that the Court would ever amount to much. Adams turned next to his secretary of state, John Marshall, who accepted.

Several weeks before the switch in administrations, the Federalist-dominated Congress passed the District of Columbia Act, which authorized the appointment of forty-two new justices of the peace. President Adams made the appointments, much to the displeasure of the Jeffersonians waiting in the wings. This series of events was possible because Congress convened annually in December in those days, which meant that members defeated in the November election (the "lame ducks") were still on hand to make laws. The newly elected Congress would not convene until after the presidential inauguration in March of

The role of the Supreme Court in governing the nation is one of the distinguishing characteristics of the American government. (iStock)

Whose Constitution Is It?

What standard should guide justices of the Supreme Court in deciding what the Constitution means? One approach criticizes the justices for too often substituting their own values in place of those the Constitution explicitly contains. Because the Constitution says nothing about abortion, for instance, and because there is no evidence that those who wrote either the document of 1787 or later amendments intended to include abortion as a protected liberty, they believe the Court was plainly wrong when it ruled in *Roe v. Wade* (1973) that the Constitution protects the right to abortion (see Chapter 3). In place of excessive judicial creativity, the Court relies on "original intent."[1] According to this view, the Supreme Court's task is to give the Constitution the meaning intended by those who wrote it. Whether abortions should be legal thus becomes a question for voters and legislators, not judges.

Others disagree and advance a different approach. Often the original intent is neither knowable nor clear, they argue. Even if it is, whose intent is supposed to matter most—those who wrote the words in the Constitution, those who voted on them at the Philadelphia Convention or (with respect to amendments) in Congress, or those in state ratifying conventions and legislatures? These questions aside, must the nation always be locked into an old way of thinking until the Constitution is formally amended? The Fourteenth Amendment, for example, commands that no state deny to any person the "equal protection of the laws." In its historic decision in *Brown v. Board of Education of Topeka* (1954), discussed in Chapter 3, the Supreme Court concluded that these words prohibited racial segregation in public schools. Yet the same Congress that wrote and proposed the Fourteenth Amendment almost a century earlier also mandated racially segregated schools for the District of Columbia. It is hard to argue that the framers of the Fourteenth Amendment intended to ban a practice they were themselves requiring. Does this mean that the 1954 decision was wrong? No—because the Constitution must be adaptive. According to opponents of "originalism," the Court's task should be one of applying principles, not specific intents. This approach sees in the Constitution the general principle of human dignity. One generation's understanding of human dignity will probably not be the same as another's. The question becomes not what the words meant in 1787 or 1868, but what the words mean in our own time.[2]

Even many proponents of original intent do not disagree with the result of *Brown*. Rather, they say that the Court can be faithful to the intent of the Fourteenth Amendment and still invalidate laws that require racial segregation because the framers of the Fourteenth Amendment, in laying down a command of "equal protection," did not foresee the harmful consequences of forced segregation.

If justices of the Supreme Court interpret the Constitution according to their understanding of the basic principles that the Constitution contains, how do they discover those principles? Why is their view of the values protected by the Constitution somehow superior to the views of state legislators or members of Congress? Should the fundamental law of the land be developed by elected representatives or by appointed judges?

1 Robert H. Bork, *The Tempting of America* (New York: Free Press, 1990), 143–160.

2 William J. Brennan Jr., "The Constitution of the United States: Contemporary Ratification," *American Constitutional Law,* edited by Alpheus T. Mason and D. Grier Stephenson Jr. 16th ed. (New York: Longman, 2011).

---

the following year, a practice that was not changed until ratification of the Twentieth Amendment in 1933.

In the waning hours of the Adams administration, John Marshall—who was still serving as secretary of state—failed to deliver all of the commissions of office to the would-be justices of the peace. Upon assuming office on March 4, 1801, Jefferson held back delivery to some of Adams's appointees and substituted a few of his own. Later that year, William Marbury and three others whom Adams had named as justices of the peace filed suit against Secretary of State James Madison in the Supreme Court. They wanted the Supreme Court to issue a ***writ of mandamus*** to Madison, directing him to hand over the undelivered commissions. (A writ of mandamus is an order issued by a court to a public official, directing performance of a ministerial, or nondiscretionary,

writ of mandamus

Order by a court to a public official to perform a nondiscretionary or ministerial act

act.) Thus, a case was initiated that tested the power of the Supreme Court over another branch of government.

When the Court heard the arguments in the case of *Marbury v. Madison* in February 1803, the Jefferson administration displayed its hostility to Marshall and the other Federalist justices by boycotting the proceeding.[7] By then it was apparent that Marshall and the five associate justices were in a predicament. If the Court issued the writ, Jefferson and Madison would probably disregard it. There would be no one to enforce the order, and the Court would seem powerless and without authority. For the Court to decide that Marbury and the others were not entitled to their judgeships would be an open acknowledgment of weakness and error.

Marshall's decision skillfully avoided both dangers and claimed added power for the Supreme Court, even though Marbury walked out the door empty-handed. First, in a lecture on etiquette to his cousin the president, Marshall made it clear that Marbury was entitled to the job. Second, he ruled that courts could examine the legality of the actions of the head of an executive department. Third, and dispositive, Marshall announced that Marbury was out of luck because the writ of mandamus he requested was not the proper remedy.

Why? Marshall acknowledged that Section 13 of the 1789 Judiciary Act gave the Supreme Court authority to issue a writ as part of the Court's original, as opposed to appellate, jurisdiction. (A court has **original jurisdiction** when a case properly starts in that court and **appellate jurisdiction** when the case begins elsewhere and comes to a higher court for review.) Marshall pointed out that the Supreme Court's original jurisdiction was specified in Article III of the Constitution and included no mention of writs of mandamus. By adding to the Court's original jurisdiction, Section 13 appeared unwarranted by the Constitution. Was the Court to apply an unconstitutional statute? No. To do so would make the statute (and Congress) superior to the Constitution. Section 13, therefore, was void, and the Court was obliged to say so.

1.5b The Significance of *Marbury*

Marbury v. Madison remains important because of what Chief Justice Marshall said about the Constitution and the Supreme Court. First, officers of the government were under the law and could be called to account in court. Second, statutes contrary to the Constitution were not valid laws. Third, the Court claimed for itself the authority to decide what the Constitution means and to measure the actions of other parts of the government against that meaning. This is the power of **judicial review**: Judges holding lifetime appointments can block an electorally responsible agency of government. Alternatively, the law-making body (Congress) would be the judge of its own authority. Fourth, Marshall was answering the rumblings of dissent heard in the **Kentucky and Virginia Resolutions** of 1798. Written, respectively, by Jefferson and Madison (the latter had by now become a foe of strong central government) as an attack on Federalist Party policies, these resolutions claimed for the states final authority to interpret the Constitution. In the words of those resolutions lay the seeds for dismemberment of the Union. Marshall's reply was that the Court would have the final say on the meaning of the Constitution.

1.5c Judicial Review and the Framers

The novelty of the *Marbury* case is that it marked the first instance in which the Supreme Court declared an act of Congress to be in violation of the Constitution. Did the framers intend the Court to have such power? The question cannot be answered with certainty. Some members of the Philadelphia Convention seemed

Marbury v. Madison

Landmark decision [5 U.S. (1 Cranch) 137 (1803)] by the Supreme Court in 1803 establishing the Supreme Court's power of judicial review

original jurisdiction

Authority of a court over cases that begin in that court; courts of general jurisdiction have original jurisdiction over most criminal offenses, the original jurisdiction of the U.S. Supreme Court is very small

appellate jurisdiction

Includes cases a court receives from lower courts; congress defines the appellate jurisdiction of the U.S. Supreme Court

judicial review

The authority of courts to set aside a legislative act as being in violation of the Constitution

Kentucky and Virginia Resolutions

A challenge to national supremacy, these state documents declared states to be the final authority on the meaning of the Constitution

to assume that the Court could set aside laws that ran counter to the Constitution. In *Federalist* No. 78, Alexander Hamilton made an argument in support of judicial review that Marshall followed closely in his *Marbury* ruling. References to judicial review abound in the records of the state ratifying conventions, and some state courts made use of the power well before Marshall did. Moreover, several Supreme Court decisions prior to *Marbury* assumed the existence of judicial review but neither explained nor applied it. Still, if the Court were to possess such a potentially important power, it is strange that the Constitution would not mention it. Neither does the Constitution say anything about how its words are to be interpreted—a question that still divides political leaders and legal scholars. (See "Politics and Ideas: Whose Constitution Is It?")

It is probably safe to say that Marshall's opinion in *Marbury* would not have come as a great surprise to the authors of the Constitution; however, it is also probably true that they did not envision the Court becoming a major policy-maker—a role that the doctrine of judicial review makes possible and that the Court enjoys today, as Chapters 3 and 12 show. In fairness to Marshall, he viewed judicial review as a modest power. Whereas Marshall was not hesitant to strike down state laws that he felt conflicted with the Constitution, it was not until the infamous *Dred Scott* case in 1857—twenty-two years after Marshall's death—that the Supreme Court again set aside an act of Congress as violating the Constitution.[8] (Inflaming abolitionist sentiment on the eve of the Civil War, this decision denied congressional authority to prohibit slavery in the territories and asserted that African Americans were not intended to be citizens under the Constitution.)

Because of judicial review, the changes wrought by custom and formal amendment, and the needs of an expanding nation, what Americans mean by "the Constitution" today is vastly different from the document that emerged from the convention in Philadelphia in 1787. Yet the Constitution, coupled with a commitment to constitutionalism, continues to play a vital role in the third century of American government.

CHAPTER REVIEW

1. The Constitution of the United States is a living document—the charter of the nation—and thus has a presence that gives it a special place in American government.

2. The Declaration of Independence attempted to justify revolution against Great Britain by explaining the purposes of government. The Articles of Confederation represented the first effort at establishing a central government for the newly independent states, but the plan proved to be defective.

3. The Philadelphia Convention in 1787 produced a plan for a new national government that had to be approved by conventions in nine states before going into effect.

4. The Constitution was designed to achieve both effective and limited government: effective by granting powers sufficient for a strong union and limited by restraining and arranging those powers to protect liberty.

5. The possibility of amendment helps explain how the Constitution remains current in its third century. The Constitution has also been remade through interpretation by the courts and through custom and usage.

6. *Marbury v. Madison* brought judicial review to the Constitution in 1803. As a result, the Supreme Court sits as the final authority on the meaning of the Constitution.

KEY TERMS

Readings for Further Study

A Machine That Would Go of Itself, by Michael Kammen (Piscataway, NJ: Transaction, 2006), explores the role of constitutionalism in American life.

Decisions of the Supreme Court interpreting the Constitution are readily found in edited form in casebooks such as Lee Epstein and Thomas G. Walker, *Constitutional Law for a Changing America*, 8th ed. (Washington, DC, CQ Press, 2013).

An explanation of the Constitution, section by section, appears in Sue Davis and J. W. Peltason, *Corwin and Peltason's Understanding the Constitution*, 17th ed. (Belmont, CA: Wadsworth, 2008).

Useful insight into American political thought in the founding era can be gleaned from Gordon S. Wood, *The Creation of the American Republic, 1776–1787*, (Chapel Hill, University of North Carolina Press, 1998).

The Federalist essays are widely available in several editions.

The best collection of antifederalist literature is Herbert J. Storing, ed., *The Complete Anti-Federalist*, 3 vols. (Chicago: University of Chicago Press, 2007).

A wide range of writings from the founding era is collected in Bruce Frohnen, ed., *The American Republic*: Primary Sources (Indianapolis: Liberty Fund, 2002).

Constitutional development since colonial days is the subject of Alfred H. Kelly, Winfred A. Harbison, and Herman Belz, *The American Constitution*, 7th ed., 2 vols. (New York: Norton, 1991).

Notes

1. See Max Farrand, *The Records of the Federal Convention of 1787*, 4 vols. (New Haven, CT: Yale University Press, 1911).

2. John Quincy Adams, *The Jubilee of the Constitution* (New York: Samuel Colman, 1839), p. 55.

3. *Heart of Atlanta Motel v. United States*, 379 U.S. 274 (1964). This is a citation to a Supreme Court decision. "U.S." stands for the *United States Reports*, the official publication containing decisions by the Supreme Court. The number 379 preceding "U.S." and the number 274 following "U.S." indicate the volume and page, respectively, of the *reports* in which the case can be found. For more information about Supreme Court decisions, see Chapter 12.

4. *McCulloch v. Maryland*, 17 U.S. (4 Wheaton) 316, 415 (1819) (emphasis deleted). "Wheaton" was the name of the Supreme Court's reporter of decisions at this time. Until 1875, when the use of "U.S." became the rule, citations to Supreme Court decisions contained the reporter's name. Hence, this case was in volume 4 of the reports published by Henry Wheaton.

5. Marcia Coyle, "No Set Procedure for Amendments," *National Law Journal*, June 1, 1992, p. 10.

6. Richard Hofstadter, *The Idea of a Party System* (Berkeley: University of California Press, 1969), p. 128.

7. 5 U.S. (1 Cranch) 137 (1803).

8. *Scott v. Sanford*, 60 U.S. (19 Howard) 393 (1857).

POP QUIZ

1. The Declaration of Independence contains a strong belief that government is the creation and servant of the _____.

2. Under the Articles of Confederation the _____ retained most political power.

3. Supporters of the proposed Constitution called themselves _____.

4. The _____ authorizes Congress to pass laws allowing it to carry into execution its expressed powers.

5. The British Constitution can be changed by an act of Parliament.   T   F

6. Virtual unanimity existed in the colonies in favor of declaring independence in 1776.   T   F

7. One of the few successes of Congress under the Articles of Confederation was the Northwest Ordinance.   T   F

8. As written, the Constitution facilitates the political parties and interest groups, called *factions* by Madison.   T   F

9. The Constitution of the United States is longer than most state constitutions.   T   F

10. Prior to the American Revolution, what did British leaders in London do?

    A) attempted to force the colonies to raise armies for self defense

    B) repealed the Townshend Acts, allowing the colonies to tax

    C) gave the colonies power to appoint their own governors

    D) attempted to bring the colonies under more direct control

11. Which of the following is not a major theme of the Declaration of Independence?

    A) Humankind shares equality.

    B) Government is a divinely ordained compact between people and God.

    C) The rights that all people intrinsically possess constitute a higher law binding government.

    D) Governments are bound by their own laws.

12. Which of the following was one of the major deficiencies of the Articles of Confederation?

    A) too great a policy-making role for the national courts

    B) the ability of the states to declare war separately

    C) the ease by which the Articles could be amended by the states

    D) the absence of sufficient power in the central government

13. One of the few successes of the Articles of Confederation was the _____.

    A) Annapolis Convention

    B) Northwest Ordinance

    C) Townshend Acts

    D) three-fifths compromise

14. In order for the new Constitution to go into effect, it had to be approved by which of the following?

    A) all of the state legislatures

    B) seven of the thirteen state legislatures

    C) popularly elected conventions in nine states

    D) popularly elected conventions in all of the states

15. The Kentucky and Virginia Resolutions of 1798 did which of the following?

    A) called for the Supreme Court to have the power of judicial review

    B) favored decentralized over centralized judicial review

    C) claimed for the states the final authority to interpret the Constitution

    D) called for Congress to have the power of judicial review

Answers:
1. people   2. states   3. Federalists   4. necessary and proper clause (or elastic clause)   5. T   6. F   7. T   8. F   9. F   10. D   11. B   12. D   13. B   14. C   15. C

Chapter

02

Federalism: States in the Union

In This Chapter

(Shutterstock)

Chapter Objectives

The Constitution established a national government with power dispersed among separate branches. The document also created a second kind of power diffusion: the sharing of power between the national government and individual states. This sharing of power is the principal characteristic of a "federal" system. At its root, federalism is the product and symbol of the continuing struggle between the value of unity and the value of diversity as they compete for dominance in the political system.

This chapter considers the meaning of federalism and why comprehending it is crucial to a full understanding of American government. Continuing tension between national and state governments requires a look at the place of state governments in the Constitution and their role in American politics. The chapter discusses the legal, fiscal, and political relationships among national, state, and local governments.

The national government has progressively become more dominant, but the chapter concludes by reviewing federalism as a complex, adaptable system of relationships in which states have begun to assume a more energetic and vigorous role in domestic policy.

The Idea of Federalism

Federalism is a system of government in which the national government *and* state governments share governmental power within the same political system. As the terrorist attacks on the World Trade Center and Pentagon in 2001, the devastation of Hurricane Katrina in 2005, the recent crises in the financial sector, the BP oil spill of 2010, and concerns about illegal immigration have all demonstrated, a single event may trigger action by officials at both levels of government.

In a federal system, both the national and state governments have jurisdiction over individuals. For example, in preparation for the tax-filing deadline each year, individual citizens perform tasks resulting directly from the existence of a federal system. Taxpayers must file returns with the national government; and in most states (those that choose to have income taxes), they must file returns with state governments as well. The duty of filing national and state tax returns illustrates an important point about federalism: Individuals receive services both from Washington and their state capitals, and they must consequently send money to two different levels of government.

The federal system is a compromise between a strong central government and a league of separate states. Because the states ultimately had to approve any change to the new constitution being created in 1787, the challenge for the framers was clear: How could a stronger national government be created without, at the same time, instilling so much fear in the states that the proposed new structure would be rejected? The states, after all, were already in place. The framers pressed for change, but not so much change that their efforts would fail. The result was a federal system.

2.1a   Confederate, Unitary, and Federal Forms of Government

As Figure 2.1 illustrates, the powers of states and the powers of a central or national government can assume different combinations in different political systems. A **confederation** is a loose collection of states in which principal power lies at the level of the individual state rather than at the level of the central or national government. Individual states, not the central government, have jurisdiction over individuals. As discussed in Chapter 1, the Articles of Confederation made up such a system when they were in force during the decade before the Philadelphia Convention of 1787. Under the Articles, the states retained many important powers.

In contrast to a confederation, a **unitary system** of government is one in which principal power within the political system lies at the level of a national or central government rather than at the level of some smaller unit, such as a state or province. Individual citizens have direct allegiance to the national or central government, which possesses ultimate power to make all political choices and determine public policy. The government of France is an example of a unitary system. The fifty American states are themselves unitary governments with respect to their own local governments. As later discussion in this chapter will make clear, principal power *within* each state lies with the state government rather than with local governments.

Confederations are founded on the political idea of diversity and local control. Such structures allow individual states to pursue diverse approaches to policy matters. On the matter of voting rights, for example, one state might allow every citizen over the age of eighteen to vote, another might require that voters own property, and a third might make the right to vote contingent on passing a literacy test. According

---

federalism

A system of government in which both the national and state governments share power within the same political system

confederation

A loose association of states in which dominant political power lies with the member states and not with the central government

unitary system

A system of government in which principal power lies at the level of a national or central government rather than at the level of some smaller unit (a state or a province) within the political system

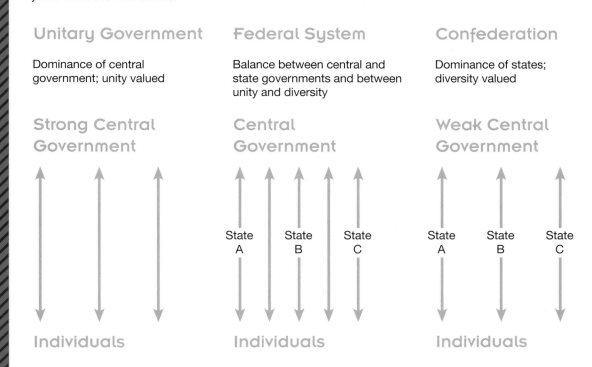

Figure 2.1 | Unitary, Federal, and Confederate

The central government has jurisdiction over individuals in a unitary government. If states or provinces exist, they are symbolic or administrative units with no real power. In a confederation, states are dominant and have jurisdiction over individuals. In a federal system, the central and state governments both have jurisdiction over individuals.

Unitary Government	Federal System	Confederation
Dominance of central government; unity valued	Balance between central and state governments and between unity and diversity	Dominance of states; diversity valued

Strong Central Government	Central Government	Weak Central Government
	State A State B State C	State A State B State C
Individuals	Individuals	Individuals

to the idea of diversity, individual states know best their own people and their own needs. Consequently, individual states ought to have their own powers to pursue individual approaches to the problems they face. On the issue of voter eligibility, consider this: The state of North Dakota does not require its citizens to register to vote. The government of that state has determined that this system is effective at encouraging residents to vote without creating any unintended problems. This is possible, in part, due to a relatively sparse population that allows for very small voting precincts. The much more populous state of New York, on the other hand, has determined that registration twenty-five days before an election is necessary to avoid potential problems with voter fraud. The federal nature of American government allows for such diversity.

Unitary structures rest on the value of unity. Such structures assume that there is a national interest in meeting needs and problems in a particular way. Individuals are citizens of the nation (not of separate states); procedures and approaches to policy problems ought to be uniform rather than individualized and disparate. In the voting rights example, voter qualifications would be determined at the central level in the interest of a unified voting rights policy for all citizens of the nation.

In creating a federal system, the framers of the Constitution sought to change the political structure of a loose collection of states so that the value of unity might be more easily achieved. Although they were moved by a mix of considerations in the move to a national government, the most important were probably the economy, foreign policy, and the military.[1] Foreign and military policies are areas in which centralized approaches are essential to success. Diverse approaches in these areas (e.g., if North Carolina and Massachusetts were to conduct their own foreign policies) would surely make any kind of union among the states impossible. Indeed, this was a major fault of the Articles of Confederation. The weak central government provided by the Articles had no real way to prevent the states from going in separate directions. At the same time, the framers had to acknowledge the continuing existence of diverse states—and their diverse approaches to some areas of public policy.

2.1b   Unity and Diversity in the Federal System

Diversity among the states can be measured in numerous dimensions. States differ in historical traditions, unemployment rates, economic development, ethnic composition, social welfare spending, federal funding, age distributions, religious affiliations, voter turnout rates, degrees of political party competitiveness, and even physical environments.[2] That states differ in physical size and population is readily evident. For example, Rhode Island is a state of just over 1,000 square miles; Alaska, by far the largest state, comprises more than 570,000 square miles. About 541 Rhode Islands could fit into Alaska. California, a state with 38 million people, has about sixty-six times the number of people living in Wyoming.

Per capita income is another measure of state differences. For example, Connecticut in 2013 had a per capita income that was almost double the per capita income of Mississippi.[3] Such basic factors of wealth help to determine how much individual states can tax and how much they can spend on programs such as education and public assistance.

To what degree should physical, economic, and social differences among the states allow diverse public policies, and when should national values prevail? The minimum drinking age and marijuana laws are contemporary issues that illustrate the search for an appropriate balance between state and national approaches to public policy—more than two centuries after the framers originally wrestled with the problem. The repeal of Prohibition in 1933 granted to the states the power to regulate alcohol in whatever ways they saw fit. States had various minimum drinking ages ranging from eighteen to twenty-one. By the early 1980s, the problem of drunk driving had received national attention. People under age twenty-one were found to be responsible for a disproportionate number of alcohol-related traffic fatalities and injuries. In response to growing pressure from groups such as Mothers Against Drunk Driving (MADD), Congress enacted a measure withholding a portion of national highway funds from

MADD's then-president Millie Webb holds an image of her late nineteen-month-old nephew Mitchell Pewitt as she speaks during MADD's twentieth-anniversary rally. (AP World Wide Photo)

individual states unless the states raised their minimum drinking age to twenty-one. Whether there should be a national drinking age or whether the individual states ought to decide their own minimum drinking age is a classic example of the types of debates that arise in a federal system. Is the value of unity (a national approach) more or less important than the value of diversity (individual state approaches) in a matter that has been the states' own prerogative for more than half a century?

Debate over the decriminalization or legalization of marijuana for medicinal or recreational use illustrates the same question. Although national laws prohibiting the use of certain narcotics have existed since 1914, it was not until the early 1970s that the national "War on Drugs" took its present form, with the establishment of a comprehensive drug policy and creation of the federal Drug Enforcement Administration. Concerns about high enforcement and incarceration costs, lack of effective prevention efforts, and questions surrounding the costs and benefits of marijuana for some medicinal uses led several states to balk at the federal policy. In 1996, California voters passed a law making it legal—under state law—for residents to possess marijuana for personal medicinal use. Since then twenty other states and the District of Columbia have passed similar laws, creating an awkward situation where medical marijuana use is a violation of federal law, but not state law, in over one-third of the country. The states of Washington and Colorado have approved marijuana for recreational use as well as medical use. The Supreme Court has upheld the federal government's authority to regulate marijuana, but the tension between federal and state law has made marijuana decriminalization a hot political issue in the twenty-first century. Should there be a uniform national law on marijuana use, or should states decide for themselves the acceptable use of this drug within their borders?

2.1c   A Comparative Perspective on Federalism

Federalism is not unique to the United States. Other countries that have federal constitutional systems include Australia, Brazil, India, Malaysia, Nigeria, Pakistan, Switzerland, and Venezuela. Although such countries may differ in size, wealth, and military power, what is common among them is their attempt to pull together disparate groups while at the same time acknowledging the groups' separate identities. The search for the appropriate balance in power between the states and the national government in the United States resonates in other federal systems as well.

Daniel Elazar, the renowned federalism scholar, wrote that "[f]ederalism has to do with the need of people and polities to unite for common purposes yet remain separate to preserve their respective integrities. It is rather like wanting to have one's cake and eat it too."[4] Groups in federal systems might be cultural or language minorities, people living in geographical units whose history predates the creation of the federal system, or different religious denominations in which no single one is dominant. Federal systems have pulled together, or tried to, French and English speakers, Lithuanians and Ukrainians, and Pennsylvanians and New Yorkers. Such groups get together for purposes such as a common defense or a common currency, but they retain their separate identities for other purposes, such as education or law enforcement.

The relative power of the central government and constituent groups will vary among countries, but federal systems generally have a dynamic quality in which there

> **D**espite their name, the Antifederalists actually favored federalism. A collection of their views on the need for strong government can be found at this site.
>
> http://www.bvtlab.com/78q88

is a continuing search for the appropriate balance between national purposes and group needs. Some of the world's great political conflicts are essentially struggles to define this balance. For example, debate over the political status of French-speaking Quebec—the only one of Canada's ten provinces with a French majority—has strained Canadian politics for years. Whether Quebec can, or will, go it alone remains a troubling issue for Canada.

The dissolution of the Soviet Union is an illustration of how changes in a federal system can have momentous implications for world politics. The Soviet Union, a military superpower, was comprised of fifteen republics held together by the Communist Party and backed by the threat of military force. Unchallenged central control made the system federal in name only. Worsening economic conditions, the emergence of ethnic demands, and attempts at liberal reforms showed cracks in the system. After an attempted coup by Communist Party hard-liners failed in 1991, the central government's power over the fifteen Soviet republics dwindled sharply. Individual republics declared their independence, and what was left of the Soviet Union quickly unraveled. The Soviet government officially disbanded several months after the failed coup and was replaced by the Commonwealth of Independent States in which the republics retained their independent status.[5] Today, the former Soviet republics are largely autonomous states, allying themselves when appropriate via international treaties and organizations, but displaying few traces of the once forced federal relationship.

2.2 States in the Constitutional System

That there are fifty states is a historical accident. If wars had been lost instead of won, if treaties and land purchases had not been made, if rivers coursed through different areas, the number, names, and sizes of states would be different. States are integral parts of our social and political consciousness. State boundaries are superimposed on satellite pictures of weather patterns. State universities enjoy great attention through the exploits of their athletic teams, and children in elementary schools throughout the land spend time trying to memorize the names of state capitals. The existence of states is a ubiquitous part of American life.

States play a crucial role in the American political system. They administer social welfare policies, grapple with regional problems, amend the Constitution, and shape electoral contests at the national level. States act in some measure as administrative units to help carry out national social welfare programs substantially funded by Congress, such as the Supplemental Nutrition Assistance Program (SNAP), Medicaid, and Temporary Assistance for Needy Families (TANF). Through the device of the **interstate compact**, states can enter into formal agreements with other states to deal with policy problems that cross state lines. An example is the agreement between New York and New Jersey to establish the New York Port Authority to regulate transportation in the New York City area. States also play a role in the process of formally amending the Constitution. Although controversy between states has raged over a variety of proposed amendments—involving issues like abortion, flag burning, and a balanced budget—no formal change to the Constitution can be made without the states considering, debating, and voting on the issue.

interstate compact

A formal agreement between states designed to solve a problem faced by more than one state when such an agreement is necessary because political problems are not limited by geographic boundaries

With the exception of the president and vice president of the United States, every elected official in the country is chosen either by all the voters in a particular state (the governor or a U.S. senator) or by voters in part of a state (U.S. representatives or state legislators). Every elected official, except for the president and vice president, has a geographic constituency that is either a state or part of a state, such as a county or a congressional district. This simple but crucial fact helps to explain much legislative behavior at the national level, such as when members of Congress press for national legislation that helps industries in their home states or oppose the closing of military bases in their districts.

The **Electoral College**, a political institution that—following the mandate in the Constitution—determines the winner in presidential elections, is another illustration of the role of the

State governments act as administrators to carry out national social welfare policies such as welfare benefits, SNAP, EBT (Electronic Benefit Transfer), Medicaid, and TANF programs. (AP World Wide Photo)

states. Presidents are elected not by a plurality (the highest number) of votes cast by voters throughout the United States, but by a majority of Electoral College votes. Each state has a number of electoral votes equal to the number of its members in the House and Senate combined. Because the number of representatives is determined by population, the states with larger numbers of people have a larger number of electoral votes. California, for example, has fifty-five electoral votes, whereas Delaware has only three. In every state but two, the presidential candidate receiving the largest number of popular votes in that state receives all of that state's electoral votes.[6]

In effect, on the day of the presidential election, fifty-one separate elections are taking place (in the fifty states and the District of Columbia). Voters choose among slates of electors committed to one or another of the candidates. When the popular votes in each state are counted, state-by-state Electoral College vote totals are combined to determine the presidential victor. After the election, victorious electors officially cast their presidential votes in their respective state capitals. From the perspective of federalism, the important point is that *states as states* play a crucial role in electing the person who holds the most important political office in the land. Presidential candidates must appeal not to an amorphous mass of citizens but to Texans, North Carolinians, Californians, and Virginians.

The center of the U.S. population changes as more and more people follow the sun and move to the South and the West. Florida, California, and Texas have gained population, while New York, Ohio, Pennsylvania, Illinois, and Michigan have suffered relative losses. Such population changes have implications for power shifts in the U.S. House and in the Electoral College. Table 2.1 shows the shifts in regional power between 1950 and 2015. Since the 2010 census, more than one in four members of the U.S. House come from California, Texas, or Florida, and the presidential candidate winning California receives 20 percent of the electoral votes needed to win the presidency.

Electoral College

Institution established by the Constitution for electing the president and vice president and whose members— electors chosen by the voters—actually elect the president and vice president

table 2.1 | Shifts in Regional Power: 1950 and 2015, as Measured by the Size of State Delegations in the U.S. House of Representatives

Shifts and changes in population between 1950 and 2015 meant that over the past sixty-five years parts of the East and the Midwest have lost seats in the House of Representatives, while the West and South have gained seats. The apportionment of the 435 House seats is calculated for each state following the census every ten years. A state may increase its population but lose a seat if the rate of gain in other states is much greater.

Region/State	1950	2015	Region/State	1950	2015
Mountains and Plains	**29**	**36**	**Midwest**	**117**	**85**
Montana	2	1	Minnesota	9	8
Wyoming	1	1	Wisconsin	10	8
North Dakota	2	1	Michigan	17	14
South Dakota	2	1	Iowa	8	4
Nebraska	4	3	Illinois	26	18
Kansas	6	4	Indiana	11	9
New Mexico	2	3	Ohio	23	16
Arizona	2	9	Missouri	13	8
Utah	2	4	**East**	**127**	**87**
Idaho	2	2	Maine	3	2
Colorado	4	7	New Hampshire	2	2
South	**128**	**152**	Vermont	1	1
West Virginia	6	3	Massachusetts	14	9
Virginia	9	11	Connecticut	6	5
Oklahoma	8	5	Rhode Island	2	2
Arkansas	7	4	New York	45	27
Kentucky	9	6	Pennsylvania	33	18
North Carolina	12	13	New Jersey	14	12
Tennessee	10	9	Maryland	6	8
South Carolina	6	7	Delaware	1	1
Texas	21	36	**West**	**34**	**75**
Louisiana	8	6	Washington	6	10
Mississippi	7	4	Oregon	4	5
Alabama	9	7	California	23	53
Georgia	10	14	Nevada	1	4
Florida	6	27	Arkansas	N/A	4
			Hawaii	N/A	2

N/A = not applicable

As Chapter 1 made clear, the states were clearly dominant under the Articles of Confederation. The national government quite literally started out from nothing; yet we have today a national government whose actions—from delivering Social Security checks to regulating the safety of toys and power plants—pervade the daily lives of citizens. How did this change come about? Massive technological, communication, and economic changes have transformed the nation over the past two centuries. War and depression have made their own contributions to the shift in focus of demands and expectations.

The conflict between unity and diversity, which gave birth to the federal system, also shaped the relationships between the national and state governments in the early decades of the new nation. The national government cooperated with the states in a variety of areas. Because economic development was among the highest of priorities for the new nation, the national government provided funds and technical assistance to the states for construction of roads and canals. Land grants to states in the West for educational purposes signaled greater cooperation between the national government and the states to come.[7]

Despite the cooperation, however, sharp conflicts also occurred between the national government and the states in the early decades of the Republic. The Kentucky and Virginia Resolutions, adopted by the legislatures of those states in 1798, held that the Constitution created a compact among the states and that the power of the national government was sharply limited by the states. In 1819 the state of Maryland contested the right of the national government to establish a national bank (leading to the Supreme Court case *McCulloch v. Maryland*, discussed in the following section), and in 1832 the South Carolina legislature declared a national tariff law null and void. The very existence of national power was at issue in these instances of nation/state conflict.

The federal system was ultimately tested in war. The early skirmishes between the national government and the states paled in significance compared to the Civil War. At one level, the war was about the question of slavery; at another level, the war was about the question of federalism. Could a state (or several states) leave the Union and, in effect, unravel the work of the Constitutional Convention of 1787? From the perspective of federalism, the most important consequence of the war was preservation of the Union. President Lincoln is best known as emancipator of the slaves, but his sharp and unyielding refusal to allow dissolution of the Union was crucial in the evolution of federalism. The significance of Lincoln's stance cannot be overstated. Lincoln, the chief executive in a national government that had not even existed a century earlier, used *national* resources in a major war effort to resist by brute force the claims of the seceding states—four of which predated the national government itself.

The end of the Civil War marked the beginning of a rapid change in the character of the nation's economy. Transcontinental railroads pulled the nation together and brought farmers, producers, and sellers closer to buyers and consumers. Major new industries—such as steel, oil, and, later, the automobile—began to emerge. With them came new forms of economic organization. Corporations crossed state boundaries in their activities and their effects. Control and regulation of economic matters increasingly eluded the grasp of any single state, resulting in political demands by the states that the national government confront the problems that economic monopolies left in their trail.

Later, in the twentieth century, the economy plunged into the Great Depression of the 1930s. Farm and industrial prices collapsed, factories closed, banks failed, homes were foreclosed, and unemployment rates rose dramatically. State and local governments were overwhelmed by the needs and demands of millions of Americans who clearly needed help to survive. National problems seemed to require national solutions. As never before, the national government embarked on a series of social welfare policies—known as the New Deal—that both improved the economic conditions of many and generated expectations that the national government could solve a variety of social problems in the future. Today many domestic programs administered by the states or their localities are funded by the national government.

Finally, the national government is responsible for national security and relations with other nations. In the twentieth century, the Cold War and the increasing interdependence of the world economy combined to make the national government's conduct of foreign affairs important on a continuing basis.

A twenty-two-year-old mother with her children camped in a resettlement camp for migrants during the Great Depression. (Library of Congress)

Although the Cold War has ended, demands for a revitalized military establishment remain strong; and the need for national government policies to enhance the nation's competitiveness in the global economy have become more acute.

The seemingly inexorable rise in the power of the national government has been accompanied by political demands that state and local governments assume a larger presence in the making of policy decisions affecting them. For example, **New Federalism**—a term most closely associated with the Republican administrations of Richard Nixon (1969–1974) and Ronald Reagan (1981–1989)—calls for state and local governments to assume a much greater role than they traditionally had during the explosions of national policy initiatives that took place during the Democratic administrations of Franklin Roosevelt (1933–1945) (the New Deal) and Lyndon Johnson (1963–1969) (the Great Society).[8] New Federalism took on a new life during the George W. Bush (2001–2009) administration, this time in the form of calling for state self-reliance during crises and scaling back federal environmental regulations. New Federalism holds that not only should state and local governments be entrusted with greater responsibilities but that they should also be allowed to follow their own best judgment in making decisions. Giving state and local governments more discretion in how they spend national grant money is an illustration. This view of federalism dovetails with the traditional Republican Party "grassroots" philosophy that the government in the best position to make good policy choices is the government "closest" to the people. Whether nationally defined policy goals, such as the amelioration of poverty, can (or should) accommodate state and local policies that may diverge from those goals is an old question in federalism.

2.2b Express and Implied Powers

The search for the right balance between state and national power remains an enduring issue in the federal system. What powers do the states have in their relationships to each other and to the national government? What powers does the national government have over the states? The Republic has struggled with these questions since 1787. The Constitution prohibits the exercise of some powers by

New Federalism

A view of federalism that posits an expanded role for state and local governments and holds that state and local governments should be entrusted with greater responsibilities

one or both levels of national and state governments; for example, states may not coin money. In addition, national and state governments share some *concurrent* powers, such as the power each has to tax the same individual's income. However, the most important point about national and state powers is the distinction between *delegated* and *reserved* powers.

In accepting the Constitution, the people in the states—through the ratification process—delegated important powers to the new national government. The statement of these powers is contained in Article I, Section 8, of the Constitution (see the Appendix). **Delegated powers** are ordinarily divided into two types: express powers and implied powers. **Express powers** are specifically enumerated as belonging to Congress. Among these are the powers to levy and collect taxes, to borrow money, to regulate interstate commerce, to coin money, to declare war, and to raise and support armies.

However, the last statement of power listed in Article I, Section 8, also delegates to the national government **implied powers**, which by their very nature have been subject to intense dispute. As discussed in Chapter 1,

Keep up-to-date on the latest developments in state politics at the Council of State Governments website.

http://www.bvtlab.com/727EB

this provision is also known as the elastic or necessary and proper clause and delegates to Congress the power "to make all Laws which shall be necessary and proper for carrying into Execution the foregoing Powers, and all other Powers vested by this Constitution in the Government of the United States, or in any Department or Officer thereof." Obviously, what is "necessary and proper" in a particular circumstance is a matter open to varying interpretations. A narrow interpretation would constrict the powers of the national government, whereas a broad interpretation would enlarge them.

The first time the clause was specifically interpreted was in *McCulloch v. Maryland*, one of the most famous and consequential Supreme Court decisions ever made.[9] The case represented an ideological division over the powers of the national government and the place of the states in the Union. Conflicting political objectives were sought in terms of opposing theories of federalism. Congress had chartered a national bank. Some states opposed the bank because it competed with state-chartered banks. Hoping to put the national bank out of business, Maryland imposed a tax on the new bank. McCulloch, its cashier, refused to pay. As part of its case, Maryland argued not only that a state could tax a nationally chartered bank but also that Congress had no authority to charter a bank in the first place because banking was not a power delegated to Congress. Instead, Maryland claimed, banking was a power the Constitution reserved for the states.

Contrary to Maryland's claims, Chief Justice John Marshall (1801–1835) declared that Congress possessed ample constitutional authority to charter a bank, even though such a power was not expressly listed in the Constitution. In Marshall's view, the power to establish a bank was implied in the express powers, such as the powers to tax and to coin money. A bank was a means to achieving the ends spelled out in the Constitution. Marshall's interpretation of the necessary and proper clause clearly allowed expansive power to the national government. In his memorable words,

> Let the end be legitimate, let it be within the scope of the Constitution, and all means which are appropriate, which are plainly adapted to that end, which are not prohibited, but consistent with the letter and spirit of the constitution, are constitutional.

delegated powers

Legal authority that the people in the states granted to the national government for certain purposes by ratifying the Constitution; can be either express or implied

express powers

Powers specifically enumerated in the Constitution as belonging to the national government

implied powers

Powers of national government that are not specifically cited in the Constitution but that are implicit in powers expressly granted by the Constitution

McCulloch v. Maryland

Supreme Court case in 1819 that established the constitutionality of a national bank and solidified national power by confirming that the federal government can exercise implied powers to carry out legitimate and otherwise constitutional ends

Furthermore, Marshall held that Maryland could not tax the bank because it was an instrument of the national government. In a conflict between an act of Congress and a state law, the former would prevail. No single part of the political community could be allowed to subvert a policy undertaken by the whole community represented in Congress.

Because of the brevity of the Constitution, many of its clauses and phrases are ambiguous and give little or no direction as to what is "legitimate" in a particular circumstance. The framers could not address every problem or clarify every uncertainty. According to Marshall's decision in *McCulloch*, the Constitution created a stronger national government by delegating to it express and implied powers. Exactly how strong it was to be or how it would evolve was left for later generations to decide.

2.2c   Reserved Powers: What Do the States Do?

If the new government was to be more powerful and the states were, nonetheless, to continue to exist, what powers were left to the states? Although simpler in theory than in practice, the principle is that states can do all things not specifically prohibited to them and not delegated exclusively to the national government. These remaining powers are known as **reserved powers**. State and local governments are responsible for delivering the vast majority of public services. About 2.7 million civilian employees work for the national government, a number that has decreased slightly since a peak of 3.1 million in 1990. However, growth in government employment has occurred at the state and local levels. The most recently reported figures, in 2012, indicate that state and local governments employ just over 19.2 million people—about seven times the number of civilian employees working for the national government.[10] This number of employees indicates that states and localities play a large role in providing public services.

The **Tenth Amendment** states that "the powers not delegated to the United States by the Constitution, nor prohibited by it to the States, are reserved to the States respectively, or to the people." Politicians and groups whose political ideas are served by advocating "states' rights" have frequently pointed to the Tenth Amendment as support for their claims. However, that amendment, unlike the Articles of Confederation, does not contain the word *expressly* in citing powers delegated to the national government. Such delegated powers therefore include the implied powers cited by Chief Justice Marshall in *McCulloch v. Maryland*.

Among powers reserved for the states are "police" responsibilities for the health, safety, and welfare of citizens. For civilized life to be possible, people must be able to carry on their day-to-day activities with the reasonable assurance that physical threats to their health and well-being are kept to an absolute minimum. For example, among the health responsibilities of states are those such as dealing with outbreaks of contagious diseases, the disposal of wastes, cleanliness in public eating establishments, and the administration of networks of state hospitals and mental institutions.

In one of their most visible roles, the states also have primary responsibility for preventing and prosecuting criminal activities. Most of this work occurs at the level of local governments whose organization, powers, and functions are constitutionally subject to control by state governments. Some crimes, such as airline hijacking, kidnapping, tampering with U.S. mail, and counterfeiting money, are violations of national law enforced by the national government. However, most law enforcement officers in the country are state agents and local personnel who act as agents of the state. From state police officers to county sheriffs who track down suspected criminals

reserved powers

Powers not specifically prohibited to the states and not delegated to the national government by the Constitution

Tenth Amendment

Amendment ratified in 1791 that reserves to the states powers not prohibited to them and not delegated to the national government by the Constitution

to the local police who deal with matters such as burglary and domestic violence, most law enforcement responsibilities lie at the state and local levels. Most suspected rapists, murderers, thieves, burglars, muggers, and assorted swindlers are pursued only by state and local law enforcement personnel, prosecuted only in state courts, and incarcerated only in state prisons.

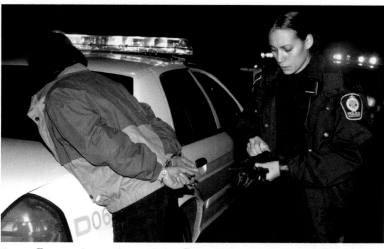

State officers, such as police and sheriffs, track down suspected criminals—rapists, murderers, thieves, burglars, muggers, and assorted swindlers. These suspects are tried and prosecuted primarily in state courts and incarcerated primarily in state prisons. (Shutterstock)

Sometimes these state police powers and national policy interests come into conflict. The Constitution grants the national government control over immigration via the power to "establish a uniform Rule of Naturalization" in Article I, Section 8. Despite a thorough set of federal immigration laws, some states, frustrated by increases in illegal immigration, have enacted their own statutes. In 2010 Arizona passed a law making it a state crime to be in the country illegally, banning undocumented immigrants from working in the state, authorizing police to arrest individuals they suspect of having committed a deportable offense upon probable cause, and requiring police to check the immigration status of everyone they detain. In the 2012 case *Arizona v. United States*, the Supreme Court held the first three of these provisions to be unconstitutional because they are preempted by federal laws and sent the fourth back for further review by the lower courts.[11]

Most individuals encounter state power in a direct and personal way many times in their lives. A variety of inoculations and vaccinations may be required by the state before entrance into the elementary school system. To drive a car, you must apply for a state driver's license and pass a driver's test administered by a state officer. Individuals who wish to marry must apply for a state marriage license, and the ceremony is performed either by a state public official (such as a justice of the peace) or by an individual (often a religious leader, like a minister, priest, or rabbi) who acts as an agent of the state in performing the ceremony. In divorce, the contesting parties must go through some state judicial proceeding to legally dissolve the relationship; and when the custody of children is at issue, state courts are called on to make the decision.

States also play a regulatory role in a variety of matters having to do with business and commerce within the state. From laws on safety to zoning practices to requirements for filing periodic tax and information reports—practically no enterprise can escape the touch of the state. Entrance into many professions is controlled by state licensing boards, which set rules, regulations, and standards that are supposed to ensure the quality of services delivered to citizens, but which also serve to limit entry into the profession. Such licensing procedures touch barbers, lawyers, medical specialists, dietitians, cosmetologists, real estate agents, and even taxidermists.

Perhaps the most visible and pervasive role of the state is in the area of public education. State policies of universal education have emerged from a belief in the importance of schools for improving literacy, inculcating civic and cultural values, and generally enhancing the capabilities of citizens. In administering educational systems, local school districts are agencies of the state. Curricula, certification of teachers, length of the school year, and policy on truancy are all matters of state power and

Handling a Hurricane: Federalism and Disaster Relief

In August 2005 a Category 5 hurricane formed in the Atlantic Ocean. Dubbed Hurricane Katrina, the storm caused severe damage all along the Gulf Coast, affecting Florida, Mississippi, and especially the city of New Orleans, Louisiana. According to a report from the National Hurricane Center, at least 1,833 people died as a result of the storm, many thousands more lost their homes and/or businesses, and the financial damages were in excess of $81 billion.[1] Several years after Katrina struck, many of those affected remained without adequate housing; and many communities, particularly in New Orleans, had not been rebuilt.

The emergency response to Katrina involved dozens of government agencies. Due to our federal system of government, agencies at all three levels—national, state, and local—were involved in the rescue efforts. Initially a matter of local responsibility, the scope of this disaster quickly led the federal government to declare a national emergency and to instruct the Federal Emergency Management Agency (FEMA) to take the lead. An agency within the Department of Homeland Security, FEMA has as its mission "to lead the effort to prepare the nation for all hazards and effectively manage federal response and recovery efforts following any national incident."[2] In this case, that responsibility included coordinating the efforts of numerous agencies, such as the U.S. Army Corps of Engineers, as well as cooperating with state and local agencies like the Louisiana Department of Health and Hospitals, and nongovernmental agencies like the American Red Cross.

The difficulty of coordinating all of these agencies—each with its own goals, training, and procedures—led to inefficiencies, redundancies, and criticism. At the heart of the matter was whether or not FEMA had mishandled the relief efforts, in effect making the situation worse than it should have been. Politicians and media pundits accused FEMA Director Michael Brown of incompetence, and the director soon resigned under pressure. However Brown claimed that the disaster agency had itself been a disaster even before he had taken control. Polls conducted in the weeks following the hurricane suggested that a majority of Americans thought state and local officials and the residents of New Orleans, as well as President Bush and FEMA, had failed to respond well.[3] Whoever was to blame, the American public was left with the impression that their government, at many levels, had let them down.

What is the proper balance of responsibility between federal, state, and local levels of government in disaster relief? Should the federal government's superior financial resources supersede concerns about over-centralization? Should the federal government foot the bill but then defer to the potentially greater expertise of state and local agencies when it comes to implementation? How did the public react to the government's failure to respond promptly to this emergency? A majority of the New Orleans population is African American. This fact, combined with an inadequate government response, led 60 percent of African Americans (but only 12 percent of whites) to conclude that race was a factor in the government's slow response.[4] What factors point to support, or lack of support, for this claim? With the benefit of hindsight, was the government's response to Hurricane Katrina appropriate or inappropriate? Why?

1   Richard D. Knabb, Jaime R. Rhome, and Daniel P. Brown, National Hurricane Center, "Tropical Cyclone Report: Hurricane Katrina," August 10, 2006, http://www.nhc.noaa. gov/pdf/TCR-AL122005_Katrina.pdf (October 5, 2006).

2   "About FEMA," August 3, 2006, http://www.fema.gov/about/index. shtm (October 5, 2006).

3   The Gallup Poll, "Blacks Blast Bush for Katrina Response," September 14, 2005, http://www.galluppoll. com/content/?ci=18526&pg=1, (October 6, 2006).

4   Ibid.

(iStock)

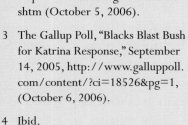

concern. Some of the great policy debates of the past generation have focused on the role of the states in education. Should prayers be said aloud in the schools, or should a moment of silence for "meditation" be allowed at the beginning of each school day? Should schools be desegregated, and if so, how? Should the busing of schoolchildren be required to achieve integration? Should states be required to equalize expenditures among wealthier and poorer school districts? The *national* government can pursue *national* approaches, but its stress on unity can limit or threaten diversity among the states. Educational policy debates illustrate the vitality of the federal system. When should the national government have its way, and when should the states be allowed to go their separate ways? In recent years, the federal No Child Left Behind law has challenged traditional answers to these questions.

2.2d   Local Government: A Political Landscape of Contrasts

One of the reserved powers of the states is their control over the structure and powers of local governments. The Constitution makes no mention of city or other local governments, only of the nation's capital, the "Seat of Government." This fact makes local governments "creatures of the state." The relationships between state legislatures (traditionally with a rural bias) and local governments, especially those of larger cities, have frequently been stormy. Through much of the nineteenth century, state legislatures kept local governments on a tight leash by determining with great specificity their powers, functions, and procedures. In the late nineteenth century and the first half of the twentieth century, however, many local governments—particularly those of larger cities—were granted **home rule**: the power to determine, within broad limits, their own powers and functions. In the 1960s local governments (again, those of larger cities, in particular) increasingly developed relationships—generally created by flows of cash—directly with the national government. Nonetheless, all local governments are, according to the Constitution, agents of the state, performing what are constitutionally state functions.

As shown in Table 2.2, more than ninety thousand local governments exist in the United States. These local governments perform many of the unglamorous services essential to civilized life, such as collecting trash, pursuing criminals, putting out fires, and providing drinking water. Local governments range in size from huge cities like New York with more than eight million people (more than in forty entire states) to small villages and hamlets with fewer than one hundred inhabitants. Governments at the local level differ in their structure. Some have a **mayor-council** form of government, which mirrors the executive-legislative structure at the state and national levels. Others have a **council-manager** form in which appointed managers look after the day-to-day operations of the government. Still others have a commission form of government in which power is diffused, and no single individual is in charge. Some local governments are "general purpose"—that is, they are responsible for a wide variety of functions including police protection, housing, social services, and parks administration. School districts and special districts overlap these general-purpose governments and are limited to a single function, such as education, mosquito control, fire protection, or transportation.

Although residents do not usually pay much attention to local government, they can and do get intensely interested during a local crisis or controversy. For example, when the water supply becomes polluted with toxic waste, citizens get involved. School board meetings can be drab affairs, but they can become arenas of excitement and drama when matters such as sex education programs or higher taxes to fund a new school are at stake. Similarly, most local zoning board hearings are routine and

home rule

A legal status in which local governments, especially large cities, can determine for themselves within broad parameters their own powers and functions without interference from the state government

mayor-council

A form of government at the local level that mirrors the executive-legislative structure at the state and national levels where the mayor has executive powers and the council has legislative powers

council-manager

A form of government at the local level where an elected council exercises legislative powers and hires a city manager to perform executive and administrative duties

table 2.2 | Governmental Units in the Federal System

The federal system contains many governments, but they do not all do the same things. The national government, all state governments, and many local governments are general-purpose governments; that is, they perform a wide variety of functions. A city government, for example, will typically provide police protection and numerous social services. School districts and special districts geographically overlap with general-purpose governments and perform only a single function, such as education, water distribution, fire protection, or sewage treatment. The largest growth in number of governmental units in recent years has occurred in special districts, due to the fact that they enable local areas to collectively provide services that they could not afford individually. Moreover, the particular tasks of special districts often stretch beyond the boundaries of local general-purpose governments. Finally, some local governments, such as towns or townships, have not been given power by their state constitutions and governments to perform such functions.

1	National government
50	State governments
90,056	Local governments
3,031	Counties (called parishes in Louisiana)
16,360	Towns and townships
19,519	Municipal governments
12,880	School districts
38,266	Special districts

SOURCE: U.S. Census Bureau, 2012 Census of Governments, September 2013.

sparsely attended, but proposals such as a hamburger chain seeking to locate near a predominantly residential area, or the efforts of a chemical company to place a toxic waste facility in or near a town, are issues that practically guarantee action by affected residents. In terms of size, structure, function, and degree of citizen interest, local governments are a mosaic of contrasts.

2.3 Government Relationships in the Federal System

The existence of different levels of government within a federal system means that federalism is about *relationships* among governments.[12] Because these governmental relationships are intangible and constantly shifting and changing, trying to understand them is not an easy task. Unlike the presidency, for example, federalism is not an institution with a physical place where its work is done; however, one way to understand federalism is to picture it as a series of *legal*, *fiscal*, and *political* relationships among levels of government.

The federal system can at first appear to be a jumble of intangible relationships without obvious order or meaning. The effort to create models is an attempt to create pictures or portraits that bring some order to the complexity and chaos. Two models are particularly important.

The first is **dual federalism**, a model positing the view that national and state governments are separate and independent from each other, with each level exercising its own powers in its own jurisdiction. This model, supporting the rights of the states, was important as a judicial theory of federalism in the nineteenth and early twentieth centuries. In *Hammer v. Dagenhart*[13] (a decision the justices later overturned) the Supreme Court ruled that Congress could not ban shipment across state lines of products made with child labor because labor regulation was a state power only.

Dual federalism was never a completely realistic description of the relationship between the nation and the states. For example, in the nineteenth century the national government gave land to the states to use for educational purposes. Indeed, some of the nation's great universities today are among the "land grant" institutions that resulted from this policy. The model does reflect, however, the fact that the state and national governments in much of the nineteenth and early twentieth centuries did not interact with each other with the regularity taken for granted today. Dual federalism is also known as the "layer cake" model because the separate levels of government in the model are likened to distinct layers of a cake.

The second model is **cooperative federalism**. In this model, national and state governments share a number of tasks that had previously been the exclusive domain of only one level of government. Cooperative federalism is sometimes called "marble cake" federalism because it is a view of federalism that likens the intertwining relationships between the national and state and local governments to the intertwining flavors in a marble cake.[14] Cooperative federalism best describes the system that developed as a result of the expansion of national government roles in the twentieth century, particularly after implementation of the New Deal and Great Society programs. Across a wide range of public policies, despite occasional conflict, all levels of government work closely with one another. Minnesotans and Georgians are also Americans, and that fact helps to explain the intermingling of governmental functions. Interstate highways are largely funded by federal grants, but the highways are built and patrolled by the states. National and state governments jointly fund medical care for the poor. National, state, and local law enforcement authorities regularly combine forces in pursuit of criminals such as drug smugglers, bank robbers, and suspected murderers whose escape routes take them across state lines. State and local health authorities call on the expert services of the national Centers for Disease Control and prevention when outbreaks of contagious or mysterious diseases threaten communities. State environmental and health agencies work with national units, such as the Environmental Protection Agency or the Nuclear Regulatory Commission, when problems with toxic or radioactive waste arise.

The relationships are not always smooth and free of conflict. State and local officials criticize the national government for cuts in funding; FBI agents may run up against local police policies that, in the agents' view, hinder efficient law enforcement work; state and local officials may confront national regulations that they see as either pointless or unnecessarily encumbering. In recent years, tensions between local, state,

dual federalism

A model of federalism in which national and state governments are separate and independent from each other, with each level exercising its own powers in its own jurisdiction

cooperative federalism

A model of federalism that features intertwining relationships and shared areas of responsibility between the national and state and local governments and national approaches to tightened airport security and other homeland security measures have been emblematic of this ongoing struggle. Nonetheless, cooperative federalism is a portrait of the federal system in which officials from different levels of government work together regularly.

2.3b Legal Relationships

One consequence of having different levels of government in the same political system is the potential for conflict over who has the power to do what. Legal conflicts between the national and state governments have both a rich past and a continuing vibrancy. The Supreme Court has played a major role in answering the questions that such conflicts raise.

The Court has interpreted the Constitution to mean that utilizing diverse approaches among the states in some matters is constitutionally unacceptable. It has generally supported the national government and national constitutional values in conflicts with the states. Its interpretation of the interstate commerce clause is a good example. The "regulation of interstate commerce" is one of the most important powers that the Constitution grants to Congress. This provision has allowed Congress to shape national economic and even social policy. States do have a role to play. They can enact legislation affecting commerce to protect the health and safety of citizens. States can also act in the absence of congressional action or when not prohibited by Congress. When Congress does act, the Supreme Court has generally allowed wide latitude to national legislation that limits state power in interstate commerce. For example, upholding the reach of congressional power in the Civil Rights Act of 1964, the Court held that hotels and local restaurants could not discriminate on the basis of race in their services because travelers and food served were part of inter-

(iStock)

state commerce.[15] More recently, however, the Court has indicated a willingness to restrict the definition of interstate commerce, thereby limiting congressional power to create gun-free school zones, for example, or to limit violence against women.[16] In 2012, the Court refused to accept the national government's argument that the commerce clause gave Congress the power to require individuals to purchase health insurance, though the Court majority concluded that the Patient Protection and Affordable Care Act (see discussion in Chapter 12) was constitutional as a result of Congress's taxing powers.[17]

Through its interpretation of the due process clause of the Fourteenth Amendment, the Court has also applied most of the limitations on the power of the national government contained in the first eight amendments to the activities of the states themselves. These amendments were added to the Constitution in the early years of the new government to assuage fears that the new national government might be a powerful threat to individual liberties. Ironically, the Court has applied these limitations to the states as well. For example, states must now provide counsel for people accused of crimes and may not sponsor prayer in the public schools.[18]

The Court's interpretation of the Fourteenth Amendment's equal protection clause has also limited state power. For example the Court's reapportionment decision, which required equal populations in state legislative districts, shifted political power from rural to urban areas.[19] The Court has even shaped the structure of local government. As an example, the Court found New York City's Board of Estimate—a local government body with substantial powers over land use, the city's budget, and other matters—in violation of its "one person, one vote" rulings.[20] The five boroughs of New York had equal representation on the board, despite great population differences among the boroughs. The Court's decision was the impetus behind the elimination of the Board of Estimate and a major restructuring of New York City's government.

Using the equal protection clause, the Court has also held that the states cannot exclusively determine for and by themselves the shape of their own school systems— even though public education has been traditionally among the reserved powers of the states. In *Brown v. Board of Education*,[21] the Court unanimously declared that racially segregated school systems are unconstitutional. Thus, some constitutional values have been deemed so important that they must be nationally determined and, if necessary, enforced by national power.

Despite the support the Court has generally given to the national government, the constitutional power of the states in conflicts with the national government is not a predetermined issue. In some recent cases the Court has weakened the power of the states and slighted the principle of federalism; in others the Court has asserted a constitutional role for the states, protecting them from incursions of congressional power. The issue of who should set minimum wages and maximum hours for the employees of state governments and their political subdivisions is an example of a case that has gone back and forth with regard to who has jurisdiction. Although the Court upheld that private employers could set wages and hours a half-century ago, it declared in 1976 that states were immune to such requirements. The Court reversed itself, however, in 1985 by ruling in *Garcia v. San Antonio Metropolitan Transit Authority* that Congress may apply minimum-wage and maximum-hour legislation to state employees.[22] Three years later, in *South Carolina v. Baker*, the Court ruled that Congress could tax state and local government bearer bonds,[23] a decision that limits the tax immunity of state and local governments. The *Garcia* and *South Carolina* decisions made state and local officials wonder whether the Court had "abandoned" Tenth Amendment protection of state powers.[24]

However, assuaging such fears, the Court ruled in 1991 that a congressional statute banning age discrimination does not overrule a provision in the Missouri Constitution requiring state judges to retire at age seventy. In other words, the state of Missouri can reasonably determine for itself mandatory retirement policies for state officials.[25] The Court also ruled, in 1992, that Congress cannot require a state to "take title" to radioactive waste produced within its borders if the state does not make provision for its disposal.[26] Additionally, in 1997 the Court struck down a congressional attempt to require local law enforcement officials to perform background checks on handgun purchasers and, in 2000, ruled unconstitutional Congress's effort to prevent states from disclosing a driver's personal information without the driver's consent.[27]

Looming on the forefront of federalism is the issue of same-sex marriage—a legal arrangement that some state supreme courts have ruled must be permitted under their constitutions. Though marriage is currently in the domain of state law, the national attention this issue has gained in recent years has led some groups on both sides of the debate to push for national uniformity. The Court's decisions on this issue in 2013, while striking down a federal law that defined marriage as only a union between a man and a woman, maintained that marriage rules are properly an area of

Some state supreme courts have ruled that same-sex marriages are constitutional. Marriage is currently in the domain of state law, but the strong attention the issue has gained in recent years has led many interest groups to push for national uniformity. (Shutterstock)

state law. These cases indicate that states continue to draw on powers reserved for them in the Constitution.[28] The search for the proper legal balance between state and national power continues to be a point of contention; the line between them has not disappeared.

2.3c Fiscal Relationships

Federalism is about more than just legal relationships. Cooperative fiscal relationships have become the single most important characteristic of federalism in the twentieth and twenty-first centuries, with money acting as a kind of glue that binds the different levels of government together. It is now commonplace to cite the ratification of the **Sixteenth Amendment** in 1913, which granted Congress the power to tax incomes, as a significant event contributing to the national government's unparalleled capacity to raise revenue. This capacity to raise funds reinforced the unprecedented emergence of public expectations for national government action in the Great Depression. The national government was cast in the role of banker, doling out money to deal with social and economic ills that states had either ignored or found too large for local solutions.

Terms and conditions vary enormously from one program to another, but cash grants from the national government to state and local governments are usually divided into two groups: categorical grants-in-aid and block grants. A **categorical grant-in-aid**, the predominant form of national aid, is a transfer of cash from the national government to state or local governments for some specific purpose—usually with the accompanying requirement that state and local governments match the national money with some funds of their own. The purposes of these grants are determined by the national government, and state and local governments have little or no discretion or flexibility in how the funds can be spent. If the money is given for highways, it cannot be spent on libraries or airports. Some of these grants are given to state and local governments on the basis of formulas that take into account factors such as population, poverty, and income levels. Others distribute money for specific projects in response to applications from state or local governments.

Categorical grants are available in practically every policy area, including highways, health, education, and nutrition. The *Catalog of Federal Domestic Assistance* reports that there are 2,284 grant programs;[29] however, a small number of grants make up a large proportion of total grant dollars. The grants for health programs, including Medicaid (medical benefits for the poor), and income security programs (such as welfare payments) will make up almost 73 percent of the grant total in 2015.[30]

A **block grant** is a transfer of cash from the national government to state and local governments that allows the recipients greater discretion in its use. Instead of defining with great specificity how the money must be spent, the national government permits expenditures in some broad policy area, such as community development, social services, or criminal justice. An increase in this type of grant has been a major federalism priority of Republican administrations because block grants allow greater discretion at the state and local levels. State and local governments prefer the

Sixteenth Amendment

Amendment to the Constitution, ratified in 1913, that gave Congress the power to tax incomes and thereby massively increase the potential revenue available to the national government

categorical grant-in-aid

Transfers of cash from the national to state and/or local governments for some specific purpose, usually with the accompanying requirement that state and local governments match the national money with some funds of their own

block grant

Transfers of cash from the national to state and local governments in which state and local officials are allowed discretion in spending the money within some broad policy area, such as community development or social services

Changing State Constitutions

In contrast to the U.S. Constitution, state constitutions are newer, longer, and more frequently changed. Of the forty-five states admitted to the union before 1900, thirteen adopted one or more constitutions in the twentieth century. Of the fifty states, thirty-one have adopted two or more constitutions, with Louisiana having approved its eleventh in 1975. Among the most recent is the Georgia constitution (the state's tenth) adopted in 1983. Only one state constitution still in force—Massachusetts's, adopted in 1780—predates the U.S. Constitution.

With about 8,300 words, only Vermont's constitution is nearly as short as the U.S. Constitution. Alabama's has 350,000 words, Texas's over 100,000, and Oklahoma's about 94,000. Much of the length of state constitutions is due to amendments. The length of state constitutions means that they are usually far more detailed than the U.S. Constitution. The abundant detail is explained by a fundamental difference in the way Americans view their national and state constitutions. The former has been largely concerned with the structure, operation, and powers of the government. Since the early nineteenth century the latter have reflected battles within the states over economic and social issues—matters of less interest to the national government before 1890. State constitutions also reflect struggles over legislative apportionment and the franchise. Since constitutions were more permanent than statutes, contending political groups attempted to write their preferred policies into a state's higher law. Moreover, state courts could not invalidate a constitutional provision as being in conflict with the state's constitution. This is why many state constitutions today read more like statutes.

The detail in state constitutions also means that they are changed frequently. The California constitution has been amended over five hundred times, and even the new Georgia constitution has had eighteen amendments added within six years of its adoption. Since 1776, some 232 constitutional conventions have been held by the states to propose new constitutions or major alterations to existing ones. Between 1900 and 1997, forty-three of the fifty states took some kind of official action to amend their constitutions, resulting in the adoption of 644 constitutional amendments—an average of nearly 13 per state. Approximately one-sixth of the 644 were "local" amendments that affected only part of a state, but the remaining amendments had statewide applications. In both categories, the amendments typically involved finance, taxation, and debt.

States vary in the way constitutional amendments are proposed, although each state makes proposing an amendment a separate step from ratifying it. While all allow the legislature (like Congress) to propose amendments, eighteen permit a constitutional initiative. This allows voters to begin the process of constitutional change by collecting the required number of signatures on a petition. Some states, however, restrict the kind of amendment that may be proposed by an initiative. Amendments may also be proposed by convention. Indeed, the constitutions of fourteen states now require the periodic submission to the voters of the question of whether a constitutional convention should be held. By whatever means proposed, ratification of amendments in almost all states occurs following a majority vote by the electorate.

This chapter explains that much of the change in the national constitution has come about not through formal amendment but by judicial interpretation. Should Americans prefer more frequent change of the national Constitution by amendment, as is now done in the states? Should the people vote directly on changes to the national Constitution as they routinely do on changes to state constitutions?

---

flexibility allowed by block grants to the more rigid procedural requirements that accompany categorical grants.

In 1922, the national government granted to the states the relatively paltry sum of $122 million, the major proportion of which was spent on highway construction.[31] Figure 2.2 shows the sharp increase in such aid over the past several decades. Reflecting the explosion of Great Society grant programs in the 1960s, national aid in current dollars almost quintupled between 1965 and 1975, from $11 billion to $50 billion, and it almost tripled again in the decade and a half after 1975.

Figure 2.2 | National Aid to State and Local Governments since 1960, in Current and Constant Dollars, in Billions

National aid to state and local governments rose sharply after 1960 to a high point in 1980 of $264.7 billion in constant 2009 dollars and then fell in constant dollars through the 1980s. In the early 1990s, aid began to rise again, in both current and constant dollars. In 2015, the amount in constant dollars is estimated at eleven times the amount of aid in 1960.

SOURCE: *Office of Management and Budget.*

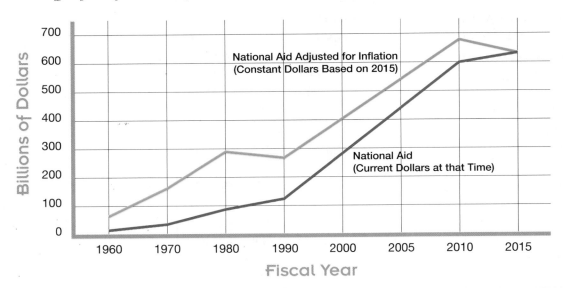

Figure 2.2 shows that national aid has continued to rise in the 2000s; however, the growth area in national government dollars is in programs providing payments for individuals, such as Medicaid. In 1960, 35 percent of federal grant dollars were spent on payments for individuals.

By 2015 that proportion increased to about 71 percent.[32] The proportional drop in grant programs that allow state and local governments to spend money, such as funding for capital projects, forced those governments to depend increasingly on their own resources to support programs that had previously been aided by Congress.

2.3d Political Relationships

The federal system can be viewed as a series of legal and fiscal relationships. However, a third way to look at the federal system is to see it as an arena for political relationships among officials at all levels of government who lobby and cajole one another and who bargain and negotiate with one another. The cast of political players includes members of Congress representing states and local districts, the president, governors, state legislators, mayors, county and township commissioners, and national, state, and local bureaucrats. These officials band together into groups such as the National Governors Association, the National Conference of State Legislatures, and the United States Conference of Mayors—all of which participate in federal system politics.

The range and variety of political relationships are enormous because officials at all levels in the federal system press for their own interests as they see them. Scarce resources, the search for the appropriate balance between state and national power, and social and economic differences among the states all drive these political relationships. Sometimes local or state officeholders will make demands on the national government as a group. In the competition for dollars, for example, mayors want more federal money. In the battle over which level of government has the power to do what, governors want fewer federal regulations and more state flexibility in deciding regulatory policy.

Many of the political relationships in the federal system derive from economic differences between regions and states and their localities as they compete with each other to press their individual interests. Economic development and the creation of new jobs are always among the highest priorities of state officials. New businesses and jobs can bolster tax collections, help political incumbents keep their posts, and make the state more attractive to outsiders. Understandably, states are in constant competition with each other to attract new industry and to retain the industry they have. Domestic and foreign corporations that are planning new plant sites are wooed by governors, economic development staffs, and local officials, all of whom cite favorable tax provisions, excellent physical facilities, and a skilled and dependable workforce as reasons the new plant should be located in their state.

State officials lobby to get what they see as their fair share of the huge budget expenditures of the national government. Associations of state and city officials and organizations such as the Northeast-Midwest Institute promote the economic interests of the regions they represent. Members of Congress want for their states and districts the "plums" of national policy, such as military contracts, but not the undesirable consequences of national policy, such as nuclear waste dumps. Competition among the states for national defense dollars is especially keen. Military installations and work on new weapons systems may bring millions of dollars into a state each year, and efforts to close facilities or cut weapons development meet with predictable opposition from state officials and congressional representatives. Understandably, Mississippi's members of Congress think that naval ships built in Mississippi are better than ships built in Virginia.

Other policy examples—beyond the struggle for money—also illustrate the conflicts between states, and between states and the national government. The long history of slavery and discrimination against blacks in the South created epic battles between the Southern states and the national government. Fights over school integration over the past generation illustrate the durability of the struggle. The issue did not reach the same intensity in states with different traditions and different avenues of economic development. Some of the great battles in Congress over environmental policy are conflicts between members of Congress trying to represent the interests

Members of Congress come into conflict over many issues, including environmental policy. These policies affect protected areas of the United States such as Yellowstone National Park. (Shutterstock)

BVT *Lab*

Flashcards are available for this chapter at www.BVTLab.com.

Chapter 02 | Federalism: States in the Union | 66

of their states. Californians want stricter auto emissions standards to ameliorate their problem of dirty air, but autoworkers in Michigan fear the economic consequences of stricter standards for their industry. As these illustrations suggest, political relationships in the federal system shape many public policies.

The Supreme Court created a political hot potato for all three levels of government in 2005 when it clarified and, by doing so, expanded the governmental power of eminent domain in the case *Kelo v. City of New London*.[33] The takings clause of the Fifth Amendment has long been interpreted to provide governments the power to seize private property for public use in exchange for just compensation. In the *Kelo* case, however, the Court presented a very broad interpretation of "public use" that enables governments to take private property and resell it to other private entities as long as there is a "public purpose." Fearing this decision would lead cities to condemn private homes in favor of shopping malls (which produce more tax revenue), citizens of many states and localities demanded that their governments pass laws or ordinances to limit the use of this broad power.

2.4   Federalism Today

In the second decade of the twenty-first century, the federal system appears to be a curious blend of contrasts, as each level of government asserts its role. The states are now innovators in a variety of public policy areas, including education, welfare, and the environment. Policy innovation is not a new role for the states. States had, in the past, experimented with new ideas that were later accepted as national policy. For example, a variety of states enacted old-age pension laws several years before Congress mandated Social Security as a national policy in 1935. Similarly, the state of Wisconsin had a program of unemployment compensation that predated national policy on the matter.[34]

Some states are now experimenting with market-like approaches in public education by allowing parents to choose the schools their children will attend; other state courts are mandating more equal educational expenditures across school districts. The latest round of welfare reform (requiring welfare recipients to work) was actually presaged by states that had already begun to experiment with such programs.[35] Across a range of environmental policies—including auto and power plant emissions, recycling, and water quality—some states have set more stringent standards than the national government. Federal budget cuts help to explain this increased vigor of the states. As the national government has wrestled with its own budget deficit, the states have expanded their policy role.

During the early 1990s, tensions grew between the national and state and local governments. The national government cut funding going to state and local governments, while, at the same time, it increased the number of regulations applied to state and local governments. Critics of this strategy called the national actions "unfunded mandates." Examples of these regulations, which result in higher costs that state and local governments must pay, include the federal mandate that local school districts remove asbestos materials from school buildings and the requirement that municipalities monitor a large list of pollutants in drinking water.[36] Protecting water supplies and the health of schoolchildren are worthwhile objectives, but which level of government should pay to meet the costs of national policy mandates?[37] States were being asked to do more to achieve policy objectives set by the national government—but with fewer federal resources. By 1995, however, the national government seemed to have gotten the message. Congress passed the Unfunded Mandates Reform Act that year; though not a panacea, the legislation led to the review of over 350 intergovernmental mandates during its first five years of operation. The Congressional Budget Office reports that the number of mandates that could be defined as unfunded declined steadily over that time period.[38]

Governors, state legislators, and mayors are more active than they used to be; many of them believe, however, that the national government is curtailing their powers and responsibilities and denying them sufficient resources to perform the tasks they are asked to do. The national government has increasingly preempted state and local action in a variety of areas. For example, the national government has told the states to stay out of the economic regulation of buses, trucks, and airlines. The rise in federal demands and the scarcity of dollars at all levels have increased tensions among governments in the federal system. State and local governments have assumed a prominent role in policy making; yet the lively debate over which level of government should have the power to do what, whether national or state action is more appropriate, and who should pay the costs in light of budget deficits illustrates the continuing vitality of the federal system.

CHAPTER REVIEW

1. Federalism is a system of government in which a central or national government and regional or state governments exercise governmental power within the same political system. Federalism is a compromise between a confederation, in which states hold principal power, and a unitary form of government, in which a central government is dominant. Countries throughout the world have federal systems, and some of the most bitter and consequential conflicts in other countries are battles to redefine the shape of federal systems.

2. In policy, the amendment process, and elections, states play an important role; but the national government has become more dominant in the federal system over the past two centuries. The Constitution delegates express powers to the national government, and the Supreme Court has given expansive interpretation to the implied powers clause in the document. Powers not delegated to the national government are reserved for the states and include police powers, ensuring the health, safety, and education of citizens. Also among state powers is control over local governments, which vary greatly in size, structure, and functions.

3. Two models of the federal system are dual federalism and cooperative federalism. The federal system can be seen as a series of legal, fiscal, and political relationships among governments. Through its interpretation of the Constitution, the Supreme Court has generally supported national constitutional values and the national government. At the expense of support for capital and other programs, an increasingly greater proportion of national aid to state and local governments goes to payments for individuals. Officials at all levels press for the interests of their governments in political relationships with other officials in the federal system.

4. States are now vigorous policy innovators, but budget deficits and the rise in national regulations have increased tensions in the federal system.

KEY TERMS

Readings for Further Study

Laurence J. O'Toole and Robert K. Christensen, eds., *American Intergovernmental Relations: Foundations, Perspectives, and Issues*, 5th ed. (Washington, D.C.: CQ Press, 2012) offers a contemporary view of federalism.

The Council of State Governments (Lexington, Kentucky) publishes biennially *The Book of the States*, a compendium of demographic, structural, and policy data about the states.

Articles describing and analyzing state and local governments in the federal system can be found in the journals *Publius* and *National Civic Review* and in the magazine *Governing*.

Iwan W. Morgan and Philip J. Davies, eds., offer a comparative perspective on federalism during the George W. Bush administration in *The Federal Nation: Perspectives on American Federalism* (New York: Palgrave, 2009).

David Osborne provides case studies of policy vigor in the states in *Laboratories of Democracy: A New Breed of Governor Creates Models for National Growth* (New York: McGraw-Hill, 1990).

Osbourne and Ted Gaebler's *Reinventing Government* (New York: Plume, 1993) presents an entrepreneurial approach to state and local governance that has been successful in providing policy makers with workable approaches in contemporary federalism.

Politics in the American States: A Comparative Analysis, 10th ed. (Los Angeles: Sage/CQ Press, 2013), edited by Virginia Gray, Russell L. Hanson, and Thad Kousser, is one of the best scholarly comparisons of state policy.

Alice Rivlin's *Reviving the American Dream: The Economy, the States, and the Federal Government* (Washington, D.C.: The Brookings Institution, 1993) presents provocative proposals to reorder policy responsibilities between the national and state governments.

Robert F. Nagel's *The Implosion of American Federalism* (New York: Oxford University Press, 2002) offers a critical look at contemporary American federalism.

Notes

1. John P. Roche, "The Founding Fathers: A Reform Caucus in Action," *American Political Science Review 55* (1961): 804; William H. Riker, *Federalism: Origin, Operation, Significance* (Boston: Little, Brown, 1964).

2. For a seminal discussion of different political cultures among the states, see Daniel J. Elazar's *American Federalism: A View from the States*, 3rd ed. (New York: Harper & Row, 1984), pp. 114–142.

3. Bureau of Economic Analysis, U.S. Department of Commerce, Interactive Data, http://www.bea.gov/iTable/iTable.cfm?reqid=70&step=1&isuri=1&acrdn=3 (July 16, 2014).

4. Daniel J. Elazar, *Exploring Federalism* (Tuscaloosa, AL: University of Alabama Press, 1987), p. 33.

5. See Gregory Gleason's *Federalism and Nationalism: The Struggle for Republican Rights in the USSR* (Boulder, CO: Westview Press, 1990) for discussion of Soviet federalism prior to the creation of the Commonwealth of Independent States.

6. The two exceptions are Maine and Nebraska, which allocate electoral votes on the basis of candidate victories in congressional districts.

7. See Daniel J. Elazar's "Federal-State Cooperation in the Nineteenth-Century United States," *Political Science Quarterly 79* (1964): 248–265.

8. For an examination on the differences between the Nixon and Reagan approaches to New Federalism, see Timothy Conlan's *New Federalism: Intergovernmental Reform from Nixon to Reagan* (Washington: Brookings Institution, 1988).

9. 17 U.S. (4 Wheaton) 316 (1819).

10. U.S. Census Bureau, http://www2.census.gov/govs/apes/12stlus.txt (July 16, 2014).

11. 567 U.S. _____ (2012).

12. For a comprehensive view of government relationships in the federal system on which this section draws, see Laurence J. O'Toole and Robert K. Christensen, eds., *American Intergovernmental Relations: Foundations, Perspectives, and Issues*, 5th ed. (Washington: CQ Press, 2012).

13. 247 U.S. 251 (1918).

14. The classic statement of the model can be found in Morton Grodzins, "The Federal System," in *President's Commission on National Goals, Goals for Americans* (Englewood Cliffs, NJ: Prentice-Hall, 1960), pp. 265–282.

15. See *Heart of Atlanta Motel v. United States*, 379 U.S. 274 (1964), and *Katzenbach v. McClung*, 379 U.S. 294 (1964).

16. See *United States v. Lopez*, 514 U.S. 549 (1995), and *United States v. Morrison*, 529 U.S. 598 (2000), respectively.

17. *National Federation of Independent Businesses v. Sebelius*, 567 U.S. ____ (2012).

18. *Gideon v. Wainwright*, 372 U.S. 335 (1963); *Engel v. Vitale*, 370 U.S. 421 (1962).

19. *Baker v. Carr*, 369 U.S. 186 (1962); *Reynolds v. Sims*, 377 U.S. 533 (1964).

20. *Morris v. Board of Estimate*, 489 U.S. 103 (1989).

21. 347 U.S. 483 (1954).

22. *National League of Cities v. Usery*, 426 U.S. 833 (1976); *Garcia v. San Antonio Metropolitan Transit Authority*, 469 U.S. 528 (1985).

23. 485 U.S. 505 (1988).

24. See, for example, David E. Nething, "States Must Regain Their Powers," *State Government 63* (January–March 1990): 6–7.

25. *Gregory v. Ashcroft*, 59 U.S.L.W. 4687 (1991).

26. *New York v. United States*, 60 U.S.L.W. 4603 (1992).

27. See *Printz v. United States*, 521 U.S. 898 (1997), and *Reno v. Condon*, 528 U.S. 141 (2000).

28. See Charles Wise and Rosemary O'Leary, "Is Federalism Dead or Alive in the Supreme Court? Implications for Public Administrators," *Public Administration Review 52* (November–December 1992): 559–572.

29. Catalog of Federal Domestic Assistance, https://www.cfda.gov/ (July 17, 2014).

30. Office of Management and Budget, *Analytical Perspectives, Budget of the United States Government, Fiscal Year 2015*, http://www.whitehouse.gov/omb/budget/Analytical_Perspectives/ (July 17, 2014).

31. Advisory Commission on Intergovernmental Relations, *Categorical Grants: Their Role and Design* (Washington: Government Printing Office, 1978), p. 16.

32. Office of Management and Budget, *Analytical Perspectives, Fiscal Year 2015*, p. 245.

33. 545 U.S. 469 (2005).

34. Arthur M. Schlesinger Jr., *The Coming of the New Deal* (Boston: Houghton Mifflin, 1965), pp. 301–303.

35. Elaine Stuart, "Roaring Forward," *State Government News* (January/February 1999): 10–14.

36. Ibid., 28–29.

37. Timothy J. Conlon, "And the Beat Goes On: Intergovernmental Mandates and Preemption in an Era of Deregulation," *Publius 21* (Summer 1991): 50–53.

38. Congressional Budget Office, *CBO's Activities Under the Unfunded Mandates Reform Act, 1996–2000* (May 2001).

POP QUIZ

1. The fifty American states are themselves _____ governments because the principal power within each state lies with the state government.

2. The Supreme Court case of_____ v. _____ interpreted the necessary and proper clause as allowing expansive power to the national government.

3. A model of federalism that views national and state governments as separate and independent from each other is called _____.

4. The most predominant form of national aid to the states takes the form of _____ _____.

5. The federal system is a compromise between a strong central government and a league of separate states.   T   F

6. States act in some measure as administrative units to carry out national social welfare programs.   T   F

7. Among the powers reserved for the states is the responsibility for preventing and prosecuting criminal activities.   T   F

8. Studies have shown that citizen interest in the affairs of local government is almost nonexistent.   T   F

9. Through a process of cooperative agreements, the states have the power to regulate interstate commerce.   T   F

10. Federalism is the product and symbol of the continuing ideological struggle between the values of _____ and _____.

    A) freedom, equality

    B) unity, diversity

    C) justice, protection

    D) individualism, nationalism

11. The government of France is a _____ system.

    A) confederate

    B) unitary

    C) federal

    D) decentralized

12. Federal systems are found in _____.

    A) Africa

    B) South Asia

    C) North America

    D) All of the above

13. The states play a crucial role in all except which of the following activities?

    A) administering social welfare policies

    B) regulating interstate commerce

    C) amending the Constitution

    D) shaping electoral contests at the national level

14. The Supreme Court case of *McCulloch v. Maryland* confirmed the national government's _____ powers.

    A) delegated

    B) express

    C) implied

    D) reserved

15. According to the text, the most visible and pervasive role of the state is in the area of _____.

    A) interstate commerce

    B) education

    C) health

    D) business regulation

Answers:
1. unitary   2. *McCulloch; Maryland*   3. dual federalism
4. categorical grants-in-aid   5. T   6. T   7. T   8. F   9. F
10. B   11. B   12. D   13. B   14. C   15. B

Chapter

03

Civil Liberties and Civil Rights

In This Chapter

(Shutterstock)

Chapter Objectives

Chapter 1 explained that a constitution can be a mainstay of rights. Beyond organizing and granting authority, constitutions place limits on what governments may do. Collectively, these limits are known as civil liberties and civil rights. Civil liberties are legally enforceable freedoms to act or not to act and to be free from unwarranted official intrusion into one's life. They include (but are not limited to) the First Amendment's guarantees of free expression and religious freedom and the Fourth, Fifth, Sixth, and Eighth Amendments' strictures governing police and courts in fighting crime.

Civil rights relate to participation—citizens' rights under the law to take part in society on an equal footing with others. They embrace the guarantees of the three Civil War amendments to the Constitution (the Thirteenth, Fourteenth, and Fifteenth), as well as laws passed to give those amendments meaning and force.

Civil rights are assurances that people are not penalized because of criteria (such as race or gender) that society decides should be irrelevant in making public policy. Yet, even after more than 225 years' experience as a nation, we continue to disagree over what liberty and equality mean in practice. Which rights and liberties do you exercise most frequently? Are there any that deserve more protection than they are currently afforded? What happens when civil rights and liberties come into conflict with one another?

The Bill of Rights: Securing the Blessings of Liberty

As explained in Chapter 1, when the Constitution left the hands of the framers in 1787 there appeared to be too few restrictions on what the national government could do, leaving individual liberty without sufficient protection. Several of the state conventions that ratified the proposed Constitution did so with the provision that a "bill of rights" would soon be added. In 1791, the Bill of Rights, comprising the first ten amendments, was ratified (see Table 3.1).

3.1a Applying the Bill of Rights to the States

Nearly 180 years elapsed before most of the rights spelled out in the Bill of Rights applied fully to state governments. This was because, as Chief Justice John Marshall (1801–1835) held for the Supreme Court, the Bill of Rights was not intended to apply to the states.[1] As a result, at first disputes between states and their citizens were controlled by the federal constitution to only a small degree. For most abuses of power, citizens had recourse only to their state constitutions and state courts; the ratification of the **Fourteenth Amendment** (see Appendix) in 1868, however, laid the groundwork for a drastic change in the nature of the Union. First, the amendment's language is directed to *state* governments, so aggrieved persons have the federal Constitution as an additional shield between themselves and their state governments. Second, the words of the amendment are ambiguous. What, for instance, is the "liberty" the amendment protects?

The Supreme Court was initially hesitant to use the Fourteenth Amendment as a vehicle through which to make the Bill of Rights applicable to the states. Within a century, however, the Court did just that. Without an additional formal amendment of the Constitution, the Court "incorporated" or absorbed the Bill of Rights into the Fourteenth Amendment in a series of about two dozen cases, beginning in 1897 and largely concluding in 1969. The most recent right to be incorporated was the Second Amendment's right to bear arms, which was not applied to the states until 2010.[2] Today almost all of the provisions in the first eight amendments—whether involving free speech or the rights thought necessary for a fair trial—apply with equal rigor to both state and national officials and the laws they make. Only the Sixth Amendment's stipulation about a trial's location, the Seventh's stipulation for a jury trial in most civil suits, the Eighth's ban on excessive bail and fines, and the Third Amendment still apply only to the national government. Of these, only the Eighth is substantively important (the Ninth and Tenth Amendments, although part of the Bill of Rights, do not lend themselves to absorption into the Fourteenth Amendment).

3.1b The Fragility of Civil Liberties

Charters of liberty, like a bill of rights, are commonplace today in the constitutions of many governments. Yet even a casual observer of world affairs knows that civil liberties are more likely to be preserved (or suspended) in some countries than in others. Even in the United States, the liberties enshrined in the Bill of Rights have meant more in some years than in others because of changing interpretations by the Supreme Court. For example, the Fourth Amendment's ban on "unreasonable searches and seizures" did not apply for a long time to electronic surveillance unless police physically trespassed on a suspect's property. This meant that state and federal agents could eavesdrop electronically in many situations without fear of violating the Constitution. In 1967, however, the Court ruled that the Fourth

Fourteenth Amendment

Ratified in 1868, the amendment altered the nature of the Union by placing significant restraints on state governments

table 3.1 | Content of the Bill of Rights

Consisting of barely 450 words, the Bill of Rights (Amendments I through X) was intended to remedy a defect critics found in the Constitution of 1787. In September 1789 Congress proposed twelve amendments for approval by the states. As the eleventh state (three-fourths of fourteen), Virginia's ratification in December 1791 made the Bill of Rights officially part of the Constitution. The remaining three states—Connecticut, Georgia, and Massachusetts—did not ratify until the 150th anniversary of the Bill of Rights in 1941. One amendment was never ratified. It dealt with apportionment of the House of Representatives and is now obsolete. The other amendment was not ratified until 1992—more than two hundred years after it was proposed! The Twenty-seventh Amendment—called the "lost amendment"—delays any increase in congressional salaries until a congressional election has intervened.

Amendment I	Nonestablishment of religion; free exercise of religion; freedoms of speech, press, petition, and peaceable assembly
Amendment II	Keep and bear arms
Amendment III	No quartering of troops
Amendment IV	No unreasonable searches and seizures; standards for search warrants
Amendment V	Indictment by grand jury; no double jeopardy or self-incrimination; no deprivation of life, liberty, or property without due process of law; compensation for taking of private property
Amendment VI	Speedy and public trial by impartial jury in state and district where crime was committed; nature and cause of accusation; confrontation of accusers; compulsory process for witnesses; assistance of counsel
Amendment VII	Jury trial in certain civil cases
Amendment VIII	No excessive bail or fines; no cruel and unusual punishments
Amendment IX	Recognition of the existence of rights not enumerated
Amendment X	Reserved powers of the states

Amendment covered most electronic searches, too, as long as there was a "reasonable expectation of privacy."[3] In 2014, the Court specifically extended this privacy right to cover the data stored on cell phones.[4] The words in the Bill of Rights have not changed, but the meaning attributed to those words has changed in the context of Supreme Court decisions.

Exactly why civil liberties thrive in one place or time and not another is a complex phenomenon. However, this much is certain: Civil liberties are fragile. The most frequent and sometimes the most serious threats to civil liberties have come not from people intent on throwing the Bill of Rights away but from well-meaning and overzealous people who find the Bill of Rights a temporary bother, standing in the way of objectives—often laudatory ones—they want to reach. Put another way, constitutional protections are sometimes worth the least when they are needed most. When public opinion calls for a "crack down" on certain rights, such demands are felt in judicial chambers just as they are heard in legislative halls. Unsupported, courts and the Bill of Rights alone cannot defend civil liberties.

Free Expression: Speech, Press, and Assembly

The place of the **First Amendment** in the Bill of Rights is symbolic. Its liberties are fundamental because they are essential to the kind of nation the framers envisioned.

3.2a The Value of Free Expression

Free expression serves several important objectives. First, *free expression is necessary to the political process set up by the Constitution*. It is difficult to imagine government being responsive to a majority of the political community if the members of that community are afraid of saying what they think. It is even more difficult to imagine members of a political minority trying to persuade the majority without the right to criticize political officeholders. For democratic politics to work, free speech must prevail.

Second, in politics, as in education, *free expression allows the dominant wisdom of the day to be challenged*. Open discussion and debate aid the search for truth and thus foster intelligent policy making. Whether the question is safeguarding the environment or probing the causes of birth defects, free speech encourages both investigation of the problem and examination of possible solutions.

Third, *free expression aids self-development*. Intellectual and artistic expression may contribute to realizing one's full potential as a human being. If government has the authority to define what kind of art is "acceptable," other kinds will be discouraged or suppressed altogether. Freedom of expression does not guarantee success as a poet, artist, or composer, but it does guarantee each person's right to try.

Free expression has its risks, however. There are no assurances that open debate and discussion will produce the "correct" answer or the wisest policy. Letting people speak their minds freely will surely stretch out the time it takes for a political community to decide what to do. Free speech can also threaten social and political stability. Although there are risks in silencing dissent, risks exist in permitting it, also. Nations in upheaval rarely tolerate vocal dissent against official policy. On balance, however, the American people—through their public officials and judges—seem willing to accept these risks most of the time.

3.2b The Test of Freedom

Even though the First Amendment has been part of the Constitution from almost the beginning, freedom's record has not been free of blemishes. The ink had hardly dried on the Bill of Rights when Congress passed the Sedition Act of 1798, making it a crime to publish "false, scandalous, and malicious" statements about government officials. The law was not challenged in the Supreme Court even though at least ten individuals were convicted before it expired in 1801. Scattered instances of suppression occurred on both sides during the Civil War, but the next major nationwide attacks on speech were directed at virtually anyone or anything pro-German during World War I and on socialist ideas during the "Red Scare" that followed. Only then did the Supreme Court first interpret the free speech clause of the Constitution.

During World War I, Charles Schenck was found guilty of violating the Espionage Act by printing and circulating materials designed to protest and obstruct the draft. Announcing the **clear and present danger test**, Justice Oliver Wendell Holmes (1902–1932) ruled that the First Amendment provided no shield for Schenck's words: "The question … is whether the words are used in such circumstances and are of such a nature as to create a clear and present danger that they will bring about the substantive evils that Congress has a right to prevent. It is a question of proximity and degree."[5]

First Amendment

The part of the Bill of Rights containing protections for political and religious expression

clear and present danger test

Guideline devised by the Supreme Court in *Schenck v. United States* [249 U.S. 47 (1919)] to determine when speech could be suppressed under the First Amendment

Although Schenck lost his case, Holmes's reasoning remained important. Only when harmful consequences of speech were imminent could government act to suppress it. As Justice Louis Brandeis (1916–1939) later declared, "If there be time to expose through discussion the falsehood and fallacies, to avert the evil by the processes of education, the remedy to be applied is more speech, not enforced silence."[6] Since 1969 the clear and present danger test has evolved into the **incitement test**, stressing the Court's insistence that harmful consequences (such as a riot) be exceedingly imminent.[7]

Some settings and speech content also allow for limitations on First Amendment speech rights. In a 2007 case, the Supreme Court held that the characteristics of the school environment made it consti-

Since the Bill of Rights was enacted, freedom of speech has been, and still remains, a subject of controversy. (AP World Wide Photo)

tutionally permissible for school administrators to demand that students remove a banner reading "BONG HiTS 4 JESUS" from a public forum without infringing on the students' speech rights.[8] On the other hand, the Court has held that concern about a lack of decency and respect in location choice does not limit free expression protections. In the 2011 case *Snyder v. Phelps*, the Court concluded that the hateful signs that members of the Westboro Baptist Church display at military funerals are protected from liability claims by the First Amendment.[9]

3.2c Gags

Of the possible restrictions on speech today, the Court is least likely to approve a **prior restraint**. This is official censorship *before* something is said or published, or censorship that halts publication already under way. Prior restraints are especially dangerous to free expression because government does not have to go to the trouble of launching a prosecution and convicting someone at a trial. Even when *The New York Times* and the *Washington Post* reprinted verbatim parts of a purloined classified study of the Defense Department's decision-making on Vietnam, the Supreme Court (in the "Pentagon Papers" case) refused to ban further publication.[10] Most of the justices admitted that the government could make it a crime to publish such materials, but concluded that there could be no restraints in advance. Likewise, the justices will only rarely approve a pretrial gag on media reports about a crime, even if such suppression would help protect another constitutional right: the right to a fair trial.

3.2d Obscenity and Libel

Descriptions and depictions of various sexual acts have presented a special problem. Unlike cases involving other types of speech, the Court has required no evidence that obscene materials are in fact harmful. Yet the Court steadfastly regards **obscenity** as unprotected speech because of the widespread public view that exposure to obscenity is deleterious. The justices have had a hard time writing a clearly understood definition of what is obscene. Justice Potter Stewart (1958–1981) once admitted, "I know

incitement test

The Court's current test for First Amendment restrictions that asks whether a speech act attempts or is likely to incite lawless action

prior restraint

Official censorship before something is said or published, or censorship that halts publication already under way is usually judged unconstitutional today under the First Amendment

obscenity

As applied by the Supreme Court, certain pornographic portrayals of sexual acts not protected by the First Amendment (The Supreme Court's current definition of the legally obscene appeared in *Miller v. California* [413 U.S. 5 (1973)].)

it when I see it." Under the current standard, the Court will uphold an obscenity conviction if

> (a) "the average person, applying contemporary community standards," would find that the work, taken as a whole, appeals to the prurient interest, (b) ... the work depicts or describes, in a patently offensive way, sexual conduct specifically defined by the applicable state law, and (c) ... the work, taken as a whole, lacks serious literary, artistic, political, or scientific value.[11]

The target seems to be "hard-core" pornography. Within limits, the "community" to which the Court refers is local and not national, making the definition of obscenity variable. The policy thus allows one locale to suppress sexually explicit materials while another tolerates them. For example, the Court recently upheld a city ordinance that prohibited nudity in public places, including erotic dancing establishments.[12] Obscenity continues to trouble the nation. Films, videos, and magazines portraying explicit sex are big business. Many think the Supreme Court's definition is both too lax and insufficiently enforced. Although reluctant to advocate censorship, some feminists object to obscenity because it degrades women and may even contribute to sexual crimes against women. The Court, however, continues to err on the side of liberty in this issue—even when ruling on a subject as universally condemned as child pornography. In a series of recent cases, the Court held that the federal Child Online Protection Act and its revisions (measures designed to restrict child pornography on the Internet) have been too sweeping, failing to meet the Court's "least restrictive means" test for limiting free speech.[13] Moving beyond pornography, a majority of justices applied similar logic to video games in 2011 when they struck down a California law banning the sale of violent video games to minors.[14] The Court held that video games are protected by the First Amendment and that the law was not narrowly tailored and failed to provide a compelling state interest to limit their sale.

The First Amendment protects the freedom to assemble. (Shutterstock)

Like obscenity, the First Amendment does not protect **libel**. Involving published defamation of a person's character or reputation, libel may subject a publisher or television network to damage suits involving thousands or even millions of dollars. Beginning in 1964, however, the Supreme Court made it very difficult for public figures and public officials to bring successful libel suits against their critics because the court felt that the democratic process needs robust and spirited debate, which might be muted by threat of legal action. In such situations, public figures and officials initiating libel suits must be able to prove "actual malice"—that is, that the author published information knowing it was false or not caring whether it was true or false.[15]

libel

Defamation of a person's character or reputation, not protected by the First Amendment (*New York Times Co. v. Sullivan* [376 U.S. 254 (1964)] makes it difficult for public figures and officials to bring successful libel suits against their critics.)

BVT Lab
Improve your test scores.
Practice quizzes are
available at
www.BVTLab.com.

People often convey ideas and attempt to build support for a cause by holding a meeting or a rally. This is an example of the freedom of assembly that the First Amendment protects. Sometimes assembly involves **symbolic speech** in which words, pictures, and ideas are not at issue, but action is. A person may *do* something to send a message, usually in a dramatic, attention-getting manner. It might be a sit-in at the mayor's office to protest a budget cut, or a sit-down on a public road leading to a nuclear power plant under construction. In some instances, demonstrators may be constitutionally punished for such nontraditional forms of expression—not because of the ideas expressed but because of the harm that results from the *mode* of expression. It is not the message but the medium that can be the basis of a legitimate arrest.

Yet in a 1989 decision that generated a storm of controversy, the Supreme Court overturned the conviction of Gregory Lee Johnson for burning the American flag in violation of a Texas law.[16] In a demonstration at Dallas City Hall during the Republican National Convention in 1984, protesters chanted, "America, the red, white, and blue, we spit on you," as Johnson doused the flag with kerosene and set it ablaze. Short of a protest that sparks a breach of the peace or causes some other kind of serious harm, the Court held (5–4) that a state could not criminalize the symbolic act of flag burning. The Court's reasoning was that government protects the physical integrity of the flag because the flag is a symbol of the nation. Just as people may verbally speak out against what they believe the nation "stands for," they may also express the same thought by defacing or destroying the symbol of the nation. The following year, the Court held that the First Amendment also barred Congress from criminalizing flag burning, a decision that sparked a renewed drive

Flag burning is considered an extension of freedom of speech. (Shutterstock)

to amend the Constitution.[17] The drive failed in 1990 when Congress failed to pass a constitutional amendment by the required two-thirds vote in both houses.

The Court has also invalidated a city ordinance that outlawed cross burning and other forms of symbolic hate speech directed against certain minorities.[18] The ordinance was defective because it was content based. Some, not all, hate messages were banned. The decision may be far-reaching because it calls into question the constitutionality of similar bans at public universities. In 2014, the Court struck down a Massachusetts law that attempted to limit speech near women's health clinics. The Court held that the law's attempt to create a buffer zone around the clinics was overbroad and violated the speech rights of those wishing to make known their views on abortion.[19]

3.3   Religious Freedom

Guarantees of religious freedom form the first lines of the First Amendment. Ahead of other protections are an assurance of free exercise and a prohibition of an established religion. Removing religion from the reach of political majorities

symbolic Speech

A speech act that centers on action or performance to communicate a point rather than on words

reflected practical needs in 1791. The United States was already one of the world's most religiously diverse countries.

3.3a Religion and the Constitution

The Constitution is intentionally a nonsectarian document. It had to be if the framers were to secure ratification after 1787 and if the new government were to avoid the religious divisiveness that had plagued Europe before and after the Protestant Reformation, as well as the American colonies. Even though a few states still maintained established (state-supported) churches in 1791, the First Amendment said that the nation could not have one.

The United States is even more religiously diverse today. About 83 percent of the population identifies with a particular religion.[20] More than seventeen distinct religious groups claim more than one million members each, with dozens more having smaller memberships.[21] Within this context, the religion clauses have the same objectives, but they work in different ways. The **free exercise clause** preserves a sphere of religious practice free of interference by government. The idea is that people should be left to follow their own dictates of belief or nonbelief. The **establishment clause** keeps government from becoming the tool of one religious group against others. Government cannot be a prize in a nation of competing faiths.

Even though both religion clauses work to guard religious freedom, they concern different threats and so at times seem to pull in opposite directions. Rigorous protection of free exercise may appear to create an established religion. Rigorous enforcement of the ban on establishment may seem to deny free exercise.[22]

3.3b Aid to Sectarian Schools

The Supreme Court has never limited the First Amendment's ban on the literal establishment of an official state church. How much involvement between church and state is too much, however? Coins, for example, display the motto "In God We Trust." A troublesome area for almost a half-century has been public financial support for sectarian schools. The current standard for determining when government has violated the establishment clause in this context dates from a 1971 decision by the Supreme Court.[23] To pass scrutiny under the *Lemon* test, a law must have, first of all, a *secular purpose*. Second, the primary effect of the law must be *neutral*, neither hindering nor advancing religion. Third, the law must not promote *excessive entanglement* between church and state by requiring government to become too closely involved in the affairs of a religious institution. Using these criteria, the Court has upheld some, but not most, forms of state aid that have been challenged. Generally, direct grants of money from a government agency to a religious institution are the least likely to be found acceptable under the Constitution. However, in 2011—drawing a distinction between direct and indirect state contributions—the Supreme Court let stand an Arizona law that provided tax credits for individual contributions to religiously affiliated schools.[24]

3.3c Prayer in Public Schools

Whether or not religious observances can take place in public schools is another thorny issue. Even though we don't tend to think of schools as part of the government, public schools are funded through tax dollars and are governed by elected school boards—they are government-run institutions. Because of strong emotions on both sides of the prayer in schools issue, the Court's decisions have stirred up controversy. In 1962, the justices outlawed a nondenominational prayer prescribed by the

free exercise clause

Provision of the First Amendment guaranteeing religious freedom

establishment clause

Provision of the First Amendment barring government support of religion

***Lemon* test**

A standard announced in *Lemon v. Kurtzman* [403 U.S. 602 (1971)] to determine when a statute violates the establishment clause (The law in question must have a secular purpose and a neutral effect and must avoid an excessive entanglement between church and state.)

Board of Regents for opening daily exercises in the public schools of New York State. The following year, a Pennsylvania statute mandating daily Bible readings in public schools met a similar fate.[25] Reactions to these decisions in Congress and the nation were anything but dispassionate. After the New York prayer case, the U.S. House of Representatives unanimously passed a resolution to have the motto "In God We Trust" placed behind the Speaker's desk in the House chamber. The motto is still there for all to see during televised sessions of Congress.

Of course, the Supreme Court has never said that students cannot pray in school—students have been doing that before exams for years—but the Court has remained firm in its opposition to state-sponsored religious activities in public schools. For example, an Alabama statute authorizing a period of silence at the start of the school day for "meditation or voluntary prayer" was seen by most justices as constitutionally defective because the law endorsed religion as a preferred activity.[26] A bare majority of the Court even found an invocation offered by a rabbi at a public middle school commencement constitutionally objectionable. Although student attendance at the

The Supreme Court has held that state-sponsored religious activities in public schools are unconstitutional. (iStock)

ceremony was optional, the prayer nonetheless carried "a particular risk of indirect coercion" of religious belief, according to Justice Anthony Kennedy.[27] For the four dissenters, Justice Antonin Scalia asserted that the nation's long tradition of prayer at public ceremonies was a compelling argument that the school had not violated the establishment clause. In 2000, the Court maintained course by finding a student-led prayer played over a public address system prior to a school football game to be in violation of the establishment clause.[28]

3.3d Religious Observances in Official Settings

Because of the impressionable nature of children, the Court has been quickest to strike down religious influences in elementary and secondary schools. Elsewhere, the justices sometimes look the other way. In 1983, the Court approved Nebraska's practice of paying the state legislature's chaplain out of public funds.[29] In a narrowly decided 2014 case, the Court upheld ceremonial invocations at the beginning of local government meetings—even though plaintiffs in the case objected to the specifically Christian nature of most of these prayers.[30] (Both houses of the United States Congress also have chaplains who pray at the beginning of each day's session.) In 1984, a bare majority allowed city officials in Pawtucket, Rhode Island, to erect a municipally owned Christmas display, including a crèche, in a private park. However, the Court has placed some limits on official observances of religious holidays, finding unacceptable a privately owned crèche displayed in the county courthouse in Pittsburgh, Pennsylvania. Above the crèche was a banner proclaiming *"Gloria in Excelsis Deo"* (Latin for "Glory to God in the highest"). Yet in the same case, the Court found acceptable a nearby display that combined an eighteen-foot menorah and a forty-five-foot tree decorated with holiday ornaments. The justices explained that the crèche and banner impermissibly "endorsed" religion, but that the menorah and tree only "recognized" the religious nature of the winter holidays.[31]

In 2004, a Californian named Michael Newdow brought suit on behalf of his daughter to oppose the recitation of the Pledge of Allegiance and its phrase "under God" in a public school setting. Although the Court dismissed the case without deciding its merits, the issue sparked renewed public debate over the boundaries of church and state.[32] In 2005 the Court held that a display of the Judeo-Christian Ten Commandments in a Kentucky courthouse violated the establishment clause because it violated the requirement of government neutrality. Employing the *Lemon* test, the majority of justices found that the display lacked a primary secular purpose.[33] On the same day, however, the Court handed down another decision in which it found acceptable a display of the Ten Commandments at the Texas state capitol.[34] The justices found the passive nature of the display and its location and historical presence to be the key factors distinguishing it from the Kentucky case. Such decisions point to the difficulty in deciding how much separation the establishment clause commands between government and religion.

3.3e Free Exercise of Religion

Contemporary free exercise problems typically arise from the application of a law that by its own words has nothing to do with religion, yet that causes hardship for some religious groups by commanding them to do something that their faith forbids (or by forbidding them to do something that their faith commands). This kind of conflict often occurs with small separatist groups whose interests are overlooked when laws are made. Relying on the free exercise clause, they ask to be exempted on religious grounds from obeying the law. For example, a nearly unanimous bench in 1972 exempted members of the Old Order Amish and the Conservative Amish Mennonite churches from Wisconsin's compulsory school attendance law.[35] Like most states, Wisconsin required school attendance until age sixteen. The Amish were religiously opposed to formal schooling beyond the eighth grade. The justices found a close connection between the faith of the Amish and their simple, separatist way of life. The law not only compelled them to do something at odds with their religious tenets but also threatened to undermine the Amish community. On balance, in the Court's view, the danger to religious freedom outweighed the state's interest in compulsory attendance.

At other times, however, the Court has been less hospitable to free exercise claims. In 1990, the justices ruled against two members of the American Indian Church who were fired from their jobs as drug counselors in a clinic in Oregon after they ingested peyote (a hallucinogen) as part of a religious ritual. Oregon officials then denied them unemployment compensation because their loss of employment resulted from "misconduct." Under state law, peyote was a "controlled substance" and its use was forbidden. The two ex-counselors cited scientific and anthropological evidence that the sacramental use of peyote was an ancient practice and was not harmful. The Court, however, decided that Oregon had not violated the First Amendment. When action based on religious belief runs afoul of criminal law, the latter prevails.[36] Even though Congress attempted to reverse this ruling with the Religious Freedom Restoration Act in 1993, the Court found that this act exceeded congressional authority.[37]

Most recently, the Court defended the free exercise rights of a private company when it decided the case *Burwell v. Hobby Lobby*.[38] In a 5–4 decision, the Court ruled that the Affordable Care Act could not compel businesses to provide employees with insurance coverage for certain types of contraception over the religious objections of the business owners.

3.4   Fundamentals of American Criminal Justice

The American system of criminal justice insists not simply that a person be proved guilty but also that the guilt is proven in the legally prescribed way. This is the concept of **legal guilt**, inherent in the idea of "a government of laws and not of men."[39] Courts sit not just to make sure that wrongdoers are punished but also to see that law enforcement personnel obey the commands of the Bill of Rights. The precise meaning of these commands at a given time represents the prevailing judgment on the balance to be struck between two values: the liberty and the safety of each citizen. The first focuses on fairness to persons accused of crimes and emphasizes that preservation of liberty necessitates tight controls on law enforcement officers, even if some guilty persons go unpunished. The second focuses on crime control, emphasizing that too many rules hamstring police and judges, give lawbreakers the upper hand, and disserve honest citizens. Tension between the two values persists.

Inconvenient as they may be, the strictures of the Bill of Rights deliberately make government's crime fighting tasks harder to perform. Yet, holding police to standards of behavior set by the Constitution protects the liberty of everyone. Otherwise, officials would have the power to do whatever they wanted to whomever they wanted, whenever they wanted. Without limits to authority, America would be a far different place in which to live.

3.4a   Presumption of Innocence and Notice of Charges

The idea that a person is "innocent until proved guilty" is often misunderstood. It does not mean that the police and prosecuting attorney think that the accused person is innocent, for putting obviously innocent people through the torment of a criminal trial would be a gross injustice. Instead, the **presumption of innocence** lays the burden of proof on the government. It is up to the state to prove the suspect's guilt "beyond a reasonable doubt." Along with a convincing case of factual guilt, the prosecution must also demonstrate criminal intent, or *mens rea*.

A suspect is entitled to know what the state intends to prove and, therefore, what he or she must defend against. The state must go beyond saying merely that someone is a thief. The charge must explain, among other things, (1) what was stolen, (2) approximately when it was stolen, (3) by whom, and (4) from whom it was stolen. This principle also means that criminal laws must be as specific as possible so that citizens can have fair notice of what conduct is prohibited. The greater the vagueness in a law, the greater the danger of arbitrary arrests and convictions is.

The basic fairness component of advance notice is why the Constitution prohibits **ex post facto laws**, criminal laws that apply retroactively. The Constitution also forbids a bill of attainder for a similar reason. A **bill of attainder** is a law that imposes punishment but bypasses the procedural safeguards of the legal process. Thus, a person might not have the opportunity for even a simple defense.

legal guilt

The concept that a defendant's factual guilt be established in accordance with the laws and the Constitution before criminal penalties can be applied

presumption of innocence

A concept in criminal procedure that places the burden of proof in establishing guilt on the government

ex post facto laws

Laws that make an act a crime after it was committed or increase the punishment for a crime already committed—prohibited by the Constitution

bill of attainder

A law that punishes an individual and bypasses the procedural safeguards of the legal process—prohibited by the Constitution

3.4b Limits on Searches and Arrests

The **Fourth Amendment** denies police unbounded discretion to arrest and search people and their possessions. Many searches and some arrests cannot take place at all until a judge has issued a **warrant**, or official authorization. To obtain a warrant, the police must persuade a judge that they have very good reason (called **probable cause**) for believing that someone has committed a crime or that evidence exists in a particular location. Warrantless searches of arrested suspects or automobiles are permitted in certain circumstances, but police officers who have made a warrantless search must still convince a judge afterward that they had probable cause to act. In 2009, the Court clarified that warrantless automobile searches are only permissible if there are safety concerns or if there is a reasonable belief that the car contains evidence relevant to the specific crime for which the suspect is being arrested.[40] In 2013, the Court concluded that the use of a trained police dog (for the purpose of detecting narcotics) on a person's front porch was also the type of search that required a warrant.[41]

Electronic surveillance is usually considered to be a search, in the constitutional sense. Under current law, practically all such "bugging" must be done on the authority of a warrant—except for exceptional situations involving agents of foreign powers.[42] Advances in surveillance technology continue to push the boundaries of the Fourth Amendment. In 2001, the Court held that heat-sensing equipment that detects whether a private home is radiating abnormal levels of heat (which might indicate the use of heat lamps for growing marijuana plants) could not be used without a warrant.[43] Similarly, in 2012 a Court majority held that police could not install a GPS device on a vehicle in order to track its owner without a warrant.[44]

Once a valid arrest has been made, however, police have a right to search a detained individual. In a 2012 case, the Court ruled that a man arrested for failing to appear at a court hearing to pay a fine could be subjected to a strip search.[45] This search was found acceptable in order to ensure the safety of the correctional facility where he was being detained, regardless of the reason for the initial arrest. The following year the Court extended the logic of diminished privacy rights for those held in custody when it upheld the constitutionality of a Maryland law that allows officers to collect DNA samples from those charged with violent crimes.[46]

What happens when a judge concludes that police officers have acted improperly when making an arrest or conducting a search? In such instances, the **exclusionary rule** may come into play. This judge-made rule puts teeth into the Fourth Amendment by denying government, in many situations, the use of evidence gained as a result of the violation of the suspect's rights. The rule lies at the heart of the clash between the values of fairness and crime control.[47]

3.4c Assistance of Counsel and Protection Against Self-Incrimination

Other constitutional restraints are at work in the police station and in the court-room. As interpreted by the Supreme Court, the Fifth Amendment denies government the authority to coerce confessions from suspects or to require suspects to testify at their own trials. These restraints conform to presumption of innocence. The state must make its case—it may not compel the suspect to do its work. Under *Miranda v. Arizona*,[48] judges exclude almost all confessions, even if no physical coercion is present, unless police have first performed the following actions:

1. Advised the suspect of his or her right to remain silent (that is, the right not to answer questions)

Fourth Amendment

Part of the Bill of Rights that prohibits unreasonable searches and seizures of persons and their property

warrant

Official authorization for government action

probable cause

A standard used in determining when police can conduct arrests and searches

exclusionary rule

Rule developed in *Mapp v. Ohio* [367 U.S. 643 (1961)] that prevents the state from bringing evidence against a defendant when that evidence was obtained illegally

2. Warned the suspect that statements he or she might make may be used as evidence at a trial

3. Informed the suspect of his or her right to have a lawyer present during the interrogation

4. Offered the services of a lawyer free of charge during the interrogation to suspects financially unable to retain one

If a suspect refuses to talk to the police, the police may not continue the interrogation. If a suspect waives these *Miranda* **rights** and agrees to talk, the state must be prepared to show to

The Supreme Court found that the foreign nationals detained at the Guantanamo Bay facilities were denied the writ of habeas corpus. (AP World Wide Photo)

a judge's satisfaction that the waiver was done "voluntarily, knowingly, and intelligently." As it is, many defendants decide that it is in their interest to accept a **plea bargain**—a deal with the prosecutor to obtain fewer or lesser charges or a lighter sentence in exchange for a guilty plea. Guilty pleas allow most criminal cases to be settled without going to trial, so the legal use of confessions continues. In 2010, the Court clarified that simply remaining silent for a period of time is not the same as invoking the right to remain silent; therefore, law enforcement can continue to question a suspect even if he or she does not initially respond.[49]

For a long time, the **Sixth Amendment's** assurance of counsel, or legal assistance, remained more promise than substance. Many defendants simply could not afford to hire an attorney, and some courts provided free counsel for the poor only in **capital cases** (cases in which the death penalty might be imposed). Until the 1970s, for example, 75 percent of people accused of **misdemeanors** (less serious offenses, punishable by a jail term of less than one year) went legally unrepresented. Since the 1930s the Supreme Court has greatly expanded the Sixth Amendment right. Today all persons accused of **felonies** (serious offenses, punishable by more than one year in jail) and all accused of misdemeanors for which a jail term is imposed must be offered counsel, at the government's expense if necessary.[50]

The ongoing war on terrorism has led to a reexamination of several of these criminal defense concerns. In 2004, the Court handed down a series of decisions that among other things, concluded that the government may detain enemy combatants indefinitely during times of war, but that those being held, whether U.S. citizens or foreign nationals, must be given the opportunity to challenge their detention in court.[51] In 2008 the Court exercised its power of judicial review in finding that parts of the Detainee Treatment Act of 2005 and the Military Commissions Act had unconstitutionally denied the writ of habeas corpus to foreign nationals detained in the American facilities at Guantanamo Bay.[52] The ongoing and contentious nature of these cases speaks to the currency and importance of establishing clear and fair rules for the criminally accused.

Still, none of the right-to-counsel rulings create full equality in access to legal assistance. The Constitution, after all, does not guarantee a "perfect" trial, only a "fair" one. Indigents must be content with public defenders and court-appointed attorneys paid from public funds. Public defenders carry heavy caseloads; their time is spread thin; and compared to others in their profession, they are underpaid. In federal courts

---

***Miranda* rights**

Requirements announced in *Miranda v. Arizona* [384 U.S. 436 (1966)] to protect a suspect during a police interrogation

plea bargain

A deal with the prosecutor to obtain fewer or lesser charges or a lighter sentence

Sixth Amendment

Provision of the Bill of Rights assuring, among other things, the right to counsel

capital case

A criminal proceeding in which the defendant is on trial for his or her life

misdemeanor

Less serious criminal offense, usually punishable by not more than one year in jail

felony

A serious criminal offense, usually punishable by more than one year in prison

BVT Lab

Visit www.BVTLab.com to explore the student resources available for this chapter.

they are now responsible for over half of all defense work. They can cope with their caseloads only with the help of plea bargains. Defendants retaining counsel at their own expense also fare differently. Only a few can afford the best.

3.4d Limits on Punishment

Guilty verdicts by juries or through guilty pleas usually result in the punishment of the accused. Generally the Constitution leaves the particulars of the sentence to legislators and judges, subject to the **Eighth Amendment's** prohibition of **"cruel and unusual punishment."** In the Supreme Court's view, this means first that certain kinds of penalties (torture, for example) may not be imposed at all; second, that certain acts or conditions (such as alcoholism) may not be made criminal;[53] and third, that penalties may not be imposed capriciously. Indeed, the Eighth Amendment comes into play most frequently when someone has been sentenced to death. In only a few noncapital cases has the Court overturned a sentence because it was too extreme.[54] Most recently, in 2012, the Court found that sentencing a juvenile to life in prison without parole violated the Eighth Amendment.[55] More typically, though, the Court is reluctant to find the length of sentences to be cruel and unusual; in 2003 the Court upheld the use of "three strikes" laws (by which criminals are given long sentences, such as twenty-five years to life) for a third felony offense, regardless of its severity.[56]

Between 1930 and mid-2014 there were approximately 5,243 legal executions in the United States, with about 75 percent of these occurring before 1972. Today, thirty-two of the fifty states—as well as the federal government—allow capital punishment; however, the states vary widely in terms of the number of executions carried out, as Figure 3.1 shows. Nationally, about 3,070 persons were on "death row" as of mid-2014.[57] Opponents of the death penalty would like the Supreme Court to impose more restrictions on the states. Death penalty opponents claimed a rare victory in 2005 when the Court held that the execution of defendants under the age of eighteen was a cruel and unusual punishment.[58] Even if executions are not inherently "cruel and unusual," many believe that they are racially discriminatory because African Americans are more likely than whites to be sentenced to die, as are killers of whites versus killers of African Americans.[59] Others conclude that the sentencing process is fundamentally flawed because it results in caprice. One study found little or no difference between the facts of murder cases in which the death penalty was imposed and in which it was not.[60]

The constitutionality of capital punishment remains a contentious issue. In 2008, the Court rejected an argument that lethal injection as a method of capital punishment subjected the condemned to cruel and unusual punishment. However, it overturned a Louisiana law that allowed for the death penalty as a punishment for the rape of a child because "evolving standards of decency" preclude death as a punishment for a crime that does not itself cause a death.[61]

Eighth Amendment

The part of the Bill of Rights that prohibits "cruel and unusual punishment," which is often at issue in death penalty cases

cruel and unusual punishment

Prohibited by the Eighth Amendment—at issue in capital cases

Ninth Amendment

Part of the Bill of Rights that cautions that the people possess rights not specified in the Constitution

| 3.5 | A Right to Privacy |

Some liberties Americans enjoy are not specifically mentioned in the Constitution, as the **Ninth Amendment** cautions. One such judicially discovered civil liberty is the right to privacy, announced in 1965.[62] With far-reaching implications, this decision invalidated a Connecticut statute that prohibited the use of birth control devices.

Figure 3.1 | Executions by State, 1976–2014*

In Furman v. Georgia, *408 U.S. 238 (1972), the Supreme Court ruled 5–4 that the death penalty, as then administered, was cruel and unusual punishment in violation of the Eighth Amendment. Too much discretion in the hands of juries and judges had made application of the death penalty capricious. Most states then reinstated capital punishment (as did Congress for aircraft hijacking) with more carefully drawn statutes to meet the Court's objections in* Furman. In Gregg v. Georgia, *428 U.S. 152 (1976), a majority of the Supreme Court concluded that the death penalty was not inherently cruel and unusual and upheld a two-step sentencing scheme designed to set strict standards for trial courts. A jury would first decide the question of guilt and then in a separate proceeding impose punishment. Of the thirty-two states that now permit capital punishment, two (New Hampshire and Kansas) executed no one between 1976 and 2014. The states of Texas, Virginia, Oklahoma, and Florida accounted for approximately 60 percent of the executions during that time span. Twenty states executed 98 convicted capital felons in 1999—the largest number of executions in a single year since 1951, when 105 persons were put to death.*

* Data are current through 17 July 2014.   SOURCE: Death Penalty Information Center.

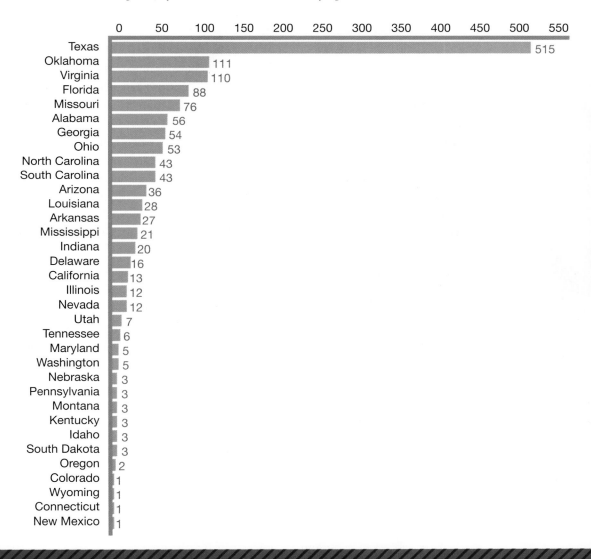

Several decisions that followed led to *Roe v. Wade*,[63] the landmark abortion case. Throwing out the abortion laws of almost all the states, the Court recognized a woman's interest in terminating her pregnancy, the state's interest in protecting her health, and the state's interest in protecting "prenatal life." According to the seven-justice majority, the Constitution prohibited virtually all restrictions on abortions during the first trimester of pregnancy, allowed reasonable medical regulations to guard the woman's health in the second trimester (but no outright prohibitions of abortion), and permitted the state to ban abortions only in the third trimester after the point of fetal "viability" (except when the pregnancy endangered the woman's life). For fifteen years after *Roe*, Congress and some state legislatures tried to limit the availability of abortion and to discourage its use; however, the Supreme Court invalidated most restrictions, reasoning that the right to an abortion was a fundamental right, and thus the government had to show compelling reasons when the right was curtailed.

In 1989, opponents of abortion won a significant victory in the Supreme Court. In a case from Missouri, five justices upheld (among other things) a requirement for fetal viability testing prior to the twenty-fourth week of pregnancy—something the Court previously would doubtlessly have struck down.[64] Moreover, the Court discarded *Roe*'s trimester-based analysis of the abortion right, but stopped short of overruling *Roe*. In 1992, the Court upheld parts of a Pennsylvania statute that imposed several conditions before a woman could obtain an abortion.[65] These included informed consent provisions, a twenty-four-hour waiting period, parental consent for minors, and record-keeping regulations for medical personnel. However, the Court refused to accept a requirement for spousal notification because it imposed an "undue burden" on the abortion right.

(Shutterstock)

The decisions in the Missouri and Pennsylvania cases have led to four conclusions. First, abortion is no longer a fundamental right, but it does enjoy modest constitutional protection. Second, and as a consequence of the first, total or near-total bans on abortion are almost certainly unconstitutional. Third, it remains to be seen what additional abortion regulations the Court is prepared to accept. Fourth, except for outright bans, a woman's freedom to terminate a pregnancy now depends largely on what her state legislature, Congress, and the executive branch allow. That being said, in 2000 the Court further defined the scope of legislative restrictions by ruling unconstitutional a Nebraska statute that criminalized late-term abortions that used a specific medical procedure (called "partial birth" by its opponents).[66] In a follow-up case in 2007, however, the Court refused to strike down a more narrowly worded federal law banning the procedure.[67] The right to choose abortion again came into play in 2010, when antiabortion legislators threatened to block passage of the healthcare reform bill until they were assured that limits on federal funding of abortion would be kept in place.[68]

Roe v. Wade

Supreme Court decision [410 U.S. 113 (1973)] establishing a constitutional right to abortion

How Much Affirmative Action?

Suppose that a school board and a teachers' union agree to increase the number of minority faculty members in public schools. In this district there has been no prior racial discrimination; the union and the school officials simply conclude that it is good publicity to hire more minority teachers. Suppose, also, that the agreement protects minority teachers by providing that if layoffs become necessary, the percentage of minority teachers would not be reduced. Next assume that budget reductions force layoffs, with the result that white teachers with greater seniority are laid off before minority teachers with less. In a 1986 case with similar facts from Jackson, Michigan,[1] the Supreme Court ruled that racially preferential firing was not permissible unless identifiable victims of past discrimination were being protected. Most justices thought the Michigan plan went too far by imposing undue burdens on particular individuals in order to achieve the laudable objective of racial equality. Yet, a majority believed that racially preferential hiring was permissible under certain circumstances. According to Justice Sandra Day O'Connor, "A public employer, consistent with the Constitution, may undertake an affirmative action program which is designed to further a legitimate remedial purpose and which implements that purpose by means that do not impose disproportionate harm on the interests, or unnecessarily trammel the rights, of innocent individuals."

In another situation, suppose that a city government requires contractors receiving city business to subcontract out a certain percentage of the dollar amount of each contract to one or more minority-owned businesses. Called a set-aside quota, the plan is designed to assist minorities by overcoming their exclusion in past years from the construction trade. Modeling its program on a 10 percent set-aside mandated by Congress and upheld by the Supreme Court in 1980,[2] the city council in Richmond, Virginia, adopted a 30 percent set-aside plan in 1983. In 1989, however, the Supreme Court ruled that the quota violated the Fourteenth Amendment's equal protection clause.[3] According to Justice O'Connor, "To accept Richmond's claim that past societal discrimination alone can serve as a basis for rigid racial preferences would be to open the door to competing claims for 'remedial relief' for every disadvantaged group. The dream of a Nation of equal citizens in a society where race is irrelevant to personal opportunity and achievement would be lost in a mosaic of shifting preferences based on inherently unmeasurable claims of past wrongs" The ruling in the *Richmond* case has had a widespread impact—36 states and 190 cities had similar remedial programs.

In a situation like the Michigan case, should consideration of race be permitted in hiring but not in firing? In his dissent in the layoff case, Justice John Paul Stevens compared the Michigan plan to a contract that gives added job protection to computer science or foreign-language teachers. Should race-based classifications be regarded differently from those that are skill-based? In the *Richmond* case, do you agree with the Court's decision? Should it make any difference that a bare majority of Richmond's city council was African American at the time the council adopted the set-aside quota? The Court has also addressed affirmative action in college admissions (see the section titled "Affirmative Action" later in this chapter). Do your views on affirmative action differ depending on whether it involves school or work? Why or why not?

1   *Wygant v. Jackson Board of Education,* 476 U.S. 267 (1986).

2   *Fullilove v. Klutznick,* 448 U.S. 448 (1980).

3   *Richmond v. J. A. Croson Co.,* 488 U.S. 469 (1989).

3.5b   Personal Autonomy and Sexual Orientation

For many people, the principle of personal autonomy, which lies at the heart of privacy cases, suggests that government should leave people alone in their choices about sexual relations. Nonetheless, all states today have laws regulating private behavior and personal relations to some extent. Sexual privacy has been an issue of particular concern among members of the LGBTQ community (those who identify as lesbian, gay, bisexual, transgender, or queer), who have been the group most frequently affected by state forays into sexual privacy. In some locales, same-sex couples may not

In some areas, same-sex couples may not adopt or have legal custody of children. (iStock)

adopt or have legal custody of children. While twenty-one states and numerous cities have banned discrimination based on gender identity and/or sexual orientation, it remains legal in many places to engage in sexual orientation discrimination in housing and public accommodation practices.[69]

The two most salient issues regarding government regulation of sexual orientation have been anti-sodomy laws and laws recognizing or banning same-sex marriages and domestic partnerships. Before 2003, five states outlawed sodomy (oral or anal sex) between persons of the same gender, and twelve more states outlawed sodomy regardless of gender. Although the Supreme Court found such policies acceptable under the Constitution in 1986, ten years later it found that a Colorado constitutional amendment that prohibited laws barring discrimination against homosexuals was in violation of the equal protection clause of the Fourteenth Amendment.[70] In 2003, the Court went a step further, directly overturning the 1986 decision and declaring that laws prohibiting sexual acts between same-sex partners violated the due process clause of the Fourteenth Amendment.[71]

Regarding same-sex marriage, in 1996 Congress passed the Defense of Marriage Act, which provided a federal definition of marriage that specifically excluded same-gender couples. Forty-one states passed similar laws, many of which have now been challenged in the courts.[72] In 2004, the Massachusetts Supreme Judicial Court brought more attention to this controversy when it held that a proposed state law creating civil unions for same-sex couples was discriminatory and that the state must give same-sex couples the same marriage rights as opposite-sex couples. In reaction to this decision, eleven states modified their statutes or constitutions in November 2004 to specifically forbid same-sex marriage. In May 2008, the California Supreme Court found the state's ban on same-sex marriage to be unconstitutional, and the state began issuing marriage licenses to same-sex couples in June of that year. However in November 2008, California voters went to the polls and a narrow majority voted for a ballot initiative that revised the state constitution in order to re-institute the ban. The initiative was subsequently challenged in federal court on the grounds that it served no legitimate state interest and that gays and lesbians should be treated as a protected class with constitutional protections from discrimination. The trial court decided that the law was unconstitutional, and when the governor and attorney general refused to defend the law, the Supreme Court held that the district court decision must stand, making same-sex marriage legal in the nation's largest state.[73] In 2011, New York joined New Hampshire, Massachusetts, Connecticut, Iowa, and Vermont as states legalizing same-sex marriage. President Barack Obama (2009–) made headlines in May 2012 when he became the first president to take a public position in favor of same-sex marriage. Then, in 2013, a big change occurred. In the case *United States v. Windsor* the Supreme Court held the federal Defense of Marriage Act unconstitutional.[74] Finding that this law resulted in discrimination against a class of persons that many states sought to protect, the Court majority concluded that it must be invalidated on equal protection grounds. As a majority of Americans now believe same-sex marriages should be recognized by the law as valid, and as other states and the federal government grapple with their own laws and constitutional amendments, this issue promises to be one of evolving debate in the years to come. It also appears to be an issue of generational divide. While 55 percent of Americans overall support legal same-sex marriage, that figure rises to 78 percent among the eighteen- to twenty-nine-year-old demographic.[75]

3.6 Racial Equality

The United States is racially and ethnically wealthy because of centuries of immigration from virtually every part of the globe. The nation's motto (*E Pluribus Unum*—"out of many, one") symbolizes this coming together of peoples as much as it does the union of the states. Some groups have encountered massive discrimination, however; racial, religious, and ethnic stigmas have been real barriers for many. Perhaps because of color—and certainly because of centuries of slavery—African Americans have had the biggest challenge overcoming discrimination in America. Latinos, whose numbers in this nation have increased in recent years, have faced some of the same obstacles to equality.

3.6a Equality: A Concept in Dispute

A word like *equality* can mean different things to different people. For believers in **equality of opportunity**, it is enough if government removes barriers of discrimination that have existed in the past. If life is like a marathon, all people should be allowed to participate by having a number and a place at the starting line. Others think government should promote **equality of condition**. To do this, policies should seek to reduce or even eliminate handicaps that certain runners face because of the lingering effects of past discriminations. The marathon can hardly be fair, they say, if some runners start out with their shoelaces tied together or have to wear ill-fitting shoes. Accordingly, the government will have to redistribute income and resources, collecting from those who have more and giving to those who have less. Head Start programs for preschool children and need-based scholarships for

Head Start programs for preschool children are intended to further equality of condition. Actress Jennifer Garner reads to children in a Head Start program. (AP World Wide Photo)

equality of opportunity

A standard that calls for government to remove barriers of discrimination, such as segregation laws or racially exclusive hiring practices, that have existed in the past

equality of condition

A standard, beyond equality of opportunity, that requires policies (such as redistribution of income and other resources) that seek to reduce or eliminate the effects of past discrimination

table 3.2 | Chronology of Major Civil Rights Decisions, Laws, and Amendments

The drive for political equality for all Americans has been a long process and remains incomplete. Congressional statutes and Supreme Court decisions since the Civil War have been important in achieving equality.

1865 Thirteenth Amendment abolishes slavery and "involuntary servitude"

1868 Fourteenth Amendment prohibits state action denying any person "the equal protection of the laws"

1870 Fifteenth Amendment removes race as a qualification for voting

1875 Civil Rights Act bans racial discrimination in places of public accommodation

1883 Civil Rights cases hold 1875 statute unconstitutional

1896 *Plessy v. Ferguson* upholds constitutionality of state law requiring racial segregation on trains in "separate but equal" facilities

1920 Nineteenth Amendment extends franchise to women

1954 *Brown v. Board of Education of Topeka* declares unconstitutional racially segregated public schools; *Plessy v. Ferguson* reversed

1957 Congress establishes the Civil Rights Commission

1963 Congress passes the Equal Pay Act

1964 Congress passes the Civil Rights Act: Title II outlaws racial discrimination in places of public accommodation; Title IV allows the Justice Department to sue school districts on behalf of African American students seeking integrated education; Title VI bans racial discrimination in federally funded programs; Title VII prohibits most forms of discrimination (on the basis of race or gender) in employment and creates the Equal Employment Opportunity Commission

Twenty-fourth Amendment eliminates poll taxes in federal elections

1965 Congress passes the Voting Rights Act; President Johnson bans racial discrimination by federal contractors

1968 Civil Rights Act's Title VIII prohibits most forms of discrimination in sale or rental of housing

1971 Twenty-sixth Amendment lowers national voting age to 18

1972 Congress submits Equal Rights Amendment to states for ratification

1978 *Regents v. Bakke* invalidates a medical school admissions program that reserved a specific number of seats for minority applicants

1979 *Steelworkers v. Weber* upholds legality of a voluntary affirmative action plan for industrial apprenticeships that gives preference to African American workers over white workers with greater seniority

1982 Ratification of Equal Rights Amendment fails; Congress extends and amends Voting Rights Act; Title IX of Educational Amendments bars sex discrimination in "any education program or activity receiving Federal financial assistance"

1989 *Richmond v. J. A. Croson Co.* invalidates a municipally mandated 30 percent set-aside quota for racial minorities

1990 Congress enacts the National Hate Crimes Statistics Act, which requires the Justice Department to gather data on crimes motivated by prejudice about race, religion, ethnicity, or sexual orientation; the Americans with Disabilities Act becomes law

1991	Congress enacts a civil rights bill designed to modify several 1989 Supreme Court decisions that had made on-the-job discrimination more difficult to prove, and affirmative action plans easier to challenge in court
2003	The Supreme Court finds the University of Michigan's law school admission process, which uses race as affirmative criteria, acceptable because it is narrowly tailored
2006	Congress reauthorizes the Voting Rights Act for an additional twenty-five years
2011	President Obama certifies the congressional act repealing the military's "Don't Ask, Don't Tell" policy (This allows gay men, lesbians, and bisexuals to serve openly in the military for the first time.)

college students are obvious devices intended to further equality of condition. Some find such policies inadequate. The effects of inequality, whether of wealth or race or gender, are too strong and pervasive. Government must, therefore, pursue **equality of result**. In the marathon, government may have to carry some runners to the finish line if they are to get there at all. Some affirmative action programs are aimed at achieving equality of result.

3.6b The Legacy: Slavery and Third-Class Citizenship

Shortly after the Civil War ended, in 1865, ratification of the **Thirteenth Amendment** banished slavery and "involuntary servitude" from the country. Following quickly were ratification of the Fourteenth and Fifteenth Amendments in 1868 and 1870 and passage of several civil rights acts. Collectively these conferred rights of citizenship on the newly freed slaves and officially removed race as a criterion for voting. Especially significant was the **equal protection clause** of the Fourteenth Amendment: "Nor shall any State deny to any person within its jurisdiction the equal protection of the laws" (see Table 3.2).

By the end of the nineteenth century, however, it was clear that the nation had abandoned the promise of full citizenship for the former slaves. Enforcement of civil rights laws became lax, and the Supreme Court made it clear that the Constitution would not stand in the way of racially discriminatory policies. In *Plessy v. Ferguson*, for example, the Court announced the **separate-but-equal doctrine** in upholding a Louisiana law that required racial segregation on trains.[76] As long as racially separate facilities were "equal," the Court maintained, the Constitution had not been violated.

Three kinds of policies then developed that denied many African Americans their rights until after the middle of the twentieth century. First, the law racially segregated virtually every aspect of life in the South (the region of the nation in which most African Americans lived). Segregation existed elsewhere, too, but it was enforced more by custom than by law. No section of the nation was immune to racist attitudes and racially motivated violence, including riots and lynchings. Segregated neighborhoods became fixtures in the North and South alike.

Second, Southern politicians systematically excluded African Americans from the political process. To get around the Fifteenth Amendment, legislatures turned to devices such as poll taxes, good character tests, and literacy tests to keep African Americans away from the ballot box. Until its use was declared unconstitutional by

equality of result

A standard, beyond equality of condition, that requires policies such as affirmative action or comparable worth that places some people on an equal footing with others

Thirteenth Amendment

The first of the Civil War amendments to the Constitution; adopted in 1865, it banned slavery throughout the United States

equal protection clause

Part of the Fourteenth Amendment that is the source of many civil rights and declares that no state shall deny to any person "the equal protection of the laws"

separate-but-equal doctrine

The standard announced by the Supreme Court in *Plessy v. Ferguson* in 1896 that allowed racially separate facilities on trains (and by implication in public services such as education), as long as the separate facilities were equal (overturned by *Brown v. Board of Education of Topeka* in 1954)

the Supreme Court,[77] the "grandfather clause" allowed whites to vote who would otherwise have been disfranchised by those same barriers. Of all the discriminatory devices, the white primary was probably the most effective. Because one party (the Democrats) was dominant in the region after 1900, the real electoral choices in state, local, and congressional races were made in the primary—not in the general election. White Democrats thus excluded African Americans from meaningful political participation by adopting party rules that allowed only whites to vote in the Democratic primaries. Even though the white primary seems an affront to the Fifteenth Amendment, it was not until 1944 that the Supreme Court ruled that such deception violated the Constitution.[78] Still, for two decades afterward most African Americans were kept from voting in many places.

Third, without the vote African Americans were shortchanged across the board in the delivery of public services such as education. Favors are rarely extended to entire groups that are permanently disfranchised, especially when they bear racial or religious stigmas as well. Thus, the spirit of *Plessy* was honored only in part; although separate, services and facilities were rarely equal.

3.6c   The Counterattack

Opponents of racism saw little hope of victory through the legislative process. At the local level, African Americans were politically powerless in the areas in which segregation was most pervasive. At the national level, Congress operated racially segregated schools in Washington, D.C., and provided separate eating and working places for African American civil servants. Even Uncle Sam's toilets were marked "Whites Only" and "Colored." The armed forces remained racially segregated until President Harry Truman (1945–1953) ordered an end to the practice in 1948.

Thus, the counterattack against racism looked to the federal judiciary and was led principally by the National Association for the Advancement of Colored People. Known by its initials, the **NAACP** was founded in 1909 to improve the social, economic, and political condition of African Americans. A separate division for litigation, called the Legal Defense Fund (LDF), began work in 1939 and had the primary responsibility of pressing the desegregation drive in courtrooms in the 1940s, 1950s, and 1960s. One prominent African American attorney in the LDF was Thurgood Marshall, later the first African American justice on the Supreme Court (1967–1991).

The National Civil Rights Museum was established in Memphis, Tennessee, in 1991. Visit this website for an interactive tour of the museum.

http://www.bvtlab.com/3833V

The assault on racial segregation reached a climax in the landmark decision of May 17, 1954: ***Brown v. Board of Education of Topeka***.[79] "Does segregation of children in public schools solely on the basis of race, even though the physical facilities and other 'tangible' factors may be equal, deprive the children of the minority group of equal educational opportunities?" asked Chief Justice Earl Warren (1953–1969). "We believe that it does. ... In the field of public education," he concluded, "the doctrine of 'separate but equal' has no place. Separate educational facilities are inherently unequal." *Plessy* was overruled.

3.6d   Putting *Brown* to Work: The Law and Politics of Integration

The Court had made its decision. What was to happen? Rather than order an immediate end to segregation, the justices announced that integration was to proceed "with all deliberate speed."[80] In most places "deliberate speed" proved to be a turtle's pace.

NAACP

National Association for the Advancement of Colored People; an organization founded to improve the social, economic, and political condition of African Americans

Brown v. Board of Education of Topeka

Landmark Supreme Court decision [347 U.S. 483 (1954)] that overturned the separate-but-equal standard of *Plessy v. Ferguson* [163 U.S. 537 (1896)] and began an end to racial segregation in public schools

A decade after the Court's historic pronouncement, less than 1 percent of the African American children in the states of the old Confederacy were attending public school with white children. In six border states and the District of Columbia the figure was much higher: 52 percent.

Several factors severely hampered quick implementation of *Brown*, making the 1954 decision a test case of the Supreme Court's power. First, some federal judges in the South were themselves opposed to integration. They did little to press for *Brown*'s speedy implementation. Second, state legislatures and local school boards usually reflected strong white opposition to *Brown*'s enforcement. Third, fear of hostile reaction by the local white community discouraged litigation. It was economically and physically risky for parents of African American children to sue local officials. Fourth, the Court received little initial support from Congress, the White House, and a large part of the organized legal community.

Significant enforcement of *Brown* and the lowering of other racial barriers did not come until civil rights activists, such as Martin Luther King Jr., riveted the nation's attention on the injustices that persisted and called for action. Congress then enacted two important pieces of legislation: the **Civil Rights Act of 1964** and the Elementary and Secondary Education Act of 1965. The importance of the first act for *Brown* came in Title VI: Every federal agency that funded local programs through grants, loans, or contracts was required to press for an end to racial discrimination. The 1965 school aid act was the first massive federal appropriation for local school systems; to keep the money, however, school systems had to move swiftly on integration. The 1964 act was the hook, and the 1965 act was the bait. Ironically, public schools in the South are now among the most integrated in the nation, whereas schools in the Northeast are among the most segregated.

3.6e   The Continuing Effects of *Brown*

Supreme Court decisions about school integration since 1971 have come largely from states outside the South. Non-Southern school systems had segregated schools, but rarely had law segregated them recently. The racial composition of these schools reflected decades of residential segregation that had resulted from economic inequities and private discrimination. This kind of "unofficial" segregation was called **de facto segregation**; but in a pair of decisions from Ohio in 1979,[81] the Supreme Court decided that "racially identifiable schools" in any district probably resulted from school board policy. What many had thought to be de facto segregation was now considered **de jure segregation**: racial separation caused by government policy. Because of the 1979 ruling, local officials now have the affirmative duty of redrawing attendance zones and busing pupils from one part of town to another.

Busing itself remains controversial. Many parents—African American and white alike—object to having their children transported farther than seems necessary. Many prefer neighborhood schools. Aside from achieving integration, scholars disagree on the effects of busing and similar measures on the schoolchildren involved, debating whether integration improves the educational performance of African American students. Although integrated schools often mean that African American parents lose control over schools in African American neighborhoods, integrated education probably prepares all students better for living in a racially diverse society. Moreover, many believe that "green follows white"—that the presence of white students assures more generous economic support of a school by local officials. Nonetheless, the Supreme Court has now taken the position that once a school district has eliminated

Civil Rights Act of 1964

Comprehensive legislation to end racial segregation in access to public accommodations and in employment in the public and private sectors

de facto segregation

Programs or facilities that are racially segregated by private choice or private discrimination, not because of law or public policy

de jure segregation

Programs or facilities that are racially segregated because of law or public policy

Segregated drinking fountains symbolized the separate worlds of the South until the 1960s. (Library of Congress)

segregation, the district ceases to be under a constitutional obligation to continue the policies that produced the integrated system, even if "re-segregation" might result.[82]

Whatever the progress has been with school integration, social segregation remains a fact in many areas of the nation. Even though the Civil Rights Acts of 1964 and 1968, respectively, prohibit racial discrimination in employment and in the sale or rental of housing (as do the laws in most states and hundreds of municipalities), African Americans remain the most segregated minority group—the group most isolated from whites.

3.6f Affirmative Action

Many people believe that ending discrimination is not enough. They believe that positive steps called **affirmative action** are also needed to overcome the residual effects of generations of racial bias. Others oppose affirmative action if it involves preferential treatment for minorities. They argue that jobs and university scholarships, for example, are finite. To give to one means to withhold from someone else. They make the case that the nonminority applicant who loses out because of race has been hurt in much the same way as a minority applicant in earlier years who was kept out because of race.

If a national consensus has developed against racial discrimination in its old forms, no firm consensus exists on affirmative action. A recent poll indicates that 58 percent of Americans favor affirmative action programs, but 37 percent oppose them; however, only 28 percent of Americans believe race should be taken into account in college admissions.[83] Even the Supreme Court has been divided, as *Regents of the University of California v. Bakke*[84] illustrates. In this landmark affirmative action case, the Supreme Court invalidated the use of a racial quota for medical school admissions at the Davis campus of the University of California, but it said that race could still be taken into account. Admissions officers may use race as one of several criteria in evaluating the record of an applicant but may not admit or exclude solely on the basis of race. In 2003, twenty-five years after *Bakke*, the Court again took up the issue, holding that the University of Michigan's undergraduate admission system unfairly allowed race to play too decisive a role because it failed to treat applicants as individuals rather than merely group members.[85] On the other hand, the Court found Michigan's law school admission process acceptable because its use of race as affirmative criteria was narrowly tailored.[86] In other cases, the Court has allowed governments and private businesses wide latitude in personnel decisions.

Title VII of the Civil Rights Act of 1964 bans job discrimination on the basis of "race, color, religion, sex, or national origin." The Court has reasoned that a law intended to end discrimination against racial minorities and women should not be used to prohibit programs designed to help those groups.[87] Finally, in its two most recent affirmative action cases, the Court has held that admissions policies can only consider race if the university can meet the "strict scrutiny" standard of showing a

affirmative action

Positive steps taken by public or private institutions to overcome the remaining effects of racial or sexual bias (Affirmative action programs attempt to achieve equality of result.)

Race and (In)Justice: Ferguson, Missouri

On August 9, 2014, at a little past noon, unarmed African American teenager Michael Brown was shot and killed by white police officer Darren Wilson in the town of Ferguson, Missouri. Beyond this simple statement of fact, we will never know for certain the specific circumstances that led to this tragedy. What we do know is this: The event crystallized for many the ongoing struggles and tensions our nation experiences when it comes to race. In the hours, days, and months following the killing of Michael Brown, many people came to Ferguson or discussed its significance. There were peaceful protests, demands for justice, damage to local businesses, violent acts, curfews, clashes between citizens and law enforcement, accusations, and frustrations. When a grand jury failed to indict Officer Wilson on November 24, 2014, it was as if the wound of Brown's death had been reopened. Missouri Governor Jay Nixon declared a state of emergency and called out the National Guard in an attempt to restore peace to the troubled community. Many took this outcome as a sign of the failure of our justice system.

Why was this event so significant? What made Michael Brown's death an issue of national, not just personal, tragedy? One answer has to do with the reality of stark differences in the American criminal justice system. African American teenagers are twenty-one times more likely to be shot and killed by police officers than white teens. Moreover, African Americans and Latinos make up 25 percent of the total U.S. population, but 58 percent of those incarcerated in our nation's prisons and jails. If these trends continue, one in three African American males born today will be imprisoned over the course of his lifetime, but only one in seventeen white men will suffer that fate.[1] On the other side of the equation, we have a law enforcement system that is largely white: 75 percent of local police officers are white. In the town of Ferguson, for example, the total population is two-thirds African American, but there are only three African Americans on the town's fifty-three-member police force.

Another reason the events in Ferguson, Missouri, became a part of the national conversation is that perceptions of the facts described above differ markedly. In the weeks following the shooting of Brown, 80 percent of African Americans, but only 37 percent of white Americans, said the event "raises important issues about race." Racial profiling, use of force, and the militarization of domestic law enforcement are also issues Americans often view differently depending on their own ascriptive identities. Sixty percent of white Americans trust the ability of police to protect them from violent crime, but less than half of nonwhite Americans feel the same way. Similar double-digit racial differences exist when Americans are polled about their confidence in the police or the criminal justice system generally. And what causes the disparate outcomes described in the previous paragraph? Fifty percent of African Americans say the cause is mostly discrimination, but only 19 percent of white Americans agree.

What does Michael Brown's homicide mean for American politics? Among other things, it reminds us that the processes and policies of our system of government have very real consequences for us. The politicians we vote for in federal, state, and local elections shape our communities and our justice system. The choices we have made over centuries and that we continue to make today have created an imperfect system that we must continue to improve. When America was founded, we endeavored to (among other things) "form a more perfect Union, establish Justice, [and] insure domestic Tranquility." Ferguson, Missouri, in 2014 reminds us of how hard we still need to work to attain those goals.

SOURCES: The Week, October 24, 2014. "Criminal Justice Fact Sheet," NAACP. org (November 25, 2014). Ibid. Bureau of Justice Statistics, http://www.bjs.gov/index.cfm?ty=tp&tid=71 (November 25, 2014). "Ferguson: A Tipping Point for Black Americans?" The Week, September 5, 2014. The Gallup Organization, "Nonwhites Less Likely to Feel Police Protect and Serve Them," November 17, 2014, http://www.gallup.com/poll/179468/nonwhites-less-likely-feel-police-protect-serve.aspx (November 25, 2014). The Gallup Organization, 2013.

1 Freeman v. Pitts, 503 U.S. 467 (1992).

compelling state interest; moreover, it is permissible for a state constitutional amendment to ban the use of race-conscious admissions policies entirely.[88]

What, then, are the limits to affirmative action under the law? There is no clear answer to this question. Generally, policies by an employer to overcome the effects of its past discrimination are permissible; indeed, they may be required. Even some policies by an employer to alleviate general "societal discrimination" for which the employer is not responsible are permissible. Hiring policies that look like "quotas" or admissions policies that assign point values to one's race have the greatest chance of being struck down.[89]

3.6g Voting Rights

Two centuries ago most Americans were denied the right to vote. The Constitution left voting qualifications to the states, with the result that women, African Americans, and even some white adult males were left out. Since the 1820s, the national trend has

The Voting Rights Act of 1965 was the most important voting legislation ever enacted by Congress. The legislation provided African Americans the right to vote without discrimination. (AP World Wide Photo)

been to chip away at these restrictions so that today almost all adult citizens in the United States have the right to vote.

As late as 1964, however, African Americans in particular were systemically denied the right to vote in most parts of the South. The response to this situation was the **Voting Rights Act of 1965**—the most important voting legislation ever enacted by Congress. Besides removing many barriers to voting, the act requires that any change in a "standard, practice, or procedure with respect to voting" in certain parts of the United States (most of them being in the South) can take effect only after being cleared by the attorney general of

the United States or by the United States District Court for the District of Columbia. The Supreme Court has interpreted "standard, practice, or procedure" to include any change in a locale's electoral system. This advance clearance requirement is satisfied only if the proposed change has neither the *purpose* nor the *effect* of "denying or abridging the right to vote on account of race or color." This means that African American voting power can in no way be weakened or diluted by any change in local election practices.

Congress made an important change in the law in 1982, banning existing electoral arrangements with a racially discriminatory effect anywhere in the United States. Conceivably, this addition to the law may produce a realignment of political power in sections of the country in which African Americans and Latinos amount to at least a sizable minority of the population, and in which local political practices dilute the political influence of these minorities. More recently, the Court ruled in 1993 that reapportionment schemes may violate the equal protection clause if they are drawn based solely on race—even when the intent is to increase racial minority representation.[90] Evidence that the Voting Rights Act continues to be controversial can be found in the 2006 congressional debates over renewing the act. Southern Republicans opposed extending the provisions requiring some states (mostly in the South) to obtain preclearance before altering their voting laws, and other legislators balked at extending

Voting Rights Act of 1965

Major legislation designed to overcome racial barriers to voting, primarily in the Southern States; it was extended again in 2006 for twenty-five years

requirements to provide ballots in multiple languages.[91] Ultimately, the act was extended for another twenty-five years, with some portions being made permanent. President George W. Bush signed the reauthorization act into law on July 27, 2006.

Provisions of this reauthorization faced legal challenges, though, and in 2009 the Supreme Court unanimously ruled that the law's "preclearance" provisions can be challenged by individual communities ("political subdivisions") seeking permanent exemption based on the argument that discrimination is no longer a concern in their locality.[92] Then, in 2013, a narrowly divided Court weakened the power of the Voting Rights Act still further. Finding the formula that identified those jurisdictions to be anachronistic and an overreach of federal power, it struck down the provision listing preclearance jurisdictions entirely. Stating that the nation had changed greatly since the act's initial passage, the Court insisted that legislation must address current conditions.[93] As a result of this decision some jurisdictions, such as Texas, have adopted new voter ID laws and redistricting maps that may not have been approved by the federal government had preclearance still been in effect. The long-term effects on voter registration and turnout remain to be seen.

The Voting Rights Act has had a far-reaching impact. African Americans in the Southern states now vote at a rate approximating that of whites. In the 2014 election for the U.S. House of Representatives, voters nationally chose forty-seven African American and twenty-nine Latino members—a number that amounts to about 17 percent of the chamber. At the time of writing, there are currently two African Americans and three Latinos serving in the U.S. Senate. Of course, it goes without saying that the 2008 presidential election was a landmark for African Americans in electoral politics. Illinois Senator Barack Obama, the son of a black father and white mother, became the first African American identified presidential nominee of a major party when he was chosen as the Democratic nominee after a hard-fought primary season. He made history again in November 2008, when he was elected as the first African American president. One of the most significant acts of President Obama's first year in office was to appoint Sonia Sotomayor to the Supreme Court, making her the first Latina Supreme Court justice.

3.7   Sexual Equality

Because the political system has been a battleground for so many years in the fight for racial equality, it is easy to suppose that sexual equality has occupied the attention of Congress and the courts for just as long. However, such has not been the case. Making the nation free of discrimination based on gender has been a national priority for only about four decades.

3.7a   The Legacy

Until recently, the legal status of women in the United States was one of substantial inequality. A wife had no legal existence apart from her husband. Without his consent, she could make no contracts that bound either of them. In response to such attitudes, the first convention on women's rights was held in 1848 in Seneca Falls, New York. Change in attitudes came slowly, however. Even the Fourteenth Amendment spoke of "male inhabitants." The **Nineteenth Amendment**, extending the franchise to women, was not ratified until 1920, after a long and turbulent

Nineteenth Amendment

Amendment ratified in 1920 that prohibits limitations on voting based on sex

The Nineteenth Amendment prohibits state and federal governments from denying citizens the right to vote because of their gender. (iStock)

suffrage movement. Not until 1971 did the Supreme Court first invalidate a law because it discriminated against women,[94] and as late as 1973 there were nine hundred gender-based federal laws still on the books.

3.7b Gender to the Forefront

Attacks on racial discrimination during the 1950s helped to turn attention to laws that penalized women because they were women. Sex discrimination became a political issue few politicians could ignore after the publication of books such as Betty Friedan's *Feminine Mystique* in 1963 and Kate Millett's *Sexual Politics* in 1971, and after the formation of the National Organization for Women (NOW) in 1966. At about the same time, the female half of the postwar "baby boom" entered college, graduate schools, and the workforce. There were more women than ever before who were at an age and place in life and career when questions of gender discrimination were very important.

Responding to inequities that had become obvious, Congress passed the Equal Pay Act in 1963, which commanded "equal pay for equal work." Title VII of the Civil Rights Act of 1964 outlawed sexual (as well as racial) bias in employment and promotion practices. Title IX of the 1972 Educational Amendments banned sex discrimination in education programs and activities at colleges receiving federal financial aid. (Title IX remains contentious because of its applicability to how universities allocate dollars between male and female athletic teams.)

As a result of changes in both laws and attitudes, sex-based retirement plans, for example, may no longer require women to make higher contributions or to receive lower monthly benefits than men just because women as a group live longer than men as a group.[95] States may no longer operate single-sex schools of nursing (and probably any other kind), even if coeducational public nursing schools also exist.[96] In the workplace, not only has sexual harassment been judged to be a violation of Title VII, but the Supreme Court also holds employers responsible under the law for not taking steps to prevent it.[97] Despite such remedies, sexual harassment continues to be a problem in many settings, as the reaction to Anita Hill's accusations against Supreme Court nominee Clarence Thomas in 1991 revealed.

Many people believe that real economic equality between the sexes will not be achieved without **comparable worth** (equal pay for jobs of equal value), a policy not required by federal law. Otherwise, they say, full-time female workers will continue to earn on average no more than about two-thirds the pay of full-time male workers.

3.8 Other Americans and Civil Rights

comparable worth

An employment policy designed to overcome the economic inequities of sexual discrimination, mandating that persons holding jobs of equal responsibility and skill be paid the same

Discrimination against women and African Americans has occupied a prominent place on the public agenda in recent years, but discrimination has claimed other victims as well. American Indians, Asian Americans, Latinos, immigrants, and Americans with disabilities have all demanded—with varying degrees of success—that public officials take steps to remedy years of neglect and unequal treatment. Sexual orientation has also been the basis for discrimination by governments, businesses, and individuals, and was discussed as an aspect of privacy earlier in this chapter.

3.8a American Indians

From an estimated sixteenth-century population of perhaps 2 million or more[98] (no one knows for certain), American Indians (also called Native Americans) numbered barely 500,000 in 1900 as war, disease, and systematic slaughter took their toll. Today,

there are over 5.2 million, about 2 percent of the total U.S. population. As a group, American Indians suffer disproportionately high rates of sickness, poverty, illiteracy, and unemployment. Not until 1924 did Congress recognize them as citizens.

In 1924, Congress recognized American Indians as citizens. (iStock)

Many American Indians have understandably resisted assimilation into the rest of the population, insisting instead on preserving their culture and heritage. Approximately one-quarter live on 325 semautonomous reservations and, in Alaska, in 223 native villages under the supervision of the Bureau of Indian Affairs in the Department of the Interior. The Indian Self-Determination and Education Assistance Act of 1975 granted American Indians greater control over their own affairs, and the Indian Bill of Rights of 1968 gave American Indians living on reservations protections similar to those found in the Constitution.

Recent policy reflects resurgent ethnic pride and new political awareness that began in the 1960s and 1970s and has been asserted by activist groups such as the National Indian Youth Council and the American Indian Movement. Such groups have not only protested inadequate national assistance and the plight of the reservation population but also have attempted, with some success, to recover through litigation ancient tribal fishing and land rights sometimes worth millions of dollars. Over the last two decades, several American Indian tribes have been granted state authorization to operate gaming facilities on reservation land, providing an important source of revenue for their communities. With this success, though, has come a backlash. Though tribes have historically operated largely autonomously of state control, state compacts authorizing gaming have resulted in large profits that the non-Indian populations of these states have seen as potential tax revenue, leading some states to seek tax rates on casino profits well in excess of standard business tax rates.

The American Civil Liberties Union is a nonprofit and nonpartisan organization that fights vigorous court battles to defend the civil rights and liberties guaranteed by the Constitution. To find out more about the organization and the issues they are currently addressing, visit this website.

http://www.bvtlab.com/7Ud79

3.8b Latinos

Numbering more than 53 million and making up about 17 percent of the population, Latinos are the nation's fastest-growing minority. In the 2010 census, the number of Americans identifying themselves as Latino was larger than the number identifying

BVT Lab

Flashcards are available for this chapter at www.BVTLab.com.

Chapter 03 | Civil Liberties and Civil Rights | 102

as African American. A majority originally came from Mexico; most of the others came from Puerto Rico, South America, and parts of Central America. Historically, Mexican Americans resided mainly in the Southwest, Cuban Americans in Florida, and Puerto Ricans in the Northeast; today, Latinos live in significant numbers throughout much of the country.

For decades, Latinos have encountered the same discriminations in voting, education, housing, and employment that have confronted African Americans, compounded by a language barrier. Amendments to the Voting Rights Act of 1965 require ballots to be printed in Spanish as well as English in areas in which Spanish-speaking people number more than 5 percent of the population. Partly as a result of this act, Latino voter registration jumped dramatically nationwide between 1972 and 2010, rising to over 51 percent of eligible Latino voters; yet Latinos are still less likely than African Americans and whites to register to vote.[99] Moreover, Title VI of the Civil Rights Act of 1964 requires public schools to provide bilingual instruction to students deficient in English. Both education and political participation are important to any group seeking to maintain ethnic identity in a diverse culture. Policies to lower language barriers have sparked a backlash among those who see non-English-speaking (particularly Spanish-speaking) persons as a threat to an American cultural identity.

3.8c Immigrants

As the Statue of Liberty signifies, America is a land of immigrants—but some have been more welcome than others. Until 1921 entry into the United States was virtually unlimited; but in that year Congress established the first of a series of ceilings on immigration that discriminated against persons from Eastern Europe and Asia, a bias not eliminated until 1965. Today the law sets a ceiling of 675,000 immigrants per year, including those admitted because of job skills and family relationships. Exceptions to the ceiling for refugees and others mean that the total number of immigrants admitted annually exceeds 1 million.

Thousands more—no one knows the exact number—successfully enter or remain in the country illegally, putting pressure on public services and, some say, taking jobs from citizens and others who legally reside in the United States. About 11 million immigrants reside in the United States illegally today. In response to these issues, Congress passed the Immigration Reform and Control Act in 1986. Among other things, the law requires employers to verify the American citizenship or legal status of all job applicants and provides stiff penalties for employers who hire illegal aliens. The 1986 law has had an unintended consequence: discrimination against persons of Latino or Asian descent. A study by the General Accounting Office (an investigatory agency of Congress, now called the Government Accountability Office) found that one in five of the 4.6 million employers surveyed admitted that the law encouraged them to discriminate against job applicants who were "foreign-appearing" or "foreign-sounding."[100] Arizona sparked immigration controversy in 2010 when it passed a law requiring law enforcement officials to determine the immigration status of anyone they reasonably suspected of being an illegal alien. Supporters argued that this misdemeanor offense merely enforces existing federal law, while opponents contended it

The number of immigrants entering the United States was virtually unlimited until 1921. (Library of Congress)

would lead to discriminatory racial profiling.[101] In 2012, The Supreme Court struck down most of the law on federalism grounds, but let stand the provision that requires state law enforcement officials to check the immigration status of people they arrest.[102] The continued influx of immigrants guarantees that "immigration reform" will continue to be an important political topic for the foreseeable future.

3.8d Americans with Disabilities

One of the nation's largest minority groups consists of the more than 56 million Americans with a physical or mental disability. The Civil Rights Act of 1964, the most comprehensive anti-discrimination legislation ever enacted by Congress, did not cover disabled Americans—long victims of bias in both the public and private sectors.

In 1990, Congress passed the Americans with Disabilities Act, which bans discrimination in employment (in businesses with more than fifteen employees) and in places of public accommodation (including not only restaurants and hotels but also establishments as varied as physicians' offices, zoos, sports arenas, and dry cleaners). Called a "bill of rights for Americans with disabilities," the law also stipulates that newly manufactured buses and railroad cars be accessible to persons in wheelchairs and that telephone companies provide service for those with hearing and speech impairments. The law's definition of Americans with disabilities goes beyond those who rely on wheelchairs or who have difficulty seeing or hearing—it includes people with mental disorders and those with AIDS (acquired immune deficiency syndrome) and HIV (the virus that causes AIDS), but not those who use illegal drugs or who abuse legal drugs such as alcohol. Although in 2001 the Supreme Court ruled that the Americans with Disabilities Act required the PGA (Professional Golfers' Association) to allow disabled persons to use golf carts during the PGA tour, the act suffered a major setback when the Court held that state employees could not sue states for failing to comply with the act.[103]

3.9 Liberties and Rights in the Constitutional Framework

Civil rights and liberties, the subjects of this chapter, are part of the framework of American constitutional government. Freedoms of political and religious expression, limits on the police, protection of privacy—all examples of civil liberties—are not only essential components of the political process but also help to define the quality of life Americans enjoy. Civil rights in turn are inspired by the bold assertion of the Declaration of Independence that "all men are created equal." Against a legacy of toleration of inequality, much of what government and private citizens have done in recent decades has been driven by an intolerance of inequality. Through application of constitutional provisions, laws, and policies, many people have tried to make the Declaration's words a reality, for women as well as men, for African Americans as well as whites. Their efforts employ the tools of politics and the major institutions of government, described in the chapters that follow.

CHAPTER REVIEW

1. Civil liberties are freedoms, protected by law, to act or not to act and to be free from unwarranted governmental intrusion in one's life. Civil rights encompass participation in society on an equal footing with others.

2. Initially the Bill of Rights restrained only the national government; however, using the Fourteenth Amendment, the Supreme Court has applied most of the protections of the Bill of Rights to the states.

3. Free expression is necessary to the democratic political process. Only in rare instances today will the Court approve restrictions on the content of what a person says.

4. The free exercise and establishment clauses have two main objectives: separation of church and state and toleration of different religious faiths.

5. Other parts of the Bill of Rights guard liberty by placing limits on what officials may do in the process of fighting crime.

6. By interpretation, the Constitution includes a right to privacy, giving people the right to make basic decisions about procreation without undue interference by government. Abortion continues to be a divisive national issue.

7. Only since the landmark case of *Brown v. Board of Education of Topeka* in 1954 has the nation made significant progress toward removing discrimination on the basis of race from American life. The Voting Rights Act of 1965 has enabled African Americans (as well as others) to participate more equally in the political process.

8. Most discrimination based on sex is generally forbidden by statute and by the Supreme Court's interpretation of the Fourteenth Amendment.

9. LGBTQ individuals, American Indians, Latinos, immigrants, and Americans with disabilities are other groups who face discrimination and present special needs.

KEY TERMS

Readings for Further Study

The Bill of Rights by Irving Brant (American Council of Learned Societies History E-Book Project, 2008) remains one of the best treatments of the origins of the liberties protected in the Constitution.

The rapidly changing field of criminal procedure and criminal justice can be followed in *CJ: Realities and Challenges*, 2nd ed., by Ruth Masters, Lori Beth Way, Phyllis B. Gerstenfeld, Bernadette T. Muscat, Michael Hooper, John P.J. Dussich, Lester Pincu, and Candice A. Skrapec (New York: McGraw-Hill, 2012).

Efforts to achieve racial equality are fully described in Richard Kluger's *Simple Justice* (New York: Vintage, 2004).

A great resource for tracing the statistical history of minority politics is Mart Martin's *The Almanac of Women and Minorities in American Politics 2002* (Boulder, CO: Westview Press, 2001).

Lisa Garcia Bedolla examines Latino politics in *Introduction to Latino Politics in the U.S.* (Boston: Polity, 2010), and Kim Geron provides another useful account in *Latino Political Power* (Boulder, CO: Lynne Rienner, 2005).

American Indian politics is discussed in John M. Meyer, ed., *American Indians and U.S. Politics* (Westport, CT: Praeger, 2002) and *American Indian Politics and the American Political System*, 3rd ed., by David E. Wilkins and Heidi Kiiwetinepinesiik Stark (Lanham, MD: Rowman & Littlefield, 2010).

The emerging field of sexual diversity and politics is well-covered in *The Politics of Gay Rights*, edited by Craig A. Rimmerman, Kenneth D. Wald, and Clyde Wilcox, (Chicago: University of Chicago Press, 2000); in *Same-Sex Marriage in the United States: The Road to the Supreme Court* by Jason Pierceson (Lanham, MD: Rowman & Littlefield, 2013); and in *Victory: The Triumphant Gay Revolution*, by Linda Hirshman (New York: HarperCollins, 2012).

Notes

1. *Barron v. Baltimore*, 32 U.S. (7 Peters) 243 (1833).

2. *McDonald v. Chicago*, 561 U.S. 3025 (2010).

3. *Katz v. United States*, 389 U.S. 347 (1967), overruling *Olmstead v. United States*, 277 U.S. 438 (1928).

4. *Riley v. California*, 573 U.S. ___ (2014).

5. *Schenck v. United States*, 249 U.S. 47 (1919).

6. *Whitney v. California*, 274 U.S. 357, 377 (1927), Justice Brandeis concurring.

7. *Brandenburg v. Ohio*, 395 U.S. 444 (1969).

8. *Morse v. Frederick*, 551 U.S. 393 (2007).

9. *Snyder v. Phelps*, 562 U.S. ___ (2011).

10. *New York Times Co. v. United States*, 403 U.S. 713 (1971).

11. *Miller v. California*, 413 U.S. 5, 8 (1973).

12. *Erie v. Pap's A.M.*, 529 U.S. 277 (2000).

13. *Reno v. ACLU*, 521 U.S. 844 (1997); *Ashcroft v. ACLU*, 535 U.S. 564 (2002); *Ashcroft v. ACLU*, 542 U.S. 656 (2004).

14. *Brown v. Entertainment Merchants Association*, 564 U.S. ___ (2011).

15. *New York Times Co. v. Sullivan*, 376 U.S. 254 (1964).

16. *Texas v. Johnson*, 491 U.S. 397 (1989).

17. *United States v. Eichman*, 496 U.S. 310 (1990).

18. *R.A.V. v. City of St. Paul*, 505 U.S.L.W. 377 (1992).

19. *McCullen v. Coakley*, 573 U.S. ___ (2014).

20. The Gallup Organization, "Religion," http://www.gallup.com/poll/1690/Religion.aspx (July 21, 2014).

21. *Statistical Abstract of the United States*, 2012.

22. For example, see *Westside Community Schools v. Mergens*, 496 U.S. 226 (1990).

23. *Lemon v. Kurtzman*, 403 U.S. 602 (1971).

24. *Arizona Christian School Tuition Organization v. Winn*, 563 U.S. ___ (2011).

25. *Engel v. Vitale*, 370 U.S. 421 (1962); *School District of Abington Township v. Schempp*, 374 U.S. 203 (1963).

26. *Wallace v. Jaffree*, 472 U.S. 38 (1985).

27. *Lee v. Weisman*, 505 U.S. 577 (1992).

28. *Santa Fe Independent School Dist. v. Doe*, 530 U.S. 290 (2000).

29. *Marsh v. Chambers*, 463 U.S. 783 (1983).

30. *Town of Greece v. Galloway*, 572 U.S. ___ (2014).

31. *Allegheny County v. American Civil Liberties Union*, 492 U.S. 573 (1989).

32. *Elk Grove Unified School District v. Newdow*, 542 U.S. 1 (2004).

33. *McCreary County v. American Civil Liberties Union of Kentucky*, 545 U.S. 844 (2005).

34. *Van Orden v. Perry*, 545 U.S. 677 (2005).

35. *Wisconsin v. Yoder*, 406 U.S. 205 (1972).

36. *Oregon Employment Division v. Smith*, 494 U.S. 872 (1990).

37. *City of Boerne v. Flores*, 521 U.S. 507 (1997).

38. 573 U.S. ___ (2014).

39. This phrase was popularized by John Adams shortly before the Revolutionary War and was later incorporated into the Massachusetts Constitution, the oldest of the American state constitutions still in force.

40. *Arizona v. Gant*, 556 U.S. 332 (2009).

41. *Florida v. Jardines*, 569 U.S. ___ (2013).

42. *United States v. U.S. District Court*, 407 U.S. 297 (1972).

43. *Kyllo v. United States*, 533 U.S. 27 (2001).

44. *U.S. v. Jones*, 566 U.S. ___ (2012).

45. *Florence v. Board of Chosen Freeholders*, 566 U.S. ___ (2012).

46. *Maryland v. King*, 569 U.S. ___ (2013).

47. See *Mapp v. Ohio*, 367 U.S. 643 (1961), and *United States v. Leon*, 468 U.S. 897 (1984).

48. 384 U.S. 436 (1966). See also *Dickerson v. United States*, 530 U.S. 428 (2000).

49. *Berghuis v. Thompkins*, 560 U.S. ___ (2010).

50. *Powell v. Alabama*, 287 U.S. 45 (1932); *Gideon v. Wainwright*, 372 U.S. 335 (1963); *Scott v. Illinois*, 440 U.S. 367 (1979).

51. *Hamdi v. Rumsfeld*, 542 U.S. 507 (2004); *Rasul v. Bush*, 542 U.S. 466 (2004).

52. *Boumediene v. Bush*, 553 U.S. 723 (2008).

53. *Robinson v. California*, 370 U.S. 660 (1962).

54. *Weems v. United States*, 217 U.S. 349 (1910); *Solem v. Helm*, 463 U.S. 277 (1983). *Harmelin v. Michigan*, 501 U.S. 957 (1991), which upheld a mandatory sentence of life imprisonment without the possibility of parole for possession of more than 650 grams of a substance containing cocaine; means that legislatures have almost complete discretion in setting punishments for noncapital offenses.

55. *Miller v. Alabama*, 567 U.S. ___ (2012).

56. *Lockyer v. Andrade* 538 U.S. 63 (2003).

57. Death Penalty Information Center, "Facts About the Death Penalty," July 17, 2014.

58. *Roper v. Simmons*, 543 U.S. 551 (2005.)

59. David C. Baldus, George Woodworth, and Charles Pulanski, "Comparative Review of Death Sentences: An Empirical Study of the Georgia Experience," *Journal of Criminal Law and Criminology 74* (1983): 661; see *McCleskey v. Kemp*, 481 U.S. 279 (1987).

60. Victor L. Streib, "Executions Under the Post-Furman Capital Punishment Statutes," *Rutgers Law Journal 15* (1984): 443.

61. *Baze v. Rees*, 553 U.S. 35 (2008); *Kennedy v. Louisiana*, 554 U.S. 407 (2008).

62. *Griswold v. Connecticut*, 381 U.S. 479 (1965).

63. 410 U.S. 113 (1973).

64. *Webster v. Reproductive Health Services*, 492 U.S. 490 (1989).

65. *Planned Parenthood of Southeastern Pennsylvania v. Casey*, 505 U.S. 833 (1992).

66. *Stenberg v. Carhart*, 530 U.S. 914 (2000).

67. *Gonzales v. Carhart*, 550 U.S. 124 (2007).

68. CNN.com, "Obama Signs Executive Order on Abortion Funding Limits," March 24, 2010.

69. Wayne van der Meide, *Legislating Equality: A Review of Laws Affecting Gay, Lesbian, Bisexual, and Transgendered People in the United States* (Washington: National Gay and Lesbian Task Force, 2000); National Gay and Lesbian Task Force, "State Nondiscrimination Laws in the U.S.," January 20, 2012.

70. *Bowers v. Hardwick*, 478 U.S. 186 (1986), and *Romer v. Evans*, 517 U.S. 620 (1996).

71. *Lawrence v. Texas* 539 U.S. 558 (2003).

72. National Gay and Lesbian Task Force, "Anti-Gay Marriage Measures in the U.S." (July 11, 2008).

73. *Hollingsworth v. Perry*, 570 U.S. ___ (2013).

74. 570 U.S. ___ (2013).

75. The Gallup Organization, "Same-Sex Marriage Support Reaches New High at 55%," May 21, 2014.

76. 163 U.S. 537 (1896).

77. *Guinn v. United States*, 238 U.S. 347 (1915).

78. *Smith v. Allwright*, 321 U.S. 649 (1944).

79. 347 U.S. 483 (1954).

80. *Brown v. Board of Education of Topeka (II)*, 349 U.S. 294 (1955).

81. *Columbus Board of Education v. Penick*, 443 U.S. 449 (1979); *Dayton Board of Education v. Brinkman*, 443 U.S. 526 (1979).

82. *Freeman v. Pitts*, 503 U.S. 467 (1992).

83. The Gallup Organization, "In U.S., Most Reject Considering Race in College Admissions," July 24, 2013.

84. 438 U.S. 265 (1978).

85. *Gratz v. Bollinger* 539 U.S. 244 (2003).

86. *Grutter v. Bollinger* 539 U.S. 306 (2003).

87. For example, see *United Steelworkers of America v. Weber*, 443 U.S. 193 (1979), and *Johnson v. Transportation Agency*, 480 U.S. 616 (1987).

88. *Fisher v. University of Texas at Austin*, 570 U.S. ___ (2013); *Schuette v. BAMN*, 572 U.S. ___ (2014).

89. *Richmond v. J.A. Croson Co.*, 488 U.S. 469 (1989).

90. *Shaw v. Reno*, 509 U.S. 630 (1993).

91. Associated Press, "House Delays Vote on Voting Rights Act Renewal" June 21, 2006, http://www.cnn.com/2006/POLITICS/06/21/voting.rights.act.ap/index.html (June, 21 2006).

92. *Northwest Austin Municipal Utility District Number One v. Holder*, 557 U.S. 193 (2009).

93. *Shelby County v. Holder*, 570 U.S. ___ (2013).

94. *Reed v. Reed*, 404 U.S. 71 (1971).

95. *Los Angeles v. Manhart*, 435 U.S. 702 (1978); *Arizona v. Norris*, 463 U.S. 1073 (1983).

96. *Mississippi University for Women v. Hogan*, 458 U.S. 718 (1982).

97. *Mentor Savings Bank v. Vinson*, 477 U.S. 57 (1986).

98. *Historical Atlas of the United States* (Washington: National Geographic Society, 1988), p. 34.

99. Mark Hugo Lopez, *The Latino Electorate in 2010: More Voters, More Non-Voters*, (Washington, DC: Pew Hispanic Center, April 26, 2011.)

100. Paul M. Barrett, "Immigration Law Found to Promote Bias by Employers," *Wall Street Journal*, March 30, 1990, p. A18.

101. CNN.com, "Thousands Descend on Phoenix to Protest Immigration Law," May 29, 2010, http://www.cnn.com/2010/US/05/29/arizona.immigration.march/ (June 8, 2010).

102. *Arizona v. United States*, 567 U.S. ___ (2012).

103. *PGA TOUR, Inc. v. Martin*, 532 U.S. 355 (2001); *Board of Trustees of University of Alabama v. Garrett*, 531 U.S. 356 (2001).

POP QUIZ

1. The purpose of protecting _____ _____ is to place certain practices beyond government's reach.

2. Of the possible restrictions on speech today, the Supreme Court is least likely to approve a _____ _____.

3. The _____ clause keeps government from becoming the tool of one religious group against others.

4. A deal with a prosecutor to obtain a lesser charge or lighter sentence in exchange for a guilty plea is called a _____ _____.

5. Affirmative action programs are often aimed at achieving equality of _____.

6. For the most part, the Supreme Court considers obscenity as unprotected speech.   T   F

7. The establishment clause forbids the creation of an official state religion.   T   F

8. A police officer must always present a warrant before any search is made.   T   F

9. The Supreme Court has required the states to formulate uniform policies toward capital punishment.   T   F

10. Civil rights refers exclusively to one's specific constitutional rights.   T   F

11. Which of the following statements does not reflect an important objective of free expression?

    A) It is necessary to the political process set up by the Constitution.

    B) It contributes to social and political stability.

    C) It allows the dominant wisdom of the day to be challenged.

    D) It aids self-development.

12. An example of symbolic speech is _____.

    A) a sit-in

    B) libel

    C) obscenity

    D) defamation of character

13. The Supreme Court has approved all except which of the following?

    A) paying a state legislature's chaplain out of public funds

    B) letting the Amish take their children out of school after the eighth grade

    C) the formation of a religious club at a public high school

    D) exempting from state law members of the American Indian Church who ingest peyote as part of a religious ritual

14. The exclusionary rule does which of the following?

    A) allows retroactive application of criminal laws in certain cases

    B) bypasses the procedural safeguards of the legal process when meting out punishment

    C) denies government the use of evidence gained as a result of the violation of the suspect's rights

    D) allows the police to search a suspect without a warrant

15. According to the Supreme Court, segregation between school districts is unconstitutional when which of the following occurs?

    A) Each district is composed of over 85 percent of one race.

    B) It is accompanied by large economic inequalities between the districts.

    C) There is evidence that school boards have caused the segregation between districts.

    D) Educational opportunities are substantially different between the districts.

Answers:
1. civil liberties   2. prior restraint   3. establishment
4. plea bargain   5. result   6. T   7. T   8. F   9. F
10. F   11. B   12. A   13. D   14. C   15. C

Chapter

04

Political
Ideologies

In This Chapter

(Shutterstock)

Chapter Objectives

Politics is about power and influence—who gets what, when, and how; but also, politics is about ideas. A political ideology is an integrated set of political ideas about what constitutes the most equitable and just political order. Political ideologies are concerned with the proper function of government, the issues of liberty and equality, and the distribution of goods and services.

All of the ideological perspectives discussed in this chapter, and given any serious attention by Americans, accept the basic ideas of democracy—representative government and individual liberty. They do not question the fundamental precepts of American political life, but they differ on matters of emphasis and degree. Although most Americans do not think in rigid ideological terms, ideology does influence how Americans think about political leaders. Politicians and policies tend to be labeled liberal, conservative, radical, or reactionary; and with some frequency we hear the terms *neoconservative* and *neoliberal* (*neo* being Greek for "new"). This chapter introduces the landscape of contemporary American political ideas and movements— liberal, conservative, neoliberal, neoconservative, socialist, and libertarian.

4.1 American Political Ideologies

Ideology "spells out what is valued and what is not, what must be maintained, and what must be changed."[1] Most political leaders and most Americans share elements of or identify with mainstream ideologies. Generally identified as *liberal* or *conservative*, these ideological positions do not challenge the existing political order. Neither liberals nor conservatives want to make major changes in our political and social order. They accept capitalism American-style as a successful economic system, and the economic marketplace as the chief instrument for the distribution of economic goods. At the same time, liberals and conservatives accept most of the economic reforms of the New Deal (explained later in this chapter)—Social Security, unemployment insurance, and agricultural subsidies—as a permanent part of our political system. Their differences are over matters of emphasis and degree.

A political ideology is an integrated set of political ideas that influences how Americans think about political leaders. (AP World Wide Photo)

By contrast, radical ideologies—such as *democratic socialism* and *libertarianism*—challenge much of the existing social and political order. Democratic socialists do not accept the capitalist system or what they consider to be the inordinate power of the big corporations. Socialists want to remove most of the major economic decisions on investments, wages, and prices from the private sector and place them in the hands of government. Libertarians seek to establish an economic system free of governmental interference and regulation and to dismantle most of the existing welfare state programs. These ideologies challenge many of the existing arrangements in our political system.

Exotic as socialism or libertarianism may seem to most Americans, these ideologies and movements operate within the framework of our democratic system. Democratic socialists and libertarians believe in peaceful change and accept the rules of the game. They frequently enter candidates in elections—although those candidates rarely win, and then typically just at the state and local levels. Because their ideas challenge the dominant ideologies of our time, it is important to understand their criticisms and their prescriptions for the future, just as it is important to understand beliefs that are more widely held.

4.2 Liberalism

liberalism

An ideology that regards the individual as a rational being capable of overcoming obstacles to a better world and supporting changes in the political and economic status quo

One influential American ideology is **liberalism**. Liberalism begins with the assumption that individuals are, in the main, rational beings capable of overcoming obstacles to progress without resorting to violence. The roots of liberalism can be traced to the great English philosopher John Locke (1632–1704). Locke, who believed in

BVT Lab

Improve your test scores. Practice quizzes are available at www.BVTLab.com.

Chapter 04 | Political Ideologies | 113

the natural goodness of human beings, developed the **contract theory** of the state. According to Locke's theory, the state gains its legitimacy from the consent of the governed and is formed primarily to protect individuals' rights to life, liberty, and property. Locke's ideas of limited government, resting on the consent of the governed, became the textbook of the American Revolution. Locke was an inspiration to Thomas Jefferson, one of the most important early American liberal thinkers.

4.2a Classical Liberalism: Thomas Jefferson and Andrew Jackson

Contemporary American liberalism is vastly different from what was known in the nineteenth century as **classical liberalism** (see Table 4.1). Liberals of that time, going back to Thomas Jefferson and Andrew Jackson, believed that a government that governed least governed best. Those nineteenth-century liberals felt that government should step out of the way so that the new entrepreneurs of the young Republic—the small business owners and farmers—could have an opportunity to compete in the economic system. Jefferson shared Locke's view that government must treat property rights with particular care. Jefferson had high praise for Adam Smith's *Wealth of Nations* (1776), the bible of capitalism. In his first inaugural address, Jefferson stated:

> A wise and frugal government, which shall restrain men from injuring one another, shall leave them otherwise free to regulate their own pursuits of industry and improvement and shall not take from the mouth of labor the bread it has earned. This is the sum of good government.[2]

President Andrew Jackson's (1829–1837) struggle against the wealth and power of a national bank was a classic example of the nineteenth-century liberal creed in action. Jackson also opposed extensive government expenditures on roads and canals. He believed that such expenditures "would make the federal government a partner with business in the financial prosperity of the upper class."[3] Speaking for the liberal reformers of his day, Jackson declared that a strong central government "is calculated to raise around the administration a moneyed aristocracy dangerous to the liberties of the country."[4] Like Jefferson, Jackson believed that liberty was the absence of government interference in the rights of all citizens to enjoy the fruits of their labor and prosperity.

4.2b Populism and Progressivism: The Repudiation of Classical Liberalism

In the latter part of the nineteenth century, liberal attitudes toward government began to change. In the decades following the Civil War, American farmers—the backbone of support for Jeffersonian and Jacksonian liberalism—suffered through a perpetual economic crisis. Agricultural prices fell and interest rates rose. The target of liberal reform became the railroads and the banks, not the government. Out of this turmoil evolved a new liberal movement, known as **populism**. The populists, who formed their own political party in the 1880s, called for further democratization of government through the secret ballot, direct election of senators, and voter initiatives and referenda. They also advocated fundamental economic reforms that would strengthen government's role, including nationalization of the railroads and the telegraph, a graduated income tax, free coinage of silver, and a vastly expanded supply of paper money. The Populist Party did not supplant either of the two major parties; however, its ideas—particularly with the nomination of William Jennings Bryan as the Democratic presidential candidate in 1896—profoundly affected the Democratic Party in the twentieth century.

contract theory

Theory holding that the state gains its legitimacy from the consent of the governed and is formed primarily to protect the rights of individuals to life, liberty, and property

classical liberalism

A view, dating from the nineteenth century, that government should play a minimal role in society and should permit maximum economic freedom for the individual

populism

a political movement that sets the interests of the masses or common people against those of the political elite or the wealthy

table 4.1 | Key Ideas of American Ideologies

Different forms of liberalism and conservatism have defined much of the ideological debate in American politics; other ideologies challenged and influenced mainstream ideas.

Ideology	Key Ideas and Policies
Liberalism	
Classical Liberalism	Minimal government; protection of property rights
Populism	Democratization of government; economic reform
Progressivism	Social programs to cope with problems caused by industrialization; public limits on private corporate power
Contemporary Liberalism	The positive state; faith in solving problems collectively through government; programs to provide for the economic well-being of the nation, including the basic material needs of each individual; tolerance of various lifestyles
Neoliberalism	Creation, not redistribution, of wealth; free trade; reform of entitlement programs; a strong but economical defense
Conservatism	
Early American Conservatism	Sanctity of private property; distrust of unchecked popular rule; duty of government to promote a healthy economic environment and a virtuous citizenry
Industrial Age Conservatism	Laissez-faire economics; individualism; social Darwinism
Contemporary Conservatism	Reduced spending on social programs; revamping tax policies to encourage economic growth; strong military defense; little positive action to redress racial and gender discrimination; duty of government to promote a virtuous citizenry
Neoconservatism	Skepticism of government's ability to solve social and economic problems; acceptance of a modest welfare state; opposition to racial and gender quotas to redress discrimination; creation, not redistribution, of wealth; assertive foreign policy
Challenges to the Status Quo	
Democratic Socialism	Public ownership of basic industries, banks, agricultural enterprises, and communications systems; wage and price controls; redistribution of wealth to achieve true economic equality; expanded welfare programs
Libertarianism	Minimal government; protection of property rights and freedom of individuals; no governmental regulation of the economy; noninterventionist foreign policy; drastic reduction in defense spending

In urban America, among the middle classes, there was also a growing movement for social and economic reform known as **progressivism**. Progressives supported government programs to ease the problems of industrialization, including worker's compensation, a ban on child labor, regulation of corporations, and a minimum wage. Progressives achieved their major successes during the presidential administrations of Theodore Roosevelt (1901–1909) and Woodrow Wilson (1913–1921). During Roosevelt's years in office, Congress passed the Hepburn Act, which regulated the railroads, and the Pure Food and Drug Act and the Meat Inspection Act, which eliminated many of the unhealthy practices of food and drug industries.

Woodrow Wilson signed into law bills regulating the banking industry, restricting unfair business competition, and establishing an eight-hour day for railroad workers. The populist and progressive belief that government could remedy the economic ills of the

Progressives supported government programs, including worker's compensation, to ease the problems of industrialization. Picketing hospital workers are shown at a rally outside Temple University Hospital in Philadelphia. (AP WorldWide Photo)

nation by limiting the power and wealth of private corporations and banks had a profound effect on American liberalism. The rise of populism and progressivism signaled a decline in the faith of liberalism in laissez-faire (minimal government regulation of economic affairs) and began a new era of belief in the power and virtues of a strong central government.

Wilson felt that Jefferson would have understood the need for more activist government. He said,

> If Jefferson were living in our day, he would see what we see: that the individual is caught in a great confused nexus of all sorts of complicated circumstances, and that to let him alone is to leave him helpless.[5]

4.2c Contemporary Liberalism: The Welfare State and Beyond

The administration of President Franklin D. Roosevelt (1933–1945) took the concerns of the populists and progressives a step further. Roosevelt's New Deal program reflected the change in the constituency of liberalism. In contrast to the nineteenth-century liberal, who addressed the needs of the entrepreneurial class, New Deal liberals were concerned about the farmers, the unemployed, and the labor union movement. Carrying on the populist and progressive tradition, liberals no longer saw government as a threat to liberty or as the inevitable partner of the rich and powerful. In a complex industrial age—particularly one racked by the Great Depression of the 1930s—liberals believed that government action should ensure the economic well-being of the nation and should provide basic material guarantees (food, shelter, healthcare, and education) for every individual. The New Deal included programs to ensure protection for the unemployed, pensions for the elderly, and guaranteed prices for the farmers. It symbolized the idea of the positive or interventionist state, which became the hallmark of contemporary liberalism.

In the 1960s, President Lyndon Johnson's Great Society moved beyond the New Deal. Civil rights laws protected the rights of minorities, Medicare and Medicaid laws provided health insurance for the elderly and the poor, and funds aided impoverished elementary and secondary school districts. In the 1970s, liberals proposed a broad range of programs to protect the environment, to assist consumers, and to expand welfare benefits through the food stamp program.

progressivism

An urban reform movement of the late nineteenth and early twentieth centuries that called for direct primaries, restrictions on corporations, and improved public services and that was influential in the administrations of Theodore Roosevelt and Woodrow Wilson

Liberals today believe that a strong central government is necessary to protect individuals from the inequities of a modern industrial and technological society, and that the growth of government has enhanced—not diminished—individual freedom. Although the positive state is central to the contemporary liberal creed, liberals do not believe that government should displace private enterprise. Most liberals are capitalists, if not forthrightly so. In fact, many argue that American capitalism has survived because government has humanized the industrial order, and that Franklin Roosevelt's New Deal saved capitalism from repudiation during the 1930s. Liberals argue that the positive state cushions the inequalities of power and wealth that arise in any capitalist system. They see government as correcting the injustices of the marketplace, not supplanting it. Liberals recognize that in any society there will be some inequalities of wealth and income, but they feel that government must intervene to redress the most excessive inequalities. Thus, in debates over tax laws, liberals frequently support shifting more of the burden to people in the upper income brackets.

The World's Smallest Political Quiz is a tool designed to assess one's political ideology. The quiz was created by a Libertarian organization.

Does that make it too biased, or is it useful?

Visit this site and decide for yourself.

http://www.bvtlab.com/8GAMr

The idea of a benevolent government that offers services to the disadvantaged (unemployment insurance) as well as to the middle class (Social Security) has been for generations the centerpiece of American liberalism. Liberal ideas fueled the administrations of Presidents Franklin Roosevelt, Harry Truman, John Kennedy, and Lyndon Johnson. Johnson, for one, saw the United States as "an endless cornucopia." His Great Society began a virtual torrent of new government programs: rent supplements for the poor, scholarships for college students, aid to the arts and humanities, higher pensions for government workers and veterans, aid to children with disabilities, and a massive food stamp program. These programs assisted the poor and the disadvantaged as well as many in the middle and upper income brackets.

In the 1970s and early 1980s, the growth rate of the economy declined while the demand for government services continued. Unlike his predecessors, President Jimmy Carter (1977–1981) did not offer a new set of governmental programs and benefits. Hampered by the problems of inflation and an energy shortage, Carter could offer few initiatives. His administration stirred little enthusiasm among liberals.

Liberals remain wedded to the idea of affirmative government. In the early 1980s, some began to discuss the idea of an industrial policy. Championed by liberal economic thinkers such as Robert Reich and Felix Rohatyn, an **industrial policy** involves a partnership in economic decision-making among government officials, labor unions, and public interest groups. President Bill Clinton (1993–2001) endorsed this approach in a slightly modified form in his 1992 election campaign and later named Reich secretary of labor.

In matters involving national security and personal morality, however, liberals seek to restrict the role of government. Liberals extend broad tolerance to different lifestyles and dispute government efforts to impose a single standard of religious practice or sexual morality. Consequently, liberals are at the forefront of opposition to constitutional amendments that might sanction prayer in schools or limit the rights of women to obtain an abortion.

industrial policy

Proposals for partnership in economic decision-making among government officials, corporate leaders, union officials, and public interest groups

Since the Vietnam War, liberals have backed away from an interventionist, military-oriented foreign policy. In January 1991, most congressional liberals voted against authorizing President Bush to use military force in the Persian Gulf and preferred the continuation of economic sanctions against Iraq. Liberals are also critical of large defense budgets and became, in recent years, the most vocal critics of the Iraq and Afghanistan Wars.

In general, liberals favor government programs and budgeting priorities that put domestic social programs before those of the Pentagon. Their belief in a strong activist government concentrates primarily on domestic issues (see Table 4.2). Recently, liberals have been outspoken on the issue of universal healthcare—health insurance coverage as a right for all Americans—and achieved at least a partial victory in 2010 with the passage of the Patient Protection and Affordable Care Act and the Health Care and Education Reconciliation Act.

Who are the liberals? They are usually found in the Democratic Party, although historically the Democrats have harbored some conservatives and the Republicans a

table 4.2 | Milestones in American Liberalism

1690	John Locke's *Second Treatise on Government* published.
1776	Adam Smith's *Wealth of Nations*, Thomas Paine's *Common Sense*, and the Declaration of Independence published.
1832	President Andrew Jackson vetoes a bill to recharter the Bank of the United States.
1892	First Populist Party convention held.
1896	William Jennings Bryan wins Democratic presidential nomination; the Democratic Party adopts much of the Populist program.
1909	Herbert Croly's *Promise of American Life* published; a group of African American leaders, including W. E. B. DuBois, meets at Niagara Falls, Canada, and inaugurates the modern civil rights movement.
1913–1916	President Woodrow Wilson steers his New Freedom program through Congress.
1933–1936	President Franklin Roosevelt's New Deal reforms inaugurate the modern welfare state.
1954	The Supreme Court declares racial segregation *unconstitutional* in *Brown v. Board of Education of Topeka*.
1964	Congress passes the landmark Civil Rights Act of 1964.
1965	President Lyndon Johnson successfully pushes his Great Society programs through Congress.
1972	Liberal Democratic candidate George McGovern loses presidential election to conservative Republican incumbent Richard Nixon in a landslide.
1992	Bill Clinton wins the presidency while making universal healthcare a cornerstone of his campaign.
2010	President Barack Obama and a Democratic majority in Congress pass the Affordable Care Act, providing all Americans the opportunity to purchase health insurance.
2010	President Barack Obama announces plans to end the Iraq War. U.S. troops leave by end of 2011.
2012	President Barack Obama announces his support for same-sex marriage rights.

handful of liberals. Some liberals also support third parties, such as the Green Party. The association of liberals with Democrats is in part due to the fact that the constituency of the Democratic Party—minorities, the labor movement, feminists, and the poor—supports a wide range of liberal welfare programs. **Americans for Democratic Action** (ADA) has historically been the best-known pressure group for contemporary liberalism. Founded in 1947, ADA presidents have included Senators Hubert Humphrey (D–MN)* and George McGovern (D–SD), both one-time nominees of the Democratic Party for president. Headquartered in Washington, D.C., the ADA is an advocate of legislation designed to reduce economic inequality and defense spending and to protect consumers. It opposes laws that encroach on civil rights and civil liberties. Each year it rates members of Congress on a broad spectrum of liberal issues. In recent years, the popularity of the ADA among liberals has been surpassed by the upstart progressive organization MoveOn. Founded in 1998, MoveOn now boasts a membership of over seven million.

4.2d   Neoliberalism: Adjusting Liberalism to the Twenty-First Century

During the administrations of Franklin Roosevelt, Harry Truman, and John Kennedy, liberalism focused on economic issues and emphasized government's obligation to assist those on the lower end of the income scale. In recent decades, liberalism has shifted its focus somewhat and reached into social and foreign policy issues. However, it did so at a political cost. The strong association of liberalism with the civil rights movement hurt the liberal image among Southerners who identified with the old, white-dominated political order and among Northern whites living in urban enclaves who also felt threatened by African American advancement. Many voters also associated liberalism with controversial Supreme Court decisions legalizing abortion and banning school prayer. After the Vietnam War, liberals were highly critical of American military intervention and the level of defense spending, alienating some voters who considered them "soft" on defense. Although liberal candidates were quite successful in congressional and state elections, such negative associations dogged them at the presidential level.

Stunned by these successive presidential defeats, a group of young journalists and elected officials attempted to sharpen and modernize the focus of contemporary liberalism. The leader of the movement was Charles Peters, the editor of the *Washington Monthly* (see Table 4.3), who adopted the label "neoliberal." **Neoliberalism** calls for a shift in the emphasis of liberalism from the redistribution of wealth to the promotion of wealth, for a far less critical attitude toward American capitalism, and for policies that promote greater government and business cooperation.

Neoliberals do not repudiate the New Deal and Great Society legacies; they simply feel that the emphasis of liberal reform should be different. They argue that liberals must confront public distrust of government. As a writer for the *Washington Monthly* put it, "Any time a liberal politician says the word 'program,' most voters hear 'bureaucracy' and right away get turned off."[6]

Neoliberals direct their attention not to the expansion of government services, but to their effective delivery. Neoliberals criticize government unions and the size and costs of government bureaucracy. Neoliberals also call for the reform of entitlement spending programs such as Social Security that go to people who are already well protected by private pensions and their own investments. The neoliberals criticize civil service and military retirement benefits for being far more generous than

---

Americans for Democratic Action

The best-known pressure group for contemporary liberalism

neoliberalism

A pragmatic form of liberalism that emphasizes such beliefs as the promotion of wealth rather than its redistribution and the reform of military practices rather than the simple reduction of military spending

---

* "D–MN" is a journalistic designation used for members of the U.S. Senate and House of Representatives: "D" or "R" indicates political party, followed by the member's home state.

table 4.3 | A Guide to Contemporary Political Ideas and Leaders

American ideologies are expressed through a variety of journals, writers, and political leaders.

Ideology	Major Journal	Leading Spokesperson	Political Leader
Liberalism	*The American Prospect*	Robert Reich	Barack Obama
Neoliberalism	*Washington Monthly*	Charles Peters	Robert Rubin
Conservatism	*National Review*	Rush Limbaugh	Sarah Palin
Neoconservatism	*Weekly Standard*	William Kristol	Marco Rubio
Democratic Socialism	*Dissent*	Cornel West	Bernard Sanders
Libertarianism	*Reason*	Ron Paul	Rand Paul

those in the private sector. They believe that increases in spending for these programs should be based not on the cost of living but on the rate of real growth in the economy.

Traditional liberals take issue with the neoliberal emphasis on government efficiency. They emphasize older liberal issues such as the problem of personal income inequality, which has become more pronounced in recent decades. Traditional liberals would like to increase the top income tax rate, which is currently 39.6 percent. They unapologetically champion the cause of affirmative government and the positive state. Arthur Schlesinger Jr., a prominent liberal spokesperson for over a generation, argued for greater government investment in research and development and in education; in the rehabilitation of our bridges, dams, and highways; and in the protection against toxic waste, acid rain, and global warming. "The markets," wrote Schlesinger, "will solve none of these problems."[7]

Some traditional liberals feel that Michael Dukakis's emphasis on competency rather than ideology during the 1988 presidential campaign was, in fact, a neoliberal theme that failed to ignite the electorate. By contrast Bill Clinton, in 1992 and 1996, and Al Gore, in 2000, were able to blend older, more populist ideas—such as raising taxes for the rich—with neoliberal themes such as a partnership between government and business. John Kerry's presidential campaign spotlighted both traditional liberal values, like affordable healthcare, and neoliberal ideas about fiscal responsibility; but these issues took a backseat to foreign policy in 2004. The year 2008 saw a return to more traditional liberal positions when the Democratic Party nominated Barack Obama (D–IL) as its presidential candidate. An analysis of Senate roll call votes from 2007 led the *National Journal* to identify Obama as the nation's most liberal senator.[8]

The election of Barack Obama as president in 2008 (and reelection in 2012) brought about a return to more traditional liberal positions. (Shutterstock)

4.3 Conservatism

In contrast to liberalism's confidence in the capacity of individuals to overcome obstacles collectively, political conservatism reflects doubt and distrust. **Conservatism** emphasizes the value of tradition and established practices as guides for the future. It finds its origins in the writings of Edmund Burke (1729–1797), whose most famous work, *Reflections on the Revolution in France* (1790), is considered the first major statement of conservative principles. A leading figure in the British Parliament, Burke was appalled by the excesses of the French Revolution and by its rejection of tradition. Burke was suspicious of any generation's claim that it could remake society, believing that the experience of past generations was the most reliable guide to good government. Customs, traditions, and laws embodied the wisdom of the past and should not be carelessly discarded. Thus, argued Burke, people should act with deliberation, seeking change only when necessary. Burke believed that society grew slowly and with purpose; therefore, the past gave continuity to present and future generations. Burke was suspicious of the general public and its capacity to appreciate tradition and custom. He believed in government by the propertied class. People were not equal in ability or talent, according to Burke, and should not be so considered when it came to the governing of society. In Burke's view, a natural inequality among people meant that a ruling class of ability and property ought to control government.

4.3a Early American Conservatism: John Adams

It was difficult to make Burkean conservatism relevant to the American experience, which had no landed aristocracy, no established church, and no royal tradition. American conservatism—although influenced by Burke—found its own voice in John Adams, the second president of the United States, who lived from 1735 to 1826. The excesses of the French Revolution, particularly its executions and confiscation of property, repelled Adams as they did Burke. Adams agreed with Burke unreservedly about the sanctity of private property (see Table 4.1); but unlike Burke, Adams did not associate property rights with a landed aristocracy. Adams believed that property should be widely held and that a propertied class would produce a natural aristocracy of talent.

Although Adams was one of the architects of the American Revolution and a passionate defender of the right of every individual to life, liberty, and property, he distrusted unchecked democratic rule as much as he did excessive power in the hands of the aristocracy. Unlimited rule of the people led to clamor for dictatorship. Adams rejected the Jeffersonian notion of the natural goodness of humankind; he felt that people were neither totally innocent nor totally depraved. Laws and government, in Adams's view, were needed to promote public virtue and to curb private greed. By public virtue Adams meant "a positive passion for the public good, the public interest, honor, power, and glory established in the minds of the people."[9] A properly balanced government could serve to suppress the evils of ambition, selfishness, self-indulgence, and corruption.

John Adams found this balance in the American Constitution. A popularly elected House would represent the people, an indirectly elected Senate would protect the rights of property, and the president would represent the whole. Thus the poor could not confiscate the property of the rich, and the rich would not be able to exploit the poor. Society would retain its balance, and liberty would be safeguarded from both the excesses of democracy and the abuses of an aristocracy. After Adams had appointed John Marshall, a conservative Federalist, to the Supreme Court in 1801,

conservatism

A defense of the political and economic status quo against forces of change, holding that established customs, laws, and traditions should guide society

Adams looked to the judicial branch as the ultimate guarantor of property rights against any attempts by legislatures to compromise them.

In the 1820s, long after he had left the presidency, Adams joined with other American conservatives—including Chief Justice Marshall and Senator Daniel Webster—in opposing the elimination of property qualifications for voting. These conservatives considered *universal suffrage* (and in that era they debated only universal *white male suffrage*) to be a threat to the Republic. In their opinion, men without property lacked the independence, judgment, and virtue to be voting members of a free republic.[10]

Chancellor James Kent of New York, one of the most famous legal scholars and jurists of the early nineteenth century, argued that "there is a tendency in the majority to tyrannize over the minority and trample down their rights; and in the indolent and profligate to cast the whole burden of society upon the industrious and virtuous."[11] The victory of Jacksonian democracy in the states during the 1820s brought an end to antidemocratic conservatism. Conservatives seemed to realize the finality of their defeat on that issue and concentrated, in the latter part of the nineteenth century, on the defense of property rights and the system of laissez-faire economics.

4.3b Conservatism and the Industrial Age: Herbert Spencer and William Graham Sumner

Industrialization following the Civil War brought a major change in American conservatism. Although conservatives of the early Republic fervently believed in property rights, the belief that government should play a limited role in the economy did not necessarily follow. Conservatives such as John Adams, John Marshall, and Alexander Hamilton supported a strong central government to defend the propertied classes from the encroachments of the more radical state governments. They defended the Bank of the United States against the attacks of the Jefferson-Jackson liberals.

As America industrialized, conservatives embraced **laissez-faire economics**—an economic system that operated free of government control. Burke and Adams regarded the state as essential to the promotion of public virtue and the protection of property; in the Industrial Age, however, the state became the object of conservative scorn. In stressing individualism, economic growth, and the limited role of government, conservatives seemed closer to Jefferson and Jackson in this regard than to Burke and Adams.

Herbert Spencer (1820–1903), an English social scientist, and William Graham Sumner (1840–1910), an American sociologist, developed the theory of economic individualism that became the keystone of late-nineteenth-century and early-twentieth-century conservatism. The theory was popularly known as **social Darwinism**. Sumner stated the case in a somewhat extreme form: People, Sumner argued, should be free to compete with each other for survival. From this economic competition, the fit will survive and the weak will perish. The result will be the betterment of humankind through the survival of superior individuals. Sumner opposed governmental aid to the needy as inconsistent with his views on social and economic evolution. Government was inefficient by nature, Sumner argued, and should be limited to fundamental concerns. Sumner wrote, "At bottom there are two chief things with which government has to deal. They are, the property of men and the honor of women. These it has to defend against crime."[12]

Although these views were far too extreme—even for the nineteenth century—Spencer and Sumner made a great impact on conservative thinking. Conservatives of the Industrial Age did not emphasize the individual's obligation to the state or the state's obligation to promote public virtue; instead, the emphasis was almost entirely on the individual. If people worked hard, they argued, people could become

laissez-faire economics

French for "leave things alone"; the view in economics that government should not interfere in the workings of the economy

social Darwinism

A set of ideas applying Charles Darwin's theory of biological evolution to society and holding that social relationships occur within a struggle for survival in which only the fittest survive

BVT *Lab*

Visit www.BVTLab.com to explore the student resources available for this chapter.

successful; and economic growth would ensue. The government need only stand out of the way. Many business leaders were attracted to this philosophy, although it did not prevent them from helping themselves to governmental favors (tariff protection or direct subsidies) when the occasion arose. These business leaders invoked conservatism to justify opposition to antitrust laws, bills regulating hours and wages, and a progressive income tax.

In short, conservatism became the ideology of America's business class. As long as most Americans shared somewhat in the growth of the American economy, they were willing to accept most of the tenets of conservatism. From the end of Reconstruction to the New Deal, Americans elected presidents (with the exceptions of Theodore Roosevelt and Woodrow Wilson) who reflected those values.

4.3c Contemporary Conservatism: A Response to the Welfare State

Conservatism since the 1980s has taken on a more positive cast with an agenda of its own—reducing social spending, reshaping the tax code, and rebuilding national defense. In economic matters, conservatives draw on many of the ideas of nineteenth-century individualism. Conservatism still remains at its core a defense of economic individualism against the growth of the welfare state. Conservatives oppose any increase in the role of the federal government over the general direction of the economy and contend that a vibrant private-sector economy can best create jobs for the poor, immigrants, and minorities. Welfare state programs, conservatives argue, only create a permanent class of the poor who are dependent on the state and have no genuine incentives to enter the working world.

Although many conservatives opposed the major civil rights laws of the 1960s on the grounds that they represented a serious encroachment on states' rights, most now accept these laws as a permanent part of our political landscape. They do, however, challenge the idea of quotas and other affirmative-action policies as a means of enforcing civil rights laws in the areas of jobs, educational opportunities, and access to federal contracts. They argue that civil rights should mean equality of treatment and not equality of results.

On social and cultural issues, conservatives remain close to Burkean ideals. Contemporary conservatives believe that the state must promote virtue and social responsibility and take appropriate measures to improve the moral climate of society. They support constitutional amendments restricting abortion and permitting prayers in public schools. They oppose the concept of civil rights for homosexuals in jobs, the military, housing, and marriage. Speaking as a modern-day Burkean, conservative philosopher and syndicated columnist George Will wrote, "Traditional conservatism has not been, and proper conservatism cannot be, merely a defense of industrialism and individualist 'free market'

Conservatives believe that the state should take part in improving the moral climate of society, such as by promoting prayer in schools. (Shutterstock)

economics. Conservatism is about the cultivation and conservation of certain values or it is nothing."[13]

As conservative causes have gained broader public support, conservatives no longer invoke the suspicion of the masses as they did in John Adams's day (see Table 4.4). Nor do they talk very much about the independence of the judicial branch as a check on the excesses of legislative power. In fact, conservatives have been particularly critical of Supreme Court decisions outlawing prayers in school and legalizing abortion.[14]

Conservatives support efforts to have such decisions overturned by constitutional amendment or weakened by legislative action. Direct democracy, so feared by the conservatives of the eighteenth and nineteenth centuries, has become an important tool of contemporary conservatives. Conservatives have successfully employed the popular initiative or referendum process (a device that permits people to vote on policy questions as well as for candidates) in California and Massachusetts as a check on the power of state legislatures to tax their own citizens.

Some conservative causes have generated intense (although not broad) rank-and-file support. In part because of conservative support for reduced taxes, prayer in school, restrictions on abortion, and opposition to same-sex marriage, conservatism has been transformed from an elitist philosophy of the propertied class to a more populist cause of the working and middle classes.

table 4.4 | Milestones in American Conservatism

1790	Edmund Burke's *Reflections on the Revolution in France* published; Alexander Hamilton, first U.S. Treasury secretary, introduces a report recommending a national bank.
1851	Herbert Spencer's *Social Statics* published.
1883	William Graham Sumner's *What Social Classes Owe to Each Other* published.
1905	Supreme Court in *Lochner v. New York* strikes down New York law limiting working hours of bakers as a violation of freedom of contract under the Fourteenth Amendment.
1920	Warren Harding elected president, marking the beginning of a new era of conservative dominance lasting until 1932.
1955	*National Review* founded, marking the beginning of the intellectual revitalization of post–World War II conservatism.
1964	Barry Goldwater receives the Republican presidential nomination, beginning the conservative ascendancy in the party.
1981	President Ronald Reagan begins his program of tax reductions, domestic spending cuts, and defense buildup.
1994	Newt Gingrich and his "Contract with America" sweep the Republican Party into the majority in both chambers of Congress for the first time in forty years.
2000	George W. Bush and Dick Cheney win the electoral vote and embark on an agenda of tax cuts, defense spending, and environmental deregulation.
2002	The Bush doctrine of preventive war is announced in National Security Strategy of the United States, with the country embarking on the Iraq War the following year.
2010	Bolstered in part by the Tea Party movement, voters return a Republican majority to both chambers of Congress in the midterm elections.

Millennials and Political Ideology

Would you describe yourself as a conservative or a liberal? How do you feel about the economy, same-sex marriage, and healthcare coverage? How do your views compare to those of your fellow college students? Since 2000, a Harvard University Institute of Politics survey has been asking young people across the country about their political views.[1] Regarding specific issues, the 2014 survey of eighteen- to twenty-nine-year-olds found that only 21 percent of respondents believed that the country is headed in the right direction, while 45 percent thought the country was off on the wrong track. In other surveys, 58 percent of millennials listed the economy as their number one political concern, followed by healthcare (7 percent); education and immigration tied for third (5 percent each). When asked to compare twenty different issue priorities, respondents deemed the issue "creating jobs and lowering the unemployment rate" to be the most important 77 percent of the time.[2]

Regarding political parties, the survey found that 24 percent of young adults identified themselves as Republicans, 37 percent as Democrats, and 38 percent as Independents. This finding represents an increase in the number of Independents and suggests that it may be important to move beyond partisan labels and take a deeper look at ideology in order to best understand the political beliefs of millennials.

In taking this deeper look, the Harvard study discovered that, in addition to the traditional progressive–conservative ideological spectrum, millennial ideologies could also be divided along a religious–passive continuum. Combining these two categories created four labels for identifying young adult ideology.

New Progressives make up 15 percent of the sample population. A strong majority of this group says that health insurance, food, and shelter should be provided for people who cannot afford them. They believe government should spend more to reduce poverty and slow down climate change.

New Conservatives make up 11 percent of this population. They believe homosexual relationships are immoral, oppose preferences for quali- fied minorities in hiring and education, and do not believe basic healthcare is a right for all people. They would like to see religious values take on a more prominent role in government.

New Religious are 28 percent of the millennial generation. These individuals have strong beliefs about religion and morality, but also see a positive role for the federal government, and are the most ethnically diverse group. They are concerned about the country's moral direction and believe in school choice, but also see healthcare as a right and believe the government should take active steps to reduce poverty.

New Passives describes about 23 percent of millennials. The least likely group to vote, they oppose both affir- mative action and a larger role for religion in government. They do not believe homosexual relationships are morally wrong.

What role did the millennial vote play during the 2014 midterm election campaign? What role will it play in the 2016 presidential election? Do you think these survey findings accurately describe your college campus? Why or why not? Which of the four categories most closely describes your political thinking?

1 Harvard University Institute of Politics, *Survey of Young Americans' Attitudes Toward Politics and Public Service,* 21st–25th Editions, April 24, 2012, to April 29, 2014.

2 Ibid., p. 9.

Who are the conservatives? In most cases their political home is in the Republican Party. Ronald Reagan was the first president since the Great Depression to identify himself openly with conservatism and conservative causes. Previous Republican presidents—Eisenhower, Nixon, and Ford—were men of the center who shunned ideology and ideological labels. Perhaps the best-known conservative journal is *National Review*, founded by William Buckley, who was one of the most prominent conservative spokespersons for over half a century.

4.3d   Neoconservatism in the Twenty-First Century

In the 1970s, a number of leading American intellectuals, many of them longtime liberals, became openly critical of the drift of contemporary liberalism; thus began the ideology labeled **neoconservatism** in the popular press. Neoconservatives feel that liberals have overestimated the ability of government to solve social problems such as industrial pollution, economic inequality, and racial discrimination. They argue that liberals have gone beyond the initial New Deal concept that government need only provide a "safety net" for the subsistence needs of society's victims—the unemployed, disabled Americans, and the elderly. Contemporary liberalism, the neoconservatives claim, transformed the New Deal's modest welfare state into a more intrusive, paternalistic state. Neoconservatives disagree with such liberal ideas as the use of racial or gender preferences as a means of assuring fairness in hiring, promotion, or acceptance to professional schools. They also reject the idea of forced school busing as a means of achieving racial balance in enrollment. They consider these ideas elitist liberal schemes not supported by the majority of Americans.

Neoconservatives feel that liberals no longer speak for the "average person" but rather for a "new class" of relatively affluent reformers—lawyers, social workers, educators, and city planners—with careers in the expanding public sector. This new liberal class intends "to propel the nation from that modified version of capitalism we call 'the welfare state' toward an economic system so regulated in detail as to fulfill many of the traditional anticapitalist aspirations of the left."[15]

Neoconservatives also argue that liberals emphasize policies (such as higher taxes on the upper class) that are aimed not at creating wealth but only at redistributing it. Skeptical about government's ability to erase economic inequalities, neoconservatives stress policies such as lower taxes on large incomes and less regulation of business to promote economic growth. Such growth, they feel, would more likely broaden economic opportunity and create greater social stability. Likewise, they are suspicious of policies that polarize one class or group against another—such as racial busing that pits the white working-class communities in the large cities against the poor African American community—and gender and racial quotas that place the interests of women and minorities above those of white males.

In short, neoconservatives feel that modern liberals have promised too much to too many groups and that a government that promises too much cannot deliver, becoming "overloaded." As a result, they argue, government loses its authority and cannot govern effectively. Neoconservatives differ from traditional conservatives in that neoconservatives support, in principle and practice, a modest welfare state (Social Security, unemployment insurance, and Medicare). In fact, neoconservatives argue that a properly constructed welfare state strengthens citizens' loyalty to the existing capitalist system and is thus a stabilizing force.

Neoconservatives have engendered some resentment among many members of the Old Right, sometimes dubbed paleoconservatives (*paleo* from the Greek meaning "ancient"), who decry the neoconservative accommodation to the welfare state and remain hostile to government efforts to establish social and economic equality. The paleoconservatives believe that religious traditions embodied in the church and family should be the basis of a stable and ordered society. The welfare state philosophy of the New Deal and Great Society is, according to them, an effort to create a secular moral order. By defending the New Deal legacy, the paleoconservatives charge the neoconservatives with defending not only a misguided political idea but also a religious heresy.

The sudden collapse of communism in 1989 opened up new fissures in contemporary conservatism. With the unraveling of the Soviet Union, some paleoconservative leaders—such as journalist Patrick Buchanan, who challenged President George H. W. Bush in the 1992 primaries—sounded older conservative themes of isolationism and America first. Neoconservatives, in turn, strongly supported continued American

neoconservatism

A belief associated with many former liberal intellectuals that contemporary liberalism has transformed the modest New Deal welfare state into an intrusive, paternalistic state

leadership in world affairs. George W. Bush (2001–2009) surrounded himself with a number of neoconservative advise, such as Paul Wolfowitz, and embarked on his presidency with a promise of "compassionate conservatism."

Neoconservatism has emerged as an influential intellectual and political force. Its ideas influenced the Reagan administration and both Bush administrations and have brought about a more respectful hearing for conservatism in general among academics and intellectuals.

4.4   Ideological Challenges to the Status Quo

Not all American ideologies fit comfortably under the rubrics *liberal* and *conservative*. Some challenge dominant opinion and propose policies that are outside today's mainstream. Yet the fact that they represent a minority point of view does not make them unimportant. The history of American political thought is full of examples of "extreme" ideas that gained acceptability and entered the mainstream.

4.4a   Democratic Socialism: A Radical Challenge to American Capitalism

Democratic socialism is an economic system in which the basic industries, banks, agricultural systems, and communication networks are owned and controlled by the government at either the local or national level. While a private sector of the economy may continue to exist under socialism, major industries and corporations would be owned by the state; thus, the government would be responsible for planning and directing the economy. Key decisions concerning investments, prices, and wages would be placed in the hands of public institutions. What separates democratic socialists from communists, who also believe in the principle of public ownership, is that democratic socialists reject the idea of violent revolution. Instead, democratic

Among other things, democratic socialism requires government ownership and control of the major industries, utilities, and transportation systems—such as the subway, which is vital in a busy metropolis like New York City. (Shutterstock)

democratic socialism

An economic system in which the major industries are owned by a democratically elected government responsible for planning and directing the economy socialists advocate the adoption of socialism through peaceful and constitutional means; they support the basic democratic rights embodied in our Constitution.

Economic equality is an essential idea in socialism. Socialists argue that capitalism in America—despite its success in creating wealth—has failed to solve the fundamental problem of poverty. Equality of opportunity is not enough, socialists argue. A genuinely democratic society must produce equality of results. Socialists wish to replace a society based on competition with a society based on cooperation. The socialist ideal sees individuals motivated not by profit and personal gain, but by a sense of social responsibility.

In short, democratic socialism requires the following:

1. Government ownership and control of the major industries, utilities, and transportation systems

2. A limit on individual wealth and property

3. A welfare system that guarantees all persons decent healthcare, an education, and adequate food and shelter

4. Extensive governmental regulation of the economy

Democratic socialism was a powerful force in Western Europe throughout the twentieth century; but in the United States, socialism and social democratic parties have had little success. In the early years of the twentieth century, the Socialist Party, headed by Eugene V. Debs and later by Norman Thomas, gained some influence and support. During the Great Depression, the millions of unemployed provided the socialists with a major opportunity. In 1932, in the last significant showing of the Socialist Party in a presidential election, Norman Thomas gained about 2 percent of the popular vote; but the election of Franklin Roosevelt and acceptance of his New Deal welfare measures stole much of the socialists' thunder. Irving Howe, co-chair of the Democratic Socialists of America, admitted in 1984, "The Socialist Party fell apart because it could not come to terms with Roosevelt."[16]

The "Migrant Mother" photo of destitute thirty-two-year-old Florence Thompson, mother of seven children, has become one of the most recognized documentary-type photographs of the Depression Era, circa 1930. (Library of Congress)

The Democratic Socialists of America, the successor to the Socialist Party of Debs and Thomas, no longer expects to galvanize broad mass support behind its banners. Instead, it operates within a number of liberal organizations, including the Democratic Party, to influence their ideas and direction.

The issues that faced the socialist movement in the pre–New Deal days were relatively simple and dramatic: The elderly needed a guaranteed pension; the unions needed government guarantees of their rights to organize and bargain; and the unemployed needed some form of protection. The New Deal established programs to deal with these issues, and the subsequent questions of their financing and administration were no longer dramatic. What, then, is the social democratic program in the post–New Deal, post–welfare state era?

Full employment, guaranteed by the government, has become a major demand of contemporary socialists. This requires a reduction of the workweek from forty to

BVT Lab

Flashcards are available
for this chapter at
www.BVTLab.com.

Chapter 04 | Political Ideologies | 128

thirty-five hours so that more people can work fewer hours, with the government compensating workers with tax credits for any wages they lose by a reduction of their hours. Socialists call for a massive public works program for rebuilding America's *infrastructure* (roads, bridges, sewage systems) in order to create millions of new jobs for the currently unemployed. Because full employment can stimulate inflation, the socialists would also employ controls on wages, prices, incomes, rents, and dividends.

Sensitive to the issue that socialism spawns bureaucracy and centralization, American socialists support a system of public ownership characterized by worker-owned or community-controlled businesses and factories. Nevertheless, Americans remain resistant to the idea of socialism, associating it with either the authoritarian communism that plagued Eastern Europe or, in its democratic form, with the sluggish economy that characterized pre-Thatcherite Great Britain. In the present era, socialism presents more of an intellectual challenge to American capitalism than a serious political threat. Nonetheless, in 1990, longtime socialist Bernard Sanders—not running under the Democratic banner—was elected to the House of Representatives from Vermont. He was the first independent socialist elected to Congress in over half a century. In 2004, he returned to Congress for his eighth consecutive term, winning 68 percent of the votes. In 2006, Sanders ran as an independent candidate for the U.S. Senate. Sanders squared off against a Republican candidate for the open seat, and Vermonters elected the independent socialist to the Senate with 65 percent of the vote. He won reelection in 2012 by an even wider margin and is considering running for president in 2016.

The international Occupy movement, sometimes called the "99 Percent" movement, that started in 2011 in the United States bears some resemblance to democratic socialism, although it does not call for government ownership of industry the way that socialism does. A protest against the powerful influence of Wall Street and mega-corporations, the growth in income inequality, and what the movement's supporters see as an increasingly undemocratic government, the Occupy movement has a diverse set of goals and demands. It remains to be seen whether this movement will be successful in its goals of reducing economic inequalities and holding government more accountable to the citizenry.

Members of National Nurses United labor union show their support for Occupy Wall Street in Foley Square in New York City on October 5, 2011. (Wikimedia Commons)

4.4b   Libertarianism: A Revival of Classical Liberalism

Although the Libertarian Party remains on the fringe of American politics, its ideas have stimulated considerable interest. The intellectual roots of libertarianism can be traced to the classical liberal movement of the eighteenth and nineteenth centuries and the ideas of Thomas Jefferson and Andrew Jackson. In the 2012 presidential election, the Libertarian Party candidate, former Republican governor of New Mexico Gary Johnson, polled about 1.2 million votes—just under 1 percent of the total votes cast.

Like classical liberalism, **libertarianism** holds that the state must be kept extremely small. The essential role of government should be only the protection of the following human rights:

1. The right to life, by which libertarians mean protection against the use of force by others

2. The right to liberty, meaning the freedoms of speech, press, and assembly and protection against any government restrictions on ideas, books, films, or other means of communication

3. The right to property, by which libertarians support legislation that protects the property rights of individuals against confiscation, robbery, trespass, libel, fraud, and copyright violations[17]

Libertarians also oppose the interference of government in the private lives of citizens. They seek, for example, the repeal of all laws that involve so-called victim-less crimes (prostitution, pornography, gambling). They seek an unfettered, free-market economy and oppose laws regulating the price of milk as well as those that prohibit the use of marijuana. Unlike the liberals, who support laws expanding the role of government in the economy, and social conservatives, who support legislation outlawing abortion and pornography, the libertarians oppose with equal fervor laws that regulate either the moral or the economic life of individuals.

Libertarians favor nonintervention in the affairs of other nations. They believe that military alliances and arms aid only lead to war, and that

Libertarians feel that the government should not prohibit the use of marijuana or otherwise interfere in the private lives of citizens. (Shutterstock)

wars and war preparation bring about a vast increase in the power of government. One leading libertarian theorist argued that the United States should revoke all its military and political commitments to other countries.[18]

Libertarians call for a drastic reduction in the defense budget and a defense policy designed solely to defend the territory of the United States. Accordingly, the military draft is considered a form of involuntary servitude. Because proponents of the libertarian movement and the Libertarian Party have no immediate prospect of coming into power, their positions remain free of the need to compromise. In the 2012 presidential campaign, candidate Gary Johnson called for a drastic reduction in military spending, a constitutional amendment on marriage equality to legalize same-sex marriage, simplification of the immigration process, a broad expansion of civil liberties, and the decriminalization of drugs.[19]

libertarianism

A belief that the state should regulate neither the economic nor the moral life of its citizens

Although the Libertarian Party remains a minor party, its ideas have influenced both major parties. The Republican Party has taken a much more aggressive stand against the social programs of the 1960s and 1970s. It has also championed the reduction of income tax rates and the deregulation of business and industry.

Are your congressional representatives and senators generally liberal, or are they mostly conservative?

Americans for Democratic Action is an organization that attempts to answer that question by assigning each legislator a "Liberal Quotient" score based on their voting record.

http://www.bvtlab.com/3A8Dp

The Democratic Party has supported broader freedom from government interference in the areas of abortion, school prayer, and LGBTQ issues. Nevertheless, Americans have generally been reluctant to follow radical or revolutionary movements. Perhaps they perceive libertarianism as an interesting criticism, but they are not yet prepared to accept its far-reaching solutions.

The most recent form of libertarianism to capture America's imagination has been a blend of conservative and libertarian positions coalescing under the umbrella of the Tea Party movement. Formally founded in 2009 as the Tea Party Patriots, this organization takes its name from the Boston Tea Party—the colonial American rebellion against British-imposed taxes. Sponsoring local chapters in many states throughout the country, Tea Party activists call for "promoting the principles of fiscal responsibility, constitutionally limited government, and free markets."[20] Although not founded to run candidates for office, the movement's popularity and the passion of its adherents were considered to have a significant effect on the outcome of a number of congressional elections in 2010, 2012, and 2014.

CHAPTER REVIEW

1. People do not simply dispute issues that reflect their own self-interest. They also disagree—sharply, at times—about what constitutes a good society. Since the American and French revolutions, disputes between liberals and conservatives have occupied center stage in Western democracies and in the United States, in particular; but liberalism and conservatism have often changed colors and even exchanged attitudes.

2. Nineteenth-century liberals Thomas Jefferson and Andrew Jackson equated the idea of a powerful state with the protection of the wealthy merchant classes, but liberalism changed in the Industrial Age. Deeply affected by the populist and progressive movements, liberalism saw government as an important vehicle for the protection of the many from exploitation by the few. Liberals and neoliberals today still regard governmental programs and intervention as the key to solving our economic problems; but in matters of personal morality, liberals hark back to an earlier age. Their opposition to governmental interference in matters of abortion and school prayer is reminiscent of Jefferson's concerns.

3. Conservatives in the early days of the American republic were the supporters of a strong government. They believed that only a government of a talented and propertied elite could preserve the sacred rights of all people. As the voting franchise was extended to more and more people, conservatives lost their faith in central government and focused on the rights of property, independent of the state, and the rights of individuals to be free of governmental interference. With their opposition to abortion, pornography, and LGBTQ rights, conservatives remain true in matters of moral and social policy to the old Burkean belief that the state can promote social virtue. The central controversy between liberals and conservatives today is not over whether government should be strong or weak but when it should be strong or weak.

4. Libertarianism and democratic socialism advocate fundamental alterations in the status quo. Social democrats focus on the good of the whole society and envision a system under which all people will be equal economically and politically. They support a broad program of governmental control that includes ownership of the major corporations and industries. Unlike the libertarians, who see the state as the greatest threat to human liberty, the social democrats see the state as the greatest hope for human equality.

5. Libertarians, in their opposition to the very idea of big government, hark back to the nineteenth-century liberals. They are opposed to government interference in the setting of agricultural price supports as well as in the prohibition of illegal drugs. They believe that government should exist primarily to defend the rights to life, liberty, and property, and to defend the homeland from attack.

KEY TERMS

Readings for Further Study

A broad overview of political ideologies can be found in Leon P. Baradat, *Political Ideologies: Their Origins and Impact*, 11th ed. (Upper Saddle River, NJ: Pearson, 2012), and in John Andrew Heywood, *Political Ideologies: An Introduction*, 5th ed. (New York: Palgrave Macmillan, 2012).

Both David F. Ericson and Louisa Bertch Green, eds., *The Liberal Tradition in American Politics* (New York: Routledge, 1999) and Charles W. Dunn and J. David Woodard, *The Conservative Tradition in America* (Lanham, MD: Rowman & Littlefield, 2003) provide a valuable collection of important historical readings.

Alpheus T. Mason and Gordon E. Baker, *Free Government in the Making*, 4th ed. (New York: Oxford University Press, 1985) supplements readings on American political thought with helpful essays.

Readers interested in exploring socialist thought should consult Michael Newman, *Socialism: A Very Short Introduction* (New York: Oxford University Press, 2005).

Those interested in a greater understanding of libertarianism should see Jacob H. Huebert, *Libertarianism Today* (Santa Barbara: Praeger, 2010).

For a discussion of neoliberal and neoconservative thought, consult David Harvey, *A Brief History of Neoliberalism* (New York: Oxford University Press, 2007) and Francis Fukuyama, *America at the Crossroads: Democracy, Power, and the Neoconservative Legacy* (New Haven: Yale University Press, 2007).

For an overview of the impact of the contemporary ideological debate on American politics, see Morris P. Fiorina, *Culture War? The Myth of a Polarized America*, 3rd ed. (New York: Pearson Longman, 2010) and Thomas Frank, *What's the Matter With Kansas?* (New York: Henry Holt and Company, 2005).

For an understanding of the Tea Party movement, see Theda Skocpol and Vanessa Williamson, *The Tea Party and the Remaking of Republican Conservatism.* (New York: Oxford University Press, 2012).

The Occupy movement is explored in *The Occupy Handbook*, edited by Janet Byrne (New York: Back Bay Books, 2012).

Notes

1. Roy C. Macridis, *Contemporary Political Ideologies* (Boston: Little, Brown, 1983), p. 9.

2. Quoted in Walter E. Volkomer, ed., *The Liberal Tradition in American Thought* (New York: Capricorn Books, 1969), p. 104.

3. Robert V. Remini, *Andrew Jackson and the Course of American Freedom, 1822–1832*, vol. 2 (New York: Harper & Row, 1981), p. 116.

4. Ibid., p. 33.

5. Quoted in Arthur A. Ekrich Jr., *Progressivism in America* (New York: New Viewpoints, 1974), p. 170.

6. Paul Glastris, "The Phillips Curve," *Washington Monthly* (June 1990): 54.

7. Arthur Schlesinger Jr., "The Liberal Opportunity," *The American Prospect* (Spring 1990): 15.

8. *National Journal*, "Obama: Most Liberal Senator in 2007," January 31, 2008.

9. Quoted in James M. Burns, *The Vineyard of Liberty* (New York: Knopf, 1982), p. 225.

10. Clinton Rossiter, *Conservatism in America*, 2nd ed., rev. (Cambridge, MA: Harvard University Press, 1982), p. 118.

11. Quoted in Jay Sigler, ed., *The Conservative Tradition in American Thought* (New York: Capricorn Books, 1969), p. 118.

12. Quoted in Rossiter, *Conservatism in America*, p. 138.

13. George Will, *Statecraft as Soulcraft: What Government Does* (New York: Simon & Schuster, 1983), pp. 119–120.

14. *Engel v. Vitale*, 370 U.S. 421 (1962); *Roe v. Wade*, 410 U.S. 113 (1973); *Wallace v. Jaffree*, 472 U.S. 38 (1985).

15. Irving Kristol, *Reflections of a Neoconservative: Looking Back, Looking Ahead* (New York: Basic Books, 1953), p. 212.

16. "Voices from the Left: A Conversation Between Michael Harrington and Irving Howe," *The New York Times Magazine*, June 17, 1984, p. 28.

17. John Hospers, "What Libertarianism Is," in Tibor Machan, ed., *The Libertarian Alternative: Essays in Social and Political Philosophy* (Chicago: Nelson-Hall, 1974), p. 13.

18. Murray Rothbard, *For a New Liberty: The Libertarian Manifesto*, rev. ed. (New York: Collier, 1978), p. 291.

19. Gary Johnson 2012, http://www.garyjohnson2012.com/front (July 18, 2012).

20. "Tea Party Patriots Mission Statement and Core Values," http://www.teapartypatriots.org/Mission.aspx (June 8, 2010).

POP QUIZ

1. Classical liberals believed that the government that governed _____ governed _____.

2. _____ direct their attention not to the expansion of government services but to their effective delivery.

3. Contemporary conservatism remains at its core a defense of economic individualism against the growth of the _____ _____.

4. Democratic socialists believe that a genuinely democratic society must produce equality of _____.

5. Both liberals and conservatives accept most of the economic reforms of the New Deal.   T   F

6. Populists and progressives advocate economic reforms that would strengthen the government's role.   T   F

7. Neoliberals have repudiated the New Deal and Great Society legacies while emphasizing the promotion of wealth.   T   F

8. Early American conservatives believed that only men who owned property should be allowed to vote.   T   F

9. Democratic socialism essentially supports the democratic process and the ideals of capitalism.   T   F

10. Which of the following is true of radical ideologies such as democratic socialism and libertarianism?

    A) They accept the basic principles of capitalism as a successful economic system.

    B) They challenge much of the existing social and political order.

    C) They function outside of the democratic process.

    D) They have become a major challenge to liberalism and conservatism in America.

11. Classical liberals such as Thomas Jefferson and Andrew Jackson believed which of the following?

    A) in a strong central government

    B) that unregulated capitalism resulted in rule by a moneyed aristocracy

    C) that liberty was the absence of government interference with the rights of citizens

    D) that government expenditures should be limited to infrastructure projects such as roads and canals

12. Which of the following was true of New Deal, contemporary liberalism?

    A) It changed the constituency of liberalism to include the entrepreneurial class.

    B) It is based on the belief that government should provide basic material guarantees for every individual.

    C) It favored a decreased role of government in the economy.

    D) It repudiated the ideals of capitalism.

13. Which of the following is true of neoliberals?

    A) They favor policies that call for greater government and business cooperation.

    B) They support expanding the size and role of government unions.

    C) They prefer reducing defense spending to military reforms.

    D) They favor tying civil service and military benefits to the cost of living.

14. Which of the following is true of neoconservatives?

    A) They support racial and sexual quotas.

    B) They stress policies that lower taxes on large incomes.

    C) They call for more regulation of business to promote economic growth.

    D) They support the idea of the welfare state in principle, but not in practice.

15. The intellectual roots of libertarianism can be traced to which of the following?

    A) populism and progressivism

    B) the philosophy of Edmund Burke

    C) classical liberalism

    D) the New Deal

Answers:
1. least, best   2. Neoliberals   3. welfare state   4. results
5. T   6. T   7. F   8. T   9. F   10. B   11. C   12. B
13. A   14. B   15. C*

Chapter
05

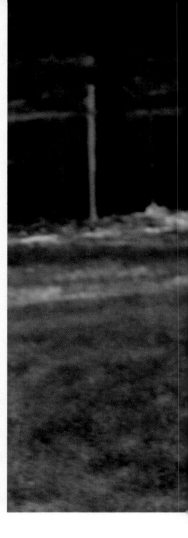

Public Opinion and Political Participation

In This Chapter

(Shutterstock)

Chapter Objectives

This chapter examines what the American people actually think about politics, how they come to think what they do, and how they translate their thoughts into politically relevant actions. Chapter 4 described the major patterns of American political beliefs in philosophical and historical terms. In this chapter, we concern ourselves with the extent to which the general public actually subscribes to those beliefs—leading into an examination of how people learn to think about politics.

What influences encourage people to become Democrats, independents, or Republicans and determine their opinions on political issues?

These topics are discussed in the sections on political socialization. The chapter concludes with a discussion of how political beliefs are translated into political actions, ranging from voting to protest demonstrations and civil disobedience.

Republican Senator of Texas Ted Cruz at Republican Leadership Conference on April 17, 2015. He announced he would run for the Republican Party nomination in the 2016 U.S. Presidential election on March 23, 2015. (Wikimedia Commons)

5.1   Public Opinion: What Americans Think About Politics

What Americans *think* about politics is important because it determines, in part, how they act politically. The diverse but predominantly moderate character of Americans' political views and the relatively modest intensity with which most people advance their views set the tone for the whole political process. To understand how people think about politics is to understand an essential element of the environment within which the political process functions.

5.1a The Character of Public Opinion

Public opinion may sound like a simple and stable concept, but it is actually complex and ever changing. **Public opinion** is a combination of the views, attitudes, and ideas held by individuals in a community. There is no single public opinion; there is, rather, a wide variety of viewpoints. Different publics or groups of people think differently about political questions. Some people hold very sophisticated views about politics; others do not. Some people devote their entire lives to politics; others hardly ever think about politics.

Certain facets of public opinion are remarkably constant. Love of country and pride in the nation's accomplishments, for instance, are attitudes that are almost always present and widely shared. Other facets of public opinion are *dynamic*—fluctuating considerably in response to social, political, and economic events. Some opinions are held *intensely*; others seem to be little more than *casual preferences*. An opinion that is intensely held is more likely to influence what a person thinks about political candidates and how that person might get involved politically.

The politically sophisticated and the general public observe the same political world. However, much of the public sees it—to borrow an expression from the Bible—"through a glass darkly." Politicians and political commentators can argue at length about what they see as the major political issues of the time, but much of this seems to pass by most of the public. As explained in the following sections, a substantial share of the American public does not care much about politics, knows relatively

public opinion

The array of beliefs and attitudes that people hold about political and related affairs

little about it, and does not think about it in very sophisticated terms. Still, few would say that public opinion is unimportant. Indeed, political analysts and politicians are very concerned about what the public thinks.

5.1b How Much Americans Care and Know About Politics

Polling—the process of using social science methods to get an accurate sense of the public's view on an issue—has been an important facet of American politics since the 1930s. The first public opinion pollsters assumed that the public cared and was reasonably well-informed about politics; however, they were startled to find that many Americans cared little and knew less about what went on in the political arena. More recent surveys have done little to contradict these early findings or show any recent increase in public interest and information—a surprising finding given the rising level of education and the proliferation of the media, particularly television and Internet news, over the last few decades.

This is not to say that the public as a whole is essentially uninterested in politics; indeed, a substantial number of people indicate a considerable degree of interest. For example, a 2014 survey found that 48 percent of the public said that they followed government and public affairs "most of the time," 29 percent only "some of the time," and 22 percent "only now and then" or "hardly at all."[1] These results fall short of the democratic ideal of a keenly interested electorate, but are reasonably reassuring in that most people do seem to be at least somewhat interested in politics.

The meaningfulness of such expressions of interest is called into question, however, by the public's level of information about politics. A 2014 survey indicated that 42 percent of Americans did not know which party had a majority of seats in Congress; and in another survey, 22 percent of Americans had never heard of Senate Majority Leader Harry Reid (D–NV). A 2011 study found that 24 percent of Americans could not name the country from which the United States gained its independence following the Revolutionary War.[2]

5.1c What Americans Hold in Common

On many fundamental political matters, the majority of Americans are in substantial agreement. First of all, Americans are proud of their country and emotionally attached to it and its symbols. The majority of Americans—about 85 percent—say they are either "extremely proud" or "very proud" to be an American, with another 11 percent identifying as "moderately proud." Only 5 percent of Americans say they are "only

Of Americans polled, 96 percent say they are proud of their country. (Shutterstock)

a little" or "not at all proud."[3] Studies consistently show that the percentages of people expressing enthusiasm and pride for their country are, in fact, higher in the United States than in almost any other country.

Americans are also positive about their country's political, social, and economic institutions. When asked how much confidence they had in their country's public and private institutions, Americans consistently responded more favorably than citizens from four European democracies (Figure 5.1). Although some Americans are critical of their nation's institutions, what is most striking is that Americans are clearly less critical than people in other countries. Americans consistently have more confidence in even

polling

The process of using social science methods to get an accurate sense of the public's view about an issue or set of issues

Figure 5.1 | Confidence in Public Institutions: A Comparative Perspective

Americans consistently express greater confidence in their country's political, social, and economic institutions than do citizens of other democratic countries.

SOURCE: The Gallup Organization, "Confidence in Institutions," June 2014, http://www.gallup.com/poll/1597/Confidence-Institutions.aspx (August 7, 2014) and European Commission, "Eurobarometer Report Numbers 64–81, June 2006–July 2014, http://ec.europa.eu/public_opinion/archives/eb_arch_en.htm (August 7, 2014).

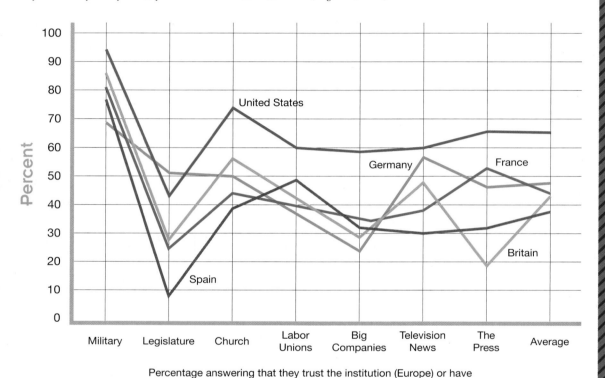

Percentage answering that they trust the institution (Europe) or have "a great deal," "quite a lot," or "some" confidence in it (U.S.).

those institutions that are sometimes singled out as objects of public disdain—such as the media, labor unions, and Congress—than do their European counterparts.

Why are Americans generally so proud of their country and positive about its institutions? One reason is that they have been taught all their lives to think of America as the best (see the section on political socialization later in this chapter); the roots of American pride run deeper than that, however. Americans also take pride in their country because they are generally raised to hold certain basic values and to believe that the United States, among all nations, is particularly dedicated to the fulfillment of those values. The Declaration of Independence exemplifies these values:

> WE hold these Truths to be self-evident, that all Men are created *equal,* that they are endowed by their Creator with certain unalienable Rights, that among these are *Life, Liberty, and the Pursuit of Happiness.* That to secure these rights, Governments are instituted among Men, deriving their just *Powers* from the *Consent of the Governed.*

Textbooks and Children's Ideas About American Politics

American students typically spend a dozen or more years of their lives poring over textbooks of various sorts. Some of these books have little to do with politics: math books, chemistry books, foreign language books. Many of them, however, do deal directly or indirectly with topics related to politics: social studies books, history books, American government books, economics books, and sociology books.

Because students spend so much time reading them, textbooks seem likely to significantly affect how students think about politics. Further, the books may be particularly influential because of the way students are likely to approach them. Students treat the material in textbooks as information they need to know, rather than as information to be read critically or thought about afterward in depth. Almost as soon as the material is known, it starts to be forgotten. As the specific facts fade, what tends to be remembered is a general impression— a color and tone and feeling that can persist for years.

The influence of textbooks brings up some of the most important and difficult issues of political socialization.[1] Much of political socialization occurs not in sudden and dramatic jumps from ignorance to knowledge or from ambivalence to passion but through a slow, steady gain and loss of political information and impressions. The content of school textbooks is determined by a combination of scholarly, economic, and political factors. The scholars who write the book, the editors and publishers who mold the book to help it sell, and the more or less politically accountable officials who pick the books to be used—all shape the final product. Yet who should decide which textbooks American children should read? Are not school boards democratic institutions? More generally, who should decide what children will be taught? How democratic do we want the education process to be?

Earlier textbooks often presented children with an idealized picture of American history, society, and politics ("sugarcoating," some scholars have called it); recently, however, there has been more sentiment toward giving students the "unvarnished truth." For example, over the past generation textbooks have become more multicultural—featuring more stories and descriptions of ethnic and racial minorities and women.[2] But is there such a thing as "unvarnished truth," or are there just different perspectives? Is there a "best" way to present America's diverse cultural history? Again, who should decide?

Teaching children to think critically about their country, as newer texts tend to do, is certainly an admirable goal; yet it can run counter to the goal of political socialization necessary to promote good citizenship. How does a society create in its children the appropriate balance of respect and skepticism for its basic values? To put it differently, every society wants to instill in its youth favorable feelings toward its values and institutions. Where is the line between socialization and brainwashing?

1 Joseph Moreau, *Schoolbook Nation* (Ann Arbor: University of Michigan Press, 2004).

2 Jesus Garcia, "The Changing Image of Ethnic Groups in Textbooks," *Phi Delta Kappa 75* (1993): 29–35.

To these three basic values of democracy—equality, freedom, and consent of the governed—can be added most Americans' commitment to capitalism and the free enterprise system.

- _Equality_   The majority of Americans genuinely believe in equality; and whether or not they really think people are equal, they believe that the government should treat everyone as if they were equal.[4] That being said, Americans tend to disagree on the best way for the government to treat citizens equally. For example, just 32 percent of Americans believe the government should play a major role in trying to improve the social and economic position of minorities in the United States.[5]

- _Freedom_   Americans believe in their capacity to do what is best for themselves. Hence, they think that individuals should be free to act as they please, with minimal government interference, as long as they do not interfere with other people's freedom. Surveys have long shown a strong commitment to freedom of speech, press, religion, and association.[6] For example, 92 percent of Americans responding to a poll indicated that the First Amendment protection for freedom of speech is either crucial or very important to their own sense of freedom.[7] On the other hand, when rights come into conflict, Americans are faced with tough choices regarding which freedoms to support. The issue of school prayer often pits those who favor free exercise of religion against those who oppose the establishment of religion. In a recent poll, 76 percent of Americans said they would favor a constitutional amendment to allow prayer in public schools, even though the Supreme Court has consistently found such prayer in violation of the First Amendment.[8]

- *Consent of the governed*   Americans see their acceptance of government as voluntary. About 89 percent of Americans believe that periodic elections make the government "pay attention to what the people think" at least some of the time.[9] While only 13 percent responded that they trust the government most or all of the time, just 10 percent of Americans said they never trust the government.[10] Americans also believe firmly in the idea that the majority (more than half) of the people should rule in political affairs. At the same time, however, they believe that majorities should not possess unlimited power and that the rights of a minority (less than half) of the people should be protected against the whims of the majority.

- *Capitalism and the free enterprise system*   Americans believe in the value of hard work, in private property, in economic competition, and in profit. In contrast to some other societies, most Americans tend to view hard work as a virtue and laziness as a vice—tenets of the so-called Protestant ethic. They see private property as an essential element of economic progress. They believe that competition brings out the best in people and that the most successful competitors deserve the greatest rewards. Americans' preference for freedom over equality manifests itself in the economic as well as the political sphere. This particular combination of values fits well with a free-market, entrepreneurial economy. Americans like the idea of a fair competition in which everybody starts out equally, but in which they all have the freedom to pursue their self-interest and thus end up unequally well-off, depending on how well they have pursued their self-interest. A series of Gallup polls taken over the past twenty years indicates that a consistent plurality of Americans believes the government "is trying to do too many things that should be left to individuals and businesses."[11] Regarding taxation, 52 percent of Americans polled in 2014 indicated that the amount of federal income tax they have to pay is too high.[12] On the other hand, in the very same poll 54 percent of respondents said the amount of taxes they have to pay is fair and 59 percent agreed with the statement "the money and wealth in this country should be more evenly distributed among a larger percentage of the people."[13] Polling also found that over 74 percent of respondents agreed that there is either too much or just the right amount of government regulation of business and industry.[14]

Although Americans are proud of their country and its system of government, and although they believe in the fundamental values on which it rests, they are not beyond finding fault with it. In fact, since the 1960s the American political system has struggled with a widespread undercurrent of dissatisfaction with the way in which the system is working, fueled by the urban disorder of the 1960s, the Vietnam War, the Watergate scandal, and the nation's ongoing economic problems. Between 1964 and 1994, the percentage of Americans who said they trusted the government to do what was right all or most of the time fell from 76 percent to 21 percent; and the percentage who said that public officials care what "people like me" think declined from 62 percent to 22 percent. This sense of alienation started to turn around somewhat by the beginning of the twenty-first century, however, as the trust in government number rose to 47 percent, and the percent who believed government cared about what they think rose to 34 percent by 2004.[15] By late 2008, however, the trust in government index had fallen again—this time to 26 percent. Such mood changes may not be entirely unrelated to Americans' pocketbooks. In 2008, due to the economic downturn of the early 2000s, only 8 percent of Americans believed the economy was getting better; 87 percent believed it was getting worse. By 2012, though, a majority of Americans believed that the economy was recovering.[16] These figures coincided with the public's rising approval ratings for the president (50 percent).[17] Then, as the economic recovery fell short of expectations in 2013 and 2014, so fell President Obama's approval ratings in those years.[18] This connection between trust in the government and the success of the economy is an enduring feature of American public opinion.

Americans like the idea of a fair competition in which everybody starts out equally, but in which they all have the freedom to pursue their self-interest and thus end up unequally well-off. (Shutterstock)

5.1d Where Americans Differ

Citizens of the United States manifest considerable agreement on the general principles of democracy just described, but consensus is far from complete. The American people differ on the implications of these general principles when applied to particular cases. They also differ in their political ideologies.

The Meaning of Equality

Although Americans profess a belief in equality in the abstract, just what this means and to whom it applies are matters for disagreement. First, as we discussed in Chapter 3, does equality mean equality of opportunity or equality of result? That is, should everybody have an equal chance to pursue an education and earn a high income, or should everybody get the same education and earn the same income? Americans seem to lean away from equality of result. Only 19 percent believe the government should "take active steps in every area it can to try and improve the lives of its citizens."[19]

Second, just which "men" are equal? Some Americans do not believe that men and women are equal. According to a 2008 survey, 7 percent think, "Women's place is in the home rather than business, industry, or government."[20] Even into contemporary times, a substantial percentage of Americans have not regarded African Americans and whites as equals. In a 1990 survey, 78 percent of whites thought that African Americans were more likely to prefer living on welfare than whites; 62 percent thought African Americans less likely to be hardworking; 56 percent thought African

BVT *Lab*

Improve your test scores. Practice quizzes are available at www.BVTLab.com.

Americans more prone to violence; and 53 percent thought African Americans less intelligent. African Americans see this sense of racial inequality from a different perspective. In a 2013 poll, 74 percent of whites thought an African American had as good of a chance as a white American to get a job for which they were qualified, but 59 percent of African Americans felt this was not the case. Additionally, 80 percent of whites believed that African American children have the same chance as white children to get a good education, whereas only 55 percent of African Americans share this view.[21]

Limits of Freedom

Although Americans believe in freedom as a general principle, they do see it as having definite limits. More than 95 percent endorse the principle of freedom of expression in the abstract, but percentages drop sharply with the possibility that "bad" or "dangerous" ideas will be expressed.[22] For many Americans, freedom of expression does not extend to speaking, writing, or teaching when the ideas are unpopular ones—for example, antireligious or racist.[23] Further, some Americans do not agree that people should be able to express their views any way they want. The Supreme Court's decisions in 1989 and 1990 upholding the rights of protesters to burn the American flag set off a bitter national debate. A constitutional amendment to criminalize the act has been introduced in Congress nearly every session since. In the wake of the war on terrorism, Americans have expanded their view on what expressions are potentially dangerous and how restrictive the government should be in response. Some have argued that the 2001 Patriot Act went too far in restricting civil liberties, but by 2006, only 30 percent of Americans thought the act needed major changes or should be eliminated entirely.[24] Even a decade after the 9/11 attacks, 25 percent of Americans responded that "the government should take all steps necessary to prevent terrorist acts, even if their "basic civil liberties would be violated."[25]

Majority Rule Versus Minority Rights

The American people's adherence to the ideals of majority rule and minority rights sometimes loses something in the translation to everyday political questions. Slightly more than half of the respondents in one survey held that only people who were well informed about issues should be allowed to vote in elections in which questions relating to "tax-supported undertakings" are at issue, and in a 2014 survey 34 percent of respondents held that only people who pay taxes should have the right to vote.[26] The idea that any citizen should be able to grow up to be president is endorsed in the abstract but rejected by some in practice. In April 2008, 35 percent of Americans did not think the country was ready for a woman president and 22 percent did not think the country was ready for a black president.[27] Of course, the Democratic Party put those attitudes to the test when Senators Hillary Clinton (D–NY) and Barack Obama (D–IL) campaigned throughout the entire presidential primary season. By June of that year, Obama had

(Shutterstock)

secured enough delegates to become his party's nominee and the first black presidential candidate to represent one of the two main political parties. His election victory in November 2008 may have finally put the question about race to rest, and Hillary Clinton's possible nomination in 2016 could do the same for the gender question.

Free Enterprise in Practice

As enamored with the free enterprise system as Americans are, their affection for it still has some limits. About 62 percent of Americans express quite a lot or a great deal of confidence in small business owners, but only about 21 percent have that same degree of confidence in big business.[28] In light of the recent financial sector crises, 61 percent of Americans approved of increased government regulation of banks and financial institutions.[29] Americans are particularly wary of big business, with almost half of respondents in a 2014 poll saying they would like to see big business have less influence on the nation than it does now and only 6 percent wishing it had more influence.[30]

Political Ideology

Perhaps the most important matter on which Americans differ is political ideology. American politics is often portrayed as a controversy between liberals and conservatives. As discussed in Chapter 4, with the rise of neoconservatism, neoliberalism, and the return to classical liberal principles in libertarianism, particularly in recent years, the reality has become much more complicated. Commentators have also distinguished among the different dimensions of liberalism and conservatism: economic, social, and cultural. Such debates have certainly occupied the attention of the intellectual elites, but what is striking is how far removed they are from the concerns of most Americans. Even the most basic notions of liberalism and conservatism meet with limited recognition. Only about half of U.S. citizens recognize the terms *liberalism* and *conservatism* and have some general sense of what they mean.[31] In a 2012 national survey, about 23 percent of the respondents declined to place themselves on a liberal–conservative scale when asked to do so because they said they did not know or had not thought that much about it, and another 24 percent responded that they were "middle of the road."[32] Studies of people's answers to questions raising liberal-conservative issues have long shown little consistency between answers, suggesting that many people do not think about politics in ideologically coherent terms.[33] First of all, such findings are important because they suggest that a good share of the population does not really have a grasp on the debate between liberals and conservatives. Second, the findings raise questions about the meaningfulness of the American public's responses to questions about their political ideology. When people are unsure of what they are being asked, a safe response is often in the middle.

Figure 5.2 shows how over the last four decades more Americans have characterized themselves as conservatives than as moderates or liberals. This trend peaked in 1994, when 36 percent of Americans identified themselves as conservative and only 14 percent as liberal. The years since then have shown a small reversal, yet still 11 percent more Americans said they were conservative than liberal in 2012. When given the opportunity to clarify the degree of their ideology, however, Americans reveal that their ideological beliefs are, for the most part, mild. Both liberals and conservatives were more likely to indicate that they were "slightly ideological" than "extremely so." In fact, no more than 4 percent of respondents in any of the survey years indicated that they were "extremely liberal" or "extremely conservative."

What these findings really mean is difficult to interpret without some sense of what the American public means when it uses the words *liberal* and *conservative*.

Figure 5.2 | Americans Rate Themselves on the Liberal–Conservative Scale, 1972–2012

While the number of Americans identifying themselves as conservatives has remained higher than the number identifying themselves as liberals over the last forty years, only a slim majority of Americans identify with either label.

SOURCE: *American National Election Studies, 2008, 2012.*

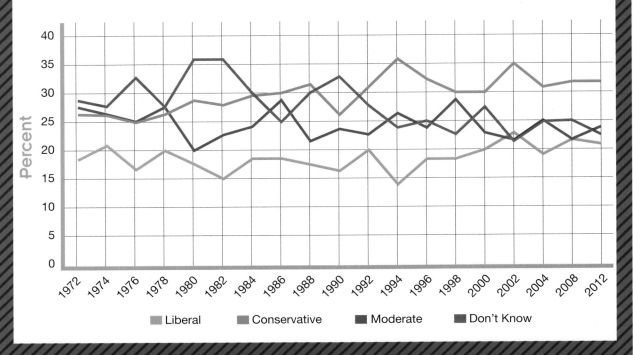

Different people appear to mean different things by them. When a national election survey asked people what they had in mind when they said that someone's political views were liberal or conservative, the most common responses described liberals as people who are open to change and new ideas, for government action to help solve social problems, allied with working people, inclined to spend government money, and somewhat rash. In contrast, conservatives were viewed as resistant to change, for free enterprise solutions, allied with big business and the rich, against government spending, and cautious.[34]

What about the people who don't think in terms of—or even recognize—liberal and conservative labels? Political scientists have tried to plumb political thinking to get at the mental images of these people. What they have found does not paint an encouraging portrait. Many Americans seem to respond to political issues on an essentially individual basis, without any broad or overarching political philosophy to guide them. Instead, their responses are shaped by their sense of identification with one or another political party or group, by their feelings about whether "it's good times" or "it's hard times," or by their feelings about a particular candidate or public figure.[35]

Economic Status and Ideology

Conventional wisdom has it that political ideology is closely tied to economic status, with the less well-off holding liberal beliefs and the better-off aligning themselves with a conservative viewpoint. How well does this relationship hold up in America? Figure 5A shows the relationship between the respondent's professed political ideology and the income of the respondent's family.

The poorest Americans are not the most likely group to identify themselves as liberal. These citizens are more likely to identify as moderate or conservative than liberal. In the second and third groups, liberals and conservatives are closer to even. In the highest income category, liberals reach their highest total—but so do conservatives. Conservative views outnumber both of the others in only the highest income category, and there does seem to be support for the claim that wealthier individuals are more likely to be conservative. Additionally, the higher income groups are more likely to express an ideological identity: 70 percent of the wealthiest group identified with one of the three categories, but only 59 percent of the poorest group did. One striking feature of these data

is the relative weakness of the ideological differences between the income groups. More than 33 percent of the poorest Americans describe themselves as conservative. In the wealthiest group, over 30 percent describe themselves as liberal. Surprisingly, then, not everybody who pays (through taxes) for liberal government programs opposes them; and not everybody who might benefit from them supports them. Clearly, economic standing alone does not determine the ideological views of the American public.

What other factors might determine how liberal or conservative a person is? How do you think the other ideological viewpoints discussed in Chapter 4 might relate to economic status?

Figure 5A | Political Ideology and Income

Poor people tend to be less ideological and rich people tend to be more conservative, but all income levels have substantial numbers of conservatives, and the richest group has the highest percentage of liberals.

SOURCE: *General Social Survey, 2012.*

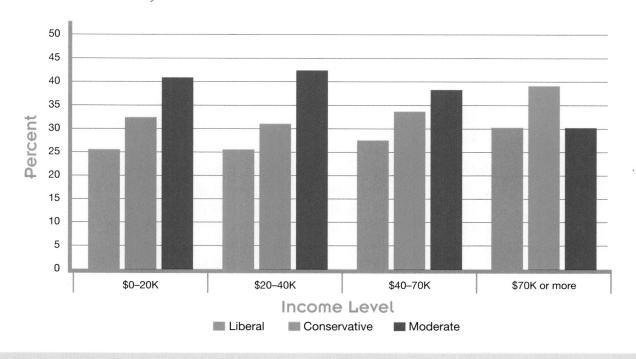

However, there may be an important qualification: The level of coherence in public thinking may be at least partially dependent on how politicians handle issues in campaign and policy-making discussions. When candidates and public figures address the public on issues, the public does seem to respond by becoming more conscious of and concerned about those issues. For example, in the relatively placid 1950s, candidates and parties did little to bring issue differences to the attention of the public, and the public showed little awareness of issues or coherence in its thinking about them. From the mid-1960s into the 1970s, however, candidates began to discuss compelling issues such as the Vietnam War and urban disorder; and the public seemed to respond with increased awareness and coherence.[36]

More recent research has called into question the degree and meaningfulness of the changes observed in the 1960s and 1970s, suggesting that they may result from changes in the way questions were asked and that much of the research into this area may be fatally flawed. It may be that the public's level of sophistication about politics has always been low and that it has changed little over the last fifty years. Whatever apparent increases in liberal-conservative thinking there have been may result from the public merely parroting the heightened liberal-conservative rhetoric of candidates without really understanding it.[37]

The political beliefs of the American public establish patterns that help to shape politics. The general agreement on principles such as freedom and majority rule defines the boundaries within which the game of American politics is played. These limits help to blunt any potential for political instability or violence. Commitments to ideas such as equal opportunity tend to define the basic objectives of the political system. The relatively low level of ideological thinking provides political leaders with room to maneuver and thereby fosters political stability.

Nevertheless, differences in ideological perspective result in fundamental conflicts that the political process must resolve. For instance, how actively should the government promote the interests of disadvantaged or oppressed groups? Where should the government strike the balance between promoting social change and maintaining social stability? How the public thinks about politics defines, in part, some of the most fundamental principles and problems of American democracy.

5.2 The Sources of Public Opinion: Political Socialization

Given the importance of public opinion, it is useful to comprehend why the public thinks as it does about politics. The origins of public opinion lie in history and philosophy, as discussed in Chapter 4. However, knowing where ideas come from does not explain how people come to hold certain beliefs; understanding that phenomenon requires a discussion of political socialization.

Political socialization is the process by which citizens come to think what they do about politics. Through political socialization, citizens internalize—or incorporate into their own thinking—beliefs, feelings, and evaluations (judgments on whether something is good or bad) about the political world in which they live. Think of the tremendous range of knowledge, feelings, and evaluations that people have about politics, and think of the many sources from which they all come; political socialization is obviously a long and complicated process.

political socialization

The process by which citizens acquire politically relevant knowledge, beliefs, attitudes, and patterns of behavior

Most of what people think and feel about politics has been learned from somebody else, but to leave it at that would deny the dynamic nature of the process and ultimately the possibility of any political change. That is, if all people simply stuck with what they have been taught about politics, nobody would ever think of anything new; and nothing would ever change. Clearly, then, some people break away from rigid adherence to old ideas and put thoughts together in new ways; but even those people start somewhere, building upon what already exists. Thus, political socialization is important to both stability and change in American politics.

5.2a The Processes of Political Socialization

How do people learn about politics? Psychologists say that people tend to repeat behavior patterns that are rewarded and not to repeat patterns that are not rewarded or that are punished. Much of what people know about politics they learn through explicit teaching. Information is presented to them, and they are either rewarded for learning it (by a higher grade or the praise of teachers or parents, for example) or punished for not learning it (by a lower grade or the criticism of teachers or parents). The mechanisms of learning are really the domain of psychology. Listed below are some of the basic processes that political scientists have identified as important in political socialization.

- *Social learning theory* People experience subtle rewards and punishments from the psychological attachments they form to particular people around them, some of whom they admire, others of whom they dislike. Because people like to have favorable images of themselves, they may attempt to boost their self-images by acting like people they admire or by avoiding the behavior of those they do not like. Thus, a little boy may parrot his mother's views about the president, or a rebellious teenager may criticize a candidate that her disliked father holds dear.

- *Transfer theory* People may carry over attitudes developed in a narrower setting, such as the family or school, to the broader political setting. A boy who dislikes his father may rebel against political authority more generally.

- *Cognitive development theory* What people can learn about politics depends on the stage of their mental development. Some things can be learned only early in life, while others can be learned only later on. An adult immigrant newly arrived in America may never develop the deep emotional attachment to the nation felt by a person who has grown up in this country from birth. By contrast, a first grader lacks the intellectual capacity to master the intricacies of federalism.[38]

These different theories of how people learn about politics are not competing but are rather complementary. Social learning sometimes occurs through explicit teaching. The possibilities of transference, social learning, and explicit teaching probably all vary, depending on the intellectual development of the learner. Political socialization is too complex to be accounted for by any one theory or explanation.

5.2b The Agents of Political Socialization

Agents of socialization are the people and institutions from which we learn. A person growing up in the United States learns about politics from many teachers. A comprehensive list would be too long to include here, but it is possible to identify a few of

agents of socialization

A "teacher" in the process of political socialization, for example, the family, the school, a peer group, or the mass media

the most important agents. (Another important agent, the mass media, is discussed in the next chapter.)

- *The Family*   Under almost any realistic theory of political socialization, the family is uniquely situated to be a potent agent. The young individual who, according to developmental theory, is most vulnerable to socialization spends much time with the family. Thus, the family has the first chance at influencing political development. Psychological attachments are often strong and therefore conducive to the transference of attitudes toward authority, which influences attitudes and behavior relating to participation and partisanship. Although much learning takes place in the family, how much of that learning is political is difficult to pinpoint and varies from family to family. Politics is not of paramount interest to most Americans and thus is not usually at the top of the typical family's agenda for discussion. As such, it is not surprising that children sometimes grow up to be politically different from their parents. Research indicates that the transmission of political attitudes from parents to their children is substantial only when the attitudes relate to topics that regularly come up for discussion in the family.[39]

- *The School*   The school is also a prime agent of political socialization. Education can be related to many political orientations—political participation, political knowledgeability, and political tolerance, among others. Certainly the school is the primary explicit teacher of information about politics and government. A good share of the learning fades away, as every student well knows, unless it is periodically reinforced by additional education, exposure to the media, political discussion, or repeated use.

  However, schools involve more than just the presentation of facts; they are complex and diverse bundles of experiences and impressions. Students encounter teachers, books, authority figures and role models (such as principals and coaches), and their fellow students or peers. Some of the people students encounter may be very much like themselves, and some may be different. Meeting students of different races or religions in the school setting often provides children with their first real encounter with social diversity. Students may involve themselves in low-level political activities: class and club elections, student government, protests against school policies, and so on. They acquire not just facts but also subtle impressions about the way things are and the way things ought to be. They develop feelings about social and political involvement and what they can hope to accomplish through the political process.[40]

School is a prime agent of political socialization. (Shutterstock)

- *Peer Groups*   Peer groups are groups of people, roughly equal in social position, who interact with one another. Students who go to school together, people who work together in an office or factory or bowl on the same team, the neighbors on the block—all are peer groups. Social pressures on group members to conform can be quite powerful. Group members adopt "proper" attitudes and behavior because they seek the boost to their self-image that comes with the approval of others—or because they fear that nonconformity will lead to ostracism. Because other things are usually more important, peer groups do not always set norms relating to politics. However, when they do, the political consequences can be significant.[41]

5.2c The Development of a Political Self

How does political learning actually take place? How do politically blank infants develop into full-blown political beings? Probably the first political thought to blossom in the mind of a small child in the United States is a psychological attachment to America. This is by no means a sense of what America is, just a feeling of belonging to it. In families where partisanship is important, a primitive sense of "I'm a Republican" or "I'm a Democrat" may appear. A sense of an external authority—above the authority of the parents—that must be obeyed also emerges. This is most often attached to two specific figures: the president and the police officer. The president is the focal point of the American political system; thus, it is not surprising that this focused attention influences even very small children. The police officer gains attention as a less remote figure of considerable authority who moves about in a child's world. Perhaps the most striking feature of these early images is their positive character. Small children tend to idealize political authorities, attributing to them all possible virtues.[42]

Peers can act as agents of political socialization and influence your development and opinions. (Shutterstock)

As children grow, their political orientations evolve. In school they begin to acquire substantial new knowledge pertinent to politics. Much of this they soon forget, but some of it becomes part of their lasting store of information. Their conceptions of politics become less personal and more institutional. For example, the president is important not so much as a person but as a position. Idealization of political authority fades to realism: Public figures have flaws, they make mistakes, and people criticize them. Once in school, where teachers may try to minimize classroom conflict by downplaying partisan differences, children tend to become less partisan.

As partisanship declines, the ability to deal with the political world on a more abstract level increases. Children develop intellectually and morally to the extent that they can begin to look at politics in a more sophisticated and structured way. The critical age at which political thinking really starts to blossom seems to be about twelve. Within a couple more years, children's thinking becomes nearly as abstract and sophisticated as that of adults. Also, with increasing exposure to the sometimes unattractive facets of political life, realism often fades into cynicism. By the late teens, most individuals have established a political identity.

Political socialization does not end at the age of twenty-one, however; learning about politics continues through adulthood. As people age, their needs and concerns

Public Opinion and Terrorism: American Government in the Eyes of the World

As soon as the terrorist attacks hit the United States on September 11, 2001, Americans and governments and citizens throughout the world began to react to the unfolding events. Many of these reactions were captured in opinion polls conducted by the news media and by independent polling agencies. Although reactions were initially quite uniform, cleavages soon began to emerge around the world.

Reaction to the American government's initial response to the 9/11 terrorist attacks varied around the world. (Wikimedia Commons)

A majority of Americans supported the government's initial responses. The president's approval ratings (in response to the question "Do you approve or disapprove of the way George W. Bush is handling his job as president?") initially jumped from 51 percent, just prior to September 11, to 86 percent a few days later. This figure rose to 90 percent in the following weeks and remained there for longer than any previous president since the Gallup Organization started measuring approval ratings in the 1940s. Throughout the weeks that followed 9/11, Americans also indicated strong support for Congress (84 percent), military action in Afghanistan (88 percent), and the use of ground troops (80 percent). When it came to the next steps, however, diversity of opinion—a hallmark of democracy—began to return to American politics. Although support for the government's overall actions was high, about half of the nation (49 percent) believed that the government's repeated warnings about the possibility of further terrorist attacks didn't help but "just scared people." When political leaders began to speculate about the need to restrict personal freedoms, such as personal privacy, in order to prevent future acts of terror, 60 percent of Americans opposed making it easier for legal authorities to read mail and e-mail or tap phones without a person's knowledge.

Around the world reactions have been even more varied. Although countries almost universally condemned the terrorist attacks against the United States, opinions were wide ranging regarding America's military response. In the weeks following the attacks of September 11 and the October 7 launch of a military response, America's closest traditional allies tended to be the most supportive. British Prime Minister Tony Blair made his nation's support evident, and the British people followed suit: 93 percent favored arresting anyone found to be aiding terrorists, and 70 percent believed the United States and its allies should "be prepared to take military action" against nations harboring the terrorists responsible for the attacks. Britons were wary, however, of the consequences of such actions—78 percent believed any military response would create a wider conflict between "the Western world and the Islamic world."

The people of many other nations were deeply split over support for the military response. The Russians—a newly acquired and still cautious ally—expressed confidence in the Bush administration's ability to handle the situation; only 42 percent approved of the military strikes against Afghanistan, however. The Russian people had experienced firsthand the misery of a protracted Afghan war in the 1980s, and many (60 percent) believed the actions of the United States would threaten Russian security. Some (54 percent) blamed terrorism and the Taliban regime for the military conflict, but others (30 percent) held American leadership and American society responsible. One of the main concerns expressed in the Russian press and elsewhere was that the United States was engaging in actions that would not solve the problem of terrorism, and was doing so without providing evidence of al Qaeda's guilt to the rest of the world.

Finally, the citizens of several nations stood opposed to nearly all American military efforts, some believing the United States should have pursued a diplomatic solution and others asserting that America's foreign policy and global capitalism were merely reaping what they had sown. Although the official government responses of nations such as Egypt and Pakistan, for example, were initially supportive of American strikes against Afghanistan, the people of these countries demonstrated opposition through anti-American street protests and peace vigils. Why such a reaction? One factor is that many nations in the Middle East and Asia have large Muslim populations that expressed concerns that an attack on one Muslim nation could spread to others. This was the case in Turkey, where 80 percent of Turkish citizens opposed an American military response in Afghanistan.

In the years since 9/11, this division between America and the Arab and broader Muslim world has deepened as American military efforts turned from Afghanistan to Iraq—with increasing hints that Iran might be a future target, as well. Though attitudes toward the American people and the values of freedom and democracy remained largely favorable, a 2004 survey of six Arab nations indicated declining attitudes, overall, over the previous two years. Opposition to American terrorism policy ranged from 75 to 96 percent and opposition to American Iraq policy ranged from 78 to 98 percent. A 2008 poll indicated that American leadership received only a 17 percent approval rating in the Middle East—the lowest of any region and only about half of the world average. Although still lower than in most parts of the world, and still the only region where more respondents disapprove than approve, approval of American leadership by Arab nations did increase significantly with the election of President Barack Obama.

Do you remember the attacks on America? How did you or your family initially react? What policy approaches have you approved of and disapproved of since then? Are the world's citizens correct to criticize American foreign policy, or are their perspectives too limited by the information they receive? Is there such a thing as an objective, or "correct," view of politics?

SOURCES: The Gallup Organization, "Reactions to the Attacks on America and U.S.-Led Response," October 9, 2001, http://www.gallup.com/poll/releases/pr010914f.asp (November 4, 2001); The Gallup Organization, "Attack on America: Key Trends and Indicators," October 23, 2001, http://www.gallup.com/poll/releases/pr010926c.asp (October 30, 2001); CNN. Com, "World Reacts to War on Terror," http://www.cnn.com/ (November 3, 2001); and World Press Review, "After September 11: A New Worldview," http://www.worldpress.org/specials/wtc/front.htm (November 3, 2001); Zogby International, "Impressions of America 2004: How Arabs View America, How Arabs Learn About America," 2004; The Gallup Organization, "U.S. Leadership Approval Lowest in Europe, Mideast," April 2, 2008, http://www.gallup.com/poll/105967/US-Leadership-Approval-Lowest-Europe-Mideast (July 15, 2008); The Gallup Organization, "Global Image of U.S. Leadership Rebounds," April 10, 2014, http://www.gallup.com/poll/168425/global-image-leadership-rebounds.aspx (September 10. 2014).

evolve; for example, from their own education to their children's education and, later in life, to their own healthcare. People's social environments change; their family roles shift from child to parent to grandparent; the school years recede into the past, and peer groups switch from fellow students to fellow workers to fellow retirees. Broader social change affects political learning, too, as large-scale social transformations—such as the civil rights movement and the women's movement—alter the expectations that people have of themselves and of society. Major unresolved issues revolve around how much childhood socialization persists into adulthood, and how much adult political learning is constrained by what has been learned as a child.[43]

5.2d Diversity in Socialization

Socialization is not an identical process for all Americans. American society includes many subsocieties with their own distinctive political subcultures or shared patterns of political attitudes and behavior—many of which are racially and ethnically based. African Americans constitute one of the largest distinctive subcultures. Although African Americans and white Americans view many issues similarly, significant divisions exist—particularly with regard to equality and the government. For example, 85 percent of whites believe that equal housing opportunities exist for African Americans, but only 56 percent of African Americans hold this view. While 68 percent of African Americans believe they are treated less fairly by the justice system, only 25 percent of whites believe this is true.[44] When the nation reacted strongly to the killing of young African American Michael Brown by a white police officer in Ferguson, Missouri, in 2014, it was not surprising that responses differed by race: 59 percent of whites say

BVT Lab

Visit www.BVTLab.com to explore the student resources available for this chapter.

Chapter 05 | Public Opinion and Political Participation | 152

they have a great deal or quite a lot of confidence in the police, but only 37 percent of African Americans share this view.[45]

Latino and Asian subcultures are harder to characterize, partly because neither is a single subculture but rather a collection of them. The rapidly growing Latino subculture encompasses the Mexican-oriented culture of the Southwest, the Cuban-oriented culture of south Florida, and the Puerto Rican culture of New York and other large cities. Similarly, the Asian subculture includes the long-established Chinese communities of San Francisco, Los Angeles, and New York City and the more recently established communities of immigrants from Vietnam, Laos, and other Southeast Asian countries.

The different regions of the United States, to some degree, also constitute distinctive subcultures with unique patterns of political thought and behavior. The South is perhaps the most distinct from the others, owing to the continuing legacy of slavery and subsequent racial strife, as well as its more rural, agricultural subculture. Earlier studies of socialization found children in the South to differ from those in the North, but these differences seem to be fading.

In fact, the general trend seems to be away from clear-cut differentiation and toward greater homogeneity. Some attribute this trend to the "nationalization" of American culture and politics, which tends to blur regional differences. Americans in all parts of the country eat the same fast food and buy the same national-brand products. Most important politically, they read the same wire-service news stories, national news magazines, and Internet news sites; and they watch the same network and cable news broadcasts. As a result, public opinion in the United States is becoming more and more uniform from region to region.

One other aspect of diversity in political socialization involves gender differences. Much of the early research on political socialization portrayed females as less political than males and traced those differences back to the childhood years.[46] The changing social and economic role of women from the eighteenth century to today is both a cause and a result of changes in the political interest, competence, and involvement of women.[47] The move toward more equal roles for men and women fostered by feminist movements is likely to manifest itself in, and benefit from, less political difference between young males and females.

5.3 Political Participation

So far we have examined what Americans think about politics and why they think what they do. The next step in our discussion is to focus on what Americans do about what they think. In other words, how is public opinion translated into political participation? Of course, putting it in those terms suggests that political participation stems exclusively from political considerations such as concern about issues and ideology. Such considerations are only part of the story.

5.3a Motives for Political Participation

The conventional image of political participation is that of concerned citizens trying to advance their views by engaging in political activity. This is no doubt an accurate picture for some people. However, substantial numbers who are relatively unconcerned about politics nevertheless participate, and substantial numbers of people who are concerned about politics do not participate. Obviously, other factors must also motivate political participation.

Some participation is sparked by *political motivations*. **Political efficacy** is a person's sense of being able to accomplish something politically. It involves judgments both about one's own competence in the political arena (sometimes called internal efficacy) and about the responsiveness of the political system to one's efforts (external efficacy). People with a very strong sense of efficacy are more likely to be politically active than those with a weak sense of efficacy. Other citizens are motivated to become involved by a **sense of duty**. They may care less about the issues or be put off by politics, but they have been socialized to think that good citizens get involved in politics. People with a strong sense of duty are more likely to participate politically than those without it.

Party identification, the psychological attachment that many Americans feel toward a particular political party, also provides a strong impetus for political action. The highest rates of political activity are observed

Keep your finger on the pulse of American public opinion with the latest polls from the Gallup Organization.

http://www.bvtlab.com/a7e8t

among people with a strong commitment to one or another of the political parties. A person who strongly supports programs advocated by the Democratic Party, for example, will probably work to promote a Democratic victory. Yet someone who sees little difference between the parties and who cares little about issues may not even vote.

Other factors spurring people on to political involvement are essentially non-political or *social motivations*. Many people engage in political activity for its social rewards: meeting people, making friends, and developing new relationships. People low in self-esteem or lacking in confidence may attempt to bolster their self-image by taking on the social opportunities and challenges that political activity offers. In other cases, concern about an issue may initially mobilize a citizen into political involvement; but even when the concern fades away, the social connection keeps the person going.[48] This is not to say that political activity so inspired is of no political consequence; the labor, the money, or the vote of such a person counts the same as that of the most ideological partisan. Rather, the point is that not all political actions can be understood simply in terms of political motives.

5.3b Forms of Participation

Any American who wants to become politically involved has a broad range of options, from merely glancing at the TV news occasionally all the way to running for president of the United States. Some of these forms of participation are the focus of other chapters in this book. Participation related to campaigns and elections will be discussed in greater detail in Chapter 8. Much political activity occurs within the framework of interest groups and political parties. These facets of participation will be examined closely in Chapter 7. The rest of this section focuses on some of the most important other ways in which Americans can participate politically.

Following Politics

Just paying attention to politics constitutes a simple form of political participation. For many Americans, politics is—if nothing more—an entertaining spectator sport. As noted earlier in this chapter, almost two-thirds of Americans say they follow government and public affairs "most" or "some" of the time. How actively they pursue public affairs is suggested by this statistic: 58 percent of the American people say

political efficacy

A person's sense of being able to accomplish something politically, an important determinant of political participation

sense of duty

A motivating factor, felt by some citizens, to get involved in politics

party identification

Psychological attachment that a citizen may feel toward a particular political party

Even simply following political progression online can be a form of participating. (iStock)

they watch television news, 44 percent receive news via the Internet or on a mobile device, and 34 percent listen to radio news.[49]

Contacting Public Officials

One of the most direct ways to convey a political message is to deliver it straight to a politician or governmental authority. Not many Americans do this very often, and the numbers seem to be declining. One study indicates that 23 percent fewer citizens wrote to their legislators between the 1970s and 1990s.[50] Another study shows that while 22 percent of respondents twenty-six and older had contacted a public official in the past year, only 11 percent of those twenty-five and younger had.[51] So where does all that mail to public officials come from? First, an occasional letter from even a small proportion of a large number of constituents can generate a lot of mail—as the caseworker in almost any congressional office can confirm. Beyond that, it appears that a small group of letter writers writes a large number of letters. One study estimated that two-thirds of all mail to public officials comes from just 3 percent of the population.[52]

Direct, face-to-face contact with members of Congress and other public officials is harder to assess. One estimate is that about 20 percent of Americans directly contact public officials about an issue or problem.[53] Another standard strategy for contacting public officials is the petition—a right protected by the First Amendment. A petition is a written statement requesting that the government follow some course of action, circulated among and signed by a group of citizens. More than one-third of Americans (35 percent) claim that they have signed a petition in the last twelve months.[54] Writing letters and signing petitions have both changed significantly in recent years. As the Internet and social media have greatly reduced the costs of both circulating and sending such messages, participation has increased.[55] That being said, the interest in and impact of both sending and receiving such messages remain a topic deserving of continued study.

Protests Within and Beyond the Law

Abstract theories of representative democracy and the original Constitution itself focus on the election of representatives as the principal means of communication between citizens and government. The First Amendment to the Constitution—in its guarantees of freedom of speech, assembly, and petition—reminds us of other forms of political expression, however. These guarantees reflect a political tradition in which political protest sometimes assumes an important role and embodies the view that at least some such actions are legitimate.

Political protest can assume many different forms, some of which are discussed below.

- *Marches and rallies* Marches and demonstrations have a long-standing tradition in American politics. Perhaps the most famous example was the great March on Washington in August 1963. This landmark event in the civil rights movement, which brought more than 250,000 peaceful demonstrators to the National Mall, culminated with Dr. Martin Luther King Jr.'s historic "I Have a Dream" speech from the steps of the Lincoln Memorial. The Vietnam War brought numerous marchers to Washington in the late 1960s and early 1970s. In recent years, protesters have come from the right in the form of the Tea Party and from the left in the form of the Occupy movement.

- *Boycotts*   Boycotts, the refusal of citizens to buy a particular product or use a certain service, are another important tool of protest. In the late 1950s, the refusal of African Americans in the South to ride in the rear of buses exerted economic pressure on municipalities and attracted public attention to their cause. Some 38 percent of American people twenty-six and older, and 30 percent of those twenty-five and younger, say that they have participated in a boycott in the past year.[56]

- *Picketing*   Groups of protesters standing in front of a retail store or office building, placards in hand, are a common sight in the American political scene. One of the most frequent uses of picketing in recent years has been for pro-environmental or animal causes—such as pickets in front of World Trade Organization meetings or protests against human use of animal fur or other inhumane animal treatment.

Boycotts and protests are examples of political expression. (Shutterstock)

Protest demonstrations are one of the most visible, though certainly not the most common, forms of political participation in America. Accurate estimates of the extent of protest are notoriously difficult to obtain because people are sometimes reluctant to admit their participation to researchers. That being said, this is one area in which younger people are more likely than their older peers to be involved. Only 5 percent of those twenty-six and older have protested in the past year, but 11 percent of those twenty-five and younger have.[57]

Estimates of participation are even more difficult when it comes to actions that involve violence and crime.

- *Political violence*   On some occasions, American citizens have engaged in violent outbursts with political connotations. At the very founding of the United States, Massachusetts farmers led by Daniel Shays forced the closing of local and state courts before the rebellion was forcibly put down by the state militia. The antidraft riots of the Civil War, the urban ghetto riots of the 1960s, and the antiwar violence of the Vietnam War era resulted in widespread personal injury and destruction of property for political ends. In the spring of 1992 there was a large-scale riot in Los Angeles, following the announcement of not guilty verdicts in the cases of four police officers accused of brutally beating a young African American motorist, Rodney King. The riot resulted in the destruction of more than $500 million in property and the loss of more than ninety lives.

- *Politically motivated crimes*   Although riots and other violent outbursts have at least the appearance of spontaneity, other politically relevant acts are clearly premeditated criminal violence. The civil rights movement, in particular, spawned a number of violent reactions: the death of four African

American children in a fire-bombed church; the murder of three young civil rights workers—Andrew Goodman, James Chaney, and Michael Schwerner—in Mississippi in 1963; and the assassination of Dr. Martin Luther King Jr. in Memphis in 1968.

Many types of political protest are perfectly legal—particularly as long as they do not endanger the well-being of others. Peaceful marches and demonstrations certainly fall into this category. Others are clearly illegal: Most people would probably agree that rioting and assassination fall into the latter category because they destroy both life and property. Nevertheless, the line between legitimate and illegitimate political protest is sometimes hard to define. Further, some acts of political protest, even if illegal, are undertaken on the basis of a moral justification. These are acts of **civil disobedience**—deliberate violations of the law as a means of asserting the illegitimacy of the law or calling attention to a higher moral principle. Civil rights activists in the South in the 1950s and 1960s organized sit-ins at lunch counters and other facilities designated for whites only with the explicit intention of being arrested. They saw such action as a way of calling attention to unjust laws and, more generally, to their unjust treatment.

A related strategy is the practice of **passive resistance**, in which protesters do not actively oppose government, but rather refuse to cooperate by doing nothing. For example, protesters may not struggle with angry white citizens or police, but simply lie down in the face of attack or arrest and force the police to drag them off to the police van and jail. Beginning in September 2011, groups of protesters identifying as part of the Occupy movement began using tactics of civil disobedience to protest a wide range of economic disparities in cities throughout the United States. Dr. Martin Luther King Jr. provided a good explanation of the moral legitimacy of an illegal action in a famous letter that he wrote from a Birmingham jail:

One of the most tragic politically motivated crimes that our country has known was the terrorist attacks on September 11, 2001. Strong restrictions placed around air travel were a result of that day. (AP World Wide Photo)

> I submit that an individual who breaks a law that conscience tells him is unjust, and willingly accepts the penalty by staying in jail to arouse the conscience of the community over its injustice is in reality expressing the very highest respect for law.

Civil disobedience is thus characterized by a moral justification, a willingness to accept whatever penalty the action incurs, and as a critical element, some would add, an intention to avoid physical harm to others. Only a small proportion of Americans (2 percent) say that they have broken the law in a protest for a political or social cause.[58] However, civil disobedience is widely recognized as an acceptable strategy in extreme circumstances. When asked whether people should obey the law without exception, or whether there are exceptional occasions on which people should follow their consciences even if it means breaking the law, 42 percent of a national sample supported obeying the law, whereas 57 percent opted for following one's conscience.[59]

civil disobedience

A form of political protest in which advocates of a cause deliberately break a law as a means of asserting its illegitimacy or drawing attention to their cause

passive resistance

A form of civil disobedience in which protesters do not actively oppose government's attempts to control them, but rather refuse to cooperate by doing nothing—for example, by going limp when police try to pick them up or insisting on being carried to a police van rather than walking

What determines the forms of political participation in which citizens tend to engage? In probably the most thorough study of political participation in America yet done, Sidney Verba and Norman Nie identified six categories of citizen participation and determined the kinds of people who fell into each.[60]

The choice is up to you to follow the law or your own conscience when you feel it is necessary. For example, African American Rosa Parks decided to follow her conscience and did not give up her seat on the bus. (Wikimedia Commons)

1. *Inactives*   These people, making up about 22 percent of the population, take virtually no part in political life. Lower-status social and economic groups, African Americans, women, the youngest, the oldest, and the least concerned about politics are particularly likely to fall into this category.

2. *Voting specialists*   About 21 percent of the population do little more politically than vote regularly. This group is distinctive primarily due to its strong sense of partisanship. It seems that some citizens who might otherwise be inactive get firmly attached to a party and that connection is enough to bring them to the polls at most elections.

3. *Parochial participants*   About 4 percent of the population contact public officials when they have a particular personal problem and seek governmental assistance in solving it. Such activity is more common among lower-status groups, Catholics, and urban dwellers than among higher-status, Protestant, and rural citizens. Such people show little partisan or ideological involvement, but they can sometimes make a difference in what government does.

4. *Communalists*   Another 20 percent of the population has little involvement in electoral politics apart from voting, but they do engage in group and community activities with the aim of solving social problems. This group is highly involved in politics but decidedly nonpartisan and nonconflictual in its orientation. This group is very much an upper-status group socially and economically, predominantly white, Protestant, and more small-town and rural than urban.

Are you registered to vote?

You can register using the Election Assistance Commission's National Mail Voter Registration form at this website:

http://www.bvtlab.com/78P86

5. *Campaigners*   In sharp contrast to the preceding group, this 15 percent of the population engages in little group activity but much campaign activity. This pattern stems, in part, from a highly partisan and more conflictual orientation to politics. The group tends to be of higher status; but African Americans and Catholics are also campaigners, as are urban and suburban dwellers.

6. *Complete activists*   About 11 percent of the population do it all: voting, contacting, group activities, and campaigning. This is a group highly attuned to politics, predominantly upper-status and middle-aged.

What difference does it make that different groups tend to participate in different ways? Public officials are bombarded with messages from the public and people claiming to represent the public. Public officials have preconceptions and make judgments about the forms of political participation to which they need to be most

BVT *Lab*

Flashcards are available
for this chapter at
www.BVTLab.com.

attentive. Because different kinds of people tend to participate in numerous ways, officials get varying impressions of public opinion depending on the forms of participation to which they pay attention. A senator who focuses on constituency service by reading all the mail from parochial participants will get a different sense of the public's mind than one who hobnobs with campaign workers and financial supporters. The people staging a sit-in in front of a congressional representative's district office have very different things on their minds from those who pulled the lever in the voting booth a couple of Novembers earlier. For politicians assessing public opinion, the medium of participation in large measure determines the message.

5.3d The Impact of Political Participation

Does political activity really make any difference? The stereotypical notion of democracy is that the people's wishes become the law of the land. However, the democratic process cannot be that simple. On some issues, many people do not know what they want. Even if they do, they may not be moved to express their preferences via the political process. Politicians—whether they are presidents, Senate or House members, or Supreme Court justices—may be attentive to what the "public" wants, but such preferences are rarely the only factors they take into account. First of all, our nation is comprised of many publics, not just one. Further, constitutional constraints, legal constraints, budgetary constraints, foreign policy constraints on domestic policy, and domestic policy constraints on foreign policy also impact the decisions government officials can make.

Little wonder, then, that most studies of the relationship between public opinion and public policy have found the connection to be a relatively loose one.[61] Public opinion is usually sufficiently amorphous, officials' perceptions of it sufficiently cloudy, and more tangible pressures sufficiently strong to ensure that officials are not severely constrained by public opinion. When there is a clearly expressed body of opinion on a salient issue, the relationship between public opinion and public policy can be substantial, however.[62] For example, growing public concern over drugs in the late 1980s led politicians to move anti-drug legislation to the top of the agenda. In 1989, the much-publicized oil spill from the tanker *Exxon Valdez* into Prince William Sound on the Alaska coast reenergized the flagging environmental movement and sparked a flurry of environmental legislation in the early 1990s. After a series of energy crises in early 2001, 21 percent of Americans in a nationwide poll mentioned energy as the most important problem facing the country.[63] In the wake of recent terrorist attacks, 46 percent of Americans in an October 2001 poll indicated that terrorism was the most important problem.[64] In 2006, Americans named the Iraq War as the most important problem facing the country.[65] From 2008 through 2012, the struggling economy was the number one concern of the largest number of Americans—but non-economic concerns began to dominate beginning in 2013. In 2014, dissatisfaction with government was the most frequently mentioned concern of those polled, and less than 1 percent of Americans named the threat of terrorism as the most important problem.[66]

5.3e The Rationality of Political Participation

rational actor model

A perspective that looks at politics as a system in which individuals and organizations pursue their self-interests, defined in terms of costs and benefits, and choose to do those things that give them the greatest benefit at the least cost

Does it make sense to participate politically? Over fifty years ago, Anthony Downs pioneered a new field of political analysis in an important and influential book called *An Economic Theory of Democracy*.[67] He examined political activity in terms of the so-called **rational actor model**. In this model, a citizen rationally weighs the costs and the benefits of participating. If the benefits exceed the costs, the citizen participates;

if not, the citizen does not. Focusing on voting, Downs pointed out that getting registered, keeping informed, and going to the polls all take a substantial amount of time. The benefits, by contrast, are actually quite low. What politicians from one party or the other actually do after an election may not be very different from what their opponents would have done. Even more important, one individual's vote is very unlikely to determine whether his or her favored candidate wins. These factors make the expected benefit of voting relatively small.

In 2011–2012, Americans expressed their dissatisfaction with the wealth disparity, generally—and the financial sector, specifically—via the Occupy movement. (Shutterstock)

A similar analysis could be made of most other individual political actions. When weighed against the low probability of any benefit, the costs of individual political actions make them appear to be of dubious rationality. One possible exception is what Verba and Nie call *parochial participation*. When focused on a narrow personal objective, and with the expenditure of a fair amount of effort directed toward a particular decision maker, the individual may stand a fair chance of achieving success.[68] Collective activities may also be more effective. Joining together allows costs to be shared and resources to be pooled. All other things being equal, many citizens will probably be more influential than one.

Finally, even political protest may prove to be a rational strategy. Minority and dissident groups often lack political clout because they lack resources and thus cannot afford the costs of participation. One political scientist has called this the "problem of the powerless."[69] A rational strategy for such people is to attract the attention of those with resources and draw them into the cause. A minimal expenditure of resources is required to engage in unusual or dramatic activities, such as sit-ins and demonstrations, which call public attention to the plight of the protesters. Such activities constitute, to borrow one apt description, the use of "protest as a political resource."[70]

CHAPTER REVIEW

1. Public opinion is complicated because our nation consists of not one public but many, and because opinion varies over time and in intensity and sophistication. Americans differ widely in their interest in and sophistication about politics; most of them have relatively little day-to-day concern with, knowledge about, or real understanding of what goes on in the political world. Americans do agree on certain basic values. However, they disagree about exactly what many of these values mean in particular circumstances and about political ideology.

2. Political socialization is the process by which young Americans are taught about political life in the United States. Through various processes of socialization, young people acquire the information and the ability to reason about politics. The values that they draw on as political actors are learned from their parents, schools, peers, and the mass media.

3. Americans involve themselves in politics in many ways for a variety of reasons. Involvement can range from simply following politics and voting to intense immersion in campaigns, community activities, or more dramatic forms of participation such as protest marches, sit-ins, and demonstrations. The impact of participation on policy is often weak, however; and much political participation is hard to justify in purely rational terms.

KEY TERMS

agents of socialization. 147

civil disobedience .156

party identification 153

passive resistance 156

political efficacy 153

political socialization. 146

polling. 137

public opinion 136

rational actor model 158

sense of duty 153

Classic works on public opinion include Walter Lippmann's *Public Opinion* (CreateSpace, 2012) and one of the first major reports on survey research into public opinion, *Voting: A Study of Opinion Formation in a Presidential Campaign*, by Bernard R. Berelson, Paul F. Lazarsfeld, and William N. McPhee (Chicago: University of Chicago Press, 1986).

Rosalee A. Clawson and Zoe M. Oxley's *Public Opinion: Democratic Ideals, Democratic Practice*, 2nd ed. (Washington, D.C.: CQ Press, 2012) provides a more recent overview of public opinion, and *Polling and the Public*, 8th ed., by Herbert Asher (Washington, DC: CQ Press, 2010) addresses the more scientific aspects of opinion polls.

Perhaps the major contributor to our understanding of basic American political values is Herbert McClosky, who has written (with Alida Brill) *Dimensions of Tolerance* (New York: Russell Sage, 1983) and (with John Zaller) *The American Ethos* (Cambridge, MA: Harvard University Press, 1984).

James G. Gimpel, J. Celeste Lay, and Jason E. Schuknecht, *Cultivating Democracy: Civic Environments and Political Socialization in America* (Washington, DC: Brookings Institute, 2003), provides a good overview of the topic of political socialization.

An excellent recent study of civic engagement in America is Robert D. Putnam, *Bowling Alone* (New York: Touchstone, 2000).

Perhaps the best overall empirical studies of political participation in all its facets are *Political Participation in America: Political Democracy and Social Equality* (New York: Harper & Row, 1987) by Sidney Verba and Norman Nie; *Voice and Equality: Civic Volunteerism in American Politics* (Cambridge: Harvard University Press, 2006) by Sidney Verba, Kay Lehman Schlozman, and Henry Brady; and *The Unheavenly Chorus: Unequal Political Voice and the Broken Promise of American Democracy* (Princeton: Princeton University Press, 2012) by Kay Lehman Schlozman, Sidney Verba, and Henry E. Brady.

How Americans talk to each other about politics is covered in *Talking Together: Public Deliberation and Political Participation in America* (Chicago: University of Chicago Press, 2009) by Lawrence R. Jacobs, Fay Lomax Cook, and Michael X. Delli Carpini.

1. Pew Research Center, June, 2014, "Beyond Red vs. Blue: The Political Typology."

2. Pew Research Center; The Gallup Organization, "Favorability: People in the News," http://www.gallup.com/poll/1618/Favorability-People-News.aspx (August 7, 2014), and Marist Poll, "Independence Day—Seventeen Seventy When?," July 1, 2011, http://maristpoll.marist.edu/71-independence-day-dummy-seventeen-seventy-when/print/ (August 7, 2014).

3. The Gallup Organization, 2013.

4. ABC News/*Washington Post Poll*, Survey 77.

5. The Gallup Organization 2013.

6. Herbert McClosky and Alida Brill, *Dimensions of Tolerance: What Americans Believe About Civil Liberties* (New York: Russell Sage Foundation, 1983), pp. 48–135.

7. The Gallup Organization, "Question Profile," November 12, 2003, http://brain.gallup.com/documents/question.aspx?question=146243 (October 10, 2006).

8. The Gallup Organization, "Question Profile," August 11, 2005, http://brain.gallup.com/documents/question.aspx?question=153996 (October 10, 2006).

9. American National Election Studies, 2008.

10. CNN/Opinion Research Corporation Poll, July 18–20, 2014.

11. The Gallup Organization, 2014.

12. Ibid.

13. The Gallup Organization, 2013.

14. The Gallup Organization, 2013.

15. American National Election Studies, 2008.

16. NBC News/*Wall Street Journal Poll*, June 20–24, 2012.

17. The Gallup Organization, 2012.

18. The Gallup Organization, 2014.

19. The Gallup Organization, 2013.

20. Ibid.

21. The Gallup Organization, "Race Relations," 2014, http://www.gallup.com/poll/1687/Race-Relations.aspx (August 14, 2014).

22. For perhaps the most thorough analysis of the gap between support for freedom of speech in the abstract and support for it in particular situations, see McClosky and Brill, *Dimensions of Tolerance*, pp. 48–58.

23. National Opinion Research Center, General Social Survey, 2012, http://www3.norc.org/GSS+Website/Browse+GSS+Variables/Subject+Index/ (July 23, 2012).

24. The Gallup Organization, 2006.

25. The Gallup Organization, 2012.

26. James W. Prothro and Charles M. Grigg, "Fundamental Principles of Democracy," *Journal of Politics 22* (1960): 276–294; YouGov, February 20, 2014, "Should Only Taxpayers Have a Vote?" https://today.yougov.com/news/2014/02/20/should-only-taxpayers-have-vote/ (August 14, 2014).

27. CNN/*Essence Magazine*/Opinion Research Corporation Poll, April 2008.

28. The Gallup Organization, 2014.

29. *USA Today*/Gallup Poll, August 27–30, 2010.

30. The Gallup Organization, 2014.

31. Eric R. A. N. Smith, *The Unchanging American Voter* (Berkeley: University of California Press, 1989), pp. 56–58.

32. American National Election Studies, 2012.

33. The path-breaking study on attitude consistency, in particular, and mass political ideology, more generally, is Philip Converse's "The Nature of Belief Systems in Mass Publics," in David Apter, ed., *Ideology and Discontent* (New York: Free Press, 1964). For perhaps the best overview of the long and complicated series of challenges and counterchallenges to Converse's work over the last twenty-five years, see Smith, *The Unchanging American Voter*.

34. American National Election Survey, 1988.

35. Angus Campbell, Philip E. Converse, Warren E. Miller, and Donald E. Stokes, *The American Voter* (New York: Wiley, 1960); Norman H. Nie, Sidney Verba, and John R. Petrocik, *The Changing American Voter*, enlarged ed. (Cambridge, MA: Harvard University Press, 1979).

36. Nie, Verba, and Petrocik, *The Changing American Voter*.

37. The best summary of, and most substantial contribution to, this recent research is Smith, *The Unchanging American Voter*. On the role of political rhetoric, see especially pp. 45–104.

38. Robert D. Hess and Judith V. Torney, *The Development of Political Attitudes in Children* (Garden City, NY: Doubleday/Anchor Books, 1967), pp. 24–26, offers a good overview of psychological theories of socialization.

39. M. Kent Jennings and Richard Niemi, *Generations and Politics* (Princeton, NJ: Princeton University Press, 1981), pp. 76–114.

40. David C. Bricker, *Classroom Life as Civic Education* (New York: Teachers College Press, 1989), is a discussion of some of these issues.

41. Theodore M. Newcomb, "Persistence and Regression of Changed Attitudes: Long-Range Studies," *Journal of Social Issues 19* (1963): 3–14.

42. Fred I. Greenstein, *Children and Politics* (New Haven, CT: Yale University Press, 1965).

43. Roberta S. Sigel, ed., *Political Learning in Adulthood* (Chicago: University of Chicago Press, 1989) provides a good overview of adult political socialization and research on the topic.

44. The Gallup Organization, "Race Relations," 2014, http://www.gallup.com/poll/1687/Race-Relations (September 10, 2014).

45. The Gallup Organization, "Gallup Review: Black and White Attitudes Toward Police," August 20, 2014, http://www.gallup.com/poll/175088/gallup-review-black-white-attitudes-toward-police.aspx?utm_source=alert&utm_medium=email&utm_campaign=syndication&utm_content=morelink&utm_term=Politics, (September 10, 2014).

46. See, for example, Fred L. Greenstein, "Sex-Related Political Differences in Childhood," *Journal of Politics 23* (1961): 353–371.

47. Ethel Klein, *Gender Politics* (Cambridge, MA: Harvard University Press, 1984), pp. 117–119.

48. Samuel J. Eldersveld, *Political Parties: A Behavioral Analysis* (Chicago: Rand McNally, 1964), pp. 290–292.

49. The Pew Research Center for the People & the Press, 2010.

50. Robert D. Putnam, *Bowling Alone* (New York: Touchstone, 2000), p. 45.

51. Mark Hugo Lopez, et al., *The 2006 Civic and Political Health of the Nation: A Detailed Look at How Youth Participate in Politics and Communities*, October 2006, http://www.civicyouth.org (August 2, 2012).

52. Philip E. Converse, Aage R. Clausen, and Warren E. Miller, "Electoral Myth and Reality: The 1964 Election," *American Political Science Review 59* (June 1965): 321–336.

53. Sidney Verba and Norman Nie, *Political Participation in America: Political Democracy and Social Equality* (New York: Harper & Row, 1972), p. 31.

54. The Roper Center, "Social Capital Community Benchmark Survey," 2000.

55. See American National Election Study, 2012.

56. Lopez, et al.

57. Ibid.

58. Norman Ornstein, Andrew Kohut, and Larry McCarthy, The People, the Press, and Politics: The Times Mirror Study of the American Electorate (Boston: Addison-Wesley, 1988).

59. International Social Survey Program: Role of Government III, 1996.

60. Verba and Nie, *Political Participation in America*, pp. 56–81. If a particular characteristic is not mentioned, the group is about average for that characteristic.

61. Perhaps the most famous study is Warren E. Miller and Donald E. Stokes, "Constituency Influence in Congress," *American Political Science Review 57* (1963): 45–56.

62. Benjamin L. Page and Robert Y. Shapiro, "Effects of Public Opinion on Policy," *American Political Science Review 77* (1983): 175–190, show how changes in public policy between 1935 and 1979 in the United States related to changes in public opinion, particularly when there were large and enduring changes in public opinion on salient issues.

63. The Gallup Organization, 2001.

64. Ibid.

65. The Gallup Organization, 2006.

66. The Gallup Organization, 2008–2014.

67. New York: Harper & Row, 1957.

68. Verba and Nie, *Political Participation in America*, pp. 104–106.

69. James Q. Wilson, "The Strategy of Protest: Problems of Negro Civic Action," *Journal of Conflict Resolution 3* (September 1961): 291.

70. Michael Lipsky, "Protest as a Political Resource," *American Political Science Review 62* (1968): 1144.

POP QUIZ

1. Although Americans profess a belief in equality, they seem to lean away from equality of _____.

2. Groups of people, roughly equal in social position, that interact with one another are called _____ _____.

3. _____ _____ is a person's sense of being able to accomplish something politically.

4. According to the _____ _____ _____ the expected benefit of voting is relatively small.

5. Americans tend to support equality of opportunity over equality of result.   T   F

6. The effect of school as an agent of political socialization is sudden and dynamic as the child enters grade school.   T   F

7. Once in school, children tend to become less partisan.   T   F

8. The highest rates of political activity are among people with a strong commitment to a political party.   T   F

9. Most studies have shown a strong relationship between public opinion and public policy.   T   F

10. A recent survey found that a plurality of the public says they follow government and public affairs _____.

   A) most of the time

   B) some of the time

   C) only now and then

   D) hardly at all

11. In recent years, American public opinion has done which of the following?

   A) shifted to the right

   B) shifted to the left

   C) stayed essentially centrist

   D) has become less ideologically oriented

12. Which of the following best describes the first political thoughts acquired by a small child?

   A) a psychological attachment to America

   B) a primitive sense of party identification

   C) a sense of external authority above parental authority

   D) all of the above

13. Acts of civil disobedience have been justified on the basis of _____.

   A) legality

   B) effectiveness

   C) morality

   D) popularity

14. According to Verba and Nie, the category of citizen participation that comprises about 4 percent of the population; consists of mainly lower-status groups, Catholics, and urban dwellers; and shows little partisan or ideological involvement is _____.

   A) inactives

   B) parochial participants

   C) communalists

   D) campaigners

15. According to the rational actor model, which of the following activities would be considered the most rational and effective form of political participation?

   A) voting

   B) letter writing to public officials

   C) collective activities

   D) political assassination

Chapter

06

Politics and
the Media

In This Chapter

(Shutterstock/Wikimedia Commons)

Chapter Objectives

Most of the chapters in this book focus on political institutions and leaders and the things they do. This chapter, however, focuses on part of American corporate life called the "mass media." Of special interest are journalists: people who gather, write, edit, report, and produce the news that people read in newspapers, hear on the radio, watch on television, and browse on the Internet.

Of course, nobody votes for journalists. They are not public officials. They do not make laws. They do not work for the government. So why do the mass media rate a chapter in a book on American government? The mass media have a chapter all to themselves because newspapers, radio, television, and the Internet matter politically. In carving out a specific guarantee for freedom of the press, the First Amendment of the Constitution gives a strong hint that the news media are supposed to matter.

They are the means by which much political information and many political ideas reach the American people. They often provide the forums for clashes between ideologies. In short, they help to define political reality for the nation. Understanding the business of print and electronic journalism is now a necessary part of understanding American government.

The job of the White House press secretary is to move information in two directions—from the president to the people and from the people to the president. Josh Earnest, Barack Obama's press secretary, regularly stands before the White House press corps (a select group of respected **journalists**) to describe the president's actions and answer questions. He is also responsible for informing and updating the executive branch of the government on the news stories being reported in the press. Few in the White House, on Capitol Hill, or in any statehouse or city hall are unconcerned about or uninterested in the news business. All want to know what has become news and how others have reacted to the news.

Political leaders since George Washington's time have known that access to knowledge and control of communication matter in a democracy. Essential to both today are the **mass media**: newspapers, magazines, radio, television, and the Internet. The word *media* in this context refers to the *means* of communication with large numbers of people. In recent years, this has also meant taking a leading role in the development of new media—such as cable and satellite television and radio, websites, and video streaming via the Internet. Growing numbers of Americans are even getting up-to-the-minute news via Twitter and other smartphone-based applications. The media now offer the American people rapid access to large amounts of news about public affairs. Indeed, the distribution of news and opinions is so important that the press occupies a special place in the constitutional system.

6.1 The "Fifth Branch"

The press is sometimes called the **fifth branch** of government—after Congress, the president, the Supreme Court, and the bureaucracy. This classification reflects the fact that the mass media can serve as an additional check on the powers of public officials through their discovery and coverage of news and commentary on events. However, because the media are mainly businesses that exist to make money, it is essential to know something about these commercial enterprises. Like government, the news media have changed greatly over the course of the past two centuries.

6.1a The Dynamics of an Industry

Newspapers have been part of American culture since early colonial days. In an era during which news could travel only as fast as the fastest horse, these were four-page weeklies with type painstakingly set by hand. It was through the medium of these early papers that news about skirmishes with the British at Lexington and Concord and copies of the Declaration of Independence circulated up and down the eastern seaboard in 1775 and 1776. Publication of *The Federalist Papers* and much of the rest of the debate over ratification of the Constitution, discussed in Chapter 2, took place in the press.

Telegraphy, larger and faster presses, lower unit production costs, and improved literacy made possible the rapid growth of newspapers in the nineteenth century. The "penny press" (named for its price) became the main contact for many Americans with events around the nation and the world. No doubt the intensity of feeling about slavery and secession, in both the North and South, on the eve of the Civil War was due in part to the pervasiveness of the press. Growth of the industry later opened

journalists

People who gather, write, and report the news for newspapers, magazines, radio, television, and the Internet

mass media

Instruments such as newspapers, magazines, radio, television, and the Internet that provide the means for communicating with large numbers of people in a short period of time

fifth branch

Refers to the press in its role as a check on public officials, after the other four branches (Congress, the president, the Supreme Court, and the bureaucracy)

the door to the increased political influence of publishers and editors such as Joseph Pulitzer and William Randolph Hearst.

Yet eighteenth- and nineteenth-century newspapers were distant cousins in size and circulation to today's computer-composed, mass-produced daily papers that frequently fill one hundred pages or more, contain news and photographs transmitted digitally, and have accompanying websites that allow Americans to read the "paper" on their e-readers and smartphones. As Table 6.1 suggests, print journalism has experienced changes brought about by advances in technology, altered lifestyles, competition from television, radio, and the Internet, and other economic forces. A typical trend over the past several years for many leading newspapers has been declining print circulation accompanied by increases in digital circulation—though the latter can be difficult to quantify consistently.[1]

(iStock)

Magazines are another form of print journalism that became popular in the nineteenth century. Over seven thousand periodicals other than newspapers are published in the United States, with a growing number available digitally. While most are small or have little to do with public affairs, political news and opinion are the main content of many. Mass circulation weekly news magazines include *Time* and *Newsweek*. Others, such as *Washington Monthly*, *The American Prospect*, and *National Review* (described in

table 6.1 | American Daily Newspapers Since 1900

Daily newspaper circulation since 1990 has decreased even as the population has increased. Fewer than half of American households seem to have regular access to a daily print newspaper. Also, the decline among dailies has been greater for afternoon than morning papers.

Year	Number of Daily Papers	Circulation	Circulation as Percent of Number of Households*
1900	2,226	15,102,000	95
1920	2,042	27,791,000	114
1930	1,942	39,589,000	132
1940	1,878	41,132,000	118
1950	1,772	53,829,000	124
1960	1,763	58,882,000	112
1970	1,748	62,108,000	99
1980	1,745	62,200,000	77
1990	1,611	62,300,000	67
2000	1,480	55,800,000	53
2011	1,382	44,421,000	38

* A "household" is the Census Bureau's term for a living unit.

SOURCES: Bureau of the Census, Statistical Abstract of the United States.

Chapter 4) are journals of opinion and target different political audiences. While nearly all major print magazines also have a web presence, other magazines—such as *Slate*, *The Huffington Post*, and *Salon*—are found only on the internet and have never existed in print form.

The year 1920 marked the beginning of radio as a mass medium. Within a decade, as Table 6.2 shows, radios were common household appliances. Not far behind was television. Its astonishing growth since 1950 now permits almost all households to be served by many stations. Thanks to cable and satellite systems, many homes now have hundreds of stations from which to choose.

table 6.2 | Growth of Radio and Television in the United States

Nearly half of all American households owned a radio set by 1930, enabling Franklin Roosevelt to become the first "media president." Though World War II delayed the commercial development of television, TV sets are now as common in U.S. homes as refrigerators. The average number of television sets in American homes is 2.8.

(A) Radio

Year	Number of AM Stations	Number of FM Stations	Households with at Least One Radio Set (%)
1922	30	0	0.2
1930	618	0	46.0
1940	847	3	82.8
1950	2,144	753	94.0
1960	3,483	906	95.0
1970	4,288	2,542	99.0
1980	4,689	4,546	99.9
1990	4,977	5,694	99.9
2000	4,783	5,766	99.9
2010	4,786	9,717	99.9
2014	4,721	10,704	99.9

(B) Television

Year	TV Stations*	Households with at Least One TV Set (%)
1950	104	9
1960	626	87
1970	881	95
1980	1,132	98
1990	1,446	98
2000	1,585	98
2010	1,784	98
2014	1,782	98

* Includes commercial and educational stations on VHF and UHF channels.

SOURCES: Bureau of the Census, Statistical Abstract of the United States; Federal Communications Commission.

BVT Lab
Improve your test scores.
Practice quizzes are
available at
www.BVTLab.com.

171 | Politics and the Media | Chapter 06

Beginning in the 1970s, cable services developed. They did not transmit over the air, like ordinary television stations had; instead, they transmitted by satellite directly to cable companies in hundreds of cities and towns. Over the last thirty years cable, digital satellite, and other subscription services have drastically changed the way Americans view television. Rather than offering only local stations and a few large networks for free, subscription television now provides access to hundreds of stations broadcast from around the world and serves interests ranging from the very broad to the quite narrow. All American television programming completed the switch from analog to digital delivery in 2009. This transition, prompted by the government's Federal Communications Commission and federal law, provides a much more efficient delivery format. Today, over 157 million televisions, for an average of nearly 1.4 per household, are equipped with some type of paid premium service.

In recent years, the growth of cable has produced several new networks devoted exclusively to news. CNN, MSNBC, CNBC, and Fox News have become worldwide sources for news. Many world leaders, including American presidents, have been known to tune in to these stations, especially when following critical events as they unfold at almost any point on the globe. For example, millions of Americans—including many political leaders—watched the coverage on these networks nearly around the clock on September 11, 2001, in a search for answers regarding terrorist attacks on the World Trade Center and Pentagon. Government agencies sometimes find cable news a more accurate source of timely information than their own official sources. That so many leaders might rely on the same source at the same time could have a major impact in the management of international crises and in other situations calling for rapid decision making.

The impact of cable and satellite television continues to be felt. The proliferation of channels, along with the widespread use of DVD players and subscription streaming-video on-demand services like Netflix and Hulu, is the major reason that the share of the viewing audience claimed by the major broadcast networks (NBC, ABC,

The Daily Show *with Jon Stewart is a primary source for political communication to young adults today. (Wikimedia Commons)*

CBS, and Fox) has declined steadily. By 2001, cable network news had surpassed the broadcast networks, claiming nearly 60 percent of the total news audience. Today, 55 percent of Americans say television is their main source of news.[2]

As a result of the phenomenal growth of the video industry, television has largely displaced radio as a major source of news. Except for a few all-news stations, the radio industry invests little in national news reporting beyond providing a headline service interspersed in music and talk shows. Indeed, television has surpassed the newspaper as the primary source of national news for most Americans, although newspapers remain the main source for local news.

The average American spends seventy minutes a day with some form of news media. Thirty-two of those minutes are spent watching television news, fifteen are spent listening to the radio, ten are spent reading a print newspaper, and thirteen are spent getting news online.[3] The Internet is the news source growing fastest in popularity; in 2011, 41 percent of Americans—including 65 percent of those eighteen to twenty-nine years old—said the Internet was a major source for national and international news.[4] Of course, when topics beyond just the news are considered, television is the clear winner. The average American watches almost three hours of television per day.[5] Over 98 percent of households have at least one television, and 93 percent of Americans view television on at least a weekly basis.[6]

Most Americans get at least some news on a daily basis.[7] Of Americans, 58 percent watch television news daily, 31 percent read a daily newspaper, 34 percent listen to the radio, and 34 percent get daily news online.[8] Easy access to information and entertainment, however, does not guarantee attentiveness to public affairs. While young Americans from 1941 to 1975 knew as much about issues and followed major news events as closely as their elders, this is no longer the case. Younger people are now far less attentive to public affairs. Even though someone who is twenty-one years old is more likely than someone who is fifty years old to have used a computer, to have gone to college, or to currently be reading a book, the younger individual is likely to be substantially less aware of current events and public figures. As Table 6.3 suggests, one implication of such differences is that Americans in different age groups

table 6.3 | News Consumption "Yesterday"

Younger Americans read newspapers and watch news on television less than older Americans. Younger Americans also "consume" such news far less regularly than they did a few decades ago. In the category of Internet news usage, however, Americans under fifty seem to be leading the way.

Read a Newspaper Yesterday	1960	1990	2000	2012
All respondents 21 and older*	71%	44%	46%	23%
Under 35**	67%	30%	29%	8%
35–49***	73%	44%	43%	14%
50+	74%	55%	58%	37%

Watched TV News Yesterday	1960	1990	2000	2012
All respondents 21 and older*	55%	53%	55%	55%
Under 35**	52%	41%	44%	34%
35–49***	52%	49%	51%	52%
50+	62%	67%	67%	69%

Read News Online or Digitally Yesterday	1960	1990	2000	2012
All respondents 21 and older*	—	—	33%	50%
Under 30	—	—	46%	61%
31–49	—	—	37%	59%
50+	—	—	20%	35%

* For the year 2012, the age range for this category is 18 and older.
** For the years 2000 and 2012, the age range for this category is under 30.
*** For the years 2000 and 2012, the age range for this category is 30–49.

SOURCES: The Age of Indifference: A Study of Young Americans and How They View the News. (Washington, DC: Times Mirror Center for The People & The Press, 1990), p. 20; The Pew Research Center for the People and the Press, "In Changing News Landscape, Even Television Is Vulnerable," September 27, 2012, http://www.people-press.org/files/legacy-pdf/2012%20News%20Consumption%20Report.pdf (September 19, 2014); and U.S. Census Bureau, Statistical Abstract of the United States, 2008.

may be consuming different types of news. Older Americans are the most likely to be aware of events reported on televised news, whereas younger Americans are more likely to be aware of news reported online.

6.1b The Constitutional Basis of the Press

It is not by chance that the media count politically. The Constitution confers on journalists explicit recognition and protection: "Congress shall make no law," the First Amendment declares, "abridging the freedom of … the press." This restraint has also applied to state and local governments since 1931.[9] As explained in Chapter 3, aside from obscenity and libel, prevailing interpretations of the Constitution by the Supreme Court tolerate almost no restrictions on the content of what editors decide to publish. "A free press is indispensable to the workings of our democratic society," Justice Felix Frankfurter (1939–1962) once declared. The point to remember is that the Constitution creates the *opportunity* for the press to play an active role in public affairs. What the role actually becomes, however, is left up to reporters, editors, and publishers—and to their readers and viewers.

Protection of the press from most governmental restraints is necessary because its involvement with "the workings of our democratic society" guarantees conflict between journalists and government. "Politics and media are inseparable," veteran CBS correspondent Walter Cronkite observed. "It is only the politicians and the media that are incompatible."[10] The First Amendment anticipates a common failing: the tendency to attempt to silence those who criticize or disagree. In personal relations, this tendency may only be annoying; in political relations between leaders and citizens, it can prove deadly to democracy.

6.1c The Federal Communications Commission

While the news media enjoy constitutionally protected freedom, some of the media are freer than others. This is because electronic journalism operates under legal restraints that do not (and could not constitutionally) apply to print journalism.

With the development of radio early in the twentieth century, the nation faced a choice. Table 6.4 shows how the political implications of the new medium, soon followed by television, became apparent. The new medium could be left to grow almost unregulated, like newspapers; or it could be operated mainly by government, as is done now in most places in the world (France and Great Britain, for example) even where some privately owned stations are permitted. Because of the ideological preference for free enterprise, public ownership in the United States was never a serious possibility. Because of the potential for chaos on the airwaves, complete freedom for broadcasters was unacceptable as well. Congress chose a middle route of private ownership under government supervision.

Initial regulation was in the hands of the Department of Commerce, but Congress created the Federal Radio Commission in 1927 with the power to issue station licenses, allocate frequencies, and fix transmitting power. Present regulation of all wired and wireless communication, including transmission via satellite, is the responsibility of the **Federal Communications Commission (FCC)**, established in 1934 as the successor to the Radio Commission. The FCC has broad rule-making authority, which it has employed to require radio and television stations to operate "in the public interest." For instance, stations are limited in the number of commercials that may be broadcast per hour, a certain amount of time must be set aside for public service and public affairs programming, and obscenity and "filthy words" are prohibited.[11] The

Federal Communications Commission (FCC)

An agency of the national government that regulates the telecommunications industry in the United States, including the licensing and operation of all radio and television stations

Media Monopolies?

America today teems with information. As Tables 6.1 and 6.2 suggest, print and electronic media are within easy reach of almost everyone. However as depicted in Figure 6A, multiple outlets do not themselves ensure diversity of news and opinion. Indeed, *concentration* is the word that best applies to the mass media today. This economic reality raises questions about the role of the media in a democratic political system.

Most newspapers and radio and television stations rely on relatively few sources of national and international news. Wire services such as the Associated Press and United Press International are indispensable for daily newspapers and for locally produced newscasts. They are often the only sources for news of statewide interest. Only the largest newspapers will maintain reporters in Washington, the state capital, and abroad as independent sources. The largest television audiences belong to the more than seven hundred commercial stations affiliated with one of the four major broadcast networks: ABC, CBS, Fox, and NBC. Public television stations—funded by private contributions, state appropriations, and since 1967 the federally chartered and congressionally supported Corporation for Public Broadcasting—divide a much smaller audience. Network programming typically accounts for about 65 percent of a local station's airtime, with much of the rest consisting of reruns of discontinued network shows.

Among newspapers, competition for reporting news and setting advertising rates has all but disappeared in many sections of the nation. Today, only a dozen or so American cities have separately owned and fully competitive daily newspapers, compared to 502 cities in 1923.

Chain ownership is quickly dominating newspaper and television business. Locally owned newspapers and television stations may soon be a thing of the past. Media mergers over the past two decades mean that today just nine corporations control over half of the broadcast media in America.[1] In 2001, the ten largest media companies earned revenues totaling over ninety-eight billion dollars—an amount greater than the next ninety largest companies combined.[2] Today, only five corporations control a majority of the

Figure 6A | Channels Receivable per TV Household

In 2000 some 69 percent of American households with television sets could receive 26 or more channels. By 2014, the average home received 189 channels, despite regularly watching only 17 of them.

SOURCES: *Pew Research Center for the People & the Press; The Nielsen Company, "Changing Channels: Americans View Just 17 Channels Despite Record Number to Choose From," May 6, 2014, http://www.nielsen.com (September 19, 2014).*

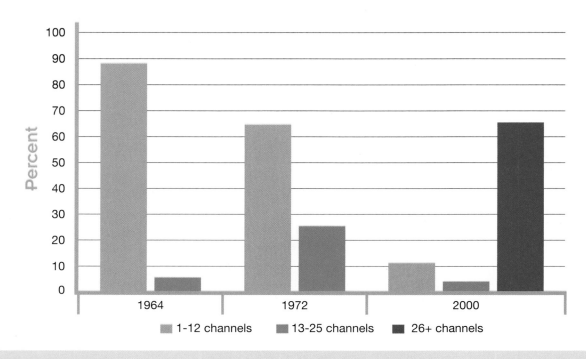

media in the United States.[3] This consolidation trend is not limited to traditional media. Even the Internet has not escaped the move toward mega-media corporations. Between 1999 and 2001, the number of companies controlling 60 percent of online time shrank from 110 down to only 14.[4] Some media corporations own several outlets of the same type—newspapers or television stations. Many stress cross-media ownership, combining newspapers, radio, television, cable, and Internet services. Time Warner, for example, owns hundreds of magazine publishing companies (Real Simple, *Sports Illustrated*), cable and broadcast television stations (HBO, CNN, CW, and film companies (DC Entertainment, Warner Bros.)). Disney owns the ABC network, television stations, radio stations, book and magazine publishing companies, and cable channels.[5]

Aside from antitrust restraints, which apply to all businesses, additional limitations on media concentrations come in the form of regulations issued by the Federal Communications Commission. The most significant of these limitations include rules that prevent a single company's stations from reaching more than 35 percent of viewers and prevent a single company from owning more than one of the four major networks; a rule limiting the number of television stations a company can own across the country; and rules limiting the number of media sources (radio, TV, and newspaper) a company can own in a single market.[6]

Alongside these restrictions is the growth of satellite technology and cable television, the former now serving 30 percent of American households and the latter 68 percent.[7] Satellites decrease the cost of transmitting news over vast distances and increase a local station's news sources. Aside from one of the four major networks, a station may have a contract with CNN, may receive "feeds" direct from government agencies, and may exchange stories with other local stations. For viewers, cable television at first glance means greater choice; yet many of the cable channels are themselves owned by the media conglomerates.

If concentrations in ownership are easy to measure, their effects are not. One view argues that an information conglomerate's "most powerful influence … is the power to appoint media leaders" such as editors, producers, and publishers.[8] To what degree does the economic reality of media corporations tend to decrease the diversity of news and opinion Americans that read, see, and hear? Does concentration of ownership increase the political power of these corporations?

1 Paul Wellstone, "Growing Media Consolidation Must Be Examined to Preserve Our Democracy," *Federal Communications Law Journal* 52 (2000): 551–554.

2 "100 Leading Media Companies," *Advertising Age* (August 19, 2002).

3 Ben H. Bagdikian. *The New Media Monopoly,* 7th ed. (Boston: Beacon Press, 2004).

4 Press Release, *Jupiter Media Metrix,* June 4, 2001.

5 "Who Owns What," *Columbia Journalism Review,* http://www.cjr.org/owners/ (February 24, 2015).

6 Yochi J. Dreazen, "FCC Will Simultaneously Review All of Its Media-Ownership Rules," *Wall Street Journal,* June 18, 2002, http://online.wsj.com/article_email/0SB1024337625179502320.html (September 18, 2002).

7 The Gallup Organization, "Americans Inventory Their Gadgets," December 23, 2005, http://www.gallup.com/poll/20593/Americans-Inventory-their-Gadgets.aspx?ci=20593 (accessed October 20, 2006; now discontinued).

8 Bagdikian, *The New Media Monopoly.*

justification for such governmental intrusion has been that frequencies (and therefore the number of stations) are finite and that the airwaves are public property.[12]

Today, the FCC is composed of five commissioners appointed by the president and confirmed by the Senate for seven-year terms. Since the 1970s, the FCC has moved toward less regulation of radio and television, adopting the view that the marketplace and not the commissioners should dictate development of the industry, with the commission confining itself to licensing stations, assigning frequencies, and policing their use. Among the regulations, two have been very significant for news reporting.

6.1d The Equal-Time Rule

The **equal-time rule**, from section 315 of the Communications Act of 1934, requires stations to give or sell time to one political candidate if the station has given or sold time to another candidate for the same office. The time must not only be equal in

equal-time rule

A provision of the Communications Act of 1934 that requires radio and television stations to give or sell equivalent time to one political candidate if the station has given or sold time to another candidate for that office

table 6.4 | Radio, Television, the Internet, and Politics: Milestones

Commercial radio has been part of American culture since the 1920s. Television became widespread after World War II ended in 1945. The Internet emerged as an important news source in the 1990s. All three media are politically important today.

1920	KDKA in Pittsburgh announces election results in the presidential race between Warren Harding and James Cox.
1923	President Calvin Coolidge's opening address to Congress is broadcast by a series of radio stations, linked by telephone lines, as far west as Dallas.
1927	Congress establishes the Federal Radio Commission, assuring private ownership of the broadcast industry, with government regulation.
1928	General Electric Co. and the Radio Corporation of America begin experimental television transmissions.
1933	President Franklin Roosevelt delivers his first "fireside chat" to Americans via radio.
1934	Congress establishes the Federal Communications Commission, replacing the Federal Radio Commission.
1939	NBC begins limited regular television programming.
1940	The Democratic and Republican conventions are televised.
1943	The FCC requires NBC to sell its second ("blue") network, which becomes ABC.
1947	President Harry Truman's State of the Union message is the first complete presidential address transmitted on television.
1948	President Truman is the first to sit in the White House and watch his opponent nominated on television.
1949	The FCC introduces the fairness doctrine.
1951	The Supreme Court rules that movies qualify for First Amendment protection.
1952	Richard Nixon's "Checkers speech" on television helps convince Dwight Eisenhower to keep him as his running mate; the Republican Party makes first use of TV commercials in a presidential campaign.
1960	Candidates John Kennedy and Richard Nixon meet in the first televised debate between presidential candidates.
1961	President Kennedy institutionalizes "live" televised White House press conferences.
1963	Evening network news programs expand from fifteen to thirty minutes.
1964	Television networks call the results of the presidential election between President Lyndon Johnson and Senator Barry Goldwater before the polls have closed on the West Coast.
1965	The networks provide regular coverage of the Vietnam fighting on the evening news; first regular transmission of television signals via satellite begins.
1979	U.S. House of Representatives approves live television coverage of its sessions (now carried on C-SPAN, a cable channel).
1980	Cable News Network (CNN)—a twenty-four hour, all-news, cable-only service—begins operation.
1984	TV networks cease "gavel-to-gavel" coverage of presidential nominating conventions.
1986	U.S. Senate approves television coverage of its sessions.
1987	The FCC repeals the fairness doctrine.
1991	Live media coverage of the Persian Gulf War allows Americans a view of the conflict as it unfolds.

1996	Congress passes the Communications Decency Act to regulate Internet content. (It was later held unconstitutional, in part, by the Court.)
2003	Over half of all American households have access to the Internet.
2009	All broadcast television stations in the Unite States stop analog use and begin broadcasting only in a digital format.

length but must also be at a similar time of the day. A station cannot give a candidate for school board five minutes of airtime at 8:00 a.m. and then relegate an opponent to 2:30 a.m. During the 1980 and 1984 presidential campaigns, for example, television stations had to cease showing old movies starring Ronald Reagan. That would have amounted to free time, which could have been demanded in equal quantities by his Democratic opponents, Jimmy Carter and Walter Mondale. In 1984 the FCC decided that the rule does not apply to televised debates among candidates, thus allowing a station to invite some candidates and not others. This ruling allowed networks to invite only President Barack Obama and former Massachusetts Governor Mitt Romney to the 2012 presidential debates, despite protestations by excluded third-party candidates.

> The Federal Communications Commission is responsible for regulating the mass media. You can read about the agency's latest activities and its current priorities at this site:
>
> http://www.bvtlab.com/79F8H

6.1e The Fairness Doctrine

The **fairness doctrine** was an FCC regulation that applied throughout the year, not just during political campaigns. Stations had to devote a "reasonable" percentage of airtime to a discussion of public issues and had to ensure fair coverage for each side. If a station presented only one side of an issue, advocates for the other side had a legal right to be heard. If, in the discussion of an issue, the honor or integrity of a person or group was attacked, the station had to notify the person or group and supply both a transcript of the attack and an opportunity to respond on the air. Moreover, if a station endorsed a candidate for public office, the same requirements for notice and reply applied. It was to avoid conflict with the fairness doctrine that television networks routinely allowed a "Democratic response" following an address by a Republican president, a practice that has survived the demise of the doctrine itself. For a time, public broadcasting stations were treated differently and prohibited by law from editorializing at all on the air, a restriction the Supreme Court voided in 1984.[13]

Given the trend toward deregulation of the broadcast industry, it was not surprising that the FCC repealed the fairness doctrine in 1987. The FCC concluded that the doctrine was unconstitutional and that expansion of cable television had largely undercut the original rationale for treating radio and television stations differently from newspapers. Most communities now have access to more television channels than newspapers, meaning that the potential for competition among viewpoints is now greater in electronic than print journalism. That being said, access to more channels does not necessarily mean access to media owned by a wider variety of

fairness doctrine

A regulation of the Federal Communications Commission that required radio and television stations to devote some airtime to a balanced discussion of public issues; abolished in 1987

individuals or companies. As "Politics and Economics: Media Monopolies?" indicates, fewer regulations on media ownership can have a dampening effect on competition.

6.1f Regulating the Internet

While the FCC is responsible for regulating interstate and international communication within the United States, its jurisdiction does not extend to global communications such as the Internet. As the Internet becomes an increasingly important force in mass media, the federal government will face challenges in its attempt to regulate Internet content. Efforts to crack down on Internet fraud have been handled by the Federal Trade Commission and have met with some degree of success. The Supreme Court, however, has found that the First Amendment protects nearly all nonfraudulent commercial and private uses of this medium. In 1996, Congress passed the Communications Decency Act in an attempt to limit postings of obscene and offensive materials on websites. As discussed in Chapter 3, the Court held that this and subsequent congressional efforts have been overbroad limitations on protected speech. Since efforts to restrict offensive materials have been unsuccessful, any regulation of news content seems highly unlikely to pass constitutional muster. For now, almost anything goes on the Internet.

The media can help identify and define issues that people regard as important, such as the struggling economy, the healthcare law, same-sex marriage, and marijuana legalization. (Wikimedia Commons)

6.2 Politics and the Press

Understanding why the press matters politically requires a look at several roles the media play in American politics. The media serve as *vehicles* of direct communication, as *gatekeepers* of political knowledge and attitudes, as *spotlights* on issues, and as *talent scouts* in campaigns.

6.2a Direct Communication: The Media as Vehicles

With heavy doses of entertainment and information in abundance, the mass media understandably have real significance for politics and government in the United States. Radio, television, and the Internet have become *vehicles*, making it possible for a president or

Confidentiality of News Sources and Information

Government cannot constitutionally prevent reporters from publishing news, but protection of a reporter's news sources and information remains uncertain. The success of much investigative journalism depends on the willingness of people with information to share it with journalists. For a variety of reasons, however, these news sources do not want their identities revealed. Some may fear embarrassment or the loss of a job; in the case of disclosure of criminal wrongdoing, they may be concerned about their physical safety. With no assurance of confidentiality, news sources might dry up, resulting in a loss of news to the public. Moreover, without some legal protection, officials could harass reporters they do not like by hauling them into court.

When it becomes apparent that reporters possess information, such as the names of witnesses, that law enforcement agents do not have, many people believe that journalists should have to testify just like ordinary citizens. Moreover, they say, because government officials rely on the press for a favorable public image, abuses would rarely, if ever, occur. Besides, sources do not disappear simply because the assurance of confidentiality is not absolute. In 1972, the Supreme Court ruled 5 to 4 in *Branzburg v. Hayes*[1] that the First Amendment does not protect the identity of a reporter's sources, but most states have enacted shield laws that give varying degrees of protection to news sources. Some protect only a journalist's sources, while others protect undisclosed information too. Congress has not passed a **shield law** for federal investigations.

The Supreme Court has also ruled in a case from Stanford University that the First Amendment does not shield newspaper offices from police searches, even when the newspaper, broadcast station, or its staff is not accused of wrongdoing.[2] Following violent demonstrations on the campus, the *Stanford Daily* published photographs of the clash. Police concluded that the newspaper's files might contain other evidence to help identify rioters and searched the premises. In reaction to the Stanford case, Congress passed the Privacy Protection Act of 1980, which prohibits unannounced searches of news media offices and those of authors and researchers by federal, state, and local police departments. There are three exceptions: when a reporter may have committed a crime, when the desired information is classified or otherwise related to national defense, or when someone's physical safety is at risk. The 1980 act has not ended newsroom searches, but it has reduced their frequency.[3]

More recently, news leaks regarding the war on terrorism have led government officials to seek out the informant on their own, rather than going after the journalists. On June 19, 2002, CNN first reported that the National Security Agency had intercepted conversations regarding an imminent terrorist attack prior to September 11, 2001. Since the intelligence community had only shared this classified information with a limited number of individuals—namely, the Senate Intelligence Committee—the FBI investigation focused on the senators rather than the news media.[4]

Another unusual twist on the issue of source confidentiality came in July 2003, when journalist Robert Novak wrote a column for the *Washington Post* in which he identified former ambassador Joseph Wilson's wife, Valerie Plame, as a CIA agent. The revelation was controversial because revealing the identity of an intelligence agent is illegal due to the security risk it creates and because many suspected that members of the Bush administration had leaked the information in retaliation for published criticism by Wilson. Although Novak cooperated with the special prosecutor assigned to investigate the leak, another reporter in possession of the leaked information, Judith Miller, refused to identify her sources and spent almost three months in jail as a result. Eventually, the investigation revealed that three administration officials had provided the classified information on Plame to reporters: President Bush's senior policy adviser Karl Rove, Vice President Cheney's chief of staff I. Lewis "Scooter" Libby, and Deputy Secretary of State Richard Armitage.[5]

Whether in shielding the identity of sources or investigatory material, should journalists have legal protection denied to other citizens? Should government officials be held to different standards? How might threats to national security change your views?

1 408 U.S. 665 (1972).

2 *Zurcher v. Stanford Daily,* 436 U.S. 547(1978).

3 Jane E. Kirtlet, "Dealing with Newsroom Searches," *National Association of Broadcasters InfoPalt* (October/November 1988).

4 Kate Snow, "FBI Seeks Senators' Records in 9/11 Leak Probe," CNN.com, August 24, 2002.

5 CBS News, "Armitage on CIA Leak: 'I Screwed Up,'" September 7, 2006, http://www.cbsnews.com/stories/2006/09/07/eveningnews/main1981433.shtml (October 23, 2006).

shield laws

Statutes that protect the identity of journalists' news sources or their knowledge of criminal acts

other national political leader to speak simultaneously and directly to virtually everyone in the land. "No mighty king, no ambitious emperor, no pope, no prophet ever dreamt of such an awesome pulpit, so potent a magic wand," observed CBS veteran news director Fred W. Friendly.[14] Former senator J. William Fulbright (D–AR) even claimed that television had changed the constitutional system by doing "as much to expand the powers of the president as would a constitutional amendment formally abolishing the co-equality of the three branches of government."[15]

Among recent presidents, Ronald Reagan and Bill Clinton have appeared the most comfortable communicating directly with the American people via television. Regardless of preferences, circumstances often force presidents into the national spotlight. During his first several months in office, George W. Bush gave relatively few nationally televised addresses—preferring to communicate less formally or through his press secretary at the time, Ari Fleischer. After the 9/11 tragedies, however, Bush was compelled to deliver a series of difficult televised addresses. By many accounts, these tragedies turned a reluctant speechmaker into a formidable public communicator.

6.2b Political Knowledge and Attitudes: The Media as Gatekeepers

As *gatekeepers*, editors and journalists in newsrooms across the land decide in large measure what the American people will receive information about. Just because the media report a lot of news, however, does not mean that Americans are always eager to receive it—or even when they are eager recipients, they aren't always successful at remembering most of what they read or see.[16] It was shown in Chapter 5 that many Americans do not know very much about their political leaders and what they do

Former President Ronald Reagan (Wikimedia Commons)

or how the American political system works. In part, this is because most of the time spent watching television, reading newspapers, or browsing the Internet is not spent watching or reading the news. Only about 35 percent of Americans report that they follow national political news very closely.[17]

Even when people pay attention to the news, they do not retain large amounts of specific information for very long. Given the number of events and situations that are televised, written about, and talked about, one day's news is overtaken by the next.

The mass media also influence political attitudes—what people think about their political leaders and institutions. Of course, the formation of political attitudes is complex, stretching from childhood to old age; and the media are part of this process. News stories contribute to emotions and impressions that can matter politically, apart from whatever facts are transferred from the screen or page to the brain. Feelings of outrage, sadness, pride, trust, or distrust can linger long after the specific content of a news story has been forgotten.

It makes a difference, then, how journalists keep watch over public life when pointing to shortcomings, corruption, failures, and successes. One study of network television news coverage of the White House found that stories reflecting favorably on the president and his policies were outnumbered by those that reflected unfavorably on the administration.

The author suggested that this fact accounts for the difficulty recent presidents have had in maintaining their popularity past the initial "honeymoon" stage.[18] President Clinton was an amazing exception to this rule, leaving office after eight years with an approval rating higher than when he started. This was not due to favorable news stories (indeed, a vast number of stories centered on the scandals that led to his impeachment), but rather to a favorable economy. Americans consistently gave high marks to Clinton's job performance, but low marks to the president "as a person."[19] The media were initially critical of George W. Bush's job performance but rallied around him after the 9/11 attack, possibly in response to a perceived need for national unity. Although this supportive media attitude lasted for some time, questions began to emerge about the necessity—and success—of the Iraq War; and the media returned to their more critical role.

6.2c Issue Making and Issue Reporting: The Media as Spotlights

Just as the media can act as gatekeepers, they can be *spotlights* as well. Sometimes journalists talk about their work as if television, newspapers, and the Internet were mirrors of society. That would mean that life in its many varieties and experiences would be reflected in the programs people watch and the articles they read. Most of the humdrum of daily living, however, goes unnoticed and unreported by the media. Indeed, many people watch television to escape, not relive, such humdrum. Rather than thinking of the media as "mirroring" society, it is probably more helpful to think about the media as spotlighting or highlighting parts of it.

The media help to identify and define the issues people regard as important. Moreover, prominent coverage of a topic, such as drunk driving, day after day may heighten the importance people assign to it—just as an absence of coverage can lead people to believe that a problem, such as hunger, is no longer serious. Footage of drug sales on street corners in broad daylight, for instance, is almost certain to produce some kind of response from the mayor or police chief. More media attention results, then, because officials are now considering the problem and deciding what action, if any, to take. Journalists and government officials will sometimes collaborate to "manufacture" an issue. For example, the staff of a congressional committee might share information with reporters about waste and cost overruns in the military. The objective is to generate widespread feeling that new policies are needed to cope with a recently "discovered" problem.[20]

Especially when the news is not favorable, journalists may run afoul of officials. When investigating a story on local corruption, for instance, reporters will need "inside" sources to provide information and insight. These sources, understandably, will not want their names made public. Yet if the story leads to arrests by the police, witnesses will have to be called. Should reporters nonetheless be allowed to protect the identity of their sources? This is the question probed in "Contemporary Controversies: Confidentiality of News Sources and Information."

Spotlighting issues may affect political attitudes by **priming** the public. Priming occurs when the news media, especially television, set the terms by which the public judges its leaders. The way in which the media present an issue, such as protecting the environment, can make it appear to be the business of a particular official, such as the president. If viewers and readers then regard the problem as important—as they probably will if it appears to be a problem of presidential magnitude—they are likely to judge officials according to how well they think the latter have responded to the challenge.[21] The media do not tell the people what to think. Rather, American media are significant because they tell the people what (and whom) to think about.

BVT *Lab*

Visit www.BVTLab.com to explore the student resources available for this chapter.

181

Chapter 06 | Politics and the Media

priming

Occurs when the news media, especially television, set the terms by which the public judges its leaders

6.2d Candidates and Campaigns: The Media as Talent Scouts

Just as every aspiring singer and shortstop wants to be noticed and taken seriously, candidates for political office want "good press." Political parties have historically been intermediaries, or linkages, between governors and the governed. To a degree, the two major parties still perform these functions; as parties have weakened, however, the media have come to occupy an ever-larger political role in campaigns, partially displacing the parties themselves. Today voters receive more political information from the media than from political parties. More voters can see a presidential candidate simultaneously in a single appearance on television than during a three-week whistle-stop train tour of the nation one hundred years ago. Good reporting can help voters understand a candidate's stand on the issues.

Former President Richard Nixon election flyer distributed on behalf of his campaign for Congress, 1946 (Wikimedia Commons)

All too often, however, the media treat campaigns as if they were little more than horse races. News stories identify "serious" contenders and "front-runners," those whose campaigns have "momentum," as well as those who have "peaked too soon" or are "has-beens." Candidates want to do well at the start, with their early successes featured in the news.[22]

Sometimes this means getting more votes than any of the other candidates, or it may mean getting more votes than journalists expected. News accounts may then affect outcomes in later primaries because they affect the support that flows toward or away from a candidate. On the other side—especially in state and local races, where turnouts are usually lower than in national elections—a lack of media attention can leave voters in the dark about who the candidates are and where they stand on the issues.

Moreover, given the legal constraints on campaign gifts and spending, news stories that place candidates in a favorable light can add up to free advertising. Particularly for campaigns run on a financial shoestring, journalists are indispensable in bringing candidates' views and personalities to the attention of the electorate. Without such "free publicity," for example, third-party candidates like Gary Johnson (Libertarian Party) and Jill Stein (Green Party) would not have been able to reach as many potential voters. This "free" media attention comes at a price, however. When candidates have to rely on journalists to present their message, they often find themselves at the mercy of the journalists' perspective. Once most mainstream media outlets decided Johnson and Stein were not serious contenders for the presidency, they devoted significantly less attention to these candidates, possibly reducing public support for these presidential hopefuls.

6.2e Believability

Whether functioning as vehicles, gatekeepers, spotlights, or talent scouts, many news media receive respectable marks from the public for "believability"—whether people are inclined to accept what they read and see as true. Thus believability makes news reporting more important politically. Polls done a half-century ago indicated that, at the time, about one person in three thought that the news media were inaccurate. A

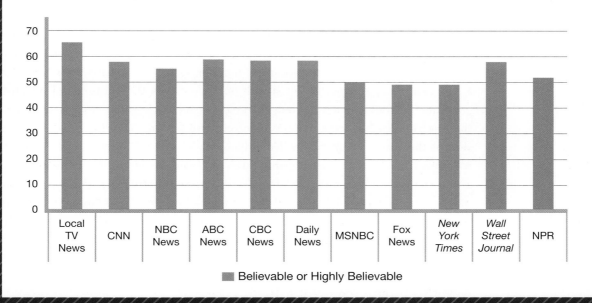

Figure 6.1 | Believability Ratings for Selected Mass Media

In a 2012 survey, respondents were asked to rate the believability of selected mass media organizations on a four-point scale. They were told that a 4 meant "you can believe all or most of what they say" and 1 meant "you can believe almost nothing of what they say." The graph shows the degree of believability (score of 3) and the high believability (score of 4). Percentages shown in the graph are based on total responses of 1, 2, 3, and 4 and exclude responses of "never heard of" and "can't rate."

SOURCE: The Pew Research Center for the People and the Press, "Further Decline in Credibility Ratings for Most News Organizations," August 16, 2012, http://www.people-press.org/files/2012/08/8-16-2012-Media-Believability1.pdf (September 24, 2014).

■ Believable or Highly Believable

survey performed in 1986 yielded similar figures.[23] By 2014, however, 60 percent of those polled said they had not very much or no confidence that the news media report the news fairly and accurately.[24] With reference to *particular* news sources, the believability scores are sometimes higher, as Figure 6.1 indicates. Yet nearly 80 percent of Americans see the press as influenced by powerful people and organizations.[25]

6.3 | Tools of the Trade: Politicians and the "Fifth Branch"

If politicians need the mass media, the media also need candidates and officials. The relationship between the two is *symbiotic*: It is advantageous to both, with each contributing something to the needs of the other. In dealing with the media, politicians have several tools that they can use to their own advantage as journalists compete with each other for page space and airtime. "What producers and reporters want more than anything else," admitted Fred Friendly, "is to get on the air."[26]

6.3a Access

Journalists rely on candidates and officials for access to news and news sources. Access, in turn, promotes their stature and advancement in the profession. For example, reporters assigned to cover the White House—who are usually among the first to learn what is happening, who are called on at presidential news conferences, or who have their telephone calls returned—are envied by their peers and valued by their employers.

Access sometimes takes the form of being the recipient of a **leak**. A leak is rarely accidental. It is a deliberate release of information by an official to a reporter for a specific purpose. Besides doing the journalist a favor, the official may be trying to embarrass a supervisor, impress the journalist, expose bad management or corruption, provide damaging details to discredit a policy, or test the political waters for a new idea. Leaks can spring from the pettiest personal motives or from the loftiest patriotic sentiments. They counterbalance an agency's tight control of information.

In 1986, for instance, the *Washington Post* angered high officials in the Defense Department by revealing the location, number, cost, and test flight routine of the air force's hitherto super-secret stealth bomber—even the existence of which the government would not acknowledge. The story made it clear that this was information the *Post* had acquired from persons involved with the project.[27] (See also the discussion of the Plame affair in the "Confidentiality of News Sources and Information" feature.) The source of a leak is only rarely revealed. By contrast, the **exclusive** is an acknowledged interview that an official grants to one or more journalists. The subject may be the First Lady, the president, or the chief justice of the United States. Such people consent to interviews infrequently. Being scarce, interviews are, therefore, marks of status and recognition every reporter covets; yet both leaks and exclusives sometimes create ethical and legal dilemmas for journalists.

6.3b Public Announcements

In contrast to leaks and exclusives, news releases, press conferences, and news briefings are aimed at all interested reporters. These devices make news by virtue of their happening. Written by an official's press secretary, the **news release** is a ready-made story distributed for the purpose of attracting media attention to some event or situation. The **press conference** and **news briefing** are similar. In the first, an official or a candidate stands before reporters, cameras, and microphones and answers questions. With his quick wit and disarming smile, President John Kennedy (1961–1963) was the first to make the televised White House press conference a regular event. It was a forum in which he excelled.

In a briefing, an official makes an announcement or attempts to explain a policy. In international hostage situations, for instance, much of the news originates from regular briefings given to reporters at the State Department. **Backgrounders** are like briefings, except that reporters may not cite the source. They permit officials to make statements without having their names attached to what is reported. Each form of public announcement attempts to create a newsworthy event that qualifies for press coverage. Officials may achieve much the same result by agreeing to appear on Sunday interview shows such as *Face the Nation* and *Meet the Press*. Often, statements made on these programs generate front-page stories in Monday's newspapers or become trending topics in social media.

leak

The deliberate release of information by an official to a journalist for a specific purpose

exclusive

An interview that an official or other individual grants to one or more journalists that provides information not generally made available to all media

news release

A story written by a press agent for distribution to the media

press conference

A meeting of journalists and an official or other person at which the latter answers the questions posed by the former

news briefing

An announcement or explanation of policy by an official

backgrounders

News briefings in which reporters may not reveal the identity of the source of their information

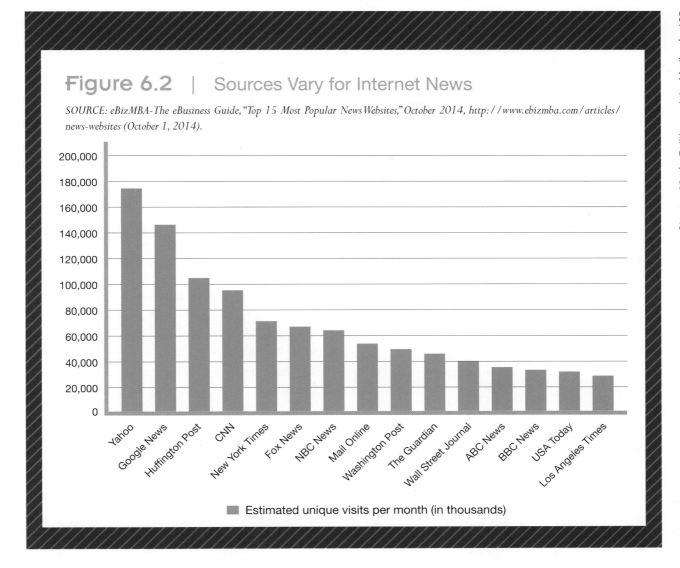

Figure 6.2 | Sources Vary for Internet News

SOURCE: eBizMBA-The eBusiness Guide, "Top 15 Most Popular News Websites," October 2014, http://www.ebizmba.com/articles/news-websites (October 1, 2014).

■ Estimated unique visits per month (in thousands)

6.3c Other Media Events

Like news releases, letters can make news. Rather than simply letting it be known that a senator is concerned about, say, unfair trade restrictions abroad, the senator can write a letter to the secretary of commerce and release a copy to the press. Reporters might have trouble writing a story about a vague concern, but a letter is concrete. Moreover, like an event, it is something to report.

Designed for television, the **visual** features someone's appearance at an appropriate location. For a state legislator who wants to launch a campaign against potholes, merely complaining may go unheard; but if she stands in a pothole (after alerting camera crews, of course), she will be hard to miss. Television reporters do their own visuals. When a story breaks at the White House, network correspondents take turns doing their "stand-ups" with the lovely mansion as a backdrop.

Important for newspapers, but especially so for television, **photo opportunities** are events staged not so much for the purpose of dramatizing an issue as for creating visible activity. They show an official or candidate *doing something*—providing footage for the evening news or a good shot for tomorrow's front page. When a foreign leader comes to Washington to confer with the president, little may be released about what

visual

An image or series of images representing news in action; a visual depiction of a political act, such as campaigning, which may carry more impact than words alone

photo opportunity

An event scheduled to give newspaper reporters and television crews a chance to photograph someone

is actually discussed. Instead, viewers will see the two chatting informally over coffee, taking a stroll in the Rose Garden on the White House grounds, or tossing horseshoes at Camp David.

6.3d A Right to Know?

All of these "tools of the trade" involve officials providing news of one kind or another to the media. There are plenty of other occasions, however, when reporters want information but can find no one to provide it. "A free press and a purposeful government are destined always to be involved in a war of sorts," observed one former White House aide.[28] Although the Constitution protects the reporter's right to print news, there is not an equal right in all situations to acquire it. The press "is free to do battle against secrecy and deception in government," Justice Potter Stewart once said, "but the press cannot expect from the Constitution any guarantee that it will succeed."[29]

For instance, how much access should journalists have to ongoing military operations? Traditionally, journalists have witnessed most American military operations, even if dispatches might be delayed or censored for security reasons. The Vietnam War ushered in the first major television coverage of day-to-day combat, with evening news shows displaying in vivid color battle scenes that had occurred within twenty-four hours of airtime. In contrast with World War II, there were virtually no government-imposed restrictions on what could be shown. Some people believe that the daily scenes of battlefield carnage, combined with questioning by journalists of war aims, gradually undermined American resolve to continue the fighting.[30]

Although the exact role television played in changing public attitudes about the war will probably never be known, the Vietnam experience has prompted officials in the Defense Department to rethink the custom of open media access to combat areas. No such free access exists in authoritarian countries, and even democracies such as Israel and Great Britain permit only limited access. Tighter controls, the argument goes, reduce the need for outright censorship and avoid unfavorable coverage as well as the inconvenience of having reporters underfoot. Taking a cue from other nations, and the negativity surrounding the Vietnam conflict, the American military took a very limiting stance on reporter access during the Grenada and Panama invasions of the 1980s and the Gulf War of 1991.

The government walks a fine line when censoring certain content on TV and the Internet while maintaining the press's constitutional rights and freedoms. (Wikimedia Commons)

During the American government's "war on terrorism, which began in late 2001, the Defense Department has taken a somewhat more inclusive position on media access. The military has allowed a select number of journalists to accompany fighting units in "embedded" positions. In other words, the reporters have observed the conflict directly, alongside troops and with all of the related dangers. While this approach has led to some excellent, up-close coverage, some worry that the Defense Department may be extending an open invitation in certain situations only so that the decision to restrict access elsewhere won't be questioned. This issue made the headlines again during the Iraq War when media outlets were warned against depicting caskets of American soldiers and when efforts were made to restrict photos of prison abuse by American soldiers at Abu Ghraib. When actions are committed in secret, without press coverage, Americans are prevented from forming objective opinions. As Michael Getler, ombudsman of the *Washington Post*, has remarked, "We don't know what we don't know."[31]

6.4 Are the Media Biased?

Politicians, including most American presidents, have long complained about news coverage. Are the media biased? Most Americans apparently think so. Of Americans, 67 percent believe there is political bias in media coverage.[32] That being said, Americans do not agree on the direction of the bias: Polling found that 44 percent believe the media has a liberal bias and 19 percent see it as too conservative.[33] Some bias is probably unavoidable in reporting the news. The bias is both *personal* and *structural*. It results from the political attitudes of reporters and editors as well as from the nature of the news-reporting business itself.

6.4a The Journalists

Vice President Spiro Agnew (1969–1973) once publicly accused the news media of controlling news. "A small group of men, numbering perhaps no more than a dozen anchormen, commentators, and executive producers," argued Agnew, "settle upon the film and commentary that is to reach the public. They decide what forty to fifty million Americans will learn of the day's events in the nation and the world."[34]

Of course the people who write news influence it. Reporters and commentators are not value-free machines that simply grind out a product. Their attitudes and outlooks are bound to affect what Americans read and see, even if journalists make every effort to be accurate. Who are the journalists staffing the major newspapers and network news bureaus? Generally, they tend to come from small towns, largely in the Midwest, rather than the cities and suburban communities of the Northeast or the West. Many of them went to state colleges, not to Ivy League or other highly selective private institutions. They probably majored in journalism or English rather than in philosophy, economics, or political science. Few have been politically active in the sense of strongly identifying with and working for a party and its candidates.

Are Internet media credible?

Decide for yourself. Self-styled cyberjournalist Matt Drudge has been criticized by some and lauded by others. Check out this website.

http://www.bvtlab.com/w8a4v

Can Political News Be Both Entertaining and Informative?

Most of the facts and figures about media used in this chapter are based on nationwide polls of adults in general. It may not surprise you to learn that there are generational differences in preferred news sources. A report by the Pew Research Center for the People and the Press found that about 40 percent of young people (aged eighteen to twenty-nine) got at least some of their political news from comedy shows like *The Colbert Report* or *The Daily Show* with Jon Stewart. This figure is more than twice as high as for Americans aged fifty and older.[1] The popularity of satirical news has had an important effect on ratings as well. During the 2004 Democratic and Republican conventions, ratings for *The Daily Show* were higher than those for more conventional counterparts on Fox News Channel and CNN.[2]

Is all of this comedy and satire good for young adults? Survey results suggest that, at the very least, it is better than no news at all. Of young viewers, 27 percent indicated that they learned things about the presidential campaign from watching comedy and late-night shows that they had not known before.[3] Although anyone wishing to be an informed citizen should seek out news from a variety of sources, it appears that comedy shows may be a legitimate part of that repertoire. A poll that tested respondents' knowledge of political campaigns found that viewers of *The Daily Show* scored 16 percent higher than respondents who did not watch any late-night comedy programs.[4] The organization conducting the poll, however, was quick to point out that *The Daily Show* was probably not solely responsible for the greater knowledge and that the findings were likely the result of viewers' prior knowledge combined with information learned from the show.

What media sources do you turn to for political news? Are they the same sources your parents use? What might be the disadvantages of seeking all of your political news from comedy sources?

1 The Pew Research Center for the People and the Press, "Americans Spending More Time Following the News," September 12, 2010, http://www.people-press.org/2010/09/12/americans-spending-more-time-following-the-news/ (August 6, 2012).

2 Erika Chavez, "Young Want Political News Served with a Side of Irony," *Sacramento Bee,* August 30, 2004.

3 The Pew Research Center for the People and the Press, "Cable and Internet Loom Large in Fragmented Political News Universe," January 11, 2004, http://people-press.org/reports/display.php3?ReportID=200 (October 9, 2004).

4 National Annenberg Election Survey, "*Daily Show* Viewers Knowledgeable About Presidential Campaign, National Annenberg Election Survey Shows," September 21, 2004.

When they vote, journalists overwhelmingly favor Democratic or otherwise liberal candidates. Moreover, they tend to be suspicious of most politicians—whether Democratic or Republican, liberal or conservative. As one scholar has concluded, journalists distrust politicians because politicians have to compromise. Compromise "tends not to involve the clear and snappy opposition of right and wrong that is the stuff of television drama." There is a journalistic idea "of the individual good citizen, independent of special interests and party loyalties, making up his own mind about the measures and candidates that will best promote the public good."[35]

Suspicion of politicians, in turn, leads to suspicion of "the establishment"—the people in power. In a campaign, the underdog may be more appealing than the supposed front-runner. With numerous exposés to their credit, uncovering corruption and shady deals by public officials, journalists may see themselves as a permanent "loyal opposition" or "watchdog" apart from the competition between the ins and outs of the two-party system. Surely the important role of newspaper sleuths in uncovering and probing the Watergate scandal during the early 1970s has only strengthened this perception.

Without a watchful press, President Richard Nixon (1969–1974) and "all the president's men" would probably have survived the impeachment controversy that led to his resignation in August 1974.[36] However the press was far less vigilant, collectively, in the late 1980s in reporting the growing insolvency of the savings and loan industry—a fiasco that Americans are continuing to pay for through their tax dollars. Whether because the subject was so complex, involved so many people and institutions, or seemingly lacked drama and interest, journalists initially ignored the topic while Congress, the executive branch, and the regulatory agencies allowed the problem to fester. Finding it to be a more gossipy, attention-grabbing story, the media devoted a great deal of attention to the extramarital scandals of the Clinton presidency during the 1990s.

(iStockphoto)

Other forces tend to compensate for a liberal bias, to the extent it exists in the national press. Editorial endorsements from the "front office" usually go to conservatives, and reporters in towns and small cities may have a more conservative outlook, too. (Still, the more liberal urban papers have larger circulations.) Moreover, reactions of advertisers, viewers, readers, and officials have to be considered. Editors and producers, for example, may want to curry favor with sponsors by avoiding subjects or ideas that sponsors might find offensive. In addition, the media mergers that have occurred over the past two decades mean that a large number of media outlets are owned by a small number of megacorporations—a trend that may be leading to more favorable coverage of big business and more conservative coverage generally.

Another concern is that because journalists rely on officials for access to information, journalists may become "lap dogs" by placing favorable slants on stories they write. Conservative officials and causes may, therefore, get more balanced treatment than they would otherwise receive. Some critics say that these considerations mean that certain issues may be neglected altogether or covered only in a shallow fashion. The result is that people are poorly informed by a bland style of reporting that succeeds only because it is marginally acceptable to most and offensive to only a few. Still, a tradition of journalistic professionalism argues strongly for both *depth* and *evenhandedness* in news coverage.

6.4b Deciding What Becomes News

Since literally thousands of events occur in the world every day, space and time constraints mean that most of them go unreported. Selecting what becomes news— the process of **agenda setting**—is especially critical in television. Approximately twenty minutes are available for news during a thirty-minute news show, allowing for ten to fifteen stories at most. This means that even the major stories are usually allotted only two to three minutes each. The news reported last evening on television could easily fit on the front page of this morning's newspaper. If a "big story" is in the news, other stories are crowded out. Once cut, these would-be stories may never

agenda setting

The process by which the news media select and focus on a small number of stories from a large number of possibilities—shaping, in part, Americans' opinions about what is important

have a second chance to appear. Expanded coverage is possible only on more lengthy programs such as *PBS NewsHour* on public television.

What factors seem to guide this inevitable selection? Some events seem destined to become news: natural disasters and political "turning points" such as elections, revolutions, and military invasions. Other events or circumstances will become news if they happen to appeal to the people responsible for selecting stories or if they have a high interest among the reading and viewing audience. Still others qualify as news

Political cartoons are a part of the mass media that are meant to entertain, inform, and critique. Find your favorite cartoonist at this website.

http://www.bvtlab.com/49KmF

because they are "scoops"—attention-getting stories made public by a single newspaper or station. A day's delay might give the competition the chance to claim a scoop as its own. Aside from scoops, there seems to be substantial agreement among the networks on what constitutes the most newsworthy events. One study found that two of three major networks carried the same lead story on the evening news 91 percent of the time, and in only 7 percent of the programs did two run the same lead story without the third network placing it somewhere in the program.[37]

About half of network news stories originate from or focus on Washington. This is not only because it is the nation's capital—and thus the location of many stories reporters deem important—but also because staff, equipment, and circuits are already there. Reporting stories from Washington is, therefore, relatively easy and cost-efficient. Within Washington, however, news coverage is not equally dispersed. About half the stories deal primarily with the "golden triangle"—the White House, the Department of Defense, and the Department of State. Reporters and technicians assigned just to cover the White House number more than two hundred. Congress receives somewhat less coverage, with the Senate drawing more attention than the House. Regulatory agencies and the Supreme Court receive the least coverage. Moreover, two-thirds of the stories on the presidency—but only half of those on Congress—are accompanied by film or video. Presidential stories typically run more than twice the length of those on Congress and tend to come earlier in the broadcast.[38] Of course, these figures are dependent on the relative levels of congressional and White House initiative, as well as the number of international crises, and are therefore subject to some variation from year to year. Campaign reporting by the four broadcast networks tilts even more sharply toward the presidency.

What accounts for this disparate treatment? It is partly a function of the stories journalists think are most important. Also, the executive branch, though many times larger than Congress, is more easily personified. One can associate the president or the secretaries of state and defense with policies in a way that is not as conveniently done in Congress with its 100 senators and 435 representatives. Moreover, much congressional time is consumed with deliberation. This is often not as dramatic to report as an initial proposal to Congress that originated in the White House or an executive decision based on legislation Congress has passed. Imbalance in coverage between presidential and congressional races on the networks is largely explained by the difficulty ABC, CBS, Fox, and NBC have in holding the interests of viewers (and, therefore, their audiences) in one state when discussing the House and Senate races of another state. The solution for the networks is obvious: ignore most of the congressional races most of the time.

Television coverage of Congress is technically easier now that both the House (since 1979) and Senate (since 1986) permit television cameras in their chambers. Thus coverage of the legislative process has increased, especially on locally produced newscasts. Aside from interviews with individual legislators, networks and local stations can pick up statements from floor debates to include on news programs. This is an opportunity that has not gone unnoticed, as some members have learned to "play" to the cameras, even before a virtually empty room. Indeed, continuous television in Congress now means that floor debates sometimes resemble a video equivalent of the telephone answering machine. Even in the momentous debate in the House and Senate, in January 1991, over the use of force in the Persian Gulf crisis, most members with something to

By 1986, both the House and Senate were finally allowing cameras into their chambers so that news teams could cover debates. (Wikimedia Commons)

say filed into their respective chamber at the designated time, made a speech that was recorded for posterity, and then returned to their offices or homes to watch, on television, their colleagues doing the same.

Yet, just because something can be considered newsworthy is not necessarily reason enough why it *should* become news. Journalistic ethics play a role, too. To what extent, for instance, should journalists probe the private lives of officials and candidates? This was the question posed when the *Miami Herald* published reports in 1987 accusing Democratic presidential front-runner Gary Hart of improprieties in spending a weekend with a woman who was not his wife. When made aware of additional damaging information in the possession of the *Washington Post* a few days later, candidate Hart announced his withdrawal from the race.[39] The media's success with Hart laid the groundwork for their approach to the Monica Lewinsky scandal during the Clinton administration. Issues that would have been deemed "off limits" in a previous generation made their way, for good or ill, into prime-time news coverage. Some people argue that the lives of candidates should be like a "fishbowl" or an "open book." Others say that one's personal life should not be the public's business unless it reflects on a candidate's qualifications to be president or to hold another public office.

6.4c Deciding How the News Appears

Journalists describe or portray events in different ways, with different emphases. This process of shaping stories is sometimes called **framing**. In one of the televised debates in 1976 between President Gerald Ford (1974–1977) and challenger Jimmy Carter (1977–1981), for example, Ford slipped up by saying that Poland was not under Soviet domination. In surveys immediately after the debate, viewers were almost evenly divided when asked which candidate had done the better job; but over the next twenty-four hours, as news reports about the debate emphasized Ford's blunder, reaction shifted dramatically in Carter's favor. Some people later admitted to changing their minds, saying that the news stories about the debate led them to conclude that their initial judgments (favoring Ford) must have been wrong. The "newsworthy" part of the debate had become Ford's blooper.[40]

Today candidates are reluctant to leave interpretation of events solely to journalists. In the 2012 presidential campaign debates between President Barack Obama and former Massachusetts governor Mitt Romney, for example, the candidates had barely begun when the "spin doctors" went to work. Viewers were presented with ample

framing

The way that the media present a story, consisting of angle, tone, and point of view

live feedback in the form of tweets and on-screen messages. As soon as each debate ended, there was "post-debate quarterbacking" from officeholders and campaign officials from each party who crowded around the press to provide instant analysis of what "really happened." Unlike the usual press conference, however, there were more interviewees than interviewers. Do the spin doctors make a difference? Unless one candidate commits a major blunder, as Ford did in 1976, most viewers will probably not be greatly swayed by post-debate commentary. Still, it probably shapes the opinions of some, and neither campaign wants to leave the other free to provide an unanswered interpretation of events.

More than print journalism, television news reporting calls for *interpretation* of events, rather than a bare statement of what happened. This is also the case with stories on programs such as *60 Minutes*. Because of the need to hold a viewing audience to a particular channel, television news is purposely designed to be gripping and dramatic. An executive producer of the *NBC Nightly News* once made this point a requirement for his staff:

> Every news story should, without any sacrifice of probity or responsibility, display the attributes of fiction, of drama. It should have structure and conflict, problem and denouement, rising action and falling action, a beginning, middle, and an end. These are not only the essentials of drama; they are the essentials of narrative.[41]

What if an event lacks the elements of fiction, drama, or conflict? The item might be passed over entirely or, if reported, given the added drama it needs. Reporting the news may well mean molding it, too. The irony is that politicians often succeed by managing conflict and reconciling differences among groups. Journalists succeed by capitalizing on conflict and magnifying those differences.[42]

Because news reporting is a business, stations sell time on news programs just as they do during weekend football games and afternoon soap operas. Newspapers and websites sell ad space. Understandably, media executives are acutely conscious of circulation figures and **Nielsen ratings**. Such numbers largely determine commercial revenue, and therefore profits. Economic considerations understandably dictate that the media attract as many viewers and readers as possible.

6.4d The Impact of the Visual

Television's unique quality is its capacity to transmit images into virtually every home in the land simultaneously. Thus, television gives a special meaning to the old saying that a picture is worth a thousand words. A news article about a plane crash will not have the same effect as color video of the same scene. Consider, for example, the emotionally moving nature of the photographs and video of the World Trade Center collapse. The tragedy seemed all the more real, and near, because it was on television.

The *visual* also becomes a factor in the selection of stories and in the way those stories will be presented. Television news editors prefer stories that can be easily visualized. Similarly, they prefer to cover the parts of a story that display movement. Televised reports on political campaigns, for instance, typically emphasize what candidates are *doing* more than what they are *saying*. Instead of the issues that divide candidates, viewers may get an eyeful of colorful rallies, parades, flag-waving, and handshaking. One may see a lot of activity without necessarily *learning* very much about a candidate or the substance of the campaign. Sometimes, knowledge that voters glean about the candidates is more likely to have come from the candidates' own advertisements than from news reports on their campaigns.

Nielsen ratings

Surveys conducted by the A.C. Nielsen Company to measure the size of television audiences

Likewise, television's preference for action shapes the way candidates conduct their campaigns. Appearances must be timed so that coverage can make the evening news. A prepared statement on grain subsidies or interest rates will not draw nearly the attention generated by a ride on a tractor across a wheat field or a visit to the home of a farmer whose house and farm are about to be foreclosed. Including such visuals in newscasts is far easier today than it was a generation ago because of the miniaturization of cameras and other devices that have largely replaced bulkier and more cumbersome equipment. Because television favors images over words, candidates learn to include "sound bites"

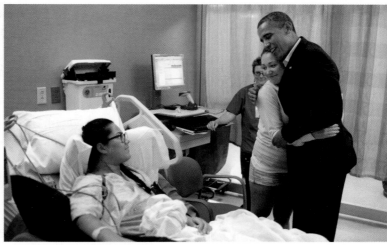

President Barack Obama hugs Stephanie Davies, who helped keep her friend, Allie Young, left, alive after she was shot during the theater shooting on July 20, 2012, in Aurora, Colorado. The president visited patients and family members affected by the shooting on July 22, 2012, at the University of Colorado Hospital. (Wikimedia Commons)

in their speeches—one or two catchy sentences or phrases designed for the brief coverage television provides. With the advent of streaming video on the Internet, viewers can now watch these sound bites over and over at their own leisure when visiting media websites. Such use further enhances the value of a good sound bite—and the cost of an embarrassing one.

In politics, television has clearly benefited some political leaders more than others. One of the earliest examples of television's impact occurred in 1960 when Senator John Kennedy (D–MA) debated Vice President Richard Nixon (1953–1961) in the first televised debate between presidential candidates. While transcripts of the debates show plainly how the candidates differed on some of the issues, many viewers were struck more by what they saw than by what they heard. Nixon went into the debate widely perceived as the "candidate of experience" even though both he and Kennedy had entered Congress in the same year. While Kennedy had served in the Senate as well as the House, many thought that he was inexperienced and maybe just a little too youthful and immature for the presidency. The September debate, the first of four that fall, shook both sets of preconceptions. Perhaps the perfect television candidate, Kennedy seemed mature, firm, vigorous, and at ease. Nixon appeared drooped, tired, nervous, and even haggard. In short, Kennedy *looked* presidential and thus achieved on television, in an instant, what it would have otherwise taken weeks of campaigning to accomplish.

It is likely that the televised debates in the 2000 election also helped one candidate and hurt the other, largely due to the inability of each to meet with viewers' and the media's preconceived expectations and the impact of the visual. Vice President Al Gore, assumed to be the more practiced and qualified statesperson, did not dominate his opponent the way many had predicted he would. On the other hand, Governor George W. Bush—depicted in the media as an inexperienced leader with a poor grasp on foreign policy—held his own. Gore's visual image reinforced descriptions of him as stiff and wooden. Bush's expressive face allowed viewers to develop a sense of being personally connected with the candidate. Thus, even though the content of the debates resulted in a draw at best for Bush, the fact that he performed better than many in the media had predicted and provided viewers with a more human visual image led to a boost in his poll numbers following each debate.[43] By the 2004

BVT *Lab*

Flashcards are available for this chapter at www.BVTLab.com.

Chapter 06 | Politics and the Media | 194

debates, public expectations of Bush had risen, so when his answers seemed less developed and appealing than his opponent's, viewers concluded that Senator John Kerry (D–MA) was the winner. Ultimately, the debate victory meant little, however, as the election victory went to the perceived loser of the debates for the third time in the last six presidential elections.

The 2008 debates gave both Senators Obama and McCain an opportunity to talk about their own brands of change. Facing a country mired in financial crisis, and in which only 7 percent of the populace said they were satisfied with the way things were going, both candidates made efforts to distinguish themselves from the unpopular Bush administration. Senator Obama stressed middle-class tax cuts and foreign policy diplomacy, while Senator McCain emphasized offshore oil drilling and reducing wasteful spending.

The 2012 election was, in many ways, a referendum on President Obama's first term, with the president listing his successes and Governor Romney pointing out the president's failures. Though a majority of viewers felt Obama came up short in the first debate, they saw Obama as the victor in the second and third. This result left many Americans feeling that the overall debate outcome was essentially a tie.

While reactions to a debate do not necessarily translate into votes, a televised debate presents an opportunity for voters to sense which candidate they would rather see as the nation's leader during the next four years. As voters form impressions of candidates, few doubt that the visual component of television plays an important role.

6.4e A Public Trust

If bias exists in news reporting, does this mean that journalists have somehow betrayed a trust? Are journalists worthy of the protections accorded them by the First Amendment? If Americans of President Washington's time were alive today, they would probably confess that they expected bias in the news. The press then, as well as throughout the nineteenth century, was far more biased, inaccurate, partisan, and vitriolic than almost any newspaper widely available today.

The First Amendment does not assume a bias-free press any more than the Constitution assumes pure and ambition-free politicians. Recall the constitutional system of checks and balances discussed in Chapter 1. At the heart of this arrangement, the media amount to another kind of check and balance. Just as the Constitution allows ambition to counter ambition, so the First Amendment allows one opinion to combat another; one claim of truth, perspective, and opinion to compete with another. In this way, the media best serve democratic politics.

CHAPTER REVIEW

1. The media today are characterized by less diversity in ownership and in the production of news. While Americans have access to more television channels than ever before, most national news originates from several networks and major newspapers. Moreover, the number of daily newspapers is declining. The First Amendment makes possible an important role for the media by prohibiting most restrictions on what is published. The electronic media, however, are subject to special kinds of regulations that do not apply to the print media. That being said, a constitutional method of regulating new media sources, such as the Internet, has proven more elusive.

2. The mass media—newspapers, magazines, radio, television, and the Internet—are vital links between citizens and their government. As observers of the political arena, the media serve as vehicles, gatekeepers, spotlights, and talent scouts.

3. The relationship between politics and media is symbiotic. While officials need the media, individual reporters depend on candidates and officeholders for access to news sources and newsmakers.

4. Bias in journalism may result from the political views of the people who report, publish, and broadcast the news and from the structure of the news media. Half of network news stories focus on Washington, and of these about half deal mainly with the executive branch. The visual nature of television not only influences which events will be deemed newsworthy but also influences the ways political campaigns are conducted and the ways officials attempt to gain publicity.

KEY TERMS

Readings for Further Study

Two good, up-to-date texts that approach the topic of American politics through the lens of the mass media are Amber E. Boydstun's *Making the News: Politics, the Media, and Agenda Setting* (Chicago: University of Chicago Press, 2013) and *Making Sense of Media and Politics* by Gadi Wolfsfeld (New York: Routledge, 2011).

Two of the leading contemporary researchers in the field of politics and the media are Doris Graber and Shanto Iyengar. Graber's recent works include *Mass Media and American Politics*, 9th ed. (Washington, D.C.: CQ Press, 2014) and *Media Power in Politics*, 6th ed. (Washington, D.C.: CQ Press, 2010). Iyengar has written *News That Matters: Television and American Opinion*, rev. ed. (Chicago: University of Chicago Press, 2010) with Donald R. Kinder and Benjamin I. Page and *Media Politics: A Citizen's Guide*, 2nd ed. (New York: Norton, 2011).

The Boys on the Bus (New York: Random House, 2003) by Timothy Crouse is a classic case study of journalists in the 1972 presidential contest.

A more recent look at journalists is provided by Beth J. Harpaz's *The Girls in the Van* (New York: St. Martin's Press, 2002), which follows Hillary Clinton's 2000 Senate campaign.

For details on legal regulation of both print and electronic journalism, see T. Barton Carter, Marc A. Franklin, Amy Kristin Sanders, and Jay B. Wright's *The First Amendment and the Fourth Estate: The Law of Mass Media*, 11th ed. (Mineola, NY: Foundation Press, 2011) and *The First Amendment and the Fifth Estate: Regulation of Electronic Mass Media*, 7th ed. (Mineola, NY: Foundation Press, 2007).

Michael Parenti's *Inventing Reality: The Politics of News Media*, 2nd ed. (New York: St. Martin's Press, 1993) argues that journalism is the tool of established economic and political interests in the United States.

Ben H. Bagdikian's *The New Media Monopoly* (Boston: Beacon Press, 2004) addresses some of the problems associated with media consolidation.

The Power of the Press: The Birth of American Political Reporting by Thomas C. Leonard (New York: Oxford University Press, 2000) is a study of the rise of political journalism in the nineteenth century.

In *Democracy and the News* (New York: Oxford University Press, 2004), Herbert J. Gans explores the relationship between democracy and the news media in light of new media developments such as cable and satellite television and the Internet. Also see *After Broadcast News: Media Regimes, Democracy, and the New Information Environment* by Bruce A. Williams and Michael X. Delli Carpini (New York: Cambridge University Press, 2012).

Finally, the writers of the satirical news program *The Daily Show* have written *America: The Book* (New York: Warner Books, 2006) as a parody of an American government textbook. Not to be outdone, Stephen Colbert followed up with *I Am America (And So Can You!)* the following year (New York: Grand Central, 2007).

1. Sam Kirkland, "Digital Circulation Figures Are an Absolute Mess," Poynter. May 5, 2014, http://www.poynter.org/latest-news/mediawire/250218/digital-circulation-figures-are-an-absolute-mess/ (September 19, 2014).

2. The Gallup Organization, "TV Is Americans' Main Source of News," 2013. http://www.gallup.com/poll/163412//americans-main-source-news.aspx (July 12, 2013).

3. The Pew Research Center for the People and the Press, "Americans Spending More Time Following the News," September 12, 2010, http://www.people-press.org/2010/09/12/americans-spending-more-time-following-the-news/ (August 2, 2012).

4. The Pew Research Center for the People and the Press, "Internet Gains on Television as Public's Main News Source," January 4, 2011, http://www.people-press.org/2011/01/04/internet-gains-on-television-as-publics-main-news-source/ (August 2, 2012).

5. U.S. Bureau of Labor Statistics, *American Time Use Survey*, June 22, 2012.

6. U.S. Census Bureau, *Statistical Abstract of the United States*, 2012.

7. U.S. Census Bureau, *Statistical Abstract of the United States*, 2003.

8. The Pew Research Center for the People and the Press, "Americans Spending More Time Following the News," September 12, 2010, http://www.people-press.org/2010/09/12/americans-spending-more-time-following-the-news/ (2 August 2012).

9. *Near v. Minnesota*, 283 U.S. 697 (1931).

10. James F. Fixx, ed., *The Mass Media and Politics* (New York: Arno Press, 1972), p. ix.

11. *Federal Communications Commission v. Pacifica Foundation*, 438 U.S. 726 (1976).

12. *Red Lion Broadcasting Co. v. Federal Communications Commission*, 395 U.S. 367 (1969).

13. *Federal Communications Commission v. League of Women Voters*, 468 U.S. 364 (1984).

14. Quoted in Newton Minnow et al., *Presidential Television* (New York: Basic Books, 1973), p. vii.

15. U.S. Congress. Senate. Committee on Commerce. Subcommittee on Communication. *Hearings on S.J. Res. 209.* 91st Cong. 2nd Sess. 1970, p. 15.

16. Charles Atkin, "A Conceptual Model for Information Seeking, Avoiding, and Processing," in *New Models for Mass Communication Research*, ed. Peter Clarke (Beverly Hills, CA: Sage, 1973), pp. 205–242.

17. The Gallup Organization, 2011.

18. Fred Smoller, "The Six O'Clock Presidency," *Presidential Studies Quarterly 26* (1986): 42–44.

19. The Gallup Organization, "Clinton Leaves Office With Mixed Public Reaction," January 12, 2001, http://www.gallup.com/poll/releases/pr010112.asp (September 14, 2002).

20. Fay Lomax Cook, et al., "Media and Agenda Setting: Effects on the Public, Interest Group Leaders, Policy Makers, and Policy," *Public Opinion Quarterly 47* (1983): 32–33.

21. Shanto Iyengar and Donald R. Kinder, *News That Matters* (Chicago: University of Chicago Press, 1987), pp. 98–111.

22. Richard Joslyn, *Mass Media and Elections* (Reading, MA: Addison-Wesley, 1984), p. 215.

23. *The People and the Press* (Los Angeles: Times Mirror, Inc., 1986), p. 20.

24. The Gallup Organization, 2014.

25. The Pew Research Center for the People and the Press, "Widely Criticized, but Trusted More than Other Information Sources," September 22, 2011, http://www.people-press.org/2011/09/22/press-widely-criticized-but-trusted-more-than-other-institutions/ (August 3, 2012).

26. "The New Face of TV News," *Time*, February 25, 1980.

27. *Washington Post*, August 22, 1986, p. A1. For a discussion of leaks prior to the American raid on Libya in 1986, see David C. Martin and John Walcott, *Best Laid Plans: The Inside Story of America's War Against Terrorism* (New York: Harper & Row, 1988), pp. 269–271.

28. Douglass Cater, *Power in Washington* (New York: Random House, 1964), p. 235.

29. Potter Stewart, "Or of the Press," *Hastings Law Journal 26* (1975): 634.

30. Edward J. Epstein, *Between Fact and Fiction: The Problems of Journalism* (New York: Random House/Vintage Books, 1975), pp. 210–232.

31. "Press Coverage and the War on Terrorism: Assessing the Media and the Government," Brookings/Harvard Forum transcript, January 9, 2002, http://www.brook.edu/dybdocroot/comm/transcripts/20020109.htm (September 15, 2002).

32. The Pew Research Center for the People and the Press, "Database," January 2012, http://www.people-press.org/question-search/?qid=1804630&pid=51&ccid=51#top (October 2, 2014).

33. The Gallup Organization, 2014.

34. *Collected Speeches of Spiro Agnew* (New York: Audubon Books, 1971), p. 89.

35. Austin Ranney, "The Cook Lectures: Politics in the Television Age," *Law Quadrangle Notes 26* (1982): 19. See also Austin Ranney, *Channels of Power* (New York: Basic Books, 1983), pp. 55–63.

36. Carl Bernstein and Bob Woodward, *All the President's Men* (New York: Simon and Schuster, 1974).

37. Joe Foote and Michael Steele, "Degree of Conformity in Lead Stories in Early Evening Network TV Newscasts," *Journalism Quarterly 63* (1986): 21.

38. Lynda Kaid and Joe Foote, "How Network Television Coverage of the President and Congress Compare," *Journalism Quarterly 62* (1985): 59.

39. Paul Taylor, "Hart to Withdraw from Presidential Campaign," *Washington Post*, May 8, 1987, p. Al. Hart later reentered the race and competed in some of the 1988 primaries before withdrawing again.

40. Frederick T. Steeper, "Public Responses to Gerald Ford's Statements on Eastern Europe in the Second Debate," in *The Presidential Debates: Media, Electoral, and Policy Perspectives*, ed. George F. Bishop, et al. (New York: Praeger, 1978), pp. 81–101.

41. Reuven Frank, quoted in Edward Jay Epstein, *News from Nowhere* (New York: Random House/Vintage Books, 1973), pp. 4–5.

42. Herbert Schmertz, "The Media and the Presidency," *Presidential Studies Quarterly 26* (1986): 21.

43. The Gallup Organization, "Major Turning Points in 2000 Election: Primary Season, Party Conventions, and Debates," November 7, 2000, http://www.gallup.com/poll/releases/pr001107c.asp (September 16, 2002).

POP QUIZ

1. People who gather, write, and report the news for the mass media are called _____.

2. The equal-time rule requires _____ and _____ stations to give or sell equivalent time to a political candidate if the station has given or sold time to another candidate for the same office.

3. The_____ _____ was a regulation of the FCC that required radio and television stations to devote some airtime to a balanced discussion of public issues.

4. Priming occurs when the news media, especially _____, set the terms by which the public judges its leaders.

5. A news release is a story written by a press agent for distribution to the _____.

6. Visuals allow the public to see political candidates and their characteristics.   T   F

7. Journalistic ethics do not play a role in the bias of the media.   T   F

8. Economics plays a role in what stories the media will cover.   T   F

9. The bias of the media is affected by the attitudes and outlooks of journalists.   T   F

10. A visual is a scheduled event to give newspaper reporters and television crews a chance to photograph someone.   T   F

11. An announcement or explanation of policy to the media is called a _____.

    A) news briefing

    B) press conference

    C) news release

    D) news framing

12. When candidates answer questions given by journalists, they are at a _____.

    A) news briefing

    B) press conference

    C) news release

    D) news framing

13. Favorable stories equal free advertising for _____.

    A) candidates

    B) journalists

    C) television

    D) radio

14. Since the 1960s, _____ have been using the media to directly communicate with the American people.

    A) presidents

    B) mayors

    C) journalists

    D) executives

15. The _____ requires radio and television stations to give or sell equivalent time to one political candidate if the station has given or sold time to another candidate for that office.

    A) equal-time rule

    B) fair candidate rule

    C) airtime doctrine

    D) fairness doctrine

Answers:
1. journalists   2. radio and television   3. fairness doctrine
4. television   5. media   6. T   7. F   8. T   9. T   10. F
11. A   12. B   13. A   14. A   15. A

Chapter
07

Interest Groups and Political Parties

In This Chapter

(Shutterstock)

Chapter Objectives

People get involved in politics not just as individuals but also as groups. This chapter examines the uniquely important role that two kinds of groups—interest groups and political parties—play in the American political system. The first part of the chapter focuses on interest groups, their activities, and the reasons behind differences in their effectiveness. This discussion sets the stage for an examination of some of the major interest groups on the American political scene today and an evaluation of the role that interest groups play.

The second part of the chapter focuses on parties, which differ from interest groups in that political parties run candidates for public office. By trying to elect members to office, the party serves a variety of important political functions, for example, channeling and clarifying political consensus and conflict, training political leaders, and organizing elections and government.

The American parties form a loosely organized two-party system, a system that is in transition. Are the parties in trouble? What does the future hold for them? These questions are considered in this chapter.

Interest groups are associations of people who hold common views and who work together to influence what government does. Their interest is in a position, benefit, or advantage (such as favorable treatment under the tax laws) that they want to protect and perhaps enlarge. Interest groups look out for their members' political interests by campaigning for policies that promote their goals and by opposing policies that work against those goals. The American Federation of Labor and Congress of Industrial Organizations (AFL-CIO), one of the largest groups of unionized labor in the nation, obviously seeks to win favorable wage and job benefits from companies employing its members; however, it also exists to ensure that government protects its unionizing activities and adopts policies on issues such as trade, interest rates, and education that promote the well-being of its members.

Interest groups have been a prominent feature of American politics since the earliest years of the Republic. During the thick of the public debate over the adoption of a new constitution in 1787, James Madison wrote in *Federalist* No. 10 about the divisions he saw as naturally developing in a society:

> A zeal for different opinions concerning religion, concerning government, and many other points … have, in turn, divided mankind into parties, inflamed them with mutual animosity, and rendered them much more disposed to vex and oppress each other than to cooperate for the common good. … The regulation of these various and interfering interests forms the principal task of modern legislation and involves the spirit of party and faction in the necessary and ordinary operations of government.

Compared to other countries, interest groups in the United States play a particularly prominent role in political life. Chapter 5 reported Verba and Nie's finding that roughly 30 percent of Americans (communalists and complete activists) engage in group activities and that joining and working through groups to solve community problems is more common in the United States than in other democracies. It is not

Interest groups are associations of people who hold common views and work together to influence government decisions. (Shutterstock)

interest groups

Associations of people who hold common views and who work together to influence what government does

surprising, therefore, that scholars studying the American social and political system have focused on interest groups as a uniquely important element of American life. As noted in "Politics and Ideas: Pluralism and Elitism," many see these groups as the basic building blocks of American political life. Perhaps the dominant view is of America as a **pluralist democracy**: American society is made up of many different groups, each looking to secure its members' interests. The principal task of government is, therefore, one of managing the interplay of group interests.

Why American society and politics should be so group-conscious is hard to say. Probably the best explanation is that America is the coming together of so many diverse groups—the "**melting pot**" of different races, nationalities, religions, cultures, and languages—that the variety itself constantly calls attention to the existence and the activities of groups. Beyond being one of the most universally identified features of American politics and society, interest groups are also among the most controversial. Interest groups have long been praised as one of the most important contributors to the success of American democracy. As interest groups have become more visible, more sophisticated in their tactics, and more powerful, they are now sometimes condemned as one of the greatest threats to the continuing viability of the American political system. These are concerns that we will return to later.

7.1a Characteristics of Interest Groups

A stunning variety of organizations fit under the general definition of interest group. The different forms and features that interest groups assume can have an impact on a group's political effectiveness. Of course, no determinant of effectiveness is absolute. A group's influence must be measured relative to the groups with which it contends. Several major characteristics distinguish interest groups and affect their influence.

One of the most obvious characteristics is size. Interest groups vary dramatically in size. All other things being equal, the bigger the group, the more effective it is likely to be. Large groups can mobilize more members, raise more money to support lobbying activities and favored political candidates, and swing more votes in an election. Although, as will be seen shortly, being large is not an unequivocal advantage for an interest group, given a democracy's reliance on plurality and majority decision-making, being large is generally better than being small. Sometimes, when an interest group is large or a number of interest groups band together in a common cause, the result is referred to as a **movement**, as in the civil rights movement, environmental movement, feminist movement, or Tea Party movement.

Interest groups vary in membership procedures. Some groups enroll members formally, as when labor unions ask workers to join and pay dues. Other groups rest on a more informal notion of membership in which people just think of themselves as belonging. People may never go to church, but nevertheless think of themselves as Catholics. Even this informal sense of membership can vary. Some groups evoke in their membership a very strong sense of identification with the group, whereas others do so only weakly. For still other groups, membership is not even a choice of the individual involved—people belong by the fact of having a particular characteristic. African Americans and women are often identified as important interest groups, but most African Americans and most women belong to no race- or gender-based organization. They may not even think of themselves as belonging to some large group. Rather, they are labeled as a member of the group simply because they possess a particular characteristic. Generally speaking, the stronger the bonds of the individual members to the group, the more effective the group will be.[1]

pluralist democracy

A system in which the people rule and have their interests protected through the interaction of many different social, political, and economic groups, and in which the principal task of government is to manage group conflict and cooperation

melting pot

Characterization of America as the coming together of a wide variety of racial, ethnic, and religious groups

movement

An effort to attain an end through an organized set of actions and individuals

Pluralism and Elitism

Pluralism is one of the fundamental ideas of American politics. It is hard to appreciate this unique American contribution to political thought without understanding a little about the political perspective with which it so sharply contrasts. Elitism holds that power in a society is concentrated in the hands of a small group of powerful people, a ruling class. This "elite" is often seen as exercising its power in ways that work to its own benefit and to the disadvantage of those whom it rules, the "masses." Other commentators portray elites as more benevolent, using their power to improve the lot of the less fortunate and to promote democratic values. The major American contributor to

elitist theory was C. Wright Mills.[1] He saw real power in the United States as concentrated in the hands of the highest political, military, and corporate leaders. Mills did not argue for malevolent conspiracy. Rather, he saw the leaders of these institutions as coming from similar backgrounds, sometimes trading positions, interacting with one another, and therefore tending to hold similar values. Foremost among them was a belief in a strong and stable society.

Pluralism, in contrast, sees power as dispersed among many different centers of power, the leaders of various groups that make up society: labor organizations, professional associations, veterans, industries, and the like. Sometimes these centers of power are in agreement, but other times they are not. In any case, collective action is difficult without a reasonable amount of consensus among the groups about what should be done.

This need for consensus compels politics to be moderate and stable. For example, laws passed since the early 1970s to reduce harmful automobile emissions were not imposed on the nation by a single small elite. The laws do not represent a "perfect" solution but rather a compromise among many groups: environmentalists, healthcare specialists, the elderly, automobile manufacturers and dealers, labor unions, and petroleum companies.

What evidence of a power elite do you see in American society? Who is in it? To what ends does it use its power? What evidence do you see of pluralism in American society? What are the dominant groups? How do they use their power? How do the recent Tea Party and Occupy movements fit into this discussion?

1 *The Power Elite* (Oxford: Oxford University Press, 2000).

Membership in some interest groups can be involuntary—people belong simply by sharing a particular characteristic, such as women in the military. (Wikimedia Commons)

Groups also differ in how well they are organized, and the success of an interest group in advancing its interests depends in some measure on this criteria on. A strong network of communication and control can amplify the power of one group, whereas poor internal organization and an inability to coordinate common efforts can dissipate the influence of another. Groups also differ in how democratic they are. Some groups are run as virtual autocracies with the leadership exerting almost dictatorial control over the group; others are very democratic. The relationship between how democratic a group is and its effectiveness is an uncertain one. Groups run democratically may benefit from the additional commitment that broad membership participation engenders, as long as members can reach substantial consensus in the group. When a lack of consensus hinders decision-making, however, the group may suffer from a lack of common purpose. Conversely, groups run by narrow elites may benefit from singleness of purpose but suffer a lack of support if members feel estranged from the leadership.

How connected a group is to politics can also affect its influence. Some interest groups have little if any connection to politics. They are generally not concerned with political issues or involved in political activity. A town's bowling league rarely has anything to do with politics. Indeed, it would probably suffer as an organization if it became embroiled in partisan political struggles. Its political significance lies in its potential to become politically active should its interests somehow be threatened in the political arena. Legislation to outlaw bowling as an immoral pastime would undoubtedly inspire it to take up the cudgels of politics. However, under normal circumstances it stands completely aside from the political fray. Other interest groups exist solely to pursue political ends. A political action committee, about which we will say more later, exists in most cases solely for the purpose of channeling money to political candidates sympathetic to the interests of the group. Between these two extremes reside many organizations that are involved in politics to a greater or lesser degree. The more closely a group is tied to political issues, personalities, and organizations, the more likely it is to be effective politically.

Finally, groups differ in terms of their adherence to the essentially mainstream views of society. Some groups pursue a course outside the American mainstream. For example, the American Nazi Party leaned to the right of the mainstream and the Communist party to the left of it. Where a group stands in relation to the consensus of American politics has considerable effect on how influential it will be. The most passionate, best-organized interest group in the country will make little headway if it pursues policies that are far off the beaten track of American politics. Groups that argue for complete elimination of income taxes, for example, are likely to make less headway than those that argue for modest reform in the current system.

7.1b What Interest Groups Do

Interest groups engage in a broad range of activities to protect and advance the well-being of their members. Foremost among these activities is the attempt to influence public opinion. Many interest groups try to create public support or sympathy for their political goals. The major channel for accomplishing this is the mass media. When a group's political interests are threatened, representatives of the group use the media to make the group's views known. Interviews on radio and television news broadcasts, quotations in newspaper and magazine articles, letters to the editor, blog posts, and essays for newspaper op-ed pages are all tools of influence for interest groups. In recent years, interest groups have developed the use of an individual (as opposed to mass) medium to influence public opinion. This is the **direct mail** method, in which computers generate thousands of personally addressed letters soliciting support and financial contributions from potentially sympathetic citizens. Even more recently, savvy interest groups have begun direct *e-mail* efforts—targeting potential donors, providing them with a secure method of payment, and saving a stamp in the process.

Interest groups, of course, are involved in the electoral process through the votes their members cast. More important, interest group members can work in the campaigns of their favored candidates. In recent years, interest groups have been deeply involved in the financing of political campaigns, usually through **political action committees** or **PACs**. PACs are organizations devoted to channeling money from members of interest groups to political candidates sympathetic to the groups' policy preferences. By law, PACs must register with the Federal Election Commission (FEC), have at least fifty contributors, and make contributions to at least five candidates for federal office. No contributor can give any one PAC more than $5,000 per calendar year, and no PAC can give any one candidate more than $5,000 per election. Until recently, individuals were limited in their total contributions to candidates, parties, and committees to $123,200 over a two-year campaign cycle. In 2014, however, the Supreme Court case *McCutcheon v. FEC* held that

direct mail

Method of contacting citizens by mail, rather than through personal contact or the mass media

political action committee (PAC)

Political organization set up to channel campaign money from a group to political candidates sympathetic to the group's political views

Figure 7.1 | The Proliferation of PACs, 1974–2014

The number of political action committees has soared since the post-Watergate campaign reforms made them the preferred vehicle for channeling money from interest group members to political candidates.

SOURCE: Federal Election Commission, 2014.

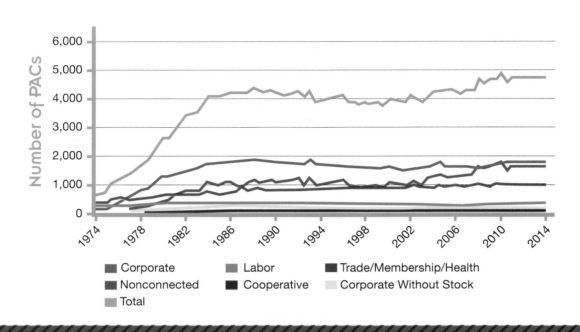

limiting an individual's overall contributions was a violation of First Amendment freedom of speech guarantees.[2] So, while per-candidate limits still exist, individuals can give money to as many different candidates and PACs as they choose. There is also no limit on how much PACs may raise or give in total. Nor is there any limit on the total amount that a candidate can accept from different PACs. In addition to making direct contributions to candidates, PACs may also spend as much money as they want on independent activities in behalf of one or more candidates, usually purchasing advertising in the broadcast or print media.

PACs blossomed as a result of the **Federal Election Campaign Act**, passed in 1971 and amended significantly in 1974 in an attempt to prevent the misuse of campaign funds brought to light in the Watergate scandal. A few PACs existed previously; but the 1974 act, by setting limits of $1,000 on individual contributions and $5,000 on group contributions, made group contributions more attractive and led to a proliferation of PACs. From 1974 to 2014, the number of PACs increased from about 600 to over 4,600 (see Figure 7.1). During the same period the amount of money spent by PACs rose from about $10 million to well over $1 billion. PACs have become a controversial issue in American politics, with many questioning whether the post-Watergate reforms have not been a cure that is worse than the disease.

In an effort to rein in what many perceived as out-of-control campaign spending, Congress passed the Bipartisan Campaign Reform Act in 2002 (also known as BCRA, or the McCain-Feingold Act, after its sponsors). Among the notable features of this law

Federal Election Campaign Act

Law that regulates campaign financing, requiring full disclosure of sources and uses of campaign funds, and limits contributions to political candidates

BVT Lab

Improve your test scores. Practice quizzes are available at www.BVTLab.com.

Chapter 07 | Interest Groups and Political Parties | 207

are a disclaimer rule that requires candidates to verbally acknowledge their approval of radio and television advertisements created on their behalf and a "Millionaire's Amendment" that allows increased contribution limits for candidates running against wealthy opponents. The Supreme Court, in the case of Davis v. FEC (2008), held that this amendment was unconstitutional. The Court found the burden imposed on wealthy candidates is not justified by a compelling government interest in lessening corruption. The most controversial feature of the BCRA has been its effort to control "soft money" (unregulated) donations. Although the law closed some loopholes for PACs, it spawned a rise of "527" organizations—so called because they are defined by section 527 of the Internal Revenue Code. These organizations are not permitted any communication with a candidate or allowed to expressly attempt to elect or defeat a particular candidate; but since they are not regulated by the FEC, many contributors have used them as a way to influence politics free from monetary limitations by making independent expenditures. Again, the effort for reform seems to have been thwarted by the desire to use money to influence political outcomes.

Efforts to regulate campaign spending were dealt a blow in 2010 when the Supreme Court held in *Citizens United v. FEC* that prohibiting corporations and labor organizations from independently spending money to advocate for or against candidates for federal office was a violation of the First Amendment's free speech protections.[3] This decision has led to the rise of "super PACs"—organizations that are able to collect and spend money with practically no limitation or regulation, as long as they do not coordinate their efforts directly with political parties or candidates. In the 2014 campaign cycle, this often led to super PACs far outspending the campaign organizations of individual candidates. By October 2014, about 1,200 super PACs were registered with the Federal Election Commission.

Lobbying, the attempt to influence the shape of legislation emanating from the U.S. Congress and other political decision-making bodies, has traditionally been a mainstay of interest group activity. Lobbying involves more than just hobnobbing with legislators; in many cases, lobbyists are a major source of reliable information for the legislature. Lobbyists provide published materials and advisory letters and testify before congressional committees. They sometimes become deeply involved in the actual process of writing legislation by collaborating with members of Congress and their staffs on the drafting of bills or amendments. In some cases, they may even draft legislation themselves and pass it on to a senator or representative willing to introduce it on the floor. Modern lobbyists are a far cry from the shady figures of folklore. Some are among the most highly paid, respected, and influential figures in Washington.

Lobbyists provide published materials and advisory letters and testify before congressional committees. (Wikimedia Commons)

The idea of lobbying extends beyond the corridors and offices of Capitol Hill. The effect of a law depends not just on how the legislation is written but also on how it is translated into action. Therefore, interest group representatives keep close watch on the rules and regulations set by the many agencies of the executive branch of government and the various independent regulatory commissions. When group interests appear to be threatened, representatives swing into action. They publicize the potential threat, mobilize group and public opinion, meet with agency officials, and ask legislators sympathetic to the "true intent" of the original legislation to intercede with the erring bureaucrats.

lobbying

Attempting to influence legislation under consideration, particularly through personal contact by group representatives

Some special interest groups are focused and are a response to an immediate issue or concern, such as protests about how the government responded to the effect of the BP oil spill on New Orleans. (Wikimedia Commons)

Interest group representatives are so closely involved with legislators and administrators in the making and implementation of public policy that the threesome has come to be called the **iron triangle** of American politics.

Traditionally, the American judiciary has been seen as isolated from external political pressures. However, a more realistic appraisal is that the courts, like the other branches of government, are susceptible to the influence of interest groups in several ways. First, interest groups can affect the selection of judges who sit on state and federal benches. Most prominently, when the president nominates a candidate to fill a vacancy on the Supreme Court, interest groups line up to express their views to the Senate Judiciary Committee. For example, pro- and antiabortion rights groups and women's groups angered by Anita Hill's charges of sexual harassment lobbied vigorously after Clarence Thomas was nominated for the high court in 1991. Second, interest groups can play a role in the judicial process as parties in cases brought before the courts, either as litigants themselves or in **class action suits**. Class action suits allow litigation to be initiated on behalf of a large number of individuals without any formal connection other than their sharing a grievance against another party. Third, interest groups can encourage individuals to bring legal action and provide the financial, legal, and moral support they need to do so. Fourth, interest groups can formally make their views known to the courts, even in cases in which they are not themselves parties. This is done by filing an *amicus curiae* ("friend of the court") **brief**, in which a group offers "friendly" advice about how to decide a case.

7.1c Major Interest Groups

Americans belong to a myriad of interest groups. As noted, some are members of more than one group. The *Encyclopedia of Associations*, which confines itself to formal organizations, lists over 23,000 different national groups and over 100,000 state and local organizations. There is even a lobby for lobbyists: the Association of Government Relations Professionals. Taking into account all of the uncounted formal groups and the multitude of informal groups, there are tens of thousands more. Interest groups can be categorized by their characteristics, goals, tactics, and degrees of success. Major groups usually fit into economic, social, religious, ideological, or issue categories. Table 7.1 summarizes the major concerns of different types of interest groups and gives examples of each type of group.

Economic Groups

Interest groups frequently form around economic issues. In *Federalist* No. 10, Madison wrote, "The most common and durable source of factions has been the various and unequal distribution of property." The various ways in which people gain their livelihood lead to great diversity in the array of groups that form.

Business groups are among the most powerful of all interest groups. Perhaps business's most prominent advocate is the Chamber of Commerce of the United States, which pursues efforts to influence government on a broad front. It engages in extensive **grass roots lobbying** by encouraging its members across the country to contact their elected officials about issues of concern. However, its effectiveness is

---

iron triangle

The combination of interest group representatives, legislative committees, and government administrators seen as extremely influential in determining the outcome of political decisions

class action suit

Legal action initiated on behalf of a large number of individuals without any common interest other than their grievance against the person or institution being sued

***amicus curiae* brief**

Latin for "friend of the court"—persons, government agencies, or groups that are not parties to a case but nonetheless have an interest in its outcome can make their views known by filing this brief with the court

grass roots lobbying

Attempting to influence members of Congress by encouraging citizens in the home district or state to contact their legislators

table 7.1 | Types of Major Interest Groups

The table includes only a few of the thousands of groups that exist. In addition, note that a group may be of more than one type. This occurs when economic groups, for example, make statements about social and ideological questions.

Type	Concerns	Examples
Economic	Business, labor, agriculture, and professions	National Association of Manufacturers; American Federation of State, County, and Municipal Employees; American Bar Association; American Farm Bureau Federation
Social	Gender, race, and ethnic discrimination; economic advancement	National Organization for Women; National Association for the Advancement of Colored People; Mexican American Legal Defense and Educational Fund; National Congress of American Indians
Religious	Religious freedom; values reflected in public policy	U.S. Catholic Conference; National Council of Churches; American Jewish Committee; Mennonite Central Committee
Ideological	Political impact of specific public policy	Americans for Democratic Action; People for the American Way; Heritage Foundation; MoveOn
Single-Issue	Narrow agenda; limited political goals	Environmental Defense Fund; National Right to Life Committee; National Abortion Rights Action League
Public Interest	Broadly-defined consumer and general welfare goals	Common Cause; Public Citizen; Consumers Union; Equal Justice Foundation; League of Women Voters

sometimes diminished, due to the fact that the breadth of its membership makes it difficult for it to take stands that are satisfactory to all its members.

Business interests combine into other, larger organizations based on their special concerns. Large manufacturing companies, for example, have come together in the National Association of Manufacturers. A vast array of industry-wide trade associations, such as the American Iron and Steel Institute and the American Gas Association, represent more particular interests. At the other end of the spectrum are small businesses—the hundreds of thousands of small manufacturing concerns, neighborhood TV repair shops, and "mom and pop" grocery stores. The National Federation of Independent Business is one of the best-known small business–oriented groups. Particular professions are represented by important organizations such as the American Medical Association (the leading organization of doctors), the National Association of Realtors, and the American Bar Association. Business groups do not always speak with one voice, however, because political issues sometimes pit one business interest against another. For example, in the early 2000s, many software companies found themselves at odds with industry giant Microsoft when the latter fought against federally imposed antitrust actions.

When people think of labor as an interest group, they usually think first of its more visible side, labor as organized into unions. Individual unions themselves function as independent interest groups. The United Auto Workers, the Teamsters, and the American Federation of State, County, and Municipal Employees are just a few of the many unions recognized as politically active. The AFL-CIO is an umbrella organization of unions with a total membership of approximately 11 million that spearheads political activity on behalf of organized labor. Disagreements over strategy led several member unions to split from this parent organization in 2005 and form their own umbrella organization of about 5.5 million workers called the Change to Win federation. Organized labor was once seen as a monolithic mainstay of the Democratic coalition; but in recent years its influence has diminished, primarily because the share of the labor force belonging to unions has dropped considerably in the last fifty years. The creation of Change to Win indicates a redirection of political efforts in light of this decline in union membership.

Labor has another, less visible but numerically much larger, side than the union-ized contingent. The majority of American working people do not belong to unions. In fact, workers in the new high-technology industries are much less likely to be unionized than workers in the old smokestack industries they are supplanting. The nonunion workers' lack of organization limits their political influence. Although their more organized counterparts advance some of their interests, their opportunities for political representation are often limited to the actions of their individual members.

Farmers have long been a potent force in American politics. Even today agri-culture is a huge industry. Long-standing organized groups include the American Farm Bureau Federation and the National Grange. They lobby furiously as Congress, once every five years, revises the rules governing agricultural subsi-dies. Dwindling numbers and hard economic times, however, have conspired to reduce the political power of agricultural interests. In 1930 more than 25 percent of all Americans lived on farms; today that number has fallen to less than 1 percent. Such pressures have spawned several more radical and aggressive farm groups, such as the National Farmers Organization and the American Agriculture Movement. The heyday of the farm lobby is over, but agriculture remains a sector that cannot be ignored.

Social Groups

Birth, not choice, determines membership in some interest groups. One of these groups, women, composes one of the potentially largest interest groups in the United States. Slightly more than half of the American population is female, but relatively few belong to politically relevant women's organizations. The most prominent organiza-tion is the National Organization for Women (NOW), which presses for economic and political equality of women and, particularly, freedom of choice on abortion. NOW has over five hundred thousand members, about one out of every three hundred American women. Within such a group, the sense of identification can run strong, although it may not run as strong in the female population as a whole.

The women's movement is closely tied to politics in that many of its goals relate to political issues. The increasing number of female candidates running for public office has also strengthened ties. For many years the legitimacy of female involvement in politics was impugned by the old saying that "a woman's place is in the home," but today women are increasingly accepted as equal participants in the American polit-ical process. Perhaps the best indication of change is the growing number of women who have been elected to public office in the past forty years (see Figure 7.2). The nomination of the first major party female candidate for president or vice president occurred in 1984, when Geraldine Ferraro was the Democratic candidate for vice

president. Senator Hillary Clinton's (D–NY) bid for the Democratic Party's presidential nomination in 2008 came up just short, but it solidified her position as a key contender in future races. In 2014, there were seventy-nine women in the House of Representatives and twenty in the Senate. The percentage of female state legislators was 24.2 percent in 2014, more than five times what it was in 1971.

Certainly the most prominent of all biologically based interest groups in recent American history is the African American population. Whereas African Americans constitute only about 13 percent of the American population,

A growing number of women have been elected to public offices within the last forty years. (Wikimedia Commons)

they gain considerable influence from two sources: their strong sense of group identification and the close ties between the group and the world of politics. Shut out from the social and economic establishment, African Americans had little recourse but to pursue advancement through the political system, which in itself has given their cause a special political legitimacy. Further, forceful African American leaders, such as Dr. Martin Luther King Jr. and the Reverend Jesse Jackson, have not hesitated to spur African Americans to political action. The National Association for the Advancement of Colored People (NAACP) remains perhaps the most visible African American interest organization. Although only a small percentage of African Americans (less than 2 percent) belong to the NAACP, it is the most widely recognized formal African American organization in America, with a membership of about three hundred thousand.

Although the United States is far from total resolution of its racial problems, the African American civil rights movement has, over the long term, met with considerable success. This success is at least partly due to the fact that the movement's goals are not an attack on fundamental values but rather a push for broader realization of traditional American social, political, and economic equality. In recent years, a major effort has been aimed at encouraging African Americans to use their hard-won right to vote and get more African Americans elected to public office. All told, the United States now has more than nine thousand elected African American officials[4] (see Figure 7.2). The number of African Americans in the House of Representatives has risen from seventeen in 1981 to forty-three in 2014.

Another prominent ethnic group is the growing Latino segment of the American population—primarily Mexican Americans, Cuban Americans, and Puerto Ricans. Although Latinos in the United States currently number about 54 million, they confront a situation similar to what African Americans faced forty years ago. Like African Americans, Latinos lag in educational level and are only now developing a strong sense of collective political identity. Fewer Latinos are registered to vote (only 52 percent of the 24.8 million eligible Latinos); and those who are registered do not always vote (48 percent, compared to 64 percent for whites and 66 percent for African Americans in 2012).[5] Those who cast ballots do not necessarily vote for Latino candidates. Latinos lack a cohesive national organization on the order of the

Figure 7.2 | Female, African American, and Latino National and State Legislators and Executives, 1975–2014

The increasing numbers of women, African Americans, and Latinos elected to public offices such as the U.S. Senate and House and state legislatures and to state executive offices in the last forty years demonstrates how the political process has opened up to members of these groups.

SOURCES: *Statistical Abstract of the United States, 2012; Center for the American Woman and Politics, 2014; NALEO Educational Fund, 2014 Vital Statistics on American Politics, 4th ed., 1999–2000.*

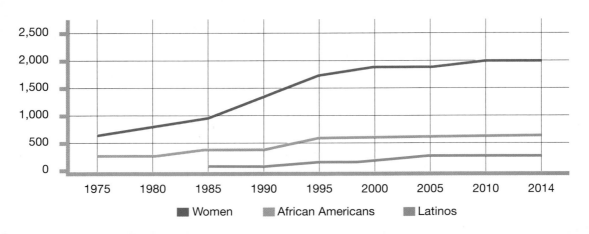

NAACP. As a result, there are fewer elected Latino leaders (see Figure 7.2). Outside the Southwest and a few big cities, Latinos are seldom recognized as a significant political bloc. However, the Latino people have considerable political potential. They are concentrated in a number of big states that can be critical to victory in a presidential election. Partly because of this fact, the number of Latinos in the House jumped from six to twenty-eight between 1981 and 2014.

Religious Groups

Although the Constitution provides for separation of church and state, the religious freedom the Constitution also guarantees inevitably results in the existence of religious groups that are active on a wide variety of political issues. This involvement has engendered some controversy. The **Christian Right**, as fundamentalist groups are often called, has worked for a constitutional amendment to allow prayer in the public schools, tax credits for private school tuition, and the teaching of creationism in public schools, and against laws favoring the rights of women and homosexuals and the teaching of anything but abstinence in sex education.

The religious right loomed as a major factor in American politics through the early 1980s; however, its visibility receded in the late 1980s after revelations of sexual and financial misconduct by such well-known figures as Jim and Tammy Bakker and Jimmy Swaggart. Since then, though, conservative Christians have been working quietly but diligently around the country to elect their adherents to state and local offices and have virtually taken over the Republican Party organization in several

Christian Right

Conservative, religiously based groups that involve themselves in the political process states. Perhaps the most prominent organization spearheading this activity is television evangelist Pat Robertson's Christian Coalition. The Christian Right was credited with playing an important role both in the election of a Republican congressional majority in 1994 and the election of George W. Bush in 2000 and 2004. In 2008, Christian conservatives made former Arkansas Governor Mike Huckabee a viable candidate in the Republican presidential primary. Other more socially liberal denominations such as the United Church of Christ, in effect an emerging "Christian Left," have involved themselves in controversies over arms control, human rights abroad, and U.S. policy in Central America, among others.

No issue in recent years has drawn religious groups more into the political fray than abortion. The Catholic Church and the Christian Right have both worked hard to make abortion a political issue through support of sympathetic candidates and demonstrations outside abortion clinics. A particularly dramatic example by the Roman Catholic Church was its use of the threat of excommunication against Catholics who support or even tolerate abortion.

Ideological Groups

Some groups pursue an explicitly political agenda almost exclusively. When that agenda is broad, the group is characterized as an ideological one. Such groups typically have a clear philosophy of governmental action and evaluate public policy proposals in those terms. Perhaps the best example is the Americans for Democratic Action (ADA), a relatively small group with about 65,000 members that has long espoused a liberal perspective on American politics. Thus, it has become a beacon to those on the American left and an enemy to those on the right. The ADA is best known for the ratings of members of the

Rush Limbaugh is a conservative political commentator. Conservatism is an ideological political group. (AP World Wide Photo)

House and the Senate, which it publishes every year as a way of calling attention to individual legislators' fidelity to liberal values. In recent election cycles, the organization MoveOn has played a growing role in supporting progressive causes by making use of the Internet and electronic mailing lists to build a network of supporters and contributors. At the other end of the political spectrum, Tea Party organizations around the country have backed an array of conservative or libertarian candidates and causes, with a particular focus on reducing taxes and budget deficits.

Single-Issue Groups

In contrast to the broad political agenda of ideological groups, single-issue groups have narrower agendas and more limited political goals. One of the most visible of all the narrow single-issue groups has been the antiabortion, or right-to-life, movement. Groups such as the National Right to Life Committee have been single-minded in their attempts to ban abortion. These groups regard the issue of abortion as the overriding issue of contemporary politics—a so-called litmus test of whether a candidate should be supported. The uncompromising position of antiabortion groups has spawned some similarly uncompromising reactions from single-interest abortion-rights groups. The most prominent among these groups is the National Abortion and Reproductive Rights Action League, which claims some 250,000 members.

Single-issue groups are a controversial political phenomenon. Advocates contend that there are indeed some overriding moral issues that people should rightly pursue

Outbreaks of E. coli *in spinach and other produce in 2008 and 2009 provide an example of an issue that may rally public interest groups. Public interest groups focus on issues of product safety and the effectiveness of government regulation of public utilities and industry. (iStock)*

to the exclusion of everything else. Others see single-issue groups as a threat to democracy because they refuse the compromise that helps to make a democratic system work.

Public Interest Groups

With so many interest groups vying for advantage in the political arena, it sometimes seems that everybody's individual political interests get served, but not the public's as a whole. Thus, organizations have formed to represent broad-based notions of the public's interest. These groups focus on issues such as product safety and the effectiveness of government regulation of public utilities and industry. Perhaps the most prominent such group is Common Cause, the self-styled "citizens' lobby" founded in 1970. It has taken on a broad range of issues, including that of campaign financing.

7.2   Perspectives on Interest Groups

Given the visibility and the pervasiveness of interest groups in American democracy, it is not surprising that they evoke strong reactions from both the general public and political experts. Some citizens view interest groups in highly positive terms, seeing them as essential elements of a successful democracy. Others take a dimmer view, finding them to be perpetual and inevitable dangers to the common good.

7.2a Interest Groups as the Foundation of Democracy

Classical democratic theory demands that citizens be interested in politics, informed about politics, rational in their political judgments, and active in the political process. As Chapter 5 made clear, many people fall short of these expectations. The question is how American democracy can continue to function, and even prosper, in the face of this disparity.

Some observers see interest groups as the answer. As noted earlier, the United States is a pluralist society. Most Americans belong to at least one formal group as well as to a number of other groups. The leaders of these various interest groups act on behalf of their members to protect and advance their causes. Because there are so many groups, sheer force of competition prevents any single group or handful of groups from dominating the others. Thus, every member of society has his or her interests protected without having to be politically active. Democracy functions through representation—not just formal representation via elected officials, but also representation of individual citizens by the leaders of the interest groups.

Further, because most Americans belong to several groups, political disputes seldom run along the same lines. To illustrate, one woman may be a white, Catholic homemaker, whereas her neighbor is a white, Protestant, public school teacher. The two will probably agree about property taxes but disagree about tuition tax credits for parents with children in private schools. Political scientists call this tendency for different coalitions to form on different issues **cross-cutting cleavage** and see it as a

cross-cutting cleavage

The overlapping of interest group membership from individual to individual, with the result that society rarely finds the same people lined up on opposite sides on all the issues and is thus protected against political polarization

brake on polarizing conflict in society. These two elements, competition between interest groups and cross-cutting cleavages, contribute to an equitable and stable society. Indeed, some scholars laud the pluralistic character of American society as an essential factor in the success of its democratic system.[6]

Not surprisingly, critics have found flaws in this flattering portrait of American politics. Not every citizen belongs, in any meaningful way, to a significant interest group; and group leaders do not necessarily represent the best interests of all the group members. In fact, the structure of some interest groups may be very undemocratic. Also, pure competition cannot exist among all the interest groups in a society. Some groups are big and powerful and can dominate; others are small and weak and can be dominated. After all, with what does a small and powerless interest group have to bargain? It is very hard for a group to enter into negotiations with nothing and emerge with something. Thus, "pluralist democracy" may, in reality, turn out to be **interest group elitism**. The elites within interest groups pursue their own interests rather than their members' interests; and the elite interest groups—the biggest and most powerful groups—pursue their interests at the expense of the small and powerless groups.

7.2b Interest Groups Versus the Public Interest

Interest groups are most widely reviled when they are seen as using the political process to achieve selfish objectives. A manufacturing group that resists regulation by the Consumer Product Safety Commission may claim that it is only defending the public's right to buy whatever it wants at the lowest possible price. Instead, the public may perceive the group as demanding the right to make money by producing shoddy and unsafe goods. This kind of spectacle is no doubt one of the greatest frustrations of democratic government and has caused many people to favor tighter regulation of lobbying and other interest group activities. What is the "common good"? Who gets to define it? Should the common good never be impaired in the slightest, even to do a great good for a small number? Does a common good exist, in fact, apart from the outcome of the democratic process that defines it?

Interest group obstructionism of the majority may seem indefensible until it is our own interests upon which that majority is about to trample. A person might protest loudly when import quotas on automobiles make imported cars more expensive and push up prices of domestic models. That same person would probably think differently if he or she worked in a

The healthcare bill was an example of an interest group gridlock. (Shutterstock)

Detroit auto assembly plant or owned a Ford dealership. The real quarrel of those who decry interest group activities may not be with interest groups themselves but rather with the political processes that strike the balance between majority and minority interests.

7.2c Interest Group Gridlock

Pluralist theory envisions a myriad of interests doing battle in the political arena and the government emerging with policies that, although probably not ideal for any, are

BVT *Lab*

Visit www.BVTLab.com to explore the student resources available for this chapter.

Chapter 07 | Interest Groups and Political Parties | 215

interest group elitism

The idea that the leaders of interest groups may act in ways that promote their own interests rather than the interests of the broader membership of the group

acceptable to all. What if no consensus could be reached, however? Critics charge that a pluralistic system could arrive at a virtual state of paralysis, in which an overabundance of interest groups develops, each refusing to compromise. One commentator has called this situation *interest group gridlock,* analogous to the traffic gridlock that often develops in large cities.[7] In an analogy to the clogged arteries that threaten many people's health, another commentator has characterized these stalemates as "demosclerosis"—a state in which the political process is so clogged by the piling up of numerous permanent commitments to interest groups that the government lacks the resources to deal with new problems that arise.[8] Interest group gridlock and demosclerosis may be stark warnings of the dangers of pluralism run amok. The hope of democracy is that good "traffic regulation" by public officials and a more moderate diet for interest groups can help to smooth the way for the successful development of public policy.

7.3 Political Parties

A **political party** is an organization that seeks to influence public policy by putting its own members into positions of governmental authority. In the United States and other democratic nations where most important public officials are chosen by popular election, this means placing a party member's name on the ballot, identifying the candidate as a member of that party, and then working to elect the party member to the office. Parties and interest groups are alike in that their members may share common political views or objectives and may engage in collective political activities. They differ in that interest groups do not run their own candidates for public office. Further, there are many interest groups, each with narrower agendas; however, there are just two major parties, each with a broader agenda.

7.3a What Parties Do

In the pursuit of elective office, parties can perform several important functions that help to bring order to the electoral process and coherence to government. First, by making themselves visible actors on the stage of politics and trying to gain public support, parties accomplish several important **socialization functions**. Because people tend to identify with political parties, parties provide a psychological hook that pulls people into the world of politics. Parties also help to structure people's perceptions of politics. They provide important cues to citizens as they perceive and try to make sense of the political world around them. Parties educate citizens about politics and mobilize them into political action. In their attempts to attract voters to their causes, parties tell voters about what is going on in politics, how it affects them, and why they should get involved. Finally, whereas candidates and issues come and go from one election to the next, parties tend to persist. By providing relatively fixed reference points in a changing political scene, parties help people keep their political bearings and thus help to maintain political and social stability.

Winning elective office requires getting votes. Given the wide range of voters' interests, a single issue will probably not appeal to enough voters to win. The party, therefore, must put together a package of positions on a variety of issues that will attract sufficient numbers of voters. In doing so, parties accomplish four important **electoral functions**. The first is to integrate interests. It is unlikely that any one candidate will

political party

A group that seeks to influence public policy by placing its own members in positions of governmental authority

socialization functions

With reference to political parties, the ways in which parties, by seeking to win elections, help to socialize voters into politics and form public opinion

electoral functions

With reference to political parties, the ways in which parties, by seeking to win elections, help to bring order to campaigns and elections

offer everything that every voter seeks; however, candidates who satisfy needs common to large numbers of voters will receive their support. Second, the set of alternatives from which voters can pick is simplified. Because substantial numbers of voters find their views reflected by one or the other of the coalition candidates, fewer candidates are needed on the ballot. Third, the parties complement the legally established process for choosing public officials. By setting up procedures for determining who will represent a party in a campaign and for supporting these candidates in the election, parties fill important gaps in the

Green Party presidential candidate Jill Stein speaks at Texas Tech University in 2012. (Wikimedia Commons)

selection process. Finally, parties are a prime means of recruiting and training political leaders. Parties provide many people with an entry into politics and opportunities to develop their political skills.

Once a political party achieves electoral victory, it confronts the task of governing. By trying to achieve what they have proposed during the campaign, parties accomplish two important **governmental functions**. First, they organize government and give coherence to governmental policy. Because the founders saw centralized political power as a threat to individual freedom, the Constitution dispersed power to avoid the tyranny of the majority. Power was broken up by function in the separation of powers in the federal system and by geography. Experience soon showed, however, that this fragmentation of power led to a lack of coordination, stagnation, and even paralysis in government. Political parties evolved as a new source of coordination in the political system. With like-minded individuals pursuing common objectives dispersed throughout the executive, legislative, and judicial branches of the national and state governments, coherence and coordination were restored to policy making.[9]

Second, parties help make government responsible to the people. Because parties are stable features on the American political scene, the electorate can reward a party that does a good job of governing and punish a party that does not. Thus, even though the public is not in a position to supervise every detail of governmental action, parties allow the public to exert some degree of oversight and control over what the government does.

7.4 Basic Characteristics of the American Party System

Political parties exist under almost every form of government. However, the particular shape a party system assumes varies from one country to another. In the United States, the party system is characterized by having just two major parties and a loose relationship between the national, state, and local parties and the three components that make up the party: the formal party organization, the party in the electorate, and the party in the government.

governmental functions

With reference to political parties, the ways in which parties, by seeking to win elections, help to organize the government, give coherence to public policy, and make government responsible to the people

Economic Status and Party Identification

Traditional wisdom portrays the Democrats as the party of the economically less well-off and the Republicans as the party of the more economically successful. How well does this image square with current reality? Figure 7A shows the relationship between party identification and income. Interestingly, about one-third of Americans at every income level identify themselves as purely Independent—not leaning toward the Democrats or the Republicans. Apart from this fact, the trends anticipated by the traditional image of the parties do appear. Far more of the poorest people are Democrats than Republicans, and more of the wealthiest people are Republicans than Democrats. However, a significant number of the poorest people are Republicans, and an even larger number of the wealthiest people are Democrats. Thus, economic status has some effect, but party choice in the United States is not made on the basis of economic self-interest alone.

Why is the Democratic Party traditionally associated with the less well-off and the Republican Party with the better-off? Why does party affiliation not divide more clearly along economic lines—that is, why are some poorer people Republicans and some richer people Democrats?

Figure 7A | Party Identification by Income

SOURCE: Pew Research Center for the People & the Press, "A Closer Look at the Parties in 2012," August 23, 2012.

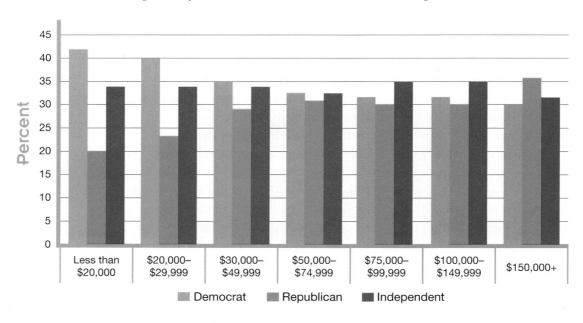

7.4a A Two-Party System

From its beginnings, the United States has had a two-party system. Never have there been more than two large and enduring political organizations at the same time. Party fortunes, of course, have ebbed and flowed. At some times, minor parties have flourished. At other times, some people have feared that one party would rule the nation unchallenged; but the minor parties have always faded, the party with the overwhelming majority has faltered, or the opposition party has rebounded.

Why does this pattern consistently recur? One theory is based on the old saying that "there are two political parties because there are two sides to every question." This explanation sounds good, but many political questions have more than two sides. Also, unless there are fewer sides to political questions in the United States than in other countries, every country should have a two-party system. Many of them do not.

Another old adage may come closer to the truth: "There are two political parties because there are two sides to every office—inside and outside." In the American system, where most offices are contested on an individual basis (i.e., one person wins a single office such as mayor or governor or congressional representative), winning usually requires simply getting more votes than anybody else. This is called **plurality election**. Plurality elections contrast with **majority elections**, in which the victor must receive more than half of all the votes. A **run-off election** is required under a system of majority elections if more than two candidates run and none gets a majority. With plurality or majority elections, most electoral contests in the United States have a single winner and one or more losers—one "in" and one or more "outs." Because the only way for an outsider to displace an insider is to win more votes, the natural tendency is for political organizations to form around those in power and those out of power.

An alternative electoral system is **proportional representation**, whereby offices, such as seats in a legislature, are awarded in proportion to the percentage of votes a party receives. Proportional representation may encourage the growth of more than two parties because a party may place third or fourth in an election and still win seats. Proportional representation is relatively rare in the United States; it is more common in other countries, such as France and Italy.

The plurality election system is not the only reason the United States has a two-party system. Undoubtedly other factors enter in as well, including the predominantly centrist distribution of opinion, the impact of history, and the absence of consistently intense ethnic and religious divisions that might lead to chronic political fragmentation. However, the electoral system has certainly played a significant role in shaping the basic structure of the American party system.

This discussion of the two-party system should not obscure the fact that third parties do have a place in the American political system. As shown in Figure 7.3, third parties have existed for a long time. Although most third parties have been little more than temporary vehicles for a particular candidate or issue, they nevertheless have played an important role in influencing the actions of the major parties. They have raised issues that the major parties were eventually forced to address. For example, the abolitionist parties of the mid-nineteenth century forced slavery onto the agendas of the major political parties. Persistent advocacy of egalitarian ideas such as female suffrage, government regulation of big business, Social Security, and low-cost healthcare by the Populists, Progressives, and Socialists laid the groundwork for much of the New Freedom of Woodrow Wilson, the New Deal of Franklin Roosevelt, and the Great Society of Lyndon Johnson.

In a few cases, the presence of third parties in the field has tipped the balance from one of the major parties to the other. In 1912, in the middle of a long period of Republican

Both major political parties draft statements of beliefs, called platforms, every presidential election year. You can find the most recent Democratic and Republican platforms at the below websites.

Republican platform

http://www.bvtlab.com/QqM67

Democratic platform

http://www.bvtlab.com/96WR7

plurality election

Election in which a candidate wins simply by getting more votes than any other candidate, even if it is less than a majority of the votes

majority election

Election in which a candidate wins by getting more than one-half of the votes cast

run-off election

An election pitting the leading candidates of a previous election against each other when the previous election has not produced a clear-cut winner

proportional representation

A system for allocating seats in a legislative body in which the number of seats a party gets out of the total is based on the percentage of votes that the party receives in an election

Figure 7.3 | American Political Parties Since 1789

The chart indicates the years during which parties either ran presidential candidates or held national conventions. The life-span for many political parties can only be approximated because parties existed at the state or local level before they ran candidates in presidential elections and continued to exist at local levels after they ceased running presidential candidates. For example, in the year 2012, at least a dozen parties ran a candidate for president in one or more states; but only five candidates were on the ballot in over half of the states: Mitt Romney (Republican), Barack Obama (Democrat), Gary Johnson (Libertarian), Jill Stein (Green), and Virgil Goode (Constitution).

SOURCES: Congressional Quarterly's Guide to the U.S. Elections, *2nd ed. (Washington, D.C.: Congressional Quarterly, 1985), p. 224;* Congressional Quarterly Weekly Report, *November 5, 1988, p. 3184; Federal Election Commission, "1992 Official Presidential General Election Results," Press Release of January 14, 1993; Federal Election Commission, http://www.fec.gov/.*

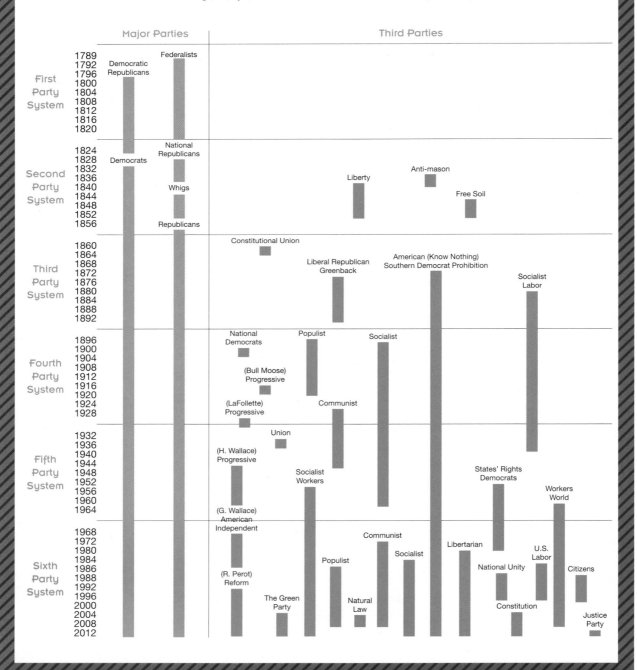

dominance, former President Theodore Roosevelt's Bull Moose Party garnered 27 percent of the popular vote and eighty-eight electoral votes, siphoning off enough votes from the Republican incumbent William Howard Taft to give the Democrat Woodrow Wilson the victory. (This was, by the way, the only time in American history that a **third party** actually outpolled one of the major parties in a presidential election.) In 1968, American Independent candidate George Wallace won 14 percent of the popular vote and forty-six electoral votes, probably drawing off enough votes from Democrat Hubert Humphrey to give Republican Richard Nixon the victory.

In 1992, independent presidential candidate Ross Perot, running under the banner of his United We Stand movement, garnered 19 percent of the popular vote, making his the most successful third-party movement in recent American history. Because Perot seemed to draw votes almost equally from Bush and Clinton, it is unlikely that he changed the outcome of the election. However, Perot participated in the three presidential debates and was instrumental in making deficit reduction and economic revival major issues in the campaign. Perot ran again in 1996, but only managed to gain about half of the total vote that he had earned in 1992. In 2000, Pat Buchanan ran on the Reform Party ticket, and Ralph Nader ran as a Green Party candidate. The two combined to garner over 3.3 million votes in a very tight election. Since Nader, who generated about 2.9 million of those votes, was a decidedly liberal candidate, some have suggested that he cost Gore the election. Such conclusions, however, overlook the fact that many Nader voters were disenchanted with the two-party system and might not have voted at all if Bush and Gore were the only choices available. The lesson Americans took away from that election, though, may have been that it is risky to vote for a minor party candidate during a close presidential race. In 2004, Pat Buchanan backed the incumbent Republican president and the Green Party refused to nominate Ralph Nader, choosing to go

Patrick Buchanan ran on the Reform Party ballot in 2000, but backed the Republican president in 2004. (Wikimedia Commons)

instead with a candidate who vowed to campaign only in states where the outcome was not expected to be close. Ultimately, less than one percent of the popular vote went to minor party candidates in 2004. This trend continued into 2008 and 2012. Given the many contrasts between the two major party candidates, voters largely stuck with the Democratic and Republican choices in 2008 and 2012, not providing more than 1 percent of the vote for any third party candidate.

7.4b A Complex Party Structure

An American political party is not a single organization but rather a broad family of related formal organizations and informal groupings. It is complex, not in the sense that it is particularly hard to understand, but in that it is made up of many different parts. Perhaps the most useful way to think about all these parts and the relationships between them is to imagine the party as being divided along two dimensions: a vertical dimension corresponding to the levels of government in the United States and a horizontal dimension corresponding to the different components that make up a party.

Parties and the Levels of Government: National, State, and Local

Because party organizations tend to develop and operate around institutions of government, it is only natural that their structure tends to parallel that of government. One of the most important divisions of government in the United States is the federal system.

third party

In the American political context, a minor party that attracts only a small share of the electorate's vote and is a party other than the two major parties that have dominated politics through most of American history

Just as the American government is divided into national, state, and local institutions, so also are parties divided into national, state, and local organizations and groupings. As in the government, the relationship among the levels is not a strictly hierarchical one; each level retains some level of independence and autonomy from the others.

Parties and Their Components: Formal, Electoral, and Governmental

Even at any one level of government, a political party is not just a single organization. Rather, it has at least three distinguishable sectors or components: the formal party organization, the party in the electorate, and the party in the government.[10] The **formal party organization** is the party narrowly construed and that which most people would think of if asked to define political party. It consists of the people who actually work for the party as leaders or followers, professionals or volunteers, and members of committees or attendees of meetings.

The formal structure of American parties parallels the structure of federalism. Power is vested at both the national and state levels. Ultimate authority lies with the party's **national convention**, which meets prior to the presidential election every four years. Because political parties exist to contest elections, most of what the convention does is related to the upcoming presidential campaign: writing a **platform** (a statement of the party's proposed program) and selecting the party's candidates for president and vice president. These activities are discussed in more detail in Chapter 8.

Some of the convention's activities have a more strictly organizational slant. The convention is the ultimate authority in setting the party's rules; and it formally designates the **national committee**, the permanent body that oversees the party's affairs on an ongoing basis. Each state's members on the national committee are usually picked by state party organizations in conventions or primaries. The national committee, in turn, formally elects the party chairperson. The national chairperson supervises the work of the headquarter staff, a role that has become more significant in recent years, for reasons to be seen shortly. In the presidential election year of 2012, the Democratic Party chairperson was Debbie Wasserman Schultz, a member of Congress from Florida. The Republican Party was led by Reince Priebus, an attorney and former chair of the Wisconsin Republican Party.

For years, state and local parties were the bedrock of the American party system, often due to the influence of state and local "political machines." A **political machine** is a political organization that recruits and controls its membership through the use of its governmental authority to bestow benefits on its supporters and withhold them from its opponents. This patronage includes benefits such as obtaining government jobs, government contracts, and "favors." To gain benefits, people had to support the machine by voting for its candidates and campaigning for the machine. The great urban political machines, in large part, have faded from the American political scene, although the use of public power to perpetuate partisan dominance lives on in many municipalities and some states.

The structure of the state and local parties is, in many respects, similar to that of the national parties with state party conventions and **state committees** that are usually made up of representatives from the state's counties or congressional districts. The party typically elects a state chairperson, who is in charge of the day-to-day operations of the party. Underlying the statewide party organization is a hierarchy of

---

What issues affect the public in your state?

The Public Interest Research Group's website is a good starting point for answering this question.

http://www.bvtlab.com/BH8T9

---

formal party organization

One of the three components or distinguishable sectors of a political party; the official structure of a political party and includes people who officially belong to it, elected and appointed officers, and committees

national convention

The quadrennial meeting of an American political party that focuses on the upcoming presidential election

platform

A broad statement of the philosophy and program under which a party's candidates run for election

national committee

The body responsible for guiding political party organization on an ongoing basis

political machine

Political organization that recruits and controls its membership through the use of its governmental authority to give benefits (jobs, contracts, etc.) to its supporters and deny them to its opponents

state committee

The body responsible for guiding a state political party organization on an ongoing basis

county, city, ward (or district), and precinct committees and chairpersons. In some locales this organization constitutes a formidable political force, while elsewhere the structure is moribund, with many of the positions not even filled.

There is more to a party than just its formal organization. A party includes, not in any formal sense but psychologically and socially, the citizens in the electorate who support it. This **party in the electorate** can be viewed in two different ways. At the individual level, the defining component of the connection of an individual to a party is party identification, "a psychological identification" or "sense of individual attachment to a party," independent of "legal recognition or even without a consistent [voting] record of party support."[11] Appropriate to the definition, party identification has typically been measured simply by asking people whether they think of themselves as Republicans, Democrats, Independents, and so on, and following up with questions about strength of feeling. Thus, the party in the electorate is really defined by people who claim to think of themselves as belonging to the party. Figure 7.4 shows how the distribution of party identification has varied over the last fifty years.

Individuals who identify with a party relate to it, not just as individuals, but also as members of the various groups to which they belong. Parties, in other words, can be seen as coalitions of the various social, economic, regional, and religious groups. The Democratic Party was traditionally seen as the party of the working class, the rural and southern constituents, and Catholics, whereas the Republican Party has been seen as the party of the upper classes, big businesses, and Protestants. These relationships have changed in recent years as new political battles have reshaped party lines, but the fact remains that both parties must rely on their appeal to large groups of the electorate to maintain their appeal. Thus, the party in the electorate also includes these groups that are thought of as belonging to the party's **coalition**.

Finally, there is the **party in the government**. Once a party's candidates are elected, the elected officials (at least in theory) need to organize themselves and work together to implement the policies on the basis of which they campaigned. Thus, the party in government consists of the elected candidates of a party—president, governors, mayors, senators, members of the House, state legislators, city council members—as well as the organizations these officials establish and the leaders they designate to help carry out their work. The most visible of these are the legislative party meetings (caucuses, as the Democrats call them, and conferences, as the Republicans call them), the congressional campaign committees, and the majority and minority leaders and whips. The party in government also includes, however, the less visible and informal "executive party" created by the president and governors who tend to appoint members of their own party to administrative positions, and even the shadowy "judicial party" suggested by patterns of party-oriented bloc voting in some courts.[12]

7.5 American Political Parties: Past, Present, and Future

The health of the American party system has been one of the most talked-about political subjects over the last forty years. To understand the current state of the American party system and what its future may be, it is necessary to understand a little about the history of the American party system.

party in the electorate

The individual citizens throughout the country who identify with a political party

coalition

A subgroup of a party, based on common social, economic, and religious characteristics

party in the government

One of the three components or sectors of a political party; the party as embodied in those of its members who have been elected or appointed to public office, the organizations they establish, and the leaders they choose to help them carry out their work

Figure 7.4 | Party Identification of the American Electorate, 1960–2014

The Democratic Party held a substantial edge in party identification from the 1960s into the 1970s, but Republican resurgence beginning in the 1980s eroded that edge. Today, more Americans identify as Independents than with either party.

SOURCE: *American National Election Studies, 2006; The Gallup Organization, 2014.*

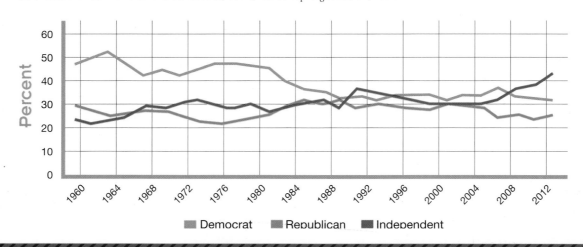

7.5a Parties Past

Political parties emerged early in the history of the American republic and have existed ever since. American history up through 1968 can be divided into six major **party systems** (see Figure 7.3). The first party system (1789–1824), which developed from the pre-Revolutionary alignment of parties paralleling the British system of the period (conservative Tories and progressive Whigs), pitted Federalists against Antifederalists. The two parties disagreed primarily on whether the new government should be relatively centralized and elite (the Federalist view) or decentralized and democratic (the Antifederalist view). The Federalist Party faded away after 1800; but the Democratic Republicans, as the Antifederalists came to be called, continued on to govern through a period of comparatively little national political conflict between 1815 and 1825, called the Era of Good Feelings.

By the mid-1820s, the weak framework of the Democratic Republican Party began to fall apart. Andrew Jackson emerged from this factional conflict as the founder of the Democratic Party, which continues as an active party today, making it the oldest party in the world. The Democrats confronted a new Whig party in the second party system (1824–1860). The Democrats were the party of lower-class rural and urban "working people" and old-fashioned machine politics, whereas the Whigs were the party of business and political reform. Slavery destroyed the Whig-Democratic party alignment; through the 1850s, both parties split into northern and southern branches over the issue that would soon tear apart the nation as well.

Beginning in 1860, under the third party system (1860–1896), former Whigs, led by Abraham Lincoln of Illinois, combined with some progressive remnants of the northern

party system

Period during which the pattern of support for political parties based on a particular set of important political issues remains reasonably stable

Democrats to form the new Republican Party, built on opposition to slavery and also on the idea of government as a promoter of commerce. The Democratic Party receded into the Confederacy during the Civil War. After the war and the restoration of the union, the Democrats reemerged on the national scene to compete vigorously with the Republicans for the favor of business. The pro-business tilt of the third party system fostered progressive and populist sentiment for more regulation of big business and protection of common people's interests.

Andrew Jackson, as depicted on the U.S. twenty-dollar bill, was the founder of the Democratic Party. Founded in the mid-1820s, the U.S. Democratic Party is still active, making it the oldest in the world today. (iStock)

These sentiments, fired by a series of disastrous recessions and depressions, came to a head in the election of 1896, when the populist Democrat William Jennings Bryan challenged the candidate of the business establishment, Republican William McKinley. The failure of the populist challenge marked the beginning of the fourth party system (1896–1932), throughout which the Republicans dominated the national political scene and allowed the capitalist system free reign. Only when former Republican President Teddy Roosevelt's progressive Bull Moose Party split Republican ranks were the Democrats able to put their candidate, Woodrow Wilson, into the White House from 1912 to 1920.

The onset of the Great Depression in 1929, in part the result of the lack of restraint placed on the free enterprise system, drove Republican President Herbert Hoover from office. Franklin Delano Roosevelt swept into the White House in 1932 on a flood tide of national discontent and despair. In a bold effort to use the power of the federal government to end the depression and restore economic prosperity, he ushered in a new era of governmental involvement in economic affairs and government responsibility for ensuring the people's basic well-being. FDR also initiated a period of Democratic dominance that constituted the fifth party system (1932–1968).

In each of these years—1824, 1860, 1896, and 1932—a new party system evolved from an old one in a relatively short period of turmoil and change called "realignment." **Realignment** occurs when a reasonably stable pattern of party support, based on a particular set of important political issues, is replaced by a new pattern of party support based on a new set of issues. Because realignments are such landmark events in the American party system, scholars have devoted much effort to determining when and why they occur. They have identified a number of significant changes that seem to accompany realignment, most notable of which is the period before each realignment in which the old party structure seems to fall apart, or **dealign**. Why do realignments occur? As the preceding discussion suggests, the single most important factor may be the emergence of some new issue that cuts across the existing party lines and divides the electorate in some new way—for example, slavery in the third party system, and the Great Depression and the role of the federal government in the economy in the fifth party system. Also, quite clearly, realignments have tended to come at approximately thirty-six-year intervals.

realignment

A major change in the pattern of support for political parties and the important issues on which that pattern of support is based

dealignment

Period during which the partisan ties of the public diminish and the party system breaks down

Beginning in the mid-1960s, the fifth party system began to falter. This was most evident in the woes of the Democratic Party, whose long-standing dominance began to unravel. Consistent with the pattern of a major partisan shift every thirty-six years, the Democratic Party, which had won the White House in every election over the thirty-six years from 1932 to 1968 except 1952 and 1956—seven of nine elections— lost the 1968 election; and over the next twenty years it would win only one of five more. The only bright spot for the Democrats was that they did manage, mostly, to hold on to their majorities in the House and Senate throughout the period; the one exception being the Republican's majority in the Senate from 1981 to 1987, which primarily was a result of the Reagan victory in 1980.

Reagan's presidential inauguration, 1981 (Wikimedia Commons)

That exception alone set political analysts abuzz. Dealignment was clearly underway. While some saw realignment into a new Republican majority in the offing, others worried that the party system was confronting an even more fundamental crisis—the possibility of complete collapse.

Certainly, beginning in the 1960s, both parties were beset by signs of deterioration. At the national level, the national party headquarters, the national chairperson, and the national committee seemed increasingly irrelevant to the course of American politics and to political campaigns, specifically. Their principal function seemed to be to organize the national party convention once every four years. The title of a study published in 1964 seemed to sum up their plight, "Politics Without Power: The National Party Committees."[13]

The party in the electorate, the mass base of the political parties, also showed signs of weakening. Through the early 1960s, more than 75 percent of the American people said that they identified strongly or weakly with one or the other of the parties and less than 25 percent described themselves as Independents. Beginning about 1964, attachments to parties started to weaken substantially. By the late 1970s only about 60 percent said that they identified with a party, and more than a third said they were Independents. Not only were people less likely to identify with the parties, voters were also less likely to see the parties in favorable terms and to vote according to their party identification.

Trouble loomed, as well, for the other aspect of the party in the electorate, the party coalitions. The coalitions that had supported the major parties, particularly the Democratic coalition, seemed to be coming apart. At its peak in the Johnson landslide, the Democratic Party had expanded to encompass not just the Roosevelt New Deal coalition of the working class, unions, the poor, urban residents, citizens of the South, Catholics, Jews, and liberals, but also African Americans. The Republican Party was left as the party of the upper class, big business, and people residing in the suburbs. Clearly through the 1970s and peaking in 1980, the Democratic coalition fell into disarray, as working-class people, Catholics and some Jews, and white Southerners were drawn away in the Reagan landslide and left the Democratic Party looking more and more like the party of liberals and African Americans—two groups too small to have much of a future as a winning coalition for the party.

The parties in government also suffered their own difficulties through the 1970s and 1980s as party discipline and coordination seemed to deteriorate. Party discipline seemed to sag in the Congress, as members less dependent on the party for help in getting reelected increasingly broke party ranks when local needs or special interest groups dictated.[14] Party coordination between the executive branch and the legislative branch suffered as presidents and members of their own party in Congress were often at odds on legislation.

What caused the parties to go into **decline**? A number of governmental, electoral, and socialization changes seem to have contributed to the deteriorating condition of American political parties since the mid-1960s. As noted earlier, patronage was one of the traditional reservoirs of party strength. It provided party leaders with bargaining chips to use in the game of politics, but reformers intent on reducing the power of the bosses and increasing the competence and integrity of public employees pushed for the establishment of a system of civil service. As more public jobs fell under civil service, politicians found themselves with fewer "goodies" to give out and were, thus, less able to marshal political support.

Another governmental change that hurt the parties was the rise of the public welfare system. The parties of earlier years built support by serving as a kind of informal welfare system for their supporters. A faithful party member in financial trouble could seek help in the form of money, food, or shelter from the neighborhood party organization. People came to owe the party. With the rise of the modern welfare system, the government itself formally began to ensure a minimal level of well-being among citizens. Consequently, the party lost its exclusive role as a source of help and its ability to put people in its debt.

Electoral changes played an important part in hurting the parties, as well. In earlier years, political parties were an essential part of the electoral apparatus of the United States. To get a message to the electorate, a candidate needed an army of workers to fan out over the constituency—buttonholing passersby, knocking on doors, handing out party literature, and twisting arms. Modern technology provides less labor-intensive alternatives. Nowadays, with a string of appearances on television news programs and in campaign advertisements, a candidate can make more frequent and seemingly more "personal" contact with far more voters than could an army of party workers on the streets. Computerized direct mailing and e-mailing techniques and smart use of social media like Facebook and Twitter can yield large sums of money, which can be used to buy more television time and send out more mail, which can generate more money, and so on. Simply put, candidates no longer need to rely as much on parties and party workers to serve as their intermediaries with the public.

Traditionally, parties have also been important sources of campaign funds for their candidates. Today, however, members of Congress benefit from the support of the PACs, and presidential candidates can rely on public financing. Access to these new sources of money has made candidates less dependent on parties for help and has, consequently, contributed to the weakening of the parties. Also, in an earlier era, parties tightly controlled the process by which candidates for public office were selected. Party leaders got together in party **caucuses** (meetings) or conventions to pick the party's candidates. However, political reformers fought to open up the nomination process to represent a broader cross section of the population, leading to selection of convention delegates by open conventions or primary elections.

decline

The idea that the American political parties are collapsing and may, perhaps, eventually disappear

caucus

A meeting of members of a political party or the members of a party in a legislature—also referred to as a party caucus; in some states used to select delegates to the national conventions, which nominate presidential candidates

Delegates from the state of Ohio listen to chairman of the Republican National Committee Reince Priebus during the abbreviated opening session of the Republican National Convention in Tampa, Florida, on August 27, 2012. (AP World Wide Photo)

Parties long existed as standing armies of campaign workers, ready to step into political battle on behalf of the party candidates. Now, more and more candidates are relying not on the party machinery but on their own personal organizations for campaign assistance. Although candidates obviously want to capitalize on their party's name, many run without the aid of the party machinery. Once in office, they are likely to feel little obligation to help the party. Single-issue groups also pose a challenge to the existing party system by threatening to siphon off precious campaign resources and public support. The antiabortion movement is perhaps the most prominent recent example.

Finally, most people acquire their sense of party identification through socialization by their parents, but that process of transmission has appeared to break down in recent years. Between the 1950s and the 1970s, the percentage of young people adopting the same party as their parents dropped by about 15 percent. Expansion of the Vietnam War tarnished both parties, the Republican Party was scarred by the Watergate scandal, and the Democratic Party suffered from the economically difficult Carter years. Party disenchantment in one generation sows party disenchantment in the next. Thus, it is not hard to understand why the ranks of the party faithful dwindled and the ranks of the Independents swelled.

Many of these changes were viewed with concern; analysts were not clear whether what was occurring was dealignment leading toward realignment or dealignment leading toward collapse. The deeper concern was that the weakening or disappearance of political parties might impair the functioning of our democratic system. Think of all the valuable functions parties perform, and then think about what might happen if the parties were not around to perform them.

Just as the idea that the parties were dead or dying began to gain widespread currency, a new group of commentators rose to argue that the parties were making a comeback. Led by Xandra Kayden and Eddie Mahe Jr.'s *The Party Goes On: The Persistence of the Two-Party System in the United States*,[15] a number of new studies found evidence of the parties in **resurgence**. The major center of revitalization in the formal party organizations has been within the national party organizations, particularly the national party headquarters supervised by the national chairperson and operated on a day-to-day basis by an increasingly professional, sophisticated, and well-paid staff. These staff employ modern data technology to gather and analyze polling results, conduct direct mail and e-mail campaigns, and raise money.

Although the American public has not flooded back to embrace the political parties, the trend against them has at least been arrested, perhaps even slightly reversed. There is also some evidence that the party coalitions are reforming along somewhat different lines. The Democratic Party has suffered from the loss of the white South and some working-class Catholic and union support, but it has gained a new constituency in female and racial and ethnic minority voters. The Republican Party has gained substantially among working-class whites and in the South.

resurgence

The idea that American political parties, following a period of decline from the 1960s to the early 1980s, are now making a comeback, gaining in organizational, electoral, and governmental strength

The primary reason for party resurgence is that the parties, instead of standing on the sidelines and allowing themselves to be kept out of the game, have at last recognized the changing environment of the American political system and adjusted their activities accordingly. For example, they have recognized that modern political campaigns depend less on armies of party volunteers tramping from door to door and more on money and the media. Thus, they have moved to become a major source of political money, in effect not fighting the PACs but joining them. They have seen how candidates must rely on a modern media campaign and have moved to provide candidates with the training and production services that they need to conduct such campaigns. They know that candidates want to use polling results and social media, so they share polling results and social media strategies and technologies.

7.5c Parties Future

Realignment, dealignment, and resurgence—it is hard enough to say where the American party system is now, much less where it is going. The Democrats' victory in the 1992 presidential election did not make the task any easier. Certainly some sort of realignment took place in the transition from the fifth party system's clear Democratic dominance to what seemed to be a sixth party system starting in 1968 of divided government—Republican domination of the presidency and Democratic domination of Congress. Was 1992 a return to Democratic dominance? Events since 1992 suggest that, despite Clinton's victory in 1992, we were still very much in the era of divided government. United Democratic governance lasted only until the 1994 midterm elections when the Republican Party won majorities in both the House and Senate. Clinton won reelection in 1996; his last six years in office were a continuation of the dealignment era's divided government pattern, although this time with a Democratic president and Republican Congress.

At first, the 2000 election looked to be another opportunity for realignment as the Republicans gained unified control of the government for the first time since the Eisenhower administration. George W. Bush's opportunity to lead a united Congress, however, was even shorter-lived than Clinton's had been. After the election, the Senate stood evenly divided, with fifty Democrats and fifty Republicans. The Republicans maintained a procedural majority because Vice President Dick Cheney, in his role as president of the Senate, could break any tie votes. In May 2001, however, Jim Jeffords, a third-term senator from Vermont, left the Republican Party. This action provided Democrats with a fifty to forty-nine majority and returned the nation to divided party government. Since the Republicans reestablished their majority in 2002, the 2004 election was seen by many as a potential turning point. Republican victory would solidify arguments for the party's resurgence, while a Democratic victory in the presidential race could spell a return to divided government. Although the campaign was neck and neck up to the very end, the Republican Party emerged victorious, winning the presidency and strengthening majorities in both the House and Senate. The year 2006 spelled a reversal of fortune for the Republicans with Democrats regaining the majority in both the House and the Senate for the first time in a dozen years. The Democratic victory created another period of divided government, once again calling into question the future direction and momentum of American political parties.

The 2008 campaign was another important moment for the two political parties. Barack Obama and the Democratic Party rode to victory on a wave of dissatisfaction with a faltering economy. Gaining support from new voters and younger voters, turnout was the highest it had been in four decades; and the Democrats gained seats in both the House and Senate, as well as claiming a decisive victory in the presidential race.

BVT *Lab*

Flashcards are available for this chapter at www.BVTLab.com.

Chapter 07 | Interest Groups and Political Parties | 230

The Republican Party's only modest success was in maintaining at least forty Senate seats—the number required to make a viable filibuster threat.

Partly as a result of the 2008 election, and partly in reaction to "big government" proposals to stimulate a stalled economy, a movement adopting the moniker "tea party" emerged in 2009. By mid-2010, an organization called the Tea Party Patriots could boast of hundreds of local chapters and over one hundred thousand members nationwide. The organization identifies its core values as fiscal responsibility, constitutionally limited government, and free markets.[16] Is this "party" more like a political party, or more like an interest group? Thus far, they have campaigned on behalf of (or against) particular candidates, but have not sought recognition on the ballot. Officially, the Tea Party remains non-partisan, but whether it will emerge as a third party in the future remains to be seen. In any event, the movement's priorities likely helped the Republicans gain a majority in the House of Representatives in 2010. The movement was not well-represented by either candidate in the 2012 presidential election—where President Obama handily defeated Mitt Romney. Tea Party adherents did play a role in securing some Republican seats in the 2014 midterm elections, but some of the Republican primary candidates they supported held extreme positions that likely worked to the advantage of the Democrats in other districts.

Is the recent resurgence of the parties just the last gasp of a dying system? Some critics think that it is and that the two-party system is really on its last legs;[17] however, the parties' comeback probably represents a broader and more permanent change. Through much of American history, political parties were decentralized because political power in the United States was decentralized. Political power has become more centralized; and parties, although slow to react, have now adapted to that new reality with stronger central party organizations. It makes little sense to think that parties will move again toward decentralization unless the government does—and that does not appear to be in the offing. Similarly, the resurgence of the national party organizations occurred in response to the rise of the modern media campaign and the increased demand for campaign money. It would make sense to think that the organizations would again wither away only if the media and money somehow became less important, but there is no sign that such changes are on the immediate horizon.

Of course, this analysis does not take into account the many other factors that might change and affect the parties, either strengthening or weakening them. The recent episode of decline and resurgence, though, does teach us something about parties that is useful when contemplating their future: The parties have demonstrated an ability to adapt to changing circumstances—not always quickly, not always entirely successfully, but eventually and sufficiently. Unforeseen social and political changes involving circumstances hardly envisioned in this chapter may occur and lay the parties low again; past experience, however, suggests that parties—perhaps not exactly as we know them today, but parties nevertheless—will adapt again.

CHAPTER REVIEW

1. Groups are an essential element in the functioning of the American democratic system. A group's political effectiveness depends on its size, the strength of its members' identification, its proximity to politics, its internal organization, and its closeness to the broader societal consensus.

2. Interest groups engage in a wide array of politically relevant activities. They press their views on their own membership, the general public, and the political elites of the legislative, executive, and judicial branches. One of their most potent weapons of late has been the political action committee (PAC).

3. Some of the major group participants in the American political process are based on different interests: economically based groups, such as the Chamber of Commerce of the United States and the AFL-CIO; socially based groups, such as the National Organization for Women (NOW) and the National Association for the Advancement of Colored People (NAACP); ideological groups, such as the liberal Americans for Democratic Action; single-issue groups, such as the right-to-life and pro-choice movements; and public interest groups, such as Common Cause, the "citizens' lobby."

4. The role that interest groups play in a democratic society is as controversial as it is pervasive. Pluralistic theory sees interest groups as working to overcome the deficiencies of individual citizens and to perpetuate a functioning democracy. Other perspectives see interest groups as failing to serve their own members' interests, the public interest, or both.

5. In a democracy, political parties try to influence public policy by backing members as candidates in elections to public offices. In the course of getting their members elected to public office, political parties perform a number of important functions for the system of government: socializing citizens, pulling together the diverse interests contending in a society, simplifying the alternatives confronting the voters, structuring campaigns and elections, recruiting and training political leaders, and organizing and coordinating government.

6. The American party system is a two-party system, probably due primarily to the plurality election system commonly used in the United States and the generally centrist distribution of political beliefs in America. The parties are characterized by a relatively loose relationship among their component parts—divided into national, state, and local at one level and into formal party organization, the party in the electorate, and the party in the government at another level.

KEY TERMS

Readings for Further Study

James Madison's *Federalist* No. 10 remains mandatory reading for anyone interested in exploring the role of groups in American political life.

A more modern, yet classic, study is *The Governmental Process* (Berkeley: Public Policy Press, 1993) by David Truman.

Interest groups are important elements in the pluralist perspective on American democracy. Robert A. Dahl sets out that perspective most clearly in *Who Governs?* 2nd ed. (New Haven, CT: Yale University Press, 2005). Another important work is *Interest Group Politics*, 8th ed. (Washington, D.C.: CQ Press, 2011) edited by Allan J. Cigler and Burdett A. Loomis.

As a central feature of American politics, parties are one of the most written-about of all American political institutions. V. O. Key Jr. provides a classic description of the role that parties play in the American political system in *Politics, Parties, and Pressure Groups*, 5th ed. (New York: Crowell, 1964).

Jeffrey M. Stonecash's *Political Parties Matter: Realignment and the Return of Partisan Voting* (Boulder: Lynne Rienner, 2005) offers a historical perspective on the parties, centering on the notion of realignment.

Good overviews of the changing role of American parties are *The State of the Parties*, 6th ed. (Lanham, MD: Rowman & Littlefield, 2010), edited by John C. Green and Daniel J. Coffey, and Marjorie Randon Hershey's *Party Politics in America*, 16th ed. (New York: Pearson, 2014).

Theda Skocpol and Vanessa Williamson give an account of the most recent party and interest group phenomenon in *The Tea Party and the Remaking of Republican Conservatism* (New York: Oxford, 2013).

A good account of the future of political parties is Larry J. Sabato and Bruce Larson, *The Party's Just Begun*, 2nd ed. (New York: Longman, 2009). Theodore J. Lowi and Joseph Romance debate the fundamentals of a two-party system in *A Republic of Parties?* (Lanham, MD: Rowman & Littlefield, 1998).

Notes

1. The ideas in this section and the next are drawn in part from the seminal discussion of group influences in politics in Angus Campbell, Philip E. Converse, Warren E. Miller, and Donald E. Stokes, *The American Voter* (New York: Wiley, 1960), pp. 295–332.

2. 572 U.S. ___ (2014).

3. *Citizens United v. FEC*, 558 U.S. 50 (2010).

4. Statistical Abstract of the United States, 2012.

5. U.S. Census Bureau, "The Diversifying Electorate—Voting Rates by Race and Hispanic Origin in 2012," May 2013.

6. The leading advocate of this point of view is Robert A. Dahl. See, for example, his classic book *Who Governs?* (New Haven, CT: Yale University Press, 1961).

7. Robert J. Samuelson, "Interest Group Gridlock," *National Journal* (September 25, 1982): 1642.

8. Jonathan Rauch, "Demosclerosis," *National Journal* (September 5, 1992): 1998–2003.

9. V. O. Key, Jr., *Politics, Parties, and Pressure Groups*, 5th ed. (New York: Crowell, 1964), p. 656.

10. This distinction is another legacy of V. O. Key Jr., originated in his *Politics, Parties, and Pressure Groups*. (New York: It has now been widely adopted by students of the American party system. See, for example, Frank J. Sorauf and Paul Allen Beck, *Party Politics in America*, 6th ed. (Glenview, IL: Scott, Foresman, 1988).

11. Campbell, et al., *The American Voter*, pp. 121–122.

12. Sorauf and Beck, *Party Politics in America*, pp. 396–446.

13. Cornelius P. Cotter and Bernard C. Hennessy (New York: Atherton, 1964).

14. William J. Keefe, *Parties, Politics, and Public Policy in America* (Hinsdale, MN: Dryden Press, 1976), pp. 139–140; Barbara Sinclair Deckard, "Political Upheaval and Congressional Voting: The Effects of the 1960s on Voting Patterns in the House of Representatives," *Journal of Politics 38* (1976): 326–345.

15. New York: Basic Books, 1985.

16. Tea Party Patriots, "Mission Statement and Core Values," http://www.teapartypatriots.org/Mission.aspx (June 14, 2010).

17. Theodore Lowi, "The Party Crasher," *The New York Times Magazine* (August 23, 1992): 28–33.

POP QUIZ

1. Interest groups, legislators, and administrators are sometimes called the _____ _____ of American politics.

2. America has been known as the _____ _____ society because it consists of people of all races and nationalities.

3. The tendency for different coalitions to form on different issues is called _____ _____.

4. One of the _____ functions of parties is to educate citizens and mobilize them into political action.

5. The increase in party identification since 1978 has primarily benefited the _____ Party.

6. Most PACs are registered with the Federal Election Commission.   T   F

7. The influence of the Christian Right declined dramatically in the late 1980s.   T   F

8. Political parties are formally sanctioned in Article III, Section 4 of the Constitution.   T   F

9. Third parties have had very little influence on the American political system.   T   F

10. The increase in the number of single-issue interest groups has contributed to the resurgence of political parties based on new coalitions.   T   F

11. The major means by which interest groups try to create public support or sympathy for their political goals is/are _____.

    A) the mass media

    B) direct mail

    C) opinion leaders

    D) political action committees

12. The iron triangle of American politics consists of which of the following?

    A) interest group representatives, legislators, and judges

    B) Congress, the presidency, and the Supreme Court

    C) interest group representatives, legislators, and administrators

    D) interest group representatives, PACs, and political candidates

13. In recent years the most important political issue concerning religious groups has been _____.

    A) the Middle East conflict

    B) abortion

    C) school prayer

    D) poverty

14. When a pluralistic system becomes paralyzed from too many interest groups refusing to compromise, this is known as interest group _____.

    A) gridlock

    B) anarchy

    C) elitism

    D) cleavage

15. Each party system evolved from its predecessor in a relatively short period of political turmoil and change called _____.

    A) factionalization

    B) dealignment

    C) realignment

    D) anarchy

ANSWERS:
1. iron triangle   2. melting pot   3. cross-cutting cleavage
4. socialization   5. Republican   6. T   7. T   8. F   9. F
10. F   11. A   12. C   13. B   14. A   15. C

Chapter

08

Campaigns and Elections

In This Chapter

Chapter Objectives

In a campaign and the election that concludes it, all the actors in the political process come into vigorous interplay. Parties begin selecting and promoting candidates. Interest groups mobilize their forces to ensure that their interests will be remembered. The mass media put politics more clearly and consistently at center stage. As a result, the public, whose interest in political affairs is generally limited, now turns its attention to the candidates vying for public office.

This chapter examines the process from the perspectives of the two principal types of players in the drama: voters and candidates. For voters, the basic questions are whether to vote and how to vote. Candidates, whether presidential or congressional, must devise strategies that will bring voters to the polls and attract their votes. They must pull together the financial resources and organization needed for a credible campaign, obtain the nomination of their parties, and compete against the other party's candidate in the general election campaign.

8.1 The Voter's Perspective: To Vote or Not to Vote

As discussed in Chapter 5, politics is not usually a matter of concern to most citizens. Their interest is most aroused around Election Day—when they begin to take note of the campaign, think about going to the polls to cast their ballots, and

First Lady Michele Obama campaigning in Las Vegas on October 26, 2012 (Shutterstock)

sometimes engage in activities related to the campaign. Many begin to follow it on television or in newspapers and talk about it with family and friends; some try to influence the way in which someone else will vote. A somewhat smaller number wear buttons, display stickers or signs on their cars or houses, post about candidates or positions on social media, and attend campaign meetings, rallies, speeches, or dinners. A few actually work for or give money to a candidate or party. Even with these other kinds of campaign-related activities, voting remains the most frequent act of political participation and the most meaningful act as well. In a representative democracy, voting forges the essential link between the citizens and their government. In the end, then, it comes down to two basic decisions: whether to vote and how to vote.

8.1a Voting Requirements and Eligibility

Not everyone is in a position to decide to vote. The law excludes some people. In fact, for more than one hundred years after the founding of the United States, a majority of the American people were not eligible to vote. During that period the states controlled who could or could not vote, and they typically limited the electorate to white males over the age of twenty-one. Since then the United States has made great strides in eliminating restrictions on voting.

Racial barriers to voting began to fall first. The **Fifteenth Amendment** (1870) outlawed denying the right of citizens to vote on the grounds of "race, color, or previous condition of servitude." Nevertheless, after the Civil War the South created a new system of inferior status for African Americans, which came to be called "Jim Crow." Jim Crow included several elements limiting African American voting. One element was the white primary. As discussed in Chapter 3, in the one-party South of the post-Reconstruction era, winning the Democratic primary was equivalent to an election because the general election was nearly always a rout of the disfavored Republicans. The Democratic Party routinely excluded African Americans from its primaries, thus effectively barring them from any meaningful role in the electoral process. The Supreme Court in *Smith v. Allwright* struck down the white primary in 1944.

Another element of Jim Crow was the **poll tax**, which stipulated that in order to vote, citizens had to pay a tax. This tax was often enforced cumulatively, meaning that people had to pay the tax for every previous election in which they had not voted. Because African Americans had not been able to vote in many previous elections, they were confronted with large cumulated poll taxes that they could not pay. Thus, they were excluded from voting. However, the **Twenty-fourth Amendment** prohibited

Fifteenth Amendment

Outlawed race-based restrictions on voting

poll tax

A tax on voting, applied discriminatorily to African Americans under "Jim Crow" in the post–Civil War South

Twenty-fourth Amendment

Adopted in 1964, this amendment forbids the use of poll taxes in federal elections. Since 1966 the Court has applied this proscription to state elections as well.

poll taxes in federal elections in 1964, and the Supreme Court's decision in *Harper v. Virginia State Board of Elections*, in 1966, prohibited them in state elections.

A third element of Jim Crow was the literacy test. In order to vote, a person had to demonstrate the ability to read. Many African Americans at that time were illiterate, so they were, thereby, excluded. This requirement was prohibited by the **Voting Rights Act of 1965**, which waived literacy tests for anyone with a sixth-grade education. The Voting Rights Act of 1965 and subsequent amendments in 1982 and 2006 took other important steps to protect African American voting rights, as discussed in Chapter 3.

While African American participation declined under Jim Crow, political pressures to grant **female suffrage**, the right of women to vote, increased. This movement, stirred to life in the early nineteenth century, achieved its first major success when the territory of Wyoming granted suffrage to women in 1869. Activists first coalesced into two competing organizations with somewhat different styles—the more militant National Woman Suffrage Association led by Susan B. Anthony and the more conservative American Woman Suffrage Association led by Lucy Stone. The two groups joined forces in 1890. Final success was not achieved on the national level until 1920, when the states ratified the **Nineteenth Amendment**, which gave women the right to vote.

The last major broadening of the electorate occurred in 1971, when the **Twenty-sixth Amendment** reduced the voting age from twenty-one to eighteen. In the midst of the Vietnam War, the argument that people old enough to die for their country ought to be able to vote in their country's elections was very persuasive. In addition, both Republicans and Democrats hoped to capitalize on the large bloc of new voters. In combination with the coming of age of the post–World War II baby boom generation, the lowering of the voting age produced one of the greatest expansions of the electorate in American history.

The laws of the United States generally exclude from voting people who are not citizens of this country. Some other voting laws differ widely from state to state. In most states, people who have been convicted of a felony or who are confined in prisons and mental institutions cannot vote. Most jurisdictions also typically exclude citizens who have not resided within their boundaries for a minimum amount of time. This law is intended to ensure that citizens are reasonably permanent residents of the community. Impediments to voting imposed by lengthy **residence requirements** were weakened substantially by the **Voting Rights Act of 1970**, which mandated that states require no more than thirty days' residency to establish eligibility to vote in presidential elections. Today the thirty-day maximum is standard for all elections, even though some states have selected shorter periods.

Beyond meeting the basic qualifications, potential voters in most places in the United States (all states except North Dakota) are required to **register**—that is, to enter their names on the local government's list of those eligible to vote in a particular area, usually by visiting a government office. This requirement poses enough of an inconvenience that many people do not bother. Recent studies have shown, in fact, that the registration requirement may reduce electoral participation by as much as 10 to 15 percent.[1] Because registration reduces voting, it has long been the target of political reformers. Some places now permit registration by mail or via the Internet, and a few allow citizens to register on Election Day, even at the same time and place as they vote. Such arrangements seem to make a difference. Eight states have implemented these same-day registration laws, with advocates claiming a significant reduction in voters being turned away at the polls for lack of registration.[2]

Recognizing the important role played by registration laws, Congress passed the National Voter Registration Act of 1993, also known as the "Motor Voter" law

BVT *Lab*

Improve your test scores. Practice quizzes are available at www.BVTLab.com.

239

Chapter 08 | Campaigns and Elections

Voting Rights Act of 1965

Major legislation designed to overcome racial barriers to voting, primarily in the southern states—extended in 1982 for twenty-five years and again in 2006

female suffrage

The right of women to vote, which was bestowed nationally by the Nineteenth Amendment in 1920

Nineteenth Amendment

Constitutional amendment of 1920 giving women the right to vote

Twenty-sixth Amendment

Constitutional amendment adopted in 1971 that fixed the minimum voting age at eighteen years

residence requirements

State laws designed to limit the eligible electorate by requiring citizens to have been a resident of the voting district for a fixed period of time prior to an election

Voting Rights Act of 1970

The law that limited residence requirements to thirty days for presidential elections, further ensuring voting rights

register

To place one's name on the list of citizens eligible to vote

Voters are required to register if they wish to vote. The inconvenience of this alone deters many residents from voting at all; therefore, many states have passed legislation to allow same-day registration. (iStock)

since it required voter registration to be made available at the state Departments of Motor Vehicles. Over fifteen million Americans registered to vote via their state motor vehicle agency in 1997–98. Partly as a result of this new law, registration rates climbed to over 70 percent in 1998, the highest level in a congressional election year since 1970. It is important to note that this piece of legislation passed was during a period of unified Democratic government. Many prior proposals had failed primarily because of Republican opposition. The historical pattern has been for Republicans to oppose such measures and for Democrats to support them. The Democrats generally emphasize the virtues of higher turnout, whereas the Republicans worry about opening the door to fraud.[3] These positions are also consistent with strategic considerations for each party, as demographic data suggest that increased registration and turnout would help Democrats and hurt Republicans.

8.1b Who Votes?

Voting turnout varies with people's social characteristics and psychological and political attitudes, as well as with the circumstances of voting. Voting participation used to vary dramatically across a wide variety of social groupings in the United States. Whites were much more likely to vote than African Americans, men were more likely to vote than women, and so on. In recent years there has been a general convergence in the voting rates among various groups of citizens. This is partly due to the success of the long struggle to ensure equal access to the voting booth. Just as significant, the broader trend toward social and economic equality has tended to promote political equality.

Two social characteristics show the strongest relation to voting turnout: age and education. (A third important factor is discussed in "Politics and Economics: Turnout, Choice, and Economic Status.") The older a person is, the more likely that person is to vote. One reason is that older people move less often and therefore do not need to re-register as often. Young people are more likely to be away from their place of residence—for example, at college or in the military. Because voting by absentee ballot takes more forethought and is more difficult than voting in person, young people are more likely to be discouraged from voting. They are also more preoccupied with getting a start in life than with relatively remote political concerns. As people grow older, they have more time and inclination to participate in politics and consequently build a habit of voting.

The more educated a person is, the more likely he or she is to vote. Slightly

Voting turnout varies with people's social characteristics, psychological and political attitudes, and circumstances of voting. (iStock)

Turnout, Choice, and Economic Status

Economic status influences voter turnout. For example, as Figure 8A shows, the higher a citizen's income, the more likely the citizen is to vote. This pattern emerges, in part, because higher income encourages many of the factors that promote voting, particularly education, political interest, and efficacy.

Voting choice is also influenced by economic status. As Figure 8B shows, in 2012 the higher a citizen's income, the more likely the citizen was to vote for Mitt Romney. This tendency of higher-income people to favor Republican candidates has also been observed in many previous elections. It results primarily because higher-income people tend to identify with the Republican Party, as discussed in Chapter 7, and because Republican identifiers tend to vote for Republican candidates.

These two factors combine to hurt Democratic candidates and help Republican candidates. Democratic candidates have a greater following among lower-income people, but those people turn out to vote less often. Republican candidates have a greater following among higher-income people, who vote more often. This is one reason why the Republicans, even as the minority party in terms of population, have been so successful in getting their candidates elected to public office.

What other reasons are there for the Republicans' success in winning elections, even though they have been in the minority for so long?

SOURCES: U.S. Census Bureau, Current Population Survey, November 2012; The New York Times, President Exit "Polls," 2012.

Figures 8A and 8B | The Higher the Income of a Voter's Family, the More Likely That Citizen Is to Vote

Figure 8A | Voting Turnout by Family Income, 2012

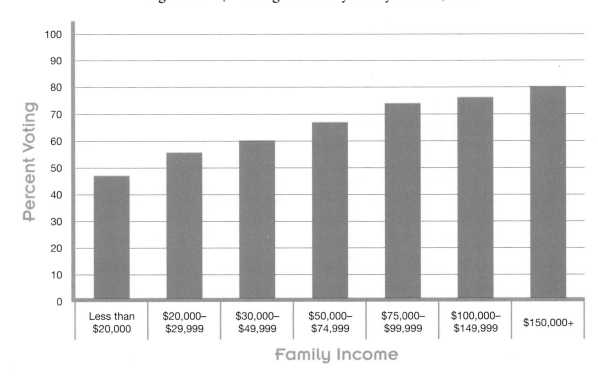

Continued on next page

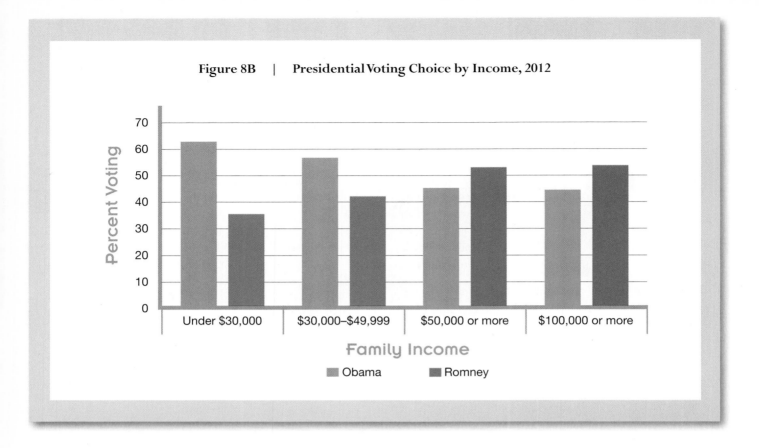

Figure 8B | Presidential Voting Choice by Income, 2012

more than 37 percent of the voting-age population with less than a high school education voted in 2012, whereas over 75 percent of those with a college degree or graduate-school education voted. Education plays such a big role because it stimulates political interest and provides the information that people need to be effective participants in the political process. Differences in education have undoubtedly contributed to voting differences between social groups in the past. African Americans and women voted less often than white males, in part because they did not enjoy the benefits of education that white males did. With the recent expansion of educational opportunities for minorities and women, levels of voting for these groups have approached those for white males. In fact, the Census Bureau reported that in the 2012 presidential election women voted at a significantly higher rate than men—64 percent to 60 percent.

Psychological influences play a role as well. Not surprisingly, the greater a person's interest in politics, the more likely the person is to vote. The more a citizen thinks he or she can accomplish politically (i.e., the more political efficacy he or she has), the greater the likelihood the person will vote. Partisanship is a powerful motivating force. The stronger a person's attachment to a political party, the more inclined that person will be to vote. Conservatives and liberals are slightly more likely to vote than moderates, probably because they tend to be more interested and partisan. However, some psychological factors thought to have a major impact on turnout really do not. Surprisingly, despite much attention in the late 1960s and early 1970s, trust—defined as reliance on the integrity of public officials—has little effect. Overall, in 2012, about 57.5 percent of eligible voters cast a ballot for president.

Finally, primarily as a result of differences in psychological factors, turnout varies substantially across the different types of elections. In elections that the public finds interesting and important, so-called **high-stimulus elections**, turnout is usually relatively high; in less interesting, **low-stimulus elections**, it is usually low.[4] Presidential

high-stimulus election

Election that the public finds interesting and important

low-stimulus election

Election that the public finds uninteresting or unimportant

Figure 8.1 | Turnout in Presidential and Congressional Elections, 1790–2014

Since the end of the nineteenth century, the long-term historical trend for voter turnout has been downward. Turnout for midterm congressional elections is lower than in presidential elections.

SOURCES: *Harold W. Stanley and Richard G. Niemi,* Vital Statistics on American Politics *(Washington, D.C.: CQ Press, 1990); Federal Election Commission; United States Election Project, http://www.electproject.org/home/voter-turnout/voter-turnout-data (November 5, 2014).*

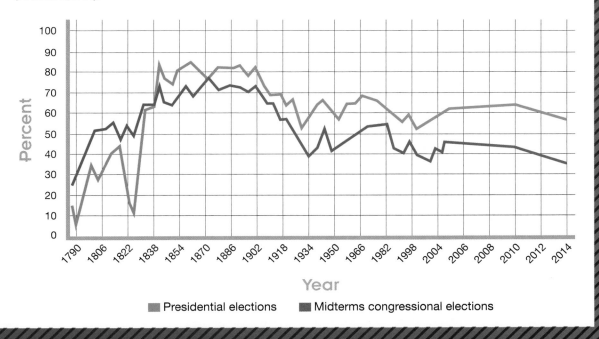

Presidential elections   Midterms congressional elections

elections are generally higher stimulus than congressional elections, and general elections are usually higher stimulus than the primary elections that precede them. Turnout in recent presidential elections has averaged between 50 and 60 percent, while turnout in congressional elections has run between 35 and 40 percent. Voting rates in presidential general elections also typically far exceed the turnout rates of 30 percent or less observed in primary elections.

8.1c Declining Turnout

Although presidential voting nearly reached the 60 percent mark in 2008, the highest level since 1968, this figure fell slightly in 2012, and there remains a troubling long-term trend toward lower voter turnout in the United States, as shown in Figure 8.1. After an explosion in the early nineteenth century, owing to the expansion of the electorate discussed earlier in this chapter, voter turnout by the 1990s had fallen to one of its lowest points in the last 150 years and had sagged substantially since its post–World War II peak in 1960. Although the long-term trend in turnout is striking, it is not necessarily ominous. The greatest part of the decline took place in the late-nineteenth and early-twentieth centuries. Some theorists attribute this to growing disaffection for the political system,[5] but other factors were probably involved.

Campaign and Electoral Reform: A Comparative Perspective

Opponents of campaign and electoral reform often contend that changing the current system will upset the finely tuned balance of the American political system and impair the functioning of democracy. Proponents point, however, to other countries with different systems that work just fine.

One criticism of American presidential campaigns is that they go on too long, close to two years counting the run-up to the primaries and then the general election campaign. Congressional campaigns, in a sense, never stop. As soon as members of Congress take office in January, they must begin to look to the next election "only" twenty-two months away. Clearly other nations, particularly those with parliamentary systems, accomplish the process much more quickly. The best example is Great Britain where the span from the announcement of an election to the new government's taking office is little more than a month.

Another area of comparison is in campaign finance. The United States has partial public funding of presidential campaigns and no public funding of congressional campaigns. Acceptance of public funding binds presidential candidates to some limits, but there are no limits on what congressional candidates can spend. Even the effort to limit presidential spending, however, can be partially circumvented by a wealthy candidate who can decline public funds—such as George W. Bush in the 2000 and 2004 election cycles—or a well-funded one like Barack Obama in 2008 and 2012 and Mitt Romney in 2012. Britain, Israel, and Japan have no public funding whatsoever. Britain and Japan do impose limits on spending while Israel does not. Denmark, France, Italy, and Germany all have public funding based on strength in the previous election or a reimbursement according to strength in the current election.

A third point of comparison is in the use of television in campaigns. Of the eight countries just mentioned, the United States is the only one that does not provide free television time to candidates for public office (apart from debates between candidates, which broadcasters cover, at their discretion, as news events). Most of the countries above provide free and equal time in proportion to the parties' strength in the previous election.

Do the successes of other countries with shorter campaigns and different arrangements for campaign finance and television use mean that such reforms would work well in the United States? What differences between the United States and these other countries might make the impact of such reforms differ?

The widespread imposition of voter registration systems lowered turnout, both by excluding fraudulent votes and by discouraging some honest ones.[6] Moreover, Jim Crow laws in the South wiped out the gains made among African American voters in the years after the Civil War.

The Nineteenth Amendment, which enlarged the electorate by giving women the right to vote, temporarily reduced turnout. Many women had never voted before and did not immediately begin to exercise the right. As women, particularly younger women, got used to the newly opened political world, turnout climbed steadily through the 1930s. World War II disrupted voting interest, but interest bounced back in the 1950s. Demographic and institutional changes reduced voter turnout in the 1960s and 1970s. The maturation of the postwar baby boom and the reduction of the voting age from twenty-one to eighteen added millions of new voters; but because younger citizens are not as likely to vote as older people, this actually decreased the figures for turnout as a percentage of the voting-age population.

Yet many observers still believe that deep-seated psychological inclinations account for some of the contemporary decrease. Some blame political alienation or distrust. They argue that the American people are discouraged by what they see going on in politics and are increasingly inclined, therefore, not to vote. However, as noted earlier, trust does not seem to have much effect on voting; so an increase in distrust does not necessarily imply a decrease in voting. In fact, many of the new voters in the 2000s seem to have been motivated more by the emergence of a national campaign by the Green Party than anything else. On the other hand, decreasing partisanship and external political efficacy clearly relate to voting turnout.[7] Young people are less partisan, and less partisan people are less likely to vote. It may, therefore, be that weakening partisanship is due to the influx of young people into the electorate, resulting in a decline in voting.

Some commentators view the long-term decline in voter turnout with alarm. The success of democracy, they argue, depends on the enthusiastic participation of its citizens; thus, declining electoral involvement is not a good sign. However, other commentators believe that less than total participation may be desirable

American people are discouraged by what they see going on in politics and are more inclined not to vote. However, an increase in distrust does not necessarily imply a decrease in voting. Many new voters seem to have been motivated more by the emergence of a national campaign by the Green Party than anything else. (iStock)

because it can give a democracy room for compromise and flexibility.[8] Nonvoting may not imply a lack of trust or support for the political system but is perhaps a passive nonvote of confidence. In other words, staying home on Election Day may just be a way of saying that everything is all right.

8.2 The Voter's Perspective: How to Vote

Just as various political, social, and psychological factors contribute to citizens' decisions about whether to exercise their voting rights, different elements help determine for whom they cast their ballots. Analysts have identified three major factors that seem to influence how people vote: parties, candidates, and issues.

8.2a Parties

For many years, affiliation with a political party was regarded as the mainstay of voting decisions in the United States. For some people, all that mattered was that a candidate belonged to "their" party. However, voter allegiance was not the only impact of strong party affiliation. In many instances party identification colored the way in which a voter looked at the pivotal elements of a presidential election. Party continues to play an important role in American electoral behavior. The 2012 presidential race illustrates the strong relationship between how people vote and their sense of partisanship. Eighty-seven percent of Democrats reported plans to vote for the candidate of their party, while only 8 percent planned to cross party lines to vote for Romney. Moreover, 90 percent of Republicans planned to vote for the candidate of their party, while only 6 percent planned to defect to Obama.[9]

Yet, as established in Chapter 7, there can be little doubt that party has weakened as a reference point for many American voters in recent years. As party has become less important to voters, it has become a less important determinant of their voting decisions, which has left more room for candidate characteristics and issues to have an influence.

8.2b Candidates

Opinions about the candidates themselves play a powerful role in influencing how voters ultimately vote. Because partisanship is fairly stable, assessments of the candidates are major contributors to changes in presidential voting from one election to the next.[10] When it comes to qualities of the candidate, voters seem to put the greatest weight on three factors:

- *Experience*   The public shows a marked preference for someone with substantial political experience. Hence, the public leans very much toward incumbent presidents, vice presidents, senators, and governors from large states. The only recent presidents without substantial national political experience prior to taking office were Dwight Eisenhower (1953–1961), who had extensive military experience, and Jimmy Carter (1977–1981), the governor of a smaller state, Georgia. Although Bill Clinton (1993–2001) was the governor of a small southern state, he had been active on the national scene for many years as a leader in the National Governors Association and the Democratic Leadership Council. In the 2008 campaign, many of John McCain's advertisements focused on the candidate's long tenure in the Senate as compared to his opponent's much shorter tenure. By 2012, however, President Obama could point to four years in the White House, so lack of experience was no longer an issue. Having served as governor of a populous state, Mitt Romney could boast of political experience as well.

- *Leadership*   The public is partial toward candidates who seem able to take command of a situation, who do not wallow in pessimism or indecision, and who act when the time is right. President Carter suffered in the 1980 campaign because in the face of economic problems and the Iranian hostage crisis, he was not seen as taking decisive and effective action. Twelve years later, in 1992, George H. W. Bush was hurt by the widespread public perception that he had no plan for addressing the economic problems besieging the country. His son must have learned a lesson from this as his efforts to project the image of a strong, decisive leader consistently resulted in high marks on this quality in opinion polls. Senator Hillary Clinton (D–NY) capitalized on this public attitude early in the Democratic primary in 2008, when her campaign ran a commercial suggesting that she was the candidate voters should trust in an emergency.

- *Personal qualities*   At the same time that voters want someone who will be a strong leader, they are also inclined to want an attractive and "nice" person in the White House. Eisenhower, Kennedy (1961–1963), and Reagan (1981–1989) all benefited from attractive personalities. Bill Clinton's campaign in 1992 mounted a major effort to offset early perceptions of him as dishonest and untrustworthy—"Slick Willy"—with an image-rebuilding effort that campaign insiders dubbed the "Manhattan Project" after the World War II program to develop the atomic bomb.[11] Not only did Clinton overcome negative public perception to win the election in 1992 and reelection in 1996, but when he left office in January 2001, despite eight years of investigation that ultimately led to his impeachment, 65 percent of the American public approved of the way he handled his job as president.[12] In 2008, Barack Obama struck millions of Americans as an inspiring source of positive change, and his powerful speeches created the biggest stir about personality since the Reagan era. Eighty-one percent of respondents in a mid-2012 poll found Barack Obama "likable" and only 64 percent found Mitt Romney to be so.[13]

8.2c Issues

Today more than ever, issues seem to drive the public toward a particular electoral choice. A 2004 poll suggested that voters saw whether or not a candidate shared their values as the defining issue in the presidential race between Kerry and Bush.[14] In 2012, voters gave that edge to Obama over Romney by a margin of 53 to 45 percent.[15] Even observers who have previously minimized the importance of issues now concede that issues can make a difference when the public knows and cares about them and when the candidates differentiate themselves on issues. Single-issue groups, described in Chapter 7, play a big role in emphasizing particular concerns. Opponents of gun control or tax increases, for example, can "target" an official for defeat. Even without the participation of single-issue groups, social issues such as crime control and foreign policy issues such as military intervention in the Middle East usually receive considerable attention in a campaign.

Single-issue groups hold great sway over whether a candidate will gain a citizen's vote. It doesn't matter if a candidate supports or opposes the use of nuclear weapons, abortion, gun control, or other controversial issues; he or she can still be dropped from the race for office. (Wikimedia Commons)

More often, though, the voter's focus is on economic issues. Year in and year out, the mainspring issue driving most electoral decisions seems to be the economy. Even the earliest voting studies that discovered issues to be relatively unimportant found that bread-and-butter economic issues did make a difference. Personal economic well-being seems to influence how Americans vote. Figure 8.2 relates the percentage of the popular vote for president received by the incumbent party to an indicator of how much a citizen's disposable income had increased during the election year. Clearly, the better off people are during an election year, the more likely they are to vote for the party holding the White House.

Some political commentators pointed to Ronald Reagan's celebrated question near the end of his 1980 election debate with Jimmy Carter—"Are you better off now than you were four years ago?"—as the symbolic turning point of that campaign. The statistical evidence suggests that the Reagan campaign may have been right in emphasizing the role of the economy. The same was true for the 1992 presidential election—exit polls showed Bush running far ahead of Clinton (62 percent to 24 percent) among voters who thought their family's financial situation had improved over the preceding four years, and the two candidates were dead even (at 41 percent each) among those who thought things had stayed the same. Clinton outpolled Bush 61 percent to 14 percent among those who felt they were worse off; and fortunately for Clinton, those voters outnumbered by a margin of four to three voters who felt they were better off—enough to give Clinton the victory. Clinton benefited from an economic upturn during his first administration, and the fact that a majority of Americans in the fall of 1996 believed that national economic conditions were improving helped him retain office. However, although an even higher percentage of Americans thought the economy was getting better in fall

2000, Al Gore was unable to translate his connection to the incumbent Democratic administration into electoral victory.[16] In 2008, a national recession allowed Barack Obama to gain ground by distancing himself from the Bush administration in a way that his Republican opponent could not. When the economy began to rebound by 2012, the incumbent Obama was able to take advantage of that change, as well.

This is not to say that economics is the only issue that sways voters. Other issues have some impact. No doubt the candidates' differences on same-sex marriage, healthcare, and foreign policy influenced some voters to opt for Romney or Obama in 2012.

In talking about parties, candidates, and issues separately, this discussion runs the risk of oversimplification. In reality, the relationship among parties, issues, and candidates as influences on the vote is complex. Voters may take a position on an issue because it is the position of their party, or they may choose their party on the basis of its position on issues. Voters may tend to prefer certain candidates because they are the candidates of their party and reject other candidates because they are candidates of the other party; or they may judge a party according to how much they like its

Economic issues are not the only ones to sway voters. Here, supporters of healthcare reform rally in front of the Supreme Court in Washington, D.C., on March 28, 2012. (AP World Wide Photo)

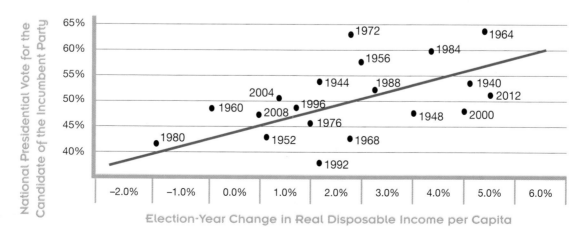

Figure 8.2 | The Economy and Presidential Voting

The better the economy, the better the candidate of the incumbent party does in the presidential election. The diagonal line shows the basic trend in the relationship—that is, how much, on average, voting is related to improvements in the economy. In 2008, the economy was the number one issue mentioned by voters in preelection polls. Thus, it should not be surprising that the candidate representing the incumbent party lost in a landslide.

SOURCE: Updated from Edward Tufte, Political Control of the Economy (Princeton, NJ: Princeton University Press, 1978), p. 123.

candidates. Finally, voters may like candidates because they agree with their positions on certain issues, or voters may adopt certain positions on issues because they like the candidates who advocate them. Thus, voter decision-making is based on the interplay of a number of factors—and not just on those factors alone.

8.3   The Candidate's Perspective: Running for President

While voters need to decide whether and how to vote, a more complicated set of choices confronts candidates. Their basic decisions include whether or not to run and how to attract enough votes to win. To achieve the latter, contemporary presidential candidates must make scores of strategic decisions, carve out a clear position as a serious contender early on, raise large amounts of money, choose the right campaign consultant, decide which issues to raise, select the primaries and caucuses on which to concentrate, garner enough delegates in the national convention to secure the nomination, choose a running mate, and win states with enough electoral votes to win the electoral college. These tasks are compounded by the fact that a candidate must also outmaneuver opponents who are working equally hard to attract voters.

8.3a Who Runs for President?

In American political folklore, anyone can grow up to be president whether they have humble beginnings, like Abraham Lincoln, or high social and economic status, like Franklin Roosevelt. Is such folklore actually true? In fact, the Constitution lays down few requirements. The person must be a natural-born citizen of the United States, a resident of the United States for at least fourteen years, and at least thirty-five years of age. The **Twenty-second Amendment** (1951), ratified in the aftermath of Franklin Roosevelt's unprecedented four elections to the presidency, imposes one more restriction: An individual cannot be elected to the presidency more than twice, or more than once if the individual has completed more than two years of another president's term.

(iStock)

Despite the relatively small set of formal qualifications, however, evidence suggests that the path to power is fairly steep and narrow. The key to attaining the highest political office in the United States is to have held other reasonably high political offices. Consider the twenty-four individuals who have run for the presidency under the banner of the major parties in the last seventeen elections. Eight of them had been governors of their states, eight had previously served as vice president, and thirteen had served in the U.S. Senate. Only one, Dwight Eisenhower, had never held an elective office. However, the best assurance of being elected president is to already *be* president. In the thirty elections in which an incumbent president sought reelection, the incumbent was successful in twenty-one, or 70 percent of the time. This statistic probably stems in part from the incumbent president's unique ability to manipulate events in his favor and the high visibility and name recognition a president enjoys.

What other qualities put an individual in line to be considered for the highest office in the land? Recent history suggests several qualities are prevalent. For one,

Twenty-second Amendment

Ratified in 1951, this amendment restricts the president to two terms in office

An Election Gone Wrong?

The Constitution charges the American states with the responsibility of regulating the time, place, and manner of elections. Traditionally, this has meant that each state establishes its own rules and designs its own ballots. Since the presidential election is combined with state and local races, county election boards often end up designing ballots of their own, following state guidelines. Typically this is not an issue of concern; but controversy arose on November 7, 2000, when one county's choice of ballot design seemed to determine the outcome of an extremely close presidential election.

Palm Beach County, Florida, voters were confronted with a "butterfly ballot" (so called because the pages on either side of the center punch card resemble wings) that listed presidential candidate names alternately on both the left and right sides of the holes. The Republican Party candidates were listed first on the left side, and the Democratic Party candidates second; but in between the two, the Reform Party candidates were listed on the *right* side. Many voters claimed to be confused as a result of this ballot—a claim that seemed well-supported by the election results. In Palm Beach County, 5,330 voters punched holes for both Al Gore and Pat Buchanan. Did some, or even most, of these voters intend to select Al Gore? We will never know for certain. But after careful analysis of the Florida vote, it seems possible that this ballot irregularity cost Al Gore the presidency.

A study commissioned by *USA Today* and several other papers concluded that George W. Bush still would have been victorious even if a hand recount of all the Florida votes had taken place. The study also noted, however, that a majority of Florida voters probably intended to vote for Al Gore. In an election as close as the presidential race in 2000, a poorly designed ballot in a single county can have an enormous effect. As a result of these complications, Congress passed the Help America Vote Act in 2002, which provided funds to states so that they could update and streamline voting and ballot counting procedures.

Should the federal government regulate ballots? Should it provide suggested guidelines to the states? What standards are needed to guarantee a fair and accurate election? What do ballots look like in your county? Do you find them confusing or easy to use?

---

the presidency was historically a white, male, Protestant preserve. This was not seriously challenged until 2008, when the Democratic primary elections ensured change by presenting a Caucasian woman (Hillary Clinton) and an African American identified man (Barack Obama, whose father was a black man from Kenya) as their top two contenders. In addition, most presidents in recent times have been from at least reasonably well-off, Protestant backgrounds and have been reasonably well educated. Not until 1960, with the election of John F. Kennedy, did a Catholic become president; and there was not another Catholic on a major party ticket until John Kerry in 2004. Joe Biden became the first Catholic elected vice president in 2008, and the Republican nomination of Paul Ryan in 2012 meant both vice-presidential candidates were Catholic that year. No Jew has ever been elected president, and Joe Lieberman became the first Jewish vice-presidential candidate of a major party in 2000. Mitt Romney's 2012 Republican nomination was the first of a Mormon. This growing diversity in nominees for the nation's highest offices reflects changes in both the demographics and the cultural acceptance of diversity in America.

In this age of media politics, an attractive image is clearly an important asset; perhaps, however, the most important quality of all is determination. Securing a major party's presidential nomination nowadays typically takes months, even years, of grinding work. In some cases candidates start campaigning in January of the year before the presidential election year and continue nonstop for almost the next two years. Presidential hopeful Gary Hart vividly illustrated the kind of ordeal that a modern presidential candidate has to endure when he revealed that some mornings, during his 1984 campaign, he would awaken in a strange hotel room and have to reach for the phone book in order to remember what city he was in.

8.3b The Media Campaign

The primary determinant of the shape of the modern political campaign is the mass media. Candidates used to be concerned primarily with mobilizing the party organization behind their efforts. Now their principal concern is mobilizing the media, particularly television, to bring their name and "image" before the public. Such efforts assume three principal forms. The first form is the expenditure of most of the campaign treasury on political advertisements. Precious paid television time is generally devoted to short advertisements that focus on simple images and issues, rather than longer speeches that focus on in-depth discussions of public policy. Campaign debates waged in one-minute, thirty-second, and even fifteen-second spots have drawn considerable criticism for oversimplifying campaign issues. Ross Perot's 1992 and 1996 campaigns defied traditional practice by spending millions of dollars on half-hour blocks devoted to detailed discussions of economic problems and solutions—and defied conventional wisdom by drawing large viewing audiences.

Another way candidates bring their names before the media is to structure traditional campaign events—such as speeches, rallies, and news conferences—in order to get media attention. These activities, once the core of the traditional political campaign, are now used mainly as "media events," or opportunities to attract coverage by the news media.

A third strategy is for candidates to try to get as much free television time as possible on regular news and interview broadcasts. Extended nationally televised appearances on the nightly network news broadcasts, traditional news interview programs such as *Nightline*, and, more recently, the "softer" interview shows such as *The View* are the candidate's dream—but these coveted appearances are hard to come by.

(Shutterstock)

The bread and butter of free television time comes in two forms: the "sound bite" on the national network news broadcasts and the daily stream of interviews on local TV stations as candidates travel around the country. Sound bites are short, taped excerpts from statements that a candidate makes. Candidates hope to get at least one sound bite on the network news broadcasts every night during the course of the campaign and attempt, thus, to say things in ways that are "sound biteable" to the TV crews covering them.

Another major development of recent years has been the rise of the professional **media consultant**. In the past, candidates tended to rely on party leaders or a personal coterie to plan and execute their campaign strategy. The current trend, however, is toward reliance on professional campaign consultants. Such individuals, while certainly oriented more toward one party or philosophy than another, make themselves available for hire to candidates able to pay for their services. One of the best known and most successful media consultants in recent years is James Carville, who led Bill Clinton's media campaign in 1992 and then served as senior political advisor to President Clinton.

media consultant

An expert hired by a political candidate to give advice on the use of the mass media, particularly television and direct mail, in a campaign for public office

BVT Lab

Visit www.BVTLab.com to explore the student resources available for this chapter.

The media typically concentrate not on the issues of the campaign but on the strategies, tactics, and likely outcome of the campaign. Politicians and commentators call such a focus the horse race. Poll results are tracked throughout the campaign to see who is in the lead and to test the potential effect of various moves by the candidates. Some critics have argued that the emphasis placed on the polls in the mass media serves to make polls the makers, rather than the measurers, of public opinion. Polling results showing a candidate doing better than expected tend to increase that candidate's credibility, and thereby contribute to further gains in the polls. Polling results showing a candidate lagging far behind may lead the public to write off that candidate as a wasted vote. Also, a poor showing in the polls can cause potential contributors to cut the flow of money to a candidate. Politicians, particularly those trailing in the polls, like to say, "The only poll that counts is the one on Election Day"; yet preelection polls may encourage shifts in opinion that are translated into shifts in voting on Election Day. In 1992, interest in the election was heightened as public opinion polls showed the race between Bush and Clinton tightening in the last two weeks of the campaign, only to have the drama diminish as the apparent Bush surge fell back in the last few days before the voting. In 2000, the race was tight right down to the wire; opinion polls during the last two weeks before the election consistently found the race too close to call. In this case the polls were right. The election turned out to be one of the tightest in recent history, with only a few hundred votes separating Bush and Gore in some key states.

The 2000 race for the presidency between George W. Bush and Al Gore came down to only a few hundred votes. The news media risked its credibility when it inaccurately claimed Al Gore to have won Florida's votes. A recount named Bush the winner of the votes in Florida. (Wikimedia Commons)

In recent years, the media and the polls have become controversial even on Election Day itself. Modern sampling techniques and **exit polls** (interviews with voters leaving the polls) often enable analysts to predict the winner long before polls everywhere have closed. For example, in 1988 CBS and ABC projected George Bush as the victor over Michael Dukakis at 9:20 p.m. Eastern Standard Time, well before many voters in Western states had voted. Do early predictions about who is winning or losing dissuade those who have not yet voted from doing so, create a "bandwagon" effect for the projected winner, or do they incur sympathy votes for the projected loser? The evidence on these questions is mixed, but there are some signs that early projections do reduce turnout. In the 2000 election, the media caused an even bigger uproar, first by declaring Al Gore the winner of Florida's twenty-five electoral votes, then by retracting and declaring Bush the winner of both Florida and the national election, and then—finally—by admitting that the race was too close to call. In its race to break an important story, the news media risked its credibility with the public.

As the media have come more and more to shape the modern presidential campaign, and as dissatisfaction with modern campaigns has grown, the media have become the object of blame for the problems and the target of reform. As reasonable and laudable as the proposed media reforms sound, many of them collide with the First Amendment principles of freedom of the press and speech, potentially infringing on broadcasters' rights as journalists and the candidates' rights to express themselves freely. Below are some of the specific proposals that have been advanced in recent years.

exit poll

A poll of voters taken as they leave a polling place and usually conducted by the media to get an advance indication of voting trends and facilitate analysis of the reasons behind the outcome of the election

- Requiring broadcasters to give more free time to candidates, thus reducing the candidates' need for money to spend on advertising

Low Voter Turnout: A Comparative Perspective

The public debate about low voter turnout in the United States and what to do about it takes place against an international backdrop that offers some unflattering comparisons. As Figure 8C shows, the United States ranks near the bottom of democratic countries in the percentage of its voting-age population that actually votes.

All kinds of explanations relating to distrust of government and lack of confidence in American political institutions have been offered to account for the low rate of turnout in the United States. The evidence shows, however, that these factors have little impact and

that, in any case, trust and confidence in government are higher in the United States than in many other countries.

Turnout is lower in the United States than elsewhere primarily because there are more obstacles and fewer incentives to vote than elsewhere. The primary obstacle is, of course, the American system of voter registration. In fact, in many other democratic countries, registration is automatic. In Germany, Italy, and Sweden, for example, citizens who move are required to report their new address to the government. Once they do this, their voting rights are automatically canceled at their old polling place and reinstated at their new one. Other countries (for example, Australia, Belgium, Greece, and Spain) have given people an incentive to vote by establishing penalties for nonvoting that, even if rarely enforced, seem to boost turnout by 10 percent. Perhaps the most effective sanctions are found in Italy. Italian citizens who fail to vote have "DID NOT VOTE" stamped on their identification

papers, which can be a significant embarrassment and disadvantage in dealing with government officials.[1]

Despite such evidence, solutions to low voter turnout may take time to materialize. The American government took steps to address the registration concern with passage of the National Voter Registration Act in 1993. Although this effort to simplify the process resulted in higher registration rates, voter turnout in the 2012 presidential election was still less than 54 percent of the voting-age population.

Voting is the defining act of a democracy. While such problems as voter fraud cannot be ignored, the United States might take a lesson from many of its sister democracies: Low turnout is not an intractable given, but a problem that can be addressed by reducing obstacles and increasing incentives.

1 David Glass, Peverill Squire, and Raymond Wolfinger, "Voter Turnout: An International Comparison," Public Opinion (December, 1983): 49–55.

Senior student Sarah Carlton, age twenty-one, updates her voter registration at Westminster College in Fulton, Missouri. (AP World Wide Photo)

Continued on next page

Figure 8C | Percentage of Voting-Age Population That Votes in Twenty-one Western Countries

The United States ranks near the bottom of democratic countries in the percentage of the voting-age population that actually votes, primarily because it places more obstacles in front of, and offers fewer incentives to, voters.

SOURCE: *International Institute for Democracy and Electoral Assistance,"Voter Turnout,"http://www.idea.int/vt/ (November 12, 2014).*

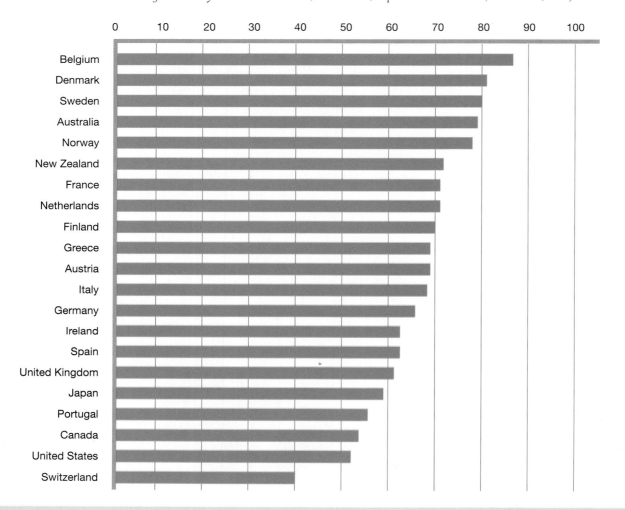

- Establishing rules for political advertising on television, thus possibly forcing broadcasters and candidates to present only spots of one minute or more and prohibiting any unfair or negative elements

- Conditioning federal campaign funding for presidential candidates on their agreement to participate in at least four televised debates

- Challenging television news organizations to devote more time to the substance of the campaign and less to the horse race

- Prohibiting television news organizations from projecting winners before all polls have closed, or creating, as an alternative, a uniform national poll-closing time

8.3c Campaign Finance

Financing campaigns has always been an issue for presidential candidates. The rate at which modern, media-based, jet-borne, poll-addicted campaigns consume money has made the problem even greater. The Federal Election Commission (FEC) reports that in congressional races alone candidates spent over $2 billion in the 2012 election cycle. With the demands for more money have come growing public concern and increased legislative action to prevent political money from tainting the electoral and governmental processes.

In 1971 Congress passed the **Federal Election Campaign Act** (FECA). The unfolding of the Watergate scandal in 1974 and other subsequent developments have led to amendments to FECA. Current campaign finance law requires full disclosure of the sources and uses of campaign funds on the theory that requiring candidates to disclose where their money came from will encourage them to behave more ethically. Thus, candidates must file a complete accounting with the FEC of where they get their money and how they spend it.

The law bans direct contributions to candidates by corporations and labor unions, although such organizations can set up political action committees (PACs) through which their employees or members can contribute. (For more on PACs, see Chapter 7.) The law also places limits on campaign contributions. Currently individuals may give up to $5,200 per candidate in each election cycle, but thanks to a recent Supreme Court ruling there is no longer an overall cap.[17] In other words, a wealthy donor could contribute that full $5,200 to each candidate throughout the nation. An individual cannot give more than $5,000 to a PAC per election per year, and a PAC cannot give more than $5,000 to one candidate in a federal election. However, there are no limits on the total a PAC can contribute to all federal candidates or on the total a candidate can receive from all PACs. National party committees can also spend about six cents per member of the voting population on the presidential election campaign.

> **F**rom where does all the money for a political campaign come?
>
> Find out who contributes to your favorite (or least favorite!) candidates at the Center for Responsive Politics.
>
> http://www.bvtlab.com/6Y8RN

The Revenue Act of 1971 created a system of public financing for presidential campaigns. Every taxpayer had the option of earmarking $1 of federal income tax for the **Presidential Election Campaign Fund**. This earmark has since been raised to $3. The money generated is distributed directly to presidential candidates according to specific formulas that tie amounts that can be spent to the rate of inflation. Before the party conventions, candidates are eligible for federal matching funds. To receive these funds, candidates must raise at least $5,000 in each of at least twenty states. Contributions are limited to $250 per contributor. Once a candidate has qualified, the federal government will match all individual contributions up to a specified amount if the candidate agrees to hold total spending under a limit. After the party conventions, major-party candidates who give up the right to accept any contributions from the public whatsoever can opt for federal financing of their campaigns, up to limits set by the law. Since the Revenue Act of 1971 was passed, all major-party presidential candidates have opted for federal funding—until 2008, when Senator Barack Obama decided to forego this option, citing a broken system that needed to be fixed. Senator McCain initially accepted, and then later rejected, the spending limits and the $84.1 million dollars from the federal government that came with it. The 2012 presidential campaign marked the first time that neither major-party candidate accepted public funding for either the primary or general election.

Federal Election Campaign Act

Law passed in 1971 and amended several times that regulates campaign financing and requires full disclosure of sources and uses of campaign funds and limits contributions to political candidates

Presidential Election Campaign Fund

Pool of money available that is collected from a $3 check-off on the federal income tax form and is available to presidential candidates for campaign expenses

Individual, PAC, and party contributions, as well as federal funds, are not the only money that can be spent on a candidate's behalf. Independent of the official campaign, individuals and PACs can spend as much as they want on behalf of a presidential candidate on such things as their own political advertisements and direct mail. Also, candidates willing to forego federal funding can spend as much of their own money as they want. In 1992 Independent candidate Ross Perot was estimated to have spent at least $60 million of his own money in his bid to win the White House. Candidates who do opt for federal funding are limited to spending $50,000 of their own money.

The problems concerning PACs have led some recent candidates to reject financial support from them. Many critics now call for the abolition of PACs or for tighter controls on them, but these actions would raise serious questions about freedom of speech. As a result, PACs may be a permanent fixture of American politics. How candidates manage their relationships with them, however, is another, less predictable matter. Proposals for PAC reform include increasing the amounts that individuals can give to candidates and restoring tax deductions for political contributions.

The major loophole in the controls on money that can be spent on a candidate's behalf was a seemingly innocuous amendment to the campaign finance laws passed by Congress in 1979—the so-called **soft money** loophole. The tight controls on party spending imposed by the FECA laws in the early 1970s had the effect of drastically reducing the money that the national party could give to state and local parties to help pay for grass roots activities supporting the presidential campaign— handing out buttons and bumper stickers, for example. In 1979 Congress moved to solve this problem by allowing the national parties to raise and spend money, without any restrictions, for state and local parties, routine operating expenses, and "party-building" activities, as long as the expenditures were not directly related to any federal campaign.

The parties soon began to exploit this exception to the hilt. Within the law, they moved to solicit unlimited contributions from individuals, corporations, and unions. Within the law, they cleverly spent the money in ways that technically were not directly associated with federal candidates, but clearly helped the candidates and freed up other party funds to help them. Under the new law, parties have to report virtually nothing about how the money is raised or spent.

Many critics, led by such organizations as Common Cause, see the soft money exception as an evasion of the entire structure of campaign finance law. These organizations have prodded the FEC to scrutinize more closely whether state and local expenditures are too closely tied to federal candidates and to rewrite the rules governing the raising and spending of soft money. The FEC has been slow to make changes; however, one reform that stands some chance of being implemented is fuller disclosure of the sources and uses of soft money—partly because the parties have already begun to do this on a limited, voluntary basis in an attempt to head off more restrictive reforms. Some would like to see the 1979 amendment that opened the soft money loophole repealed, but such repeal seems unlikely given that so many of the legislators voting on the issue benefit from the soft money system. Indeed, the Bipartisan Campaign Reform Act of 2002 closed many loopholes, but its failure to tighten restrictions on uncoordinated expenditures (see Chapter 7) led to the formation of new groups and a new approach to soft money spending.

8.3d Getting Nominated

The modern-day orientation toward the media, supported by unending efforts to raise money, is superimposed over the traditional political events that in the heyday

soft money

A category of campaign money that was created by an amendment to the campaign finance laws in 1979, allowing the national parties to raise and spend money, essentially without restriction, for state and local parties, routine operating expenses, and party-building activities, as long as the expenditures are not directly related to any federal campaign

of political parties were the central mechanisms by which candidates were selected: primaries, caucuses, and conventions.

The most visible part of the presidential nominating process in recent years has been the long string of **primary elections** and party caucuses, extending from the Iowa caucuses and the New Hampshire primary in early February, to the big primaries in such populous states as Illinois and New York in March and April, to the latecomers like New Jersey and Montana in June. Primary elections are intraparty elections in which a political party selects the candidates it will run for office in the final interparty **general election**. Primary elections differ from state to state in terms of who is allowed to vote. In an **open primary**, any voter regardless of party affiliation can participate in the selection of the party's candidates. In a **closed primary**, only voters registered as members of the party can participate in the selection process for that party. Some states express their presidential preferences in caucuses, or small party meetings. **Caucuses** typically include discussion time before voting, thus giving them a more deliberative character than the simple voting of a primary election. Each state and each party has its own set of rules for caucuses, but the process often includes a series of conversations about the candidates in which efforts are made to come to consensus by persuading the supporters of less popular candidates to join the cause of candidates with greater support. The process continues until one or more candidate(s) reaches a previously agreed to threshold of support, or until the state's delegates are divided proportionately.

The earliest presidential primaries and caucuses are the most important because they quickly sort out the field into contenders and also-rans. Most important in this respect is the New Hampshire primary, which provides the first real electoral test of the candidates' popular appeal. Candidates in the earliest contests run not so much against one another as against the expectations that the press and polls have created about how those candidates should fare. After the early contests shape the field, the political battles move out onto a broader plain.

In 2008, the process worked as expected for the Republican Party with John McCain securing enough delegates to cause his main rivals to drop out of the race and he to become his party's presumptive nominee by early March. The race on the Democratic side, however, was much lengthier with Senators Clinton and Obama battling it out through the entire season of primaries and caucuses. Many observers attributed the long primary season to the Democratic Party's awarding of state delegates proportionately. Unlike the Republicans' winner-take-all approach, any Democratic candidate securing at least 15 percent of a state's vote is eligible to receive delegates. This process allowed both candidates to continue accruing delegates, even in states where their opponent won the plurality of votes.

The 2012 primary season was much less eventful for the Democrats because incumbent president Barack Obama did not face any serious primary challengers. The Republican contest was essentially wrapped up by the end of April when the front-runner, Mitt Romney, received over half of his party's delegates.

The protracted series of primaries and caucuses leading up to the party conventions seems excessive to many observers. The crucial early events, which set the tone for the rest of the campaign, take place in relatively small and unrepresentative states. Some see this as a good thing. A long primary season with many of the early events centered in small states keeps the political process open by giving less well-known candidates with limited resources a chance to break into the political arena. Others see this as a disadvantage. They say the American political process is served less well by the election of obscure outsiders than by that of better-known insiders who

primary election

Preliminary election in which a party picks delegates to a party convention or its candidates for public office

general election

Election, which occurs in November, to choose the candidates who will hold public office, following primary elections held during the spring and summer

open primary

A primary election in which any voter, regardless of party affiliation, can participate

closed primary

A primary election in which only the members of the party holding the election are allowed to participate

caucus

A meeting of members of a political party (the members of a party in a legislature are also referred to as a party caucus), used in some states to select delegates to the national conventions, which nominate presidential candidates

The 2012 primary season was essentially over for the Republican Party by the end of April when front-runner Mitt Romney received over half of his party's delegates. (Shutterstock)

understand how to make the system work as soon as they take office.

One reform proposal suggests that the primary process be compressed in time and broadened in representation by instituting either a one-day national primary or a series of regional primaries. Advocates argue that such moves would speed up the nominating process and give the citizens of every state, not just those with early delegate-selection procedures, the opportunity to play a meaningful role in the selection of presidential candidates. The one-day national primary strikes many as a radical change, giving only the best-known and most prosperous candidates a real chance at the nomination. A reasonable compromise between the current fragmented system and a single national primary has been proposed—a series of **regional primaries** in different areas of the country, perhaps spaced two weeks apart over two months. Lesser-known candidates would then have the opportunity to build from small beginnings in their home regions.

The state caucuses and primaries culminate in the selection of delegates to the national **party conventions** held in August and September of the presidential election year. It is here that the party nominees are finally selected. In the past, the outcome of the nominating contest was often in doubt as delegates wrangled over disputes about rules, credentials, and party platforms, and as decisions were made in "smoke-filled rooms" by party elites. In recent years conventions have become more sedate. The publicity surrounding the selection of delegates has made the convention process almost perfunctory. The parties have tried hard to settle differences in advance of—or off of—the convention floor, lest public bickering paint an inharmonious picture of the party on television screens across the country. As the parties have tried to control and exploit media coverage of their conventions, the "news value" of these political events has declined; and the television networks have given them less coverage.

One of the most important strategic decisions a presidential candidate must make by the end of the convention is selection of a vice-presidential running mate. Much political folk wisdom revolves around this choice, particularly the need to **balance the ticket** geographically or ideologically. The idea is to pick a running mate who differs from the presidential candidate in a way that makes the ticket attractive to a broader range of voters. Thus, southern outsider Jimmy Carter picked northern insider Walter Mondale in 1976, western outsider Ronald Reagan picked eastern insider George Bush in 1980, and eastern liberal Michael Dukakis picked southern conservative Lloyd Bentsen in 1988. Bill Clinton broke with this practice in 1992 when he chose Al Gore, a moderate white southern male like himself, as his running mate. In 2000, Al Gore attempted to purify a candidacy tainted by connection to campaign finance scandals and chose Joe Lieberman, a Senator whose ethical standards were above reproach. George W. Bush, perceived by some as being an intellectual lightweight, chose the more cerebral Dick Cheney to balance his ticket. In 2004, John Kerry of Massachusetts went the regional route, selecting North Carolina Senator John Edwards to provide the ticket with broader appeal in the South. In 2008, Barack Obama selected Delaware Senator Joe Biden to give his ticket more experience in the field of foreign policy. John McCain selected

regional primary

A primary election held across an entire geographic area (for example, the South or the West) rather than within a single state

party convention

Regularly scheduled general meeting of a political party that is held for the purpose of ratifying party policies and deciding on party candidates

balance the ticket

A political party's effort to appeal to a wider cross-section of voters by providing regional or ideological balance in its nominations for president and vice president

Alaska Governor Sarah Palin in order to shore up support from the more conservative wing of the Republican Party. In 2012, Mitt Romney also catered to conservative Republicans with his choice of running mate, Paul Ryan. Unlike McCain, though, Romney avoided accusations that he had chosen an inexperienced political lightweight by selecting Wisconsin Representative Ryan, a member of Congress since 1999 who had already held important leadership roles, such as chair of the House Budget Committee.

The vice presidency has long been the object of political scorn. Nevertheless, the offer of the vice-presidential nomination is something that few politicians would sneer at. The amenities that go with the job are first-class, and recent presidents have gone to special lengths to see that their seconds have meaningful work. Perhaps most important is the fact mentioned earlier: The vice presidency is the most direct stepping-stone to the White House. Of the forty-five people who have served as vice president, fourteen have gone on to become president. No job in the world gives its holder better odds of becoming president. However, the

Vice President Joe Biden (Shutterstock)

ascent typically comes by death of the president rather than election. Since 1800, only two incumbent vice presidents have gone on to win a presidential election: Martin Van Buren in 1836 and George Bush in 1988.

8.3e The Electoral College

The main factor driving strategic decisions in the general election is the **Electoral College**. The election of the president of the United States is an indirect process: Citizens' votes elect electors; and those electors, constituted as the Electoral College, elect the president. Each state gets a number of electors equal to the combined number of its representatives in the Senate and House. Thus, every state gets at least three electors, with additional electors depending on the size of its population. The District of Columbia currently gets three electors under the terms of the **Twenty-third Amendment** (1961). (Table 8.1 shows the number of electoral votes for each state.) The Electoral College has 538 in all, with 270 needed to win the presidency. There is no constitutional requirement about how states choose their electors; such choices are left to the discretion of each state's legislature. All but two of the states have chosen to award all their electoral votes to the candidate (actually the slate of electors for that candidate) who wins a plurality in the state. The exceptions are Maine and Nebraska, which award two electoral votes to the statewide winner and the rest of their electoral votes by congressional district.

The members of the Electoral College never actually meet in one place. Electors from each state meet in their state capitals to cast their ballots on or about December 15 of the election year. The results are sent to the U.S. Senate; and the president of the Senate (who is, of course, the vice president of the United States) presides over the counting of the results in the presence of the Senate and House of Representatives. A presidential candidate who has a majority (more than 50 percent) of the electoral votes is elected outright. If no candidate has a majority, the House of Representatives—with each state delegation casting a single vote—elects a president by majority from among the top three contenders. If no president can be elected by this process, the vice president becomes acting president. A vice-presidential candidate who has a

Electoral College

This institution was established by the Constitution for electing the president and vice president. Electors chosen by the voters actually elect the president and vice president. Each state has a number of electors equal to the total number of its senators and representatives, while the District of Columbia (under the terms of the Twenty-third Amendment) has three electors.

Twenty-third Amendment

Constitutional amendment adopted in 1961 granting the District of Columbia three electors in the Electoral College

table 8.1 | Electoral Votes, 2012 Presidential Election

State	Romney	Obama	State	Romney	Obama
AK	3	—	MT	3	—
AL	9	—	NC	15	—
AR	6	—	ND	3	—
AZ	11	—	NE	5	—
CA	—	55	NH	—	4
CO	—	9	NJ	—	14
CT	—	7	NM	—	5
DC	—	3	NV	—	6
DE	—	3	NY	—	29
FL	—	29	OH	—	18
GA	16	—	OK	7	—
HI	—	4	OR	—	7
IA	—	6	PA	—	20
ID	4	—	RI	—	4
IL	—	20	SC	9	—
IN	11	—	SD	3	—
KS	6	—	TN	11	—
KY	8	—	TX	38	—
LA	8	—	UT	6	—
MA	—	11	VA	—	13
MD	—	10	VT	—	3
ME	—	4	WA	—	12
MI	—	16	WI	—	10
MN	—	10	WV	5	—
MO	10	—	WY	3	—
MS	6	—	**TOTAL**	**206**	**332**

majority is elected outright. If no candidate has a majority, the Senate picks the vice president from the top two contenders by majority vote of individual members. In the days following the 2000 election, Al Gore found himself with 267 electoral votes and George W. Bush had 246—with disputed Florida returns still in question. The need for the House of Representatives to decide the outcome was averted when the Supreme Court ruled against additional recounts and Bush was declared the winner in Florida, allowing him to clear the threshold with 271 electoral votes. Though still close, the 2004 contest was more decisive, with Bush beating Kerry 286–252. In 2008, Barack Obama claimed 365 electoral votes to McCain's 173, providing the most decisive electoral outcome since 1996. In 2012, Obama was reelected with 332 electoral votes to Romney's 206.

The Electoral College has been, perhaps, the most prominent target of the advocates of electoral reform. Because the number of senators as well as the number of representatives determines a state's representation, small states are represented out of proportion to their populations. Electors are chosen state by state by plurality election, so a winner's advantage and a loser's disadvantage, no matter how slim, are magnified in the extreme. The greatest gains can be made at the smallest cost with narrow victories in big states, so candidates often focus their efforts almost entirely in the larger states. Further, persons chosen as electors for a particular presidential ticket are under no effective legal obligation to actually cast their ballots for that ticket (the **faithless elector** problem).

Worst of all, to some people, is the prospect of a popular-minority president—a president who gets fewer popular votes than the opponent but still wins the presidency. This has happened four times in American history. In 1824 Andrew Jackson received more votes than John Quincy Adams, but the House chose Adams as president. In 1888, popular-vote winner Grover Cleveland lost to Benjamin Harrison. In 1876, the Democratic candidate Samuel J. Tilden outpolled Republican Rutherford B. Hayes; but a Republican-controlled commission appointed to settle a dispute over the electoral votes of three southern states awarded them—and thus the White House—to Hayes. The 2000 presidential contest provides the most recent occurrence, when Gore received 50,992,335 popular votes to George W. Bush's 50,455,156, making Gore the popular-vote winner but electoral-vote loser.

Eugene Miller, one of Ohio's twenty electors, signs his name on one of the certificates of votes during the Electoral College of Ohio proceedings at the Ohio Statehouse, on Monday, December 15, 2008. (AP World Wide Photo)

To repair all these alleged defects, reformers have come up with a variety of changes. The most sweeping proposal is to do away with the Electoral College entirely and to replace it with **direct popular election** of the president and vice president. Thus, whichever candidate received the largest percentage of the total national popular vote would win the White House. Such a process solves all the problems cited so far, but critics of direct national election see it as jeopardizing the delicate balance of the American political system. Simple plurality election would mean that presidents could be elected with the support of far less than half the people. Instituting a requirement of a majority of the votes to be elected might often mean a runoff election. That, in turn, would encourage more candidates to run in the first-round election. The result might be the end of the two-party, middle-of-the-road approach that has so long characterized American politics. Critics of the popular election can easily point to one of the Electoral College's greatest virtues: With only the four exceptions cited, it almost always produces a clear-cut winner.

Seeing problems with both the current Electoral College and direct popular election, moderate reformers propose to steer a course somewhere between the two. One idea for reducing the impact of the statewide winner-take-all system with the resultant candidate emphasis on big states is to move to a winner-take-all system on the level of congressional districts, as Maine and Nebraska have done. This would reduce the tendency of large blocs of votes to be awarded on the basis of narrow popular-vote margins. Solutions to the faithless elector problem propose requiring electors to vote for the presidential candidate under whose banner they were elected or to do away with electors completely and simply tally up electoral votes.

Another call for reform focuses on the problems generated by a president who is compelled to spend the last half of a first term running for a second term. Critics of the current law, which limits a president to two full four-year terms, contend that single-term presidents do not have enough time to master the job and that first-term

faithless elector

A person who is chosen to vote for particular presidential and vice-presidential candidates in the Electoral College but who, nevertheless, votes for different presidential and vice-presidential candidates

direct popular election

Selection of officials on the basis of those receiving the largest number of votes cast, sometimes referring to a proposal to choose the president and vice president on this basis rather than through the Electoral College

presidents who aspire to a second term are diverted from their duties by their efforts to get reelected. Defenders of the status quo argue that the limitation of two four-year terms gives good presidents plenty of time to achieve their objectives and allows the public ample opportunity to vote out poor presidents. A president limited to a single term, they say, would become an instant lame duck. A compromise would be to allow the president one longer term, for example, a term of six years (see "A Six-Year Term for Presidents?" in Chapter 10).[18]

8.3f Campaign Strategies

Presidential campaigns must pay careful attention to several strategic problems. One such problem is that of image. Most candidates seek to establish their image in the public mind. For an incumbent, the choice is usually an easy one: to exploit

Look at maps, examine party success over time, and compare vote totals for every presidential election at Dave Leip's *Atlas of U.S. Presidential Elections.*

http://www.bvtlab.com/776aj

as much as possible the resources of the presidency. Presidents often try to look fully occupied with governing the country and too busy to engage in partisan politics. For opponents the choices are more difficult. Should the challenger go on the attack against the incumbent president or play the role of the statesperson instead? If the president is popular, the electorate may take the former as an attack on the country; however, the latter course is likely to attract little attention. Neither of these does the challenger much good.

How much focus should be placed on issues is another strategic problem. Should the candidate present specific proposals regarding national problems or instead project a broad and necessarily fuzzy vision of the future? The American people continually decry candidates who do not take clear positions on issues because they deny voters a choice. It is sobering to note, however, that the two candidates in postwar history who gave the public the clearest choices, the conservative Barry Goldwater in 1964 and the liberal George McGovern in 1972, went down in two of the biggest defeats in American electoral history.

Nowhere are the questions of images and issues raised more directly and dramatically than in presidential debates. For an incumbent, a debate is close to a no-win

Sen. Amy Klobuchar (D-MN, on left) delivers gumbo to Sen. Mary Landrieu's (D-LA, on right) office after the New Orleans Saints defeated the Minnesota Vikings. Landrieu lost her seat to Bill Cassidy (R-LA) in one of 2014's most competitive Senate races. (Wikimedia Commons)

proposition. It gives publicity to the opponent, puts the challenger on an equal footing with the president, and risks embarrassment either by an inadvertent slip or by an aggressive challenger. Only the desire not to appear intimidated keeps a president from opting out of debates completely. As a result, incumbents usually want as few debates and as much structure as possible. For a non-incumbent, a debate represents perhaps the best strategic opportunity of the campaign. It provides the greatest media exposure, "presidential" standing, a chance to flush the president (if the incumbent is the opponent) out of the Rose Garden, and an opportunity to display one's intellectual, political, and rhetorical wares.

The 1992 debates provided a case study on many of these issues. George Bush, as an incumbent tied to a weak economy facing an experienced and articulate debater in Bill Clinton, initially tried to avoid debates as long as possible. Clinton's taunts that Bush was afraid to debate (accompanied by Clinton supporters dressed in chicken suits haunting Bush campaign appearances) and Clinton's persistent lead in the polls forced Bush campaign advisers to go with a heavy debate schedule as one of their few hopes of turning the election around.

In the debates, Clinton appeared presidential and Bush failed to deliver either a negative knockout punch or a positive vision of his plans for a second term. In fact, many saw Bush's fumbling response in the second debate to a young woman's question about how the bad economy had affected him personally as a clear sign that he was not going to be able to turn the election around. Bill Clinton, who followed up with a more articulate and sensitive response to that question, and Ross Perot, who scored overall with his homespun rhetoric and humorous one-liners, emerged as the overall winners.

The questions of campaign strategy are numerous and complex. The most vexing fact, however, is that strategy is always at the mercy of events. An unforeseen event can make a candidate look like a hero or a fool. A serious economic dislocation, a negative revelation about an associate, an outbreak of violence halfway around the world—any of these things can make one candidate look inept and another candidate look "presidential." Because incumbent presidents have the power to take action rather than just talk about events, they generally gain some advantage in such circumstances. If events prove to be intractable, incumbent presidents can suffer badly. Jimmy Carter's futile struggle to free the hostages from the American embassy in Tehran, Iran, during the 1980 campaign and George Bush's poor economic record in 1992 stand as recent examples. Sometimes there is little anyone, even the president of the United States, can do to overcome events.

8.4   The Candidate's Perspective: Running for Congress

Running for Congress is much like running for president, except the stage is smaller, of course—a state (for the Senate) or a congressional district (for the House) instead of the entire country. The basic strategic elements are the same: the problem of getting money; the two-phase contest of getting the nomination and then winning the election; the impact of party, candidate appeal, and issues; the growing importance of the media; the long hours on the campaign trail; and so on. However, different aspects tend to be particularly problematic.

8.4a Campaign Finance

Like presidential campaigns, House and Senate elections have become big-money enterprises. Candidates need money for television advertising, direct mail operations to get their messages across and raise more money, polling to see how their messages are playing, and expensive media consultants. According to Federal Election Commission statistics, candidates for the House and Senate in the 2014 midterm elections spent about $1.3 billion on their contests. This figure represents a 50 percent increase in spending over the 2000 midterm election cycle.[19]

Although public financing is an important resource for presidential elections, congressional campaigns continue to operate without it. This leaves, as the primary resources for most congressional campaigns, money donated or spent by individuals, parties, and PACs. Recent congressional elections have seen widespread efforts by candidates and parties to get around the restrictions imposed by federal campaign finance laws. Foremost among such efforts was the increasing use of independent PAC expenditures to avoid the legal limits on direct contributions to candidates and the use of soft money by parties. Since the Court's 2010 decision in *Citizens United*, the spending by non-affiliated independent expenditure groups known as super PACs has shown a dramatic increase.[20]

A key question is whether this money actually helps a candidate. Research suggests that it helps challengers more than officeholders. The more money a challenger spends, the more likely he or she is to defeat the incumbent. Such a tendency is probably due to the fact that money can be used to buy the name recognition and visibility necessary to offset the advantages of incumbency. Incumbents who spend a lot of money, however, do not fare as well as those who spend less. This is probably because incumbents tend to spend a lot of money only when they find themselves facing a serious challenge.[21]

As in presidential campaigns, financing is a frequent target for reform in congressional campaigns. The focuses for reform are similar in some respects—for example, too much PAC money, particularly for incumbents, and too much soft money. However, the problems for congressional elections are exacerbated by the lack of public financing of congressional campaigns. This makes congressional candidates much more dependent than presidential candidates on problematic sources of funds. Thus, the most significant campaign reform in congressional campaigns would be to institute public funding—a change that would be supported by about 50 percent of Americans.[22] Congress has struggled repeatedly over the last several years to institute this reform, but so far it has been unable to arrive at any plan agreeable to both Democrats and Republicans. Many Democrats and Republicans now say they want public financing; the bone of contention lies over whether spending limits should be imposed. Democrats want limits because they fear the wealth and fund-raising potential of some Republican candidates. Republicans, on the other hand, oppose limits because they think outspending firmly entrenched Democratic incumbents is the only way to dislodge them.

Even the modest reforms of the Bipartisan Campaign Reform Act of 2002 were struck a blow in 2008, when the Supreme Court found one of its provisions—the so-called "Millionaire's Amendment"—unconstitutional. The Court said the provision, which provided candidates with higher party contribution limits when their opponents exceeded certain self-financing thresholds, was an infringement of First Amendment speech rights.[23]

8.4b Incumbency

Incumbency is even more of an asset to members of Congress than it is to presidents. In 2014 more than 95 percent of all representatives who ran for reelection won. In the Senate, incumbency is also an important advantage, although the retention rates are typically somewhat lower. In 2014, though, the success rate for incumbent

Midterm Elections: Reflection and Change

On November 4, 2014, American voters went to the polls to cast their ballots in elections for all 435 members of the U.S. House of Representatives and about one-third of the U.S. Senate. Dubbed midterm elections, these federal elections come in even-numbered years when there is not a presidential election. These elections are typically characterized by relatively low turnout and serve both as an opportunity for the nation to reflect on the performance of the incumbent president and his or her party, and the as beginning of speculation about the upcoming presidential race. The 2014 midterms were no exception to these trends. Only 36.6 percent of eligible voters cast a ballot—as opposed to the 57.5 percent who voted in the 2012 presidential election. The lack of a presidential race, combined with the lack of competitiveness and voter interest that characterizes many congressional races, produces far fewer voters.

Despite low turnout, midterm elections often serve as a referendum on the president. In six of the last seven second-term midterm elections, the president's party has lost congressional seats. On average, the opposition party gains six Senate seats and twenty-nine House seats during the sixth year of a presidency; 2014 was fairly typical in this regard. President Obama's Democratic Party lost at least fourteen seats in the House and at least seven in the Senate. This shift resulted in the largest number of Republican House seats since just after World War II and a new Republican majority in the Senate. These changes likely mean that President Obama will have a more difficult time achieving his legislative agenda during the last two years of his presidency. Though the Democrats held majorities in both chambers during the first two years of his presidency, President Obama faced a Republican majority in the House of Representatives over the next four years and will face unified opposition during his last two years in office.

The media attention around midterm elections—especially during a president's second term—often focuses on potential contenders for the White House. In this regard, as well, 2014 was no exception. On the Democratic side, former secretary of state and former senator Hillary Clinton has been the presumed "front-runner" for the Democratic nomination. Despite not being up for election in 2014, Clinton garnered a large amount of media attention throughout the campaign season and will likely continue to make moves that draw headlines if she intends to return to the White House. On the Republican side, three incumbent senators have all been rumored to be considering presidential runs. Marco Rubio (R–FL), Rand Paul (R–KY), and Ted Cruz (R–TX) have all championed causes from the more conservative, Tea Party wing of the Republican Party. In order to gain positive attention and emerge as likely presidential candidates, these three will have to walk a fine line. They will need to work with the more mainstream leadership in their party in order to realize achievements that show they can be leaders who accomplish things, but they will also need to stick to their right-wing principles to avoid being seen as sell-outs by their core constituencies.

What lies ahead for the 114th Congress (2015–16)? It is possible that Congress will interpret this election as a demand for change. After all, nearly two-thirds of Americans say they are dissatisfied with how well the system of government works, 80 percent have a more negative than positive view of Congress, and only 28 percent say they trust the legislative branch of government.[1] On the other hand, it is also possible that both political parties will place their desire to score partisan victories above their desire to govern effectively. In the weeks following the election, President Obama signaled his desire to avoid working with an obstinate Congress by issuing executive orders to change immigration policy (see the story below) and Republican Speaker of the House John Boehner (R–OH) filed a federal lawsuit against the Obama administration. Boehner's pursuit of this legal action—which claims the White House has acted unconstitutionally in implementing parts of the Affordable Care Act—comes despite polls showing that 57 percent of Americans oppose a lawsuit and two-thirds oppose impeachment efforts against the president.[2] How will this battle between Congress and the president play out during the last two years of the Obama administration? Pay attention to the news to find out.

1 The Gallup Organization, 2013, 2014.

2 CNN.com, July 31, 2014.

BVT *Lab*

Flashcards are available
for this chapter at
www.BVTLab.com.

senators was almost 95 percent as well. Of course, political movements can challenge the incumbency advantage from time to time. The Tea Party movement and other anti-incumbency sentiment led to the defeat of over sixty incumbent legislators who were seeking reelection during the 2010 midterm elections.

The main reason for the frequent difference between the House and Senate return rates is that about five out of six congressional districts are **safe seats**. That is, House districts tend to be homogeneous, and the division of party affiliation within them is lopsided enough that one or the other party is virtually assured of victory. Because senators represent states, their "districts" are often more heterogeneous, with a more even division between the parties. For both representatives and senators, incumbents are usually much better known than their challengers.[24]

As described in Chapter 9, incumbents in Congress continually boost themselves by taking credit for every beneficial activity the federal government undertakes in their states and districts. Incumbents, also, generally have a much easier time raising campaign funds. For example, in recent elections, more than 80 percent of all PAC money contributed to House campaigns went to incumbents. In addition, members of Congress are in a good position to use the resources of their offices to get reelected. One of the most valuable resources they have is the franking privilege, the right to send out official mail without any postage. Senators and representatives frequently use this privilege to send out newsletters extolling their activities on behalf of the district or questionnaires soliciting the public's opinion on current issues. In almost every case, the name and face of the legislator are prominently displayed. Another valuable resource is staff. Most members of Congress use much of their staff's time to perform constituency services—mostly running interference through the Washington bureaucracy for constituents with problems. Needless to say, the hope is that the satisfied home voters will remember the favors on Election Day.

Critics charge that the high rates of reelection for incumbents have led to legislative stagnation and unresponsiveness. One solution that has attracted broad attention in recent years is **term limits**, restricting the number of terms a person can serve in the House or Senate (for example, to twelve years). Term limits were on the ballot in fourteen states in 1992 and won in all fourteen. In 1995, the Supreme Court held that these restrictions were unconstitutional at the federal level, although limitations on state level officials now exist in over twenty states.[25] Another solution is to reduce the advantages that come with a seat in the House or Senate, in particular to limit the amount of mail members of Congress may send at public expense under their franking privilege. A series of revisions to the franking privilege in the late 1990s require members of Congress to deduct franking costs from their official budgets, even though there is no restriction on the amount of their budgets they can use for mailings.

8.4c Parties, Candidates, and Issues

After incumbency, the single most important determinant of voting in congressional races is party. Both party and incumbency provide "low-cost" information cues to people facing a voting decision. The candidate's party is supplied on the ballot. The incumbent's name and generally positive reputation are known. Either may be used with little time and effort in information gathering—and either one may be substituted for the other.[26]

Earlier discussion indicated that the issues themselves usually do not play a major role in presidential campaigns. The same is even truer of congressional campaigns. The major problem is information, or rather a lack of it. If, as in many contests, voters do not even recognize the names of the candidates, they obviously know even

safe seats

Congressional districts in which the division of voters between the parties is so lopsided as to virtually ensure one party of victory

term limits

Laws restricting the number of terms an elected representative may serve— the Court has struck down state efforts to limit terms for federal offices, but has allowed state laws that limit terms for elected officials at the state level

less about the candidates' positions and voting records on the issues.[27] Of course, the impact of issues can soar when differences between the candidates are sharp and well publicized on matters of importance. The only issue that consistently achieves salience with the public is the economy. In both presidential and midterm election years, the better the economy is doing, the better the congressional candidates of the president's party do.[28]

The other major factor in congressional voting, as in presidential voting, is the candidates themselves. Candidates for the House rest their appeal on such general qualities as trust and competence, and voters seem to respond most favorably to them.[29] Senate candidates, in contrast, are evaluated in more specific terms of experience and ability, qualities that are closer to those by which presidential candidates are judged.[30] This difference in factors affecting voting decisions between House and Senate candidates is probably due to the fact that Senate candidates are generally better known than House candidates. Negative campaigning is as much a trend and an issue for congressional campaigns as it is for presidential ones.

The impact of issues can soar when differences between the candidates are sharp and well publicized on matters of importance, such as immigration. (Shutterstock)

The success of the congressional candidates from each party may be affected by the popularity of their party's president or presidential candidate. In the years when congressional elections coincide with a presidential election, a presidential candidate whose popularity appears to give a boost to his party's candidates for the House and Senate is said to have coattails. Ronald Reagan was said to have coattails in 1980 because his appeal seemed to help Republican congressional candidates to do better than had been expected. In contrast, in 1988 George Bush was said to have no coattails because his party picked up no seats. In two of the last five presidential elections, the winning candidate's party actually lost seats in Congress—an effect known as negative coattails. In midterm elections, the Congressional vote is often interpreted as a referendum on how the president is doing. Historically, the president's party has tended to lose congressional seats in midterm elections. A gain or a small loss for the president's party is interpreted as an endorsement of the president and a big loss as repudiation. In the 2006 midterm elections, President Bush's Republican Party lost thirty-four seats; and in the 2010 midterm elections, President Obama's Democratic Party lost sixty-nine seats. The 2010 midterm elections proved to be the largest swing in recent years, with the Republicans gaining seventy seats and regaining the majority in the House of Representatives. The news only got worse for President Obama in the 2014 midterm elections. His party lost its majority in the Senate—and in the House, Republicans made enough gains to secure their largest majority since just after World War II.

CHAPTER REVIEW

1. The American voter confronts two fundamental decisions on Election Day: whether or not to vote and, if so, how to vote. Qualifications for voting and registration in most states define the boundaries of the electorate. Beyond that, voting turnout varies substantially with social characteristics and psychological outlook toward politics.

2. The voter's decision about how to vote is similarly influenced by a broad range of factors. Throughout much of American history, partisanship has established a baseline in the division of the vote; but in recent years, opinions about candidates and issues have caused voters to break from party lines.

3. Presidential candidates confront a challenge that is difficult in both strategic and physical terms. Strategically, a candidate for president confronts two separate contests: the intraparty race for the nomination and the interparty race for the White House. Physically, the candidate faces a grueling journey that begins not long after one presidential election and ends in elation or disappointment on election night four years later.

4. Congressional candidates confront a similar range of problems in getting elected. Money is an even greater problem because public financing has not yet come to congressional campaigns. Private contributions, particularly from PACs, remain a major source of political lifeblood. Because congressional elections are generally less visible than presidential campaigns, personalities and issues usually count for less and party and incumbency for more.

KEY TERMS

The voter's side of campaigns and elections is explored in two major works on voting, the classic *The American Voter* by Angus Campbell, Philip E. Converse, Warren E. Miller, and Donald E. Stokes (Chicago: University of Chicago Press, 1980), and in *The Changing American Voter*, rev. ed., by Norman Nie, Sidney Verba, and John Petrocik (Cambridge, MA: Harvard University Press, 1979). The former is based on surveys from the 1950s, and the latter on updates ; the latter also and challenges, in some cases, the earlier study with surveys from the 1960s and 1970s. The ideas in these volumes have been updated with the publication of *The American Voter Revisited* (Ann Arbor: University of Michigan Press, 2008) by Michael Lewis-Beck, William G. Jacoby, Helmut Norpoth, and Herbert F. Weisberg.

Examinations of more recent elections include Michael Nelson, *The Elections of 2012* (Washington, D.C.: CQ Press, 2013), *Political Behavior of the American Electorate*, 13th ed. (Washington, D.C.: CQ Press, 2014) by William H. Flanigan and Nancy H. Zingale, and *The American Campaign* by James E. Campbell (College Station: Texas A&M University Press, 2008).

Two excellent studies of voting turnout are Raymond Wolfinger and Steven Rosenstone, *Who Votes?* (New Haven, CT: Yale University Press, 1980) and Ruy A. Teixeira *The Disappearing American Voter* (Washington, D.C.: Brookings, 1992). A recent study on how the electorate can be changed is Lisa Garcia Bedolla and Melissa R. Michelson's *Mobilizing Inclusion: Transforming the Electorate Through Get-Out-the-Vote Campaigns* (New Haven , CT: Yale University Press, 2012).

The literature on presidential campaigns and elections is rich indeed. Virtually every election spawns at least one substantial account of what "really" went on. Most notable is the *Making of the President* series by Theodore H. White, particularly the classic *The Making of the President 1960* (New York: Atheneum, 1988).

An interesting philosophical question is raised in Martin P. Wattenberg's *Is Voting for Young People?*, 3rd ed. (New York: Pearson, 2011). Russell J. Dalton takes up a similar theme in *The Good Citizen: How a Younger Generation Is Reshaping American Politics* (Washington, D.C.: CQ Press, 2008).

Notes

1. Steven Rosenstone and Raymond Wolfinger, "The Effect of Registration Laws on Voter Turnout," *American Political Science Review 72* (1978): 22–45; G. Bingham Powell Jr., "American Voter Turnout in Comparative Perspective," *American Political Science Review 80* (1986): 35; Brennan Center for Justice, *Voting Law Changes in 2012*, http://brennan.3cdn.net/92635ddafbc09e8d88_i3m6bjdeh.pdf (August 9, 2012).

2. Pew Center for the States, *Electionline Weekly*, March 27, 2008, http://www.pewcenteronthestates.org/uploadedFiles/wwwpewcenteronthestatesorg/Reports/Electionline_Reports/electionline%20Weekly%2003%2027%2008.pdf (August 16, 2008).

3. Federal Election Commission, *The Impact of the National Voter Registration Act on the Administration of Elections for Federal Office, 1997–1998*, http://www.fec.gov/pages/9798NVRAexec.htm (August 26, 2001).

4. Angus Campbell, "Surge and Decline: A Study of Electoral Change," in *Elections and the Political Order*, eds. Angus Campbell, Philip E. Converse, Warren E. Miller, and Donald E. Stokes (New York: Wiley, 1966), p. 41.

5. Walter Dean Burnham, "The Changing Shape of the American Political Universe," *American Political Science Review 59* (1965): 7–28.

6. Philip E. Converse, "Change in the American Electorate," in *The Human Meaning of Social Change*, eds. Angus Campbell and Philip E. Converse (New York: Russell Sage Foundation, 1972), pp. 281–286.

7. Paul Abramson, *Political Attitudes in America* (San Francisco: Freeman, 1983), pp. 291–306.

8. This argument is most often associated with Bernard Berelson, *Voting* (Chicago: University of Chicago Press, 1954), pp. 305–323.

9. The Gallup Organization, August 2012.

10. Donald Stokes, "Some Dynamic Elements of Contests for the Presidency," *American Political Science Review 60* (1966): 19–28.

11. "Manhattan Project, 1992," *Newsweek* special election edition (November/December 1992): 40–56.

12. The Gallup Organization, 2001.

13. The Gallup Organization, "Likeability Top Characteristic for Both Romney and Obama.

14. The Gallup Organization, 2004.

15. The Gallup Organization, "Likeability Top Characteristic for Both Romney and Obama," June 26, 2012.

16. The Gallup Organization, 2001.

17. *McCutcheon v. Federal Election Commission*, 572 U.S. ___ (2014).

18. Tom Wicker, "Six Years for the President?" *The New York Times Magazine* (June 26, 1983): 16.

19. Center for Responsive Politics, http://www.opensecrets.org (November 12, 2014).

20. *Citizens United v. Federal Election Commission*, 558 U.S. 50 (2010).

21. Gary Jacobson, *Money in Congressional Elections* (New Haven, CT: Yale University Press, 1980), p. 49.

22. The Gallup Organization, "Half in U.S. Support Publicly Financed Federal Campaigns," June 24, 2013.

23. *Davis v. FEC*, 554 U.S. 724 (2008).

24. Edie N. Goldenberg and Michael W. Traugott, *Campaigning for Congress* (Washington, DC: Congressional Quarterly, 1984), p. 136.

25. *U.S. Term Limits, Inc. v. Thornton*, 514 U.S. 779 (1995).

26. Barbara Hinckley, *Congressional Elections* (Washington, DC: Congressional Quarterly, 1981), p. 68.

27. Thomas Mann and Raymond Wolfinger, "Candidates and Parties in Congressional Elections," *American Political Science Review 74* (1980): 629.

28. Edward Tufte, *Political Control of the Economy* (Princeton, NJ: Princeton University Press, 1978), pp. 113, 120.

29. Richard Fenno, *Home Style: House Members in Their Districts* (Boston: Little, Brown, 1978), pp. 54–61.

30. Hinckley, *Congressional Elections*, pp. 79–82.

POP QUIZ

1. Two social characteristics that show the strongest relation to voting turnout are _____ and _____.

2. The three virtues that voters seem to consider most important in a candidate are attractive personal qualities, _____, and _____.

3. Today, presidential candidates tend to rely on more professional _____ _____ to plan and execute their campaign strategy.

4. A major loophole in the controls on money that can be spent on a presidential candidate's behalf is the ability of state and local parties to raise _____ _____.

5. A presidential candidate whose popularity appears to give a boost to his party's candidates for the House and Senate is said to have _____.

6. Studies have shown that younger people are more likely to vote than older people.   T   F

7. In recent years, political party affiliation has become a less important determinant of voting decisions.   T   F

8. Candidates tend to favor long television advertisements in order to maximize public exposure and issue formulation.   T   F

9. An incumbent president has little to gain in accepting a debate with his opponent.   T   F

10. Candidates for the House and Senate receive only a small amount of public financing, too little to run a successful campaign.   T   F

11. The two social characteristics that show the strongest relation to voting are _____ and _____.

    A) party identification, income

    B) race, religion

    C) age, education

    D) sex, regional habitat

12. In recent years, which of the following is true of serious contenders for the presidency?

    A) They have most often come from the successful side of mainstream America.

    B) They usually come from the House of Representatives.

    C) They have never, until George Bush, served as vice president.

    D) They have rarely had college educations.

13. Which of the following is true of the Federal Election Campaign Act?

    A) It creates a system of public financing for presidential campaigns through the federal income tax system.

    B) It limits the amount of money a PAC can contribute to all federal candidates.

    C) It requires all contributions to be funneled through the state and local political party.

    D) It requires full disclosure of sources and uses of campaign funds.

14. Which of the following applies to presidential debates?

    A) They are most advantageous for nonincumbents.

    B) They are required by law before a candidate can receive federal funds.

    C) They have had little impact on the outcome of presidential elections.

    D) All of the above

15. Which of the following is true of midterm congressional elections?

    A) They usually result in a gain for the president's party.

    B) They are often viewed as a referendum on how the president is doing.

    C) They usually result in high voter turnout.

    D) They have historically favored the Republican Party.

Answers:

1. age, education   2. experience, leadership   3. campaign consultants   4. soft money   5. coattails   6. F   7. T   8. F   9. T   10. F   11. C   12. A   13. D   14. A   15. B

Chapter
09

Congress

In This Chapter

(Wikimedia Commons)

Chapter Objectives

Thanks to the Constitution, Congress is the chief law-making body in the land. Because it is the branch of government established in Article I of the Constitution, Congress is sometimes called the "first branch." Of the three branches, Congress is also called the "people's branch" because its members are the public officials who seem most immediately responsive to changes in the public's moods and opinions. Americans have demonstrated significant mood changes in recent years. In 1994 voters chose a majority Republican House and Senate for the first time in forty years. In 2006 the public mood swung back in the other direction, creating Democratic majorities in both chambers again. The 2010 midterm elections provided yet another swing. Republicans reduced the Democratic majority in the Senate by several seats and regained a majority in the House of Representatives. In the 2014 midterms, Republicans added to their majority in the House and regained control of the Senate, as well.

Congress is also the branch of the national government in which the political ideas of Americans are most visibly represented. Few legislative bodies possess greater authority over the lives, property, and happiness of a nation. Congress makes, or at least ratifies, fundamental decisions about national policy—for instance, whether the United States will have a military draft. Congress determines the fraction of every person's income the government will collect as taxes and the purposes for which that money will be spent.

Key to understanding the first branch is understanding the 535 individuals who serve in Congress: 435 as members of the House of Representatives and 100 as members of the Senate. Knowing who they are, what their job is like, what forces influence what they do, and how Congress is organized helps to explain how laws are passed.

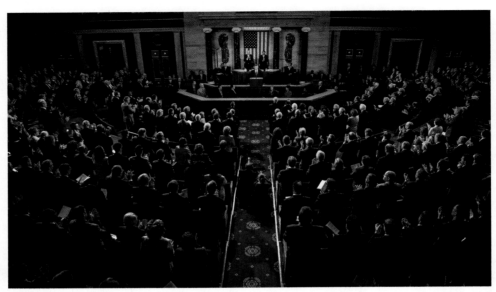

Of the three government branches, Congress is sometimes called the "first branch." It is also called the "people's branch" because its members are the public officials who seem most immediately responsive to changes in the public's moods and opinions. (iStock)

9.1   The Constitutional Powers of Congress

The very first words of the Constitution declare, "All legislative powers herein granted shall be vested in a Congress which shall consist of a Senate and a House of Representatives." What are those powers? As summarized in Table 9.1, Congress may levy taxes, borrow and spend money, regulate foreign and interstate commerce, coin money, declare war, maintain the armed services, and establish federal courts inferior to the Supreme Court, to name but a few. Perhaps the most important grant of power is in the **necessary and proper clause**, which authorizes Congress to "make all laws which are necessary and proper for carrying into execution the foregoing powers and all other powers vested by this Constitution in the government."

In *McCulloch v. Maryland*,[1] Chief Justice Marshall, speaking for the Supreme Court, found ample power in this clause for Congress to use all appropriate means to achieve its enumerated goals. In this case, discussed in Chapter 2, the Court supported the congressional power to create a national bank, even though this explicit power was not mentioned in the Constitution. Marshall made it clear that the necessary and proper clause added implied powers to those enumerated in the Constitution. With few exceptions, the powers of Congress have been construed broadly ever since. That being said, the current Supreme Court has demonstrated a greater willingness than its recent predecessors to rein in congressional power.[2] Even with these occasional setbacks, however, the powers granted by the necessary and proper clause remain vast.

The Constitution does, however, impose some constraints. First, the enumeration of specific powers limits what Congress can do to those powers and others implied from them. Second, Article I, Section 9, contains eight specific limitations,

necessary and proper clause

Also called the "elastic clause," Article I, Section 8, of the Constitution, is the source of "implied powers" for the national government, as explained in *McCulloch v. Maryland* [17 U.S. (4 Wheaton) 316 (1819)].

table 9.1 | The Constitutional Powers of Congress

Article I of the Constitution grants many powers to Congress. In most cases, both houses must act, but in a few instances the Constitution specifies that one house or the other has a special role.

Responsibilities of Both House and Senate	Responsibilities of Senate Only	Responsibilities of House Only
Levy taxes	Try impeachments	Bring impeachments
Borrow and spend money	Ratify treaties	Originate tax bills
Regulate commerce	Confirm all federal judges, ambassadors, cabinet members, and other officials	
Regulate currency		
Establish postal system		
Provide for patents and copyrights		
Establish federal courts below Supreme Court		
Declare war		
Maintain armed forces		
Govern the nation's capital		
Oversee national property		
Make laws "necessary and proper" to carry out above powers		

including a ban on **bills of attainder** (legislative acts that declare an individual guilty and mete out punishment without a trial) and **ex post facto laws** (laws that make an act a crime after it was committed or increase the punishment for a crime already committed). As described in Chapter 3, the Bill of Rights places a set of personal liberties beyond the reach of Congress. For example, Congress cannot establish a state religion or abolish jury trials in criminal cases without violating the First and Sixth amendments. In the area of economic and social policy, Congress is given a wide berth. For example, Congress can decide whether to regulate certain industries or to continue price supports for certain farm commodities.

The Constitution requires Congress to share many of its powers. This is the principle of **checks and balances** discussed in Chapter 1. The Senate ratifies treaties, but the president or his advisers negotiate them. Congress may pass laws, but the president can veto them (and can be overruled by a two-thirds vote in each chamber). The Supreme Court can also declare them unconstitutional. In foreign policy the president and Congress battle for control. Although Congress can declare war, the president commands the armed forces and can send them anywhere on the globe.

Congress also shares power within itself, for it is divided into two chambers—the Senate and the House of Representatives. The House, according to one of the founders, George Mason, "was to be the grand depository of the Democratic principles of government." Each state was granted representation in the House according to its proportion of the national population, and members were selected by direct election. In 1964 the Supreme Court, in *Wesberry v. Sanders*,[3] took the principle a step

bill of attainder

A law, prohibited by the Constitution, that punishes an individual and bypasses the procedural safeguards of the legal process

ex post facto law

A law that makes an act a crime after it was committed or increases the punishment for a crime already committed, both of which are prohibited by the Constitution

checks and balances

The system of separate institutions sharing some powers that the Constitution mandates for the national government, the purpose of which is to keep power divided among the three branches: legislative, executive, and judicial

Speaker of the House John Boehner speaking at the Values Voter Summit in Washington, DC. (Wikimedia Commons)

further, requiring that each congressional district within the states be apportioned on the basis of equal population.

The delegates to the Constitutional Convention assumed that the House, being the most democratic of our institutions, would also be the most impulsive. Thus the Senate was meant to constrain the excesses of popular government. As James Madison put it, "The use of the Senate is to consist in its proceeding with more coolness, with more system, and with more vision than the popular branch."[4]

Apportioned two for each state, senators were originally elected by the state legislatures with the expectation that they would be more conservative and partial to entrenched economic interests. With direct election of senators required in 1913 by the **Seventeenth Amendment**, the Senate also became subject to the mass electorate; and the distinction the founders considered to be so important faded away.

Differences between the House and the Senate remain, however, as Table 9.2 indicates. Almost all members of the House represent only part of a state, whereas each senator represents an entire state. Although the Constitution assigns both equal weight in writing laws, it commands unique duties to each. The Senate has the sole power to try impeachments, to confirm presidential nominations, and to ratify treaties. The House must originate tax bills (and, by custom, appropriation bills) and bring impeachments. Although neither chamber has ever consistently dominated the other, the prestige of a senator is greater than that of a House member. The reasons are obvious—there are fewer senators, and their terms are three times longer (six years versus two years). Representatives frequently give up their House seats to run for the Senate, but the reverse is seldom done.

9.2   The Members of Congress

The powers that the Constitution bestows on Congress present the opportunity for congressional action and influence on national policy. Much of what Congress actually does, however, is not specified in the Constitution but is largely a product of the values and interests of the 535 members who sit in the House and the Senate.

9.2a Who Are They?

The constitutional requirements for membership in Congress are simple. A House member must be twenty-five years old, a U.S. citizen for seven years, and a resident of the state (not the district) he or she represents. A senator must be thirty years of age, a U.S. citizen for nine years, and a resident of the state he or she represents. Although these requirements open the door to most of the adult population of the country, in practice the people who eventually go to Congress do not represent a cross-section of the adult population. Members of Congress are predominantly

Seventeenth Amendment

Ratified in 1913, it provides for the direct popular election of United States senators.

table 9.2 | Differences Between the House and the Senate

Although the House and the Senate are alike in many ways, differences give each a special character. In addition, the Constitution assigns to the Senate particular confirmation and treaty-ratifying powers and to the House the right to originate tax bills.

Senate	House of Representatives
Senators represent entire states, with each state differing in population from other states.	Members represent only part of a state (unless a state is assigned only one representative); House districts are equal in population.
Senate contains 100 members.	House contains 435 members.
Senators serve six-year terms.	Representatives serve two-year terms.
Floor debate important in shaping outcome of legislation	Committee work important in shaping outcome of legislation
Unlimited debate	Limited debate
Riders (nongermane amendments) permitted	Riders prohibited
More prestige, media coverage, and visibility	Less prestige, media coverage, and visibility
Larger staff for each senator, with size determined by population of state and distance from Washington, D.C.	Smaller staffs of equal size for each member
Casework less important	Casework more important
Fewer committees	More committees
Source of many presidential aspirants	Few presidential aspirants
Vice president is presiding officer.	House elects presiding officer (Speaker). Rules Committee is important.

white and upper middle class. In the 114th Congress (2015–2016), the majority are lawyers or people who came from banking or business. Some members—such as Jason Chaffetz (R–UT), a former college football player, and Sean Duffy (R–WI), former cast member of *The Real World*—have cashed in on their celebrity status to gain election to Congress.

From its beginnings, Congress was predominantly a men's club. The percentage of women serving in Congress in 1991 (5.8 percent) was only slightly higher than the percentage serving in 1953 (3 percent). Dubbed "the year of the woman," the 1992 election brought twenty-four new women to the House and four new women to the Senate. In the 114th Congress, women make up about 19 percent of the House and 20 percent of the Senate. This will be the first time that women have held more than a hundred legislative seats. These percentages are likely to continue to grow in the coming years as more women are elected to state legislatures, a common launching ground for a congressional race.

African Americans were barely represented in Congress a generation ago. Between 1900 and 1928, there were no African Americans in Congress; and until the passage of the Voting Rights Act of 1965, there were no African Americans representing the South. Judicial interpretation of the Voting Rights Act has required that minorities be given maximum opportunity to elect their own to Congress. Consequently, in the 1992 election thirteen new African Americans and six new Latinos won election to the House. In the 114th Congress, there are forty-three African Americans in the House. African Americans still constitute only 10 percent of Congress, although they make up about 13 percent of our population. In 2006 Minnesota voters sent Keith Ellison to Congress. Ellison, an African American, became the first Muslim elected to the House of Representatives. In 2012, Hawaii voters elected Tulsi Gabbard, the first Hindu American in Congress, and Wisconsin voters elected Tammy Baldwin, the first openly gay person in the U.S. Senate. Table 9.3 profiles members of Congress by age, gender, and ethnicity.

Keith Ellison, an African American, became the first Muslim elected to the House of Representatives. (Wikimedia Commons)

9.2b How Do They See Their Roles?

The great eighteenth-century English political thinker Edmund Burke felt that an elected representative should seek to represent not his constituents' views but rather his own conscience and the broad interests of the nation. "Your representative owes you," said Burke, "not his industry only, but his judgment; and he betrays, instead of serving you, if he sacrifices it to your opinion."[5] Such an understanding is known as the **trustee role**. Those who see themselves as simply voting their constituents' desires perform the **delegate role**. Most legislators combine both roles into what is known as the **politico style** of representation. These members consider both their constituents' opinions and their own view of the national interest in making up their minds. The weight assigned to each varies with the issue involved. On bread-and-butter questions, such as public works and farm supports, members are more likely to follow their constituents' views than on issues they might consider moral questions such as abortion or same-sex marriage.

9.2c How Long Do They Stay?

In the early years, few members considered an actual career in Congress. Washington in the 1800s was a provincial, mosquito-ridden town, and most members lived in boardinghouses. Until after the Civil War it was not uncommon for half the members of the House to be first-timers. Nor was it unusual for a representative or senator to resign midterm to pursue a more lucrative profession. Few served longer than two terms.

Toward the end of the nineteenth century, more members began to see service in Congress as a career. As the role of the national government expanded, the business of Congress seemed more urgent and exciting. Between 1850 and 1950 the average tenure for both senators and representatives increased, and the percentage of first-term members declined. In the 1970s those trends began to flatten. Fewer members seemed interested in a lengthy congressional career, and the number of House members with twenty or more years' service decreased by half. In the 113th Congress, the average House member had served 9.1 years and the average Senator 10.2 years. Although voters continue to reelect incumbents, this does not mean that Americans are satisfied with the job of Congress as a whole. Consistently the lowest rated of the three branches of government, Congress reached a historic low in November 2013, when a nationwide poll indicated that only 9 percent of Americans approved of the job the legislature was doing.[6]

9.2d How Much Do They Do?

Today's legislators work almost eleven hours a day when Congress is in session, which adds up to approximately three hundred working days a year. The business of Congress

trustee role

The concept that legislators should vote on the basis of their consciences and the broad interests of the nation, not simply on the views of their constituents

delegate role

A concept of legislative work as simply voting the desires of one's constituents, regardless of one's own personal views

politico style

A manner of representation in which members of Congress attempt to strike a balance between the interests of their constituents and the dictates of their own judgment and conscience

table 9.3 | Profile of the 114th Congress (2015–2016)

	Senate	House
Average Age	62.2	56.7
Men/Women	80/20	351/84
African Americans	0	47
Latinos	3	28
Asian Americans and Pacific Islanders	2	10
American Indians	0	1

SOURCE: *Congressional Research Service, 2014.*

has expanded in both volume and complexity. No longer does Congress have the luxury to ruminate over the two or three issues of the day. In the Sixteenth Congress, when James Monroe (1817–1825) was president, 480 bills were introduced. In the 113th Congress (2013–2014), over 5,000 measures were introduced; and they were longer and more intricate and involved practically every area of our economic and social life. Only about 200 of those bills were eventually passed and enacted into law.

Legislators' schedules are long, fragmented, and unpredictable. On any particular day they may breakfast with a reporter; attend several committee hearings; meet with constituents, lobbyists, or officials on legislative issues; discuss pending legislation with other members or staff; and attend floor debate. Evenings are often consumed with meetings, receptions, and fund raisers. Most of this is crammed into four working days so that members may return home for a weekend of campaigning. A survey of members showed that one-half had no personal time and one-third had no time for family.[7]

9.2e What Do They Do?

The imperative of getting reelected motivates most members of Congress; therefore, they must cultivate the support and the trust of their constituents. How they do that is described by political scientist Richard Fenno as a member's *home-style*, which involves the following: (1) the members' allocation of time and resources to their district, (2) their personal style, and (3) their explanations of their Washington activities. Sophisticated use of the **franking privilege** (free postage for official business) has become an increasingly effective method of members for keeping their constituents informed. By 1990, the cost of the congressional frank exceeded $100 million. Public outrage at such costs led to reform legislation that curtailed the privilege somewhat. In 2013, Congress spent $11.3 million on franking.

A recent phenomenon is satellite-feed video, whereby members can send prepackaged statements directly to a local television channel or stream them directly to their own websites. Both parties have high-tech studios on Capitol Hill. For example, in the Hart Office Building the Senate Republicans have studios, film-editing rooms, and dishes on the roof so that Senators can do call-in shows or interviews for local cable channels.[8] With an advanced copy of the president's State of the Union address, members can send their taped reaction to the speech to local television stations in time for the eleven o'clock news.

franking privilege

A congressional benefit that permits members to send out official mail using their signature rather than postage

Congress Shows Several Members the Door

Americans often muse about "crooked politicians." In fact in recent polls, 54 percent of Americans indicated that they believe that most members of Congress are corrupt.[1] While "most" is likely an overstatement, Congress seems to have gotten the message and demonstrated its concern for ethics in recent years when investigations led to the departure of several scandal-plagued incumbents.

The largest single scandal involved legislators who had financial ties to Jack Abramoff, a Washington lobbyist convicted of bribing legislators in exchange for influence on legislation. Abramoff's crimes included giving large campaign donations and other gifts to legislators, who then agreed to support bills or make statements on behalf of Abramoff's clients.[2] Representative Bob Ney (R–OH) and House majority leader Tom DeLay (R–TX) both resigned in 2006 and faced criminal charges as a result of their involvement in the conspiracy. Other Representatives with ties to Abramoff managed to avoid resignation. Richard Pombo (R–CA) stayed in office, though

the scandal ultimately contributed to a failed reelection bid; and John Doolittle (R–CA) managed to get reelected, despite a tarnished image, but did not run for reelection in 2008.

There were multiple legislative scandals in the 113th Congress (2013–2014). In 2013 former representative Jesse Jackson Jr. (D–IL) pled guilty to misusing about $750,000 in campaign funds for personal expenses. Later that year Representative Trey Radel (R–FL) entered a guilty plea after purchasing cocaine from an undercover agent. In 2014 married representative Vance McAllister (R–LA) was videotaped kissing an aide in his office. Finally, in 2014 Representative Michael Grimm (R–NY) faced twenty charges related to over $1 million of unreported income while operating a restaurant. Of these scandal-plagued politicians, only Grimm returned to the 114th Congress.

Representatives Jackson and Grimm have not been the only legislators to face ethics charges related to money in recent years. In June 2007, Representative William Jefferson (D–LA) was convicted by a grand jury after $90,000 in alleged bribe money was found in his freezer. Jefferson retained his seat and sought reelection in 2008 despite having been stripped of his committee posts by his own party. He lost his reelection bid and was sentenced to thirteen years in prison. In 2008, Senator Ted Stevens (R–AK) won his party primary handily, despite facing a felony indictment for concealing over a quarter of a million dollars in gifts from oil executives. By the time he fought a close battle in the November 2008 election, he had already been convicted

of seven charges. In 2010, Representative Charles Rangel (D–NY) was forced to give up his powerful role as chair of the Ways and Means Committee in the midst of an ethics investigation regarding failure to pay taxes and inappropriate receipt of gifts. He was found guilty of eleven charges and censured by Congress but did not resign; in fact, he ran for reelection in 2012 and 2014—winning both times. Since the House Ethics Committee only investigates current members, some have found leaving office to be the easiest way to end unwanted probes. Representative Michele Bachmann (R–MN) took this route in 2013 amid investigations of improper use of campaign funds during her 2012 presidential bid. As the 113th Congress drew to a close at the end of 2014, five members left office while still under investigation for wrongdoing.[3]

What is the proper role for ethics in politics? Are members of Congress held to higher ethical standards than the rest of society? Should they be? Who suffers when a member of Congress leaves office amid scandal? Who suffers when they don't leave?

1   The Gallup Organization, 2014.

2   CNN.com, "GOP Lawmaker Tied to Convicted Lobbyist Pleads Guilty," September 15, 2006, http://www.cnn.com/2006/POLITICS/09/15/ney.investigation/index.html, (September 15, 2006).

3   *Roll Call,* "5 House Members Leave Congress with Open Ethics Reviews," (November 12, 2014).

pork barrel politics

The effort to enact legislation favoring a legislator's home district, often in the form of costly government spending that may not be advantageous to the country as a whole

Members use a variety of methods to gain recognition and build support back home. They fight hard to see to it that their states or districts get their share of the governmental pie. Known as **pork barrel politics**, the process involves gaining federal funds for such things as sewage plants, housing units, and dams.

As eager as legislators are to denounce the size of the federal budget, they are far more anxious to secure a new federal office building, a bridge, or a hospital in their own districts. One cannot denounce Congress, however, because the public at large shares the hypocrisy. Constituents expect their representatives in Washington both to cut the budget and to gain them a slice of the pork.

Beyond legislative work, each member is also expected to serve as an **ombudsman**, or go-between, who intervenes with the federal bureaucracy on behalf of individual constituents. Such intervention is called **casework** and may include helping a student who requests information on a government scholarship program, a soldier interested in an early discharge, or someone

During the recent years of large deficits and budget cutbacks, legislation often requires that sacrifices, rather than rewards, be shared. (iStock)

with a tax or immigration problem. The staff usually handles such matters through phone calls to the appropriate agency. If the case is difficult or involves influential people in the state or district, a member will deal with it personally.

9.2f How Do They See Each Other?

Legislative norms are the standards or unwritten rules of acceptable behavior in Congress. Some of these norms operate differently in each chamber, and time has altered others. First among the most important norms is **reciprocity**. Members are expected to extend support to other members in the expectation that the favor will be returned. An urban representative may support a farm bill in exchange for a rural member's vote for the food stamp program. This practice is known as **logrolling**. Among the general public it is considered vaguely disreputable, but members consider such conduct perfectly acceptable.

During the recent years of large deficits and budget cutbacks, legislation often requires that sacrifices rather than rewards be shared. In a form of negative logrolling, members will accept across-the-board reductions that limit all programs or benefits. If members can claim that everyone is taking their lumps, they can more easily avoid blame.[9]

Second, since political conflict is inherent in Congress, members are expected to extend as much *personal courtesy* to each other as is possible. On the floor of Congress, colleagues refer to each other as "the gentleman from …" or "the gentlewoman from … ." Members who engage in personal attacks on their colleagues are frequently rebuked.

Historically, because of the Senate's smaller size, its members have gotten to know each other better than those in the House. This tendency has changed somewhat in recent years. The necessities of dealing with larger staffs, media demands, and frequent traveling have made it difficult for senators to establish close friendships. The Senate's "club-iness" and sense of esprit de corps have consequently declined.[10]

Third, members are expected to specialize in one or two subjects, usually matters within their assigned committees. This gives Congress a degree of expertise on complex issues ranging from defense spending to healthcare. Specialization also makes a legislator's job manageable, allowing members to allocate their time and energy more efficiently. The degree of specialization is greater in the House than

ombudsman

A person who intervenes with the bureaucracy on behalf of individual citizens

casework

The congressional task of handling requests by constituents for information or assistance with the federal bureaucracy

legislative norms

The unwritten rules of acceptable behavior in Congress

reciprocity (or logrolling)

A practice whereby two or more members of Congress exchange support for legislation important to each other

the Senate. Large staffs do an enormous amount of legwork, enabling a Senator to become knowledgeable on a broad range of issues.[11]

In the 1950s, when older, conservative, and generally Southern members dominated Congress, junior members were expected to serve a period of apprenticeship. They were expected to work hard, stay out of floor debates, and defer to their seniors—in brief, they were to be seen and not heard. Today a more independent and outspoken membership rarely observes such deference. The liberal members elected in the 1960s and 1970s and the conservatives elected in the 1980s and 1990s were independent and impatient. In the House, new members who recognize the need for some period of apprenticeship see it as months, not years. Junior senators feel no obligation to serve an apprenticeship, and senior members no longer expect it of them.

9.3 The Structure of Congress

Congress contains a complex network of party organizations, committees, subcommittees, and supporting agencies. Understanding each part of this network is important to comprehending the whole.

9.3a Party Leadership: The House

The **Speaker of the House** is the presiding officer of the House of Representatives. The position, established by the Constitution (Article I, Section 2) is, according to the Presidential Succession Act of 1947, next in line to succeed the president after the vice president. Although formally elected by the entire House membership, the majority party nominates the Speaker; and all majority-party members routinely vote for him or her. When the president and the Speaker are of the same party, the Speaker is expected to mobilize support for the president's program in the House and to represent House opinion to the president, seeing to it that unnecessary clashes are avoided.

The Speaker's power once rivaled that of the president; toward the end of the nineteenth century, the Speaker was frequently referred to as a czar. The office reached its pinnacle under Speaker Joseph Cannon (R–IL; 1903–1911). Cannon had the power to make committee assignments and appoint and remove committee chairpersons. His impact on national policy was unmistakable. A staunch reactionary, Cannon helped to stifle much of President Theodore Roosevelt's (1901–1909) reform program on child labor, lower tariffs, and banking. In the 1910–1911 session of Congress, a rising tide of progressivism (see Chapter 4) swept the House; a revolt arose against Cannon, in particular, and the powers of the Speaker, in general. The Speaker lost the power to make committee assignments and appoint committee chairpersons; and for some years after the revolt, the Speaker once again became a figurehead.

In 1975 the House Democrats increased the substantive power of the Speaker considerably. The Speaker became the chair of the party's Steering and Policy Committee, with the power to nominate all Democratic members of the **Rules Committee**, which clears major legislation going to the House floor and is generally considered one of the most desirable and powerful committees. During his brief tenure as Speaker, Jim Wright (D–TX; 1987–1989) aggressively exploited the new powers of the office to speed his legislative priorities through the House. He exerted tight control of scheduling and used the Rules Committee to restrict the

Speaker of the House

The presiding officer of the House of Representatives, who is selected by the majority party

Rules Committee

Powerful House committee that clears most important bills for floor consideration and decides the rule under which bills should be considered; also, the committee of a party convention that recommends changes in the way a party conducts its affairs

amendments offered on the House floor. Wright referred pieces of major legislation to multiple committees with strict deadlines for consideration—a device known as "multiple referrals." He oversaw the passage of major trade legislation, a farm credit bill, and catastrophic health insurance. Wright resigned from the House in 1989 under fire for ethics violations. Yet, in two years he had transformed the office from a consensus builder to an agenda setter.[12] When the 2006 midterm elections swept the Democrats back into power in the House, after a period of twelve years of Republican majorities, Representatives elected Nancy Pelosi (D–CA) Speaker, making her the first woman to hold that post. Pelosi replaced Denny Hastert (R–IL), who had held this position since 1999. The Republican majority elected in 2010 made John Boehner (R–OH) Speaker, a position he still holds in the 114th Congress.

The **majority leader** is the Speaker's chief deputy and the second most powerful figure in the majority party. Elected by the party caucus, the formal organization of House Democrats and House Republicans, the majority leader is the party's leader on the floor of the House, its chief spokesperson, and defender of the party's record from partisan attacks. He or she assists the Speaker in scheduling legislation and deciding party strategy in floor debates. Owing to his or her influence with the Speaker, the majority leader can help colleagues schedule legislation for floor consideration. When the president is of the same party, the majority leader confers regularly with the president and frequently works to advance the president's programs. At the outset of the 113th Congress, the majority leader was Eric Cantor (R–VA). But when Cantor lost his party primary to a right-wing challenger in June 2014, Republicans selected Kevin McCarthy (R–CA) to succeed him in that role. Cantor was the first sitting majority leader to lose a primary since the office was created in 1899.[13]

Party whips, such as Steve Scalise, have to act as an assistant majority or minority leader by encouraging party discipline and floor attendance during important votes. They are the heart of political party communication. (Wikimedia Commons)

The leader of the loyal opposition in the House is the **minority leader**, a post filled in the 114th Congresses by former Speaker Nancy Pelosi (D–CA). Being the leader of a minority can be dispiriting because one's party does not control the committee agenda and frequently loses votes on the floor.

The **party whip** acts as an assistant majority or minority leader. The party caucus chooses the whips. Although they have little independent power, they serve their party leadership by encouraging party discipline and floor attendance during important votes. This makes the whips the heart of the party communication system. They poll members on crucial legislation and, when possible, pressure uncommitted members to follow the party line. They have the major responsibility of ensuring that the necessary members are present during important votes. The House majority whip's office is a large intelligence-gathering organization that includes a chief deputy whip, seven deputy whips, more than thirty at-large whips, and more than twenty assistant whips. In the 114th Congress, Democratic representatives selected Steny Hoyer (D–MD) to be their party whip; Steve Scalise (R–LA) is the Republican whip for the 114th.

The Democratic Caucus, which is comprised of all Democratic House members, elects Democratic leadership, approves committee assignments, and enforces party rules and discipline. It is composed of a number of task forces that report on important current policy issues. In the 114th Congress, the Democratic Caucus focused on a few key issues, covering topics such as the economy and immigration reform.

majority leader (House)

Leader and chief spokesperson for the majority party in the House

minority leader (House)

Leader and chief spokesperson for the minority party in the House

party whip

Member of each party's leadership responsible for party discipline and attendance for key votes

The Republican caucus, known as the **Conference**, organizes the Republican membership of the House. The members elect Republican leadership, approve committee assignments, and shape communications and strategy for the party. The major arm of the Conference is the House Republican Policy Committee. This is a fifty-six-member committee that develops policy and legislative proposals. This work helps guide and focus party priorities for the legislative term.

9.3b Party Leadership: The Senate

Because the Senate has fewer members, party organization in the Senate is not as elaborate as it is in the House. Moreover, a tradition of independence cuts against attempts to regiment the membership along party lines. The **president of the Senate** and chief presiding officer is the vice president of the United States, but the role is entirely ceremonial. It involves presiding over Senate sessions, which rarely occur, and voting only to break a tie, which happens infrequently. In addition to the vice president, the Constitution also provides for a **president pro tempore** who may preside over the Senate in the absence of the vice president. An important exception to this general rule occurred in early 2001, when Vice President Dick Cheney cast tie-breaking votes multiple times in a Senate that was evenly divided between the parties. In practice, the task of presiding over the Senate debates is given to a dozen or so junior senators in the majority party who serve about a half-hour each day. Since 1945 the post of president pro tempore has been regarded as largely honorific and given to the senior majority party member.

The **majority leader** is the leader of the majority party in the Senate and elected at the beginning of each session. The **minority leader**, who leads the minority party, is also elected by party colleagues; however, the majority leader is the dominant figure. As the floor leader, the majority leader is recognized first in debate, influences who will be recognized, and controls the scheduling of bills for floor consideration. Like the House Speaker, the majority leader may influence committee assignments of new senators and of other senators seeking to gain more desirable committee positions.

The Senate is far more difficult to lead than the House. Its one hundred members, elected for six years, have a strong sense of independence and expect more deference to their wishes from the leadership than do House members. Only by a vote of sixty members can debate be terminated, and most routine Senate business is conducted by unanimous consent. Much of the majority leader's time is spent accommodating the hectic schedules of the individual senators. Rising constituent demands involve more service and visits to home states. The need for aggressive self-promotion and perpetual campaigning requires much from senators. They must not only make frequent home visits but also engage in a constant round of media appearances, speeches, and fund-raising activities. Former majority leader Robert Byrd (D–WV) once explained his role as "a traffic cop, babysitter, welfare worker, minister, lawyer, umpire, referee, punching bag, target, lightning rod, and the cement that holds his party group together."[14] Thus, an effective majority leader must be a consummate diplomat—nurturing inflated egos, accommodating individual agendas, and smoothing ruffled feathers in order to pass important legislation.

Senators have to be great multitaskers. Between service and visits to home states, they must aggressively self-promote and campaign. They must also engage in a constant round of media appearances, speeches, and fund-raising activities. (iStock)

Conference

The Republican leadership committee in the House

president of the Senate

A largely ceremonial role held by the vice president of the United States

president pro tempore

The presiding officer of the Senate in the absence of the vice president—largely honorific post and usually given to the senior majority party member

majority leader (Senate)

Leader and chief spokesperson for the majority party in the Senate

minority leader (Senate)

Leader and chief spokesperson for the minority party in the Senate

The function of the party leader goes beyond managing the business of the Senate. The party leader is also a media personality and spokesperson for the party. Senator Harry Reid (D–NV) carried this burden from the beginning of 2007 until the end of 2014. When the Republicans regained the majority in the Senate after the 2014 midterm elections, Senator Mitch McConnell (R–KY) became majority leader and Reid was relegated to the role of Senate minority leader.

The whip system in the Senate is smaller and less institutionalized than in the House. The *Senate whips* basically serve the floor leaders as vote counters and are not major power brokers. Both the Senate majority and minority whips are elected by their caucus on a secret ballot prior to the beginning of each new Congress.

9.3c The Committee System

Contemporary law making involves an understanding of numerous complex subjects. Members of Congress cannot be expected to master the details of the hundreds of bills that come before them. Through the committee system, they can gain specialized knowledge of particular areas of policy and legislation.

There are three classes of committees. **Standing committees** (twenty in the House and sixteen in the Senate—see Table 9.4) are at the center of the congressional process. They alone can approve

Former U.S. president Bill Clinton was named co-chair of the Interim Haiti Reconstruction Commission. Such committees are created to study special problems not covered by other committees. (AP World Wide Photo)

legislation and send it to the House or Senate floor for consideration. **Joint committees** are permanent committees made up of members from both houses. **Special or select committees** are created periodically to study particular problems or new areas of legislation not covered by the standing committees. For example, in 2007 the House of Representatives established a Select Committee on Energy Independence and Global Warming. This committee was eliminated at the beginning of 2011.

The concept of seniority, or privileges based on length of service, permeates Congress and is essential to understanding the committee system. **Congressional seniority** is based on length of continuous service in Congress. Seniority can affect committee assignments, the amount of office space a member is granted, and even the deference shown a member during floor debate. Committee seniority is determined by the years of continuous service on a particular committee. The committee chair is usually the member of the majority party with the longest consecutive service on the committee. A member who switches committees must start at the bottom of the committee ladder. This adherence to seniority has been challenged and revised in recent years. In 1995, a newly elected Republican majority disregarded seniority in making many of its committee leadership selections.

Members consider desirable committee assignments crucial to their reelection. After each congressional election, freshmen representatives and senators scramble to gain assignments suitable to their political fortunes and interests. Incumbents maneuver to gain more prestigious assignments. Assignments are first handled by a committee or committees in each chamber by each party, approved by the party caucuses (Democrats only), and then, in what is always a formality, approved again by the full Senate and House. Several criteria govern these assignments. For example, House Democrats rarely allow any member serving on what they call the "exclusive" committees (Ways and

standing committees

The permanent committees of Congress that alone can approve legislation and send it to the floor of the House or Senate

joint committees

Permanent committees of Congress made up of members from both houses

special or select committees

Committees of Congress created periodically to study particular problems or new areas of legislation

congressional seniority

Based on a member's length of continuous service in the Congress, it can affect committee assignments, the amount of office space granted, and even the deference shown a member during floor debate.

Means, Rules, and Appropriations) to serve on any other standing committee. Both Republicans and Democrats in the Senate agree that no member will receive two major committee assignments until every member has received one. Almost every senator now has the opportunity to serve on one of the four most prestigious committees (Appropriations, Armed Services, Finance, and Foreign Relations).

Members concerned primarily with reelection seek to join committees whose work has a direct impact on their constituents. A representative or senator from an area with considerable defense installations and large military contracts will probably seek membership on the Armed Services Committee, which handles the defense budget. Westerners are attracted to the House Natural Resources and Senate Energy and Natural Resources committees, whose jurisdictions include mining, government lands, immigration, and environmental laws. Members from states that produce crops heavily dependent on government support programs (wheat, peanuts, tobacco, and sugar) seek membership on the agriculture committees. Those interested in influencing national policy seek membership on committees that consider broad public issues such as education, foreign policy, and civil rights. Some members, as they become more senior and more entrenched at home, seek to expand their influence within their respective chambers. They are drawn to committees that decide matters of importance to practically every member, such as the tax-writing committees (Senate Finance and House Ways and Means, as well as the Joint Taxation Committee), the spending committees (Appropriations and Budget), and, in the House, the scheduling committee (Rules).

Members of Congress concerned with reelection join committees whose work has a direct impact on their constituents. Examples are the House Natural Resources and Senate Energy and Natural Resources committees, whose jurisdictions include mining, government lands, immigration, and environmental laws. (iStock)

Members cannot passively wait for their assignments. They must make their preferences known, urge senior members from their own states to lobby for them, personally meet with the chair or ranking minority member of the committee, and cultivate the support of the party leadership. Election results are barely known in November when senators and representatives descend on Washington to compete for the choicest committee seats. Committee assignments, one of the few benefits the congressional leadership can control, are employed, when possible, to promote party loyalty and responsibility. At one time, committee chairs gained their position by sheer dint of seniority and ran their committees like feudal baronies. They appointed subcommittee chairs, abolished or created subcommittees, decided whether to call committee meetings, and hired staff. Although the chairs still retain many of these powers (influencing the agenda, hiring staff, controlling committee funds), they are no longer the autocrats of yesteryear.

The reforms of the 1970s limited and defined the chairs' power. In the House, they lost the power to prevent committees from meeting, to designate subcommittee chairs, and to refer legislation to subcommittees. In the Senate, chairs no longer control all staff appointments; consequently, they have lost their influence over this important group of experts. Chairs do not want to appear to be obstructing legislation strongly supported by a majority of the caucus for fear of losing their positions; although it is far from absolute, however, chairs still hold considerable power. To get

table 9.4 | Committees in Congress

Standing Committees

House	Senate
Agriculture	Agriculture, Nutrition, and Forestry
Appropriation	Appropriations
Armed Services	Armed Services
Budget	Banking, Housing, and Urban Affairs
Education and the Workforce	Budget
Energy and Commerce	Commerce, Science, and Transportation
Ethics	Energy and Natural Resources
Financial Services	Environment and Public Works
Foreign Affairs	Finance
Homeland Security	Foreign Relations
House Administration	Health, Education, Labor, and Pensions
Judiciary	Homeland Security and Government Affairs
Natural Resources	Judiciary
Oversight and Government Reform	Rules and Administration
Rules	Small Business and Entrepreneurship
Science, Space, and Technology	Veterans' Affairs
Small Business	
Transportation and Infrastructure	
Veterans' Affairs	
Ways and means	

Special/Select Committees

House	Senate
Permanent Select Committee on Intelligence	Indian Affairs
	Select Committee on Ethics
	Select Committee on Intelligence
	Special Committee on Aging

Joint Committees

Joint Economic Committee

Joint Committee on Taxation

Joint Committee on Printing

Joint Committee on the Library

things done, they must use all their diplomatic and legislative skills. Former House Rules Committee chair Joe Moakley (D–MA) put it this way: "The days of snarling chairmen who look through junior members are long gone. To survive, you have to be gracious even when you say no."[15] Nor can chairs exercise their authority behind closed doors. The Legislative Reorganization Act of 1970 opened up the committee process, which had previously been conducted away from the direct scrutiny of the public and the media (as well as the lobbyists). Open committee hearings are now required in most cases, and committee roll-call votes are available to the public.

9.3d Subcommittees

Most of the standing congressional committees are divided into subcommittees. In the 113th Congress there were 104 subcommittees in the House and 68 in the Senate. House committee chairs previously controlled their subcommittees by packing them with members who would follow their lead. Under such circumstances, subcommittees would rarely report to the full committee legislation that the chair opposed. When the era of the autocratic chair came to an end, however, the trend in the House toward "subcommittee government" began.

Mike Conaway is committee chair of the House Committee on Agriculture and is a member of the Committee on Armed Services, Committee on Ethics, and Permanent Select Committee on Intelligence. (Wikimedia Commons)

In 1973 the House Democratic Caucus adopted a subcommittee "bill of rights." Democrats on every committee were given the authority to select subcommittee chairs, establish subcommittee jurisdiction, and provide the budgets for running the subcommittees. It required that all committees with more than twenty members establish at least four subcommittees, ending the Ways and Means Committee's unique practice of operating without subcommittees. Subcommittee chairs and the ranking minority members were allowed to hire staff to work directly for them on their subcommittee.

Subcommittees assumed greater independence, conducting legislative hearings once held primarily by the full committee. Whereas subcommittees conducted only 30 percent of the legislative hearings in the early 1950s, by the mid-1970s the figure had risen to 90 percent. Subcommittees were also drafting more legislation and frequently gaining full committee approval. Subcommittee chairs were replacing committee chairs as the managers of legislation on the floor.

This movement toward subcommittee government is less prevalent in the Senate, where subcommittees primarily hold hearings and key votes are taken in the full committee. In the Senate Commerce, Judiciary, and Labor committees, subcommittees have gained greater autonomy.[16]

The more democratic subcommittee government came with a cost. As more members exercised initiative and fewer could deliver the votes and call the shots, the committee system became increasingly unwieldy. With additional centers of power in Congress, party leaders had a far more difficult time building coalitions and constructing compromises.

9.3e Congressional Staff and Agencies

legislative assistant (LA)

A congressional aide who analyzes bills, drafts laws, writes speeches, and prepares position papers

administrative assistant (AA)

Top aide to a member of Congress who frequently acts on behalf of the legislator in dealing with staff, colleagues, constituents, and lobbyists

One hundred years ago senators and members of Congress performed their duties with only a few clerks, paid from members' own personal funds. In 2015, about thirty thousand people were employed by the legislative branch to work, for instance, on Capitol Hill as personal staff to representatives and senators or as committee staff—all paid from public funds. This burgeoning congressional bureaucracy reflects the complexity of modern government. The issues have grown more intricate, the congressional workload has expanded, and Congress has felt the need to match the expertise of the executive branch. A typical congressional office will include a **legislative assistant (LA)** to analyze bills, draft laws, write speeches, and prepare position papers, and an **administrative assistant (AA)** to act as the legislator's alter ego in dealing with colleagues, constituents, and lobbyists. In addition, most legislators have offices in their home states or districts to provide efficient constituent service and a personal touch.

Two Ideologues Leave the House

Ideologues can rarely be called great architects of legislation, although they can have an important effect on a legislative body and on the national political conversation. Consider two recent members of the House of Representatives: Ron Paul and Dennis Kucinich. Standing at opposite ends of the political spectrum, Representative Dennis Kucinich (D–OH) and Representative Ron Paul (R–TX) were ideologues—people for whom it is more important to defend principles than to resolve differences. Kucinich served in the House for eighteen years, losing a primary re-election bid in 2012 after redistricting combined his district with that of a fellow incumbent; and Paul served in three separate stints, totaling 23 years between 1976 and 2012.

Paul, a Texas obstetrician, became known for holding the most libertarian, anti–big government views in Congress. In fact, these firmly held convictions prompted him to leave the Republican Party for a time—running as the Libertarian Party's candidate for president in 1988. Although Paul ran as a Republican when he returned to Congress in 1996, and unsuccessfully sought the Republican nomination for the presidency in 2008 and 2012, he was never comfortable with the breadth of the Republican agenda, particularly its social conservatism. Identifying himself at various times as a Libertarian and Constitutionalist, Paul was outspoken in his support of free-market policies and decreases in taxes and spending and his opposition to the Iraq War and nearly all social welfare policies.

In his later years in Congress, these positions made Paul a favorite of the newly emerging Tea Party movement. Even though his extreme positions on what he saw as basic principles of economics and government often placed him at odds with the majority of the American public and sometimes forced his fellow Republicans into difficult positions, his charismatic personality, impressive intellect, and unwavering stances made him a popular figure at Libertarian rallies and on college campuses alike. Always more focused on principles than on electoral or legislative success, Paul remarked that "Politicians don't amount to much, but ideas do." In the 2010 election, Paul's son Rand Paul won a Senate seat in Kentucky, and the Pauls become the first simultaneous father-son House-Senate duo in American history.[1]

While sharing only a few of Ron Paul's views (although both opposed the Iraq War), liberal Representative Dennis Kucinich employed some of the same techniques. Although they were polar opposites on many issues, ranging from Social Security to healthcare reform, Kucinich and Paul were both outspoken critics of colleagues with whom they disagreed, and both mastered the use of social media to develop a national following beyond the halls of Congress and the confines of their congressional districts.[2] After first gaining notoriety as the youngest mayor of a major city when he took the helm in Cleveland in 1978, Kucinich turned to national politics in the 1990s. A ventriloquist and a vegan, Kucinich was never one to stick to the mainstream. He advocated for the creation of a Department of Peace and for mandatory pre-kindergarten. He sought a federal ban on the death penalty and the elimination of all nuclear weapons. Like Paul, he also made unsuccessful bids for the presidency, seeking the Democratic nomination in 2004 and 2008.

Both Paul and Kucinich paid a price for their extremism, as creating enemies within their own parties sometimes led to a lack of support for the measures they, themselves, proposed. Never afraid to stand their ground, they stuck to principle—and often found themselves the lone opposition to popular issues. Some critics say these maverick legislators are more interested in using the House as a platform for their ideas than in forging coalitions and compromises. Do legislators such as Paul and Kucinich raise important issues, or do they merely obstruct the business of Congress? Is it more important for a legislator to compromise and pass legislation, or to always stick firmly to a principle? What other legislators retired in 2012? What views did they hold?

1 "The Antiwar, Anti-Abortion, Anti-Drug-Enforcement-Administration, Anti-Medicare Candidacy of Dr. Ron Paul," New York Times, (July 22, 2007).

2 "Colorful Kucinich Calls It Quits," Sacramento Bee, (May 20, 2012).

Who are these staff people? They are relatively young (average age slightly under forty), well educated (close to half have postgraduate or professional degrees), and predominantly male (about 68 percent).[17] In an earlier time they may have been political operatives or cronies of the legislator, but today they are bright university graduates. The experience of being a staffer can be both exhilarating and precarious. Staffers are frequently in the center of dramatic legislative battles, but they have no civil service protection and can be fired by their representative or senator without cause or notice.

Unlike the personal staffers, whose job it is to serve the member and his or her political interest, the *committee staffers* are responsible for developing the legislation that comes from the committees. The committee chair, subcommittee chair, or ranking minority party member appoint these committee staffers. They, in turn, organize hearings, conduct research, assist in the drafting of legislation, and prepare the reports that accompany bills sent out of committee. The chief committee aides—those most familiar with the details of a particular bill—may accompany the committee chair when the bill is debated on the floor. Because a member's time is stretched thin, staffers may act as stand-ins for the legislators themselves, negotiating with lobbyists, executive branch officials, and even other legislators to gain support for a particular bill. Like the rest of the congressional bureaucracy, the congressional committee staffs grew from about four hundred in 1947 to over twenty-five hundred by the 2000s—an increase of over 600 percent.

You can search through the full text of federal legislation and track bills through the legislative process at Congress.gov—a service of the Library of Congress.

http://www.bvtlab.com/43k77

Has this expansion of staff solved the congressional need for more information? Some argue that members have become too dependent upon committee staff. Frequently, staffers are the only ones who understand increasingly complex legislation, such as the Patient Protection and Affordable Care Act of 2010. Others argue that more staff generate more legislation, diluting a member's ability to concentrate on what is important. Has the Congress simply transferred its dependency for information from the executive branch to its own staff?[18]

In addition to staff, three agencies provide Congress with research and analysis of policy options:

1. *The Congressional Research Service (CRS)* serves the entire Congress—members, committees, and aides. On request, it conducts legal research and policy analysis and digests and summarizes legislation. Congress created the CRS to remedy the dearth of information at Congress's disposal as compared to the information resources long available to the president.

2. *The Government Accountability Office (GAO),* known as the watchdog agency, reports to Congress on the efficiency and performance of federal programs. With over thirty-two hundred employees, its task is to determine whether a program is achieving the objectives that Congress has prescribed. Previously known as the General Accounting Office, the name was changed in 2004 to better reflect the agency's activities, which now extend well beyond mere financial audits.

3. *The Congressional Budget Office (CBO)* provides essential analysis of the economy and the federal budget for Congress. Specifically, it provides an assessment of the inflationary impact of major bills, projects the five-year costs of proposed legislation, and forecasts economic trends. The CBO gives Congress

an independent base of economic and budgetary expertise to challenge the economic assumptions behind the president's budget.

9.4 | Congressional Procedures: How a Bill Becomes a Law

Ultimately, Congress impacts American government because it is the chief law-making body. Presidents, parties, and interest groups may propose a host of programs; yet unless Congress acts favorably, each proposal remains an idea, not a law. The legislative process in Congress is an obstacle course (see Figure 9.1). A bill can be stalled or defeated at various points along the way, and most are. Of the over five thousand bills introduced in the 113th Congress, only about two hundred eventually became law.

9.4a Committee to Floor Debate

The objective of guiding a bill through Congress is to have both houses pass the bill in identical form. Only then can it go to the president for signing. At the initial stage of the legislative process, only a member of the House or the Senate may introduce a bill, although the proposal frequently originates in the executive branch, an interest group, or a member's staff. Once a bill is introduced, it is sent to the appropriate committee; should a committee refuse to consider the bill, it is consigned to an early death. If the bill is considered, it is usually assigned to a subcommittee for study; and the process begins. The subcommittee may then hold hearings inviting government officials and other experts to testify. These hearings serve not only to obtain information but also to test public opinion, build support for the measure, or perhaps delay ultimate consideration. Except in the case of national security matters, most hearings are open to the public. When the hearings are complete, the bill is **marked up**. This is the process whereby the subcommittee decides on the bill's precise language and on amendments. Like hearings, most mark-up sessions are open to the public.

The bill, if approved by the subcommittee, then goes to the full committee for consideration. If the full committee approves the bill (it may mark up the bill or add its own amendments), it sends the bill to its respective chamber for consideration. Bills voted out of committee are often accompanied by an extensive report that explains the bill's purpose, the committee amendments, its effect on existing law, and its probable costs.

9.4b Floor Debate: The House

Bills finally reported out of committee are listed on one of the House calendars. Tax and appropriation bills are placed on the **Union Calendar**. Non-money bills go to the **House Calendar**. Private bills, such as one that granted citizenship to a 111-year-old Albanian woman so that she could vote in a free election before she died, are placed on the **Private Calendar**.

The Speaker and the majority leader determine when bills are called off the calendar and placed on the House floor. Bills on the Private Calendar can be heard only on certain days of the month; they are brought directly to the floor, usually by unanimous consent, and passed with little debate. The Speaker may also bring other minor bills directly to the floor by a suspension of the rules. Under this procedure, which requires a two-thirds vote of the House, debate is limited to forty minutes; no amendments are

mark-up

The process in which a legislative committee sets the precise language and amendments of a bill

Union Calendar

The House schedule for the consideration of tax and appropriation bills

House Calendar

The legislative schedule in the House of Representatives for non-money bills

Private Calendar

The schedule for House bills that concerns personal rather than general legislative matters

Figure 9.1 | How a Bill Becomes Law

At each step along the way a bill can be stymied, making this journey a genuine obstacle course.

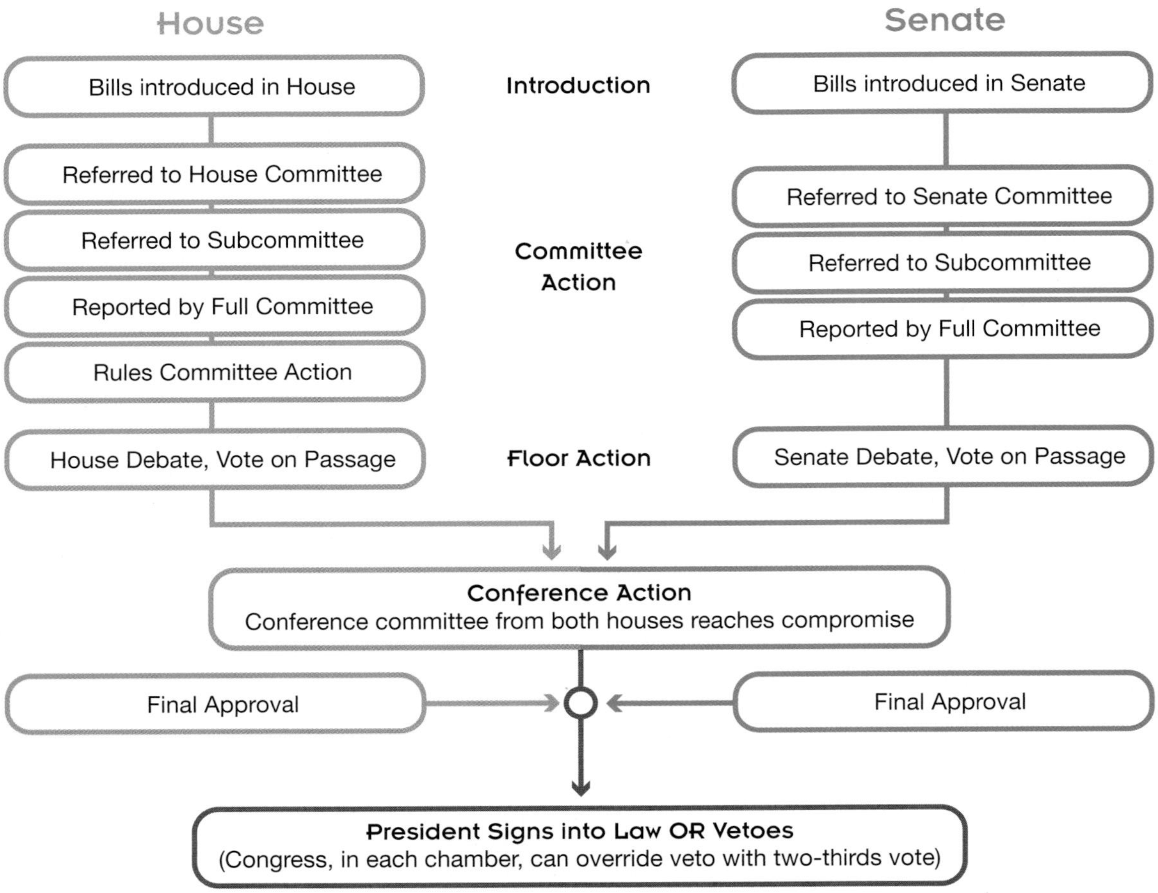

House   **Senate**

Introduction

- Bills introduced in House — Bills introduced in Senate
- Referred to House Committee — Referred to Senate Committee

Committee Action

- Referred to Subcommittee — Referred to Subcommittee
- Reported by Full Committee — Reported by Full Committee
- Rules Committee Action

Floor Action

- House Debate, Vote on Passage — Senate Debate, Vote on Passage

Conference Action
Conference committee from both houses reaches compromise

Final Approval ○ Final Approval

President Signs into Law OR Vetoes
(Congress, in each chamber, can override veto with two-thirds vote)

---

closed rule

An order from the House Rules Committee that prohibits amendments to a bill under consideration on the House floor

open rule

An order from the House Rules Committee whereby amendments to a bill are permitted on the floor

modified rule

An order from the House Rules Committee allowing a limited number of amendments to a bill during floor consideration

allowed. Other matters are considered privileged and can be brought to the House floor at almost any time, but most major bills must take the route from the committee to the House floor via the Rules Committee. The Rules Committee decides the amount of time the House will spend debating a bill and dictates the amending process. The committee may send a bill to the floor with a **closed rule**, prohibiting all amendments except those from the committee that reported the bill; an **open rule**, permitting any amendments from the floor; or a **modified rule**, allowing a limited number of amendments. Tax bills, reported out of the Ways and Means Committee, are usually given the privilege of a closed rule. The Speaker appoints all of his or her party's members on the Rules Committee, and the committee is thus an arm of the leadership.

When floor debate begins, the Speaker has a member of the Rules Committee from each party explain the rule under which the bill will be debated and voted. Usually the Rules Committee specifies from one to two hours of debate, but it will grant controversial bills of particular importance up to ten hours. Debate begins with a statement from the floor manager of the bill, who is by custom the chairperson of the committee or subcommittee that reported the bill. The floor manager has the responsibility of guiding the bill to passage. Frequently debate is conducted in the **Committee of the Whole**. This device allows the House to conduct business more quickly by relaxing the formal rules and allowing a quorum of only 100, instead of the usual 218; but the full House must approve decisions made by the Committee of the Whole before they are official.

After general debate covering the pros and cons of the bill, the amending process begins. Here the fate of a bill may be decided. Opponents of the bill may try to amend it beyond recognition or else add objectionable provisions destined to kill it. The House rules require that amendments be germane to the bill under consideration. Amendments are debated no more than ten minutes—five minutes for the sponsors and five for the opponents.

An electronic voting system, installed in 1973, makes time-consuming roll-call votes unnecessary. Members may insert a plastic card into one of forty voting machines and vote "yes," "no," or "present" (abstaining). The vote is recorded on an electronic display board on the wall of the chamber, and the process takes about fifteen minutes. A series of bells that ring through the halls and offices of Congress alerts members to floor votes.

9.4c Floor Debate: The Senate

The Senate, being smaller, has a more flexible set of procedures. First, the Senate has only two calendars: an **Executive Calendar** for presidential nominations and treaties and a Calendar of General Orders for all other legislation. Second, there is no equivalent of the House Rules Committee. Thus the Senate imposes no time limits on general debate, no five-minute rule on amendments, and no restrictions on the number of amendments. In addition, amendments need not be germane to the bill under consideration.

Nongermane amendments, called **riders**, allow a proposal to bypass a hostile Senate committee that otherwise would have considered and probably killed it. The rider must then only survive the conference committee if the complete bill passes the Senate. Riders are also used to force the president to accept a program that would be vetoed were it to reach him as a separate piece of legislation. Attaching the rider to necessary legislation, such as a general appropriations bill that the president will feel compelled to sign, does this. One may wonder how, with such permissive rules, the Senate ever accomplishes anything. The answer is that through the mechanism of **unanimous consent agreements**, terms of Senate debates are limited. These agreements, usually secured by the majority leader in cooperation with the minority leader, are carefully negotiated to accommodate the desires of senators who wish to speak or offer amendments.

The best-known technique for forestalling the work of the Senate is the **filibuster**—a continuing debate designed to prevent passage of a bill. A single senator or a group of senators can conduct a filibuster. The filibuster is essentially a political device to stop a bill that the minority does not have the votes to defeat, to win concessions on a bill, or to arouse public opposition to it. Owing to the time constraints on a busy Senate (more committee meetings, more recorded votes, more bills considered), even the threat to delay business by a filibuster can force a concession on a bill. Defenders argue that the filibuster protects minority rights and requires the Senate to consider not only the extent of opposition but its depth and intensity as well. Critics claim that the filibuster thwarts majority will and allows a small minority to exercise disproportionate influence on a bill or even to defeat it altogether.

Committee of the Whole

A parliamentary device used by the House of Representatives to facilitate floor consideration of a bill; when the House dissolves itself into the Committee of the Whole, it can suspend formal rules and consider a bill with a quorum of 100 rather than the usual 218

Executive Calendar

One of two registers of business in the U.S. Senate that contains presidential nominations and treaties

riders

Provisions, usually attached to appropriation bills, which "ride" into law on the backs of necessary pieces of legislation, forcing the president to veto the entire bill in order to kill the amendment

unanimous consent agreement

A common mechanism used by the Senate leadership to limit Senate debate

filibuster

Continuing debate designed to prevent consideration of a particular bill; a technique used in the Senate

Until 1917 the Senate had no way of ending debate except through unanimous consent. At that time the Senate adopted Rule 22, a **cloture** (debate-ending) rule that allowed two-thirds of the senators present to end debate. In 1975 the rule was amended so that sixty members (or three-fifths of the membership) can shut off debate. Once cloture is invoked, the Senate can continue consideration of the bill for only thirty additional hours. Prior to the 1970s, a filibuster was a rare event, used primarily by southern Democrats to block civil rights legislation. Now it is almost commonplace and occurs on a wide range of issues. Cloture votes, which numbered six in the 90th Congress (1967–1969), rose steadily beginning in the 1970s, and sky-rocketed starting in the mid-2000s. In the recently completed 113th Congress, there were nearly two hundred cloture votes—almost double the previous record. In an effort to overcome their inability to invoke cloture for a large number of executive and judicial appointees, in 2013 Senate Democrats chose what is sometimes referred to as the "nuclear option." They changed the rules to allow for a simple majority to end a filibuster for these nominations. While this move created a temporary solution, some fear it may lead to more partisan extremism in the future.

In 2012 Representative Barney Frank (D–MA) became the first member of Congress to marry someone of the same gender while in office. His husband, Jim Ready, appears at left in this photo. (iStock)

9.4d The Conference Committee: Resolving Senate-House Differences

Rarely do the Senate and House pass bills in identical form. If one house makes only minor changes in a bill passed by the other, the chamber that initially passed the bill will usually agree to the changes and send the bill on to the president for signature. But when there are major differences over a bill, a **House-Senate Conference Committee** must reconcile them. The House Speaker and the Senate presiding officers name the conferees on the recommendation of the chairperson of the committee that reported the bill. The majority from each delegation must be from the majority party in that chamber. Each chamber has one vote in the conference, which is determined by a vote of the majority of its delegation. When the conference finishes its job, it sends the conference report or compromise bill back to the House and Senate for approval. Approval of the conference report by both houses constitutes final approval of the bill.

Numerous traps await a bill before it gets to the president's desk. Bills must pass the Senate and the House within the two-year period that makes up a particular Congress; otherwise, the bill must start through the obstacle course anew with the

cloture

Rule 22 of the Senate in which discussion on a piece of legislation can be suspended after no more than thirty hours of debate by a vote of sixty members

House-Senate Conference Committee

A joint committee designed to reconcile differences between the House and Senate versions of a bill

E very year the United States Congress passes hundreds of laws.

Where do they end up?

In the United States Code, an extensive resource that is updated annually and accessible at this website:

http://www.bvtlab.com/4KCNp

BVT Lab

Flashcards are available
for this chapter at
www.BVTLab.com.

Chapter 09 | Congress | 295

next Congress. It can be buried in committee or by the House Rules Committee, stifled by a Senate filibuster, or caught in a conference committee deadlock. Sponsors of a bill must know congressional procedure, be sensitive to key personalities such as the Speaker or the important committee chairs, and must, at each crucial point, weave a majority coalition for the bill.

9.5   Congress and the Political System

The legislative process alone does not explain why some bills become law and others do not. Congress is also part of the broader political system. Everything it does affects citizens, as well as one or more interest groups and governmental agencies. These different constituencies labor mightily to influence congressional decisions.

9.5a Lobbies

As the range of government programs, subsidies, and entitlements has grown, so has the number of interest groups with a stake in them. The result has been the proliferation of lobbies and lobbyists, as described in Chapter 7. Critics feel that lobbies distort the political process and give particular groups inordinate influence over legislation.

Lobbyists are most successful in affecting **distributive policies** (special interest subsidies such as water reclamation projects, farm price supports, and new post offices). These programs usually provoke little opposition because they are perceived as providing considerable benefits at little relative cost. As a result, the entire Congress rarely pays close attention to such questions. Lobbyists can then concentrate their efforts on a key subcommittee or committee, simplifying its task. Open committee sessions allow lobbyists to monitor congressional action quite carefully. Rather than waiting outside a closed door while a committee mark-up session is going on, a lobbyist may be right in the committee room suggesting precise legislative language or a compromise amendment.

Lobbies have the most difficulty affecting **redistributive policies**, those that produce benefits to some segments of society at substantive cost to others. These include broad budget decisions that place social programs against defense spending or proposals for tax reform. Such issues are frequently resolved on the floor of Congress, not in committee. Because they usually involve conflicts among interest groups, the result is often a compromise with no single lobby getting exactly what it wants.

Contemporary lobbying must go beyond working the halls of Congress; moving legislation often requires affecting public opinion. Therefore, lobbyists must employ the techniques of mass marketing: targeted mailings and e-mailings, television advertising, and slick public relations campaigns. In twenty-four hours the National Rifle Association can generate millions of e-mails and faxes opposing a gun control measure; AARP—the retirees' lobby—swamped former Speaker Jim Wright in one day with over fifteen million postcards and letters warning against tampering with the cost-of-living formula for Social Security.[19] Much of the increase in lobbying is a result of the weakened power of the committee chairs and the decentralization of power in Congress. Now that there are more committee members and staffers to be persuaded, more lobbyists are required to do the job.

distributive policies

Programs such as water reclamation projects that provide considerable benefits for a few people and relatively small costs for many, usually provoking little opposition

redistributive policies

Programs such as tariffs or tax reforms that produce considerable benefits to some segments of society but high costs to others

Interest groups are not the only lobbying forces in Congress. The bureaucracy itself exercises considerable influence on the congressional process. Together with interest groups and congressional committees, bureaucratic agencies often develop informal partnerships called subgovernments or **iron triangles**. Each group scratches the back of the other. The agency gets its budget from the committee and political support from the interest group. The interest group gets favorable legislation from the committee and sympathetic treatment from the agency. The congressional committee members get campaign reelection support from the interest group and conscientious constituency service from the bureaucracy. These subgovernments have special influence over distributive policy.

The veterans' programs provide an example of such interplay. In this case, the subgovernment includes the veterans' groups, the veterans' committees of Congress, and the Department of Veterans Affairs (see Figure 9.2). Together these pieces of the subgovernment conspire to protect veterans' programs from the budget-cutter's scalpel. Veterans' benefits are usually not matters at the top of the president's agenda, nor are they issues that excite broad congressional interest. They are, in fact, typical of the type of distributive policies that are shaped by subgovernments.

To function effectively, an iron triangle requires that the participants be shielded from the glare of publicity. Over the past two decades the environment has changed, and the effectiveness of these subgovernments has declined. The media are more aggressive in covering Congress, the number of lobbies with competing interests in legislation has increased, and new public interest lobbies watch for special interest favoritism; no committee has exclusive control over such broad issues as energy, foreign trade, and the environment. In a period of tight budgets, fewer issues can be classified as distributive, providing benefits to a few without significant and visible costs to the many.[20]

9.6   What Role for a Changing Congress?

Largely through its own efforts, Congress democratized its rules and opened up its procedures. The seniority system is no longer sacred. Committee chairs do not control their committees. Committee sessions are now accessible to the public. Junior members can make an immediate impact, often serving as subcommittee chairs; and the creation of the Congressional Budget Office, plus the addition of more professional staffers, has put Congress in the position to challenge the expertise of the executive branch.

Many people welcome the resurgence of congressional will as a necessary corrective to the presidential excesses that produced the Vietnam War and the Watergate scandal. They argue that the openness of Congress is essential to a democratic society, but other observers question whether Congress has gone too far in its reassertion of power and independence. Congress cannot control inflation, negotiate arms agreements, or solve our trade deficit. Congressional leaders feel that the American government functions best under the leadership of the president. Only the president,

iron triangle

The combination of interest group representatives, legislators, and government administrators seen as extremely influential in determining the outcome of political decisions

they argue, can define national objectives that can arouse a majority of citizens. The historic statements of national policy, so the argument goes, were presidential not congressional: the Monroe Doctrine, the Emancipation Proclamation, and the War on Poverty. Although Congress cannot lead, it does have an important role to play. It provides more citizen access to policy making and offsets the impersonality of the bureaucracy. In a larger sense, Congress brings the parochialism of Main Street, the suburban kaffeeklatsch, and the union hall to Washington's corridors of power. The many and often-confusing voices with which Congress speaks are the clatter of the democratic process.

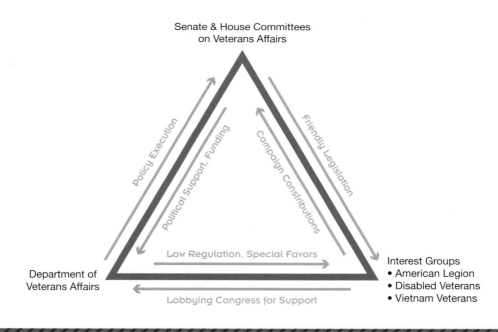

Figure 9.2 | The "Iron Triangle" and Veterans' Policy

The triangular relationship among congressional committees, bureaucratic agencies, and interest groups indicates how relatively few people can determine public policy on some questions. The relationship does not mean that the groups are always in agreement, but it does mean that the dominant opinion represented will usually have the largest say in setting veterans' policy. Sometimes the components in the triangle are more numerous. A proposed change in educational benefits, for example, would involve higher-education lobbies and other committees and agencies. A change in job-training policy for veterans would involve the Labor Department as well as the labor committees in Congress.

Senate & House Committees
on Veterans Affairs

Policy Execution

Political Support, Funding

Campaign Constributions

Friendly Legislation

Low Regulation, Special Favors

Department of
Veterans Affairs

Lobbying Congress for Support

Interest Groups
• American Legion
• Disabled Veterans
• Vietnam Veterans

CHAPTER REVIEW

1. Since 1819 the Supreme Court has granted Congress great leeway in legislating on social and economic matters. Both houses have equal weight in writing laws; but the Senate—owing to its longer member terms, its special responsibilities (ratifying treaties and confirming presidential appointments), and its smaller size—seems to command somewhat greater prestige.

2. The task of members of Congress has many dimensions: mastering fields of legislation, bringing back a share of federal benefits for their state or district, meeting the needs of individual constituents, learning the norms and rules of their respective chambers, and voting on a wide variety of legislative questions. It is a demanding, complex, full-time job.

3. Power in the contemporary Congress is no longer the exclusive prerogative of a few senior members. In the House, much of the power has flowed to the subcommittees. Individual senators have become increasingly assertive. Junior members feel little obligation to serve a period of apprenticeship. Congress, as a result, is both more democratic and more unwieldy.

4. Leadership in Congress is based largely on persuasion and ability. Autocratic leaders are increasingly rare. The influence of the caucus requires that most congressional leaders be sensitive to the concerns of the rank-and-file members.

5. Before a bill can become a law, it must pass through a complete obstacle course. At each crucial point, successful sponsors must weave a majority coalition for their bill.

6. Congress, although influenced by presidential leadership, is not the president's rubber stamp and initiates much legislation on its own.

KEY TERMS

Readings for Further Study

For a comprehensive overview of Congress, consult Roger H. Davidson, Walter J. Oleszek, Frances E. Lee, and Eric Schickler *Congress and Its Members*, 14th ed. (Washington, D.C.: CQ Press, 2013), and Morris P. Fiorina, *Congress: Keystone of the Washington Establishment*, 2nd ed. (New Haven, CT: Yale University Press, 1989).

The most complete review of the rules and processes of Congress is Walter J. Oleszek's *Congressional Procedures and the Policy Process*, 9th ed. (Washington, D.C.: CQ Press, 2013).

An excellent history of development and change in Congress is Nelson W. Polsby's *How Congress Evolves: Social Bases of Institutional Change* (New York: Oxford, 2005).

A collection of highly readable essays on the problems of the contemporary Congress can be found in Lawrence C. Dodd and Bruce I. Oppenheimer, eds., *Congress Reconsidered*, 10th ed. (Washington, D.C.: CQ Press, 2012).

Up-to-date information and lively accounts of individual senators and representatives are available in Michael Barone's and Grant Ujifusa's *Almanac of American Politics* (Washington, D.C.: National Journal), published every two years.

A valuable collection of historical data appears in Norman J. Ornstein, Thomas E. Mann, and Michael J. Malbin, *Vital Statistics on Congress, 2008* (Washington, D.C.: Brookings Institution Press, 2008).

Notes

1. 17 U.S. (4 Wheaton) 316 (1819).

2. For example, *United States v. Lopez*, 514 U.S. 549 (1995) and *United States v. Morrison*, 529 U.S. 598 (2000).

3. 376 U.S. 1 (1964).

4. Quoted in Roger J. Davidson and Walter J. Oleszek, *Congress and Its Members*, 3rd ed. (Washington, DC: Congressional Quarterly, 1990), p. 23.

5. David J. Vogler, *The Politics of Congress*, 4th ed. (Boston: Allyn & Bacon, 1983), p. 76.

6. The Gallup Organization, "Congress and the Public," 2014.

7. Hedrick Smith, *The Power Game: How Washington Works* (New York: Ballantine Books, 1989), p. 108; Davidson and Oleszek, "Congress and Its Members," pp. 124–227.

8. Davidson and Oleszek, Congress and Its Members, pp. 130–131.

9. R. Kent Weaver, "The Politics of Blame Avoidance," *The Brookings Review 5* (Spring 1987): 43–47.

10. Barbara Sinclair, *The Transformation of the U.S. Senate* (Baltimore, MD: Johns Hopkins University Press, 1989), pp. 98–100.

11. Andy Plattner, "The Lure of the Senate: Influence and Prestige," *Congressional Quarterly Weekly Report* (May 25, 1985): 991–998.

12. Roger H. Davidson, "The New Centralization on Capitol Hill," *Review of Politics 50* (1988): 358–359.

13. "House majority leader's shocking defeat," This Week, (June 20, 2014).

14. Quoted in Samuel C. Patterson, "Party Leadership in the U.S. Senate," *Legislative Studies Quarterly 14* (1989): 409.

15. *Congressional Quarterly Weekly Report* (December 8, 1990): 406.

16. Lawrence Dodd and Bruce Oppenheimer, "The House in Transition: Change and Consolidation," in *Congress Reconsidered*, 2nd ed. (Washington, DC: Congressional Quarterly, 1981), p. 42; Davidson and Oleszek, "Congress and Its Members," p. 230.

17. "Congressional Staffers: Who Are the People Behind the Scenes in Washington?" The Huffington Post, June 17, 2011, http://www.huffingtonpost.com/2011/06/17/congressional-staffers-infographic_n_879000.html (August 17, 2012).

18. Michael L. Mezey, "The Legislature, the Executive, and Public Policy: The Futile Quest for Congressional Power," in James A. Thurber, ed., *Divided Democracy* (Washington, DC: Congressional Quarterly, 1991), p. 107.

19. Smith, *The Power Game*, p. 383.

20. Morris P. Fiorina, *Congress: Keystone of the Washington Establishment*, 2nd ed. (New Haven, CT: Yale University Press, 1989), pp. 122–123.

POP QUIZ

1. Members of Congress who primarily vote according to their constituents' desires follow the _____ role of representation.

2. The _____ Committee clears all major legislation going to the floor of the House.

3. Congressional _____ can affect committee assignments, office space, and even deference shown a member on the floor.

4. The agency that reports to Congress on the efficiency and performance of federal programs is called the _____ _____ _____.

5. The informal partnerships between interest groups, congressional committees, and bureaucratic agencies are called _____ _____.

6. By 2007 the percentage of African Americans in Congress finally came to equal the percentage of African Americans in the population as a whole.   T   F

7. Party whips in the House act as the heart of the party communication system.   T   F

8. A member who switches committees is able to transfer his seniority from the old committee to the new.   T   F

9. Committee staffers are responsible for developing the legislation that comes from the committees.   T   F

10. Once an effective and often-used strategy, the filibuster has been rarely used since the Senate adopted Rule 22 on cloture.   T   F

11. Most members of Congress see themselves as following the _____ role.

    A) trustee

    B) delegate

    C) politico

    D) party

12. Legislative norms include _____.

    A) reciprocity

    B) personal courtesy

    C) subject specialization

    D) all of the above

13. Why are members of Congress motivated to choose a particular committee?

    A) To enhance their reelection prospects

    B) To shape national policy

    C) To gain influence within Congress

    D) All of the above

14. What does it mean when a bill is marked up?

    A) The bill's language and amendments have been decided upon.

    B) The bill is being delayed by a filibuster.

    C) The bill is being called up to bypass the Rules Committee.

    D) The bill is bottled up in the Rules Committee.

15. Which of the following is true of the Conference Committee?

    A) It reconciles differences between the two parties in the House.

    B) It has become primarily a formality.

    C) It is often the scene of very hard bargaining and compromise.

    D) It is closed to the public.

Answers:
1. delegate   2. Rules   3. seniority   4. Government Accountability Office   5. iron triangles or subgovernments   6. F   7. T   8. F   9. T   10. F   11. C   12. D   13. D   14. A   15. C

Chapter

10

The Presidency

In This Chapter

Chapter Objectives

The American presidency is an awe-inspiring and complex office. Its demands are numerous and often contradictory. The president is expected to be honest and trustworthy, yet tough if not ruthless; to be a moral leader who is above politics, as well as a political operator who can achieve results; to control government spending and taxes and yet provide extensive governmental services; and to preserve American honor against international threats and yet keep the peace. When presidents extend their power, they are chastised for being imperial; when they fail to offer decisive leadership, they are considered weak and ineffective.

Even the most powerful American presidents have rarely been able to dictate the political agenda. They have had to lead; and leadership in a democratic society requires an ability to persuade without being tiresome, a capacity to administer without getting lost in details, and a sense of when to compromise and when to stand one's ground. The office is a complex mixture of authority and constraints, too subtle to capture in any one theoretical model. Some presidents have mastered the office; some have been mastered by it.

Commentators on the presidency in the 1950s and 1960s stressed its great powers and the capacity of its occupant to accomplish great things. Franklin D. Roosevelt (1933–1945) was the model—a president who dominated Congress, shepherded through an ambitious reform agenda, centralized decision-making in his own hands, fully exercised his powers as commander in chief, and inspired the nation with his speeches. Roosevelt's presidency influenced many to regard the office in heroic terms.

The fall from political grace of Lyndon Johnson (1963–1969) over Vietnam and Richard Nixon (1969–1974) over Watergate led later scholars of the office to warn against the dangers of an imperial presidency. Responding to the mood of the general public, Congress in the mid-1970s passed a series of laws constraining the president's power. The two presidents of that period, Gerald Ford (1974–1977) and Jimmy Carter (1977–1981), thus besieged, appeared to be weak. Although weakened by the Iran-contra affair toward the end of his term, President Ronald Reagan (1981–1989) restored some personal power to the office, but not its institutional authority. George Bush (1989–1993), who was unable to exert the mastery over domestic and economic policy that he had shown in the Desert Storm operation, was defeated for reelection. Bill Clinton (1993–2001), although elected twice, tarnished the image of the presidency when his difficulties with marital fidelity and misleading testimony led him to become only the second president to be impeached by the House of Representatives. New directions in American foreign policy, particularly in regard to terrorism and war, largely shaped the presidency of George W. Bush (2001–2009). President Barack Obama's (2009–) challenges have ranged from handling a massive recession to winding down two wars. It remains to be seen how history will judge his efforts.

President Barack Obama (Shutterstock)

chief of state

The role the president plays as the ceremonial head of the nation that can also make the president a symbol of national unity during times of crisis

head of government

The chief executive officer of a government—The president is the head of government in the United States.

10.1 The President and Symbolic Leadership

America has no purely symbolic head of state. Unlike most Western democracies, America does not separate the ceremonial **chief of state** from the actual **head of government**. We have no constitutional monarch, as in Great Britain, the Netherlands, and Sweden, and no ribbon-cutting ceremonial president, as in Germany, Italy, and Israel. The American president is both monarch and prime minister, reigning as well as ruling.

As the head of state, the president in a single week may meet with the winners of the high school Voice of Democracy essay contest, honor the teacher of the year, and prepare a humorous speech for the Washington Gridiron Club. Although a president usually spends no more than one or two hours a week on such activities, they are not as trivial as they may sound. Such ceremonies are important to a nation's morale, its sense of unity, and its recognition of common values.

The ceremonial presidency also has a political dimension. Because the president is our only symbolic head of state, the office carries with it a considerable fund of public goodwill and support. Presidents, no matter how narrow their election victory, find that in the weeks and months after assuming office they are the objects of public adoration. According to opinion polls, their approval rating is rarely as high again.

During this honeymoon period some presidents have successfully translated public goodwill into notable political victories. Franklin Roosevelt, in his first hundred days, persuaded Congress to pass the bulk of his economic recovery program. Lyndon Johnson, soon after succeeding John Kennedy (1961–1963), pushed through Congress the far-reaching Civil Rights Act of 1964 (see Chapter 3). Ronald Reagan, in the months following his first inauguration, won major victories on budget and tax issues.

In times of international crisis, the public will often rally to support the office. When the nation perceives itself to be threatened or to have been wronged, the president is the symbol of unity. After the Japanese attack on Pearl Harbor in 1941, Franklin Roosevelt's popularity rose 12 percent. After the Korean War broke out in 1950, Harry Truman's (1945–1953) rose 9 percent. Even after the ill-fated Bay of Pigs invasion in Cuba in 1961, John Kennedy's support increased 12 percent. After the hostages were seized in Iran in 1979, Jimmy Carter's popularity increased a dramatic 31 percent. Immediately after hostilities commenced in the Gulf War in 1991, George H. W. Bush's approval rating soared to 89 percent. His son's turn-around was even more dramatic. George W. Bush saw his approval rating move from 51 percent just before September 11, 2001, to 90 percent just after. Yet, when the United States became bogged down in a seemingly interminable war in Iraq, Bush's approval rating dipped to an abysmal 28 percent.

The fusion of symbolic and political authority in this office can result, however, in a distorted public image of what its occupant can achieve. Just as the public will rally to the president in a time of crisis, so will people frequently blame the president when events sour. Presidential popularity is often directly related to whether the news is good or bad. In other words, given the symbolic nature of the office, the public may both credit and blame a president for events over which he or she has little control.

Since the presidency has both symbolic and substantive power, a paradox is built into the office. The president is expected to be both the symbol of national unity and the intensely political leader of the executive branch. Inevitably, the president must promote solutions to problems that will alienate some faction of the public, and symbolic leadership will be sacrificed by the need for substantive leadership. The result is that presidential popularity frequently will decline from the beginning of a president's term to the end of it.

Dwight Eisenhower (1953–1961), Ronald Reagan (1981–1989), and Bill Clinton (1993–2001) were exceptions to the rule; they seemed to be able to reconcile the two roles. All three completed two full terms and left office as popular as they entered (see Table 10.1). Eisenhower avoided taking on issues that he knew would cost him support, such as civil rights, and jealously protected his political goodwill. Reagan took controversial positions, but his reassuring personality and rhetorical skills generated much public trust. Clinton was often mired in personal scandal, but

BVT Lab
Improve your test scores. Practice quizzes are available at www.BVTLab.com.

305

Chapter 10 | The Presidency

table 10.1 | Public Approval Ratings of Presidents Roosevelt to Obama

Public approval ratings usually vary widely during a president's time in office. Sometimes they reflect the president's handling of events. At other times, they reflect public frustration over events largely out of a president's control.

	Beginning of Term	End of Term	High	Low	Average
Franklin Roosevelt*	—	—	84	54	75
Harry Truman	87	31	87	23	43
Dwight Eisenhower	68	59	79	49	65
John Kennedy	72	58	83	56	71
Lyndon Johnson	79	49	80	35	55
Richard Nixon	59	24	68	24	49
Gerald Ford	71	53	71	37	47
Jimmy Carter	66	34	75	21	47
Ronald Reagan	51	63	68	35	52
George H. W. Bush	51	49	89	32	61
Bill Clinton	58	65	73	37	55
George W. Bush	57	32	90	25	49
Barack Obama**	67	—	69	38	47

*Polls taken 1938–1943 only.
**Numbers are through November 2014 only.

SOURCE: The Gallup Organization, 2014.

the public was largely able to separate their disapproval of the president's personal life from their enthusiasm for his leadership skills and success in guiding the economy. All three were fortunate in avoiding protracted and unresolved military conflicts and in presiding over a period of general prosperity. The latter, above all, may be the key to presidential popularity.

| 10.2 | The President and the Constitution |

To understand the presidency, one must start with the Constitution. As with members of Congress, discussed in Chapter 9, the Constitution is specific with regard to who may be president.

Only **natural-born citizens**, not **naturalized citizens**, qualify. Article II is the only place in which the Constitution distinguishes between one kind of citizenship and another. (A natural-born citizen is one who has American citizenship by birth, although it is unclear whether a person born abroad of American parents qualifies as natural-born within the meaning of the Constitution. A naturalized citizen is an alien who has become a citizen by virtue of a procedure established by Congress.)

natural-born citizen

A person actually born in the United States

naturalized citizen

A person, born in another country, who becomes a citizen of the United States by a procedure set by Congress

Election 2008: A Presidential Election Breaks New Ground

On January 20, 2009, Barack Obama was sworn in as the forty-fourth president of the United States. Having a new president is always an important event in and of itself, but the path to the presidency in 2008 was unprecedented in many ways. In terms of experience, the election marked the first time in over fifty years that neither an incumbent president nor vice president appeared on one of the major party tickets.

The campaign also featured a degree of diversity never before seen in a national political race. In the Republican presidential primary, former New York Mayor Rudolph "Rudy" Giuliani was labeled an early front-runner. Had he stayed in the race and won the nomination, he would have become the first Catholic Republican nominee for president. Another serious contender for the nomination was former Massachusetts Governor Mitt Romney, who would

have been the first member of the Church of Jesus Christ of Latter-Day Saints (Mormon) to head a major party ticket (a distinction he achieved in 2012). In the end, though, it was Arizona Senator John McCain who won the Republican nomination. At age seventy-two, McCain became the oldest nonincumbent to run as a major party presidential nominee. In a move seen by some as a deliberate effort to woo female voters from the Democratic Party, McCain nominated little known Alaska Governor Sarah Palin as his vice-presidential running mate.

On the Democratic side, the two front-running candidates made history in a number of ways. New York Senator Hillary Clinton became the first woman to actively campaign throughout the entire primary season, winning more primaries than any other previous woman in the process. In the end, Clinton was narrowly defeated by Illinois Senator Barack Obama, who became the first African American major party candidate for president. Obama named Delaware Senator Joseph Biden as his running mate.

The campaign featured unique elements as well, most notably the disruptions caused by a struggling national economy. As Congress pondered a $700 billion bailout of the banking sector, Senator McCain temporarily suspended his campaign just two days before the first scheduled debate in order to direct all of his attention toward the crisis. Although the debate went on as scheduled, its intended focus

on foreign policy was largely subsumed by questions about the economy.

Finally, the election itself—on November 4, 2008—was special in that it mobilized more Americans to cast ballots than ever before, including over 50 percent of those aged eighteen to twenty-nine for the largest youth vote since 1972. When all the votes had been counted, Barack Obama became the first African American elected president, as well as the first president born in Hawaii; and Joe Biden became the first Catholic vice president.[1] Over 70 percent of those polled indicated that Obama's election was one of the two or three most important advances for African Americans over the past century.[2] The American electorate wanted change, and a solid majority decided Obama was the candidate for the job.

What do you remember most about the 2008 presidential election? What other important events can you recall, or have you read about, from previous presidential races? What changes did you see in the 2012 race? If you were eligible to vote, did you? Why or why not?

1 Ed Rollins "Election 2008 Is Heading for the History Books," 2008, http://www.cnn.com/2008/POLITICS/10/26/rollins.historic/index.html (November 8, 2008).

2 The Gallup Organization, "Americans See Obama Election as Race Relations Milestone," 2008, http://www.gallup.com/poll/111817/Americans-See-Obama-Election-Race-Relations-Milestone.aspx (November 7, 2008).

Moreover, a president must be thirty-five years of age or older and a resident of the United States for at least fourteen years.

Unlike representatives, who serve terms of two years, and senators, who serve terms of six, presidents have four-year terms. Although the Constitution in 1787 placed no limit on the number of terms a president could serve, George Washington's preference for a maximum of two terms set a tradition that remained unbroken until Franklin Roosevelt ran for his third term in 1940 and was then elected to a fourth term in 1944. Mainly in response to Roosevelt's multiple terms, the **Twenty-second Amendment** (1951) banned any future president from being elected president "more than twice." This amendment prohibits not only a third successive term but also an additional term even if a gap exists between the first two.

10.2a Executive Power

The Constitution confers many powers on the Congress, but few substantive powers on the president. Indeed, Article I, which established Congress, is more than two times the length of Article II, which created the presidency. Section 1 of Article II begins with the **vesting clause**: "The executive Power shall be vested in a President of the United States." What do these words define? Does the phrase *executive Power* give the president an inherent authority to meet emergencies in the absence of any specific constitutional or legislative mandate?

Presidents have interpreted this power differently throughout history. At one extreme, President William Howard Taft (1909–1913) construed his powers narrowly. Taft claimed, "The president can exercise no power which cannot be fairly and reasonably traced to some specific grant of constitutional or legislative power." By contrast, President Theodore Roosevelt (1901–1909), Taft's predecessor, argued that the president could "do anything that the needs of the nation demanded unless such action was forbidden by the Constitution or by the laws."[1] Roosevelt's broad interpretation of the office became known as the **stewardship theory**, and Taft's narrow interpretation as the **constitutional theory**.

Between these somewhat extreme views is the more balanced approach of Supreme Court Justice Robert H. Jackson, put forth in the steel seizure case: "When the President acts in absence of either a congressional grant or denial of authority... there is a zone of twilight in which he and Congress may have concurrent authority." Jackson implied that the Court would decide such constitutional boundary disputes on the basis of "the imperatives of events and contemporary imponderables rather than on abstract theories of law."[2]

Justice Jackson was close to the mark. Presidents since George Washington (1789–1797) have all possessed nearly identical formal constitutional powers, yet some have been far more influential than others. The reason comes from the *plasticity* of the presidency—the tendency of the office to be molded according to the energy and personality of its occupant in combination with the needs and challenges of the day.

10.2b The Power of Appointment

Section 2 of Article II states that the president "shall nominate, and by and with the Advice and Consent of the Senate, shall appoint Ambassadors, other public Ministers and Consuls, Judges of the Supreme Court, and all other Officers of the United States." For positions that require confirmation, the Senate generally allows presidents to select people with whom they feel comfortable personally and ideologically. The Senate restricts itself in most cases to the personal qualifications of the nominee and to any possible conflicts of interest.

The president's power to appoint affects the judicial branch, as well, because the president appoints Supreme Court justices and all federal judges. These judges serve until they retire or, in rare circumstances, are impeached. Franklin Roosevelt's nine appointments to the Supreme Court changed its character for a generation, and Ronald Reagan's three appointments and George H. W. Bush's two gave the Court a decidedly conservative cast in the early 1990s. Although this was tempered somewhat by Clinton's two appointments, the balance of the Court remained an important

Twenty-second Amendment

Ratified in 1951, it limits the president to two terms in office.

vesting clause

As the first clause of Article II, its statement confers executive power in the president.

stewardship theory

An expansive theory of presidential power, put forth by Theodore Roosevelt, that holds that the president can undertake any act as long as it is not prohibited by a specific provision of the Constitution or statutory law

constitutional theory

The concept, associated with President William Howard Taft, that the president cannot exercise any power unless it is based on a specific constitutional provision or legislative grant

issue through the 1996, 2000, and 2004 elections, an unusually lengthy period when no justices retired (see Chapter 12). This drought finally ended in 2005–2006 when George W. Bush appointed two new justices after Justice Sandra Day O'Connor retired and Chief Justice William Rehnquist passed away.

10.2c The Removal Power

The Supreme Court in *Myers v. United States*[3] declared that the president's power to remove non–civil service appointees was unrestricted and beyond the reach of Congress. Later the Court ruled in *Humphrey's Executor v. United States*[4] that President Roosevelt could not fire a member of the Federal Trade Commission (FTC), an independent regulatory commission, because of policy differences. The FTC Act specified that the president could only remove a commissioner for "inefficiency, neglect of duty, or malfeasance in office." The Court ruled that the president's removal powers applied only to "purely executive offices." The FTC (and by inference all independent regulatory commissions) was a "quasi-legislative" and "quasi-judicial" agency, according to the Court; and the president's removal authority did not apply. (These commissions are discussed in greater detail in Chapter 11.)

Presidents cannot dismiss career civil servants except for cause (misconduct, inefficiency, incompetence, or criminal conduct). They can, however, transfer or demote them, subject to the procedures of the civil service laws. Presidents can also work through the budgetary process to reduce or eliminate funding for a particular agency, thus eliminating numerous jobs.

10.2d The Power to Pardon

Article II, Section 2, gives the president the exclusive power to grant "Reprieves and Pardons for Offenses against the United States, except in Cases of Impeachment." The power includes the president's right to grant a full pardon, a conditional pardon, clemency for a class of people (amnesty), a commutation or reduction of a sentence, and the remission of fines. This power is limited to violations of federal laws and does not apply to state or local laws.

The use of this power rarely gains headlines, but it did in 1974, 1992, and 2001. On September 8, 1974, President Ford granted a complete pardon to former President Richard Nixon for any misdeeds that he might have committed during his presidency, which, of course, included the Watergate affair. Many criticized Ford's action as improper because formal charges had yet to be brought against Nixon. Without the benefit of trial, many argued, the full facts in Nixon's case and in the whole Watergate affair were unlikely to be uncovered. Others thought that Ford spared the country the unpleasant and disruptive sight of a former president placed on trial. On Christmas Eve 1992, President Bush pardoned former Secretary of Defense Caspar Weinberger and five others involved in the Iran-contra affair. The special prosecutor in the case, Lawrence E. Walsh, called the pardons a "cover-up" of misdeeds. Bush argued that Walsh's prosecutions did not represent legitimate law enforcement but were

President Richard Nixon's resignation, August 9, 1974 (Wikimedia Commons)

A "New Kind of War"—The Ongoing War on Terrorism

When President George W. Bush (2001–2009) spoke to New York leaders in the wake of the September 11 attacks, he stated, "My resolve is steady and strong about winning this war that has been declared on America. It's a new kind of war. And I understand it's a new kind of war. And this government will adjust." These comments acknowledge the need for adaptation in light of a significant change. America has officially declared war five times and has been involved in numerous military conflicts, but the ongoing war on terrorism represents the first time that our nation has embarked on a war with a concept rather than a nation. What is a war on terrorism, and where does the authority to conduct such a war reside?

Article I, Section 8 of the U.S. Constitution states in part that "The Congress shall have Power ... To declare War ... and make Rules concerning Captures on Land and Water." On the other hand, Article II of the Constitution begins by vesting the executive power in the president. While it is widely agreed that the framers of the Constitution intended to provide the president with the authority to repel sudden attacks, but also intended to reserve for Congress the power to move the nation from a state of peace to a state of war, there is a large gray area in the middle of these two objectives. The distinction between presidential and congressional powers has proved difficult to maintain in practice.

Examples of congressional action in response to the terrorist attacks consist of a joint resolution authorizing the president to use military force; the Air Transportation Safety and System Stabilization Act, which, in part, provided economic subsidies for the struggling airline industry; the Patriot Act and its amendments, which authorized law enforcement agencies to develop a number of new tools for combating and preventing future terrorist attacks; and creation of the independent and bipartisan National Commission on Terrorist Attacks upon the United States (also known as the 9/11 Commission). In October 2006, a divided Congress passed the Military Commissions Act, which expanded the detention and interrogation powers (including the power to suspend the writ of habeas corpus) of military tribunals trying "alien unlawful enemy combatants engaged in hostilities against the United States."[1]

Presidential actions taken by President Bush included creating the new Department of Homeland Security; securing the diplomatic and military support of other world leaders; and, in coordination with his National Security Council, directing the military actions of Operation Enduring Freedom. Other actions have been taken by executive branch agencies that receive funding and authority from Congress and are, ultimately, under the direction of the president and his appointees. When the Federal Aviation Administration, for example, greatly expanded its Federal Air Marshal program, it did so with the approval of its parent agency, the Department of Transportation, and the funding of Congress. Opinion polls suggest that the American public wants Congress to become even more involved in making decisions about military action: 76 percent of Americans think the president should be required to seek congressional approval before using military aircraft to bomb suspected terrorists, and 79 percent believe he should be required to have Congress's approval to send armed forces into action abroad.

In addition to granting powers, the Constitution also limits governmental power by placing many individual liberties off-limits from government control. Even though most Americans have welcomed increased security measures, it is unlikely that many Americans would willingly sacrifice all their freedoms just to decrease threats to their security. Fortunately, the Constitution and its amendments—through such guarantees as free speech, free press, due process, and equal protection—assure us that we will not have to make such choices.

What else makes the war on terrorism a "new kind of war"? Is our Constitution equipped to handle such a war, or are changes necessary? When faced with a decision between maintaining fundamental freedoms for all Americans and increasing security to reduce the risk of future terrorist attacks, what criteria should we employ? Should our constitutional protections extend to non-citizens? Who in American government should make these decisions, and how do we know when they are making the right choices? Has the war on terrorism changed under President Obama? If so, how? If not, why not?

1 Military Commissions Act of 2006.

SOURCES: George W. Bush, "President Pledges Assistance for New York in Phone Call with Pataki, Giuliani," September 13, 2001, http://www.whitehouse.gov/news/releases/2001/09/20010913-4.html (November 4, 2001); The Gallup Organization, "Public Wants Congress to Approve Military Action, Bombings," July 7, 2008.

"the criminalization of policy differences." Just prior to leaving office on January 20, 2001, Clinton pardoned billionaire Marc Rich, who had been living in Switzerland since 1983 to avoid federal charges of tax evasion and other misdeeds. After the public learned that Rich's ex-wife had donated about $1 million to the Democratic Party, the House Committee on Oversight and Government Reform began an investigation of the pardon. Notwithstanding the merits of their decisions, Ford, Bush, and Clinton were acting within their constitutional powers. The courts have established that a presidential pardon might be granted prior to a conviction or even an indictment.[5]

10.3 The President and the Executive Branch

In order to formulate and implement policy, presidents must appoint a considerable number of senior officials to whom they will turn for support and assistance. Who are these people? They include cabinet secretaries, undersecretaries, and the administrators and deputies of the various independent agencies—all of whom require Senate confirmation. These officials, plus about sixty senior White House aides whom the president can appoint without Senate confirmation, make up **the administration**—the people who direct government policy on the president's behalf.

10.3a The Cabinet

Despite its prestige, the president's cabinet (see Table 10.2) is not a collective high-level decision-making body. Because ours is not a parliamentary government, the president is not obligated to share responsibility with the cabinet. Its officers serve at the president's discretion, and the president is under no obligation to consult with them individually or collectively.

Individual officers can have great significance for the president. As will be discussed in Chapter 11, they serve as the president's arm in controlling the massive federal bureaucracy and in imposing his political priorities upon it. The cabinet also provides a mechanism for bringing into the administration people who represent different social, economic, and political constituencies. Often presidents will make appointments from constituent groups who did not support them but whose support they need.

After several years in office, presidents become more concerned with controlling the bureaucracy than with decorating their cabinet with people whose value is more symbolic than substantive. Thus, they look for cabinet officers who may be less well known but will be more loyal.

The selection of the right cabinet is a difficult problem. Few cabinet officers, whatever their temperament or background, can serve simply as the president's loyal agent. They must also represent to the president the perspective of their department and the *constituent groups* it serves. For example, the secretary of labor should have a good working relationship with organized labor; the secretary of the interior should have a solid relationship with the developers or the environmentalists, preferably both; and the secretary of agriculture must have a good rapport with farmers and the agribusiness community.

Not all cabinet officers are created equal. The cabinet is often divided into an **inner cabinet** and an **outer cabinet**.[6] The inner group consists of secretaries of state, defense, and the treasury, as well as the attorney general. These people handle issues of broad importance: national security, the economy, and the administration of justice.

the administration

The president plus senior officials such as cabinet officials, undersecretaries, and the administrators and deputies of the various independent agencies

inner cabinet

Cabinet officers whose departments handle issues of broad national importance, including the secretaries of state, defense, and the treasury, and the attorney general

outer cabinet

Cabinet officers whose departments deal with sharply defined programs and are subject to considerable pressure from client groups

table 10.2 | The Cabinet, 2015

The cabinet comprises the heads of the fifteen executive departments and certain other officials in the executive branch to whom the president has accorded cabinet rank. The vice president also participates in meetings of the cabinet, and from time to time the president may invite others to participate in the discussion of particular subjects.

Secretary of Commerce	Secretary of Health and Human	Secretary of Veterans Affairs
Secretary of Treasury	Services	Director of the Office of
Secretary of Defense	Secretary of Housing and Urban	Management and Budget
Secretary of Labor	Development	Administrator, Environmental
Secretary of Interior	Secretary of Transportation	Protection Agency
Secretary of Agriculture	Secretary of Energy	Vice President
Secretary of State	Secretary of Education	Ambassador, United States
	United States Ambassador to the	Trade Representative
	United Nations	Attorney General
	Secretary of Homeland Security	President's Chief of Staff
		Administrator
		Small Business Administration

SOURCE: http://www.whitehouse.gov/administration/cabinet

Of necessity, they have a direct and close working relationship with the president. The outer group is made up of the remaining members. These officers deal with sharply defined programs and are subject to considerable pressure from client groups. Only when a crucial issue arises will they gain frequent access to the president, and such instances are the exception. This lack of access by members of the outer Cabinet often leads to a sense of isolation from the president, gravitation toward the constituent interests served by their departments, and a strained relationship with the White House staff.

To avoid such problems, President Reagan established the Economic Policy Council and the Domestic Policy Council, chaired, respectively, by the treasury secretary and the attorney general. The councils consisted of relevant cabinet officers and senior White House aides. They were designed to coordinate policy and to keep members of the outer cabinet in close contact with the president. When these councils met to make a crucial policy decision, the president would chair the meeting. Satisfied with this arrangement, subsequent presidents have maintained this system, though the Economic Policy Council was replaced by the National Economic Council in 1993.

From the president's perspective, the ideal cabinet member should be clearly in charge of his or her department, sensitive to the department's constituency, able to distinguish between

President Barack Obama's inner cabinet meeting (Wikimedia Commons)

POLITICS & IDEAS

A Six-Year Term for Presidents?

In 1913, the Senate passed a resolution favoring a single six-year term for the president. Earlier presidents had advocated it as well. Although the idea has never been adopted, it continues to arouse interest. Is it a good idea? People who favor the proposal argue that it would free the president of reelection concerns and allow him or her to rise above partisan politics. A president could escape the lure of political expediency. Had not President Nixon been so concerned with reelection, some

speculate, the Watergate affair might not have happened.

Should a president be above politics and unconcerned about reelection? Some commentators say no. The prospect of an election concentrates the mind of a political leader on issues of importance to the general public. In a democracy this should not be a fault. A concern for reelection would prevent presidents from becoming too isolated from the mood of the country. Besides, a single six-year term would make a president a "lame duck" from the very first day in the White House.

Another argument for the proposal maintains that presidents are rarely effective over two terms. Once reelected to a second term, particularly if by a wide margin, presidents can become intoxicated with their own power and overreach their authority. Four modern

presidents made such miscalculations early in their second terms. Franklin Roosevelt introduced his court-packing scheme to Congress; Lyndon Johnson began escalating American involvement in Vietnam; Richard Nixon engaged in a cover-up of the Watergate affair; and Ronald Reagan became entangled in the Iran-contra affair.

Another argument against the idea came from Woodrow Wilson, who maintained that six years is too long for an ineffective president and too short for an outstanding one. Would a single six-year term allow a president to act like a statesman, or would it contribute to his isolation from the public? Do limits on presidential terms (including the Twenty-second Amendment limiting presidents to two terms) thwart democracy, or do they protect us from potential usurpers of power?

---

the president's interest and those of that constituency, and able to work well with Congress. Obviously, the job requires well-developed administrative and political skills. President Clinton was anxious to have a cabinet that "looked like America." Thus, out of sixteen cabinet-rank positions, Clinton appointed five women, four African Americans, and two Hispanics. However, his cabinet included a higher percentage of millionaires than did President Bush's cabinet. President George W. Bush indicated his priorities by affording cabinet-level status to the director of the Office of Management and Budget, the director of the National Drug Control Policy, and the U.S. Trade Representative. After the September 2001 terrorist attacks, Bush created the Office of Homeland Security. President Obama, whose lack of national experience had been a campaign issue for his opponents, named to his cabinet a number of former senators, governors, and other seasoned politicians, including Senator Hillary Rodham Clinton—his chief rival during the 2008 Democratic primaries—as secretary of state.

10.3b The White House Staff

Prior to the presidency of Franklin Roosevelt, White House aides played no role in policy. They were clerks—managers of files, appointments, and correspondence. Cabinet officers were the president's primary source of advice and counsel. Today the president's closest confidants are rarely cabinet members, who spend much of their time managing their departments. Presidents now rely heavily on their White House staffs. They select for senior White House positions people with whom they are comfortable and with whom they share a common background and political perspective. The loyalty of these people is not to a political party, an ideology, or their own political careers but to the president, first and last.

Responsibilities of senior White House aides involve the following tasks:

- Giving the president broad-gauged advice not influenced by a departmental or interest group perspective

- Setting legislative strategy

- Keeping check on the bureaucracy

- Reviewing the performance of cabinet and subcabinet officials

- Planning the president's time

- Saying no for the president to people who want something that he or she cannot give

Presidents manage the White House to suit their own personalities. Eisenhower and Nixon preferred a formalistic system and a highly structured staff. Eisenhower, who had spent most of his adult life in the military, was comfortable with a clear chain of command. At the opposite end of the spectrum was the competitive style of Franklin Roosevelt. Roosevelt had no rigid chain of command and was, in fact, his own chief of staff. He insisted on surrounding himself with strong-minded generalists who had divergent points of view and who could work on a variety of problems.

Although the elder President Bush appointed a chief of staff, John Sununu, Bush's style was closer to Roosevelt's than Nixon's. Bush relied upon a process known as **multiple advocacy**, which was designed to allow the president to hear all sides of an issue. White House aides would stage policy debates for the president's benefit. Dubbed "scheduled train wrecks," these debates would involve senior officials with sharply differing views on such issues as clean air proposals. President Bush, who relished these debates, would take notes, interrupt with questions, and afterward solicit the views of others in the administration or Congress. With his passion for secrecy and surprise, Bush would often conceal his final decision from everyone until he was ready for a public announcement.

10.3c The Executive Office of the President

Across a small side street from the White House is an imposing Victorian building that houses part of the **Executive Office of the President (EOP)**. The EOP was created in 1939 as the managerial arm of the modern presidency when a presidential commission uttered its famous recommendation: "The president needs help." In its early years, the EOP consisted of six administrative assistants and three advisory bodies—the National Resources Planning Board, the Liaison Office for Personnel Management, and the Office of Government Reports—all of which are now defunct.

The structure of the EOP reflects the dominant issues of the time. In the 1940s its agencies, such as the Office of Defense Mobilization, mirrored concerns with war and defense planning. In the 1960s and 1970s, the EOP agencies (Cost of Living Council, Council on Environmental

multiple advocacy

A system of advising the president in which all sides of an issue are presented

Executive Office of the President (EOP)

Created in 1939 to serve as the managerial arm of the presidency, it includes such agencies as the National Security Council, the Office of Management and Budget, and the Council of Economic Advisers.

(Wikimedia Commons)

Quality, Energy Resources Council) paralleled the national concern with the problems of energy, the environment, and inflation.

During the Reagan years the EOP was pared back. One of its permanent agencies, the **Office of Management and Budget (OMB)**, became one of its most important. Created in 1921 as the Bureau of the Budget and renamed the Office of Management and Budget in 1970, the OMB has three major responsibilities:

1. Helping the president to develop the annual budget that gets submitted to Congress

2. Serving as a clearinghouse for legislative proposals submitted to the president by the various departments and ensuring that all such proposals are consistent with presidential objectives

3. Monitoring the implementation of the president's programs and making sure they are administered efficiently

Secretary of Health and Human Services Sylvia Mathews Burwell (Wikimedia Commons)

Presidents usually employ the OMB to suit their own needs. Because the Nixon administration was interested in controlling the bureaucracy and in mobilizing the executive branch to support its programs, the OMB had the primary responsibility of supervising administration programs in some detail. Under Ford and Carter, the OMB played a relatively minor role.

During the Reagan and elder Bush administrations, OMB enjoyed a significant comeback. Richard Darman, Bush's OMB director, was a powerful member of Bush's administration, shaping the contours of the budget and negotiating budget and tax policy with Congress. Shaun Donovan has been President Obama's OMB director since July 2014. As long as budgetary politics dominate a president's agenda, the OMB will remain a vital arm of the presidency.

The **National Security Council (NSC)**, established by the National Security Act of 1947, is an essential part of the EOP. It is designed to provide the president with advice and policy coordination on questions of national security. Its members are the president, the vice president, the secretary of state, the secretary of defense, and other officials the president may wish to add. As with the OMB, presidents use the NSC to suit their own styles.

Truman and Eisenhower employed the NSC to coordinate policy, but not to formulate it. Both relied on strong secretaries of state for policy advice. Under President Kennedy the council fell into disuse and was rarely convened. Instead, Kennedy relied on the NSC staff headed by the national security adviser to provide him with information and expertise.

When President Nixon appointed Dr. Henry Kissinger to be his national security adviser in 1969, the role of the NSC grew substantially. With Nixon's encouragement, Kissinger and his staff not only dominated policy making but also became deeply involved in the actual conduct of foreign policy, shutting the State Department out of Nixon's major diplomatic initiatives. Kissinger conducted the negotiations that led to Nixon's historic visit to China, the Vietnam armistice, and the SALT I treaty.

The NSC's involvement in foreign policy operations reached its height during the Iran-contra affair. Congressional restrictions had barred direct aid to the Nicaraguan contras, who were fighting to overturn the pro-Soviet Sandinista government. Frustrated by the restrictions, President Reagan authorized the NSC staff to seek contra assistance from friendly governments such as Israel and Saudi Arabia. Marine

Office of Management and Budget (OMB)

An agency in the Executive Office of the President that provides the president with budgetary information and advice and is responsible for compiling the president's annual budget proposal to Congress

National Security Council (NSC)

Designed to provide the president with advice and policy coordination on questions of national security, NSC's members include the president, the vice president, the secretaries of state and defense, and any other officials the president may add.

Condoleezza Rice and Angelina Jolie during World Refugee Day at the National Geographic Society (Wikimedia Commons)

Lt. Col. Oliver North, a senior NSC staffer, supervised this effort as well as those of private domestic groups seeking to provide funds for the contras. The president also authorized the NSC to oversee the secret sale of arms to Iran to encourage the release of our hostages. Without the president's apparent knowledge, part of the profits of that sale were diverted to contras. The affair seriously diminished Reagan's public support and resulted in extensive congressional investigations and lengthy criminal trials.

A presidential commission to examine the Iran-contra affair was appointed by Reagan and headed by former Texas senator John Tower. The Tower Commission recommended that the NSC "focus on advice and management, not implementation and execution." The first President Bush's NSC adviser Brent Scowcroft, a member of the Tower Commission, appeared to follow this advice and kept the NSC out of covert operations. Under Scowcroft, the NSC functioned as an honest broker, coordinating advice from the bureaucracy and providing the president with policy options. When George W. Bush appointed Condoleezza Rice to be his national security adviser, she became both the first woman and first African American to hold this post. General James L. Jones, Tom Donilon (a former deputy adviser to Jones), and Susan Rice (the former U.S. ambassador to the United Nations) have served as Barack Obama's national security advisers.

The **Council of Economic Advisers (CEA)**, established by the Employment Act of 1946, is another permanent part of the EOP. Consisting of three members and a small staff, its chairperson, usually a prominent academic economist, is the predominant figure. The CEA's primary task is to analyze economic issues, make economic forecasts, and prepare the president's annual economic report to Congress. The CEA can be an important source of economic advice for the president; however, it must share economic policy making with the OMB, the Treasury Department, and the Federal Reserve Board.

The effectiveness of the CEA depends largely on the ability of the chair to gain the president's confidence and to translate obscure economic jargon into language the president can readily understand. President Reagan had little interest in the intricacies of economic policy; he let the CEA wither on the vine and even considered its abolition. George H. W. Bush, who had a fascination with details, frequently consulted with the CEA and let its chair become a major player in his administration.[7] Clinton, who had promised in his campaign to focus on economic issues "like a laser," established a new National Economic Council to coordinate overall economic policy. It would have a status similar to the National Security Council. The chair of the CEA would now have to compete with yet another source of economic policy making. George W. Bush and Barack Obama relied on the CEA and many other economic experts as they led the country through the storms of recession.

Council of Economic Advisers (CEA)

Established by the Employment Act of 1946 as a part of the Executive Office of the President, CEA consists of a chairperson, usually a prominent academic economist, and two other members who have the primary task of analyzing economic issues for the president.

Find out about presidential history and current executive policy agendas at the official White House website.

http://www.bvtlab.com/Ma878

10.3d The Vice President

Until 1941 vice presidents merely served in the ceremonial role as president and chief presiding officer of the Senate and had little influence on decisions in the White House. The office was a frequent target of ridicule and disdain, even by its occupants. The first vice president, John Adams, called it "the most insignificant office that ever the invention of man contrived or his imagination conceived."

Later vice presidents continued to find the job deeply frustrating. Harry Truman was not even aware of the existence of the secret atomic bomb project when he succeeded to the presidency upon Roosevelt's death. Richard Nixon, Eisenhower's vice president for two terms, served as partisan "hit man," making attacks on the Democrats that Eisenhower felt were beneath the dignity of the president to do himself. This same demeaning task Nixon later assigned to his own vice president, Spiro Agnew. Lyndon Johnson, who had been the powerful Senate majority leader, was given largely ceremonial responsibilities as John Kennedy's vice president. Johnson, a proud and sensitive man, felt humiliated in the job and considered himself merely a spectator in the Kennedy administration.

The experience of Walter Mondale as Jimmy Carter's vice president gave fresh hope that the office could become a vital part of the executive branch. Mondale served as President Carter's intimate adviser. He had an office in the White House West Wing, close to the president, and was given access to all important meetings and policy papers. Mondale had a private lunch every Monday with Carter so that he could give the president confidential and candid advice. By all accounts, Mondale was involved in all major policy decisions. The Carter-Mondale arrangement converted the vice presidency from an office without a role into that of a senior policy adviser to the president. The importance of the office was again revived when Dick Cheney stepped into the role in 2001. Publicly stating that he had no further political ambitions of his own, he became a key adviser to the presi-

Vice President Joe Biden speaks during a welcome home ceremony at Fort Bragg, N.C., Wednesday, April 8, 2009. Biden welcomed home the XVIII Airborne Corps from Iraq after their second deployment. (AP World Wide Photo)

dent. Since George W. Bush had been elected with little foreign policy experience, Cheney's previous experience in Congress and as secretary of defense added weight to the administration in this important area.

10.3e Presidential Succession

Should a president be impeached and convicted, resign, or die in office, the vice president automatically becomes president and fills the remainder of the term. Should a president become disabled and unable to fulfill presidential duties, the **Twenty-fifth Amendment**, ratified in 1967, provided a mechanism whereby the vice president could serve as an acting president. Presidents can declare themselves disabled and can authorize the vice president to assume the presidency. Alternatively, the vice president and a majority of the cabinet can declare that the president is disabled, in which case the vice president also assumes the job. The president may claim at any time, however, that the disability is over and resume the office. Should

Twenty-fifth Amendment

Ratified in 1967, it provides the mechanism for the vice president to assume the presidency in the event of a presidential disability and the selection of a replacement for the vice president should that office become vacant.

President Barack Obama discusses his jobs plan, the American Jobs Act, in a speech delivered to a joint session of the 112th United States Congress on September 8, 2011. Vice President Joe Biden and House Speaker John Boehner are seated behind the President. (Wikimedia Commons)

the vice president and a majority of the cabinet disagree, the issue goes to Congress. If both houses decide by a two-thirds vote that the president is unfit to resume duties, the vice president continues as acting president.

The Twenty-fifth Amendment also established a mechanism to fill a vacancy in the vice presidency. During our nation's history, six vice presidents have died in office, two have resigned, and nine have succeeded to the presidency—in each case leaving the office vacant. The amendment now eliminates the possibility that the vacancy will stand for long. The president is authorized in the event of a vacancy to nominate a vice president, subject to confirmation by both houses of Congress. This procedure was first used in October 1973, when Spiro Agnew resigned because of allegations of misconduct. President Nixon selected Gerald Ford as vice president.

In the unlikely event of a simultaneous double vacancy in the presidency and the vice presidency, the **Presidential Succession Act of 1947** applies. It establishes the following line of succession: (1) the Speaker of the House; (2) the president pro tempore of the Senate; and (3) the cabinet secretaries in the chronological order of the establishment of their departments, beginning with the secretary of state and ending with the secretary of homeland security.

10.4 The President and Congress: Foreign Policy

Presidential Succession Act of 1947

Established the line of presidential succession after the vice president as follows: the Speaker of the House, the president pro tempore of the Senate, and the Cabinet secretaries in the order of the establishment of their departments

In foreign policy the Constitution divides formal power between the president and Congress, but the president does maintain the initiative. The president negotiates treaties, mediates disputes, and proclaims friendship with new governments or works covertly to undermine them. Congress may reject these initiatives by refusing to ratify treaties, discouraging foreign arms sales, or outlawing covert activities. However, when presidents put their prestige on the line, as the elder President Bush did in securing support for his Gulf War policy, they generally prevail. Why is that? Congress fears eroding presidential influence in international negotiations, a fear that presidents use to their own advantage. Congress also lacks access to classified information and often defers to executive expertise. The reality is that Congress can influence foreign relations, but only the president can conduct them; thus the extent of Congress's influence is subject to the ebb and flow of history.

During the period from Pearl Harbor (1941) to the end of the Vietnam War (1973), the president dominated foreign policy, and congressional rebukes were rare and ineffective. The unpopularity of the Vietnam War, however, produced a subsequent public disdain for future military involvements and with it an end to the era of presidential domination. The president still had the leading role in foreign policy but no longer controlled the play.

Over President Nixon's veto in 1973, Congress passed the War Powers Resolution, requiring congressional approval after sixty days of any presidential decision to send troops into combat. In 1974 Congress passed the Hughes-Ryan Amendment, requiring congressional notification of covert operations conducted by the CIA. Emboldened by its newfound authority, Congress actually banned covert action in Angola from 1978 to 1983 and during the 1980s limited covert aid to the Nicaraguan contras. Presidential leadership in foreign policy now requires considerable skill and subtlety. Congress can be very independent unless a president carefully consults it and develops strong public support for his policies. That being said, threats to American national security are never taken lightly. When these risks are perceived, as in the early 2000s, Congress typically reacts by giving the president broad authority to act. Thus, George W. Bush received overwhelming Congressional support for his plan to invade Iraq. As with Vietnam, however, when the perceived threat recedes and public support for military actions begins to erode, presidents are often left on their own to defend their actions. Presidents since Nixon have uniformly disfavored the War Powers Resolution, questioning its authority. President Obama ignored it entirely in 2011 when he did not seek congressional approval after sixty days for troops he sent to Libya and in 2014 when he announced airstrikes and extended military action against the Islamic State of Iraq and Syria (ISIS).[8]

During the period from Pearl Harbor (1941) to the end of the Vietnam War (1973), the president dominated foreign policy, and congressional rebukes were rare and ineffective. (iStock)

10.4a Negotiating Treaties

By the terms of Article II of the Constitution, the president negotiates and signs treaties, subject to a vote of approval by two-thirds of the Senate. During the course of our history, the Senate has approved the vast majority of treaties. The most notable defeat came in 1919, when the Senate refused to ratify the Treaty of Versailles, which formally ended World War I and would have brought the United States into the League of Nations. This defeat provided a profound object lesson for future presidents.

President Woodrow Wilson (1913–1921), who negotiated the Treaty of Versailles, did not include a single senator from either party in the negotiating delegation, nor did he provide the Senate with information on the progress of the negotiations. In shutting the Senate out of the negotiating process, Wilson failed to build broad bipartisan support for the treaty.

Presidents Franklin Roosevelt and Harry Truman were careful to avoid Wilson's mistake and included both Democratic and Republican members of the Senate Foreign Relations Committee in the negotiations for the United Nations Treaty (1945) and the North Atlantic Treaty Organization (1949). During the decade that followed World War II, the Senate ratified without reservations or significant opposition mutual security treaties with over forty nations. Since then the Senate has become more jealous of its prerogatives; approval of important treaties is now rarely routine and often requires presidential concessions.

10.4b Executive Agreements

Presidents can avoid the political brambles of Senate ratification by entering into treaties with foreign governments. These agreements do not require Senate approval.

Theoretically, a treaty involves a legal relationship between nations, whereas an **executive agreement** is merely an understanding between heads of state. In practice, however, no distinction can be observed; and the Supreme Court has provided no clear guidelines.

In the early years of the Republic, executive agreements involved relatively minor matters, such as the settlement of claims American citizens had against foreign governments. Beginning with Franklin Roosevelt, however, executive agreements became a serious tool of foreign policy. In September 1940, Roosevelt agreed to trade fifty American destroyers to Great Britain in exchange for leases of naval bases on British territory in Newfoundland and the Caribbean. Toward the end of World War II, Roosevelt concluded a secret executive agreement with Joseph Stalin granting the Soviet Union territory and rights in the western Pacific previously belonging to China and Japan. In exchange Stalin agreed to enter the war against Japan.

Such secret agreements, unusual even in wartime, have now become almost commonplace. Of the 4,359 agreements in force in 1972, almost four hundred were classified and kept from Congress. Many involved commitments and informal alliances with other nations such as Spain, Laos, and Ethiopia.

To remedy what Congress considered an abuse of executive power, it passed the **Case Act** (1972), which placed some restrictions on the use of executive agreements, particularly secret ones. The Case Act requires that the secretary of state submit to the Senate the final text of any executive agreement. Should the agreement concern sensitive national security matters, it can be submitted in private to the Senate Foreign Relations Committee and the House Foreign Affairs Committee. The Case Act is largely symbolic and does not give Congress the power to alter or reject executive agreements. Moreover, compliance with the act is not easy to obtain. A 1976 Senate study disclosed that the executive branch had delayed submitting a number of executive agreements by almost a year and avoided submitting others by renaming them "arrangements."[9]

executive agreements

Agreements between heads of state that, unlike treaties, do not require approval by the Senate—there are no clear legal distinctions between the substance of a treaty and that of an executive agreement

Case Act

Requires the secretary of state to submit to the Senate the final text of any executive agreement and allows agreements concerning sensitive national security matters to be submitted privately to the Senate Foreign Relations and House Foreign Affairs committees

commander-in-chief clause

Article II, Section 2 of the U.S. Constitution names the president as the civilian head of U.S. military forces

10.5 The President and Congress: The War Power

The war power is also divided in the Constitution. The formal power to declare war was given to Congress (Article I, Section 8: "The Congress shall have the power … To declare war"), and thus the power to initiate war rests with it alone. The framers of the Constitution were careful, however, to leave the president with some independent war-making authority. At the urging of James Madison and Elbridge Gerry, the Constitutional Convention changed the original phrase from "make war" to "declare war." In changing this language, the framers intended to leave the president with the power *to repel sudden attacks on the United States, its territories, its possessions, or its armed forces.* The **commander-in-chief clause** (Article II, Section 2) was not designed to alter this relationship nor to grant the president additional war-making powers. The clause simply established the principle of civilian control over the military. The president was to be, in Alexander Hamilton's words, "the first general and admiral."

10.5a The Mexican and Civil Wars

Presidents have used the power to control the armed forces in order to manipulate Congress and preempt the war power itself. In 1846, for example, President

James Polk (1845–1849) ordered troops into the territory disputed by the United States and Mexico and set the stage for the Mexican War. The troops occupied high ground overlooking a Mexican village and aimed their artillery on the town square. The Mexican government, feeling threatened by the maneuver, responded militarily. Congress, at Polk's request, passed a declaration of war. Several years later the House of Representatives, feeling deceived by Polk's maneuver, passed a resolution that condemned him for a war "unnecessarily and unconstitutionally begun."

When Abraham Lincoln became president (1861–1865), he used the war power in a manner more consistent with the original understanding of the framers. After the attack on Fort Sumter (1861), which began the Civil War, Lincoln announced a blockade of the southern ports, increased the size of the army and navy, instructed the Treasury Department to spend $2 million to purchase military supplies, and in certain areas suspended the writ of habeas corpus (a judicial safeguard against unlawful imprisonment). Congress, which was not in session, had authorized none of these steps. On July 4, 1861, Congress, back in session, ratified all of Lincoln's actions except the suspension of the writ of habeas corpus and the naval blockade. The Supreme Court in the Prize Cases[10] declared that Lincoln was within his constitutional powers "in suppressing an insurrection."

10.5b The Two World Wars

Twice in the twentieth century (1917 and 1941) Congress formally declared war and delegated vast discretionary powers to the president. During World War I Congress granted President Wilson almost dictatorial control over the economy. This included the power to seize mines and factories, fix prices, license the distribution of foodstuffs, and take over railroads and telephone lines. Although Wilson did not exercise all this authority, he did assume unprecedented control over prices, consumption, and industrial production.

Congress granted Franklin Roosevelt similar authority during World War II; but Roosevelt, who had a broad and expansive view of the office, asserted wartime powers independent of Congress. The most dramatic and controversial of Roosevelt's actions came early in World War II. On February 19, 1942, Roosevelt decreed that 112,000 persons of Japanese descent living in the Pacific Coast region (70,000 of whom were American citizens) be removed from their homes, stripped of their jobs and property, and sent to detention camps. Concern about sabotage was the justification, although there was no evidence of its likelihood; yet many of these people remained in the camps for the duration of the war. Congress later passed a law embodying the president's order and, in effect, ratifying it. In *Korematsu v. United States*[11] the Supreme Court upheld the exclusion program as within the combined war powers of Congress and the president. The entire case, repudiated by a government commission years later and the subject of renewed litigation

On February 19, 1942, Roosevelt decreed that 112,000 persons of Japanese descent living in the Pacific Coast region (70,000 of whom were American citizens) be removed from their homes, stripped of their jobs and property, and sent to detention camps. (Wikimedia Commons)

in the 1980s, serves as a reminder of how difficult it is in time of war to maintain democratic standards and values.

10.5c The Cold War

Only when America became a global power after World War II did presidents assert independent war-making powers, in the context of the Cold War with the Soviet Union. The most dramatic example came in June 1950, when President Truman, on his own independent authority, ordered American ground, air, and naval forces to aid the government of South Korea against an invasion of North Korean forces. Truman declined to ask Congress for a resolution authorizing this decision and simply cited his powers as commander in chief. Because the Korean invasion did not involve a sudden attack on American troops, citizens, or territory, Truman's unilateral action fell outside the framers' original understanding of the war power. Although Congress later implicitly ratified the decision by voting military appropriations for the war, Truman had nevertheless initiated America's involvement in a war that lasted three years and cost thirty thousand American lives.

During the next two decades, presidential war-making authority grew, nurtured by a new political consensus. Unlike the Americans of the eighteenth and nineteenth centuries who believed in having no permanent military alliances, limited international interests, and a small standing army, Americans of the mid-twentieth century concluded that only through collective security and armed strength could war be prevented. Given this political climate, presidents felt emboldened to establish overseas bases, station troops abroad, and even send them into combat—all on the presidents' own authority. Congress did little to object.

In 1955 President Eisenhower requested from Congress a joint resolution authorizing him to use military force to protect Taiwan from a possible invasion by the People's Republic of China. The resolution stated that the president had the authority "to employ the Armed Forces as he deems necessary" to defend Taiwan. This undated check to the president to make war on his own terms passed Congress overwhelmingly. The comments of House Speaker Sam Rayburn (D–TX) reflected the measure of congressional acquiescence to presidential authority in those Cold War years. "If the President had done what is proposed here without consulting Congress," Rayburn acknowledged, "he would have had no criticism from me."[12]

10.5d The Vietnam Trauma

As hundreds of thousands of American troops entered the Vietnam War in the mid-1960s, presidential control of the war-making authority continued to go unchallenged. An alleged attack on two American destroyers by North Vietnamese patrol boats off their coastal waters triggered action from President Lyndon Johnson, who sought broad authority from Congress. At Johnson's request, Congress passed the **Gulf of Tonkin Resolution** (1964), which stated:

> The United States is, therefore, prepared, as the president determines, to take all necessary steps including the use of armed forces to assist any member or protocol state of the Southeast Asia Collective Defense Treaty requesting assistance in defense of its freedom.

Gulf of Tonkin Resolution

A congressional resolution passed in 1964 granting President Johnson the authority to undertake military activities in Southeast Asia

The resolution passed unanimously in the House and with only two dissenting votes in the Senate, recognizing the president's claim to unilateral war-making authority.

As the Vietnam War lost public support, Congress sought to regain its constitutional authority largely through its control of spending power; but the task was

BVT Lab

Visit www.BVTLab.com to explore the student resources available for this chapter.

Chapter 10 | The Presidency | 323

arduous and the results were ambiguous. In 1970, Congress, fearing an extension of the war, barred the use of funds to "finance the introduction of the ground troops into Laos or Thailand." President Nixon circumvented the law, however, by ordering continued aerial bombing and paramilitary activities in Laos. After he authorized an invasion of Cambodia that year, Congress responded by prohibiting the use of funds for ground combat troops in that beleaguered country. Although Nixon eventually withdrew the ground troops from Cambodia, he continued the bombing.

The Paris Peace Accords (1973) ended direct American combat involvement in Vietnam but not the bombing of Cambodia and Laos. Thus, the war continued—but with very little congressional support. Finally, in June 1973, Congress was able to use its power of the purse to control the power of the sword. President Nixon, weakened and distracted by the Watergate scandal, signed an appropriation bill that prohibited the further use of funds for all combat activities in Indochina as of August 15, 1973. However, the bill was signed only after American combat activities against the North Vietnamese had ended— and nine years after Congress had passed the Gulf of Tonkin Resolution.

10.5e The War Powers Resolution

Chastened by the Vietnam experience and anxious to recapture its war-making authority, Congress passed the War Powers Resolution in the fall of 1973 over President Nixon's veto. The resolution specified that the president could not commit troops to combat beyond sixty days unless authorized by Congress. It also stipulated that before introducing troops into combat, the president had to consult with Congress in every possible instance.

Both hawks and doves criticized the War Powers Resolution. Senator Barry Goldwater (R–AZ) argued that the sixty-day cut off provision was an unconstitutional interference with the president's powers as commander in chief. Senator Thomas Eagleton (D–MO) claimed that the resolution placed no defined limits on when a president could take the country to war without prior congressional approval. So far the resolution has had little effect on presidential behavior, confirming neither the fears of its critics nor the hopes of its sponsors.

For years supporters of the resolution were concerned about the failure of presidents to abide fully by its provisions were the Congress to challenge the president. The effectiveness of the resolution depends on how seriously Congress takes its responsibilities. Congress was not tested until January 12, 1991, when it granted President George H. W. Bush the power, as authorized under the War Powers Resolution, to begin military operations to enforce the United Nations Security Council's resolutions demanding Saddam Hussein's military withdrawal from Kuwait. There was no way of knowing at the time that this military action would set the stage for another conflict with Iraq a decade later.

10.5f The Iraq War

After the 9/11 attack the pendulum of war power quickly swung back in the direction of the president. George W. Bush acted decisively, and with congressional approval, by invading Afghanistan, a country that had harbored members of the al Qaeda terrorist network. In September 2002, he also issued a revised version of the National Security Strategy of the United States, a document that outlines the country's approach to defense. Among the new features of the Bush administration's plan was something called the Doctrine of Preemption. This stated that America's strategy would now be to attack potential enemies before they had the opportunity to attack the United States. The document also named Iraq, Iran, and North Korea as

Engineering Aide First Class Scott Lyerla, assigned to Naval Mobile Construction Battalion One Five (NMCB-15), maintains security for his convoy with an M-60 machine gun while driving through Al Hillah, Iraq. (Wikimedia Commons)

part of an "axis of evil" that potentially threatened the United States.

George W. Bush argued that immediate action needed to be taken against Iraq because according to intelligence reports (later proven inaccurate), Iraq possessed and was continuing to develop weapons of mass destruction. Seeing no success from U.N. sanctions, Bush asked for and received broad authority from Congress to take action against Iraq. Although the American military swiftly defeated the armies of Saddam Hussein, maintaining the long-term stability of the region proved much more difficult. As costs and casualties continued to mount, however, there was little Congress could do. Once it had granted authority for military action, the only remaining congressional power was over spending; but with every proposed cut portrayed as risking American lives, it was clearly not feasible for Congress to exercise this authority either. Barack Obama announced plans to end the war shortly after taking office in 2009; and American troops completed their withdrawal on December 18, 2011, over eight years after the war began. Over 4,409 American troops were killed in Iraq and over 31,000 were wounded.[13] Information about Iraqi deaths has been more difficult to calculate, but the most thoroughly documented approach indicates that between 108,000 and 118,000 Iraqi civilians died in the conflict.[14]

As long as American foreign policy requires global political commitments and a powerful mobile military, any limits on the president's role as commander in chief will be difficult for Congress to impose. The era of American isolation and neutrality has long passed, and along with it a small standing army. Contemporary presidents shape a large defense budget, select major weapons systems, control access to classified information, and send large carrier task forces around the globe. Thus, congressional attempts to reassert authority meet with mixed results.

10.6 The President and Congress: Domestic Policy

In domestic policy, as well as foreign, the relationship between the president and Congress is rarely easy and never a predetermined fact. Presidents' capacities to push their legislative programs through Congress are strong indications of their powers and often determine their historical impact on the office. Few presidents have been able to dominate Congress; and those who have, have done so only for short periods. Presidents with an ambitious domestic agenda and aspirations beyond maintaining the status quo have a particular need for congressional support. Getting such support requires great skill, a sense of what the public will support, and a capacity to persuade 535 independent-minded senators and representatives. What are the political ingredients that enable presidents to be successful leaders of Congress? Recent experience suggests several.[15]

10.6a Legislative Skills

A president must know the legislative environment. One of Franklin Roosevelt's advisers once explained that a president must understand who influences whom, who the key players are on an issue, and what a group wants that others can be persuaded either to accept or to tolerate. Lyndon Johnson made it his business to know as much as he could about the key members of Congress. By contrast, Jimmy Carter, whose legislative performance was less than spectacular, was unfamiliar with the ways of Washington and held himself aloof from the congressional leadership.

A president needs a good sense of timing. Presidents must know when to lead and when to pause. For example, wars often deplete the national energy for reform, and Congress itself can reflect such a national mood. Postwar presidents Warren Harding (World War I), Truman (World War II), and Eisenhower (Korea) were unable to get much reform legislation from Congress. Harding and Eisenhower did not even try, but Truman did and found the going very difficult. Clinton pushed for healthcare reform before Americans had reached consensus on the type of change they wanted, but George W. Bush's plan for tax cuts was well received.

Presidents must establish their priorities and know where to concentrate their energies. Presidents will not get everything they ask from Congress; therefore, they must put forward programs that are not only important but that also have a chance of success. Early successes may build a reputation for political mastery that can be translated into future legislative victories. Ronald Reagan focused on the budget and taxes in his first year and achieved astonishing success.

Clinton failed to heed "Jefferson's advice" early in his first term when he presented Congress and its slim Democratic majority with a sweeping plan for healthcare reform. (Wikimedia Commons)

Presidents must have a high-quality legislative liaison office. Presidents cannot personally keep in touch with all members of Congress. An effective liaison office gives members more access to the White House, if not to the president directly. It also provides the president with vital intelligence: How many votes are there for a particular bill? Which members need to be persuaded? What particular favors can be granted dissenters to sway their votes? The liaison office can build crucial loyalty and support for presidents and their policies.

Presidents must consult with party leaders in the opposition as well as in their own party when they are developing major policy initiatives. A president needs to have a strong working relationship with those who can report the mood of Congress. Jimmy Carter failed to consult with the appropriate congressional leaders when he unveiled his energy program in 1977. To the surprise of very few, Congress extensively revised and rewrote it.

Wise presidents remember Jefferson's advice: Great innovations should not and cannot be forced upon slender majorities. Major innovations require broad bipartisan support or else they will fail. Truman worked closely with leading senior Republicans in Congress in order to gain support for the United Nations treaty, the Marshall Plan (economic rehabilitation aid to Western Europe after World War II), and the North Atlantic Treaty Organization. Presidents Kennedy and Johnson, in building a consensus for their civil rights program, cultivated relationships with Republican leaders in both houses. President Reagan's strong working relationship with conservative southern Democrats in the House (known as "Boll Weevils") was

BVT *Lab*

Visit www.BVTLab.com to explore the student resources available for this chapter.

Chapter 10 | The Presidency | 326

essential to his legislative success in 1981 and 1982. Clinton failed to heed this advice early in his first term when he presented Congress and its slim Democratic majority with a sweeping plan for health care reform. Rejection of this plan forced Clinton to be more cautious later in his administration.

10.6b The Presidential Veto

The president has a number of constitutional and statutory powers available in dealing with Congress, but none is more important than the veto. According to Article I, Section 7, the president may veto a congressional bill within ten days after it reaches the president's desk. The president then returns the bill to the congressional chamber of origin with a message explaining the reasons and perhaps suggesting changes that could make the bill acceptable. Congress may override the veto by a two-thirds majority of each house of Congress. The bill then becomes a law without presidential approval. Should Congress announce its adjournment during the ten-day period, the president may employ a pocket veto by simply killing the bill without a formal message and without the need of returning it to Congress. Congress cannot override a pocket veto. Presidents cannot veto constitutional amendments, but they can veto joint resolutions that are formal expressions of congressional opinion and have the force of law. Table 10.3 summarizes presidential vetoes and overrides since Franklin Roosevelt.

The president, unlike a number of state governors, does not possess an item veto, which allows an executive to veto sections of a bill and sign the remaining portion. President Reagan, for one, was a vocal supporter of the item veto, the implementation of which would require a constitutional amendment. Under certain conditions, the president can refuse to spend part of an appropriations bill. Occasionally, a president may sign a bill and at the same time note that certain provisions are unconstitutional and cannot be enforced. The president's authority to do this has yet to be tested in court, however. As discussed in Chapter 9, a common congressional technique for avoiding a veto is to attach amendments (riders) to an appropriations bill. Frequently, the president cannot afford to veto such a bill without having the government run out of money. During the Vietnam War, Congress attached such riders to defense bills restricting the president's authority. President Nixon, in need of the appropriations to continue funding the war, was forced to accept these riders, which he otherwise surely would have vetoed.

In April 1996, Congress passed the Line Item Veto Act in an effort to allow the president the authority for item vetoes. After President Clinton first used this authority in early 1997, several members of Congress who had voted against the bill challenged the constitutionality of the law in court. In 1998, the Supreme Court held that the law violated the presentiment clause of Article I of the Constitution. Thus, the president's line item veto authority was short-lived.[16] In 2004, George W. Bush became the first president since John Quincy Adams to complete a full four-year term in office without vetoing a single piece of legislation. Although Bush eventually vetoed bills in his second term, starting with the rejection of a bill on stem cell research, he preferred the more subtle—and more legally dubious—strategy of appending signing statements to bills with which he disagreed. Standing on his right to refuse to enforce legislation he deemed unconstitutional, Bush issued over 150 signing statements, challenging over 1,100 sections of legislation during his eight years in office, leading to an investigation by the American Bar Association, which approved a resolution condemning the practice.[17]

table 10.3 | Presidential Vetoes and Overrides

The veto remains one of the president's most significant constitutional powers. Yet the president does not possess authority for an item veto—the power to reject part of a bill; the president must accept or reject the entire bill.

	Total Vetoes	Pocket Vetoes	Vetoes Overridden
Franklin Roosevelt (1933–1945)	65	263	9
Harry Truman (1945–1953)	250	70	12
Dwight Eisenhower (1953–1961)	181	108	2
John Kennedy (1961–1963)	21	9	—
Lyndon Johnson (1963–1969)	30	14	—
Richard Nixon (1969–1974)	43	17	7
Gerald Ford (1974–1977)	66	18	12
Jimmy Carter (1977–1981)	31	18	2
Ronald Reagan (1981–1989)	78	39	9
George H. W. Bush (1989–1993)	46	17	1
Bill Clinton (1993–2001)	37	1	2
George W. Bush (2001–2009)	12	0	4
Barack Obama (2009–)*	3	—	—

*Through March 2015

SOURCE: United States Senate, http://www.senate.gov/reference/Legislation/Vetoes/vetoCounts.htm (November 26, 2014).

10.6c Executive Privilege

Control over policy requires control over information. Thus, since George Washington's time, presidents have claimed that personal communications with their advisers were immune from congressional or judicial scrutiny. Presidents have argued that they need the protection of confidentiality to ensure that they will receive frank and candid advice. The right of the president to refuse information requested by Congress and the courts is called executive privilege.

During the Watergate affair President Nixon attempted to enlarge the power of executive privilege. Nixon asserted that it included the authority to withhold from Congress and the courts information in the possession of any employee of the executive branch. In 1973, Nixon maintained that even the papers and tapes of conversations under subpoena by the Watergate special prosecutor were protected by executive privilege. Nixon's lawyer maintained that a president's claim of executive privilege was absolute and not subject to review by the courts or Congress. This broad definition suffered a setback from the Supreme Court in *United States v. Nixon*[18] when it ruled that although the president did enjoy a right to executive privilege, the privilege was not absolute. The Court concluded that the need for the tapes and papers as evidence in the Watergate trial outweighed the president's claim of confidentiality and ordered Nixon to produce the tapes and papers.

In the criminal trial of Admiral John Poindexter, District Court Judge Harold H. Greene ordered President Reagan to turn over his personal diaries to the court. Judge Greene read the diaries *in camera* (in his private chambers), weighing the former

United States v. Nixon addressed only the president's right to withhold information from the courts. Since the Watergate scandal, Congress has become more assertive against such claims and suspicious that they were used to cover up maladministration. (iStock)

president's claim of executive privilege against Poindexter's assertion that he could not get a fair trial without access to them. After reviewing one hundred diary entries, Judge Greene declared that the diaries furnished "no new insights" into the Iran-contra affair and concluded that Reagan's claim of executive privilege outweighed Poindexter's need for the material.[19]

United States v. Nixon and the Poindexter case addressed only the president's right to withhold information from the courts and not the right to withhold information from Congress. Since the Watergate scandal, Congress has become more assertive against such claims and suspicious that they were used to cover up maladministration, if not corruption. In 1982 there were, in fact, charges of collusion between top officials of the Environmental Protection Agency (EPA) and corporations cited for allegedly dumping toxic waste. When EPA director Anne Burford refused to hand over to a House subcommittee documents relating to the enforcement of the toxic waste program, the House voted her in contempt of Congress.

President Reagan, claiming executive privilege for Burford, had the Department of Justice challenge the contempt citation in federal court. The federal judge of the case, reluctant to enter into this unchartered area of law, urged both sides to settle their differences out of court. The judge stated, "When constitutional disputes arise concerning the respective powers of the legislative and executive branches, judicial intervention should be delayed until all possibilities for settlement have been exhausted."[20] As a result of the political controversies that developed around the toxic waste program, Burford resigned; and President Reagan released all the documents to the relevant congressional committees. Presidents have to consider whether the assertion of a particular claim of executive privilege outweighs the political costs of withholding the information. In the matter of Anne Burford, President Reagan felt that the costs of asserting the privilege were too high.

In 2012, President Obama asserted executive privilege to avoid sharing with Congress documents related to Operation Fast and Furious—a bungled effort by the Bureau of Alcohol, Tobacco, and Firearms in which thousands of illegal firearms were sold in hopes of developing evidence against Mexican drug cartels.

10.6d Impeachment

In the struggle between the president and Congress, presidential impeachment and removal from office is the ultimate congressional weapon. Article II, Section 4, of the Constitution states: "The President, Vice President and all Civil Officers of the United States shall be removed from Office on Impeachment for, and Conviction of, Treason, Bribery, or other high Crimes and Misdemeanors."

The actual impeachment resembles a criminal indictment in which the House acts as the grand jury. The investigation is done by the House Judiciary Committee, which votes on whether to recommend impeachment to the full House. The House can vote to impeach by a simple majority. The question of guilt or innocence is then determined by a trial, conducted by the Senate. The chief justice of the United States serves as the

The President and Economic Policy Making

Nowhere is the gap greater between what the public expects and what the president can do than in economic policy. Accustomed to general prosperity, the American public demands full employment, stable prices, and an increased standard of living. Presidents who fail to provide all of these things usually do not get reelected. Herbert Hoover, Gerald Ford, Jimmy Carter, and George H.W. Bush—all defeated incumbents—stand as examples. Hoover presided over the Great Depression; Ford served during a period of high unemployment; Carter contended with double-digit inflation; and Bush served during a recession and a slow recovery.

How much blame presidents should share for such conditions is unclear. They act under severe constraints, and it may seem unfair that they must take responsibility for things they cannot control. What are some of these constraints? First, the president can propose a budget and tax plan, but the Congress must approve them. The president must deal with a complex congressional budgeting process and the powerful special interests that influence Congress. Often the budget the president does finally get from Congress does not resemble the one requested (see Chapter 14). Second, the president's budget must be prepared sixteen months before its enactment; during that period the economy can change dramatically. Third, the president must share power with the Federal Reserve Board, which sets interest rates and controls the supply of money in the economy. Fourth, much of the budget (approximately 75 percent) is controlled by legislation that is supported by powerful interests and hard to change— Social Security payments, Medicare, Medicaid, military pensions, and farm support subsidies, to name a few. The interest on the national debt, another legal obligation, now consumes about 6 percent of the budget.

In addition to the problems of budget making, the president must contend with the economy itself, which is complex and unpredictable. The cycles of inflation and recession frequently elude economists' crystal balls. In addition, America is part of the international economic system and is affected by events beyond the president's reach. The sharp increase in oil prices by the Organization of Petroleum Exporting Countries (OPEC) contributed to the high inflation of the 1970s.

Over the past three decades, Japan, Western Europe, and South Korea have emerged as major economic powers, providing steep competition for key American industries such as steel, automobiles, textiles, and electronics. In the 1980s, America became dependent on Japanese purchases of government bonds to assist in financing its deficits, and upon Japanese investments in the private sector to help in sustaining its economic growth. Changes in the behavior and economic fortunes of countries such as Japan, and more recently China, can have a significant impact on our economy. The downturn in several Asian economies in the late 1990s, for example, created significant fluctuations in the American stock market.

Over the past three decades, presidents have devoted increased time and energy to economic policy. Their economic advisers have become major players in the administration. The role of the OMB director in providing the president with budgetary advice and negotiating the budget with Congress has grown. The treasury secretary, who must advise the president on international economic policy and the supervision of the savings and loan industry, is usually a close confidant of the president. The president must also develop a good working relationship with the chair of the Federal Reserve Board. Whether or not the economic conditions that prevail during an administration are the results of the president's policy, the public will hold the president accountable.

presiding judge over the proceedings involving the president or the vice president, and a vote of two-thirds of the Senate is required for conviction and removal.

President Andrew Johnson (1865–1869) was impeached in 1868 by an overwhelming majority in the House, but escaped conviction in the Senate by one vote. More than a century later, in 1974, President Richard Nixon faced a serious threat of impeachment. After eight months of hearings, the House Judiciary Committee voted three articles of impeachment, charging Nixon with (1) obstruction of justice for encouraging perjury, destruction of evidence, and interfering with investigations by the FBI; (2) abuse of power for authorizing the FBI and IRS to harass his political

Immigration Reform: Laws and Executive Orders

Obama announced an executive action on November 20, 2014. This order instructed the relevant federal agencies to take three sets of actions. First, it redirected the nation's deportation efforts to focus solely on criminals and threats to national security. Second, it expanded opportunities to stay in the United States for people born in the United States to undocumented immigrants. Third, the president developed a process for undocumented immigrants who have been in the country for at least five years and whose children are legal residents to remain in the country and receive work permits. While the plan does not grant amnesty or provide citizenship, it removes the threat of deportation for up to five million undocumented immigrants.

What is the difference between an executive order and a law? And why did the president issue the former, rather than call on Congress to pass the latter? The answer to the first question is factual, but an answer to the second is more speculative. A law must be passed by both chambers of Congress and signed by the president. If the president vetoes the legislation, a congressional supermajority can override that action. Laws are meant to change public policy. Executive orders, on the other hand, are designed to give guidance to those in the government on how to carry out existing policies. In use since the presidency of George Washington, these orders are an important tool for enabling our chief executive to "execute" the laws.

One answer to the second question is partisan politics. Legislation passed by the Democrat-led Senate was not voted on by the Republican-led House of Representatives. While both Democrats and Republicans acknowledge that the current immigration system is flawed, they differ in their preferences for solving the problem. Many Democrats want a policy that grants amnesty and a path to citizenship for those already in the country, but they are aware that too lenient a policy may encourage increases in undocumented immigration in the future. Furthermore, they must avoid policies that strike voters as unfair. Many Republicans say that the focus should be on deportation and securing borders, but they also know that this message can easily slide into racism and xenophobia. Republicans must focus on solutions rather than blame to avoid alienating the growing number of Hispanic voters, many of whom may otherwise be attracted to conservatism.

Despite these differing approaches, most Americans agree on the basic facts. We know that there are roughly 11.3 million undocumented immigrants in the United States. While many remain undetected, millions have been identified and are in various stages of the deportation process. During the first six years of the Obama administration, over 2.1 million undocumented immigrants were deported to their country of origin.[1] There is also bipartisan agreement that the eight million or so unauthorized workers in the United States aid the American economy because they "fill the growing gap between expanding low-skilled jobs and the shrinking pool of native-born Americans who are willing to take such jobs."[2] Simply removing all undocumented immigrants is not a viable economic solution. Finally, we know that our current laws are not effectively addressing the situation. Many people want to legally immigrate to the United States and many Americans want them to do so. But the State Department reports that 4.4 million potential immigrants have started the legal immigration process, and the wait for a visa can take decades.[3] Clearly, this is a policy area ripe for reform.

Will the two parties—and two policy-making branches of government—work together to develop a comprehensive plan for immigration reform in 2015? A majority of Americans say it is more important for political leaders in Washington to compromise to get things done rather than stick to their beliefs and risk doing little.[4] Only time will tell whether Congress and the president will listen to this preference. But until the two sides in this struggle acknowledge the need for compromise, America will limp along with a broken system—and immigrants will continue to cross our borders seeking opportunity.

1   The Week, September 26, 2014.

2   Maria Santana, "5 Immigration Myths Debunked," November 20, 2014, http://money.cnn.com/2014/11/20/news/economy/immigration-myths/ (November 26, 2014).

3   Ibid.

4   The Gallup Organization, 2013.

opponents; and (3) contempt of Congress for refusal to comply with congressional subpoenas for tapes and papers relevant to the impeachment investigation. Before the House had an opportunity to vote on the Judiciary Committee report, Nixon resigned the presidency.

The Nixon experience helped to clarify the question of what is an impeachable offense. Treason and bribery are clear offenses, and Nixon was charged with neither. What, however, constitutes a "high crime and misdemeanor"? The framers, especially Alexander Hamilton and James Madison, believed that the phrase included the abuse of political power. By including the abuse of power in the articles of impeachment, the House Judiciary Committee accepted the view of Madison and Hamilton that high crimes and misdemeanors involve "the violation of some public trust." Nixon's attempt to use the FBI and the IRS against his political enemies was considered by the committee a threat to political order and therefore an impeachable offense.

10.6e The Clinton Impeachment

The most recent case of presidential impeachment came in December 1998, when the House of Representatives passed two articles of impeachment against President Bill Clinton. The story of Clinton's impeachment begins in 1994, when an independent counsel was assigned the task of investigating a Clinton real estate investment known as Whitewater. Although the Whitewater investigation never led to charges against Clinton, Independent Counsel Kenneth Starr asked for and received authority to investigate additional leads on potential misdeeds that had turned up during the course of the Whitewater investigation. At the same time, Paula Jones, a former Arkansas state worker, was suing Clinton for sexual harassment. In January 1998, Clinton gave a deposition in that case in which he was asked questions about a number of possible improprieties, among them an affair with former White House intern Monica Lewinsky. At about the same time, Kenneth Starr, acting on a tip from Lewinsky's former friend Linda Tripp, sought authority to extend his investigation to cover possible wrongdoings (perjury, obstruction of justice) regarding the Lewinsky affair. In August 1998, President Clinton testified before a grand jury about his relationship with Lewinsky and allegations of his efforts to cover up that relationship. In his testimony, Clinton admitted that the relationship had been inappropriate. As a result, in September

Former White House intern Monica Lewinsky and her attorney in 1998: Among other charges, former President Bill Clinton was charged with lying about his relations with Lewinsky. (AP World Wide Photo)

1998, Starr issued to Congress a several-thousand-page report, which recommended impeachment based on inconsistencies between Clinton's January and August testimonies. In November and early December, the House wrestled with the gravity of the president's wrongdoing. Had he just been misleading and immoral, as the Democrats claimed; or did Clinton's actions constitute the kind of "high crimes and misdemeanors" that the Constitution outlined as impeachable offenses, as the Republicans claimed? Ultimately, a Republican-led House of Representatives that voted almost entirely along party lines voted to approve one article of impeachment that charged the president with lying under oath and another that charged him with obstruction of justice. In early 1999, this action created the need for an impeachment trial in the

BVT Lab

Flashcards are available for this chapter at www.BVTLab.com.

Senate, where two-thirds of the Senate could vote to convict and remove the president from office. By the time the final vote was taken on February 12, Congress, the president, and the American people were all weary of the issue. In the final tally, the Senate rejected both articles of impeachment. Ten different Republicans voted against either one or both of the articles, and not a single Democrat voted in favor of either. Was this impeachment the pursuit of justice against a president who was acting above the law, or a mere partisan attack? The debate still goes on.

10.7   The President and the Media

Presidents and the media are usually involved in a love-hate relationship that resembles a bad marriage. They need each other, yet they have difficulty living together. Practically every president has complained about the press. George Washington charged that the unfavorable stories about his administration were "outrages of common decency." President Thomas Jefferson, a champion of a free press, stated, "Even the least informed of the people have learned that nothing in a newspaper is to be believed." Richard Nixon, who suffered serious criticism of his Vietnam policy, had a considerable number of Washington reporters on his "enemies list." During the Iran-contra affair, Ronald Reagan claimed that reporters were circling the White House like "sharks." George H. W. Bush championed this slogan during his unsuccessful 1992 reelection campaign: "Annoy the media. Reelect Bush/Quayle." The media found virtually nothing off-limits during the Clinton administration, as discussion of his possible sexual improprieties became a frequent story in the national news.

Listen to recorded speeches by every U.S. president since Benjamin Harrison at the Vincent Voice Library.

http://www.bvtlab.com/TY2X8

Such conflict is built into the relationship. Chief executives are advocates of their own administration and want to see it portrayed favorably. They also feel the responsibility of suppressing information that, in their eyes, could damage national security. Presidents, therefore, are inclined to control the content and timing of information about their administrations. Reporters, in contrast, want to get their hands on as much interesting and relevant information as possible, regardless of its sensitivity. Many a president has had the day ruined by seeing material from a highly classified document cited in the morning papers.

Editors want stories that sell newspapers or improve television ratings. Trivial stories, such as Nancy Reagan's purchase of expensive china for the White House or the dating lives of the Bush daughters, will often receive more attention than a complex and important issue.

As much as presidents may grouse about the media, they are not above using it for their own purposes. Michael Deaver, a senior aide to President Reagan, spent much of his time constructing effective visual backgrounds for presidential stories on the nightly news.

10.7a Phases of the Relationship

The relationship between the president and the media can go through a series of phases. The first is cooperation and occurs in the early honeymoon stage of an administration. Presidents in this phase woo the media, grant numerous interviews, have nationally syndicated columnists for dinner, may visit influential reporters in their homes, and see to it that a reporter's calls to the White House are returned. During this time, stories frequently appear about what a breath of fresh air the administration has brought to Washington.

The second phase begins after the administration has settled in, begun to develop some internal conflicts, seen some sensitive information leak, suffered through its first crisis, and received its first series of negative stories. It is at this point that the relationship turns to one of conflict. Presidents will try more vigorously to control leaks, may deny critical reporters access to top officials, and favor those writers who support the administration. After enjoying a honeymoon with the press and beginning to see stories critical of his leadership, President Kennedy said he was "reading more and enjoying it less."

The third phase can be described as detachment. The president becomes less accessible to the press, holds fewer press conferences, and mainly appears before sympathetic audiences. In the final months of his administration, Lyndon Johnson, under constant attack for his Vietnam policy, spoke primarily at

President Barack Obama plays basketball with White House staffers while on vacation on Martha's Vineyard, Aug. 26, 2009. (Wikimedia Commons)

military installations. Besieged by negative stories during the Iran-contra affair, President Reagan went months without holding a news conference. Clinton did the same in the wake of the Monica Lewinsky scandal. In this phase the media become more aggressive in seeking out stories. Their sources may be largely those outside the White House or from disgruntled former officials. Consequently, the stories may grow more negative. By the end of a presidential term, the relationship has exhausted itself.[21]

10.7b The Imperial President Versus the Imperial Media

Both the president and the media have powerful weapons at their disposal in dealing with each other. Presidents can decide what format to use in presenting their case to the public—a prime-time news conference, a fireside chat, or an off-the-record briefing. They can orchestrate their public appearances for the maximum visual effect. They can leak information to those reporters they favor and withhold it from those they disdain.

The media, in turn, can do extensive investigative reporting and take advantage of leakers in the administration who want to undercut a particular presidential policy. Reporters can pressure presidents to release information through the Freedom of Information Act and barrage them with persistent questions at press conferences. They can portray presidential scandals as dramatic and initiate "who-done-its"—as was done in Watergate, Iran-contra, and Whitewater—whetting the public appetite for more information and placing the administration on the defensive.

The contest is usually a standoff. No president has been able to manage the press, and the media cannot make or break a president. The vast majority of American newspapers opposed Franklin Roosevelt and endorsed his opponents. Many Washington reporters had slight regard for Ronald Reagan's ability or wisdom. Yet such media opinions had little or no effect upon the ultimate judgment of the American people.

CHAPTER REVIEW

1. Because the president is the ceremonial head of state as well as the actual governmental leader, the office of the presidency has strong symbolic power. The president can use this power to rally the country in times of crisis, but the power and visibility of the office can also mean that the public will hold the president responsible for events over which the president may have no control.

2. The actual nature of the "executive power," which the Constitution grants to the president, is not clear, and presidents have given it different interpretations. The general contours of the specific powers of appointment, removal, and pardon, however, are quite clear and leave little room for ambiguity.

3. Although presidents have the complete power to appoint all their top advisers, they must be careful to appoint those who will both carry out their policies and run their department effectively.

4. In foreign policy, the Constitution divides power between the president and Congress. The president retains the initiative, but Congress can limit the president's options—and in the period since Vietnam, it has. To lead in foreign policy, presidents cannot simply impose their will; they must persuade both the public and Congress to accept their leadership.

5. In domestic policy, the task of presidential leadership is even more difficult. The president must be able to develop a close working relationship with Congress and have a clear sense of priorities and the public mood.

6. Conflict is inherent in the relationship between the president and the media. Presidents want the media to portray their administrations favorably, and the media are anxious for news that gains public attention regardless of how presidents and their administrations are characterized.

KEY TERMS

Case Act 320

chief of state 304

commander-in-chief clause 320

constitutional theory 308

Council of Economic Advisers (CEA) 316

executive agreements 320

Executive Office of the
　　President (EOP) 314

Gulf of Tonkin Resolution 322

head of government 304

inner cabinet 311

multiple advocacy .314

National Security Council (NSC) 315

natural-born citizen 306

naturalized citizen .306

Office of Management and
　　Budget (OMB) 315

outer cabinet 311

Presidential Succession Act of 1947 318

stewardship theory 308

the administration .311

Twenty-fifth Amendment 317

Twenty-second Amendment 308

vesting clause 308

Readings for Further Study

For a broad overview of the presidency consult Joseph A. Pika and John Anthony Maltese, *The Politics of the Presidency*, rev. 8th ed. (Washington, D.C.: CQ Press, 2013), and George C. Edwards III and Stephen J. Wayne, *Presidential Leadership: Politics and Policy Making*, 9th ed. (Independence, KY: Cengage, 2014).

Two excellent examinations of the role of personality in the presidency are Fred I. Greenstein's *The Presidential Difference*, 3rd ed. (Princeton: Princeton University Press, 2009) and James David Barber's *The Presidential Character* (New York: Longman, 2008).

A highly readable collection of essays on the contemporary presidency can be found in Michael Nelson, ed., *The Presidency and the Political System* 10th ed. (Washington, D.C.: CQ Press, 2013).

A useful general reference is Michael Genovese, ed., *Encyclopedia of the American Presidency*, (New York: Facts On File, 2009).

The complex relationship among the president, Congress, and the people is explored in Samuel Kernell's *Going Public*, 4th ed. (Washington, D.C.: CQ Press, 2006).

Notes

1. Quoted in Christopher H. Pyle and Richard M. Pious, *The President, Congress, and the Constitution* (New York: Free Press, 1984), pp. 68, 70.

2. Ibid., p. 130.

3. 272 U.S. 52 (1926).

4. 295 U.S. 602 (1935).

5. Louis Fisher, *The Politics of Shared Power: Congress and the Executive*, 2nd ed. (Washington, D.C.: Congressional Quarterly, 1987), p. 11.

6. Thomas E. Cronin, *The State of the Presidency*, 2nd ed. (Boston: Little, Brown, 1980), pp. 253–296.

7. Paul Strobin, "In the Loop," *National Journal* (March 24, 1990): 715–718.

8. Rich Lowry, "Obama Kills the War Powers Act," *National Review Online*, June 7, 2011.

9. Thomas M. Franck and Edward Weisband, *Foreign Policy by Congress* (New York: Oxford University Press, 1979), p. 142.

10. 67 U.S. (2 Black) 635 (1863).

11. 323 U.S. 214 (1944).

12. *Congressional Record* (January 25, 1955): 672.

13. U.S. Department of Defense, "Operation Iraqi Freedom U.S. Casualty Status," http://www.defense.gov/news/casualty.pdf (August 22, 2012).

14. Iraq Body Count, http://www.iraqbodycount.org/ (August 22, 2012).

15. The following discussion derives from Reo M. Christenson, "Presidential Leadership of Congress," in *Rethinking the Presidency*, ed. Thomas E. Cronin (Boston: Little, Brown, 1982), pp. 255–271.

16. *Clinton v. City of New York*, 524 U.S. 417 (1998).

17. *Boston Globe*, "Bar Group Will Review Bush's Legal Challenges," June 4, 2006, http://www.boston.com/news/nation/articles/2006/06/04/bar_group_will_review_bushs_legal_challenges/ (June 5, 2006); CNN.com, "Signing Statements Add Presidential Spin to New Laws," June 19, 2007; Signing Statements: George W. Bush, http://www.coherentbabble.com/signingstatements/signstateann.htm (August 16, 2008).

18. 418 U.S. 683 (1974).

19. *The New York Times*, March 22, 1990, p. A1.

20. *Congressional Quarterly Weekly Report*, February 12, 1983, p. 334.

21. Michael Baruch Grossman and Martha Joynt Kumar, *Portraying the President: The White House and the News Media* (Baltimore, MD: Johns Hopkins University Press, 1981), ch. 11.

POP QUIZ

1. A third presidential term is forbidden by the _____ Amendment.

2. The group of cabinet members who handle issues of broad importance such as national security, economy, and justice is called the _____ _____.

3. Presidents can avoid the need for Senate ratification of treaties by entering into _____ _____ with foreign governments.

4. The president does not possess a/an _____ veto, allowing him to veto sections of a bill.

5. The third and last phase of the relationship between the president and the media is characterized by _____.

6. The Senate has the right to refuse a presidential appointment even if only on the grounds of opposition to a particular policy.   T   F

7. The primary responsibility of the Council of Economic Advisers is to help the president develop the annual federal budget.   T   F

8. During World War I, Congress granted President Wilson almost dictatorial control over the economy.   T   F

9. The president of the United States, unlike many governors, does not possess a line item veto.   T   F

10. A president's endorsement of a candidate has little influence on voters.   T   F

11. Which of the following is true of presidential pardon power?

    A) It applies equally to federal and state and local laws.

    B) It does not include clemency for a class of people.

    C) It rarely gains headlines.

    D) It may not be granted prior to a conviction or indictment.

12. The executive office responsible for the formulation, coordination, and implementation of economic and domestic policy is the _____.

    A) Office of Management and Budget

    B) National Security Council

    C) Council of Economic Advisers

    D) Office of Policy Development

13. The constitutional power to declare war belongs to the _____.

    A) courts

    B) Congress

    C) president

    D) military

14. Which of the following is true of the Gulf of Tonkin Resolution?

    A) It gave President Johnson broad authority to use military force in Southeast Asia.

    B) It was passed unanimously in the House, but defeated in the Senate.

    C) It was revoked by Congress only three months after being passed.

    D) It requires the president to consult with Congress before introducing troops into combat.

15. The gap between what the public expects and what the president can do is greatest when it comes to

    A) economic policy.

    B) foreign policy.

    C) environmental policy.

    D) military policy.

Answers:
1. Twenty-second   2. inner cabinet   3. executive agreements
4. line item   5. detachment   6. T   7. F   8. T   9. T
10. T   11. C   12. D   13. B   14. A   15. A

Chapter 11

Bureaucracies

In This Chapter

(iStock)

Figure 11.1 shows a schematic organization of the United States government. It does not display actual patterns of authority or the real size (in numbers of people or dollars spent) of various units, but it does provide a general outline of the branches of government. In terms of numbers of people employed and dollars spent, the executive branch is the largest. It includes the president and his Executive Office staff, as well as bureaucracies such as executive departments (Department of Defense), independent establishments (National Aeronautics and Space Administration), and government corporations (U.S. Postal Service). Because the president and his staff are politically separate in many ways from executive departments, independent agencies, and government corporations, these latter units are sometimes called a **fourth branch** of government.[2]

11.1c Distinguishing Characteristics of Bureaucracies

The most distinguishing characteristic of bureaucracies is that only they are responsible for executing public policies. The bureaucratic units in the fourth branch are also fundamentally different from the other three branches in size, diversity of purpose, physical dispersion, and relative anonymity. Approximately 64,000 people work in the legislative and judicial branches, a number that is dwarfed by the nearly 2.7 million civilian employees in the executive branch.

Bureaucracies are as diverse as the public purposes of government. Getting satellites into orbit (National Aeronautics and Space Administration), protecting consumers from deceptive advertising (Federal Trade Commission), and collecting taxes (Internal Revenue Service in the Department of the Treasury) are public services executed by individual bureaucracies. The degree of diversity among bureaucratic units in the fourth branch is so vast that it makes the other three branches appear almost monolithic in comparison.

The Capitol, the White House, and the Supreme Court Building are familiar Washington landmarks. However, the bureaucracy has no such single physical symbol. Rather, individual bureaucracies are dispersed throughout the Washington area. Some are

fourth branch

Viewed as separate from the presidency, the collection of executive departments, independent establishments, and government corporations

Figure 11.1 | The Government of the United States

The fourth branch is comprised of executive departments, independent establishments, and government corporations. Although the president appears to be in command of the executive departments and other agencies, his actual control is measured by the degree of influence he is able to have on their decisions and programs. Most bureaucrats have civil service status and cannot be dismissed at the president's discretion. Only a relatively few administrative heads serve "at the pleasure of the president."

SOURCE: *U.S. Government Manual, 2013.*

The Constitution

Legislative Branch

Congress (Senate & House)

Architect of the Capitol
Congressional Budget Office
Government Accountability Office
Government Printing Office
Library of Congress
United States Botanic Garden

Executive Branch

The President
The Vice President
Executive Office of the President

Council of Economic Advisers
Council on Environmental Quality
National Security Council
Office of Administration
Office of Management and Budget
Office of National Drug Control Policy
Office of Science and Technology Policy
Office of the United States Trade Representative
Office of the Vice President
White House Office

Judicial Branch

The Supreme Court of the United States

Administrative Office of the United States Courts
Federal Judicial Center
Territorial Courts
United States Courts of Appeals
United States Court of Appeals for Veterans Claims
United States District Courts
United States Court of Federal Claims
United States Court of International Claims
United States Sentencing Commission
United States Tax Court

Fourth Branch

Executive Departments

Department of Agriculture
Department of the Interior
Department of Commerce
Department of Defense
Department of Education
Department of Energy
Department of Health and
  Human Services
Department of Homeland Security
Department of Housing and
  Urban Development
Department of Justice
Department of Labor
Department of State
Department of Transportation
Department of the Treasury
Department of Veterans Affairs

Independent Establishments and Government Corporations

Administrative Conference of the United States
African Development Foundation
Broadcasting Board of Governors
Central Intelligence Agency
Commodity Futures Trading Commission
Consumer Financial Protection Board
Consumer Product Safety Commission
Corporation for National and Community Service
Defense Nuclear Facilities Safety Board
Environmental Protection Agency
Equal Employment Opportunity Commission
Export-Import Bank of the United States
Farm Credit Administration
Federal Communications Commission
Federal Deposit Insurance Corporation
Federal Election Commission
Federal Housing Finance Agency
Federal Labor Relations Authority
Federal Maritime Commission
Federal Mediation and Conciliation Service
Federal Mine Safety and Health Review Commission
Federal Reserve System
Federal Retirement Thrift Investment Board
Federal Trade Commission
General Services Administration
Inter-American Foundation
Merit Systems Protection Board
National Aeronautics and Space Administration
National Archives and Records Administration

National Capital Planning Commission
National Credit Union Administration
National Foundation on the Arts and the Humanities
National Labor Relations Board
National Mediation Board
National Railroad Passenger Corporation (Amtrak)
National Science Foundation
National Transportation Safety Board
Nuclear Regulatory Commission
Occupational Safety and Health Review Commission
Office of the Director of National Intelligence
Office of Government Ethics
Office of Personnel Management
Office of Special Counsel
Overseas Private Investment Corporation
Peace Corps
Pension Benefit Guaranty Corporation
Postal Regulatory Commission
Railroad Retirement Board
Securities and Exchange Commission
Selective Service System
Small Business Administration
Social Security Administration
Tennessee Valley Authority
Trade and Development Agency
United States Agency for International Development
United States Commission on Civil Rights
United States International Trade Commission
United States Postal Service

housed in highly visible and well-known places, such as the Pentagon or the J. Edgar Hoover FBI Building. Discovering where most bureaucracies are located, however, requires initiative and enterprise. Indeed, 86 percent of bureaucrats work outside Washington in thousands of regional and field offices throughout the nation.

Most bureaucracies usually carry on their work with little sustained public awareness. The president performs his tasks in what seems like a fishbowl. Congress receives enormous media attention, and major Supreme Court

Aerial view of the Pentagon (Wikimedia Commons)

decisions are given extensive news coverage as well. Except for some highly visible cabinet secretaries, however, most bureaucrats work with relative anonymity. Their names and exactly what they do are unknown to most citizens.

In the early decades of the nineteenth century, only several thousand people worked for the executive branch. That number grew to about a quarter of a million by the beginning of the twentieth century. Executive branch employment expanded rapidly during the New Deal decade of the 1930s and reached its highest point ever, at almost 4 million, by the end of World War II. For several decades, the number of civilians working in the executive branch remained fairly stable, at about 3 million people. Over the past several years, it has declined slightly to about 2.8 million.

Many government employees, as clerks and office workers, do not fit into the stereotypical view of bureaucrats. Someone working for the federal government performs practically every occupation. Executive branch employees include engineers, accountants, investigators, biologists, mathematicians, librarians, and veterinarians. Many blue-collar occupations are represented as well. The range of jobs in the federal service suggests the wide variety of public purposes. Generalizations about bureaucrats and bureaucracy, therefore, almost always refer in fact to *some* bureaucrats, *some* bureaucracies, or a *portion* of the federal service.

11.2 Executive Branch Organization: Types of Bureaucracies

Individual bureaucracies are generally created in response to specific political pressures in a particular area of public policy. A mix of diverse demands and expectations in the political struggle to define the public purposes government ought to pursue produces an array of organizational types of bureaucracies.[3] In terms of size and visibility, five types are particularly important: the Executive Office of the President, executive departments, independent agencies, independent regulatory commissions, and government corporations.

11.2a The Executive Office of the President

The president has a variety of personal and institutional staff advisers, working in organizations such as the Office of Management and Budget, the National Security

Council, and the Council of Economic Advisers. Beyond the economic and foreign policy advice they offer, executive office units are resources the president can use in his attempts to influence other bureaucracies in the executive branch.

11.2b Executive Departments

As a group, the executive departments are generally the largest and most visible bureaucracies in the national government. The heads of these departments make up the **president's cabinet**, a source of collective advice that the president may or may not seek as he sees fit. Cabinet status is naturally conferred on organizations whose governmental purposes, such as national defense, are crucial by any standard. Beyond the groups that carry out these crucial activities, just what organizations deserve cabinet status is a political question.

For example, following President Reagan's endorsement of the idea, Congress in 1988 gave cabinet status to the Veterans Administration. Creation of the Department of Veterans Affairs reflected the considerable political clout of veterans' groups in their demand for representation in the cabinet. As recognition of the high place environmental issues have on the nation's policy agenda, President Clinton early in his administration pushed for legislation to elevate the Environmental Protection Agency to cabinet status. The absence of departments of science and consumer affairs suggests the crucial role that political support plays in awarding public purposes a place in the cabinet. President George W. Bush's early effort to create five Centers for Faith-Based and Community Initiatives within existing cabinet departments was a signal of his priorities for the nation.

(Shutterstock)

Table 11.1 shows that executive departments differ in their dates of creation, number of employees, and amounts of money they spend. Each department has a unique organizational history, and the dates of creation listed in the table mark either the beginning of cabinet status or significant organizational change. For example, the Department of Defense was created in 1949 following the consolidation of the departments of the Army, Navy, and Air Force into the National Military Establishment in 1947, even though the nation had a Department of War (the army) beginning in 1789.

In terms of number of employees, as Table 11.1 shows, the Department of Defense exceeds all the others. With about 772,000 civilian employees (the additional 2.2 million active and reserve military personnel are not included in the table), the Defense Department alone accounts for almost one-fourth of the total number of civilians working for the national government. Health and Human Services, largely because of the huge Social Security program, typically accounts for the largest single chunk of money that the government spends. In recent budgets the Treasury Department has also seen high levels of spending, due to the enormous bailout of the financial sector and lending market that this agency has been responsible for overseeing.

Executive departments have presidentially appointed secretaries and assistant secretaries who provide direction, but these departments are really organizational "umbrellas" or "holding companies" within which a variety of smaller bureaucratic units are located. For example, the Federal Bureau of Investigation (FBI) is a unit

president's cabinet

Political institution comprised mainly of executive department heads that collectively serve as a source of advice for the president

table 11.1 | The Executive Departments

Executive departments vary widely in terms of employees and budgets. Expenditures are not always related to size of staff, as the numbers for the departments of Defense and Health and Human Services show.

	Date of Creation	Employees	Expenditures (in billions)
Defense	1949*	772,601**	$739.7
Veterans Affairs	1988	304,665	$141.1
Homeland Security	2003	183,455	$48.1
Treasury	1789	110,099	$532.3
Justice	1870	117,916	$33.5
Agriculture	1862	106,867	$152.1
Interior	1849	70,231	$13.0
Health and Human Services	1979	69,839	$909.7
Transportation	1966	57,972	$79.5
Commerce***	1913	56,856	$11.9
State	1789	39,016	$28.9
Labor	1913	17,592	$148.0
Energy	1977	16,145	$44.6
Housing and Urban Development	1965	9,585	$60.8
Education	1979	4,452	$79.4

* The War Department, predecessor of the Defense Department, was created in 1789.
** Number includes civilian employees only.
*** A Department of Commerce and Labor existed between 1903 and 1913.

SOURCE: Statistical Abstract of the United States, 2012.

within the Department of Justice. The Federal Aviation Agency (FAA), which is responsible for the safety of airports and airliners, is located within the Department of Transportation. The National Institutes of Health (NIH), overseeing what is probably the largest life sciences research program in the world, is an agency within the Department of Health and Human Services. The NIH has as its public purpose the satisfaction of one of the most persistent public expectations of the twenty-first century, namely, that government discover the causes and cures of disease. Although it is only part of a cabinet department, the NIH itself spends more money than the Department of State and employs more people than the Department of Education.

11.2c Independent Agencies

A third major type of bureaucratic unit is the **independent agency**. Among the best examples of such agencies are the National Aeronautics and Space Administration (NASA) and the Peace Corps. These units are called independent because they are located outside executive departments. The president can hire and fire their heads, and the amount of money these agencies spend must go through the regular appropriations process whereby the president and Congress make final expenditure decisions.

independent agency

A type of bureaucratic unit organizationally located outside of an executive department and generally headed by a single individual

Another type of bureaucracy is an independent agency, such as the National Aeronautics and Space Administration (NASA). (Shutterstock)

The determination of whether an agency shall be placed inside or outside an executive department is strongly influenced by political considerations. Some groups may want an agency serving its purposes to be more highly visible, be unfettered by cabinet control, or have more direct access to the president. Agencies can also be granted independent status because of the judgment that no executive department would be an appropriate home for the agency. For example, NASA was established as an independent unit to avoid the inter–military service rivalry that marred the early space program and to give the nation's space program a nonmilitary cast.

11.2d Independent Regulatory Commissions

A fourth type of unit is the **independent regulatory commission**. As the title suggests, commissions comprised of usually five to eleven people, rather than single individuals, head such units. The commission device was justified on the grounds that a group of experts in a particular field of economic activity, relatively insulated from partisan political considerations, could make reasonable and fair judgments on the basis of their technical knowledge.[4] The Interstate Commerce Commission, created in 1887, served as an organizational model for subsequent regulatory efforts.

Like independent agencies, independent regulatory commissions lie outside executive departments. However, the independence of the commissions has greater significance, for they have a special status that insulates them to some degree from control by the president. The terms of the commissioners are fixed, so the president may appoint new commissioners only when vacancies occur. Often their terms are longer than the president's. In addition, the Supreme Court has ruled that the president can remove commissioners only for causes specified in statutory law governing the commission. Because the commissions are not purely "executive" agencies, the president's controls over them are more limited.[5]

11.2e Government Corporations

A fifth type of bureaucratic unit is the **government corporation**. Examples of government corporations include the National Railroad Passenger Corporation (Amtrak), the Federal Deposit Insurance Corporation, and the National Park Foundation. Government corporations provide services—such as rail transportation, offering insurance, or producing electric power—that are also provided by private corporations. In the provision of these services, government corporations generally produce much of their own revenue. For example, people must pay a specific fee to enter a national park.

Historically, certain types of essentially commercial enterprises have been judged to be of sufficient public importance to merit substantial government involvement. A system of insuring bank deposits is such an enterprise. Compared to other public bureaucracies, such corporations have been granted a degree of financial and operational flexibility because of the essentially commercial character of their work. Because they generally rely on user fees, they are not tied to the regular appropriations process as are other types of bureaucracies.[6]

independent regulatory commission

A type of bureaucratic unit organizationally located outside of an executive department, headed by a group of individuals called a commission, and charged with regulating a specific industry or economic practice

government corporation

A type of bureaucratic unit that offers some service for which the benefiting individual or institution must pay directly

11.3 The Search for Competence in the Civil Service

In assessing bureaucrats and their role, two questions are particularly important. First, how can the nation ensure that bureaucrats are competent? Second, to whom are bureaucrats responsive in the political system? The issue of responsiveness has become particularly important as government has grown over the last half-century, but concern over competence is as old as the Republic itself.

President Washington stressed the importance of "fitness of character" in appointments to high office. His ideal appointees tended to be educated members of the upper classes who looked on government as a high calling. When the Jeffersonians took control from the Federalists after the election of 1800, many moderate Federalists remained on the job. This era has been called one of "government by gentlemen" because the "business of governing was prestigious, and it was anointed with high moral imperatives of integrity and honor."[7]

11.3a The Spoils System

The early period of integrity and honor is not nearly as widely known as the famous, or infamous, **spoils system**, the practice of making appointments to government jobs on the basis of party loyalty and support in election campaigns. The term *spoils system* comes from a statement made by Senator William L. Marcy of New York during a Senate debate over a presidential appointment in 1832: "They see nothing wrong in the rule that to the victor belong the spoils of the enemy."[8]

The beginning of the spoils system is traditionally associated with the presidency of Andrew Jackson (1829–1837), which began a period of "government by the common man," a reaction against the elitism of government service in earlier decades.[9] The spoils system led to wholesale changes in government personnel after presidential elections. Government posts were openly bargained for and traded. Presidents spent much of their time, not pondering great affairs of state, but dealing with people whose needs were much more simple—they wanted government jobs. The result was a view of government as an employment agency and a perception, continuing even today, of government and politics as a corrupt and dirty business.

In an irony of history, the single most important contributor to the demise of the spoils system was an individual who sorely wished to take advantage of it. Charles Guiteau asked President James Garfield (1881) for an appointment as consul to Paris. When he did not receive a government job, Guiteau shot the president, who died several months later. In galvanizing public opinion, an assassin's bullet accomplished what for so long had eluded reasoned debate.

President Andrew Jackson (Library of Congress)

11.3b The Pendleton Act and the Merit Principle

President Garfield's assassination, combined with public reaction against scandals and corruption in the preceding Grant and Hayes administrations, led to the passage of the single most significant piece of legislation affecting public service. The **Pendleton Act** of 1883 established a Civil Service Commission whose task was to introduce the concept of merit as a condition of government employment. Merit was to

spoils system

The practice of making appointments to government jobs on the basis of party loyalty and support in election campaigns

Pendleton Act

Legislation passed in 1883 that created a Civil Service Commission charged with the task of using merit, rather than partisan political connections, as a condition of government employment

be determined by competitive examinations that tested an individual's ability to perform the job in question. Expertise replaced partisan political connections as the criterion for selection. In the beginning, the Pendleton Act covered only about 10 percent of all government positions. However, as a result of a variety of executive and legislative actions over the past century, the vast majority of government jobs are now filled on the basis of merit. This emphasis on merit has been so strong that in 1939 Congress enacted the **Hatch Act**, which banned civil servants from participation in partisan political activity.

President Garfield's assassination led to the passage of the single most significant piece of legislation affecting public service, the Pendleton Act of 1883. (Wikimedia Commons)

People become government employees through a variety of avenues. The military services have their own system of recruitment. Similarly, other agencies—such as the Postal Service, the FBI, and the State Department's Foreign Service—each have their own separate systems of hiring and merit. Most government jobs, however, are covered by the civil service system administered by the Office of Personnel Management. This agency has assumed most of the functions of the Civil Service Commission, which was abolished in 1978. For many positions, particularly at lower levels, competitive examinations are required. For others, individuals are rated on the basis of their experience and qualifications.

Clerical and administrative personnel within the competitive service are classified in a "general schedule" (GS) that is divided into fifteen "grades," with stages within each grade. Specific grades are based on the experience and qualifications of individuals, as well as the job responsibilities they are assigned. Lower grades are assigned to individuals who perform clerical, secretarial, or administrative support tasks. College graduates generally begin at grade five or above, whereas grades thirteen, fourteen, and fifteen are "midlevel management positions."[10] Individuals with higher-level positions beyond GS-15 are generally in the Senior Executive Service discussed below. Presidential appointments are in a separate Executive Schedule.

The FBI is another example of a bureaucratic agency. (Getty Images News)

Hatch Act

Legislation that prohibits civil servants from participating in partisan political activity

11.3c The Civil Service Reform Act of 1978

As a candidate for the presidency, Jimmy Carter made reform of the federal bureaucracy one of his campaign themes. Among the most significant pieces of legislation enacted during his term was the **Civil Service Reform Act** of 1978, the most far-reaching attempt to change the civil service since the Pendleton Act. The act was intended to defend the merit principle and to provide incentives for high-quality work. It established a system of merit pay for midlevel managers and provided protections for whistle-blowers, individuals in the bureaucracy who report waste or fraud. The act also created the **Senior Executive Service (SES)**, a group of about eight thousand high-level civil servants who might be given bonuses, transferred among agencies, or demoted—all depending on their performance.[11]

President Carter established the **Office of Personnel Management (OPM)** as the government's principal personnel agency with ultimate responsibility for hiring and maintaining the highest-quality work force. He also redesignated the Civil Service Commission as the **Merit Systems Protection Board**, charged with protecting individual employees against violations of the merit principle or actions taken against whistle-blowers.

The 1978 reform has not lived up to its promise, however. In the decade following passage of the act, the merit pay system was hobbled by a lack of adequate funds and perceptions of inequity in merit pay awards.[12] Hopes that the SES would become a prestigious and respected group of senior civil servants were not fulfilled. SES members expressed dissatisfaction with their political superiors, their compensation, and the generally unfavorable public perceptions of the federal civil service.[13] Some changes in these attitudes started to occur by the 1990s. For example, senior civil servants generally expressed satisfaction with their salaries after a generous pay raise in 1991.[14] The history of the 1978 act, nonetheless, shows that efforts to reform the civil service system are at once difficult and durable.

11.4 The Search for Bureaucratic Responsiveness: The Political Environment of Bureaucracies

Who determines what bureaucrats do is a matter of critical importance in any discussion of bureaucracy. Because the political system is one of dispersed power, the work of bureaucrats is shaped by a variety of individuals and institutions, including the president, Congress, the courts, and interest groups. Both the president and Congress can point to specific clauses in the Constitution that give each a claim to control over the bureaucracy. Conflict about who ought to control the bureaucracy is, therefore, inevitable.

11.4a The President

As the title "chief executive" suggests, the individual most responsible for the performance and actions of bureaucrats in the executive branch is the president of the United States. The Constitution charges the president with the responsibility to "take care that the Laws be faithfully executed." In addition, the Constitution authorizes the president to make appointments of department heads and allows the president to "require the opinion, in writing, of the principal officer in each of the executive Departments, upon any subject relating to the Duties of their respective Offices."

Civil Service Reform Act

Legislation designed to improve the level of performance of civil servants by creating incentives for high-quality work, protecting whistle-blowers, and making it easier to fire inadequate employees

Senior Executive Service (SES)

Created by the Civil Service Reform Act of 1978, a class of civil servants drawn from the highest grades and who might be given bonuses, transferred among agencies, or demoted—all depending on the quality of their work

Office of Personnel Management (OPM)

Created in 1981 as part of the Executive Office of the President, focuses on the formulation, coordination, and implementation of domestic and economic policy, and provides staff support for the Economic and Domestic Policy Councils

Merit Systems Protection Board

An agency charged with protecting individual employees against violations of the merit principle or actions taken against whistle-blowers

Despite such constitutional authority, incoming presidents have discovered that they have to work hard to achieve bureaucratic responsiveness to their demands and requests.[15] The relationship sometimes resembles more of a struggle among contestants than the easy downward flow of power suggested by neat organization charts.

Presidential control of bureaucracy is difficult for a variety of reasons. First, the sheer size and diversity of the executive branch means that close presidential control and direction of every bureaucrat is a literal impossibility.[16] Much of the work of government has a dynamic of its own; and each day, without direct presidential attention, the assigned tasks must be accomplished.

Second, as specialists in some area of public policy, bureaucrats tend to be committed to their own work rather than to the person of the president. Such commitment is strengthened by the fact that they usually hold relatively permanent positions, whereas presidents are in office for a much shorter period of time. Perhaps most important, bureaucrats, taking advantage of the dispersion of power in the political system, can make alliances with other groups and institutions. Congress, its committees, and political interest groups are among the main sources of power bureaucrats can tap in their struggles with the president.

Bureaucrats can delay action, take no action, or offer alternatives in response to a presidential request; but presidents determined to get action have at their disposal a variety of tools to make bureaucrats responsive. First, the president has the power to make some three thousand appointments to the departments and agencies. These individuals, who include cabinet secretaries, assistant secretaries, and the heads of independent agencies, are the people the president depends on to carry forward his programs in the executive branch. President Reagan, for example, skillfully used his appointments to help shape his public policy goals. President Bill Clinton won the presidency with the promise of new public policies to produce jobs and higher growth in a lagging economy. Meeting that promise depended, in some measure, on the people Clinton chose to fill important executive branch posts in his administration.

Second, presidents can use the budget process to propose cuts or increases in the financing of specific bureaucracies. Although the president cannot independently determine expenditures, his proposals can significantly affect the size of bureaucratic budgets. For example, in his budget proposals, President George W. Bush was the single most important individual shaping Defense Department spending and proposals to shift resources to new civilian technologies. Finally, subject to congressional approval, presidents can reorganize agencies to make them more compliant to their wishes. Using this power, presidents can abolish agencies, create new ones, and rearrange lines of responsibility among existing agencies.

11.4b Congress

The president's most powerful competitor in the effort to ensure bureaucratic responsiveness is Congress. According to the Constitution, presidential appointments shall be made "by and with the Advice and Consent of the Senate." The document also grants to Congress taxing powers to provide for "the general welfare of the United States." The Constitution

The president's most powerful competitor in the effort to ensure bureaucratic responsiveness is Congress. Here President Barack Obama speaks to a joint session of Congress regarding health-care reform (Wikimedia Commons)

grants what is probably the most potent power of Congress over bureaucracy by stating "no money shall be drawn from the Treasury, but in Consequence of Appropriations made by Law." Like the president and the president's staff, Congress cannot hope to oversee consistently and in any detailed fashion the daily operations of every bureaucratic unit. However, a Congress determined to make a difference can substantially shape bureaucratic behavior.

Congress is granted taxing powers to provide for the general welfare of the United States and the potent power over bureaucracy "that no money shall be drawn from the United States Treasury, but in consequence of appropriations made by law." (iStock)

First, Congress has the ultimate responsibility for the creation and abolition of agencies. Second, the Senate must confirm presidential appointments, particularly those at the highest bureaucratic levels. Although presidents generally get approval for their appointees, the Senate occasionally exercises its constitutional right to reject nominees. The possibility of Senate rejection no doubt eliminates some candidates from consideration at the outset. Third, congressional power to enact a budget means that Congress may substantially shape both the amount and the purpose of money bureaucrats spend. Finally, pursuant to its constitutional authority to enact laws, Congress can use its power to investigate bureaucratic behavior. In hearings before its committees, Congress can question bureaucrats about allegations of abuse of the purpose of specific legislation.

Congress engages in efforts to control bureaucracies partly because of self-interest. Reelection of its members frequently depends on what bureaucrats do and how they do it. Indeed, one observer argues that the growth of big government and the expansion of bureaucratic involvement in the lives of citizens are, in no small measure, the responsibility of Congress itself. According to this view, members of Congress find electoral profit in "pork-barreling" and "casework" activities.[17] Pork-barreling refers to the attempt by members of Congress to get as many federal dollars and projects to flow into their districts as possible. Casework refers to services to individual constituents who are having difficulties with government agencies, ranging from a lost Social Security check to getting a passport.

11.4c The Case of the Veto

As society has become increasingly technological and interdependent, Congress has delegated more generous discretionary authority to the president and executive agencies to grapple with the technical and complicated issues confronting government. To temper executive discretion, Congress also provided for a **legislative veto**. Under this provision, a vote by one or both houses of Congress—or even by a congressional committee in some instances—can halt an executive initiative, bypassing the president in the process. In this way, rather than initially specifying what could be done, Congress reserved for itself the right to react to what had been done. Congress has written legislative veto power into many laws, among which are statutes governing the rule-making powers of regulatory agencies. In one of its best-known exercises of legislative veto power, Congress invalidated a proposed agency regulation that would have required used-car dealers to give potential buyers more extensive information about the cars. Critics of legislative veto power charged that the provision allowed Congress

legislative veto

Congressional power, which the Supreme Court ruled unconstitutional in 1983, to halt an executive initiative by a vote of one or both houses or by a congressional committee

In May 2010, a Rush Limbaugh advertisement on a radio truck near Diablo Stadium was seen during the "Stand With Arizona" Tea Party rally in Tempe, Arizona. The "Buy-cott Arizona" and "Stand With Arizona" campaigns were responses to that state's immigration law. (AP World Wide Photo)

to interfere with executive prerogatives. In 1983, in *Immigration and Naturalization Service v. Chadha,*[18] the Supreme Court declared the legislative veto unconstitutional because it violated the separation of powers mandated by the Constitution.

However, the Court's ruling did not settle the matter, for "the decision has been eroded by open defiance and subtle evasion."[19] The legislative veto power continues to be written into some statutes. In addition, informal arrangements provide that agencies will not take certain actions without consulting Congress. For example, NASA and the House Appropriations Committee have agreed that they will not exceed spending ceilings on NASA programs without informal committee approval. The legislative veto continues because bureaucrats need to exercise some discretion as they administer federal programs, but Congress needs to place limits on that discretion without always resorting to the cumbersome process of enacting laws. The continuing use of the legislative veto is the practical result of these realities.

11.4d Interest Groups

Bureaucracies are engaged in day-to-day execution of public purposes; thus, political interest groups understandably try to shape what bureaucrats do. Practically every bureaucratic unit has the strong support of some group. In some cases, groups have what amounts to a proprietary interest in specific departments and agencies. Veterans' groups consider the Department of Veterans Affairs "theirs," and farmers view the Department of Agriculture in much the same way. In other cases, groups compete as they press their claims on the same agency. The Environmental Protection Agency (EPA) is consistently in the middle of a crossfire of conflicting demands from environmental groups, which charge that the EPA is not enforcing environmental laws vigorously enough, and industrial groups, which argue that the EPA is enforcing such laws too vigorously. Debate over public purposes naturally extends to the work of bureaucracies.

Groups can make direct appeals to the bureaucrats themselves, for example, by commenting on proposed regulations; and groups can also make claims on bureaucracies through other institutions, such as the mass media, the courts, and Congress. Groups can use press conferences or advertising campaigns to influence bureaucratic decisions, or they can ask the courts to order bureaucracies to halt "unfavorable" actions or begin "favorable" actions. Most important, groups can try to influence Congress to use its substantial powers to bring about the kind of bureaucratic activity that groups see as favorable to their own interests.

One of the most familiar models of decision making in American government is the **iron triangle**, comprised of interest groups, relevant congressional committees, and one or more executive branch agencies (see Chapter 9, Figure 9.2, for an

iron triangle

The combination of interest group representatives, legislators, and government administrators seen as extremely influential in determining the outcome of political decisions

example of the iron triangle and veterans' policy). Iron triangles characterize the decision-making process for many areas of public policy. One triangle, for example, consists of the Defense Department, congressional armed services committees, and corporate contractors who manufacture weapons systems.

Each of the sides of these triangles depends on, and can support, the other two because the triangles are held together by large doses of mutual self-interest. The development of a new aircraft or the continued production of an older one, for example, is a decision heavy with political and economic significance. Congressional appropriations for production not only satisfy units in the Department of Defense but also please aircraft companies, their suppliers and contractors, unions, and local communities—all of which benefit when government money is spent. Defense cuts strain these relationships. Attempts to cancel development of a new plane or to shift the contract for production to another company (and perhaps a different section of the country) are sure to provoke resistance from those who have the most to lose.

11.4e The Courts

The courts play a more passive role in the political environment of bureaucracies and can significantly shape, in a variety of ways, what bureaucrats do. First, the courts can determine the constitutionality of some congressional or presidential action and can affect, therefore, the work of bureaucrats. More than a half-century ago, the Supreme Court ruled that Congress had unconstitutionally delegated its own powers to the National Recovery Administration, a New Deal agency created to help relieve the economic crisis in the Great Depression.[20] Although the Court since the New Deal has generally allowed Congress to determine the matter of delegation, controversial subjects, such as the legislative veto and claims of executive privilege, have been tested in the courts in recent years.

Second, the courts attempt to ensure procedural fairness in the efforts of bureaucratic units to promulgate rules and regulations. If the courts determine that a group has not been given adequate notice or the right to comment, the rule may be struck down.

Third, in discerning congressional intent behind legislation that is either vague or ambiguous, the courts can decide what bureaucracies can or cannot do. For example, if Congress in statutory law bans the use of public funds in "programs where abortion is a method of family planning," can the Department of Health and Human Services (HHS) issue rules that forbid medical personnel in federally funded clinics from even *discussing* with patients abortion as an option? Although President Clinton later lifted the ban, in 1991 the Supreme Court in *Rust v. Sullivan* upheld the HHS regulations banning such discussion as a plausible interpretation of the congressional statute.[21] When Congress is not precise in what a bureaucracy should or could do in a specific instance, the courts ultimately decide the legitimacy of bureaucratic action.

Finally, as another example of judicial power over bureaucracies, the courts can determine whether rules issued by regulatory agencies are reasonable in light of available evidence. The courts must wait for cases to come to them, but judges can powerfully shape the work of bureaucrats.

Want to work for a federal agency?

Find out how at the Office of Personnel Management's website.

http://www.bvtlab.com/a8P8m

BVT Lab
Visit www.BVTLab.com to explore the student resources available for this chapter.

353

Chapter 11 | Bureaucracies

11.5 Bureaucrats and Government Regulation

Because of the great diversity among public purposes, bureaucrats engage in a wide range of activities, from doing research on AIDS to collecting taxes to building space stations. Issuing rules and regulations that affect a large number of individuals and companies throughout the nation has been the most controversial activity of bureaucrats over the past several decades. Regulations have produced sharp debate because of the costs and behavior changes they impose on the people affected. A review of regulatory policy illustrates the role of bureaucrats in public policy and the intensely political environment that shapes their work.

11.5a Regulation in Perspective

The Environmental Protection Agency has the Herculean task of producing regulations required by the Clean Air Act amendments that Congress enacted in 1990. For example, in the effort to limit the release of ozone-depleting chlorofluorocarbons (CFCs) into the atmosphere, Congress required the EPA to produce regulations on the servicing of motor vehicle air conditioners. The EPA rules are highly detailed and technical and provide an illustration of the role of bureaucrats in translating ideas into action—in this instance producing specific requirements that will change behavior to protect the ozone layer.[22]

Evidence of regulations in a wide range of policy areas is all around us. Electricity used in millions of homes may be produced by nuclear power plants regulated by the Nuclear Regulatory Commission. Radio and television stations are regulated by the Federal Communications Commission. The Food and Drug Administration certifies the safety of prescription drugs. The EPA sets detailed standards for safe drinking water. The physical safety of workplaces is regulated by the Occupational Safety and Health Administration. Baby cribs and toys are subject to regulation by the Consumer Product Safety Commission. Although these are all examples of national agencies, the federal nature of American government means that many of these regulatory bodies have state-level counterparts as well. Most states, for example, control and regulate the sale of alcoholic beverages through a state agency.

Government regulations touch people's lives at the most basic levels. For example, it was once noted that more than three hundred federal regulations shape what goes into a pizza and how it may be sold.[23] Ingredients must meet specified nutritional requirements to pass federal inspection. Regulations similarly affect other common foods.

The hamburger, an American staple, is shaped by forty-one thousand federal and state regulations.[24] Few people who eat pizza or hamburgers are aware of or give much thought to the dense network of rules that surrounds their meals. For those who produce and market pizza and hamburgers, however, these regulations are a constant reminder of the pervasiveness of government in even the ordinary activities of life. Such rules are intended to protect consumers from unsafe products and to try to ensure nutritional, high-quality meals.

(Shutterstock)

One of the continuing issues in regulatory policy debate is whether regulatory agencies go beyond congressional intent in their creation of rules. Congress has delegated much authority to these agencies due to the fact that members of Congress have neither the time nor the expertise to draft such rules. How to place limits on experts without crippling their expertise is an ongoing issue in the relationship between legislators and policy makers.

11.5b Regulatory Agencies and Types of Regulations

Regulations are rules devised by government to shape the actions of individuals and groups to achieve purposes mandated by law.[25] With the increase in public expectations and the general expansion of government activity, rules and regulations cover practically every commercial activity and achieve a variety of policy goals. More than one hundred agencies have regulatory powers.

The distinction between economic regulation and social regulation is useful in understanding the regulatory goals of government. In **economic regulation**, a government agency issues rules that shape the structure of some industry or ban or encourage certain business practices. For example, the Federal Trade Commission is charged with limiting monopolistic practices. In **social regulation**, agencies issue rules that are designed to achieve social goals, such as fair treatment in employment, clean air, or safe workplaces.[26] For example, the Equal Employment Opportunity Commission is charged with limiting employment discrimination. The consequence is the enhancement of the political and social status of some groups, such as women and African Americans.

Regulatory agencies perform both **quasi-legislative** and **quasi-judicial** functions. In their quasi-legislative roles, agencies issue rules that, like legislation, apply to whole classes of people. For example, rules of the Securities and Exchange Commission (SEC) against stock market trading on the basis of insider information apply to all individuals and firms in the securities industry. As quasi-judicial bodies, agencies, like courts, can make decisions in individual cases. Because of action by the SEC, for instance, "junk bond" trader Michael Milken agreed in 1990 to pay $600 million in fines and compensation to investors for securities law violations.

As another example, consumers or competitors can complain to the Federal Trade Commission that a company is engaged in deceptive advertising. The commission can investigate the charge with an **administrative law judge**, who hears the case in what amounts to a trial proceeding. Administrative law judges were mandated by the Administrative Procedure Act of 1946 as part of a general effort to provide procedural protections for individuals and groups in agency proceedings. Administrative law judges hold an insulated status in agencies to protect their judicial function, and their findings in particular cases can be appealed to the commission and, if necessary, to the federal courts.

Table 11.2 lists selected regulatory agencies, their dates of creation, and their purposes. Major government initiatives to regulate the economy first occurred in the decades around the beginning of the twentieth century. As industrialization proceeded in the late nineteenth century, the relationships between the buyers and sellers of goods and services became increasingly national in scope. The growth of corporations and nationalization of the economy brought a variety of unsavory practices, such as price gouging, and structures, such as monopolies, to the marketplace. Such iniquities led to demands that government remedy the imbalance between producers and purchasers. These problems frequently crossed state lines; and in many instances, redress involved the national government.

regulations

Rules devised by government agencies that shape the actions of individuals and groups in order to achieve purposes mandated by law

economic regulation

Type of regulation in which a government agency issues rules that shape the structure of some industry, such as limiting entrance into the broadcast industry, or banning or encouraging certain business practices

social regulation

Type of regulation in which a government agency issues rules designed to achieve noneconomic policy goals, such as fair treatment in employment, clean air, or safe workplaces

quasi-legislative

A function of regulatory agencies in which they can make rules that, like legislation, apply to whole classes of people

quasi-judicial

A function of regulatory agencies in which, like a court, they can make decisions in individual cases

administrative law judge

An officer with relatively independent status in a regulatory agency who presides over and makes findings in judicial proceedings in which the agency's actions in individual cases are at issue

table 11.2 | Selected Regulatory Agencies

Establishment of regulatory agencies has come in waves or groups, as Congress has responded to persistent political demands.

Agency	Date of Creation	Purpose
Interstate Commerce Commission (ICC)	1887	To regulate interstate surface transportation, including trains, trucks, buses, and water carriers
Federal Trade Commission (FTC)	1914	To protect economic competition against monopoly or restraints on trade, and to protect against unfair or deceptive trade practice
Food and Drug Administration (FDA)	1930*	To protect the health of citizens against impure and unsafe foods, drugs, cosmetics, and other potential hazards
Federal Communications Commission (FCC)	1934	To regulate interstate and foreign communications by radio, television, wire, satellite, and cable
Securities and Exchange Commission (SEC)	1934	To provide protection for investors and to ensure that securities markets are fair and honest and, when necessary, to provide the means to enforce securities laws through sanctions
National Labor Relations Board (NLRB)	1935	To safeguard employees' rights to organize, to determine through elections whether workers want unions as their bargaining representatives, and to prevent and remedy unfair labor practices
Equal Employment Opportunity Commission (EEOC)	1964	To eliminate discrimination in employment on the basis of race, color, religion, sex, national origin, disability, or age
Occupational Safety and Health Administration (OSHA)	1970	To develop, promulgate, and enforce occupational safety and health standards
Environmental Protection Agency (EPA)	1970	To control and abate pollution in the areas of air, water, solid waste, pesticides, radiation, and toxic substances
Consumer Product Safety Commission (CPSC)	1972	To protect the public against unreasonable risks of injury from consumer products, to develop consumer product safety standards, and to promote product safety and research
Nuclear Regulatory Commission (NRC)	1974**	To license and regulate the civilian use of nuclear energy to protect public health and safety and the environment
Federal Energy Regulatory Commission (FERC)	1977***	To set rates and charges for the transportation and sale of natural gas and oil by pipeline and for the transmission and sale of electricity and the licensing of hydroelectric power projects

* Assumed functions placed in the Department of Agriculture in 1906.

** Assumed many of the functions given to the Atomic Energy Commission in 1946.

*** Assumed many of the functions of the Federal Power Commission created in 1920.

SOURCE: Some statements of purpose were taken, with some modifications, from U.S. Government Manual, 2007–2008.

Establishment of regulatory agencies has come in waves or groups as Congress has responded to persistent political demands. The first wave occurred around the turn of the twentieth century and dealt with the unprecedented size and impact of major industrial corporations and with the problems encountered by the buyers and sellers of goods and services. The second, in the 1930s, sprang from the economic dislocation caused by the Great Depression. The third, in the 1960s and 1970s, came in response to demands to remedy inequalities and to protect the environment and the workplace.

In 1887, Congress created the Interstate Commerce Commission to regulate the railroads. The commission device was justified on the grounds that a group of technical experts in a particular field of economic activity, who were relatively insulated from partisan political considerations, could make reasonable and fair judgments. New industries and new demands for regulation came in the twentieth century, and the Interstate Commerce Commission served as a model for subsequent regulatory efforts. Other enactments followed, such as the Sherman Antitrust Act (1890) and the Federal Trade Commission Act (1914), which tried to limit the growing economic power of trusts and large corporations. The goal of regulation was to establish government as a counterweight to the concentration of economic power in a small number of businesses.

Another kind of regulation tried to protect consumers of specific products. In the ideal free market, companies compete with each other to sell products at the lowest price to consumers who make their purchase choices based on full information about the relative merits of the products. However, in the real world consumers either do not have access to such information or do not take the trouble to get it. Regulation of consumer products means that government action compensates for such market failures. Largely in response to publicity about unsavory practices in particular industries, Congress enacted the Pure Food and Drug Act (1906) and the Meat Inspection Act (1907) to protect unwary consumers. Such regulation continues, as contemporary rules on pizza and hamburgers suggest.

The next period of new regulatory activity occurred during the explosion of government initiatives during the New Deal of the 1930s. Regulation increased as part of the general response of government to the Great Depression. The drive for active government brought entire industries under federal regulation. Among the regulatory agencies created were the Securities and Exchange Commission for financial exchange markets, the Federal Communications Commission for electronic communications, and the Civil Aeronautics Board for the airline industry.[27] In the effort to combat unfair labor practices, the National Labor Relations Board was established to regulate employer-employee relationships in businesses in interstate commerce.

Until the past generation, most government regulations had predominantly economic goals. The objects of regulation were relationships among businesses—rates, business practices, and entry into an industry. However, in the 1960s and 1970s, new regulatory efforts went beyond economic concerns to encompass such social goals as affirmative action, worker safety, environmental protection, and consumer product safety. Among the regulatory agencies established were the Equal Employment Opportunity Commission to fight discrimination in the workplace, the Environmental Protection Agency to limit environmental pollution, the Occupational Safety and Health Administration to promote worker safety, and the Consumer Product Safety Commission to protect consumers from unsafe products. Social regulation has been the lightning rod drawing most of the conflict over regulation since the 1960s.

Regulation and Cost-Benefit Analysis

Regulations obviously cost money. Regulatory agencies require buildings, people, and sometimes sophisticated equipment and research capabilities—all of which must be funded by tax dollars. Agency rules can also require that other people spend money. The protection of workers may require that companies make expensive physical alterations in the workplace. Environmental quality standards may require that manufacturing plants install special equipment to reduce air emissions. Companies may be forced to spend scarce research and development dollars to meet mandated consumer product safety standards. One of the most durable and volatile issues in regulatory policy debate is whether these costs are worth the effort.

Cost-benefit analysis is one of the techniques used to assess the impact of regulations. In theory, cost-benefit analysis should enable government officials to determine whether regulations are worth their costs. The technique can take complicated mathematical forms. In general, the costs of a regulation are tallied and then compared with the benefits the regulation is designed to gain. For example, are the benefits of the lives saved from cleaner air worth the costs of EPA enforcement activities and air scrubbers used in manufacturing plants? The matter is complicated by the fact that progressively higher standards may require geometrically higher costs. For example, cleaning the air of 90 percent of its particulate matter may be equal to or less than the cost of cleaning the next 5 percent.

Efforts to make cost-benefit analyses an integral part of rule making have been controversial. In 1981 President Reagan issued an executive order requiring that agencies assessing proposed or existing regulations be guided by an analysis of costs and benefits. According to the order, agencies can make rules only if "the potential benefits to society for the regulation outweigh the potential costs to society." Agencies proposing major rules—rules having an impact of $100 million or more on the economy—must submit to the Office of Management and Budget (OMB) a regulatory impact analysis before the rule goes into effect. Critics in Congress charged that the OMB used its powers of reviewing regulatory costs and benefits to delay or weaken proposed rules designed to enhance worker or consumer safety or to meet environmental goals. In the George H. W. Bush administration, the White House Council on Competitiveness, headed by Vice President Dan Quayle, assumed the role of regulatory watchdog as it diluted rules it judged to be too costly. The OMB and the Competitiveness Council were strongly supported by those who wanted to keep in check what they saw as unreasonably costly regulations; but the sharp criticism of the limits these agencies placed on regulations illustrates the political debate that can swirl around cost-benefit analysis.

The existence of the debate indicates that cost-benefit analysis does not offer easy answers for public officials. Efforts to tally costs and benefits can become mired in questions such as how much a life is worth or how the benefit of a smogless day can be calculated. Political interests are highly resistant to conclusions that do not support their positions, regardless of how mathematically sound they appear. Acknowledging the limitations of cost-benefit analysis, what questions can be asked about any proposed rule to assess its worth?

11.5c The Regulatory Process

Regulatory agencies make rules that can have real consequences easily discernible to most people. For example, almost everyone has had the experience of struggling to open a "childproof" aspirin bottle, yet almost no one thinks about the circuitous route such regulations travel before they touch us. Figure 11.2 shows where regulations come from. All regulations ultimately have their roots in the Constitution, which grants Congress the power to pass laws and to establish agencies to accomplish specific purposes. Each act of Congress is published in the form of a **slip law**, which is the written text of the legislation. Depending on the subject matter, slip laws can range from a single page to several hundred pages in length. The slip laws passed by each session of Congress are bound together to form a volume of ***U.S. Statutes-at-Large***. Laws currently in effect are classified by subject matter, such as transportation, labor,

slip law

The written text of an act of Congress

U.S. Statutes-at-Large

Chronological compilation, by year, of slip laws passed in each session of Congress

or public health and welfare, in the **U.S. Code**, a collection of dozens of volumes periodically revised to reflect changes in legislation.

Once established, agencies must abide by stringent procedural requirements in their promulgation of rules and regulations. To provide adequate notice and opportunity for hearing under the provisions of the Administrative Procedure Act of 1946, agencies must publish proposed rules to allow anyone affected to comment on them. Such rules appear in the **Federal Register**, a daily government publication (now easily accessible on the Internet) that also contains presidential proclamations and executive orders. On any given day the *Federal Register* may be several hundred pages in length, a fact that suggests the complexity and scope of the federal regulatory effort. All rules and regulations currently in effect are compiled by agency and subject matter in the **Code of Federal Regulations (CFR)**, a collection divided into fifty titles and consisting of over two hundred volumes, revised annually on a staggered basis. The regulations are arranged topically in the *CFR* just as statutes are arranged topically in the *U.S. Code*.

Regulations setting acceptable contaminant levels in drinking water traversed this process, as did those requiring childproof aspirin bottles to prevent accidental poisoning. In 1972 Congress enacted the Consumer Product Safety Act, which gave wide-ranging powers on consumer safety to the Consumer Product Safety Commission (CPSC). The act entered the *U.S. Statutes-at-Large* and the *U.S. Code*.[28] By publishing proposed rules in the *Federal Register*, receiving comment, and then issuing final rules, the commission establishes safety standards that a large number of consumer products must meet. The standards are compiled in the *Code of Federal Regulations*. The congressional act that established the CPSC is only twenty-seven

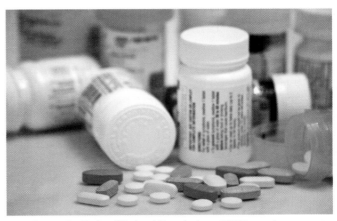

According to the Code of Federal Regulations (CFR), *regulations require childproof aspirin bottles to prevent accidental poisoning. (iStock)*

pages in length; yet an entire volume of the *Code of Federal Regulations*, which is more than six hundred pages long, is devoted to the commission and its rules. Among the detailed safety standards in the *CFR* are twenty-one pages on poison prevention packaging requirements, including rules on aspirin bottles.

Agencies themselves may go through a complicated internal sequence of steps before they issue a rule.[29] A variety of groups and individuals within the agency, including lawyers, technicians, scientists, and economists, shape the proposed regulation. The proposed rule is then reviewed by the Office of Management and Budget, after which it appears as a proposal in the *Federal Register*. After a period for public comment to take public reaction into account, the regulation is published as a final rule in the *Federal Register*. The process may not end here; for affected parties, such as a trade association, might contest the rule in the courts or try to get Congress to change the enabling statute. Because regulators make choices, their work is naturally and continually shaped by the political demands of groups affected by those choices.

11.5d The Ebb and Flow of Regulatory Debate

Regulations have been a controversial political issue because they symbolize government interference in the daily lives of individuals and businesses. Some economic regulation, in fact, actually benefited the regulated industries by limiting competition and supporting the prices of services. In the name of economic efficiency and increased competition, some industries have been deregulated. For example, as part

U.S. Code

Compilation of laws currently in effect, classified by subject matter, such as transportation or labor

Federal Register

A daily government publication that contains proposed and final regulations, presidential proclamations, and executive orders

Code of Federal Regulations (CFR)

Compilation of U.S. administrative rules currently in effect, classified by agency and subject matter

Figure 11.2 | Where Regulations Come From

Regulatory authority lies in the Constitution, which authorizes Congress to enact and the president to approve the creation of departments and programs. A new piece of legislation appears first as a slip law and then in U.S. Statutes-at-Large *and the* U.S. Code. *Established by such legislation, agencies issue and enforce regulations. These in turn appear in the* Federal Register *and later in the* Code of Federal Regulations. *Regulations may be contested in the courts.*

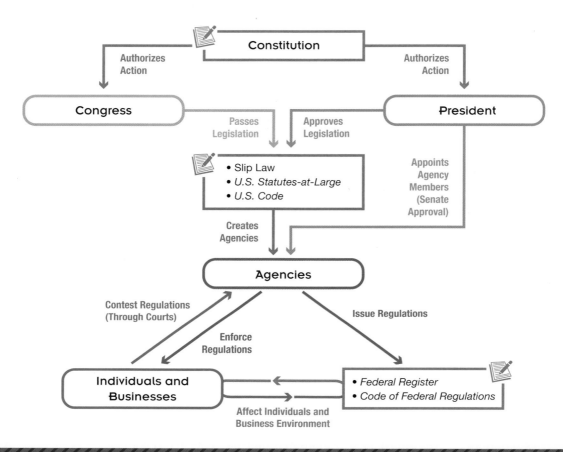

of the general effort to lighten the regulatory burden, the Civil Aeronautics Board, which sets airline routes and rates, was eliminated in 1985. Congressional enactments also limited the regulatory role of the Interstate Commerce Commission before finally eliminating the agency in 1995.

In response to criticism of regulation, recent presidents have made regulatory reform a policy objective. Emphasizing the view that regulatory costs threaten economic productivity,[30] President Reagan, in particular, made **deregulation** a major theme in his call to "roll back" the growth of government. He created a presidential task force on regulatory relief and appointed to regulatory agencies people who shared his interest in reducing the impact of regulations. The budgets of regulatory agencies were cut, and many new proposed regulations were suspended. The Office of Management and Budget assumed an active role in assessing the costs and benefits

deregulation

Process of reducing the number and scope of government regulations

of new rules; however, as "Politics and Economics: Regulations and Cost-Benefit Analysis" suggests, OMB review of regulations has been controversial.

As the 1980s wore on, critics saw deregulatory efforts as attempts to strip government of its power to pursue worthy economic and social goals.[31] A turning point came early in the decade in the battle between Congress and President Reagan over the EPA. In 1980, Congress gave to the EPA the task of cleaning up toxic waste dumps with money drawn from a "super-fund" financed by a tax on chemicals. Within a short time critics charged that the EPA was being too responsive to the interests of the chemical companies and was not vigorously enforcing the toxic waste law. The House of Representatives cited the head of the EPA (a Reagan appointee) for contempt of Congress for refusing to make available agency documents. Six congressional committees began investigations amid intense criticism that the agency reflected the Reagan administration's neglect of environmental concerns. To contain the political damage, the White House made sweeping changes in the agency's leadership and released the requested documents. The struggle uncovered the deep political support for strong governmental action in environmental protection.

Feeling overregulated? Did you know that the government invites comments from the public on *newly proposed regulations*?

Use this website to search new rules and participate in the federal rule-making process.

http://www.bvtlab.com/6w887

By the mid-1980s, regulation as a volatile political issue temporarily receded, and renewed receptivity to government regulation became more evident. In 1986, Congress broadened environmental regulations on drinking water and toxic wastes.[32] Later in the decade some critics argued that the financial disaster of the collapse of savings and loan institutions could have been avoided had the regulatory atmosphere not been so lax.[33] As a lagging economy dogged his presidency, President Bush, in his 1992 State of the Union address, called for a "moratorium on any new federal regulations that could hinder growth." Predictably, the moratorium drew fire from consumer and environmental groups and support from those charging that regulations pose a costly burden. The scope of regulatory activity was an issue in the 1992 presidential campaign; and Bill Clinton's victory promised, as a contrast to the Bush moratorium, greater receptivity in the White House to consumer and environmental regulations. However, a knotty task that the Clinton administration confronted was making regulation more vigorous to protect the environment, workers, and consumers without limiting job growth and economic productivity.[34] By adopting many tenets of a market-driven approach to public management, known as "reinventing government," the Clinton administration was largely able to succeed in its objectives.[35]

Regulatory bureaucrats caught in the middle of the crossfire of conflict

Regulatory bureaucrats caught in the middle of the crossfire of conflict surrounding regulations are really at the center of a debate over the appropriate role of government. Environmentalists want to protect endangered species and wilderness areas, but loggers fear a loss of jobs. (iStock)

surrounding regulation are really at the center of a debate over the appropriate role of government. The attempt to ban unsafe toys may be hailed by consumer groups, but criticized by manufacturers. Environmentalists want to protect endangered species and wilderness areas, but loggers fear a loss of jobs. Citizens with disabilities promote efforts to make buildings more accessible, but corporations and universities have worried about the high financial costs of providing such accessibility. Health groups vigorously support efforts to regulate cigarette advertising, but the tobacco industry views such regulation as a threat. Businesses cite the high financial burden of some worker safety requirements, but labor unions see efforts to limit such rules as increasing physical risks to workers. The contests over changes in regulatory efforts are more than differences over financial costs. The intensity of the debate may ebb and flow; however, conflict over regulations springs from disagreement over what government should do, who should benefit from government action, and whether compromises among competing goals can be achieved.

11.6　Bureaucracies: Targets and Mirrors of Conflict

For much of the past generation, bureaucrats have been the target of biting criticism from elected officials, candidates for public office, and private citizens. Like lightning rods, bureaucrats have drawn criticism aimed at government in general.

Four charges summarize the criticism. First, bureaucrats waste or defraud precious public resources. Second, they wrap much of their work in what appears to be endless amounts of **red tape**, which can be defined as "unnecessary" procedural requirements that impede needed action. Third, bureaucrats do work that either duplicates or conflicts with the work of other bureaucrats. Fourth, and perhaps most important, they play an independent and "political" role in public policy—that is, through their use of discretion, unelected bureaucrats make choices that either directly counter or go beyond the wishes of elected politicians.

Every large organization has individuals who work diligently and conscientiously and others whose work is either haphazard or detrimental to the goals of the organization. Given the size of the national government, it is inevitable that waste and fraud exist, but there is no agreement on their extent. The national government spends huge amounts of time and money trying to limit waste and ensure integrity of work. The battle is always being fought.[36]

The criticism of red tape can be more accurately leveled at groups in the political system generally, rather than at individual bureaucrats. One observer has argued, "One person's red tape may be another's treasured safeguard."[37] That is, what appears to be red tape is really the result of conflicting expectations on the parts of different groups in the political system. For example, advocates of nuclear power may decry the long bureaucratic process of hearings, certifications, and licensing procedures that accompanies the construction of a nuclear power plant. Environmentalists and some local residents may see such procedures as absolutely essential to public health and safety. Perhaps red tape is more a reflection of the attempt to satisfy political values in our society, such as consideration of different points of view, than it is an effort by bureaucrats to paralyze action.[38]

Similarly, charges that bureaucrats engage in work that duplicates or conflicts with the work of other bureaucrats can be explained in large measure by outside expectations. For example, in granting college funds to veterans, the Department of Veterans

red tape

Bureaucratic rules and procedures that seem to complicate and delay needed action unnecessarily

Affairs (DVA) may be duplicating the educational programs of the Department of Education; yet the political expectation that the DVA serve veterans encourages that agency to assume educational functions of its own. Similarly, the Agriculture Department represents the economic demands of tobacco farmers, while Health and Human Services represents the demands of health groups. The conflicting demands of different groups in society are largely reflected in conflict among different groups of bureaucrats.

The most serious criticism of bureaucrats, however, is that even though they are unelected, they independently make choices affecting public policy and play an unintended political role in the process. However, three qualifications need to be made about their political role. First, in executing policy purposes, bureaucrats obviously strive to achieve their institution's goals. For example, an administrator at the NIH may stress the importance of additional funding for cancer research or defense analysts may call for the construction of a new weapons system. Executing policy is bureaucrats' work; bureaucrats, not surprisingly, want the most favorable environment possible in which that work can proceed.

Second, bureaucrats cannot always exercise discretion in translating ideas into action. The Internal Revenue Service, for example, cannot decide to tax certain income groups at rates

The Department of Agriculture often confronts the economic demands of tobacco farmers. (iStock)

higher or lower than those prescribed by law. The greater the specificity of the idea written into law, the lower the degree of discretion bureaucrats have in translating that idea into action.

Third, if the law is vague or ambiguous, bureaucratic discretion is inevitable. In much legislation, Congress cannot possibly provide for every contingency or circumstance. Such detailed decisions fall to bureaucrats. For example, the Social Security Administration (SSA), in administering benefits to disabled Americans, must determine just what constitutes disability in individual cases. Depending on how rigorous that determination is, the SSA, in effect, can make public policy toward citizens with disabilities.[39]

In many areas of public policy, different groups and institutions have conflicting ideas on what government ought to do; they are interested in bureaucracy because they want to get their ideas translated into action. In large measure, the issue of bureaucratic responsiveness centers on the determination of whose ideas ought to be translated into action. In an enlightening and provocative statement, a civil servant in the EPA declared during a controversy over environmental policy: "I signed an oath of office, and it was not to the president. It was to the American people."[40] The statement implies that control over the bureaucracy comes to those who can successfully claim to determine what "the American people" want. The search for that determination, like the struggle to control bureaucracy, lies at the heart of political conflict.

CHAPTER REVIEW

1. The principal task of bureaucracy is the translation of policy ideas into action. Bureaucrats are people appointed to positions in the executive branch. Individuals responsible for executing public policies work relatively anonymously in bureaucracies. Compared to the other branches of government, bureaucracies are much larger, more diverse in purpose, and physically dispersed. The 2.8 million government employees work in a great variety of occupations.

2. Executive Office units advise and serve the president. The executive departments generally contain a large number of smaller bureaucratic units. Independent agencies are placed outside the executive departments, generally in response to political demands for greater visibility. More insulated from presidential control than other bureaucracies, independent regulatory agencies monitor various sectors of the economy. Government corporations are public bodies engaged in essentially commercial enterprises.

3. Government service was seen as a high calling in the early decades of the Republic. In the spoils system, government jobs were rewards for political service. The Pendleton Act of 1883 established the merit principle as the basis for government employment. The Civil Service Reform Act of 1978 attempted to protect the merit system and rid the system of abuses, but its success has been questioned.

4. The president can shape bureaucracies by exercising his appointment, budget proposal, and reorganization powers. Congress can contest the president in the struggle to control bureaucracy through its statutory, budget, confirmation, and investigative powers. In iron triangles, interest groups can work with members of Congress to make claims on bureaucracies. The courts can shape the work of bureaucracies by declaring laws unconstitutional, ensuring procedural fairness, interpreting statutes, and judging the reasonableness of agency actions.

5. Regulation is a major policy of government that affects practically everyone in some way. Economic regulation centers on specific industries, and social regulation tries to achieve a variety of social goals. Major regulatory initiatives were made in the late nineteenth and early twentieth centuries, during the New Deal, and in the 1960s and 1970s. Regulatory agencies issue rules pursuant to powers they receive from congressional enactments. Debates over the regulatory roles of government ebb and flow with the debates over the appropriate roles of government and who should bear the costs of government action.

6. Bureaucracies have been targets of sharp criticism over the past generation. Depending on the amount of discretion Congress allows in law, bureaucrats can potentially make policy. The issue of bureaucratic responsiveness centers principally on determining whose policy ideas should be implemented.

KEY TERMS

Readings for Further Study

The United States Government Manual (Washington, D.C.: Government Printing Office) is a basic reference work that contains a history, relevant congressional enactments, and an organization chart for each bureaucratic unit.

Donald F. Kettl's *The Politics of the Administrative Process*, 6th ed. (Washington, D.C.: CQ Press, 2014) is a comprehensive and erudite review of bureaucracies in the policy process.

A classic work on the obstacles to the implementation of policies is Jeffrey L. Pressman and Aaron B. Wildavsky's *Implementation*, 3rd ed. (Berkeley: University of California Press, 1984).

A look at change over time and the role of today's bureaucracy is found in Donald F. Kettl's *The Transformation of Governance: Public Administration for Twenty-first Century America* (Baltimore: The Johns Hopkins University Press, 2005).

William T. Gormley Jr. and Steven J. Balla's *Bureaucracy and Democracy*, 3rd ed. (Washington, DC: CQ Press, 2012) reviews and analyzes efforts to control bureaucracy in a democratic society.

Richard A. Harris and Sidney Milkis's *The Politics of Regulatory Change: A Tale of Two Agencies*, 2nd ed. (New York: Oxford University Press, 1996), examines the Federal Trade Commission and the Environmental Protection Agency within the context of regulatory politics.

A. Lee Fritschler and Catherine E. Rudder's *Smoking and Politics: Policymaking and the Federal Bureaucracy*, 6th ed. (Englewood Cliffs, NJ: Prentice-Hall, 2006) is an illuminating analysis of the Federal Trade Commission's attempt to regulate cigarette advertising.

John A. Rohr's *Civil Servants and Their Constitutions*, (Lawrence: University Press of Kansas, 2002) explores the relationship between the bureaucracy and the public.

Notes

1. A more extended discussion can be found in H. H. Gerth and C. Wright Mills, eds., *From Max Weber: Essays in Sociology* (New York: Oxford University Press, 1958), pp. 196–198.

2. For an example of use of the phrase, see Kenneth J. Meier's *Politics and the Bureaucracy: Policymaking in the Fourth Branch of Government*, 3rd ed. (Pacific Grove, CA: Brooks/Cole, 1993).

3. Harold Seidman, *Politics, Position, and Power: The Dynamics of Federal Organization*, 3rd ed. (New York: Oxford University Press, 1980), p. 321.

4. For a more detailed assessment of the commission form, see Marver H. Bernstein's *Regulating Business by Independent Commission* (Princeton, NJ: Princeton University Press, 1966), pp. 23–30.

5. *Humphrey's Executor v. United States*, 295 U.S. 602 (1934).

6. See Seidman, *Politics, Position, and Power*, pp. 265–276.

7. Frederick C. Mosher, *Democracy and the Public Service*, 2nd ed. (New York: Oxford University Press, 1982), pp. 58, 60.

8. U.S. Civil Service Commission, *Biography of an Ideal: A History of the Federal Civil Service* (Washington, DC: Government Printing Office, 1973), pp. 16–17.

9. Mosher, *Democracy and the Public Service*, pp. 64–66.

10. Many individuals who were formerly in grades sixteen, seventeen, and eighteen (which have been abolished) are now members of the Senior Executive Service. See Meier, *Politics and the Bureaucracy*, pp. 34–36.

11. Patricia W. Ingraham and David H. Rosenbloom, "Symposium on the Civil Service Reform Act of 1978: An Evaluation," *Policy Studies Journal* 17 (1988–1989): 311–312, provide a more complete list of the act's goals. The symposium contains a series of articles assessing the act from various perspectives (pp. 311–447).

12. U.S. General Accounting Office, *Pay for Performance* (Washington, DC: Government Printing Office, 1989), p. 12.

13. U.S. General Accounting Office, *The Public Services: Issues Affecting Its Quality, Effectiveness, Integrity, and Stewardship* (Washington, DC: Government Printing Office, 1989), p. 34.

14. U.S. General Accounting Office, *Senior Executive Service: Opinions About the Federal Work Environment* (Washington, DC: Government Printing Office, 1992), p. 4.

15. For a concise history of presidential efforts to get control of bureaucracy, see Francis E. Rourke, "Responsiveness and Neutral Competence in American Bureaucracy," *Public Administration Review 52* (November–December 1992): 539–546.

16. Herbert Kaufman, "Fear of Bureaucracy: A Raging Pandemic," *Public Administration Review 41* (January–February 1980): 3–4.

17. Morris P. Fiorina, *Congress: Keystone of the Washington Establishment*, 2nd ed. (New Haven, CT: Yale University Press, 1989), pp. 40–47 and 85–94.

18. 462 U.S. 919 (1983).

19. Louis Fisher, *Constitutional Dialogues: Interpretation as a Political Process* (Princeton, NJ: Princeton University Press, 1988), p. 225. This discussion of the persistence of the legislative veto draws on Fisher's analysis, pp. 226–228. See also Fisher's *Constitutional Conflicts Between Congress and the President* (Lawrence: University Press of Kansas, 1991), pp. 146–152.

20. *Schecter Poultry Corp. v. United States*, 295 U.S. 495 (1935).

21. 59 U.S.L.W. 4451.

22. 57 *Federal Register* 31242 (July 14, 1992).

23. "A Pizza With the Works—Including 310 Regulations," *U.S. News & World Report* (May 31, 1982): 25, 55.

24. "Your Hamburger: 41,000 Regulations," *U.S. News & World Report* (February 11, 1980): 64.

25. This definition draws on Kenneth J. Meier's *Regulation: Politics, Bureaucracy, and Economics* (New York: St. Martin's Press, 1985), pp. 1–2.

26. See *Federal Regulatory Directory*, 6th ed. (Washington, DC: Congressional Quarterly, 1990), pp. 2, 5–13.

27. To deregulate and allow the operation of market incentives in the airline industry, the Civil Aeronautics Board has since been abolished.

28. The act transferred responsibility for poison prevention packaging from the EPA and the Department of Health, Education, and Welfare to the new commission.

29. For example, see Gary C. Bryner's *Bureaucratic Discretion: Law and Policy in Federal Regulatory Agencies* (New York: Pergamon, 1987), pp. 98–105.

30. For a critique of regulation, see Murray L. Weidenbaum's *The Future of Business Regulation: Private Action and Public Demand* (New York: AMACOM, 1979).

31. See Susan J. Tolchin and Martin Tolchin's *Dismantling America: The Rush to Deregulate* (Boston: Houghton Mifflin, 1983).

32. Michael E. Kraft, "Environmental Gridlock: Searching for Consensus in Congress," in Norman J. Vig and Michael E. Kraft, eds., *Environmental Policy in the 1990s* (Washington, DC: Congressional Quarterly, 1990), pp. 110–111.

33. Jeff Gerth, "Regulators Say 80's Budget Cuts May Cost U.S. Billions in 1990," *The New York Times*, December 19, 1989, pp. Al, B10.

34. For a discussion of the debate over regulations in the campaign, see Gerald F. Seib and Bob Davis, "Bush and Clinton Joust Over How to Regulate U.S. Business Activity," *Wall Street Journal*, September 23, 1992, pp. Al, A6.

35. David Osborne and Ted Gaebler, *Reinventing Government* (Reading, MA: Addison-Wesley, 1992).

36. See the discussion in Herbert Kaufman's *Red Tape: Its Origins, Uses, and Abuses* (Washington, DC: Brookings Institution, 1977), pp. 50–54.

37. Ibid., p. 4.

38. Ibid.

39. See, for example, Susan Gluck Mezey's *No Longer Disabled: The Federal Courts and the Politics of Social Security Disability* (Westport, CT: Greenwood, 1988).

40. Hugh B. Kaufman, quoted in Cass Peterson, "A Nagging Voice from E.P.A. Depths Now Singing from the Catbird Seat," *Washington Post,* February 14, 1983, p. A9.

POP QUIZ

1. The most distinguishing characteristic of bureaucracies is that only they are responsible for _____ public policies.

2. One of the most important determinants of what purposes deserve Cabinet status is _____.

3. The practice of making appointments to government jobs on the basis of party loyalty is called the _____.

4. _____ has the ultimate responsibility for the creation and abolition of agencies.

5. Often justified as a safeguard against abuse, bureaucracies have been criticized for wrapping their work in endless amounts of _____.

6. In American government the term *bureaucrat* generally refers to any individual who works in the executive branch of government.   T   F

7. Independent agencies are outside executive departments and their heads cannot be fired by the president.   T   F

8. According to the Hatch Act, civil servants are banned from participation in partisan political activity.   T   F

9. Salaries for public officials are usually equal or above the compensation rates for equivalent positions in the private sector.   T   F

10. When laws are vague or ambiguous, bureaucratic discretion is inevitable.   T   F

11. According to Max Weber, an ideal bureaucracy consists of _____.

   A) expertise

   B) impersonal rules

   C) a hierarchical division of labor

   D) all of the above

12. Which of the following makes independent agencies independent?

   A) They are outside the regular appropriations process.

   B) The president cannot hire or fire their heads.

   C) They are located outside of the executive departments.

   D) They are not influenced by interest groups.

13. Government employment during the administration of George Washington was characterized by _____.

   A) corruption

   B) political spoils

   C) integrity and honor

   D) lack of respect and prestige

14. Which of the following is one of the tools that the president has to make bureaucrats more responsive?

   A) Propose cuts or increases in the budgets of bureaucracies.

   B) Create or abolish agencies.

   C) Investigate bureaucratic power.

   D) All of the above

15. Which of the following is the most serious criticism of bureaucrats?

   A) They waste and defraud public resources.

   B) They affect public policies and play an unintended political role.

   C) They wrap their work in unnecessary amounts of red tape.

   D) They do work that duplicates or conflicts with other bureaucrat's work.

Chapter

12

The Supreme Court and American Judiciary

In This Chapter

(Shutterstock)

Chapter Objectives

One of the distinguishing characteristics of American government is the major role the Supreme Court and other courts play in governing the nation. Because of the importance of the issues that confront American judges, their decisions weigh heavily in shaping the liberties, fortunes, and quality of life of many citizens. Chief among courts is the United States Supreme Court, the third branch of government.

The Supreme Court enjoys prominence because of the Constitution and because Americans have been reluctant to place their fate entirely in the hands of elected officials and popular majorities. The Court, therefore, sits as an institution primarily responsible for interpreting the law of the land. Yet because the Court appears anti-democratic in a government that strives to be democratic, Americans have also been wary of giving judges too much power.

Explaining what judges do, discerning the Supreme Court's place in American government, and exploring how the Court decides cases are the objectives of this chapter.

12.1 The National Court System

A look at almost any recent term of the Supreme Court turns up decisions on subjects as varied as presidential powers, crime, taxation, religious freedom, and racial and sexual equality. The fact that the Supreme Court confronts important issues makes the Court similar to other major political institutions in Washington; however, three factors distinguish the Supreme Court and other courts from the rest of the national government:

1. The judiciary operates only in the context of cases.

2. The cases develop in a strictly prescribed fashion.

3. Judges rely heavily on reason in justifying what they do.

The judiciary is distinctive because it is the part of government that speaks the language of the fundamental values of the political system.

12.1a Cases: Raw Material for the Judiciary

The judiciary acts by deciding **cases**. A case is a dispute handled by a court. Like most disputes, there are at least two opposing parties. A case may pit one individual against another, a government agency against an individual, a corporation against the government, and so forth. Cases are criminal or civil.

Criminal cases result when the government begins legal action against someone following commission of a crime. A **crime** is a public wrong. That is, it is an offense, such as murder, against society at large—even though it may have been committed against only a single individual. **Civil cases** encompass all noncriminal legal actions and commonly include attempts to redress a private wrong or to settle a private dispute. Divorces and recovery of damages following an automobile accident, for example, present civil law questions. They involve efforts by one party to enforce a right or to be compensated for harm caused by another.

By deciding cases, courts, like other governmental institutions, attempt to resolve conflicts peacefully. It is only a slight exaggeration to say that disputes that bring a regiment of soldiers into the streets of some countries summon a battalion of lawyers into the courtrooms of America.

12.1b Fifty-one Judicial Systems

Topped by the Supreme Court, the national court system contains both state courts and federal courts. The latter, in turn, consist of district courts, courts of appeals, and a few special courts.

References to **state courts** and **federal courts** can be confusing to anyone not familiar with the political features of American federalism (see Chapter 2). Concisely put, each state has its own system of courts, and the national government has its own system of courts (see Figures 12.1 and 12.2). The national courts are usually referred to, somewhat misleadingly, as "federal courts."

The two types of courts hear different kinds of cases. Almost all divorce and personal injury cases, for example, are heard in state courts, as are violations of state criminal laws. Antitrust actions and violations of federal criminal laws, by contrast, are adjudicated in federal courts. Someone charged with robbing a corner grocery will be tried in state court; someone charged with robbing a post office will be tried in federal court. The dual system of courts means that almost everyone in any of the fifty states is simultaneously within the jurisdiction, or reach, of two judicial systems, one

case

A controversy to be decided by a court

criminal case

Judicial proceedings that the government begins against an individual following commission of a crime

crime

A public wrong; an offense, such as murder, against society at large—even though it may have been committed against only a single individual

civil case

Noncriminal legal action, such as divorces or attempts to recover damages following an automobile accident

state courts

Courts of the fifty states, as opposed to the federal, or national, courts

federal courts

The courts of the United States, as distinguished from the courts of the fifty states

state and the other federal. **Jurisdiction** refers to the authority a court has to entertain a case. The term has two basic dimensions: who and what. The first identifies the parties who may take a case into a particular court. The second refers to the subject matter the parties can raise in their case.

The role of the Supreme Court is to have the final say on interpreting the constitution. (Wikimedia Commons)

State and federal courts have at least two important points in common. First, the U.S. Constitution binds all American courts. Second, the U.S. Supreme Court may decide cases that originate in both systems. Because the Supreme Court hears only a tiny fraction of all the cases looked at by judges each year across the land, however, the quality of justice in the nation depends largely on what these other courts and judges do. The Supreme Court weighs heavily in American politics, not because it can literally oversee what every other court does, but because these other courts consider the Supreme Court's decisions binding on questions of national law and policy.

12.1c State and Local Courts

State and local courts are organized according to the laws and constitutions of the fifty states. The resulting variety only serves to make them interesting, not insignificant. They handle the great bulk of legal business. The total number of cases filed in state courts each year exceeds 96 million.[1] Criminal cases make up about 20 percent of that total. Most crimes committed each year are violations of state laws and are tried in state courts, as are most disputes over estates, contracts, and property. As will be explained, a relative few are ever candidates for review by the U.S. Supreme Court. Most Americans who go to court, then, go to state courts and only state courts.

The judicial systems of most states are divided into four levels (see Figure 12.2). At the bottom are **courts of limited jurisdiction**, which hear cases in villages, towns, and cities involving small claims, traffic violations, domestic matters, juvenile affairs, and minor criminal offenses. Such courts are variously labeled municipal court, county court, magistrate's court, traffic court, or recorder's court. Usually a judge sitting without a jury decides such cases. On the next tier are **courts of general jurisdiction**; usually one such court is located in each county. These courts receive appeals from the bottom tier and serve as trial courts for serious criminal offenses and civil suits involving substantial amounts of money. Again, the names vary from state to state: superior court, county court, or court of common pleas. Above these courts in many states, especially the more populous, are one or more **intermediate appellate courts**, which are labeled superior court or court of appeals; they accept appeals from the courts of general jurisdiction. At the top of the state system of courts is a **court of last resort**, usually called the supreme court. Most states have only one "supreme court," but Texas and Oklahoma have two, with one specifically designated to hear appeals in criminal cases. (In New York the highest court is called the Court of Appeals, and a supreme court is a court of general jurisdiction.)

Unlike federal judges, who are appointed for life and removable only by impeachment, most state judges are elected. In some states, judges run in nonpartisan elections or in partisan elections just as legislative candidates do. In other states the governor appoints

jurisdiction

Authority of a court or other agency to act

courts of limited jurisdiction

The lowest-level court in a state's judicial system that hears particular kinds of cases involving small claims, traffic violations, and minor criminal infractions

courts of general jurisdiction

The basic unit of a court system, receiving appeals from courts of limited jurisdiction and serving as trial courts for serious criminal offenses and civil suits involving substantial amounts of money

intermediate appellate courts

Courts between courts of general jurisdiction and the court of last resort; in the federal court system, the courts of appeals

court of last resort

The highest court within a particular judicial system, such as a state supreme court, to which a litigant may appeal a case

Figure 12.1 | The United States Court System

Almost all cases the Supreme Court decides each year are part of its appellate jurisdiction. These cases begin in the state and federal courts.

SOURCE: *Administrative Office of the United States Courts.*

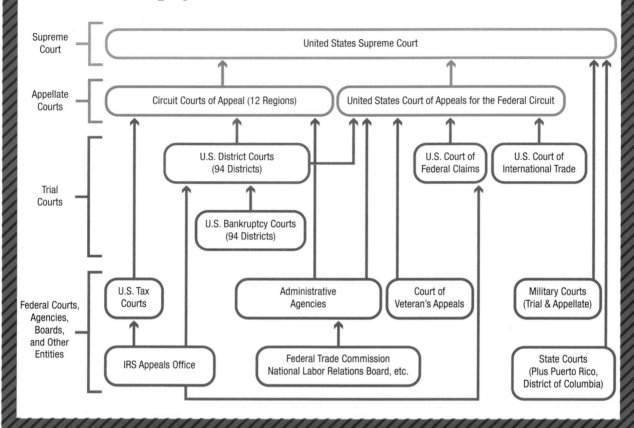

judges from a list of nominees provided by a panel of lawyers and other citizens. The latter method is called the **Missouri Plan**, after the state that pioneered its use. Following initial election or appointment, judges may then be subject to retention votes every five or ten years. That is, instead of running for reelection like other officeholders, judges have their names placed on a ballot alongside the question, "Shall Judge X be continued in office for another term?" A negative vote creates a vacancy, and a new election is held or a new appointment is made. At present, nineteen states use a single method for selecting judges; in the remaining states judges are selected by one of two (or even three) methods, depending on the court involved.

Whether a judge is chosen by election or the Missouri Plan, the people can unseat state judges at the polls. Critics say that this possibility undercuts judicial independence, making judges too dependent on the voters and perhaps afraid to render unpopular decisions. Others reply that the

The vast majority of court cases take place in our nation's state court system. Find out about your state's court system through the National Center for State Courts at this website.

http://www.bvtlab.com/GJ8nb

Missouri Plan

Method of selecting state judges, involving appointment from a list of recommended nominees and a later retention vote by the electorate

Figure 12.2 | Typical Organization of State Courts

Each state has its own system of state courts. No system is exactly like another, but all are organized in a hierarchy similar to that pictured here. All states have courts of limited jurisdiction, courts of general jurisdiction, and a court of last resort. In Texas and Oklahoma, there are two separate courts of last resort—one for criminal appeals and one for all other types of cases. Most, but not all, states have at least one intermediate appellate court. In the twelve states that have no intermediate court, cases move on appeal from courts of general jurisdiction to the court of last resort.

SOURCE: *National Center for State Courts.*

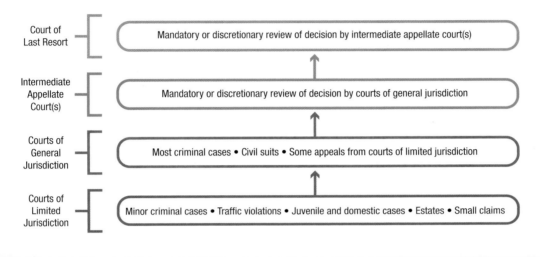

Court of Last Resort — Mandatory or discretionary review of decision by intermediate appellate court(s)

Intermediate Appellate Court(s) — Mandatory or discretionary review of decision by courts of general jurisdiction

Courts of General Jurisdiction — Most criminal cases • Civil suits • Some appeals from courts of limited jurisdiction

Courts of Limited Jurisdiction — Minor criminal cases • Traffic violations • Juvenile and domestic cases • Estates • Small claims

---

people should retain control over all public officials, even judges. Experience shows that judges elected on partisan ballots are more likely than those chosen on nonpartisan ballots or under an appointment/retention plan to be turned out of office by the voters.

12.1d United States District Courts

Of all federal courts, the Constitution only provides for the Supreme Court. Article III left the creation of other ("inferior") courts to the discretion of Congress. Plausibly, Congress could have permitted the existing state courts to handle national business but chose instead, in the Judiciary Act of 1789, to organize a separate court system for the nation as a whole.

Almost all federal cases (over 390,000 annually, excluding bankruptcy filings) begin in the ninety-four **United States district courts**, staffed by 678 judges. There are eighty-nine district courts in the fifty states, plus one each in the District of Columbia, Guam, Puerto Rico, the Virgin Islands, and the Northern Mariana Islands. Each state has at least one district court, and no district crosses a state line. Some states have two or three districts; and the populous states of California, New York, and Texas have four each (see Figure 12.3).

The jurisdiction of district courts extends to cases that arise under the Constitution, laws, and treaties of the United States, as well as admiralty and maritime cases. Questions of state law (such as liability in an automobile accident) may get into

United States district courts

Trial courts in the federal court system in which almost all federal cases begin; courts of general jurisdiction

Figure 12.3 | Geographic Boundaries of U.S. Courts of Appeals and U.S. District Courts

The map shows how the ninety-four U.S. district courts and thirteen U.S. courts of appeals exist with the court systems of the fifty states and the District of Columbia.

SOURCE: *Administrative Office of the United States Courts.*

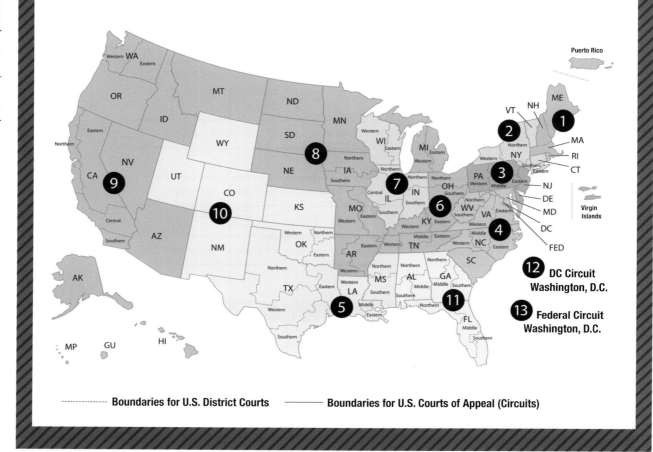

---------- **Boundaries for U.S. District Courts** ———— **Boundaries for U.S. Courts of Appeal (Circuits)**

district court through diversity jurisdiction. This occurs when the parties to a case are citizens of different states and when the amount at issue is greater than $50,000. As a way of reducing the volume of cases in the district courts, Congress has considered repealing diversity jurisdiction altogether. Should this happen, cases now qualifying for diversity jurisdiction would be decided by state courts, entirely outside the federal court system.

12.1e United States Courts of Appeals

Thirteen **United States courts of appeals**, staffed by 179 judges, occupy a middle position in the hierarchy of the federal judiciary. Twelve of these courts have a regional jurisdiction or circuit, as Figure 12.3 shows.

Although district judges sit individually in most cases, appeals judges normally sit in panels of three. In special situations, cases are heard *en banc*, with most of a circuit's bench sitting at once. Cases in the courts of appeals number more than 55,000

United States courts of appeals

Intermediate appellate courts in the federal court system, just below the Supreme Court

annually. Most are appeals from disappointed parties in the district courts and the U.S. Tax Court (see Figure 12.1). Under exceptional circumstances, cases may go from district courts directly to the Supreme Court, bypassing a court of appeals. Another large source of work for the appeals courts comes in the form of reviewing rulings of various administrative and regulatory agencies of the national government, such as the Federal Communications Commission, the Federal Trade Commission, and the National Labor Relations Board. The Court of Appeals for the District of Columbia Circuit hears more of these agency cases than any of the other appeals courts, making this court one of the most influential in the land.

The thirteenth appeals court is the newest; and unlike the other twelve, it has a different—and a national—jurisdiction. The Court of Appeals for the Federal Circuit accepts appeals in patent cases from any district court, as well as all appeals from the Claims Court, the Court of International Trade, and the Court of Veterans Appeals. For most litigants, the courts of appeals are the courts of last resort in the federal judicial system, due to the fact that the Supreme Court accepts relatively few cases.

12.1f Special Courts

Congress has created other tribunals to hear particular kinds of cases in which considerable specialization and expertise are desirable. Into this category fall the following:

1. The *Court of Federal Claims* hears suits involving monetary damages against the U.S. government.

2. The *Court of International Trade* adjudicates controversies concerning the classification and valuation of imported merchandise.

3. The U.S. *Tax Court* decides disputes between taxpayers and the Internal Revenue Service.

4. The *Appeals for Veterans Claims* reviews decisions on benefits and entitlements from the Board of Veterans Appeals in the Department of Veterans Affairs. The newest special court, it heard its first case in 1990.

5. The *Appeals for the Armed Forces* reviews judgments handed down by courts-martial in the several branches of the armed forces.

These courts rarely make the headlines, but they are quite important. In the first four, millions of dollars may ride on the outcome of decisions. The lives and liberties of hundreds of thousands of American citizens are in the care of the fifth.

12.1g The Supreme Court of the United States

It is from these courts, state and federal, that the nine justices of the Supreme Court receive almost all the cases they decide each term. At present, some ten thousand new cases appear annually on their docket, joining about one thousand carried over from the previous term. All but a handful invoke the Court's **appellate jurisdiction**. Defined by Congress, this is the authority that the Court has to review decisions of the federal courts, as well as decisions of the highest state courts that raise **federal questions** (matters involving the interpretation of the Constitution, a statute, or a treaty of the United States). Today, almost all cases reach the Supreme Court on a *writ of certiorari* (Latin for "to be informed"). Except for a few cases involving the

appellate jurisdiction

Includes cases a court receives from lower courts—congress defines the appellate jurisdiction of the U.S. Supreme Court

federal question

An issue that involves the interpretation of the Constitution or a statute or a treaty of the United States

writ of certiorari

A petition for review by a higher court; the most common route for an appeal to reach the Supreme Court

BVT *Lab*

Improve your test scores.
Practice quizzes are
available at
www.BVTLab.com.

378

Chapter 12 | The Supreme Court and American Judiciary

Voting Rights Act, review by the Supreme Court is plainly discretionary, not obligatory. It takes a minimum of four justices (one short of a majority) to agree to accept a case for review. This **rule of four** allows the Court not only to limit the number of cases it decides but also to engage or avoid particular issues.

A very few cases each term are candidates for the Court's **original jurisdiction**, meaning that the case begins or originates with the Court. Indeed, the number of "original" cases the Court decided between 1789 and 2014 totaled only about two hundred. The Supreme Court's original jurisdiction is spelled out in Article III of the Constitution and includes four kinds of disputes:

1. _Cases between one of the states and the U.S. government_ For example, in _United States v. Maine_,[2] the justices ruled that the national government—not the states—had control of oil deposits more than three miles offshore.

2. _Cases between two or more states_ In 1967, Michigan and Ohio each claimed the same piece of mineral-rich territory in Lake Erie; and in a series of cases, Arizona and California have battled each other over water resources.[3]

3. _Cases involving foreign ambassadors, ministers, or consuls_ The framers wanted cases that could involve the nation's relations with other countries to be heard initially by the highest court.

4. _Cases begun by a state against a citizen of another state or against another country_ The **Eleventh Amendment**, however, requires suits initiated against a state by a citizen of another state or of a foreign country to begin in the courts of that state. The Eleventh Amendment came about because of a 1793 decision by the Supreme Court that a citizen of South Carolina could sue the state of Georgia in the federal courts.[4]

Only controversies between states qualify today exclusively as original cases in the Supreme Court. The justices have been content for Congress to grant concurrent original jurisdiction to the U.S. district courts for cases in the other three categories. As such, although one of these cases _could_ begin in the Supreme Court, in almost every instance the case will begin in a district court—unless it involves a dispute between two states of the Union.

The Supreme Court is headed administratively by the chief justice of the United States (the position has been filled since September 2005 by John G. Roberts). Through the years, the Court has usually been known by the name of the chief justice (the Marshall Court, for example); however, the chief's vote in cases counts no more than the vote of any of the eight associate justices. The chief justice also presides over the judicial Conference of the United States, which is composed of representatives of the lower federal courts and makes recommendations to those courts, as well as to Congress, with regard to staffing needs and operating efficiency.

12.1h Federal Judicial Selection

The Constitution gives the president power to appoint federal judges, subject to confirmation by a majority vote of the Senate. In practice, presidents rarely know, personally, any of the district or appeals judges they appoint. Judges on the district, appeals, and Supreme Court benches serve "during good behavior," a provision of the Constitution that effectively ensures lifetime tenure with removal only by impeachment. In contrast to presidents and members of Congress, the Constitution spells out no qualifications, such as age or citizenship, for any federal judge. Federal judges do not even have to be lawyers, although since 1789 each has had legal training of some

rule of four

Procedure of the
U.S. Supreme Court by
which the affirmative votes
of four justices are needed to
accept a case for decision

original jurisdiction

Authority of a court over
cases that begin in that
court, such as courts of
general jurisdiction having
original jurisdiction over
most criminal offenses—the
original jurisdiction of the
U.S. Supreme Court is very
small

Eleventh Amendment

The first reversal of a
Supreme Court decision
[_Chisholm v. Georgia_, 2 U.S.
(2 Dallas) 419 (1793)] by
constitutional amendment,
denying federal courts
jurisdiction in suits against
a state brought by citizens
of another state or a foreign
country

kind. Today, it would be unthinkable for the Senate to approve a nominee who is not a law school graduate and a member of the bar.

Presidents overwhelmingly appoint members of their own political party to the federal bench (during the past one hundred years, only in the Taft, Hoover, and Ford administrations has the figure dropped below 90 percent). The choices for the district courts are usually made by officials in the Justice Department working with political leaders from the state in which the appointment is to be made. A state's U.S. senators (one or both)—particularly if they are of the same party as the president— traditionally play a prominent role in the selection. There is some truth in the wisecrack that a federal judge is a lawyer who knows a senator. In contrast, appointment of appeals judges reflects more national and less local influence, with the attorney general and other officials in the Justice Department having a large say in the selection. District judges are obvious choices for appeals posts because they have observable judicial "track records."

You can read the latest Supreme Court opinions, find biographical sketches of the current justices, and even see the Court's upcoming calendar at the Supreme Court website.

http://www.bvtlab.com/79868

Under present policy of the Senate Judiciary Committee, a "blue slip" (indicating disapproval) from a home-state senator is sufficient to block a judicial nominee outright if the administration fails to consult with home-state senators before naming a candidate. This is an example of **senatorial courtesy**, the practice that allows home-state senators considerable control over the fate of presidential nominees. If a senator submits a blue slip after having been consulted, the committee considers the senator's objections but does not always reject the nominee.

An additional screening role is played by the Standing Committee on the Federal Judiciary of the American Bar Association (ABA), the largest organization of lawyers in the country. Before the president sends a nominee's name to the Senate, the attorney general submits the name to the ABA committee for review. This committee then finds the candidate "well-qualified," "qualified," or "not qualified." Only occasionally will presidents nominate someone the committee considers not qualified; and some nominees are, nonetheless, confirmed by the Senate when they do. The ABA's participation in the review process is significant because it means that a private organization, in effect, shares the confirmation role the Constitution assigns to the Senate. The committee's screening attracts the most attention when the president nominates an individual to the Supreme Court.

In contrast to the other federal courts, vacancies on the Supreme Court occur relatively infrequently. Including the six original seats George Washington (1789–1797) filled, 112 persons have served on the Court through 2014. Supreme Court nominations are far more likely to personally occupy a president's time and attention. Such focus is not simply because the Supreme Court decides important questions but also because, once appointed, justices tend to stay on the Court a long time— usually far longer than the president who named them remains in the White House. The following five considerations most often are at work as presidents make up their minds about whom to appoint:

1. _Professional qualifications_   How respected is the nominee?

2. _Acceptability to the Senate_   Will he or she be confirmed?

3. _Ideological fit_   Will the nominee support the president's program?

senatorial courtesy

Custom in the Senate to reject, for federal office, a nominee who is unacceptable to a senator from the nominee's state when the senator and president are of the same party

4. _Personal friendship_   Does the president want an old friend on the Court?

5. _Region, race, religion, gender, and other background factors_   Does a particular group need "representation" on the Court?

Since Washington's time, presidents have wanted a Court supportive of their administrations; yet they are not always successful in picking "right-thinking" justices. President Dwight Eisenhower (1953–1961) once remarked that appointing Earl Warren (1953–1969) as chief justice was "the biggest damnfool mistake I ever made" after Warren turned out to be more liberal than Ike had supposed. President Richard Nixon (1969–1974) hardly approved of Justice Harry A. Blackmun's (1970–1994) authorship of the 1973 abortion decision,[5] and presidents Ronald Reagan and George H. W. Bush were disappointed when three of their appointees (Justices Sandra O'Connor [1981–2006], Anthony Kennedy [1988–], and David Souter [1990–2009]) voted against administration positions on school prayer.[6]

Particular background factors have frequently been important in aiding or hurting one's chances to become a Supreme Court justice. Most presidents have taken geographical region into account. Moreover, religion, race, and gender have sometimes been important considerations as well. Even so, Supreme Court justices have hardly been representative of American society. Of the 112 justices who sat through 2014, all but twenty-two were Protestant males of Anglo-Saxon origin. Justice Antonin Scalia (1986–) is the Court's first Italian American member. Justice Thurgood Marshall (1967–1991) was the first African American member of the Court, and Justice O'Connor was its first female member. Clarence Thomas became the second African American to serve in 1991, and Ruth Bader Ginsburg (1993–) became the second woman in 1993. Barack Obama became the first president to appoint two women to the Court when he nominated Sonia Sotomayor (also the Court's first Hispanic justice) in 2009 and Elena Kagan in 2010. Most of the 112 have come from economically comfortable and civic-minded families. All have been lawyers or have held law degrees. About one-third graduated from the most prestigious colleges and universities in the United States. Most have been active in public affairs or have held political office; but some, including Justice Byron White (1962–1993), had no prior judicial experience. Only three chief justices (out of a total of seventeen since 1789) have been "elevated" directly from associate justice. All other chief justices were nominated from outside the Court.

Whatever a president's motivations, the Senate must still vote to confirm the nominee. Such approval has been forthcoming most of the time, but on twenty-six occasions the Senate has not given it. In this century, four presidents—Herbert Hoover (1929–1933), Lyndon Johnson (1963–1969), Richard Nixon (1969–1974), and Ronald Reagan (1981–1989)—have had their choices blocked by the Senate. Nixon, in fact, struck out twice in succession before the Senate handily confirmed Judge Harry Blackmun, his third nominee for the same vacancy. When Reagan picked Judge Robert Bork to succeed retiring justice Lewis Powell (1972–1987), the Senate said no. Reagan's second choice, Judge Douglas Ginsburg, withdrew his name from consideration after acknowledging disclosures that he had smoked marijuana as a student in the 1960s and as a member of the Harvard law faculty in the 1970s. Powell's seat remained vacant until early 1988 when the Senate confirmed Reagan's third choice, Judge Anthony M. Kennedy.

Although most presidents can expect to fill a vacancy or two, especially if they serve two terms, the period from 1994 to 2005 marked the longest drought in new appointees since 1823. In 2005, President George W. Bush finally had an opportunity to make appointments. Justice O'Connor announced her retirement in the summer of that year, and Chief Justice William Rehnquist died after a long battle with cancer on September 3, 2005. Bush nominated John R. Roberts, an appellate court judge who was raised Catholic in Buffalo, New York, and graduated from Harvard Law School, to be the next chief justice. The Senate confirmed him in a 78–22 vote. Bush then nominated White House Counsel Harriet Miers to the post of associate justice. Concerns about her abilities and qualifications from across the political spectrum led Bush to withdraw her nomination before it could be voted on. He then nominated appellate court judge Samuel Anthony Alito Jr. to the post. A native of New Jersey, Alito received his law degree from Yale University. His 58–42 confirmation vote by the Senate made him the second Italian American justice and created a Catholic majority on the Court for the first time.

President George W. Bush watches as U.S. Supreme Court Justice Samuel Alito Jr. is sworn in by U.S. Chief Justice John Roberts, Wednesday, February 1 2006. (Wikimedia Commons)

12.2   What Courts Do

In the process of deciding cases, the Supreme Court and other courts perform several functions—including constitutional interpretation, statutory interpretation, fact determination, clarification of the boundaries of political authority, education and value application, and legitimization. Not all courts perform each function in every case, and some courts do more of one than another. As will be noted, fact determination is largely, though not exclusively, the province of trial courts. Appellate courts are heavily engaged in constitutional and statutory interpretation.

12.2a Constitutional Interpretation

American government is constitutional government—government according to basic institutions, procedures, and values inscribed in a written document. The Constitution of the United States is not without ambiguity, however. Because some of its provisions are not clear and because the framers could not possibly have anticipated all contemporary issues, the document invites interpretation. This need for interpretation, in turn, guarantees disagreement over what the correct interpretation should be.

> IT IS EMPHATICALLY THE PROVINCE AND DUTY OF THE JUDICIAL DEPARTMENT TO SAY WHAT THE LAW IS.
>
> MARBURY v. MADISON
> 1803

Inscription on the wall of the Supreme Court Building from Marbury v. Madison, in which Chief Justice John Marshall outlined the concept of judicial review (Wikimedia Commons)

Interpretation involves the power of **judicial review**, first formally declared by the United States Supreme Court in the 1803 case of *Marbury v. Madison*.[7] Judicial review provides a court with the authority to set aside decisions made by elected representatives of the people if the court concludes that a law violates the Constitution. Judicial review allows contending political groups to continue their political skirmishes in the context of cases built around opposing interpretations of particular clauses of the

judicial review

The authority of courts to set aside a legislative act as being in violation of the Constitution

Constitution. Groups whose issues have not prevailed in executive offices or legislative chambers often resort to the courts. Whether the question involves education, immigration, or criminal justice, one side seeks to persuade the constitutional umpire that the other has broken the rules.

12.2b Statutory Interpretation

Many cases require courts to interpret statutes passed by Congress or state legislatures. In a typical term, about half the cases the Supreme Court decides involve the meaning the justices give to words the legislators have written. At first glance this task seems avoidable. Why are legislators not able to say exactly what they mean? Sometimes legislators expect judges to fill in the blanks, so to speak. Legislators will write laws that set up certain standards for judges to apply, or as a way of avoiding controversy legislators will deliberately choose language that is vague. In addition, ambiguities can arise that the people who wrote the law simply did not anticipate. Judges will often try to discover the **legislative intent** of a law by trying to figure out what the legislators who wrote the law would have wanted.

One of the first pages in this book refers to a copyright. The holder of the copyright has exclusive use and control of the work for a specified period of time. In this century, copyrights have been extended to motion pictures and television programs. When Congress last rewrote the Copyright Act in 1976, provision was made for "fair use." Fair use allows one to legally make copies of protected material "for purposes such as criticism, comment, news reporting, teaching, … scholarship, or research"—all without violating the copyright or paying a fee to the holder of the copyright. Is in-home videotaping of television programs an example of fair use, or an infringement of copyright? Congress decreed only that certain factors are to be taken into account in deciding whether something amounts to fair use leaving the task of adding precision to judges. With fuzzy guidance, different courts arrived at different conclusions. In the end, the Supreme Court announced that in-home videotaping of copyrighted materials was fair use within the meaning of the statute.[8]

12.2c Fact Determination

Often the meaning of statutes and constitutional passages may be clear, and cases turn on the facts instead. Through fact determination, judges select from competing testimony and evidence which facts they accept as true and which they reject as false. This task is inescapable because the judicial process in the United States is adversarial. That is, cases pit one side against the other. Each side attempts to build the stronger argument to persuade the judge or jury to accept its version of the truth. Fact discretion is perhaps most visible in a **trial court**, the arena in which the issues and merits of a case are heard for the first time. In the federal court system, trial courts are the district courts. In state court systems, trials occur in both the courts of limited and general jurisdiction (see Figures 12.1 and 12.2).

12.2d Clarification of the Boundaries of Political Authority

As explained in Chapter 1, the Constitution mandates separation of powers—the division of political functions among the three branches of government. It is not obvious, however, where the legitimate power of one branch stops and another's begins. Courts sometimes try to resolve this built-in tension. In 1952, for example, President Harry Truman (1945–1953) directed the secretary of commerce to seize and operate the nation's steel mills. Labor disputes in the steel industry threatened the supply of war materials needed for American troops in the Korean conflict. Truman based his actions

legislative intent

A legislature's understanding of the meaning of a law and what it is designed to accomplish

trial court

A court of limited or general jurisdiction in which the disputed facts of a case are heard and decided

not on any statutory authority but on the president's responsibility for national security as commander-in-chief of the armed forces. Voting 6 to 3, the Supreme Court held that Truman had exceeded his powers under the Constitution. Although Congress might provide for such a takeover of industries by statute, Congress had not done so. Furthermore, the Court found nothing in the Constitution authorizing the president to act on his own.[9]

President Harry Truman (Library of Congress)

12.2e Education and Value Application

In deciding cases, judges teach and apply values. Even an ordinary criminal trial involves a judgment on what kinds of behaviors are acceptable or unacceptable, on the part of both the suspect and the police. One of the hallmarks of constitutional government, after all, is that limits apply not just to the governed but to the governors as well. The constitutions and statutes of the state and national governments all represent value choices that define the kind of nation its citizens expect to enjoy. Judicial opinions give judges an opportunity to articulate those values. Of course, no one pretends that judicial opinions are widely read by the general public. They are, however, read and studied by journalists, scholars, and other opinion leaders, who in turn inform the public and help shape the attitudes Americans have about the courts and the issues judges confront.

12.2f Legitimization

Because of the powers of judicial review, courts are expected to make sure that actions of public officials conform to the Constitution and statutes. In the great majority of cases, judges uphold the challenged laws or policies, thus placing a "seal of approval" on what others have done. Securing legitimacy may be crucial when a policy emerges from a long and loud national debate. Winners look to the judiciary for support; losers look to the judiciary for redress. Both typically see the courts as offering "the final word." During the civil rights movement of the 1960s, for example (see Chapter 3), Congress took the bold and controversial step of banning racial discrimination in restaurants, hotels, theaters, and other privately owned places of public accommodation. During debate on the bill in 1963 and 1964, opponents argued that the ban would be an unjustified intrusion into the right of owners of businesses to run their enterprises as they wished. The Supreme Court's decision upholding the constitutionality of the law virtually ended the controversy. Within a matter of months, most public agitation over the legitimacy of the new policy simply ceased.[10] A ruling can, however, inflame an issue, not soothe it. On occasion it may appear that the judges have thrust a broom handle into a hornet's nest, as the abortion controversy illustrates.

12.3   The Supreme Court at Work

Cases decided by the Supreme Court move through five distinct stages: petition for review, briefs on the merits, oral argument, conference and decision, and assignment and writing of opinions.

Anti-Abortion Activists March In Washington. (Getty Images News)

12.3a Petition for Review

Litigants who lose in lower courts begin climbing the steep slope toward the Supreme Court when their lawyers file documents called **briefs** with the Court's clerk. In these petitions for review, the opposing parties attempt to convince the justices that the issues the case raises are so important (or unimportant) that they deserve (or do not deserve) the Court's attention. As discussed previously, the Court will not accept a case unless a minimum of four justices agrees that the case warrants review.

From the thousands of cases on its docket each term, the justices will typically decide no more than 150 with full opinion (and only 80–90 in recent years), in accordance with the procedure laid out below. Other cases may be decided "summarily," without opinion by a directive affirming or reversing the lower court. Except for cases carried over into the following year's term, the justices deny review in all other cases. The result is that the lower court's decision stands (see Figure 12.4).

What factors seem to guide the Court in selecting cases for decision? Although the justices rarely explain their reasons for rejecting cases, chances for review by the nation's highest court are significantly increased if one or more of the following is present:

- The United States is a party to the case and requests Supreme Court review.

- The case presents a question that has been decided differently by different courts of appeals.

- The case involves an issue some of the justices are eager to resolve.

- A lower court has made a decision clearly at odds with established Supreme Court interpretation of a law or constitutional provision.

- The Court's workload permits accepting another case for decision.

- The case presents an issue of overriding importance to the nation.

Even if a case fits into one of the categories listed, the Supreme Court will not necessarily grant review. Because the Court's docket contains thousands of cases each term, a litigant's chances of having a case heard by the justices are usually very slim. Claims that someone will "take this all the way to the Supreme Court" are, therefore, more threat than promise.

briefs

Documents filed with a court containing the arguments of the parties in a case

Figure 12.4 | Caseload in the U.S. Supreme Court, 1950–2012

Figure 12.4 shows the number of cases appealed to the Supreme Court in each of seven years and the number of cases decided with full opinion. The justices decide other cases summarily each term. The number of summary decisions each term sometimes equals the number of cases decided with full opinion. The volume of cases has grown almost eightfold since 1950, while the number of cases decided has varied only modestly. Indeed, since 1988 when 171 decisions were issued, the Court has been deciding fewer cases, a trend aided by the virtual elimination of the Court's obligatory appellate jurisdiction in 1988. Almost all of each year's cases come from the lower federal courts and the state supreme courts. Only a handful, at most, of original cases appears each term. A minimum of four justices must agree to hear a case.

SOURCE: *Administrative Office of the United States Courts.*

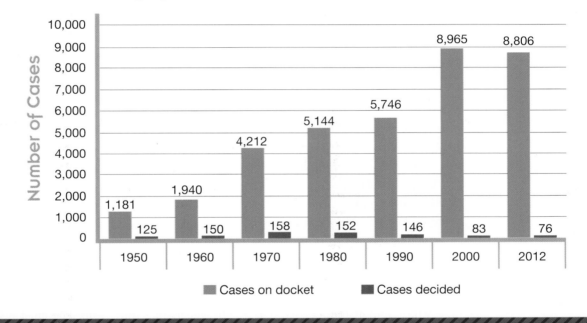

12.3b Briefs on the Merits

Once the Court has placed a case on its "decision calendar," attorneys for the opposing sides file a second round of briefs. This time the arguments focus on the decision the justices should make, not on whether they should accept the case. **Amicus curiae** briefs supplement briefs of opposing counsel. Submitted by "friends of the court," these documents come from interest groups and others who are not parties to the case, but who have a stake in its outcome.

One lawyer whose briefs the justices routinely read with extra care is the **solicitor general of the United States**—the third-ranking official in the Justice Department and the government's lawyer before the Supreme Court. In cases in which the government has lost in a lower court, the "S.G." decides whether the United States will petition the Supreme Court for review. If so, the solicitor general is responsible for both written briefs and oral argument supporting the government's position. The job is important because the United States is a party in about half the cases that confront the justices.

amicus curiae

Latin for "friend of the court," referring to persons, government agencies, or groups that are not parties to a case but nonetheless have an interest in its outcome and that make their views known by filing an *amicus curiae* brief with the court hearing the case

solicitor general of the United States

In the Supreme Court, the lawyer for the United States who decides which cases the government will appeal to the Supreme Court

In her position as solicitor general of the United States, Elena Kagan was the third-ranking official in the Justice Department and the government's lawyer before the Supreme Court. (Getty Images News)

Five solicitors general have gone on to serve as Supreme Court Justices, most recently Elena Kagan (2010–).

12.3c Oral Argument

The most public part of the Court's work is **oral argument**. On about forty days (always Mondays, Tuesdays, and Wednesdays), starting in October and concluding in late April, opposing lawyers face the justices. Cases are routinely allotted one hour with each side receiving thirty minutes. Oral argument, a spontaneous event, gives each justice an opportunity to ask questions about the case. Although not every justice asks a question in every case, Justice Clarence Thomas (1991–) has been noted to be unusually reticent. During a seven-year period between 2006 and 2013, he did not utter a single word during oral argument.[11] Sometimes, questioning from the bench is lively and intense; at other times, the justices may barely seem interested. At all times, they rock back and forth in their leather swivel chairs, occasionally pass notes and whisper among themselves, and send pages on errands to fetch documents and law books. The justices attach great importance to the oral argument step of the decision-making procedure. Whether such arguments change many minds, however, is a question only the justices can answer.

An appearance before the Supreme Court can be intimidating even for the most seasoned advocates. Standing at the small lectern before the raised bench, an attorney can feel very lonely. Heightening the tension are the time limits, which the Court rigidly enforces. When five minutes remain, the marshal flicks a switch that turns on a white light at the lectern. A red light signals that time is up. The chief justice may allow counsel to complete a sentence or to answer a question, but Chief Justice Charles Evans Hughes (1910–1916, 1930–1941) is said to have cut off one attorney in the middle of the word *if*.

12.3d Conference and Decision

On Wednesday afternoons, after argument has finished at three o'clock, and all day on Fridays, the justices convene in a small room adjacent to the chief justice's chambers to discuss the cases they heard that week. They also act on petitions for review. The importance of oral argument may be enhanced because the spoken words are fresh on the justices' minds when they take up a case in conference. The usual practice is for the chief justice to lay out his or her views first, followed by each associate justice, starting with the most senior. By the time all have had their say, each justice's position is often clear. If not, a vote is taken. These votes, recorded by each justice in a leather-bound docket book, are tentative. The decision does not become final until it is announced in court, weeks or even months later.

In contrast to the openness of oral argument, the conferences are closed. No pages or law clerks are present in the room, only the justices. If something is needed, the most junior justice acts as messenger and goes to the door. What happens inside the room

oral argument

Event in which opposing counsel verbally presents their views to the court during the decision-making process of a court

The Supreme Court and Economic Policy

Although Supreme Court decisions today may affect the economy, just as they affect American life in other ways, between the years 1890 and 1937 the justices (and lower court judges, too) played a far more active role in economic affairs. Then judges routinely reviewed the constitutionality of many kinds of social and economic laws that are now accepted without question.

In the decades after the Civil War, Congress and state legislatures passed hundreds of laws regulating working conditions, prices, wages and hours, and health standards in an effort to cope with the harmful effects of growth and industrialization. Opponents of such legislation advanced the arguments of laissez-faire economics, claiming that government regulation of business and economy should be kept to a minimum. Soon justices of the Supreme Court decided that freedom from economic regulation was a constitutionally protected liberty. This did not mean that the Court turned aside all legislative attempts to improve the life of working people, but it did mean that the justices had what amounted to the last word on which regulatory policies were acceptable and which were not. For example, *Lochner v. New York* struck down a law that set a maximum number of working hours for bakery employees, and *Hammer v. Dagenhart* invalidated a congressional act banning interstate shipment of goods manufactured with child labor.

The Court's role as economic censor came under sharp attack when laissez-faire economics faced the realities of the Great Depression in the 1930s. As states and the national government responded with policies to deal with economic dislocation, the Court proved to be a stumbling block. In 1935 and 1936, the justices invalidated ten acts of Congress, cutting the heart out of President Franklin Roosevelt's New Deal program of economic recovery.

After his landslide reelection in 1936, Roosevelt proposed legislation (dubbed by its enemies the "court-packing plan") that would permit him to appoint one additional justice for every sitting justice over the age of seventy, up to a total bench size of fifteen. Under the guise of aiding the justices with their work, the plan was actually a ploy to create seats for new justices who would support the president's programs. The plan never became law, but one or more justices quickly changed their positions in economic regulation cases to give the president the majority he needed. Tagged "the switch in time that saved nine," in *National Labor Relations Board v. Jones & Laughlin Steel Corporation* the Court upheld by a vote of 5 to 4, the far-reaching Wagner Labor Act of 1935, which created the National Labor Relations Board and guaranteed to unions the right of collective bargaining. The law remains the foundation of American labor policy. Thanks to changed views and a series of retirements and new justices, the Court soon made it clear that it was retreating from its old role as economic censor. Since that time, the Court has by and large left economic policy making to the president, Congress, and the states.

Recently, however, the Court has hinted that limits may still exist to a state's regulatory powers over property owners. Does the Constitution require the Court to keep its hands off economic policy?

is very secret. In fact, the Court has the best secrecy record in Washington. Leaks, as prevalent in the nation's capital as the summer humidity, are so rare at the Court that they make headlines when they occur. Confidentiality is crucial—not just because it gives the justices freedom to talk and maneuver amid the most controversial issues of the day, but also because political and economic fortunes often hang in the balance.

12.3e Assignment and Writing of Opinions

On Saturday or early in the week after the standard two-week session of oral argument, the chief justice circulates an assignment list to the justices. If part of the majority, the chief justice makes the opinion assignment in a particular case. If not, the task falls to the senior associate justice in the majority. The goal is an **opinion of the Court**, which is an explanation and justification of the decision agreed to by at least a bare majority of the justices. Between assignment of the opinion and announcement of the

opinion of the Court

Statement representing the views of a majority of the judges of the Court

decision in open court, vigorous give-and-take routinely goes on among the justices. The justice writing an opinion has a draft printed in the Court's own print shop and done in strictest secrecy. Copies circulate among the other justices. Those in the majority will insist on changes. It is not unusual for an opinion to go through a dozen or more rewrites. Each opinion of the Court, therefore, represents the consensus of the majority, not merely the views of its author. Justices in the majority may write one or more **concurring opinions** when they reject the majority's reasoning, while accepting its result; or they simply may have other thoughts to add.

In only about a third of the cases each term do all nine justices agree on the result. For the rest, justices in the minority typically write one or more **dissenting opinions**. These help to explain what divides the Court and are written for the express purpose of undercutting the logic and/or exposing the folly that dissenting justices find in the majority viewpoint.

Majority, concurring, and dissenting opinions are later collected and published as the *United States Reports*. This is the official record of the Court's work; it currently comprises over five hundred volumes.

12.3f Law Clerks

Assisting the justices are law clerks, recent law school graduates who typically serve a justice for a year. The justices use their clerks in a variety of ways: to do research, summarize *certiorari* petitions, and write and critique drafts of opinions. Justice Blackmun confessed that his clerks managed to entice him to an Orioles baseball game at least once a term! Diversions aside, a clerk's day is long and includes evenings and weekends. Nonetheless, the opportunities for close association with the justices can be rewarding. Of the justices on the Court in 2015, three (John Roberts, Elena Kagan, and Stephen Breyer) are former clerks.

12.4 The Supreme Court and American Government: An Assessment

Early in our nation's history, the justices assumed a prominent role in governing the nation. However, this role has never been free from controversy. For most of its history, the Court has seen itself as the guardian of preferred values. Years ago, for instance, the justices routinely censored social and economic legislation that they thought interfered unduly with property rights. In the years since President Franklin Roosevelt (1933–1945) confronted the justices in the "court-packing" fight of 1937 (see "Politics and Economics: The Supreme Court and Economic Policy"), the Court's decisions have emphasized civil liberties and civil rights instead. Now about half the cases each term involve a provision of the Bill of Rights or the Fourteenth Amendment.

12.4a Judicial Review and Democracy

As explained in Chapter 1 and as noted earlier in this chapter, the authority to interpret the Constitution carries with it the power of judicial review. Some critics assert that judicial review is antidemocratic because judges invalidate decisions made by elected representatives of the people. Moreover, they say that judicial review

concurring opinion

A statement issued separately by a judge voting with the majority

dissenting opinion

A statement issued by a judge explaining his or her disagreement with the majority position

United States Reports

The official, published decisions of the United States Supreme Court

The Supreme Court and "Obamacare"

When, after years of negotiation and compromise, Congress finally passed and President Obama signed into law the Patient Protection and Affordable Care Act in 2010, the exhaustive *legislative* battle for healthcare reform was finally over. Yet the battle in the *judiciary* was just beginning. Opponents, who rejected a larger government role in healthcare, derisively referred to the new law as "Obamacare" and filed suit in federal court as soon as the law was passed.

The act, which went into effect in 2014, requires states to coordinate health insurance exchanges, requires insurers to accept dependents up to age twenty-six, and prevents insurance companies from denying applicants with pre-existing conditions. It also contains a provision known as the "individual mandate." This was the most controversial aspect of the new law, in that it requires all Americans (except those with income or religion exemptions) to either have at least a minimal amount of health insurance or pay a penalty to the Internal Revenue Service. Less-wealthy Americans will be eligible for tax credits to purchase insurance plans.

The Supreme Court accepted the case on *writ of certiorari* from the Eleventh Circuit Court of Appeals. Over the course of three days in March 2012, the justices heard oral testimony in the case of *National Federation of Independent Business v. Sebelius*.[1] Americans, in a 2012 poll, were somewhat evenly split in their views of the law, with 45 percent viewing it favorably and 44 percent unfavorably.[2] Despite a majority of Americans believing that the federal government has a responsibility to make sure all Americans have healthcare coverage, only 20 percent believed the individual mandate would pass constitutional muster.[3]

On June 28, 2012, Chief Justice Roberts announced the historic decision. By a vote of 5–4, the Court upheld nearly all of the law, including the individual mandate. (The portion of the law struck down removes the federal government's ability to reduce state Medicaid funding to states that refuse to expand coverage.) Writing for the majority in a complex opinion, Roberts reasoned that the individual mandate was a constitutional use of Congress's *taxing* power. This outcome was a surprise to many, who assumed the Court would strike down the mandate and base its decision on the commerce clause or the necessary and proper clause. However, a majority of justices did not find that route acceptable; and the typically conservative Roberts found himself siding, for the first time, with the four more liberal justices (Ginsburg, Breyer, Sotomayor, and Kagan) in a 5–4 decision.

Did the Court reach the correct conclusion? If you were a Supreme Court justice, how would you have decided this case? On what parts of the Constitution would you base your decision? Does healthcare seem more like a basic human right that everyone should have, or more like an option for those who can afford it? How would you design a healthcare system? What outcomes would result from your answers?

1   567 U.S. ___ (2012).

2   "Americans, Views on the Healthcare Law," June 22, 2012, The Gallup Organization, http://www.gallup.com/poll/155300/Gallup-Editors-Americans-Views-Healthcare-Law.aspx (June 25, 2012).

3   Ibid.

encourages citizens to rely on judges and not the political process to protect their rights. Without judicial review, elected officials would have to give more thought to the constitutionality of their actions. Besides, critics maintain, individual rights survive in nations like Great Britain, where judges exercise no judicial review at all.

Others reply that the very idea of a written constitution means that a majority is not always supposed to get what it wants. Democracy American-style stresses not just majority rule but also minority rights. Judicial review is but one of several constitutional features designed to control government power. Although citizens' control over their leaders through election is the primary check on government, judicial review can be an additional safeguard. Whatever the experience in other countries, enforcement of limits on government in this country seems to require the existence of institutions—like the federal courts—that are not directly accountable to the people.

12.4b Influences on Supreme Court Decision-Making

What are some of the major factors that shape the Supreme Court's decisions? In the face of Chief Justice Marshall's broad self-denial that "courts are the mere instruments of the law, and can will nothing,"[12] political leaders have long recognized that justices do not make decisions in a vacuum. Surely, "judicial decisions are not babies brought by constitutional storks."[13] Individual and institutional forces, as well as legal and extralegal factors, affect what the Court does.[14]

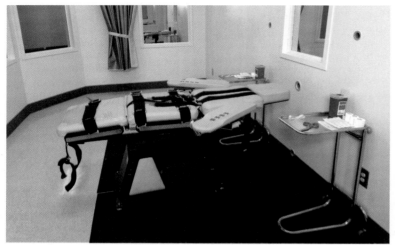

A justice's own personal political ideas may help determine his or her decisions. A justice who is against capital punishment is more inclined to regard the death penalty as cruel and unusual punishment than one who is for capital punishment. (Wikimedia Commons)

Foremost perhaps are the justices' own *political ideas*. A jurist adamantly opposed to capital punishment, for example, will be more inclined than one who is not to regard the death penalty as one of the "cruel and unusual punishments" prohibited by the Eighth Amendment. A justice who does not place high value on the free exchange of views will probably not be a strong defender of the First Amendment's guarantee of free speech. Indeed, research indicates that judicial decisions of most justices reflect a generally consistent ideological position.[15]

Role perception,[16] akin to but different from political ideas, is another factor that affects decision-making. What does being a justice mean to an individual named to the Supreme Court? Some justices have been result oriented—that is, they see their task as one of writing certain political ideas into their decisions. Other justices are process oriented; they are hesitant to interfere with majority rule. Although they are prepared to apply the constitutional brakes to runaway legislatures, they are less inclined to do so than their result-oriented colleagues. Instead, they believe that judges should allow maximum discretion to the people's elected representatives.

Jurists most eager to apply judicial review are **judicial activists**. Those most reluctant to do so are **judicial restraintists**. Yet even by practicing judicial restraint, the Court makes policy. Judicial restraint results in upholding the judgment made by some other part of the political system. By affirming someone else's judgment, the Court is legitimating it and making the original judgment the Court's own. When the Court upholds the validity of a search of someone's home by police, for example, it is accepting the police officer's understanding of the Fourth Amendment (see Chapter 3).

Whether an activist or restraintist, no justice today writes on a blank slate. Although a new case is rarely identical to one the Court has decided in years gone by, prior decisions in similar cases called **precedents** may point the way to the decision the Court should render. When courts adhere to legal principles established in prior cases, they are following the doctrine of *stare decisis* (Latin for "let the decision stand"). *Stare decisis* does not mean that the Supreme Court must rule as it ruled one hundred years ago, or even ten years ago; it does result, however, in the reluctance of justices to overrule decisions that are already "on the books." They do so only when a legal principle seems plainly wrong or when public necessity dictates a change.

The power of precedent was an acknowledged factor in 1992 when five justices rejected the first Bush administration's request to overrule the 1973 landmark decision *Roe v. Wade*,[17] which created a constitutionally protected right to abortion.

judicial activists

Judges who are least hesitant to invoke judicial review to strike down an act of Congress or of a state legislature

judicial restraintists

Judges who are reluctant to invoke judicial review to strike down an act of Congress or of a state legislature

precedents

Prior decisions of courts that are cited as authority by other courts

stare decisis

A legal doctrine that suggests courts should follow precedent as a general rule, breaking with previously legal principles only on rare occasions

Three of the five (O'Connor, Kennedy, and Souter) indicated that they would not have sided with the majority position in *Roe* had they been on the Court in 1973. Nineteen years later, however, they believed that the Court should not turn back the clock.[18] In 2000, the Court upheld the judicially created requirement of *Miranda*

warnings, even though several of the justices had elsewhere opposed the judicial activist stance taken in the *Miranda* decision.[19]

The Court's own decision-making process, described earlier in this chapter, also shapes its decisions. Briefs and oral argument inform the justices and define the issues the case presents. Briefs and arguments may even supply the reasoning the Court uses in justifying its decision. Articles in *law reviews*, the scholarly journals law schools publish, may also be of influence. Justices, like everyone else, are sensitive to evaluations of their work by others, and they pay attention to suggestions for evolution in the law that find their way into print. Moreover, because all justices participate in each case, *collegial interaction* becomes a factor. Discussion in

Border patrol agent reads the Miranda *rights to a suspected criminal. In 2000: The Court upheld the judicially created requirement of* Miranda *warnings, even though several of the justices had elsewhere opposed the judicial activist stance taken in the* Miranda *decision. (Wikipedia photo)*

conference and persuasive comment by one justice on an opinion drafted by another contribute to the form a decision eventually takes and sometimes cause a justice to change positions in a case.[20]

Finally, justices are aware of *public opinion*. Although Justice John Paul Stevens (1975–2010) may have been correct in asserting that "it is the business of judges to be indifferent to unpopularity,"[21] public attitudes count, nevertheless, in judicial decisions in at least two ways. First, public attitudes may influence the meaning justices give certain provisions in the Constitution. In the case of capital punishment, for example, most states reenacted death penalty laws after the Supreme Court set rigorous new standards for capital punishment in 1972 (see Chapter 3).[22] State legislatures, in effect, were telling the Court that they did not think capital punishment was "cruel and unusual" but instead was a form of punishment the American people accepted. These new laws probably made it easier for some justices to decide, in 1976, that capital punishment is not cruel and unusual.[23] Second, courts matter in American government ultimately because their decisions are accepted and applied, if grudgingly, by the rest of the political system. Thus, public reaction to judicial decisions may affect compliance with them.

12.4c Checks on Judicial Power

Supreme Court justices and other federal judges enjoy substantial independence from outside political control. Thanks to the Constitution, they never face the voters in an election and may not have their salaries decreased by Congress. Although the Court is a potent institution in American government, it does not enjoy unlimited power. Through *constitutional amendment*, Congress and the states may correct the Supreme Court's interpretation of the Constitution. Admittedly, amending the Constitution is not easy, but the justices have been reversed by amendment four times. The Eleventh Amendment (restricting federal court jurisdiction over the states) overturned *Chisholm v. Georgia*.

The Fourteenth Amendment (granting both national and state citizenship to all persons born or naturalized in the United States) countered the infamous *Dred Scott* decision, which had held that the Constitution did not intend for African Americans to be citizens. The Sixteenth Amendment (allowing for a national tax on incomes) reversed *Pollock v. Farmers' Loan and Trust Co.,* and the Twenty-sixth Amendment (establishing a nationwide voting age of eighteen) set aside *Oregon v. Mitchell.* [24]

The Fourteenth Amendment (granting both national and state citizenship to all persons born or naturalized in the United States) countered the infamous Dred Scott *decision, which had held that the Constitution did not intend for African Americans to be citizens. (iStock)*

Similarly, *statutory amendment* allows Congress to correct the Court's interpretation of a statute. Although passing a law is easier than amending the Constitution, it still is not an easy task, as Chapter 9 made clear.

Impeachment of justices by Congress may be only a "scarecrow," as President Thomas Jefferson (1801–1809) once said, but it is a weapon available in extraordinary situations. On grounds of misconduct, Congress has removed eight judges of lower federal courts through impeachment, including U.S. district court judge G. Thomas Porteous of Louisiana in 2010; however, a Supreme Court justice has never been removed. In fact, the Senate has held no impeachment trial for a justice since the Jefferson administration attempted to have Supreme Court Justice Samuel Chase (1796–1811) removed in 1805. The House of Representatives might have begun impeachment proceedings against Justice Abe Fortas (1965–1969) after certain improprieties came to light, but Fortas resigned.[25] Six other federal judges have either been acquitted by the Senate or had charges against them dismissed before a Senate trial began.

Congress may attack the Court by *withdrawing jurisdiction* to hear certain types of cases. Because Article III grants appellate jurisdiction to the Supreme Court "with such exceptions, and under such regulations as the Congress shall make," opponents of particular judicial doctrines can try to prevent certain types of cases from reaching the Court altogether. Such extreme measures are frequently threatened, but only very rarely carried out. Congress may also *change the size* of the Court, which was the heart of President Franklin Roosevelt's "court-packing" proposal in 1937. Although the plan failed, the Court changed its interpretation of the Constitution to uphold the president's New Deal program (see "Politics and Economics: The Supreme Court and Economic Policy").

Appointment of new justices by the president can place new ideas as well as new personalities on the bench. *Senate confirmation*, however, may limit the range of a president's choices; however, judicial vacancies occur irregularly as well as infrequently. For example, President Nixon was able to name four justices between 1969 and 1971, whereas President Carter (1977–1981) was able to name none.

To be effective, Supreme Court decisions require *compliance*. Judges possess very little power to actually coerce obedience. Therefore, courts depend on others to obey and to carry out their decisions. An absence of widespread compliance with the

Supreme Court's school integration decision of 1954[26] (see Chapter 3) meant that for nearly a decade the decision went largely unenforced. Reaction to this decision was a reminder that the Supreme Court needs the support of both state and federal courts, as well as other agencies of government, to carry out its judgments. Hostile reaction to the 1954 school decision highlighted an additional check: *litigation*. African American families were sometimes afraid to initiate legal action against local officials who continued to disregard the Supreme Court's decision. Without a case, no court could act. Unlike legislators, who may introduce bills, judges do not initiate the cases they decide.

As cases bring issues old and new to the Court each term, the justices play a part in American government. For more than two hundred years the Supreme Court has conducted a dialogue with the people that reflects the public's historic attraction to, and suspicion of, majority rule. "The people have seemed to feel that the Supreme Court," wrote Justice Robert H. Jackson (1941–1954), "whatever its defects, is still the most detached, dispassionate, and trustworthy custodian that our system affords for the translation of abstract into concrete constitutional commands."[27] The justices are the keepers of American constitutional morality. That truth is both a source of and limit on their power.

BVT Lab

Flashcards are available for this chapter at www.BVTLab.com.

CHAPTER REVIEW

1. As the highest court in the land, the Supreme Court of the United States annually confronts a variety of important political issues that appear in the form of cases. The system of courts in the United States consists of the federal courts and the courts of the fifty states. Major federal courts include the district courts and the courts of appeals, in addition to the United States Supreme Court. Supreme Court justices and all federal judges are appointed by the president and confirmed by a majority of the Senate.

2. In deciding cases, the Supreme Court and other American courts engage in constitutional and statutory interpretation, fact determination, clarification of the boundaries of political authority, education and value application, and legitimization.

3. Cases decided by the Supreme Court proceed through five major stages: petition for review, briefs on the merits, oral argument, conference and decision, and assignment and writing of the opinion of the Court.

4. The decisions of the Supreme Court are the products of several factors and have been a source of controversy during most of American history. Although the Court enjoys considerable political independence from Congress and the president, external checks on judicial power do exist.

KEY TERMS

Readings for Further Study

A helpful survey of the role of the Court during much of the nation's history is Robert G. McCloskey's *The American Supreme Court*, 5th ed. (Chicago: University of Chicago Press, 2010).

Henry J. Abraham's *Justices, Presidents, and Senators*, 5th ed. (Lanham, MD: Rowman & Littlefield, 2007), is the standard work on appointment of Supreme Court justices.

Behind Bakke: Affirmative Action and the Supreme Court, by Bernard Schwartz (New York: New York University Press, 1988), takes a close look at how the Court reached its decision in a single case.

David M. O'Brien's *Storm Center: The Supreme Court in American Politics*, 10th ed. (New York: Norton, 2014), explores the broader political environment in which the Supreme Court operates.

Important decisions of the Supreme Court interpreting the Constitution are readily found in edited form in casebooks such as *Constitutional Law in Contemporary America* (New York: Oxford University Press, 2010) by David Schultz, John R. Vile, and Michelle D. Deardorff, or *Constitutional Law for a Changing America*, 8th ed. (Washington, DC: CQ Press, 2013) by Lee Epstein and Thomas G. Walker.

The Supreme Court Compendium, 6th ed. (Washington, D.C.: CQ Press, 2015) by Lee Epstein, Jeffrey A. Segal, Harold J. Spaeth, and Thomas G. Walker contains information on almost all aspects of the Court's work.

Notes

1. Court Statistics Project, *Examining the Work of State Courts: An Overview of 2012 State Trial Court Caseloads* (National Center for State Courts, 2014).

2. 420 U.S. 515 (1975).

3. *Michigan v. Ohio*, 386 U.S. 1029 (1967); *Arizona v. California*, 460 U.S. 605 (1983).

4. *Chisholm v. Georgia*, 2 U.S. (2 Dallas) 419 (1793).

5. *Roe v. Wade*, 410 U.S. 113 (1973).

6. *Lee v. Weisman*, 60 U.S.L.W. 4723 (1992); Marcia Coyle, "The Court Confounds Observers," *National Law Journal*, July 13, 1992, p. 1.

7. The *Marbury* case and the concept of judicial review are discussed in Chapter 1.

8. *Sony Corporation v. Universal City Studios*, 464 U.S. 417 (1984).

9. *Youngstown v. Sawyer*, 343 U.S. 579 (1952).

10. *Heart of Atlanta Motel v. United States*, 379 U.S. 274 (1964).

11. Adam Liptak, "Justice Clarence Thomas Breaks His Silence," *The New York Times*, January 14, 2013.

12. *Osborn v. Bank of the United States*, 22 U.S. (9 Wheaton) 738, 866 (1824).

13. Max Lerner, quoted in Henry J. Abraham's, *The Judicial Process*, 5th ed. (New York: Oxford University Press, 1986), p. 348.

14. Tracey E. George and Lee Epstein, "On the Nature of Supreme Court Decision Making," *American Political Science Review 86* (1992): 323.

15. David W. Rhode and Harold J. Spaeth, "Ideology, Strategy, and Supreme Court Decisions: William Rehnquist as Chief Justice," *Judicature 72* (1989): 247; Harold J. Spaeth and Stuart H. Teger, "Activism and Restraint: A Cloak for the Justices' Policy Preferences," in Stephen C. Halpern and Charles M. Lamb, eds., *Supreme Court Activism and Restraint* (Lexington, MA: Lexington Books, 1982), pp. 277–301.

16. Harold J. Spaeth, *Supreme Court Policy Making* (San Francisco: Freeman, 1979), pp. 109–139; Mark W. Cannon and David M. O'Brien, eds., *Views from the Bench* (Chatham, NJ: Chatham House, 1985), pp. 253–302.

17. 410 U.S. 113 (1973).

18. *Planned Parenthood of Southeastern Pennsylvania v. Casey*, 60 U.S.L.W. 4795 (1992).

19. *Dickerson v. United States*, 530 U.S. 428 (2000), and *Miranda v. Arizona*, 384 U.S. 436 (1966).

20. Walter F. Murphy, *Elements of Judicial Strategy* (Chicago: University of Chicago Press, 1964), ch. 3.

21. "Reflections on the Removal of Sitting Judges," *Stetson Law Review 13* (1984): 215, 217.

22. *Furman v. Georgia*, 408 U.S. 238 (1972).

23. *Gregg v. Georgia*, 428 U.S. 153 (1976).

24. 2 U.S. (2 Dallas) 419 (1793); 60 U.S. (19 Howard) 393 (1857); 158 U.S. 601 (1895); 400 U.S. 112 (1970).

25. Bruce Allen Murphy, *Fortas: The Rise and Ruin of a Supreme Court Justice* (New York: William Morrow, 1988).

26. *Brown v. Board of Education*, 347 U.S. 483 (1954).

27. *The Supreme Court in the American System of Government* (Cambridge, MA: Harvard University Press, 1955), p. 23.

POP QUIZ

1. Almost all divorce and personal injury cases are heard in _____ courts.

2. The _____ Court hears suits involving monetary damages against the United States government.

3. Today, almost all cases reach the Supreme Court on a *writ of* _____.

4. Petitions for review filed by lawyers with the Supreme Court's clerk are called _____.

5. Congress and the states may correct the Supreme Court's interpretation of the Constitution through a _____ _____.

6. The judiciary operates only in the context of cases.   T   F

7. Most federal and state judges are appointed for life and can be removed only by impeachment.   T   F

8. About half the cases the Supreme Court decides involve the meaning the justices give to words legislators have written.   T   F

9. Supreme Court conferences and deliberations are open to the public.   T   F

10. The most often used check on judicial power has been impeachment.   T   F

11. Which of the following applies to state courts that serve as trial courts for serious criminal offenses?

   A) They are courts of limited jurisdiction.

   B) They are courts of general jurisdiction.

   C) They are intermediate appellate courts.

   D) They are courts of last resort.

12. The Supreme Court's original jurisdiction includes which of the following types of cases?

   A) Cases between one of the states and the United States government

   B) Cases between two or more states

   C) Cases involving foreign ambassadors, ministers, or consuls

   D) All of the above

13. Fact discretion is most visible in _____.

   A) the Supreme Court

   B) legislative courts

   C) trial courts

   D) intermediate appellate courts

14. Documents submitted to the Court from interest groups and others who are not parties to the case but have a stake in its outcome are called _____.

   A) *amicus curiae* briefs

   B) *writs of certiorari*

   C) arraignments

   D) dissenting opinions

15. Checks on judicial power include which of the following?

   A) constitutional amendment

   B) impeachment

   C) withdrawing jurisdiction

   D) all of the above

Answers:
1. state   2. Claims   3. *certiorari*   4. briefs
5. constitutional amendment   6. T   7. F   8. T   9. F
10. F   11. B   12. D   13. C   14. A   15. D

Chapter

13

Government and Public Policy

In This Chapter

(Shutterstock)

Chapter Objectives

Public policy is collectively what governments do. This chapter begins by addressing what public policy is and how it relates to the political process. We will then learn to think about public policies so that what appears to be a chaotic mass of procedures, institutions, and personalities is more understandable. Finally, given the fact that government does so many different things, this chapter will attempt to differentiate among different kinds of public policies.

Public policy can be defined in a variety of ways, but the simplest is that "public policy is whatever governments choose to do or not to do."[1] Financing cancer research, providing a Social Security system, cutting or raising taxes, initiating or halting development of a new weapons system, and attempting to clean up toxic waste dumps are all examples of public policies. This chapter will introduce the process of public policy; the following three chapters will address economic, domestic, and foreign policies, respectively.

13.1a Conflict Over the Ends of Government

Government is always subject to conflicting demands due to the great differences among citizens in economic status, occupations, and political ideas. Different groups will likely press for public policies in their own interests, regardless of the effect those policies might have on other groups. The use of rules, procedures, representatives, and institutions is important to such groups only toward the end of achieving public policies favorable to them.

The results of public policy mirror conflicts in demands. No governmental action can affect all citizens in exactly the same way. Whatever government does will have varying consequences for different groups. For example, placing limits on Medicare spending will provide some relief to taxpayers by reducing pressure for higher taxes, but those same limits will place economic strains on hospitals and other health-care providers. Increasing the money supply to reduce interest rates will help first-time home buyers by making mortgages easier to afford, but doing so will hurt senior citizens who depend on higher interest rates to bolster their investment income. Differences in demands and in the consequences of government action create political conflict. At issue in the public policy debate is which groups shall win and which shall lose in the effort to shape government actions to their own interests.

Increasing the money supply to reduce interest rates will help first-time home buyers by making mortgages easier to afford, but doing so will hurt senior citizens who depend on higher interest rates to bolster their investment income. (Wikimedia Commons)

13.1b Perspectives on Policy Making

The nature of politics and policy is such that a variety of models or explanations has been offered as accurate or desirable portrayals of public policy making. Among the most familiar is the **systems model**, which holds that policy is the product of an interlocking relationship between the political system and its social, cultural, and economic environment.[2] From its environment the political system receives "inputs" in the form of demands and supports. Through its decision-making process, the political system then converts demands into "outputs," which are authoritative or official decisions. These decisions may, in turn, affect the environment and shape new inputs into the system. For example, demands that government reduce the burden of

public policy

Whatever governments choose to do or not to do

systems model

A model of policy making that holds that policy is the product of an interlocking relationship between institutions of government and their social, economic, and political environment

regulations may result in government decisions to eliminate some regulations. These decisions may penalize people who benefited under the old regulations, and those people may then clamor for reinstatement. As another illustration, a court decision that weakens the constitutional claim to the right to have an abortion may shift much of the political battle over abortion to state legislatures.

Other models view policy making from different perspectives. The **bureaucratic model** posits the crucial role of bureaucracies and the commitment and expertise they can provide in making policy. Some models use ideological frameworks with an economic focus to explain how policies are or should be made. The **Marxism model** holds that public policy decisions in non-Marxist regimes reflect the interests of the ruling economic class at the expense of the workers. The **free-market capitalism model** sees a limited role for government, a role in which the natural forces of supply and demand are allowed to prevail in the marketplace. Other models might be discussed as well; the interplay of interests and passions that drives policy debate and the rich complexity of making public policy have produced numerous models of policy making.

Two of the most useful perspectives are elitism and pluralism. They are particularly helpful in understanding the maze of public policy because they address a fundamental question about which there has been much debate: *Who* makes public policy decisions?

Elitism holds that public policy decisions are made by a relatively small group of individuals acting in their own self-interest.[3] The theory takes a variety of forms, depending on who is included in the elite. Some elements of the mass media, big business, and the military have been variously portrayed as making up the elite. According to the model, members of the elite—on issues of importance to them—make public policy judgments in the interest of the elite rather than in the interest of the mass of citizens.

Some elements of the mass media, big business, and the military have been variously portrayed as making up the elite. (iStock)

bureaucratic model

A model of policy making that holds that bureaucracies play a crucial role in making policy because of their commitment and the expertise they can provide

Marxism model

A model of policy making that holds that public policy decisions in non-Marxist regimes reflect the interests of the ruling economic class at the expense of workers

free-market capitalism model

A model of policy making that posits a limited role for government so that the natural forces of supply and demand are allowed to prevail in the marketplace

elitism

A model of policy making that holds that public policy decisions are made by a relatively small group of individuals acting in their own self-interest rather than in the interest of the mass of citizens

table 13.1 | Selected Perspectives on Policy Making

Given the complexity of making policy and the sharp conflicts that can drive policy debate, a variety of models, interpretations, and approaches have been offered as portraits of how policy is or should be made.

I. Models of the Policy making Process

Systems model	Policy is the product of an interlocking relationship between institutions of government and their surrounding social, economic, and political environment.
Bureaucratic model	Because of their commitment and the expertise they can provide, bureaucracies play a crucial role in making policy.
Marxism model	Public policy decisions reflect the interest of the ruling class at the expense of workers.
Free market capitalism model	The natural forces of supply and demand are allowed to work in the marketplace, and government plays only a limited role in shaping those forces.

II. Interpretations of Who Makes Public Policy

Elitism	Public policy decisions are made by a relatively small group of individuals acting in their own self-interest rather than the interest of all citizens.
Pluralism	Public policy decisions are the result of struggle among contesting groups, with the various interests among the masses reflected and represented in the policy process.

III. Approaches to How Public Policy Is Made

Rational comprehensive approach	Decision makers should identify problems, rank the values they wish to achieve, consider various policy alternatives that can attain these values, assess the cost and benefits of each alternative, and select and implement the policy strategy that can best achieve the stated values with the highest benefits and lowest costs. Critics of the model argue that information in the real world of policy making is limited and uncertain and that the clash of interests in the policy process makes any ranking of values impossible.
Incrementalism	Since present decisions are only marginally different from past decisions, policy makers focus on proposed marginal changes in existing policies. A capacity to achieve agreement among contesting interests defines a good public policy. Critics of the model argue that the tie to past policies reduces the possibility of new policy approaches and that the sensitivity to political power and the emphasis on agreement risk the exclusion of interests without political power.

pluralism

A model of policy making that holds that public policy decisions are the result of struggles among contesting groups that reflect the various interests among citizens

Pluralism holds that public policy decisions are the result of struggle among contesting groups rather than a single elite.[4] The groups represent various interests in society and press for decisions responsive to those interests. Policy is determined not by a single set of values as in elitism but by a contest of conflicting values held by various groups. Even though the number of participants in the making of public policy is small, they reflect and convey the broad range of positions held by the mass

Figure 13.1 | The Systems Model of Policy Making

The systems model describes policy making in terms of the relationship between a political system and its environment. "Inputs" (demands and supports) are converted into "outputs" (policy decisions). By affecting the environment of the political system, these outputs may generate new inputs.

SOURCE: James E. Anderson, Public Policymaking, 4th ed. (Boston: Houghton Mifflin, 2000), p. 18.

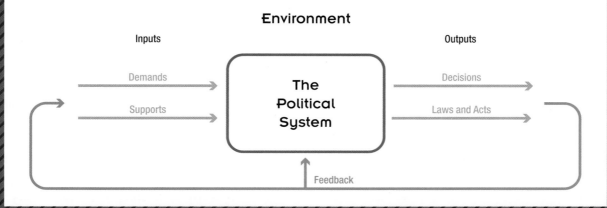

of citizens. Competing elites with different values ensure democratic responsiveness. In the pluralist view, government is a broker among groups, seeking to satisfy as many as possible. Conflicts among groups produce a balance so that no single group dominates. This is sometimes called the *countervailing theory of pressure politics*.

A second issue is how decisions are made.[5] Two contrasting perspectives are the rational-comprehensive approach and incrementalism. The **rational-comprehensive model** involves a sequence of steps for "rational" decisions. Decision makers identify problems, rank the values they wish to achieve, consider various policy alternatives that can attain these values, assess the costs and benefits of each alternative, and select and implement the policy strategy that can best achieve the stated values with the highest benefits and lowest costs. This model has been criticized for imposing unrealistic demands on people making policy decisions. Critics argue that information in the real world of policy making is limited and uncertain, and the clash of interests makes impossible any ranking of values.

Incrementalism is an alternative model that takes these criticisms into account. In the view of critics, the tie to past policies reduces the possibility of new policy approaches. Policy makers do not begin with a clean slate but rather focus on proposed marginal changes in existing policies. Deciding on budgets is an example. Rather than creating an entirely new budget each year, budget makers focus on proposed marginal changes from the previous year's budget. The same goes for policies like environmental regulation. A change to emissions standards for next year is likely to be greatly influenced by the existing standards. Imagine how difficult it would be to conduct business if future rules were often radically different from present rules.

By highlighting marginal changes in existing policies, incrementalism poses lower information demands. In addition, incrementalism holds that a capacity to achieve agreement among contesting interests defines good public policy.

rational-comprehensive model

A model of decision making that holds that policy makers should identify problems, consider various policy alternatives and their costs and benefits, and select and implement the policy strategy with the highest benefits and the lowest costs

incrementalism

A model of decision making that holds that new policies should differ only marginally from existing policies

This definition of good policy is in sharp contrast to the rational-comprehensive emphasis on the search for costs and benefits of alternative policy approaches.[6]

Incrementalism has been criticized for being too conservative in its implications. In addition, the sensitivity to political power and the emphasis on agreement in the model risk the exclusion of interests without power. In the effort to be realistic and pragmatic, incrementalism neglects some interests in the search for the appropriate purposes of government.

Despite these criticisms, incrementalism does raise important questions in public policy. Under what circumstances is the political system capable of fundamental rather than incremental changes in policy? What does it take to make a substantial break with the past? Change in the number of people insured by the Social Security system and increases in taxes to pay for the program have been incremental over the past eighty-five years, as Figure 13.2 shows; but the decision to establish the system in 1935 was a fundamental break with the past. Decisions to create new agencies (or abolish existing ones) or to initiate new programs (or terminate current ones) are fundamental rather than incremental. The circumstances allowing such decisions can be the threat of crisis or substantial changes in technology, in social or economic values, or in the alignment of political power. The model of incrementalism may be as important for the questions it raises about policy as it is for the explanations it offers.[7]

Whether looking at incrementalism or another policy making model, it is good to remember that models are learning tools. By abstracting from reality, they try

Figure 13.2 | Incrementalism and Social Security Taxes

The creation of the Social Security program in 1935 was a fundamental change in government policy. Once Social Security was established, changes in the rates of taxes to pay for the program occurred in incremental steps over time. Short of an emergency of the magnitude of the Great Depression, it is unlikely that there will be any drastic and abrupt changes in the program. Rather, adjustments will come gradually.

SOURCE: *Data from* Social Security Bulletin, Annual Statistical Supplement, 2005, *p. 87, and from Social Security Online, http://www.socialsecurity.gov/OACT/ProgData/taxRates.html (December 12, 2014).*

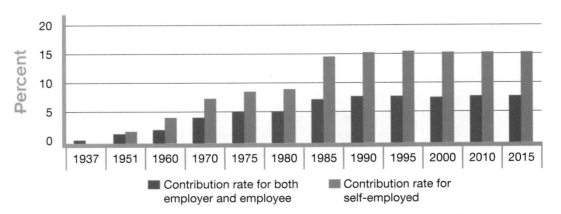

The tax rates of 7.65 percent for employees and employers and 15.3 percent for the self-employed will remain in effect for future years unless Congress and the president decide to change Social Security tax rate policy.

to explain why things happen as they do. The utility of a model lies in increasing our understanding of reality, yet no single model describes completely a complex political system. Thinking of events in terms of two or three models may be a better way to think about how policy is made and about who is influential in shaping policy.

13.1c Stages in the Policy Process

In the real world of politics and conflict, the making of public policy frequently appears to be full of chaos. Groups demand or oppose, members of Congress respond or criticize, presidents agree or refuse, judges rule or defer, bureaucrats proceed or halt, and the mass media report or ignore. The making of public policy is not like a play where all the actors follow a predetermined script. Rather, in the making of policy, a group leader or a congressional representative may say and do things without knowing how others will respond or whether they will respond at all. In the efforts to shape policy, hope, uncertainty, and chance all play a role. Consequently, the policy process may seem to be a confusing clash of ideas, events, and personalities.

Public policy analysts try to break down the process of making policy into definable stages to order and make sense out of what appears to be chaotic.[8] Figure 13.3 portrays the stages in the evolution of public policies. In the real world, policies do not evolve in such neatly defined and apparently simple stages. Participants in the process make demands, offer responses, and make decisions without consciously following some analytical framework. Nonetheless, identification of these stages helps to make the evolution of public policies and the role of government procedures and institutions in the process more understandable.

As Figure 13.3 shows, there are five stages in the evolution of policies:

1. A problem or issue must somehow get on the agenda of government.

2. Specific proposals to do something about the problem are discussed.

3. Government officials adopt a policy by choosing some specific strategy for action from among the proposals discussed.

4. Bureaucrats implement or translate into action the adopted proposal.

5. The policy is evaluated to determine whether or not it succeeded in solving or ameliorating the originally defined problem.

Stage 1: Getting Issues on the Agenda of Government

The **policy agenda** of government is comprised of the list of issues that engage the attention of elected officials. Obviously, governments cannot simultaneously deal with every conceivable problem. Like individuals, governments must make choices on which matters will get their attention at particular times. Issues get on the policy agenda in a variety of ways. No single explanation can capture the rich complexity of the process.[9]

Factors that contribute to moving some particular issue onto the government agenda include technological change, the demands of politically emerging groups, the evolution of social values, the threats of crisis or war, changing economic conditions, and the political will of a strong leader. Sometimes the mass media can create issues by focusing attention on particular concerns. For example, the Watergate affair, which resulted in the resignation of President Richard Nixon, became a matter of nearly constant public discussion between 1972 and 1974 as the press revealed wrongdoing. More recently, the Clinton impeachment, the 9/11 tragedy and subsequent

policy agenda

The public issues that engage the attention of elected officials

Figure 13.3 | Stages in the Policy Process

Although policies do not always develop in the neatly defined stages outlined below, an awareness of what happens in each stage helps us understand the process that occurs as government attempts to solve problems and accomplish goals. Any number and combination of persons and events can bring concerns to the attention of political leaders (stage 1). Policy makers in the executive and legislative branches then study the range of choices open to them to meet those concerns (stage 2). A variety of public officials may be involved in selecting a course of action or in deciding to do nothing at all (stage 3). The policy then becomes the responsibility of bureaucrats to administer (stage 4). Finally, evaluation occurs. Does the plan work? Is it worth its costs (stage 5)? The evaluation may become a factor in encouraging further policy making by government.

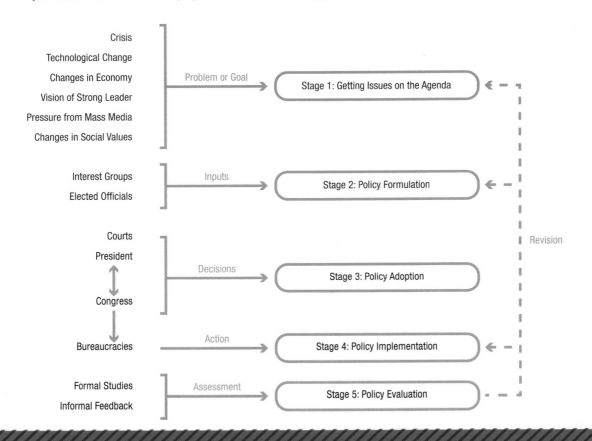

war on terrorism, and the recent economic recession have been events that have played major roles in the government's agenda.

Further, the issues on the policy agenda are always changing. Those that get resolved or lose relevance in a changing society are simply no longer discussed. For example, slavery was the most bitterly divisive issue of the nineteenth century, yet one consequence of the Civil War was that slavery is no longer a matter of public debate. Some issues in their demise simply give rise to other issues. Slavery is no longer an issue, but the economic and social status of African Americans is a matter of continuing policy debate and discussion.

Different sets of issues have dominated policy discussion at different times. The severe economic problems of the Great Depression of the 1930s moved government officials to spend much of their efforts on programs to deal with high unemployment, bank failures, and factory closings. During the 1960s, poverty, hunger, and despair in urban ghettos were targets of major policy initiatives before the war in Vietnam intervened. In the 1970s, concern about the quality of the nation's physical environment emerged as a major policy issue. The Arab oil embargo of that decade also put a sudden end to cheap energy; consequently, the competition between the search for new energy sources and the quest for environmental quality dominated the agenda of those years.

The Arab oil embargo of the 1970s put a sudden end to cheap energy; consequently, the competition between the search for new energy sources and the quest for environmental quality dominated the agenda of those years. (Wikimedia Commons)

Thus far in the twenty-first century, two issues seem to be overwhelming and affecting practically all others on the policy agenda: the use of money as a public resource and the role of the United States in the international arena. Domestically, how much the government should spend (and on what), how much and whom government should tax, the impact of budget deficits and surpluses on the economy, and how far the reach of the federal government (as opposed to that of states and private parties) should extend in such areas as Social Security, welfare, health care, and global climate change are the questions that drive most policy debate. In foreign affairs, how to respond to terrorism, whether and how to take unilateral military action in a world of increasing multinational organization, and the ethical responsibilities of superpower status are the concerns driving policy. The policy agenda of government is like a kaleidoscope: the turn of decades results in constantly shifting patterns of issue concerns.

Stage 2: Policy Formulation

Once an issue gets on the agenda of government, public debate centers on specific proposals on what government ought to do and how to do it.[10] To say that government ought to "do something" about budget deficits, the needs of children in poverty, climate change, or drug abuse is only a beginning. To achieve results requires a specific **policy strategy**, some specific course of action designed to deal with the originally defined problem.

If the budget deficit is a problem, should we increase taxes, decrease spending, or press for a balanced budget amendment? If the needs of children in poverty are a problem, should we increase family assistance payments, track down absent fathers, or build orphanages? If climate change is a problem, should we ban the use of certain fuels, or should we tax their use to pay for research on alternative energies? If drug abuse is a problem, should we open more treatment centers, eradicate drug-producing crops around the world, or legalize the use of drugs? Of course, several policy strategies to deal with a problem might be pursued simultaneously, but the relative emphasis on one or another strategy can provoke intense controversy.

Confused by the contradictory claims politicians sometimes make about public policy?

The Annenberg Political Fact Check is a nonpartisan and nonprofit effort to investigate the factual accuracy of claims political leaders make. Check out the website and check up on the politicians!

http://www.bvtlab.com/nb76h

policy strategy

A specific course of action designed to deal with a public problem

BVT *Lab*

Visit www.BVTLab.com to explore the student resources available for this chapter.

Chapter 13 | Government and Public Policy | 408

Questions of what government should do, who should benefit, and who should bear the costs of such action make up the raw material of policy debate. Groups with different ideological beliefs are likely to propose different solutions to policy problems. To reduce budget deficits, for example, conservatives are likely to propose cuts in social welfare spending and liberals are likely to propose cuts in defense spending or the closing of tax loopholes for the wealthy. The groups that benefit from one proposal will suffer under the other. The demands of interest groups, debates in Congress, requests by bureaucracies, conflicts between political parties and candidates, presidential speeches, and reporting in the mass media all focus on the question of what government ought to do in some specific policy area.

Stage 3: Policy Adoption

Although an issue can get on the policy agenda and various policy strategies can be debated and discussed, nothing happens until institutions of government **adopt a policy** that started as a proposal. At some point a formal, authoritative decision must be made on the action government will take to address a particular concern. Ultimately, the institutions of government exist to make such formal, authoritative decisions.

Formal adoption occurs in several ways. A bill passed by both houses of Congress and duly signed by the president is an example of formal adoption. For example, if growing budget deficits are deemed an important issue on the policy agenda, one specific strategy to deal with the problem might be a tax bill designed to raise revenue. If both houses can agree on a bill and if the president concurs on the wisdom and necessity of the measure, the resulting law is the formal adoption of a strategy for action. Similarly, decisions by the Supreme Court and the declaration of regulations by bureaucracies are also illustrations of adoption in the making of policy. If the Court requires busing to eliminate racially segregated schools, it is—by making an authoritative, formal decision—in effect adopting a strategy for action. If a regulatory agency requires the installation of air bags in automobiles, it too is adopting a strategy for action.

| nterested in an internship or career in public policy?

The National Association of Schools of Public Affairs and Administration offers these suggestions and starting points for you.

http://www.bvtlab.com/N8k8r

Adopting some policy strategy does not end the debate, however. The losers (both inside and outside the government) in the adoption process may retreat to other units in the political system and seek to have the decision changed or revised. A tax law may become an issue in a subsequent electoral campaign, or a regulatory decision on air bags may end up in the courts. Alternatively, those who have lost may simply wait for another day, when events or changing times or different officials will allow their position another hearing. In the short run, few issues are resolved by the adoption of some particular strategy for action. Rather, the discussion usually continues as revisions are proposed or as the consequences of the adopted strategy become matters of debate. The wheel of policy making turns endlessly. Moreover, failure to adopt a policy proposal is, in itself, policy making. It represents a formal, authoritative decision to leave policy where it was before the debate began, with the effect that taxes do not go up or air bags are not required.

policy adoption

A formal, authoritative decision, such as the enactment of legislation, made by institutions of government to address an issue on the policy agenda

Stage 4: Policy Implementation

Policy debate is really debate over *ideas*. For example, Congress and the president may decide that sending retired persons monthly checks funded by people currently employed is a good idea and formally adopt a strategy. However, that idea or strategy for action must be *implemented* before anything happens. A bureaucracy must be charged with the task of actually getting the right checks to the right people. Bureaucracies play the central role in this stage in the policy process, for they are ultimately responsible for **policy implementation**, or translating policy ideas

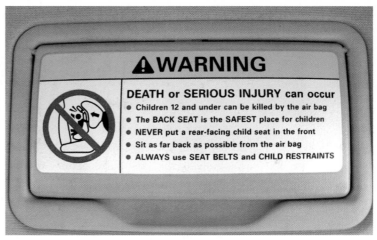

If a regulatory agency requires the installation of air bags in automobiles, it is adopting a strategy for action. (iStock)

into action. The difficulties and obstacles that frequently accompany the implementation process are suggested by the expressive (if lengthy) subtitle of a classic book: *How Great Expectations in Washington Are Dashed in Oakland; Or, Why It's Amazing That Federal Programs Work at All, This Being a Saga of the Economic Development Administration as Told by Two Sympathetic Observers Who Seek to Build Morals on a Foundation of Ruined Hopes.*[11] Clearly, implementation is neither automatic nor predictable.[12]

Given the vast differences among policy ideas, not every policy can be implemented in exactly the same way. Different bureaucracies have very different problems in their implementation tasks. For example, getting astronauts to the moon and back was a clear task with a sharply defined end; and once the task was accomplished, the implementation process ended. By contrast, collecting taxes and funding medical care for the elderly are ongoing programs that are never completed. Moreover, Congress and the president give some bureaucracies very little discretion in implementing policy ideas, while they give other bureaucracies vague, broad mandates. The Social Security Administration has no freedom in determining who among the elderly should get how much each month; but the Consumer Product Safety Commission has flexibility in determining which consumer products will become subject to new regulations.

Continuing debate frequently accompanies the implementation process. In the judgment of the opponents of some particular policy strategy, a bureaucracy may outrun, or even contradict, the intent of Congress. For example, efforts in Congress to invalidate regulations of the Federal Trade Commission by legislative veto were attempts to put controls on the agency. Alternatively, a bureaucracy may not be vigorous enough in discharging its task. For example, in 2001, some members of Congress charged the Environmental Protection Agency with being too vigorous in enforcement of prohibitions in rural areas, but far too lax in enforcing violations in places with greater political clout, like the metro Washington, D.C., area.[13] A bureaucracy can be caught in the same crossfire of conflicting demands that were present in the debate before a strategy was formally adopted. On pollution control policy, for example, the EPA can be in the middle of conflict between environmentalists and business interests fearful of the costs of environmental regulations. In any case, the implementation stage in policy is frequently a continuation of the political struggle that surrounds an issue from the time it first gets on the policy agenda.

policy implementation

The translation of policy ideas into action

Stage 5: Policy Evaluation

The final analytical stage in the evolution of policies is evaluation.[14] This stage logically follows from the others because of the reasonable expectation that we ought to know whether a particular policy strategy "worked." Determining whether the formally adopted, implemented strategy in fact ameliorated or solved the originally defined problem is the goal of **policy evaluation**. However, the expectation that policy strategies ought to be evaluated definitively is more easily stated than actually met.

(Shutterstock)

Formal evaluation of policies has received increased attention since the late 1960s. As the national government attempted to do more policy making, criticism surfaced that government did not deliver on its promises. Consequently, demands for policy evaluation intensified. The techniques of such formal evaluation range from simple before-and-after studies to more sophisticated controlled experiments. Do innovative education programs (new curricular efforts, charter schools, the expenditure of additional funds, etc.), in fact, improve learning skills among disadvantaged children? Do rehabilitation programs (employment, training, special counseling, etc.), in fact, reduce the likelihood that individuals released from prison will commit crimes again? In a controlled experiment, do individuals who receive a guaranteed income behave any differently from another group of individuals who do not?

Such questions are legitimate, but formal evaluation efforts almost never give unequivocal answers that end debate over the policy. In fact, debate frequently swirls about evaluation results, especially if the answers do not coincide with the expectations of the people who want the policy to work. Unfavorable results can almost always be explained away by citing inadequate research instruments, insufficient time to assess the policy, or inaccurate interpretations of the findings.[15] For example, people who want school vouchers to work might criticize negative findings on vouchers because the study was based on too short a time span. Evaluation results are more likely to continue, rather than end, policy debate.

Not every government policy goes through a formal evaluation procedure. There may be insufficient time and money as well as analytical difficulties. For example, are nuclear weapons policies preventing nuclear war? The answer may be that they are for now; but if such a war should occur, the assertion would obviously be proved wrong, with dire consequences few wish to even contemplate. In this instance, the policy relies on hope rather than on unattainable evaluation results. In the absence of a cure for cancer or HIV/AIDS, is the nation's medical research policy working? No reasonable person would suggest that cancer or HIV/AIDS research should be halted

This image, from a scanning electron micrograph, shows HIV-1 budding (in green) from cultured lymphocyte, or white blood cell. (Wikimedia Commons)

policy evaluation

The act of determining whether a formally adopted and implemented policy ameliorated or solved a public problem

The Road to a New Cabinet Department

America's response to the 9/11 terrorist attacks illustrates both the speed with which public policy can be enacted and the hurdles that must be overcome in the public policy process. On September 20, 2001—just nine days after the tragedy—President George W. Bush announced that he would be establishing an Office of Homeland Security, headed by Pennsylvania Governor Tom Ridge, in an effort to prevent future terrorist attacks on the United States. Although the office was established quickly via an executive order on October 8, 2001, the president's goal of making the office a cabinet-level department would require a much longer route. The first step of the policy process, getting the issue on the policy agenda, was certainly the easiest. Domestic security was in the forefront of every government official's mind in the autumn of 2001.

President Bush delivered the second stage, developing a policy strategy, during his address. He proposed a course of action to address the problem of terrorism. Specifically, he suggested a cabinet-level office designed to prevent future terrorist attacks, reduce American vulnerability, and help in recovery efforts for attacks that do occur.[1] In this case, strategy development occurred very quickly; this speed was a result of the gravity of the problem the policy addressed.

Policy adoption became a sticking point for homeland security. Although President Bush was able to swiftly establish an executive office without the need of additional approval, creation of a full-blown cabinet department requires a congressional act. Thus, on June 24, 2002, Representative Dick Armey (R–TX) introduced the Homeland Security Act of 2002 in the House of Representatives. Although the Republican-led House of Representatives voted to approve the bill just one month later (quick adoption by congressional standards), the Democratic majority in the Senate voiced reservations about the extent of the proposed department's powers. Senator Robert Byrd (D–WV) cautioned that "Congress must never act recklessly," as he and others voiced concerns about civil service employee protections in light of the bill's proposed merger of twenty-two federal agencies into a single department.[2] Eventual adoption would depend on the ability of Congress and the president to reach a compromise. This compromise was finally reached when the Senate passed a revised bill on November 19, 2002, and President Bush signed it into law.

Policy implementation has involved a large-scale restructuring of existing offices and agencies, affecting over 170,000 federal employees. Even though an executive office was already in place, coordinating and organizing such a large number of workers into four newly created divisions has taken a considerable amount of time. Initial stages of policy implementation tend to be measured in months, but completion of large-scale policy changes can sometimes take years.

The final stage of the process, policy evaluation, started to take place as soon as President Bush announced his intentions. From the moment his speech ended, journalists, politicians, and policy analysts have been assessing success and failure. In addition to formal evaluation, such as the annual appropriations process in Congress, informal evaluation of Homeland Security is likely to occur every time American security is threatened. Although policies are tested constantly, only time can tell whether they will ultimately succeed or fail.

The speed of the public policy process varies. What aspects seem too fast? Too slow? Which perspective on policy making, discussed earlier in this chapter, provides the best description of efforts to create a Department of Homeland Security?

1 The Department of Homeland Security, http://www.white house.gov/deptofhomeland/ (September 23, 2002).

2 "Democrats Urged to Act on Homeland Security Bill," September 18, 2002, http://www.cnn.com/2002/ALLPOLITICS/09/18/homeland.security.ap/index.html (September 23, 2002).

because individuals continue to die of the disease. Again, hope for success sustains the policy, yet the very existence of some policies constitutes almost a definition of success. The Social Security program, for example, is working as long as the checks are regularly sent out.

Although most policies are not evaluated formally, they are often appraised *informally* during the process of implementation. Some informal assessments of government programs include congressional budget and authorization hearings, the sharp policy conflicts between opposing candidates in electoral campaigns, presidential speeches to set the nation's policy priorities, and the eternal demands of interest groups. Ultimately, most evaluation of government policies is the product of the endless interplay of political passions at the root of all political conflict.

13.2 The Purposes and Presence of the National Government

Readers of newspapers and viewers of television newscasts are told almost daily of a bewildering array of national government actions. The Air Force presses to keep a new bomber program alive. NASA announces plans for a mission to Mars. The Nuclear Regulatory Commission publishes a new set of rules on certification procedures for the operation of nuclear power plants. The Supreme Court hands down a decision on the constitutionality of a campaign finance law. Congress continues to wrestle with budget deficits. The president's budget director defends a plan to eliminate the inheritance tax. This blizzard of activity reflects the pervasiveness of the national government as well as the complexity and scope of its work.

13.2a Views of Public Policy

No single set of categories can adequately capture everything government does. However, some divisions among policies can help make the scope of government activity more comprehensible. The identification of policy categories defines patterns of government action to clarify what government does and how it goes about its work.

Foreign policies can have important domestic consequences. For example, international trade policy with Japan can affect the prices of goods , such as cars and cell phones, in the United States. (Wikimedia Commons)

Perhaps the most common sets of policy categories are **foreign policy**, decisions about relations with other nations, and **domestic policy**, decisions about matters affecting citizens within the United States. Some foreign policies can have important domestic consequences. For example, international trade policy with Japan can affect the prices of goods in the United States. In general, however, public officials make foreign policy decisions in ways different from those used in social welfare policies. The president is less constrained by other officials and groups in the international arena than he is in seeking changes in the Social Security system. Interest groups tend to be less concerned about foreign policies than about domestic policies, which affect them more immediately and directly.[16] Domestic policy can be further subdivided into functional areas, such as education, health, transportation, energy, and environment.

foreign policy

A nation's collective decisions about relations with other nations

domestic policy

A category of public policy that is comprised of policy decisions about matters affecting individuals within a political system

13.3   Politics and Economic Self-Interest

The presence or absence of *economic self-interest* can also be a useful criterion for differentiating policies. Economic self-interest plays little or no role in the disposition of issues such as abortion, the legal drinking age, same-sex marriage, and the draft. In each of these cases, money would not resolve the conflict. Some people, for example, vehemently believe that abortion is an undeniable evil while others see abortion as an inalienable right of women. Proponents of abortion argue that women should be able to decide not to have children for economic as well as personal reasons. However, money concerns are not paramount in this debate.

Another category includes government actions on matters in which money plays a central role. For example, debates over taxes and budget deficits are essentially economic questions. Who shall pay for government, and who shall receive how much out of it? Which states shall receive more than others in federal grants? Which groups shall bear the brunt of cuts in social welfare spending? Does inflation merit more government action and attention than unemployment?

Finally, in some policy debates economic self-interest and assertions of principle are mixed. Money plays an important but not exclusive role in these issues. Policies on civilian nuclear power, civil rights, and pornography are examples. Electric power companies have an economic interest in favorable governmental policies on nuclear plant construction. Similarly, groups like women, African Americans, and Americans with disabilities see active civil rights policies

The protection of legal and constitutional rights, through such measures as the Americans with Disabilities Act, has been a principal focus of national government activities in recent years. (iStock)

on hiring and promotion as favorable to their economic self-interest; but assertions of principle also play an important role in the debates. The opponents of civilian nuclear power see nuclear power plants as a threat to public health and the quality of the environment. Civil rights advocates see the enhanced status of certain groups as a matter of right and justice. Finally, while the producers and sellers of pornography assert the principle of freedom of speech, their opponents see the defense of pornography (from which money is made) as a defense of economic self-interest.

13.3a Categories of National Government Policies

No single set of categories can adequately capture everything government does. However, even though overlaps occur, some divisions among policies can help make the scope of government activity more comprehensible. Over time the national government has taken on new functions and responsibilities in response to crises, changing technologies, citizen demands, and political pressures. Six substantive categories can help to bring some order to the scope of national government policies.

BVT *Lab*

Flashcards are available
for this chapter at
www.BVTLab.com.

Chapter 13 | Government and Public Policy | 414

Foreign and Defense Policies   The oldest functions of the national government are to conduct relationships with foreign nations, such as trade negotiations with Mexico and Canada, and to maintain national security against threats from other nations, using physical force if necessary, such as the use of troops in the 1991 Persian Gulf War or the Iraq War (2003–2011).

Social Welfare   In terms of the amount of money spent by the national government, the growth of social welfare activities was the most significant policy change in the role of government in the twentieth century. Like a huge check processor, the national government takes money from taxpayers or borrows it and disburses cash or in-kind benefits, such as the Supplemental Nutrition Assistance Program, to millions of people who qualify because of old age, disability, unemployment, or poverty.

Protection of Legal and Constitutional Rights   The protection of legal and constitutional rights has been one of the principal sets of national government activities over the past generation. Supreme Court justices, presidents, and members of Congress have all brought to bear, to varying degrees, the power and influence of the national government to protect the rights of a variety of groups, such as political, religious, and ethnic minorities; the LGBT community; Americans with disabilities; and people accused of crimes.

Promotion of Science and Technology   Basic research, new technologies, and changing public expectations have drawn the national government into efforts to achieve certain public policy goals with the help of science and technology. Examples of such policies include the civilian space program, continuing research efforts on diseases such as HIV/AIDS and cancer, the use of stem cells in research, therapeutic cloning, and the development of new civilian technologies to help the nation become more competitive in the world economy of the twenty-first century.

Regulation   Regulations are among the tools government uses to shape sectors of the economy. However, because their purposes go beyond economic goals, regulations can be considered a specific category of policy. As the chapter on bureaucracies indicated, government regulations are designed to structure relationships in specific industries, such as broadcasting and the marketing of securities, or to ensure social objectives, such as clean air and worker safety.[17]

Economic Policies   Given a national budget that now exceeds $3.5 trillion, what the national government does (or does not do) in its spending, taxing, and borrowing policies has enormous consequences for the economy. Spending on education and on transportation and communication networks will shape the kind of economy the nation has in coming decades. Tax laws that eliminate or create tax deductions and tax credits influence investment decisions made by individuals and corporations. Large deficits can encourage higher interest rates, just as higher government spending can reduce unemployment rates. Through its control of the money supply, the Federal Reserve can also affect interest and unemployment rates and private investment decisions. Government efforts to shape the economy through its spending, taxing, borrowing, and money supply decisions make up a major part of the policy agenda.

CHAPTER REVIEW

1. Public policy is whatever government chooses to do or not to do. Ultimately, political activity springs from conflict within society over what government ought to do and for whom or to whom it ought to do it. The elitism and pluralism models offer different explanations of who should make public policy decisions. The rational-comprehensive approach and incrementalism raise fundamental questions about how decisions are made.

2. Definable stages of policy making: getting issues onto the agenda of government, formulating policy proposals, formally adopting policy, implementing policy, and evaluating policy.

3. Public policies can be distinguished from one another in a variety of ways. Economic self-interest is a useful criterion in distinguishing among policies. Six substantive categories differentiate national government policies: foreign and defense policies, social welfare, protection of legal and constitutional rights, promotion of science and technology, regulation, and economic policies.

KEY TERMS

Readings for Further Study

A good overview of public policy analysis and the stages of the public policy process can be found in James E. Anderson's *Public Policymaking*, 8th ed. (Boston: Cengage, 2015).

John Kingdon's *Agendas, Alternatives, and Public Policies*, 2nd ed. (New York: Longman, 2010) is an interesting discussion of the changing shape of the public policy agenda.

An excellent account of policy making, and an attempt to explain the apparent contradictions involved in the process, is Deborah A. Stone's *Policy Paradox: The Art of Political Decision Making*, 3rd ed. (New York: Norton, 2012).

The theories behind public policy are addressed in Paul A. Sabatier and Christopher M. Weible, eds., *Theories of the Policy Process: Theoretical Lenses on Public Policy* (Boulder, CO: Westview Press, 2014), and in Thomas A. Birkland, *An Introduction to the Policy Process*, 3rd ed. (Armonk, NY: M.E. Sharpe, 2010).

The causes for the rise and fall of public policies over time are explored in Frank R. Baumgartner's and Bryan D. Jones, *Agendas and Instability in American Politics*, 2nd ed. (Chicago: University of Chicago Press, 2009).

Two quarterly journals of the Policy Studies Organization, the *Policy Studies Journal* and the *Review of Policy Research*, are sources of current scholarship on the field of policy analysis and on specific policy areas.

Notes

1. Thomas R. Dye, *Understanding Public Policy*, 10th ed. (Englewood Cliffs, NJ: Prentice-Hall, 2001), p. 2.

2. For a comprehensive statement of the systems model, see David Easton, *A Systems Analysis of Political Life* (Chicago: University of Chicago Press, 1979).

3. For a classic statement on elitism, see C. Wright Mills, *The Power Elite*, 2nd ed. (New York: Oxford University Press, 2000).

4. An analysis of pluralism that helped set the terms of the debate with elitism is Robert Dahl's *Who Governs? Democracy and Power in an American City* (New Haven, CT: Yale University Press, 1961).

5. For a review of different analytical approaches to decision making, see James W. Fesler and Donald F. Kettl, *The Politics of the Administrative Process* (Chatham, NJ: Chatham House, 1996).

6. The classic argument for incrementalism and its comparison to the rational-comprehensive approach is Charles Lindblom's "The Science of 'Muddling Through,'" *Public Administration Review 19* (1959): 79–88.

7. For a review of the criticisms of the rational-comprehensive approach and incrementalism, see Amitai Etzioni, "Mixed-Scanning: A 'Third' Approach to Decision-Making," *Public Administration Review 27* (1967): 385–392.

8. James E. Anderson, *Public Policymaking*, 5th ed. (Boston: Houghton Mifflin, 203), pp. 30–31.

9. See John W. Kingdon, *Agendas, Alternatives, and Public Policies*, 2nd ed. (New York: Addison-Wesley, 1995).

10. For a discussion of the contributions and limits of knowledge in efforts to resolve policy problems, see Peter deLeon's *Advice and Consent: The Development of the Policy Sciences* (New York: Russell Sage, 1988).

11. Jeffrey L. Pressman and Aaron B. Wildavsky, *Implementation*, 3rd ed. (Berkeley: University of California Press, 1984).

12. On the heightened attention that policy analysts have given to implementation over the last two decades, see Dennis Palumbo's *Public Policy in America: Government in Action*, 2nd ed. (Stamford, CT: Thomson, 1997).

13. "EPA Criticized for Selective Enforcement," *Environment and Climate News*, September 2001.

14. See Pressman and Wildavsky's *Implementation* for a discussion of the relationship between evaluation and implementation, pp. 181–205.

15. See, for example, Dye's *Understanding Public Policy*.

16. See, for example, Aaron Wildavsky, "The Two Presidencies," *Trans-Action* (December 1966): 7–14.

17. For a discussion of the purposes of regulation, see *Federal Regulatory Directory*, 10th ed. (Washington, DC: CQ Press, 2001).

POP QUIZ

1. Debates over procedures and rules are really debates over _____.

2. A specific course of action designed to deal with the originally defined problem is called a policy _____.

3. The _____ model of policy making holds that policy is the product of an interlocking relationship between institutions of government and their surrounding social, economic, and political environment.

4. One approach to policy making is that of _____, in which policy decisions vary only marginally from previous policy.

5. The goal of _____ _____ is to determine whether the formally adopted, implemented strategy did in fact solve the original problem

6. Policies that are designed to protect some common good always affect everyone in the same way. T F

7. The political will of a strong leader may help move some particular issue onto the government agenda. T F

8. When a policy is formally and legally implemented, debate over the issue usually ends. T F

9. It is required by law that every government policy go through a formal evaluation procedure. T F

10. Which of the following is true of public policy making?

    A) It is nonconflictual in a democratic system.

    B) It is involves debate over rules but not procedures.

    C) It is has varying consequences for different groups.

    D) It is designed to protect the common good.

11. The decision to deal with the drug abuse problem by opening more treatment centers would be an example of a policy _____.

    A) agenda
    B) strategy
    C) adoption
    D) implementation

12. The idea that policy decisions reflect the interest of the ruling class at the expense of the workers is a tenet of the _____ model.

    A) elitism
    B) pluralism
    C) Marxism
    D) free-market capitalism

13. Bureaucracies play a central role in the policy process during the _____ stage.

    A) agenda building
    B) policy proposal
    C) policy adoption
    D) implementation

14. The final analytical stage in the evolution of policies is _____.

    A) evaluation
    B) agenda building
    C) implementation
    D) adoption

15. Which of the following is true of policy evaluation?

    A) It is required by law.
    B) It formally ends the policy debate.
    C) It usually occurs informally during the implementation process.
    D) It has become increasingly accurate with precise measures.

Answers:
1. policy 2. strategy 3. systems 4. incrementalism 5. policy evaluation 6. F 7. T 8. F 9. F 10. C 11. B 12. C 13. D 14. A 15. C

Chapter

14

Public Policy and Economics

In This Chapter

(Shutterstock)

Chapter Objectives

Economic issues are typically high on the political agenda because they affect so many people and often lead to sharp conflicts that the political process must resolve. This chapter defines fiscal and monetary policy, describes elements of economic policy, and outlines the tenets of three major schools of thought about economic policy: Keynesian economics, monetarist economics, and supply-side economics.

Given the importance of national budget policy in the twenty-first century, the chapter then pays special attention to spending choices in fiscal policy by surveying major categories of spending and addressing the issue of the deficit and why government expenditures are so hard to control. The chapter concludes with a review of how budget decisions are made and a discussion of the eternal search, driven by the persistence of high deficits, for better procedures in deciding how money will be spent.

14.1 Government and Economic Policy

Some of the sharpest conflicts in a society are economic—who gains and who loses, who gives and who receives, who has and who has not. These issues affect the lives and well-being of millions of Americans. Further, with the development of an increasingly interdependent world economy, these issues affect billions of people around the world as well.

In its broadest sense, **economic policy** refers to the decisions a government makes that affect the production, distribution, and consumption of goods; the provision of services; the flow of income; and the accumulation of wealth. In a complex and interdependent modern economy, such as that of the United States, virtually everything the government does has economic consequences. For example, President Kennedy's 1961 declaration to put a man on the moon by 1970 set off an explosion of research in metallurgy, electronics, and computers during the 1960s. This research, in turn, sparked the growth of new high-tech industries and the introduction of consumer goods such as the personal computer.

Nevertheless, the term *economic policy* is usually confined to decisions government makes with the explicit intention of influencing the economy. These decisions inevitably address fundamental questions about the role that government should play in the economy and society and about the kind of economy and society the United States should have.

14.1a Basic Issues of Economic Policy

Economic questions have been part of American politics since the earliest days of the Republic. As Chapter 1 explained, unpopular British tax policies helped to spark the drive for independence before 1776. Barriers to trade and threats to creditors contributed to the call for a new and stronger national government in 1787. Political conflicts today over taxes, deficits, surpluses, the national debt, trade, and alternative strategies for ensuring prosperity demonstrate the durability of economic issues on the nation's policy agenda. Current controversies illustrate five important economic issues that have recurred as themes through American history, from the beginning to the present.

First, *should government involve itself in economic affairs at all?* As discussed in Chapter 4, one long-standing philosophical view is that the government should stay out of economics and business. Known as **laissez-faire** (French for "leave things alone"), this idea maintains that completely free economic competition among individuals, each pursuing his or her own self-interest, will work naturally to the benefit of all.[1] Under laissez-faire, most economic regulations, such as regulation of the securities business, simply would not exist. This view contrasts

Economics issues, such as energy sources, are politically important because they affect so many people and often lead to conflicts. (iStock)

starkly with **socialism**, which holds that people will be best off if economic decision making is completely under the control of the government and if government owns and operates most of the major industries. Although Americans have always favored laissez-faire much more than socialism, they divide over just where to strike the balance between the two.

The United States has the world's largest national economy. Its nominal gross domestic product (GDP) was estimated to be $16.8 trillion in 2013. (Shutterstock)

Second, even if government does involve itself in economic affairs, *should it try to stabilize the economy, or should it remain neutral?* Over the course of American history, the economy has gone through periodic booms and busts. When the economy goes into a slump—a **recession** when the slump is relatively minor and short-lived, or a **depression** when it is serious and sustained—or when it accelerates too quickly, some people argue that the government should not interfere but should rather allow the economy to correct itself in time. Others want the government to moderate the trends. Before the arrival of the New Deal during the Great Depression of the 1930s, the view that government should remain neutral prevailed. Since then the judgment that government should take an active role in stabilizing the economy has been dominant. Today, the increasingly global nature of the American economy means that foreign, as well as domestic, policies are a part of this active governmental role.

Third, if government is to maintain economic stability, *which policies will achieve that goal?* Some economists believe that government should adjust its spending and taxing decisions when the economy needs to accelerate or to slow down. Others think the government should try to shape general economic activity by adjusting the money supply and interest rates to influence the willingness of individuals and companies to borrow money.

Fourth, aside from policies that affect the general health of the economy, *should government promote or discourage particular types of economic activity?* Some people believe that government should subsidize heavy industry, such as steel mills and shipyards, because they are vital in times of war. A variation on this theme, often favored by the neoliberals discussed in Chapter 4, is the idea of developing a national "industrial policy" that plots out cooperation between government and industry in identifying and supporting particularly promising new products and industries. Others believe that certain industries, such as textile plants, need government help to protect them from foreign competition because these industries provide employment to many Americans. If necessary, government should engage in **protectionism** by restricting the flow of foreign goods into the United States. Advocates of **free trade**, by contrast, argue that a nation's economy will be better off in the long run if local producers who cannot compete with more efficient foreign producers are allowed to die a natural economic death. A recent twist—called **outsourcing**—has seen American corporations establishing factories in foreign countries in order to take advantage of cheaper labor markets. While such practices often create inexpensive products for American consumers, many worry about the negative effect exporting jobs has on employment rates in America.

socialism

The view in economics that economic decision making should be completely under the control of political authority

recession

A minor and relatively short period of economic decline

depression

A period of serious and sustained economic decline

protectionism

Opposite of *free trade;* belief that government should protect American business and industry by restricting the flow of foreign goods into the United States

free trade

Belief that America's economic interests are best served by allowing foreign producers to sell their goods without restriction in the United States

outsourcing

Establishment, by American corporations, of factories and offices in foreign countries to take advantage of cheaper labor markets

Free trade advocates believe that local producers who can't compete with foreign producers should be allowed to go out of business. (Shutterstock)

The possibilities of success and failure suggest a fifth concern: *Should government foster economic equality among its citizens?* There is little support in this country for the idea that the government should ensure complete economic equality among all citizens. However, it is a principal tenet of contemporary liberalism that no citizen should be allowed to fall below a certain economic minimum. This view accounts for social welfare programs such as nutrition assistance and medical care for the poor. A more conservative position is that government should see that every citizen has equal opportunity and then let economic forces work in their natural way. Extreme conservatives may find even this an unjustified intrusion into the economy.

Each of these five questions asks whether government should play an active or passive role. How each is answered has profound consequences for the kind of society in which Americans live. Should taxes be raised or lowered? Should the supply of money be expanded or contracted? Should social welfare spending be increased or cut? Should the national government embark on a major program of capital investment or not? Such questions dominate most policy debate in the 2000s. This debate was on the front burner of American politics in both the 2008 and 2012 election cycles, when economic crises in the lending and financial sectors led politicians to scramble for solutions.

14.1b Fiscal and Monetary Policy

Economic policies are of two major types: fiscal and monetary. The two are conceptually and practically distinct although political decision makers certainly must take the relationship between them into account. Some regulatory policy also involves economic issues, as discussed in the chapter on bureaucracies.

Determinations of how much and whom to tax, and how much and on what to spend, constitute the **fiscal policy** of the United States. The president makes tax and spending proposals and signs, if he agrees, legislation the Congress passes. The Constitution gives Congress the power "to lay and collect taxes, duties, imposts, and excises, to pay the debts and provide for the common defense and general welfare of the United States," and "to borrow money on the credit of the United States." Taken individually, decisions on these questions constitute much of the routine business of government. Should the savings from military spending cuts be put into constructing new bridges and highways? Should government raise the personal income tax or the corporate income tax to pay for new programs? Taken as a whole, these decisions by the president and Congress exert a powerful influence on the economic life of the nation.

Monetary policy, the second major type of economic policy, is the determination of how much money should circulate in the economy and what the cost of borrowing money, or the interest rate, should be. The Constitution gives Congress the power "to coin money, regulate the value thereof, and of foreign coin." In the landmark case of *McCulloch v. Maryland*,[2] the Supreme Court recognized Congress's "implied power" to determine monetary policy when it held that the Congress could charter a national bank, even though the Constitution did not explicitly give it that power

fiscal policy

Governmental decisions about taxing and spending that affect the economic life of a nation

monetary policy

Government decisions about how much money should circulate in the economy and what the cost of borrowing money, the interest rate, should be (see Chapter 2). In other words, Congress possesses the power to set monetary policy for the United States. Pursuant to this power, Congress created the Federal Reserve System and delegated to it the power to make these decisions on the supply of money and the cost of borrowing.

The making of economic policy illustrates the classic interplay between institutions and ideas. In fiscal policy, the president and his **Office of Management and Budget (OMB)**, an Executive Office agency that puts together the president's annual budget proposal, interact with Congress and its committees to produce a national budget. In monetary policy, the Federal Reserve shapes the economy by manipulating the money supply and interest rates. As the box "Politics and Economics: The Ideology of Economic Policy" shows, officials in these government institutions choose from among competing economic doctrines in the proposals and decisions they make. Conflicting ideas are the roots of economic policy debate.

14.2   The Deficit and the National Budget

Grappling with fiscal policy choices—that is, what taxes to raise or lower, what spending to increase or cut—has dominated the policy agenda in recent decades. Taxing and spending issues touch the president at almost every turn in his efforts to initiate and shape policy. Congress spends much of its time wrestling with the size and shape of the national budget. Sometimes elected officials find it easier to approve spending increases than tax increases, and the resulting budget deficits loom as a serious policy issue—Americans bristle at the prospect of making larger and larger payments for the interest on the national debt. Other times elected officials respond to budget difficulties and the economy by cutting spending programs and lowering taxes, pleasing some citizens but creating economic crises for others. This chapter will analyze the former problem—deficit spending.

College students can readily understand the concepts of deficit and debt. A deficit occurs when expenditures exceed revenues, such as income from a part-time job. (Shutterstock)

14.2a The Deficit as a Political Issue

College students can readily understand the concepts of deficit and debt. A **deficit** occurs when expenditures (tuition, room, meals, and so forth) exceed revenues (income from a part-time job and money from parents, for example). A student makes up the difference by borrowing money. **Debt** is the sum of the deficits of prior years. A student who borrows $2,000 each year for four years graduates with a debt of $8,000. This debt will not be erased until the student earns enough money to meet both current expenses and payments on those college loans.

Office of Management and Budget (OMB)

An agency in the Executive Office of the President that provides the president with budgetary information and advice and is responsible for compiling the president's annual budget proposal to Congress

deficit

An excess of government expenditures over revenues

debt

The total amount of money that the national government owes to lenders, such as banks, individual and foreign investors, insurance companies, and the variety of financial institutions that purchase government securities

A tax cut and higher defense spending during the administration of fortieth U.S. president Ronald Reagan contributed to the deficit of the 1980s. (Shutterstock)

The federal government today is in a similar position because the government's expenses routinely exceed revenues. Demands on government a century ago were not nearly so great as they are now. The national government in the nineteenth century had an almost embarrassing **surplus** (an excess of revenue over expenses) of funds. Difficult as it may be to believe, the national government had a budget surplus in seventy-one of the one hundred years between 1800 and 1900. In 1834 the total public debt was about $37,000, a sum translating to less than a penny per citizen.[3] Even though the national government regularly ran surpluses in the nineteenth century, the existence of government deficits and debt today is really not a new phenomenon. What is new is the size and persistence of the debt. Deficits have now become the norm in budget policy. Although a strong economy allowed the national government to run a surplus in the late 1990s, there was a budget deficit every year between 1970 and 1997, and again every year beginning in 2002.

Annual deficits and the federal debt increased substantially from the 1970s through the 1990s. In 1965 the annual deficit was a relatively modest $1.4 billion, but by 1975 the deficit began to exceed $50 billion annually. By 1985 the deficit was more than $200 billion. Over the relatively short period of ten years, annual budget deficits quadrupled.[4] Inflation accounts for some of this increase, but a tax cut pressed by President Reagan in 1981 and higher defense spending in the 1980s contributed substantially to the growth in deficits. Although there was a brief respite during the economic boom of the late 1990s, by 2002 deficit numbers again began to swell. The deficit for fiscal year 2015 is estimated at over $560 billion.[5]

Even a budget surplus, however, does not mean the government is debt free. The accumulated federal debt—the total amount of money government owes to lenders, such as government trust funds, banks, insurance companies, and the various financial institutions that purchase government securities—has also increased sharply over the past four decades. Federal debt rose from $322 billion in 1965 to almost $1 trillion in 1980. The debt was $3 trillion in 1990 and grew to over $17 trillion in 2014—over $50,000 for every person in the country.[6]

Some of the debate over the deficit is colored by the belief that government ought to be guided by traditional values in the matter of money—"living within one's own means."

Think it's easy to balance the budget?

Try it yourself by playing the budget simulation game at this website.

http://www.bvtlab.com/h8RS8

However, as in other matters, economists disagree over the extent to which the deficit poses a problem. Some argue that government deficits are essential to stimulate consumer demand in a failing or even sluggish economy. That is, by cutting taxes or increasing spending, government pumps money into the private economy to allow the kind of consumer spending that counters a depressed economy. Some maintain that the nation has had large deficits in the past, particularly in wartime, and those deficits actually spurred the economy.

Many other economists argue, however, that large deficits that are the product of a fundamental imbalance between revenues and expenditures can have the effect of slowing down consumer spending and economic growth. Government

surplus

An excess of government revenues over government expenditures

The Ideology of Economic Policy

In recent American history, several philosophies of economic policy have vied for acceptance as official government doctrine. The dominant perspective among Democrats since the New Deal has been Keynesian economics. For many years the primary challenge has come from advocates of monetarism, usually traditional conservative Republicans. Beginning in the Reagan years, some less orthodox Republican conservatives embraced the new (or at least newly packaged) doctrine of supply-side economics.

Keynesian Economics

The brilliant British economist John Maynard Keynes saw the health of an economy as dependent on the relationship between overall supply and demand in the economy. Supply is the total amount of goods and services produced in the economy; demand is the total amount of goods and services consumed. Economic problems arose, he argued, when supply and demand were not in balance. If supply exceeded demand, businesses would build up a backlog of unsold goods, cut back production, and lay off workers. Thus, supply exceeding demand would lead to unemployment. If demand exceeded supply, buyers would bid up the prices of goods; inflation would result. Only if supply and demand were in balance would the economy experience maximum employment and minimum inflation.

Keynes argued that in complex modern economics, supply and demand would not automatically balance and that the imbalance would lead to economic problems. Keynes's solution was to have the government use its fiscal policy to bring the two into balance. If supply exceeded demand and unemployment threatened, the government could spend more than it received in taxes—that is, it could engage in deficit spending and bring total demand, and hence employment, up to the optimum level. If demand exceeded supply and inflation loomed, the government could collect more in taxes than it spent—that is, it could run a surplus—and bring total demand, and hence inflation, down. In other words, Keynesians emphasize using government fiscal policy to adjust the level of demand to the point of balance with supply that will yield a low-inflation, high-employment economy.

Monetarism

Monetarists focus, as the name implies, on monetary policy. They see monetary policy, rather than fiscal policy, as the best way to control the level of demand for goods and services. If the Federal Reserve lets the amount of money grow too large and the cost of money (i.e., the interest rate) fall too low, consumers and business managers will borrow and spend so much money that demand will exceed supply and inflation will result. If money is in short supply and interest rates are high, consumer and business spending and borrowing will decline, supply will exceed demand, and unemployment will result.

One widely recognized monetarist prescription, advanced by the prominent economist Milton Friedman, is that growth in the money supply should be steady and gradual, roughly in pace with the growth in the amount of goods and services the economy produces. Anything more will lead to inflation, anything less to unemployment. Further, many monetarists, being conservative and suspicious of active governmental involvement in the economy, prefer adherence to this general rule rather than "politically" exercised discretion about monetary policy.

Supply-Side Economics

As one might expect, supply-side economics focuses on how much is produced in the economy rather than on how much is demanded, as in the Keynesian and monetarist perspectives. According to supply-side economics' leading theoretician, Arthur Laffer, government can affect the balance of supply and demand in the economy better by adjusting supply than by adjusting demand. In fact, government is seen as having created the imbalance by setting taxes so high (particularly for the highest income groups) that people have little incentive to work or to invest and thereby produce. Only if government reduces taxes sufficiently to restore incentives and make money available will people begin to work harder, invest more, and produce more. The stimulus to economic activity created by lower tax rates will, according to the supply-siders, be so great that tax revenues will actually increase as a result of higher employment and consumption.

Supply-side concerns have played an important role in recent debates over whether to reduce the deficit by taxing the rich. Rejecting liberal concerns about increasing inequality in income distribution, supply-siders have argued that income tax rates on the rich and rates for capital gains taxes on everyone should be kept low. Their argument is that the rich especially are more likely than the poor to invest their money (rather than spend it), thereby stimulating greater production and prosperity.

Compare these economic theories to the plans being offered by the president and congressional leaders? What similarities and differences do you see? What examples of successes and failures of these policies can you point to? Which approach seems most likely to achieve positive results in today's economy? Why?

borrowing to cover deficits results in government competition with all other potential borrowers in the economy, such as corporations that want to build plants or individuals who want to buy houses or cars. The deficit raises the cost of capital and the cost of doing business.

Most politicians and economists believe that persistent large deficits can lead to severe economic consequences. The long-term health of a society depends on its ability and willingness to save and invest for future growth. Resources must be invested in basic research, new products, new technologies, and education. If present consumption limits the amount of saving possible for such investment, the society risks a decline in the standard of living. The Congressional Budget Office reports that among the world's most developed countries the United States has had the greatest decline in national saving as a percentage of gross domestic product."[7] Congressional Budget Office, Assessing the Decline in the National Saving Rate (Washington, DC: Government Printing Office, 1993), pp. 2–3. National savings rates were compared for the period 1960 to 1989. This downward trend continued throughout the 1990s. See Bureau of Economic Analysis, "Note on the Personal Saving Rate," Survey of Current Business (February 1999): 8–9." on page 424 Americans saved about 5 percent of their disposable income in 2014.[8] Federal budget deficits and the national debt are major contributors to a low national saving rate.

Persistent deficits figured prominently as a political issue in the 1992 presidential campaign. Third-party candidate Ross Perot skillfully used television to criticize both major parties for inaction on the deficit and the resulting public debt. Perot clearly struck a chord with voters. He received 19 percent of the popular vote in the election, the best showing for a third-party candidate in eighty years.[9] Although he received less than half that vote when he ran again in 1996, the Reform Party that he and his followers created indicated the importance of economic reform to many Americans.

Perot's electoral strength placed pressure on elected officials to grapple seriously with the deficit. That task is not easy. A booming economy, like the one the United States enjoyed in the mid and late 1990s, can replace deficits with surpluses for a time, allowing politicians to delay making difficult economic decisions. Eventually, though, the dynamic nature of a macroeconomy ensures that challenges will return.

At the beginning of the 2000s, economic downturns signaled the return of deficits and the tough policy choices that accompany them. By 2010, another political movement—the Tea Party—had emerged to challenge incumbent politicians to take the dangers of debt and deficit seriously.

Reducing the deficit is difficult because of the sharp conflict over the alternative ways of doing it—and the pain that lower deficits leave in their wake. Choosing among cutting expenditures, increasing taxes, or some combination of the two is really the essence of politics. For example, elimination of the revenue-sharing program through which the national government granted funds to local governments lowered the deficit somewhat. However, elimination of the program also forced local governments

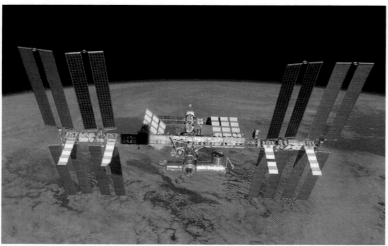

Building an orbiting space station would be of great economic benefit to some contractors and some states but would cost other states tax dollars without immediate benefit. (Wikimedia Commons)

to decide whether to increase their own taxes or cut services for local residents. As another example, building an orbiting space station or the superconducting super collider would be of great economic benefit to some contractors and some states, but at the same time it would cost the government tax dollars. Political leaders also face trade-off decisions regarding Social Security and Medicare. As the baby boom generation has begun retiring, these programs are paying out money to more individuals than the number they are collecting from, which may create a need to either increase the tax burden on working-age Americans or decrease benefits to those of retirement age. Neither option is likely to be popular because these decisions also mean that either the deficit or taxes will be higher. Raising taxes will cut the deficit, but higher taxes also mean less money in the pockets of consumers. Researchers want more government money to do their work. Social welfare advocates want more spending on poverty programs. The beneficiaries of government spending—such as military contractors, researchers, and state and local governments—obviously press to maintain and even increase their benefits. At the same time, taxpayers do not welcome proposals to raise federal revenues by increasing taxes.

These ongoing battles took a back burner in 2008 and 2009, as a national economic downturn reached crisis stage. Years of deregulation and poor decision making in the lending industry finally took their toll, as banks and other financial institutions teetered on the brink of collapse. The resulting tightening of credit markets threatened to shut down the American economy on a large scale. Concerns over banking and credit instability sent the American stock markets into free fall, losing one-third of their value in a matter of days. By early October 2008, Congress passed a law allowing Treasury Secretary Henry Paulson to spend $700 billion to purchase shares in private banks. The move was intended to restore confidence and loosen up credit availability, but not to make this partial nationalization permanent. The government began selling its shares after a few years, after banks had an opportunity to recover and stabilize.[10]

14.2b Major Components of the National Budget

Money's rise to the top of the policy agenda has deep roots in the past. Since the Great Depression of the 1930s, government has treated the economic and social needs of groups such as the elderly, the disabled, and the poor as public problems. Meeting these welfare demands has meant the expenditure of huge amounts of public money. War and the threat of war have also made their own heavy demands on public funds. Paying interest on borrowed money has itself become a major category of spending.

Figure 14.1 offers a graphic and useful summary of major budgetary trends over the past several decades. The figure divides the budget into five proportional categories: national defense, human resources, physical resources, net interest payments, and all other expenditures, which include programs such as cancer research, space exploration, highway construction, and environmental protection.

National Defense

The national government has a constitutional responsibility to provide for the nation's security. Consequently, spending on defense has always consumed a significant portion of the budget. For example, of the $10.8 million that the national government spent in 1800, more than 55 percent went to the War Department (army) and the navy.[11]

(Wikimedia Commons)

BVT Lab
Improve your test scores. Practice quizzes are available at www.BVTLab.com.

Chapter 14 | Public Policy and Economics | 427

Figure 14.1 | Federal Government Expenditures

Payments for individuals (identified here as human resources) and national defense are the largest categories of federal expenditures. National defense consumed 17 percent of the budget in 2014.

SOURCE: U.S. Office of Management and Budget, Historical Tables, Budget of the United States Government, Fiscal Year 2015 (Washington, D.C.: Government Printing Office, 2014).

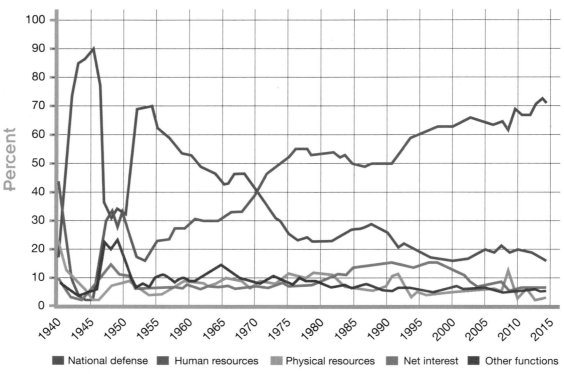

Federal Government Expenditures

Figure 14.1 shows that at the height of World War II in 1945 almost 90 percent of the budget went to defense. After a postwar drop and then an increase in the early 1950s during the Korean conflict, the proportion of federal dollars going to defense began a general decline from almost 70 percent in 1954 to less than 23 percent in 1980. In absolute dollars, the amount spent on national defense increased over this period; yet defense expenditures consumed an increasingly smaller proportion of the total budget. Other expenditure items in the budget were growing at a faster rate, and the proportional decline in defense spending became a major political issue.

One of Ronald Reagan's (1981–1989) priorities was strengthening defense; and, as Figure 14.1 shows, the proportional amount of federal spending going to national defense increased in the 1980s. However, the breakup of the Soviet Union and the end of the Cold War weakened the military's claim on the budget beginning in the early 1990s, and the proportion of the budget spent on defense went down accordingly. In 2000, the national government spent just 16 percent of its budget on national defense, but this percentage rose to over 20 percent as President George W. Bush retooled the nation's military and intelligence sectors to more effectively address the threat of terrorism.

Payments for Individuals

Payments for individuals, the second major spending category in the budget, includes social support programs that are primarily a legacy of the New Deal of the 1930s and the Great Society of the 1960s. Sometimes called human resources, such programs include Social Security, Medicare, unemployment compensation, the Supplemental Nutrition Assistance Program (SNAP), Medicaid, and supplemental security income. Retired and disabled citizens receive monthly checks through the Social Security program. Medicare provides medical care for the elderly and the disabled. The short-term unemployed receive weekly checks through the unemployment compensation program. Individuals in need receive food, medical care, or cash through programs such as SNAP, Medicaid, or supplemental security income. In administering these programs, the national government takes money from some groups in the form of retirement contributions or taxes and transfers it to other groups either in the form of cash, such as Social Security checks, or in the form of in-kind payments, such as SNAP benefits.

This category of spending, compared to national defense, is a relatively new one for the national government. Only within the past half-century has the national government administered social support programs on such a comprehensive scale. This category has grown proportionally faster than any other since the 1940s, as Figure 14.1 graphically illustrates. In 1942 payments for individuals made up less than 20 percent of all federal spending, a proportion that increased to 38 percent in 1970. This category of spending consumed over 70 percent of the budget in 2015. Such growth has prompted reformers to suggest privatizing some of these programs. One study, for example, argues that transforming the government-run Social Security program into individually controlled private retirement accounts can reduce government spending while providing an efficient and solvent method for individual financial security during old age.[12]

Interest Costs

The third major category of spending, **net interest**, represents the cost that government must pay the public for the use of borrowed money to cover budget deficits. Most individuals have, at one time or another, encountered the inevitability of making interest payments on goods they purchase. For example, most people who wish to buy a new home simply do not have enough cash to cover the full purchase price. If they want to buy a $100,000 home, they may have to borrow $80,000 from a bank or mortgage company to add to the resources they have to make the purchase. College students often take out student loans to pay for college; even if their payments are deferred until they graduate,

If someone wants to buy a $100,000 home, they may have to borrow $80,000 from a bank or mortgage company to add to their existing resources in order to make the purchase. (Shutterstock)

net interest

Charges that the government must pay to the public for the use of money borrowed to cover budget deficits and added to the interest paid to government trust funds to create total interest costs

they will eventually have to pay the money back—with interest. Borrowing money is really nothing more than using money that belongs to others. Of course, the right to use this money comes at a price, which is the payment of interest.

Money is among the most expensive items individuals can buy; and how much it costs depends on interest rates, which are in constant flux. If a home purchaser borrows $80,000 at 9 percent interest to be repaid over thirty years, the total repayment at the end of that period will amount to more than $230,000, or almost three times the original $80,000 borrowed! The amount of interest paid will vary with interest rates and the time period of the loan, but this simple example illustrates the high cost of using other people's money.

Students march in "jazz funeral" form, a funeral with music, to protest state budget cuts for the University of New Orleans. (Wikimedia Commons)

Individuals borrow money because they want things that cost more than the cash they have on hand. Governments borrow money for much the same reason. Because the money demands on government exceed the amount of money government receives in taxes, borrowing money from individual investors and financial institutions that buy government securities must cover the resulting deficit. As the deficits rise, so too must the cost of borrowing money. In 1965 the government paid $8.6 billion in net interest, about 7 percent of total federal expenditures in that year. Though only about 6.5 percent of expenditures, interest payments alone were $250 billion in 2015.

14.2c Mandatory Programs in the Budget

When the president and Congress begin to work on budget proposals every year, they do not begin with a clean budgetary slate. Present and future budgets build on past budgets in increments. This theory of **incrementalism** holds that "the largest determining factor of the size and content of this year's budget is last year's budget."[13] Expenditures are difficult to control largely because present decisions are shaped by past decisions. Budget makers cannot decide to reduce total spending from $1.9 trillion to, say, $500 billion in a single year. Just as a rapidly moving freight train cannot be stopped quickly (and without much screeching of brakes), so too budget expenditures cannot be massively and rapidly reduced from one year to the next.

Much of the budget is comprised of **mandatory programs** in which spending automatically increases from one year to the next without specific annual appropriations action by Congress. **Social entitlements**, programs in which eligible citizens receive benefits to which they are entitled by law, are a main source of mandatory programs and include Social Security, Medicare, Medicaid, public assistance programs, unemployment compensation, and retirement programs for federal employees. The largest of the mandatory programs is Social Security, which alone accounts for over 20 percent of the total budget. According to the Congressional Budget Office, "managing the growth of federal spending ... will be largely a matter of controlling the growth of mandatory outlays."[14] In a creative attempt at reducing these costs to the government, George W. Bush recommended allowing individuals to retain control over a portion of their payroll taxes in personal retirement

incrementalism

A model of decision making that holds that new policies differ only marginally from existing policies

mandatory programs

Government programs, such as Social Security expenditures, in which spending automatically increases from one year to the next without specific annual appropriations action by Congress

social entitlements

Programs, such as Social Security and Medicaid, whereby eligible individuals receive benefits according to law

accounts.[15] Though the plan was not approved, it brought the issue of mandatory spending to the forefront of American politics.

Social Security provides a good illustration of the concept of mandatory spending. Congress and the president do not decide every year whether or not the nation should have a Social Security program. Once the program was established, it became a solid rock on the political landscape, and it continues to give eligible individuals benefits year after year. A person who has made contributions to the Social Security system via payroll taxes becomes automatically eligible for Social Security benefits upon retirement at age sixty-five. Social Security expenditures are determined by the demographic movement of individuals into retirement age and by increases in payments because of inflation. Congress and the president could substantially reduce those benefits, but only at very high political and social costs.

A related program that illustrates the difficulty of cutting the budget from one year to the next is net interest. By law, interest on the debt must be paid. Failure to make such interest payments would destroy investor confidence in government securities and result in economic consequences too grave to contemplate. Thus, Congress and the president do not have much choice in the matter of paying interest. The amount paid in a given year will depend on interest rates and the size of deficits. Because of the necessity to pay interest and the existence of mandatory programs, budget makers cannot easily make proportionally large spending cuts from one year to the next.

In 2014, President Barack Obama's Office of Management and Budget estimated that about 63 percent of the 2015 budget would be comprised of mandatory programs. Net interest payments and mandatory programs together would account for almost 70 percent of the total budget in 2015. Some changes can be made in social entitlements, but the programs cannot be cut drastically; and interest must be paid. The concept of mandatory spending illustrates the obstacles Congress and the president face in their attempts to cut deficits.

14.3 The President and Congress in the Budgeting Process

Most individuals know very little about the details of the national budget or how various governmental institutions work together to arrive at specific taxing and spending policies. However, taxpayers are acutely aware of the degree to which their withholding taxes reduce their salaries, and beneficiaries of public programs notice even small changes in their benefits. From the perspective of individuals or specific groups, the politics of money is about maintaining or increasing the benefits of government spending while shifting the tax costs to someone else. If politics is the process of making choices among conflicting perceptions of national purpose, with different consequences for different people, then choices on the collection and use of public money are intensely political decisions.[16]

Budgets are essential because human wants must be tamed by the scarcity of resources. If human wants were limited, or if resources were unlimited, budgets would be unnecessary. However, because neither condition exists, the president and Congress are inevitably forced to wrestle with the necessity of coming up with a **budget**, or a planned statement of revenues and expenditures. One scholar has cited

budget

A planned statement of expenditure that includes specific categories of spending

"the twin functions of a budget process as an opportunity for claiming resources and as a procedure for rationing limited resources among claimants."[17] Budgeting lies at the intersection of the inevitability of demands and the necessity to impose constraints on those demands. Continuing budget deficits are simply a reflection of the political fact that satisfying demands is more appealing than the distasteful business of imposing constraints.

Because the money pie cannot be expanded infinitely, making budget policy is a battle over the shares of the pie that different programs should receive. In addition to the inevitability of disagreement, putting together a budget is a complicated process for several reasons. First, determining how much government will collect in taxes and how much it will spend in a given year is largely a matter of estimation. Budget makers cannot accurately predict the flow of dollars into and out of the federal treasury in a particular year. Such dollar flows are greatly influenced by the performance of the nation's economy, a matter over which the

The U.S. Treasury Department's Bureau of the Public Debt continually updates the national debt down to the last penny.

http://www.bvtlab.com/E8B97

president and Congress have little short-term control. Second, budgeting is complicated and difficult because constructing a budget is a highly decentralized process. That is, a large number of individuals and groups, both inside and outside government, help to shape the budget. The president and his Office of Management and Budget, the executive agencies, Congress and a variety of its committees and their staffs, interest groups, and sometimes even the courts—all contribute to the making of budget decisions. At the center of political conflict, the budget process reflects the decentralization inherent in the political system itself. The process would certainly be more tidy and efficient if only one individual or committee could make all budget determinations, but the framers of the Constitution did not intend such a system. Especially in the budget process, ambition counters ambition, resulting in inevitable disorder and complexity.[18]

14.3a The Stages of Budgeting

The most important governmental actors in the budgetary process are the president and his staff, Congress and its committees, and the executive agencies. Budgeting can be divided into three separate stages, with each of these three groups playing a primary role in one of them.[19]

1. *Presidential proposal* The president and his staff compile agency requests for funds, shape those requests to fit presidential priorities, and then submit to Congress a proposed Budget of the United States Government.

2. *Congressional response* Congress and its various committees review the presidential budget proposals and mold them to meet congressional priorities. If the president agrees with those congressional actions, they then become law.

3. *Agency expenditure of funds* The executive agencies spend the money pursuant to budget laws enacted by Congress and signed by the president.

fiscal year

For budget and accounting purposes in the national government, the twelve-month period beginning on October 1 and ending on September 30 of the following calendar year

Each stage occurs every year. Actual expenditures take place during a **fiscal year**, which for U.S. government budget and accounting purposes is a twelve-month period beginning each year on October 1 and ending on September 30 of the following calendar year. The calendar year designation given to the fiscal year is the calendar year in which the fiscal year ends. For example, fiscal year 2016 begins on October 1, 2015, and ends on September 30, 2016. Starting the fiscal year on October 1, rather

Corporations and the Economy

Throughout American political history government regulation of the private economic sector (or lack thereof) has been a source of conflict and occasional corruption. One of the most famous incidents of economic misconduct, the Teapot Dome scandal of the 1920s, resulted in a prison sentence for a cabinet official. Secretary of the Interior Albert Fall leased federal oil reserves to his friends in the oil industry without seeking competitive bids and received kickbacks in return.

More recent examples of economic fraud are the corporate accounting debacles of the early 2000s. Created in 1934 as a response to the uncontrolled market forces that led to worldwide depression, the Securities and Exchange Commission (SEC) was designed to enforce laws requiring accurate and public disclosures of financial health by companies offering publicly traded securities, or stocks. One such rule requires companies to register with the SEC, a process that involves "a description of the company's properties and business; a description of the security to be offered for sale; information about the management of the company; and financial statements certified by independent accountants."[1] During late 2001 and early 2002, several corporations, including giants Enron and WorldCom, were found to have violated this rule by providing false financial reports. In other words, false accounting claims vastly overstated the projected earnings of the corporations, leading to artificially inflated stock

Enron filed the largest bankruptcy in history and laid off thousands of workers who lost 401(k) savings loaded in Enron stock. (AP World Wide Photo)

prices. When the companies could no longer hide their insolvency, the false claims became public, the corporations filed for bankruptcy, many stockholders lost their investments, and many employees lost their jobs.

One of the most troubling aspects of this situation was that highly respected accounting firms, such as Arthur Andersen, played a big role in the fraudulent action. Accountants are supposed to provide independent audits of corporate financial claims; in these cases, however, the accounting firms shared in the guilt. In response to these corrupt practices, Congress passed—and the president signed—the Public Company Accounting Reform and Investor Protection Act in 2002, a measure designed to provide increased supervision over corporate accounting and stiffer penalties for misconduct—including twenty-year

prison sentences for chief financial officers certifying false reports. In signing the new law, President Bush warned: "No boardroom in America is above or beyond the law."[2]

Can the government prevent corporate corruption through tougher regulation? Does the government have a duty to protect citizens from fraud? What role should the government play in the economic sphere?

1 Securities and Exchange Commission, "The Investor's Advocate: How the SEC Protects Investors and Maintains Market Integrity," December 1999, http://www. sec.gov/about/whatwedo.shtml (September 27, 2002).

2 Suzanne Malveaux, "Bush Signs Bill to Stop 'Book Cooking,'" CNN.com, July 30, 2002.

Figure 14.2 | Major Steps in the Budgeting Process

The steps in the budgeting process for each fiscal year take two and a half years to complete. If appropriation action is not completed by September 30, Congress enacts temporary appropriations (i.e., a continuing resolution).

SOURCES: *Adapted from U.S. Office of Management and Budget,* Analytical Perspectives, Budget of the United States Government, Fiscal Year 2011 *(Washington, D.C.: Government Printing Office, 2010); and information contained in U.S. Office of Management and Budget,* Budget System and Concepts, Fiscal Year 2009 *(Washington, D.C.: Government Printing Office, 2008).*

Steps in the Budgeting Process for Fiscal Year 2017

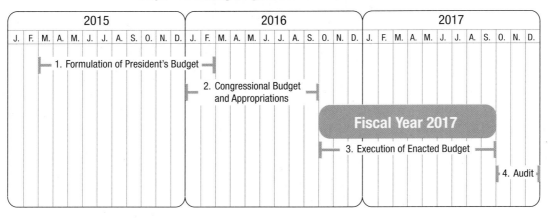

than January 1, is based on the assumption that Congress will make budget decisions in the nine-month period between the beginning of its session in January and October 1, the beginning of the fiscal year. That Congress does not always meet this deadline exemplifies the problems Congress has in making difficult budget choices.

As Figure 14.2 shows, the three stages of the budgeting process take a total of more than two years to complete. For example, the president and his staff began to formulate proposals for fiscal year 2016 in spring 2014, about eighteen months before the beginning of the fiscal year in October 2015. Given uncertainties in estimating receipts and expenditures, planning for a fiscal year so long in advance is obviously no easy task. The second stage of congressional action begins in February 2015, eight months before the start of fiscal 2016. Agencies actually spend the money in the fiscal year itself, October 1, 2015, through September 30, 2016.

Not all budgetary action by all three sets of budgetary actors concentrates on a single fiscal year at a time. At a single point in a given calendar year, each of the three stages may be in progress for three different fiscal years. In spring 2014, for example, agencies were actually spending money in fiscal year 2014, Congress was reviewing presidential proposals for year fiscal 2015, and the president and his staff were beginning to plan for 2016. The need for planning and executing money decisions seems to be eternal, and so does the process of putting together a budget.

The president is the single most important individual in the process of constructing a budget for the national government. The president's central role in the budgetary process springs from his unique position in the political system. More than the words and actions of any other person, what presidents say about the budget and the priorities their words and actions establish are especially important in shaping subsequent debate about the budget.

The president is guaranteed a central role in the budgetary process because of two important powers. First, with the help of the Office of Management and Budget, the president proposes a budget to Congress. Proposal power does not mean that presidents will necessarily get what they want. Congress can and does work its own will on the budget. The power to propose is a significant one because the president's budget proposal sets the tone of debate and becomes the standard against which congressional changes are measured.

The president's budget proposals are really political statements because, if enacted, they inevitably have different consequences for different groups. Depending on their budget priorities, presidents can propose more (or less) spending on defense or housing or education. They can propose changes in eligibility standards for entitlement programs with the hope of saving money in future years. They can propose tax cuts or increases with consequences for the general health of the economy, the size of the deficit, and the economic status of different income groups. Presidents can do all of these things with the great flair of publicity—natural to the office of the presidency—that brings guaranteed and immediate attention to their proposals. President Barack Obama announced his economic plan for fiscal year 2015 in his State of the Union address in January 2014. The plan contained a wide range of initiatives to rebuild infrastructure, stimulate economic growth and new jobs by providing incentives for innovation, meet domestic energy needs, and provide education and training opportunities. Members of Congress can oppose presidential initiatives, but the president's proposals define the budget policy debate.

In addition to the authority to make budget proposals, the president has the constitutional power to *veto budget bills passed by Congress*. Appropriations bills go through the legislative process and must ultimately be signed by the president before they become law and actual spending proceeds. The president may be opposed to an appropriations bill that Congress submits because it diverges too much from the president's original proposal. However, the president must veto the entire bill rather than portions of it. Congress can try to override the veto with an extraordinary majority (a two-thirds vote in each chamber), or Congress may try to recast the bill in terms more agreeable to the president. No other person has such power as the president to stop the budgetary process in its tracks. The ever-present threat of a presidential veto dramatizes the critical role that the president plays in the budget process. Congress, however, has substantial powers of its own to shape budgetary choices.[20]

14.3c **Congress and Budgeting**

Congressional power to make decisions on the budget is firm and clear. The Constitution states, "No money shall be drawn from the Treasury, but in Consequence of Appropriations made by Law." Presidential proposals cannot become law in the absence of congressional action. The first budgetary stage of presidential proposal is a triumph of simplicity compared to the second stage of congressional action.

BVT *Lab*

Visit www.BVTLab.com
to explore the student
resources available for
this chapter.

Chapter 14 | Public Policy and Economics | 436

Congress is a much more complicated institution than the presidency. By definition, the president is one individual to whom responsibility for budget proposals can be easily assigned. Congress is a fragmented institution with 535 individuals representing different parts of the nation and inevitably reflecting conflicting views; through voting, however, each of these individuals can help to shape the budget that emerges from Congress.

Most of the important work of budget review and decision in Congress is done in committee. In addition to the authorizing committees (such as Agriculture and Armed Services), each chamber also has "money" committees, such as those on the budget, appropriations, and revenue (called Ways and Means in the House and Finance in the Senate). Each one of these committees can affect the budget in some way. Under the best of circumstances, the process of making budget decisions is never easy because the demand for government services always outruns the supply of money to fund those services. This fundamental difficulty is heightened in Congress by the large number of individuals and committees, each moved by diverse and conflicting interests, with the capacity to shape the budget.

House Armed Services Committee chairman Mac Thornberry, R-Texas, speaks with reporters in the Rayburn House Office Building on Monday, Feb. 2, 2015. (AP World Wide Photo)

For most government programs, Congress must take two separate steps before money can actually be spent. The first step is program **authorization**, or the congressional decision to create (or continue) a program and the agency administering it. Such authorizations begin in substantive legislative committees, such as the Agriculture, Armed Services, and Interstate and Foreign Commerce committees. Authorizing legislation ordinarily contains statements of program and agency goals, as well as enabling powers to carry the program forward. Authorizations may be for one year, for several years, or open-ended. The legislation also contains a statement of money authorized to be spent on the program. For example, an authorization measure may state that an expenditure not exceeding $700 million is authorized for the following fiscal year for, say, certain pollution abatement activities carried out by the Environmental Protection Agency. No money can be legally spent, however, as the result of such an authorization measure. Agencies do not have the legal right to actually spend money unless Congress takes the second step of appropriating funds pursuant to the authorization.

This second step is program **appropriations**, the congressional decision to fund an authorized program with a specific sum of money. Such appropriations decisions are shaped by recommendations from the Appropriations Committee in each chamber. The actual amount appropriated need not be the same as the amount authorized. For example, although $700 million may be authorized for pollution abatement, only $600 million may be actually appropriated.

The authorization-appropriations sequence does not apply to all government programs. For example, the authorization (creation and subsequent amendment) of most entitlement programs includes, in effect, a permanent appropriation to fund

authorization

Congressional enactment that creates or continues a policy program and the agency administering it

appropriation

Congressional enactment that funds an authorized program with a specific sum of money

the program. By establishing the Social Security program, Congress has pledged that individuals reaching a certain age and meeting eligibility requirements will receive monthly checks. Congress can change the rules, but the amount of money spent in a given fiscal year is not dependent on specific congressional action for that year.

14.4   The Search for Better Budget Procedures

The deficit is proof of the extraordinary difficulty Congress and the president have in coming to grips with decisions on cutting expenditures and raising taxes. The substantive issues are so difficult that policy makers have naturally considered whether different budget procedures might make their task easier. Would tough budget decisions be made more readily if procedures for arriving at them were different?

Proposed budget changes come in a variety of forms. The most controversial budget reforms are proposals to give the president **line-item veto** power and to add an amendment to the Constitution requiring a balanced budget. Under current rules, the president must sign or veto an entire bill sent by Congress. An appropriations bill may contain many specific programs, and the president must either accept or reject all of them in the bill. The line-item veto would give the president the power to reject some items in the bill and to allow others to become law. Governors in forty-three states have line-item veto power, which proponents argue increases the managerial capability chief executives should have. With this power, its supporters say, presidents would not be forced to accept wasteful spending projects that members of Congress pack into a bill. Riding a wave of reform, Republicans in the 104th Congress passed the Line Item Veto Act in 1996 in order to provide the president with this power. President Clinton's first exercise of this power, however, was met with a legal challenge; and in 1998, the Supreme Court ruled the act invalid for its circumvention of the law-making procedure set forth in the Constitution. Although the law was struck down, the idea remains alive. Amendments have been introduced in recent years to change the Constitution in order to allow for a presidential line-item veto. Such a reform is not without its congressional detractors, though. Many members fear that the line-item veto would result in a discernible shift in budgetary power from Congress to the president. Given the much larger number of options the power would afford, presidential flexibility in determining the shape of the budget would greatly increase. Congressional ability to mold the budget would correspondingly diminish.

The size of deficits and a growing public debt have also sparked interest in a constitutional amendment that would require a balanced budget. Proponents of a **balanced budget amendment** argue that only a constitutional mandate will force Congress and the president to produce balanced budgets. Opponents hold that the amendment risks tax increases and major reductions in a wide range of politically popular programs. Several times over the last decade, balanced budget amendment proposals have failed to get the constitutionally required two-thirds vote of the House and Senate before being sent on to the states for ratification. In 1992 Congress considered an amendment proposal that would have mandated a three-fifths majority, except in a military emergency, in the House and Senate to allow deficit spending. The amendment did not receive the necessary two-thirds vote in either chamber;

line-item veto

Most state governors have this power, through which a chief executive, reacting to a bill passed by the legislature, may accept some items in the bill while also rejecting other items in the same bill. The president does not have this power.

balanced budget amendment

A proposal for a constitutional amendment that would require the federal government to operate with a budget in which revenues equaled or exceeded expenditures

BVT *Lab*

Flashcards are available
for this chapter at
www.BVTLab.com.

438 | Public Policy and Economics

Chapter 14 |

however, the amendment had substantial support, a sign that the political frustration of dealing with persistent deficits has led to a serious search for extraordinary constitutional remedies. Such efforts, although still pursued in every Congress, have lost some momentum in the past few years.

Although the line-item veto power and the balanced budget amendment remain proposals, Congress and the president have passed three laws resulting in fundamental changes in the process of deciding on budget expenditures while wrestling with the pain of reducing deficits.

The Congressional Budget and Impoundment Control Act of 1974

Before 1974, Congress reviewed the president's budget in a highly decentralized, piecemeal fashion. Budget totals resulted from a process of summing up the work of separate committees rather than any conscious effort to consider the budget comprehensively. Nor was there institutionalized consideration of the relationship between spending and expected revenue, a violation of sound budget practice.

With increasing frequency, appropriations bills were not enacted by the beginning of the fiscal year. In the absence of appropriations laws, some agencies were forced to operate under a **continuing resolution**, a temporary funding measure passed by Congress. In addition, the relentless growth of the budget produced demands for more budgetary information, and the regularity of annual deficits sparked heated battles within Congress and between Congress and the president over who was to blame for the budgetary "red ink." In fact, in an unprecedented use of presidential impoundment powers, President Nixon refused to spend billions of dollars already appropriated. He did so on the grounds that he was forced to take action to limit spending because Congress had not done so.

As a response to these problems, the **Congressional Budget and Impoundment Control Act of 1974** changed the fiscal year from a July 1–June 30 sequence to an October 1–September 30 sequence in order to give Congress more time to review the president's budget. The act also created the **Congressional Budget Office (CBO)**, a congressional staff unit with the responsibility of providing Congress with needed information about the budget and the analytical expertise to sharpen budgetary choices for Congress; placed limits on the president's impoundment powers; created budget committees in both the House and Senate to provide a mechanism for comprehensive budget review by Congress; and established a timetable (revised by subsequent legislation) for the congressional budget review process.

The president submits his proposed budget to Congress early in the calendar year. Congressional committees review the programs within their jurisdictions and offer budget estimates to the budget committees by mid-March. With the help of the CBO, the budget committees pursue a more comprehensive budget review and report to the House and Senate a budget resolution containing targets for total revenues, total expenditures, and money to be spent in functional categories across the budget for the next fiscal year. The resolution is to be adopted by the full House and Senate by April 15. Legislation on appropriations and revenue is then to proceed in light of the budget targets set in the resolution. Congressional money decisions and budget targets are to be reconciled in time for spending to begin at the start of the fiscal year on October 1; however, in some years Congress has not been able to meet these procedural deadlines required by law. For example, in the fall of 1990 not a single one of the appropriations measures was enacted by the time the new fiscal year had begun.

continuing resolution

Legislative action taken by Congress to allow spending to proceed at the previous year's level when Congress has not met the deadline for reaching agreement on appropriations for the next fiscal year

Congressional Budget and Impoundment Control Act of 1974

Legislation that significantly changed congressional budget procedures by creating budget committees, establishing a budget decision timetable, changing the fiscal year, placing limits on presidential impoundments, and establishing the Congressional Budget Office

Congressional Budget Office (CBO)

A congressional staff unit that provides Congress with budgetary expertise, independent of the president's budget staff, to help Congress clarify budgetary choices

President Barack Obama meets with the National Commission on Fiscal Responsibility and Reform, a bipartisan panel tasked with finding ways to reduce federal deficits. (AP World Wide Photo)

Gramm-Rudman-Hollings

In response to the problem of deficits, Congress enacted the Balanced Budget and Emergency Deficit Control Act of 1985, more popularly known as Gramm-Rudman-Hollings after the senators who sponsored the legislation. The act, as later amended, mandated progressive annual cuts in the deficit and set into motion a process of automatic across-the-board spending cuts to achieve a balanced budget by 1993. The president ordered the cuts through the process of **sequestration**. Some programs—such as Social Security, Medicaid, and interest payments on the debt—were exempted from the cuts.

Gramm-Rudman-Hollings was enacted in the hopes of forcing Congress and the president to reduce the deficit. One problem with the deficit targets is that they encouraged the use of budget-reducing "gimmicks," which made it appear that cuts were made when in fact they were not. An example of a gimmick is pushing back a government payday several days from the fiscal year in question (say October 1) to the prior fiscal year (say September 29) so that the payroll will not be counted as expenditure in the fiscal year under review. However, since the money was spent anyway, if only at a different time, the cut was not real. The deficits continued, so Congress and the president tried a new law in 1990.

Budget Enforcement Act of 1990

Congress made fundamental changes in Gramm-Rudman-Hollings and tried a new approach to the deficit in the **Budget Enforcement Act of 1990**. The 1990 act shifts the emphasis of congressional action from deficit reduction to the control of spending.[21] Rather than being driven by overall deficit targets, Congress is limited by caps on discretionary spending and by constraints on changes in mandatory spending.

For fiscal years 1991 through 1993, the law placed caps on spending in each of the three categories of defense, international, and domestic discretionary—that is, nonmandatory—spending. The budget for the Federal Bureau of Investigation is an example of domestic discretionary spending because Congress can change FBI budget amounts from one year to the next. Medicare payments to hospitals to fund health care for the elderly is an example of mandatory spending because eligible individuals automatically and regularly receive benefits without specific congressional

sequestration

The process through which the president makes budget cuts in government programs to meet the mandates in law requiring ceilings on specific categories of spending

Budget Enforcement Act of 1990

Legislation that fundamentally changed budget deficit reduction efforts from the focus on deficit targets contained in Gramm-Rudman-Hollings to a focus on ceilings or caps on specific categories of spending

House Commerce, Justice, Science, and Related Agencies subcommittee Chairman Rep. Frank Wolf, R–VA (right) asks a question of FBI director Robert Mueller, back to camera, on Capitol Hill in Washington, D.C., on April 6, 2011, during the subcommittee's hearing on the FBI's budget. (AP World Wide Photo)

authorizing action from one year to the next. If discretionary spending exceeded the ceilings, then sequestration cuts were to be made within the category in which excess spending occurred. Under the law, all discretionary spending was combined into a single category in fiscal years 1994 and 1995. In addition, mandatory program increases had to be balanced by cuts in nonexempt programs or by revenue increases. Cuts were not required during war or a downturn in economic growth.[22] These complex budgeting limits felt less restrictive during the economic upturn of the mid and late 1990s. The return to deficit spending in 2002, however, reminded the government that it is crucial to have these rules in place for handling the less rosy economic forecasts that are often lurking just around the corner.

The rules of the Budget Enforcement Act were extended several times and then eventually replaced by a concept in the 2000s called PAYGO, or "pay as you go." This means that items added to a budget that result in additional spending must be accompanied by corresponding cuts or increases in revenue to offset their effects. This approach to handling the difficulties and temptations of deficit spending was codified as the **Statutory Pay-As-You-Go Act** in 2010. It maintains a similar—though more extensive—series of exemptions as previous laws. Despite these statutory efforts at limiting deficit spending, the practice continues.

Almost no one is satisfied with the procedures for considering and passing a budget. Elected officials and their staffs spend inordinate amounts of time dealing with budget issues. Congress has missed budget deadlines, government agencies have sometimes closed down temporarily for lack of spending authority, and deficits continue. Critics wonder, "Is this any way to run a government?" Efforts to tinker with existing procedures will continue, and proposals for new ones are inevitable;[23] however, tinkering with procedures is a symptom of a deeper political problem. Continuing entitlement programs at current levels, reducing the debt, and avoiding both tax increases and deep cuts in general government spending cannot all be achieved simultaneously. Such budgetary pressures have placed obvious strains on procedures for deciding budget policy. Ultimately, those pressures and strains emerge from the intense political resistance to spending cuts or tax increases. As recent budget proposals illustrate, harnessing wants with available resources remains the quintessential challenge to government in the 2000s.

Statutory Pay-As-You-Go Act

Law passed in 2010 that requires budget increases to be offset by either reductions elsewhere or increased revenues

CHAPTER REVIEW

1. Conflict over economic policy has been at or near the top of the political agenda throughout American history. Government makes two major types of economic policy: fiscal and monetary. Fiscal policy assesses the impact on the economy as a whole of governmental decisions to tax, spend, and borrow; monetary policy concerns the availability and cost of money and credit in the economy.

2. Budget deficits, the dominant economic policy issue Congress and the president faced for much of the past few decades, can be reduced by cutting expenditures, increasing taxes, or some combination of these two strategies. Payments for individuals make up the largest category in the national budget. The cost of borrowing money has become a significant national expenditure. Much of the budget is comprised of mandatory spending.

3. Given the decentralization of power in the political system, no single individual or group alone can decide the size and shape of the budget. The president has the power to make budget proposals, but money can be spent only after Congress reviews and revises those proposals and enacts them into law. Deficits persist despite procedural changes. Continuing calls to revise procedures are a consequence of the collision between the necessity to impose constraints and the political resistance to spending cuts or tax increases.

KEY TERMS

Readings for Further Study

For a thorough understanding of economic policy making, there is no better starting point than a good text on economics, such as Paul A. Samuelson and William D. Nordhaus's *Economics*, 19th ed. (New York: McGraw Hill, 2010).

Analyses of current economic problems, along with an excellent compendium of useful economic data, are found in the *Economic Report of the President*, written by the president's Council of Economic Advisers, and available online: http://www.gpo.gov/fdsys/browse/collection.action?collectionCode=ERP.

Comprehensive information on the budget can be found in a document the Office of Management and Budget produces each year as the president submits a budget to Congress. The Budget of the United States Government contains extensive analysis of budgetary issues, detailed personnel and budgetary data for each agency in the government, and a variety of historical tables. The Congressional Budget Office also issues periodic reports that analyze the president's proposals, assess the state of the economy, and offer Congress spending and revenue options to reduce the deficit. See: http://www.whitehouse.gov/omb/budget.

The New Politics of the Budgetary Process, 5th ed. (New York: Longman, 2003) by Aaron Wildavsky and Naomi Caiden is a superb analysis of the political environment of budgeting and the enormous changes that have taken place since Wildavsky first wrote on the topic in 1964.

Irene S. Rubin takes up the topic of balanced budgets in *Balancing the Federal Budget* (New York: Chatham House, 2003).

An updated look at budgetary rules and politics is *The Federal Budget: Politics, Policy, and Process*, 3rd ed. (Washington, D.C.: Brookings, 2007) by Allen Schick with Felix LoStracco.

Two good recent texts focusing on economic policy are James J. Gosling's *Economics, Politics and American Public Policy* (Armonk, NY: M. E. Sharpe, 2007), and Jeffrey E. Cohen's, *Politics and Economic Policy in the United States*, 2nd ed. (Boston: Houghton Mifflin, 2000).

Finally, George C. Wilson's *This War Really Matters* (Washington, D.C.: CQ Press, 2000) is an inside look at the budget battles over defense spending.

Notes

1. Eighteenth-century English economist Adam Smith called this idea the "invisible hand" in his classic *Wealth of Nations*.

2. 17 U.S. (4 Wheaton) 316 (1819).

3. Citizens for Budget Reform, "National Debt," http://www.budget.org/NationalDebt/Debt/ (September 25, 2002).

4. U.S. Office of Management and Budget, *Budget Baselines, Historical Data, and Alternatives for the Future* (Washington, DC: Government Printing Office, 1993), pp. 278–279.

5. U.S. Office of Management and Budget, *Historical Tables*, http://www.whitehouse.gov/omb/budget/Historicals (December 15, 2014).

6. Ibid.

7. Congressional Budget Office, *Assessing the Decline in the National Saving Rate* (Washington, DC: Government Printing Office, 1993), pp. 2–3. National savings rates were compared for the period 1960 to 1989. This downward trend continued throughout the 1990s. See Bureau of Economic Analysis, "Note on the Personal Saving Rate," *Survey of Current Business* (February 1999): 8–9.

8. Bureau of Economic Analysis, "National Income and Product Accounts Table," November 25, 2014, http://www.bea.gov/, (December 15, 2014).

9. In 1912, after a split in the Republican Party, Theodore Roosevelt, a former president, received 27 percent of the popular vote as the candidate of the Progressive Party.

10. *Sacramento Bee*, "U.S. Public to Acquire Stake in Banks," 2008, http://www.sacbee.com (October 15, 2008).

11. U.S. Bureau of the Census, *Historical Statistics of the United States: Colonial Times to 1970*, pt. 2 (Washington, DC: Government Printing Office, 1975), pp. 1114–1115.

12. See, for example, June O'Neill, "The Trust Fund, the Surplus, and the Real Social Security Problem," *The Cato Project on Social Security Privatization 26* (April 9, 2002).

13. Aaron Wildavsky and Naomi Caiden, *The New Politics of the Budgetary Process*, 4th ed. (New York: Addison Wesley, 2000).

14. Congressional Budget Office, *Reducing the Deficit: Spending and Revenue Options* (Washington, DC: Government Printing Office, 1993), p. 225.

15. *A Blueprint for New Beginnings* (Washington, DC: Government Printing Office, 2001), pp. 45–48.

16. For the argument that "budgeting is at its very core political," see Donald F. Kettl, *Deficit Politics: Public Budgeting in Its Institutional and Historical Context* (New York: Macmillan, 1992), pp. 156–157.

17. Allen Schick, *Congress and Money: Budgeting, Spending, and Taxing* (Washington, DC: Urban Institute, 1980), p. 570.

18. See "Madisonian Budgeting, or Why the Process Is So Complicated," in Joseph White and Aaron Wildavsky, *The Deficit and the Public Interest: The Search for Responsible Budgeting in the 1980s* (Berkeley: University of California Press, 1989), pp. 1–17.

19. An excellent brief review of the budget process can be found in *The Budget System and Concepts, Budget of the United States Government, Fiscal Year 2005* (Washington, DC: Government Printing Office, 2004).

20. For a good review of relationships between the branches in the budgetary process, see *The Federal Budget: Politics, Policy, and Process*, 3rd ed. (Washington, DC: Brookings, 2007), by Allen Schick.

21. Congressional Budget Office, "The 1990 Budget Package: An Interim Assessment," December 1990, p. 2 (mimeo).

22. U.S. House of Representatives, Committee on Ways and Means, *Background Material on the Federal Budget and the President's Proposals for Fiscal Year 1994* (Washington, DC: Government Printing Office, 1993), pp. 71, 82.

23. For a summary discussion of budget process reforms, see *Broken Purse Strings: Congressional Budgeting 1974 to 1988* (Washington, DC: Urban Institute, 1988), pp. 109–129, by Rudolph G. Penner and Alan J. Abramson.

POP QUIZ

1. _____ is French for "leave things alone." It is the belief that government should not interfere in the workings of the economy.

2. The _____ ____ _____ _____ _____ is the Executive Office agency that provides the president with budgetary information.

3. _____ is the sum of the deficits of prior years.

4. The president has the power to _____ budget bills passed by the Congress.

5. The _____ _____ amendment is a proposed amendment to the Constitution that would require the federal government to operate with a budget in which revenues equaled or exceeded expenditures.

6. Free trade is the belief that American interests are better served by allowing foreign producers to sell their goods without restriction. T F

7. Monetary policy involves government decisions about how much money should circulate and what the interest rate should be. T F

8. Social Security, Medicare, and the Supplemental Nutrition Assistance Program are all examples of payments for individuals. T F

9. Line-item veto would give the president the power to accept some items in a bill and reject other items in the same bill. T F

10. Gramm-Rudman-Hollings mandated sequestration to achieve a balanced budget by 1991. T F

11. Government involvement in the economy has increased dramatically since which of the following occurred?

    A) The line-item veto was first utilized by President Clinton.

    B) Establishment of the Congressional Budget Office (CBO)

    C) Ratification of the Gramm-Rudman-Hollings Act

    D) The New Deal and Great Depression

12. The fiscal policy of the government entails which of the following?

    A) the submission of governmental budgets on a twelve-month time frame starting with October 1 and ending with September 30 of every year

    B) manipulating the money supply and interest rate

    C) decisions about taxing and spending that affect the economic life of a nation

    D) excesses in government revenues over government expenditures

13. Deficit is an excess of government's _____.

    A) revenues over expenditures

    B) expenditures on national defense

    C) expenditures on Social Security

    D) expenditures over revenues

14. Mandatory programs are government programs where which of the following occurs?

    A) Individual state participation is mandated by federal law.

    B) Spending is restricted to only programs mandated by federal law.

    C) Spending automatically increases without any action by the Congress.

    D) Spending is restricted to congressionally mandated programs.

15. The following are all examples of attempts to control the national debt except _____.

    A) balanced budget amendment

    B) socialism

    C) line-item veto

    D) PAYGO

Chapter
15

Domestic Policy

In This Chapter

Chapter Objectives

Americans typically divide the substance of public policy into two categories—foreign and domestic. While foreign policy will be the focus of the next chapter, in this chapter we explore a few of the thousands of **domestic policies** the American government enacts each year. In the 2015 fiscal year, domestic programs accounted for about $3 trillion in government spending. As explained in the previous chapter, much of this money (over two-thirds) is committed to nondiscretionary programs, such as Social Security, that have grown and changed incrementally over a long period of time.

However, some of the financial commitment—such as recent job creation efforts—is dedicated to new and developing programs. Thus, on an annual basis, Americans must face tough decisions about which programs to expand and which to abandon, when to continue with an existing approach and when to change course, and when to embark on something entirely new.

Since we cannot address the entire gamut of domestic policies in the space of a single chapter, we focus on two significant policy areas and explore them in detail. First, social welfare programs are examined. Ranging from mandatory entitlements that benefit everyone directly, such as Social Security, to need-based efforts that are targeted at specific segments of society, such as welfare. These programs aim to ameliorate economic inequality.

domestic policy

A category of public policy that is comprised of policy decisions on matters affecting individuals within a political system

Second, this chapter addresses environmental policy. As the human population continues to grow and consume resources, Americans will be faced with more and more challenges in our efforts to devise a sustainable environmental policy that provides for the needs of human, plant, and animal ecosystems.

15.1 Debates Over Public Purposes

Differences over what government should do beyond protection of the nation against external threat and protection of individual citizens from each other are at the core of political conflict. Should the government fund programs for farmers, for the elderly, for the poor? Should the government subsidize the work of defense contractors, universities, and medical researchers? Should the government give aid to the middle class in the form of favorable tax policies and pensions?

Over the past century, enormous changes in the role of government have produced new relationships between the government and citizens. How these changes occur is an important issue in the analysis of policies. What government should do, who should gain the benefits of government action, and who should pay the costs are common questions in policy debate.

As explained in the policy process chapter, new demands and new issues get on the policy agenda in a variety of ways. Changes in the social and economic environment produce new groups and new problems and, consequently, new issues. Industrialization, the rise of corporations, and the emergence of a national economy shaped the post–Civil War period. The resulting stresses and strains changed relationships among groups, which then

Somebody must pay for farm programs, retirement pensions, and food and nutrition programs. Here farmer Rob Wheeler speaks at the "Keep Local Farms" program launch and urges consumers to chip in and help save the region's dairy farms, which are struggling with record-low prices being paid for their milk. (AP World Wide Photo)

resorted to asking the government for help. Crises can also indelibly change the policy agenda. The Great Depression in the 1930s so threatened the nation's political and social institutions that the government enacted welfare and regulatory policies radically different from those of the past.

Debate over the appropriate role of the government frequently begins with the perceptions of the *self-interests* of various groups and individuals. Farmers want help in their battles against falling agricultural prices. Consumers want help in their battles against shoddy or dangerous products. The elderly want help in the economic uncertainties of retirement. Corporations want help in their battles against competitors.

Through political parties, the mass media, and interest groups, demands for help are made on government institutions. In the process, self-interest is frequently cloaked in the mantle of the *national interest*. That is, groups often claim that what is good for them is really good for the nation. Determining whether groups are right in such claims is the substance of much political debate. Since most politicians desire reelection, they do their best to satisfy (or even create) demands that the government provide help. These demands are frequently in intractable conflict. Somebody must pay for farm programs, retirement pensions, and food and nutrition programs. Conflicts between the houses of Congress or between Congress and the president reflect these struggles.

Yet policies are not always the precise result of a collision of differing perceptions of self-interest. Some groups in and out of government favor certain policies because they are "right" and "fair." For example, the poor and the destitute lack the resources to exercise their economic claims on government. The idea that the government provide needy citizens with life's basic necessities has a powerful appeal and political support that goes beyond self-interest.

15.1a Social Welfare Policies

The expression **social welfare** has no precise definition. It is burdened by the unfavorable connotations frequently attached to the word *welfare*. To some, welfare simply means public money given to people whose desire to live off the public dole is greater than their desire to work for a living. However, within the category of social welfare policy are a large number of public programs serving heterogeneous groups of people.

The Census Bureau defines the concept of social welfare as "all governmental programs directed specifically toward promoting the well-being of individuals and families."[1] This definition catches within its net a large number of programs. The breadth of the concept signals the wide-ranging presence of government in the lives of citizens.

The data in Table 15.1 illustrate the growth of government social welfare spending since the start of the Great Depression. In 1929, government at all levels spent less than 4 percent of the gross national product (GNP) on social welfare programs. By 2010, this proportion had more than tripled. At 5.7 percent, social insurance programs constitute the second largest category of social welfare spending. Medical programs, now the largest category, include Medicare and have been the fastest growing part of the social welfare budget in recent years. Public aid, comprised of programs intended for the poor, such as Supplemental Nutrition Assistance Program (SNAP) and Supplemental Security Income (SSI), is the third largest category. These are means-tested programs and are discussed later in this chapter. Recipients qualify for support only if their incomes are below a certain level. Social insurance and public aid are **social entitlements**, which are programs in which individuals receive benefits they are entitled to by law.

Social insurance alone accounts for about 40 percent of all social welfare expenditures. Social insurance, medical and health, and public aid combined account for about 93 percent of total social welfare spending, while veterans' affairs, education, and other programs make up the rest. A review of how the national government became so heavily committed to providing social welfare offers insights on how issues move onto the policy agenda.

To some, welfare simply means public money given to people whose desire to live off the public dole is greater than their desire to work for a living. For others, it is the only way to feed and clothe their children. (Shutterstock)

social welfare

Governmental programs, such as social insurance and poverty programs, directed specifically toward promoting the well-being of individuals and families

social entitlements

Programs, such as Social Security and Medicaid, whereby eligible individuals receive benefits according to law

table 15.1 | Gross Domestic Product and Social Welfare Expenditures, 1929–2010

In 1929, government at all levels spent less than 4 percent of GNP on social welfare programs. By the mid-1960s, government social welfare spending accounted for more than 10 percent of GDP. The largest category of social welfare spending is comprised of federal social insurance programs, followed by health and medical programs. Social welfare spending as a percentage of GDP gives an indication of how much society's total output of goods and services is devoted to these programs.

	1929		1940		1950		1960	
GNP	$101,000	(100)	$95,100	(100)	$266,800	(100)	$506,700	(100)
Total welfare	$3,921	(3.9)	$8,795	(9.2)	$23,508	(8.8)	$52,293	(10.3)
Social insurance	$342	(0.3)	$1,272	(1.3)	$4,947	(1.7)	$19,307	(3.8)
Education	$2,434	(2.4)	$2,561	(2.7)	$6,674	(2.5)	$17,626	(3.5)
Public aid	$60	(0.1)	$3,597	(3.8)	$2,496	(0.9)	$4,101	(0.8)
Health and medical programs	$351	(0.3)	$616	(0.6)	$2,064	(0.8)	$4,464	(0.9)
Veterans' programs	$658	(0.6)	$629	(0.7)	$6,866	(2.6)	$5,479	(1.1)
Housing	—		$4	*	$15	*	$177	*
Other social welfare	$76	(0.1)	$116	(0.1)	$448	(0.2)	$1,139	(0.2)

	1970		1980		1990		2000	
GNP	$1,023,100	(100)	$2,718,900	(100)	$5,800,500	(100)	$9,951,500	(100)
Total welfare	$145,979	(14.3)	$492,213	(18.1)	$566,100	(9.8)	$1,027,827	(10.3)
Social insurance	$54,691	(5.3)	$229,754	(8.5)	$282,096	(4.8)	$445,450	(4.5)
Education	$50,846	(5.0)	$121,050	(4.5)	$12,286	(0.2)	$21,851	(0.2)
Public aid	$16,488	(1.6)	$72,703	(2.7)	$63,481	(1.1)	$106,285	(1.1)
Health and medical programs	$10,030	(1.0)	$26,762	(1.0)	$188,808	(3.3)	$427,194	(4.3)
Veterans' programs	$9,078	(0.9)	$21,466	(0.8)	$17,687	(0.3)	$25,004	(0.3)
Other social welfare	$4,145	(0.4)	$13,599	(0.5)	$1,742	*	$2,043	*

	2010**	
GNP	$14,498,900	(100)
Total welfare	$2,076,109	(14.3)
Social insurance	$928,660	(5.7)
Education	$56,757	(0.4)
Public aid	$217,858	(1.5)
Health and medical programs	$892,410	(6.2)
Veterans' programs	$51,429	(0.4)
Other social welfare	$28,005	(0.2)

Note: All monetary amounts are in millions. Percent of GNP/GDP appears in parentheses. Figures prior to 1970 measure gross national product rather than gross eomestic product.

*Less than 0.05 percent   **Some data are for 2009

SOURCES: For 1929 and 1940, Social Security Administration. Data for 1950 and 1960 are taken from Social Security Administration, Social Security Bulletin: Annual Statistical Supplement, 1990 (Washington, D.C.: Government Printing Office, 1990), p. 100. All other data are from U.S. Census Bureau, Statistical Abstract of the United States (Washington, D.C.: Government Printing Office).

At the beginning of the Republic in the late eighteenth century, the national government was miniscule. The pervasive presence of the national government in the twenty-first century symbolizes the drastic changes in the relationship between government and individuals over the past two hundred years. Such changes did not come gradually. Rather, the national government's presence grew in relatively short bursts of activity, resulting in an ever-larger government that maintained its size in succeeding decades.

The domestic activities of the national government before the twentieth century were relatively limited. There were no Social Security programs, no health programs such as Medicare and Medicaid, no unemployment compensation programs, no food stamp/SNAP programs, no poverty programs, and no programs to meet the special needs of the elderly or of individuals with disabilities. There were no public programs to help nineteenth-century factory workers who lost their jobs or were disabled or to help families who lost a breadwinner. The national government taxed relatively little, spent relatively little, and did relatively little. It was, consequently, a shadow rather than an omnipresent force in the daily lives of most citizens. Today a widely held expectation is that the national government should assume major responsibilities for social welfare. However, this contemporary expectation contrasts sharply with the political attitudes that were dominant a century ago.

15.2a The Philosophy of Social Darwinism

The dominant philosophy that shaped attitudes on the role of government in the late nineteenth century was **social Darwinism**, a set of ideas that applied Charles Darwin's theory of biological evolution to society. Darwin's theory held that physical changes in living organisms evolved as responses to the demands of survival and that organisms that adapted most successfully to their environments were most likely to survive. The theory of social Darwinism held that social relationships took place within a "struggle for survival" and that in this struggle only the "most fit" survive. Just as living organisms evolved to higher states, so too does society as a whole progress to a higher state as natural selection proceeds.

The theory seemed to offer intellectual justification for limited government and the unfettered growth and expansion of big industry and business in the late nineteenth century.[2] Since society could best progress to higher forms through its natural processes of competition and survival with no outside interference, government should not act on behalf of those too weak to survive on their own. Herbert Spencer, a British philosopher whose name is closely associated with social Darwinism, argued that government should limit itself to protecting the rights of individuals to pursue their own ends. In this view, government should not assume the role of providing for social welfare because such action would interfere with natural forces acting to improve society as a whole.[3]

Herbert Spencer, a British philosopher, argued that government should limit itself to protecting the rights of individuals to pursue their own ends. (Wikimedia Commons)

social Darwinism

A set of ideas applying Charles Darwin's theory of biological evolution to society and holding that social relationships occur within a struggle for survival in which only the fittest survive

15.2b The Progressive Era

Social Darwinism, as a set of ideas about society and the role of government, was dominant in the generation after the Civil War. Rapid urbanization, nationalization of the economy, and bigness in industry meant an end to the relative self-sufficiency individuals enjoyed in a less complicated agricultural society. The concentration of large numbers of people in urban areas strained the ability of local governments to provide essential services and bred a variety of social problems such as poverty and inadequate housing. Increasingly large and faceless companies provided goods and services to consumers who had little power to influence corporate decisions. Similarly, the availability of jobs and the quality of the work environment were matters over which workers had little control.

Opinions vary on whether too many or too few people qualify for public assistance. The actual number of those receiving welfare (via TANF) is available from the Department of Health and Human Services.

http://www.bvtlab.com/367f7

Such conditions gave rise to questions about the consequences of unfettered free enterprise. The limited role that government played at all levels increasingly became a matter of policy debate. It was in this environment of rapid social and economic change that reform movements began. This period of reform, named the **Progressive Era** by historians, generally spanned the last decade of the nineteenth century and the years of the twentieth century before World War I.

Progressive public policy goals included the replacement of corrupt politics by civil service systems, the regulation of monopolies, and the protection of consumers against unsafe products. Progressives also pressed for a more substantive role for government in aiding specific groups who suffered due to rapid industrialism.[4] Most of the initiatives for such social welfare legislation came at the state, rather than the national, level. Laws on minimum wages, worker's compensation, and pensions all directly countered the social Darwinist view that government ought to play a minimal role in social and economic relationships. Progressive efforts at the state level to redress the economic and social imbalances created by rapid industrialization and urbanization laid the groundwork for the revolutionary change in the national government role that was to come.

15.2c The New Deal Policy Revolution

The **New Deal** spanned the first two terms of President Franklin D. Roosevelt (1933–1945). His revolutionary initiatives established the pervasive and active national government role taken for granted today.

The easy tranquility of the national government during the 1920s was exploded by the Great Depression, a period of massive and severe economic hardship that rivaled the Civil War in its cataclysmic impact on the nation's political institutions. Banks failed, companies went bankrupt, home and farm mortgages were foreclosed, industrial production plummeted, and unemployment soared. Millions of people lost jobs, homes, and bank accounts, with the attendant social misery such losses inevitably bring.[5] Few government programs existed to cushion the shock of this economic disaster. Whatever government programs existed (almost entirely at the state and local level) were simply overwhelmed by the sharp and sweeping economic decline. In responding to the economic crisis of the Great Depression, the national government for the first time assumed the active and extensive role now expected.

Progressive Era

An urban reform movement of the late nineteenth and early twentieth centuries that called for direct primaries, restrictions on corporations, and improved public services that was influential in the administrations of Theodore Roosevelt and Woodrow Wilson

New Deal

The first two terms of President Franklin D. Roosevelt (1933–1945), whose revolutionary policy initiatives established a pervasive and active role for the national government

The Depression's impact on the public policy agenda was clear and unmistakable. Roosevelt was determined to take immediate and forceful action to bolster the nation's confidence in the government's ability to deal with the crisis. On the day after his inauguration as president, Roosevelt called Congress into special session, "convened in an atmosphere of wartime crisis." Congress gave every indication of wanting to be led, and the president accommodated this desire by sending to Capitol Hill a flurry of proposals for action. By the end of the special session, the famous "100 days," Congress passed every one of Roosevelt's fifteen proposals.[6]

Enacted during the New Deal was the insurance of bank deposits by the Federal Deposit Insurance Corporation, Social Security for the aged, unemployment compensation, and minimum wage and maximum-hours requirements. Designed to relieve the suffering of practically every social group touched by the Depression, these programs are all now embedded in the policy role of government. *Public expectations that government "do something" about social and economic problems flowered during the Roosevelt presidency.* An interlocking relationship between heightened public demands and government efforts to meet those demands developed. Government in Washington would no longer be distant, relaxed, and indifferent.

15.2d Expansion of the National Role in the Great Society

The New Deal firmly established the national government as the most important participant in ensuring the social and economic welfare of individuals. During subsequent decades, major New Deal programs such as Social Security, federal insurance for bank deposits, and unemployment compensation have been changed in incremental steps; but the existence of such programs is no longer seriously debated.

The next period of major change in the role of the national government occurred during the **Great Society** of Lyndon Johnson's presidency (1963–1969). Johnson assumed office after the assassination of President John F. Kennedy in November 1963, an event that seared the nation nearly as much as the attack on Pearl Harbor in 1941. National grief turned into popular support for proposals that Johnson pressed as unfinished business of the slain president. This support combined with Johnson's landslide victory over conservative Barry Goldwater and huge gains by the Democratic Party in Congress in 1964 to produce fertile ground for further growth of the national government's role.

President Lyndon B. Johnson, who succeeded to the presidency after the assassination of John F. Kennedy in 1963, expanded the role of the national government with the Great Society. (Wikimedia Commons)

The Civil Rights Act of 1964 and the Voting Rights Act of 1965 finally provided by law rights long denied to African Americans. The Equal Opportunity Act and the Food Stamp Act of 1964 explicitly dealt with the plight of poor Americans. The Elementary and Secondary Education Act of 1964 provided federal aid for the disadvantaged in the nation's schools. Perhaps the most significant change in the social welfare role of the national government was the amendment of the Social Security Act in 1965 to provide health care for the aged (Medicare) and the poor (Medicaid).

The Great Society was the last major period in which the national government embarked on new social welfare initiatives. Growing budget deficits and foreign policy concerns, coupled with the election of conservative leaders such as Nixon, Reagan, and the two Bushes, made continued expansion of social welfare programs both unpopular and unlikely. By the mid-1990s, in fact, efforts to reduce the scope of the federal role emerged. Most notably, attempts to reduce federal domestic spending focused on a restructuring of social insurance programs, which are described in the next section.

Great Society

President Lyndon Johnson's term for an egalitarian society that aggressive governmental action to help the poor and disadvantaged would attempt to create in the 1960s

15.3   The National Government as Social Insurer

The principal consequence of the New Deal policy revolution is that the national government has assumed a major responsibility for the social welfare of individuals who are old, disabled, or unemployed. Rather than relying on private charities or state and local programs, people are *insured*, in effect, by the national government against the potentially harsh social and economic consequences that old age, disability, and unemployment can bring.

A significant feature of **social insurance programs** is that they serve all eligible people, regardless of income levels. To be sure, millions of individuals would fall into officially defined poverty in the absence of these programs, but the receipt of social insurance benefits is not dependent on income. An elderly person need not be poor to receive Social Security benefits, and people who have lost relatively high-paying jobs can be eligible for unemployment compensation. The beneficiaries of social insurance programs are individuals from practically all income levels, a fact that helps to explain the staunch political support on which these programs rest.

15.3a Social Security

The **Social Security Act of 1935** was probably the most significant piece of domestic legislation ever enacted. Passed in the New Deal, the act provided for a system of old age insurance financed by taxes on workers and employers and a variety of categorical grants to the states to provide programs for cash assistance to the unemployed, dependent children, and the blind, disabled, and aged. The 1935 act has been amended many times, but it is significant because it firmly established for the first time a social welfare role for the national government.

Administered by the Social Security Administration in the Department of Health and Human Services, "Social Security" is really a bundle of separate programs rather than a single one. Within the Social Security umbrella are insurance programs for retired workers and their spouses (old age insurance), survivors of retired workers (survivors' insurance), and individuals with disabilities and their dependents (disability insurance). The total package is generally known by the acronym *OASDI* (old age, survivors', and disability insurance). The evolution of these programs is a classic example of **incrementalism**, a process through which policies once established are changed piecemeal over time. The number of workers covered, the amount of benefits, and the level of payroll taxes to pay for these Social Security programs have all increased incrementally over the past half-century.

In terms of expenditures—number of people receiving benefits, number of workers covered, and intensity of political support—the Social Security umbrella of programs is the national government's largest and single most important domestic policy. The OASDI consumed more than 23 percent of all federal expenditures in fiscal year 2014. More than 56 million people are OASDI beneficiaries. Benefits vary for different groups and are indexed to increase each year; in 2013 retired workers received an average monthly benefit of about $1,334.[7] Figure 15.1 offers clues on the economic importance of Social Security to older Americans. Social Security benefits, as a proportion of income, rise as people get older and are the largest source of income for Americans over the age of sixty-five—facts that help explain the potent political support for the program.

In the original 1935 act, only workers in commerce and industry were insured; but in classic incremental fashion, other occupational groups—including self-employed

---

social insurance programs

Welfare programs that provide cash or services to the aged, the disabled, and the unemployed, regardless of income level

Social Security Act of 1935

Landmark legislation that firmly established for the first time a social welfare role for the national government by providing old age insurance and grants to the states to provide programs for cash assistance to the unemployed, dependent children, and the blind, disabled, and aged

incrementalism

A model of decision making that holds that new policies differ only marginally from existing policies

farmers, military personnel, self-employed professionals, and even the president and vice president of the United States and members of Congress—have been progressively brought into the system. Coverage is now practically compulsory. Virtually every worker and employer in the United States must pay a payroll tax to fund the program.

These statistics suggest the potentially volatile political consequences that any change in Social Security can have. Practically no one can avoid being touched by the program in some tangible and specific way, either by receiving welcome benefit checks or by paying unwelcome taxes. The potential

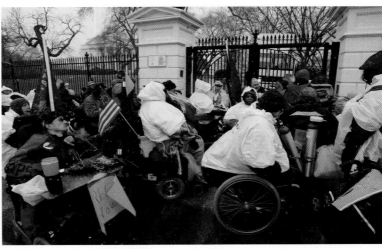

Members of the American Disabled for Attendant Programs Today (ADAPT) protest in front of the White House. They want legislation that provides alternatives to institutionalizing people who can be served in the community. (AP World Wide Photo)

for intergenerational conflict in such a system is obvious. Younger workers may resent what they consider an increasingly rapacious payroll tax bite for a program that, they fear, may not even still be in existence when they retire. Retired workers may view the program differently. Since they paid taxes into the system during their working years, they feel they are simply getting back in benefits what they rightly deserve. Given the very scope of the program, its crucial importance to so many people, and the potential for group conflicts, presidents and members of Congress pondering program changes are in a political minefield.

By the late 1970s and early 1980s, it had become clear that major changes were essential if the program was to survive. Projections showed that expenditures (benefits) would soon exceed revenues (payroll taxes). A declining birthrate and a longer life expectancy meant that the number of retirees (beneficiaries) was growing faster than the number of workers paying taxes to fund the program. In addition, increases in benefit levels caused by inflation outpaced revenues.

The political consequences of the Social Security system "going broke" were too horrendous to contemplate. Unlike means-tested programs (to be discussed shortly) for which only lower-income people qualify, almost everyone expects to benefit directly from Social Security. This fact gives Social Security a political base far broader than that enjoyed by any means-tested welfare policy.

As a result of such concerns, the future of Social Security has been an almost constant topic on the American political scene for the past three decades. In the 1980s, adjustments—such as raising the payroll tax rate and gradually increasing the retirement age—were made to insure solvency in the system as baby boomers began to approach retirement age. During the 1990s, issues fluctuated between fears that the system would run out of money and concerns that the system's surplus funds were being used inappropriately. By the 2004 presidential election, both major-party candidates found themselves making pledges to ensure the security of the Social Security system. One recent proposal suggests turning over control of at least part of the system's funds to individual contributors to manage as they see fit. This would make Social Security function more like a private pension plan. Such proposals are

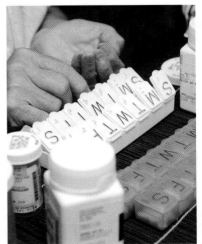

A declining birth rate and a longer life expectancy meant that the number of retirees (beneficiaries) was growing faster than the number of workers paying taxes to fund the Social Security program. (Shutterstock)

Figure 15.1 | Shares of Income for the Older Population

Older Americans rely heavily on Social Security income. Social Security benefits are the principal source of income for Americans over the age of sixty-five.

SOURCES: *Social Security Administration,* Income of the Population 55 and OLDER, 2012 *(Washington, D.C.: Social Security Administration, 2014).*

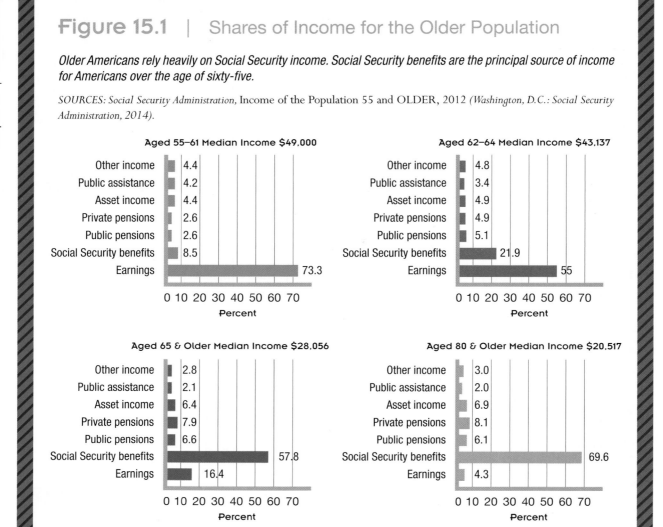

Aged 55–61 Median Income $49,000

	Percent
Other income	4.4
Public assistance	4.2
Asset income	4.4
Private pensions	2.6
Public pensions	2.6
Social Security benefits	8.5
Earnings	73.3

Aged 62–64 Median Income $43,137

	Percent
Other income	4.8
Public assistance	3.4
Asset income	4.9
Private pensions	4.9
Public pensions	5.1
Social Security benefits	21.9
Earnings	55

Aged 65 & Older Median Income $28,056

	Percent
Other income	2.8
Public assistance	2.1
Asset income	6.4
Private pensions	7.9
Public pensions	6.6
Social Security benefits	57.8
Earnings	16.4

Aged 80 & Older Median Income $20,517

	Percent
Other income	3.0
Public assistance	2.0
Asset income	6.9
Private pensions	8.1
Public pensions	6.1
Social Security benefits	69.6
Earnings	4.3

tempting because they offer contributors greater control; individuals could choose to invest in high-yielding securities, for example. They are also hazardous because high rates of return tend to be accompanied by higher risks as well. During economic downturns, pension plans often take a hard financial hit.

15.3b Medicare

The second major social insurance policy of the national government is **Medicare**, a program enacted in the Great Society in 1965 and administered by the Centers for Medicare and Medicaid Services in the Department of Health and Human Services. Medicare is essentially a public health insurance program for the elderly and disabled. Rather than providing cash benefits to individuals like other Social Security programs, Medicare pays the providers of health care (hospitals, physicians, and other health professionals) for services given to patients who are aged, disabled, or afflicted with terminal illness. The program now insures about fifty million people. In the past, the elderly and Americans with disabilities who were in need of medical care relied

Medicare

A public health insurance program in which government pays the providers of health care for medical services given to patients who are aged or disabled

on families, private insurance plans, or the help of charities or friends—or they went without medical care. However, Medicare has become a major source of health care funding for the elderly and disabled. In fiscal year 2014 the national government spent an estimated $519 billion on Medicare, or almost 15 percent of total federal expenditures.

Medicare is a program with multiple parts. Part A is Hospital Insurance (HI), funded by a portion of the Social Security tax paid into a hospital trust fund. After a patient pays a deductible,

Medicare now insures about fifty million people. In the past, the elderly and Americans with disabilities who were in need of medical care relied on families, private insurance plans, or the help of charities or friends—or they went without medical care. (Shutterstock)

Medicare covers hospital costs for two months, with patients sharing costs after that period. Part B of the program is Supplementary Medical Insurance (SMI): After the patient pays a deductible amount, SMI funds physician and outpatient services. SMI, which is voluntary, is funded by premiums paid by enrollees and general revenues from the federal treasury.[8]

Medicare was enacted after a bitter political struggle in which opponents of the measure argued that health insurance was "socialized medicine" and unwarranted interference in the relationship between patients and physicians. Providing health care for the elderly and people with disabilities has proved, however, to be a highly popular program. Still, assumption of a major medical insurance role by the national government has inevitably created policy debates over costs—how high they should be and who should pay them. Efforts to ensure the financial soundness of Medicare are complicated by rising medical costs. Congress has attempted to control expenditures by placing ceilings on some of the medical costs the program will pay and by offering financial incentives to hospitals to keep costs low.

The original Medicare plan has been supplemented with additional coverage areas over the past few decades. One area in which many Americans wanted to see the program expand was prescription drug coverage for the elderly. The rising costs of prescription drugs place a particularly large burden on the elderly, many of whom have modest incomes and require multiple long-term prescriptions. To address these concerns, Medicare Part D went into effect in 2006 in order to provide prescription drug benefits for Medicare recipients. The most recent changes to Medicare—an expansion of this prescription drug coverage and adjustments to the Medicare tax, among other items—made up a portion of the 2010 Patient Protection and Affordable Care Act.

15.3c Unemployment Compensation

A third major social insurance policy is **unemployment compensation**, a program of temporary financial assistance for the unemployed first enacted in the original Social Security Act of 1935 and administered by the states and the Office of Workforce Security in the Department of Labor. Massive unemployment was one of the severe economic and social problems that sparked the assumption of a much greater social welfare role by government in the Great Depression. The problem obviously continues, for changes in the economy and the decline of some industries mean that official unemployment rates exceeding 5 percent are not unusual. During times of

unemployment compensation

A social insurance policy that grants temporary financial assistance to the unemployed recession, the rate can go much higher. It went over 10 percent in 2009 and remained over 8 percent through 2012 before finally falling back under 6 percent by late 2014.

One of the most significant public policy changes in the past half-century is that unemployed workers now receive cash benefits for a short period of time while they seek other employment. For example, as foreign competition and changes in the international economy have racked their industries, unemployed steel and autoworkers have been beneficiaries of the program. Unemployment compensation is designed not for the chronically unemployed but for those who need financial assistance to keep afloat between jobs. Both the national and state governments tax employers to pay for the benefits and the administrative costs of the program. Eligibility requirements and benefit levels vary among the states. In general, an unemployed person receives weekly checks up to twenty-six weeks and up to thirteen additional weeks in states where unemployment rates are particularly high.

15.4 Public Policy and Economic Inequality

In addition to social insurance, the second major category of social welfare policy at the national level is comprised of programs explicitly designed to aid the poor. Table 15.2 offers a summary portrait of both types of programs. Each of these two categories of programs serves different groups of people and is shaped by different kinds of political pressures. In general, social insurance programs tend to be the larger of the two types in terms of the number of beneficiaries and the amount of money spent. Given their broader constituencies, these programs also tend to receive much stronger political support.

Programs specifically intended for the poor—and only the poor—are known as **means-tested programs** because the receipt of benefits is completely dependent on income level. Under these programs, individuals receive benefits only if they qualify by having little or no income. Unlike social insurance, beneficiaries of means-tested programs do not pay money into the programs before they receive benefits. Children whose parents have little or no income and the chronically unemployed are among the beneficiaries of such programs.

15.4a Measures of Economic Inequality

Political equality amid sharp economic inequality remains one of the great ironies of the American experience. Economic inequality is a fact of life supported by even casual observation. Differences in the clothes people wear, the food they eat, the entertainments they pursue, the cars they buy, and the houses they live in—all suggest great differences in economic status. One familiar measure of income disparity is a division of families into five groups (or quintiles) according to the proportion of total money income each group receives.

Perfect income equality would mean that each fifth of the population of families receives 20 percent of all money income—that is, each quintile of families receives an equal slice of the money pie. However, great income inequality persists. Table 15.3 shows that the lowest fifth of families received just 3.2 percent of aggregate income in 2013, while the highest fifth received 51 percent in the same year. The table also shows that the lowest three-fifths of families have lost ground, from a combined 32 percent of aggregate income in 1971 to 25.9 percent in 2013. In the same period

means-tested programs

Type of social welfare program in which government provides cash or in-kind benefits to individuals who qualify by having little or no income

table 15.2 | Major Social Welfare Programs

Social insurance and means-tested programs are major categories of social welfare programs. Social insurance programs are generally funded by specific taxes and have the retired, the aged, individuals with disabilities, and the unemployed as their beneficiaries. Means-tested programs are designed for needy individuals, are funded by general revenues, and usually involve the states in their administration.

NOTE: All data from Office of Management and Budget, Historical Tables, http://www.whitehouse.gov/omb/budget/Historicals (December 19, 2014).

Social Insurance

Program	Date Enacted	Benefits	Funding Sources	Estimated Cost in Billions, 2015
Social Security (old age, survivors', and disability insurance)	1935	Monthly checks for retired and disabled workers, their dependents, and survivors of retired workers	Social Security tax, paid by workers and employers	$896
Medicare	1965	Medical care for aged and disabled	Social Security tax, premiums paid by beneficiaries, general revenues	$526
Unemployment compensation	1935	Weekly checks for short-term unemployed workers	State and national taxes on employers	$47

Means-Tested Programs

Program	Date Enacted	Benefits	Funding Sources	Estimated Cost in Billions, 2015
Temporary Assistance for Needy Families (TANF)	1935	Monthly checks for needy children and parents	National and state general revenues	$33
Supplemental Security Income	1972	Monthly cash payments for needy aged, blind, and disabled	National general revenues and state supplements	$54
Medicaid	1965	Medical care for needy individuals and families	National and state general revenues	$336
Food stamps/ SNAP	1964	Monthly food cards for needy individuals and families	National general revenues and some state funds	$100

the highest fifth increased aggregate income from 43.5 to 51 percent. A domestic policy question is the degree to which such growing income inequality will develop into a trenchant political issue in the twenty-first century. The Occupy movement that started in 2011—with its emphasis on the stark contrast between incomes of the top 1 percent of the population and those of the bottom 99 percent—is an example of how dissatisfaction with income inequality can manifest into a political agenda.

Another measure of economic inequality is the proportion of the total population classified as poor in the United States. The term *poverty* is a human construct that does not have the same meaning in all societies. People are poor according to some economic standard against which they are judged, and those standards may vary greatly across the planet. A poor family in America may have a consistent diet of rice and potatoes, but those in nations who have little or no food at all may consider such a diet a rich one.

The concept of **relative deprivation** indicates how variable definitions of poverty can be.[9] According to this concept, individuals with less money will feel poor or deprived relative to those who have more. Of course, the greater the material wealth in a particular society, the more likely individuals will feel poor if they do not possess material goods in the same degree as others in the society. The substantial political and economic obstacles to fundamental changes in the distribution of income suggest the persistence of poverty defined relatively.

Another approach consists of some absolute standard below which individuals can be defined as poor. The United States government has constructed a standard to measure the extent of poverty and its changes over time. Based on a Department of Agriculture finding on how much families spend on food, the Social Security Administration in 1964 established a **poverty threshold**—an income level below which individuals are defined as poor. That income level is different for families of different sizes and changes each year with changes in the consumer price index (CPI). By 2013 the average poverty threshold for a family of four was $23,624. Families with money income below this level are defined as poor.

Figure 15.2 shows the number of poor people in the United States between 1960 and 2013 on the basis of this poverty threshold. In 1960 almost 40 million people, or 22.2 percent of the total population, were defined as poor. Both the absolute number and the proportion of poor people declined until the early 1970s, before rising again beginning in the 1980s. In 2013 there were over 45 million poor people in America. At 14.5 percent, the proportion of Americans who were poor in 2013 was at one of its highest points since 1965.

Like almost all other social measures, the official definition of poverty has been subject to criticism. In particular, critics have charged that the income standard used by the government overestimates the number of poor people. First, only money income (such as wages and cash benefits from government) is included in the standard. Not included are noncash benefits, such as SNAP (food stamps), Medicare and Medicaid health benefits, and subsidized housing benefits, which many of the poor receive from the government. Counting such noncash benefits as income, critics argue, would greatly reduce the number of people officially defined as poor. On the other hand, when the Census Bureau makes adjustments for out-of-pocket costs, like those for medical care, the percentage of poor people shows an increase over the official measure, even when noncash benefits are included as income.[10]

While aggregate numbers on poverty are open to criticism, no one questions the fact that poverty occurs disproportionately among different groups. Figure 15.3 displays poverty rates for selected groups in selected years since 1959. The graph

relative deprivation

A definition of poverty that holds that individuals with less, regardless of their absolute income level, will feel poor or deprived relative to those who have more

poverty threshold

Income level differentiated by family size and annually adjusted for inflation, below which government defines individuals as being poor

table 15.3 | Aggregate Family Income by Quintiles

In the years between 1971 and 2013, the bottom four quintiles of families received a declining share of aggregate income, while the top quintile increased their share of aggregate income.

	1971	1981	1991	2001	2013
Lowest fifth	4.1%	4.1%	3.8%	3.5%	3.2%
Second fifth	10.6%	10.1%	9.6%	8.7%	8.4%
Third fifth	17.3%	16.7%	15.9%	14.6%	14.4%
Fourth fifth	24.5%	24.8%	24.4%	23.0%	23.0%
Highest fifth	43.5%	44.3%	46.5%	50.1%	51.0%

SOURCE: U.S. Census Bureau, Income and Poverty in the United States: 2013.

Figure 15.2 | Number and Proportion of Poor People in the United States, Selected Years, 1960–2013

Although the absolute number of poor people remains high, the percentage of poor in the population has been below 15 percent in recent years.

SOURCE: U.S. Census Bureau, Income and Poverty in the United States: 2013
(Washington, D.C.: Government Printing Office, 2014).

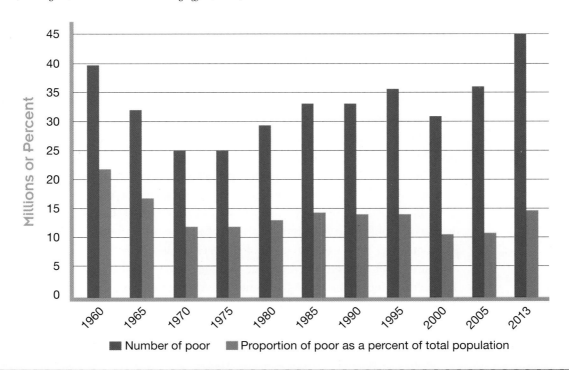

■ Number of poor ■ Proportion of poor as a percent of total population

Chapter 15 | Domestic Policy | 462

BVT *Lab*
Visit www.BVTLab.com
to explore the student
resources available for
this chapter.

shows that the poverty rate for whites tends to fall below the overall poverty rate, while the proportion of African Americans in poverty is consistently higher than the rate for the total population. The *absolute number* of whites in poverty exceeds the number of poor African Americans, but a higher *proportion* of the African American population is poor. In 1959 less than 20 percent of whites but more than 50 percent of African Americans were defined as poor. By 2013, less than 10 percent of whites but over 27 percent of African Americans still fell below the poverty threshold. Persons identifying themselves as Hispanic or Latino have poverty rates higher than whites but slightly lower than African Americans. Poverty among children has fluctuated but is consistently at a higher rate than among the population as a whole. The group that has experienced the most consistent positive gains over the past several decades is the elderly. Although this group has historically experienced poverty at above average rates, recently that trend has begun to reverse itself. Today, whites and the elderly are among the groups least likely to be poor.

As Figure 15.3 indicates, poverty among children continues to exceed the overall poverty rate. The figure does not show that poverty rates differ among children of different races. The Census Bureau reports the startling fact that in 2013 more than one-third of African American (38.3 percent) children and nearly one-third of Hispanic (30.4 percent) children under the age of eighteen were poor.

15.4b Poverty as a Political and Social Problem

Widespread poverty in a land of affluence has been a vexing political and social problem, especially since the national government assumed a massive social welfare role over a half-century ago. Economic inequality persists despite the huge sums of money spent by the national government over the past half-century to ameliorate economic distress among citizens in need. Why people are poor is an issue that has bitterly divided citizens, politicians, policy analysts, and academics. No single reason can adequately explain the existence of poverty among such a large number of people.

Social scientists have generally offered two sets of explanations for why people are poor. The first holds that people are poor because they lack *personal qualities*, such as ambition or intelligence, which make successful competition in the economic marketplace possible. A second explanation centers on the kind of social, economic, and cultural environment that is likely to be fertile ground for poverty. In this view, poverty is the result of, for example, the absence of a good education, a weak or crumbling family structure, disability, or the lack of job opportunities. Sorting out these distinctions is no easy task. As an example, continuing failure to find a job can weaken ambition to go on.

The population of poor people in the United States is a constantly changing kaleidoscope, for individuals are falling into and climbing out of officially defined poverty from one year to the next. Personal crises, like the death of the family income-earner or loss of a job, can at least temporarily make some individuals poor. A rising unemployment rate increases the level of poverty, while falling unemployment has the opposite effect. Indeed, employment is no guarantee against poverty. In 2012 about 7.1 percent of the labor force, 10.6 million Americans, were classified as the **working poor**. These people worked or looked for work for at least half the year and yet were still officially defined as poor because their low earnings were not enough to pull their families above the poverty line.[11]

Some proportion of the poor are in what some poverty analysts call an **underclass**, comprised of individuals isolated from the rest of society and for whom poverty is a continuing way of life. Chronic unemployment, unstable family environments,

working poor

Individuals who, despite being employed or seeking employment, are still defined as poor because their low earnings are not enough to put them above the poverty threshold

underclass

A proportion of the poor comprised of individuals isolated from the rest of society and for whom poverty is a continuing way of life

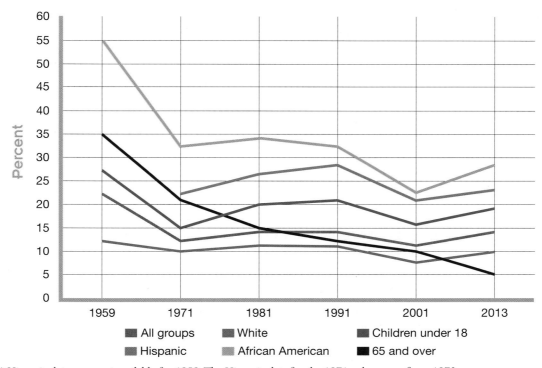

Figure 15.3 | Poverty Rates for Selected Groups, Selected Years, 1959–2013

Although poverty rates are lower than they were in 1959, substantial differences among groups remain.

SOURCE: *U.S. Census Bureau,* Income and Poverty in the United States: 2013 *(Washington, DC: Government Printing Office, 2014).*

Legend: All groups, White, Children under 18, Hispanic, African American, 65 and over

* Hispanic data were not available for 1959. The Hispanic data for the 1971 column are from 1972.

welfare dependency, and a high incidence of crime are all characteristics of under-class poverty. Whether the growth of the underclass can be attributed to systemic economic changes that have resulted in fewer blue-collar jobs and more unemployment, self-destructive behavior patterns among the underclass poor, or some combination of economic and behavioral factors is an issue that reflects the general debate over the causes of poverty.[12]

Grappling with poverty in some way is the object of a range of government policies, including income transfer programs such as Social Security; but two categories of policy strategies illuminate government approaches. The first are **curative strategies** designed to get at the "root" causes of the problem, so that individuals can get out of poverty and lead productive, self-sufficient lives.[13] Expenditures on education, particularly targeted to the disadvantaged, are an example. In addition, employment training seeks to give individuals the skills necessary for a measure of economic success. Perhaps the most controversial example was the community action program of Lyndon Johnson's War on Poverty in the mid-1960s. That effort sought to involve the poor in initiating and coordinating local community efforts to combat poverty. The

curative strategies

Policy strategies designed to reach the fundamental causes of poverty and to enable individuals to get out of poverty and lead productive, self-sufficient lives

A range of government policies seeks to deal with poverty. (Shutterstock)

program began with the high hopes and optimism so characteristic of the Great Society; however, political support evaporated when some local community action groups, in their efforts to exert political power, criticized what they saw as the insensitivity of elected officials.[14]

The second category of antipoverty strategies is **alleviative** in approach;[15] that is, these strategies do not seek to cure poverty but simply to make it more bearable. Rather than trying to lift people out of poverty, such programs give cash or *in-kind* (noncash) *benefits* to poor individuals or families to help keep them afloat financially. Various forms of housing assistance, the school lunch program, and emergency fuel assistance fall into this category. In terms of expenditures, these programs as a group make up the national government's principal policy strategy for dealing with poverty. Illustrations of major means-tested programs whose principal aim is the alleviation of poverty are discussed in the following sections.

15.4c Temporary Assistance for Needy Families

One of the oldest alleviative poverty programs at the national level is **Temporary Assistance for Needy Families (TANF)**, first enacted (under the name Aid to Families with Dependent Children [AFDC]) as part of the landmark Social Security Act of 1935. The program originally provided cash benefits for needy children under the age of sixteen, but subsequent amendments have raised the age limit and extended benefits to one adult relative or to both parents in needy families. TANF is a program administered by the states under the Office of Family Assistance in the Department of Health and Human Services and jointly funded about equally by state and federal revenues. The states themselves determine eligibility standards and payment levels within guidelines established by the national government. Monthly benefits vary widely among the states. For example, the maximum monthly payment for a family of three in 2011 was $170 in Mississippi, $185 in Tennessee, $638 in California, and $923 in Alaska.[16]

The number of TANF recipients grew tremendously from its beginnings until the reform efforts of the 1990s. Just over half a million individuals received benefits in the first year of the program in 1936, but that number increased to almost 8.5 million in 1970. In fact, the number grew by 3.5 million between 1969 and 1971. The rate of growth declined in the early 1970s, and even the absolute number of beneficiaries declined in some later years. In 1994 the program hit its peak with 14.4 million individuals receiving cash benefits. Due to the reform described below, the caseload figures declined in the early 2000s and were about 3.5 million in 2014.[17]

Welfare was among the most controversial poverty programs because of the widely held perception that it creates a "welfare dependency" that is passed on from one generation of families to the next, with little hope of breaking out of what seems like a vicious cycle. Conservatives saw welfare as subsidizing the undeserving, while liberals decried the insensitivity of bureaucrats administering the program and the insufficiency of resources devoted to it.

alleviative strategies

Policy strategies designed to make poverty more bearable for individuals rather than designed to attack poverty by reaching its fundamental causes

Temporary Assistance for Needy Families (TANF)

Social welfare program, administered by the states and jointly funded by state and national revenues, that provides cash assistance, in participating states, to needy children and one adult relative or an unemployed parent

Political Ideologies and the Welfare State

Policy debate is fundamentally a collision of ideas on what the appropriate role of government should be. Nowhere has the collision of ideas been more evident than in debate over social welfare. The scope of government expenditures, the number of people directly touched, and the shape of political discourse throughout this and most of the previous century all attest to the central place of the issue in our politics.

The contemporary welfare state is primarily the handiwork of political liberals, of whom most have been in the Democratic Party. Viewing government as helper, provider, and protector of the disadvantaged, liberals successfully initiated and extended the programs that collectively make up the welfare state. In the liberal view, a significant government presence is right, just, and necessary to help redress the economic imbalances in a capitalist system.

Conservatives have generally opposed the creation and extension of social welfare programs, from the original Social Security Act in the New Deal to the Medicare program in the Great Society. They believe that such programs entrust government with decisions that should be left to individuals and groups in the private marketplace. Government intervention smothers initiative, risks values like independence, and threatens to overwhelm citizens in mindless bureaucracy and red tape.

Liberals and conservatives have been the major contestants in this battle of ideas, but other ideologies have contributed their own perspectives to the debate over government's social welfare role. Neoliberals see some welfare policies as too generous to middle-class recipients. Neoconservatives accept the necessity of a modest welfare state, but they argue that government's capacity to solve social problems has often been overestimated and that public programs frequently do not make good on their promises. Ideologies on the margins of political debate raise even more fundamental concerns. Democratic socialists press for much greater government control of the economy and a comprehensive welfare system. At the opposite end of the spectrum, libertarians argue that government should be limited to protecting the nation from external attack and preserving the individual rights of citizens. They question the very existence of a contemporary welfare state.

Today, few people seriously contest a fundamental social welfare role for government. Liberals and conservatives battle over whether more or less money should be spent on social welfare programs. However, social welfare policy debate has taken some new twists and turns. To maintain political support for welfare and to limit long-term dependency, liberals accepted a work requirement and time limit for welfare recipients in the 1996 Welfare Reform Act. Conservatives, for example, by supporting voucher programs to allow the poor to purchase their own housing, have tried to blend their traditional support for market incentives with acceptance of social welfare policies.

The shape of social welfare lies at the center of battles over budget deficits now common in American politics. Budget makers wrestle with the question of whether deficits can be eliminated without some reductions in social welfare spending. Conflicting ideas over what is appropriate government action complicate this debate over deficits. On what criteria should judgments on cuts or increases in social welfare programs be made? What solutions do you see to the enduring problem of poverty in America?

Concerns from both ends of the political spectrum and the goal of making welfare less of an alleviative and more of a curative antipoverty strategy led Congress to pass the Personal Responsibility and Work Opportunity Reconciliation Act of 1996. Known more commonly as the **Welfare Reform Act**, this piece of legislation fundamentally altered welfare. First, in changing the acronym from AFDC to TANF, the law stressed the temporary nature of the cash payment program. In an effort to break the cycle of poverty, the act placed a two consecutive-year limit on receipt of benefits and a five-year lifetime limit. As recipients reached these limits, the states removed them from the rolls. The reform also required recipients to work at least part-time while receiving benefits, providing some exemptions for education and job training. While

Welfare Reform Act

A 1996 law that fundamentally altered the AFDC welfare program by renaming it TANF and placing work and training requirements, as well as time limits, on its use the reform effort has been undeniably successful at reducing welfare caseloads and expenditures (at least partially as a result of its strict time limitations), it remains to be seen whether this harsh approach to poverty will be successful at reducing poverty in America over the long run.

15.4d Supplemental Security Income

President Nixon's proposal to guarantee incomes for poor families seemed to violate a widely held public expectation that incomes should be earned rather than simply granted. In this view, both economic efficiency and simple fairness demand that incomes be rewards for contributions to society rather than guarantees unrelated to any such contributions. However, in 1972 Congress enacted what amounts to a guaranteed income program for certain groups. Under the **Supplemental Security Income (SSI)** program, administered by the Social Security Administration, the national government guarantees a certain level of income for the needy among the aged, blind, and disabled. In 2013 the program spent over $54 billion to serve over 8.4 million needy people. The national government's successful enactment of SSI shortly after the bitter battle over a proposal to guarantee incomes for poor families suggests the warm political support enjoyed by certain categories of individuals. In effect, SSI represents a national commitment to support aged, blind, and disabled poor people who are clearly unable to support themselves.

15.4e Medicaid

Medicaid is a means-tested program, enacted in the Great Society, designed to provide medical care for the needy. Unlike TANF and SSI, **Medicaid** provides the poor with **in-kind benefits** rather than cash. That is, the needy receive a service (medical care) rather than cash, and money from the program goes directly to the providers (hospitals, physicians, etc.) of that service. The program funded medical care for more than 56 million needy people in 2012. Like TANF, Medicaid is funded jointly by state and federal revenues and administered by individual states within guidelines established by the national government. The Centers for Medicare and Medicaid Services is the unit in the national government responsible for the program. While specific rules of eligibility are highly complex, individuals who receive TANF and SSI benefits are generally eligible for Medicaid services. The rapid growth in Medicaid costs has become a political issue. In 2014 the program cost about $308 billion, a hefty sum in a year of fiscal strains. The Affordable Care Act created an option for states to begin expanding Medicaid coverage to cover all residents up to 133 percent of the poverty line in 2014. Though not all states have chosen to participate, this option will bring continued change to the Medicaid program in the coming years.

15.4f The Supplemental Nutrition Assistance Program

Like Medicaid, the **Supplemental Nutrition Assistance Program**, or **SNAP** (formerly known as the *food stamp program*), was enacted in the 1960s to provide in-kind benefits to the needy rather than cash. The Food and Nutrition Service in the Department of Agriculture administers this program through state and local welfare offices. In this case, beneficiaries receive coupons (now typically in the form of debit cards) that they trade for food items at grocery stores or supermarkets. The coupons represent money, but they can be used only to purchase food. The national government pays for the cost of the cards but shares the administrative costs of the program with the states. Individuals and families who meet an income test qualify for SNAP. Like TANF beneficiaries, the number of food stamp recipients grew tremendously over time,

Supplemental Security Income (SSI)

Social welfare program administered by the Social Security Administration whereby the national government guarantees a certain level of income for the needy, aged, blind, and disabled

Medicaid

A means-tested medical care program providing in-kind medical benefits for the poor

in-kind benefits

Noncash benefits, such as medical care services, that the needy receive from some social welfare programs

Supplemental Nutrition Assistance Program (SNAP)

A means-tested program (formerly known as the food stamp program) that provides the eligible needy with cards that can be used only to purchase food

BVT Lab

Flashcards are available
for this chapter at
www.BVTLab.com.

467

Chapter 15 | Domestic Policy

from less than one-half million people in the mid-1960s to more than 22 million in 1981.[18] In response to charges of waste and fraud in the program, eligibility rules were tightened in the early 1980s and the number of beneficiaries declined. However, rules were made more liberal later in the decade. The program is highly sensitive to changes in the economy. With higher unemployment rates, more people depend on the program for help. In 2008, what had originally been called the food stamp program was renamed SNAP. In 2014, national and state governments spent over $74 billion for about 46.5 million SNAP beneficiaries.[19]

15.4g Social Welfare Policy and Future Challenges

Since the late 1960s, social welfare debate has generally revolved not around new program initiatives but around the ways in which the nation can pay for existing programs, which consume ever-greater resources. If Presidents Roosevelt and Johnson attempted to expand the national government role in social welfare, Presidents Reagan and Clinton tried to find economically possible and politically acceptable limits to that role. Changing economic conditions and how policy makers like President Barack Obama decide to deal with budget deficits and demands for federal spending in other sectors, such as military and defense policy, will determine the shape of social welfare policies in the twenty-first century. How much should social welfare cuts contribute to deficit reduction and other spending needs, or should social welfare programs be immune to cuts? If cuts are made, which groups—the elderly, or the working poor, or children, for example—should bear the brunt of the social and economic costs of the changes? The future shape of social welfare policies depends on how elected officials, interest groups, and individual voters respond to such questions.

15.5 Environmental Policy

While the previous section focused on the service-providing aspects of domestic policy via social welfare, this section addresses the regulatory aspects of the government's role in domestic policy via the environment. Over the past several decades, environmental protection has emerged as a highly visible political issue. Limiting pollution of the land, air, and water about us is a major policy objective at all levels of government. Public policies to protect the environment try to cope with the by-products of technological change, such as air pollution in a nation so dependent on the automobile. At the same time, environmental policy relies on scientific research and technological advances to limit pollution, such as the installation of catalytic converters in cars to reduce auto exhaust emissions, or the promotion of hybrid vehicles. Science and technology can also help to identify environmental problems, but the uncertainty of risk complicates regulatory efforts to reduce pollution.

15.5a Environmentalism on the Policy Agenda

The imposing catalogue of threats to the environment helps to explain the deep well of political support for environmental protection efforts. Toxic waste dumps throughout the country contain used chemicals and other waste products of industrial production that can pose serious health threats. Burning fossil fuels to produce electricity emits into the atmosphere particles that are encircled by water droplets and carried by winds for hundreds of miles. They fall in the form of acid rain and

Nuclear Power and the Environment

The high promise and menacing threat of nuclear energy have posed stark policy questions over the past sixty years. Flowing from basic research in particle physics, the ability to create nuclear fission reactions with enormous releases of energy led to development of weapons capable of almost incomprehensible destruction at the end of World War II. Nuclear technology also seemed to hold promise as a boundless source of energy to meet the nation's growing need for electrical power; the bubble broke in 1979, however, when an accident at the Three Mile Island nuclear power plant led to a partial meltdown of the reactor. The accident so shook public confidence in nuclear reactor safety that the industry has not yet recovered. No new nuclear power plants have been ordered since. Anxieties about nuclear power were exacerbated by the more serious accident in 1986 at the Chernobyl nuclear plant in the Ukraine, which was then part of the Soviet Union.

In a classic illustration of the promise and threat that science and technology pose for public policy, nuclear power is at the same time pressed as a solution to some environmental problems but feared to be a creator of others. For example, many climatologists argue that extensive use of fossil fuels like coal and oil releases into the atmosphere carbon dioxide that, along with other gases such as methane and nitrous oxides, acts like a shield that traps heat from the sun. This global warming creates the risk of dramatic climatic changes that can turn fertile farm land into desert and that can put coastal regions under water by melting polar ice and raising ocean levels. A greater reliance on nuclear power plants to produce electricity would reduce fossil fuel damage to the atmosphere, but public anxiety about the safety of nuclear plants makes greater reliance on nuclear energy a controversial option. In fact, at the same time that fears about global warming emerged, New York State negotiated with the Long Island Lighting Company to close down the Shoreham nuclear power plant. Long Island residents and state and local elected officials opposed the plant because of fears that evacuation of the surrounding densely populated areas could not be quickly and reasonably accomplished in the event of a nuclear accident. Thus, a newly constructed, $5.5 billion dollar plant never became operational. The decision not to use a facility that would reduce dependence on fossil fuels and that might help limit global warming illustrates the tough policy choices posed by nuclear energy. To many Long Islanders the decision was a wise move greeted by relief. To nuclear power advocates, closing down a perfectly good nuclear plant was folly.

Another tough environmental policy issue concerns the management of nuclear waste. Spent nuclear fuel remains highly radioactive, and potentially quite dangerous, for several hundred thousand years. Since no one wants this dangerous by-product near them, finding locations for safe storage of nuclear waste has been a troubling domestic policy problem. In 2002, after a decades-long, $4 billion scientific study, President Bush signed legislation establishing a new waste facility at Yucca Mountain, Nevada. The plan was for the waste depository to be maintained by the Department of Energy's Office of Civilian Radioactive Waste Management, making it the nation's "first long-term geologic repository for spent nuclear fuel and high-level radioactive waste."[1] Supporters of the project claim that a central location at a remote and secure site provides the safest solution for the problem of radioactive waste. Critics argue that an accident could endanger millions of lives (Yucca Mountain is just one hundred miles from Las Vegas) and that transporting radioactive waste from all over the country exacerbates the risks of radioactive contamination. Despite years of planning and development, the site remains years away from opening; and in 2009, after years of budget reductions for the project, the Obama administration announced it would look for a new site for a repository. In light of the promise and problems of nuclear energy, should more nuclear power plants be built, should more be closed down, or should we use less energy?

1 Office of Civilian Radioactive Waste Management, "The Yucca Mountain Project," http://www.ymp.gov/ (October 13, 2002).

kill forests and water life. Burning fossil fuels and the massive burning of tropical forestland for development dumps carbon dioxide into the atmosphere that traps the sun's heat and risks causing global warming with potentially dire consequences for the earth's climate. Scientists have also detected deterioration in the layer of ozone in the stratosphere high above the earth's surface. Ozone protects the planet from the damaging effects of the sun's ultraviolet radiation. Depletion of the protective ozone layer risks ultraviolet radiation damage to crops and an increase in the incidence of skin cancer.

Radon, a colorless, odorless gas, seeps into millions of homes from decaying uranium in the earth and threatens occupants with higher risks of lung cancer. The mountains of solid waste the nation produces pose a national problem touching every community. Great strides have been made in limiting air pollution; but the

Environmental Protection Agency reported in 2014 that even though air quality has improved over the past twenty years, more than seventy-five million people live in counties where the air is unhealthy at times due to high levels of pollutants—a consequence of the ninety-four million tons of pollution released into the air annually.[20]

(Shutterstock)

One reason this catalogue of dangers seems so imposing is that we now have a more refined capacity to detect environmental changes and minute quantities of potentially harmful substances. Sophisticated instruments and proce-dures allow environmental scientists to detect radon, pesticide residues, and tears in the ozone layer. In part, environmental issues get on the policy agenda because new knowledge pushes them there.

Protecting the environment has potent political support in the first decades of the twenty-first century. Campaigning politicians from across the political spectrum seek to align themselves with the environmentalist cause. The 2000 presidential campaign featured both a major-party candidate, Al Gore, who had made environmentalism a key feature of his political career, and the emergence of a formidable third party, the Green Party, which placed environmental policy at the core of its political agenda. Significant majorities of Americans judge that high environmental standards are necessary to deal with a deteriorating environment, even if that means setting higher emissions and pollution standards for business and spending more money on the development of renewable energy resources.[21] This intense concern for environmental issues—focusing on topics such as logging in the national forests, the safety risks of offshore oil drilling, and cleaner fuel technology—continued through the early 2000s, with 66 percent of the public saying that they worry either a great deal or a fair amount about the quality of the environment in 2014.[22] The executive agency that has the task of meeting these public demands may have the toughest job in Washington.

The Endangered Species Act created federal protections for species at risk of extinction. The U.S. Fish and Wildlife Service maintains a searchable database of these threatened and endangered animals and plants at this website:

http://www.bvtlab.com/7DSBt

The EPA administers laws that try to protect air, water, and land by regulating emission standards, toxic wastes, pesticides, radiation standards, and potentially dangerous substances. (Wikimedia Commons)

15.5b The Environmental Protection Agency and Government Regulation

The political environment of the **Environmental Protection Agency (EPA)** contains a mix of pressures and constraints that severely tax efforts to meet the policy goal of environmental protection. The agency must deal with a staggering array of potential threats to the environment, including thousands of sources of pollution throughout the nation. Public and environmental interest group expectations for agency action are high, but so are the anxieties of businesses and industries that see environmental regulation as an economic cost that someone must pay.

The Environmental Protection Agency was established in 1970 by pulling together into a single unit the antipollution programs then spread among several agencies. More than four decades after its creation the EPA is one of the biggest, and probably the most visible, regulatory agencies, employing over eighteen thousand people and (in fiscal year 2014) spending about $8.2 billion annually. The agency must administer laws that try to protect air, water, and land—a daunting task that encompasses regulation of auto emission standards, toxic wastes, pesticides, radiation standards, and potentially dangerous substances such as asbestos, mercury, and radon. The demands on the EPA are a recipe of political passions, economic considerations, and scientific findings, a mix that makes the EPA's task at once fascinating and frustrating.

Since much of the EPA's work is based on research and technological innovation, science and technology help to structure its decisions. For example, for fiscal year 2015 the EPA requested from Congress about $200 million for efforts to reduce greenhouse gas emissions.[23]

Science and technology inevitably play a role in EPA decisions. Substances posing health and environmental threats are frequently invisible, their consequences long-term, and their structures and incidence discoverable only by highly trained investigators in fields such as chemistry and the life sciences. Does the runoff of pesticides into rivers ultimately damage human health? What will global warming do to climate patterns and ecosystems? How much of a carcinogen must an individual ingest before serious health effects occur? Ultimately, much of the EPA's work is comprised of **risk assessment**, or estimating the degree of environmental risk a pollutant or ecosystem change poses, and **risk management**, or making decisions that try to reduce or contain the identified risk.[24] Even with the trappings of scientific research, however, risk assessment retains a large measure of uncertainty. Different models and different data sets can produce different answers to the question of whether a contaminant in minute amounts causes cancer.

Environmental Protection Agency (EPA)

An independent agency that controls and abates air and water pollution and protects the environment from pollution by solid wastes, pesticides, radiation, and toxic substances

risk assessment

The process of estimating the potentially dangerous consequences of damage that might be caused by a particular practice, such as smoking, or by the use of a particular product, such as the impact of the burning of fossil fuels on global warming

risk management

The process of making decisions that try to reduce or contain identified risks

Scientific research can help the EPA ask the appropriate questions and frame the debate; but if action is to be taken and environmental goals are to be reached, the agency must issue specific regulations that limit pollution by trying to change the behavior of individuals, companies, and governments. Regulatory agencies such as the EPA ultimately receive all their power from Congress, which adopts policies through the statutes it enacts. As the policy process chapter explained, the implementation of policies or the translation of policy ideas into action is left to bureaucrats. Congress identifies problems and establishes policy goals but delegates to regulatory agencies the power to write rules that specify in greater detail the definitions, criteria, and standards of behavior

Toyota Motor Corporation produced the Prius, one successful example of a full hybrid electric mid-size car. The EPA and California Air Resources Board (CARB) also rate the Prius as among the cleanest vehicles sold in the United States based on smog forming and toxic emissions. (Shutterstock)

necessary to meet congressional intent. For example, bringing to bear its highly technical expertise, the Nuclear Regulatory Commission issues detailed rules guiding the operation of nuclear power plants. As another illustration, the Environmental Protection Agency specifies maximum contaminant levels in drinking water. Congress may be very vague or very explicit in its statutes directing the work of regulatory agencies. Individuals in regulatory agencies with scientific and technical expertise are ultimately given the tasks of specifying, detailing, and defining in matters such as safe nuclear reactor procedures and acceptable drinking water contaminant levels.

Environmental regulations at once promise environmental benefits and impose monetary costs. Clean air and clean water are not free, and much debate ensues over who ought to pay how much. Heightened by media attention to toxic waste dumps, contaminated water, and carcinogens in the air, the EPA faces passionate demands from environmental groups to take aggressive action. At the same time, the agency is required by law or by presidential executive order to take into account economic considerations to ensure that the presumed benefits of environmental rules outweigh their costs. The EPA is, therefore, frequently in the middle of the political struggle over the appropriate role for government in environmental regulation, an issue that reverberates in other areas of government regulation as well.

15.5c The Future of Environmental Policy

As America looks forward, environmental policy challenges abound. Our government's difficult task of balancing interests is, perhaps, highlighted best in this arena. The EPA and other federal agencies will continue to negotiate the conflicts between those seeking to preserve natural habitats and those wishing to pursue economic development of resources. Should we preserve the pristine environment of the Alaskan arctic wilderness, or should we utilize this resource by drilling for oil there? Should we increase regulations and raise environmental standards for industries, even if this means economic hardship for some businesses and more expensive products for consumers? Should we join international efforts to slow the advance of global warming, or should we study the issue further before taking any action? These are among the difficult questions American environmental policy must confront in the coming decades.

CHAPTER REVIEW

1. Government policies provide benefits to every income group. Social insurance and means-tested programs designed for the poor are the principal social welfare policies of the national government.

2. The philosophy of social Darwinism held that only a limited government role would allow society to progress, but substantial change in the activities of government began to occur in the Progressive Era. The real revolution in the social welfare role of the national government took place in the New Deal presidency of Franklin D. Roosevelt, who initiated a variety of new policies designed to cushion the economic hardship of the Great Depression. President Johnson's Great Society was the latest period of major new social welfare initiatives.

3. Social insurance programs, including Social Security and Medicare, tend to be the largest social welfare programs. The size of social insurance programs and the fact that their beneficiaries come from across the income spectrum mean that such programs can draw on widespread political support.

4. Poverty can be measured either relatively or according to some absolute standard. The causes and extent of poverty are continuing matters of debate, but official estimates based on an absolute income standard indicate that 14.5 percent of the population in 2013 was poor. Programs designed to ameliorate poverty include Temporary Assistance for Needy Families, Medicaid, food stamps/SNAP, and Supplemental Security Income. In these "means-tested" programs, the national government, in most cases in cooperation with the states, grants cash or in-kind benefits to individuals who qualify on the basis of income.

5. Spending on some social welfare programs has been the target of budget cuts over the past two decades, but resistance to further cuts indicates the well of public support for a substantial social welfare policy role for the government. Many social welfare problems persist, but the future shape of social welfare programs depends on Americans' willingness to continue to support them in the face of other perceived fiscal needs.

6. Environmental protection efforts draw on a deep well of political support to deal with the varied threats to environmental quality. The Environmental Protection Agency, with the challenging task of administering the nation's environmental laws, confronts in its regulatory work a mix of political passions, economic considerations, and scientific data.

KEY TERMS

Michael Harrington's *The Other America: Poverty in the United States*, reprint ed. (New York: Touchstone Books, 1997) was influential in moving poverty onto the policy agenda when it was first published in the early 1960s. This study is updated by *Rediscovering the Other America: The Continuing Crisis of Poverty and Inequality in the United States*, edited by Keith M. Kilty and Elizabeth A. Segal (Binghampton, NY: Haworth Press, 2003).

William Julius Wilson's *When Work Disappears: The World of the New Urban Poor* (New York: Vintage Books, 1997); Herbert J. Gans's *The War Against the Poor: The Underclass and Antipoverty Policy* (New York: Basic Books, 1996); and David K. Shipler's *The Working Poor: Invisible in America* (New York: Vintage, 2005) are good discussions of poverty and public policy.

An effort to understand issues of the contemporary working poor is *Nickel and Dimed: On (Not) Getting by in America* by Barbara Ehrenreich (New York: Picador, 2011).

The history of social welfare policy is described in Walter I. Trattner's *From Poor Law to Welfare State: A History of Social Welfare in America*, 6th ed. (New York: Free Press, 1999).

A good textbook approach to social welfare policy is *Social Welfare: Politics and Public Policy* by Diana M. Dinitto and David H. Johnson (Upper Saddle River, NJ: Prentice Hall, 2011).

An analysis of recent efforts to reform the welfare system is found in *Work Over Welfare: The Inside Story of the 1996 Welfare Reform Law* by Ron Haskins (Washington, DC: Brookings Institution Press, 2007) and in *Stretched Thin: Poor Families, Welfare Work, and Welfare Reform* by Sandra Morgen, Joan Acker, and Jill Weigt (Ithaca, NY: Cornell University Press, 2009).

Environmental policy is explored from a historical perspective in Samuel P. Hays's *A History of Environmental Politics Since 1945* (Pittsburgh: University of Pittsburgh Press, 2000).

One of the most influential books in the development of an environmental movement in America when it was first released in 1962 was Rachel Carson's *Silent Spring* (Boston: Houghton Mifflin, 2002).

The process of environmental policy making is explored in Daniel J. Fiorino's *Making Environmental Policy* (Berkeley: University of California Press, 1995) and in Steven Cohen's *Understanding Environmental Policy*, 2nd ed. (New York: Columbia University Press, 2014).

A good text that explores the future of environmental policy is *Environmental Policy: New Directions for the Twenty-First Century*, 8th ed., by Norman J. Vig and Michael E. Kraft, eds (Washington, DC: CQ Press, 2012).

Finally, the relationship between technical experts and environmental policy advocates is examined in Frank Fischer's *Citizens, Experts, and the Environment: The Politics of Local Knowledge* (Durham, NC: Duke University Press, 2000).

Notes

1. U.S. Bureau of the Census, *Historical Statistics of the United States: Colonial Times to 1970*, vol. 1 (Washington, DC: Government Printing Office, 1975), p. 332.

2. Richard Hofstadter, *Social Darwinism in American Thought*, rev. ed. (Boston: Beacon Press, 1955), p. 44.

3. Herbert Spencer, *Social Statics* (London: 1851; New York: Augustus M. Kelley, 1969), p. 323. For a review of the criticisms of social Darwinism, see Hofstadter, *Social Darwinism*, especially pp. 200–204.

4. Richard Hofstadter, *The Age of Reform* (New York: Knopf, 1955), p. 240.

5. See William E. Leuchtenburg, *The Perils of Prosperity, 1914–32*, 2nd ed. (Chicago: University of Chicago Press, 1993).

6. William F. Leuchtenburg, *Franklin D. Roosevelt and the New Deal* (New York: Harper & Row, 1963), pp. 43, 61.

7. Social Security Administration, *Annual Statistical Supplement to the Social Security Bulletin, 2014* http://www.ssa.gov/policy/docs/statcomps/supplement/2014/index.html (December 18, 2014).

8. For details on the program, see the Medicare website, located at http://www.medicare.gov/.

9. See Edward C. Banfield, *The Unheavenly City Revisited* (Prospect Heights, IL: Waveland Press, reissue 1990), pp. 129–130.

10. U.S. Census Bureau, *Income, Poverty, and Health Insurance Coverage in the United States: 2008* (Washington, DC: Government Printing Office, 2012).

11. For more detail on the working poor, see U.S. Bureau of Labor Statistics, *A Profile of the Working Poor, 2012* (Washington, DC: Government Printing Office, 2014).

12. See William Julius Wilson, *When Work Disappears: The World of the New Urban Poor* (New York: Vintage Books, 1997) and Herbert J. Gans, *The War Against the Poor: The Underclass and Antipoverty Policy* (New York: Basic Books, 1996).

13. For a discussion of curative strategies, see Thomas R. Dye, *Understanding Public Policy*, 10th ed. (Englewood Cliffs, NJ: Prentice-Hall, 2002).

14. For an interesting account of the community action program, see Daniel P. Moynihan, *Maximum Feasible Misunderstanding: Community Action in the War on Poverty* (New York: Free Press, 1970).

15. See Dye, *Understanding Public Policy*.

16. Office of Family Assistance, "Temporary Assistance For Needy Families Program, Tenth Report to Congress," http://www.acf.hhs.gov/programs/ofa/resource/tenth-report-to-congress, Figure 12-H (December 26, 2014).

17. The Administration for Children and Families, *TANF Caseload Data, 2014,* http://www.acf.hhs.gov/programs/ofa/resource/caseload-data-2014 (December 26, 2014).

18. Social Security Bulletin, *Annual Statistical Supplement, 1989*, p. 343.

19. Food and Nutrition Service, http://www.fns.usda.gov/sites/default/files/pd/SNAPsummary.pdf (December 26, 2014).

20. Environmental Protection Agency, *Air Quality Trends*, http://www.epa.gov/airtrends/aqtrends.html (December 26, 2014).

21. The Gallup Organization, "Environment-Unfriendly Policies Have Yet to Damage Bush's Ratings," April 17, 2001, http://www.gallup.com (October 12, 2002).

22. The Gallup Organization, "Environment," March 9, 2014, http://www.gallup.com/poll/1615/Environment.aspx (December 26, 2014).

23. Environmental Protection Agency, "FY 2015 EPA Budget in Brief," http://www2.epa.gov/sites/production/files/2014-03/documents/fy15_bib.pdf (December 26, 2014).

24. These definitions are adapted from Science Advisory Board, *Reducing Risk: Setting Priorities and Strategies for Environmental Protection* (Washington, DC: Environmental Protection Agency, 1990), p. 2.

POP QUIZ

1. _____ _____ are governmental programs directed specifically toward promoting the well-being of individuals and families (for example, social insurance).

2. The set of ideas that applied the theory of biological evolution to society and held that societal relationships occur within a struggle for survival in which only the fittest survive is known as _____ _____.

3. _____ is a public health insurance program in which government pays the providers of health care for medical services given to patients who are aged or disabled.

4. _____ _____ are policy strategies designed to make poverty more bearable for individuals rather than designed to attack poverty by reaching its fundamental causes.

5. The independent agency that controls and abates air and water pollution and protects the environment from pollution from solid wastes, pesticides, radiation, and toxic substances is the _____ _____ _____.

6. The Progressive Era was a time when people applied Charles Darwin's theory of biological evolution to society and held that societal relationships occur within a struggle for survival in which only the fittest survive.   T   F

7. The Great Society was the policy initiatives enacted during the first two terms of President Franklin D. Roosevelt in an effort to relieve the suffering of those touched by the Depression.   T   F

8. Medicare is a public health insurance program in which government pays the providers of health care for medical services given to patients who are aged or disabled.   T   F

9. The Welfare Reform Act abolished the requirement that welfare recipients work at least part time in order to receive benefits.   T   F

10. Risk assessment is the process of making decisions that try to reduce or contain identified risks.   T   F

11. All of the following are programs initiated during the Great Society except the _____.

    A) Civil Rights Act

    B) Elementary and Secondary Act

    C) Social Security Act

    D) Food Stamp Act

12. The public health insurance program in which government pays the providers of health care for medical services given to patients who are aged or disabled is known as _____.

    A) Medicaid

    B) Supplemental Medical Insurance

    C) Social Security

    D) Medicare

13. Means-tested programs are a type of social welfare program in which government provides cash or in-kind benefits to individuals who qualify with which of the following?

    A) having little or no income

    B) having worked a minimum of ten years

    C) having invested a set amount

    D) having lived long lives

14. All *except* which of the following are attempts at welfare reform?

    A) putting two-year limits on receiving benefits

    B) providing unemployment compensation

    C) changing the title from AFDC to TANF

    D) requiring recipients to work at least part time

15. The process of making decisions that try to reduce or contain identified risks is called _____.

    A) risk assessment

    B) curative strategies

    C) alleviative strategies

    D) risk management

Answers:
1. Social welfare   2. social Darwinism   3. Medicare
4. Alleviative strategies   5. Environmental Protection Agency
6. F   7. F   8. T   9. F   10. F   11. C   12. D   13. A
14. B   15. D

Chapter

16

Foreign Policy

In This Chapter

(Sh

Chapter Objectives

Foreign and defense policy are central concerns of the American government. The president spends well over half his time on these issues. Defense and security spending consumes about 16 percent of the total budget, representing about 53 percent of the discretionary part of the federal budget; and American military expenditures account for about 39 percent of all such expenditures worldwide.[1] The advent of nuclear, biological, and chemical weapons of mass destruction has raised the stakes of policy to enormous levels. Whereas a mistake in domestic policy can be serious, one in foreign and defense policy can be fatal.

During this period of endless crisis, personalities and events have influenced American policies and political institutions. Of particular importance are the roles of the president, Congress, and various agencies. This chapter also explores the effects of special economic and ethnic interests on defense and diplomacy as well as the major problems facing America as the world's twenty-first century superpower fighting a war on terrorism.

16.1 America's Role in the World

Prior to World War II American involvement in world affairs had been sporadic. American participation in World War I was followed by our rejection of the League of Nations treaty and a withdrawal from active leadership in world affairs. Until the Japanese attack on Pearl Harbor on December 7, 1941, George Washington's advice, given in his farewell address, to "steer clear of permanent alliances with any portion of the foreign world" made good sense to most Americans. Especially in the 1920s and 1930s, **isolationism** was the American credo in **foreign policy**. This was the belief in noninvolvement in the affairs of other countries, especially staying aloof from armed conflict elsewhere in the world.

Foreign and defense policy are central concerns of the American government. (Shutterstock)

America emerged from World War II as the predominant industrial and military power. In the post–World War II era a new American credo was born: **internationalism**. This was the belief in the necessity of involvement in the affairs of other countries in order to protect the nation's political and economic security. Most Americans became convinced that peace abroad and liberty at home required our permanent involvement in global affairs. Accepting this new role, America took the lead in 1945 to form the United Nations. However, the breakdown of Soviet-American relations in 1946 and 1947 illustrated that the new era of internationalism meant not only responsibility but conflict and tension as well. After surviving the tense **Cold War**, which lasted for more than four decades, America emerged as the seeming victor of the struggle at the end of the 1980s. The collapse of the Soviet empire, however, did not mean smooth sailing ahead for American foreign policy. The post–Cold War era has seen America's role in the world change and expand in unanticipated directions. Some have welcomed America's leadership in global policy, which has included foreign aid contributions intended to stimulate developing economies. Others have found America's new internationalism domineering, paternalistic, and unwanted. A few have even taken extreme and unjust measures to express their anger at America—such as the terrorist attacks on the World Trade Center and Pentagon. Today, the challenge of American foreign policy is to provide political and economic leadership while insuring national security. A solid majority of Americans (66 percent) favors this leadership role, but the percentage of Americans favoring a more limited role has risen from 20 percent to 32 percent over the past decade.[2]

16.1a The Cold War and the Post–Cold War Era

Although the United States and the Soviet Union had been allies during World War II, the rupture of relations between them had numerous causes that were steeped in mistrust and ideological division. Given the historic record, each nation had ample reasons to suspect the other.

Along with Britain and France, America had intervened militarily in Russia soon after the communist revolution of 1917 to obstruct that revolution and aid the Russian anticommunist forces. Although this intervention was brief and unsuccessful,

isolationism

A belief that America should not involve itself in the quarrels of Europe and Asia and should pursue a policy of military nonintervention

foreign policy

Efforts to pursue national objectives beyond the geographic boundaries of the nation by engaging either diplomatically or militarily with one or more foreign nations or multinational organizations

internationalism

A foreign policy perspective that concludes that America's interests in peace abroad and liberty at home require its permanent involvement in world affairs

Cold War

An era of intense ideological tension between the Soviet Union and its allies and the United States and its allies lasting from roughly the end of World War II to the collapse of the Soviet Union in 1991

it symbolized America's hostility toward this new revolutionary state. Finally, in 1933, America formally recognized the Soviet Union on the unrealized expectation of expanded trade; and during World War II, the countries became allies. That alliance was never easy. America delayed opening a second front in Western Europe, leaving the Soviets alone on the continent to face the German army. While the United States worked closely with Great Britain on the atomic bomb project, it refused even to inform the

Soviets about the project until the bomb was used against Japan. Immediately after the war ended in Europe, President Harry Truman (1945–1953) abruptly curtailed providing military supplies, through a program known as lend-lease, to the Soviet Union. Thus the Soviets contended that they were never treated as a genuine ally by the United States.

Ideological differences added to the lack of trust. From the outset of their revolution, the Soviets believed that the Western capitalist states were hostile and would give them grudging acceptance, at best. From the American perspective, Soviet communism presented a profound challenge to our institutions and values.

The failure of the United States and the Soviet Union to agree on the disposition of Germany resulted in the creation of two German states. The German capital was divided in half—into East Berlin and West Berlin—and separated by the Berlin Wall. (iStock)

The Soviets emphasized economic development above all and saw no function for representative democracy, freedom of speech and religion, free enterprise, or independent trade unions.

Through this prism of mutual distrust the United States and the Soviet Union found it difficult to resolve the complex issues created by the defeats of Germany and Japan. As the Soviet army pushed German forces out of Poland, Romania, and Bulgaria in 1945, the Soviets imposed communist regimes on those countries. American suspicion of Soviet motives and hostility to the communist social system made it impossible to accept with tranquility Soviet control of Eastern Europe, now described as being sealed from the West by an "iron curtain." Most American leaders were convinced by 1946 that Soviet domination of Eastern Europe was a first step toward the control of all Europe.

The Soviets resented American insistence on free elections in Eastern Europe, arguing that they had a legitimate claim to dominant political influence in bordering countries vital to their security. The failure of the two superpowers to agree on the Eastern European issue also meant failure to agree on the disposition of Germany. As a result, the occupation zones in Germany evolved into separate German states—one allied with the West (the Federal Republic of Germany) and the other controlled by the Soviet Union (the German Democratic Republic). By 1947 Europe appeared to be permanently divided into an American sphere in Western Europe and a Soviet sphere in Eastern Europe. The Cold War would produce several tense moments in the decades to follow. President Truman's approach to the situation was to send economic aid to countries at the risk of being influenced or destabilized by the Soviet Union. His plan of opposing Soviet aggression came to be known as the **Truman Doctrine** and was a guiding principle of American foreign policy during the Cold War. The Truman administration was also responsible for the **Marshall Plan** (named for Secretary of State George C. Marshall), a multiyear, multibillion-dollar program designed to help strengthen

Truman Doctrine

A policy, proclaimed by President Harry Truman in 1947, in which the United States would oppose the expansion of communism anywhere in the world

Marshall Plan

A multibillion-dollar American program begun after World War II for the economic rehabilitation of Western Europe

Contrasting Approaches to Foreign Policy: Idealism, Realism, and Isolationism

American foreign policy is a complex mixture of domestic pressures, geopolitical interests, and ideas. Over the course of this century several fundamental ideas about foreign policy have emerged and have found articulate spokespersons and advocates.

One of those ideas is the concept of realism, which accepts conflict as a permanent part of international politics. Realists believe that foreign policy can, at best, limit conflict, not eliminate it. Peace and national self-interest, from the realist view, are best assured by constructing a stable balance of power. Since not all conflicts threaten the balance of power, realists support a policy of limits: A nation should only commit itself to those struggles where vital interests are at stake and when it has the means to prevail. President Theodore Roosevelt (1901–1909) was one of the earliest exponents of realism.

Roosevelt asserted America's primary interest in the Caribbean, where he could exclude the European powers without dragging the country into a major war. In 1903, he promoted Panama's rebellion from Colombia and then acquired the Canal Zone from Panama. In 1905, he placed the finances of Santo Domingo under American control to prevent any European country from asserting authority over that beleaguered country. Critics argued that such realism had only short-term benefits, brought America few friends, and encouraged the belief that military threats could solve all problems.

The idealist approach to foreign policy begins with the assumption that human nature is basically good and that war and other forms of conflict are not the normal condition of humankind. Political idealism holds that the goal of American foreign policy should be to promote the principles of universal peace, human rights, and democracy. President Woodrow Wilson (1913–1921) is the American statesperson most closely identified with this school of thought. In the years 1914–1916, Wilson sent American troops to Mexico, Haiti, and the Dominican Republic—not, as had Roosevelt, to stave off European intervention, but to establish democratic governments.

After war broke out in Europe in 1914, Roosevelt, then a private citizen, urged American intervention to prevent Germany from dominating Europe and thus upsetting the balance of power on that continent. Wilson was reluctant to intervene until Germany began unrestricted submarine warfare against American merchant ships. Then he justified involvement upon the most lofty of ideals. In asking Congress for a declaration of war, Wilson claimed that America would fight for "the ultimate peace of the world and for the liberation of its peoples ... the world must be made safe for democracy." When World War I ended, Wilson insisted upon a peace settlement, known as the Fourteen Points, that would require a global peacekeeping entity (the League of Nations), arms limitations, open diplomacy, and the self-determination of nations. The eventual treaty, signed in Versailles in 1919, embodied few of these principles except for the creation of the League of Nations and was rejected by the United States Senate.

In twenty years Europe was embroiled in another war. Critics argued that Wilson's efforts at peacemaking did not end European habits of power politics, hostile alliances, and imperialist politics. Such moralistic policies, critics contended, only lead to futile crusades and endless wars.

The doctrine of isolationism has deep roots in American history, going back to George Washington's admonition in his farewell address. According to the isolationist credo, America should be a beacon light of liberty for all humanity, but not attempt to impose its way of life on other societies. America would only be contaminated by its involvement in the power struggles of the world. One of the leading spokespersons for isolationism prior to World War II was President Herbert Hoover (1929–1933). Hoover saw no clear moral choice between imperialist Britain and communist Russia on one side and Nazi Germany and fascist Italy on the other. Hoover feared that permanent involvement in the affairs of the world would so enlarge the role of the government and the military in the life of the nation as to constitute a threat to our liberty. Most Americans spurned Hoover's advice, believing that America must play a continual role in the international community.

Do you see the influences of realism, idealism, or isolationism in contemporary foreign policy?

European economies, most of which had been devastated by World War II. The Marshall Plan became an American–Western European endeavor. After American aid of $12 billion over five years, European economies began to stabilize, forming the basis for a generation of Western European prosperity and democracy and further solidifying bonds to the United States.

The Soviets responded to the Truman Doctrine and the Marshall Plan by tightening their control over Eastern Europe, making both diplomatic and personal relationships between the two sides of Europe difficult. Such actions led America to develop a new foreign policy tack. Containment of the Soviet Union—holding communist political power within existing borders—became the hallmark of American foreign policy.

In April 1949, a total of twelve nations (the United States, Britain, France, Italy, the Netherlands, Belgium, Canada, Iceland, Luxembourg, Denmark, Norway, and Portugal) formed the **North Atlantic Treaty Organization (NATO)** and declared that an attack on one member would be considered an attack on all. NATO, the first mutual defense treaty signed by the United States since 1800, provided an American guarantee for the defense of Western Europe against a Soviet attack. The Soviet empire provided a counterbalance to NATO with the Warsaw Pact, established in 1955, and providing Eastern Europe with the same sort of alliance that NATO provided for the West. Interestingly, NATO never had to be used for the purposes of an all-out war during this era. Since the collapse of the Soviet empire, NATO has been expanded. It now contains nineteen member states, including some from the former Soviet Union's sphere of influence.

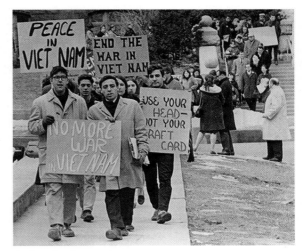

(Wikimedia Commons)

Although it was called the Cold War, this period also saw real military conflict, most notably in Korea and Vietnam. The Korean conflict (1950–1953) saw the American military deployed to the Korean peninsula when communist forces from North Korea crossed into South Korea. President Truman, following his containment policy, withdrew troops after the border between the two Koreas was resecured. The Vietnam conflict (1961–1973) also involved discord between communist and noncommunist factions in an Asian nation. This time the strategy was not as simple, and the result not as pleasing, for the American military. After nearly a decade of heavy fighting, and the loss of more than fifty thousand American lives, the Nixon administration reached a cease-fire agreement and began to withdraw the American military in 1973, leaving the war-ravaged country to continue the conflict on its own. South Vietnamese forces eventually fell to the communist North Vietnamese in 1975.

The Vietnam War profoundly altered the public's patience with the costs of containment policy. If America's leaders were to maintain some semblance of this policy, a new strategy had to be developed. President Nixon and his National Security Adviser Henry Kissinger attempted to shape a policy that would accommodate itself to these new realities. Known as **détente** (a French word meaning "relaxation" or "calm"), this approach was designed to ease tensions between the United States and the Soviet Union. Rather than containing Soviet influence by elaborate and costly means, Nixon and Kissinger hoped that diplomacy could persuade the Soviets to limit their own behavior. Although détente did not live up to the expectations of either side, it did result in some important outcomes. It established a precedent for arms limitations negotiations; and it reduced American global commitments by advocating the

North Atlantic Treaty Organization (NATO)

Multinational organization formed in 1949 to provide for mutual defense against foreign attacks

détente

A French word meaning "relaxation" that was applied to Soviet-American relations in the early 1970s

Nixon Doctrine—a claim that America would no longer be responsible for providing, as it did in Korea and Vietnam, the military personnel to protect its allies.

While American efforts such as détente had some effect at easing Cold War tensions, the end of the war itself was largely a result of changes in Soviet policy. When Mikhail Gorbachev assumed power in the Soviet Union in 1985, Soviet-American relations began a period of profound alteration. With the Soviet economy in shambles, Gorbachev realized that his country required fundamental reform and could no longer afford the military and economic costs of competition with the West. In 1987, both countries signed the Intermediate -Range Nuclear Forces (INF) Treaty, which banned an entire category of nuclear weapons (missiles with ranges between 300 and 3,400 miles) and provided for intrusive on-site inspection procedures. Gorbachev had made virtually all the concessions. Even President Ronald Reagan, who early in his administration had dubbed the Soviet Union an "evil empire," concluded, as he left office, that a fundamental shift had occurred in Soviet policy.

Where does foreign policy come from?

One of the most influential bodies in the development of American foreign policy strategy is the National Security Council, which consists of the president and key advisers and is headed by the National Security Adviser. See what this organization is up to at this site:

http://www.bvtlab.com/8n886

It was, however, a series of cataclysmic events in the first two years of the George H. W. Bush administration that altered the political map of Europe and brought the Cold War to an end. In April 1989, the noncommunist Polish Solidarity movement was legalized, with Gorbachev's consent, and swept to an election victory that June. Throughout the autumn and winter of 1989, Hungary, Czechoslovakia, and Romania followed suit. By the end of 1989, the governments of all the Soviet Union's East European allies had collapsed. New regimes asked the Soviet Union to withdraw its military forces. The Warsaw Pact was in shambles and ceased to exist, for all intents and purposes.

Underscoring this was an agreement signed in the summer of 1990 between President Bush and West German Chancellor Helmut Kohl for a united Germany within the NATO alliance. The division of Europe into two armed camps marked the ending of the Cold War, but that did not mean the end of international conflict. The Iraqi invasion of Kuwait in August 1990 and the Gulf War that followed reminded the world of that grim fact. Without two rival superpowers, however, a major burden of responding to international politics seemingly fell to the United States alone—a reminder that American leadership in world affairs would not end with the Cold War.

During the 1990s and the early years of the twenty-first century, America has been in the process of redefining its role to accommodate the changing international sphere. Presidents Bush, Clinton, the second Bush, and Obama established a large role for American diplomacy and military presence around the world. In addition to the Gulf War, the first President Bush involved America in military actions in Panama and Somalia. President Clinton continued American efforts in Somalia and sent troops to Haiti and Bosnia, in addition to continuing bombings of Iraq. President George W. Bush campaigned for office as something of an isolationist; but when confronted with the tragedy of international terrorism, he responded by using the U.S. military in Afghanistan and Iraq. President Obama entered office promising a new tenor to American foreign

Nixon Doctrine

Proclaimed by President Nixon in 1969, a policy stipulating that the United States will support its allies with economic and military aid but that the allies should provide the bulk of the personnel for their own defense

The U.S. vs. ISIS: A New Direction in the War on Terror?

In June 2013, President Barack Obama announced a shift in the ongoing war on terrorism. He stated that the extensive powers granted to the executive, the expanding use of drones to target enemies abroad, and the seemingly permanent detention of suspected terrorists put the United States at risk of living in a state of perpetual war. He intended to reduce or eliminate all of these approaches. Unfortunately, new threats and growing instability in the Middle East prevented a lasting shift away from war.

President Obama was awarded the Nobel Peace Prize in 2009 largely based on the perception that he would take the United States in a more peaceful direction than had his predecessor, George W. Bush. While the Iraq War that started in 2003 did eventually wind down at the end of 2011, new developments in international aggression have made it challenging for the president to avoid military conflict. Notably, in June 2014 an organization known as ISIS—the Islamic State of Iraq and Syria—announced its existence as a state.[1] Though earlier versions of this extremist rebel group had been around for over a decade, 2014 marked a turn in its strategy. Calling itself simply the Islamic State, the group of violent Sunni Muslims announced a caliphate—a single religious state that would place the world under Islamic religious control—and began a series of well-publicized kidnappings and subsequent beheadings of Western civilians. These actions captured media attention around the world and called out for a response from the United States—a frequent target of ISIS attacks and messages.

In 2014 President Obama responded to these terrorist acts and the territorial gains made by ISIS with Operation Inherent Resolve—a plan for a multiyear military action designed to contain and weaken ISIS. Though the president was adamant about avoiding the use of American ground troops, the actions—which include airstrikes, military advisers, and support for groups opposing ISIS—will likely cost billions of dollars and lead to many lost lives. ISIS has the explicit goal of waging war against Western democracies like the United States and has recruited an army to help carry out that goal. The threat is clear; the most effective response is less so.

Has President Obama's approach to ISIS been successful? How do we measure success in such circumstances? Was it the *right* choice to make? Neither George W. Bush nor Barack Obama entered office with plans of conducting multiple wars in the Middle East, yet both did. How much flexibility do presidents have to pursue their own path in foreign policy and how much are they limited by the circumstances in which they find themselves?

1   ISIS is also known as ISIL—the Islamic State of Iraq and the Levant. The latter term refers to a geographic region that covers parts of Syria as well as several other eastern Mediterranean countries.

SOURCE: *"Redefining the War on Terrorism,"* The Week, *June 7, 2013.*

policy—moving to shut down the military prison at Guantanamo Bay and to bring an end to the wars in Afghanistan and Iraq. Although implementing such changes proved difficult, the world recognized Obama's efforts for change; and, in 2009, he became the fourth U.S. president to receive the Nobel Peace Prize. To be sure, some recent efforts were humanitarian in nature, and many were multinational efforts. Their sheer quantity, though, underscores the growing burden of American foreign policy in the post–Cold War world of the twenty-first century. Recently, even the idea that the Cold War is over has been cast into doubt. With aggressive military moves in the Crimea by Vladimir Putin—a Russian leader who has been in power as either president or prime minister for over fifteen years—50 percent of Americans say they are worried that Cold War tensions will again emerge between the United States and Russia.[3]

16.2   The Policy Machinery

Since the Vietnam War, there has been no clear public consensus on foreign policy. Global containment was discredited by Vietnam, and the end of the Cold War has left policy makers without a clear political strategy. Consequently, every major foreign and defense policy initiative is subject to searching examination. President Carter was barely able to get the Panama Canal treaty, which returned control of the canal to Panama, through the Senate; he also had great difficulty in gaining Senate support for SALT (Strategic Arms Limitation Treaty) II. Despite his impressive election victories, President Reagan had no easy victories in Congress. His defense buildup was reduced, aid to the Nicaraguan contras was seriously circumscribed, and the MX missile program was severely limited. The vote to authorize the first President Bush to use military force against Iraq was marked by strong partisan cleavages. Even the second President Bush, who received incredible public support in the wake of the 9/11 attacks, faced significant opposition when he sought approval for large-scale military actions against Iraq.

Nonetheless, foreign policy in the nuclear age still carries a large presidential stamp. Since 1945, the major policy initiatives (the Truman Doctrine, the Marshall Plan, NATO, the Korean intervention, the Vietnam War, détente, the Gulf War, and the war on terrorism) have come from the White House. Gaining support for policy initiatives is increasingly difficult, however. Not only is Congress more independent, but the bureaucracy itself is, also, not easily corralled. Each agency frequently has its own perspective, with a cabinet secretary who may be its vigorous advocate.

The president, frequently operating through the National Security Council (NSC), attempts to control the play. The following sections explore and analyze the elaborate machinery of agencies and departments that the president seeks to dominate. They are responsible for the day-to-day operations of policy.

16.2a Department of State

Although the conduct of crisis diplomacy and the overall direction of foreign policy come from the White House, the **Department of State** has the primary responsibility for the routine daily functions of foreign policy. The department's activities include maintaining diplomatic relations with over 180 countries; operating over 300 embassies, consulates, and other posts around the world; representing the United States in scores of international organizations; being involved in the negotiations of treaties and other agreements with foreign nations; monitoring human rights policies of both our allies and our adversaries; supervising foreign aid programs; promoting cultural and educational exchanges; and making policy recommendations to the president and being responsible for their implementation.

Heading the department is the secretary of state, who reports directly to the president. This position is currently held by former Senator John Kerry. Beneath the secretary are the deputy secretary of state, six undersecretaries, and a counselor. Below that level, the department is a mix of geographic and functional bureaus (see Figure 16.1). The *geographic* bureaus (such as African, European and Eurasian, Near Eastern, Western Hemisphere, East Asian, and South and Central Asian) have within them scores of country desks that are responsible for monitoring events around the world. The *functional* bureaus—which include Intelligence and Research, War Crimes Issues, and Counterterrorism—are responsible for specialized areas of policy. They inevitably involve other departments. For example, the Political-Military

Department of State

Responsible for the routine daily functions of foreign policy; the department that represents the United States abroad; involved in international negotiations, supervising foreign aid and programs, promoting cultural and educational exchange, and making policy recommendations to the president

Figure 16.1 | United States Department of State

In addition to its headquarters in Washington, known as Foggy Bottom, the State Department has over 140 embassies abroad, more than 100 consulates, and 8 special missions to international organizations. Yet as measured by its budget and personnel, it is among the smaller executive departments. Of particular importance are functional bureaus and geographic bureaus.

SOURCE: *Adapted from U.S. Department of State, Department Organization Chart, http://www.state.gov/r/pa/ei/rls/dos/99494.htm (December 29, 2014).*

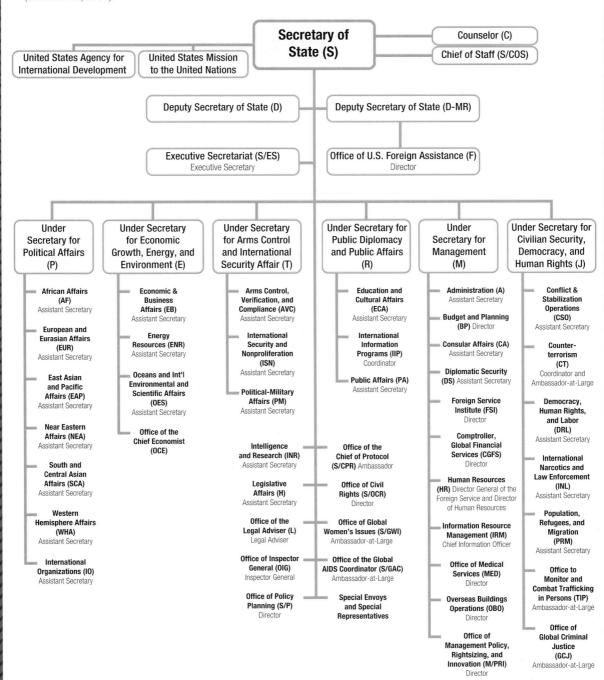

The Department of State has the responsibility for the routine daily functions of foreign policy. Some of the department's activities include maintaining diplomatic relations with over 180 countries; operating over 300 embassies, consulates, and other posts around the world; and representing the United States. Pictured is the U.S. Embassy in Budapest. (Wikimedia Commons)

Affairs Bureau frequently interacts with the Pentagon and is crucial to Department of State (also known as State Department) participation in the development of military policy.

Attached to the State Department are the U.S. permanent representative to the United Nations and the **United States Agency for International Development (USAID)**. In 1999 the United States Information Agency, which became the **Bureau of International Information Programs (IIP)**, was integrated into the department. USAID coordinates economic assistance programs, and IIP directs communications programs that provide information about the United States worldwide.

An elite corps of employees, known as foreign service officers (FSOs), staffs the State Department. They are selected through a rigorous series of written and oral exams. Few people would dispute the talent and ability of the FSOs, but they have been criticized for their caution, conformity, and elitism. These tendencies may be reinforced by the "up or out" promotion system in which a senior officer must advance beyond his or her present rank or be discharged.

Over the years the State Department has had difficulty leading foreign policy within the executive branch. In the modern age of diplomacy, the State Department must share its own field of foreign policy making with the Defense Department, the Central Intelligence Agency, and the NSC.

16.2b Central Intelligence Agency

Established in 1947, the **Central Intelligence Agency (CIA)** was originally charged with gathering information and coordinating all intelligence operations in the federal government. As tensions increased during the Cold War, the CIA shifted its primary task from the collection of intelligence information to the conduct of secret political activities. Its early operations involved aiding in the installation of pro-American governments in Iran (1953) and Guatemala (1954). Covert activities became such an important part of the CIA between 1962 and 1970 that they consumed 52 percent of the agency's total budget and 55 percent of its personnel.[4]

(iStock)

In the early 1970s, public disclosure of CIA abuses put the agency on the defensive, thus weakening its political support. The abuses involved unsuccessful efforts to assassinate Fidel Castro in the early 1960s and an attempt to prevent Marxist-leaning Salvador Allende from taking office as

---

United States Agency for International Development (USAID)

Agency of the State Department that coordinates economic assistance programs

Bureau of International Information Programs (IIP)

An agency of the State Department that directs overseas information programs

Central Intelligence Agency (CIA)

Agency, established by the National Security Act of 1947, that is responsible for gathering information and coordinating foreign intelligence operations in the federal government

BVT *Lab*

Improve your test scores. Practice quizzes are available at www.BVTLab.com.

487 | Foreign Policy | Chapter 16

president of Chile in 1970 after he had been legally elected. Congress then took steps to limit such activities. The Hughes-Ryan Amendment of 1974 required that the president notify Congress when a covert action was undertaken and certify its importance "to the national interests of the United States."

Presidents Ford and Carter set firm limits on CIA operations by placing covert activities under close presidential control. They prohibited such extreme measures as assassination and forbade any CIA operations within the United States. President Reagan, however, felt that the CIA had been unduly restricted. In 1981, he appointed William J. Casey as director of the CIA with the explicit mandate to revitalize the agency. Reagan amended the Ford and Carter orders and allowed some domestic CIA operations as long as their focus was on gathering significant foreign intelligence data.

The Reagan administration was far less reluctant than its predecessors to approve covert operations. The CIA increased its flow of small arms and other military equipment to the Afghan rebels combating the Soviet invaders. It provided millions of dollars in arms to Iranian paramilitary groups opposing the Khomeini government in Tehran. It also trained the personal security forces of Liberian dictator Samuel K. Doe. The CIA's most ambitious operation, however, involved the support of Nicaraguan exile groups, known as *contras*, seeking to overthrow the Marxist Sandinista government. Congress raised serious objections to this operation and barred funds, in 1982, "for the purpose of overthrowing the government of Nicaragua." In 1986, Congress, under considerable pressure from President Reagan, however, appropriated $100 million in *contra* aid. Only later did it come to light that some of the funds received from arms sales to Iran may have been diverted to the *contras*.

Although the current functions of the CIA are difficult to identify due to the classified nature of much of the intelligence-gathering work, the agency does make some of its activities public. For example, one recent effort has been the collection of intelligence on foreign terrorist groups. Although the budget of the CIA and its number of employees is not made public, documents leaked by former CIA and National Security Agency (NSA) employee Edward Snowden revealed that the 2013 CIA budget was $14.7 billion.[5]

The dilemma that CIA covert operations pose for our democratic society is severe. Can the American government conduct a secret foreign policy without subverting the principles of democratic control? Should it stand by helpless if international terrorists operate without constraints? There are no simple answers.

16.2c Department of Defense

The **Department of Defense (DoD)**, housed in the famous Pentagon building, is a mammoth organization. It was created in 1947 and reorganized in 1949 to reduce interservice rivalry and to provide more coherence for national security policy. DoD is comprised of three basic organizations: the Office of the Secretary of Defense (OSD), the **Joint Chiefs of Staff (JCS)**, and the separate armed services, which are headed by a civilian service secretary and a uniformed service chief.

Overseeing this organization, the secretary of defense is one of the most powerful cabinet secretaries. The defense secretary has the challenging task of advising the president on crucial military decisions, serving as the link between the military leadership and the president, and building a policy consensus within the department. Frequently this task brings the secretary of defense into conflict with the secretary of state, who may emphasize diplomacy over force, arms control over military buildups, or alliance solidarity over unilateral U.S. military action.

Department of Defense (DoD)

Established by the National Security Act of 1947 and responsible for formulating military policy and maintaining the armed forces

Joint Chiefs of Staff (JCS)

Heads of the various armed services and their chair who advise the president and the secretary of defense on important military questions

Chair of the Joint Chiefs of Staff General Martin E. Dempsey (right) and Field Marshal Mohammed Hussein Tantawi at the Egyptian Ministry of Defense in Cairo, Egypt, on February 11, 2012. (Wikimedia Commons)

Such conflict was apparent from time to time in the second Bush administration. Secretary of Defense Donald Rumsfeld demonstrated a preference for an aggressive military response in the war on terrorism, even when this meant the United States must act unilaterally. This approach was sometimes at odds with the more cautious, diplomatic route preferred by former Secretary of State Colin Powell, himself a retired Army general and former chairperson of the Joint Chiefs of Staff; yet the approach seemed to work well for Secretary of State Condoleezza Rice. Nevertheless, when Republicans suffered setbacks in the 2006 midterm elections and voters expressed dissatisfaction with the Iraq War as a reason for the change, President Bush replaced Rumsfeld with former CIA director Robert Gates. Gates proved so successful in this office that he achieved the rare feat of retaining it despite a partisan change in the presidency with the election of Barack Obama. When Gates retired in 2011, Obama appointed another former CIA Director—Leon Panetta—to fill the post. Former Senator Chuck Hagel succeeded Panetta in 2013.

The Joint Chiefs of Staff (JCS) consist of a chairperson, the chiefs of staff of the Army and the Air Force, the chief of naval operations, and the commandant of the Marine Corps. Until recently, the JCS advised the president and the secretary of defense on important military questions and also served as heads of their various services. A former chairperson of the JCS, General David Jones, argued that the service chiefs were unable to separate themselves from the interests of their individual service and to give objective advice on matters involving the defense budget. Another defense critic argued that the requirements of satisfying each individual service have weakened our capacity to prosecute war successfully.[6] Thus, giving every service a mission assignment often took precedence over designing strategy. The failure of President Carter's Desert One Operation to rescue American hostages in Tehran in 1980 was attributed to the fact that every service had to be given a piece of the action.

How much does America spend on National Defense?

Find the answer and historical analysis by consulting this page from the Congressional Budget Office:

http://www.bvtlab.com/8Tb7c

To improve the situation, Congress passed the Goldwater-Nichols Department of Defense Reorganization Act in 1986. It made the chair of the Joint Chiefs the principal military adviser to the secretary of defense and the president. Since the chair headed no specific service, he or she was expected to provide objective military advice and to avoid the bland consensus that could come from the Joint Chiefs. To reduce service rivalry further, the actual command of combat forces rests with nine unified commanders. The 2002 Unified Command Plan, which revised the previous structure, divided responsibility between five geographic and four structural unified commands.[7]

Figure 16.2 | Department of Defense

The Defense Department is practically an empire unto itself. The massive Pentagon office building covers 34 acres and contains a workforce of over 25,000 people. Approximately 2.8 million people are employed by Defense, over two-thirds of them in the armed forces. The Defense Department is divided mainly into the Office of the Secretary of Defense, the Joint Chiefs of Staff, and the three service departments.

SOURCE: Department of Defense, Organization Chart, http://odam.defense.gov/Portals/43/Documents/Functions/Organizational%20 Portfolios/Organizations%20and%20Functions%20Guidebook/DoD_Organization_March_2012.pdf (December 29, 2014).

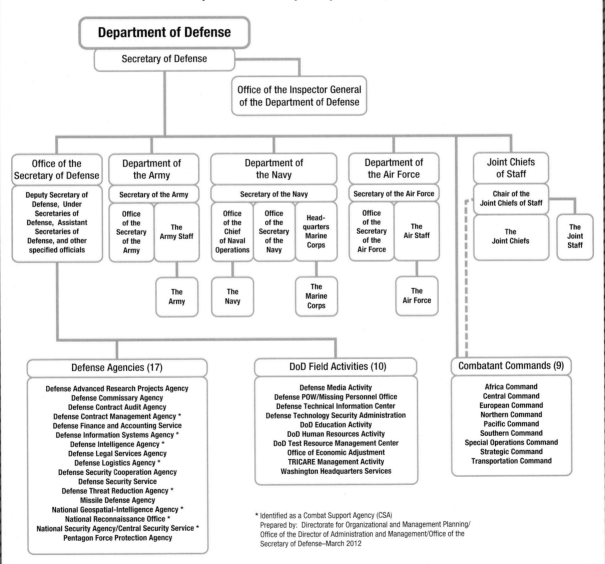

Organization of the Department of Defense (DoD)

Can Presidents Take the Country to War on Their Own Authority

The Gulf War was no minor military operation, certainly as compared to the American interventions in Grenada (1983) and Panama (1989). It involved over 500,000 troops, several carrier battle groups, and an extensive air armada. Could President George H. W. Bush have committed such forces to battle, as did President Truman in Korea, without prior congressional approval? The issue was never politically joined, as Congress did authorized President Bush to use military force against Iraq on January 12, 1991. Nonetheless, President Bush had maintained that he had ample constitutional authority to initiate such action without a congressional mandate. Was he correct? This question remains a vital one for American foreign policy. The second President Bush faced a similar question—ironically enough, also with Iraq. Like his father, George W. Bush took the constitutionally assured route, receiving permission from Congress to invade Iraq on October 10, 2002.

In the following selections, excerpted from the 1991 congressional debate on this question, Robert W. Merry argues that constitutional history and political necessity both require that the president receive authorization from the Congress before taking the country to war. On the other

hand, *Senator Jesse Helms (R–NC) in his speech to the Senate during the January 12 debate argues that the president had ample authority to make war without prior congressional consent.*

Congressional Record—Senate

Jesse Helms

On August 27, 1787, the Constitutional Convention meeting in Philadelphia adopted without debate the words of Article II, section 2, clause 1, that the President is "Commander in Chief of the Army and Navy of the United States." He is also the head of the militia of the several States, if federalized.

Thus, the Constitution made the President the only Commander in Chief of the Armed Forces of this Nation. The President is, therefore, obligated to protect the interests of the United States, to defend the rights of its citizenry, and to preserve the national security by whatever means are necessary.

Thirteen years later, at the beginning of the second decade of the Constitutional Republic, Congressman John Marshall, before he was appointed Chief Justice, declared on the floor of the House of Representatives, "the President is the sole organ of the Nation in its external relations, and its sole representative with foreign nations."

There is no historical evidence that Chief Justice Marshall ever changed his mind. The phrase "sole organ of the Nation in its external relations" was emphatically restated by the U.S. Supreme Court in 1936 (*U.S. v. Curtiss Wright Corp.*). This view has never been repudiated by the Court.

On the other hand, the Constitution fails to provide for 535 other Commanders in Chief.

Article III, section 8, clauses 11–16, specifically enumerate the war powers of the Congress in the Constitution. Congress is given the power: First, to declare war; second, to raise and support armies; third, to provide and maintain a navy; fourth, to make laws regulating the Armed Forces; and fifth, to support the militia of the Federal States. These specific powers encompass the sole authority of the U.S. Congress with regard to war.

Thus, Congress can in no way limit or authorize the President's constitutional authority as Commander in Chief. Congress has attempted to do that in the War Powers Act, an act which I strongly opposed at the time of its passage in 1973, and which no Chief Executive has ever accepted; but I believe that the War Powers Act is plainly unconstitutional.

In the short time that the Convention spent debating the subject, the Founders made a careful distinction between making war and declaring war. James Madison and Elbridge Gerry were responsible for enlarging the Presidential prerogative to enable the Chief Executive to meet the demands of national security.

As Madison warned in *Federalist No. 48*, encroachments by one branch upon another branch will upset the delicate balance of the tripartite constitutional system. Thus, it is exceedingly important to hold the branches to their intended functions with respect to the conduct of American foreign relations.

What the Framers originally intended ... was to make a careful distinction between declaring war and making war. The Constitution is silent on whether the President is required to make war after Congress declares war; at the same time, it is silent on whether the President is prohibited from making war if Congress has not declared war. Clearly, common sense requires that the President seek the agreement and cooperation of Congress in any endeavor that commits the lives and fortunes of the American people.

The powers to declare and make war are inherent powers of national sovereignty. The President has welcomed the cooperation of the United Nations and our allies in the United Nations who have supported us with diplomacy and by conducting troops. But the U.S. Constitution is superior to any obligations that we may or may not have undertaken by assenting to the U.N. Charter. No treaty can compel us, either in fact or in intention, to set aside any provision of the U.S. Constitution. The power to declare and make war therefore remains with the United States, and has not been delegated to the United Nations.

The U.S. Constitution was carefully crafted to allow much room for judgment. And in matters of war, the power to declare war does indeed lie with Congress ... nobody disputes that. But Congress has used that power only five times. On the other hand, the power to make war clearly belongs to the Commander in Chief, and we do not have but one Commander in Chief at a time.

From the Congressional Record, *January 12, 1991, p. S387*

President, Congress, and War Powers

Robert W. Merry

When presidents commit the country to military campaigns of such force, should they seek from Congress a declaration of war?

There are two elements to the question: the constitutional and the political.

Though the president is the country's commander in chief, the Constitution vests with Congress the power to "declare war." This division was a bold innovation when the Founding Fathers wrote it; at the time, all other governments vested the warmaking power solely in the executive.

But the Founders considered that approach dangerous. As James Madison wrote, "The Constitution supposes ...

the executive is the branch of power most interested in war and most prone to it. It has accordingly, with studied care, vested the question of war in the legislature."

Through the country's 200-year saga, Congress has declared war five times: the War of 1812, the Mexican War (1846), the Spanish-American War (1898), World War I (1917), and World War II (1941). And yet the forces of history have fostered a constant growth in presidential prerogative in this crucial area.

"With few exceptions, the power to initiate and wage war has shifted to the executive branch," historian Louis Fisher wrote in 1972. This was particularly true after 1945, when the cold war and the advent of nuclear weapons and intercontinental missiles raised questions about the ability of Congress to act with sufficient speed in a modern global crisis.

Thus, we had the Korean and Vietnam conflicts, two major wars waged without any formal congressional approval. Congress provided financial support, of course, and passed vague expressions of assent such as the 1964 Tonkin Gulf Resolution.

But at the base of all this was the question of whether the government had simply decided to ignore the Constitution. What precisely did the congressional power to declare war mean? Did it confer any obligation on the executive branch to seek formal congressional assent before going to war? Did it impose obligations on Congress to assert its prerogative in such momentous matters?

In light of the past 45 years, these might seem like mere academic discussion points .... But the political dimension renders them far more serious than that. In the 1950s and 60s, with World War II fresh in the nation's consciousness, the American people were inclined to delegate to

the executive broad discretion in the use of military force. And Congress pretty much went along. Thus, when President Dwight D. Eisenhower sent 14,300 marines to Lebanon in 1958, it caused hardly a political ripple in the United States. Johnson's Dominican Republic action generated far more domestic criticism, but the operation's success staved off any lasting political harm.

All that changed in the post-Vietnam era. Congress is more protective of its foreign policy prerogatives these days, more inclined to assert itself on operational matters and to criticize the president on delicate matters of state. In recent years, we have seen a House Speaker from the congressional majority party, Texas Democrat Jim Wright, virtually take control of the country's Central American policy.

All this underscores the political danger inherent in foreign military operations. When the stark realities become evident with the first signs of difficulty, the president becomes vulnerable to congressional second-guessing and naysaying. One could argue that the military challenge is daunting enough, without adding this political component.

And getting Congress aboard in the early days of national resolve is one way to lessen the political danger later on. It has been said that the postwar era was too dangerous and unstable to allow for consistent fealty to constitutional niceties such as the right of Congress to declare war. But that era is history now, and so perhaps it would be proper—and politically prudent—to return to the Constitution.

From Congressional Quarterly Weekly Report, *August 25, 1990.*

16.2d The Role of Congress

Given the different philosophies, interests, and objectives of the 535 representatives and senators, there are practical limits on congressional power in this field. Congress cannot forge a coherent foreign policy, it cannot negotiate with foreign powers, it cannot respond quickly to international crises, and it cannot conduct the day-to-day business of foreign relations. Congress can, however, tell the president what the executive branch cannot do. In the 1970s, it limited the president's authority to conduct arms sales, to intervene in Angola, to continue the bombing of Cambodia and Laos during the Vietnam War, and to send troops into combat for longer than sixty days without congressional approval. Congress serves as a check or constraining force in foreign policy—and to its critics, it plays largely a negative role. As one former senator pointed out, foreign policy is a geopolitical chess game, and chess is not a team sport.[8]

Congress is poorly equipped to conduct foreign policy for three reasons: *parochialism*, *organizational weakness*, and *lack of information*. Parochialism is found in the constituency focus of the members. As a result, their attention to foreign policy can be only brief and determined by the newsworthy nature of the issue. Organizational weakness is found in the fragmented and diffuse centers of congressional decision making. Over half of the standing committees in the House and Senate have jurisdiction over some area of foreign policy. No individual, set of individuals, or particular committee can speak for the entire Congress. Congress does not have the same resources as the executive branch for obtaining information and often must rely, therefore, upon the other branch.[9] It is, in part, because of these institutional weaknesses that Congress often abdicates the authority that it does have, turning over the reins of foreign policy almost entirely to the president. On October 10, 2002, Congress passed a joint resolution authorizing the president to deploy U.S. armed forces in order to conduct military actions against Iraq with very little congressional oversight. The fact that the House and Senate only asked the president to report his actions to them from time to time after the United States started a military campaign, and that they authorized a broad use of force, indicates how difficult Congress finds it to limit the president in foreign and defense policy. After such authority is granted, the congressional role is largely limited to funding and oversight. In the Iraq War, for example, Congress continued to demonstrate its support for the conflict by passing supplemental spending bills. It also demonstrated its concern over the Abu Ghraib prison abuses and inadequate prewar intelligence estimates by holding committee hearings, issuing committee reports, and introducing resolutions on the chamber floors.

16.3 Domestic Policy and National Security

In general, the public is more concerned with domestic questions than foreign and defense issues, but leaders cannot conduct national security policy in a political vacuum. Public opinion sets the outer limits of what is politically possible. Moreover, ethnic and economic interests exercise considerable influence on specific policies. The 9/11 attacks brought foreign policy and national security to the forefront of national attention for the first time in a decade or more, but it remains to be seen what the long-term effect on the relationship between domestic policy and national security will be.

Public opinion surveys generally show the American people to be uninformed about the complexities and details of foreign policy. On specific issues, public opinion changes frequently, is affected by current events, and—in the short term—accepts dramatic decisions made by the president. Does public opinion, then, have any influence on foreign policy?

Public moods or general attitudes, rather than opinions on specific questions, are what really influence policy. Such moods set limits within which foreign policy decisions are made. After the Japanese attacked Pearl Harbor in 1941, the public mood shifted from isolationism to internationalism. This internationalist mood became the broad consensus that provided the basis of public support for the United Nations, the Marshall Plan, NATO, and other initiatives of that period.[10]

The Vietnam War created a split in the internationalist consensus between liberal and conservative internationalists. Opposed to America's participation in that war and disillusioned with military power, liberal internationalists supported such cooperative goals as increasing assistance to the developing nations, reaching accommodation with the Soviet Union, negotiating arms control, and combating world hunger. Conservative internationalists stressed competition, opposed détente with the Soviet Union, and emphasized military defense and the use of force to protect our allies and interests abroad.[11]

In the years that have followed the Vietnam War, the public mood has vacillated. In the mid-1970s, less than 50 percent of the public approved of the use of American troops to support even such allies as Western Europe and Japan from a Soviet attack. The seizure of American hostages in Iran and the Soviet invasion of Afghanistan in 1979, however, created a shift toward conservative internationalism; by 1980 a majority of Americans supported the use of troops to defend Western Europe and Japan.

The invasions of Grenada (1983) and Panama (1989), designed to oust dictatorships and install friendly democratic governments, found broad public support. These actions, however, were brief, involved relatively few troops, and resulted in minor casualties. Although the Gulf War in 1991 involved an enormous commitment of land, air, and naval forces, victory was so swift and decisive that public support never wavered. On the other hand, the Korean and Vietnam experiences revealed that Americans soon become impatient with protracted and unresolved land wars. American support for the war on terrorism, in all of its evolving phases, has been mixed. Support for the initial strikes against the Taliban government in Afghanistan in late 2001 was very high. In November 2001, 62 percent of Americans believed the United States should "mount a long-term war to defeat global terrorist networks."[12] As the scope of conflict broadened in the months that followed, however, support for military action decreased. By October 2002, only a slim majority (53 percent) supported an invasion of Iraq, and that majority disappeared entirely when qualifiers were added to the question. For example, only 37 percent of Americans would support such an invasion if the United Nations opposed the action, and only one-third

A first lieutenant looks at possible enemy positions during Operation Saray Has, near Forward Operating Base Naray, Afghanistan. (Wikimedia Commons)

BVT *Lab*

494

Chapter 16 | Foreign Policy

Visit www.BVTLab.com
to explore the student
resources available for
this chapter.

would support the invasion if they knew there would be five thousand U.S. casualties.[13] By October 2006, with American casualties continuing to rise, no weapons of mass destruction found, and military skirmishes continuing to destabilize Iraq, 58 percent of Americans believed that sending troops to Iraq had been a mistake. Furthermore, 64 percent of Americans believed the war was going very or somewhat badly for the United States, and more Americans thought the Iraqi insurgents were winning the war. Over half of Americans surveyed (54 percent) believed the United States should withdraw either immediately or within one year, despite President Bush's plan to remain through at least 2011. Finally, 52 percent of Americans believed the war with Iraq actually made the United States *less* safe from terrorism.[14] These opinions likely made an important difference in the 2006 midterm elections, where exit polls indicated voter dissatisfaction with the Bush administration's Iraq policy and voters made Democrats the majority party in both the House and Senate. Immediately following the election, Secretary of State Donald Rumsfeld resigned and key senators from both parties indicated an unwillingness to confirm President Bush's nominee John Bolton as the American ambassador to the United Nations.

By the summer of 2010, nearly nine years after the 9/11 attacks, there were 5,545 U.S. military fatalities in the combined Iraq and Afghanistan operations. A consistent majority of Americans indicated a preference to see the Iraq War come to a close, with 62 percent indicating opposition to the war and 58 percent concluding that the war had been a mistake.[15] When President Obama moved to officially end the Iraq War by removing all U.S. troops by December 2011, 75 percent of Americans approved of this decision.[16] By the time the Afghanistan War drew to a close at the end of 2014, it had become the longest military conflict in American history and had cost a total of nearly $1 trillion.[17] With the growing threat posed by the Islamic State, it seems that U.S. military intervention in the Middle East will continue for the foreseeable future.

How do such moods affect foreign policy? They can place limits on the choices available to policy makers. The American public is clearer about what they do not want than about what should be done. During the late 1960s and early 1970s, public opinion opposed continued American involvement in the Vietnam War; but it gave no clear indication, however, as to how the Nixon administration should end that involvement. The government faces a similar situation today: Most Americans want a change in America's involvement in the Middle East, but they remain somewhat divided on exactly what that change should be.

16.3b Multinational Corporations and Banks

Multinational corporations are large corporations based in one country that have considerable assets and numerous subsidiaries in others. The leading American giants are Walmart, ExxonMobil, Chevron, Berkshire Hathaway, and Apple.[18] These corporations command greater resources than many of the countries in the United Nations. Their sales today outrank all but the richest nations of the world. ExxonMobil, for example, made over $32 billion in profits in 2013 and its revenues are approximately 2.5 percent of the U.S. gross domestic product.

In 1975, the United States, through the CIA, actively opposed the Soviet- and Cuban-backed faction in Angola, known as the MPLA. The Gulf Oil Company, with extensive oil investments in Angola, however, made its royalty payments to the MPLA in amounts that far exceeded the budget of the CIA operation. When the State Department protested, Gulf temporarily suspended its payments. They were eventually resumed after the MPLA had triumphed over the pro-Western faction, and Gulf Oil continued to develop a cooperative relationship with the Marxist MPLA

multinational corporations

Large companies that carry on business in two or more countries simultaneously

government.[19] In 2000, multinational corporations successfully lobbied for the passage of a bill providing permanent normalized trade relations (PNTR) with China. America had held the giant Asian country at arm's length in the past, due to a poor human rights record; but corporations lobbied diligently for America to reduce trade barriers. These efforts, in addition to $58 million in campaign contributions, may have played an important role in the policy change. The new trade status resulted in $123.9 billion in trade between the two nations in 2000, a 22 percent jump over the previous year.[20] By 2013, that figure had surpassed the $440 billion mark.[21]

Pictured here is the interior of a Walmart store in China. Walmart is a multinational corporation, a large corporation based in one country that has considerable assets and numerous subsidiaries in others. (Wikimedia Commons)

American banks have also become heavily involved in overseas activities. In 1980 American banks had made $280 billion in overseas loans, a large portion of which went to developing nations and Eastern Europe. By the end of 2005, American banks claimed over $1.29 trillion in international investment, with some of the recent growth coming in the form of loans to Western Europe and the Caribbean.[22] Are loans of this nature and magnitude in the interests of the American people? Critics of the banks contend that loans to unstable developing governments unnecessarily risk important investment capital. Supporters argue they can help development schemes and add to stability in these parts of the world.

The volume of these debts underscores the growing interdependence of the world economy. For example, what would happen if a major debtor nation defaulted on its loans? Clearly it could throw many of the major banks, and perhaps the entire international economy, into turmoil. Indeed this was just the risk the world economy faced in the late 1990s when several East Asian countries became mired in economic turmoil. It was only the proffering of over $200 billion in aid packages from the International Monetary Fund that prevented a much deeper and more widespread crisis.

While foreign loans and investments gave American banks and corporations a stake in the economies of these countries, the leverage of the multinational corporations can work both ways—opening the door to foreign influence over the American economy as well. Japanese companies, for example, made large investments in the United States, buying Columbia Records and the Rockefeller Center. The Japanese automobile and electronics industries depend heavily upon their American customers. Japanese companies contribute to state political campaigns, and the Japanese government spends millions each year lobbying Congress against legislation that would limit the market for Japanese goods. Over the past decade, as Japan's

ExxonMobil Research and Development Headquarters in Shanghai, China (Wikimedia Commons)

economy has stumbled, other nations, notably China, have followed this lead by investing in America, adding to the complexity of American foreign policy.

16.3c The Military-Industrial Complex

In his farewell address, President Eisenhower warned the American people "against the acquisition of unwarranted influence, whether sought or unsought, by the military-industrial complex. The potential for disastrous use of misplaced power exists and will persist." What is the military-industrial complex? Does its influence distort our national security policy?

Few observers deny the existence or importance of the **military-industrial complex**. It includes the Pentagon, major corporations whose profits depend on large defense contracts, members of Congress whose states and districts include these contractors or military installations, unions whose members depend on defense work, and the numerous defense scientists and academic strategists whose work is funded by the military.

Critics find that the influence of the military-industrial complex distorts defense policy and weakens our economy. They charge that by absorbing so much of the country's scientific and engineering talent, it erodes our ability to compete with other industrialized countries in the application of advanced technology to consumer products.

Second, critics argue that the military-industrial complex favors the production of weapons that are too expensive and often obsolete. Much of the blame for this centers on Congress, which frequently funds weapons systems regardless of their military value, simply because they are produced in the districts of influential members.

Several of the nation's largest corporations—Boeing, United Technologies, Lockheed Martin, Honeywell International, and Raytheon, for example—each have revenues in excess of $20 billion and gain a large percentage of their sales from the federal government, most of it related to defense.[23] These companies also operate some of the largest PACs in America and channel their contributions to members of Congress on the Appropriation and Armed Forces Committees. In the 2012 election cycle, defense corporations spent over $27 million in campaign and soft money contributions, with about 40 percent going to Democrats and 60 percent to Republicans.[24] Although it may be unfair to claim defense industry lobbying is the sole cause of defense spending, America spends an average of $1.2 million per minute on defense.[25]

Although many Americans anticipated a decreased need for military spending after the end of the cold war, such a windfall has not occurred. Throughout the 1990s, Defense Department officials and defense industry lobbyists insisted that America's economic well-being depended on a smoothly functioning international system, which could require the use of military power. The 9/11 attacks convinced many of this need. In fiscal year 2014, America devoted $51 billion exclusively to **homeland security**.[26]

Learning to live with the military-industrial complex is a formidable challenge to the American political system. In the era of the Founders, large standing armies, entangling alliances, and centralized governments were evils to be avoided, not accommodated.

military-industrial complex

The Pentagon, defense contractors, unions in the defense industry, members of Congress whose states or districts receive considerable military funds, and academic strategists whose work is funded by the military

homeland security

The effort of protecting United States soil, particularly from foreign or terrorist attack

16.4 Current Issues in Foreign and Defense Policy

Faced with the limits of power and yet still burdened with the obligations of a superpower, America confronts issues that defy any easy or quick solutions. Policy makers face painful choices. They must recognize the demands of Congress and the public, the concerns of our allies, the unpredictable social forces in the developing world, and the ever-present dangers of nuclear arms and other weapons of mass destruction.

Shaping the defense budget in an era of fiscal austerity involves annual struggles with Congress. Dealing with the Western European allies who have grown prosperous and independent since the days of the Marshall Plan requires greater patience and tact. Confronting threats to the peace, such as international terrorist attacks, and the proliferation of nuclear weapons may take a measured balance of military force and shrewd diplomacy. Those problems will occupy our policy makers for some time to come.

16.4a 9/11 and the Ongoing War on Terrorism

When terrorists hijacked four airplanes to use as weapons against America on September 11, 2001, they did much more than kill thousands of innocent human beings. They prompted a new era of American foreign and defense policy, known generally as the war on terrorism. In the months following the attack, the Bush administration used military force to drive the Taliban government (which had been harboring the al Qaeda terrorist network responsible for the attack) from power in Afghanistan, identified several other potentially threatening countries as an "axis of evil," and prepared for a military invasion of Iraq, which it accused of amassing chemical and biological weapons. Although an independent commission appointed by President Bush later determined that Iraq had not possessed weapons of mass destruction, the administration continued to defend the invasion on the basis of Iraq posing an imminent terrorist threat.

In addition to these highly visible actions, the Bush administration also developed a broad strategy for approaching world affairs. Unveiled in September 2002, President Bush's *National Security Strategy of the United States of America* called for "a distinctly American internationalism that reflects the union of our values and our national interests."[27] The

A firefighter surveys the remaining shell and tons of debris of the World Trade Center in New York City on September 25, 2001. Clearing the rubble from the collapsed twin towers and other surrounding buildings was a daunting task for the hundreds of workers at the site of the terrorist attack. (Wikimedia Commons)

document, which was further revised in 2006 and again in 2010, set forth three goals: political and economic freedom, peaceful interstate relations, and respect for human dignity. The Bush administration hoped to attain these goals through a strong, worldwide military presence, encouraging free trade and economic development, and transforming national security institutions.

An example of this last point is the creation of a Department of Homeland Security. Although President Bush was able to create an Office of Homeland Security within the executive branch, he needed congressional approval to make this office a permanent, cabinet-level department. The struggles he encountered in this effort are illustrative of the difficulty in changing America's formal institutions. Congressional Democrats opposed Bush's proposal, in part, because by reclassifying 170,000 federal employees, the proposal removed their job security. President Bush argued that national security should not be hamstrung by labor disputes, but Democrats were concerned that the Republican administration would use the reduced job protection clause to unfairly weed out employees for political reasons. As late Senator Arthur Vandenberg (R–MI) famously noted in regard to American foreign policy, "Politics ends at the water's edge." While this claim may have held true in an earlier era, the shape and direction of American defense policy in the twenty-first century continue to be a matter of domestic political difference.

16.4b International Organization and the Developing World

Another challenge of twenty-first century foreign policy is the great economic disparity between wealthy countries and poor countries. The latter group of countries, commonly referred to as **developing nations**, find themselves in the difficult position of attempting to gain an economic foothold and maintain political stability in a world where many other countries already have established themselves in the global market. Recognition of this difficult situation by the international community has resulted in two organizations whose mission is to help alleviate this problem. The two agencies, both part of the United Nations, are the **International Monetary Fund (IMF)** and the **World Bank**.

G7 finance ministers (front row) and central bank governors (back row) gather for a group picture during meetings at the U.S. Treasury Department in Washington. (Wikimedia Commons)

The IMF was created in 1945 to help U.N. member nations overcome problems in their balance of payments and to help avoid another worldwide depression like the one that dominated the 1930s. Starting with just 45 member nations, the IMF today consists of 188 countries and has resources (which it calls quotas) of $362 billion.

The IMF seeks to achieve its economic objectives through increased international trade, monetary stability and cooperation, and making by funds available to nations experiencing debt crises.[28] Although its objectives are noble, some have criticized the organization and tactics of the IMF. For example, critics note that the members representing the wealthier, industrialized nations of the IMF executive board often control the decisions responsible for conducting the organization's day-to-day business. Some have argued that the United States, for example, takes a carrot-and-stick approach to funding decisions, rewarding nations that fall in line with American policy interests and punishing those that do not, regardless of the economic results on which the agency is supposed to focus.[29]

Closely related to the IMF, the World Bank was created in 1944 to provide loans to poor countries, with a goal of promoting worldwide economic growth and reducing poverty. In 2014 the World Bank loaned about $65 billion to developing nations. As signs of its success, the organization points to increases in life expectancy and literacy rates and decreases in infant mortality around the globe.[30] Like the IMF, however, this body has its critics. One charge is that the bank's narrow focus on economic development sometimes causes it to make decisions that are at odds with other important concerns, such as environmental protection.

developing nations

Nations whose standard of living lags far behind that of the industrialized states

International Monetary Fund (IMF)

A specialized agency of the United Nations designed to promote international monetary cooperation

World Bank

A specialized agency of the United Nations that makes loans to poorer nations for economic development

So how does all of this affect American foreign policy? To start with, in an increasingly interconnected world, decisions that affect one nation, or group of nations, are likely to have an impact on every other country as well. If the problems of overpopulation, malnutrition, and underemployment go unattended in the developing world, the chances of civil wars, regional conflicts, and revolutions in those areas will increase. It is unlikely that such regional instability will fail to adversely affect the political stability of the industrialized world as well. Second, as the world's second largest economy—recently surpassed by China—the United States plays a particularly crucial role in shaping the global economy. With such power comes responsibility. One of the challenges for American foreign policy in the twenty-first century will be deciding which values should drive our economic relations with the rest of the world.

BVT Lab

Flashcards are available for this chapter at www.BVTLab.com.

CHAPTER REVIEW

1. The foreign policy consensus after World War II represented a shift from isolationism to internationalism. During the Cold War years, this internationalism was characterized by the doctrine of containment. After the Cold War ended in 1989–90, the United States had to develop a new approach to foreign policy, this time as the world's primary superpower.

2. Although the president no longer monopolizes foreign and defense policy making, he is the major actor and the primary initiator. Congress, though it cannot direct policy, can place important constraints on policy. Neither can the State Department dominate the foreign policy bureaucracy. As military action and covert activities have become an integral part of policy implementation, the Defense Department and the CIA have staked a permanent claim to much of the foreign policy turf.

3. A number of domestic constituencies, largely economic, have developed a strong interest in particular aspects of foreign and defense policy. Although their influence is considerable, it is difficult for them to overcome the determined will of the president.

4. Contemporary concerns, such as the war on terrorism and the economies of developing nations, defy solutions that can be reduced to simple formulas or doctrines. Every choice a policy maker makes may involve antagonizing an ally, a domestic constituency, members of Congress, or even part of the executive bureaucracy itself.

KEY TERMS

Readings for Further Study

For a comprehensive overview of American foreign policy since 1945 see *American Foreign Policy Since World War II*, 19th ed. (Washington, DC: CQ Press, 2012) by Steven W. Hook and John W. Spanier and *The Wise Men: Six Friends and the World They Made* (New York: Simon & Schuster, 2012) by Walter Isaacson and Evan Thomas.

Joseph S. Nye *The Paradox of American Power: Why the World's Only Superpower Can't Go It Alone* (New York: Oxford University Press, 2003) explores the difficulties of the United States' emerging role as the world's sole superpower.

An excellent account of presidents' actions in foreign and defense policy throughout American history is Louis Fisher's *Presidential War Power*, 3rd ed. (Lawrence: University Press of Kansas, 2013).

The process of defense budgeting is described insightfully in George C. Wilson's *This War Really Matters: Inside the Fight for Defense Dollars* (Washington, DC: CQ Press, 2000).

Emerging problems of a global economy are explored in Joseph E. Stiglitz's *Globalization and Its Discontents* (New York: W.W. Norton, 2003).

American policy toward developing nations is explored by Robert Chase, ed., *The Pivotal States: A New Framework for U.S. Policy in the Developing World* (New York: W.W. Norton, 2000).

Notes

1. Office of Management and Budget, *Fiscal Year 2015 Summary Tables,* http://www.whitehouse.gov/sites/default/files/omb/budget/fy2015/assets/tables.pdf (December 29, 2014); Global Issues, "World Military Spending" June 30, 2013, http://www.globalissues.org/article/75/world-military-spending (December 29, 2014).

2. The Gallup Organization, "Growing Minority Wants Minimal U.S. Role in World Affairs," February 21, 2011.

3. The Gallup Organization, "Half of Americans Say U.S. Headed Back to Cold War," March 27, 2014, http://www.gallup.com/poll/168116/half-americans-say-headed-back-cold-war.aspx (December 29, 2014).

4. Charles W. Kegley and Eugene R. Wittkopf, *American Foreign Policy: Pattern and Process*, 4th ed. (New York: St. Martin's Press, 1991), p. 342; Foreign Policy Association, "International Defense Industry," http://www.fpa.org/newsletter_info2584 (November 1, 2004).

5. *Washington Post*, "CIA Is Largest U.S. Spy Agency, According to Black Budget Leaked by Edward Snowden," August 30, 2013, http://www.washingtonpost.com/world/national-security/cia-is-largest-us-spy-agency-according-to-black-budget-leaked-by-edward-snowden/2013/08/29/d8d6d5de-10ec-11e3-bdf6-e4fc677d94a1_story.html (December 29, 2014).

6. David C. Jones, "Why the Joint Chiefs of Staff Must Change," in *Understanding U.S. Strategy: A Reader*, ed. Terry L. Heyns (Washington, DC: National Defense University Press, 1983), pp. 304–325; Edward Luttwak, *The Pentagon and the Art of War* (New York: Simon and Schuster, 1985).

7. Department of Defense, "Unified Command Plan," http://www.defense.gov/specials/unifiedcommand/ (October 16, 2002).

8. John G. Tower, "Congress Versus the President," *Foreign Affairs 60* (1981–1982): 18.

9. Martin E. Goldstein, *America's Foreign Policy: Drift or Decision* (Wilmington, DE.: Scholarly Resources, Inc., 1984), p. 367.

10. Gabriel A. Almond, *The American People and Foreign Policy* (New York: Praeger, 1962), p. 53.

11. William Schneider, "Conservatism, Not Internationalism: Trends in Foreign Policy Opinion, 1974–1982," in *Eagle Defiant: United States Foreign Policy in the 1980s*, eds. Kenneth Oye, Robert J. Lieber, and Donald Rothchild (Boston: Little, Brown, 1983), p. 45.

12. The Gallup Organization, "Americans on Iraq: Military Action or Diplomacy?" October 8, 2002, http://www.gallup.com/poll/tb/goverPubli/20021008.asp (October 17, 2002).

13. The Gallup Organization, "Top Ten Findings About Public Opinion and Iraq," October 8, 2002, http://www.gallup.com/poll/releases/pr021008.asp (October 17, 2002).

14. The Gallup Organization, "Americans' Views of Situation in Iraq Deteriorate Further," October 25, 2006, http://www.galluppoll.com/content/Default.aspx?ci=25132 (October 30, 2006).

15. CNN/Opinion Research Corporation Poll, May 21–23, 2010; Gallup Poll, July 10–12, 2009.

16. The Gallup Organization, "Iraq," http://www.gallup.com/poll/1633/Iraq.aspx (September 17, 2012).

17. *Financial Times*, "$1tn Cost of Longest U.S. War Hastens Retreat From Military Intervention," December 14, 2014, http://www.ft.com/intl/cms/s/2/14be0e0c-8255-11e4-ace7-00144feabdc0.html#slide0 (December 29, 2014).

18. Fortune 500 2014, http://money.cnn.com/magazines/fortune/fortune500/ (December 29, 2014).

19. Richard J. Barnet, *Real Security: Restoring American Power in a Dangerous Decade* (New York: Simon & Schuster, 1981), p. 69.

20. The Center for Responsive Politics, "A Passage to China Update: House Approves PNTR," May 24, 2000, http://www.opensecrets.org (October 17, 2002); "Anxious Eyes on Beijing—and Washington," *BusinessWeek*, April 30, 2001.

21. U.S. Census Bureau, https://www.census.gov/foreign-trade/balance/c5700.html (December 29, 2014).

22. Financial Markets Center, *Capital Flows Monitor*, (April 27, 2006).

23. Fortune 500 2014 http://money.cnn.com/magazines/fortune/fortune500/ (December 29, 2014).

24. The Center for Responsive Politics, https://www.opensecrets.org/industries/indus.php?ind=D (December 29, 2014).

25. Sean Kennedy, "National Debt Reaching Critical Mass, Military Spending Bloats Budget," June 24 2010, http://business.gather.com/viewArticle.action?articleId=281474978325767 (July 13, 2010).

26. Office of Management and Budget, *Historical Tables*, http://www.whitehouse.gov/omb/budget/Historicals (December 29, 2014).

27. George W. Bush, *The National Security Strategy of the United States of America* (Washington, DC: Government Printing Office, 2002), p. 1.

28. International Monetary Fund, "The IMF at a Glance," http://www.imf.org/external/np/exr/facts/glance.htm (December 29, 2014).

29. Gustavo Gonzalez, "Aid to Brazil, Uruguay Fails to Dampen Criticism of IMF," *Third World Network Online*, http://www.twnside.org.sg/title/twr143g.htm (October 20, 2002).

30. The World Bank, "Annual Report 2014," http://www.worldbank.org/en/about/annual-report (December 29, 2014).

POP QUIZ

1. The _____ _____ is a specialized agency of the United Nations that makes loans to poorer nations for economic development.

2. General moods are important because they can place limits on the choices available to _____.

3. Public support never wavered during the _____ _____ in 1991.

4. Congress can limit the president's authority to conduct _____ _____.

5. The Department of _____ was established by the National Security Act in 1947.

6. Internationalism dominated American thought in the 1920s and 1930s. T   F

7. America took a lead role and formed the United Nations in 1945. T   F

8. One of the causes of the Cold War was that America insisted on free elections in Eastern Europe. T   F

9. The Marshall Plan was an American program begun after World War II for the economic rehabilitation of Western Europe. T   F

10. The Soviet Union responded to the Truman Doctrine and the Marshall Plan by tightening their control over Western Europe. T   F

11. A French word meaning "relaxation" that was applied to American-Soviet relations is _____.

    A) détente

    B) louver

    C) frettage

    D) révolue

12. One of the events that ended the Cold War was the unification of _____.

    A) Poland

    B) Germany

    C) Russia

    D) Spain

13. Right below the secretary of state is/are the _____.

    A) undersecretary

    B) coordinator

    C) bureaus

    D) deputy secretary of state

14. This organization coordinates economic assistance programs:

    A) Office of International Programs

    B) Agency for International Development

    C) World Bank

    D) Secretary of Economics

15. The CIA aided in the installment of a pro-American government in _____.

    A) Iraq

    B) Hungary

    C) Turkey

    D) Iran

Answers:
1. World Bank   2. policy makers   3. Gulf War   4. arms sales
5. Defense   6. F   7. T   8. T   9. T   10. F   11. A
12. B   13. D   14. B   15. D

Appendix

The Declaration of Independence

When in the Course of human events, it becomes necessary for one people to dissolve the political bands which have connected them with another, and to assume among the powers of the earth, the separate and equal station to which the Laws of Nature and of Nature's God entitle them, a decent respect to the opinions of mankind requires that they should declare the causes which impel them to the separation.

We hold these truths to be self-evident, that all men are created equal, that they are endowed by their Creator with certain unalienable Rights, that among these are Life, Liberty and the pursuit of Happiness.—That to secure these rights, Governments are instituted among Men, deriving their just powers from the consent of the governed, that whenever any Form of Government becomes destructive of these ends, it is the Right of the People to alter or to abolish it, and to institute new Government, laying its foundation on such principles and organizing its powers in such form, as to them shall seem most likely to effect their Safety and Happiness. Prudence, indeed, will dictate that Governments long established should not be changed for light and transient causes; and accordingly all experience hath shewn, that mankind are more disposed to suffer, while evils are sufferable, than to right themselves by abolishing the forms to which they are accustomed. But when a long train of abuses and usurpations, pursuing invariably the same Object evinces a design to reduce them under absolute Despotism, it is their right, it is their duty, to throw off such Government, and to provide new Guards for their future security.—Such has been the patient sufferance of these Colonies: and such is now the necessity which constrains them to alter their former Systems of Government. The history of the present King of Great Britain is a history of repeated injuries and usurpations, all having in direct object the establishment of an absolute Tyranny over these States. To prove this, let Facts be submitted to a candid world.

He has refused his Assent to Laws, the most wholesome and necessary for the public good.

He has forbidden his Governors to pass Laws of immediate and pressing importance, unless suspended in their operation till his Assent should be obtained; and when so suspended, he has utterly neglected to attend to them.

He has refused to pass other Laws for the accommodation of large districts of people, unless those people would relinquish the right of Representation in the Legislature, a right inestimable to them and formidable to tyrants only.

He has called together legislative bodies at places unusual, uncomfortable, and distant from the depository of their public Records, for the sole purpose of fatiguing them into compliance with his measures.

He has dissolved Representative Houses repeatedly, for opposing with manly firmness his invasions on the rights of the people.

He has refused for a long time, after such dissolutions, to cause others to be elected; whereby the Legislative Powers, incapable of the Annihilation, have returned to the People at large for their exercise; the State remaining in the mean time exposed to all the dangers of invasion from without, and the convulsions within.

He has endeavored to prevent the population of these States; for that purpose obstructing the Laws of Naturalization of Foreigners; refusing to pass others to encourage their migrations hither, and raising the conditions of new Appropriations of Lands.

He has obstructed the Administration of justice, by refusing his Assent to Laws for establishing Judiciary powers.

He has made Judges dependent on his Will alone, for the tenure of their offices, and the amount and payment of their salaries.

He has erected a multitude of New Offices, and sent hither swarms of Officers to harass our People, and eat out their substance.

He has kept among us, in times of peace, Standing Armies, without the Consent of our Legislatures.

He has affected to render the Military independent of and superior to the Civil Power.

He has combined with others to subject us to a jurisdiction foreign to our constitution, and unacknowledged by our laws; giving his Assent to their acts of pretended Legislation:

For Quartering large bodies of armed troops among us:

For protecting them, by a mock Trial, from punishment for any Murders which they should commit on the Inhabitants of these States:

For cutting off our Trade with all parts of the world:

For imposing Taxes on us without our Consent:

For depriving us in many cases, of the benefits of Trial by Jury:

For transporting us beyond Seas to be tried for pretended offences:

For abolishing the free System of English Laws in a Neighboring Province, establishing therein an Arbitrary government, and enlarging its Boundaries so as to render it at once an example and fit instrument for introducing the same absolute rule into these Colonies:

For taking away our Charters, abolishing our most valuable Laws, and altering fundamentally the Forms of our Governments:

For suspending our own Legislatures, and declaring themselves invested with power to legislate for us in all cases whatsoever.

He has abdicated Government here, by declaring us out of his Protection, and waging War against us.

He has plundered our seas, ravaged our Coasts, burnt our towns, and destroyed the lives of our people.

He is at this time transporting large Armies of foreign Mercenaries to compleat the works of death, desolation and tyranny, already begun with circumstances of Cruelty & perfidy, scarcely paralleled in the most barbarous ages, and totally unworthy the Head of a civilized nation.

He has constrained our fellow Citizens taken Captive on the high Seas to bear Arms against their Country, to become the executioners of their friends and Brethren, or to fall themselves by their Hands.

He has excited domestic insurrections amongst us, and has endeavoured to bring on the inhabitants of our frontiers, the merciless Indian Savages, whose known rule of warfare, is an undistinguished destruction of all ages, sexes and conditions.

In every stage of these Oppressions We have Petitioned for Redress in the most humble terms: Our repeated Petitions have been answered only by repeated injury. A Prince whose character is thus marked by every act which may define a Tyrant, is unfit to be the ruler of a free people.

Nor have We been wanting in attentions to our British brethren. We have warned them from time to time of attempts by their legislature to extend an unwarrantable jurisdiction over us. We have reminded them of the circumstances of our emigration and settlement here. We have appealed to their native justice and magnanimity, and we have conjured them by the ties of our common kindred to disavow these usurpations, which, would inevitably interrupt our connections and correspondence. They too have been deaf to the voice of justice and of consanguinity. We must, therefore, acquiesce in the necessity, which denounces our Separation, and hold them, as we hold the rest of mankind, Enemies in War, in Peace Friends.

We, therefore, the Representatives of the United States of America, in General Congress, Assembled, appealing to the Supreme Judge of the world for the rectitude of our intentions, do, in the Name, and by Authority of the good People of these Colonies, solemnly publish and declare, That these United Colonies are, and of Right ought to be Free and Independent States; that they are Absolved from all Allegiance to the British Crown, and that all political connection between them and the State of Great Britain, is and ought to be totally dissolved; and that, as Free and Independent States, they have full Power to levy War, conclude Peace, contract Alliances, establish Commerce, and to do all other Acts and Things which independent States may of right do. And for the support of this Declaration, with a firm reliance on the protection of divine Providence, we mutually pledge to each other our Lives, our Fortunes and our sacred Honor.

John Hancock, Josiah Bartlett, Wm Whipple, Saml Adams, John Adams, Robt Treat Paine, Elbridge Gerry, Steph. Hopkins, William Ellery, Roger Sherman, Samel Huntington, Wm Williams, Oliver Wolcott, Matthew Thornton, Wm Floyd, Phil Livingston, Frans Lewis, Lewis Morris, Richd Stockton, Jno Witherspoon, Fras Hopkinson, John Hart, Abra Clark, Robt Morris, Benjamin Rush, Benja Franklin, John Morton, Geo Clymer, Jas Smith, Geo. Taylor, James Wilson, Geo. Ross, Caesar Rodney, Geo Read, Thos M:Kean, Samuel Chase, Wm Paca, Thos Stone, Charles Carroll of Carrollton, George Wythe, Richard Henry Lee, Th. Jefferson, Benja Harrison, Thos Nelson, Jr., Francis Lightfoot Lee, Carter Braxton, Wm Hooper, Joseph Hewes, John Penn, Edward Rutledge, Thos Heyward, Junr., Thomas Lynch, Junior., Arthur Middleton, Button Gwinnett, Lyman Hall, Geo Walton.

The Constitution of the United States

We the People of the United States, in Order to form a more perfect Union, establish Justice, insure domestic Tranquility, provide for the common defense, promote the general Welfare, and secure the Blessings of Liberty to ourselves and our Posterity, do ordain and establish this Constitution for the United States of America.

Article I

Section 1 All legislative Powers herein granted shall be vested in a Congress of the United States, which shall consist of a Senate and House of Representatives.

Section 2 The House of Representatives shall be composed of Members chosen every second Year by the People of the several States, and the Electors in each State shall have the Qualifications requisite for Electors of the most numerous Branch of the State Legislature.

No person shall be a Representative who shall not have attained to the Age of twenty five Years, and been seven Years a Citizen of the United States, and who shall not, when elected, be an Inhabitant of that State in which he shall be chosen.

Representatives and direct Taxes shall be apportioned among the several States which may be included within this Union, according to their respective Numbers, which shall be determined by adding to the whole Number of free Persons, including those bound to Service for a Term of Years, and excluding Indians not taxed, three fifths of all other Persons. The actual Enumeration shall be made within three Years after the first Meeting of the Congress of the United States, and within every subsequent Term of ten Years, in such Manner as they shall by Law direct. The Number of Representatives shall not exceed one for every thirty Thousand, but each State shall have at Least one Representative; and until such enumeration shall be made, the State of New Hampshire shall be entitled to chuse three, Massachusetts eight, Rhode-Island and Providence Plantations one, Connecticut five, New-York six, New Jersey four, Pennsylvania eight, Delaware one, Maryland six, Virginia ten, North Carolina five, South Carolina five, and Georgia three.

When vacancies happen in the Representation from any State, the Executive Authority thereof shall issue Writs of Election to fill such Vacancies. The House of Representatives shall chuse their Speaker and other Officers; and shall have the sole Power of Impeachment.

Section 3 The Senate of the United States shall be composed of two Senators from each State, chosen by the Legislature thereof, for six Years; and each Senator shall have one Vote.

Immediately after they shall be assembled in Consequence of the first Election, they shall be divided as equally as may be into three Classes. The Seats of the Senators of the first Class shall be vacated at the Expiration of the second Year, of the second Class at the Expiration of the fourth Year, and of the third Class at the Expiration of the sixth Year, so that one-third may be chosen every second Year; and if Vacancies happen by Resignation, or otherwise, during the Recess of the Legislature of any State, the Executive thereof may make temporary Appointments until the next Meeting of the Legislature, which shall then fill such Vacancies.

No Person shall be a Senator who shall not have attained to the Age of thirty Years, and been nine Years a Citizen of the United States, and who shall not, when elected, be an Inhabitant of that State for which he shall be chosen.

The Vice President of the United States shall be President of the Senate, but shall have no vote, unless they be equally divided.

The Senate shall chuse their other Officers, and also a President pro tempore, in the Absence of the Vice President, or when he shall exercise the Office of President of the United States.

The Senate shall have the sole Power to try all Impeachments. When sitting for that Purpose, they shall be on Oath or Affirmation. When the President of the United States is tried, the Chief Justice shall preside: And no Person shall be convicted without the Concurrence of two thirds of the Members present.

Judgment in Cases of Impeachment shall not extend further than to removal from Office, and disqualification to hold and enjoy any Office of honor, Trust, or Profit under the United States: but the Party convicted shall nevertheless be liable and subject to Indictment, Trial, Judgment and Punishment, according to Law.

Section 4   The Times, Places and Manner of holding Elections for Senators and Representatives, shall be prescribed in each State by the Legislature thereof; but the Congress may at any time by Law make or alter such Regulations, except as to the Places of chusing Senators.

The Congress shall assemble at least once in every Year, and such Meeting shall be on the first Monday in December, unless they shall by Law appoint a different Day.

Section 5   Each House shall be the Judge of the Elections, Returns and Qualifications of its own Members, and a Majority of each shall constitute a Quorum to do Business; but a smaller number may adjourn from day to day, and may be authorized to compel the Attendance of absent Members, in such Manner, and under such Penalties, as each House may provide.

Each House may determine the Rules of its Proceedings, punish its Members for disorderly Behaviour, and, with the Concurrence of two thirds, expel a Member.

Each House shall keep a Journal of its Proceedings, and from time to time publish the same, excepting such Parts as may in their Judgment require Secrecy; and the Yeas and Nays of the Members of either House on any question shall, at the Desire of one fifth of those Present, be entered on the Journal.

Neither House, during the Session of Congress, shall, without the Consent of the other, adjourn for more than three days, nor to any other Place than that in which the two Houses shall be sitting.

Section 6   The Senators and Representatives shall receive a Compensation for their Services, to be ascertained by Law, and paid out of the Treasury of the United States. They shall in all Cases, except Treason, Felony and Breach of the Peace, be privileged from Arrest during their Attendance at the Session of their respective Houses, and in going to and returning from the same; and for any Speech or Debate in either House, they shall not be questioned in any other Place.

No Senator or Representative shall, during the Time for which he was elected, be appointed to any civil Office under the Authority of the United States, which shall have been created, or the Emoluments whereof shall have been increased, during such time; and no Person holding any Office under the United States shall be a Member of either House during his Continuance in Office.

Section 7   All Bills for raising Revenue shall originate in the House of Representatives; but the Senate may propose or concur with Amendments as on other Bills.

Every Bill which shall have passed the House of Representatives and the Senate, shall, before it become a Law, be presented to the President of the United States: If he approve he shall sign it, but if not he shall return it, with his Objections to that House in which it shall have originated, who shall enter the Objections at large on their Journal, and proceed to reconsider it. If after such Reconsideration two thirds of that House shall agree to pass the Bill, it shall be sent, together with the Objections, to the other House, by which it shall likewise be reconsidered, and if approved by two thirds of that House, it shall become a Law. But in all such Cases the Votes of both Houses shall be determined by yeas and Nays, and the Names of the Persons voting for and against the Bill shall be entered on the Journal of each House respectively. If any Bill shall not be returned by the President within ten Days (Sundays excepted) after it shall have been presented to him, the Same shall be a Law, in like Manner as if he had signed it, unless the Congress by their Adjournment prevent its Return, in which Case it shall not be a Law.

Every Order, Resolution, or Vote to which the Concurrence of the Senate and House of Representatives may be necessary (except on a question of Adjournment) shall be presented to the President of the United States; and before the Same shall take Effect, shall be approved by him, or being disapproved by him, shall be repassed by two thirds of the Senate and House of Representatives, according to the Rules and Limitations prescribed in the Case of a Bill.

Section 8   The Congress shall have Power To lay and collect Taxes, Duties, Imposts and Excises, to pay the Debts and provide for the common Defense and general Welfare of the United States; but all Duties, Imposts and Excises shall be uniform throughout the United States;

To borrow Money on the credit of the United States;

To regulate Commerce with foreign Nations, and among the several States, and with the Indian Tribes;

To establish an uniform Rule of Naturalization, and uniform Laws on the subject of Bankruptcies throughout the United States;

To coin Money, regulate the Value thereof, and of foreign Coin, and fix the Standard of Weights and Measures;

To provide for the Punishment of counterfeiting the Securities and current Coin of the United States;

To establish Post Offices and post Roads;

To promote the Progress of Science and useful Arts, by securing for limited Times to Authors and Inventors the exclusive Right to their respective Writings and Discoveries;

To constitute Tribunals inferior to the supreme Court;

To define and punish Piracies and Felonies committed on the high Seas, and Offences against the Law of Nations;

To declare War, grant Letters of Marque and Reprisal, and make Rules concerning Captures on Land and Water;

To raise and support Armies, but no Appropriation of Money to that Use shall be for a longer Term than two Years;

To provide and maintain a Navy;

To make Rules for the Government and Regulation of the land and naval Forces;

To provide for calling forth the Militia to execute the Laws of the Union, suppress Insurrections and repel Invasions;

To provide for organizing, arming, and disciplining the Militia, and for governing such Part of them as may be employed in the Service of the United States, reserving to the States respectively, the Appointment of the Officers, and the Authority of training the Militia according to the discipline prescribed by Congress;

To exercise exclusive Legislation in all Cases whatsoever, over such District (not exceeding ten Miles square) as may, by Cession of particular States, and the acceptance of Congress, become the Seat of Government of the United States, and to exercise like Authority over all Places purchased by the Consent of the Legislature of the State in which the Same shall be, for the Erection of Forts, Magazines, Arsenals, dock-Yards, and other needful Buildings; And

To make all Laws which shall be necessary and proper for carrying into Execution the foregoing Powers, and all other Powers vested by this Constitution in the Government of the United States, or in any Department or Officer thereof.

Section 9 The Migration or Importation of such Persons as any of the States now existing shall think proper to admit, shall not be prohibited by the Congress prior to the Year one thousand eight hundred and eight, but a Tax or duty may be imposed on such Importation, not exceeding ten dollars for each Person.

The Privilege of the Writ of Habeas Corpus shall not be suspended, unless when in Cases of Rebellion or Invasion the public Safety may require it.

No Bill of Attainder or ex post facto Law shall be passed.

No Capitation, or other direct, Tax shall be laid unless, in Proportion to the Census or enumeration herein before directed to be taken.

No Tax or Duty shall be laid on Articles exported from any State.

No Preference shall be given by any Regulation of Commerce or Revenue to the Ports of one State over those of another: nor shall Vessels bound to, or from, one State, be obliged to enter, clear, or pay Duties in another.

No Money shall be drawn from the Treasury, but in Consequence of Appropriations made by Law; and a regular Statement and Account of the Receipts and Expenditures of all public Money shall be published from time to time.

No Title of Nobility shall be granted by the United States: And no Person holding any Office of Profit or Trust under them, shall, without the Consent of the Congress, accept of any present, Emolument, Office, or Title, of any kind whatever, from any King, Prince, or foreign State.

Section 10 No State shall enter into any Treaty, Alliance, or Confederation; grant Letters of Marque and Reprisal; coin Money; emit Bills of Credit; make any Thing but gold and silver Coin a Tender in Payment of Debts; pass any Bill of Attainder, ex post facto Law, or Law impairing the Obligation of Contracts, or grant any Title of Nobility.

No State shall, without the Consent of the Congress, lay any Imposts or Duties on Imports or Exports, except what may be absolutely necessary for executing its inspection Laws: and the net Produce of all Duties and Imposts, laid by any State on Imports or Exports, shall be for the Use of the Treasury of the United States; and all such Laws shall be subject to the Revision and Controul of the Congress.

No State shall, without the Consent of Congress, lay any Duty of Tonnage, keep Troops, or Ships of War in time of Peace, enter into any Agreement or Compact with another State, or with a foreign Power, or engage in War, unless actually invaded, or in such imminent Danger as will not admit of delay.

Article II

Section 1 The executive Power shall be vested in a President of the United States of America. He shall hold his Office during the Term of four Years, and, together with the Vice President, chosen for the same Term, be elected, as follows:

Each State shall appoint, in such Manner as the Legislature thereof may direct, a Number of Electors, equal to the whole Number of Senators and Representatives to which the State may be entitled in the Congress; but no Senator or Representative, or Person holding an Office of Trust or Profit under the United States, shall be appointed an Elector.

The Electors shall meet in their respective States, and vote by Ballot for two Persons, of whom one at least shall not be an Inhabitant of the same State with themselves. And they shall make a List of all the Persons voted for, and of the Number of Votes for each; which List they shall sign and certify, and transmit sealed to the Seat of the Government of the United States, directed to the President of the Senate. The President of the Senate shall, in the Presence of the Senate and House of Representatives, open all the Certificates, and the Votes shall then be counted. The Person having the greatest Number of Votes shall be the President, if such Number be a Majority of the whole Number of Electors appointed; and if there be more than one who have such Majority, and have an equal Number of Votes, then the House of Representatives shall immediately chuse by Ballot one of them for President; and if no Person have a Majority, then from the five highest on the List the said House shall in like Manner chuse the President. But in chusing the President, the Votes shall be taken by States, the Representation from each State having one Vote; a quorum for this Purpose shall consist of a Member or Members from two-thirds of the States, and a Majority of all the States shall be necessary to a Choice. In every Case, after the Choice of the President, the Person having the greatest Number of Votes of the Electors shall be the Vice President. But if there should remain two or more who have equal Votes, the Senate shall chuse from them by Ballot the Vice President.

The Congress may determine the Time of chusing the Electors, and the Day on which they shall give their Votes; which Day shall be the same throughout the United States.

No person except a natural born Citizen, or a Citizen of the United States, at the time of the Adoption of this Constitution, shall be eligible to the Office of President; neither shall any Person be eligible to that Office who shall not have attained to the Age of thirty-five Years, and been fourteen Years a Resident within the United States.

In Case of the Removal of the President from Office, or of his Death, Resignation, or Inability to discharge the Powers and Duties of the said Office, the Same shall devolve on the Vice President, and the Congress may by Law provide for the Case of Removal, Death, Resignation, or Inability, both of the President and Vice President, declaring what Officer shall then act as President, and such Officer shall act accordingly, until the Disability be removed, or a President shall be elected.

The President shall, at stated Times, receive for his Services a Compensation, which shall neither be increased nor diminished during the Period for which he shall have been elected, and he shall not receive within that Period any other Emolument from the United States, or any of them.

Before he enter on the Execution of his Office, he shall take the following Oath or Affirmation:—"I do solemnly swear (or affirm) that I will faithfully execute the Office of President of the United States, and will to the best of my Ability, preserve, protect and defend the Constitution of the United States."

Section 2 The President shall be Commander in Chief of the Army and Navy of the United States, and of the Militia of the several States, when called into the actual Service of the United States; he may require the Opinion, in writing, of the principal Officer in each of the executive Departments, upon any subject relating to the Duties of their respective Offices, and he shall have Power to Grant Reprieves and Pardons for Offences against the United States, except in Cases of Impeachment.

He shall have Power, by and with the Advice and Consent of the Senate, to make Treaties, provided two thirds of the Senators present concur; and he shall nominate, and by and with the Advice and Consent of the Senate, shall appoint Ambassadors, other public Ministers and Consuls, Judges of the supreme Court, and all other Officers of the United States, whose Appointments are not herein otherwise provided for, and which shall be established by Law: but the Congress may by Law vest the Appointment of such inferior Officers, as they think proper, in the President alone, in the Courts of Law, or in the Heads of Departments.

The President shall have Power to fill up all Vacancies that may happen during the Recess of the Senate, by granting Commissions which shall expire at the End of their next Session.

Section 3   He shall from time to time give to the Congress Information of the State of the Union, and recommend to their Consideration such Measures as he shall judge necessary and expedient; he may, on extraordinary Occasions, convene both Houses, or either of them, and in Case of Disagreement between them, with Respect to the Time of Adjournment, he may adjourn them to such Time as he shall think proper; he shall receive Ambassadors and other public Ministers; he shall take Care that the Laws be faithfully executed, and shall Commission all the Officers of the United States.

Section 4   The President, Vice President and all civil Officers of the United States, shall be removed from Office on Impeachment for, and Conviction of, Treason, Bribery, or other high Crimes and Misdemeanors.

Article III

Section 1   The judicial Power of the United States shall be vested in one supreme Court, and in such inferior Courts as the Congress may from time to time ordain and establish. The Judges, both of the supreme and inferior Courts, shall hold their Offices during good Behaviour, and shall, at stated Times, receive for their Services, a Compensation, which shall not be diminished during their Continuance in Office.

Section 2   The judicial Power shall extend to all Cases, in Law and Equity, arising under this Constitution, the Laws of the United States, and Treaties made, or which shall be made, under their Authority;—to all Cases affecting Ambassadors, other public Ministers and Consuls;—to all Cases of admiralty and maritime Jurisdiction;—to Controversies to which the United States shall be a Party;—to Controversies between two or more States; between a State and Citizens of another State—between Citizens of different states,—between Citizens of the same State claiming Lands under Grants of different States, and between a State, or the Citizens thereof, and foreign States, Citizens or Subjects.

In all Cases affecting Ambassadors, other public Ministers and Consuls, and those in which a State shall be Party, the supreme Court shall have original Jurisdiction. In all the other Cases before mentioned, the supreme Court shall have appellate jurisdiction, both as to Law and Fact, with such Exceptions, and under such Regulations as the Congress shall make.

The Trial of all Crimes, except in Cases of Impeachment, shall be by Jury; and such Trial shall be held in the State where the said Crimes shall have been committed; but when not committed within any State, the trial shall be at such Place or Places as the Congress may by Law have directed.

Section 3   Treason against the United States, shall consist only in levying War against them, or in adhering to their Enemies, giving them Aid and Comfort. No Person shall be convicted of Treason unless on the testimony of two Witnesses to the same overt Act, or on Confession in open Court.

The Congress shall have power to declare the Punishment of Treason, but no Attainder of Treason shall work Corruption of Blood, or Forfeiture except during the Life of the Person attainted.

Article IV

Section 1 Full Faith and Credit shall be given in each State to the public Acts, Records, and judicial Proceedings of every other State. And the Congress may by general Laws prescribe the Manner in which such Acts, Records and Proceedings shall be proved, and the Effect thereof.

Section 2 The Citizens of each State shall be entitled to all Privileges and Immunities of Citizens in the several States.

A Person charged in any State with Treason, Felony, or other Crime, who shall flee from Justice, and be found in another State, shall on Demand of the executive Authority of the State from which he fled, be delivered up, to be removed to the State having Jurisdiction of the Crime.

No Person held to Service or Labour in one State, under the Laws thereof, escaping into another, shall, in Consequence of any Law or Regulation therein, be discharged from such Service or Labour, but shall be delivered up on Claim of the Party to whom such Service or Labour may be due.

Section 3 New States may be admitted by the Congress into this Union; but no new State shall be formed or erected within the Jurisdiction of any other State, nor any State be formed by the Junction of two or more States, or Parts of States, without the Consent of the Legislatures of the States concerned as well as of the Congress.

The Congress shall have Power to dispose of and make all needful Rules and Regulations respecting the Territory or other Property belonging to the United States; and nothing in this Constitution shall be so construed as to Prejudice any Claims of the United States, or of any particular State.

Section 4 The United States shall guarantee to every State in this Union a Republican Form of Government, and shall protect each of them against Invasion; and on Application of the Legislature, or of the Executive (when the Legislature cannot be convened) against domestic Violence.

Article V

The Congress, whenever two-thirds of both Houses shall deem it necessary, shall propose Amendments to this Constitution, or, on the Application of the Legislatures of two-thirds of the several States, shall call a Convention for proposing Amendments, which, in either Case, shall be valid to all Intents and Purposes, as Part of this Constitution, when ratified by the Legislatures of three-fourths of the several States, or by Conventions in three-fourths thereof, as the one or the other Mode of Ratification may be proposed by the Congress; Provided that no Amendment which may be made prior to the Year One thousand eight hundred and eight shall in any Manner affect the first and fourth Clauses in the Ninth Section of the first Article; and that no State, without its Consent, shall be deprived of its equal Suffrage in the Senate.

Article VI

All Debts contracted and Engagements entered into, before the Adoption of this Constitution, shall be as valid against the United States under this Constitution, as under the Confederation.

This Constitution, and the Laws of the United States which shall be made in Pursuance thereof; and all Treaties made, or which shall be made, under the Authority of the United States, shall be the supreme Law of the Land; and the Judges in every State shall be bound thereby, any Thing in the Constitution or Laws of any State to the Contrary notwithstanding.

The Senators and Representatives before mentioned, and the Members of the several State Legislatures and all executive and judicial Officers, both of the United States and of the several States, shall be bound by Oath or Affirmation, to support this

Constitution; but no religious Test shall ever be required as a Qualification to any Office or public Trust under the United States.

Article VII

The Ratification of the Conventions of nine States, shall be sufficient for the Establishment of this Constitution between the States so ratifying the Same.

Done in Convention by the Unanimous Consent of the States present the Seventeenth Day of September in the Year of our Lord one thousand seven hundred and Eighty seven, and of the Independence of the United States of America the Twelfth. In Witness whereof We have hereunto subscribed our Names.

Geo. Washington, President and deputy from Virginia; Delaware: Geo. Read,* Gunning Bedford, Jr., John Dickinson, Richard Bassett, Jaco. Broom; Maryland: James McHenry, Daniel of St. Thomas' Jenifer, Danl. Carroll; Virginia: John Blair, James Madison, Jr.; North Carolina: Wm. Blount, Richd. Dobbs Spaight, Hu Williamson; South Carolina: J. Rutledge, Charles Cotesworth Pinckney, Charles Pinckney, Pierce Butler; Georgia: William Few, Abr. Baldwin; New Hampshire: John Langdon, Nicholas Gilman; Massachusetts: Nathaniel Gorham, Rufus King; Connecticut: Wm. Saml. Johnson, Roger Sherman,* New York: Alexander Hamilton; New Jersey: Wil. Livingston, David Brearley, Wm. Paterson, Jona. Dayton; Pennsylvania: B. Franklin,* Thomas Mifflin, Robt. Morris,* Geo. Clymer,* Thos. FitzSimons, Jared Ingersoll, James Wilson, Gouv. Morris.

Articles in Addition to, and Amendment of, the Constitution of the United States of America, Proposed by Congress, and Ratified by the Legislatures of the Several States, Pursuant to the Fifth Article of the Original Constitution.

Amendment I [1791]

Congress shall make no law respecting an establishment of religion, or prohibiting the free exercise thereof, or abridging the freedom of speech, or of the press; or the right of the people peaceably to assemble, and to petition the Government for a redress of grievances.

Amendment II [1791]

A well regulated Militia, being necessary to the security of a free State, the right of the people to keep and bear Arms shall not be infringed.

Amendment III [1791]

No Soldier shall, in time of peace be quartered in any house, without the consent of the Owner, nor in time of war, but in a manner to be prescribed by law.

Amendment IV [1791]

The right of the people to be secure in their persons, houses, papers, and effects, against unreasonable searches and seizures, shall not be violated, and no Warrants shall issue, but upon probable cause, supported by Oath or affirmation, and particularly describing the place to be searched, and the persons or things to be seized.

Amendment V [1791]

No person shall be held to answer for a capital or otherwise infamous crime, unless on a presentment or indictment of a Grand Jury, except in cases arising in the land or naval forces, or in the Militia, when in actual service in time of War or public danger; nor shall any person be subject for the same offence to be twice put in jeopardy of life or limb; nor shall be compelled in any criminal case to be a witness against himself, nor be deprived of life, liberty, or property, without due process of law; nor shall private property be taken for public use, without just compensation.

Amendment VI   [1791]

In all criminal prosecutions, the accused shall enjoy the right to a speedy and public trial, by an impartial jury of the State and district wherein the crime shall have been committed, which district shall have been previously ascertained by law, and to be informed of the nature and cause of the accusation; to be confronted with the witnesses against him; to have compulsory process for obtaining witnesses in his favor, and to have the Assistance of Counsel for his defence.

Amendment VII   [1791]

In Suits at common law, where the value in controversy shall exceed twenty dollars, the right of trial by jury shall be preserved, and no fact tried by a jury, shall be otherwise reexamined in any Court of the United States, than according to the rules of the common law.

Amendment VIII   [1791]

Excessive bail shall not be required, nor excessive fines imposed, nor cruel and unusual punishments inflicted.

Amendment IX   [1791]

The enumeration in the Constitution, of certain rights, shall not be construed to deny or disparage others retained by the people.

Amendment X   [1791]

The powers not delegated to the United States by the Constitution, nor prohibited by it to the States, are reserved to the States respectively, or to the people.

Amendment XI   [1795]

The Judicial power of the United States shall not be construed to extend to any suit in law or equity, commenced or prosecuted against one of the United States by Citizens of another State, or by Citizens or Subjects of any Foreign State.

Amendment XII   [1804]

The Electors shall meet in their respective states and vote by ballot for President and Vice-President, one of whom, at least, shall not be an inhabitant of the same state with themselves; they shall name in their ballots the person voted for as President, and in distinct ballots the person voted for as Vice-President, and they shall make distinct lists of all persons voted for as President, and of all persons voted for as Vice-President, and of the number of votes for each, which lists they shall sign and certify, and transmit sealed to the seat of the government of the United States, directed to the President of the Senate;—the President of the Senate shall, in the presence of the Senate and House of Representatives, open all the certificates and the votes shall then be counted;—The person having the greatest number of votes for President, shall be the President, if such number be a majority of the whole number of Electors appointed; and if no person have such majority, then from the persons having the highest numbers not exceeding three on the list of those voted for as President, the House of Representatives shall choose immediately, by ballot, the President. But in choosing the President, the votes shall be taken by states, the representation from each state having one vote; a quorum for this purpose shall consist of a member or members from two thirds of the states, and a majority of all the states shall be necessary to a choice. And if the House of Representatives shall not choose a President whenever the right of choice shall devolve upon them, before the fourth day of March next following, then the Vice-

President shall act as President, as in the case of the death or other constitutional disability of the President.——The person having the greatest number of votes as Vice-President, shall be the Vice-President, if such number be a majority of the whole number of Electors appointed, and if no person have a majority, then from the two highest numbers on the list, the Senate shall choose the Vice-President; a quorum for the purpose shall consist of two-thirds of the whole number of Senators, and a majority of the whole number shall be necessary to a choice. But no person constitutionally ineligible to the office of President shall be eligible to that of Vice-President of the United States.

Amendment XIII   [1865]

Section 1   Neither slavery nor involuntary servitude, except as a punishment for crime whereof the party shall have been duly convicted, shall exist within the United States, or any place subject to their jurisdiction.

Section 2   Congress shall have power to enforce this article by appropriate legislation.

Amendment XIV   [1868]

Section 1   All persons born or naturalized in the United States, and subject to the jurisdiction thereof, are citizens of the United States and of the State wherein they reside. No State shall make or enforce any law which shall abridge the privileges or immunities of citizens of the United States; nor shall any State deprive any person of life, liberty, or property, without due process of law; nor deny to any person within its jurisdiction the equal protection of the laws.

Section 2   Representatives shall be apportioned among the several States according to their respective numbers, counting the whole number of persons in each State, excluding Indians not taxed. But when the right to vote at any election for the choice of electors for President and Vice-President of the United States, Representatives in Congress, the Executive and Judicial officers of a State, or the members of the Legislature thereof, is denied to any of the male inhabitants of such State, being twenty-one years of age, and citizens of the United States, or in any way abridged, except for participation in rebellion, or other crime, the basis of representation therein shall be reduced in the proportion which the number of such male citizens shall bear to the whole number of male citizens twenty-one years of age in such State.

Section 3   No person shall be a Senator or Representative in Congress, or elector of President and Vice-President, or hold any office, civil or military, under the United States, or under any State, who, having previously taken an oath, as a member of Congress, or as an officer of the United States, or as a member of any State legislature, or as an executive or judicial officer of any State, to support the Constitution of the United States, shall have engaged in insurrection or rebellion against the same, or given aid or comfort to the enemies thereof. But Congress may by a vote of two-thirds of each House, remove such disability.

Section 4   The validity of the public debt of the United States, authorized by law, including debts incurred for payment of pensions and bounties for services in suppressing insurrection or rebellion, shall not be questioned. But neither the United States nor any State shall assume or pay any debt or obligation incurred in aid of insurrection or rebellion against the United States, or any claim for the loss or emancipation of any slave; but all such debts, obligations, and claims shall be held illegal and void.

Section 5   The Congress shall have the power to enforce, by appropriate legislation, the provisions of this article.

Amendment XV [1870]

Section 1 The right of citizens of the United States to vote shall not be denied or abridged by the United States or by any State on account of race, color, or previous condition of servitude—

Section 2 The Congress shall have power to enforce this article by appropriate legislation.

Amendment XVI [1913]

The Congress shall have power to lay and collect taxes on incomes, from whatever source derived, without apportionment among the several States, and without regard to any census or enumeration.

Amendment XVII [1913]

The Senate of the United States shall be composed of two Senators from each State, elected by the people thereof, for six years; and each Senator shall have one vote. The electors in each State shall have the qualifications requisite for electors of the most numerous branch of the State legislatures.

When vacancies happen in the representation of any State in the Senate, the executive authority of such State shall issue writs of election to fill such vacancies: Provided, That the legislature of any State may empower the executive thereof to make temporary appointments until the people fill the vacancies by election as the legislature may direct.

This amendment shall not be so construed as to affect the election or term of any Senator chosen before it becomes valid as part of the Constitution.

Amendment XVIII [1919]

Section 1 After one year from the ratification of this article the manufacture, sale, or transportation of intoxicating liquors within, the importation thereof into, or the exportation thereof from the United States and all territory subject to the jurisdiction thereof for beverage purposes is hereby prohibited.

Section 2 The Congress and the several States shall have concurrent power to enforce this article by appropriate legislation.

Section 3 This article shall be inoperative unless it shall have been ratified as an amendment to the Constitution by the legislatures of the several States, as provided in the Constitution, within seven years from the date of the submission hereof to the States by the Congress.

Amendment XIX [1920]

The right of citizens of the United States to vote shall not be denied or abridged by the United States or by any State on account of sex.

Congress shall have power to enforce this article by appropriate legislation.

Amendment XX [1933]

Section 1 The terms of the President and Vice-President shall end at noon on the 20th day of January, and the terms of Senators and Representatives at noon on the 3d day of January, of the years in which such terms would have ended if this article had not been ratified; and the terms of their successors shall then begin.

Section 2 The Congress shall assemble at least once in every year, and such meeting shall begin at noon on the 3d day of January, unless they shall by law appoint a different day.

Section 3 If, at the time fixed for the beginning of the term of the President, the President elect shall have died, the Vice-President elect shall become President. If a President shall not have been chosen before the time fixed for the beginning of his term, or if the President elect shall have failed to qualify, then the Vice-President shall act as President until a President shall have qualified; and the Congress may by law provide for the case wherein neither a

President elect nor a Vice-President elect shall have qualified, declaring who shall then act as President, or the manner in which one who is to act shall be selected, and such person shall act accordingly until a President or Vice-President shall have qualified.

Section 4 The Congress may by law provide for the case of the death of any of the persons from whom the House of Representatives may choose a President whenever the right of choice shall have devolved upon them, and for the case of the death of any of the persons from whom the Senate may choose a Vice-President whenever the right of choice shall have devolved upon them.

Section 5 Sections 1 and 2 shall take effect on the 15th day of October following the ratification of this article.

Section 6 This article shall be inoperative unless it shall have been ratified as an amendment to the Constitution by the legislatures of three-fourths of the several States within seven years from the date of its submission.

Amendment XXI [1933]

Section 1 The eighteenth article of amendment to the Constitution of the United States is hereby repealed.

Section 2 The transportation or importation into any State, Territory, or Possession of the United States for delivery or use therein of intoxicating liquors, in violation of the laws thereof, is hereby prohibited.

Section 3 This article shall be inoperative unless it shall have been ratified as an amendment to the Constitution by conventions in the several States, as provided in the Constitution, within seven years from the date of the submission hereof to the States by the Congress.

Amendment XXII [1951]

Section 1 No person shall be elected to the office of the President more than twice, and no person who has held the office of President, or acted as President, for more than two years of a term to which some other person was elected President shall be elected to the office of the President more than once. But this Article shall not apply to any person holding the office of President when this Article was proposed by the Congress, and shall not prevent any person who may be holding the office of President or acting as President, during the term within which this Article becomes operative from holding the office of President or acting as President during the remainder of such term.

Section 2 This article shall be inoperative unless it shall have been ratified as an amendment to the Constitution by the legislatures of three-fourths of the several states within seven years from the date of its submission to the states by Congress.

Amendment XXIII [1961]

Section 1 The District constituting the seat of Government of the United States shall appoint in such manner as the Congress may direct:

A number of electors of President and Vice President equal to the whole number of Senators and Representatives in Congress to which the District would be entitled if it were a State, but in no event more than the least populous State; they shall be in addition to those appointed by the States, but they shall be considered, for the purposes of the election of President and Vice President, to be electors appointed by a State; and they shall meet in the District and perform such duties as provided by the twelfth article of amendment.

Section 2 The Congress shall have power to enforce this article by appropriate legislation.

Amendment XXIV   [1964]

__Section 1__   The right of citizens of the United States to vote in any primary or other election for President or Vice President, for electors for President or Vice President, or for Senator or Representative in Congress, shall not be denied or abridged by the United States or any State by reason of failure to pay any poll tax or other tax.

__Section 2__   The Congress shall have the power to enforce this article by appropriate legislation.

Amendment XXV   [1967]

__Section 1__   In case of the removal of the President from office or of his death or resignation, the Vice President shall become President.

__Section 2__   Whenever there is a vacancy in the office of the Vice President, the President shall nominate a Vice President who shall take office upon confirmation by a majority vote of both houses of Congress.

__Section 3__   Whenever the President transmits to the President pro tempore of the Senate and the Speaker of the House of Representatives his written declaration that he is unable to discharge the powers and duties of his office, and until he transmits to them a written declaration to the contrary, such powers and duties shall be discharged by the Vice President as Acting President.

__Section 4__   Whenever the Vice President and a majority of either the principal officers of the executive departments, or of such other body as Congress may by law provide, transmit to the President pro tempore of the Senate and the Speaker of the House of Representatives their written declaration that the President is unable to discharge the powers and duties of his office, the Vice President shall immediately assume the powers and duties of the office as Acting President.

Thereafter, when the President transmits to the President pro tempore of the Senate and the Speaker of the House of Representatives his written declaration that no inability exists, he shall resume the powers and duties of his office unless the Vice President and a majority of either the principal officers of the executive department, or of such other body as Congress may by law provide, transmit within four days to the President pro tempore of the Senate and the Speaker of the House of Representatives their written declaration that the President is unable to discharge the powers and duties of his office. There upon Congress shall decide the issue, assembling within forty-eight hours for that purpose if not in session. If the Congress, within twenty-one days after receipt of the latter written declaration, or, if Congress is not in session, within twenty-one days after Congress is required to assemble, determines by two-thirds vote of both houses that the President is unable to discharge the powers and duties of his office, the Vice President shall continue to discharge the same as Acting President; otherwise, the President shall resume the powers and duties of his office.

Amendment XXVI   [1971]

__Section 1__   The right of citizens of the United States, who are eighteen years of age or older, to vote shall not be denied or abridged by the United States or by any State on account of age.

__Section 2__   The Congress shall have power to enforce this article by appropriate legislation.

Amendment XXVII   [1992]

No law, varying the compensation for the services of the Senators and Representatives, shall take effect, until an election of Representatives shall have intervened.

Glossary

a

administration, the

The president plus senior officials such as cabinet officials, undersecretaries, and the administrators and deputies of the various independent agencies

administrative assistant (AA)

Top aide to a member of Congress who frequently acts on behalf of the legislator in dealing with staff, colleagues, constituents, and lobbyists

administrative law judge

An officer with relatively independent status in a regulatory agency who presides over and makes findings in judicial proceedings in which the agency's actions in individual cases are at issue

affirmative action

Positive steps taken by public or private institutions to overcome the remaining effects of racial or sexual bias (Affirmative action programs attempt to achieve equality of result.)

agenda setting

The process by which the news media select and focus on a small number of stories from a large number of possibilities—shaping, in part, Americans' opinions about what is important

agents of socialization

A "teacher" in the process of political socialization, for example, the family, the school, a peer group, or the mass media

alleviative strategies

Policy strategies designed to make poverty more bearable for individuals rather than designed to attack poverty by reaching its fundamental causes

Americans for Democratic Action

The best-known pressure group for contemporary liberalism

amicus curiae

Latin for "friend of the court," referring to persons, government agencies, or groups that are not parties to a case but nonetheless have an interest in its outcome and that make their views known by filing an *amicus curiae* brief with the court hearing the case

amicus curiae brief

Latin for "friend of the court"—persons, government agencies, or groups that are not parties to a case but nonetheless have an interest in its outcome can make their views known by filing this brief with the court

Annapolis Convention

The meeting of delegates from five states, held in Annapolis, Maryland, in 1786, to consider a common policy for trade among the American states; it resulted in a recommendation for a constitutional convention the following year

Antifederalists

In the first years of government under the Constitution, Antifederalists in Congress were persons who opposed ratification of the Constitution in 1787 and 1788 and opposed policies associated with a strong central government such as a national bank

appellate jurisdiction

Includes cases a court receives from lower courts; congress defines the appellate jurisdiction of the U.S. Supreme Court

appropriation

Congressional enactment that funds an authorized program with a specific sum of money

Articles of Confederation

This first plan of a national government for the thirteen American states was replaced by the Constitution; under the Articles, the states retained most political power

authorization

Congressional enactment that creates or continues a policy program and the agency administering it

b

backgrounders

News briefings in which reporters may not reveal the identity of the source of their information

balanced budget amendment

A proposal for a constitutional amendment that would require the federal government to operate with a budget in which revenues equaled or exceeded expenditures

balance the ticket

A political party's effort to appeal to a wider cross-section of voters by providing regional or ideological balance in its nominations for president and vice president

bill of attainder

A law, prohibited by the Constitution, that punishes an individual and bypasses the procedural safeguards of the legal process

block grant

Transfers of cash from the national to state and local governments in which state and local officials are allowed discretion in spending the money within some broad policy area, such as community development or social services

briefs

Documents filed with a court containing the arguments of the parties in a case

Brown v. Board of Education of Topeka

Landmark Supreme Court decision [347 U.S. 483 (1954)] that overturned the separate-but-equal standard of Plessy v. Ferguson [163 U.S. 537 (1896)] and began an end to racial segregation in public schools

budget

A planned statement of expenditure that includes specific categories of spending

Budget Enforcement Act of 1990

Legislation that fundamentally changed budget deficit reduction efforts from the focus on deficit targets contained in Gramm-Rudman-Hollings to a focus on ceilings or caps on specific categories of spending

bureaucracy

An organization that exists to accomplish certain goals or objectives called public purposes and that consists of a group of people hired and arranged in a hierarchy because of specific duties they can perform

bureaucratic model

A model of policy making that holds that bureaucracies play a crucial role in making policy because of their commitment and the expertise they can provide

bureaucrats

Individuals working in the executive branch of government who have received their positions on the basis of some type of appointment

Bureau of International Information Programs (IIP)

An agency of the State Department that directs overseas information programs

C

capital case

A criminal proceeding in which the defendant is on trial for his or her life

capitalism

An economic system based on private ownership of property and free economic competition among individuals and businesses

case

A controversy to be decided by a court

Case Act

Requires the secretary of state to submit to the Senate the final text of any executive agreement and allows agreements concerning sensitive national security matters to be submitted privately to the Senate Foreign Relations and House Foreign Affairs committees

casework

The congressional task of handling requests by constituents for information or assistance with the federal bureaucracy

categorical grant-in-aid

Transfers of cash from the national to state and/or local governments for some specific purpose, usually with the accompanying requirement that state and local governments match the national money with some funds of their own

caucus

A meeting of members of a political party (the members of a party in a legislature are also referred to as a party caucus), used in some states to select delegates to the national conventions, which nominate presidential candidates

Central Intelligence Agency (CIA)

Agency, established by the National Security Act of 1947, that is responsible for gathering information and coordinating foreign intelligence operations in the federal government

checks and balances

The system of separate institutions sharing some powers that the Constitution mandates for the national government; its purpose is to keep power divided among the three branches: legislative, executive, and judicial

chief of state

The role the president plays as the ceremonial head of the nation that can also make the president a symbol of national unity during times of crisis

Christian Right

Conservative, religiously based groups that involve themselves in the political process

civil case

Noncriminal legal action, such as divorces or attempts to recover damages following an automobile accident

civil disobedience

A form of political protest in which advocates of a cause deliberately break a law as a means of asserting its illegitimacy or drawing attention to their cause

Civil Rights Act of 1964

Comprehensive legislation to end racial segregation in access to public accommodations and in employment in the public and private sectors

Civil Service Reform Act

Legislation designed to improve the level of performance of civil servants by creating incentives for high-quality work, protecting whistle-blowers, and making it easier to fire inadequate employees

class action suit

Legal action initiated on behalf of a large number of individuals without any common interest other than their grievance against the person or institution being sued

classical liberalism

A view, dating from the nineteenth century, that government should play a minimal role in society and should permit maximum economic freedom for the individual

closed primary

A primary election in which only the members of the party holding the election are allowed to participate

closed rule

An order from the House Rules Committee that prohibits amendments to a bill under consideration on the House floor

cloture

Rule 22 of the Senate in which discussion on a piece of legislation can be suspended after no more than thirty hours of debate by a vote of sixty members

clear and present danger test

Guideline devised by the Supreme Court in *Schenck v. United States* [249 U.S. 47 (1919)] to determine when speech could be suppressed under the First Amendment

coalition

A subgroup of a party, based on common social, economic, and religious characteristics

Code of Federal Regulations (CFR)

Compilation of U.S. administrative rules currently in effect, classified by agency and subject matter

Cold War

An era of intense ideological tension between the Soviet Union and its allies and the United States and its allies lasting from roughly the end of World War II to the collapse of the Soviet Union in 1991

collective goods

Something of value that, by its nature, can be made available only to everybody or not to anyone at all

colony

A territory under the direct control of a parent state

commander-in-chief clause

Article II, Section 2 of the U.S. Constitution names the president as the civilian head of U.S. military forces

commerce clause

Found in Article I, Section 8, of the Constitution, this clause gives Congress the authority to regulate the country's economic environment

Committee of the Whole

A parliamentary device used by the House of Representatives to facilitate floor consideration of a bill; when the House dissolves itself into the Committee of the Whole, it can suspend formal rules and consider a bill with a quorum of 100 rather than the usual 218

comparable worth

An employment policy designed to overcome the economic inequities of sexual discrimination, mandating that persons holding jobs of equal responsibility and skill be paid the same

concurring opinion

A statement issued separately by a judge voting with the majority

confederation

A loose association of states in which dominant political power lies with the member states and not with the central government

Conference

The Republican leadership committee in the House

Congressional Budget and Impoundment Control Act of 1974

Legislation that significantly changed congressional budget procedures by creating budget committees, establishing a budget decision timetable, changing the fiscal year, placing limits on presidential impoundments, and establishing the Congressional Budget Office

Congressional Budget Office (CBO)

A congressional staff unit that provides Congress with budgetary expertise, independent of the president's budget staff, to help Congress clarify budgetary choices

congressional seniority

Based on a member's length of continuous service in the Congress, it can affect committee assignments, the amount of office space granted, and even the deference shown a member during floor debate.

conservatism

A defense of the political and economic status quo against forces of change, holding that established customs, laws, and traditions should guide society

constitutionalism

The belief in limiting governmental power by a written charter

constitutional theory

The concept, associated with President William Howard Taft, that the president cannot exercise any power unless it is based on a specific constitutional provision or legislative grant

continuing resolution

Legislative action taken by Congress to allow spending to proceed at the previous year's level when Congress has not met the deadline for reaching agreement on appropriations for the next fiscal year

contract theory

Theory holding that the state gains its legitimacy from the consent of the governed and is formed primarily to protect the rights of individuals to life, liberty, and property

cooperative federalism

A model of federalism that features intertwining relationships and shared areas of responsibility between the national and state and local governments

council-manager

A form of government at the local level where an elected council exercises legislative powers and hires a city manager to perform executive and administrative duties

Council of Economic Advisers (CEA)

Established by the Employment Act of 1946 as a part of the Executive Office of the President, CEA consists of a chairperson, usually a prominent academic economist, and two other members who have the primary task of analyzing economic issues for the president

court of last resort

The highest court within a particular judicial system, such as a state supreme court, to which a litigant may appeal a case

courts of general jurisdiction

The basic unit of a court system, receiving appeals from courts of limited jurisdiction and serving as trial courts for serious criminal offenses and civil suits involving substantial amounts of money

courts of limited jurisdiction

The lowest-level court in a state's judicial system that hears particular kinds of cases involving small claims, traffic violations, and minor criminal infractions

crime

A public wrong; an offense, such as murder, against society at large—even though it may have been committed against only a single individual

criminal case

Judicial proceedings that the government begins against an individual following commission of a crime

cross-cutting cleavage

The overlapping of interest group membership from individual to individual, with the result that society rarely finds the same people lined up on opposite sides on all the issues and is thus protected against political polarization

cruel and unusual punishment

Prohibited by the Eighth Amendment—at issue in capital cases

curative strategies

Policy strategies designed to reach the fundamental causes of poverty and to enable individuals to get out of poverty and lead productive, self-sufficient lives

d

dealignment

Period during which the partisan ties of the public diminish and the party system breaks down

debt

The total amount of money that the national government owes to lenders, such as banks, individual and foreign investors, insurance companies, and the variety of financial institutions that purchase government securities

decline

The idea that the American political parties are collapsing and may, perhaps, eventually disappear

de facto segregation

Programs or facilities that are racially segregated by private choice or private discrimination, not because of law or public policy

deficit

An excess of government expenditures over revenues

de jure segregation

Programs or facilities that are racially segregated because of law or public policy

delegated powers

Legal authority that the people in the states granted to the national government for certain purposes by ratifying the Constitution; can be either express or implied

delegate role

A concept of legislative work as simply voting the desires of one's constituents, regardless of one's own personal views

democracy

A system of government based on majority rule, protection of minority and individual rights, and the equality of all citizens before the law

democratic socialism

An economic system in which the major industries are owned by a democratically elected government responsible for planning and directing the economy

Department of Defense (DoD)

Established by the National Security Act of 1947 and responsible for formulating military policy and maintaining the armed forces

Department of State

Responsible for the routine daily functions of foreign policy; the department that represents the United States abroad; involved in international negotiations, supervising foreign aid and programs, promoting cultural and educational exchange, and making policy recommendations to the president

depression

A period of serious and sustained economic decline

deregulation

Process of reducing the number and scope of government regulations

détente

A French word meaning "relaxation" that was applied to Soviet-American relations in the early 1970s

developing nations

Nations whose standard of living lags far behind that of the industrialized states

direct mail

Method of contacting citizens by mail, rather than through personal contact or the mass media

direct popular election

Selection of officials on the basis of those receiving the largest number of votes cast, sometimes referring to a proposal to choose the president and vice president on this basis rather than through the Electoral College

dissenting opinion

A statement issued by a judge explaining his or her disagreement with the majority position

distributive policies

Programs such as water reclamation projects that provide considerable benefits for a few people and relatively small costs for many, usually provoking little opposition

domestic policy

A category of public policy that is comprised of policy decisions on matters affecting individuals within a political system

dual federalism

A model of federalism in which national and state governments are separate and independent from each other, with each level exercising its own powers in its own jurisdiction

economic policy

Decisions a government makes that affect the production, distribution, and consumption of goods; the provision of services; the flow of income; and the accumulation of wealth

economic regulation

Type of regulation in which a government agency issues rules that shape the structure of some industry, such as limiting entrance into the broadcast industry, or banning or encouraging certain business practices

Eighth Amendment

The part of the Bill of Rights that prohibits "cruel and unusual punishment," which is often at issue in death penalty cases

Electoral College

Institution established by the Constitution for electing the president and vice president and whose members—electors chosen by the voters—actually elect the president and vice president

electoral functions

With reference to political parties, the ways in which parties, by seeking to win elections, help to bring order to campaigns and elections

Eleventh Amendment

The first reversal of a Supreme Court decision [*Chisholm v. Georgia*, 2 U.S. (2 Dallas) 419 (1793)] by constitutional amendment, denying federal courts jurisdiction in suits against a state brought by citizens of another state or a foreign country

elitism

A model of policy making that holds that public policy decisions are made by a relatively small group of individuals acting in their own self-interest rather than in the interest of the mass of citizens

Environmental Protection Agency (EPA)

An independent agency that controls and abates air and water pollution and protects the environment from pollution by solid wastes, pesticides, radiation, and toxic substances

equality of condition

A standard, beyond equality of opportunity, that requires policies (such as redistribution of income and other resources) that seek to reduce or eliminate the effects of past discrimination

equality of opportunity

A standard that calls for government to remove barriers of discrimination, such as segregation laws or racially exclusive hiring practices, that have existed in the past

equality of result

A standard, beyond equality of condition, that requires policies such as affirmative action or comparable worth that places some people on an equal footing with others

equal protection clause

Part of the Fourteenth Amendment that is the source of many civil rights and declares that no state shall deny to any person "the equal protection of the laws"

equal-time rule

A provision of the Communications Act of 1934 that requires radio and television stations to give or sell equivalent time to one political candidate if the station has given or sold time to another candidate for that office

establishment clause

Provision of the First Amendment barring government support of religion

exclusionary rule

Rule developed in *Mapp v. Ohio* [367 U.S. 643 (1961)] that prevents the state from bringing evidence against a defendant when that evidence was obtained illegally

exclusive

An interview that an official or other individual grants to one or more journalists that provides information not generally made available to all media

executive agreements

Agreements between heads of state that, unlike treaties, do not require approval by the Senate—there are no clear legal distinctions between the substance of a treaty and that of an executive agreement

Executive Calendar

One of two registers of business in the U.S. Senate that contains presidential nominations and treaties

Executive Office of the President (EOP)

Created in 1939 to serve as the managerial arm of the presidency, it includes such agencies as the National Security Council, the Office of Management and Budget, and the Council of Economic Advisers

exit poll

A poll of voters taken as they leave a polling place and usually conducted by the media to get an advance indication of voting trends and facilitate analysis of the reasons behind the outcome of the election

ex post facto laws

Laws that make an act a crime after it was committed or increase the punishment for a crime already committed—prohibited by the Constitution

express powers

Powers specifically enumerated in the Constitution as belonging to the national government

f

fairness doctrine

A regulation of the Federal Communications Commission that required radio and television stations to devote some airtime to a balanced discussion of public issues; abolished in 1987

faithless elector

A person who is chosen to vote for particular presidential and vice-presidential candidates in the Electoral College but who, nevertheless, votes for different presidential and vice-presidential candidates

Federal Communications Commission (FCC)

An agency of the national government that regulates the telecommunications industry in the United States, including the licensing and operation of all radio and television stations

federal courts

The courts of the United States, as distinguished from the courts of the fifty states

Federal Election Campaign Act

Law that regulates campaign financing, requiring full disclosure of sources and uses of campaign funds, and limits contributions to political candidates

federalism

A system of government in which both the national and state governments share power within the same political system

Federalist, The

A series of eighty-five essays written by Alexander Hamilton, John Jay, and James Madison and published in New York newspapers in 1787 and 1788, urging ratification of the Constitution

Federalists

A term for persons who advocated ratification of the Constitution in 1787 and 1788 and generally favored a strong central government; it was also the name of the dominant political party during the administrations of Presidents George Washington and John Adams

federal question

An issue that involves the interpretation of the Constitution or a statute or a treaty of the United States

Federal Register

A daily government publication that contains proposed and final regulations, presidential proclamations, and executive orders

felony

A serious criminal offense, usually punishable by more than one year in prison

female suffrage

The right of women to vote, which was bestowed nationally by the Nineteenth Amendment in 1920

Fifteenth Amendment

Outlawed race-based restrictions on voting

fifth branch

Refers to the press in its role as a check on public officials, after the other four branches (Congress, the president, the Supreme Court, and the bureaucracy)

filibuster

Continuing debate designed to prevent consideration of a particular bill; a technique used in the Senate

First Amendment

The part of the Bill of Rights containing protections for political and religious expression

fiscal policy

Governmental decisions about taxing and spending that affect the economic life of a nation

fiscal year

For budget and accounting purposes in the national government, the twelve-month period beginning on October 1 and ending on September 30 of the following calendar year

foreign policy

Efforts to pursue national objectives beyond the geographic boundaries of the nation by engaging either diplomatically or militarily with one or more foreign nations or multinational organizations

formal party organization

One of the three components or distinguishable sectors of a political party; the official structure of a political party and includes people who officially belong to it, elected and appointed officers, and committees

franking privilege

A congressional benefit that permits members to send out official mail using their signature rather than postage

free exercise clause

Provision of the First Amendment guaranteeing religious freedom

free-market capitalism model

A model of policy making that posits a limited role for government so that the natural forces of supply and demand are allowed to prevail in the marketplace

free trade

Belief that America's economic interests are best served by allowing foreign producers to sell their goods without restriction in the United States

Fourteenth Amendment

Ratified in 1868, the amendment altered the nature of the Union by placing significant restraints on state governments

Fourth Amendment

Part of the Bill of Rights that prohibits unreasonable searches and seizures of persons and their property

fourth branch

Viewed as separate from the presidency, the collection of executive departments, independent establishments, and government corporations

framing

The way that the media present a story, consisting of angle, tone, and point of view

g

general election

Election, which occurs in November, to choose the candidates who will hold public office, following primary elections held during the spring and summer

government

The political and administrative organization of a state, nation, or locality

governmental functions

With reference to political parties, the ways in which parties, by seeking to win elections, help to organize the government, give coherence to public policy, and make government responsible to the people

government corporation

A type of bureaucratic unit that offers some service for which the benefiting individual or institution must pay directly

grass roots lobbying

Attempting to influence members of Congress by encouraging citizens in the home district or state to contact their legislators

Great Compromise

An agreement at the Constitutional Convention in 1787, arranged by the delegation from Connecticut, proposing to accept representation by population in the House and by states in the Senate; sometimes called the Connecticut Compromise

Great Society

President Lyndon Johnson's term for an egalitarian society that aggressive governmental action to help the poor and disadvantaged would attempt to create in the 1960s

Gulf of Tonkin Resolution

A congressional resolution passed in 1964 granting President Johnson the authority to undertake military activities in Southeast Asia

h

Hatch Act

Legislation that prohibits civil servants from participating in partisan political activity

head of government

The chief executive officer of a government—The president is the head of government in the United States.

high-stimulus election

Election that the public finds interesting and important

Hobbes, Thomas

Seventeenth-century English political philosopher who wrote about the basis of sovereignty residing in a social contract

homeland security

The effort of protecting United States soil, particularly from foreign or terrorist attack

home rule

A legal status in which local governments, especially large cities, can determine for themselves within broad parameters their own powers and functions without interference from the state government

House Calendar

The legislative schedule in the House of Representatives for non-money bills

House-Senate Conference Committee

A joint committee designed to reconcile differences between the House and Senate versions of a bill

i

ideology

A set of ideas concerning the proper political and economic system in which people should live

implied powers

Powers of national government that are not specifically cited in the Constitution but that are implicit in powers expressly granted by the Constitution

incitement test

The Court's current test for First Amendment restrictions that asks whether a speech act attempts or is likely to incite lawless action

incrementalism

A model of decision making that holds that new policies differ only marginally from existing policies

independent agency

A type of bureaucratic unit organizationally located outside of an executive department and generally headed by a single individual

independent regulatory commission

A type of bureaucratic unit organizationally located outside of an executive department, headed by a group of individuals called a commission, and charged with regulating a specific industry or economic practice

industrial policy

Proposals for partnership in economic decision-making among government officials, corporate leaders, union officials, and public interest groups

in-kind benefits

Noncash benefits, such as medical care services, that the needy receive from some social welfare programs

inner cabinet

Cabinet officers whose departments handle issues of broad national importance, including the secretaries of state, defense, and the treasury, and the attorney general

interest group elitism

The idea that the leaders of interest groups may act in ways that promote their own interests rather than the interests of the broader membership of the group

interest groups

Associations of people who hold common views and who work together to influence what government does

intermediate appellate courts

Courts between courts of general jurisdiction and the court of last resort; in the federal court system, the courts of appeals

internationalism

A foreign policy perspective that concludes that America's interests in peace abroad and liberty at home require its permanent involvement in world affairs

International Monetary Fund (IMF)

A specialized agency of the United Nations designed to promote international monetary cooperation

interstate compact

A formal agreement between states designed to solve a problem faced by more than one state when such an agreement is necessary because political problems are not limited by geographic boundaries

iron triangle

The combination of interest group representatives, legislators, and government administrators seen as extremely influential in determining the outcome of political decisions

isolationism

A belief that America should not involve itself in the quarrels of Europe and Asia and should pursue a policy of military nonintervention

j

Joint Chiefs of Staff (JCS)

Heads of the various armed services and their chair who advise the president and the secretary of defense on important military questions

joint committees

Permanent committees of Congress made up of members from both houses

journalists

People who gather, write, and report the news for newspapers, magazines, radio, television, and the Internet

judicial activists

Judges who are least hesitant to invoke judicial review to strike down an act of Congress or of a state legislature

judicial restraintists

Judges who are reluctant to invoke judicial review to strike down an act of Congress or of a state legislature

judicial review

The authority of courts to set aside a legislative act as being in violation of the Constitution

jurisdiction

Authority of a court or other agency to act

k

Kentucky and Virginia Resolutions

A challenge to national supremacy, these state documents declared states to be the final authority on the meaning of the Constitution

l

laissez-faire

French for "leave things alone" and the view, in economics, that government should not interfere in the workings of the economy

leak

The deliberate release of information by an official to a journalist for a specific purpose

legal guilt

The concept that a defendant's factual guilt be established in accordance with the laws and the Constitution before criminal penalties can be applied

legislative assistant (LA)

A congressional aide who analyzes bills, drafts laws, writes speeches, and prepares position papers

legislative intent

A legislature's understanding of the meaning of a law and what it is designed to accomplish

legislative norms

The unwritten rules of acceptable behavior in Congress

legislative veto

Congressional power, which the Supreme Court ruled unconstitutional in 1983, to halt an executive initiative by a vote of one or both houses or by a congressional committee

Lemon test

A standard announced in *Lemon v. Kurtzman* [403 U.S. 602 (1971)] to determine when a statute violates the establishment clause

libel

Defamation of a person's character or reputation, not protected by the First Amendment (*New York Times Co. v. Sullivan* [376 U.S. 254 (1964)] makes it difficult for public figures and officials to bring successful libel suits against their critics.)

liberalism

An ideology that regards the individual as a rational being capable of overcoming obstacles to a better world and supporting changes in the political and economic status quo

libertarianism

A belief that the state should regulate neither the economic nor the moral life of its citizens

line-item veto

Most state governors have this power, through which a chief executive, reacting to a bill passed by the legislature, may accept some items in the bill while also rejecting other items in the same bill. The president does not have this power.

lobbying

Attempting to influence legislation under consideration, particularly through personal contact by group representatives

Locke, John

English political philosopher whose ideas about political legitimacy influenced the American founders

low-stimulus election

Election that the public finds uninteresting or unimportant

m

majority election

Election in which a candidate wins by getting more than one-half of the votes cast

majority leader (House)

Leader and chief spokesperson for the majority party in the House

majority leader (Senate)

Leader and chief spokesperson for the majority party in the Senate

mandatory programs

Government programs, such as Social Security expenditures, in which spending automatically increases from one year to the next without specific annual appropriations action by Congress

Marbury v. Madison

Landmark decision [5 U.S. (1 Cranch) 137 (1803)] by the Supreme Court in 1803 establishing the Supreme Court's power of judicial review

mark-up

The process in which a legislative committee sets the precise language and amendments of a bill

Marshall Plan

A multibillion-dollar American program begun after World War II for the economic rehabilitation of Western Europe

Marxism model

A model of policy making that holds that public policy decisions in non-Marxist regimes reflect the interests of the ruling economic class at the expense of workers

mass media

Instruments such as newspapers, magazines, radio, television, and the Internet that provide the means for communicating with large numbers of people in a short period of time

mayor-council

A form of government at the local level that mirrors the executive-legislative structure at the state and national levels where the mayor has executive powers and the council has legislative powers

McCulloch v. Maryland

Supreme Court case in 1819 that established the constitutionality of a national bank and solidified national power by confirming that the federal government can exercise implied powers to carry out legitimate and otherwise constitutional ends

means-tested programs

Type of social welfare program in which government provides cash or in-kind benefits to individuals who qualify by having little or no income

media consultant

An expert hired by a political candidate to give advice on the use of the mass media, particularly television and direct mail, in a campaign for public office

Medicaid

A means-tested medical care program providing in-kind medical benefits for the poor

Medicare

A public health insurance program in which government pays the providers of health care for medical services given to patients who are aged or disabled

melting pot

Characterization of America as the coming together of a wide variety of racial, ethnic, and religious groups

Merit Systems Protection Board

An agency charged with protecting individual employees against violations of the merit principle or actions taken against whistle-blowers

military-industrial complex

The Pentagon, defense contractors, unions in the defense industry, members of Congress whose states or districts receive considerable military funds, and academic strategists whose work is funded by the military

minimalist state

A government that restricts its activities to providing only goods that the free market cannot produce

minority leader (House)

Leader and chief spokesperson for the minority party in the House

minority leader (Senate)

Leader and chief spokesperson for the minority party in the Senate

Miranda rights

Requirements announced in *Miranda v. Arizona* [384 U.S. 436 (1966)] to protect a suspect during a police interrogation

misdemeanor

Less serious criminal offense, usually punishable by not more than one year in jail

Missouri Plan

Method of selecting state judges, involving appointment from a list of recommended nominees and a later retention vote by the electorate

modified rule

An order from the House Rules Committee allowing a limited number of amendments to a bill during floor consideration

monetary policy

Government decisions about how much money should circulate in the economy and what the cost of borrowing money, the interest rate, should be

movement

An effort to attain an end through an organized set of actions and individuals

multinational corporations

Large companies that carry on business in two or more countries simultaneously

multiple advocacy

A system of advising the president in which all sides of an issue are presented

n

NAACP

National Association for the Advancement of Colored People; an organization founded to improve the social, economic, and political condition of African Americans

national committee

The body responsible for guiding political party organization on an ongoing basis

national convention

The quadrennial meeting of an American political party that focuses on the upcoming presidential election

National Security Council (NSC)

Designed to provide the president with advice and policy coordination on questions of national security, NSC's members include the president, the vice president, the secretaries of state and defense, and any other officials the president may add

natural-born citizen

A person actually born in the United States

naturalized citizen

A person, born in another country, who becomes a citizen of the United States by a procedure set by Congress

necessary and proper clause

The "elastic clause" of Article I, Section 8, of the Constitution; this is the source of "implied powers" for the national government, as explained in *McCulloch v. Maryland* [17 U.S.(4 Wheaton) 316 (1819)]

neoconservatism

A belief associated with many former liberal intellectuals that contemporary liberalism has transformed the modest New Deal welfare state into an intrusive, paternalistic state

neoliberalism

A pragmatic form of liberalism that emphasizes such beliefs as the promotion of wealth rather than its redistribution and the reform of military practices rather than the simple reduction of military spending

net interest

Charges that the government must pay to the public for the use of money borrowed to cover budget deficits and added to the interest paid to government trust funds to create total interest costs

New Deal

The first two terms of President Franklin D. Roosevelt (1933–1945), whose revolutionary policy initiatives established a pervasive and active role for the national government

New Federalism

A view of federalism that posits an expanded role for state and local governments and holds that state and local governments should be entrusted with greater responsibilities

New Jersey Plan

Introduced in the Constitutional Convention in opposition to the Virginia Plan, it emphasized the dominance of the states

news briefing

An announcement or explanation of policy by an official

news release

A story written by a press agent for distribution to the media

Nielsen ratings

Surveys conducted by the A.C. Nielsen Company to measure the size of television audiences

Nineteenth Amendment

Amendment ratified in 1920 that prohibits limitations on voting based on sex

Ninth Amendment

Part of the Bill of Rights that cautions that the people possess rights not specified in the Constitution

Nixon Doctrine

Proclaimed by President Nixon in 1969, a policy stipulating that the United States will support its allies with economic and military aid but that the allies should provide the bulk of the personnel for their own defense

North Atlantic Treaty Organization (NATO)

Multinational organization formed in 1949 to provide for mutual defense against foreign attacks

Northwest Ordinance

This major statute, enacted by Congress in 1787 under the Articles of Confederation, provided for the development and government of lands west of Pennsylvania

O

obscenity

As applied by the Supreme Court, certain pornographic portrayals of sexual acts not protected by the First Amendment (The Supreme Court's current definition of the legally obscene appeared in *Miller v. California* [413 U.S. 5 (1973)].)

Office of Management and Budget (OMB)

An agency in the Executive Office of the President that provides the president with budgetary information and advice and is responsible for compiling the president's annual budget proposal to Congress

Office of Personnel Management (OPM)

Created in 1981 as part of the Executive Office of the President, focuses on the formulation, coordination, and implementation of domestic and economic policy, and provides staff support for the Economic and Domestic Policy Councils

ombudsman

A person who intervenes with the bureaucracy on behalf of individual citizens

open primary

A primary election in which any voter, regardless of party affiliation, can participate

open rule

An order from the House Rules Committee whereby amendments to a bill are permitted on the floor

opinion of the Court

Statement representing the views of a majority of the judges of the Court

oral argument

Event in which opposing counsel verbally presents their views to the court during the decision-making process of a court

original jurisdiction

Authority of a court over cases that begin in that court, such as courts of general jurisdiction having original jurisdiction over most criminal offenses—the original jurisdiction of the U.S. Supreme Court is very small

outer cabinet

Cabinet officers whose departments deal with sharply defined programs and are subject to considerable pressure from client groups

outsourcing

Establishment, by American corporations, of factories and offices in foreign countries to take advantage of cheaper labor markets

party convention

Regularly scheduled general meeting of a political party that is held for the purpose of ratifying party policies and deciding on party candidates

party identification

Psychological attachment that a citizen may feel toward a particular political party

party in the electorate

The individual citizens throughout the country who identify with a political party

party in the government

One of the three components or sectors of a political party; the party as embodied in those of its members who have been elected or appointed to public office, the organizations they establish, and the leaders they choose to help them carry out their work

party system

Period during which the pattern of support for political parties based on a particular set of important political issues remains reasonably stable

party whip

Member of each party's leadership responsible for party discipline and attendance for key votes

passive resistance

A form of civil disobedience in which protesters do not actively oppose government's attempts to control them, but rather refuse to cooperate by doing nothing—for example, by going limp when police try to pick them up or insisting on being carried to a police van rather than walking

Pendleton Act

Legislation passed in 1883 that created a Civil Service Commission charged with the task of using merit, rather than partisan political connections, as a condition of government employment

photo opportunity

An event scheduled to give newspaper reporters and television crews a chance to photograph someone

platform

A broad statement of the philosophy and program under which a party's candidates run for election

plea bargain

A deal with the prosecutor to obtain fewer or lesser charges or a lighter sentence

pluralism

A model of policy making that holds that public policy decisions are the result of struggles among contesting groups that reflect the various interests among citizens

pluralist democracy

A system in which the people rule and have their interests protected through the interaction of many different social, political, and economic groups, and in which the principal task of government is to manage group conflict and cooperation

plurality election

Election in which a candidate wins simply by getting more votes than any other candidate, even if it is less than a majority of the votes

policy adoption

A formal, authoritative decision, such as the enactment of legislation, made by institutions of government to address an issue on the policy agenda

policy agenda

The public issues that engage the attention of elected officials

policy evaluation

The act of determining whether a formally adopted and implemented policy ameliorated or solved a public problem

policy implementation

The translation of policy ideas into action

policy strategy

A specific course of action designed to deal with a public problem

political action committee (PAC)

Political organization set up to channel campaign money from a group to political candidates sympathetic to the group's political views

political efficacy

A person's sense of being able to accomplish something politically; an important determinant of political participation

political machine

Political organization that recruits and controls its membership through the use of its governmental authority to give benefits (jobs, contracts, etc.) to its supporters and deny them to its opponents

political party

A group that seeks to influence public policy by placing its own members in positions of governmental authority

political socialization

The process by which citizens acquire politically relevant knowledge, beliefs, attitudes, and patterns of behavior

politico style

A manner of representation in which members of Congress attempt to strike a balance between the interests of their constituents and the dictates of their own judgment and conscience

politics

The process of peacefully reconciling social and economic differences

polling

The process of using social science methods to get an accurate sense of the public's view about an issue or set of issues

poll tax

A tax on voting, applied discriminatorily to African Americans under "Jim Crow" in the post–Civil War South

populism

A political movement that sets the interests of the masses or common people against those of the political elite or the wealthy

pork barrel politics

The effort to enact legislation favoring a legislator's home district, often in the form of costly government spending that may not be advantageous to the country as a whole

positive state

A government that helps provide the goods, services, and conditions for a prosperous, equitable society

poverty threshold

Income level differentiated by family size and annually adjusted for inflation, below which government defines individuals as being poor

precedents

Prior decisions of courts that are cited as authority by other courts

Presidential Election Campaign Fund

Pool of money available that is collected from a $3 check-off on the federal income tax form and is available to presidential candidates for campaign expenses

Presidential Succession Act of 1947

Established the line of presidential succession after the vice president as follows: the Speaker of the House, the president pro tempore of the Senate, and the Cabinet secretaries in the order of the establishment of their departments

president of the Senate

A largely ceremonial role held by the vice president of the United States

president pro tempore

The presiding officer of the Senate in the absence of the vice president—largely honorific post and usually given to the senior majority party member

president's cabinet

Political institution comprised mainly of executive department heads that collectively serve as a source of advice for the president

press conference

A meeting of journalists and an official or other person at which the latter answers the questions posed by the former

presumption of innocence

A concept in criminal procedure that places the burden of proof in establishing guilt on the government

primary election

Preliminary election in which a party picks delegates to a party convention or its candidates for public office

priming

Occurs when the news media, especially television, set the terms by which the public judges its leaders

prior restraint

Official censorship before something is said or published, or censorship that halts publication already under way; is usually judged unconstitutional today under the First Amendment

Private Calendar

The schedule for House bills that concerns personal rather than general legislative matters

probable cause

A standard used in determining when police can conduct arrests and searches

Progressive Era

An urban reform movement of the late nineteenth and early twentieth centuries that called for direct primaries, restrictions on corporations, and improved public services that was influential in the administrations of Theodore Roosevelt and Woodrow Wilson

progressivism

An urban reform movement of the late nineteenth and early twentieth centuries that called for direct primaries, restrictions on corporations, and improved public services and that was influential in the administrations of Theodore Roosevelt and Woodrow Wilson

proportional representation

A system for allocating seats in a legislative body in which the number of seats a party gets out of the total is based on the percentage of votes that the party receives in an election

protectionism

Opposite of *free trade;* belief that government should protect American business and industry by restricting the flow of foreign goods into the United States

public opinion

The array of beliefs and attitudes that people hold about political and related affairs

public policy

Whatever governments choose to do or not to do

public purpose

A goal or objective of a bureaucracy

q

quasi-judicial

A function of regulatory agencies in which, like a court, they can make decisions in individual cases

quasi-legislative

A function of regulatory agencies in which they can make rules that, like legislation, apply to whole classes of people

r

rational actor model

A perspective that looks at politics as a system in which individuals and organizations pursue their self-interests, defined in terms of costs and benefits, and choose to do those things that give them the greatest benefit at the least cost

rational-comprehensive model

A model of decision making that holds that policy makers should identify problems, consider various policy alternatives and their costs and benefits, and select and implement the policy strategy with the highest benefits and the lowest costs

realignment

A major change in the pattern of support for political parties and the important issues on which that pattern of support is based

recession

A minor and relatively short period of economic decline

reciprocity (or logrolling)

A practice whereby two or more members of Congress exchange support for legislation important to each other

redistributive policies

Programs such as tariffs or tax reforms that produce considerable benefits to some segments of society but high costs to others

red tape

Bureaucratic rules and procedures that seem to complicate and delay needed action unnecessarily

regional primary

A primary election held across an entire geographic area (for example, the South or the West) rather than within a single state

register

To place one's name on the list of citizens eligible to vote

regulations

Rules devised by government agencies that shape the actions of individuals and groups in order to achieve purposes mandated by law

relative deprivation

A definition of poverty that holds that individuals with less, regardless of their absolute income level, will feel poor or deprived relative to those who have more

republican (or representative) government

A style of government in which people elect representatives to make decisions in their place

reserved powers

Powers not specifically prohibited to the states and not delegated to the national government by the Constitution

residence requirements

State laws designed to limit the eligible electorate by requiring citizens to have been a resident of the voting district for a fixed period of time prior to an election

resurgence

The idea that American political parties, following a period of decline from the 1960s to the early 1980s, are now making a comeback, gaining in organizational, electoral, and governmental strength

riders

Provisions, usually attached to appropriation bills, which "ride" into law on the backs of necessary pieces of legislation, forcing the president to veto the entire bill in order to kill the amendment

risk assessment

The process of estimating the potentially dangerous consequences of damage that might be caused by a particular practice, such as smoking, or by the use of a particular product, such as the impact of the burning of fossil fuels on global warming

risk management

The process of making decisions that try to reduce or contain identified risks

Roe v. Wade

Supreme Court decision [410 U.S. 113 (1973)] establishing a constitutional right to abortion

rule of four

Procedure of the U.S. Supreme Court by which the affirmative votes of four justices are needed to accept a case for decision

Rules Committee

Powerful House committee that clears most important bills for floor consideration and decides the rule under which bills should be considered; also, the committee of a party convention that recommends changes in the way a party conducts its affairs

run-off election

An election pitting the leading candidates of a previous election against each other when the previous election has not produced a clear-cut winner

S

safe seats

Congressional districts in which the division of voters between the parties is so lopsided as to virtually ensure one party of victory

senatorial courtesy

Custom in the Senate to reject, for federal office, a nominee who is unacceptable to a senator from the nominee's state when the senator and president are of the same party

Senior Executive Service (SES)

Created by the Civil Service Reform Act of 1978, a class of civil servants drawn from the highest grades and who might be given bonuses, transferred among agencies, or demoted—all depending on the quality of their work

sense of duty

A motivating factor, felt by some citizens, to get involved in politics

separate-but-equal doctrine

The standard announced by the Supreme Court in *Plessy v. Ferguson* in 1896 that allowed racially separate facilities on trains (and by implication in public services such as education), as long as the separate facilities were equal (overturned by *Brown v. Board of Education of Topeka* in 1954)

sequestration

The process through which the president makes budget cuts in government programs to meet the mandates in law requiring ceilings on specific categories of spending

Seventeenth Amendment

Ratified in 1913, it provides for the direct popular election of United States senators.

Shays' Rebellion

A revolt by farmers from Massachusetts in 1786–1787 over the lack of economic relief, which led many to believe that a stronger central government was necessary

shield laws

Statutes that protect the identity of journalists' news sources or their knowledge of criminal acts

Sixteenth Amendment

Amendment to the Constitution, ratified in 1913, that gave Congress the power to tax incomes and thereby massively increase the potential revenue available to the national government

Sixth Amendment

Provision of the Bill of Rights assuring, among other things, the right to counsel

slip law

The written text of an act of Congress

social Darwinism

A set of ideas applying Charles Darwin's theory of biological evolution to society and holding that social relationships occur within a struggle for survival in which only the fittest survive

social entitlements

Programs, such as Social Security and Medicaid, whereby eligible individuals receive benefits according to law

social insurance programs

Welfare programs that provide cash or services to the aged, the disabled, and the unemployed, regardless of income level

socialism

The view in economics that economic decision making should be completely under the control of political authority

socialization functions

With reference to political parties, the ways in which parties, by seeking to win elections, help to socialize voters into politics and form public opinion

social regulation

Type of regulation in which a government agency issues rules designed to achieve noneconomic policy goals, such as fair treatment in employment, clean air, or safe workplaces

Social Security Act of 1935

Landmark legislation that firmly established for the first time a social welfare role for the national government by providing old age insurance and grants to the states to provide programs for cash assistance to the unemployed, dependent children, and the blind, disabled, and aged

social welfare

Governmental programs, such as social insurance and poverty programs, directed specifically toward promoting the well-being of individuals and families

soft money

A category of campaign money that was created by an amendment to the campaign finance laws in 1979, allowing the national parties to raise and spend money, essentially without restriction, for state and local parties, routine operating expenses, and party-building activities, as long as the expenditures are not directly related to any federal campaign

solicitor general of the United States

In the Supreme Court, the lawyer for the United States who decides which cases the government will appeal to the Supreme Court

Speaker of the House

The presiding officer of the House of Representatives, who is selected by the majority party

special or select committees

Committees of Congress created periodically to study particular problems or new areas of legislation

spoils system

The practice of making appointments to government jobs on the basis of party loyalty and support in election campaigns

standing committees

The permanent committees of Congress that alone can approve legislation and send it to the floor of the House or Senate

stare decisis

A legal doctrine that suggests courts should follow precedent as a general rule, breaking with previously legal principles only on rare occasions

state committee

The body responsible for guiding a state political party organization on an ongoing basis

state courts

Courts of the fifty states, as opposed to the federal, or national, courts

Statutory Pay-As-You-Go Act

Law passed in 2010 that requires budget increases to be offset by either reductions elsewhere or increased revenues

stewardship theory

An expansive theory of presidential power, put forth by Theodore Roosevelt, that holds that the president can undertake any act as long as it is not prohibited by a specific provision of the Constitution or statutory law

Supplemental Nutrition Assistance Program (SNAP)

A means-tested program (formerly known as the food stamp program) that provides the eligible needy with cards that can be used only to purchase food

Supplemental Security Income (SSI)

Social welfare program administered by the Social Security Administration whereby the national government guarantees a certain level of income for the needy, aged, blind, and disabled

surplus

An excess of government revenues over government expenditures

t

Temporary Assistance for Needy Families (TANF)

Social welfare program, administered by the states and jointly funded by state and national revenues, that provides cash assistance, in participating states, to needy children and one adult relative or an unemployed parent

Tenth Amendment

Amendment ratified in 1791 that reserves to the states powers not prohibited to them and not delegated to the national government by the Constitution

term limits

Laws restricting the number of terms an elected representative may serve—the Court has struck down state efforts to limit terms for federal offices, but has allowed state laws that limit terms for elected officials at the state level

third party

In the American political context, a minor party that attracts only a small share of the electorate's vote and is a party other than the two major parties that have dominated politics through most of American history

Thirteenth Amendment

The first of the Civil War amendments to the Constitution; adopted in 1865, it banned slavery throughout the United States

symbolic speech

A speech act that centers on action or performance to communicate a point rather than on words

systems model

A model of policy making that holds that policy is the product of an interlocking relationship between institutions of government and their social, economic, and political environment

three-fifths compromise

A temporary resolution to the controversy over slavery, this agreement allowed slave-holding states to count each slave as three-fifths of a person for purposes of congressional representation

trial court

A court of limited or general jurisdiction in which the disputed facts of a case are heard and decided

Truman Doctrine

A policy, proclaimed by President Harry Truman in 1947, in which the United States would oppose the expansion of communism anywhere in the world

trustee role

The concept that legislators should vote on the basis of their consciences and the broad interests of the nation, not simply on the views of their constituents

Twenty-fifth Amendment

Ratified in 1967, it provides the mechanism for the vice president to assume the presidency in the event of a presidential disability and the selection of a replacement for the vice president should that office become vacant

Twenty-fourth Amendment

Adopted in 1964, this amendment forbids the use of poll taxes in federal elections. Since 1966 the Court has applied this proscription to state elections as well.

Twenty-second Amendment

Ratified in 1951, this amendment restricts the president to two terms in office

Twenty-sixth Amendment

Constitutional amendment adopted in 1971 that fixed the minimum voting age at eighteen years

Twenty-third Amendment

Constitutional amendment adopted in 1961 granting the District of Columbia three electors in the Electoral College

U

unanimous consent agreement

A common mechanism used by the Senate leadership to limit Senate debate

underclass

A proportion of the poor comprised of individuals isolated from the rest of society and for whom poverty is a continuing way of life

unemployment compensation

A social insurance policy that grants temporary financial assistance to the unemployed

Union Calendar

The House schedule for the consideration of tax and appropriation bills

unitary system

A system of government in which principal power lies at the level of a national or central government rather than at the level of some smaller unit (a state or a province) within the political system

United States Agency for International Development (USAID)

Agency of the State Department that coordinates economic assistance programs

United States courts of appeals

Intermediate appellate courts in the federal court system, just below the Supreme Court

United States district courts

Trial courts in the federal court system in which almost all federal cases begin; courts of general jurisdiction

United States Reports

The official, published decisions of the United States Supreme Court

U.S. Code

Compilation of laws currently in effect, classified by subject matter, such as transportation or labor

U.S. Statutes-at-Large

Chronological compilation, by year, of slip laws passed in each session of Congress

V

vesting clause

As the first clause of Article II, its statement confers executive power in the president.

Virginia Plan

The first plan of union proposed at the Constitutional Convention in 1787; it called for a strong central government

visual

An image or series of images representing news in action; a visual depiction of a political act, such as campaigning, which may carry more impact than words alone

Voting Rights Act of 1965

Major legislation designed to overcome racial barriers to voting, primarily in the Southern States; it was extended again in 2006 for twenty-five years

Voting Rights Act of 1970

The law that limited residence requirements to thirty days for presidential elections, further ensuring voting rights

W

warrant

Official authorization for government action

Welfare Reform Act

A 1996 law that fundamentally altered the AFDC welfare program by renaming it TANF and placing work and training requirements, as well as time limits, on its use

working poor

Individuals who, despite being employed or seeking employment, are still defined as poor because their low earnings are not enough to put them above the poverty threshold

World Bank

A specialized agency of the United Nations that makes loans to poorer nations for economic development

writ of certiorari

A petition for review by a higher court; the most common route for an appeal to reach the Supreme Court

writ of mandamus

Order by a court to a public official to perform a nondiscretionary or ministerial act

Index

thirteenth edition

THE AMERICAN
PAGEANT

A HISTORY OF THE REPUBLIC

VOLUME I: TO 1877

DAVID M. KENNEDY
STANFORD UNIVERSITY

LIZABETH COHEN
HARVARD UNIVERSITY

THOMAS A. BAILEY

HOUGHTON MIFFLIN COMPANY
BOSTON   NEW YORK

Publisher: Charles Hartford
Senior Sponsoring Editor: Sally Constable
Development Editor: Lisa Kalner Williams
Senior Project Editor: Rosemary R. Jaffe
Senior Designer: Henry Rachlin
Senior Art and Design Coordinator: Jill Haber
Senior Composition Buyer: Sarah Ambrose
Senior Photo Editor: Jennifer Meyer Dare
Senior Manufacturing Coordinator: Marie Barnes
Senior Marketing Manager: Sandra McGuire

Credits for photographs are found following the Appendix at the end of the book.

Custom Publishing Editor: Peter Nowka
Custom Publishing Production Manager: Christina Battista
Project Coordinator: Jen Feltri

Cover Design: Althea Chen
Cover Image: Stephanie Asher/iStockphoto

This book contains select works from existing Houghton Mifflin Company resources and was produced by Houghton Mifflin Custom Publishing for collegiate use. As such, those adopting and/or contributing to this work are responsible for editorial content, accuracy, continuity and completeness.

Printed in the United States of America.

ISBN-13: 978-0-618-95873-3
ISBN-10: 0-618-95873-8
1021085

4 5 6 7 8 9 – CCI – 09 08

Houghton Mifflin
Custom Publishing

222 Berkeley Street • Boston, MA 02116

Address all correspondence and order information to the above address.

ABOUT THE AUTHORS

David M. Kennedy is the Donald J. McLachlan Professor of History at Stanford University, where he has taught for more than three decades. Born and raised in Seattle, he received his undergraduate education at Stanford and did his graduate training at Yale in American Studies, combining the fields of history, economics, and literature. His first book,

Birth Control in America: The Career of Margaret Sanger (1970) was honored with both the Bancroft Prize and the John Gilmary Shea Prize. His study of World War I, *Over Here: The First World War and American Society* (1980; rev. ed., 2005) was a Pulitzer Prize finalist. In 1999 he published *Freedom from Fear: The American People in Depression and War, 1929–1945*, which won the Pulitzer Prize for History, as well as the Francis Parkman Prize, the English-Speaking Union's Ambassador's Prize, and the Commonwealth Club of California's Gold Medal for Literature. At Stanford he teaches both undergraduate and graduate courses in American political, diplomatic, intellectual, and social history, and in American literature. He has received several teaching awards, including the Dean's Award for Distinguished Teaching. He has been a visiting professor at the University of Florence, Italy, and in 1995–1996 served as the Harmsworth Professor of American History at Oxford University. He has also served on the Advisory Board for the PBS television series, *The American Experience*, and as a consultant to several documentary films, including *The Great War, Cadillac Desert,* and *Woodrow Wilson*. From 1990 to 1995 he chaired the Test Development Committee for the Advanced Placement United States History examination. He is an elected Fellow of the American Academy of Arts and Sciences and of the American Philosophical Society and serves on the board of the Pulitzer Prizes.

Married and the father of two sons and a daughter, in his leisure time he enjoys hiking, bicycling, river-rafting, sea-kayaking, and fly-fishing.

Lizabeth Cohen is the Howard Mumford Jones Professor of American Studies in the history department of Harvard University. Previously she taught at New York University (1992–1997) and Carnegie Mellon University (1986–1992). Born and raised in the New York metropolitan area, she received her A.B. from Princeton University and her M.A. and Ph.D. from the University of California at Berkeley. Her first book, *Making a New Deal: Industrial Workers in Chicago, 1919–1939* (1990) won the Bancroft Prize in American History and the Philip Taft Labor History Award, and was a finalist for the Pulitzer Prize. Her article, "Encountering Mass Culture at the Grassroots: The Experience of Chicago Workers in the 1920s," (1989) was awarded the Constance Roarke Prize of the American Studies Association. Her most recent book, *A Consumers' Republic: The Politics of Mass Consumption in Postwar America* explores how an economy and culture built around mass consumption have shaped social life and politics in post–World War II America. An article related to this book, "From Town Center to Shopping Center: The Reconfiguration of Community Marketplaces in Postwar America," (1996) was honored with the ABC-CLIO, *America: History and Life* Award for the journal article that most advances previously unconsidered topics. At Harvard, she teaches courses in twentieth-century America, material culture and the built environment, and gender, urban, and working-class history and directs the Charles Warren Center for Studies in American History. Before attending graduate school, she taught history at the secondary level and worked in history and art museums. She continues to help develop public history programs for general audiences through museums and documentary films, most recently *Tupperware!*, shown on PBS. She is married to an historian of modern France, with whom she has two daughters. For leisure, she enjoys swimming and bicycling with her family, watching films, and reading fiction.

Thomas A. Bailey (1903–1983) taught history for nearly forty years at Stanford University, his alma mater. Long regarded as one of the nation's leading historians of American diplomacy, he was honored by his colleagues in 1968 with election to the presidencies of both the Organization of American Historians and the Society for Historians of American Foreign Relations. He was the author, editor, or co-editor of some twenty books, but the work in which he took most pride was *The American Pageant*, through which, he liked to say, he had taught American history to several million students.

CONTENTS

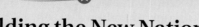

PART TWO

✪

Building the New Nation
1776–1860
164

APPENDIX

MAPS

CHARTS AND TABLES

PREFACE

For this thirteenth edition of *The American Pageant*, we have worked together closely to incorporate the most recent scholarship about American history, and to preserve the readability that has long been the *Pageant*'s hallmark. We are often told that the *Pageant* is the sole American history text that has a distinctive personality—defined by clarity, concreteness, a consistent chronological narrative, strong emphasis on major themes, avoidance of clutter, access to a variety of interpretive perspectives, and a colorful writing style leavened, as appropriate, with wit. That personality, we strongly believe, is what has made the *Pageant* both appealing and useful to countless students for more than five decades.

Our collaboration on the *Pageant* reflects our respective scholarly interests, which are complementary to a remarkable degree. David Kennedy is primarily a political and economic historian, while Lizabeth Cohen's work emphasizes social and cultural history. Together, we have revised the *Pageant* chapter by chapter, even paragraph by paragraph, guided by our shared commitment to tell the story of the American past as vividly and clearly as possible, without sacrificing a sense of the often sobering seriousness of history, and of its sometimes challenging complexity.

Changes in the Thirteenth Edition

The eleventh edition of the *Pageant* introduced essays designed to encourage students to think coherently about six eras in American history. Those essays, revised for this edition, seek to demonstrate that the study of history is not just a matter of piling up mountains of facts, but is principally concerned with discovering complex patterns of change over time, and organizing seemingly disparate events, actions, and ideas into meaningful chains of cause and consequence. The twelfth edition introduced an additional feature, "Examining the Evidence." It is intended to deepen students' understanding of the historical craft in another way, by conveying how historians develop interpretations of the past through research in many kinds of primary sources.

To acquaint students further with the various sorts of evidence that underlie all historical accounts, the thirteenth edition adds five new "Examining the Evidence" inserts to the twenty-one existing ones, offering more examples of the diverse materials from which historical interpretations are constructed. Students will learn in this edition about the insights historians derive from a wide range of historical artifacts: what a letter from a black freedman to his former master in 1865 reveals about his family's enslavement as well as their hopes for a new life, or how a song popular during World War I contains clues to soldiers' experience in the military; why the Gettysburg Address sheds light not only on President Lincoln's brilliant oratory but also his vision of the American nation; what the manuscript census teaches us about immigrant households on the Lower East Side of New York in 1900; and how a new kind of architectural structure—the shopping mall—changed both consumers' behavior and politicians' campaign tactics after World War II. Other featured sources include maps, furniture, clothing, private correspondence, travelogues, paintings and photographs, court decisions, political broadsides and cartoons, novels, motion pictures, newspapers, public opinion polling, and transcripts of important diplomatic conferences and political meetings.

This edition also contains three new "Makers of America" essays, highlighting the ordinary Americans who fought for the North and South during the Civil War, the intellectuals of the late nineteenth century who developed a distinctly American philosophy known as "Pragmatism," and the scientists and engineers whose research brought the United States to the forefront of scientific knowledge by the late twentieth century. We seek with these additions to show that Americans have forged their group identities through their shared experiences, intellectual interests, and technical skills as well as through their ethnicity and neighborhoods. Along with the twenty-nine existing "Makers" essays, these additions help constitute a comprehensive mosaic of the diverse peoples and groups that have composed our strikingly pluralistic society.

Readers will also find in this edition of the *Pageant* enriched discussion of the experiences and contributions of women, the Seven Years' War, the election of 1800, law and the national economy in the antebellum period, the Compromise of 1850, the rise of colleges and universities, American involvement in Asia, the Spanish-American War, and the Cold War.

Our greatest attention in this revision has gone to expanding two areas of inquiry that are often overlooked in U.S. history textbooks: the cultural innovations and intellectual doctrines that have engaged Americans, and the international context in which U.S. history has unfolded. We hope to instill in readers greater appreciation for the contributions of American writers, artists, and thinkers, while also conveying how extensively the American experience was shaped by this country's interaction with other nations on the world stage. We are deeply indebted to the wise counsel of two professional colleagues as we undertook these revisions: the intellectual historian David Hollinger and the international historian Frank Ninkovitch.

In addition, many new box-quotes bring more varied perspectives to the events chronicled in the *Pageant's* historical narrative. We have also compressed and reorganized the material concerning United States foreign involvements from 1890–1909 into a single Chapter 27. Treatment of the post–World War II period has been expanded to include an additional chapter, as that era lengthens in time. The final chapter has been thoroughly revised, to portray the present state of the nation in historical perspective. Updated "Varying Viewpoints" essays reflect new interpretations of significant trends and events. Selecting visual material that illuminates complex and important historical ideas continues to be a high priority for us, and readers will find many new and revised maps and charts, as well as fresh documentary images. Completely updated bibliographies are located at the end of the book, along with a revised Appendix, containing abundant statistical data on many aspects of the American historical experience.

Goals of *The American Pageant*

Like its predecessors, this edition of *The American Pageant* tries to cultivate in its readers the capacity for balanced judgment and informed understanding about American society by holding up to the present the mirror and measuring rod that is the past. The book's goal is not to teach the art of prophecy but the much subtler and more difficult arts of seeing things in context, of understanding the roots and direction and pace of change, and of distinguishing what is truly new under the sun from what is not. The study of history, it has been rightly said, does not make one smart for the next time, but wise forever.

We hope that the *Pageant* will help to develop those intellectual assets in its readers, and that those who use the book will take from it both a fresh appreciation of what has gone before and a seasoned perspective on what is to come. And we hope, too, that readers will take as much pleasure in reading *The American Pageant* as we have had in writing it.

Supplements Available with *The American Pageant*, Thirteenth Edition
The **history companion**

The Houghton Mifflin History Companion is a collection of resources designed to complement the use of *The American Pageant*. It is organized according to the chapters in the text and has four parts: the **Instructor Companion** website, the **Instructor Companion CD-ROM**, the **Student Study Companion**, and the **Student Research Companion**.

The Instructor Companion website and **Instructor Companion CD-ROM** feature the **Instructor's Resource Guide**, primary sources with instructor notes, in addition to hundreds of maps, images, audio and video clips, and PowerPoint slides for classroom presentation. The Instructor Companion CD-ROM offers the same collection of maps and images with additional audio and video clips for classroom use, the **Quizbook**, and **HM Testing**™, a computerized version of the Quizbook with flexible test-editing capabilities.

The Student Study Companion is a free, online study guide to accompany *The American Pageant*. The Study Companion contains a variety of tutorial resources including the **Guidebook**, "Examining the Evidence" exercises, ACE quizzes with feedback, annotated links to history sites, chronology exercises, flashcards, and other interactivities.

The Student Research Companion is a free, online tool with a wealth of interactive maps and primary sources. Students can use the maps for research, classroom assignments, or review of their geography skills. Primary sources provide a real-world introduction to historical evidence. The sources include headnotes that provide pertinent background information and questions that students can answer and e-mail to their instructors.

The American Spirit, **Eleventh Edition, Volumes I and II** are print primary source readers compiled and edited by David M. Kennedy and Thomas A. Bailey and designed to accompany *The American Pageant*.

Please contact your local Houghton Mifflin sales representative for more information about these learning and teaching tools in addition to the *Rand McNally Atlas of American History*, **WebCT** and **Blackboard cartridges**, and **Transparencies for United States History**.

Acknowledgments

Many people have contributed to this revision of *The American Pageant*. Foremost among them are the countless students and teachers who have written unsolicited letters of comment or inquiry. We have learned from every one of them, and encourage all readers to offer us suggestions for improving future editions. Several colleagues have also given us the benefit of their assistance, including:

Linzy Brekke-Aloise, *Harvard University*
Yonatan Eyal, *Harvard University*
David Holland, *Stanford University*
David Hollinger, *University of California, Berkeley*
David Hunter, *San Bernardino City Unified Schools*
Robert MacDougall, *Harvard University*
Frank Ninkovich, *St. John's University*
Kimberly Sims, *Harvard University*
Ruth Suyama, *Los Angeles Mission College*
F. Walter VanderHeijden, *Hempfield High School*
Daniel Wewers, *Harvard University*

Our warm thanks to each of them.

David M. Kennedy

Lizabeth Cohen

Sail, sail thy best, ship of Democracy,
Of value is thy freight, 'tis not the Present only,
The Past is also stored in thee,
Thou holdest not the venture of thyself alone, not of
*   the Western continent alone,*
Earth's résumé entire floats on thy keel, O ship, is
*   steadied by thy spars,*
With thee Time voyages in trust, the antecedent
*   nations sink or swim with thee,*
With all their ancient struggles, martyrs, heroes, epics,
*   wars, thou bear'st the other continents,*
Theirs, theirs as much as thine, the destination-port
*   triumphant. . . .*

Walt Whitman
Thou Mother with Thy Equal Brood, 1872

THE AMERICAN PAGEANT

FOUNDING THE
NEW NATION

꘎

c. 33,000 B.C.–A.D. 1783

The European explorers who followed Christopher Columbus to North America in the sixteenth century had no notion of founding a new nation. Neither did the first European settlers who peopled the thirteen English colonies on the eastern shores of the continent in the seventeenth and eighteenth centuries. These original colonists may have fled poverty or religious persecution in the Old World, but they continued to view themselves as Europeans, and as subjects of the English king. They regarded America as but the western rim of a transatlantic European world.

Yet life in the New World made the colonists different from their European cousins, and eventually, during the American Revolution, the Americans came to embrace a vision of their country as an independent nation. How did this epochal transformation come about? How did the colonists overcome the conflicts that divided them, unite against Britain, and declare themselves at great cost to be an "American" people?

They had much in common to begin with. Most were English-speaking. Most came determined to create an agricultural society modeled on English customs. Conditions in the New World deepened their common bonds. Most colonists strove to live lives unfettered by the tyrannies of royal authority, official religion, and social hierarchies that they had left behind. They grew to cherish ideals that became synonymous with American life — reverence for individual liberty, self-government, religious tolerance, and economic opportunity. They also commonly displayed a willingness to subjugate outsiders—first Indians, who were nearly annihilated through war and disease, and then Africans, who were brought in chains

Algonquian Indians Fishing, by John White
The English watercolorist accompanied the first English expedition to Roanoke Island (later part of Virginia) in 1585. His paintings faithfully recorded the Indian way of life that was now imperiled by the arrival of the Europeans.

to serve as slave labor, especially on the tobacco, rice, and indigo plantations of the southern colonies.

But if the settlement experience gave people a common stock of values, both good and bad, it also divided them. The thirteen colonies were quite different from one another. Puritans carved tight, pious, and relatively democratic communities of small family farms out of rocky-soiled New England. Theirs was a homogeneous world in comparison to most of the southern colonies, where large landholders, mostly Anglicans, built plantations along the coast from which they lorded over a labor force of black slaves and looked down upon the poor white farmers who settled the backcountry. Different still were the middle colonies stretching from New York to Delaware. There diversity reigned. Well-to-do merchants put their stamp on New York City, as Quakers did on Philadelphia, while out in the countryside sprawling estates were interspersed with modest homesteads. Within individual colonies, conflicts festered over economic interests, ethnic rivalries, and religious practices. All those clashes made it difficult for colonists to imagine that they were a single people with a common destiny, much less that they ought to break free from Britain.

The American colonists in fact had little reason to complain about Britain. Each of the thirteen colonies enjoyed a good deal of self-rule. Many colonists profited from trade within the British Empire. But by the 1760s, this stable arrangement began to crumble, a victim of the imperial rivalry between France and Britain. Their struggle for supremacy in North America began in the late seventeenth century and finally dragged in the colonists during the French and Indian War from 1756 to 1763. That war in one sense strengthened ties with Britain, since colonial militias fought triumphantly alongside the British army against their mutual French and Indian enemies. But once the French were driven from the North American continent, the colonists no longer needed Britain for protection. More important still, after 1763 a financially overstretched British government made the fateful choice of imposing taxes on colonies that had been accustomed to answering mainly to their own colonial assemblies. By the 1770s issues of taxation, self-rule, and trade restrictions brought the crisis of imperial authority to a head. Although as late as 1775 most people in the colonies clung to the hope of some kind of accommodation short of outright independence, royal intransigence soon thrust the colonists into a war of independence that neither antagonist could have anticipated just a few years before.

Eight years of revolutionary war did more than anything in the colonial past to bring Americans together as a nation. Comradeship in arms and the struggle to shape a national government forced Americans to subdue their differences as best they could. But the spirit of national unity was hardly universal. One in five colonists sided with the British as "Loyalists," and a generation would pass before the wounds of this first American "civil war" fully healed. Yet in the end, Americans won the Revolution, with no small measure of help from the French, because in every colony people shared a firm belief that they were fighting for the "unalienable rights" of "life, liberty, and the pursuit of happiness," in the words of Thomas Jefferson's magnificent Declaration of Independence. Almost two hundred years of living a new life had prepared Americans to found a new nation.

Philadelphia, Corner of Second and High Streets
Delegates to the Constitutional Convention in 1787 gathered in Philadelphia, the largest city in North America, a vivid symbol of the rise of American society from its precarious beginnings at Jamestown and Plymouth nearly two centuries earlier.

1

New World Beginnings

33,000 B.C. – A.D. 1769

I HAVE COME TO BELIEVE THAT THIS IS A MIGHTY
CONTINENT WHICH WAS HITHERTO UNKNOWN. . . .
YOUR HIGHNESSES HAVE AN OTHER WORLD HERE.

CHRISTOPHER COLUMBUS, 1498

Several billion years ago, that whirling speck of dust known as the earth, fifth in size among the planets, came into being.

About six thousand years ago—only a minute in geological time—recorded history of the Western world began. Certain peoples of the Middle East, developing a written culture, gradually emerged from the haze of the past.

Five hundred years ago—only a few seconds figuratively speaking—European explorers stumbled

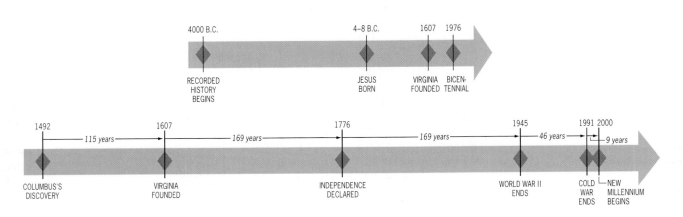

on the Americas. This dramatic accident forever altered the future of both the Old World and the New, and of Africa and Asia as well.

The Shaping of North America

Planet earth took on its present form slowly. Some 225 million years ago, a single supercontinent contained all the world's dry land. Then enormous chunks of terrain began to drift away from this colossal continent, opening the Atlantic and Indian Oceans, narrowing the Pacific Ocean, and forming the great landmasses of Eurasia, Africa, Australia, Antarctica, and the Americas. The existence of a single original continent has been proved in part by the discovery of nearly identical species of fish that swim today in the long-separated freshwater lakes of the various continents.

Continued shifting and folding of the earth's crust thrust up mountain ranges. The Appalachians were probably formed even before continental separation, perhaps 350 million years ago. The majestic ranges of western North America—the Rockies, the Sierra Nevada, the Cascades, and the Coast Ranges—arose much more recently, geologically speaking, some 135 million to 25 million years ago. They are truly "American" mountains, born after the continent took on its own separate geological identity.

By about 10 million years ago, nature had sculpted the basic geological shape of North America. The continent was anchored in its northeastern corner by the massive Canadian Shield—a zone undergirded by ancient rock, probably the first part of what became the North American landmass to have emerged above sea level. A narrow eastern coastal plain, or "tidewater" region, creased by many river valleys, sloped gently upward to the timeworn ridges of the Appalachians. Those ancient mountains slanted away on their western side into the huge midcontinental basin that rolled downward to the Mississippi Valley bottom and then rose relentlessly to the towering peaks of the Rockies. From the Rocky Mountain crest—the "roof of America"—the land fell off jaggedly into the intermountain Great Basin, bounded by the Rockies on the east and the Sierra and Cascade ranges on the west. The valleys of the Sacramento and San Joaquin Rivers and the Willamette–Puget Sound trough seamed the interiors of present-day California, Oregon, and Washington. The land at last met the foaming Pacific, where the Coast Ranges rose steeply from the sea.

Nature laid a chill hand over much of this terrain in the Great Ice Age, beginning about 2 million years ago. Two-mile-thick ice sheets crept from the polar regions to blanket parts of Europe, Asia, and the Americas. In North America the great glaciers carpeted most of present-day Canada and the United States as far southward as a line stretching from Pennsylvania through the Ohio Country and the Dakotas to the Pacific Northwest.

When the glaciers finally retreated about 10,000 years ago, they left the North American landscape transformed, and much as we know it today. The weight of the gargantuan ice mantle had depressed the level of the Canadian Shield. The grinding and flushing action of the moving and melting ice had scoured away the shield's topsoil, pitting its rocky surface with thousands of shallow depressions into which the melting glaciers flowed to form lakes. The same glacial action scooped out and filled the Great Lakes. They originally drained southward through the Mississippi River system to the Gulf of Mexico. When the melting ice unblocked the Gulf of St. Lawrence, the lake water sought the St. Lawrence River outlet to the Atlantic Ocean, lowering the Great Lakes' level and leaving the Missouri-Mississippi-Ohio system to drain the enormous midcontinental basin between the Appalachians and the Rockies. Similarly, in the West, water from the melting glaciers filled sprawling Lake Bonneville, covering much of present-day Utah, Nevada, and Idaho. It drained to the Pacific Ocean through the Snake and Columbia River systems until diminishing rainfall from the ebbing ice cap lowered the water level, cutting off access to the Snake River outlet. Deprived of both inflow and drainage, the giant lake became a gradually shrinking inland sea. It grew increasingly saline, slowly evaporated, and left an arid, mineral-rich desert. Only Great Salt Lake remained as a relic of Bonneville's former vastness. Today Lake Bonneville's ancient beaches are visible on mountainsides up to 1,000 feet above the dry floor of the Great Basin.

Peopling the Americas

The Great Ice Age shaped more than the geological history of North America. It also contributed to the origins of the continent's human history. Though recent (and still highly controversial) evidence suggests that some early peoples may have reached the Americas in crude boats, most probably came by land. Some 35,000 years ago, the Ice Age congealed much of the world oceans

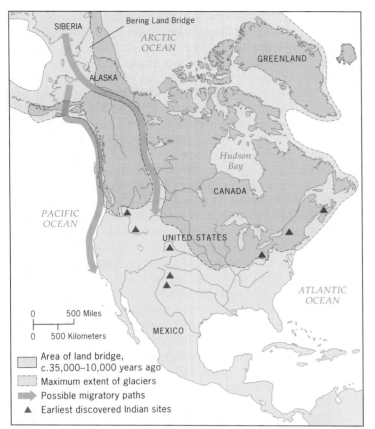

The First Discoverers of America

The origins of the first Americans remain something of a mystery. According to the most plausible theory of how the Americas were populated, for some 25,000 years, people crossed the Bering land bridge from Eurasia to North America. Gradually they dispersed southward down ice-free valleys, populating both the American continents.

Incan Culture   This mortar and corncob-shaped pestle from the Incan stronghold in present-day Peru vividly illustrate the importance of corn in Incan life.

into massive ice-pack glaciers, lowering the level of the sea. As the sea level dropped, it exposed a land bridge connecting Eurasia with North America in the area of the present-day Bering Sea between Siberia and Alaska. Across that bridge, probably following migratory herds of game, ventured small bands of nomadic Asian hunters—the "immigrant" ancestors of the Native Americans. They continued to trek across the Bering isthmus for some 250 centuries, slowly peopling the American continents.

As the Ice Age ended and the glaciers melted, the sea level rose again, inundating the land bridge about 10,000 years ago. Nature thus barred the door to further immigration for many thousands of years, leaving this part of the human family marooned for millennia on the now-isolated American continents.

Time did not stand still for these original Americans. The same climatic warming that melted the ice and drowned the bridge to Eurasia gradually opened ice-free

valleys through which vanguard bands groped their way southward and eastward across the Americas. Roaming slowly through this awesome wilderness, they eventually reached the far tip of South America, some 15,000 miles from Siberia. By the time Europeans arrived in America in 1492, perhaps 54 million people inhabited the two American continents.* Over the centuries they split into countless tribes, evolved more than 2,000 separate languages, and developed many diverse religions, cultures, and ways of life.

Incas in Peru, Mayans in Central America, and Aztecs in Mexico shaped stunningly sophisticated civilizations. Their advanced agricultural practices, based

---

*Much controversy surrounds estimates of the pre-Columbian Native American population. The figures here are from William M. Denevan, ed., *The Native Population of the Americas in 1492*, rev. ed. (Madison: University of Wisconsin Press, 1992).

EXAMINING THE EVIDENCE

Making Sense of the New World This map from 1546 by Sebastian Münster represents one of the earliest efforts to make geographic sense out of the New World (*Nouus Orbis* and *Die Nũw Welt* on the map). The very phrase *New World* suggests just how staggering a blow to the European imagination was the discovery of the Americas. Europeans reached instinctively for the most expansive of all possible terms—*world*, not simply *places*, or even *continents*—to comprehend Columbus's startling report that lands and peoples previously unimagined lay beyond the horizon of Europe's western sea.

Gradually the immense implications of the New World's existence began to impress themselves on Europe, with consequences for literature, art, politics, the economy, and, of course, cartography. Maps can only be *representations* of reality and are therefore necessarily distortions. This map bears a recognizable resemblance to modern mapmakers' renderings of the American continents, but it also contains gross geographic inaccuracies (note the location of Japan—*Zipangri*—relative to the North American west coast) as well as telling commentaries on what sixteenth-century Europeans found remarkable (note the Land of Giants—*Regio Gigantum*—and the indication of cannibals—*Canibali*—in present-day Argentina and Brazil, respectively). What further clues to the European mentality of the time does the map offer? In what ways might misconceptions about the geography of the Americas have influenced further exploration and settlement patterns?

primarily on the cultivation of maize, which is Indian corn, fed large populations, perhaps as many as 20 million in Mexico alone. Although without large draft animals such as horses and oxen, and lacking even the simple technology of the wheel, these peoples built elaborate cities and carried on far-flung commerce. Talented mathematicians, they made strikingly accurate astronomical observations. The Aztecs also routinely sought the favor of their gods by offering human sacrifices, cutting the hearts out of the chests of living victims, who were often captives conquered in battle. By some accounts more than 5,000 people were ritually slaughtered to celebrate the crowning of one Aztec chieftain.

The Earliest Americans

Agriculture, especially corn growing, accounted for the size and sophistication of the Native American civilizations in Mexico and South America. About 5000 B.C. hunter-gatherers in highland Mexico developed a wild grass into the staple crop of corn, which became their staff of life and the foundation of the complex, large-scale, centralized Aztec and Incan nation-states that eventually emerged. Cultivation of corn spread across the Americas from the Mexican heartland. Everywhere it was planted, corn began to transform nomadic hunting bands into settled agricultural villagers, but this process went forward slowly and unevenly.

Corn planting reached the present-day American Southwest by about 1200 B.C. and powerfully molded Pueblo culture. The Pueblo peoples in the Rio Grande valley constructed intricate irrigation systems to water their cornfields. They were dwelling in villages of multistoried, terraced buildings when Spanish explorers made contact with them in the sixteenth century. (*Pueblo* means "village" in Spanish.)

Corn cultivation reached other parts of North America considerably later. The timing of its arrival in different localities explains much about the relative rates of development of different Native American peoples. Throughout the continent to the north and east of the land of the Pueblos, social life was less elaborately developed—indeed "societies" in the modern sense of the word scarcely existed. No dense concentrations of population or complex nation-states comparable to the Aztec empire existed in North America outside of Mexico at the time of the Europeans' arrival—one of the reasons for the relative ease with which the European colonizers subdued the native North Americans.

The Mound Builders of the Ohio River valley, the Mississippian culture of the lower Midwest, and the desert-dwelling Anasazi peoples of the Southwest did sustain some large settlements after the incorporation of corn planting into their ways of life during the first millennium A.D. The Mississippian settlement at Cahokia, near present-day East St. Louis, was at one time home to as many as twenty-five thousand people. The Anasazis built an elaborate pueblo of more than

Cahokia This artist's rendering of Cahokia, based on archaeological excavations, shows the huge central square and the imposing Monk's Mound, which rivaled in size the pyramids of Egypt.

North American Indian Peoples at the Time of First Contact with Europeans Because this map depicts the location of various Indian peoples *at the time of their first contact with Europeans,* and because initial contacts ranged from the sixteenth to the nineteenth centuries, it is necessarily subject to considerable chronological skewing and is only a crude approximation of the "original" territory of any given group. The map also cannot capture the fluidity and dynamism of Native American life even before Columbus's "discovery." For example, the Navajo and Apache peoples had migrated from present-day northern Canada only shortly before the Spanish first encountered them in the present-day American Southwest in the 1500s. The map also places the Sioux on the Great Plains, where Europeans met up with them in the early nineteenth century—but the Sioux had spilled onto the Plains not long before then from the forests surrounding the Great Lakes. The indigenous populations of the southeastern and mid-Atlantic regions are especially difficult to represent accurately in a map like this because pre-Columbian intertribal conflicts had so scrambled the native inhabitants that it is virtually impossible to determine which groups were originally where.

six hundred interconnected rooms at Chaco Canyon in modern-day New Mexico. But mysteriously, perhaps due to prolonged drought, all those ancient cultures fell into decline by about A.D. 1300.

The cultivation of maize, as well as of high-yielding strains of beans and squash, reached the southeastern Atlantic seaboard region of North America about A.D. 1000. These plants made possible "three-sister" farming, with beans growing on the trellis of the cornstalks and squash covering the planting mounds to retain moisture in the soil. The rich diet provided by this environmentally clever farming technique produced some of the highest population densities on the continent, among them the Creek, Choctaw, and Cherokee peoples.

The Iroquois in the northeastern woodlands, inspired by a legendary leader named Hiawatha, in the sixteenth century created perhaps the closest North American approximation to the great nation-states of Mexico and Peru. The Iroquois Confederacy developed the political and organizational skills to sustain a robust military alliance that menaced its neighbors, Native American and European alike, for well over a century (see "Makers of America: The Iroquois," pp. 40–41).

But for the most part, the native peoples of North America were living in small, scattered, and impermanent settlements on the eve of the Europeans' arrival. In more settled agricultural groups, women tended the crops while men hunted, fished, gathered fuel, and cleared fields for planting. This pattern of life frequently conferred substantial authority on women, and many North American native peoples, including the Iroquois, developed matrilinear cultures, in which power and possessions passed down the female side of the family line.

Unlike the Europeans, who would soon arrive with the presumption that humans had dominion over the earth and with the technologies to alter the very face of the land, the Native Americans had neither the desire nor the means to manipulate nature aggressively. They revered the physical world and endowed nature with spiritual properties. Yet they did sometimes ignite massive forest fires, deliberately torching thousands of acres of trees to create better hunting habitats, especially for deer. This practice accounted for the open, parklike appearance of the eastern woodlands that so amazed early European explorers.

But in a broad sense, the land did not feel the hand of the Native Americans heavy upon it, partly because they were so few in number. They were so thinly spread across the continent that vast areas were virtually untouched by a human presence. In the fateful year 1492, probably no more than 4 million Native Americans

padded through the whispering, primeval forests and paddled across the sparkling, virgin waters of North America. They were blissfully unaware that the historic isolation of the Americas was about to end forever, as the land and the native peoples alike felt the full shock of the European "discovery."

Indirect Discoverers of the New World

Europeans, for their part, were equally unaware of the existence of the Americas. Blond-bearded Norse seafarers from Scandinavia had chanced upon the northeastern shoulder of North America about A.D. 1000. They landed at a place near L'Anse aux Meadows in present-day Newfoundland that abounded in wild grapes, which led them to name the spot Vinland. But no strong nation-state, yearning to expand, supported these venturesome voyagers. Their flimsy settlements consequently were soon abandoned, and their discovery was forgotten, except in Scandinavian saga and song.

For several centuries thereafter, other restless Europeans, with the growing power of ambitious governments behind them, sought contact with a wider world, whether for conquest or trade. They thus set in motion the chain of events that led to a drive toward Asia, the penetration of Africa, and the completely accidental discovery of the New World.

Christian crusaders must rank high among America's indirect discoverers. Clad in shining armor, tens of thousands of these European warriors tried from the eleventh to the fourteenth century to wrest the Holy Land from Muslim control. Foiled in their military assaults, the crusaders nevertheless acquired a taste for the exotic delights of Asia. Goods that had been virtually unknown in Europe now were craved—silk for clothing, drugs for aching flesh, perfumes for unbathed bodies, colorful draperies for gloomy castles, and spices—especially sugar, a rare luxury in Europe before the crusades—for preserving and flavoring food. Europe's developing sweet tooth would have momentous implications for world history.

The luxuries of the East were prohibitively expensive in Europe. They had to be transported enormous distances from the Spice Islands (Indonesia), China, and India, in creaking ships and on swaying camelback. The journey led across the Indian Ocean, the Persian Gulf, and the Red Sea or along the tortuous caravan routes of Asia or the Arabian Peninsula, ending at the ports of the eastern Mediterranean. Muslim middlemen exacted a heavy toll en route. By the time the strange-smelling

The New World as Paradise, by Theodore de Bry
This sixteenth-century engraving by the Flemish artist illustrates the Indian method of hunting by setting fires to drive wild game into bow range.

goods reached Italian merchants at Venice and Genoa, they were so costly that purchasers and profits alike were narrowly limited. European consumers and distributors were naturally eager to find a less expensive route to the riches of Asia or to develop alternate sources of supply.

Europeans Enter Africa

European appetites were further whetted when footloose Marco Polo, an Italian adventurer, returned to Europe in 1295 and began telling tales of his nearly twenty-year sojourn in China. Though he may in fact never have seen China (legend to the contrary, the hard evidence is sketchy), he must be regarded as an indirect discoverer of the New World, for his book, with its descriptions of rose-tinted pearls and golden pagodas, stimulated European desires for a cheaper route to the treasures of the East.

These accumulating pressures brought a breakthrough for European expansion in the fifteenth century. Before the middle of that century, European sailors refused to sail southward along the coast of West Africa because they could not beat their way home against the prevailing northerly winds and south-flowing currents.

About 1450, Portuguese mariners overcame those obstacles. Not only had they developed the caravel, a ship that could sail more closely into the wind, but they had discovered that they could return to Europe by sailing northwesterly from the African coast toward the Azores, where the prevailing westward breezes would carry them home.

The new world of sub-Saharan Africa now came within the grasp of questing Europeans. The northern shore of Africa, as part of the Mediterranean world, had been known to Europe since antiquity. But because sea travel down the African coast had been virtually impossible, Africa south of the forbidding Sahara Desert barrier had remained remote and mysterious. African gold, perhaps two-thirds of Europe's supply, crossed the Sahara on camelback, and shadowy tales may have reached Europe about the flourishing West African kingdom of Mali in the Niger River valley, with its impressive Islamic university at Timbuktu. But Europeans had no direct access to sub-Saharan Africa until the Portuguese navigators began to creep down the West African coast in the middle of the fifteenth century.

The Portuguese promptly set up trading posts along the African shore for the purchase of gold—and slaves. Arab flesh merchants and Africans themselves had traded slaves for centuries before the Europeans arrived. They routinely charged higher prices for slaves from distant

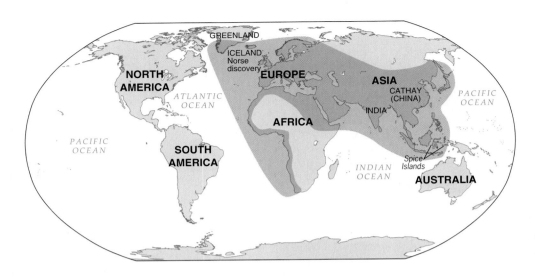

The World Known to Europe, 1492

sources, who could not easily flee to their native villages or be easily rescued by their kin. Slave brokers also deliberately separated persons from the same tribes and mixed unlike people together to frustrate organized resistance. Thus from its earliest days, slavery by its very nature inhibited the expression of regional African cultures and tribal identities.

The Portuguese adopted these Arab and African practices. They built up their own systematic traffic in slaves to work the sugar plantations that Portugal, and later Spain, established on the African coastal islands of Madeira, the Canaries, São Tomé, and Principe. The Portuguese appetite for slaves was enormous and dwarfed the modest scale of the pre-European traffic. Slave trading became a big business. Some forty thousand Africans were carried away to the Atlantic sugar islands in the last half of the fifteenth century. Millions more were to be wrenched from their home continent after the discovery of the Americas. In these fifteenth-century Portuguese adventures in Africa were to be found the origins of the modern plantation system, based on large-scale commercial agriculture and the wholesale exploitation of slave labor. This kind of plantation economy would shape the destiny of much of the New World.

The seafaring Portuguese pushed still farther southward in search of the water route to Asia. Edging cautiously

An Inhabitant of Angola, by Sir Thomas Herbert, 1634
This European depiction of a muscular and bejeweled African native appeared in one of the most vivid records of seventeenth-century travel, Herbert's account of his two-year voyage around the coast of Africa, to Persia, and as far east as the Coromandel Coast of India.

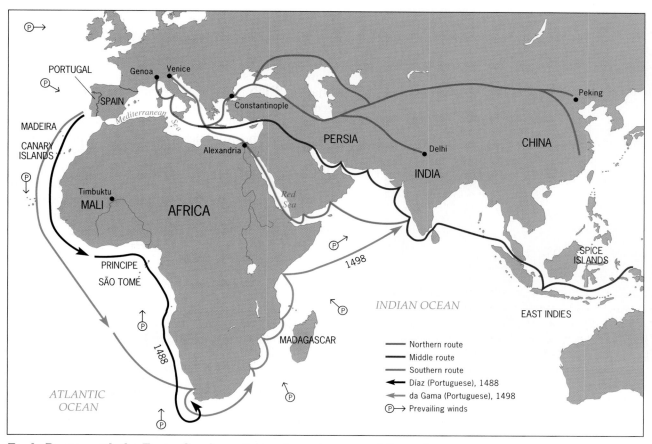

Trade Routes with the East   Goods on the early routes passed through so many hands along the way that their ultimate source remained mysterious to Europeans.

down the African coast, Bartholomeu Días rounded the southernmost tip of the "Dark Continent" in 1488. Ten years later Vasco da Gama finally reached India (hence the name "Indies," given by Europeans to all the mysterious lands of the Orient) and returned home with a small but tantalizing cargo of jewels and spices.

Meanwhile, the kingdom of Spain became united—an event pregnant with destiny—in the late fifteenth century. This new unity resulted primarily from the marriage of two sovereigns, Ferdinand of Aragon and Isabella of Castile, and from the brutal expulsion of the "infidel" Muslim Moors from Spain after centuries of Christian-Islamic warfare. Glorying in their sudden strength, the Spaniards were eager to outstrip their Portuguese rivals in the race to tap the wealth of the Indies. To the south and east, Portugal controlled the African coast and thus controlled the gateway to the round-Africa water route to India. Of necessity, therefore, Spain looked westward.

Columbus Comes upon a New World

The stage was now set for a cataclysmic shift in the course of history—the history not only of Europe but of all the world. Europeans clamored for more and cheaper products from the lands beyond the Mediterranean. Africa had been established as a source of cheap slave labor for plantation agriculture. The Portuguese voyages had demonstrated the feasibility of long-range ocean navigation. In Spain a modern national state was taking shape, with the unity, wealth, and power to shoulder the formidable tasks of discovery, conquest, and colonization. The dawn of the Renaissance in the fourteenth century nurtured an ambitious spirit of optimism and adventure. Printing presses, introduced about 1450, facilitated the spread of scientific knowledge. The mariner's compass, possibly

Christopher Columbus (1451–1506), by Ridolfo di Domenico Ghirlandaio No portrait from life exists of Columbus, so all likenesses of him, including this one, are somewhat fanciful.

borrowed from the Arabs, eliminated some of the uncertainties of sea travel. Meanwhile, across the ocean, the unsuspecting New World innocently awaited its European "discoverers."

Onto this stage stepped Christopher Columbus. This skilled Italian seafarer persuaded the Spanish monarchs to outfit him with three tiny but seaworthy ships, manned by a motley crew. Daringly, he unfurled the sails of his cockleshell craft and headed westward. His superstitious sailors, fearful of venturing into the oceanic unknown, grew increasingly mutinous. After six weeks at sea, failure loomed when, on October 12, 1492, the crew sighted an island in the Bahamas. A new world thus swam within the vision of Europeans.

Columbus's sensational achievement obscures the fact that he was one of the most successful failures in history. Seeking a new water route to the fabled Indies, he in fact had bumped into an enormous land barrier blocking the ocean pathway. For decades thereafter explorers strove to get through it or around it. The truth gradually dawned that sprawling new continents had been discovered. Yet Columbus was at first so certain

that he had skirted the rim of the "Indies" that he called the native peoples Indians, a gross geographical misnomer that somehow stuck.

Columbus's discovery would eventually convulse four continents—Europe, Africa, and the two Americas. Thanks to his epochal voyage, an interdependent global economic system emerged on a scale undreamed-of before he set sail. Its workings touched every shore washed by the Atlantic Ocean. Europe provided the markets, the capital, and the technology; Africa furnished the labor; and the New World offered its raw materials, especially its precious metals and its soil for the cultivation of sugar cane. For Europeans as well as for Africans and Native Americans, the world after 1492 would never be the same, for better or worse.

When Worlds Collide

Two ecosystems—the fragile, naturally evolved networks of relations among organisms in a stable environment—commingled and clashed when Columbus waded ashore. The reverberations from that historic encounter echoed for centuries after 1492. The flora and fauna of the Old and New Worlds had been separated for thousands of years. European explorers marveled at the strange sights that greeted them, including exotic beasts such as iguanas and "snakes with castanets" (rattlesnakes). Native New World plants such as tobacco, maize, beans, tomatoes, and especially the lowly potato eventually revolutionized the international economy as well as the European diet, feeding the rapid population growth of the Old World. These foodstuffs were among the most important Indian gifts to the Europeans and to the rest of the world. Perhaps three-fifths of the crops cultivated around the globe today originated in the Americas. Ironically, the introduction into Africa of New World foodstuffs like maize, manioc, and sweet potatoes may have fed an African population boom that numerically, though not morally, more than offset the losses inflicted by the slave trade.

In exchange the Europeans introduced Old World crops and animals to the Americas. Columbus returned to the Caribbean island of Hispaniola (present-day Haiti and the Dominican Republic) in 1493 with seventeen ships that unloaded twelve hundred men and a virtual Noah's Ark of cattle, swine, and horses. The horses soon reached the North American mainland through Mexico and in less than two centuries had spread as far as Canada. North American Indian tribes like the Apaches,

Sioux, and Blackfoot swiftly adopted the horse, transforming their cultures into highly mobile, wide-ranging hunter societies that roamed the grassy Great Plains in pursuit of the shaggy buffalo. Columbus also brought seedlings of sugar cane, which thrived in the warm Caribbean climate. A "sugar revolution" consequently took place in the European diet, fueled by the forced migration of millions of Africans to work the canefields and sugar mills of the New World.

Unwittingly, the Europeans also brought other organisms in the dirt on their boots and the dust on their clothes, such as the seeds of Kentucky bluegrass, dandelions, and daisies. Most ominous of all, in their bodies they carried the germs that caused smallpox, yellow fever, and malaria. Indeed Old World diseases would quickly devastate the Native Americans. During the Indians' millennia of isolation in the Americas, most of the Old World's killer maladies had disappeared from among them. But generations of freedom from those illnesses had also wiped out protective antibodies. Devoid of natural resistance to Old World sicknesses, Indians

died in droves. Within fifty years of the Spanish arrival, the population of the Taino natives in Hispaniola dwindled from some 1 million people to about 200. Enslavement and armed aggression took their toll, but the deadliest killers were microbes, not muskets. The lethal germs spread among the New World peoples with the speed and force of a hurricane, swiftly sweeping far ahead of the human invaders; most of those afflicted never laid eyes on a European. In the centuries after Columbus's landfall, as many as 90 percent of the Native Americans perished, a demographic catastrophe without parallel in human history. This depopulation was surely not intended by the Spanish, but it was nevertheless so severe that entire cultures and ancient ways of life were extinguished forever. Baffled, enraged, and vengeful, Indian slaves sometimes kneaded tainted blood into their masters' bread, to little effect. Perhaps it was poetic justice that the Indians unintentionally did take a kind of revenge by infecting the early explorers with syphilis, injecting that lethal sexually transmitted disease for the first time into Europe.

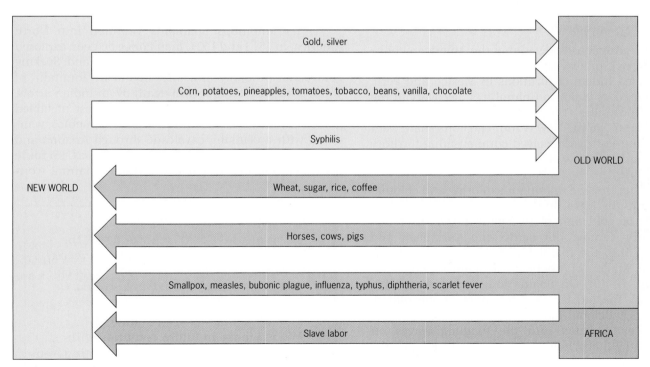

The Columbian Exchange Columbus's discovery initiated the kind of explosion in international commerce that a later age would call "globalization." (Source: Adapted from *Out of Many: A History of the American People*, Third Edition, Combined Edition by Faragher, Buhle, Czitrom, and Armitage. Copyright © 1999. By permission of Prentice-Hall, Inc., Upper Saddle River, NJ.)

The Devastation of Disease This engraving of a burial service records the horrendous impact of Old World diseases on the vulnerable Native Americans.

The Spanish *Conquistadores*

Gradually, Europeans realized that the American continents held rich prizes, especially the gold and silver of the advanced Indian civilizations in Mexico and Peru. Spain secured its claim to Columbus's discovery in the Treaty of Tordesillas (1494), dividing with Portugal the "heathen lands" of the New World. The lion's share went to Spain, but Portugal received compensating territory in Africa and Asia, as well as title to lands that one day would be Brazil.

Spain became the dominant exploring and colonizing power in the 1500s. In the service of God, as well as in search of gold and glory, Spanish *conquistadores* (conquerors) fanned out across the Caribbean and eventually onto the mainland of the American continents (see "Makers of America: The Spanish *Conquistadores*," pp. 18–19). On Spain's long roster of notable deeds, two spectacular exploits must be headlined. Vasco Nuñez Balboa, hailed as the discoverer of the Pacific Ocean, waded into the foaming waves off Panama in 1513 and boldly claimed for his king all the lands washed by that sea! Ferdinand Magellan started from Spain in 1519 with five tiny ships. After beating through the storm-lashed strait off the tip of South America that still bears his name, he was slain by the inhabitants of the Philippines. His one remaining vessel creaked home in 1522, completing the first circumnavigation of the globe.

Other ambitious Spaniards ventured into North America. In 1513 and 1521, Juan Ponce de León explored Florida, which he at first thought was an island. Seeking gold—and probably not the mythical "fountain of youth"—he instead met with death by an Indian arrow. In 1540–1542 Francisco Coronado, in quest of fabled golden cities that turned out to be adobe pueblos, wandered with a clanking cavalcade through Arizona and New Mexico, penetrating as far east as Kansas. En route his expedition discovered two awesome natural won-

Bartolomé de Las Casas (1474–1566), a reform-minded Dominican friar, wrote The Destruction of the Indies *in 1542 to chronicle the awful fate of the Native Americans and to protest Spanish policies in the New World. He was especially horrified at the catastrophic effects of disease on the native peoples:*

"Who of those in future centuries will believe this? I myself who am writing this and saw it and know the most about it can hardly believe that such was possible."

ders: the Grand Canyon of the Colorado River and enormous herds of buffalo (bison). Hernando de Soto, with six hundred armor-plated men, undertook a fantastic gold-seeking expedition during 1539–1542. Floundering through marshes and pine barrens from Florida westward, he discovered and crossed the majestic Mississippi River just north of its junction with the Arkansas River. After brutally mistreating the Indians with iron collars and fierce dogs, he at length died of fever and wounds. His troops secretly disposed of his remains at night in the Mississippi, lest the Indians exhume and abuse their abuser's corpse.

Meanwhile in South America, the ironfisted conqueror Francisco Pizarro crushed the Incas of Peru in 1532 and added a huge hoard of booty to Spanish coffers. By 1600 Spain was swimming in New World silver, mostly from the fabulously rich mines at Potosí in present-day Bolivia, as well as from Mexico. This flood of precious metal touched off a price revolution in Europe that increased consumer costs by as much as 500 percent in the hundred years after the mid-sixteenth century. Some scholars see in this ballooning European money supply the fuel that fed the growth of the economic system known as capitalism. Certainly, New World bullion helped transform the world economy. It swelled the vaults of bankers from Spain to Italy, laying the foundations of the modern commercial banking system. It clinked in the purses of merchants in France and Holland, stimulating the spread of commerce and manufacturing. And it paid for much of the burgeoning international trade with Asia, whose sellers had little use for any European good except silver.

The islands of the Caribbean Sea—the West Indies as they came to be called, in yet another perpetuation of Columbus's geographic confusion—served as offshore bases for the staging of the Spanish invasion of the mainland Americas. Here supplies could be stored, and men and horses could be rested and acclimated, before proceeding to the conquest of the continents. The loosely organized and vulnerable native communities of the West Indies also provided laboratories for testing the techniques that would eventually subdue the advanced Indian civilizations of Mexico and Peru. The most important such technique was the institution known as the *encomienda*. It allowed the government to "commend," or give, Indians to certain colonists in return for the promise to try to Christianize them. In all but name, it was slavery. Spanish missionary Bartolomé de Las Casas, appalled by the *encomienda* system in Hispaniola, called it "a moral pestilence invented by Satan."

The Conquest of Mexico

In 1519 Hernán Cortés set sail from Cuba with sixteen fresh horses and several hundred men aboard eleven ships, bound for Mexico and for destiny. On the island of Cozumel off the Yucatán peninsula, he rescued a

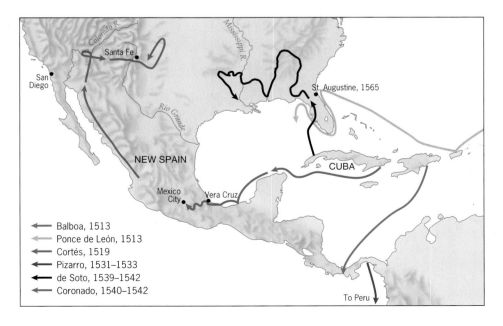

Principal Early Spanish Explorations and Conquests Note that Coronado traversed northern Texas and Oklahoma. In present-day eastern Kansas, he found, instead of the great golden city he sought, a drab encampment, probably of Wichita Indians.

The Spanish *Conquistadores*

In 1492, the same year that Columbus sighted America, the great Moorish city of Granada, in Spain, fell after a ten-year siege. For five centuries the Christian kingdoms of Spain had been trying to drive the North African Muslim *Moors* ("the Dark Ones," in Spanish) off the Iberian Peninsula, and with the fall of Granada they succeeded. But the lengthy *Reconquista* had left its mark on Spanish society. Centuries of military and religious confrontation nurtured an obsession with status and honor, bred religious zealotry and intolerance, and created a large class of men who regarded manual labor and commerce contemptuously. With the Reconquista ended, some of these men turned their restless gaze to Spain's New World frontier.

At first Spanish hopes for America focused on the Caribbean and on finding a sea route to Asia. Gradually, however, word filtered back of rich kingdoms on the mainland. Between 1519 and 1540, Spanish *conquistadores* swept across the Americas in two wide arcs of conquest—one driving from Cuba through Mexico into what is now the southwestern United States, the other starting from Panama and pushing south into Peru. Within half a century of Columbus's arrival in the Americas, the *conquistadores* had extinguished the great

Conquistadores, c. 1534
This illustration for a book called the *Köhler Codex of Nuremberg* may be the earliest depiction of the *conquistadores* in the Americas. It portrays men and horses alike as steadfast and self-assured in their work of conquest.

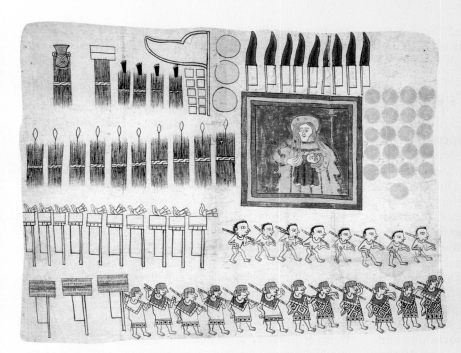

An Aztec View of the Conquest, 1531
Produced just a dozen years after Cortés's arrival in 1519, this drawing by an Aztec artist pictures the Indians rendering tribute to their conquerors. The inclusion of the banner showing Madonna and child also illustrates the early incorporation of Christian beliefs by the Indians.

Aztec and Incan empires and claimed for church and crown a territory that extended from Colorado to Argentina, including much of what is now the continental United States.

The military conquest of this vast region was achieved by just ten thousand men, organized in a series of private expeditions. Hernán Cortés, Francisco Pizarro, and other aspiring conquerors signed contracts with the Spanish monarch, raised money from investors, and then went about recruiting an army. Only a small minority of the *conquistadores*—leaders or followers—were nobles. About half were professional soldiers and sailors; the rest comprised peasants, artisans, and members of the middling classes. Most were in their twenties and early thirties, and all knew how to wield a sword.

Diverse motives spurred these motley adventurers. Some hoped to win royal titles and favors by bringing new peoples under the Spanish flag. Others sought to ensure God's favor by spreading Christianity to the pagans. Some men hoped to escape dubious pasts, and others sought the kind of historical adventure experienced by heroes of classical antiquity. Nearly all shared a lust for gold. As one of Cortés's foot soldiers put it, "We came here to serve God and the king, and also to get rich." One historian adds that the *conquistadores* first fell on their knees and then fell upon the aborigines.

Armed with horses and gunpowder and preceded by disease, the *conquistadores* quickly overpowered the Indians. But most never achieved their dreams of glory. Few received titles of nobility, and many of the rank and file remained permanently indebted to the absentee investors who paid for their equipment. Even when an expedition captured exceptionally rich booty, the spoils were unevenly divided: men from the commander's home region often received more, and men on horseback generally got two shares to the infantryman's one. The *conquistadores* lost still more power as the crown gradually tightened its control in the New World. By the 1530s in Mexico and the 1550s in Peru, colorless colonial administrators had replaced the freebooting *conquistadores*.

Nevertheless, the *conquistadores* achieved a kind of immortality. Because of a scarcity of Spanish women in the early days of the conquest, many of the *conquistadores* married Indian women. The soldiers who conquered Paraguay received three native women each, and Cortés's soldiers in Mexico—who were forbidden to consort with pagan women—quickly had their lovers baptized into the Catholic faith. Their offspring, the "new race" of *mestizos*, formed a cultural and a biological bridge between Latin America's European and Indian races.

Spanish castaway who had been enslaved for several years by the Mayan-speaking Indians. A short distance farther on, he picked up the female Indian slave Malinche, who knew both Mayan and Nahuatl, the language of the powerful Aztec rulers of the great empire in the highlands of central Mexico. In addition to his superior firepower, Cortés now had the advantage, through these two interpreters, of understanding the speech of the native peoples whom he was about to encounter, including the Aztecs. Malinche eventually learned Spanish and was baptized with the Spanish name of Doña Marina.

Near present-day Vera Cruz, Cortés made his final landfall. Through his interpreters he learned of unrest within the Aztec empire among the peoples from whom the Aztecs demanded tribute. He also heard alluring tales of the gold and other wealth stored up in the legendary Aztec capital of Tenochtitlán. He lusted to tear open the coffers of the Aztec kingdom. To quell his mutinous troops, he boldly burned his ships, cutting off any hope of retreat. Gathering a force of some twenty thousand Indian allies, he marched on Tenochtitlán and toward one of history's most dramatic and fateful encounters.

As Cortés proceeded, the Aztec chieftain Moctezuma sent ambassadors bearing fabulous gifts to welcome the approaching Spaniards. These only whetted the *conquistador's* appetite. "We Spanish suffer from a strange disease of the heart," Cortés allegedly informed the emissaries, "for which the only known remedy is gold." The ambassadors reported this comment to Moctezuma, along with the astonishing fact that the newcomers rode on the backs of "deer" (horses). The superstitious Moctezuma also believed that Cortés was the god Quetzalcoatl, whose return from the eastern sea was predicted in Aztec legends. Expectant yet apprehensive, Moctezuma allowed the *conquistadores* to approach his capital unopposed.

As the Spaniards entered the Valley of Mexico, the sight of the Aztec capital of Tenochtitlán amazed them. With 300,000 inhabitants spread over ten square miles, it rivaled in size and pomp any city in contemporary Europe. The Aztec metropolis rose from an island in the center of a lake, surrounded by floating gardens of extraordinary beauty. It was connected to the mainland by a series of causeways and supplied with fresh water by an artfully designed aqueduct.

Moctezuma treated Cortés hospitably at first, but soon the Spaniards' hunger for gold and power exhausted their welcome. "They thirsted mightily for gold; they stuffed themselves with it; they starved for it; they lusted for it like

Artists' Rendering of Tenochtitlán   Amid tribal strife in the fourteenth century, the Aztecs built a capital on a small island in a lake in the central Valley of Mexico. From here they oversaw the most powerful empire yet to arise in Mesoamerica. Two main temples stood at the city's sacred center, one dedicated to Tlaloc, the ancient rain god, and the other to Huitzilopochtli, the tribal god, who was believed to require human hearts for sustenance.

Cortés and Malinche, c. 1540 (detail) Though done by an Indian artist, this drawing identifies Malinche by her Christian name, Marina. She eventually married one of Cortés's soldiers, with whom she traveled to Spain and was received at the Spanish court.

pigs," said one Aztec. On the *noche triste* (sad night) of June 30, 1520, the Aztecs attacked, driving the Spanish down the causeways from Tenochtitlán in a frantic, bloody retreat. Cortés then laid siege to the city, and it capitulated on August 13, 1521. That same year a smallpox epidemic burned through the Valley of Mexico. The combination of conquest and disease took a grisly toll. The Aztec empire gave way to three centuries of Spanish rule. The temples of Tenochtitlán were destroyed to make way for the Christian cathedrals of Mexico City, built on the site of the ruined Indian capital. And the native population of Mexico, winnowed mercilessly by the invader's diseases, shrank from some 20 million to 2 million people in less than a century.

Yet the invader brought more than conquest and death. He brought his crops and his animals, his language and his laws, his customs and his religion, all of which proved adaptable to the peoples of Mexico. He intermarried with the surviving Indians, creating a distinctive culture of *mestizos,* people of mixed Indian and European heritage. To this day Mexican civilization remains a unique blend of the Old World and the New, producing both ambivalence and pride among people of Mexican heritage. Cortés's translator, Malinche, for example, has given her name to the Mexican language in the word *malinchista,* or "traitor." But Mexicans also celebrate Columbus Day as the *Día de la Raza*—the birthday of a wholly new race of people.

The Spread of Spanish America

Spain's colonial empire grew swiftly and impressively. Within about half a century of Columbus's landfall, hundreds of Spanish cities and towns flourished in the Americas, especially in the great silver-producing centers of Peru and Mexico. Some 160,000 Spaniards, mostly men, had subjugated millions of Indians. Majestic cathedrals dotted the land, printing presses turned out books, and scholars studied at distinguished universities, including those at Mexico City and Lima, Peru, both founded in 1551, eighty-five years before Harvard, the first college established in the English colonies.

But how secure were these imperial possessions? Other powers were already sniffing around the edges of the Spanish domain, eager to bite off their share of the promised wealth of the new lands. The upstart English sent Giovanni Caboto (known in English as John Cabot) to explore the northeastern coast of North America in 1497 and 1498. The French king dispatched another Italian mariner, Giovanni da Verrazano, to probe the eastern seaboard in 1524. Ten years later the Frenchman Jacques Cartier journeyed hundreds of miles up the St. Lawrence River.

To secure the northern periphery of their New World domain against such encroachments and to convert more Indian souls to Christianity, the Spanish began to fortify and settle their North American borderlands. In a move to block French ambitions and to protect the sea-lanes to the Caribbean, the Spanish erected a fortress at St. Augustine, Florida, in 1565, thus founding the oldest continually inhabited European settlement in the future United States.

In Mexico the tales of Coronado's expedition of the 1540s to the upper Rio Grande and Colorado River regions continued to beckon the *conquistadores'* interest northward. A dust-begrimed expeditionary column, with eighty-three rumbling wagons and hundreds of grumbling men, traversed the bare Sonora Desert from Mexico into the Rio Grande valley in 1598. Led by Don Juan de Oñate, the Spaniards cruelly abused the Pueblo peoples they encountered. In the Battle of Acoma in 1599, the Spanish severed one foot of each survivor. They proclaimed the area to be the province of New Mexico in 1609 and founded its capital at Santa Fe the following year.

The Spanish settlers in New Mexico found a few furs and precious little gold, but they did discover a wealth of

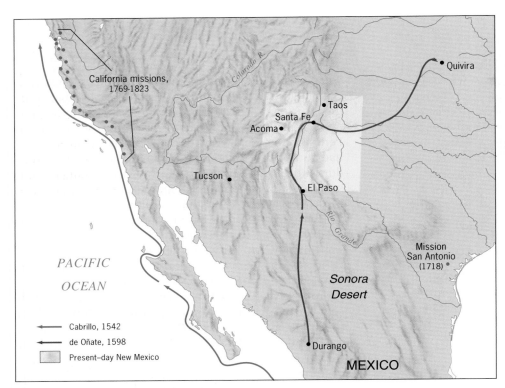

Spain's North American Frontier, 1542–1823

souls to be harvested for the Christian religion. The Roman Catholic mission became the central institution in colonial New Mexico until the missionaries' efforts to suppress native religious customs provoked an Indian uprising called Popé's Rebellion in 1680. The Pueblo rebels destroyed every Catholic church in the province and killed a score of priests and hundreds of Spanish settlers. In a reversal of Cortés's treatment of the Aztec temples more than a century earlier, the Indians rebuilt a *kiva,* or ceremonial religious chamber, on the ruins of the Spanish plaza at Santa Fe. It took nearly half a century for the Spanish fully to reclaim New Mexico from the insurrectionary Indians.

Meanwhile, as a further hedge against the ever-threatening French, who had sent an expedition under Robert de La Salle down the Mississippi River in the 1680s, the Spanish began around 1716 to establish settlements in Texas. Some refugees from the Pueblo uprising trickled into Texas, and a few missions were established there, including the one at San Antonio later

known as the Alamo. But for at least another century, the Spanish presence remained weak in this distant northeastern outpost of Spain's Mexican empire.

To the west, in California, no serious foreign threat loomed, and Spain directed its attention there only belatedly. Juan Rodriguez Cabrillo had explored the California coast in 1542, but he failed to find San Francisco Bay or anything else of much interest. For some two centuries thereafter, California slumbered undisturbed by European intruders. Then in 1769 Spanish missionaries led by Father Junipero Serra founded at San Diego the first of a chain of twenty-one missions that wound up the coast as far as Sonoma, north of San Francisco Bay. Father Serra's brown-robed Franciscan friars toiled with zealous devotion to Christianize the three hundred thousand native Californians. They gathered the semi-nomadic Indians into fortified missions and taught them horticulture and basic crafts. These "mission Indians" did adopt Christianity, but they also lost contact with their native cultures and often lost their lives as well, as the white man's diseases doomed these biologically vulnerable peoples.

The misdeeds of the Spanish in the New World obscured their substantial achievements and helped give birth to the "Black Legend." This false concept held that the conquerors merely tortured and butchered the Indians ("killing for Christ"), stole their gold, infected them with smallpox, and left little but misery behind. The Spanish invaders did indeed kill, enslave, and infect countless natives, but they also erected a colossal empire, sprawling from California and Florida to Tierra del Fuego. They grafted their culture, laws, religion, and language onto a wide array of native societies, laying the foundations for a score of Spanish-speaking nations.

Clearly, the Spaniards, who had more than a century's head start over the English, were genuine empire builders and cultural innovators in the New World. As compared with their Anglo-Saxon rivals, their colonial establishment was larger and richer, and it was destined to endure more than a quarter of a century longer. And in the last analysis, the Spanish paid the Native Americans the high compliment of fusing with them through marriage and incorporating indigenous culture into their own, rather than shunning and eventually isolating the Indians as their English adversaries would do.

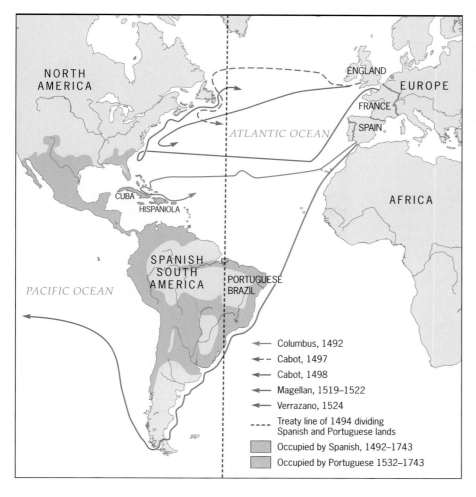

Principal Voyages of Discovery
Spain, Portugal, France, and England reaped the greatest advantages from the New World, but much of the earliest exploration was done by Italians, notably Christopher Columbus of Genoa. John Cabot, another native of Genoa (his original name was Giovanni Caboto), sailed for England's King Henry VII. Giovanni da Verrazano was a Florentine employed by France.

Chronology

c. 33,000–8000 B.C.	First humans cross into Americas from Asia
c. 5000 B.C.	Corn is developed as a staple crop in highland Mexico
c. 4000 B.C.	First civilized societies develop in the Middle East
c. 1200 B.C.	Corn planting reaches present-day American Southwest
c. A.D. 1000	Norse voyagers discover and briefly settle in northeastern North America Corn cultivation reaches Midwest and southeastern Atlantic seaboard
c. A.D. 1100	Height of Mississippian settlement at Cahokia
c. A.D. 1100–1300	Christian crusades arouse European interest in the East
1295	Marco Polo returns to Europe
late 1400s	Spain becomes united
1488	Díaz rounds southern tip of Africa
1492	Columbus lands in the Bahamas
1494	Treaty of Tordesillas between Spain and Portugal
1498	Da Gama reaches India Cabot explores northeastern coast of North America for England
1513	Balboa claims all lands touched by the Pacific Ocean for Spain
1513, 1521	Ponce de León explores Florida
1519–1521	Cortés conquers Mexico for Spain
1522	Magellan's vessel completes circumnavigation of the world
1524	Verrazano explores eastern seaboard of North America for France
1532	Pizarro crushes Incas
1534	Cartier journeys up the St. Lawrence River
1539–1542	De Soto explores the Southeast and discovers the Mississippi River
1540–1542	Coronado explores present-day Southwest
1542	Cabrillo explores California coast for Spain
1565	Spanish build fortress at St. Augustine
late 1500s	Iroquois Confederacy founded, according to Iroquois legend
c. 1598–1609	Spanish under Oñate conquer Pueblo peoples of Rio Grande valley
1609	Spanish found New Mexico
1680	Popé's Rebellion in New Mexico
1680s	French expedition down Mississippi River under La Salle
1769	Serra founds first California mission, at San Diego

For further reading, see the Appendix. For web resources, go to **http://college.hmco.com.**

2

The Planting of English America

1500–1733

. . . For I shall yet to see it [Virginia] an Inglishe nation.

Sir Walter Raleigh, 1602

As the seventeenth century dawned, scarcely a hundred years after Columbus's momentous landfall, the face of much of the New World had already been profoundly transformed. European crops and livestock had begun to alter the very landscape, touching off an ecological revolution that would reverberate for centuries to come. From Tierra del Fuego in the south to Hudson Bay in the north, disease and armed conquest had cruelly winnowed and disrupted the native peoples. Several hundred thousand enslaved Africans toiled on Caribbean and Brazilian sugar plantations. From Florida and New Mexico southward, most of the New World lay firmly within the grip of imperial Spain.

But *North* America in 1600 remained largely unexplored and effectively unclaimed by Europeans. Then, as if to herald the coming century of colonization and conflict in the northern continent, three European powers planted three primitive outposts in three distant corners of the continent within three years of one another: the Spanish at Santa Fe in 1610, the French at Quebec in 1608, and, most consequentially for the future United States, the English at Jamestown, Virginia, in 1607.

England's Imperial Stirrings

Feeble indeed were England's efforts in the 1500s to compete with the sprawling Spanish Empire. As Spain's ally in the first half of the century, England took little interest in establishing its own overseas colonies. Religious conflict, moreover, disrupted England in mid-century, after King Henry VIII broke with the Roman Catholic Church in the 1530s, launching the English Protestant Reformation. Catholics battled Protestants for decades, and the religious balance of power seesawed. But after the Protestant Elizabeth ascended to the English throne in 1558, Protestantism became dominant in England, and rivalry with Catholic Spain intensified.

Ireland, which nominally had been under English rule since the twelfth century, became an early scene of that rivalry. The Catholic Irish sought help from Catholic Spain to throw off the yoke of the new Protestant English queen. But Spanish aid never amounted to much; in the 1570s and 1580s, Elizabeth's troops

Sir Walter Ralegh (Raleigh) (c. 1552–1618), 1588
A dashing courtier who was one of Queen Elizabeth's favorites for his wit, good looks, and courtly manners, he launched important colonizing failures in the New World. For this portrait, Raleigh presented himself as the queen's devoted servant, wearing her colors of black and white and her emblem of a pearl in his left ear. After seducing (and secretly marrying) one of Queen Elizabeth's maids of honor, he fell out of favor but continued his colonial ventures in the hopes of challenging Catholic Spain's dominance in the Americas. He was ultimately beheaded for treason.

crushed the Irish uprising with terrible ferocity, inflicting unspeakable atrocities upon the native Irish people. The English crown confiscated Catholic Irish lands and "planted" them with new Protestant landlords from Scotland and England. This policy also planted the seeds of the centuries-old religious conflicts that persist in Ireland to the present day. Many English soldiers

developed in Ireland a sneering contempt for the "savage" natives, an attitude that they brought with them to the New World.

Elizabeth Energizes England

Encouraged by the ambitious Queen Elizabeth, hardy English buccaneers now swarmed out upon the shipping lanes. They sought to promote the twin goals of Protestantism and plunder by seizing Spanish treasure ships and raiding Spanish settlements, even though England and Spain were technically at peace. The most famous of these semipiratical "sea dogs" was the courtly Francis Drake. He plundered his way around the planet, returning in 1580 with his ship heavily ballasted with Spanish booty. The venture netted profits of about 4,600 percent to his financial backers, among whom, in secret, was Queen Elizabeth. Defying Spanish protest, she brazenly knighted Drake on the deck of his barnacled ship.

The bleak coast of Newfoundland was the scene of the first English attempt at colonization. This effort collapsed when its promoter, Sir Humphrey Gilbert, lost his life at sea in 1583. Gilbert's ill-starred dream inspired his gallant half-brother Sir Walter Raleigh to try again in warmer climes. Raleigh organized an expedition that first landed in 1585 on North Carolina's Roanoke Island, off the coast of Virginia—a vaguely defined region named in honor of Elizabeth, the "Virgin Queen." After several false starts, the hapless Roanoke colony mysteriously vanished, swallowed up by the wilderness.

These pathetic English failures at colonization contrasted embarrassingly with the glories of the Spanish Empire, whose profits were fabulously enriching Spain. Philip II of Spain, self-anointed foe of the Protestant Reformation, used part of his imperial gains to amass an "Invincible Armada" of ships for an invasion of England. The showdown came in 1588, when the lumbering Spanish flotilla, 130 strong, hove into the English Channel. The English sea dogs fought back. Using craft that were swifter, more maneuverable, and more ably manned, they inflicted heavy damage on the cumbersome, overladen Spanish ships. Then a devastating storm arose (the "Protestant wind"), scattering the crippled Spanish fleet.

The rout of the Spanish Armada marked the beginning of the end of Spanish imperial dreams, though

Elizabeth I (1533–1603), by Marcus Gheeraets the Younger, c. 1592 Although accused of being vain, fickle, prejudiced, and miserly, she proved to be an unusually successful ruler. She never married (hence, the "Virgin Queen"), although various royal matches were projected.

Spain's New World empire would not fully collapse for three more centuries. Within a few decades, the Spanish Netherlands (Holland) would secure their independence, and much of the Spanish Caribbean would slip from Spain's grasp. Bloated by Peruvian and Mexican silver and cockily convinced of its own invincibility, Spain had overreached itself, sowing the seeds of its own decline.

England's victory over the Spanish Armada also marked a red-letter day in American history. It dampened Spain's fighting spirit and helped ensure England's naval dominance in the North Atlantic. It started

England on its way to becoming master of the world oceans—a fact of enormous importance to the American people. Indeed England now had many of the characteristics that Spain displayed on the eve of its colonizing adventure a century earlier: a strong, unified national state under a popular monarch; a measure of religious unity after a protracted struggle between Protestants and Catholics; and a vibrant sense of nationalism and national destiny.

A wondrous flowering of the English national spirit bloomed in the wake of the Spanish Armada's defeat. A golden age of literature dawned in this exhilarating atmosphere, with William Shakespeare, at its forefront, making occasional poetical references to England's American colonies. The English were seized with restlessness, with thirst for adventure, and with curiosity about the unknown. Everywhere there blossomed a new spirit of self-confidence, of vibrant patriotism, and of boundless faith in the future of the English nation. When England and Spain finally signed a treaty of peace in 1604, the English people were poised to plunge headlong into the planting of their own colonial empire in the New World.

England on the Eve of Empire

England's scepter'd isle, as Shakespeare called it, throbbed with social and economic change as the seventeenth century opened. Its population was mushrooming, from some 3 million people in 1550 to about 4 million in 1600. In the ever-green English countryside, landlords were "enclosing" croplands for sheep grazing, forcing many small farmers into precarious tenancy or off the land altogether. It was no accident that the woolen districts of eastern and western England—where Puritanism had taken strong root—supplied many of the earliest immigrants to America. When economic depression hit the woolen trade in the late 1500s, thousands of footloose farmers took to the roads. They drifted about England, chronically unemployed, often ending up as beggars and paupers in cities like Bristol and London.

This remarkably mobile population alarmed many contemporaries. They concluded that England was burdened with a "surplus population," though present-day London holds twice as many people as did all of England in 1600.

In the years immediately following the defeat of the Spanish Armada, the English writer Richard Hakluyt (1552?–1616) extravagantly exhorted his countrymen to cast off their "sluggish security" and undertake the colonization of the New World:

"There is under our noses the great and ample country of Virginia; the inland whereof is found of late to be so sweet and wholesome a climate, so rich and abundant in silver mines, a better and richer country than Mexico itself. If it shall please the Almighty to stir up Her Majesty's heart to continue with transporting one or two thousand of her people, she shall by God's assistance, in short space, increase her dominions, enrich her coffers, and reduce many pagans to the faith of Christ."

At the same time, laws of primogeniture decreed that only eldest sons were eligible to inherit landed estates. Landholders' ambitious younger sons, among them Gilbert, Raleigh, and Drake, were forced to seek their fortunes elsewhere. Bad luck plagued their early, lone-wolf enterprises. But by the early 1600s, the joint-stock company, forerunner of the modern corporation, was perfected. It enabled a considerable number of investors, called "adventurers," to pool their capital.

Peace with a chastened Spain provided the opportunity for English colonization. Population growth provided the workers. Unemployment, as well as a thirst for adventure, for markets, and for religious freedom, provided the motives. Joint-stock companies provided the financial means. The stage was now set for a historic effort to establish an English beachhead in the still uncharted North American wilderness.

England Plants the Jamestown Seedling

In 1606, two years after peace with Spain, the hand of destiny beckoned toward Virginia. A joint-stock company, known as the Virginia Company of London, received a charter from King James I of England for a settlement in the New World. The main attraction was the promise of gold, combined with a strong desire to find a passage through America to the Indies. Like most joint-stock companies of the day, the Virginia Company was intended to endure for only a few years, after which its stockholders hoped to liquidate it for a profit. This arrangement put severe pressure on the luckless colonists, who were threatened with abandonment in the wilderness if they did not quickly strike it rich on the company's behalf. Few of the investors thought in terms of long-term colonization. Apparently no one even faintly suspected that the seeds of a mighty nation were being planted.

The charter of the Virginia Company is a significant document in American history. It guaranteed to the overseas settlers the same rights of Englishmen that they would have enjoyed if they had stayed at home. This precious boon was gradually extended to subsequent English colonies, helping to reinforce the colonists'

Sources of the Puritan "Great Migration" to New England, 1620–1650 The dark green areas indicate the main sources of the migration.

> *George Percy (1580–1631) accompanied Captain John Smith on his expedition to Virginia in 1606–1607. He served as deputy governor of the colony in 1609–1610 and returned to England in 1612, where he wrote* A Discourse of the Plantation of Virginia *about his experiences:*
>
> "Our men were destroyed with cruel diseases as swellings, burning fevers, and by wars, and some departed suddenly, but for the most part they died of mere famine. There were never Englishmen left in a foreign country in such misery as we were in this new discovered Virginia."

sense that even on the far shores of the Atlantic, they remained comfortably within the embrace of traditional English institutions. But ironically, a century and a half later, their insistence on the "rights of Englishmen" fed the hot resentment of the colonists against an increasingly meddlesome mother country and nourished their appetite for independence.

Setting sail in late 1606, the Virginia Company's three ships landed near the mouth of Chesapeake Bay, where Indians attacked them. Pushing on up the bay, the tiny band of colonists eventually chose a location on the wooded and malarial banks of the James River, named in honor of King James I. The site was easy to defend, but it was mosquito-infested and devastatingly unhealthful. There, on May 24, 1607, about a hundred English settlers, all of them men, disembarked. They called the place Jamestown.

The early years of Jamestown proved a nightmare for all concerned—except the buzzards. Forty would-be colonists perished during the initial voyage in 1606–1607. Another expedition in 1609 lost its leaders and many of its precious supplies in a shipwreck off Bermuda. Once ashore in Virginia, the settlers died by the dozens from disease, malnutrition, and starvation. Ironically, the woods rustled with game and the rivers flopped with fish, but the greenhorn settlers, many of them self-styled "gentlemen" unaccustomed to fending for themselves, wasted valuable time grubbing for nonexistent gold when they should have been gathering provisions.

Virginia was saved from utter collapse at the start largely by the leadership and resourcefulness of an intrepid young adventurer, Captain John Smith. Taking over in 1608, he whipped the gold-hungry colonists into line with the rule, "He who shall not work shall not eat." He had been kidnapped in December 1607 and subjected to a mock execution by the Indian chieftain Powhatan, whose daughter Pocahontas had "saved" Smith by dramatically interposing her head between his and the war clubs of his captors. The symbolism of this ritual was apparently intended to impress Smith with Powhatan's power and with the Indians' desire for peaceful relations with the Virginians. Pocahontas became an intermediary between the Indians and the settlers, helping to preserve a shaky peace and to provide needed foodstuffs.

Still, the colonists died in droves, and living skeletons were driven to desperate acts. They were reduced to eating "dogges, Catts, Ratts, and Myce" and even to digging up corpses for food. One hungry man killed, salted, and ate his wife, for which misbehavior he was executed. Of the four hundred settlers who managed to

The Tudor Rulers of England[*]

Name, Reign	Relation to America
Henry VII, 1485–1509	Cabot voyages, 1497, 1498
Henry VIII, 1509–1547	English Reformation began
Edward VI, 1547–1553	Strong Protestant tendencies
"Bloody" Mary, 1553–1558	Catholic reaction
Elizabeth I, 1558–1603	Break with Roman Catholic Church final; Drake; Spanish Armada defeated

*See p. 53 for a continuation of the table.

Ætatis suæ 21. Aº. 1616.

Maioaki ab Rebecka daughter to the mighty Prince Powhatan Emperour of Attanoughkomouck ab Virginia converted and baptized in the Christian faith, and Wife to the worthy Mr. Thos Rolff.

Pocahontas (c. 1595–1617)   Taken to England by her husband, she was received as a princess. She died when preparing to return, but her infant son ultimately reached Virginia, where hundreds of his descendants have lived, including the second Mrs. Woodrow Wilson.

make it to Virginia by 1609, only sixty survived the "starving time" winter of 1609–1610.

Diseased and despairing, the remaining colonists dragged themselves aboard homeward-bound ships in

The authorities meted out harsh discipline in the young Virginia colony. One Jamestown settler who publicly criticized the governor was sentenced to

"be disarmed [and] have his arms broken and his tongue bored through with an awl [and] shall pass through a guard of 40 men and shall be butted [with muskets] by every one of them and at the head of the troop kicked down and footed out of the fort."

the spring of 1610, only to be met at the mouth of the James River by a long-awaited relief party headed by a new governor, Lord De La Warr. He ordered the settlers back to Jamestown, imposed a harsh military regime on the colony, and soon undertook aggressive military action against the Indians.

Disease continued to reap a gruesome harvest among the Virginians. By 1625 Virginia contained only some twelve hundred hard-bitten survivors of the nearly eight thousand adventurers who had tried to start life anew in the ill-fated colony.

Cultural Clash in the Chesapeake

When the English landed in 1607, the chieftain Powhatan dominated the native peoples living in the James River area. He had asserted supremacy over a few dozen small tribes, loosely affiliated in what somewhat grandly came to be called Powhatan's Confederacy. The English colonists dubbed all the local Indians, somewhat inaccurately, the Powhatans. Powhatan at first may have considered the English potential allies in his struggle to extend his power still further over his Indian rivals, and he tried to be conciliatory. But relations between the Indians and the English remained tense, especially as the starving colonists took to raiding Indian food supplies.

The atmosphere grew even more strained after Lord De La Warr arrived in 1610. He carried orders from the Virginia Company that amounted to a declaration of war against the Indians in the Jamestown region. A veteran of the vicious campaigns against the Irish, De La Warr now introduced "Irish tactics" against the Indians. His troops raided Indian villages, burned houses, confiscated provisions, and torched cornfields. A peace settlement ended this First Anglo-Powhatan War in 1614, sealed by the marriage of Pocahontas to the colonist John Rolfe—the first known interracial union in Virginia.

A fragile respite followed, which endured eight years. But the Indians, pressed by the land-hungry whites and ravaged by European diseases, struck back in 1622. A series of Indian attacks left 347 settlers dead, including John Rolfe. In response the Virginia Company issued new orders calling for "a perpetual war without peace or truce," one that would prevent the Indians "from being any longer a people." Periodic punitive raids systematically reduced the native population and drove the survivors ever farther westward.

In the Second Anglo-Powhatan War in 1644, the Indians made one last effort to dislodge the Virginians.

A Carolina Indian Woman and Child, by John White The artist was a member of the Raleigh expedition of 1585. Notice that the Indian girl carries a European doll, illustrating the mingling of cultures that had already begun.

They were again defeated. The peace treaty of 1646 repudiated any hope of assimilating the native peoples into Virginian society or of peacefully coexisting with them. Instead it effectively banished the Chesapeake Indians from their ancestral lands and formally separated Indian from white areas of settlement—the origins of the later reservation system. By 1669 an official census revealed that only about two thousand Indians remained in Virginia, perhaps 10 percent of the population the original English settlers had encountered in 1607. By 1685 the English considered the Powhatan peoples extinct.

It had been the Powhatans' calamitous misfortune to fall victim to three Ds: disease, disorganization, and disposability. Like native peoples throughout the New World, they were extremely susceptible to European-borne maladies. Epidemics of smallpox and measles raced mercilessly through their villages. The Powhatans also—despite the apparent cohesiveness of "Powhatan's Confederacy"—lacked the unity with which to make effective opposition to the comparatively well-organized and militarily disciplined whites. Finally, unlike the Indians whom the Spaniards had encountered to the south, who could be put to work in the mines and had gold and silver to trade, the Powhatans served no economic function for the Virginia colonists. They provided no reliable labor source and, after the Virginians began growing their own food crops, had no valuable commodities to offer in commerce. The natives, as far as the Virginians were concerned, could be disposed of without harm to the colonial economy. Indeed the Indian presence frustrated the colonists' desire for a local commodity the Europeans desperately wanted: land.

The Indians' New World

The fate of the Powhatans foreshadowed the destinies of indigenous peoples throughout the continent as the process of European settlement went forward. Native Americans, of course, had a history well before Columbus's arrival. They were no strangers to change, adaptation, and even catastrophe, as the rise and decline of civilizations such as the Mississippians and the Anasazis demonstrated. But the shock of large-scale European colonization disrupted Native American life on a vast scale, inducing unprecedented demographic and cultural transformations.

Some changes were fairly benign. Horses—stolen, strayed, or purchased from Spanish invaders—catalyzed a substantial Indian migration onto the Great Plains in the eighteenth century. Peoples such as the Lakotas (Sioux), who had previously been sedentary forest dwellers, now moved onto the wide-open plains. There they thrived impressively, adopting an entirely new way of life as mounted nomadic hunters. But the effects of contact with Europeans proved less salutary for most other native peoples.

Disease was by far the biggest disrupter, as Old World pathogens licked lethally through biologically defenseless Indian populations. Disease took more than human life; it extinguished entire cultures and occasionally helped shape new ones. Epidemics often robbed native peoples of the elders who preserved the

> *Benjamin Franklin (1706–1790) in a 1753 letter to Peter Collinson commented on the attractiveness of Indian life to Europeans:*
>
> "When an Indian child has been brought up among us, taught our language and habituated to our customs, yet if he goes to see his relations and make one Indian ramble with them, there is no persuading him ever to return. [But] when white persons of either sex have been taken prisoners by the Indians, and lived awhile among them, though ransomed by their friends, and treated with all imaginable tenderness to prevail with them to stay among the English, yet in a short time they become disgusted with our manner of life, and the care and pains that are necessary to support it, and take the first good opportunity of escaping again into the woods, from whence there is no reclaiming them."

oral traditions that held clans together. Devastated Indian bands then faced the daunting task of literally reinventing themselves without benefit of accumulated wisdom or kin networks. The decimation and forced migration of native peoples sometimes scrambled them together in wholly new ways. The Catawba nation of the southern Piedmont region, for example, was formed from splintered remnants of several different groups uprooted by the shock of the Europeans' arrival.

Trade also transformed Indian life, as traditional barter-and-exchange networks gave way to the temptations of European commerce. Firearms, for example, conferred enormous advantages on those who could purchase them from Europeans. The desire for firearms thus intensified competition among the tribes for access to prime hunting grounds that could supply the skins and pelts that the European arms traders wanted. The result was an escalating cycle of Indian-on-Indian violence, fueled by the lure and demands of European trade goods.

Native Americans were swept up in the expanding Atlantic economy, but they usually struggled in vain to control their own place in it. One desperate band of Virginia Indians, resentful at the prices offered by British traders for their deerskins, loaded a fleet of canoes with hides and tried to paddle to England to sell their goods directly. Not far from the Virginia shore, a storm swamped their frail craft. Their cargo lost, the few survivors were picked up by an English ship and sold into slavery in the West Indies.

Indians along the Atlantic seaboard felt the most ferocious effects of European contact. Farther inland, native peoples had the advantages of time, space, and numbers as they sought to adapt to the European incursion. The Algonquians in the Great Lakes area, for instance, became a substantial regional power. They bolstered their population by absorbing various surrounding bands and dealt from a position of strength with the few Europeans who managed to penetrate the interior. As a result, a British or French trader wanting to do business with the inland tribes had little choice but to conform to Indian ways, often taking an Indian wife. Thus was created a middle ground, a zone where both Europeans and Native Americans were compelled to accommodate to one another—at least until the Europeans began to arrive in large numbers.

Virginia: Child of Tobacco

John Rolfe, the husband of Pocahontas, became father of the tobacco industry and an economic savior of the Virginia colony. By 1612 he had perfected methods of raising and curing the pungent weed, eliminating much of the bitter tang. Soon the European demand for tobacco was nearly insatiable. A tobacco rush swept over Virginia, as crops were planted in the streets of Jamestown and even between the numerous graves. So exclusively did the colonists concentrate on planting the yellow leaf that at first they had to import some of their foodstuffs. Colonists who had once hungered for food now hungered for land, ever more land on which to plant ever more tobacco. Relentlessly, they pressed the frontier of settlement up the river valleys to the west, abrasively edging against the Indians.

Virginia's prosperity was finally built on tobacco smoke. This "bewitching weed" played a vital role in putting the colony on firm economic foundations. But tobacco—King Nicotine—was something of a tyrant. It was ruinous to the soil when greedily planted in succes-

> *The wife of a Virginia governor wrote to her sister in England in 1623 of her voyage:*
>
> "For our Shippe was so pestered with people and goods that we were so full of infection that after a while we saw little but throwing folkes over board: It pleased god to send me my helth till I came to shoare and 3 dayes after I fell sick but I thank god I am well recovered. Few else are left alive that came in that Shippe."

Maryland: Catholic Haven

Maryland—the second plantation colony but the fourth English colony to be planted—was founded in 1634 by Lord Baltimore, of a prominent English Catholic family. He embarked upon the venture partly to reap financial profits and partly to create a refuge for his fellow Catholics. Protestant England was still persecuting Roman Catholics; among numerous discriminations, a couple seeking wedlock could not be legally married by a Catholic priest.

sive years, and it enchained the fortunes of Virginia to the fluctuating price of a single crop. Fatefully, tobacco also promoted the broad-acred plantation system and with it a brisk demand for fresh labor.

In 1619, the year before the Plymouth Pilgrims landed in New England, what was described as a Dutch warship appeared off Jamestown and sold some twenty Africans. The scanty record does not reveal whether they were purchased as lifelong slaves or as servants committed to limited years of servitude. However it transpired, this simple commercial transaction planted the seeds of the North American slave system. Yet blacks were too costly for most of the hard-pinched white colonists to acquire, and for decades few were brought to Virginia. In 1650 Virginia counted but three hundred blacks, although by the end of the century blacks, most of them enslaved, made up approximately 14 percent of the colony's population.

Representative self-government was also born in primitive Virginia, in the same cradle with slavery and in the same year—1619. The London Company authorized the settlers to summon an assembly, known as the House of Burgesses. A momentous precedent was thus feebly established, for this assemblage was the first of many miniature parliaments to flourish in the soil of America.

As time passed, James I grew increasingly hostile to Virginia. He detested tobacco, and he distrusted the representative House of Burgesses, which he branded a "seminary of sedition." In 1624 he revoked the charter of the bankrupt and beleaguered Virginia Company, thus making Virginia a royal colony directly under his control.

Advertisement of a Voyage to America, 1609

Early Maryland and Virginia

Absentee proprietor Lord Baltimore hoped that the two hundred settlers who founded Maryland at St. Marys, on Chesapeake Bay, would be the vanguard of a vast new feudal domain. Huge estates were to be awarded to his largely Catholic relatives, and gracious manor houses, modeled on those of England's aristocracy, were intended to arise amidst the fertile forests. As in Virginia, colonists proved willing to come only if offered the opportunity to acquire land of their own. Soon they were dispersed around the Chesapeake region on modest farms, and the haughty land barons, mostly Catholic, were surrounded by resentful backcountry planters, mostly Protestant. Resentment flared into open rebellion near the end of the century, and the Baltimore family for a time lost its proprietary rights.

Despite these tensions Maryland prospered. Like Virginia, it blossomed forth in acres of tobacco. Also like Virginia, it depended for labor in its early years mainly on white indentured servants—penniless persons who bound themselves to work for a number of years to pay their passage. In both colonies it was only in the later years of the seventeenth century that black slaves began to be imported in large numbers.

Lord Baltimore, a canny soul, permitted unusual freedom of worship at the outset. He hoped that he would thus purchase toleration for his own fellow worshipers. But the heavy tide of Protestants threatened to submerge the Catholics and place severe restrictions on them, as in England. Faced with disaster, the Catholics of Maryland threw their support behind the famed Act of Toleration, which was passed in 1649 by the local representative assembly.

Maryland's new religious statute guaranteed toleration to all Christians. But, less liberally, it decreed the death penalty for those, like Jews and atheists, who denied the divinity of Jesus. The law thus sanctioned less toleration than had previously existed in the settlement, but it did extend a temporary cloak of protection to the uneasy Catholic minority. One result was that when the colonial era ended, Maryland probably sheltered more Roman Catholics than any other English-speaking colony in the New World.

The West Indies: Way Station to Mainland America

While the English were planting the first frail colonial shoots in the Chesapeake, they also were busily colonizing the West Indies. Spain, weakened by military overextension and distracted by its rebellious Dutch provinces, relaxed its grip on much of the Caribbean in the early 1600s. By the mid-seventeenth century, England had secured its claim to several West Indian islands, including the large prize of Jamaica in 1655.

Sugar formed the foundation of the West Indian economy. What tobacco was to the Chesapeake, sugar cane was to the Caribbean—with one crucial difference. Tobacco was a poor man's crop. It could be planted easily, it produced commercially marketable leaves within a year, and it required only simple processing. Sugar cane, in contrast, was a rich man's crop. It had to be planted extensively to yield commercially viable quantities of sugar. Extensive planting, in turn, required extensive and arduous land clearing. And the cane stalks yielded their sugar only after an elaborate process of refining in a sugar mill. The need for land and for the labor to clear it and to run the mills made sugar cultivation a capital-intensive business. Only wealthy growers with abundant capital to invest could succeed in sugar.

(above) **Sugar Mill in Brazil, by Frans Post, c. 1640** (left) *Saccharum Officinarum* (sugar cane)

To control this large and potentially restive population of slaves, English authorities devised formal "codes" that defined the slaves' legal status and masters' prerogatives. The notorious Barbados slave code of 1661 denied even the most fundamental rights to slaves and gave masters virtually complete control over their

The sugar lords extended their dominion over the West Indies in the seventeenth century. To work their sprawling plantations, they imported enormous numbers of African slaves—more than a quarter of a million in the five decades after 1640. By about 1700, black slaves outnumbered white settlers in the English West Indies by nearly four to one, and the region's population has remained predominantly black ever since. West Indians thus take their place among the numerous children of the African diaspora—the vast scattering of African peoples throughout the New World in the three and a half centuries following Columbus's discovery.

African slaves destined for the West Indian sugar plantations were bound and branded on West African beaches and ferried out in canoes to the waiting slave ships. An English sailor described the scene:

"The Negroes are so wilful and loth to leave their own country, that have often leap'd out of the canoes, boat and ship, into the sea, and kept under water till they were drowned, to avoid being taken up and saved by our boats, which pursued them; they having a more dreadful apprehension of Barbadoes than we can have of hell."

The Barbados slave code (1661) declared,

"If any Negro or slave whatsoever shall offer any violence to any Christian by striking or the like, such Negro or slave shall for his or her first offence be severely whipped by the Constable. For his second offence of that nature he shall be severely whipped, his nose slit, and be burned in some part of his face with a hot iron. And being brutish slaves, [they] deserve not, for the baseness of their condition, to be tried by the legal trial of twelve men of their peers, as the subjects of England are. And it is further enacted and ordained that if any Negro or other slave under punishment by his master unfortunately shall suffer in life or member, which seldom happens, no person whatsoever shall be liable to any fine therefore."

laborers, including the right to inflict vicious punishments for even slight infractions.

The profitable sugar-plantation system soon crowded out almost all other forms of Caribbean agriculture. The West Indies increasingly depended on the North American mainland for foodstuffs and other basic supplies. And smaller English farmers, squeezed out by the greedy sugar barons, began to migrate to the newly founded southern mainland colonies. A group of displaced English settlers from Barbados arrived in Carolina in 1670. They brought with them a few African slaves, as well as the model of the Barbados slave code, which eventually inspired statutes governing slavery throughout the mainland colonies. Carolina officially adopted a version of the Barbados slave code in 1696. Just as the West Indies had been a testing ground for the *encomienda* system that the Spanish had brought to Mexico and South America, so the Caribbean islands now served as a staging area for the slave system that would take root elsewhere in English North America.

Colonizing the Carolinas

Civil war convulsed England in the 1640s. King Charles I had dismissed Parliament in 1629, and when he eventually recalled it in 1640, the members were mutinous. Finding their great champion in the Puritan-soldier Oliver Cromwell, they ultimately beheaded Charles in 1649, and Cromwell ruled England for nearly a decade. Finally, Charles II, son of the decapitated king, was restored to the throne in 1660.

Colonization had been interrupted during this period of bloody unrest. Now, in the so-called Restoration period, empire building resumed with even greater intensity—and royal involvement. Carolina, named for Charles II, was formally created in 1670, after the king granted to eight of his court favorites, the Lords Proprietors, an expanse of wilderness ribboning across the continent to the Pacific. These aristocratic founders hoped to grow foodstuffs to provision the sugar plantations in Barbados and to export non-English products like wine, silk, and olive oil.

Carolina prospered by developing close economic ties with the flourishing sugar islands of the English West Indies. In a broad sense, the mainland colony was but the most northerly of those outposts. Many original Carolina settlers, in fact, had emigrated from Barbados, bringing that island's slave system with them. They also established a vigorous slave trade in

Early Carolina Coins These copper halfpennies bore the image of an elephant, an unofficial symbol of the colony, and a prayer for the Lords Proprietors.

Carolina itself. Enlisting the aid of the coastal Savannah Indians, they forayed into the interior in search of captives. The Lords Proprietors in London protested against Indian slave trading in their colony, but to no avail. Manacled Indians soon were among the young colony's major exports. As many as ten thousand Indians were dispatched to lifelong labor in the West Indian canefields and sugar mills. Others were sent to New England. One Rhode Island town in 1730 counted more than two hundred Indian slaves from Carolina in its midst.

In 1707 the Savannah Indians decided to end their alliance with the Carolinians and to migrate to the backcountry of Maryland and Pennsylvania, where a new colony founded by Quakers under William Penn promised better relations between whites and Indians. But the Carolinians determined to "thin" the Savannahs before they could depart. A series of bloody raids all but annihilated the Indian tribes of coastal Carolina by 1710.

After much experimentation, rice emerged as the principal export crop in Carolina. Rice was then an exotic food in England; no rice seeds were sent out from

The Thirteen Original Colonies

Name	Founded by	Year	Charter	Made Royal	1775 Status
1. Virginia	London Co.	1607	1606 1609 1612	1624	Royal (under the crown)
2. New Hampshire	John Mason and others	1623	1679	1679	Royal (absorbed by Mass., 1641–1679)
3. Massachusetts	Puritans	c. 1628	1629	1691	Royal
Plymouth	Separatists	1620	None		(Merged with Mass., 1691)
Maine	F. Gorges	1623	1639		(Bought by Mass., 1677)
4. Maryland	Lord Baltimore	1634	1632	———	Proprietary (controlled by proprietor)
5. Connecticut	Mass. emigrants	1635	1662	———	Self-governing (under local control)
New Haven	Mass. emigrants	1638	None		(Merged with Conn., 1662)
6. Rhode Island	R. Williams	1636	1644 1663	———	Self-governing
7. Delaware	Swedes	1638	None	———	Proprietary (merged with Pa., 1682; same governor, but separate assembly, granted 1703)
8. N. Carolina	Virginians	1653	1663	1729	Royal (separated informally from S.C., 1691)
9. New York	Dutch	c. 1613			
	Duke of York	1664	1664	1685	Royal
10. New Jersey	Berkeley and Carteret	1664	None	1702	Royal
11. Carolina	Eight nobles	1670	1663	1729	Royal (separated formally from N.C., 1712)
12. Pennsylvania	William Penn	1681	1681	———	Proprietary
13. Georgia	Oglethorpe and others	1733	1732	1752	Royal

London in the first supply ships to Carolina. But rice was grown in Africa, and the Carolinians were soon paying premium prices for West African slaves experienced in rice cultivation. The Africans' agricultural skill and their relative immunity to malaria (thanks to a genetic trait that also, unfortunately, made them and their descendants susceptible to sickle-cell anemia) made them ideal laborers on the hot and swampy rice plantations. By 1710 they constituted a majority of Carolinians.

Moss-festooned Charles Town—also named for the king—rapidly became the busiest seaport in the South. Many high-spirited sons of English landed families, deprived of an inheritance, came to the Charleston area and gave it a rich aristocratic flavor. The village became a colorfully diverse community, to which French Protestant refugees and others were attracted by religious toleration.

Nearby, in Florida, the Catholic Spaniards abhorred the intrusion of these Protestant heretics. Carolina's frontier was often aflame. Spanish-incited Indians brandished their tomahawks, and armor-clad warriors of Spain frequently unsheathed their swords during the successive Anglo-Spanish wars. But by 1700 Carolina was too strong to be wiped out.

Early Carolina and Georgia Settlements

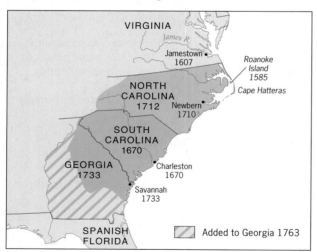

The Emergence of North Carolina

The wild northern expanse of the huge Carolina grant bordered on Virginia. From the older colony there drifted down a ragtag group of poverty-stricken outcasts and religious dissenters. Many of them had been repelled by the rarefied atmosphere of Virginia, dominated as it was by big-plantation gentry belonging to the Church of England. North Carolinians, as a result, have been called "the quintessence of Virginia's discontent." The newcomers, who frequently were "squatters" without legal right to the soil, raised their tobacco and other crops on small farms, with little need for slaves.

Distinctive traits developed rapidly in North Carolina. The poor but sturdy inhabitants, regarded as riffraff by their snobbish neighbors, earned a reputation for being irreligious and hospitable to pirates. Isolated from neighbors by raw wilderness and stormy Cape Hatteras, "graveyard of the Atlantic," the North Carolinians developed a strong spirit of resistance to authority. Their location between aristocratic Virginia and aristocratic South Carolina caused the area to be dubbed "a vale of humility between two mountains of conceit." Following much friction with governors, North Carolina was officially separated from South Carolina in 1712, and subsequently each segment became a royal colony.

North Carolina shares with tiny Rhode Island several distinctions. These two outposts were the most democratic, the most independent-minded, and the least aristocratic of the original thirteen English colonies.

Although northern Carolina, unlike the colony's southern reaches, did not at first import large numbers of African slaves, both regions shared in the ongoing tragedy of bloody relations between Indians and Europeans. Tuscarora Indians fell upon the fledgling settlement at Newbern in 1711. The North Carolinians, aided by their heavily armed brothers from the south, retaliated by crushing the Tuscaroras in battle, selling hundreds of them into slavery and leaving the survivors to wander northward to seek the protection of the Iroquois. The Tuscaroras eventually became the Sixth Nation of the Iroquois Confederacy. In another ferocious encounter four years later, the South Carolinians defeated and dispersed the Yamasee Indians.

With the conquest of the Yamasees, virtually all the coastal Indian tribes in the southern colonies had been utterly devastated by about 1720. Yet in the interior, in the hills and valleys of the Appalachian Mountains, the powerful Cherokees, Creeks, and Iroquois (see "Makers of America: The Iroquois," pp. 40–41) remained. Stronger and more numerous than their coastal cousins, they managed for half a century more to contain British settlement to the coastal plain east of the mountains.

Late-Coming Georgia: The Buffer Colony

Pine-forested Georgia, with the harbor of Savannah nourishing its chief settlement, was formally founded in 1733. It proved to be the last of the thirteen colonies to be planted—126 years after the first, Virginia, and 52 years after the twelfth, Pennsylvania. Chronologically Georgia belongs elsewhere, but geographically it may be grouped with its southern neighbors.

The English crown intended Georgia to serve chiefly as a buffer. It would protect the more valuable Carolinas against vengeful Spaniards from Florida and against the hostile French from Louisiana. Georgia indeed suffered much buffeting, especially when wars broke out between Spain and England in the European arena. As a vital link in imperial defense, the exposed colony received monetary subsidies from the British government at the outset—the only one of the "original thirteen" to enjoy this benefit in its founding stage.

Named in honor of King George II of England, Georgia was launched by a high-minded group of philanthropists. In addition to protecting their neighboring northern colonies and producing silk and wine, they were determined to carve out a haven for wretched souls imprisoned for debt. They were also determined, at least at first, to keep slavery out of Georgia. The ablest of the founders was the dynamic soldier-statesman James Oglethorpe, who became keenly interested in prison reform after one of his friends died in a debtors' jail. As an able military leader, Oglethorpe repelled Spanish attacks. As an imperialist and a philanthropist, he saved "the Charity Colony" by his energetic leadership and by heavily mortgaging his own personal fortune.

The hamlet of Savannah, like Charleston, was a melting-pot community. German Lutherans and kilted Scots Highlanders, among others, added color to the pattern. All Christian worshipers except Catholics enjoyed religious toleration. Many missionaries armed with Bibles and hope arrived in Savannah to work among debtors and Indians. Prominent among them was young John Wesley, who later returned to England and founded the Methodist Church.

Georgia grew with painful slowness and at the end of the colonial era was perhaps the least populous of the colonies. The development of a plantation economy was thwarted by an unhealthy climate, by early restrictions on black slavery, and by demoralizing Spanish attacks.

The Plantation Colonies

Certain distinctive features were shared by England's southern mainland colonies: Maryland, Virginia, North Carolina, South Carolina, and Georgia. Broad-acred, these outposts of empire were all in some degree devoted to exporting commercial agricultural products. Profitable staple crops were the rule, notably tobacco and rice, though to a lesser extent in small-farm North Carolina. Slavery was found in all the plantation colonies, though only after 1750 in reform-minded Georgia. Immense acreage in the hands of a favored few fostered a strong aristocratic atmosphere, except in North Carolina and to some extent in debtor-tinged Georgia. The wide scattering of plantations and farms, often along stately rivers, retarded the growth of cities and made the establishment of churches and schools both difficult and expensive. In 1671 the governor of Virginia thanked God that no free schools or printing presses existed in his colony.

All the plantation colonies permitted some religious toleration. The tax-supported Church of England became the dominant faith, though weakest of all in nonconformist North Carolina.

These colonies were in some degree expansionary. "Soil butchery" by excessive tobacco growing drove settlers westward, and the long, lazy rivers invited penetration of the continent—and continuing confrontation with Native Americans.

The Iroquois

Well before the crowned heads of Europe turned their eyes and their dreams of empire toward North America, a great military power had emerged in the Mohawk Valley of what is now New York State. The Iroquois Confederacy, dubbed by whites the "League of the Iroquois," bound together five Indian nations—the Mohawks, the Oneidas, the Onondagas, the Cayugas, and the Senecas. According to Iroquois legend, it was founded in the late 1500s by two leaders, Deganawidah and Hiawatha. This proud and potent league vied initially with neighboring Indians for territorial supremacy, then with the French, English, and Dutch for control of the fur trade. Ultimately, infected by the white man's diseases, intoxicated by his whiskey, and intimidated by his muskets, the Iroquois struggled for their very survival as a people.

The building block of Iroquois society was the longhouse (see photo p. 41). This wooden structure deserved its descriptive name. Only twenty-five feet in breadth, the longhouse stretched from eight to two hundred feet in length. Each building contained three to five fireplaces around which gathered two nuclear families, consisting of parents and children. All families residing in the longhouse were related, their connections of blood running exclusively through the maternal line. A single longhouse might shelter a

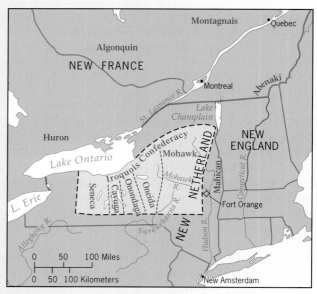

Iroquois Lands and European Trade Centers, c. 1590–1650

An Iroquois Canoe In frail but artfully constructed craft like this, the Iroquois traversed the abundant waters of their confederacy and traded with their neighbors, Indians as well as whites.

woman's family and those of her mother, sisters, and daughters—with the oldest woman being the honored matriarch. When a man married, he left his childhood hearth in the home of his mother to join the longhouse of his wife. Men dominated in Iroquois society, but they owed their positions of prominence to their mothers' families.

As if sharing one great longhouse, the five nations joined in the Iroquois Confederacy but kept their own separate fires. Although they celebrated together and shared a common policy toward outsiders, they remained essentially independent of one another. On the eastern flank of the league, the Mohawks, known as the Keepers of the Eastern Fire, specialized as middlemen with European traders, whereas the outlying Senecas, the Keepers of the Western Fire, became fur suppliers.

After banding together to end generations of violent warfare among themselves, the Five Nations vanquished their rivals, the neighboring Hurons, Eries, and Petuns. Some other tribes, such as the Tuscaroras from the Carolina region, sought peaceful absorption into the Iroquois Confederacy. The Iroquois further expanded their numbers by means of periodic "mourning wars," whose objective was the large-scale adoption of captives and refugees. But the arrival of gun-toting Europeans threatened Iroquois supremacy and enmeshed the con-

federacy in a tangled web of diplomatic intrigues. Throughout the seventeenth and eighteenth centuries, they allied alternately with the English against the French and vice versa, for a time successfully working this perpetual rivalry to their own advantage. But when the American Revolution broke out, the confederacy could reach no consensus on which side to support. Each tribe was left to decide independently; most, though not all, sided with the British. The ultimate British defeat left the confederacy in tatters. Many Iroquois, especially the Mohawks, moved to new lands in British Canada; others were relegated to reservations in western New York.

Reservation life proved unbearable for a proud people accustomed to domination over a vast territory. Morale sank; brawling, feuding, and alcoholism became rampant. Out of this morass arose a prophet, an Iroquois called Handsome Lake. In 1799 angelic figures clothed in traditional Iroquois garb appeared to Handsome Lake in a vision and warned him that the moral decline of his people must end if they were to endure. He awoke from his vision to warn his tribespeople to mend their ways. His socially oriented gospel inspired many Iroquois to forsake alcohol, to affirm family values, and to revive old Iroquois customs. Handsome Lake died in 1815, but his teachings, in the form of the Longhouse religion, survive to this day.

The Longhouse (reconstruction)
The photo shows a modern-day reconstruction of a Delaware Indian longhouse (almost identical in design and building materials to the Iroquois longhouses), at Historic Waterloo Village on Winakung Island in New Jersey. (The Iroquois conquered the Delawares in the late 1600s.) Bent saplings and sheets of elm bark made for sturdy, weather-tight shelters. Longhouses were typically furnished with deerskin-covered bunks and shelves for storing baskets, pots, fur pelts, and corn.

Chronology

1558	Elizabeth I becomes queen of England
c. 1565-1590	English crush Irish uprising
1577	Drake circumnavigates the globe
1585	Raleigh founds "lost colony" at Roanoke
1588	England defeats Spanish Armada
1603	James I becomes king of England
1604	Spain and England sign peace treaty
1607	Virginia colony founded at Jamestown
1612	Rolfe perfects tobacco culture in Virginia
1614	First Anglo-Powhatan War ends
1619	First Africans arrive in Jamestown Virginia House of Burgesses established
1624	Virginia becomes royal colony
1634	Maryland colony founded
1640s	Large-scale slave-labor system established in English West Indies
1644	Second Anglo-Powhatan War
1649	Act of Toleration in Maryland Charles I beheaded; Cromwell rules England
1660	Charles II restored to English throne
1661	Barbados slave code adopted
1670	Carolina colony created
1711-1713	Tuscarora War in North Carolina
1712	North Carolina formally separates from South Carolina
1715-1716	Yamasee War in South Carolina
1733	Georgia colony founded

3

Settling the
Northern Colonies

—◆—

1619–1700

GOD HATH SIFTED A NATION THAT HE MIGHT SEND
CHOICE GRAIN INTO THIS WILDERNESS.

WILLIAM STOUGHTON [OF MASSACHUSETTS BAY], 1699

Although colonists both north and south were bound together by a common language and a common allegiance to Mother England, they established different patterns of settlement, different economies, different political systems, and even different sets of values—defining distinctive regional characteristics that would persist for generations. The promise of riches—especially from golden-leaved tobacco—drew the first settlers to the southern colonies. But to the north, in the fertile valleys of the middle Atlantic region and especially along the rocky shores of New England, it was not worldly wealth but religious devotion that principally shaped the earliest settlements.

The Protestant
Reformation Produces Puritanism

Little did the German friar Martin Luther suspect, when he nailed his protests against Catholic doctrines to the door of Wittenberg's cathedral in 1517, that he was shaping the destiny of a yet unknown nation. Denouncing the authority of priests and popes, Luther declared that the Bible alone was the source of God's word. He ignited a fire of religious reform (the "Protestant Reformation") that licked its way across Europe for more than a century, dividing peoples, toppling sovereigns, and kindling the spiritual fervor of millions of men and women—some of whom helped to found America.

The reforming flame burned especially brightly in the bosom of John Calvin of Geneva. This somber and severe religious leader elaborated Martin Luther's ideas in ways that profoundly affected the thought and character of generations of Americans yet unborn. Calvinism became the dominant theological credo not only of the New England Puritans but of other American settlers as well, including the Scottish Presbyterians, French Huguenots, and communicants of the Dutch Reformed Church.

Calvin spelled out his basic doctrine in a learned Latin tome of 1536, entitled *Institutes of the Christian Religion*. God, Calvin argued, was all-powerful and all-good. Humans, because of the corrupting effect of original sin, were weak and wicked. God was also all-knowing—and he knew who was going to heaven and who was going to hell. Since the first moment of creation, some souls—the elect—had been destined for eternal bliss and others for eternal torment. Good works could not save those whom "predestination" had marked for the infernal fires.

But neither could the elect count on their predetermined salvation and lead lives of wild, immoral abandon. For one thing, no one could be certain of his or her status in the heavenly ledger. Gnawing doubts about their eternal fate plagued Calvinists. They constantly sought, in themselves and others, signs of "conversion," or the receipt of God's free gift of saving grace. Conversion was thought to be an intense, identifiable personal experience in which God revealed to the elect their heavenly destiny. Thereafter they were expected to lead "sanctified" lives, demonstrating by their holy behavior that they were among the "visible saints."

These doctrines swept into England just as King Henry VIII was breaking his ties with the Roman Catholic Church in the 1530s, making himself the head of the Church of England. Henry would have been content to retain Roman rituals and creeds, but his action powerfully stimulated some English religious reformers to undertake a total purification of English Christianity. Many of these "Puritans," as it happened, came from the commercially depressed woolen districts (see pp. 27–28). Calvinism, with its message of stark but reassuring order in the divine plan, fed on this social unrest and provided spiritual comfort to the economically disadvantaged. As time went on, Puritans grew increasingly unhappy over the snail-like progress of the Protestant Reformation in England. They burned with pious zeal to see the Church of England wholly de-catholicized.

The most devout Puritans, including those who eventually settled New England, believed that only "visible saints" (that is, persons who felt the stirrings of grace in their souls and could demonstrate its presence to their fellow Puritans) should be admitted to church membership. But the Church of England enrolled all the king's subjects, which meant that the "saints" had to share pews and communion rails with the "damned." Appalled by this unholy fraternizing, a tiny group of dedicated Puritans, known as Separatists, vowed to break away entirely from the Church of England.

King James I, a shrewd Scotsman, was head of both the state and the church in England from 1603 to 1625. He quickly perceived that if his subjects could defy him as their spiritual leader, they might one day defy him as their political leader (as in fact they would later defy and behead his son, Charles I). He therefore threatened to harass the more bothersome Separatists out of the land.

The Pilgrims End Their Pilgrimage at Plymouth

The most famous congregation of Separatists, fleeing royal wrath, departed for Holland in 1608. During the ensuing twelve years of toil and poverty, they were increasingly distressed by the "Dutchification" of their children. They longed to find a haven where they could live and die as English men and women—and as purified Protestants. America was the logical refuge, despite the early ordeals of Jamestown, and despite tales of New World cannibals roasting steaks from their white victims over open fires.

A group of the Separatists in Holland, after negotiating with the Virginia Company, at length secured rights to settle under its jurisdiction. But their crowded *Mayflower*, sixty-five days at sea, missed its destination and arrived off the stony coast of New England in 1620, with a total of 102 persons. One had died en route—an unusually short casualty list—and one had been born and appropriately named Oceanus. Fewer than half of the entire party were Separatists. Prominent among the nonbelongers was a peppery and stocky soldier of fortune, Captain Myles Standish, dubbed by one of his critics "Captain Shrimp." He later rendered indispensable service as an Indian fighter and negotiator.

The Pilgrims did not make their initial landing at Plymouth Rock, as commonly supposed, but undertook a number of preliminary surveys. They finally chose for their site the shore of inhospitable Plymouth Bay. This area was outside the domain of the Virginia Company, and consequently the settlers became squatters. They were without legal right to the land and without specific authority to establish a government.

Before disembarking, the Pilgrim leaders drew up and signed the brief Mayflower Compact. Although setting an invaluable precedent for later written constitutions, this document was not a constitution at all. It was a simple agreement to form a crude government and to submit to the will of the majority under the regulations agreed upon. The compact was signed by forty-one adult males, eleven of them with the exalted rank of "mister," though not by the servants and two seamen. The pact was a promising step toward genuine self-government, for soon the adult male settlers were assembling to make their own laws in open-discussion town meetings—a vital laboratory of liberty.

Plymouth Plantation
Carefully restored, the modest village at Plymouth looks today much as it did nearly four hundred years ago.

The Pilgrims' first winter of 1620–1621 took a grisly toll. Only 44 out of the 102 survived. At one time only 7 were well enough to lay the dead in their frosty graves. Yet when the *Mayflower* sailed back to England in the spring, not a single one of the courageous band of Separatists left. As one of them wrote, "It is not with us as with other men, whom small things can discourage."

God made his children prosperous, so the Pilgrims believed. The next autumn, that of 1621, brought bountiful harvests and with them the first Thanksgiving Day in New England. In time the frail colony found sound economic legs in fur, fish, and lumber. The beaver and the Bible were the early mainstays: the one for the sustenance of the body, the other for the sustenance of the soul. Plymouth proved that the English could maintain themselves in this uninviting region.

The Pilgrims were extremely fortunate in their leaders. Prominent among them was the cultured William Bradford, a self-taught scholar who read Hebrew, Greek, Latin, French, and Dutch. He was chosen governor thirty times in the annual elections. Among his major worries was his fear that independent, non-Puritan settlers "on their particular" might corrupt his godly experiment in the wilderness. Bustling fishing villages and other settlements did sprout to the north of Plymouth, on the storm-lashed shores of Massachusetts Bay, where many people were as much interested in cod as God.

Quiet and quaint, the little colony of Plymouth was never important economically or numerically. Its population numbered only seven thousand by 1691, when, still charterless, it merged with its giant neighbor, the Massachusetts Bay Colony. But the tiny settlement of Pilgrims was big both morally and spiritually.

The Bay Colony Bible Commonwealth

The Separatist Pilgrims were dedicated extremists—the purest Puritans. More moderate Puritans sought to reform the Church of England from within. Though

> *William Bradford (1590–1657) wrote in* Of Plymouth Plantation,
>
> "Thus out of small beginnings greater things have been produced by His hand that made all things of nothing, and gives being to all things that are; and, as one small candle may light a thousand, so the light here kindled hath shone unto many, yea in some sort to our whole nation."

resented by bishops and monarchs, they slowly gathered support, especially in Parliament. But when Charles I dismissed Parliament in 1629 and sanctioned the anti-Puritan persecutions of the reactionary Archbishop William Laud, many Puritans saw catastrophe in the making.

In 1629 an energetic group of non-Separatist Puritans, fearing for their faith and for England's future, secured a royal charter to form the Massachusetts Bay Company. They proposed to establish a sizable settlement in the infertile Massachusetts area, with Boston soon becoming its hub. Stealing a march on both king and church, the newcomers brought their charter with them. For many years they used it as a kind of constitution, out of easy reach of royal authority. They steadfastly denied that they wanted to separate from the Church of England, only from its impurities. But back in England, the highly orthodox Archbishop Laud snorted that the Bay Colony Puritans were "swine which rooted in God's vineyard."

The Massachusetts Bay enterprise was singularly blessed. The well-equipped expedition of 1630, with eleven vessels carrying nearly a thousand immigrants, started the colony off on a larger scale than any of the other English settlements. Continuing turmoil in England tossed up additional enriching waves of Puritans on the shores of Massachusetts in the following decade (see "Makers of America: The English," pp. 50–51). During the "Great Migration" of the 1630s, about seventy thousand refugees left England. But not all of them were Puritans, and only about twenty thousand came to Massachusetts. Many were attracted to the warm and fertile West Indies, especially the sugar-rich island of Barbados. More Puritans came to this Caribbean islet than to all of Massachusetts.

Many fairly prosperous, educated persons immigrated to the Bay Colony, including John Winthrop, a well-to-do pillar of English society, who became the colony's first governor. A successful attorney and manor lord in England, Winthrop eagerly accepted the offer to become governor of the Massachusetts Bay Colony, believing that he had a "calling" from God to lead the new religious experiment. He served as governor or deputy governor for nineteen years. The resources and skills of talented settlers like Winthrop helped Massachusetts prosper, as fur trading, fishing, and shipbuilding blossomed into important industries, especially fish and ships. Massachusetts Bay Colony rapidly shot to the fore as both the biggest and the most influential of the New England outposts.

Massachusetts also benefited from a shared sense of purpose among most of the first settlers. "We shall be as

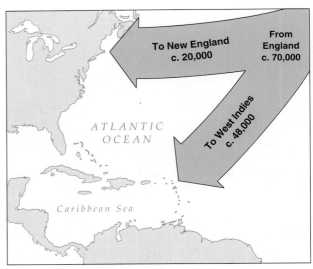

The Great English Migration, c. 1630–1642
Much of the early history of the United States was written by New Englanders, who were not disposed to emphasize the larger exodus of English migrants to the Caribbean islands. When the mainland colonists declared independence in 1776, they hoped that these island outposts would join them, but the existence of the British navy had a dissuading effect.

a city upon a hill," a beacon to humanity, declared Governor Winthrop. The Puritan bay colonists believed that they had a covenant with God, an agreement to build a holy society that would be a model for humankind.

Building the Bay Colony

These common convictions deeply shaped the infant colony's life. Soon after the colonists' arrival, the franchise was extended to all "freemen"—adult males who belonged to the Puritan congregations, which in time came to be called collectively the Congregational Church. Unchurched men remained voteless in provincial elections, as did women. On this basis about two-fifths of adult males enjoyed the franchise in provincial affairs, a far larger proportion than in contemporary England. Town governments, which conducted much important business, were even more inclusive. There all male property holders, and in some cases other residents as well, enjoyed the priceless boon of publicly discussing local issues, often with much heat, and of voting on them by a majority-rule show of hands.

Yet the provincial government, liberal by the standards of the time, was not a democracy. The able Governor Winthrop feared and distrusted the "commons" as the "meaner sort" and thought that democracy was the "meanest and worst" of all forms of government. "If the people be governors," asked one Puritan clergyman, "who shall be governed?" True, the freemen annually elected the governor and his assistants, as well as a representative assembly called the General Court. But only Puritans—the "visible saints" who alone were eligible for church membership—could be freemen. And according to the doctrine of the covenant, the whole purpose of government was to enforce God's laws—which applied to believers and nonbelievers alike. Moreover, nonbelievers as well as believers paid taxes for the government-supported church.

Religious leaders thus wielded enormous influence in the Massachusetts "Bible Commonwealth." They powerfully influenced admission to church membership by conducting public interrogations of persons claiming to have experienced conversion. Prominent among the early clergy was fiery John Cotton. Educated at England's Cambridge University, a Puritan citadel, he emigrated to Massachusetts to avoid persecution for his criticism of the Church of England. In the Bay Colony, he devoted his considerable learning to defending the government's duty to enforce religious rules. Profoundly pious, he sometimes preached and prayed up to six hours in a single day.

But the power of the preachers was not absolute. A congregation had the right to hire and fire its minister and to set his salary. Clergymen were also barred from holding formal political office. Puritans in England had suffered too much at the hands of a "political" Anglican clergy to permit in the New World another unholy union of religious and government power. In a limited way, the bay colonists thus endorsed the idea of the separation of church and state.

The Puritans were a worldly lot, despite—or even because of—their spiritual intensity. Like John Winthrop, they believed in the doctrine of a "calling" to do God's work on earth. They shared in what was later called the "Protestant ethic," which involved serious commitment to work and to engagement in worldly pursuits. Legend to the contrary, they also enjoyed simple pleasures: they ate plentifully, drank heartily, sang songs occasionally, and made love monogamously. Like other peoples of their time in both America and Europe, they passed laws aimed at making sure these pleasures stayed simple by repressing certain human instincts. In

New Haven, for example, a young married couple was fined twenty shillings for the crime of kissing in public, and in later years Connecticut came to be dubbed "the Blue Law State." (It was so named for the blue paper on which the repressive laws—also known as "sumptuary laws"—were printed.)

Yet, to the Puritans, life was serious business, and hellfire was real—a hell where sinners shriveled and shrieked in vain for divine mercy. An immensely popular poem in New England, selling one copy for every twenty people, was clergyman Michael Wigglesworth's "Day of Doom" (1662). Especially horrifying were his descriptions of the fate of the damned:

> They cry, they roar for anguish sore,
>   and gnaw their tongues for horrour. But get away
>   without delay,
>   Christ pitties not your cry:
> Depart to Hell, there may you yell,
>   and roar Eternally.

Trouble in the Bible Commonwealth

The Bay Colony enjoyed a high degree of social harmony, stemming from common beliefs, in its early years. But even in this tightly knit community, dissension soon appeared. Quakers, who flouted the authority of the Puritan clergy, were persecuted with fines, floggings, and banishment. In one extreme case, four Quakers who defied expulsion, one of them a woman, were hanged on the Boston Common.

A sharp challenge to Puritan orthodoxy came from Anne Hutchinson. She was an exceptionally intelligent, strong-willed, and talkative woman, ultimately the mother of fourteen children. Swift and sharp in theological argument, she carried to logical extremes the Puritan doctrine of predestination. She claimed that a holy life was no sure sign of salvation and that the truly saved need not bother to obey the law of either God or man. This assertion, known as *antinomianism* (from the Greek, "against the law"), was high heresy.

Brought to trial in 1638, the quick-witted Hutchinson bamboozled her clerical inquisitors for days, until she eventually boasted that she had come by her beliefs through a direct revelation from God. This was even higher heresy. The Puritan magistrates had little choice but to banish her, lest she pollute the entire Puritan experiment. With her family, she set out on foot for Rhode Island, though pregnant. She finally moved to

Anne Hutchinson, Dissenter
Mistress Hutchinson (1591–1643) held unorthodox views that challenged the authority of the clergy and the very integrity of the Puritan experiment in Massachusetts Bay Colony. An outcast in her day, she has been judged a heroine in the eye of history: this statue in her honor, erected in the nineteenth century, now graces the front of the Boston Statehouse.

New York, where she and all but one of her household were killed by Indians. Back in the Bay Colony, the pious John Winthrop saw "God's hand" in her fate.

More threatening to the Puritan leaders was a personable and popular Salem minister, Roger Williams. Williams was a young man with radical ideas and an unrestrained tongue. An extreme Separatist, he hounded his fellow clergymen to make a clean break with the corrupt Church of England. He also challenged the legality of the Bay Colony's charter, which he condemned for expropriating the land from the Indians without fair compensation. As if all this were not enough, he went on to deny the authority of civil government to regulate religious behavior—a seditious blow at the Puritan idea of government's very purpose.

Their patience exhausted by 1635, the Bay Colony authorities found Williams guilty of disseminating "newe & dangerous opinions" and ordered him banished. He was permitted to remain several months longer because of illness, but he kept up his criticisms. The outraged magistrates, fearing that he might organize a rival colony of malcontents, made plans to exile him to England. But Williams foiled them.

The Rhode Island "Sewer"

Aided by friendly Indians, Roger Williams fled to the Rhode Island area in 1636, in the midst of a bitter winter. At Providence the courageous and far-visioned Williams built a Baptist church, probably the first in America. He established complete freedom of religion, even for Jews and Catholics. He demanded no oaths regarding religious beliefs, no compulsory attendance at worship, no taxes to support a state church. He even sheltered the abused Quakers, although disagreeing sharply with their views. Williams's endorsement of religious tolerance made Rhode Island more liberal than any of the other English settlements in the New World, and more advanced than most Old World communities as well.

Those outcasts who clustered about Roger Williams enjoyed additional blessings. They exercised simple manhood suffrage from the start, though this broad-minded practice was later narrowed by a property qualification. Opposed to special privilege of any sort, the intrepid Rhode Islanders managed to achieve remarkable freedom of opportunity.

Other scattered settlements soon dotted Rhode Island. They consisted largely of malcontents and exiles, some of whom could not bear the stifling theological atmosphere of the Bay Colony. Many of these restless souls in "Rogues' Island," including Anne Hutchinson, had little in common with Roger Williams—except being unwelcome anywhere else. The Puritan clergy back in Boston sneered at Rhode Island as "that sewer" in which the "Lord's debris" had collected and rotted.

Planted by dissenters and exiles, Rhode Island became strongly individualistic and stubbornly independent. With good reason "Little Rhody" was later known as "the traditional home of the otherwise minded." Begun as a squatter colony in 1636 without legal standing, it finally established rights to the soil when it secured a charter from Parliament in 1644. A huge bronze statue of the "Independent Man" appropriately stands today on the dome of the statehouse in Providence.

New England Spreads Out

The smiling valley of the Connecticut River, one of the few highly fertile expanses of any size in all New England, had meanwhile attracted a sprinkling of Dutch and English settlers. Hartford was founded in 1635. The next year witnessed a spectacular beginning of the centuries-long westward movement across the continent. An energetic group of Boston Puritans, led by the Reverend Thomas Hooker, swarmed as a body into the Hartford area, with the ailing Mrs. Hooker carried on a horse litter.

Three years later, in 1639, the settlers of the new Connecticut River colony drafted in open meeting a trailblazing document known as the Fundamental Orders. It was in effect a modern constitution, which established a regime democratically controlled by the "substantial" citizens. Essential features of the Fundamental Orders were later borrowed by Connecticut for its colonial charter and ultimately for its state constitution.

Another flourishing Connecticut settlement began to spring up at New Haven in 1638. It was a prosperous community, founded by Puritans who contrived to set up an even closer church-government alliance than in Massachusetts. Although only squatters without a charter, the colonists dreamed of making New Haven a bustling seaport. But they fell into disfavor with Charles II as a result of having sheltered two of the judges who had condemned his father, Charles I, to death. In 1662, to the acute distress of the New Havenites, the crown granted a charter to Connecticut that merged New Haven with the more democratic settlements in the Connecticut Valley.

Far to the north, enterprising fishermen and fur traders had been active on the coast of Maine for a dozen or so years before the founding of Plymouth. After disheartening attempts at colonization in 1623 by Sir Ferdinando Gorges, this land of lakes and forests was absorbed by Massachusetts Bay after a formal purchase in 1677 from the Gorges heirs. It remained a part of Massachusetts for nearly a century and a half before becoming a separate state.

Granite-ribbed New Hampshire also sprang from the fishing and trading activities along its narrow coast. It was absorbed in 1641 by the grasping Bay Colony, under a strained interpretation of the Massachusetts charter. The king, annoyed by this display of greed, arbitrarily separated New Hampshire from Massachusetts in 1679 and made it a royal colony.

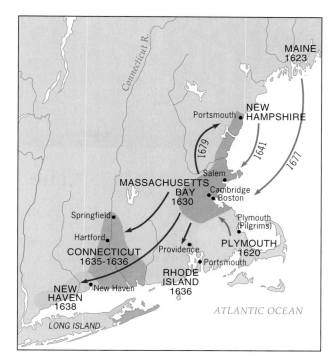

Seventeenth-Century New England Settlements
The Massachusetts Bay Colony was the hub of New England. All earlier colonies grew into it; all later colonies grew out of it.

Puritans Versus Indians

The spread of English settlements inevitably led to clashes with the Indians, who were particularly weak in New England. Shortly before the Pilgrims had arrived at Plymouth in 1620, an epidemic, probably triggered by contact with English fishermen, had swept through the coastal tribes and killed more than three-quarters of the native people. Deserted Indian fields, ready for tillage, greeted the Plymouth settlers, and scattered skulls and bones provided grim evidence of the impact of the disease.

In no position to resist the English incursion, the local Wampanoag Indians at first befriended the settlers. Cultural accommodation was facilitated by Squanto, a Wampanoag who had learned English from a ship's captain who had kidnapped him some years earlier. The Wampanoag chieftain Massasoit signed a treaty with the Plymouth Pilgrims in 1621 and helped them celebrate the first Thanksgiving after the autumn harvests that same year.

The English

During the late Middle Ages, the Black Death and other epidemics that ravaged England kept the island's population in check. But by 1500 increased resistance to such diseases allowed the population to soar, and a century later the island nation was bursting at the seams. This population explosion, combined with economic depression and religious repression, sparked the first major European migration to England's New World colonies.

Some of those who voyaged to Virginia and Maryland in the seventeenth century were independent artisans or younger members of English gentry families. But roughly three-quarters of the English migrants to the Chesapeake during this period came as servants, signed to "indentures" ranging from four to seven years. One English observer described such indentured servants as "idle, lazie, simple people," and another complained that many of those taking ship for the colonies "have been pursued by hue-and-cry for robberies, burglaries, or breaking prison."

In fact, most indentured servants were young men drawn from England's "middling classes." Some fled the disastrous slump in the cloth trade in the early seventeenth century. Many others had been forced off the land as the dawning national economy prompted landowners in southwestern England to convert from crop fields to pasture and to "enclose" the land for sheep grazing. Making their way from town to town in search of work, they eventually drifted into port cities such as Bristol and London. There they boarded ship for America, where they provided the labor necessary to cultivate the Chesapeake's staple crop, tobacco.

Some 40 percent of these immigrants of the mid-seventeenth century died before they finished their terms of indenture. (Because of the high death rate and the shortage of women, Chesapeake society was unable to reproduce itself naturally until the last quarter of the seventeenth century.) The survivors entered Chesapeake society with only their "freedom dues"—usually clothing, an ax and hoe, and a few barrels of corn.

Nevertheless, many of those who arrived early in the century eventually acquired land and moved into the mainstream of Chesapeake society. After 1660, however, opportunities for the "freemen" declined. In England the population spurt ended, and the great London fire of 1666 sparked a building boom that soaked up job seekers. As the supply of English indentured servants dried up in the late seventeenth century, southern planters looking for laborers turned increasingly to black slaves.

Town Meetinghouse, Hingham, Massachusetts
Erected in 1681, it is still in use today as a Unitarian Universalist Church, making it the oldest meetinghouse in continuous ecclesiastical use in the United States.

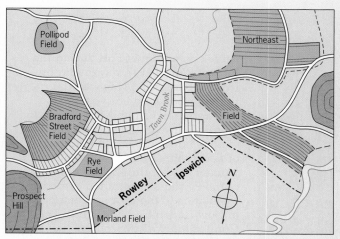

Land Use in Rowley, Massachusetts, c. 1650
The settlers of Rowley brought from their native Yorkshire the practice of granting families very small farming plots and reserving large common fields for use by the entire community. On the map, the yellow areas show private land; the green areas show land held in common.

Whereas English immigration to the Chesapeake was spread over nearly a century, most English voyagers to New England arrived within a single decade. In the twelve years between 1629 and 1642, some twenty thousand Puritans swarmed to the Massachusetts Bay Colony. Fleeing a sustained economic depression and the cruel religious repression of Charles I, the Puritans came to plant a godly commonwealth in New England's rocky soil.

In contrast to the single indentured servants of the Chesapeake, the New England Puritans migrated in family groups, and in many cases whole communities were transplanted from England to America. Although they remained united by the common language and common Puritan faith they carried to New England, their English baggage was by no means uniform. As in England, most New England settlements were farming communities. But some New England towns re-created the specialized economies of particular localities in England. Marblehead, Massachusetts, for example, became a fishing village because most of its settlers had been fishermen in old England. The townsfolk of Rowley, Massachusetts, brought from Yorkshire in northern England not only their town name but also their distinctive way of life, revolving around textile manufacturing.

Mistress Anne Pollard
Born in England, Mistress Pollard arrived in Massachusetts as a child with John Winthrop's fleet in 1630. A tavern operator and the mother of 13 children, she was 100 years old when this portrait was painted in 1721. On her death 4 years later, she left 130 descendants, a dramatic example of the fecundity of the early New England colonists.

Political practices, too, reflected the towns' variegated English roots. In Ipswich, Massachusetts, settled by East Anglian Puritans, the ruling selectmen served long terms and ruled with an iron hand. By contrast, local politics in the town of Newbury were bitter and contentious, and officeholders were hard-pressed to win reelection; the town's founders came from western England, a region with little tradition of local government. Although the Puritans' imperial masters in London eventually circumscribed such precious local autonomy, this diverse heritage of fiercely independent New England towns endured, reasserting itself during the American Revolution.

Attack on a Pequot Fort during the Pequot War of 1637, engraving by J.W. Barber, 1830   This was the first war between natives and Europeans in British North America. It culminated in the Puritan militia's vicious burning out and slaughtering of nearly three hundred Pequot men, women, and children. The defeat of the Pequots eliminated armed resistance to the new settlements of New Haven and Guildford. The Connecticut Valley would not see significant "Indian troubles" again for forty years, when the Indians of New England united in their final stand against the encroachments of English settlers, King Philip's War.

As more English settlers arrived and pushed inland into the Connecticut River valley, confrontations between Indians and whites ruptured these peaceful relations. Hostilities exploded in 1637 between the English settlers and the powerful Pequot tribe. Besieging a Pequot village on Connecticut's Mystic River, English militiamen and their Narragansett Indian allies set fire to the Indian wigwams and shot the fleeing survivors. The slaughter wrote a brutal finish to the Pequot War, virtually annihilated the Pequot tribe, and inaugurated four decades of uneasy peace between Puritans and Indians.

Lashed by critics in England, the Puritans made some feeble efforts at converting the remaining Indians to Christianity, although Puritan missionary zeal never equaled that of the Catholic Spanish and French. A mere handful of Indians were gathered into Puritan "praying towns" to make the acquaintance of the English God and to learn the ways of English culture.

The Indians' only hope for resisting English encroachment lay in intertribal unity—a pan-Indian alliance against the swiftly spreading English settlements. In 1675 Massasoit's son, Metacom, called King Philip by the English, forged such an alliance and mounted a series of coordinated assaults on English villages throughout New England. Frontier settlements were especially hard hit, and refugees fell back toward the relative safety of Boston. When the war ended in 1676, fifty-two Puritan towns had been attacked, and

twelve destroyed entirely. Hundreds of colonists and many more Indians lay dead. Metacom's wife and son were sold into slavery; he himself was captured, beheaded, and drawn and quartered. His head was carried on a pike back to Plymouth, where it was mounted on grisly display for years.

King Philip's War slowed the westward march of English settlement in New England for several decades. But the war inflicted a lasting defeat on New England's Indians. Drastically reduced in numbers, dispirited, and disbanded, they thereafter posed only sporadic threats to the New England colonists.

Seeds of Colonial Unity and Independence

A path-breaking experiment in union was launched in 1643, when four colonies banded together to form the New England Confederation. Old England was then deeply involved in civil wars, and hence the colonists were thrown upon their own resources. The primary purpose of the confederation was defense against foes or potential foes, notably the Indians, the French, and the Dutch. Purely intercolonial problems, such as runaway servants and criminals who had fled from one colony to another, also came within the jurisdiction of the confederation. Each member colony, regardless of size, wielded two votes—an arrangement highly displeasing to the most populous colony, Massachusetts Bay.

The confederation was essentially an exclusive Puritan club. It consisted of the two Massachusetts colonies (the Bay Colony and bantam-sized Plymouth) and the two Connecticut colonies (New Haven and the scattered valley settlements). The Puritan leaders blackballed Rhode Island as well as the Maine outposts. These places, it was charged, harbored too many heretical or otherwise undesirable characters. Shockingly, one of the Maine towns had made a tailor its mayor and had even sheltered an excommunicated minister of the gospel.

Weak though it was, the confederation was the first notable milestone on the long and rocky road toward colonial unity. The delegates took tottering but long-overdue steps toward acting together on matters of intercolonial importance. Rank-and-file colonists, for their part, received valuable experience in delegating their votes to properly chosen representatives.

Back in England the king had paid little attention to the American colonies during the early years of their planting. They were allowed, in effect, to become semiautonomous commonwealths. This era of benign neglect was prolonged when the crown, struggling to retain its power, became enmeshed during the 1640s in civil wars with the parliamentarians.

But when Charles II was restored to the English throne in 1660, the royalists and their Church of England allies were once more firmly in the saddle. Puritan hopes of eventually purifying the old English church withered. Worse, Charles II was determined to take an active, aggressive hand in the management of the colonies. His plans ran headlong against the habits that decades of relative independence had bred in the colonists.

Deepening colonial defiance was nowhere more glaringly revealed than in Massachusetts. One of the king's agents in Boston was mortified to find that royal orders had no more effect than old issues of the London *Gazette*. Punishment was soon forthcoming. As a slap at Massachusetts, Charles II gave rival Connecticut in 1662 a sea-to-sea charter grant, which legalized the squatter settlements. The very next year, the outcasts in Rhode Island received a new charter, which gave kingly sanction to the most religiously tolerant government yet devised in America. A final and crushing blow fell on the stiff-necked Bay Colony in 1684, when its precious charter was revoked by the London authorities.

Andros Promotes the First American Revolution

Massachusetts suffered further humiliation in 1686, when the Dominion of New England was created by royal authority. Unlike the homegrown New England Confederation, it was imposed from London. Embracing at first all New England, it was expanded two years later to include New York and East and West Jersey. The dominion also aimed at bolstering colonial defense in the event of war with the Indians and hence, from the imperial viewpoint of Parliament, was a statesmanlike move.

More importantly, the Dominion of New England was designed to promote urgently needed efficiency in the administration of the English Navigation Laws. Those laws reflected the intensifying colonial rivalries of the

The Stuart Dynasty in England*

Name, Reign	Relation to America
James I, 1603–1625	Va., Plymouth founded; Separatists persecuted
Charles I, 1625–1649	Civil wars, 1642–1649; Mass., Md. founded
(Interregnum, 1649–1660)	Commonwealth; Protectorate (Oliver Cromwell)
Charles II, 1660–1685	The Restoration; Carolinas, Pa., N.Y. founded; Conn. chartered
James II, 1685–1688	Catholic trend; Glorious Revolution, 1688
William & Mary, 1689–1702 (Mary died 1694)	King William's War, 1689–1697

*See p. 29 for predecessors; p. 110 for successors.

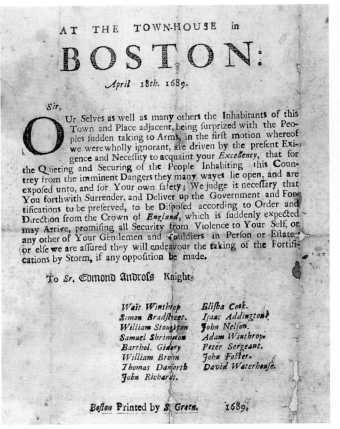

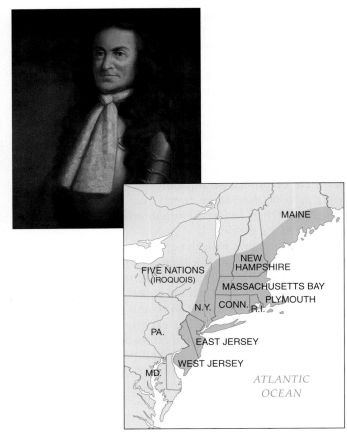

Sir Edmund Andros (1637–1714); a Boston Broadside Urging Him to Surrender, 1689; and a Map Showing Andros's Dominion of New England After being expelled from New England, Andros eventually returned to the New World as governor of Virginia (1692–1697).

seventeenth century. They sought to stitch England's overseas possessions more tightly to the motherland by throttling American trade with countries not ruled by the English crown. Like colonial peoples everywhere, the Americans chafed at such confinements, and smuggling became an increasingly common and honorable occupation.

At the head of the new dominion stood autocratic Sir Edmund Andros, an able English military man, conscientious but tactless. Establishing headquarters in Puritanical Boston, he generated much hostility by his open affiliation with the despised Church of England. The colonists were also outraged by his noisy and Sabbath-profaning soldiers, who were accused of teaching the people "to drink, blaspheme, curse, and damn."

Andros was prompt to use the mailed fist. He ruthlessly curbed the cherished town meetings; laid heavy restrictions on the courts, the press, and the schools; and revoked all land titles. Dispensing with the popular assemblies, he taxed the people without the consent of their duly elected representatives. He also strove to enforce the unpopular Navigation Laws and suppress smuggling. Liberty-loving colonists, accustomed to unusual privileges during long decades of neglect, were goaded to the verge of revolt.

The people of old England soon taught the people of New England a few lessons in resisting oppression. In 1688–1689 they engineered the memorable Glorious (or Bloodless) Revolution. Dethroning the despotic and unpopular Catholic James II, they enthroned the Protestant rulers of the Netherlands, the Dutch-born William III and his English wife, Mary, daughter of James II.

When the news of the Glorious Revolution reached America, the ramshackle Dominion of New England collapsed like a house of cards. A Boston mob, catching

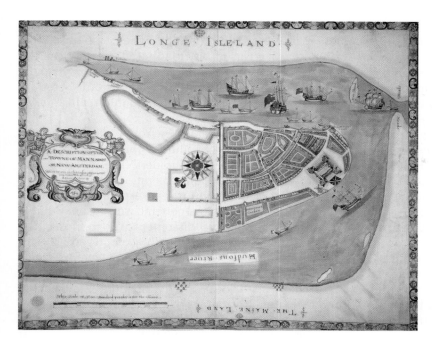

New York (then New Amsterdam), 1664
This drawing clearly shows the tip of
Manhattan Island protected by the wall
after which Wall Street was named.

the fever, rose against the existing regime. Sir Edmund Andros attempted to flee in woman's clothing but was betrayed by boots protruding beneath his dress. He was hastily shipped off to England.

Massachusetts, though rid of the despotic Andros, did not gain as much from the upheaval as it had hoped. In 1691 it was arbitrarily made a royal colony, with a new charter and a new royal governor. The permanent loss of the ancient charter was a staggering blow to the proud Puritans, who never fully recovered. Worst of all, the privilege of voting, once a monopoly of church members, was now to be enjoyed by all qualified male property holders.

England's Glorious Revolution reverberated throughout the colonies from New England to the Chesapeake. Inspired by the challenge to the crown in old England, many colonists seized the occasion to strike against royal authority in America. Unrest rocked both New York and Maryland from 1689 to 1691, until newly appointed royal governors restored a semblance of order. Most importantly, the new monarchs relaxed the royal grip on colonial trade, inaugurating a period of "salutary neglect" when the much-resented Navigation Laws were only weakly enforced.

Yet residues remained of Charles II's effort to assert tighter administrative control over his empire. More English officials—judges, clerks, customs officials—now staffed the courts and strolled the wharves of English America. Many were incompetent, corrupt hacks who knew little and cared less about American affairs. Appointed by influential patrons in far-off England, they blocked, by their very presence, the rise of local leaders to positions of political power. Aggrieved Americans viewed them with mounting contempt and resentment as the eighteenth century wore on.

Old Netherlanders at New Netherland

Late in the sixteenth century, the oppressed people of the Netherlands unfurled the standard of rebellion against Catholic Spain. After bloody and protracted fighting, they finally succeeded, with the aid of Protestant England, in winning their independence.

The seventeenth century—the era of Rembrandt and other famous artists—was a golden age in Dutch history. This vigorous little lowland nation finally emerged as a major commercial and naval power, and then it ungratefully challenged the supremacy of its former benefactor, England. Three great Anglo-Dutch naval wars were fought in the seventeenth century, with as many as a hundred ships on each side. The sturdy Dutch dealt blows about as heavy as they received.

The Dutch Republic also became a leading colonial power, with by far its greatest activity in the East Indies. There it maintained an enormous and profitable empire for over three hundred years. The Dutch East India Company was virtually a state within a state and at one time supported an army of 10,000 men and a fleet of 190 ships, 40 of them men-of-war.

Seeking greater riches, this enterprising company employed an English explorer, Henry Hudson. Disregarding orders to sail northeast, he ventured into Delaware Bay and New York Bay in 1609 and then ascended the Hudson River, hoping that at last he had chanced upon the coveted shortcut through the continent. But, as the event proved, he merely filed a Dutch claim to a magnificently wooded and watered area.

Much less powerful than the mighty Dutch East India Company was the Dutch West India Company, which maintained profitable enterprises in the Caribbean. At times it was less interested in trading than in raiding and at one fell swoop in 1628 captured a fleet of Spanish treasure ships laden with loot worth $15 million. The company also established outposts in Africa and a thriving sugar industry in Brazil, which for several decades was its principal center of activity in the New World.

New Netherland, in the beautiful Hudson River area, was planted in 1623–1624 on a permanent basis. Established by the Dutch West India Company for its quick-profit fur trade, it was never more than a secondary interest of the founders. The company's most brilliant stroke was to buy Manhattan Island from the Indians (who did not actually "own" it) for virtually worthless trinkets—twenty-two thousand acres of what is now perhaps the most valuable real estate in the world for pennies per acre.

New Amsterdam—later New York City—was a company town. It was run by and for the Dutch company, in the interests of the stockholders. The investors had no enthusiasm for religious toleration, free speech, or democratic practices; and the governors appointed by the company as directors-general were usually harsh and despotic. Religious dissenters who opposed the official Dutch Reformed Church were regarded with suspicion, and for a while Quakers were savagely abused. In response to repeated protests by the aggravated colonists, a local body with limited lawmaking power was finally established.

This picturesque Dutch colony took on a strongly aristocratic tint and retained it for generations. Vast feudal estates fronting the Hudson River, known as patroonships, were granted to promoters who agreed to settle fifty people on them. One patroonship in the Albany area was slightly larger than the later state of Rhode Island.

Colorful little New Amsterdam attracted a cosmopolitan population, as is common in seaport towns. A

New York Aristocrats
This prosperous family exemplified the comfortable lives and aristocratic pretensions of the "Hudson River lords" in colonial New York.

Peter Stuyvesant (1602–1682) Despotic in government and intolerant in religion, he lived in a constant state of friction with the prominent residents of New Netherland. When protests arose, he replied that he derived his power from God and the company, not the people. He opposed popular suffrage on the grounds that "the thief" would vote "for the thief" and "the rogue for the rogue."

French Jesuit missionary, visiting in the 1640s, noted that eighteen different languages were being spoken in the streets. New York's later babel of immigrant tongues was thus foreshadowed.

Friction with English and Swedish Neighbors

Vexations beset the Dutch company-colony from the beginning. The directors-general were largely incompetent. Company shareholders demanded their dividends, even at the expense of the colony's welfare. The Indians, infuriated by Dutch cruelties, retaliated with horrible massacres. As a defense measure, the hard-pressed settlers on Manhattan Island erected a stout wall, from which Wall Street derives its name.

New England was hostile to the growth of its Dutch neighbor, and the people of Connecticut finally ejected intruding Hollanders from their verdant valley. Three of the four member colonies of the New England Confederation were eager to wipe out New Netherland with military force. But Massachusetts, which would have had to provide most of the troops, vetoed the proposed foray.

The Swedes in turn trespassed on Dutch preserves, from 1638 to 1655, by planting the anemic colony of New Sweden on the Delaware River. This was the golden age of Sweden, during and following the Thirty Years' War of 1618–1648, in which its brilliant King Gustavus Adolphus had carried the torch for Protestantism. This outburst of energy in Sweden caused it to enter the costly colonial game in America, though on something of a shoestring.

Resenting the Swedish intrusion on the Delaware, the Dutch dispatched a small military expedition in 1655. It was led by the ablest of the directors-general, Peter Stuyvesant, who had lost a leg while soldiering in the West Indies and was dubbed "Father Wooden Leg" by the Indians. The main fort fell after a bloodless siege, whereupon Swedish rule came to an abrupt end. The colonists were absorbed by New Netherland.

New Sweden, never important, soon faded away, leaving behind in later Delaware a sprinkling of Swedish place names and Swedish log cabins (the first in America), as well as an admixture of Swedish blood.

Dutch Residues in New York

Lacking vitality, and representing only a secondary commercial interest of the Dutch, New Netherland lay under the menacing shadow of the vigorous English colonies to the north. In addition, it was honeycombed with New England immigrants. Numbering about one-half of New Netherland's ten thousand souls in 1664, they might in time have seized control from within.

The days of the Dutch on the Hudson were numbered, for the English regarded them as intruders. In 1664, after the imperially ambitious Charles II had granted the area to his brother, the Duke of York, a

Quakers in the Colonial Era Quakers, or Friends, were renowned for their simplicity of architecture, dress, manner, and speech. They also distinguished themselves from most other Protestant denominations by allowing women to speak in Quaker meetings and to share in making decisions for the church and the family.

strong English squadron appeared off the decrepit defenses of New Amsterdam. A fuming Peter Stuyvesant, short of all munitions except courage, was forced to surrender without firing a shot. New Amsterdam was thereupon renamed New York, in honor of the Duke of York. England won a splendid harbor, strategically located in the middle of the mainland colonies, and the stately Hudson River penetrating the interior. With the removal of this foreign wedge, the English banner now waved triumphantly over a solid stretch of territory from Maine to the Carolinas.

The conquered Dutch province tenaciously retained many of the illiberal features of earlier days. An autocratic spirit survived, and the aristocratic element gained strength when certain corrupt English governors granted immense acreage to their favorites. Influential landowning families—such as the Livingstons and the De Lanceys—wielded disproportionate power in the affairs of colonial New York. These monopolistic land policies, combined with the lordly atmosphere, discouraged many European immigrants from coming. The physical growth of New York was correspondingly retarded.

The Dutch peppered place names over the land, including Harlem (Haarlem), Brooklyn (Breuckelen), and Hell Gate (Hellegat). They likewise left their imprint on the gambrel-roofed architecture. As for social customs and folkways, no other foreign group of comparable size

has made so colorful a contribution. Noteworthy are Easter eggs, Santa Claus, waffles, sauerkraut, bowling, sleighing, skating, and *kolf* (golf)—a dangerous game played with heavy clubs and forbidden in settled areas.

Penn's Holy Experiment in Pennsylvania

A remarkable group of dissenters, commonly known as Quakers, arose in England during the mid-1600s. Their name derived from the report that they "quaked" when under deep religious emotion. Officially they were known as the Religious Society of Friends.

Quakers were especially offensive to the authorities, both religious and civil. They refused to support the established Church of England with taxes. They built simple meetinghouses, congregated without a paid clergy, and "spoke up" themselves in meetings when moved. Believing that they were all children in the sight of God, they kept their broad-brimmed hats on in the presence of their "betters" and addressed others with simple "thee"s and "thou"s, rather than with conventional titles. They would take no oaths because Jesus had commanded, "Swear not at all." This peculiarity often embroiled them with government officials, for "test oaths" were still required to establish the fact that a person was not a Roman Catholic.

The Quakers, beyond a doubt, were a people of deep conviction. They abhorred strife and warfare and refused military service. As advocates of passive resistance, they would turn the other cheek and rebuild their meetinghouse on the site where their enemies had torn it down. Their courage and devotion to principle finally triumphed. Although at times they seemed stubborn and unreasonable, they were a simple, devoted, democratic people, contending in their own high-minded way for religious and civic freedom.

William Penn, a wellborn and athletic young Englishman, was attracted to the Quaker faith in 1660, when only sixteen years old. His father, disapproving, administered a sound flogging. After various adventures in the army (the best portrait of the peaceful Quaker has him in armor), the youth firmly embraced the despised faith and suffered much persecution. The courts branded him a "saucy" and "impertinent" fellow. Several hundred of his less fortunate fellow Quakers died of cruel treatment, and thousands more were fined, flogged, or cast into dank prisons.

Penn's thoughts naturally turned to the New World, where a sprinkling of Quakers had already fled, notably to Rhode Island, North Carolina, and New Jersey. Eager to establish an asylum for his people, he also hoped to experiment with liberal ideas in government and at the same time make a profit. Finally, in 1681, he managed to secure from the king an immense grant of fertile land, in consideration of a monetary debt owed to his deceased father by the crown. The king called the area Pennsylvania ("Penn's Woodland") in honor of the sire. The modest son, fearing that critics would accuse him of naming it after himself, sought unsuccessfully to change the name.

Pennsylvania was by far the best advertised of all the colonies. Its founder—the "first American advertising man"—sent out paid agents and distributed countless pamphlets printed in English, Dutch, French, and German. Unlike the lures of many other American real estate promoters, then and later, Penn's inducements were generally truthful. He especially welcomed forward-looking spirits and substantial citizens, including industrious carpenters, masons, shoemakers, and other manual workers. His liberal land policy, which encouraged substantial holdings, was instrumental in attracting a heavy inflow of immigrants.

Penn's Treaty, by Edward Hicks
The peace-loving Quaker founder of Pennsylvania made a serious effort to live in harmony with the Indians, as this treaty-signing scene illustrates. But the westward thrust of white settlement eventually caused friction between the two groups, as in other colonies.

Quaker Pennsylvania and Its Neighbors

Penn formally launched his colony in 1681. His task was simplified by the presence of several thousand "squatters"—Dutch, Swedish, English, Welsh—who were already scattered along the banks of the Delaware River. Philadelphia, meaning "brotherly love" in Greek, was more carefully planned than most colonial cities and consequently enjoyed wide and attractive streets.

Penn farsightedly bought land from the Indians, including Chief Tammany, later patron saint of New York's political Tammany Hall. His treatment of the native peoples was so fair that the Quaker "broad brims" went among them unarmed and even employed them as baby-sitters. For a brief period, Pennsylvania seemed the promised land of amicable Indian-white relations. Some southern tribes even migrated to Pennsylvania, seeking the Quaker haven. But ironically, Quaker tolerance proved the undoing of Quaker Indian policy. As non-Quaker European immigrants flooded into the province, they undermined the Quakers' own benevolent policy toward the Indians. The feisty Scots-Irish were particularly unpersuaded by Quaker idealism.

Penn's new proprietary regime was unusually liberal and included a representative assembly elected by the landowners. No tax-supported state church drained coffers or demanded allegiance. Freedom of worship was guaranteed to all residents, although Penn, under pressure from London, was forced to deny Catholics and Jews the privilege of voting or holding office. The death penalty was imposed only for treason and murder, as compared with some two hundred capital crimes in England.

> In a Boston lecture in 1869, Ralph Waldo Emerson (1803–1882) declared,
>
> "The sect of the Quakers in their best representatives appear to me to have come nearer to the sublime history and genius of Christ than any other of the sects."

Among other noteworthy features, no provision was made by the peace-loving Quakers of Pennsylvania for a military defense. No restrictions were placed on immigration, and naturalization was made easy. The humane Quakers early developed a strong dislike of black slavery, and in the genial glow of Pennsylvania some progress was made toward social reform.

With its many liberal features, Pennsylvania attracted a rich mix of ethnic groups. They included numerous religious misfits who were repelled by the harsh practices of neighboring colonies. This Quaker refuge boasted a surprisingly modern atmosphere in an unmodern age and to an unusual degree afforded economic opportunity, civil liberty, and religious freedom. Even so, "blue laws" prohibited "ungodly revelers," stage plays, playing cards, dice, games, and excessive hilarity.

Under such generally happy auspices, Penn's brainchild grew lustily. The Quakers were shrewd businesspeople, and in a short time the settlers were exporting grain and other foodstuffs. Within two years Philadelphia claimed three hundred houses and twenty-five hundred people. Within nineteen years—by 1700—the colony was surpassed in population and wealth only by long-established Virginia and Massachusetts.

William Penn, who altogether spent about four years in Pennsylvania, was never fully appreciated by his colonists. His governors, some of them incompetent and tactless, quarreled bitterly with the people, who were constantly demanding greater political control. Penn himself became too friendly with James II, the deposed Catholic king. Thrice arrested for treason, thrust for a time into a debtors' prison, and afflicted by a paralytic stroke, he died full of sorrows. His enduring monument was not only a noble experiment in government but also a new commonwealth. Based on civil and religious liberty, and dedicated to freedom of conscience and worship, it held aloft a hopeful torch in a world of semidarkness.

Small Quaker settlements flourished next door to Pennsylvania. New Jersey was started in 1664 when two noble proprietors received the area from the Duke of York. A substantial number of New Englanders, including many whose weary soil had petered out, flocked to the new colony. One of the proprietors sold West New Jersey in 1674 to a group of Quakers, who here set up a sanctuary even before Pennsylvania was launched. East New Jersey was also acquired in later years by the

EXAMINING THE EVIDENCE

A Seventeenth-Century Valuables Cabinet In 1999 a boatyard worker on Cape Cod and his sister, a New Hampshire teacher, inherited a small (20-pound, 16½-inch-high) chest that had always stood on their grandmother's hall table, known in the family as the "Franklin chest." Eager to learn more about it, they set out to discover the original owner, tracing their family genealogy and consulting with furniture experts. In January 2000 this rare seventeenth-century cabinet, its full provenance now known, appeared on the auction block and sold for a record $2.4 million to the Peabody Essex Museum in Salem, Massachusetts. No less extraordinary than the price was the history of its creator and its owners embodied in the piece. Salem cabinetmaker James Symonds (1636–1726) had made the chest for his relatives Joseph Pope (1650–1712) and Bathsheba Folger (1652–1726) to commemorate their 1679 marriage. Symonds carved the Popes'

initials and the date on the door of the cabinet. He also put elaborate S curves on the sides remarkably similar to the Mannerist carved oak paneling produced in Norfolk, England, from where his own cabinetmaker father had emigrated. Behind the chest's door are ten drawers where the Popes would have kept jewelry, money, deeds, and writing materials. Surely they prized the chest as a sign of refinement to be shown off in their best room, a sentiment passed down through the next thirteen generations even as the Popes' identities were lost. The chest may have become known as the "Franklin chest" because Bathsheba was Benjamin Franklin's aunt, but also because that identification appealed more to descendants ashamed that the Quaker Popes, whose own parents had been persecuted for their faith, were virulent accusers during the Salem witch trials of 1692.

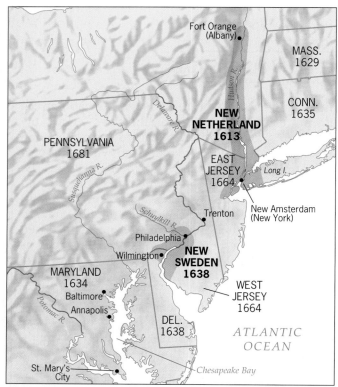

Early Settlements in the Middle Colonies, with Founding Dates

In general, the soil was fertile and the expanse of land was broad, unlike rock-bestrewn New England. Pennsylvania, New York, and New Jersey came to be known as the "bread colonies," by virtue of their heavy exports of grain.

Rivers also played a vital role. Broad, languid streams—notably the Susquehanna, the Delaware, and the Hudson—tapped the fur trade of the interior and beckoned adventuresome spirits into the backcountry. The rivers had few cascading waterfalls, unlike New England's, and hence presented little inducement to milling or manufacturing with water-wheel power.

A surprising amount of industry nonetheless hummed in the middle colonies. Virginal forests abounded for lumbering and shipbuilding. The presence of deep river estuaries and landlocked harbors stimulated both commerce and the growth of seaports, such as New York and Philadelphia. Even Albany, more than a hundred miles up the Hudson, was a port of some consequence in colonial days.

The middle colonies were in many respects midway between New England and the southern plantation group. Except in aristocratic New York, the landholdings were generally intermediate in size—smaller than in the big-acreage South but larger than in small-farm New England. Local government lay somewhere between the personalized town meeting of New England and the diffused county government of the South. There were fewer industries in the middle colonies than in New England, more than in the South.

Yet the middle colonies, which in some ways were the most American part of America, could claim certain distinctions in their own right. Generally speaking, the population was more ethnically mixed than that of other settlements. The people were blessed with an unusual degree of religious toleration and democratic control. Earnest and devout Quakers, in particular, made a compassionate contribution to human freedom out of all proportion to their numbers. Desirable land was more easily acquired in the middle colonies than in New England or in the tidewater South. One result was that a considerable amount of economic and social democracy prevailed, though less so in aristocratic New York.

Quakers, whose wings were clipped in 1702 when the crown combined the two Jerseys in a royal colony.

Swedish-tinged Delaware consisted of only three counties—two at high tide, the witticism goes—and was named after Lord De La Warr, the harsh military governor who had arrived in Virginia in 1610. Harboring some Quakers, and closely associated with Penn's prosperous colony, Delaware was granted its own assembly in 1703. But until the American Revolution, it remained under the governor of Pennsylvania.

The Middle Way in the Middle Colonies

The middle colonies—New York, New Jersey, Delaware, and Pennsylvania—enjoyed certain features in common.

Modern-minded Benjamin Franklin, often regarded as the most representative American personality of his era, was a child of the middle colonies. Although it is true that Franklin was born a Yankee in puritanical Boston, he entered Philadelphia as a seventeen-year-old in 1720 with a loaf of bread under each arm and immediately found a congenial home in the urbane, open atmosphere of what was then North America's biggest city. One Pennsylvanian later boasted that Franklin "came to life at seventeen, in Philadelphia."

By the time Franklin arrived in the City of Brotherly Love, the American colonies were themselves "coming to life." Population was growing robustly. Transportation and communication were gradually improving. The British, for the most part, continued their hands-off policies, leaving the colonists to fashion their own local governments, run their own churches, and develop networks of intercolonial trade. As people and products crisscrossed the colonies with increasing frequency and in increasing volume, Americans began to realize that—far removed from Mother England—they were not merely surviving, but truly thriving.

Chronology

1517	Martin Luther begins Protestant Reformation
1536	John Calvin of Geneva publishes *Institutes of the Christian Religion*
1620	Pilgrims sail on the *Mayflower* to Plymouth Bay
1624	Dutch found New Netherland
1629	Charles I dismisses Parliament and persecutes Puritans
1630	Puritans found Massachusetts Bay Colony
1635-1636	Roger Williams convicted of heresy and founds Rhode Island colony
1635-1638	Connecticut and New Haven colonies founded
1637	Pequot War
1638	Anne Hutchinson banished from Massachusetts colony
1639	Connecticut's Fundamental Orders drafted
1642-1648	English Civil War
1643	New England Confederation formed
1650	William Bradford completes *Of Plymouth Plantation*
1655	New Netherland conquers New Sweden
1664	England seizes New Netherland from Dutch East and West Jersey colonies founded
1675-1676	King Philip's War
1681	William Penn founds Pennsylvania colony
1686	Royal authority creates Dominion of New England
1688-1689	Glorious Revolution overthrows Stuarts and Dominion of New England

VARYING VIEWPOINTS

Europeanizing America or Americanizing Europe?

The history of discovery and colonization raises perhaps the most fundamental question about all American history. Should it be understood as the extension of European civilization into the New World or as the gradual development of a uniquely "American" culture? An older school of thought tended to emphasize the Europeanization of America. Historians of that persuasion paid close attention to the situation in Europe, particularly England and Spain, in the fifteenth and sixteenth centuries. They also focused on the exportation of the values and institutions of the mother countries to the new lands in the western sea. Although some historians also examined the transforming effect of America on Europe, this approach, too, remained essentially Eurocentric.

More recently, historians have concentrated on the distinctiveness of America. The concern with European origins has evolved into a comparative treatment of European settlements in the New World. England, Spain, Holland, and France now attract more attention for the divergent kinds of societies they fostered in America than for the way they commonly pursued Old World ambitions in the New. The newest trend to emerge is a transatlantic history that views European empires and their American colonies as part of a process of cultural cross-fertilization affecting not only the colonies but Europe and Africa as well.

This less Eurocentric approach has also changed the way historians explain the colonial development of America. Rather than telling the story of colonization as the imposition of European ways of life through "discovery" and "conquest," historians increasingly view the colonial period as one of "contact" and "adaptation" between European, African, and Native American ways of life. Scholars, including Richard White, Alfred Crosby, William Cronon, Karen Kupperman, and Timothy Silver, have enhanced understanding of the cultural as well as the physical transformations that resulted from contact. An environment of forests and meadows, for example, gave way to a landscape of fields and fences as Europeans sought to replicate the agricultural villages they had known in Europe. Aggressive deforestation even produced climatic changes, as treeless tracts made for colder winters, hotter summers, and earth-gouging floods. Ramon Gutierrez's *When Jesus Came, the Corn Mothers Went Away* (1991) has expanded the colonial stage to include interactions between Spanish settlers and Native Americans in the Southwest.

The variety of American societies that emerged out of the interaction of Europeans and Native Americans has also become better appreciated. Early histories by esteemed historians like Perry Miller exaggerated the extent to which the New England Puritan experience defined the essence of America. Not only did these historians overlook non-English experiences, they failed to recognize the diversity in motives, methods, and consequences that existed even within English colonization. The numbers alone tell an interesting story. By 1700 about 220,000 English colonists had immigrated to the Caribbean, about 120,000 to the southern mainland colonies, and only about 40,000 to the middle Atlantic and New England colonies (although by the mid-eighteenth century, those headed for the latter destination would account for more than half the total).

Studies such as Richard S. Dunn's *Sugar and Slaves* (1972) emphasize the importance of the Caribbean in early English colonization efforts and make clear that the desire for economic gain, more than the quest for religious freedom, fueled the migration to the Caribbean islands. Similarly, Edmund S. Morgan's *American Slavery, American Freedom* (1975) stresses the role of economic ambition in explaining the English peopling of the Chesapeake and the eventual importation of African slaves to that region. Studies by Bernard Bailyn and David Hackett Fisher demonstrate that there was scarcely a "typical" English migrant to the New World. English colonists migrated both singly and in families, and for economic, social, political, and religious reasons.

Recent studies have also paid more attention to the conflicts that emerged out of this diversity in settler populations and colonial societies. This perspective emphasizes the contests for economic and political supremacy within the colonies, such as the efforts of the Massachusetts Bay elite to ward off the challenges of religious "heretics" and the pressures that an increasingly restless lower class put on wealthy merchants and large landowners. Nowhere was internal conflict so prevalent as in the ethnically diverse middle colonies, where factional antagonisms became the defining feature of public life.

The picture of colonial America that is emerging from all this new scholarship is of a society unique—and diverse—from inception. No longer simply Europe transplanted, American colonial society by 1700 is now viewed as an outgrowth of many intertwining roots—of different European and African heritages, of varied encounters with native peoples and a wilderness environment, and of complicated mixtures of settler populations, each with its own distinctive set of ambitions.

For further reading, see the Appendix. For web resources, go to **http://college.hmco.com.**

American Life in the Seventeenth Century

1607–1692

BEING THUS PASSED THE VAST OCEAN, AND A SEA OF TROUBLES
BEFORE IN THEIR PREPARATION . . . , THEY HAD NOW NO FRIENDS
TO WELLCOME THEM, NOR INNS TO ENTERTAINE OR REFRESH
THEIR WEATHERBEATEN BODYS, NO HOUSES OR MUCH LESS
TOWNS TO REPAIRE TOO, TO SEEKE FOR SUCCORE.

WILLIAM BRADFORD, OF PLYMOUTH PLANTATION, C. 1630

As the seventeenth century wore on, the crude encampments of the first colonists slowly gave way to permanent settlements. Durable and distinctive ways of life emerged as Europeans and Africans adapted to the New World and as Native Americans adapted to the newcomers. Even the rigid doctrines of Puritanism softened somewhat in response to the circumstances of life in America. And though all the colonies remained tied to England, and all were stitched tightly into the fabric of an Atlantic economy, regional differences continued to crystallize, notably the increasing importance of slave labor to the southern way of life.

The Unhealthy Chesapeake

Life in the American wilderness was nasty, brutish, and short for the earliest Chesapeake settlers. Malaria, dysentery, and typhoid took a cruel toll, cutting ten years off the life expectancy of newcomers from England. Half the people born in early Virginia and Maryland did not survive to celebrate their twentieth birthdays. Few of the remaining half lived to see their fiftieth—or even their fortieth, if they were women.

The disease-ravaged settlements of the Chesapeake grew only slowly in the seventeenth century, mostly through fresh immigration from England. The great majority of immigrants were single men in their late teens and early twenties, and most perished soon after arrival. Surviving males competed for the affections of the extremely scarce women, whom they outnumbered nearly six to one in 1650 and still outnumbered by three to two at the end of the century. Eligible women did not remain single for long.

Families were both few and fragile in this ferocious environment. Most men could not find mates. Most marriages were destroyed by the death of a partner within seven years. Scarcely any children reached adulthood under the care of two parents, and almost no one knew a grandparent. Weak family ties were reflected in the many pregnancies among unmarried young girls. In one Maryland county, more than a third of all brides were already pregnant when they wed.

Yet despite these hardships, the Chesapeake colonies struggled on. The native-born inhabitants eventually acquired immunity to the killer diseases that had ravaged the original immigrants. The presence of more women allowed more families to form, and by the end of the seventeenth century the white population of the Chesapeake was growing on the basis of its own birthrate. As the eighteenth century opened, Virginia, with some fifty-nine thousand people, was the most populous colony. Maryland, with about thirty thousand, was the third largest (after Massachusetts).

★ The Tobacco Economy

Although unhealthy for human life, the Chesapeake was immensely hospitable to tobacco cultivation. Profit-hungry settlers often planted tobacco to sell before they planted corn to eat. But intense tobacco cultivation quickly exhausted the soil, creating a nearly insatiable demand for new land. Relentlessly seeking fresh fields to plant in tobacco, commercial growers plunged ever farther up the river valleys, provoking ever more Indian attacks.

Leaf-laden ships annually hauled some 1.5 million pounds of tobacco out of Chesapeake Bay by the 1630s and almost 40 million pounds a year by the end of the century. This enormous production depressed prices, but colonial Chesapeake tobacco growers responded to falling prices in the familiar way of farmers: by planting still more acres to tobacco and bringing still more product to market.

More tobacco meant more labor, but where was it to come from? Families procreated too slowly to provide it

Early Tobacco Advertising Crude woodcuts like this one were used to identify various "brands" of tobacco—one of the first products to be sold by brand-name advertising. Then, as later, advertisers sometimes made extravagant claims for their merchandise.

by natural population increase. Indians died too quickly on contact with whites to be a reliable labor force. African slaves cost too much money. But England still had a "surplus" of displaced farmers, desperate for employment. Many of them, as "indentured servants," voluntarily mortgaged the sweat of their bodies for several years to Chesapeake masters. In exchange they received transatlantic passage and eventual "freedom dues," including a few barrels of corn, a suit of clothes, and perhaps a small parcel of land.

Both Virginia and Maryland employed the "head-right" system to encourage the importation of servant workers. Under its terms, whoever paid the passage of a laborer received the right to acquire fifty acres of land. Masters—not the servants themselves—thus reaped the benefits of landownership from the headright system. Some masters, men who already had at least modest financial means, soon parlayed their investments in servants into vast holdings in real estate. They became the great merchant-planters, lords of sprawling river-front estates that came to dominate the agriculture and commerce of the southern colonies. Ravenous for both labor and land, Chesapeake planters brought some 100,000 indentured servants to the region by 1700.

> *An agent for the Virginia Company in London submitted the following description of the Virginia colony in 1622:*
>
> "I found the plantations generally seated upon mere salt marshes full of infectious bogs and muddy creeks and lakes, and thereby subjected to all those inconveniences and diseases which are so commonly found in the most unsound and most unhealthy parts of England."

These "white slaves" represented more than three-quarters of all European immigrants to Virginia and Maryland in the seventeenth century.

Indentured servants led a hard but hopeful life in the early days of the Chesapeake settlements. They looked forward to becoming free and acquiring land of their own after completing their term of servitude. But as prime land became scarcer, masters became increasingly resistant to including land grants in "freedom dues." The servants' lot grew harsher as the seventeenth century wore on. Misbehaving servants, such as a housemaid who became pregnant or a laborer who killed a hog, might be punished with an extended term of service. Even after formal freedom was granted, penniless freed workers often had little choice but to hire themselves out for pitifully low wages to their former masters.

Frustrated Freemen and Bacon's Rebellion

An accumulating mass of footloose, impoverished freemen was drifting discontentedly about the Chesapeake region by the late seventeenth century. Mostly single young men, they were frustrated by their broken hopes of acquiring land, as well as by their gnawing failure to find single women to marry.

The swelling numbers of these wretched bachelors rattled the established planters. The Virginia assembly in 1670 disfranchised most of the landless knockabouts, accusing them of "having little interest in the country" and causing "tumults at the election to the disturbance of his majesty's peace." Virginia's Governor William Berkeley lamented his lot as ruler of this rabble: "How miserable that man is that governs a people where six parts of seven at least are poor, endebted, discontented, and armed."

Berkeley's misery soon increased. About a thousand Virginians broke out of control in 1676, led by a twenty-nine-year-old planter, Nathaniel Bacon. Many of the rebels were frontiersmen who had been forced into the untamed backcountry in search of arable land. They fiercely resented Berkeley's friendly policies toward the Indians, whose thriving fur trade the governor monopolized. When Berkeley refused to retaliate for a series of brutal Indian attacks on frontier settlements, Bacon and his followers took matters into their own hands. They fell murderously upon the Indians, friendly

and hostile alike, chased Berkeley from Jamestown, and put the torch to the capital. Chaos swept the raw colony, as frustrated freemen and resentful servants—described as "a rabble of the basest sort of people"—went on a rampage of plundering and pilfering.

As this civil war in Virginia ground on, Bacon suddenly died of disease, like so many of his fellow colonists. Berkeley thereupon crushed the uprising with brutal cruelty, hanging more than twenty rebels. Back in England Charles II complained, "That old fool has put to death more people in that naked country than I did here for the murder of my father."

The distant English king could scarcely imagine the depths of passion and fear that Bacon's Rebellion excited in Virginia. Bacon had ignited the smoldering resentments of landless former servants, and he had pitted the hardscrabble backcountry frontiersmen against the haughty gentry of the tidewater plantations. The rebellion was now suppressed, but these tensions remained. Lordly planters, surrounded by a still-seething sea of malcontents, anxiously looked about for less troublesome laborers to toil in the restless tobacco kingdom. Their eyes soon lit on Africa.

Nathaniel Bacon assailed Virginia's Governor William Berkeley in 1676

"for having protected, favored, and emboldened the Indians against His Majesty's loyal subjects, never contriving, requiring, or appointing any due or proper means of satisfaction for their many invasions, robberies, and murders committed upon us."

For his part, Governor Berkeley declared,

"I have lived thirty-four years amongst you [Virginians], as uncorrupt and diligent as ever [a] Governor was, [while] Bacon is a man of two years amongst you, his person and qualities unknown to most of you, and to all men else, by any virtuous act that ever I heard of. . . . I will take counsel of wiser men than myself, but Mr. Bacon has none about him but the lowest of the people."

EXAMINING THE EVIDENCE

An Indentured Servant's Contract, 1746   Legal documents, such as this contract signed in Virginia in 1746, not only provide evidence about the ever-changing rules by which societies have regulated their affairs, but also furnish rich information about the conditions of life and the terms of human relationships in the past. This agreement between Thomas Clayton and James Griffin provides a reminder that not all indentured servants in early America came from abroad. Indentured servitude could be equivalent to an apprenticeship, in which a young person traded several years of service to a master in exchange for instruction in the master's craft. Here Clayton pledges himself to five years in Griffin's employ in return for a promise to initiate the young man into the "Mystery" of the master's craft. Why might the master's trade be described as a "mystery"? From the evidence of this contract, what are the principal objectives of each of the parties to it? What problems does each anticipate? What obligations does each assume? What does the consent of Clayton's mother to the contract suggest about the young man's situation?

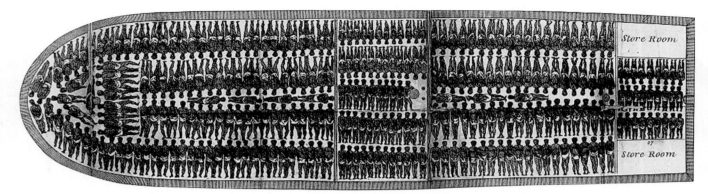

The "Middle Passage" The "middle passage" referred to the transatlantic sea voyage that brought slaves to the New World—the long and hazardous "middle" segment of a journey that began with a forced march to the African coast and ended with a trek into the American interior.

Colonial Slavery

Perhaps 10 million Africans were carried in chains to the New World in the three centuries or so following Columbus's landing. Only about 400,000 of them ended up in North America, the great majority arriving after 1700. Most of the early human cargoes were hauled to Spanish and Portuguese South America or to the sugar-rich West Indies.

Africans had been brought to Jamestown as early as 1619, but as late as 1670 they numbered only about 2,000 in Virginia (out of a total population of some 35,000 persons) and about 7 percent of the 50,000 people in the southern plantation colonies as a whole.

Hard-pinched white colonists, struggling to stay alive and to hack crude clearings out of the forests, could not afford to pay high prices for slaves who might die soon after arrival. White servants might die, too, but they were far less costly.

Drastic change came in the 1680s. Rising wages in England shrank the pool of penniless folk willing to gamble on a new life or an early death as indentured servants in America. At the same time, the large planters were growing increasingly fearful of the multitudes of potentially mutinous former servants in their midst. By the mid-1680s, for the first time, black slaves outnumbered white servants among the plantation colonies' new arrivals. In 1698 the Royal African Company, first chartered in 1672, lost its crown-granted monopoly on carrying slaves to the colonies. Enterprising

Estimated Slave Imports to the New World, 1601–1810

	17th Century	18th Century	Total	Percent
Spanish America	292,500	578,600	871,100	11.7
Brazil	560,000	1,891,400	2,451,400	33
British Caribbean	263,700	1,401,000	1,664,700	22.5
Dutch Caribbean	40,000	460,000	500,000	6.7
French Caribbean	155,800	1,348,400	1,504,200	20.3
Danish Caribbean	4,000	24,000	28,000	.4
British North America and future United States	10,000	390,000	400,000	5.4
TOTAL			7,419,400	100

This table clearly shows the huge concentration of the slave system in the Caribbean and South America. British North America's southern colonies constituted the extreme northern periphery of this system.
[Source: Philip D. Curtin, *The Atlantic Slave Trade* (Madison: University of Wisconsin Press, 1969).]

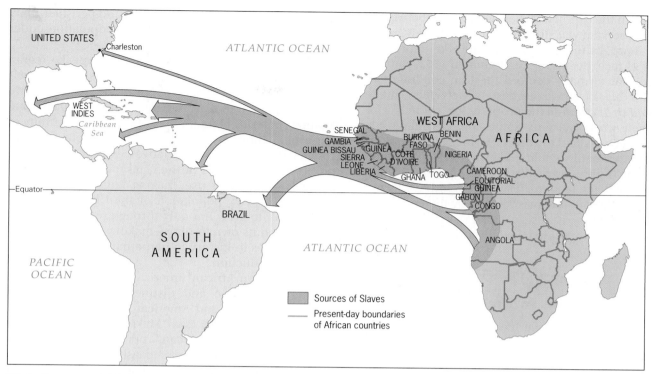

Main Sources of African Slaves, c. 1500–1800   The three centuries of the "African diaspora" scattered blacks all over the New World, with about 400,000 coming to North America.

Americans, especially Rhode Islanders, rushed to cash in on the lucrative slave trade, and the supply of slaves rose steeply. More than ten thousand Africans were pushed ashore in America in the decade after 1700, and tens of thousands more in the next half-century. Blacks accounted for nearly half the population of Virginia by 1750. In South Carolina they outnumbered whites two to one.

Most of the slaves who reached North America came from the west coast of Africa, especially the area stretching from present-day Senegal to Angola. They were originally captured by African coastal tribes, who traded them in crude markets on the shimmering tropical beaches to itinerant European—and American—flesh merchants. Usually branded and bound, the captives were herded aboard sweltering ships for the gruesome "middle passage," on which death rates ran as high as 20 percent. Terrified survivors were eventually shoved onto auction blocks in New World ports like Newport, Rhode Island, or Charleston, South Carolina, where a giant slave market traded in human misery for more than a century.

A few of the earliest African immigrants gained their freedom, and some even became slaveowners themselves. But as the number of Africans in their midst increased dramatically toward the end of the seventeenth century, white colonists reacted remorselessly to this supposed racial threat.

> *The Mennonites of Germantown, Pennsylvania, recorded the earliest known protest against slavery in America in 1688:*
>
> "There is a saying, that we should do to all men like as we will be done ourselves. . . . But to bring men hither, or to rob and sell them against their will, we stand against. . . . Pray, what thing in the world can be done worse towards us, than if men should rob or steal us away, and sell us for slaves to strange countries, separating husbands from their wives and children?"

Earlier in the century, the legal difference between a slave and a servant was unclear. But now the law began to make sharp distinctions between the two—largely on the basis of race. Beginning in Virginia in 1662, statutes appeared that formally decreed the iron conditions of slavery for blacks. These earliest "slave codes" made blacks *and their children* the property (or "chattels") for life of their white masters. Some colonies made it a crime to teach a slave to read or write. Not even conversion to Christianity could qualify a slave for freedom. Thus did the God-fearing whites put the fear of God into their hapless black laborers. Slavery might have begun in America for economic reasons, but by the end of the seventeenth century, it was clear that racial discrimination also powerfully molded the American slave system.

Africans in America

In the deepest South, slave life was especially severe. The climate was hostile to health, and the labor was life-draining. The widely scattered South Carolina rice and indigo plantations were lonely hells on earth where gangs of mostly male Africans toiled and perished. Only fresh imports could sustain the slave population under these loathsome conditions.

Blacks in the tobacco-growing Chesapeake region had a somewhat easier lot. Tobacco was a less physically demanding crop than those of the deeper South. Tobacco plantations were larger and closer to one another than rice plantations. The size and proximity of these plantations permitted the slaves more frequent contact with friends and relatives. By about 1720 the proportion of females in the Chesapeake slave population had begun to rise, making family life possible. The captive black population of the Chesapeake area soon began to grow not only through new imports but also through its own fertility—making it one of the few slave societies in history to perpetuate itself by its own natural reproduction.

Native-born African Americans contributed to the growth of a stable and distinctive slave culture, a mixture of African and American elements of speech, religion, and folkways (see "Makers of America: From African to African American," pp. 74–75). On the sea islands off South Carolina's coast, blacks evolved a unique language, *Gullah* (probably a corruption of

Rice Cultivation in the Colonial South Rice growing, imported from Africa along with African slaves to work the swampy rice fields, made South Carolina the rice basket of the British Empire.

Angola, the African region from which many of them had come). It blended English with several African languages, including Yoruba, Ibo, and Hausa. Through it many African words have passed into American speech—such as *goober* (peanut), *gumbo* (okra), and *voodoo* (witchcraft). The ringshout, a West African religious dance performed by shuffling in a circle while answering a preacher's shouts, was brought to colonial America by slaves and eventually contributed to the development of jazz. The banjo and the bongo drum were other African contributions to American culture.

Slaves also helped mightily to build the country with their labor. A few became skilled artisans—carpenters, bricklayers, and tanners. But chiefly they performed the sweaty toil of clearing swamps, grubbing out trees, and other menial tasks. Condemned to life under the lash, slaves naturally pined for freedom. A slave revolt erupted in New York City in 1712 that cost the lives of a dozen whites and caused the execution of twenty-one blacks, some of them burned at the stake over a slow fire. More than fifty resentful South Carolina blacks along the Stono River exploded in revolt in 1739 and tried to march to Spanish Florida, only to be stopped by the local militia. But in the end, the slaves in the South proved to be a more manageable labor force than the white indentured servants they gradually replaced. No slave uprising in American history matched the scale of Bacon's Rebellion.

Southern Society

As slavery spread, the gaps in the South's social structure widened. The rough equality of poverty and disease of the early days was giving way to a defined hierarchy of wealth and status in the early eighteenth century. At the top of this southern social ladder perched a small but powerful covey of great planters. Owning gangs of slaves and vast domains of land, the planters ruled the region's economy and virtually monopolized political power. A clutch of extended clans—such as the Fitzhughs, the Lees, and the Washingtons—possessed among them horizonless tracts of Virginia real estate, and together they dominated the House of Burgesses. Just before the Revolutionary War, 70 percent of the leaders of the Virginia legislature came from families established in Virginia before 1690—the famed "first families of Virginia," or "FFVs."

Yet, legend to the contrary, these great seventeenth-century merchant-planters were not silk-swathed cavaliers gallantly imitating the ways of English country gentlemen. They did eventually build stately riverfront manors, occasionally rode to the hounds, and some of them even cultivated the arts and accumulated distinguished libraries. But for the most part, they were a hard-working, businesslike lot, laboring long hours over the problems of plantation management. Few problems were more vexatious than the unruly, often surly, servants. One Virginia governor had such difficulty keeping his servants sober that he struck a deal allowing them to get drunk the next day if they would only lay off the liquor long enough to look after his guests at a celebration of the queen's birthday in 1711.

Beneath the planters—far beneath them in wealth, prestige, and political power—were the small farmers, the largest social group. They tilled their modest plots and might own one or two slaves, but they lived a ragged, hand-to-mouth existence. Still lower on the social scale

Charleston, South Carolina Founded in 1680, Charleston grew to become the bustling seaport pictured in this drawing done in the 1730s. Charleston was by then the largest city in the mostly rural southern colonies. It flourished as a seaport for the shipment to England of slave-grown Carolina rice.

From African to African American

Dragged in chains from West African shores, the first African Americans struggled to preserve their diverse heritages from the ravages of slavery. Their children, the first generation of American-born slaves, melded these various African traditions—Guinean, Ibo, Yoruba, Angolan—into a distinctive African American culture. Their achievement sustained them during the cruelties of enslavement and has endured to enrich American life to this day.

With the arrival of the first Africans in the seventeenth century, a cornucopia of African traditions poured into the New World: handicrafts and skills in numerous trades; a plethora of languages, musics, and cuisines; even rice-planting techniques that conquered the inhospitable soil of South Carolina. It was North America's rice paddies, tilled by experienced West Africans, that introduced rice into the English

diet and furnished so many English tables with the sticky staple.

These first American slaves were mostly males. Upon arrival they were sent off to small isolated farms, where social contact with other Africans, especially women, was an unheard-of luxury. Yet their legal status was at first uncertain. A few slaves were able to buy their freedom in the seventeenth century. One, Anthony Johnson of Northampton County, Virginia, actually became a slaveholder himself.

But by the beginning of the eighteenth century, a settled slave society was emerging in the southern colonies. Laws tightened; slave traders stepped up their deliveries of human cargo; large plantations formed. Most significantly, a new generation of American-born slaves joined their forebears at labor in the fields. By 1740 large groups of slaves lived together on sprawling plantations, the

(above) Africans Destined for Slavery This engraving from 1830 is an example of antislavery propaganda in the pre–Civil War era. It shows hapless Africans being brought ashore in America under the whips of slave traders and, ironically, under the figurative shadow of the national Capitol. **(right) Advertisements for Slave Sales in Charleston, South Carolina, 1753** Charleston had the largest slave market in the colonies.

(left) **Yarrow Mamout, by Charles Willson Peale, 1819** When Peale painted this portrait, Mamout was over one hundred years old. A devout Muslim brought to Maryland as a slave, he eventually bought his freedom and settled in Georgetown. (right) **The Emergence of an African American Culture** In this scene from the mid-nineteenth century, African Americans play musical instruments of European derivation, like the fiddle, as well as instruments of African origin, like the bones and banjo—a vivid illustration of the blending of the two cultures in the crucible of the New World.

American-born outnumbered the African-born, and the importation of African slaves slowed.

Forging a common culture and finding a psychological weapon with which to resist their masters and preserve their dignity were daunting challenges for American-born slaves. Plantation life was beastly, an endless cycle of miserable toil in the field or foundry from sunup to sundown. Female slaves were forced to perform double duty. After a day's backbreaking work, women were expected to sit up for hours spinning, weaving, or sewing to clothe themselves and their families. Enslaved women also lived in constant fear of sexual exploitation by predatory masters.

Yet eventually a vibrant slave culture began to flower. And precisely because of the diversity of African peoples represented in America, the culture that emerged was a uniquely New World creation. It derived from no single African model and incorporated many Western elements, though often with significant modifications.

Slave religion illustrates this pattern. Cut off from their native African religions, most slaves became Christians but fused elements of African and Western traditions and drew their own conclusions from Scripture. White Christians might point to Christ's teachings of humility and obedience to encourage slaves to "stay in their place," but black Christians emphasized God's role in freeing the Hebrews from slavery and saw Jesus as the Messiah who would deliver them from bondage. They also often retained an African definition of heaven as a place where they would be reunited with their ancestors.

At their Sunday and evening-time prayer meetings, slaves also patched African remnants onto conventional Christian ritual. Black Methodists, for example, ingeniously evaded the traditional Methodist ban on dancing as sinful: three or four people would stand still in a ring, clapping hands and beating time with their feet (but never crossing their legs, thus not officially "dancing"), while others walked around the ring, singing in unison. This "ringshout" derived from African practices; modern American dances, including the Charleston, in turn derived from this African American hybrid.

Christian slaves also often used outwardly religious songs as encoded messages about escape or rebellion. "Good News, the Chariot's Comin'" might sound like an innocent hymn about divine deliverance, but it could also announce the arrival of a guide to lead fugitives safely to the North. Similarly, "Wade in the Water" taught fleeing slaves one way of covering their trail. The "Negro spirituals" that took shape as a distinctive form of American music thus had their origins in *both* Christianity and slavery.

Indeed, much American music was born in the slave quarters from African importations. Jazz, with its meandering improvisations and complex syncopations and rhythms, constitutes the most famous example. But this rich cultural harvest came at the cost of generations of human agony.

75

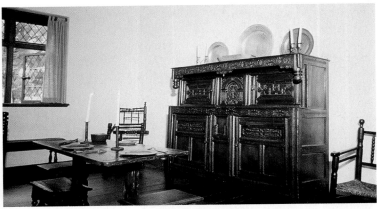

A Merchant-Planter's Home and Its Dining Room Simple by later standards, this house was home to the family of a substantial planter in the seventeenth century. It stands on land in the Virginia tidewater region first acquired by Adam Thoroughgood, who arrived in the Virginia colony as an indentured servant in 1621. By 1635, as a freeman, he had recruited 105 settlers to the colony and was rewarded, according to the practice of the headright system, with the title to some 5,250 acres along the Lynnhaven River. There his grandson erected this house in about 1680. It was continuously occupied by the Thoroughgood family for more than two centuries, until the 1920s.

were the landless whites, most of them luckless former indentured servants. Under them were those persons still serving out the term of their indenture. Their numbers gradually diminished as black slaves increasingly replaced white indentured servants toward the end of the seventeenth century. The oppressed black slaves, of course, remained enchained in society's basement.

Few cities sprouted in the colonial South, and consequently an urban professional class, including lawyers and financiers, was slow to emerge. Southern life revolved around the great plantations, distantly isolated from one another. Waterways provided the principal means of transportation. Roads were so wretched that in bad weather funeral parties could not reach church burial grounds—an obstacle that accounts for the development of family burial plots in the South, a practice unlike anything in old England or New England.

The New England Family

Nature smiled more benignly on pioneer New Englanders than on their disease-plagued fellow colonists to the south. Clean water and cool temperatures retarded

the spread of killer microbes. In stark contrast to the fate of Chesapeake immigrants, settlers in seventeenth-century New England *added* ten years to their life spans by migrating from the Old World. One settler claimed that "a sip of New England's air is better than a whole draft of old England's ale." The first generations of Puritan colonists enjoyed, on the average, about seventy years on this earth—not very different from the life expectancy of present-day Americans.

In further contrast with the Chesapeake, New Englanders tended to migrate not as single individuals but as families, and the family remained at the center of New England life. Almost from the outset, New England's population grew from natural reproductive increase. The people were remarkably fertile, even if the soil was not.

Early marriage encouraged the booming birthrate. Women typically wed by their early twenties and produced babies about every two years thereafter until menopause. Ceaseless childbearing drained the vitality of many pioneer women, as the weather-eroded colonial tombstones eloquently reveal. A number of the largest families were borne by several mothers, though claims about the frequency of death in childbirth have probably been exaggerated. But the dread of death in the birthing bed haunted many women, and it was small wonder that they came to fear pregnancy. A married woman could expect to experience up to ten pregnancies and rear as many as eight surviving children. Massachusetts governor William Phips was one of twenty-seven children, all by the same mother. A New England woman might well have dependent children living in her household from the earliest days of her marriage up until the day of her death, and child raising became in essence her full-time occupation.

The longevity of the New Englanders contributed to family stability. Children grew up in nurturing environments where they were expected to learn habits of obedience, above all. They received guidance not only from their parents but from their grandparents as well. This novel intergenerational continuity has inspired the observation that New England "invented" grandparents. Family stability was reflected in low premarital pregnancy rates (again in contrast with the Chesapeake) and in the generally strong, tranquil social structure characteristic of colonial New England.

Still other contrasts came to differentiate the southern and New England ways of life. Oddly enough, the fragility of southern families advanced the economic security of southern women, especially of women's property rights. Because southern men frequently died young, leaving widows with small children to support, the southern colonies generally allowed married women to retain separate title to their property and gave widows

Mrs. Elizabeth Freake and Baby Mary
This portrait of a Boston mother and child in about 1674 suggests the strong family ties that characterized early New England society.

New England early acquired a reputation as a healthy environment. Urging his fellow Englishmen to emigrate to Massachusetts Bay Colony in 1630, the Reverend John White described New England (somewhat fancifully) as follows:

"No country yields a more propitious air for our temper than New England. . . . Many of our people that have found themselves always weak and sickly at home, have become strong and healthy there: perhaps by the dryness of the air and constant temper[ature] of it, which seldom varies from cold to heat, as it does with us. . . . Neither are the natives at any time troubled with pain of teeth, soreness of eyes, or ache in their limbs."

the right to inherit their husband's estates. But in New England, Puritan lawmakers worried that recognizing women's separate property rights would undercut the unity of married persons by acknowledging conflicting interests between husband and wife. New England women usually gave up their property rights, therefore, when they married. Yet in contrast to old England, the laws of New England made secure provision for the property rights of widows—and even extended important protections to women within marriage.

"A true wife accounts subjection her honor," one Massachusetts Puritan leader declared, expressing a sentiment then common in Europe as well as America. But in the New World, a rudimentary conception of women's rights as individuals was beginning to appear in the seventeenth century. Women still could not vote, and the popular attitude persisted that they were morally weaker than men—a belief rooted in the biblical tale of Eve's treachery in the Garden of Eden. But a husband's power over his wife was not absolute. The New England authorities could and did intervene to restrain abusive spouses. One man was punished for kicking his wife off a stool; another was disciplined for drawing an "uncivil" portrait of his mate in the snow. Women also had some spheres of autonomy. Midwifery—assisting with childbirths—was a virtual female monopoly, and midwives often fostered networks of women bonded by the common travails of motherhood. One Boston midwife alone delivered over three thousand babies.

Above all, the laws of Puritan New England sought to defend the integrity of marriages. Divorce was exceedingly rare, and the authorities commonly ordered separated couples to reunite. Outright abandonment was among the very few permissible grounds for divorce. Adultery was another. Convicted adulterers—especially if they were women—were whipped in public and forced forever after to wear the capital letter "A" cut out in cloth and sewed on their outer garment—the basis for Nathaniel Hawthorne's famous 1850 tale *The Scarlet Letter*.

Life in the New England Towns

Sturdy New Englanders evolved a tightly knit society, the basis of which was small villages and farms. This develop-ment was natural in a people anchored by geography and hemmed in by the Indians, the French, and the Dutch. Puritanism likewise made for unity of purpose—and for concern about the moral health of the whole community. It was no accident that the nineteenth-century crusade for abolishing black slavery—with Massachusetts agita-tors at the forefront—sprang in some degree from the New England conscience, with its Puritan roots.

In the Chesapeake region, the expansion of settle-ment was somewhat random and was usually under-taken by lone-wolf planters on their own initiative, but New England society grew in a more orderly fashion. New towns were legally chartered by the colonial authorities, and the distribution of land was entrusted to the steady hands of sober-minded town fathers, or "proprietors." After receiving a grant of land from the colonial legislature, the proprietors moved themselves and their families to the designated place and laid out their town. It usually consisted of a meetinghouse, which served as both the place of worship and the town hall, surrounded by houses. Also marked out was a village green, where the militia could drill. Each family received several parcels of land, including a woodlot for fuel, a tract suitable for growing crops, and another for pasturing animals.

Towns of more than fifty families were required to provide elementary education, and roughly half of the adults knew how to read and write. As early as 1636, just

Graveyard Art These New England colonists evidently died in the prime of life. Carving likenesses on grave markers was a common way of commemorating the dead.

Now the Child being entred in his Letters and Spelling, let him learn thefe and fuch like Sentences by Heart, whereby he will be both inftructed in his Duty, and encouraged in his Learning.

The Dutiful Child's Promifes,

I Will fear GOD, and honour the KING.
I will honour my Father & Mother.
I will Obey my Superiours.
I will Submit to my Elders.
I will Love my Friends.
I will hate no Man.
I will forgive my Enemies, and pray to God for them.
I will as much as in me lies keep all God's Holy Commandments.

The New England Primer Religious instruction loomed large in early New England schools. This widely used schoolbook taught lessons of social duty and Christian faith, as well as reading and writing.

eight years after the colony's founding, the Massachusetts Puritans established Harvard College, today the oldest corporation in America, to train local boys for the ministry. Only in 1693, eighty-six years after staking out Jamestown, did the Virginians establish their first college, William and Mary.

Puritans ran their own churches, and democracy in Congregational Church government led logically to democracy in political government. The town meeting, in which the adult males met together and each man voted, was a showcase and a classroom for democracy. New England villagers from the outset gathered regularly in their meetinghouses to elect their officials, appoint schoolmasters, and discuss such mundane matters as road repairs. The town meeting, observed Thomas Jefferson, was "the best school of political liberty the world ever saw."

The Half-Way Covenant and the Salem Witch Trials

Yet worries plagued the God-fearing pioneers of these tidy New England settlements. The pressure of a growing population was gradually dispersing the Puritans onto outlying farms, far from the control of church and neighbors. And although the core of Puritan belief still burned brightly, the passage of time was dampening the first generation's flaming religious zeal. About the middle of the seventeenth century, a new form of sermon began to be heard from Puritan pulpits—the "jeremiad." Taking their cue from the doom-saying Old Testament prophet Jeremiah, earnest preachers scolded parishioners for their waning piety. Especially alarming was the apparent decline in conversions—testimonials by individuals that they had received God's grace and therefore deserved to be admitted to the church as members of the elect. Troubled ministers in 1662 announced a new formula for church membership, the Half-Way Covenant. This new arrangement modified the "covenant," or the agreement between the church and its adherents, to admit to baptism—but not "full communion"—the unconverted children of existing members. By conferring partial membership rights in the once-exclusive Puritan congregations, the Half-Way Covenant weakened the distinction between the "elect" and others, further

The Massachusetts School Law of 1647 stated,

"It being one chief project of the old deluder, Satan, to keep men from the knowledge of the Scriptures, as in former times by keeping them in an unknown tongue, it is therefore ordered that every township in this jurisdiction, after the Lord has increased them [in] number to fifty householders, shall then forthwith appoint one within their town to teach all such children as shall resort to him to write and read, whose wages shall be paid either by the parents or masters of such children, or by the inhabitants in general."

Matthew Hopkins's Witch Finder   Hopkins was a seventeenth-century English witch-hunter whose techniques included watching suspects to see if diabolical creatures, in the form of common animals, fed on the alleged witch's blood. He also urged that suspected witches be bound hand and foot and tossed in a pond. The innocent, he claimed, would sink (and often drown), while the guilty would float to the surface. His methods brought death to hundreds of women, men, and children in eastern England in the 1640s.

diluting the spiritual purity of the original settlers' godly community.

The Half-Way Covenant dramatized the difficulty of maintaining at fever pitch the religious devotion of the founding generation. Jeremiads continued to thunder from the pulpits, but as time went on, the doors of the Puritan churches swung fully open to all comers, whether converted or not. This widening of church membership gradually erased the distinction between the "elect" and other members of society. In effect, strict religious purity was sacrificed somewhat to the cause of wider religious participation. Interestingly, from about this time onward, women were in the majority in the Puritan congregations.

Women also played a prominent role in one of New England's most frightening religious episodes. A group of adolescent girls in Salem, Massachusetts, claimed to have been bewitched by certain older women. A hysterical "witch hunt" ensued, leading to the legal lynching in 1692 of twenty individuals, nineteen of whom were hanged and one of whom was pressed to death. Two dogs were also hanged.

Larger-scale witchcraft persecutions were then common in Europe, and several outbreaks had already flared forth in the colonies—often directed at property-owning women. But the reign of horror in Salem grew not only from the superstitions and prejudices of the age but also from the unsettled social and religious conditions of the rapidly evolving Massachusetts village. Most of the accused witches came from families associated with Salem's burgeoning market economy; their accusers came largely from subsistence farming families in Salem's hinterland. The episode thus reflected the widening social stratification of New England, as well as the fear of many religious traditionalists that the Puritan heritage was being eclipsed by Yankee commercialism.

The witchcraft hysteria eventually ended in 1693 when the governor, alarmed by an accusation against his own wife and supported by the more responsible members of the clergy, prohibited any further trials and pardoned those already convicted. Twenty years later a penitent Massachusetts legislature annulled the "convictions" of the "witches" and made reparations to their heirs. The Salem witchcraft delusion marked an all-time high in the American experience of popular passions run wild. "Witch-hunting" passed into the American vocabulary as a metaphor for the often dangerously irrational urge to find a scapegoat for social resentments.

The New England Way of Life

Oddly enough, the story of New England was largely written by rocks. The heavily glaciated soil was strewn with countless stones, many of which were forced to the surface after a winter freeze. In a sense the Puritans did not possess the soil; it possessed them by shaping their character. Scratching a living from the protesting earth was an early American success story. Back-bending toil put a premium on industry and penny-pinching frugality, for which New Englanders became famous. Traditionally sharp Yankee traders, some of them palming off wooden nutmegs, made their mark. Connecticut came in time to be called good-humoredly "the Nutmeg

State." Cynics exaggerated when they said that the three stages of progress in New England were "to get on, to get honor, to get honest."

The grudging land also left colonial New England less ethnically mixed than its southern neighbors. European immigrants were not attracted in great numbers to a site where the soil was so stony—and the sermons so sulfurous.

Climate likewise molded New England, where the summers were often uncomfortably hot and the winters cruelly cold. Many early immigrants complained of the region's extremes of weather. Yet the soil and climate of New England eventually encouraged a diversified agriculture and industry. Staple products like tobacco did not flourish, as in the South. Black slavery, although attempted, could not exist profitably on small farms, especially where the surest crop was stones. No broad, fertile expanses comparable to those in the tidewater South beckoned people inland. The mountains ran fairly close to the shore, and the rivers were generally short and rapid.

And just as the land shaped New Englanders, so they shaped the land. The Native Americans had left an early imprint on the New England earth. They traditionally beat trails through the woods as they migrated seasonally for hunting and fishing. They periodically burned the woodlands to restore leafy first-growth forests that would sustain the deer population. The Indians recognized the right to *use* the land, but the concept of exclusive, individual *ownership* of the land was alien to them.

The English settlers had a different philosophy. They condemned the Indians for "wasting" the earth by underutilizing its bounty and used this logic to justify their own expropriation of the land from the native inhabitants. Consistent with this outlook, the Europeans felt a virtual duty to "improve" the land by clearing woodlands for pasturage and tillage, building roads and fences, and laying out permanent settlements.

Some of the greatest changes resulted from the introduction of livestock. The English brought pigs, horses, sheep, and cattle from Europe to the settlements. Because the growing herds needed ever more pastureland, the colonists were continually clearing forests. The animals' voracious appetites and heavy hooves compacted the soil, speeding erosion and flooding. In some cases the combined effect of these developments actually may have changed local climates and made some areas even more susceptible to extremes of heat and cold.

Repelled by the rocks, the hardy New Englanders turned instinctively to their fine natural harbors. Hacking timber from their dense forests, they became experts in shipbuilding and commerce. They also ceaselessly exploited the self-perpetuating codfish lode off the coast of Newfoundland—the fishy "gold mines of New England," which have yielded more wealth than all the treasure chests of the Aztecs. During colonial days the wayfarer seldom got far from the sound of the ax and hammer, or the swift rush of the ship down the ways to the sea, or the smell of rotting fish. As a reminder of the importance of fishing, a handsome replica of the "sacred cod" is proudly displayed to this day in the Massachusetts Statehouse in Boston.

The combination of Calvinism, soil, and climate in New England made for energy, purposefulness, sternness, stubbornness, self-reliance, and resourcefulness. Righteous New Englanders prided themselves on being God's chosen people. They long boasted that Boston was "the hub of the universe"—at least in spirit. A famous jingle of later days ran,

> *I come from the city of Boston*
> *The home of the bean and the cod*
> *Where the Cabots speak only to Lowells*
> *And the Lowells speak only to God.*

New England has had an incalculable impact on the rest of the nation. Ousted by their sterile soil, thousands of New Englanders scattered from Ohio to Oregon and even Hawaii. They sprinkled the land with new communities modeled on the orderly New England town, with its central green and tidy schoolhouse, and its simple town-meeting democracy. "Yankee ingenuity," originally fostered by the flinty fields and comfortless climate of New England, came to be claimed by all Americans as a proud national trait. And the fabled "New England conscience," born of the steadfast Puritan heritage, left a legacy of high idealism in the national character and inspired many later reformers.

The Early Settlers' Days and Ways

The cycles of the seasons and the sun set the schedules of all the earliest American colonists, men as well as women, blacks as well as whites. The overwhelming majority of colonists were farmers. They planted in the spring, tended their crops in the summer, harvested in the fall, and prepared in the winter to begin the cycle anew. They usually rose at dawn and went to bed at

Life and Death in Colonial America, by Prudence Punderson Note the artist's initials, "P.P.," on the coffin. This embroidery suggests the stoic resolve of a colonial woman, calmly depicting the inevitable progression of her own life from the cradle to the grave.

dusk. Chores might be performed after nightfall only if they were "worth the candle," a phrase that has persisted in American speech.

Women, slave or free, on southern plantations or northern farms, wove, cooked, cleaned, and cared for children. Men cleared land; fenced, planted, and cropped it; cut firewood; and butchered livestock as needed. Children helped with all these tasks, while picking up such schooling as they could.

Life was humble but comfortable by contemporary standards. Compared to most seventeenth-century Europeans, Americans lived in affluent abundance. Land was relatively cheap, though somewhat less available in the planter-dominated South than elsewhere. In the northern and middle colonies, an acre of virgin soil cost about what American carpenters could earn in one day as wages, which were roughly three times those of their English counterparts.

"Dukes don't emigrate," the saying goes, for if people enjoy wealth and security, they are not likely to risk exposing their lives in the wilderness. Similarly, the very poorest members of a society may not possess even the modest means needed to pull up stakes and seek a fresh start in life. Accordingly, most white migrants to early colonial America came neither from the aristocracy nor from the dregs of European society—with the partial exception of the impoverished indentured servants.

Crude frontier life did not in any case permit the flagrant display of class distinctions, and seventeenth-century society in all the colonies had a certain simple sameness to it, especially in the more egalitarian New England and middle colonies. Yet many settlers, who considered themselves to be of the "better sort," tried to re-create on a modified scale the social structure they had known in the Old World. To some extent they succeeded, though yeasty democratic forces frustrated their full triumph. Resentment against upper-class pretensions helped to spark outbursts like Bacon's Rebellion of 1676 in Virginia and the uprising of Maryland's Protestants toward the end of the seventeenth century. In New York animosity between lordly landholders and aspiring merchants fueled Leisler's Rebellion, an ill-starred and bloody insurgence that rocked New York City from 1689 to 1691.

For their part, would-be American blue bloods resented the pretensions of the "meaner sort" and passed laws to try to keep them in their place. Massachusetts in 1651 prohibited poorer folk from "wearing gold or silver lace," and in eighteenth-century Virginia a tailor was fined and jailed for arranging to race his horse—"a sport only for gentlemen." But these efforts to reproduce the finely stratified societies of Europe proved feeble in the early American wilderness, where equality and democracy found fertile soil—at least for white people.

Chronology

1619	First Africans arrive in Virginia
1625	Population of English colonies in America about 2,000
1636	Harvard College founded
1662	Half-Way Covenant for Congregational Church membership established
1670	Virginia assembly disfranchises landless freeman
1676	Bacon's Rebellion in Virginia
1680s	Mass expansion of slavery in colonies
1689– 1691	Leisler's Rebellion in New York
1692	Salem witch trials in Massachusetts
1693	College of William and Mary founded
1698	Royal African Company slave trade monopoly ended
1700	Population of English colonies in America about 250,000
1712	New York City slave revolt
1739	South Carolina slave revolt

For further reading, see the Appendix. For web resources, go to **http://college.hmco.com**.

5

Colonial Society on the Eve of Revolution

—✦—

1700–1775

DRIVEN FROM EVERY OTHER CORNER OF THE EARTH,
FREEDOM OF THOUGHT AND THE RIGHT OF PRIVATE JUDGMENT
IN MATTERS OF CONSCIENCE DIRECT THEIR COURSE TO THIS
HAPPY COUNTRY AS THEIR LAST ASYLUM.

SAMUEL ADAMS, 1776

The common term *thirteen original colonies* is misleading. Britain ruled thirty-two colonies in North America by 1775, including Canada, the Floridas, and various Caribbean islands. But only thirteen of them unfurled the standard of rebellion. A few of the nonrebels, such as Canada and Jamaica, were larger, wealthier, or more populous than some of the revolting thirteen. Why, then, did some British colonies eventually strike for their independence, while others did not? Part of the answer is to be found in the distinctive social, economic, and political structures of the thirteen Atlantic seaboard colonies—and in the halting, gradual appearance of a recognizably *American* way of life.

Conquest by the Cradle

Among the distinguishing characteristics that the eventually rebellious settlements shared was lusty population growth. In 1700 they contained fewer than 300,000 souls, about 20,000 of whom were black. By 1775, 2.5 million people inhabited the thirteen colonies, of whom about half a million were black. White immigrants made up nearly 400,000 of the increased number, and black "forced immigrants" accounted for almost as many again. But most of the spurt stemmed from the remarkable natural fertility of all Americans, white and black. To the amazement and dismay of Europeans, the colonists were doubling their numbers every twenty-five years. Unfriendly Dr. Samuel Johnson, back in England, growled that the Americans were multiplying like their own rattlesnakes. They were also a youthful people, whose average age in 1775 was about sixteen.

This population boom had political consequences. In 1700 there were twenty English subjects for each American colonist. By 1775 the English advantage in numbers had fallen to three to one—setting the stage for a momentous shift in the balance of power between the colonies and Britain.

The bulk of the population was cooped up east of the Alleghenies, although by 1775 a vanguard of pioneers had trickled into the stump-studded clearings of Tennessee and Kentucky. The most populous colonies in 1775 were Virginia, Massachusetts, Pennsylvania, North Carolina, and Maryland—in that order. Only four communities could properly be called cities: Philadelphia, including suburbs, was first with about 34,000 residents, trailed by New York, Boston, and Charleston. About 90 percent of the people lived in rural areas.

A Mingling of the Races

Colonial America was a melting pot and had been from the outset. The population, although basically English in stock and language, was picturesquely mottled with numerous foreign groups.

Heavy-accented Germans constituted about 6 percent of the total population, or 150,000, by 1775. Fleeing religious persecution, economic oppression, and the ravages of war, they had flocked to America in the early 1700s and had settled chiefly in Pennsylvania. They belonged to several different Protestant sects—primarily Lutheran—and thus further enhanced the religious diversity of the colony. Known popularly but erroneously as the Pennsylvania Dutch (a corruption of the German word *Deutsch,* for "German"), they totaled about one-third of the colony's population. In parts of Philadelphia, the street signs were painted in both German and English.

These German newcomers moved into the backcountry of Pennsylvania, where their splendid stone barns gave—and still give—mute evidence of industry and prosperity. Not having been brought up English, they had no deep-rooted loyalty to the British crown, and they clung tenaciously to their German language and customs.

The Scots-Irish (see "Makers of America: The Scots-Irish," pp. 86–87), who in 1775 numbered about 175,000, or 7 percent of the population, were an important non-English group, although they spoke English. They were not Irish at all, but turbulent Scots Lowlanders. Over many decades, though, they had been transplanted to northern Ireland, where they had not prospered. The Irish Catholics already there, hating Scottish Presbyterianism, resented the intruders and still do. The economic life of the Scots-Irish was severely hampered, especially when the English government placed burdensome restrictions on their production of linens and woolens.

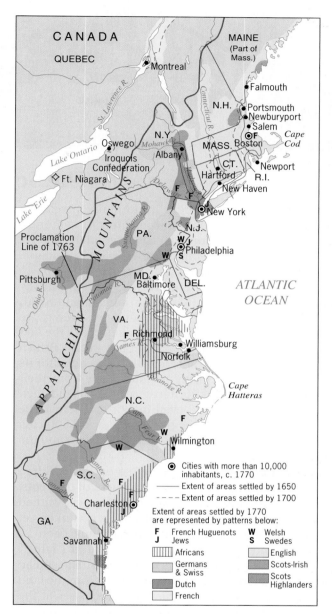

Immigrant Groups in 1775 America was already a nation of diverse nationalities in the colonial period. This map shows the great variety of immigrant groups, especially in Pennsylvania and New York. It also illustrates the tendency of later arrivals, particularly the Scots-Irish, to push into the backcountry.

Early in the 1700s, tens of thousands of embittered Scots-Irish finally abandoned Ireland and came to America, chiefly to tolerant and deep-soiled Pennsylvania. Finding the best acres already taken by Germans

The Scots-Irish

As the British Empire spread its dominion across the seas in the seventeenth and eighteenth centuries, great masses of people poured forth to populate its ever-widening realms. Their migration unfolded in stages. They journeyed from farms to towns, from towns to great cities like London and Bristol, and eventually from the seaports to Ireland, the Caribbean, and North America. Among these intrepid wanderers, few were more restless than the Scots-Irish, the settlers of the first American West. Never feeling at home in the British Empire, these perennial outsiders always headed for its most distant outposts. They migrated first from their native Scottish lowlands to northern Ireland and then on to the New World. And even in North America, the Scots-Irish remained on the periphery, ever distancing themselves from the reach of the English crown and the Anglican Church.

Poverty weighed heavily on the Scottish Lowlands in the 1600s; one observer winced at the sight of the Scots, with "their hovels most miserable, made of poles, wattled and covered with thin sods," their bodies shrunken yet swollen with hunger. But Scotland had long been an unyielding land, and it was not simply nature's stinginess that drove the Lowlanders to the ports. The spread of commercial farming forced many Scots from the land and subjected others to merciless rent increases at the hands of the landowning *lairds* (lords)—a practice called rack-renting. Adding insult to injury, the British authorities persecuted the Presbyterian Scots, squeezing taxes from their barren purses to support the hated Anglican Church.

Not surprisingly, then, some 200,000 Scots immigrated to neighboring Ireland in the 1600s. So great was the exodus that Protestant Scots eventually outnumbered Catholic natives in the several northern Irish counties that compose the province of Ulster. Still, Ireland offered only slender and temporary relief to many Scots. Although the north was prosperous compared with the rest of that unhappy nation, making a living was still devilishly hard in Ireland. Soon the Scots discovered that their migration had not freed them from their ancient woes. Their Irish landlords, with British connivance, racked rents just as ferociously as their Scottish *lairds* had done. Under such punishing pressure, waves of these already once-transplanted Scots, now called Scots-Irish, fled yet again across the sea throughout the 1700s. This time their destination was America.

Most debarked in Pennsylvania, seeking the religious tolerance and abundant land of William Penn's commonwealth. But these unquiet people did not stay put for long. They fanned out from Philadelphia into the farmlands of western Pennsylvania. Blocked temporarily by the Allegheny Mountains, these early pioneers then trickled south along the backbone of the Appalachian

This Scottish Presbyterian Church, built in 1794, still stands in Alexandria, Virginia.

This British advertisement of 1738 urged Scots-Irish Protestants to settle in colonial New York.

Georgia governor James Oglethorpe, in Scottish attire, visits Scottish settlers at New Inverness, Georgia.

range, slowly filling the backcountry of Virginia, the Carolinas, and Georgia. There they built farms and towns, and these rickety settlements bore the marks of Scots-Irish restlessness. Whereas their German neighbors typically erected sturdy homes and cleared their fields meticulously, the Scots-Irish satisfied themselves with floorless, flimsy log cabins; they chopped down trees, planted crops between the stumps, exhausted the soil fast, and moved on.

Almost every Scots-Irish community, however isolated or impermanent, maintained a Presbyterian church. Religion was the bond that yoked these otherwise fiercely independent folk. In backcountry towns, churches were erected before law courts, and clerics were pounding their pulpits before civil authorities had the chance to raise their gavels. In many such cases, the local religious court, known as the session, passed judgment on crimes like burglary and trespassing as well as on moral and theological questions. But the Scots-Irish, despite their intense faith, were no theocrats, no advocates of religious rule. Their bitter struggles with the Anglican Church made them stubborn opponents of established churches in the United States, just as their seething resentment against the king of England ensured that the Scots-Irish would be well represented among the Patriots in the American Revolution.

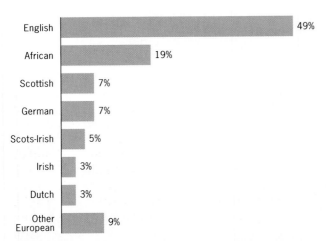

Ethnic and Racial Composition of the American People, 1790 Based on surnames. (Source: Adapted from the American Council of Learned Societies, "Report of Committee on Linguistic and National Stocks in the Population of the United States," 1932. Percentages total more than 100 percent due to rounding.)

and Quakers, they pushed out onto the frontier. There many of them illegally but defiantly squatted on unoccupied lands and quarreled with both Indian and white owners. When the westward-flowing Scots-Irish tide lapped up against the Allegheny barrier, it was deflected southward into the backcountry of Maryland, down Virginia's Shenandoah Valley, and into the western Carolinas. Already experienced colonizers and agitators

> *The young Frenchman Michel-Guillaume Jean de Crèvecoeur (1735–1813) wrote of the diverse population in about 1770:*
>
> "They are a mixture of English, Scotch, Irish, French, Dutch, Germans, and Swedes. From this promiscuous breed, that race now called Americans have arisen. . . . I could point out to you a family whose grandfather was an Englishman, whose wife was Dutch, whose son married a French woman, and whose present four sons have now four wives of different nations."

in Ireland, the Scots-Irish proved to be superb frontiersmen, though their readiness to visit violence on the Indians repeatedly inflamed the western districts. By the mid-eighteenth century, a chain of Scots-Irish settlements lay scattered along the "great wagon road," which hugged the eastern Appalachian foothills from Pennsylvania to Georgia.

It was said, somewhat unfairly, that the Scots-Irish kept the Sabbath—and all else they could lay their hands on. Pugnacious, lawless, and individualistic, they brought with them the Scottish secrets of whiskey distilling and dotted the Appalachian hills and hollows with their stills. They cherished no love for the British government that had uprooted them and still lorded over them—or for any other government, it seemed. They led the armed march of the Paxton Boys on Philadelphia in 1764, protesting the Quaker oligarchy's lenient policy toward the Indians, and a few years later spearheaded the Regulator movement in North Carolina, a small but nasty insurrection against eastern domination of the colony's affairs. Many of these hotheads—including the young Andrew Jackson—eventually joined the embattled American revolutionaries. All told, about a dozen future presidents were of Scots-Irish descent.

Approximately 5 percent of the multicolored colonial population consisted of other European groups. These embraced French Huguenots, Welsh, Dutch, Swedes, Jews, Irish, Swiss, and Scots Highlanders—as distinguished from the Scots-Irish. Except for the Scots Highlanders, such hodgepodge elements felt little loyalty to the British crown. By far the largest single non-English group was African, accounting for nearly 20 percent of the colonial population in 1775 and heavily concentrated in the South.

The population of the thirteen colonies, though mainly Anglo-Saxon, was perhaps the most mixed to be found anywhere in the world. The South, holding about 90 percent of the slaves, already displayed its historic black-and-white racial composition. New England, mostly staked out by the original Puritan migrants, showed the least ethnic diversity. The middle colonies, especially Pennsylvania, received the bulk of later white immigrants and boasted an astonishing variety of peoples. Outside of New England, about one-half the population was non-English in 1775. Of the fifty-six signers of the Declaration of Independence in 1776, eighteen were non-English and eight had not been born in the colonies.

As these various immigrant groups mingled and intermarried, they laid the foundations for a new multi-

A South Carolina Advertisement for Slaves in the 1760s   Note the reference to these slaves' origin on West Africa's "Rice Coast," a reminder of South Carolina's reliance on African skill and labor for rice cultivation. Note, too, that half the slaves were said to have survived smallpox and thus acquired immunity from further infection—and that care had been taken to insulate the others from a smallpox epidemic apparently then raging in Charleston.

The Structure of Colonial Society

In comparison to contemporary Europe, eighteenth-century America seemed like a shining land of equality and opportunity—with the notorious exception of slavery. No titled nobility dominated society from on high, and no pauperized underclass threatened it from below. Most white Americans, and even a handful of free blacks, were small farmers. Clad in buckskin breeches, they owned modest holdings and tilled them with their own hands and horses. The cities contained a small class of skilled artisans, with their well-greased leather aprons, as well as shopkeepers, tradespeople, and some unskilled day laborers. The most remarkable feature of the social ladder was its openness. An ambitious colonist, even a former indentured servant, could rise from a lower rung to a higher one, a rare step in old England.

Yet in contrast with seventeenth-century America, colonial society on the eve of the Revolution was beginning to show signs of stratification and barriers to mobility that raised worries about the "Europeanization" of America. The gods of war contributed to these developments. The armed conflicts of the 1690s and early 1700s had enriched a number of merchant princes in the New England and middle colonies. They laid the foundations of their fortunes with profits made as military suppliers. Roosting regally atop the social ladder, these elites now feathered their nests more finely. They sported imported clothing and dined at tables laid with English china and gleaming silverware. Prominent individuals came to be seated in churches and schools according to their social rank. By midcentury the richest 10 percent of Bostonians and Philadelphians owned nearly two-thirds of the taxable wealth in their cities.

The plague of war also created a class of widows and orphans, who became dependent for their survival on charity. Both Philadelphia and New York built almshouses in the 1730s to care for the destitute. Yet the numbers of poor people remained tiny compared to the numbers in England, where about a third of the population lived in impoverished squalor.

In the New England countryside, the descendants of the original settlers faced more limited prospects than had their pioneering forebears. As the supply of unclaimed soil dwindled and families grew, existing landholdings were repeatedly subdivided. The average

cultural American national identity unlike anything known in Europe. The French settler Michel-Guillaume de Crèvecoeur saw in America in the 1770s a "strange mixture of blood, which you will find in no other country," and he posed his classic question, "What then is the American, this new man?" Nor were white colonists alone in creating new societies out of diverse ethnic groups. The African slave trade long had mixed peoples from many different tribal backgrounds, giving birth to an African *American* community far more variegated in its cultural origins than anything to be found in Africa itself. Similarly, in the New England "praying towns," where Indians were gathered to be Christianized, and in Great Lakes villages such as Detroit, home to dozens of different displaced indigenous peoples, polyglot Native American communities emerged, blurring the boundaries of individual tribal identities.

size of farms shrank drastically. Younger sons, as well as daughters, were forced to hire out as wage laborers, or eventually to seek virgin tracts of land beyond the Alleghenies. By 1750 Boston contained a large number of homeless poor, who were supported by public charity and compelled to wear a large red "P" on their clothing.

In the South the power of the great planters continued to be bolstered by their disproportionate ownership of slaves. The riches created by the growing slave population in the eighteenth century were not distributed evenly among the whites. Wealth was concentrated in the hands of the largest slaveowners, widening the gap between the prosperous gentry and the "poor whites," who were more and more likely to become tenant farmers.

In all the colonies, the ranks of the lower classes were further swelled by the continuing stream of indentured servants, many of whom ultimately achieved prosperity and prestige. Two became signers of the Declaration of Independence.

Far less fortunate than the voluntary indentured servants were the paupers and convicts involuntarily shipped to America. Altogether, about fifty thousand "jayle birds" were dumped on the colonies by the London authorities. This riffraff crowd—including robbers, rapists, and murderers—was generally sullen and undesirable, and not bubbling over with goodwill for the king's government. But many convicts were the unfortunate victims of circumstances and of a viciously unfair English penal code that included about two hundred capital crimes. Some of the deportees, in fact, came to be highly respectable citizens.

Least fortunate of all, of course, were the black slaves. They enjoyed no equality with whites and dared not even dream of ascending, or even approaching, the ladder of opportunity. Oppressed and downtrodden, the slaves were America's closest approximation to Europe's volatile lower classes, and fears of black rebellion plagued the white colonists. Some colonial legislatures, notably South Carolina's in 1760, sensed the dangers present in a heavy concentration of resentful slaves and attempted to restrict or halt their importation. But the British authorities, seeking to preserve the supply of cheap labor for the colonies, especially the West Indies sugar plantations, repeatedly vetoed all efforts to stem the transatlantic traffic in slaves. Many North American colonists condemned these vetoes as morally callous, although New England slave traders benefited handsomely from the British policy. The cruel complexity of the slavery issue was further revealed when Thomas Jefferson, himself a slaveholder, assailed the British vetoes in an early draft of the Declaration of Independence, but was forced to withdraw the proposed clause by a torrent of protest from southern slavemasters.

Clerics, Physicians, and Jurists

Most honored of the professions was the Christian ministry. In 1775 the clergy wielded less influence than in the early days of Massachusetts, when piety had burned more warmly. But they still occupied a position of high prestige.

Most physicians, on the other hand, were poorly trained and not highly esteemed. Not until 1765 was the first medical school established, although European centers attracted some students. Aspiring young doctors served for a while as apprentices to older practitioners and were then turned loose on their "victims." Bleeding was a favorite and frequently fatal remedy; when the physician was not available, a barber was often summoned.

Epidemics were a constant nightmare. Especially dreaded was smallpox, which afflicted one out of five persons, including the heavily pockmarked George Washington. A crude form of inoculation was introduced in 1721, despite the objections of many physicians and some of the clergy, who opposed tampering with the will

Cotton Mather (1663–1728), Puritan clergyman and avid scientist, became frustrated with Boston residents' opposition to inoculation during the Boston smallpox epidemic of 1721. He wrote to a doctor friend,

"Never till now was that rule contested, of two evils, choose the least. . . . I would ask them whether it be not a most criminal ingratitude unto the God of Health, when He has acquainted us with a most invaluable method of the saving of our lives from so great a death, to treat with neglect and contempt, and multiply abuses on them who thankfully and in a spirit of obedience to Him, embrace His blessings?"

of God. Powdered dried toad was a favorite prescription for smallpox. Diphtheria was also a deadly killer, especially of young people. One epidemic in the 1730s took the lives of thousands. This grim reminder of their mortality may have helped to prepare many colonists in their hearts and minds for the religious revival that was soon to sweep them up.

At first the law profession was not favorably regarded. In this pioneering society, which required much honest manual labor, the parties to a dispute often presented their own cases in court. Lawyers were commonly regarded as noisy windbags or troublemaking rogues; an early Connecticut law classed them with drunkards and brothel keepers. When future president John Adams was a young law student, the father of his wife-to-be frowned upon him as a suitor.

Workaday America

Agriculture was the leading industry, involving about 90 percent of the people. Tobacco continued to be the staple crop in Maryland and Virginia, though wheat cultivation also spread through the Chesapeake, often on lands depleted by the overgrowth of tobacco. The fertile middle ("bread") colonies produced large quantities of grain, and by 1759 New York alone was exporting eighty thousand barrels of flour a year. Seemingly the farmer had only to tickle the soil with a hoe, and it would laugh with a harvest. Overall, Americans probably enjoyed a higher standard of living than the masses of any country in history up to that time.

Codfishing in Newfoundland, c. 1760   Early European explorers were awed by the enormous schools of cod on the Grand Banks offshore of Newfoundland. Fish were so numerous that they sometimes impeded the progress of sailing vessels. By the eighteenth century, New Englanders were aggressively exploiting the apparently limitless Grand Banks fishery, drying and salting huge catches for export to Europe and the West Indies. Two centuries later the accumulated predation of generations of overfishing threatened to extinguish the once-fabulous Grand Banks cod population.

Fishing (including whaling), though ranking far below agriculture, was rewarding. Pursued in all the American colonies, this harvesting of the sea was a major industry in New England, which exported smelly shiploads of dried cod to the Catholic countries of Europe. The fishing fleet also stimulated shipbuilding and served as a nursery for the seamen who manned the navy and merchant marine.

A bustling commerce, both coastwise and overseas, enriched all the colonies, especially the New England group, New York, and Pennsylvania. Commercial ventures and land speculation, in the absence of later get-rich-quick schemes, were the surest avenues to speedy wealth. Yankee seamen were famous in many climes not only as skilled mariners but as tightfisted traders. They provisioned the Caribbean sugar islands with food and forest products. They hauled Spanish and Portuguese gold, wine, and oranges to London, to be exchanged for industrial goods, which were then sold for a juicy profit in America.

The so-called triangular trade was infamously profitable, though small in relation to total colonial commerce. A skipper, for example, would leave a New England port with a cargo of rum and sail to the Gold Coast of Africa. Bartering the fiery liquor with African chiefs for captured African slaves, he would proceed to the West Indies with his sobbing and suffocating cargo sardined below deck. There he would exchange the survivors for molasses, which he would then carry to New England, where it would be distilled into rum. He would then repeat the trip, making a handsome profit on each leg of the triangle.

Manufacturing in the colonies was of only secondary importance, although there was a surprising variety of small enterprises. As a rule, workers could get ahead faster in soil-rich America by tilling the land. Huge quantities of "kill devil" rum were distilled in Rhode Island and Massachusetts, and even some of the "elect of the Lord" developed an overfondness for it. Handsome beaver hats were manufactured in quantity, despite British restrictions. Smoking iron forges, including Pennsylvania's Valley Forge, likewise dotted the land and in fact were more numerous in 1775, though generally smaller, than those of England. In addition, household manufacturing, including spinning and weaving by women, added up to an impressive output. As in all pioneering countries, strong-backed laborers and skilled craftspeople were scarce and highly prized. In early

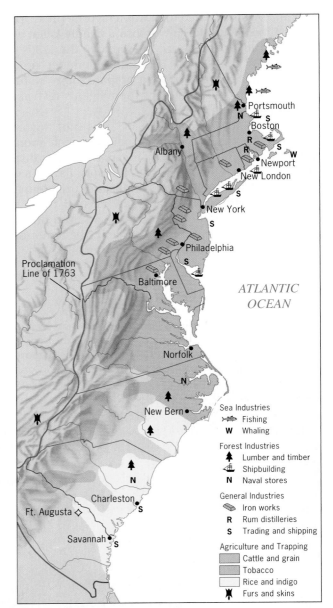

The Colonial Economy   By the eighteenth century, the various colonial regions had distinct economic identities. The northern colonies grew grain and raised cattle, harvested timber and fish, and built ships. The Chesapeake colonies and North Carolina were still heavily dependent on tobacco, whereas the southernmost colonies grew mostly rice and indigo. Cotton, so important to the southern economy in the nineteenth century, had not yet emerged as a major crop.

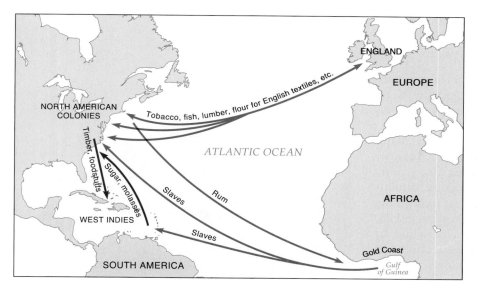

Colonial Trade Patterns, c. 1770
Future president John Adams noted about this time that "the commerce of the West Indies is a part of the American system of commerce. They can neither do without us, nor we without them. The Creator has placed us upon the globe in such a situation that we have occasion for each other."

Virginia a carpenter who had committed a murder was freed because his woodworking skills were needed.

Lumbering was perhaps the most important single manufacturing activity. Countless cartloads of fresh-felled timber were consumed by shipbuilders, at first chiefly in New England and then elsewhere in the colonies. By 1770 about four hundred vessels of assorted sizes were splashing down the ways each year, and about one-third of the British merchant marine was American-built.

Colonial naval stores—such as tar, pitch, rosin, and turpentine—were highly valued, for Britain was anxious to gain and retain a mastery of the seas. London offered generous bounties to stimulate production of these items; otherwise Britain would have had to turn to the uncertain and possibly hostile Baltic areas. Towering trees, ideal as masts for His Majesty's navy, were marked with the king's broad arrow for future use. The luckless colonist who was caught cutting down this reserved timber was subject to a fine. Even though there were countless unreserved trees and the blazed ones were being saved for the common defense, this shackle on free enterprise engendered considerable bitterness.

Americans held an important flank of a thriving, many-sided Atlantic economy by the dawn of the eighteenth century. Yet strains appeared in this complex network as early as the 1730s. Fast-breeding Americans demanded more and more British products—yet the slow-growing British population early reached the saturation point for absorbing imports from America. This trade imbalance raised a question: how could the colonists sell the goods to make the money to buy what they wanted in Britain? The answer was obvious: by seeking foreign (non-British) markets.

By the eve of the Revolution, the bulk of Chesapeake tobacco was filling pipes in France and in other European countries, though it passed through the hands of British re-exporters, who took a slice of the profits for themselves. More important was the trade with the West Indies, especially the French islands. West Indian purchases of North American timber and foodstuffs provided the crucial cash for the colonists to continue to make their own purchases in Britain. But in 1733, bowing to pressure from influential *British* West Indian planters, Parliament passed the Molasses Act, aimed at squelching North American trade with the *French* West Indies. If successful, this scheme would have struck a crippling blow to American international trade and to the colonists' standard of living. American merchants responded to the act by bribing and smuggling their way around the law. Thus was foreshadowed the impending imperial crisis, when headstrong Americans would revolt rather than submit to the dictates of the far-off Parliament, apparently bent on destroying their very livelihood.

Horsepower and Sailpower

All sprawling and sparsely populated pioneer communities are cursed with oppressive problems of transportation. America, with a scarcity of both money and workers, was no exception.

Not until the 1700s did roads connect even the major cities, and these dirt thoroughfares were treacherously deficient. A wayfarer could have rumbled along more rapidly over the Roman highways in the days of Julius Caesar, nearly two thousand years earlier. It took young Benjamin Franklin nine long, rain-drenched days in 1720 to journey from Boston to Philadelphia, traveling by sailing sloop, rowboat, and foot. News of the Declaration of Independence in 1776 reached Charleston from Philadelphia twenty-nine days after the Fourth of July.

Roads were often clouds of dust in the summer and quagmires of mud in the winter. Stagecoach travelers braved such additional dangers as tree-strewn roads, rickety bridges, carriage overturns, and runaway horses. A traveler venturesome enough to journey from Philadelphia to New York, for example, would not think it amiss to make a will and pray with the family before departing.

Where man-made roads were wretched, heavy reliance was placed on God-grooved waterways. Population tended to cluster along the banks of navigable rivers. There was also much coastwise traffic, and although it was slow and undependable, it was relatively cheap and pleasant.

Taverns sprang up along the main routes of travel, as well as in the cities. Their attractions customarily included such amusements as bowling alleys, pool tables, bars, and gambling equipment. Before a cheerful, roaring log fire, all social classes would mingle, including the village loafers and drunks. The tavern was yet another cradle of democracy.

Gossips also gathered at the taverns, which were clearinghouses of information, misinformation, and rumor—frequently stimulated by alcoholic refreshment and impassioned political talk. A successful politician, like the wire-pulling Samuel Adams, was often a man who had a large alehouse fraternity in places like Boston's Green Dragon Tavern. Taverns were important in crystallizing public opinion and proved to be hotbeds of agitation as the revolutionary movement gathered momentum.

An intercolonial postal system was established by the mid-1700s, although private couriers remained. Some mail was handled on credit. Service was slow and infrequent, and secrecy was problematic. Mail carriers,

Sign of the Pine Tree Inn, 1768 Inns like Joseph Read III's in Lisbon, Connecticut not only provided food, drink, shelter, and entertainment for colonial Americans but were also raucous arenas for debating political issues. This sign, with its yellow, circular orb (sun) over a pine tree, may have been intended as a veiled reference to the Sons of Liberty, an extra-legal resistance organization that had adopted as its symbol the Liberty Tree. The date of 1768 coincided with the British enactment of the Townshend Acts, which ignited a new wave of colonial resistance to British rule.

Estimated Religious Census, 1775

Name	Number	Chief Locale
Congregationalists	575,000	New England
Anglicans	500,000	N.Y., South
Presbyterians	410,000	Frontier
German churches (incl. Lutheran)	200,000	Pa.
Dutch Reformed	75,000	N.Y., N.J.
Quakers	40,000	Pa., N.J., Del.
Baptists	25,000	R.I., Pa., N.J., Del.
Roman Catholics	25,000	Md., Pa.
Methodists	5,000	Scattered
Jews	2,000	N.Y., R.I.
EST. TOTAL MEMBERSHIP	1,857,000	
EST. TOTAL POPULATION	2,493,000	
PERCENTAGE CHURCH MEMBERS	74%	

serving long routes, would sometimes pass the time by reading the letters entrusted to their care.

Dominant Denominations

Two "established," or tax-supported, churches were conspicuous in 1775: the Anglican and the Congregational. A considerable segment of the population, surprisingly enough, did not worship in any church. And in those colonies that maintained an "established" religion, only a minority of the people belonged to it.

The Church of England, whose members were commonly called Anglicans, became the official faith in Georgia, North and South Carolina, Virginia, Maryland, and a part of New York. Established also in England, it served in America as a major prop of kingly authority. British officials naturally made vigorous attempts to impose it on additional colonies, but they ran into a stone wall of opposition.

In America the Anglican Church fell distressingly short of its promise. Secure and self-satisfied, like its parent in England, it clung to a faith that was less fierce and more worldly than the religion of Puritanical New England. Sermons were shorter; hell was less scorching;

and amusements, like Virginia fox hunting, were less scorned. So dismal was the reputation of the Anglican clergy in seventeenth-century Virginia that the College of William and Mary was founded in 1693 to train a better class of clerics.

The influential Congregational Church, which had grown out of the Puritan Church, was formally established in all the New England colonies, except independent-minded Rhode Island. At first Massachusetts taxed all residents to support Congregationalism but later relented and exempted members of other well-known denominations. Presbyterianism, though closely associated with Congregationalism, was never made official in any colonies.

Ministers of the gospel, turning from the Bible to this sinful world, increasingly grappled with burning political issues. As the early rumblings of revolution against the British crown could be heard, sedition flowed freely from pulpits. Presbyterianism, Congregationalism, and rebellion became a neo-trinity. Many leading Anglican clergymen, aware of which side their tax-provided bread was buttered on, naturally supported their king.

Established (Tax-Supported) Churches in the Colonies, 1775*

Colonies	Churches	Year Disestablished
Mass. (incl. Me.)	Congregational	1833
Connecticut		1818
New Hampshire		1819
New York	Anglican (in N.Y. City and three neighboring counties)	1777
Maryland	Anglican	1777
Virginia		1786
North Carolina		1776
South Carolina		1778
Georgia		1777
Rhode Island	None	
New Jersey		
Delaware		
Pennsylvania		

*Note the persistence of the Congregational establishment in New England.

> *Benjamin Franklin's (1706–1790)* Poor
> Richard's Almanack *contained such
> thoughts on religion as these:*
>
> "A good example is the best sermon."
>
> "Many have quarreled about religion
> that never practiced it."
>
> "Serving God is doing good to man, but
> praying is thought an easier service,
> and therefore more generally chosen."
>
> "How many observe Christ's birthday;
> how few his precepts! O! 'tis easier to
> keep holidays than commandments."

Anglicans in the New World were seriously handicapped by not having a resident bishop, whose presence would be convenient for the ordination of young ministers. American students of Anglican theology had to travel to England to be ordained. On the eve of the Revolution, there was serious talk of creating an American bishopric, but the scheme was violently opposed by many non-Anglicans, who feared a tightening of the royal reins. This controversy poured holy oil on the smoldering fires of rebellion.

Religious toleration had indeed made enormous strides in America, at least when compared with its halting steps abroad. Roman Catholics were still generally discriminated against, as in England, even in officeholding. But there were fewer Catholics in America, and hence the anti-papist laws were less severe and less strictly enforced. In general, people could worship—or not worship—as they pleased.

The Great Awakening

In all the colonial churches, religion was less fervid in the early eighteenth century than it had been a century earlier, when the colonies were first planted. The Puritan churches in particular sagged under the weight of two burdens: their elaborate theological doctrines and their compromising efforts to liberalize membership requirements. Churchgoers increasingly complained about the "dead dogs" who droned out tedious, over-

erudite sermons from Puritan pulpits. Some ministers, on the other hand, worried that many of their parishioners had gone soft and that their souls were no longer kindled by the hellfire of orthodox Calvinism. Liberal ideas began to challenge the old-time religion. Some worshipers now proclaimed that human beings were not necessarily predestined to damnation and might save themselves by good works. Even more threatening to the Calvinist doctrine of predestination were the doctrines of the Arminians, followers of the Dutch theologian Jacobus Arminius, who preached that individual free will, not divine decree, determined a person's eternal fate. Pressured by these "heresies," a few churches grudgingly conceded that spiritual conversion was not necessary for church membership. Together, these twin trends toward clerical intellectualism and lay liberalism were sapping the spiritual vitality from many denominations.

The stage was thus set for a rousing religious revival. Known as the Great Awakening, it exploded in the 1730s and 1740s and swept through the colonies like a fire through prairie grass. The Awakening was first ignited in Northampton, Massachusetts, by a tall, delicate, and intellectual pastor, Jonathan Edwards. Perhaps the deepest theological mind ever nurtured in America, Edwards proclaimed with burning righteousness the folly of believing in salvation through good works and affirmed the need for complete dependence on God's

George Whitefield Preaching   Americans of both genders and all races and regions were spellbound by Whitefield's emotive oratory.

grace. Warming to his subject, he painted in lurid detail the landscape of hell and the eternal torments of the damned. "Sinners in the Hands of an Angry God" was the title of one of his most famous sermons. He believed that hell was "paved with the skulls of unbaptized children."

Edwards's preaching style was learned and closely reasoned, but his stark doctrines sparked a warmly sympathetic reaction among his parishioners in 1734. Four years later the itinerant English parson George Whitefield loosed a different style of evangelical preaching on America and touched off a conflagration of religious ardor that revolutionized the spiritual life of the colonies. A former alehouse attendant, Whitefield was an orator of rare gifts. His magnificent voice boomed sonorously over thousands of enthralled listeners in an open field. One of England's greatest actors of the day commented enviously that Whitefield could make audiences weep merely by pronouncing the word *Mesopotamia* and that he would "give a hundred guineas if I could only say 'O!' like Mr. Whitefield."

Triumphally touring the colonies, Whitefield trumpeted his message of human helplessness and divine omnipotence. His eloquence reduced Jonathan Edwards to tears and even caused the skeptical and thrifty Benjamin Franklin to empty his pockets into the collection plate. During these roaring revival meetings, countless sinners professed conversion, and hundreds of the "saved" groaned, shrieked, or rolled in the snow from religious excitation. Whitefield soon inspired American imitators. Taking up his electrifying new style of preaching, they heaped abuse on sinners and shook enormous audiences with emotional appeals. One preacher cackled hideously in the face of hapless wrongdoers. Another, naked to the waist, leaped frantically about in the light of flickering torches.

Orthodox clergymen, known as "old lights," were deeply skeptical of the emotionalism and the theatrical antics of the revivalists. "New light" ministers, on the other hand, defended the Awakening for its role in revitalizing American religion. Congregationalists and Presbyterians split over this issue, and many of the believers in religious conversion went over to the Baptists and other sects more prepared to make room for emotion in religion. The Awakening left many lasting effects. Its emphasis on direct, emotive spirituality seriously undermined the older clergy, whose authority had derived from their education and erudition. The schisms it set off in many denominations greatly increased the number and the competitiveness of American churches. It encouraged a fresh wave of missionary work among the Indians and even among black slaves, many of whom also attended the mass open-air revivals. It led to the founding of "new light" centers of higher learning such as Princeton, Brown, Rutgers, and Dartmouth. Perhaps most significant, the Great Awakening was the first spontaneous mass movement of the American people. It tended to break down sectional boundaries as well as denominational lines and contributed to the growing sense that Americans had of themselves as a single people, united by a common history and shared experiences.

Schools and Colleges

A time-honored English idea regarded education as a blessing reserved for the aristocratic few, not for the unwashed many. Education should be for leadership, not citizenship, and primarily for males. Only slowly and painfully did the colonists break the chains of these ancient restrictions.

Puritan New England, largely for religious reasons, was more zealously interested in education than any other section. Dominated by the Congregational Church, it stressed the need for Bible reading by the individual worshiper. The primary goal of the clergy was to make good Christians rather than good citizens. A more secular approach was evident late in the eighteenth century, when some children were warned in the following verse:

> *He who ne'er learns his A.B.C.*
> *Forever will a blockhead be.*
> *But he who learns his letters fair*
> *Shall have a coach to take the air.*

Jonathan Edwards (1703–1758) preached hellfire, notably in one famous sermon:

"The God that holds you over the pit of hell, much as one holds a spider or some loathsome insect over the fire, abhors you, and is dreadfully provoked. His wrath toward you burns like fire; he looks upon you as worthy of nothing else but to be cast into the fire."

John Adams (c. 1736–1826) the future second president, wrote to his wife:

"The education of our children is never out of my mind. . . . I must study politics and war that my sons may have the liberty to study mathematics and philosophy. My sons ought to study mathematics and philosophy, geography, natural history, naval architecture, navigation, commerce, and agriculture, in order to give their children a right to study painting, poetry, music, architecture, statuary, tapestry, and porcelain."

Education, principally for boys, flourished almost from the outset in New England. This densely populated region boasted an impressive number of graduates from the English universities, especially Cambridge, the intellectual center of England's Puritanism. New Englanders, at a relatively early date, established primary and secondary schools, which varied widely in the quality of instruction and in the length of time that their doors remained open each year. Back-straining farm labor drained much of a youth's time and energy.

Fairly adequate elementary schools were also hammering knowledge into the heads of reluctant "scholars" in the middle colonies and in the South. Some of these institutions were tax-supported; others were privately operated. The South, with its white and black population diffused over wide areas, was severely handicapped by logistics in attempting to establish an effective school system. Wealthy families leaned heavily on private tutors.

The general atmosphere in the colonial schools and colleges continued grim and gloomy. Most of the emphasis was placed on religion and on the classical languages, Latin and Greek. The focus was not on experiment and reason, but on doctrine and dogma. The age was one of orthodoxy, and independence of thinking was discouraged. Discipline was quite severe, with many a mischievous child being sadistically "birched" with a switch cut from a birch tree. Sometimes punishment was inflicted by indentured-servant teachers, who could themselves be whipped for their failures as workers and who therefore were not inclined to spare the rod.

College education—at least at first in New England—was geared toward preparing men for the ministry. After all, churches would wither if a new crop of ministers was not adequately trained to lead the region's spiritual flocks. Annoyed by this exclusively religious emphasis, many well-to-do families, especially in the South, sent their boys abroad to acquire a "real"—meaning a refined and philosophical—education in elite English institutions.

For purposes of convenience and economy, nine local colleges were established during the colonial era. Student enrollments were small, numbering about 200 boys at the most; and at one time a few lads as young as eleven were admitted to Harvard. Instruction was poor by present-day standards. The curriculum was still

Colonial Colleges

Name	Original Name (If Different)	Location	Opened or Founded	Denomination
1. Harvard		Cambridge, Mass.	1636	Congregational
2. William and Mary		Williamsburg, Va.	1693	Anglican
3. Yale		New Haven, Conn.	1701	Congregational
4. Princeton	College of New Jersey	Princeton, N.J.	1746	Presbyterian
5. Pennsylvania	The Academy	Philadelphia, Pa.	1751	Nonsectarian
6. Columbia	King's College	New York, N.Y.	1754	Anglican
7. Brown	Rhode Island College	Providence, R.I.	1764	Baptist
8. Rutgers	Queen's College	New Brunswick, N.J.	1766	Dutch Reformed
9. Dartmouth (begun as an Indian missionary school)		Hanover, N.H.	1769	Congregational

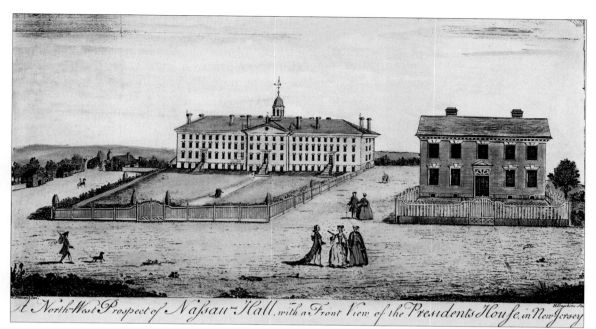

A North-West Prospect of Nassau-Hall, with a Front View of the Presidents House, in New-Jersey

The College of New Jersey at Princeton, 1764   Later known as Princeton University, it was chartered in 1746 by the Presbyterian Synod, though open to students of all religious persuasions. The fourth college to be founded in British North America, it met in Elizabeth and Newark, New Jersey, until a gift of ten acres of land precipitated a move to Princeton in 1756. All classes were held in the large building, Nassau Hall. Here the Continental Congress met for three months during the summer of 1783, making Princeton for a short time the capital of the nation. This copper engraving, based on a drawing by one of Princeton's earliest students, was part of a series of college views that reflected colonial Americans' growing pride in institutions of higher learning.

heavily loaded with theology and the "dead" languages, although by 1750 there was a distinct trend toward "live" languages and other modern subjects. A significant contribution was made by Benjamin Franklin, who played a major role in launching what became the University of Pennsylvania, the first American college free from denominational control.

A Provincial Culture

When it came to art and culture, colonial Americans were still in thrall to European tastes, especially British. The simplicity of pioneering life had not yet bred many homespun patrons of the arts. One aspiring painter, John Trumbull (1756–1843) of Connecticut, was discouraged in his youth by his father's chilling remark, "Connecticut is not Athens." Like so many of his talented artistic contemporaries, Trumbull was forced to travel to London to pursue his ambitions. Charles Willson Peale (1741–1827), best known for his portraits of George Washington, ran a museum, stuffed birds, and practiced dentistry. Gifted Benjamin West (1738–1820) and precocious John Singleton Copley (1738–1815) succeeded in their ambition to become famous painters, but like Trumbull they had to go to England to complete their training. Only abroad could they find subjects who had the leisure to sit for their portraits and the money to pay handsomely for them. Copley was regarded as a Loyalist during the Revolutionary War, and West, a close friend of George III and official court painter, was buried in London's St. Paul's Cathedral.

Architecture was largely imported from the Old World and modified to meet the peculiar climatic and religious conditions of the New World. Even the lowly log cabin was apparently borrowed from Sweden. The red-bricked Georgian style, so common in the pre-

Colonial Craftsmanship
In the "Pennsylvania Dutch" country, parents gave daughters painted wooden chests to hold their precious dowry linens at marriage. The horsemen, unicorns, and flower patterns on this dower chest confirm its origins in Berks County, Pennsylvania.

Revolutionary decades, was introduced around 1720 and is best exemplified by the beauty of now-restored Williamsburg, Virginia.

Colonial literature, like art, was generally undistinguished, and for many of the same reasons. One noteworthy exception was the precocious poet Phillis Wheatley (c. 1753–1784), a slave girl brought to Boston at age eight and never formally educated. Taken to England when twenty years of age, she published a book of verse and subsequently wrote other polished poems that revealed the influence of Alexander Pope. Her verse compares favorably with the best of the poetry-poor colonial period, but the remarkable fact is that she could overcome her severely disadvantaged background and write any poetry at all.

Versatile Benjamin Franklin, often called "the first civilized American," also shone as a literary light. Although his autobiography is now a classic, he was best known to his contemporaries for *Poor Richard's Almanack,* which he edited from 1732 to 1758. This famous publication, containing many pithy sayings culled from the thinkers of the ages, emphasized such homespun virtues as thrift, industry, morality, and common sense. Examples are "What maintains one vice would bring up two children"; "Plough deep while sluggards sleep"; "Honesty is the best policy"; and "Fish and visitors stink in three days." *Poor Richard's* was well known in Europe and was more widely read in America than anything except the Bible. Dispensing witty advice to old and young alike, Franklin had an incalculable influence in shaping the American character.

Science, rising above the shackles of superstition, was making some progress, though lagging behind that of the Old World. A few botanists, mathematicians, and astronomers had won some repute, but Benjamin Franklin was perhaps the only first-rank scientist produced in the American colonies. Franklin's spectacular but dangerous experiments, including the famous kite-flying episode proving that lightning was a form of electricity, won him numerous honors in Europe. But his mind also had a practical turn, and among his numerous inventions were bifocal spectacles and the highly efficient Franklin stove. His lightning rod, not surprisingly, was condemned by some stodgy clergymen who felt it was "presuming on God" by attempting to control the "artillery of the heavens."

Pioneer Presses

Stump-grubbing Americans were generally too poor to buy quantities of books and too busy to read them. A South Carolina merchant in 1744 advertised the arrival of a shipment of "printed books, Pictures, Maps, and Pickles." A few private libraries of fair size could be found, especially among the clergy. The Byrd family of Virginia enjoyed perhaps the largest collection in the colonies, consisting of about four thousand volumes. Bustling Benjamin Franklin established in Philadelphia the first privately supported circulating library in America, and by 1776 there were about fifty public libraries and collections supported by subscription.

Hand-operated printing presses cranked out pamphlets, leaflets, and journals. On the eve of the Revolution, there were about forty colonial newspapers, chiefly weeklies that consisted of a single large sheet folded once. Columns ran heavily to somber essays, frequently signed with such pseudonyms as *Cicero, Philosophicus,* and *Pro Bono Publico* ("For the Public Good"). The "news" often lagged many weeks behind the event, especially in the case of overseas happenings, in which the colonists were deeply interested. Newspapers proved to be a powerful agency for airing colonial grievances and rallying opposition to British control.

A celebrated legal case, in 1734–1735, involved John Peter Zenger, a newspaper printer. Significantly, the case arose in New York, reflecting the tumultuous give-and-take of politics in the middle colonies, where so many different ethnic groups jostled against one another. Zenger's newspaper had assailed the corrupt royal governor. Charged with seditious libel, the accused was

"The Magnetic Dispensary," c. 1790 This British painting made sport of the era's faddish preoccupations with electricity. Following Franklin's experiments, static electricity, generated here by the machine on the right, was employed for "medicinal" purposes as well as for tingling entertainments.

hauled into court, where he was defended by a former indentured servant, now a distinguished Philadelphia lawyer, Andrew Hamilton. Zenger argued that he had printed the truth, but the bewigged royal

> *Andrew Hamilton (c. 1676–1741) concluded his eloquent plea in the Zenger case with these words:*
>
> "The question before the court and you, gentlemen of the jury, is not of small nor private concern. It is not the cause of a poor printer, nor of New York alone, which you are now trying. No! It may, in its consequence, affect every freeman that lives under a British government on the main [land] of America. It is the best cause. It is the cause of liberty."

chief justice instructed the jury not to consider the truth or falsity of Zenger's statements; the mere fact of printing, irrespective of the truth, was enough to convict. Hamilton countered that "the very liberty of both exposing and opposing arbitrary power" was at stake. Swayed by his eloquence, the jurors defied the bewigged judges and daringly returned a verdict of not guilty. Cheers burst from the spectators.

The Zenger decision was a banner achievement for freedom of the press and for the health of democracy. It pointed the way to the kind of open public discussion required by the diverse society that colonial New York already was and that all America was to become. Although contrary to existing law and not immediately accepted by other judges and juries, in time it helped establish the doctrine that true statements about public officials could not be prosecuted as libel. Newspapers were thus eventually free to print responsible criticisms of powerful officials, though full freedom of the press was unknown during the pre-Revolutionary era.

The Great Game of Politics

American colonists may have been backward in natural or physical science, but they were making noteworthy contributions to political science.

The thirteen colonial governments took a variety of forms. By 1775 eight of the colonies had royal governors, who were appointed by the king. Three—Maryland, Pennsylvania, and Delaware—were under proprietors who themselves chose the governors. And two—Connecticut and Rhode Island—elected their own governors under self-governing charters.

Practically every colony utilized a two-house legislative body. The upper house, or council, was normally appointed by the crown in the royal colonies and by the proprietor in the proprietary colonies. It was chosen by the voters in the self-governing colonies. The lower house, as the popular branch, was elected by the people—or rather by those who owned enough property to qualify as voters. In several of the colonies, the backcountry elements were seriously underrepresented, and they hated the ruling colonial clique perhaps more than they did kingly authority. Legislatures, in which the people enjoyed direct representation, voted such taxes as they chose for the necessary expenses of colonial government. Self-taxation through representation was a precious privilege that Americans had come to cherish above most others.

Governors appointed by the king were generally able men, sometimes outstanding figures. Some, unfortunately, were incompetent or corrupt—broken-down politicians badly in need of jobs. The worst of the group was probably impoverished Lord Cornbury, first cousin of Queen Anne, who was made governor of New York and New Jersey in 1702. He proved to be a drunkard, a spendthrift, a grafter, an embezzler, a religious bigot, and a vain fool, who was accused (probably inaccurately) of dressing like a woman. Even the best appointees had trouble with the colonial legislatures, basically because the royal governor embodied a bothersome transatlantic authority some three thousand miles away.

The colonial assemblies found various ways to assert their authority and independence. Some of them employed the trick of withholding the governor's salary unless he yielded to their wishes. He was normally in need of money—otherwise he would not have come to this godforsaken country—so the power of the purse usually forced him to terms. But one governor of North Carolina died with his salary eleven years in arrears.

> *Junius, the pseudonym for a critic (or critics) of the British government from 1768 to 1772, published a pointed barb in criticizing one new appointee:*
>
> "It was not Virginia that wanted a governor but a court favorite that wanted a salary."

The London government, in leaving the colonial governor to the tender mercies of the legislature, was guilty of poor administration. In the interests of simple efficiency, the British authorities should have arranged to pay him from independent sources. As events turned out, control over the purse by the colonial legislatures led to prolonged bickering, which proved to be one of the persistent irritants that generated a spirit of revolt.*

Administration at the local level was also varied. County government remained the rule in the plantation South; town-meeting government predominated in New England; and a modification of the two developed in the middle colonies. In the town meeting, with its open discussion and open voting, direct democracy functioned at its best. In this unrivaled cradle of self-government, Americans learned to cherish their privileges and exercise their duties as citizens of the New World commonwealths.

Yet the ballot was by no means a birthright. Religious or property qualifications for voting, with even stiffer qualifications for officeholding, existed in all the colonies in 1775. The privileged upper classes, fearful of democratic excesses, were unwilling to grant the ballot to every "biped of the forest." Perhaps half of the adult white males were thus disfranchised. But because of the ease of acquiring land and thus satisfying property requirements, the right to vote was not beyond the reach of most industrious and enterprising colonists. Yet somewhat surprisingly, eligible voters often did not exercise this precious privilege. They frequently acquiesced in the leadership of their "betters," who ran colonial affairs—though always reserving the right to vote misbehaving rascals out of office.

By 1775 America was not yet a true democracy—socially, economically, or politically. But it was far more democratic than England and the European continent.

---

*Parliament finally arranged for separate payment of the governors through the Townshend taxes of 1767, but by then the colonists were in such an ugly mood over taxation that this innovation only added fresh fuel to the flames.

Colonial institutions were giving freer rein to the democratic ideals of tolerance, educational advantages, equality of economic opportunity, freedom of speech, freedom of the press, freedom of assembly, and representative government. And these democratic seeds, planted in rich soil, were to bring forth a lush harvest in later years.

Colonial Folkways

Everyday life in the colonies may now seem glamorous, especially as reflected in antique shops. But judged by modern standards, it was drab and tedious. For most people the labor was heavy and constant—from "can see" to "can't see."

Food was plentiful, though the diet could be coarse and monotonous. Americans probably ate more bountifully, especially of meat, than any people in the Old World. Lazy or sickly was the person whose stomach was empty.

Basic comforts now taken for granted were lacking. Churches were not heated at all, except for charcoal foot-warmers that the women carried. During the frigid New England winters, the preaching of hellfire may not have seemed altogether unattractive. Drafty homes were poorly heated, chiefly by inefficient fireplaces. There was no running water in the houses, no plumbing, and probably not a single bathtub in all colonial America. Candles and whale-oil lamps provided faint and flickering illumination. Garbage disposal was primitive. Long-snouted hogs customarily ranged the streets to consume refuse, while buzzards, protected by law, flapped greedily over tidbits of waste.

Amusement was eagerly pursued where time and custom permitted. The militia assembled periodically for "musters," which consisted of several days of drilling, liberally interspersed with merrymaking and flirting. On the frontier, pleasure was often combined with work at house-raisings, quilting bees, husking bees, and apple parings. Funerals and weddings everywhere afforded opportunities for social gatherings, which customarily involved the swilling of much strong liquor.

Winter sports were common in the North, whereas in the South card playing, horse racing, cockfighting, and fox hunting were favorite pastimes. George Washington, not surprisingly, was a superb rider. In the nonpuritanical South, dancing was the rage—jigs, square dances, the Virginia reel—and the agile Washington could swing his fair partner with the best of them.

Other diversions beckoned. Lotteries were universally approved, even by the clergy, and were used to raise money for churches and colleges, including Harvard. Stage plays became popular in the South but were frowned upon in Quaker and Puritan colonies and in some places forbidden by law. Many of the New England clergy saw playacting as time-consuming and

The Popular Game of Billiards
Most likely brought over by Dutch and English settlers, billiards provided amusement in local taverns throughout the colonies. By the nineteenth century Americans, like the British and French who had long dominated the sport, had become obsessed with these games of cues and balls. The most popular form of pool, eight ball, was not invented until 1900.

immoral; they preferred religious lectures, from which their flocks derived much spiritual satisfaction.

Holidays were everywhere celebrated in the American colonies, but Christmas was frowned upon in New England as an offensive reminder of "Popery." "Yuletide is fooltide" was a common Puritan sneer. Thanksgiving Day came to be a truly American festival, for it combined thanks to God with an opportunity for jollification, gorging, and guzzling.

By the mid-eighteenth century, Britain's several North American colonies, despite their differences, revealed some striking similarities. All were basically English in language and customs, and Protestant in religion, while the widespread presence of other peoples and faiths compelled every colony to cede at least some degree of ethnic and religious toleration. Compared with contemporary Europe, they all afforded to enterprising individuals unusual opportunities for social mobility. They all possessed some measure of self-government, though by no means complete democracy. Communication and transportation among the colonies were improving. British North America by 1775 looked like a patchwork quilt—each part slightly different, but stitched together by common origins, common ways of life, and common beliefs in toleration, economic development, and, above all, self-rule. Fatefully, all the colonies were also separated from the seat of imperial authority by a vast ocean moat some three thousand miles wide. These simple facts of shared history, culture, and geography set the stage for the colonists' struggle to unite as an independent people.

Chronology

1693	College of William and Mary founded
1701	Yale College founded
1721	Smallpox inoculation introduced
1732	First edition of Franklin's *Poor Richard's Almanack*
1734	Jonathan Edwards begins Great Awakening
1734-1735	Zenger free-press trial in New York
1738	George Whitefield spreads Great Awakening
1746	Princeton College founded
1760	Britain vetoes South Carolina anti–slave trade measures
1764	Paxton Boys march on Philadelphia Brown College founded
1766	Rutgers College founded
1768-1771	Regulator protests
1769	Dartmouth College founded

VARYING VIEWPOINTS

Colonial America: Communities of Conflict or Consensus?

The earliest historians of colonial society portrayed close-knit, homogeneous, and hierarchical communities. Richard Bushman's *From Puritan to Yankee* (1967) challenged that traditional view when he described colonial New England as an expanding, opening society. In this view the colonists gradually lost the religious discipline and social structure of the founding generations, as they poured out onto the frontier or sailed the seas in search of fortune and adventure. Rhys Isaac viewed the Great Awakening in the South as similar evidence of erosion in the social constraints and deference that once held colonial society together. Unbridled religious enthusiasm, North and South, directed by itinerant preachers, encouraged the sort of quest for personal autonomy that eventually led Americans to demand national independence.

Other scholars have focused on the negative aspects of this alleged breakdown in the traditional order, particularly on the rise of new social inequalities. Social historians like Kenneth Lockridge have argued that the decline of cohesive communities, population pressure on the land, and continued dominance of church and parental authority gave rise to a landless class, forced to till tenant plots in the countryside or find work as manual laborers in the cities. Gary Nash, in *The Urban Crucible* (1979), likewise traced the rise of a competitive, individualistic social order in colonial cities, marking the end of the patronage and paternalism that had once bound communities together. Increasingly, Nash contended, class antagonisms split communities. The wealthy abandoned their traditional obligations toward the poor for more selfish capitalistic social relations that favored their class peers. The consequent politicization of the laboring classes helped motivate their participation in the American Revolution.

Some scholars have disputed that "declension" undermined colonial communities. Christine Heyrman, in particular, has argued in *Commerce and Culture* (1984) that the decline of traditional mores has been overstated; religious beliefs and commercial activities coexisted throughout the late seventeenth and early eighteenth centuries. Similarly, Jack Greene has recently suggested that the obsession with the decline of deference has obscured the fact that colonies outside of New England, like Virginia and Maryland, actually experienced a consolidation of religious and social authority throughout the seventeenth and eighteenth centuries, becoming more hierarchical and paternalistic.

Like Greene, many historians have focused on sectional differences between the colonies, and the peculiar nature of social equality and inequality in each. Much of the impetus for this inquiry stems from an issue that has long perplexed students of early America: the simultaneous evolution of a rigid racial caste system alongside democratic political institutions. Decades ago, when most historians came from Yankee stock, they resolved the apparent paradox by locating the seeds of democracy in New England. The aggressive independence of the people, best expressed by the boisterous town meetings, spawned the American obsession with freedom. On the other hand, this view holds, the slave societies of the South were hierarchical, aristocratic communities under the sway of a few powerful planters.

More recently some historians have attacked this simple dichotomy, noting many undemocratic features in colonial New England and arguing that while the South may have been the site of tremendous inequality, it also produced most of the Founding Fathers. Washington, Jefferson, and Madison—the architects of American government with its foundation in liberty—all hailed from slaveholding Virginia. In fact, nowhere were republican principles stronger than in Virginia. Some scholars, notably Edmund S. Morgan in *American Slavery, American Freedom* (1975), consider the willingness of wealthy planters to concede the equality and freedom of all white males a device to ensure racial solidarity and to mute class conflict. In this view the concurrent emergence of slavery and democracy was no paradox. White racial solidarity muffled animosity between rich and poor and fostered the devotion to equality among whites that became a hallmark of American democracy.

Few historians still argue that the colonies offered boundless opportunities for inhabitants, white or black. But scholars disagree vigorously over what kinds of inequalities and social tensions most shaped eighteenth-century society and contributed to the revolutionary agitation that eventually consumed—and transformed—colonial America. Even so, whether one accepts Morgan's argument that "Americans bought their independence with slave labor," or those interpretations that point to rising social conflict between whites as the salient characteristic of colonial society on the eve of the Revolution, the once-common assumption that America was a world of equality and consensus no longer reigns undisputed. Yet because one's life chances were still unquestionably better in America than in Europe, immigrants continued to pour in, imbued with high expectations about America as a land of opportunity.

For further reading, see the Appendix. For web resources, go to **http://college.hmco.com**.

6

The Duel for North America

1608–1763

A TORCH LIGHTED IN THE FORESTS OF AMERICA
SET ALL EUROPE IN CONFLAGRATION.

VOLTAIRE, C. 1756

As the seventeenth century neared its sunset, a titanic struggle was shaping up for mastery of the North American continent. The contest involved three Old World nations—England,* France, and Spain—and it unavoidably swept up Native American peoples as well. From 1688 to 1763, four bitter wars convulsed Europe. All four of those conflicts were world wars. They amounted to a death struggle for domination in Europe as well as in the New World, and they were fought on the waters and soil of two hemispheres. Counting these first four clashes, nine world wars have been waged since 1688. The American people, whether as British subjects or as American citizens, proved unable to stay out of a single one of them. And one of those wars—known as the Seven Years' War in Europe and sometimes as the French and Indian War in America—set the stage for America's independence.

*After the union of England and Scotland in 1707, the nation's official name became "Great Britain."

France Finds a Foothold in Canada

Like England and Holland, France was a latecomer in the scramble for New World real estate, and for basically the same reasons. It was convulsed during the 1500s by foreign wars and domestic strife, including the frightful clashes between Roman Catholics and Protestant Huguenots. On St. Bartholomew's Day, 1572, over ten thousand Huguenots—men, women, and children—were butchered in cold blood.

A new era dawned in 1598 when the Edict of Nantes, issued by the crown, granted limited toleration to French Protestants. Religious wars ceased, and in the new century France blossomed into the mightiest and most feared nation in Europe, led by a series of brilliant ministers and by the vainglorious King Louis XIV. Enthroned as a five-year-old boy, he reigned for no less than seventy-two years (1643–1715), surrounded by a glittering court and scheming ministers and mistresses.

Fatefully for North America, Louis XIV also took a deep interest in overseas colonies.

After rocky beginnings, success finally rewarded the exertions of France in the New World. In 1608, the year after the founding of Jamestown, the permanent beginnings of a vast empire were established at Quebec, a granite sentinel commanding the St. Lawrence River. The leading figure was Samuel de Champlain, an intrepid soldier and explorer whose energy and leadership fairly earned him the title "Father of New France."

Champlain entered into friendly relations—a fateful friendship—with the nearby Huron Indian tribes. At their request, he joined them in battle against their foes, the federated Iroquois tribes of the upper New York area. Two volleys from the "lightning sticks" of the whites routed the terrified Iroquois, who left behind three dead and one wounded. France, to its sorrow, thus earned the lasting enmity of the Iroquois tribes. They thereafter hampered French penetration of the Ohio Valley, some-times ravaging French settlements and frequently serving as allies of the British in the prolonged struggle for supremacy on the continent.

The government of New France (Canada) finally fell under the direct control of the king after various commercial companies had faltered or failed. This royal regime was almost completely autocratic. The people elected no representative assemblies, nor did they enjoy the right to trial by jury, as in the English colonies.

The population of Catholic New France grew at a listless pace. As late as 1750, only sixty thousand or so whites inhabited New France. Landowning French peasants, unlike the dispossessed English tenant farmers who embarked for the British colonies, had little economic motive to move. Protestant Huguenots, who might have had a religious motive to migrate, were denied a refuge in this raw colony. The French government, in any case, favored its Caribbean island colonies, rich in sugar and rum, over the snow-cloaked wilderness of Canada.

France's American Empire at Its Greatest Extent, 1700

Quebec Scene, by Jean-Baptiste-Louis Franquelin, c. 1699 (detail) The metal cooking pot and the Indians' clothing and blankets show the Native Americans' growing reliance on European trade goods.

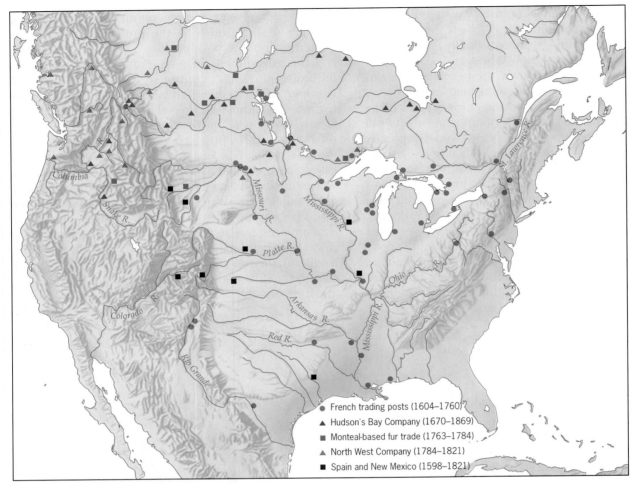

Fur-Trading Posts   To serve the needs of European fashion, fur-traders pursued the beaver for more than two centuries over the entire continent of North America. They brought many Indians for the first time into contact with white culture.

New France Fans Out

New France did contain one valuable resource: the beaver. European fashion-setters valued beaver-pelt hats for their warmth and opulent appearance. To adorn the heads of Europeans, French fur-trappers ranged over the woods and waterways of North America in pursuit of beaver. These colorful *coureurs de bois* ("runners of the woods") were also runners of risks—two-fisted drinkers, free spenders, free livers and lovers. They littered the land with scores of place names, including Baton Rouge (red stick), Terre Haute (high land), Des Moines (some monks), and Grand Teton (big breast).

Singing, paddle-swinging French *voyageurs* also recruited Indians into the fur business. The Indian fur flotilla arriving in Montreal in 1693 numbered four hundred canoes. But the fur trade had some disastrous drawbacks. Indians recruited into the fur business were decimated by the white man's diseases and debauched by his alcohol. Slaughtering beaver by the boatload also violated many Indians' religious beliefs and sadly demonstrated the shattering effect that contact with Europeans wreaked on traditional Indian ways of life.

Pursuing the sharp-toothed beaver ever deeper into the heart of the continent, the French trappers and their Indian partners hiked, rode, snowshoed, sailed, and paddled across amazing distances. They trekked in a huge arc across the Great Lakes, into present-day Saskatchewan and Manitoba; along the valleys of the

Platte, the Arkansas, and the Missouri; west to the Rockies; and south to the border of Spanish Texas (see map at left). In the process they all but extinguished the beaver population in many areas, inflicting incalculable ecological damage.

French Catholic missionaries, notably the Jesuits, labored zealously to save the Indians for Christ and from the fur-trappers. Some of the Jesuit missionaries, their efforts scorned, suffered unspeakable tortures at the hands of the Indians. But though they made few permanent converts, the Jesuits played a vital role as explorers and geographers.

Other explorers sought neither souls nor fur, but empire. To thwart English settlers pushing into the Ohio Valley, Antoine Cadillac founded Detroit, "the City of Straits," in 1701. To check Spanish penetration into the region of the Gulf of Mexico, ambitious Robert de La Salle floated down the Mississippi in 1682 to the point where it mingles with the Gulf. He named the great interior basin "Louisiana," in honor of his sovereign, Louis XIV. Dreaming of empire, he returned to the Gulf three years later with a colonizing expedition of four ships. But he failed

to find the Mississippi delta, landed in Spanish Texas, and in 1687 was murdered by his mutinous men.

Undismayed, French officials persisted in their efforts to block Spain on the Gulf of Mexico. They planted several fortified posts in what is now Mississippi and Louisiana, the most important of which was New Orleans (1718). Commanding the mouth of the Mississippi River, this strategic semitropical outpost also tapped the fur trade of the huge interior valley. The fertile Illinois country—where the French established forts and trading posts at Kaskaskia, Cahokia, and Vincennes—became the garden of France's North American empire. Surprising amounts of grain were floated down the Mississippi for transshipment to the West Indies and to Europe.

The Clash of Empires

The earliest contests among the European powers for control of North America, known to the British colonists as King William's War (1689–1697) and Queen Anne's War

Chief of the Taensa Indians Receiving La Salle, March 20, 1682, by George Catlin, 1847–1848 (detail) Driven by the dream of a vast North American empire for France, La Salle spent years exploring the Great Lakes region and the valleys of the Illinois and Mississippi Rivers. This scene of his encounter with an Indian chieftain was imaginatively re-created by the nineteenth-century artist George Catlin.

(1702–1713), mostly pitted British colonists against the French *coureurs de bois,* with both sides recruiting whatever Indian allies they could. Neither France nor Britain at this stage considered America worth the commitment of large detachments of regular troops, so the combatants waged a kind of primitive guerrilla warfare. Indian allies of the French ravaged with torch and tomahawk the British colonial frontiers, visiting especially bloody violence on the villages of Schenectady, New York, and Deerfield, Massachusetts (see the top map on p. 112). Spain, eventually allied with France, probed from its Florida base at outlying South Carolina settlements. For their part the British colonists failed miserably in sallies against Quebec and Montreal but scored a signal victory when they temporarily seized the stronghold of Port Royal in Acadia (present-day Nova Scotia).

Peace terms, signed at Utrecht in 1713, revealed how badly France and its Spanish ally had been beaten. Britain was rewarded with French-populated Acadia (which the British renamed Nova Scotia, or New Scotland) and the wintry wastes of Newfoundland and Hudson Bay. These immense tracts pinched the St. Lawrence settlements of France, foreshadowing their ultimate doom. A generation of peace ensued, during which Britain provided its American colonies with decades of "salutary neglect"—fertile soil for the roots of independence.

By the treaty of 1713, the British also won limited trading rights in Spanish America, but these later involved much friction over smuggling. Ill feeling flared up when the British captain Jenkins, encountering Spanish revenue authorities, had one ear sliced off by a sword. The Spanish commander reportedly sneered, "Carry this home to the King, your master, whom, if he were present, I would serve in like fashion." The victim, with a tale of woe on his tongue and a shriveled ear in his hand, aroused furious resentment when he returned home to Britain.

The War of Jenkins's Ear, curiously but aptly named, broke out in 1739 between the British and the Spaniards.

British Territory After Two Wars, 1713

It was confined to the Caribbean Sea and to the much-buffeted buffer colony of Georgia, where philanthropist-soldier James Oglethorpe fought his Spanish foe to a standstill.

This small-scale scuffle with Spain in America soon merged with the large-scale War of Austrian Succession in Europe, and came to be called King George's War in

Later English Monarchs*

Name, Reign	Relation to America
William III, 1689–1702	Collapse of Dominion of New England; King William's War
Anne, 1702–1714	Queen Anne's War, 1702–1713
George I, 1714–1727	Navigation Laws laxly enforced ("salutary neglect")
George II, 1727–1760	Ga. founded; King George's War; Seven Years' War
George III, 1760–1820	American Revolution, 1775–1783

*See pp. 29 and 53 for earlier monarchs.

New Englanders Capture Louisbourg, 1745   When the final peace settlement returned this fortress to France, the American colonists felt betrayed by their British masters.

America. Once again, France allied itself with Spain. And once again, a rustic force of New Englanders invaded New France. With help from a British fleet and with a great deal of good luck, the raw and sometimes drunken recruits captured the reputedly impregnable French fortress of Louisbourg, which was on Cape Breton Island and commanded the approaches to the St. Lawrence River (see the top map on p. 112).

When the peace treaty of 1748 handed Louisbourg back to their French foe, the victorious New Englanders were outraged. The glory of their arms—never terribly lustrous in any event—seemed tarnished by the wiles of Old World diplomats. Worse, Louisbourg was still a cocked pistol pointed at the heart of the American continent. France, powerful and unappeased, still clung to its vast holdings in North America.

The Nine World Wars

Dates	In Europe	In America
1688–1697	War of the League of Augsburg	King William's War, 1689–1697
1701–1713	War of Spanish Succession	Queen Anne's War, 1702–1713
1740–1748	War of Austrian Succession	King George's War, 1744–1748
1756–1763	Seven Years' War	French and Indian War, 1754–1763
1778–1783	War of the American Revolution	American Revolution, 1775–1783
1793–1802	Wars of the French Revolution	Undeclared French War, 1798–1800
1803–1815	Napoleonic Wars	War of 1812, 1812–1814
1914–1918	World War I	World War I, 1917–1918
1939–1945	World War II	World War II, 1941–1945

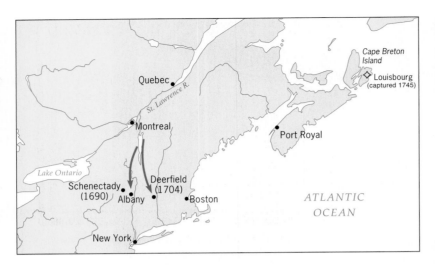

Scenes of the French Wars The arrows indicate French-Indian attacks. Schenectady was burned to the ground in the raid of 1690. At Deerfield, site of one of the New England frontier's bloodiest confrontations, invaders killed fifty inhabitants and sent over a hundred others fleeing for their lives into the winter wilderness. The Indian attackers also took over one hundred Deerfield residents captive, including the child Titus King. He later wrote, "Captivity is an awful school for children, when we see how quick they will fall in with the Indian ways. Nothing seems to be more taking [appealing]. In six months' time they forsake father and mother, forget their own land, refuse to speak their own tongue, and seemingly be wholly swallowed up with the Indians."

George Washington Inaugurates War with France

As the dogfight intensified in the New World, the Ohio Valley became the chief bone of contention between the French and British. The Ohio Country was the critical area into which the westward-pushing British colonists would inevitably penetrate. For France it was also the key to the continent that the French had to retain, particularly if they were going to link their Canadian holdings with those of the lower Mississippi Valley. By the mid-1700s, the British colonists, painfully aware of these basic truths, were no longer so reluctant to bear the burdens of empire. Alarmed by French land-grabbing and cutthroat fur-trade competition in the Ohio Valley, they were determined to fight for their economic security and for the supremacy of their way of life in North America.

Rivalry for the lush lands of the upper Ohio Valley brought tensions to the snapping point. In 1749 a group of British colonial speculators, chiefly influential Virginians, including the Washington family, had secured shaky legal "rights" to some 500,000 acres in this region. In the same disputed wilderness, the French were in the process of erecting a chain of forts commanding the strategic Ohio River. Especially formidable was Fort Duquesne at the pivotal point where the Monongahela and Allegheny Rivers join to form the Ohio—the later site of Pittsburgh.

In 1754 the governor of Virginia ushered George Washington, a twenty-one-year-old surveyor and fellow Virginian, onto the stage of history. To secure the Virginians' claims, Washington was sent to the Ohio Country as a lieutenant colonel in command of about 150 Virginia militiamen. Encountering a small detachment of French troops in the forest about forty miles from Fort Duquesne, the Virginians fired the first shots of the globe-girdling new war. The French leader was killed, and his men retreated. An exultant Washington wrote, "I heard the bullets whistle, and believe me, there is something charming in the sound." It soon lost its charm.

The Ohio Country, 1753–1754

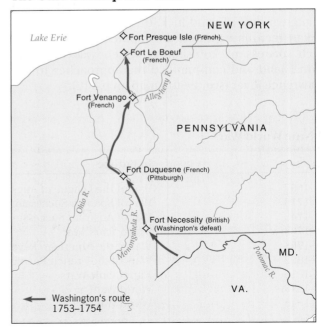

The French promptly returned with reinforcements, who surrounded Washington in his hastily constructed breastworks, Fort Necessity. After a ten-hour siege, he was forced to surrender his entire command in July 1754—ironically the fourth of July. But he was permitted to march his men away with the full honors of war.

With the shooting already started and in danger of spreading, the British authorities in Nova Scotia took vigorous action. Understandably fearing a stab in the back from the French Acadians, whom Britain had conquered in 1713, the British brutally uprooted some four thousand of them in 1755. These unhappy French deportees were scattered as far south as Louisiana, where the descendants of the French-speaking Acadians are now called "Cajuns" and number nearly a million.

Famous Cartoon by Benjamin Franklin
Delaware and Georgia were omitted.

Global War and Colonial Disunity

The first three Anglo-French colonial wars had all started in Europe, but the tables were now reversed. The fourth struggle, sometimes known as the French and Indian War, began in America. Touched off by George Washington in the wilds of the Ohio Valley in 1754, it rocked along on an undeclared basis for two years and then widened into the most far-flung conflict the world had yet seen—the Seven Years' War. It was fought not only in America but in Europe, in the West Indies, in the Philippines, in Africa, and on the ocean. The Seven Years' War was a seven-seas war.

In Europe the principal adversaries were Britain and Prussia on one side, arrayed against France, Spain, Austria, and Russia on the other. The bloodiest theater was in Germany, where Frederick the Great deservedly won the title of "Great" by repelling French, Austrian, and Russian armies, often with the opposing forces outnumbering his own three to one. The London government, unable to send him effective troop reinforcements, liberally subsidized him with gold. Luckily for the British colonists, the French wasted so much strength in this European bloodbath that they were unable to throw an adequate force into the New World. "America was conquered in Germany," declared Britain's great statesman William Pitt.

In previous colonial clashes, the Americans had revealed an astonishing lack of unity. Colonists who were nearest the shooting had responded much more generously with volunteers and money than those enjoying the safety of remoteness. Even the Indians had laughed at the inability of the colonists to pull together. Now, with musketballs already splitting the air in Ohio, the crisis demanded concerted action.

In 1754 the British government summoned an intercolonial congress to Albany, New York, near the Iroquois Indian country. Travel-weary delegates from only seven of the thirteen colonies showed up. The immediate purpose was to keep the scalping knives of the Iroquois tribes loyal to the British in the spreading war. The chiefs were harangued at length and then presented with thirty wagonloads of gifts, including guns.

The longer-range purpose at Albany was to achieve greater colonial unity and thus bolster the common defense against France. A month before the congress assembled, ingenious Benjamin Franklin published in his *Pennsylvania Gazette* the most famous cartoon of the colonial era. Showing the separate colonies as parts of a disjointed snake, it broadcast the slogan "Join, or Die."

Franklin himself, a wise and witty counselor, was the leading spirit of the Albany Congress. His outstanding contribution was a well-devised but premature scheme for colonial home rule. The Albany delegates unanimously adopted the plan, but the individual colonies spurned it, as did the London regime. To the colonists, it did not seem to give enough independence; to the British officials, it seemed to give too much. The disappointing result confirmed one of Franklin's sage observations: all people agreed on the need for union, but their "weak noddles" were "perfectly distracted" when they attempted to agree on details.

Braddock's Blundering and Its Aftermath

The opening clashes of the French and Indian War went badly for the British colonists. Haughty and bullheaded General Braddock, a sixty-year-old officer experienced in European warfare, was sent to Virginia with a strong detachment of British regulars. After foraging scanty supplies from the reluctant colonists, he set out in 1755 with some two thousand men to capture Fort Duquesne. A considerable part of his force consisted of ill-disciplined colonial militiamen ("buckskins"), whose behind-the-tree methods of fighting Indians won "Bulldog" Braddock's professional contempt.

Braddock's expedition, dragging heavy artillery, moved slowly. Axmen laboriously hacked a path through the dense forest, thus opening a road that was later to be an important artery to the West. A few miles from Fort Duquesne, Braddock encountered a much smaller French and Indian army. At first the enemy force was repulsed, but it quickly melted into the thickets and poured a murderous fire into the ranks of the redcoats. In the ensuing debate, George Washington, an energetic and fearless aide to Braddock, had two horses shot from under him and four bullets pierced his coat, and Braddock himself was mortally wounded. The entire British force was routed after appalling losses.

Inflamed by this easy victory, the Indians took to a wider warpath. The whole frontier from Pennsylvania to North Carolina, left virtually naked by Braddock's bloody defeat, felt their fury. Scalping forays occurred within eighty miles of Philadelphia, and in desperation the local authorities offered bounties for Indian scalps: $50 for a woman's and $130 for a warrior's. George Washington, with only three hundred men, tried desperately to defend the scorched frontier.

The British launched a full-scale invasion of Canada in 1756, now that the undeclared war in America had at last merged into a world conflict. But they unwisely tried to attack a number of exposed wilderness posts simultaneously, instead of throwing all their strength at Quebec and Montreal. If these strongholds had fallen, all the outposts to the west would have withered for lack of riverborne supplies. But the British ignored such sound

Detroit, 1794　A key French outpost from 1701 to 1760, Detroit fell to Britain during the Seven Years' War. The British remained at Detroit even after the American War of Independence, exciting bitter resentment in the infant American Republic (see pp. 175–176).

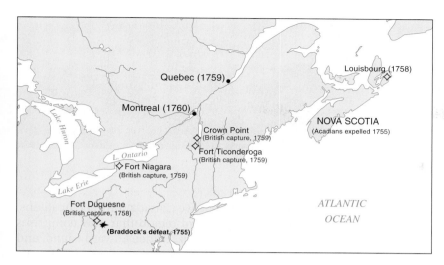

Events of 1755–1760

strategy, and defeat after defeat tarnished their arms, both in America and in Europe.

Pitt's Palms of Victory

In the hour of crisis, Britain brought forth, as it repeatedly has, a superlative leader—William Pitt. A tall and imposing figure, whose flashing eyes were set in a hawklike face, he was popularly known as the "Great Commoner." Pitt drew much of his strength from the common people, who admired him so greatly that on occasion they kissed his horses. A splendid orator endowed with a majestic voice, he believed passionately in his cause, in his country, and in himself.

In 1757 Pitt became a foremost leader in the London government. Throwing himself headlong into his task, he soon earned the title "Organizer of Victory." He wisely decided to soft-pedal assaults on the French West Indies, which had been bleeding away much British strength, and to concentrate on the vitals of Canada—the Quebec-Montreal area. He also picked young and energetic leaders, thus bypassing incompetent and cautious old generals.

Pitt first dispatched a powerful expedition in 1758 against Louisbourg. The frowning fortress, though it had been greatly strengthened, fell after a blistering siege. Wild rejoicing swept Britain, for this was the first significant British victory of the entire war.

Quebec was next on Pitt's list. For this crucial expedition, he chose the thirty-two-year-old James Wolfe, who had been an officer since the age of fourteen.

Though slight and sickly, Wolfe combined a mixture of dash with painstaking attention to detail. The British attackers were making woeful progress when Wolfe, in a daring night move, sent a detachment up a poorly guarded part of the rocky eminence protecting Quebec. This vanguard scaled the cliff, pulling itself upward by the bushes and showing the way for the others. In the morning the two armies faced each other on the Plains of Abraham on the outskirts of Quebec, the British under Wolfe and the French under the Marquis de Montcalm. Both commanders fell fatally wounded, but the French were defeated and the city surrendered (see "Makers of America: The French," pp. 116–117).

The Battle of Quebec in 1759 ranks as one of the most significant engagements in British and American history. When Montreal fell in 1760, the French flag had fluttered in Canada for the last time. By the peace settlement at Paris (1763), French power was thrown completely off the continent of North America, leaving behind a fertile French population that is to this day a strong minority in Canada. This bitter pill was sweetened somewhat when the French were allowed to retain several small but valuable sugar islands in the West Indies, and two never-to-be-fortified islets in the Gulf of St. Lawrence for fishing stations. A final blow came when the French, to compensate their luckless Spanish ally for its losses, ceded to Spain all trans-Mississippi Louisiana, plus the outlet of New Orleans. Spain, for its part, turned Florida over to Britain in return for Cuba, where Havana had fallen to British arms.

Great Britain thus emerged as the dominant power in North America, while taking its place as the leading naval power of the world.

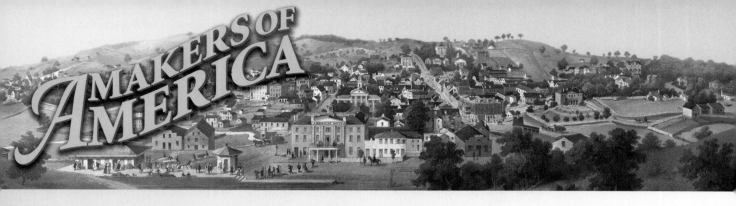

The French

At the height of his reign in the late seventeenth century, Louis XIV, France's "Sun King," turned his covetous eyes westward to the New World. He envisioned there a bountiful New France, settled by civilizing French pioneers, in the maritime provinces of Acadia and the icy expanses of Quebec. But his dreams flickered out like candles before the British juggernaut in the eighteenth century, and his former New World subjects had to suffer foreign governance in the aftermath of the French defeats in 1713 and 1763. Over the course of two centuries, many chafed under the British yoke and eventually found their way to the United States.

The first French to leave Canada were the Acadians, the settlers of the seaboard region that now comprises Nova Scotia, New Brunswick, Prince Edward Island, and part of Maine. In 1713 the French crown ceded this territory to the British, who demanded that the Acadians either swear allegiance to Britain or withdraw to French territory. At first doing neither, they managed to escape reprisals until *Le Grand Derangement* ("the Great Displacement") in 1755, when the British expelled them from the region at bayonet point. The Acadians fled far south to the French colony of Louisiana, where they settled among the sleepy bayous, planted sugar cane

(above) Acadian Architecture This architectural style was transplanted by the uprooted Acadians to the Cajun bayous of Louisiana. **(right) Franco-American Mill Workers in New England, c. 1910**

Modern-Day Quebec   A bit
of the Old World in the New.

and sweet potatoes, practiced Roman Catholicism, and spoke the French dialect that came to be called Cajun (a corruption of the English word *Acadian*). The Cajun settlements were tiny and secluded, many of them accessible only by small boat.

For generations these insular people were scarcely influenced by developments outside their tight-knit communities. Louisiana passed through Spanish, French, and American hands, but the Cajuns kept to themselves. Cajun women sometimes married German, English, or Spanish men—today one finds such names as Schneider and Lopez in the bayous—but the outsiders were always absorbed completely into the large Cajun families. Not until the twentieth century did Cajun parents surrender their children to public schools and submit to a state law restricting French speech. Only in the 1930s, with a bridge-

building spree engineered by Governor Huey Long, was the isolation of these bayou communities broken.

In 1763, as the French settlers of Quebec fell under British rule, a second group of French people began to leave Canada. By 1840 what had been an irregular southward trickle of Quebecois swelled to a steady stream, depositing most of the migrating French Canadians in New England. These nineteenth-century emigrants were not goaded by bayonets but driven away by the lean harvests yielded by Quebec's short growing season and scarcity of arable land. They frequently recrossed the border to visit their old homes, availing themselves of the train routes opened in the 1840s between Quebec and Boston. Most hoped someday to return to Canada for good.

They emigrated mostly to work in New England's lumberyards and textile mills, gradually establishing permanent settlements in the northern woods. Like the Acadians, these later migrants from Quebec stubbornly preserved their Roman Catholicism. And both groups shared a passionate love of their French language, believing it to be the cement that bound them, their religion, and their culture together. As one French Canadian explained, "Let us worship in peace and in our own tongue. All else may disappear but this must remain our badge." Yet today almost all Cajuns and New England French Canadians speak English.

North of the border, in the land that these immigrants left behind, Louis XIV's dream of implanting a French civilization in the New World lingers on in the Canadian province of Quebec. Centuries have passed since the British won the great eighteenth-century duel for North America, but the French language still adorns the road signs of Quebec and rings out in its classrooms, courts, and markets, eloquently testifying to the continued vitality of French culture in North America.

View of the Taking of Quebec, 1759   On the night of September 13, British forces scaled the rocky cliffs of Quebec and defeated the French army defending the city. The following year, Montreal, France's last bastion in North America, surrendered. Fighting continued in the Caribbean, Europe, and the Philippines for two more years, until the Treaty of Paris was signed in 1763, eliminating France as a colonial power in North America.

Restless Colonists

Britain's colonists, baptized by fire, emerged with increased confidence in their military strength. They had borne the brunt of battle at first; they had fought bravely alongside the crack British regulars; and they had gained valuable experience, officers and men alike. In the closing days of the conflict, some twenty thousand American recruits were under arms.

The French and Indian War, while bolstering colonial self-esteem, simultaneously shattered the myth of British invincibility. On Braddock's bloody field, the "buckskin" militia had seen the demoralized regulars huddling helplessly together or fleeing their unseen enemy.

Ominously, friction had developed during the war between arrogant British officers and the raw colonial "boors." Displaying the contempt of the professional soldier for amateurs, the British refused to recognize any American militia commission above the rank of captain—a demotion humiliating to "Colonel" George Washington. They also showed the usual condescension of snobs from the civilized Old Country toward the "scum" who had confessed failure by fleeing to the "outhouses of civilization." General Wolfe referred to the colonial militia, with exaggeration, as "in general the dirtiest, most contemptible, cowardly dogs that you can conceive." Energetic and hard-working American settlers, in contrast, believed themselves to be the cutting edge of British civilization. They felt that they deserved credit rather than contempt for risking their lives to secure a New World empire.

British officials were further distressed by the reluctance of the colonists to support the common cause wholeheartedly. American shippers, using fraudulent

North America Before 1754

North America After 1763 (after French losses)

papers, developed a golden traffic with the enemy ports of the Spanish and French West Indies. This treasonable trade in foodstuffs actually kept some of the hostile islands from starving at the very time when the British navy was trying to subdue them. In the final year of the war, the British authorities, forced to resort to drastic measures, forbade the export of all supplies from New England and the middle colonies.

Other colonists, self-centered and alienated by distance from the war, refused to provide troops and money for the conflict. They demanded the rights and privileges of Englishmen, without the duties and responsibilities of Englishmen. Not until Pitt had offered to reimburse the colonies for a substantial part of their expenditures—some £900,000—did they move with some enthusiasm. If the Americans had to be bribed to defend themselves against a relentless and savage foe, would they ever unite to strike the mother country?

The curse of intercolonial disunity, present from early days, had continued throughout the recent hostilities. It had been caused mainly by enormous distances; by geographical barriers like rivers; by conflicting religions, from Catholic to Quaker; by varied nationalities, from German to Irish; by differing types of colonial governments; by many boundary disputes; and by the resentment of the crude backcountry settlers against the aristocratic bigwigs.

Yet unity received some encouragement during the French and Indian War. When soldiers and statesmen from widely separated colonies met around common campfires and council tables, they were often agreeably surprised by what they found. Despite deep-seated jealousy and suspicion, they discovered that they were all fellow Americans who generally spoke the same language and shared common ideals. Barriers of disunity began to melt, although a long and rugged road lay ahead before a coherent nation would emerge.

The Reverend Andrew Burnaby, an observant Church of England clergyman who visited the colonies in the closing months of the Seven Years' War, scoffed at any possibility of unification (1760):

". . . for fire and water are not more heterogeneous than the different colonies in North America. Nothing can exceed the jealousy and emulation which they possess in regard to each other. . . . In short . . . were they left to themselves there would soon be a civil war from one end of the continent to the other, while the Indians and Negros would . . . impatiently watch the opportunity of exterminating them all together."

War's Fateful Aftermath

The removal of the French menace in Canada profoundly affected American attitudes. While the French hawk had been hovering in the North and West, the colonial chicks had been forced to cling close to the wings of their British mother hen. Now that the hawk was killed, they could range far afield with a new spirit of independence.

The French, humiliated by the British and saddened by the fate of Canada, consoled themselves with one wishful thought. Perhaps the loss of their American empire would one day result in Britain's loss of its American empire. In a sense the history of the United States began with the fall of Quebec and Montreal; the infant Republic was cradled on the Plains of Abraham.

The Spanish and Indian menaces were also now substantially reduced. Spain was eliminated from Florida, although entrenched in Louisiana and New Orleans, and was still securely in possession of much of western North America, including the vast territory from present-day Texas to California. As for the Indians, the Treaty of Paris that ended the Seven Years' War dealt a harsh blow to the Iroquois, Creeks, and other interior tribes. The Spanish removal from Florida and the French removal from Canada deprived the Indians of their most powerful diplomatic weapon—the ability to play off the rival European powers against one another. In the future the Indians would have to negotiate exclusively with the British.

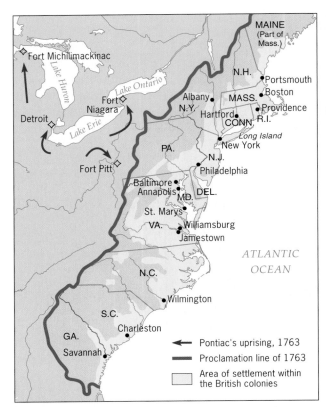

British Colonies at End of the Seven Years' War, 1763 This map, showing the colonies thirteen years before the Declaration of Independence, helps to explain why the British would be unable to conquer their offspring. The colonists were spreading rapidly into the backcountry, where the powerful British navy could not flush them out. During the Revolutionary War, the British at one time or another captured the leading colonial cities—Boston, New York, Philadelphia, and Charleston—but the more remote interior remained a sanctuary for rebels.

Sensing the newly precarious position of the Indian peoples, the Ottawa chief Pontiac in 1763 led several tribes, aided by a handful of French traders who remained in the region, in a violent campaign to drive the British out of the Ohio Country. Pontiac's warriors besieged Detroit in the spring of 1763 and eventually overran all but three British posts west of the Appalachians, killing some two thousand soldiers and settlers.

The British retaliated swiftly and cruelly. Waging a primitive version of biological warfare, one British commander ordered blankets infected with smallpox to be distributed among the Indians. Such tactics crushed the uprising and brought an uneasy truce to the frontier. His bold plan frustrated, Pontiac himself perished in 1769 at the hands of a rival chieftain. As for the British, the bloody episode convinced them of the need to stabilize relations with the western Indians and to keep regular troops stationed along the restless frontier, a measure for which they soon asked the colonists to foot the bill.

Land-hungry American colonists were now free to burst over the dam of the Appalachian Mountains and flood out over the verdant western lands. A tiny rivulet of pioneers like Daniel Boone had already trickled into Tennessee and Kentucky; other courageous settlers made their preparations for the long, dangerous trek over the mountains.

Then, out of a clear sky, the London government issued its Proclamation of 1763. It flatly prohibited settlement in the area beyond the Appalachians, pending further adjustments. The truth is that this hastily drawn document was not designed to oppress the colonists at all, but to work out the Indian problem fairly and prevent another bloody eruption like Pontiac's uprising.

But countless Americans, especially land speculators, were dismayed and angered. Was not the land beyond the mountains their birthright? Had they not, in addition, purchased it with their blood in the recent war? In complete defiance of the proclamation, they clogged the westward trails. In 1765 an estimated one thousand wagons rolled through the town of Salisbury, North Carolina, on their way "up west." This wholesale flouting of royal authority boded ill for the longevity of British rule in America.

The Seven Years' War also caused the colonists to develop a new vision of their destiny. With the path cleared for the conquest of a continent, with their birthrate high and their energy boundless, they sensed that they were a potent people on the march. And they were in no mood to be restrained.

Lordly Britons, whose suddenly swollen empire had tended to produce swollen heads, were in no mood for back talk. Puffed up over their recent victories, they were already annoyed with their unruly colonial subjects. The stage was set for a violent family quarrel.

Chronology

1598	Edict of Nantes
1608	Champlain colonizes Quebec for France
1643	Louis XIV becomes king of France
1682	La Salle explores Mississippi River to the Gulf of Mexico
1689-1697	King William's War (War of the League of Augsburg)
1702-1713	Queen Anne's War (War of Spanish Succession)
1718	French found New Orleans
1739	War of Jenkins's Ear
1744-1748	King George's War (War of Austrian Succession)
1754	Washington battles French on frontier Albany Congress
1754-1763	Seven Years' War (French and Indian War)
1755	Braddock's defeat
1757	Pitt emerges as leader of British government
1759	Battle of Quebec
1763	Peace of Paris Pontiac's uprising Proclamation of 1763

For further reading, see the Appendix. For web resources, go to **http://college.hmco.com**.

The Road to Revolution

1763–1775

THE REVOLUTION WAS EFFECTED BEFORE THE
WAR COMMENCED. THE REVOLUTION WAS IN
THE MINDS AND HEARTS OF THE PEOPLE.

JOHN ADAMS, 1818

Victory in the Seven Years' War made Britain the master of a vastly enlarged imperial domain in North America. But victory—including the subsequent need to garrison ten thousand troops along the sprawling American frontier—was painfully costly. The London government therefore struggled after 1763 to compel the American colonists to shoulder some of the financial costs of empire. This change in British colonial policy reinforced an emerging sense of American political identity and helped to precipitate the American Revolution.

The eventual conflict was by no means inevitable. Indeed, given the tightening commercial, military, and cultural bonds between colonies and mother country since the first crude settlements a century and a half earlier, it might be considered remarkable that the Revolution happened at all. The truth is that Americans were reluctant revolutionaries. Until late in the day, they sought only to claim the "rights of Englishmen," not to separate from the mother country. But what began as a squabble about economic policies soon exposed irreconcilable differences between Americans and Britons over cherished political principles. The ensuing clash gave birth to a new nation.

The Deep Roots of Revolution

In a broad sense, America was a revolutionary force from the day of its discovery by Europeans. The New World nurtured new ideas about the nature of society, citizen, and government. In the Old World, many humble folk had long lived in the shadow of graveyards that contained the bones of their ancestors for a thousand years past. Few people born into such changeless surroundings dared to question their social status. But European immigrants in the New World were not so easily subdued by the scowl of their superiors. In the American wilderness, they encountered a world that was theirs to make afresh.

Two ideas in particular had taken root in the minds of the American colonists by the mid-eighteenth century: one was what historians call *republicanism*. Looking to the models of the ancient Greek and Roman republics, exponents of republicanism defined a just society as one in which all citizens willingly subordinated their private, selfish interests to the common good. Both the stability of society and the authority of government thus depended on the virtue of the citizenry—its capacity for selflessness, self-sufficiency, and courage, and especially its appetite for civic involvement. By its very nature, republicanism was opposed to hierarchical and authoritarian institutions such as aristocracy and monarchy.

A second idea that fundamentally shaped American political thought derived from a group of British political commentators known as "radical Whigs." Widely read by the colonists, the Whigs feared the threat to liberty posed by the arbitrary power of the monarch and his ministers relative to elected representatives in Parliament. The Whigs mounted withering attacks on the use of patronage and bribes by the king's ministers—symptoms of a wider moral failure in society that they called "corruption," in the sense of rot or decay. The Whigs warned citizens to be on guard against corruption and to be eternally vigilant against possible conspiracies to denude them of their hard-won liberties. Together, republican and Whig ideas predisposed the American colonists to be on hair-trigger alert against any threat to their rights.

The circumstances of colonial life had done much to bolster those attitudes. Dukes and princes, barons and bishops were unknown in the colonies, while property ownership and political participation were relatively accessible. The Americans had also grown accustomed to running their own affairs, largely unmolested by remote officials in London. Distance weakens authority; great distance weakens authority greatly. So it came as an especially jolting shock when Britain after 1763 tried to enclose its American colonists more snugly in its grip.

Mercantilism and Colonial Grievances

Britain's empire was acquired in a "fit of absent-mindedness," an old saying goes, and there is much truth in the jest. Not one of the original thirteen colonies except Georgia was formally planted by the British government. All the others were haphazardly founded by trading companies, religious groups, or land speculators.

The British authorities nevertheless embraced a theory, called mercantilism, that justified their control over the colonies. Mercantilists believed that wealth was power and that a country's economic wealth (and hence its military and political power) could be measured by the amount of gold or silver in its treasury. To amass

gold or silver, a country needed to export more than it imported. Possessing colonies thus conferred distinct advantages, since the colonies could both supply raw materials to the mother country (thereby reducing the need for foreign imports) and provide a guaranteed market for exports.

The London government looked on the American colonists more or less as tenants. They were expected to furnish products needed in the mother country, such as tobacco, sugar, and ships' masts; to refrain from making for export certain products, such as woolen cloth or beaver hats; to buy imported manufactured goods exclusively from Britain; and not to indulge in bothersome dreams of economic self-sufficiency or, worse, self-government.

From time to time, Parliament passed laws to regulate the mercantilist system. The first of these, the Navigation Law of 1650, was aimed at rival Dutch shippers trying to elbow their way into the American carrying trade. Thereafter all commerce flowing to and from the colonies could be transported only in British (including colonial) vessels. Subsequent laws required that European goods destined for America first had to be landed in Britain, where tariff duties could be collected and British middlemen could take a slice of the profits. Other laws stipulated that American merchants must ship certain "enumerated" products, notably tobacco, exclusively to Britain, even though prices might be better elsewhere.

British policy also inflicted a currency shortage on the colonies. Since the colonists regularly bought more from Britain than they sold there, the difference had to be made up in hard cash. Every year gold and silver

> *Adam Smith (1723–1790), the Scottish "Father of Modern Economics," frontally attacked mercantilism in 1776:*
>
> "To prohibit a great people, however, from making all that they can of every part of their own produce, or from employing their stock and industry in the way that they judge most advantageous to themselves, is a manifest violation of the most sacred rights of mankind."

The Female Combatants, 1776   Britain is symbolized as a lady of fashion; her rebellious daughter, America, as an Indian princess. Their shields of Obedience and Liberty seem mutually exclusive standards.

resented its very existence—another example of how principle could weigh more heavily than practice in fueling colonial grievances.

The Merits and Menace of Mercantilism

In theory the British mercantile system seemed thoroughly selfish and deliberately oppressive. But the truth is that until 1763, the various Navigation Laws imposed no intolerable burden, mainly because they were only loosely enforced. Enterprising colonial merchants learned early to disregard or evade troublesome restrictions. Some of the first American fortunes, like that of John Hancock, were amassed by wholesale smuggling.

Americans also reaped direct benefits from the mercantile system. If the colonies existed for the benefit of the mother country, it was hardly less true that Britain existed for the benefit of the colonies. London paid liberal bounties to colonial producers of ship parts, over the protests of British competitors. Virginia tobacco planters enjoyed a monopoly in the British market, snuffing out the tiny British tobacco industry. The colonists also benefited from the protection of the world's mightiest navy and a strong, seasoned army of redcoats—all without a penny of cost.

But even when painted in its rosiest colors, the mercantile system burdened the colonists with annoying liabilities. Mercantilism stifled economic initiative and imposed a rankling dependency on British agents and creditors. Most grievously, many Americans simply found the mercantilist system debasing. They felt used, kept in a state of perpetual economic adolescence, and never allowed to come of age. As Benjamin Franklin wrote in 1775,

coins, mostly earned in illicit trade with the Spanish and French West Indies, drained out of the colonies, creating an acute money shortage. To facilitate everyday purchases, the colonists resorted to butter, nails, pitch, and feathers for purposes of exchange.

Currency issues came to a boil when dire financial need forced many of the colonies to issue paper money, which swiftly depreciated. British merchants and creditors squawked so loudly that Parliament prohibited the colonial legislatures from printing paper currency and from passing indulgent bankruptcy laws—practices that might harm British merchants. The Americans grumbled that their welfare was being sacrificed for the well-being of British commercial interests.

The British crown also reserved the right to nullify any legislation passed by the colonial assemblies if such laws worked mischief with the mercantilist system. This royal veto was used rather sparingly—just 469 times in connection with 8,563 laws. But the colonists fiercely

The Boston Gazette *declared in 1765,*

"A colonist cannot make a button, a horseshoe, nor a hobnail, but some snooty ironmonger or respectable buttonmaker of Britain shall bawl and squall that his honor's worship is most egregiously maltreated, injured, cheated, and robbed by the rascally American republicans."

Paul Revere, by John Singleton Copley, c. 1768
This painting of the famed silversmith-horseman challenged convention—but reflected the new democratic spirit of the age—by portraying an artisan in working clothes. Note how Copley depicted the serene confidence of the master craftsman and Revere's quiet pride in his work.

> *We have an old mother that peevish is*
> *   grown;*
> *She snubs us like children that scarce walk*
> *   alone;*
> *She forgets we're grown up and have sense*
> *   of our own.*

Revolution broke out, as Theodore Roosevelt later remarked, because Britain failed to recognize an emerging nation when it saw one.

The Stamp Tax Uproar

Victory-flushed Britain emerged from the Seven Years' War holding one of the biggest empires in the world—and also, less happily, the biggest debt, some £140 million, about half of which had been incurred defending the American colonies. To justify and service that debt, British officials now moved to redefine their relationship with their North American colonies.

Prime Minister George Grenville first aroused the resentment of the colonists in 1763 by ordering the British navy to begin strictly enforcing the Navigation Laws. He also secured from Parliament the so-called Sugar Act of 1764, the first law ever passed by that body for raising tax revenue in the colonies for the crown. Among various provisions, it increased the duty on foreign sugar imported from the West Indies. After bitter protests from the colonists, the duties were lowered substantially, and the agitation died down. But resentment was kept burning by the Quartering Act of 1765. This measure required certain colonies to provide food and quarters for British troops.

Then in the same year, 1765, Grenville imposed the most odious measure of all: a stamp tax, to raise revenues to support the new military force. The Stamp Act mandated the use of stamped paper or the affixing of stamps, certifying payment of tax. Stamps were required on bills of sale for about fifty trade items as well as on certain types of commercial and legal documents, including playing cards, pamphlets, newspapers, diplomas, bills of lading, and marriage licenses.

Grenville regarded all these measures as reasonable and just. He was simply asking the Americans to pay a fair share of the costs for their own defense, through taxes that were already familiar in Britain. In fact, the British people for two generations had endured a stamp tax far heavier than that passed for the colonies.

Yet the Americans were angrily aroused at what they regarded as Grenville's fiscal aggression. The new laws did not merely pinch their pocketbooks. Far more ominously, Grenville also seemed to be striking at the local

English statesman Edmund Burke (1729–1797) warned in 1775,

"Young man, there is America—which at this day serves for little more than to amuse you with stories of savage men and uncouth manners; yet shall, before you taste of death, show itself equal to the whole of that commerce which now attracts the envy of the world."

A Royal Stamp The hated Stamp Act of 1765 required stamps, certifying payment of tax, on all sorts of legal and commercial documents. This stamp was to be affixed to insurance policies and probated wills.

John Dickinson (1732–1808), a lawyer and popular essayist, advocated a middle-of-the-road response to the new British revenue acts of the 1760s that appealed to most colonists at the time:

"The constitutional modes of obtaining relief are those which I wish to see pursued on the present occasion. . . . We have an excellent prince, in whose good disposition we may confide. . . . Let us behave like dutiful children who have received unmerited blows from a beloved parent. Let us complain to our parent; but let our complaint speak at the same time the language of affliction and veneration."

liberties they had come to assume as a matter of right. Thus some colonial assemblies defiantly refused to comply with the Quartering Act, or voted only a fraction of the supplies that it called for.

Worst of all, Grenville's noxious legislation seemed to jeopardize the basic rights of the colonists as Englishmen. Both the Sugar Act and the Stamp Act provided for trying offenders in the hated admiralty courts, where juries were not allowed. The burden of proof was on the defendants, who were assumed to be guilty unless they could prove themselves innocent. Trial by jury and the precept of "innocent until proved guilty" were ancient privileges that British people everywhere, including the American colonists, held most dear.

And why was a British army needed at all in the colonies, now that the French were expelled from the continent and Pontiac's warriors crushed? Could its real purpose be to whip rebellious colonists into line? Many Americans, weaned on radical Whig suspicion of all authority, began to sniff the strong scent of a conspiracy to strip them of their historic liberties. They lashed back violently, and the Stamp Act became the target that drew their most ferocious fire.

Angry throats raised the cry, "No taxation without representation." There was some irony in the slogan, because the seaports and tidewater towns that were most wrathful against the Stamp Act had long denied full representation to their own backcountry pioneers.

But now the aggravated colonists took the high ground of principle.

The Americans made a distinction between "legislation" and "taxation." They conceded the right of Parliament to legislate about matters that affected the entire empire, including the regulation of trade. But they steadfastly denied the right of Parliament, in which no Americans were seated, to impose taxes on Americans. Only their own elected colonial legislatures, the Americans insisted, could legally tax them. Taxes levied by the distant British Parliament amounted to robbery, a piratical assault on the sacred rights of property.

Grenville dismissed these American protests as hairsplitting absurdities. The power of Parliament was supreme and undivided, he asserted, and in any case the Americans *were* represented in Parliament. Elaborating the theory of "virtual representation," Grenville claimed that every member of Parliament represented all British subjects, even those Americans in Boston or Charleston who had never voted for a member of Parliament.

The Americans scoffed at the notion of virtual representation. And truthfully, they did not really want direct representation in Parliament, which might have seemed like a sensible compromise. If they had obtained it, any gouty member of the House of Commons could have proposed an oppressive tax bill for the colonies, and the American representatives, few in number, would have stood bereft of a principle with which to resist.

Thus the principle of no taxation without representation was supremely important, and the colonists clung to it with tenacious consistency. When the British replied that the sovereign power of government could not be divided between "legislative" authority in London and "taxing" authority in the colonies, they forced the Americans to deny the authority of Parliament altogether and to begin to consider their own political independence. This chain of logic eventually led, link by link, to revolutionary consequences.

Forced Repeal of the Stamp Act

Colonial outcries against the hated stamp tax took various forms. The most conspicuous assemblage was the Stamp Act Congress of 1765, which brought together in New York City twenty-seven distinguished delegates from nine colonies. After dignified debate the members drew up a statement of their rights and grievances and beseeched the king and Parliament to repeal the repugnant legislation.

The Stamp Act Congress, which was largely ignored in England, made little splash at the time in America. Its ripples, however, began to erode sectional suspicions, for it brought together around the same table leaders from the different and rival colonies. It was one more halting but significant step toward intercolonial unity.

More effective than the congress was the widespread adoption of nonimportation agreements against British goods. Woolen garments of homespun became fashionable, and the eating of lamb chops was discouraged so that the wool-bearing sheep would be allowed to mature. Nonimportation agreements were in fact a promising stride toward union; they spontaneously united the American people for the first time in common action.

Mobilizing in support of nonimportation gave ordinary American men and women new opportunities to participate in colonial protests. Many people who had previously stood on the sidelines now signed petitions swearing to uphold the terms of the consumer boycotts. Groups of women assembled in public to hold spinning bees and make homespun cloth as a replacement for shunned British textiles. Such public defiance helped spread angry resistance throughout American colonial society.

Sometimes violence accompanied colonial protests. Groups of ardent spirits, known as Sons of Liberty and Daughters of Liberty, took the law into their own hands.

Protesting the Stamp Act   Even common household wares in the 1760s testified to the colonists' mounting rage against the Stamp Act. Many people in Britain sympathized with the Americans—and sought to profit from their anger, as this English-made teapot demonstrates.

Crying "Liberty, Property, and No Stamps," they enforced the nonimportation agreements against violators, often with a generous coat of tar and feathers. Patriotic mobs ransacked the houses of unpopular officials, confiscated their money, and hanged effigies of stamp agents on liberty poles.

Shaken by colonial commotion, the machinery for collecting the tax broke down. On that dismal day in 1765 when the new act was to go into effect, the stamp agents had all been forced to resign, and there was no one to sell the stamps. While flags flapped at half-mast, the law was openly and flagrantly defied—or, rather, nullified.

England was hard hit. America then bought about one-quarter of all British exports, and about one-half of British shipping was devoted to the American trade. Merchants, manufacturers, and shippers suffered from the colonial nonimportation agreements, and hundreds of laborers were thrown out of work. Loud demands converged on Parliament for repeal of the Stamp Act. But many of the members could not understand why 7.5 million Britons had to pay heavy taxes to protect the colonies, whereas some 2 million colonists refused to pay for only one-third of the cost of their own defense.

After a stormy debate, Parliament in 1766 grudgingly repealed the Stamp Act. Grateful residents of New York erected a leaden statue to King George III. But

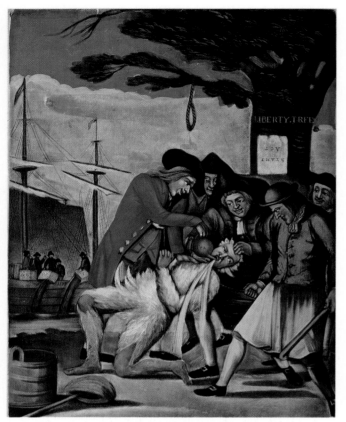

Public Punishment for the Excise Man, 1774
This popular rendering of the punishment of Commissioner of Customs John Malcomb shows him tarred and feathered and forcibly "paid" with great quantities of tea. From the Liberty Tree in the background dangles the threat of hanging, all for attempting to collect duties in Boston.

The Townshend Tea Tax and the Boston "Massacre"

Control of the British ministry was now seized by the gifted but erratic "Champagne Charley" Townshend, a man who could deliver brilliant speeches in Parliament even while drunk. Rashly promising to pluck feathers from the colonial goose with a minimum of squawking, he persuaded Parliament in 1767 to pass the Townshend Acts. The most important of these new regulations was a light import duty on glass, white lead, paper, paint, and tea. Townshend, seizing on a dubious distinction between internal and external taxes, made this tax, unlike the Stamp Act, an indirect customs duty payable at American ports. But to the increasingly restless colonists, this was a phantom distinction. For them the real difficulty remained taxes—in any form—without representation.

Flushed with their recent victory over the stamp tax, the colonists were in a rebellious mood. The impost on tea was especially irksome, for an estimated 1 million people drank the refreshing brew twice a day.

The new Townshend revenues, worse yet, were to be earmarked to pay the salaries of the royal governors and judges in America. From the standpoint of efficient administration by London, this was a reform long overdue. But the ultrasuspicious Americans, who had beaten the royal governors into line by controlling the purse, regarded Townshend's tax as another attempt to enchain them. Their worst fears took on greater reality when the London government, after passing the Townshend taxes, suspended the legislature of New York in 1767 for failure to comply with the Quartering Act.

American rejoicing was premature. Having withdrawn the Stamp Act, Parliament in virtually the same breath provocatively passed the Declaratory Act, reaffirming Parliament's right "to bind" the colonies "in all cases whatsoever." The British government thereby drew its line in the sand. It defined the constitutional principle it would not yield: absolute and unqualified sovereignty over its North American colonies. The colonists had already drawn their own battle line by making it clear that they wanted a measure of sovereignty of their own and would undertake drastic action to secure it. The stage was set for a continuing confrontation. Within a few years, that statue of King George would be melted into thousands of bullets to be fired at his troops.

Giving new meaning to the proverbial tempest in a teapot, a group of 126 Boston women signed an agreement, or "subscription list," which announced,

"We the Daughters of those Patriots who have and now do appear for the public interest . . . do with Pleasure engage with them in denying ourselves the drinking of Foreign Tea, in hopes to frustrate a Plan that tends to deprive the whole Community of . . . all that is valuable in Life."

Redcoats Landing in Boston

tax less seriously than might have been expected, largely because it was light and indirect. They found, moreover, that they could secure smuggled tea at a cheap price, and consequently smugglers increased their activities, especially in Massachusetts.

British officials, faced with a breakdown of law and order, landed two regiments of troops in Boston in 1768. Many of the soldiers were drunken and profane characters. Liberty-loving colonists, resenting the presence of the red-coated "ruffians," taunted the "bloody backs" unmercifully.

A clash was inevitable. On the evening of March 5, 1770, a crowd of some sixty townspeople began taunting and throwing snowballs at a squad of ten redcoats. The Bostonians were still angry over the death of an eleven-year-old boy, shot ten days earlier during a protest against a merchant who had defied the colonial boycott of British goods. Acting apparently without

Nonimportation agreements, previously potent, were quickly revived against the Townshend Acts. But they proved less effective than those devised against the Stamp Act. The colonists, again enjoying prosperity, took the new

Two Views of the Boston Massacre, 1770 and 1856
Both of these prints of the Boston Massacre were art as well as propaganda. Paul Revere's engraving (left) began circulating within three weeks of the event in March 1770, depicting not a clash of brawlers but armed soldiers taking aim at peaceful citizens. Absent also was any evidence of the mulatto ringleader, Crispus Attucks. Revere wanted his print to convince viewers of the indisputable justice of the colonists' cause. By the mid-1850s, when the chromolithograph (right) circulated, it served a new political purpose. In the era of the abolitionist movement, freedman Crispus Attucks held center place in the scene, which portrayed his death as an American martyr in the revolutionary struggle for freedom.

Samuel Adams (1722–1803)   A second cousin of John Adams, he contributed a potent pen and tongue to the American Revolution as a political agitator and organizer of rebellion. He was the leading spirit in hosting the Boston Tea Party. A failure in the brewing business, he was sent by Massachusetts to the First Continental Congress of 1774. He signed the Declaration of Independence and served in Congress until 1781.

Portrait Traditionally Said to Be That of Abigail Adams (1744–1818)   The wife of Revolutionary War leader and future president John Adams, she was a prominent Patriot in her own right. She was also among the first Americans to see, however faintly, the implications of revolutionary ideas for changing the status of women.

orders, but nervous and provoked by the jeering crowd, the troops opened fire and killed or wounded eleven citizens. One of the first to die was Crispus Attucks, described by contemporaries as a powerfully built runaway "mulatto" and a leader of the mob. Both sides were in some degree to blame, and in the subsequent trial (in which future president John Adams served as defense attorney for the soldiers), only two of the redcoats were found guilty of manslaughter. The soldiers were released after being branded on the hand.

The Seditious Committees of Correspondence

By 1770 King George III, then only thirty-two years old, was strenuously attempting to assert the power of the British monarchy. He was a good man in his private morals, but he proved to be a bad ruler. Earnest, industrious, stubborn, and lustful for power, he surrounded himself with cooperative "yes men," notably his corpulent prime minister, Lord North.

The ill-timed Townshend Acts had failed to produce revenue, though they did produce near-rebellion. Net proceeds from the tax in one year were a paltry £295, and during that time the annual military costs to Britain in the colonies had mounted to £170,000. Nonimportation agreements, though feebly enforced, were pinching British manufacturers. The government of Lord North, bowing to various pressures, finally persuaded Parliament to repeal the Townshend revenue duties. But the three-pence toll on tea, the tax the colonists found most offensive, was retained to keep alive the principle of parliamentary taxation.

Flames of discontent in America continued to be fanned by numerous incidents, including the redoubled efforts of the British officials to enforce the Navigation Laws. Resistance was further kindled by a master propagandist and engineer of rebellion, Samuel Adams of Boston, a cousin of John Adams. Unimpressive in appearance (his hands trembled), he lived and breathed only for politics. His friends had to buy him a presentable suit of clothes when he left Massachusetts on intercolonial business. Zealous, tenacious, and courageous, he was ultrasensitive to infractions of colonial rights. Cherishing a deep faith in the common people, he appealed effectively to what was called his "trained mob."

Samuel Adams's signal contribution was to organize in Massachusetts the local committees of correspondence. After he had formed the first one in Boston during 1772, some eighty towns in the colony speedily set up similar organizations. Their chief function was to spread the spirit of resistance by exchanging letters and thus keep alive opposition to British policy. One critic referred to the committees as "the foulest, subtlest, and most venomous serpent ever issued from the egg of sedition."

Intercolonial committees of correspondence were the next logical step. Virginia led the way in 1773 by creating such a body as a standing committee of the House of Burgesses. Within a short time, every colony had established a central committee through which it could exchange ideas and information with other colonies. These intercolonial groups were supremely significant in stimulating and disseminating sentiment in favor of united action. They evolved directly into the first American congresses.

Tea Brewing in Boston

Thus far—that is, by 1773—nothing had happened to make rebellion inevitable. Nonimportation was weakening. Increasing numbers of colonists were reluctantly paying the tea tax, because the legal tea was now cheaper than the smuggled tea, even cheaper than tea in England.

A new ogre entered the picture in 1773. The powerful British East India Company, overburdened with 17 million pounds of unsold tea, was facing bankruptcy. If it collapsed, the London government would lose heavily in tax revenue. The ministry therefore decided to assist the company by awarding it a complete monopoly of the American tea business. The giant corporation would now be able to sell the coveted leaves more cheaply than ever before, even with the three-pence tax tacked

> *Ann Hulton (d. 1779?), a Loyalist, described colonial political divisions and her hopes and fears for her own future in a letter she sent to a friend in England in 1774:*
>
> "Those who are well disposed towards Government are termed Tories. They daily increase & have made some efforts to take the power out of the hands of the Patriots, but they are intimidated & overpowered by Numbers. . . . However I don't despair of seeing Peace & tranquility in America, tho' they talk very high & furious at present. They are all preparing their Arms & Ammunition & say if any of the Leaders are seized, they will make reprisals on the friends of Government."

on. But many American tea drinkers, rather than rejoicing at the lower prices, cried foul. They saw this British move as a shabby attempt to trick the Americans, with the bait of cheaper tea, into swallowing the principle of the detested tax. For the determined Americans, principle remained far more important than price.

If the British officials insisted on the letter of the law, violence would certainly result. Fatefully, the British colonial authorities decided to enforce the law. Once more, the colonists rose up in wrath to defy it. Not a single one of the several thousand chests of tea shipped by the East India Company ever reached the hands of the consignees. In Philadelphia and New York, mass demonstrations forced the tea-bearing ships to return to England with their cargo holds still full. At Annapolis, Marylanders burned both cargo and vessel, while proclaiming "Liberty and Independence or death in pursuit of it." In Charleston, South Carolina, officials seized the tea for nonpayment of duties after intimidated local merchants refused to accept delivery. (Ironically, the confiscated Charleston tea was later auctioned to raise money for the Revolutionary army.)

Only in Boston did a British official stubbornly refuse to be cowed. Massachusetts governor Thomas Hutchinson had already felt the fury of the mob, when Stamp Act protesters had destroyed his home in 1765. This time he was determined not to budge. Ironically, Hutchinson agreed that the tea tax was unjust, but he

The Boston Tea Party, December 16, 1773
Crying "Boston harbor a teapot this night," Sons of Liberty disguised as Indians hurled chests of tea into the sea to protest the tax on tea and to make sure that its cheap price did not prove an "invincible temptation" to the people.

believed even more strongly that the colonists had no right to flout the law. Hutchinson infuriated Boston's radicals when he ordered the tea ships not to clear Boston harbor until they had unloaded their cargoes. Sentiment against him was further inflamed when Hutchinson's enemies published one of his private letters in which he declared that "an abridgement of what are called English liberties" was necessary for the preservation of law and order in the colonies—apparently confirming the darkest conspiracy theories of the American radicals.

On December 16, 1773, roughly a hundred Bostonians, loosely disguised as Indians, boarded the docked ships, smashed open 342 chests of tea, and dumped their contents into the Atlantic. A crowd of several hundred watched approvingly from the shore as Boston harbor became a vast teapot. Donning Indian disguise provided protesters with a threatening image—and a convenient way of avoiding detection. Tea was the perfect symbol to rally around as almost every colonist, rich or poor, consumed this imported, caffeinated beverage.

Reactions varied. All up and down the eastern seaboard, sympathetic colonists applauded. Referring to tea as "a badge of slavery," they burned the hated leaves in solidarity with Boston. But conservatives complained that the destruction of private property violated the law and threatened anarchy and the breakdown of civil decorum. Hutchinson, chastened and disgusted with the colonies, retreated to Britain, never to return. The British authorities, meanwhile, saw little alternative to whipping the upstart colonists into shape.

The granting of some measure of home rule to the Americans might at this stage still have prevented rebellion, but few British politicians were willing to swallow their pride and take the high road. The perilous path they chose instead led only to reprisals, bitterness, and escalating conflict.

Parliament Passes the "Intolerable Acts"

An irate Parliament responded speedily to the Boston Tea Party with measures that brewed a revolution. By huge majorities in 1774, it passed a series of acts designed to chastise Boston in particular, Massachusetts in general. They were branded in America as "the massacre of American Liberty."

Most drastic of all was the Boston Port Act. It closed the tea-stained harbor until damages were paid and order could be ensured. By other "Intolerable Acts"—as they were called in America—many of the chartered rights of colonial Massachusetts were swept away. Restrictions were likewise placed on the precious town meetings. Contrary to previous practice, enforcing officials who killed colonists in the line of duty could now be sent to Britain for trial. There, suspicious Americans assumed, they would be likely to get off scot-free. Particularly intolerable to Bostonians was a new Quartering Act, which gave local authorities the power to lodge British soldiers anywhere, even in private homes.

By a fateful coincidence, the "Intolerable Acts" were accompanied in 1774 by the Quebec Act. Passed at the same time, it was erroneously regarded in English-speaking America as part of the British reaction to the turbulence in Boston. Actually, the Quebec Act was a good law in bad company. For many years the British government had debated how it should administer the sixty thousand or so conquered French subjects in Canada, and it had finally framed this farsighted and statesmanlike measure. The French were guaranteed their Catholic religion. They were also permitted to retain many of their old customs and institutions, which did not include a representative assembly or trial by jury in civil cases. In addition, the old boundaries of the province of Quebec were now extended southward all the way to the Ohio River.

The Quebec Act, from the viewpoint of the French Canadians, was a shrewd and conciliatory measure. If Britain had only shown as much foresight in dealing with its English-speaking colonies, it might not have lost them.

But from the viewpoint of the American colonists as a whole, the Quebec Act was especially noxious. All the other "Intolerable Acts" laws slapped directly at Massachusetts, but this one had a much wider range. By sustaining unrepresentative assemblies and denials of jury trials, it seemed to set a dangerous precedent in America. It alarmed land speculators, who were distressed to see the huge trans-Allegheny area snatched from their grasp. It aroused anti-Catholics, who were shocked by the extension of Roman Catholic jurisdiction southward into a huge region that had once been earmarked for Protestantism—a region about as large as the thirteen original colonies. One angry Protestant cried that there ought to be a "jubilee in hell" over this enormous gain for "Popery."

Bloodshed

American dissenters responded sympathetically to the plight of Massachusetts. It had put itself in the wrong by the violent destruction of the tea cargoes; now Britain had put itself in the wrong by brutal punishment that seemed far too cruel for the crime. Flags were flown at half-mast throughout the colonies on the day that the Boston Port Act went into effect, and sister colonies rallied to send food to the stricken city. Rice was shipped even from faraway South Carolina.

Most memorable of the responses to the "Intolerable Acts" was the summoning of a Continental Congress in 1774. It was to meet in Philadelphia to consider ways of redressing colonial grievances. Twelve of the thirteen colonies, with Georgia alone missing, sent fifty-five well-respected men, among them Samuel Adams, John Adams, George Washington, and Patrick Henry. Intercolonial frictions were partially melted away by social activity after working hours; in fifty-four days

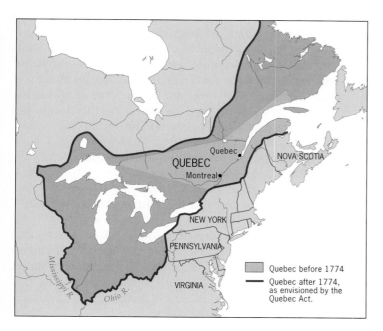

Quebec Before and After 1774 Young Alexander Hamilton voiced the fears of many colonists when he warned that the Quebec Act of 1774 would introduce "priestly tyranny" into Canada, making that country another Spain or Portugal. "Does not your blood run cold," he asked, "to think that an English Parliament should pass an act for the establishment of arbitrary power and Popery in such a country?"

A View of the Town of Concord, c. 1775   Redcoats here drill on the Concord Green, near where colonial militiamen would soon repel their advance on stores of rebel gunpowder.

George Washington dined at his own lodgings only nine times.

The First Continental Congress deliberated for seven weeks, from September 5 to October 26, 1774. It was not a legislative but a consultative body—a convention rather than a congress. John Adams played a stellar role. Eloquently swaying his colleagues to a revolutionary course, he helped defeat by the narrowest of margins a proposal by the moderates for a species of American home rule under British direction. After prolonged argument the Congress drew up several dignified papers. These included a ringing Declaration of Rights, as well as solemn appeals to other British American colonies, to the king, and to the British people.

The most significant action of the Congress was the creation of The Association. Unlike previous nonimportation agreements, The Association called for a complete boycott of British goods: nonimportation, nonexportation, and nonconsumption. Yet it is important to note that the delegates were not yet calling for independence. They sought merely to repeal the offensive legislation and return to the happy days before parliamentary taxation. If colonial grievances were redressed, well and good; if not, the Congress was to meet again in May 1775. Resistance had not yet ripened into open rebellion.

But the fatal drift toward war continued. Parliament rejected the Congress's petitions. In America chickens squawked and tar kettles bubbled as violators of The Association were tarred and feathered. Muskets were gathered, men began to drill openly, and a clash seemed imminent.

In April 1775 the British commander in Boston sent a detachment of troops to nearby Lexington and Concord. They were to seize stores of colonial gunpowder and also to bag the "rebel" ringleaders, Samuel Adams and John Hancock. At Lexington the colonial "Minute Men" refused to disperse rapidly enough, and shots were fired that killed eight Americans and wounded several more. The affair was more the "Lexington Massacre" than a battle. The redcoats pushed on to Concord, whence they were forced to retreat by the rough and ready Americans, whom Emerson immortalized:

> *By the rude bridge that arched the flood,*
> *Their flag to April's breeze unfurled,*
> *Here once the embattled farmers stood,*
> *And fired the shot heard round the world.**

The bewildered British, fighting off murderous fire from militiamen crouched behind thick stone walls, finally regained the sanctuary of Boston. Licking their wounds,

---

*Ralph Waldo Emerson, "Concord Hymn."

they could count about three hundred casualties, including some seventy killed. Britain now had a war on its hands.

Imperial Strength and Weakness

Aroused Americans had brashly rebelled against a mighty empire. The population odds were about three to one against the rebels—some 7.5 million Britons to 2.5 million colonists. The odds in monetary wealth and naval power overwhelmingly favored the mother country.

Britain then boasted a professional army of some fifty thousand men, as compared with the numerous but wretchedly trained American militia. George III, in addition, had the treasury to hire foreign soldiers, and some thirty thousand Germans—so-called Hessians—were ultimately employed. The British enrolled about fifty thousand American Loyalists and enlisted the services of many Indians, who though unreliable fair-weather fighters, inflamed long stretches of the frontier. One British officer boasted that the war would offer no problems that could not be solved by an "experienced sheep herder."

The great conservative political theorist and champion of the American cause, Edmund Burke, made a stirring speech in Britain's House of Commons in 1775, pleading in vain for reconciliation with the colonies:

"As long as you have the wisdom to keep the sovereign authority of this country as the sanctuary of liberty . . . they will turn their faces towards you. . . . Slavery they can have anywhere; freedom they can have from none but you. This is the commodity of price, of which you have the monopoly. This is the true Act of Navigation, which binds to you the commerce of the colonies, and through them secures to you the wealth of the world. Deny them this participation of freedom, and you break that sole bond which originally made, and must still preserve, the unity of the empire."

Yet Britain was weaker than it seemed at first glance. Oppressed Ireland was a smoking volcano, and British troops had to be detached to watch it. France, bitter from its recent defeat, was awaiting an opportunity to stab Britain in the back. The London government was confused and inept. There was no William Pitt, "Organizer of Victory," only the stubborn George III and his pliant Tory prime minister, Lord North.

Many earnest and God-fearing Britons had no desire whatever to kill their American cousins. William Pitt withdrew a son from the army rather than see him thrust his sword into fellow Anglo-Saxons struggling for liberty. The English Whig factions, opposed to Lord North's Tory wing, openly cheered American victories—at least at the outset. Aside from trying to embarrass the Tories politically, many Whigs believed that the battle for British freedom was being fought in America. If George III triumphed, his rule at home might become tyrannical. This outspoken sympathy in Britain, though plainly a minority voice, greatly encouraged the Americans. If they continued their resistance long enough, the Whigs might come into power and deal generously with them.

Britain's army in America had to operate under endless difficulties. The generals were second-rate; the soldiers, though on the whole capable, were brutally treated. There was one extreme case of eight hundred lashes on the bare back for striking an officer. Provisions were often scarce, rancid, and wormy. On one occasion a supply of biscuits, captured some fifteen years earlier from the French, was softened by dropping cannonballs on them.

Other handicaps loomed. The redcoats had to conquer the Americans; restoring the pre-1763 status quo would be a victory for the colonists. Britain was operating some 3,000 miles from its home base, and distance added greatly to the delays and uncertainties arising from storms and other mishaps. Military orders were issued in London that, when received months later, would not fit the changing situation.

America's geographical expanse was enormous: roughly 1,000 by 600 miles. The united colonies had no urban nerve center, like France's Paris, whose capture would cripple the country as a whole. British armies took every city of any size, yet like a boxer punching a feather pillow, they made little more than a dent in the entire country. The Americans wisely traded space for time. Benjamin Franklin calculated that during the prolonged campaign in which the redcoats captured Bunker Hill and killed some 150 Patriots, about 60,000 American babies were born.

American Pluses and Minuses

The revolutionaries were blessed with outstanding leadership. George Washington was a giant among men; Benjamin Franklin was a master among diplomats. Open foreign aid, theoretically possible from the start, eventually came from France. Numerous European officers, many of them unemployed and impoverished, volunteered their swords for pay. In a class by himself was a wealthy young French nobleman, the Marquis de Lafayette. Fleeing from boredom, loving glory and ultimately liberty, the "French gamecock" was made a major general in the colonial army at age nineteen. His commission was largely a recognition of his family influence and political connections, but the services of this teenage general in securing further aid from France were invaluable.

Other conditions aided the Americans. They were fighting defensively, with the odds, all things considered, favoring the defender. In agriculture, the colonies were mainly self-sustaining, like a kind of Robinson Crusoe's island. The Americans also enjoyed the moral advantage that came from belief in a just cause. The historical odds were not impossible. Other peoples had triumphed in the face of greater obstacles: Greeks against Persians, Swiss against Austrians, Dutch against Spaniards.

Yet the American rebels were badly organized for war. From the earliest days, they had been almost fatally lacking in unity, and the new nation lurched forward uncertainly like an uncoordinated centipede. Even the Continental Congress, which directed the conflict, was hardly more than a debating society, and it grew feebler as the struggle dragged on. "Their Congress now is quite disjoint'd," gibed an English satirist, "Since Gibbits (gallows) [are] for them appointed." The disorganized colonists fought almost the entire war before adopting a written constitution—the Articles of Confederation—in 1781.

Jealousy everywhere raised its hideous head. Individual states, proudly regarding themselves as sovereign, resented the attempts of Congress to exercise its flimsy powers. Sectional jealousy boiled up over the appointment of military leaders; some distrustful New Englanders almost preferred British officers to Americans from other sections.

Economic difficulties were nearly insuperable. Metallic money had already been heavily drained away. A cautious Continental Congress, unwilling to raise

Gilbert du Motier, Marquis de Lafayette (1757–1834), by Joseph Boze, 1790 This youthful French officer gave to America not only military service but some $200,000 of his private funds. He returned to France after the American Revolution to play a conspicuous role in the French Revolution.

anew the explosive issue of taxation, was forced to print "Continental" paper money in great amounts. As this currency poured from the presses, it depreciated until

General Washington's (1732–1799) disgust with his countrymen is reflected in a diary entry for 1776:

"Chimney corner patriots abound; venality, corruption, prostitution of office for selfish ends, abuse of trust, perversion of funds from a national to a private use, and speculations upon the necessities of the times pervade all interests."

the expression "not worth a Continental" became current. One barber contemptuously papered his shop with the near-worthless dollars. The confusion proliferated when the individual states were compelled to issue depreciated paper money of their own.

Inflation of the currency inevitably skyrocketed prices. Families of the soldiers at the fighting front were hard hit, and hundreds of anxious husbands and fathers deserted. Debtors easily acquired handfuls of the quasi-worthless money and gleefully paid their debts "without mercy"—sometimes with the bayonets of the authorities to back them up.

A Thin Line of Heroes

Basic military supplies in the colonies were dangerously scanty. While many families and towns did own firearms—widespread militia service meant men needed weapons for training—the colonists had long relied heavily on Britain for troops, armaments, and military subsidies during expensive wars against Indians, France, and Spain. The rebels were caught in an unavoidable trap: at the very moment that the supply of British funds and war materiel evaporated, the cost of home defense mounted. Sufficient stores of gunpowder, cannon, and other armaments (let alone ships to transport them) could not be found. Among the reasons for the eventual alliance with France was the need for a reliable source of essential military supplies.

Other shortages bedeviled the rebels. At Valley Forge, Pennsylvania, shivering American soldiers went without bread for three successive days in the cruel winter of 1777–1778. In one southern campaign, some men fainted for lack of food. Manufactured goods also were generally in short supply in agricultural America, and clothing and shoes were appallingly scarce. The path of the Patriot fighting men was often marked by bloody snow. At frigid Valley Forge, during one anxious period, twenty-eight hundred men were barefooted or nearly naked. Woolens were desperately needed against the wintry blasts, and in general the only real uniform of the colonial army was uniform raggedness. During a grand parade at Valley Forge, some of the officers appeared wrapped in woolen bedcovers. One Rhode Island unit was known as the "Ragged, Lousy, Naked Regiment."

American militiamen were numerous but also highly unreliable. Able-bodied American males—perhaps several hundred thousand of them—had received

Enslaved blacks hoped that the Revolutionary crisis would make it possible for them to secure their own liberty. On the eve of the war in South Carolina, merchant Josiah Smith, Jr., noted such a rumor among the slaves:

"[Freedom] is their common Talk throughout the Province, and has occasioned impertinent behavior in many of them, insomuch that our Provincial Congress now sitting hath voted the immediate raising of Two Thousand Men Horse and food, to keep those mistaken creatures in awe."

Despite such repressive measures, slave uprisings continued to plague the southern colonies through 1775 and 1776.

rudimentary training, and many of these recruits served for short terms in the rebel armies. But poorly trained plowboys could not stand up in the open field against professional British troops advancing with bare bayonets. Many of these undisciplined warriors would, in the words of Washington, "fly from their own shadows."

A few thousand regulars—perhaps seven or eight thousand at the war's end—were finally whipped into shape by stern drillmasters. Notable among them was an organizational genius, the salty German Baron von Steuben. He spoke no English when he reached America, but he soon taught his men that bayonets were not for broiling beefsteaks over open fires. As they gained experience, these soldiers of the Continental line more than held their own against crack British troops.

Blacks also fought and died for the American cause. Although many states initially barred them from militia service, by war's end more than five thousand blacks had enlisted in the American armed forces. The largest contingents came from the northern states with substantial numbers of free blacks.

Blacks fought at Trenton, Brandywine, Saratoga, and other important battles. Some, including Prince Whipple—later immortalized in Emanuel Leutze's famous painting "Washington Crossing the Delaware" (see p. 151)—became military heroes. Others served as cooks, guides, spies, drivers, and road builders.

The Flutist, by Brazilla Lew This portrait is believed to be that of an African American fifer in the Revolutionary War. Lew was a veteran of the Seven Years' War who had marched to Ticonderoga and served in the army a full seven years as front-line soldier, fifer, and drummer. In 1775, at the age of thirty-two, he fought at Bunker Hill as an enlistee in the twenty-seventh Massachusetts Regiment. A resident of Chelmsford, he was said to have taught all twelve of his children to play musical instruments.

African Americans also served on the British side. In November 1775 Lord Dunmore, royal governor of Virginia, issued a proclamation promising freedom for any enslaved black in Virginia who joined the British army. News of Dunmore's decree traveled swiftly. Virginia and Maryland tightened slave patrols, but within one month, three hundred slaves had joined what came to be called "Lord Dunmore's Ethiopian Regiment." In time thousands of blacks fled plantations for British promises of emancipation. When one of James Madison's slaves was caught trying to escape to the British lines, Madison refused to punish him for "coveting that liberty" that white Americans proclaimed the "right & worthy pursuit of every human being." At war's end the British kept their word, to some at least, and evacuated as many as fourteen thousand "Black Loyalists" to Nova Scotia, Jamaica, and England.

Morale in the Revolutionary army was badly undermined by American profiteers. Putting profits before patriotism, they sold to the British because the invader could pay in gold. Speculators forced prices sky-high, and some Bostonians made profits of 50 to 200 percent on army garb while the American army was freezing at Valley Forge. Washington never had as many as twenty thousand effective troops in one place at one time, despite bounties of land and other inducements. Yet if the rebels had thrown themselves into the struggle with zeal, they could easily have raised many times that number.

The brutal truth is that only a select minority of the American colonists attached themselves to the cause of independence with a spirit of selfless devotion. These were the dedicated souls who bore the burden of battle and the risks of defeat. Seldom have so few done so much for so many.

Chronology

1650	First Navigation Laws to control colonial commerce
1696	Board of Trade assumes governance of colonies
1763	Seven Years' War (French and Indian War) ends
1764	Sugar Act
1765	Quartering Act Stamp Act Stamp Act Congress
1766	Declaratory Act
1767	Townshend Acts New York legislature suspended by Parliament
1768	British troops occupy Boston
1770	Boston Massacre All Townshend Acts except tea tax repealed
1772	Committees of correspondence formed
1773	British East India Company granted tea monopoly Governor Hutchinson's actions provoke Boston Tea Party
1774	"Intolerable Acts" Quebec Act First Continental Congress The Association boycotts British goods
1775	Battles of Lexington and Concord

For further reading, see the Appendix. For web resources, go to **http://college.hmco.com.**

America Secedes from the Empire

1775–1783

THESE ARE THE TIMES THAT TRY MEN'S SOULS. THE SUMMER SOLDIER AND THE SUNSHINE PATRIOT WILL, IN THIS CRISIS, SHRINK FROM THE SERVICE OF THEIR COUNTRY; BUT HE THAT STANDS IT NOW, DESERVES THE LOVE AND THANKS OF MAN AND WOMAN.

THOMAS PAINE, DECEMBER 1776

Bloodshed at Lexington and Concord in April of 1775 was a clarion call to arms. About twenty thousand musket-bearing "Minute Men" swarmed around Boston, there to coop up the outnumbered British.

The Second Continental Congress met in Philadelphia the next month, on May 10, 1775, and this time the full slate of thirteen colonies was represented. The conservative element in Congress was still strong, despite the shooting in Massachusetts. There was still no well-defined sentiment for independence— merely a desire to continue fighting in the hope that the king and Parliament would consent to a redress of grievances. Congress hopefully drafted new appeals to the British people and king—appeals that were spurned. Anticipating a possible rebuff, the delegates also adopted measures to raise money and to create an army and a navy. The British and the Americans now teetered on the brink of all-out warfare.

Congress Drafts George Washington

Perhaps the most important single action of the Congress was to select George Washington, one of its members already in an officer's uniform, to head the hastily improvised army besieging Boston. This choice was made with considerable misgivings. The tall, powerfully built, dignified Virginia planter, then forty-three, had never risen above the rank of a colonel in the militia. His largest command had numbered only twelve hundred men, and that had been some twenty years earlier. Falling short of true military genius, Washington would actually lose more pitched battles than he won.

But the distinguished Virginian was gifted with outstanding powers of leadership and immense strength of character. He radiated patience, courage, self-discipline, and a sense of justice. He was a great moral force rather than a great military mind—a symbol and a rallying point. People instinctively trusted him; they sensed that when he put himself at the head of a cause, he was prepared, if necessary, to go down with the ship. He insisted on serving without pay, though he kept a careful expense account amounting to more than $100,000. Later he sternly reprimanded his steward at Mount Vernon for providing the enemy, under duress, with supplies. He would have preferred instead to see the enemy put the torch to his mansion.

The Continental Congress, though dimly perceiving Washington's qualities of leadership, chose more wisely

Washington at Verplanck's Point, New York, 1782, Reviewing the French Troops After the Victory at Yorktown, by John Trumbull, 1790
This noted American artist accentuated Washington's already imposing height (six feet two inches) by showing him towering over his horse. Washington so appreciated this portrait of himself that he hung it in the dining room of his home at Mount Vernon, Virginia.

than it knew. His selection, in truth, was largely political. Americans in other sections, already jealous, were beginning to distrust the large New England army being collected around Boston. Prudence suggested a commander from Virginia, the largest and most populous of the colonies. As a man of wealth, both by inheritance and by marriage, Washington could not be accused of being a fortune-seeker. As an aristocrat, he could be counted on by his peers to check "the excesses of the masses."

Bunker Hill and Hessian Hirelings

The clash of arms continued on a strangely contradictory basis. On the one hand, the Americans were emphatically affirming their loyalty to the king and earnestly voicing their desire to patch up difficulties. On the other hand, they were raising armies and shooting down His Majesty's soldiers. This curious war of inconsistency was fought for fourteen long months—from April 1775 to July 1776—before the fateful plunge into independence was taken.

Gradually the tempo of warfare increased. In May 1775 a tiny American force under Ethan Allen and Benedict Arnold surprised and captured the British garrisons at Ticonderoga and Crown Point, on the scenic lakes of upper New York. A priceless store of gunpowder and artillery for the siege of Boston was thus secured. In June 1775 the colonists seized a hill, now known as Bunker Hill (actually Breed's Hill), from which they menaced the enemy in Boston. The British, instead of cutting off the retreat of their foes by flanking them, blundered bloodily when they launched a frontal attack with three thousand men. Sharpshooting Americans, numbering fifteen hundred and strongly entrenched, mowed down the advancing redcoats with frightful slaughter. But the colonists' scanty store of gunpowder finally gave out, and they were forced to abandon the hill in disorder. With two more such victories, remarked the French foreign minister, the British would have no army left in America.

Even at this late date, in July 1775, the Continental Congress adopted the "Olive Branch Petition," professing American loyalty to the crown and begging the king to prevent further hostilities. But following Bunker Hill, King George III slammed the door on all hope of reconciliation. In August 1775 he formally proclaimed the colonies in rebellion; the skirmishes

Battle of Bunker Hill, June 17, 1775
This British engraving conveys the vulnerability of the British regulars to attacks by the American militiamen. Although a defeat for the colonists, the battle quickly proved a moral victory for the Patriots. Outnumbered and outgunned, they held their own against the British and suffered many fewer casualties.

were now out-and-out treason, a hanging crime. The next month he widened the chasm when he sealed arrangements for hiring thousands of German troops to help crush his rebellious subjects. Six German princes involved in the transaction needed the money (one reputedly had seventy-four children); George III needed the men. Because most of these soldiers-for-hire came from the German principality of Hesse, the Americans called all the European mercenaries Hessians.

News of the Hessian deal shocked the colonists. The quarrel, they felt, was within the family. Why bring in outside mercenaries, especially foreigners who had an exaggerated reputation for butchery?

Hessian hirelings proved to be good soldiers in a mechanical sense, but many of them were more interested in booty than in duty. For good reason they were dubbed "Hessian flies." Seduced by American promises of land, hundreds of them finally deserted and remained in America to become respected citizens.

The Abortive Conquest of Canada

The unsheathed sword continued to take its toll. In October 1775, on the eve of a cruel winter, the British burned Falmouth (Portland), Maine. In that same autumn, the rebels daringly undertook a two-pronged invasion of Canada. American leaders believed, erroneously, that the conquered French were explosively restive under the British yoke. A successful assault on Canada would add a fourteenth colony, while depriving Britain of a valuable base for striking at the colonies in revolt. But this large-scale attack, involving some two thousand American troops, contradicted the claim of the colonists that they were merely fighting defensively for a redress of grievances. Invasion northward was undisguised offensive warfare.

This bold stroke for Canada narrowly missed success. One invading column under the Irish-born General Richard Montgomery, formerly of the British army, pushed up the Lake Champlain route and captured Montreal. He was joined at Quebec by the bedraggled army of General Benedict Arnold, whose men had been reduced to eating dogs and shoe leather during their grueling march through the Maine woods. An assault on Quebec, launched on the last day of 1775, was beaten off. The able Montgomery was killed; the dashing Arnold was wounded in one leg. Scattered remnants under his command retreated up the St. Lawrence River, reversing the way Montgomery had come. French Canadian leaders, who had been generously treated by the British in the Quebec Act of 1774, showed no real desire to welcome the plundering anti-Catholic invaders.

Bitter fighting persisted in the colonies, though most Americans continued to disclaim a desire for independence. In January 1776 the British set fire to the Virginia town of Norfolk. In March they were finally

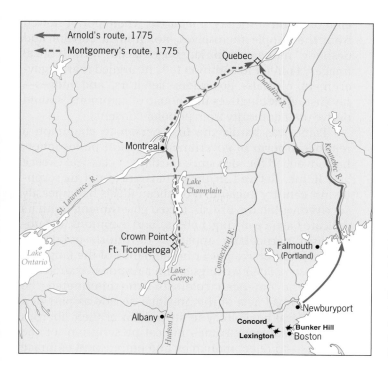

Revolution in the North, 1775–1776
Benedict Arnold's troops were described as "pretty young men" when they sailed from Massachusetts. They were considerably less pretty on their arrival in Quebec, after eight weeks of struggling through wet and frigid forests, often without food. "No one can imagine," one of them wrote, "the sweetness of a roasted shot-pouch [ammunition bag] to the famished appetite."

forced to evacuate Boston, taking with them the leading friends of the king. (Evacuation Day is still celebrated annually in Boston.) In the South the rebellious colonists won two victories in 1776—one in February against some fifteen hundred Loyalists at Moore's Creek Bridge in North Carolina, and the other in June against an invading British fleet at Charleston harbor.

Gradually the Americans were shocked into recognizing the necessity of separating from the crown. Their eyes were jolted open by harsh British acts like the burning of Falmouth and Norfolk, and especially by the hiring of the Hessians.

Thomas Paine Preaches Common Sense

Why did Americans continue to deny any intention of independence? Loyalty to the empire was deeply ingrained; many Americans continued to consider themselves part of a transatlantic community in which the mother country of Britain played a leading role; colonial unity was poor; and open rebellion was dangerous, especially against a formidable Britain. Irish rebels of that day were customarily hanged, drawn, and quartered. American rebels might have fared no better. As late as January 1776—five months before independence was declared—the king's health was being toasted by the officers of Washington's mess near Boston. "God save the king" had not yet been replaced by "God save the Congress."

In Common Sense *Thomas Paine (1737–1809) argued for the superiority of a republic over a monarchy:*

"The nearer any government approaches to a republic the less business there is for a king. It is somewhat difficult to find a proper name for the government of England. Sir William Meredith calls it a republic; but in its present state it is unworthy of the name, because the corrupt influence of the crown, by having all the places in its disposal, hath so effectively swallowed up the power, and eaten out the virtue of the house of commons (the republican part of the constitution) that the government of England is nearly as monarchical as that of France or Spain."

Portrait of Thomas Paine, by Auguste Millière.

Then in 1776 came the publication of *Common Sense,* one of the most influential pamphlets ever written. Its author was the radical Thomas Paine, once an impoverished corset-maker's apprentice, who had come over from Britain a year earlier. His tract became a whirlwind best seller and within a few months reached the astonishing total of 120,000 copies.

Paine flatly branded the shilly-shallying of the colonists as contrary to "common sense." Nowhere in the physical universe did the smaller heavenly body control the larger one. So why should the tiny island of Britain control the vast continent of America? As for the king, whom the Americans professed to revere, he was nothing but "the Royal Brute of Great Britain."

Paine and the Idea of "Republicanism"

Paine's passionate protest was as compelling as it was eloquent and radical—even doubly radical. It called not simply for independence, but for the creation of a new kind of political society, a *republic,* where power flowed from the people themselves, not from a corrupt and despotic monarch. In language laced with biblical imagery familiar to common folk, he argued that all government officials—governors, senators, and judges—not just representatives in a house of commons, should derive their authority from popular consent.

Paine was hardly the first person to champion a republican form of government. Political philosophers had advanced the idea since the days of classical Greece and Rome. Revived in the Renaissance and in seventeenth-century England, republican ideals had uneasily survived within the British "mixed government," with its delicate balance of king, nobility, and commons. Republicanism particularly appealed to British politicians critical of excessive power in the hands of the king and his advisers. Their writings found a responsive audience among the American colonists, who interpreted the vengeful royal acts of the previous decade as part of a monarchical conspiracy to strip them of their liberties as British subjects. Paine's radical prescription for the colonies—to reject monarchy and empire and embrace an independent republic—fell on receptive ears.

The colonists' experience with governance had prepared them well for Paine's summons to create a republic. Many settlers, particularly New Englanders, had practiced a kind of republicanism in their democratic town meetings and annual elections, while the popularly elected committees of correspondence during 1774 and 1775 had demonstrated the feasibility of republican government. The absence of a hereditary aristocracy and the relative equality of condition enjoyed by landowning farmers meshed well with the republican repudiation of a fixed hierarchy of power.

Most Americans considered citizen "virtue" fundamental to any successful republican government. Because political power no longer rested with the central, all-powerful authority of the king, individuals in a republic needed to sacrifice their personal self-interest to the public good. The collective good of "the people" mattered more than the private rights and interests of individuals. Paine inspired his contemporaries to view America as fertile ground for the cultivation of such civic virtue.

Yet not all Patriots agreed with Paine's ultrademocratic approach to republicanism. Some favored a republic ruled by a "natural aristocracy" of talent. Republicanism for them meant an end to hereditary aristocracy, but not an end to all social hierarchy. These more conservative republicans feared that the fervor for liberty would overwhelm the stability of the social order. They watched with trepidation as the "lower orders" of society—poorer farmers, tenants, and laboring classes in towns and cities—seemed to embrace a kind of runaway republicanism that amounted to radical "leveling." The contest to define the nature of American republicanism would noisily continue for at least the next hundred years.

Jefferson's "Explanation" of Independence

Members of the Philadelphia Congress, instructed by their respective colonies, gradually edged toward a clean break. On June 7, 1776, fiery Richard Henry Lee of Virginia moved that "these United Colonies are, and of right ought to be, free and independent states." After considerable debate, the motion was adopted nearly a month later, on July 2, 1776.

The passing of Lee's resolution was the formal "declaration" of independence by the American colonies, and technically this was all that was needed to cut the British tie. John Adams wrote confidently that ever thereafter, July 2 would be celebrated annually with fireworks. But something more was required. An epochal rupture of this kind called for some formal explanation. An inspirational appeal was also needed to enlist other British colonies in the Americas, to invite assistance from foreign nations, and to rally resistance at home.

Shortly after Lee made his memorable motion on June 7, Congress appointed a committee to prepare a more formal statement of separation. The task of drafting it fell to Thomas Jefferson, a tall, freckled, sandy-haired Virginia lawyer of thirty-three. Despite his youth, he was already recognized as a brilliant writer, and he measured up splendidly to the awesome assignment. After some debate and amendment, the Declaration of Independence was formally approved by the Congress on July 4, 1776. It might better have been called "the Explanation of Independence" or, as one contemporary described it, "Mr. Jefferson's advertisement of Mr. Lee's resolution."

Jefferson's pronouncement, couched in a lofty style, was magnificent. He gave his appeal universality by invoking the "natural rights" of humankind—not just British rights. He argued persuasively that because the king had flouted these rights, the colonists were justified in cutting their connection. He then set forth a long list of the presumably tyrannous misdeeds of George III. The overdrawn bill of indictment included imposing taxes without consent, dispensing with trial

George III (1738–1820), Studio of Alan Ramsay, c. 1767
America's last king, he was a good man, unlike some of his scandal-tainted brothers and sons, but a bad king. Doggedly determined to regain arbitrary power for the crown, he antagonized and then lost the thirteen American colonies. During much of his sixty-year reign, he seemed to be insane, but recently medical science has found that he was suffering from a rare metabolic and hereditary disease called porphyria.

by jury, abolishing valued laws, establishing a military dictatorship, maintaining standing armies in peacetime, cutting off trade, burning towns, hiring mercenaries, and inciting hostility among the Indians.*

Jefferson's withering blast was admittedly one-sided. But he was in effect the prosecuting attorney, and he took certain liberties with historical truth. He was not writing history; he was making it through what has been called "the world's greatest editorial." He owned many slaves, and his affirmation that "all men are created equal" was to haunt him and his fellow citizens for generations.

---

*For an annotated text of the Declaration of Independence, see the Appendix.

> *The American signers of the Declaration of Independence had reason to fear for their necks. In 1802, twenty-six years later, George III (1738–1820) approved this death sentence for seven Irish rebels:*
>
> "... [You] are to be hanged by the neck, but not until you are dead; for while you are still living your bodies are to be taken down, your bowels torn out and burned before your faces, your heads then cut off, and your bodies divided each into four quarters, and your heads and quarters to be then at the King's disposal; and may the Almighty God have mercy on your souls."

The formal Declaration of Independence cleared the air as a thundershower does on a muggy day. Foreign aid could be solicited with greater hope of success. Those Patriots who defied the king were now rebels, not loving subjects shooting their way into reconciliation. They must all hang together, Franklin is said to have grimly remarked, or they would all hang separately. Or, in the eloquent language of the great declaration, "We mutually pledge to each other our lives, our fortunes and our sacred honor."

Jefferson's defiant Declaration of Independence had a universal impact unmatched by any other American document. This "shout heard round the world" has been a source of inspiration to countless revolutionary movements against arbitrary authority. Lafayette hung a copy on a wall in his home, leaving beside it room for a future French Declaration of the Rights of Man—a declaration that was officially born thirteen years later.

Patriots and Loyalists

The War of Independence, strictly speaking, was a war within a war. Colonials loyal to the king (Loyalists) fought the American rebels (Patriots), while the rebels also fought the British redcoats (see "Makers of America: The Loyalists," pp. 148–149). Loyalists were derisively called "Tories," after the dominant political factions in Britain, whereas Patriots were called "Whigs," after the opposition factions in Britain. A popular definition of a Tory among the Patriots betrayed bitterness: "A Tory is a thing whose head is in England, and its body in America, and its neck ought to be stretched."

Like many revolutions, the American Revolution was a minority movement. Many colonists were apathetic or neutral, including the Byrds of Virginia, who sat on the fence. The opposing forces contended not only against each other but also for the allegiance and support of the civilian population. In this struggle for the hearts and minds of the people, the British proved fatally inept, and the Patriot militias played a crucial role. The British military proved able to control only those areas where it could maintain a massive military presence. Elsewhere, as soon as the redcoats had marched on, the rebel militiamen appeared and took up the task of "political education"—sometimes by coercive means. Often lacking bayonets but always loaded with political zeal, the ragtag militia units served as remarkably effective agents of Revolutionary ideas. They convinced many colonists, even those indifferent to independence, that the British army was an unreliable friend and that they had better throw in their lot with the Patriot cause. They also mercilessly harassed small British detachments and occupation forces. One British officer ruefully observed that "the Americans would be less dangerous if they had a regular army."

Loyalists, numbering perhaps 16 percent of the American people, remained true to their king. Families often split over the issue of independence: Benjamin Franklin supported the Patriot side, whereas his handsome illegitimate son, William Franklin (the last royal governor of New Jersey), upheld the Loyalist cause.

The Loyalists were tragic figures. For generations the British in the New World had been taught fidelity to the crown. Loyalty is ordinarily regarded as a major virtue—loyalty to one's family, one's friends, one's country. If the king had triumphed, as he seemed likely to do, the Loyalists would have been acclaimed patriots, and defeated rebels like Washington would have been disgraced, severely punished, and probably forgotten.

Many people of education and wealth, of culture and caution, remained loyal. These wary souls were satisfied with their lot and believed that any violent change would only be for the worse. Loyalists were also more numerous among the older generation. Young people make revolutions, and from the outset energetic, purposeful, and militant young people surged forward—

EXAMINING THE EVIDENCE

A Revolution for Women? Abigail Adams Chides Her Husband, 1776   In the midst of the revolutionary fervor of 1776, at least one woman—Abigail Adams, wife of noted Massachusetts Patriot (and future president) John Adams—raised her voice on behalf of women. Yet she apparently raised it only in private—in this personal letter to her husband. Private documents like the correspondence and diaries of individuals both prominent and ordinary offer invaluable sources for the historian seeking to discover sentiments, opinions, and perspectives that are often difficult to discern in the official public record. What might it suggest about the historical circumstances of the 1770s that Abigail Adams confined her claim for women's equality to this confidential exchange with her spouse? What might have inspired the arguments she employed? Despite her privileged position and persuasive power, and despite her threat to "foment a rebellion," Abigail Adams's plea went largely unheeded in the Revolutionary era—as did comparable pleadings to extend the revolutionary principle of equality to blacks. What might have accounted for this limited application of the ideas of liberty and equality in the midst of a supposedly democratic revolution?

The Loyalists

In late 1776 Catherine Van Cortlandt wrote to her husband, a New Jersey merchant fighting in a Loyalist brigade, about the Patriot troops who had quartered themselves in her house. "They were the most disorderly of species," she complained, "and their officers were from the dregs of the people."

Like the Van Cortlandts, many Loyalists thought of themselves as the "better sort of people." They viewed their adversaries as "lawless mobs" and "brutes." Conservative, wealthy, and well-educated, Loyalists of this breed thought a break with Britain would invite anarchy. Loyalism made sense to them, too, for practical reasons. Viewing colonial militias as no match for His Majesty's army, Loyalist pamphleteer Daniel Leonard warned his Patriot enemies in 1775 that "nothing short of a miracle could gain you one battle."

But Loyalism was hardly confined to the well-to-do. It also appealed to many people of modest means who identified strongly with Britain or who had reason to fear a Patriot victory. Thousands of British veterans of the Seven Years' War, for example, had settled in the colonies after 1763. Many of them took up farming on

two-hundred-acre land grants in New York. They were loath to turn their backs on the crown. So, too, were recent immigrants from non-English regions of the British Isles, especially from Scotland and Ireland, who had settled in Georgia or the backcountry of North and South Carolina. Many of these newcomers, resenting the plantation elite who ran these colonies, filled the ranks of Tory brigades such as the Volunteers of Ireland and the North Carolina Highlanders, organized by the British army to galvanize Loyalist support.

Other ethnic minorities found their own reasons to support the British. Some members of Dutch, German, and French religious sects believed that religious tolerance would be greater under the British than under the Americans, whose prejudices they had already encountered. Above all, thousands of African Americans joined Loyalist ranks in the hope that service to the British might offer an escape from bondage. British officials encouraged that belief. Throughout the war and in every colony, some African Americans fled to British lines, where they served as soldiers, servants, laborers, and spies. Many of them joined black regiments that

Loyalists Take Flight
This watercolor shows an encampment on the St. Lawrence River of Loyalists who had fled the rebellious colonies for the safe haven of Canada, where they applied to the British government for land grants.

Loyalists Through British Eyes This British cartoon depicts the Loyalists as doubly victimized—by Americans caricatured as "savage" Indians and by the British prime minister, the Earl of Shelburne, for offering little protection to Britain's defenders.

specialized in making small sorties against Patriot militias. In Monmouth, New Jersey, the black Loyalist Colonel Tye and his band of raiders became legendary for capturing Patriots and their supplies.

As the war drew to an end in 1783, the fate of black Loyalists varied enormously. Many thousands who came to Loyalism as fugitive slaves managed to find a way to freedom, most notably the large group who won British passage from the port of New York to Nova Scotia. Other African American Loyalists suffered betrayal. British general Lord Cornwallis abandoned over four thousand former slaves in Virginia, and many black Loyalists who boarded ships from British-controlled ports expecting to embark for freedom instead found themselves sold back into slavery in the West Indies.

White Loyalists faced no threat of enslavement, but they did suffer punishments beyond mere disgrace: arrest, exile, confiscation of property, and loss of legal rights. Faced with such retribution, some eighty thousand Loyalists fled abroad, mostly to Britain and the maritime provinces of Canada. Some settled contentedly as exiles, but many, especially those who went to Britain, where they had difficulty becoming accepted, lived diminished and lonely lives—"cut off," as Loyalist Thomas Danforth put it, "from every hope of importance in life . . . [and] in a station much inferior to that of a menial servant."

But most Loyalists remained in America, where they faced the special burdens of reestablishing themselves in a society that viewed them as traitors. Some succeeded remarkably despite the odds, such as Hugh Gaine, a printer in New York City who eventually reopened a business and even won contracts from the new government. Ironically, this former Loyalist soldier published the new national army regulations authored by the Revolutionary hero Baron von Steuben. Like many former Loyalists, Gaine reintegrated himself into public life by siding with the Federalist call for a strong central government and powerful executive. When New York ratified the Constitution in 1788, Gaine rode the float at the head of the city's celebration parade. He had, like many other former Loyalists, become an American.

New York Patriots Pull Down the Statue of King George III Erected after the repeal of the Stamp Act in 1766, this statue was melted down by the revolutionaries into bullets to be used against the king's troops.

figures like the sleeplessly scheming Samuel Adams and the impassioned Patrick Henry. His flaming outcry before the Virginia Assembly—"Give me liberty or give me death!"—still quickens patriotic pulses.

Loyalists also included the king's officers and other beneficiaries of the crown—people who knew which side their daily bread came from. The same was generally true of the Anglican clergy and a large portion of their congregations, all of whom had long been taught submission to the king.

Usually the Loyalists were most numerous where the Anglican Church was strongest. A notable exception was Virginia, where the debt-burdened Anglican aristocrats flocked into the rebel camp. The king's followers were well entrenched in aristocratic New York City and Charleston, and also in Quaker Pennsylvania and New Jersey, where General Washington felt that he was fighting in "the enemy's country." While his men were starving at Valley Forge, nearby Pennsylvania farmers were selling their produce to the British for the king's gold.

Loyalists were least numerous in New England, where self-government was especially strong and mercantilism was especially weak. Rebels were the most numerous where Presbyterianism and Congregationalism flourished, notably in New England. Invading British armies vented their contempt and anger by using Yankee churches for pigsties.

The Loyalist Exodus

Before the Declaration of Independence in 1776, persecution of the Loyalists was relatively mild. Yet they were subjected to some brutality, including tarring and feathering and riding astride fence rails.

After the Declaration of Independence, which sharply separated Loyalists from Patriots, harsher methods prevailed. The rebels naturally desired a united front. Putting loyalty to the colonies first, they regarded their opponents, not themselves, as traitors. Loyalists were roughly handled, hundreds were imprisoned, and a few noncombatants were hanged. But there was no wholesale reign of terror comparable to that which later bloodied both France and Russia during their revolutions. For one thing, the colonists reflected Anglo-Saxon regard for order; for another, the leading Loyalists were prudent enough to flee to the British lines.

About eighty thousand loyal supporters of George III were driven out or fled, but several hundred thousand or so of the mild Loyalists were permitted to stay. The estates of many of the fugitives were confiscated and sold—a relatively painless way to help finance the war. Confiscation often worked great hardship, as, for example, when two aristocratic women were forced to live in their former chicken house for leaning Toryward.

Washington Crossing the Delaware, by Emanuel Gottlieb Leutze, 1851   On Christmas Day, 1776, George Washington set out from Pennsylvania with twenty-four hundred men to surprise the British forces, chiefly Hessians, in their quarters across the river in New Jersey. The subsequent British defeat proved to be a turning point in the Revolution, as it checked the British advance toward Philadelphia and restored American morale. Seventy-five years later, Leutze, a German American immigrant who had returned to Germany, mythologized the heroic campaign in this painting. Imbued with the liberal democratic principles of the American Revolution, Leutze intended his painting to inspire Europeans in their revolutions of 1848. To that end, he ignored the fact that the Stars and Stripes held by Lieutenant James Monroe was not adopted until 1777; that Washington could not possibly have stood so long on one leg; that the colonists crossed the Delaware at night, not during the day; and that no African American would have been present. What Leutze did capture was the importance of ordinary men in the Revolutionary struggle and the tremendous urgency they felt at this particular moment in 1776, when victory seemed so elusive.

Some fifty thousand Loyalist volunteers at one time or another bore arms for the British. They also helped the king's cause by serving as spies, by inciting the Indians, and by keeping Patriot soldiers at home to protect their families. Ardent Loyalists had their hearts in their cause, and a major blunder of the haughty British was not to make full use of them in the fighting.

General Washington at Bay

With Boston evacuated in March 1776, the British concentrated on New York as a base of operations. Here was a splendid seaport, centrally located, where the king could count on cooperation from the numerous Loyalists. An awe-inspiring British fleet appeared off New York in July 1776. It consisted of some five hundred ships and thirty-five thousand men—the largest armed force to be seen in America until the Civil War. General Washington, dangerously outnumbered, could muster only eighteen thousand ill-trained troops with which to meet the crack army of the invader.

Disaster befell the Americans in the summer and fall of 1776. Outgeneraled and outmaneuvered, they were routed at the Battle of Long Island, where panic seized the raw recruits. By the narrowest of margins, and thanks to a favoring wind and fog, Washington escaped to Manhattan Island. Retreating northward, he crossed the Hudson River to New Jersey and finally reached the Delaware River with the British close at his heels. Tauntingly, enemy buglers sounded the fox-hunting call, so familiar to Virginians of Washington's day. The Patriot cause was at low ebb when the rebel remnants fled across the river after collecting all available boats to forestall pursuit.

The wonder is that Washington's adversary, General William Howe, did not speedily crush the demoralized American forces. But he was no military genius, and he well remembered the horrible slaughter at Bunker Hill, where he had commanded. The country was rough, supplies were slow in coming, and as a professional soldier, Howe did not relish the rigors of winter campaigning. He evidently found more agreeable the bedtime company of his mistress, the wife of one of his subordinates—a scandal with which American satirists had a good deal of ribald fun.

Washington, who was now almost counted out, stealthily recrossed the ice-clogged Delaware River. At Trenton, on December 26, 1776, he surprised and captured a thousand Hessians who were sleeping off the effects of their Christmas celebration. A week later, leaving his campfires burning as a ruse, he slipped away and inflicted a sharp defeat on a smaller British detachment at Princeton. This brilliant New Jersey campaign, crowned by these two lifesaving victories, revealed "Old Fox" Washington at his military best.

Burgoyne's Blundering Invasion

London officials adopted an intricate scheme for capturing the vital Hudson River valley in 1777. If successful, the British would sever New England from the rest of the states and paralyze the American cause. The main invading force, under an actor-playwright-soldier, General ("Gentleman Johnny") Burgoyne, would push down the Lake Champlain route from Canada. General Howe's troops in New York, if needed, could advance up the Hudson River to meet Burgoyne near Albany. A third and much smaller British force, commanded by Colonel Barry St. Leger, would come in from the west by way of Lake Ontario and the Mohawk Valley.

British planners did not reckon with General Benedict Arnold. After his repulse at Quebec in 1775, he had retreated slowly along the St. Lawrence River back to the Lake Champlain area, by heroic efforts keeping an army in the field. The British had pursued his tattered force to Lake Champlain in 1776. But they could not move farther south until they had won control of the

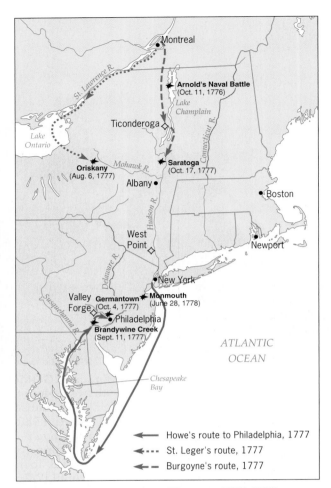

New York–Pennsylvania Theater, 1777–1778
Distinguished members of the Continental Congress fled from Philadelphia in near-panic as the British army approached. Thomas Paine reported that at three o'clock in the morning, the streets were "as full of Men, Women, and Children as on a Market Day." John Adams had anticipated that "I shall run away, I suppose, with the rest," since "we are too brittle ware, you know, to stand the dashing of balls and bombs." Adams got his chance to decamp with the others into the interior of Pennsylvania and tried to put the best face on things. "This tour," he commented, "has given me an opportunity of seeing many parts of this country which I never saw before."

lake, which, in the absence of roads, was indispensable for carrying their supplies.

While the British stopped to construct a sizable fleet, the tireless Arnold assembled and fitted out every floatable vessel. His tiny flotilla was finally destroyed

Revolutionary Standard of the Light-Horse of the City of Philadelphia, by John Folwell and James Claypoole, 1775 Silk flags like this were used to identify military units. In an exercise known as "trooping the colors," such flags were regularly paraded before the troops so that soldiers could recognize their own units in the confusion of battle.

after desperate fighting, but time, if not the battle, had been won. Winter was descending, and the British were forced to retire to Canada. General Burgoyne had to start anew from this base the following year. If Arnold had not contributed his daring and skill, the British invaders of 1776 almost certainly would have recaptured Fort Ticonderoga. If Burgoyne had started from this springboard in 1777, instead of from Montreal, he almost certainly would have succeeded in his venture. (At last the apparently futile American invasion of Canada in 1775 was beginning to pay rich dividends.)

General Burgoyne began his fateful invasion with seven thousand regular troops. He was encumbered by a heavy baggage train and a considerable number of women, many of whom were wives of his officers. Progress was painfully slow, for sweaty axmen had to chop a path through the forest, while American militiamen began to gather like hornets on Burgoyne's flanks.

General Howe, meanwhile, was causing astonished eyebrows to rise. At a time when it seemed obvious that he should be starting up the Hudson River from New York to join his slowly advancing colleague, he deliberately embarked with the main British army for an attack on Philadelphia, the rebel capital. As scholars now know, he wanted to force a general engagement with

Washington's army, destroy it, and leave the path wide open for Burgoyne's thrust. Howe apparently assumed that he had ample time to assist Burgoyne directly, should he be needed.

General Washington, keeping a wary eye on the British in New York, hastily transferred his army to the vicinity of Philadelphia. There, late in 1777, he was defeated in two pitched battles, at Brandywine Creek and Germantown. Pleasure-loving General Howe then settled down comfortably in the lively capital, leaving Burgoyne to flounder through the wilds of upper New York. Benjamin Franklin, recently sent to Paris as an envoy, truthfully jested that Howe had not captured Philadelphia but that Philadelphia had captured Howe. Washington finally retired to winter quarters at Valley Forge, a strong, hilly position some twenty miles northwest of Philadelphia. There his frostbitten and hungry men were short of about everything except misery. This rabble was nevertheless whipped into a professional army by the recently arrived Prussian drillmaster, the profane but patient Baron von Steuben.

Burgoyne meanwhile had begun to bog down north of Albany, while a host of American militiamen, scenting the kill, swarmed about him. In a series of sharp engagements, in which General Arnold was again shot in the leg at Quebec, the British army was trapped. Meanwhile, the Americans had driven back St. Leger's force at Oriskany. Unable to advance or retreat, Burgoyne was forced to surrender his entire command at Saratoga on October 17, 1777, to the American general Horatio Gates.

In this sermon, published in the Pennsylvania Gazette *on April 18, 1778, a minister decried the brutality of the British army:*

"The waste and ravage produced by this unhappy war are every where felt. Whereever our foes pervade, ruin and devastation follow after them; or rather, they march in their front, and on their right, and on their left, and in their rear they rage without controul. No house is sacred; no person secure. Age or sex, from blooming youth to decrepid age, they regard or spare not. And in the field, how many of our countrymen and friends have fallen?

Saratoga ranks high among the decisive battles of both American and world history. The victory immensely revived the faltering colonial cause. Even more important, it made possible the urgently needed foreign aid from France, which in turn helped ensure American independence.

Revolution in Diplomacy?

France, thirsting for revenge against Britain, was eager to inflame the quarrel that had broken out in America. Stripped of its North American colonies, Britain would presumably cease to be a front-rank power. France might then regain its former position and prestige, the loss of which in the recent Seven Years' War rankled deeply. For their part, the American revolutionaries badly needed help in the struggle to throw off the British yoke. The stage seemed set for the embattled new nation to make its diplomatic debut by sealing an alliance with France against the common British foe.

Yet just as they stood for revolutionary political ideas at home, the rebellious Americans also harbored revolutionary ideas about international affairs. They wanted an end to colonialism and mercantilism. They strongly supported free trade and freedom of the seas. They hoped to substitute the rule of law for the ancient reliance on raw power to arbitrate the affairs of nations. (When the new Republic's great seal proclaimed "a new order for the ages"—*novus ordo seculorum* in Latin—the sentiment was meant to apply to international as well as domestic affairs.) The Continental Congress in the summer of 1776 had accordingly drafted a "Model Treaty" to guide the American commissioners it was about to dispatch to the French court. One of the treaty's chief authors, John Adams, described its basic principles: "1. No political connection. . . . 2. No military connection. . . . 3. Only a commercial connection."

For a nascent nation struggling to secure its very existence, these were remarkably self-denying restrictions. Yet they represented an emerging school of thought, popular among enlightened figures in both Europe and America, that deemed history to have reached a momentous turning point when military conflict would be abandoned and the bonds of mutual commercial interest would guarantee peaceful relations among states. Many critics then and later have derided this dream of an imminent golden age as hopelessly naive and impractically utopian; yet it infused an element of idealism into American attitudes

Benjamin Franklin (1706–1790), by Charles Willson Peale, 1789   He left school at age ten and became a wealthy businessman, a journalist, an inventor, a scientist, a legislator, and preeminently a statesman-diplomat. He was sent to France in 1776 as the American envoy at age seventy, and he remained there until 1785, negotiating the alliance with the French and helping to negotiate the treaty of peace. His fame had preceded him, and when he discarded his wig for the fur cap of a simple "American agriculturist," he took French society by storm. French aristocratic women, with whom he was a great favorite, honored him by adopting the high *coiffure à la Franklin* in imitation of his cap.

toward international affairs that has proved stubbornly persistent.

When wily old Benjamin Franklin arrived in Paris to negotiate the treaty with France, he was determined that his very appearance should herald the diplomatic revolution the Americans hoped to achieve. In his clothing and demeanor, he affected a persona that deliberately violated every norm of diplomatic behavior. Instead of the customary ceremonial sword, he toted only a plain white walking stick. Forsaking ermined robes and fancy wigs, he sported homespun garments and a simple cap of marten fur. "Figure me," he wrote to a friend, "very plainly dress'd, wearing my thin grey strait Hair, that peeps out under my only Coiffure, a fine Fur Cap, which comes down my Forehead almost to my Spectacles. Think how this must appear among the Powder'd Heads of Paris." He shocked the royal court, besotted as it was with pomp and protocol. But ordinary Parisians adored him as a specimen of a new democratic social order, devoid of pretense and ornament. When Franklin embraced and kissed the famed French philosopher Francois Voltaire in a Paris theater, the spectators applauded wildly. Meanwhile, the diplomatic game intensified.

After the humiliation at Saratoga in 1777, the British Parliament belatedly passed a measure that in effect offered the Americans home rule within the empire. This was essentially all that the colonials had ever asked for—except independence. If the French were going to break up the British Empire, they would have to bestir themselves. Franklin now played skillfully on French fears of Anglo-American reconciliation. On February 6, 1778, France offered the Americans a treaty of alliance. It did not conform exactly to the terms of the Model Treaty Franklin had brought with him—an early example of practical self-interest trumping abstract idealism in America's conduct of foreign affairs. Against its better judgment, the young Republic concluded its first entangling military alliance and would soon regret it. But the treaty with France also constituted an official recognition of America's independence and lent powerful military heft to the Patriot cause. Both allies bound themselves to wage war until the United States had fully secured its freedom and until both agreed to terms with

After concluding the alliance, France sent a minister to America, to the delight of one Patriot journalist:

"Who would have thought that the American colonies, imperfectly known in Europe a few years ago and claimed by every pettifogging lawyer in the House of Commons, every cobbler in the beer-houses of London, as a part of their property, should to-day receive an ambassador from the most powerful monarchy in Europe."

the common enemy. With those pledges, the American Revolutionary War now became a world war.

The Colonial War Becomes a Wider War

England and France thus came to blows in 1778, and the shot fired at Lexington rapidly widened into a global conflagration. Spain entered the fray against Britain in 1779, as did Holland. Combined Spanish and French fleets outnumbered those of Britain, and on two occasions the British Isles seemed to be at the mercy of hostile warships.

Britain Against the World

Britain and Allies	Enemy or Unfriendly Powers		
Great Britain Some Loyalists and Indians 30,000 hired Hessians (*Total population on Britain's side: c. 8 million*)	Belligerents (*Total population: c. 39.5 million*)	{	United States, 1775–1783 France, 1778–1783 Spain, 1779–1783 Holland, 1779–1783
			Ireland (restive)
	Members of the Armed Neutrality (with dates of joining)	{	Russia, 1780 Denmark-Norway, 1780 Sweden, 1780 Holy Roman Empire, 1781 Prussia, 1782 Portugal, 1782 Two Sicilies, 1783 (after peace signed)

The weak maritime neutrals of Europe, who had suffered from Britain's dominance over the seas, now began to demand more respect for their rights. In 1780 the imperious Catherine the Great of Russia took the lead in organizing the Armed Neutrality, which she later sneeringly called the "Armed Nullity." It lined up almost all the remaining European neutrals in an attitude of passive hostility toward Britain. The war was now being fought not only in Europe and North America, but also in South America, the Caribbean, and Asia.

To say that America, with some French aid, defeated Britain is like saying, "Daddy and I killed the bear." To Britain, struggling for its very life, the scuffle in the New World became secondary. The Americans deserve credit for having kept the war going until 1778, with secret French aid. But they did not achieve their independence until the conflict erupted into a multipower world war that was too big for Britain to handle. From 1778 to 1783, France provided the rebels with guns, money, immense amounts of equipment, about one-half of America's regular armed forces, and practically all of the new nation's naval strength.

France's entrance into the conflict forced the British to change their basic strategy in America. Hitherto they could count on blockading the colonial coast and commanding the seas. Now the French had powerful fleets in American waters, chiefly to protect their own valuable West Indies islands, but in a position to jeopardize Britain's blockade and lines of supply. The British, therefore, decided to evacuate Philadelphia and concentrate their strength in New York City.

In June 1778 the withdrawing redcoats were attacked by General Washington at Monmouth, New Jersey, on a blisteringly hot day. Scores of men collapsed or died from sunstroke. But the battle was indecisive, and the British escaped to New York, although about one-third of their Hessians deserted. Henceforth, except for the Yorktown interlude of 1781, Washington remained in the New York area hemming in the British.

Blow and Counterblow

In the summer of 1780, a powerful French army of six thousand regular troops, commanded by the Comte de Rochambeau, arrived in Newport, Rhode Island. The Americans were somewhat suspicious of their former enemies; in fact, several ugly flare-ups, involving minor bloodshed, had already occurred between the new allies. But French gold and goodwill melted hard hearts.

Dancing parties were arranged with the prim Puritan maidens; one French officer related, doubtless with exaggeration, "The simple innocence of the Garden of Eden prevailed." No real military advantage came immediately from this French reinforcement, although preparations were made for a Franco-American attack on New York.

Improving American morale was staggered later in 1780, when General Benedict Arnold turned traitor. A leader of undoubted dash and brilliance, he was ambitious, greedy, unscrupulous, and suffering from a well-grounded but petulant feeling that his valuable services were not fully appreciated. He plotted with the British to sell out the key stronghold of West Point, which commanded the Hudson River, for £6,300 and an officer's commission. By the sheerest accident, the plot was detected in the nick of time, and Arnold fled to the British. "Whom can we trust now?" cried General Washington in anguish.

The British meanwhile had devised a plan to roll up the colonies, beginning with the South, where the Loyalists were numerous. The colony of Georgia was ruthlessly overrun in 1778–1779; Charleston, South Carolina, fell in 1780. The surrender of the city to the British involved the capture of five thousand men and four hundred cannon and was a heavier loss to the Americans, in relation to existing strength, than that of Burgoyne was to the British.

War in the South, 1780–1781

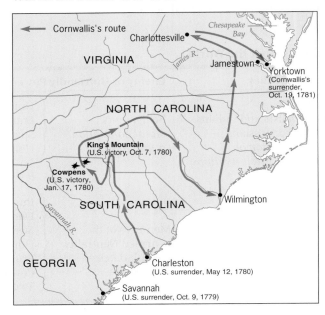

Warfare now intensified in the Carolinas, where Patriots bitterly fought their Loyalist neighbors. It was not uncommon for prisoners on both sides to be butchered in cold blood after they had thrown down their arms. The tide turned later in 1780 and early in 1781, when American riflemen wiped out a British detachment at King's Mountain and then defeated a smaller force at Cowpens. In the Carolina campaign of 1781, General Nathanael Greene, a Quaker-reared tactician, distinguished himself by his strategy of delay. Standing and then retreating, he exhausted his foe, General Charles Cornwallis, in vain pursuit. By losing battles but winning campaigns, the "Fighting Quaker" finally succeeded in clearing most of Georgia and South Carolina of British troops.

The Land Frontier and the Sea Frontier

The West was ablaze during much of the war. Indian allies of George III, hoping to protect their land, were busy with torch and tomahawk; they were egged on by British agents branded as "hair buyers" because they allegedly paid bounties for American scalps. Fateful 1777 was known as "the bloody year" on the frontier. Although two nations of the Iroquois Confederacy, the Oneidas and the Tuscaroras, sided with the Americans, the Senecas, Mohawks, Cayugas, and Onondagas joined the British. They were urged on by Mohawk chief Joseph Brant, a convert to Anglicanism who believed, not without reason, that a victorious Britain would restrain American expansion into the West. Brant and the British ravaged large areas of backcountry Pennsylvania and New York until checked by an American force in 1779. In 1784 the pro-British Iroquois were forced to sign the Treaty of Fort Stanwix, the first treaty between the United States and an Indian nation. Under its terms the Indians ceded most of their land.

Yet even in wartime, the human tide of westward-moving pioneers did not halt its flow. Eloquent testimony is provided by place names in Kentucky, such as Lexington (named after the battle) and Louisville (named after America's new ally, Louis XVI).

In the wild Illinois country, the British were especially vulnerable to attack, for they held only scattered posts that they had captured from the French. An audacious frontiersman, George Rogers Clark, conceived the idea of seizing these forts by surprise. In 1778–1779 he floated down the Ohio River with about 175 men and captured in

Joseph Brant, by Gilbert Stuart, 1786 Siding with the British, this Mohawk chief led Indian frontier raids so ferocious that he was dubbed "monster Brant." When he later met King George III, he declined to kiss the king's hand but asked instead to kiss the hand of the queen.

George Rogers Clark's Campaign, 1778–1779

quick succession the forts Kaskaskia, Cahokia, and Vincennes. Clark's admirers have argued, without positive proof, that his success forced the British to cede the region north of the Ohio River to the United States at the peace table in Paris.

America's infant navy had meanwhile been laying the foundations of a brilliant tradition. The naval establishment consisted of only a handful of nondescript ships, commanded by daring officers, the most famous of whom was a hard-fighting young Scotsman, John Paul Jones. As events turned out, this tiny naval force never made a real dent in Britain's thunderous fleets. Its chief contribution was in destroying British merchant shipping and thus carrying the war into the waters around the British Isles.

More numerous and damaging than ships of the regular American navy were swift privateers. These craft were privately owned armed ships—legalized pirates in a sense—specifically authorized by Congress to prey on enemy shipping. Altogether over a thousand American privateers, responding to the call of patriotism and profit, sallied forth with about seventy thousand men ("sailors of fortune"). They captured some six hundred British prizes, while British warships captured about as many American merchantmen and privateers.

Privateering was not an unalloyed asset. It had the unfortunate effect of diverting manpower from the main war effort and involving Americans, including Benedict Arnold, in speculation and graft. But the privateers brought in urgently needed gold, harassed the enemy, and raised American morale by providing victories at a time when victories were few. British shipping was so badly riddled by privateers and by the regular American navy that insurance rates skyrocketed. Merchant ships were compelled to sail in convoy, and British shippers and manufacturers brought increasing pressure on Parliament to end the war on honorable terms.

Yorktown and the Final Curtain

One of the darkest periods of the war was 1780–1781, before the last decisive victory. Inflation of the currency continued at full gallop. The government, virtually bankrupt, declared that it would repay many of its debts at the rate of only 2.5 cents on the dollar. Despair prevailed, the sense of unity withered, and mutinous sentiments infected the army.

> *Baron von Steuben (1730–1794), a Prussian general who helped train the Continental Army, found the Americans to be very different from other soldiers he had known. As von Steuben explained to a fellow European,*
>
> "The genius of this nation is not in the least to be compared with that of the Prussians, Austrians, or French. You say to your soldier, 'Do this' and he doeth it; but I am obliged to say, 'This is the reason why you ought to do that,' and then he does it."

Meanwhile, the British general Cornwallis was blundering into a trap. After futile operations in Virginia, he had fallen back to Chesapeake Bay at Yorktown to await seaborne supplies and reinforcements. He assumed Britain would continue to control the sea. But these few fateful weeks happened to be one of the brief periods during the war when British naval superiority slipped away.

The French were now prepared to cooperate energetically in a brilliant stroke. Admiral de Grasse, operating with a powerful fleet in the West Indies, advised the Americans that he was free to join with them in an assault on Cornwallis at Yorktown. Quick to seize this opportunity, General Washington made a swift march of more than three hundred miles to the Chesapeake from the New York area. Accompanied by Rochambeau's French army, Washington beset the British by land, while de Grasse blockaded them by sea after beating off the British fleet. Completely cornered, Cornwallis surrendered his entire force of seven thousand men on October 19, 1781, as his band appropriately played "The World Turn'd Upside Down." The triumph was no less French than American: the French provided essentially all the sea power and about half of the regular troops in the besieging army of some sixteen thousand men.

Stunned by news of the disaster, Prime Minister Lord North cried, "Oh God! It's all over! It's all over!" But it was not. George III stubbornly planned to continue the struggle, for Britain was far from being crushed. It still had fifty-four thousand troops in North America, including thirty-two thousand in the United States. Washington returned with his army to New York, there

Battle of the Chesapeake Capes, 1781 A young French naval officer, Pierre Joseph Jennot, sketched what is probably the only depiction of the epochal sea battle by a participant. The British and French fleets first engaged on September 5 and for two days chased each other while drifting one hundred miles south. On September 8, the French turned back northward and occupied Chesapeake Bay, cutting off General Cornwallis, ashore in Yorktown, from support and escape by sea. When General Washington, with more French help, blocked any British retreat by land, a doomed Cornwallis surrendered.

to continue keeping a vigilant eye on the British force of ten thousand men.

Fighting actually continued for more than a year after Yorktown, with Patriot-Loyalist warfare in the South especially savage. "No quarter for Tories" was the common battle cry. One of Washington's most valuable contributions was to keep the languishing cause alive, the army in the field, and the states together during these critical months. Otherwise a satisfactory peace treaty might never have been signed.

Blundering George III, a poor loser, wrote this of America:

"Knavery seems to be so much the striking feature of its inhabitants that it may not in the end be an evil that they become aliens to this Kingdom."

Peace at Paris

After Yorktown, despite George III's obstinate eagerness to continue fighting, many Britons were weary of war and increasingly ready to come to terms. They had suffered heavy reverses in India and in the West Indies. The island of Minorca in the Mediterranean had fallen; the Rock of Gibraltar was tottering. Lord North's ministry collapsed in March 1782, temporarily ending the personal rule of George III. A Whig ministry, rather favorable to the Americans, replaced the Tory regime of Lord North.

Three American peace negotiators had meanwhile gathered at Paris: the aging but astute Benjamin Franklin; the flinty John Adams, vigilant for New England interests; and the impulsive John Jay of New York, deeply suspicious of Old World intrigue. The three envoys had explicit instructions from Congress to make no separate peace and to consult with their French allies at all stages of the negotiations. But the American representatives chafed under this directive. They well knew that it had been written by a subservient Congress, with the French Foreign Office indirectly guiding the pen.

France was in a painful position. It had induced Spain to enter the war on its side, in part by promising to deliver British-held Gibraltar. Yet the towering rock was defying frantic joint assaults by French and Spanish troops. Spain also coveted the immense trans-Allegheny area, on which restless American pioneers were already settling.

France, ever eager to smash Britain's empire, desired an independent United States, but one independent in the abstract, not in action. It therefore schemed to keep the new Republic cooped up east of the Allegheny Mountains. A weak America—like a horse sturdy enough to plow but not vigorous enough to kick—would be easier to manage in promoting French interests and policy. France was paying a heavy price in men and treasure to win America's independence, and it wanted to get its money's worth.

But John Jay was unwilling to play France's game. Suspiciously alert, he perceived that the French could not satisfy the conflicting ambitions of both Americans and Spaniards. He saw signs—or thought he did—indicating that the Paris Foreign Office was about to betray America's trans-Appalachian interests to satisfy those of Spain. He therefore secretly made separate overtures to London, contrary to his instructions from Congress. The hard-pressed British, eager to entice one of their enemies from the alliance, speedily came to terms with the Americans. A preliminary treaty of peace was signed in 1782; the final peace, the next year.

By the Treaty of Paris of 1783, the British formally recognized the independence of the United States. In addition, they granted generous boundaries, stretching majestically to the Mississippi on the west, to the Great Lakes on the north, and to Spanish Florida on the south. (Spain had recently captured Florida from Britain.) The Yankees, though now divorced from the empire, were to retain a share in the priceless fisheries of Newfoundland. The Canadians, of course, were pro-foundly displeased.

The Americans, on their part, had to yield important concessions. Loyalists were not to be further persecuted, and Congress was to *recommend* to the state legislatures

The Reconciliation Between Britannia and Her Daughter America (detail)
America (represented by an Indian) is invited to buss (kiss) her mother.

that confiscated Loyalist property be restored. As for the debts long owed to British creditors, the states vowed to put no lawful obstacles in the way of their collection. Unhappily for future harmony, the assurances regarding both Loyalists and debts were not carried out in the manner hoped for by London.

A New Nation Legitimized

Britain's terms were liberal almost beyond belief. The enormous trans-Appalachian area was thrown in as a virtual gift, for George Rogers Clark had captured only a small segment of it. Why the generosity? Had the United States beaten Britain to its knees?

The key to the riddle may be found in the Old World. At the time the peace terms were drafted, Britain was trying to seduce America from its French alliance, so it made the terms as alluring as possible. The shaky Whig ministry, hanging on by its fingernails for only a few months, was more friendly to the Americans than were the Tories. It was determined, by a policy of liberality, to salve recent wounds, reopen old trade channels, and prevent future wars over the coveted trans-Appalachian region. This farsighted policy was regrettably not followed by the successors of the Whigs.

In spirit, the Americans made a separate peace—contrary to the French alliance. In fact, they did not. The Paris Foreign Office formally approved the terms of peace, though disturbed by the lone-wolf course of its American ally. France was immensely relieved by the prospect of bringing the costly conflict to an end and of freeing itself from its embarrassing promises to the Spanish crown.

America alone gained from the world-girdling war. The British, though soon to stage a comeback, were battered and beaten. The French savored sweet revenge but plunged headlong down the slippery slope to bankruptcy and revolution. The Americans fared much better. Snatching their independence from the furnace of world conflict, they began their national career with a splendid territorial birthright and a priceless heritage of freedom. Seldom, if ever, have any people been so favored.

Chronology

1775 Battles of Lexington and Concord
Second Continental Congress
Americans capture British garrisons at
  Ticonderoga and Crown Point
Battle of Bunker Hill
King George III formally proclaims
  colonies in rebellion
Failed invasion of Canada
	1778-
	1779 Clark's victories in the West

	1781 Battle of King's Mountain Battle of Cowpens Greene leads Carolina campaign French and Americans force Cornwallis to surrender at Yorktown
1776 Paine's *Common Sense* Declaration of Independence Battle of Trenton	**1782** North's ministry collapses in Britain
1777 Battle of Brandywine Battle of Germantown Battle of Saratoga	**1783** Treaty of Paris
	1784 Treaty of Fort Stanwix
1778 Formation of French-American alliance Battle of Monmouth	

Whose Revolution?

Historians once assumed that the Revolution was just another chapter in the unfolding story of human liberty—an important way station on a divinely ordained pathway toward moral perfection in human affairs. This approach, often labeled the "Whig view of history," was best expressed in George Bancroft's ten-volume *History of the United States of America,* published between the 1830s and 1870s.

By the end of the nineteenth century, a group of historians known as the "imperial school" challenged Bancroft, arguing that the Revolution was best understood not as the fulfillment of national destiny, but as a constitutional conflict within the British Empire. For historians like George Beer, Charles Andrews, and Lawrence Gipson, the Revolution was the product of a collision between two different views of empire. While the Americans were moving steadily toward more self-government, Britain increasingly tightened its grip, threatening a stranglehold that eventually led to wrenching revolution.

By the early twentieth century, these approaches were challenged by the so-called progressive historians, who argued that neither divine destiny nor constitutional quibbles had much to do with the Revolution. Rather, the Revolution stemmed from deep-seated class tensions within American society that, once released by revolt, produced a truly transformed social order. Living themselves in a reform age when entrenched economic interests cowered under heavy attack, progressive historians like Carl Becker insisted that the Revolution was not just about "home rule" within the British Empire, but also about "who should rule at home" in America, the upper or lower classes. J. Franklin Jameson took Becker's analysis one step further in his influential *The American Revolution Considered as a Social Movement* (1926). He claimed that the Revolution not only grew out of intense struggles between social groups, but also inspired many ordinary Americans to seek greater economic and political power, fundamentally democratizing society in its wake.

In the 1950s the progressive historians fell out of favor as the political climate became more conservative. Interpretations of the American Revolution as a class struggle did not play well in a country obsessed with the spread of communism, and in its place arose the so-called consensus view. Historians such as Robert Brown and Edmund Morgan downplayed the role of class conflict in the Revolutionary era, but emphasized that colonists of all ranks shared a commitment to certain fundamental political principles of self-government. The unifying power of ideas was now back in fashion almost a hundred years after Bancroft.

Since the 1950s two broad interpretations have contended with each other and perpetuated the controversy over whether political ideals or economic and social realities were most responsible for the Revolution. The first, articulated most prominently by Bernard Bailyn, has emphasized ideological and psychological factors. Focusing on the power of ideas to foment revolution, Bailyn argued that the colonists, incited by their reading of seventeenth-century and early-eighteenth-century English political theorists, grew extraordinarily (perhaps even exaggeratedly) suspicious of any attempts to tighten the imperial reins on the colonies. When confronted with new taxes and commercial regulations, these hypersensitive colonists screamed "conspiracy against liberty" and "corrupt ministerial plot." In time they took up armed insurrection in defense of their intellectual commitment to liberty.

A second school of historians, writing during the 1960s and 1970s and inspired by the social movements of that turbulent era, revived the progressive interpretation of the Revolution. Gary Nash, in *The Urban Crucible* (1979), and Edward Countryman, in *A People in Revolution* (1981), pointed to the increasing social and economic divisions among Americans in both the urban seaports and the isolated countryside in the years leading up to the Revolution. Attacks by laborers on political elites and expressions of resentment toward wealth were taken as evidence of a society that was breeding revolutionary change from within, quite aside from British provocations. While the concerns of the progressive historians echo in these socioeconomic interpretations of the Revolution, the neoprogressives have been more careful not to reduce the issues simplistically to the one-ring arena of economic self-interest. Instead, they have argued that the varying material circumstances of American participants led them to hold distinctive versions of republicanism, giving the Revolution a less unified and more complex ideological underpinning than the idealistic historians had previously suggested. The dialogue between proponents of "ideas" and "interests" has gradually led to a more nuanced meeting of the two views.

Most recently, scholars have taken a more trans-Atlantic view of the Revolution's origins, asking when and how colonists shifted from identifying as "British" to viewing themselves as "American." Fred Anderson has argued that long before rebellion, the Seven Years' War (1754–1763) helped create a sense of American identity, apart from Britain. Other historians such as T. H. Breen, argue that British nationalism actually intensified in the colonies over the course of the eighteenth century, as economic and cultural ties between Britain and North America strengthened through increased trade and the migration of ideas with the growth of print culture. Only when colonists realized that the British did not see them as equal imperial citizens, entitled to the same rights as Englishmen, did American nationalism emerge and Americans rebel.

For further reading, see the Appendix. For web resources, go to **http://college.hmco.com.**

BUILDING THE NEW NATION

⎯⎯⎯⎯ ⌁ ⎯⎯⎯⎯

1776–1860

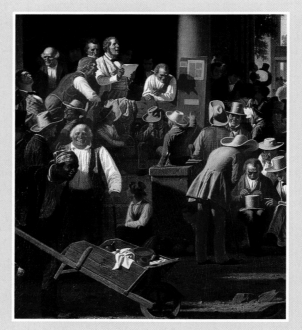

By 1783 Americans had won their freedom. Now they had to build their country. To be sure, they were blessed with a vast and fertile land, and they inherited from their colonial experience a proud legacy of self-rule. But history provided scant precedent for erecting a republic on a national scale. No law of nature guaranteed that the thirteen rebellious colonies would stay glued together as a single nation, or that they would preserve, not to mention expand, their democratic way of life. New institutions had to be created, new habits of thought cultivated. Who could predict whether the American experiment in government by the people would succeed?

The feeble national government cobbled together under the Articles of Confederation during the Revolutionary War soon proved woefully inadequate to the task of nation building. In less than ten years after the Revolutionary War's conclusion, the Articles were replaced by a new Constitution, but even its adoption did not end the debate over just what form American government should take. Would the president, the Congress, or the courts be the dominant branch? What should be the proper division of authority between the federal government and the states? How could the rights of individuals be protected against a potentially powerful government? What

The Verdict of the People (detail)
This election-day crowd exudes the exuberant spirit of the era of Andrew Jackson, when the advent of universal white male suffrage made the United States the modern world's first mass participatory democracy. Yet the black man with the wheelbarrow, literally pushing his way into the painting, is a pointed reminder that the curse of slavery still blighted this happy scene.

economic policies would best serve the infant Republic? How should the nation defend itself against foreign foes? What principles should guide foreign policy? Was America a nation at all, or was it merely a geographic expression, destined to splinter into several bitterly quarreling sections, as had happened to so many other would-be countries?

After a shaky start under George Washington and John Adams in the 1790s, buffeted by foreign troubles and domestic crises, the new Republic passed a major test when power was peacefully transferred from the conservative Federalists to the more liberal Jeffersonians in the election of 1800. A confident President Jefferson proceeded boldly to expand the national territory with the landmark Louisiana Purchase in 1803. But before long Jefferson, and then his successor, James Madison, were embroiled in what eventually proved to be a fruitless effort to spare the United States from the ravages of the war then raging in Europe.

America was dangerously divided during the War of 1812 and suffered a humiliating defeat. But a new sense of national unity and purpose was unleashed in the land thereafter. President Monroe, presiding over this "Era of Good Feelings," proclaimed in the Monroe Doctrine of 1823 that both of the American continents were off-limits to further European intervention. The foundations of a continental-scale economy were laid, as a "transportation revolution" stitched the country together with canals and railroads and turnpikes. Settlers flooded over those new arteries into the burgeoning West, often brusquely shouldering aside the native peoples. Immigrants, especially from Ireland and Germany, flocked to American shores. The combination of new lands and

new labor fed the growth of a market economy, including the commercialization of agriculture and the beginnings of the factory system of production. Old ways of life withered as the market economy drew women as well as men, children as well as adults, blacks as well as whites, into its embrace. Ominously, the slave system grew robustly as cotton production, mostly for sale on European markets, exploded into the booming Southwest.

Meanwhile, the United States in the era of Andrew Jackson gave the world an impressive lesson in political science. Between roughly 1820 and 1840, Americans virtually invented mass democracy, creating huge political parties and enormously expanding political participation by enfranchising nearly all adult white males. Nor was the spirit of innovation confined to the political realm. A wave of reform and cultural vitality swept through many sectors of American society. Utopian experiments proliferated. Religious revivals and even new religions, like Mormonism, flourished. A national literature blossomed. Crusades were launched for temperance, prison reform, women's rights, and the abolition of slavery.

By the second quarter of the nineteenth century, the outlines of a distinctive American national character had begun to emerge. Americans were a diverse, restless people, tramping steadily westward, eagerly forging their own nascent Industrial Revolution, proudly exercising their democratic political rights, impatient with the old, in love with the new, testily asserting their superiority over all other peoples—and increasingly divided, in heart, in conscience, and in politics, over the single greatest blight on their record of nation making and democracy building: slavery.

Women Weavers at Work (detail)
These simple cotton looms heralded the dawn of the Industrial Revolution, which transformed the lives of Americans even more radically than the events of 1776.

The Confederation and the Constitution

1776–1790

THIS EXAMPLE OF CHANGING THE CONSTITUTION BY
ASSEMBLING THE WISE MEN OF THE STATE, INSTEAD OF
ASSEMBLING ARMIES, WILL BE WORTH AS MUCH TO THE
WORLD AS THE FORMER EXAMPLES WE HAVE GIVEN IT.

THOMAS JEFFERSON

The American Revolution was not a revolution in the sense of a radical or total change. It did not suddenly and violently overturn the entire political and social framework, as later occurred in the French and Russian Revolutions. What happened was accelerated evolution rather than outright revolution. During the conflict itself, people went on working and praying, marrying and playing. Many of them were not seriously disturbed by the actual fighting, and the most isolated communities scarcely knew that a war was on.

Yet some striking changes were ushered in, affecting social customs, political institutions, and ideas about society, government, and even gender roles. The exodus of some eighty thousand substantial Loyalists robbed the new ship of state of conservative ballast. This weakening of the aristocratic upper crust, with all its culture and elegance, paved the way for new, Patriot elites to emerge. It also cleared the field for more egalitarian ideas to sweep across the land.

The Pursuit of Equality

"All men are created equal," the Declaration of Independence proclaimed, and equality was everywhere the watchword. Most states reduced (but usually did not eliminate altogether) property-holding requirements for voting. Ordinary men and women demanded to be addressed as "Mr." and "Mrs."—titles once reserved for the wealthy and highborn. Employers were now called "boss," not "master." In 1784 New Yorkers released a shipload of freshly arrived indentured servants, on the grounds that their status violated democratic ideals; by 1800 servitude was virtually unknown. Most Americans ridiculed the lordly pretensions of Continental Army officers who formed an exclusive hereditary order, the Society of the Cincinnati. Social democracy was further stimulated by the growth of trade organizations for artisans and laborers. Citizens in several states, flushed with republican fervor, also sawed off the remaining shackles of medieval inheritance laws, such as primogeniture, which awarded all of a father's property to the eldest son.

A protracted fight for separation of church and state resulted in notable gains. Although the well-entrenched Congregational Church continued to be legally established in some New England states, the Anglican Church, tainted by association with the British crown, was humbled. De-anglicized, it re-formed as the Protestant Episcopal Church and was everywhere disestablished. The struggle for divorce between religion and government proved fiercest in Virginia. It was prolonged to 1786, when freethinking Thomas Jefferson and his co-reformers, including the Baptists, won a complete victory with the passage of the Virginia Statute for Religious Freedom. (See the table of established churches on p. 95.)

The egalitarian sentiments unleashed by the war likewise challenged the institution of slavery. Philadelphia Quakers in 1775 founded the world's first antislavery society. Hostilities hampered the noxious trade in "black ivory," and the Continental Congress in 1774 called for the complete abolition of the slave trade, a summons to which most of the states responded positively. Several northern states went further and either abolished slavery outright or provided for the gradual emancipation of blacks. Even on the plantations of Virginia, a few idealistic masters freed their human chattels—the first frail sprouts of the later abolitionist movement.

But this revolution of sentiments was sadly incomplete. No states south of Pennsylvania abolished slavery, and in both North and South, the law discriminated harshly against freed blacks and slaves alike. Emancipated African Americans could be barred from purchasing property, holding certain jobs, and educating their children. Laws against interracial marriage also sprang up at this time.

Why, in this dawning democratic age, did abolition not go further and cleanly blot the evil of slavery from the

Elizabeth "Mumbet" Freeman (c. 1744–1829), by Susan Anne Livingston Ridley Sedgwick, 1811 In 1781, having overheard Revolutionary-era talk about the "rights of man," Mumbet sued her Massachusetts master for her freedom from slavery. She won her suit and lived the rest of her life as a paid domestic servant in the home of the lawyer who had pleaded her case.

fresh face of the new nation? The sorry truth is that the fledgling idealism of the Founding Fathers was sacrificed to political expediency. A fight over slavery would have fractured the fragile national unity that was so desperately needed. "Great as the evil [of slavery] is," the young Virginian James Madison wrote in 1787, "a dismemberment of the union would be worse." Nearly a century later, the slavery issue did wreck the Union—temporarily.

Likewise incomplete was the extension of the doctrine of equality to women. Some women did serve (disguised as men) in the military, and New Jersey's new constitution in 1776 even, for a time, enabled women to vote. But though Abigail Adams teased her husband John in 1776 that "the Ladies" were determined "to foment a rebellion" of their own if they were not given political rights, most of the women in the Revolutionary era were still doing traditional women's work.

> *The impact of the American Revolution was worldwide. About 1783 a British ship stopped at some islands off the East African coast, where the natives were revolting against their Arab masters. When asked why they were fighting, they replied,*
>
> **"America is free, Could not we be?"**

> *The Revolution enhanced the expectations and power of women as wives and mothers. As one "matrimonial republican" wrote in 1792,*
>
> "I object to the word 'obey' in the marriage-service because it is a general word, without limitations or definition. . . . The obedience between man and wife, I conceive, is, or ought to be mutual. . . . Marriage ought never to be considered a contract between a superior and an inferior, but a reciprocal union of interest, an implied partnership of interests, where all differences are accommodated by conference; and where the decision admits of no retrospect."

Yet women did not go untouched by Revolutionary ideals. Central to republican ideology was the concept of "civic virtue"—the notion that democracy depended on the unselfish commitment of each citizen to the public good. And who could better cultivate the habits of a virtuous citizenry than mothers, to whom society entrusted the moral education of the young? Indeed the selfless devotion of a mother to her family was often cited as the very model of proper republican behavior. The idea of "republican motherhood" thus took root, elevating women to a newly prestigious role as the special keepers of the nation's conscience. Educational opportunities for women expanded, in the expectation that educated wives and mothers could better cultivate the virtues demanded by the Republic in their husbands, daughters, and sons. Republican women now bore crucial responsibility for the survival of the nation.

Constitution Making in the States

The Continental Congress in 1776 called upon the colonies to draft new constitutions. In effect, the Continental Congress was actually asking the colonies to summon themselves into being as new states. The sovereignty of these new states, according to the theory of republicanism, would rest on the authority of the people. For a time the manufacture of governments was even more pressing than the manufacture of gunpowder.

Although the states of Connecticut and Rhode Island merely retouched their colonial charters, constitution writers elsewhere worked tirelessly to capture on black-inked parchment the republican spirit of the age.

Massachusetts contributed one especially noteworthy innovation when it called a special convention to draft its constitution and then submitted the final draft directly to the people for ratification. Once adopted in 1780, the Massachusetts constitution could be changed only by another specially called constitutional convention. This procedure was later imitated in the drafting and ratification of the federal Constitution.

The newly penned state constitutions had many features in common. Their similarity, as it turned out, made easier the drafting of a workable federal charter when the time was ripe. In the British tradition, a "constitution" was not a written document, but rather an accumulation of laws, customs, and precedents. Americans invented something different. The documents they drafted were contracts that defined the powers of government, as did the old colonial charters, but they drew their authority from the people, not from the royal seal of a distant king. As *written* documents the state constitutions were intended to represent a *fundamental* law, superior to the transient whims of ordinary legislation. Most of these documents included bills of rights, specifically guaranteeing long-prized liberties against later legislative encroachment. Most of them required the annual election of legislators, who were thus forced to stay in touch with the mood of the people. All of them deliberately created weak executive and judicial branches, at least by present-day standards. A generation of quarreling with His Majesty's officials had implanted a deep distrust of despotic governors and arbitrary judges.

In all the new state governments, the legislatures, as presumably the most democratic branch of government, were given sweeping powers. But as Thomas Jefferson warned, "173 despots [in a legislature] would surely be as oppressive as one." Many Americans soon came to agree with him.

The democratic character of the new state legislatures was vividly reflected by the presence of many members from the recently enfranchised poorer western districts. Their influence was powerfully felt in their several successful movements to relocate state capitals from the haughty eastern seaports into the less pretentious interior. In the Revolutionary era, the capitals of New Hampshire, New York, Virginia, North Carolina, South Carolina, and Georgia were all moved westward. These geographical shifts portended political shifts that deeply discomfited many more conservative Americans.

EXAMINING THE EVIDENCE

Copley Family Portrait, c. 1776–1777 A portrait painting like this one by John Singleton Copley (1738–1815) documents physical likenesses, clothing styles, and other material possessions typical of an era. But it can do more than that. In the execution of the painting itself, the preeminent portrait painter of colonial America revealed important values of his time. Copley's composition and use of light emphasized the importance of the mother in the family. Mrs. Copley is the visual center of the painting; the light falls predominantly on her, and she provides the focus of activity for the family group. Although Copley had moved to England in 1774 to avoid the disruptions of war, he had made radical friends in his hometown of Boston and surely had imbibed the sentiment of the age about "republican motherhood"—a sentiment that revered women as homemakers and mothers, the cultivators of good republican values in young citizens. What other prevailing attitudes, about gender and age, for example, might this painting reveal?

Economic Crosscurrents

Economic changes begotten by the war were likewise noteworthy, but not overwhelming. States seized control of former crown lands, and although rich speculators had their day, many of the large Loyalist holdings were confiscated and eventually cut up into small farms.

Roger Morris's huge estate in New York, for example, was sliced into 250 parcels—thus accelerating the spread of economic democracy. The frightful excesses of the French Revolution were avoided, partly because cheap land was easily available. People do not chop off heads so readily when they can chop down trees. It is highly significant that in the United States, economic democracy, broadly speaking, preceded political democracy.

Western Merchants Negotiating the Purchase of Tea, c. 1790–1800   Yankee merchants and shippers figured prominently in the booming trade with China in the late eighteenth century. Among the American entrepreneurs who prospered in the China trade was Warren Delano, ancestor of President Franklin Delano Roosevelt.

A sharp stimulus was given to manufacturing by the prewar nonimportation agreements and later by the war itself. Goods that had formerly been imported from Britain were mostly cut off, and the ingenious Yankees were forced to make their own. Ten years after the Revolution, the busy Brandywine Creek, south of Philadelphia, was turning the water wheels of numerous mills along an eight-mile stretch. Yet America remained overwhelmingly a nation of soil-tillers.

Economically speaking, independence had drawbacks. Much of the coveted commerce of Britain was still reserved for the loyal parts of the empire. American ships were now barred from British and British West Indies harbors. Fisheries were disrupted, and bounties for ships' stores had abruptly ended. In some respects the hated British Navigation Laws were more disagreeable after independence than before.

New commercial outlets, fortunately, compensated partially for the loss of old ones. Americans could now trade freely with foreign nations, subject to local restrictions—a boon they had not enjoyed in the days of mercantilism. Enterprising Yankee shippers ventured boldly—and profitably—into the Baltic and China Seas. In 1784 the *Empress of China*, carrying a valuable weed (ginseng) that was highly prized by Chinese herb doctors as a cure for impotence, led the way into the East Asian markets.

Yet the general economic picture was far from rosy. War had spawned demoralizing extravagance, speculation, and profiteering, with profits for some as indecently high as 300 percent. State governments had borrowed more during the war than they could ever hope to repay. Runaway inflation had been ruinous to many citizens, and Congress had failed in its feeble attempts to curb economic laws. The average citizen was probably worse off financially at the end of the shooting than at the start.

The whole economic and social atmosphere was unhealthy. A newly rich class of profiteers was noisily conspicuous, whereas many once-wealthy people were left destitute. The controversy leading to the Revolutionary War had bred a keen distaste for taxes and encouraged disrespect for the majesty of the law generally. John Adams had been shocked when gleefully told by a horse-jockey neighbor that the courts of justice were all closed—a plight that proved to be only temporary.

A Shaky Start Toward Union

What would the Americans do with the independence they had so dearly won? The Revolution had dumped the responsibility of creating and operating a new central government squarely into their laps.

Prospects for erecting a lasting regime were far from bright. It is always difficult to set up a new government and doubly difficult to set up a new type of government. The picture was further clouded in America by leaders preaching "natural rights" and looking suspiciously at all persons clothed with authority. America was more a name than a nation, and unity ran little deeper than the color on the map.

Disruptive forces stalked the land. The departure of the conservative Tory element left the political system inclined toward experimentation and innovation. Patriots had fought the war with a high degree of disunity, but they had at least concurred on allegiance to a common cause. Now even that was gone. It would have been almost a miracle if any government fashioned in all this confusion had long endured.

Hard times, the bane of all regimes, set in shortly after the war and hit bottom in 1786. As if other troubles were not enough, British manufacturers, with dammed-up surpluses, began flooding the American market with cut-rate goods. War-baby American industries, in particular, suffered industrial colic from such ruthless competition. One Philadelphia newspaper in 1783 urged readers to don home-stitched garments of homespun cloth:

> *Of foreign gewgaws let's be free,*
> *And wear the webs of liberty.*

Yet hopeful signs could be discerned. The thirteen sovereign states were basically alike in governmental structure and functioned under similar constitutions. Americans enjoyed a rich political inheritance, derived partly from Britain and partly from their own home-grown devices for self-government. Finally, they were blessed with political leaders of a high order in men like George Washington, James Madison, John Adams, Thomas Jefferson, and Alexander Hamilton.

Creating a Confederation

The Second Continental Congress of Revolutionary days was little more than a conference of ambassadors from the thirteen states. It was totally without constitutional authority and in general did only what it dared to do, though it asserted some control over military affairs and foreign policy. In nearly all respects, the thirteen states were sovereign, for they coined money, raised armies and navies, and erected tariff barriers. The legislature of Virginia even ratified separately the treaty of alliance of 1778 with France.

Shortly before declaring independence in 1776, Congress appointed a committee to draft a written constitution for the new nation. The finished product was the Articles of Confederation. Adopted by Congress in 1777, it was translated into French after the Battle of Saratoga so as to convince France that America had a genuine government in the making. The Articles were not ratified by all thirteen states until 1781, less than eight months before the victory at Yorktown.

The chief apple of discord was western lands. Six of the jealous states, including Pennsylvania and Maryland, had no holdings beyond the Allegheny Mountains. Seven, notably New York and Virginia, were favored with enormous acreage, in most cases on the basis of earlier charter grants. The six land-hungry states argued that the more fortunate states would not have retained possession of this splendid prize if all the other states had not fought for it also. A major complaint was that the land-rich states could sell their trans-Allegheny tracts and thus pay off pensions and other debts incurred in the common cause. States without such holdings would have to tax themselves heavily to defray these obligations. Why not turn the whole western area over to the central government?

Unanimous approval of the Articles of Confederation by the thirteen states was required, and land-starved Maryland stubbornly held out until March 1, 1781. Maryland at length gave in when New York surrendered its western claims and Virginia seemed about to do so. To sweeten the pill, Congress pledged itself to dispose of these vast areas for the "common benefit." It further agreed to carve from the new public domain not colonies, but a number of "republican" states, which in time would be admitted to the Union on terms of complete equality with all the others. This extraordinary commitment faithfully reflected the anticolonial spirit of the Revolution, and the pledge was later fully redeemed in the famed Northwest Ordinance of 1787.

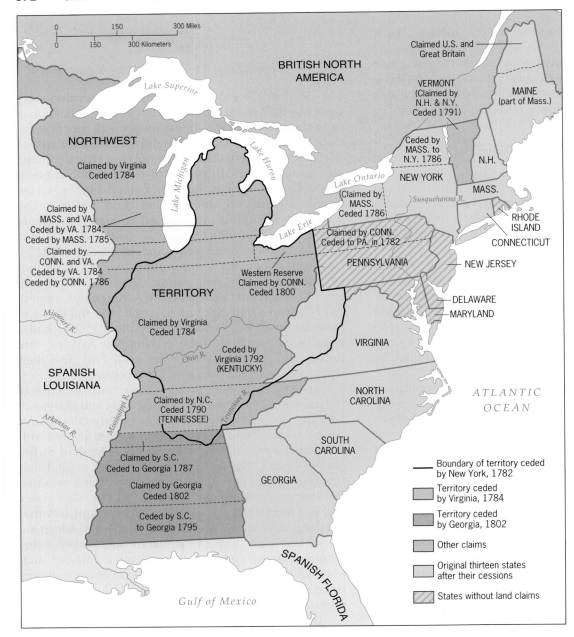

Western Land Cessions to the United States, 1782–1802

Fertile public lands thus transferred to the central government proved to be an invaluable bond of union. The states that had thrown their heritage into the common pot had to remain in the Union if they were to reap their share of the advantages from the land sales. An army of westward-moving pioneers purchased their farms from the federal government, directly or indirectly, and they learned to look to the national capital, rather than to the state capitals—with a consequent weakening of local influence. Finally, a uniform national land policy was made possible.

The Articles of Confederation: America's First Constitution

The Articles of Confederation—some have said "Articles of Confusion"—provided for a loose confederation or "firm league of friendship." Thirteen independent states were thus linked together for joint action in dealing with common problems, such as foreign affairs. A clumsy Congress was to be the chief agency of government.

There was no executive branch—George III had left a bad taste—and the vital judicial arm was left almost exclusively to the states.

Congress, though dominant, was securely hobbled. Each state had a single vote, so that some sixty-eight thousand Rhode Islanders had the same voice as more than ten times that many Virginians. All bills dealing with subjects of importance required the support of nine states; any amendment of the Articles themselves required unanimous ratification. Unanimity was almost impossible, and this meant that the amending process, perhaps fortunately, was unworkable. If it had been workable, the Republic might have struggled along with a patched-up Articles of Confederation rather than replace it with an effective Constitution.

The shackled Congress was weak—and was purposely designed to be weak. Suspicious states, having just won control over taxation and commerce from Britain, had no desire to yield their newly acquired privileges to an American parliament—even one of their own making.

Two handicaps of Congress were crippling. It had no power to regulate commerce, and this loophole left the states free to establish different, and often conflicting, laws regarding tariffs and navigation. Nor could Congress enforce its tax-collection program. It established a tax quota for each of the states and then asked them please to contribute their share on a voluntary basis. The central authority—a "government by supplication"—was lucky if in any year it received one-fourth of its requests.

The feeble national government in Philadelphia could advise and advocate and appeal. But in dealing with the independent states, it could not command or coerce or control. It could not act directly upon the individual citizens of a sovereign state; it could not even protect itself against gross indignities. In 1783 a group of mutinous Pennsylvania soldiers, whose pay was in arrears, marched to Philadelphia and made a threatening demonstration in front of Independence Hall. After Congress appealed in vain to the state for protection, its members fled to safety at Princeton College in New Jersey. The new Congress, with all its paper powers, was even less effective than the old Continental Congress, which wielded no constitutional powers at all.

Yet the Articles of Confederation, weak though they were, proved to be a landmark in government. They were for those days a model of what a loose confederation ought to be. Thomas Jefferson enthusiastically hailed the new structure as the best one "existing or that ever did exist." To compare it with the European governments, he thought, was like comparing "heaven and hell."

Statehouse in 1778, from a drawing by Charles Willson Peale, by William L. Breton, c. 1830 Originally built in the 1730s as a meeting place for the Pennsylvania colonial assembly, this building witnessed much history: here Washington was given command of the Continental Army, the Declaration of Independence was signed, and the Constitution was hammered out. The building began to be called "Independence Hall" in the 1820s.

But although the Confederation was praiseworthy as confederations went, the troubled times demanded not a loosely woven *con*federation but a tightly knit federation. This involved the yielding by the states of their sovereignty to a completely recast federal government, which in turn would leave them free to control their local affairs.

In spite of their defects, the anemic Articles of Confederation were a significant steppingstone toward the present Constitution. They clearly outlined the general powers that were to be exercised by the central government, such as making treaties and establishing a postal service. As the first written constitution of the Republic, the Articles kept alive the flickering ideal of union and held the states together—until such time as they were ripe for the establishment of a strong constitution by peaceful, evolutionary methods. Without this intermediary jump, the states probably would never have consented to the breathtaking leap from the old boycott Association of 1774 to the Constitution of the United States.

Landmarks in Land Laws

Handcuffed though the Congress of the Confederation was, it succeeded in passing supremely farsighted pieces of legislation. These related to an immense part of the public domain recently acquired from the states and commonly known as the Old Northwest. This area of land lay northwest of the Ohio River, east of the Mississippi River, and south of the Great Lakes.

The first of these red-letter laws was the Land Ordinance of 1785. It provided that the acreage of the Old Northwest should be sold and that the proceeds should be used to help pay off the national debt. The vast area was to be surveyed before sale and settlement, thus forestalling endless confusion and lawsuits. It was to be divided into townships six miles square, each of which in turn was to be split into thirty-six sections of one square mile each. The sixteenth section of each township was set aside to be sold for the benefit of the public schools—a priceless gift to education in the Northwest. The orderly settlement of the Northwest Territory, where the land was methodically surveyed and titles duly recorded, contrasted sharply with the chaos south of the Ohio River, where uncertain ownership was the norm and fraud was rampant.

Even more noteworthy was the Northwest Ordinance of 1787, which related to the governing of the Old Northwest. This law came to grips with the problem of how a nation should deal with its colonies—the same problem that had bedeviled the king and Parliament in London. The solution provided by the Northwest Ordinance was a judicious compromise: temporary tutelage, then permanent equality. First, there would be two evolutionary territorial stages, during which the area would be subordinate to the federal government. Then, when a territory could boast sixty thousand inhabitants, it might be admitted by Congress as a state, with all the privileges of the thirteen charter members. (This is precisely what the Continental Congress had promised the states when they surrendered their lands in 1781.) The ordinance also forbade slavery in the Old Northwest—a path-breaking step, though it exempted slaves already present.

The wisdom of Congress in handling this explosive problem deserves warm praise. If it had attempted to chain the new territories in permanent subordination, a second American Revolution almost certainly would have erupted in later years, fought this time by the West against the East. Congress thus neatly solved the seemingly insoluble problem of empire. The scheme worked so well that its basic principles were ultimately carried over from the Old Northwest to other frontier areas.

Surveying the Old Northwest   Sections of a township under the Land Ordinance of 1785.

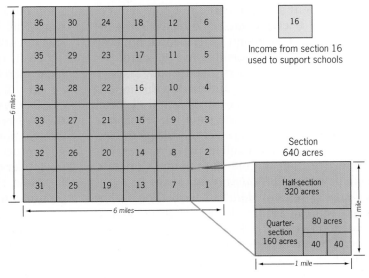

The World's Ugly Duckling

Foreign relations, especially with London, remained troubled during these anxious years of the Confederation. Britain resented the stab in the back from its rebellious offspring and for eight years refused to send a minister to America's "backwoods" capital. London suggested, with barbed irony, that if it sent one, it would have to send thirteen.

Britain flatly declined to make a commercial treaty or to repeal its ancient Navigation Laws. Lord Sheffield, whose ungenerous views prevailed, argued persuasively in a widely sold pamphlet that Britain would win back America's trade anyhow. Commerce, he insisted, would naturally follow old channels. So why go to the Americans hat in hand? The British also officially closed their profitable West Indies trade to the United States, though the Yankees, with their time-tested skill in smuggling, illegally partook nonetheless.

Scheming British agents were also active along the far-flung northern frontier. They intrigued with the disgruntled Allen brothers of Vermont and sought to annex that rebellious area to Britain. Along the northern border, the redcoats continued to hold a chain of trading posts on U.S. soil, and there they maintained their fur trade with the Indians. One plausible excuse for remaining was the failure of the American states to honor the treaty of peace in regard to debts and Loyalists. But the main purpose of Britain in hanging on was probably to curry favor with the Indians and keep their tomahawks lined up on the side of the king as a barrier against future American attacks on Canada.

All these grievances against Britain were maddening to patriotic Americans. Some citizens demanded, with more heat than wisdom, that the United States force the British into line by imposing restrictions on their imports to America. But Congress could not control commerce, and the states refused to adopt a uniform tariff policy. Some "easy states" deliberately lowered their tariffs in order to attract an unfair share of trade.

Spain, though recently an enemy of Britain, was openly unfriendly to the new Republic. It controlled the mouth of the all-important Mississippi, down which the pioneers of Tennessee and Kentucky were forced to float their produce. In 1784 Spain closed the river to American commerce, threatening the West with strangulation. Spain likewise claimed a large area north of the Gulf of Mexico, including Florida, granted to the United States by the British in 1783. At Natchez, on

Main Centers of Spanish and British Influence After 1783 This map shows graphically that the United States in 1783 achieved complete independence in name only, particularly in the area west of the Appalachian Mountains. Not until twenty years had passed did the new Republic, with the purchase of Louisiana from France in 1803, eliminate foreign influence from the area east of the Mississippi River.

disputed soil, it held an important fort. It also schemed with the neighboring Indians, grievously antagonized by the rapacious land policies of Georgia and North Carolina, to hem in the Americans east of the Appalachians. Spain and Britain together, radiating their influence out among resentful Indian tribes, prevented America from exercising effective control over about half of its total territory.

Even France, America's comrade-in-arms, cooled off now that it had humbled Britain. The French demanded the repayment of money loaned during the war and restricted trade with their bustling West Indies and other ports.

Pirates of the North African states, including the arrogant Dey of Algiers, were ravaging America's

Mediterranean commerce and enslaving Yankee sailors. The British purchased protection for their own subjects, and as colonists the Americans had enjoyed this shield. But as an independent nation, the United States was too weak to fight and too poor to bribe. A few Yankee shippers engaged in the Mediterranean trade with forged British protection papers, but not all were so bold or so lucky.

John Jay, secretary for foreign affairs, derived some hollow satisfaction from these insults. He hoped they would at least humiliate the American people into framing a new government at home that would be strong enough to command respect abroad.

The Horrid Specter of Anarchy

Economic storm clouds continued to loom in the mid-1780s. The requisition system of raising money was breaking down; some of the states refused to pay anything, while complaining bitterly about the tyranny of "King Congress." Interest on the public debt was piling up at home, and the nation's credit was evaporating abroad.

Individual states were getting out of hand. Quarrels over boundaries generated numerous minor pitched battles. Some of the states were levying duties on goods from their neighbors; New York, for example, taxed firewood from Connecticut and cabbages from New Jersey. A number of the states were again starting to grind out depreciated paper currency, and a few of them had

> Social tensions reached a fever pitch during Shays's Rebellion in 1787. In an interview with a local Massachusetts paper, instigator Daniel Shays (1747–1825) explained how the debt-ridden farmers hoped to free themselves from the demands of a merchant-dominated government. The rebels would seize arms and
>
> "march directly to Boston, plunder it, and then . . . destroy the nest of devils, who by their influence, make the Court enact what they please, burn it and lay the town of Boston in ashes."

Debtors Protest, 1787 This drawing done on the eve of the writing of the U.S. Constitution features a farmer with a plough, rake, and bottle complaining, "Takes all to pay taxes." The discontent of debt-rich and currency-poor farmers alarmed republican leaders and helped persuade them that the Articles of Confederation needed to be replaced with a new constitution.

passed laws sanctioning the semiworthless "rag money." As a contemporary rhymester put it,

> *Bankrupts their creditors with rage pursue;*
> *No stop, no mercy from the debtor crew.*

An alarming uprising, known as Shays's Rebellion, flared up in western Massachusetts in 1786. Impoverished backcountry farmers, many of them Revolutionary War veterans, were losing their farms through mortgage foreclosures and tax delinquencies. Led by Captain Daniel Shays, a veteran of the Revolution, these desperate debtors demanded that the state issue paper money, lighten taxes, and suspend property takeovers. Hundreds of angry agitators, again seizing their muskets, attempted to enforce their demands.

Massachusetts authorities responded with drastic action. Supported partly by contributions from wealthy citizens, they raised a small army. Several skirmishes occurred—at Springfield three Shaysites were killed, and one was wounded—and the movement collapsed. Daniel Shays, who believed that he was fighting anew against tyranny, was condemned to death but was later pardoned.

Shays's followers were crushed—but the nightmarish memory lingered on. The Massachusetts legislature soon passed debtor-relief laws of the kind Shays had championed, seemingly confirming Thomas Jefferson's fear of "democratic despotism." "An elective despotism was not the government we fought for," Jefferson wrote. The outbursts of Shays and other distressed debtors struck fear in the hearts of the propertied class, who began to suspect that the Revolution had created a monster of "mobocracy." Unbridled republicanism, it seemed to many of the elite, had fed an insatiable appetite for liberty that was fast becoming license. Civic virtue was no longer sufficient to rein in self-interest and greed. It had become "undeniably evident," one skeptic sorrowfully lamented, "that some malignant disorder has seized upon our body politic." If republicanism was too shaky a ground upon which to construct a new nation, a stronger central government would provide the needed foundation. A few panicky citizens even talked of importing a European monarch to carry on where George III had failed.

How critical were conditions under the Confederation? Conservatives, anxious to safeguard their wealth and position, naturally exaggerated the seriousness of the nation's plight. They were eager to persuade their fellow citizens to amend the Articles of Confederation in favor of a muscular central government. But the poorer states' rights people pooh-poohed the talk of anarchy. Many were debtors who feared that a powerful federal government would force them to pay their creditors.

Yet friends and critics of the Confederation agreed that it needed some strengthening. Popular toasts were "Cement to the Union" and "A hoop to the barrel." The chief differences arose over how this goal should be attained and how a maximum degree of states' rights could be reconciled with a strong central government. America probably could have muddled through somehow with amended Articles of Confederation. But the adoption of a completely new constitution certainly spared the Republic much costly indecision, uncertainty, and turmoil.

The nationwide picture was actually brightening before the Constitution was drafted. Nearly half the states had not issued semiworthless paper currency, and some of the monetary black sheep showed signs of returning to the sound-money fold. Prosperity was beginning to emerge from the fog of depression. By 1789 overseas shipping had largely regained its place in the commercial world. If conditions had been as grim in 1787 as painted by foes of the Articles of Confederation, the move for a new constitution would hardly have encountered such heated opposition.

A Convention of "Demigods"

Control of commerce, more than any other problem, touched off the chain reaction that led to a constitutional convention. Interstate squabbling over this issue had become so alarming by 1786 that Virginia, taking the lead, issued a call for a convention at Annapolis, Maryland. Nine states appointed delegates, but only five were finally represented. With so laughable a showing, nothing could be done about the ticklish question of commerce. A charismatic New Yorker, thirty-one-year-old Alexander Hamilton, brilliantly saved the convention from complete failure by engineering the adoption of his report. It called upon Congress to summon a convention to meet in Philadelphia the next year, not to deal with commerce alone, but to bolster the entire fabric of the Articles of Confederation.

Congress, though slowly and certainly dying in New York City, was reluctant to take a step that might hasten its day of reckoning. But after six of the states had seized the bit in their teeth and appointed delegates anyhow, Congress belatedly issued the call for a convention *for the sole and express purpose of revising* the Articles of Confederation.

Alexander Hamilton (1755–1804) clearly revealed his preference for an aristocratic government in his Philadelphia speech (1787):

"All communities divide themselves into the few and the many. The first are the rich and wellborn, the other the mass of the people. . . . The people are turbulent and changing; they seldom judge or determine right. Give therefore to the first class a distinct, permanent share in the government. They will check the unsteadiness of the second, and as they cannot receive any advantage by change, they therefore will ever maintain good government."

Every state chose representatives, except for independent-minded Rhode Island (still "Rogues' Island"), a stronghold of paper-moneyites. These leaders were all appointed by the state legislatures, whose members had been elected by voters who could qualify as property holders. This double distillation inevitably brought together a select group of propertied men—though it is a grotesque distortion to claim that they shaped the Constitution primarily to protect their personal financial interests. When one of them did suggest restricting federal office to major property owners, he was promptly denounced for the unwisdom of "interweaving into a republican constitution a veneration for wealth."

A quorum of the fifty-five emissaries from twelve states finally convened at Philadelphia on May 25, 1787, in the imposing red-brick statehouse. The smallness of the assemblage facilitated intimate acquaintance and hence compromise. Sessions were held in complete secrecy, with armed sentinels posted at the doors. Delegates knew that they would generate heated differences, and they did not want to advertise their own dissensions or put the ammunition of harmful arguments into the mouths of the opposition.

The caliber of the participants was extraordinarily high—"demigods," Jefferson called them. The crisis was such as to induce the ablest men to drop their personal pursuits and come to the aid of their country. Most of the members were lawyers, and most of them fortunately were old hands at constitution making in their own states.

George Washington, towering austere and aloof among the "demigods," was unanimously elected chairman. His enormous prestige, as "the Sword of the Revolution," served to quiet overheated tempers. Benjamin Franklin, then eighty-one, added the urbanity of an elder statesman, though he was inclined to be indiscreetly talkative in his declining years. Concerned for the secrecy of their deliberations, the convention assigned chaperones to accompany Franklin to dinner parties and make sure he held his tongue. James Madison, then thirty-six and a profound student of government, made contributions so notable that he has been dubbed "the Father of the Constitution." Alexander Hamilton, then only thirty-two, was present as an advocate of a superpowerful central government. His five-hour speech in behalf of his plan, though the most eloquent of the convention, left only one delegate convinced—himself.

Most of the fiery Revolutionary leaders of 1776 were absent. Thomas Jefferson, John Adams, and Thomas

Rising Sun Symbol at the Top of Washington's Chair
This brass sun adorned the chair in which George Washington sat during the Constitutional Convention. Pondering the symbol, Benjamin Franklin observed, "I have the happiness to know it is a rising and not a setting sun."

Paine were in Europe; Samuel Adams and John Hancock were not elected by Massachusetts. Patrick Henry, ardent champion of states' rights, was chosen as a delegate from Virginia but declined to serve, declaring that he "smelled a rat." It was perhaps well that these architects of revolution were absent. The time had come to yield the stage to leaders interested in fashioning solid political systems.

Patriots in Philadelphia

The fifty-five delegates were a conservative, well-to-do body: lawyers, merchants, shippers, land speculators, and moneylenders. Not a single spokesperson was present from the poorer debtor groups. Nineteen of the fifty-five owned slaves. They were young (the average age was about forty-two) but experienced statesmen. Above all, they were nationalists, more interested in preserving and strengthening the young Republic than in further stirring the roiling cauldron of popular democracy.

The delegates hoped to crystallize the last evaporating pools of revolutionary idealism into a stable political structure that would endure. They strongly desired a firm, dignified, and respected government. They believed in republicanism but sought to protect the

Thomas Jefferson (1743–1826), despite his high regard for the leaders at the Philadelphia convention, still was not unduly concerned about Shaysite rebellions. He wrote in November 1787,

"What country before ever existed a century and a half without a rebellion? . . . The tree of liberty must be refreshed from time to time with the blood of patriots and tyrants. It is its natural manure."

American experiment from its weaknesses abroad and excesses at home. In a broad sense, the piratical Dey of Algiers, who drove the delegates to their work, was a Founding Father. They aimed to clothe the central authority with genuine power, especially in controlling tariffs, so that the United States could wrest satisfactory commercial treaties from foreign nations. The short-sighted hostility of the British mercantilists spurred the constitution framers to their task, and in this sense the illiberal Lord Sheffield was also a Founding Father.

Other motives hovered in the Philadelphia hall. Delegates were determined to preserve the union, forestall anarchy, and ensure security of life and property against dangerous uprisings by the "mobocracy." Above all, they sought to curb the unrestrained democracy rampant in the various states. "We have, probably, had too good an opinion of human nature in forming our confederation," Washington concluded. The specter of the recent outburst in Massachusetts was especially alarming, and in this sense Daniel Shays was yet another Founding Father. Grinding necessity extorted the Constitution from a reluctant nation. Fear occupied the fifty-sixth chair.

Hammering Out a Bundle of Compromises

Some of the travel-stained delegates, when they first reached Philadelphia, decided upon a daring step. They would completely *scrap* the old Articles of Confederation, despite explicit instructions from Congress to *revise*. Technically, these bolder spirits were determined to overthrow the existing government of the United States by peaceful means.

A scheme proposed by populous Virginia, and known as "the large-state plan," was first pushed forward as the framework of the Constitution. Its essence was that representation in both houses of a bicameral Congress should be based on population—an arrangement that would naturally give the larger states an advantage.

Tiny New Jersey, suspicious of brawny Virginia, countered with "the small-state plan." This provided for equal representation in a unicameral Congress by states, regardless of size and population, as under the existing Articles of Confederation. The weaker states feared that under the Virginia scheme, the stronger states would band together and lord it over the rest. Angry debate, heightened by a stifling heat wave, led to deadlock. The danger loomed that the convention would unravel in complete failure. Even skeptical old Benjamin Franklin seriously proposed that the daily sessions be opened with a prayer by a local clergyman.

Dr. James McHenry (1753–1816), a delegate from Maryland to the Constitutional Convention of 1787, took notes on the arguments made for and against the drafting of a new constitution:

"Gov. Randolph observed that the confederation is incompetent to any one object for which it was instituted. The framers of it wise and great men; but human rights were the chief knowle[d]ge of the times when it was framed so far as they applied to oppose Great Britain. Requisitions for men and money had never offered their form to our assemblies. None of those vices that have since discovered themselves were apprehended."

Evolution of Federal Union

Years	Attempts at Union	Participants
1643–1684	New England Confederation	4 colonies
1686–1689	Dominion of New England	7 colonies
1754	Albany Congress	7 colonies
1765	Stamp Act Congress	9 colonies
1772–1776	Committees of Correspondence	13 colonies
1774	First Continental Congress (adopts The Association)	12 colonies
1775–1781	Second Continental Congress	13 colonies
1781–1789	Articles of Confederation	13 states
1789–1790	Federal Constitution	13 states

After bitter and prolonged debate, the "Great Compromise" of the convention was hammered out and agreed upon. A cooling of tempers came coincidentally with a cooling of the temperature. The larger states were conceded representation by population in the House of Representatives (Art. I, Sec. II, para. 3; see Appendix at the end of this book), and the smaller states were appeased by equal representation in the Senate (see Art. I, Sec. III, para. 1). Each state, no matter how poor or small, would have two senators. The big states obviously yielded more. As a sop to them, the delegates agreed that every tax bill or revenue measure must originate in the House, where population counted more heavily (see Art. I, Sec. VII, para. 1). This critical compromise broke the logjam, and from then on success seemed within reach.

Signing of the Constitution of the United States, 1787 George Washington presided from the dais as the Constitutional Convention's president. At a table in the front row sat James Madison, later called the Father of the Constitution, who recorded the proceedings in shorthand. Daily from 10 A.M. to 3 P.M., from late May through mid-September 1787, the fifty-five delegates wrangled over ideas for a new federal government.

One of the Philadelphia delegates recorded in his journal a brief episode involving Benjamin Franklin, who was asked by a woman when the convention ended,

"Well, Doctor, what have we got, a republic or a monarchy?"

The elder statesman answered,

"A republic, if you can keep it."

In a significant reversal of the arrangement most state constitutions had embodied, the new Constitution provided for a robust—though still legally restrained—executive in the presidency. The framers were here partly inspired by the example of Massachusetts, where a vigorous, popularly elected governor had suppressed Shays's Rebellion. The president was to have broad authority to make appointments to domestic offices—including judgeships—as well as veto power over legislation. Yet presidential power was far from absolute. The president, as commander in chief, was granted the power to wage war, but Congress retained the crucial right to *declare* war—a division of responsibilities that has been an invitation to conflict between president and Congress ever since.

The Constitution as drafted was a bundle of compromises; they stand out in every section. A key compromise was the method of electing the president indirectly by the Electoral College, rather than by direct means. While the large states would have the advantage in the first round of popular voting, as a state's share of electors was based on the total of its senators and representatives in Congress, the small states would gain a larger voice if no candidate got a majority of electoral votes and the election was thrown to the House of Representatives, where each state had only one vote (see Art. II, Sec. I, para. 2). Although the framers of the Constitution expected election by the House to occur frequently, it has happened just twice, in 1800 and in 1824.

Sectional jealousy also intruded. Should the voteless slave of the southern states count as a person in apportioning direct taxes and in according representation in the House of Representatives? The South, not wishing to be deprived of influence, answered "yes." The North replied "no," arguing that, as slaves were not citizens, the North might as logically demand additional representation based on its horses. As a compromise between total representation and none at all, it was decided that a slave might count as three-fifths of a person. Hence the memorable, if arbitrary, "three-fifths compromise" (see Art. I, Sec. II, para. 3).

Most of the states wanted to shut off the African slave trade. But South Carolina and Georgia, requiring slave labor in their rice paddies and malarial swamps, raised vehement protests. By way of compromise, the convention stipulated that the slave trade might continue until the end of 1807, at which time Congress could turn off the spigot (see Art. I, Sec. IX, para. 1). It did so as soon as the prescribed interval had elapsed. Meanwhile, all the new state constitutions except Georgia's forbade overseas slave trade.

Safeguards for Conservatism

Heated clashes among the delegates have been overplayed. The area of agreement was actually large; otherwise the convention would have speedily disbanded. Economically, the members of the Constitutional Convention generally saw eye to eye; they demanded sound money and the protection of private property. Politically, they were in basic agreement; they favored a stronger government, with three branches and with checks and balances among them—what critics branded a "triple-headed monster." Finally, the convention was virtually unanimous in believing that manhood-suffrage democracy—government by "democratick babblers"—was something to be feared and fought.

Daniel Shays, the prime bogeyman, still frightened the conservative-minded delegates. They deliberately erected safeguards against the excesses of the "mob," and they made these barriers as strong as they dared. The awesome federal judges were to be appointed for life. The powerful president was to be elected *indirectly* by the Electoral College; the lordly senators were to be chosen *indirectly* by state legislatures (see Art. I, Sec. III, para. 1). Only in the case of one-half of one of the three great branches—the House of Representatives—were qualified (propertied) citizens permitted to choose their officials by *direct* vote (see Art. I, Sec. II, para. 1).

Yet the new charter also contained democratic elements. Above all, it stood foursquare on the two great principles of republicanism: that the only legitimate government was one based on the consent of the

Strengthening the Central Government

Under Articles of Confederation	Under Federal Constitution
A loose confederation of states	A firm union of people
1 vote in Congress for each state	2 votes in Senate for each state; representation by population in House (see Art. I, Secs. II, III)
Vote of 9 states in Congress for all important measures	Simple majority vote in Congress, subject to presidential veto (see Art. I, Sec. VII, para. 2)
Laws administered loosely by committees of Congress	Laws executed by powerful president (see Art. II, Secs. II, III)
No congressional power over commerce	Congress to regulate both foreign and interstate commerce (see Art. I, Sec. VIII, para. 3)
No congressional power to levy taxes	Extensive power in Congress to levy taxes (see Art. I, Sec. VIII, para. 1)
Limited federal courts	Federal courts, capped by Supreme Court (see Art. III)
Unanimity of states for amendment	Amendment less difficult (see Art. V)
No authority to act directly upon individuals and no power to coerce states	Ample power to enforce laws by coercion of individuals and to some extent of states

governed, and that the powers of government should be limited—in this case specifically limited by a written constitution. The virtue of the people, not the authority of the state, was to be the ultimate guarantor of liberty, justice, and order. "We the people," the preamble began, in a ringing affirmation of these republican doctrines.

At the end of seventeen muggy weeks—May 25 to September 17, 1787—only forty-two of the original fifty-five members remained to sign the Constitution. Three of the forty-two, refusing to do so, returned to their states to resist ratification. The remainder, adjourning to the City Tavern, celebrated the toastworthy occasion. But no members of the convention were completely happy about the result. They were too near their work—and too weary. Whatever their personal desires, they finally had to compromise and adopt what was acceptable to the entire body, and what presumably would be acceptable to the entire country.

The Clash of Federalists and Antifederalists

The Framing Fathers early foresaw that nationwide acceptance of the Constitution would not be easy to obtain. A formidable barrier was unanimous ratification by all thirteen states, as required for amendment by the still-standing Articles of Confederation. But since absent Rhode Island was certain to veto the Constitution, the delegates boldly adopted a different scheme. They stipulated that when nine states had registered their approval through specially elected conventions, the Constitution would become the supreme law of the land in those states ratifying (see Art. VII).

This was extraordinary, even revolutionary. It was in effect an appeal over the heads of the Congress that had called the convention, and over the heads of the legislatures that had chosen its members, to the people—or those of the people who could vote. In this way the framers could claim greater popular sanction for their handiwork. A divided Congress submitted the document to the states on this basis, without recommendation of any kind.

The American people were somewhat astonished, so well had the secrets of the convention been concealed. The public had expected the old Articles of Confederation to be patched up; now it was handed a startling new document in which, many thought, the precious jewel of state sovereignty was swallowed up. One of the hottest debates of American history forthwith erupted. The antifederalists, who opposed the stronger federal government, were arrayed against the federalists, who obviously favored it.

A motley crew gathered in the antifederalist camp. Its leaders included prominent revolutionaries like Samuel Adams, Patrick Henry, and Richard Henry Lee. Their followers consisted primarily, though not exclusively, of states' rights devotees, backcountry dwellers, and one-horse farmers—in general, the poorest classes. They were joined by paper-moneyites and debtors, many of whom feared that a potent central government

Ratification of the Constitution

State	Date	Vote in Convention	Rank in Population	1790 Population
1. Delaware	Dec. 7, 1787	Unanimous	13	59,096
2. Pennsylvania	Dec. 12, 1787	46 to 23	3	433,611
3. New Jersey	Dec. 18, 1787	Unanimous	9	184,139
4. Georgia	Jan. 2, 1788	Unanimous	11	82,548
5. Connecticut	Jan. 9, 1788	128 to 40	8	237,655
6. Massachusetts (incl. Maine)	Feb. 7, 1788	187 to 168	2	475,199
7. Maryland	Apr. 28, 1788	63 to 11	6	319,728
8. South Carolina	May 23, 1788	149 to 73	7	249,073
9. New Hampshire	June 21, 1788	57 to 46	10	141,899
10. Virginia	June 26, 1788	89 to 79	1	747,610
11. New York	July 26, 1788	30 to 27	5	340,241
12. North Carolina	Nov. 21, 1789	195 to 77	4	395,005
13. Rhode Island	May 29, 1790	34 to 32	12	69,112

would force them to pay off their debts—and at full value. Large numbers of antifederalists saw in the Constitution a plot by the upper crust to steal power back from the common folk.

Silver-buckled federalists had power and influence on their side. They enjoyed the support of such commanding figures as George Washington and Benjamin Franklin. Most of them lived in the settled areas along the seaboard, not in the raw backcountry. Overall, they were wealthier than the antifederalists, more educated, and better organized. They also controlled the press. More than a hundred newspapers were published in America in the 1780s; only a dozen supported the antifederalist cause.

Antifederalists voiced vehement objections to the "gilded trap" known as the Constitution. They cried with much truth that it had been drawn up by the aristocratic elements and hence was antidemocratic. They likewise charged that the sovereignty of the states was being submerged and that the freedoms of the individual were jeopardized by the absence of a bill of rights. They decried the dropping of annual elections for congressional representatives, the erecting of a federal stronghold ten miles square (later the District of Columbia), the creation of a standing army, the omission of any reference to God, and the highly questionable procedure of ratifying with only two-thirds of the states. A Philadelphia newspaper added that Benjamin Franklin was "a fool from age" and George Washington "a fool from nature."

The Great Debate in the States

Special elections, some apathetic but others hotly contested, were held in the various states for members of the ratifying conventions. The candidates—federalist or antifederalist—were elected on the basis of their pledges for or against the Constitution.

With the ink barely dry on the parchment, four small states quickly accepted the Constitution, for they had come off much better than they expected. Pennsylvania, number two on the list of ratifiers, was the first large state to act, but not until high-handed irregularities had been employed by the federalist legislature in calling a convention. These included the forcible seating of two antifederalist members, their clothes torn and their faces red with rage, in order to complete a quorum.

Massachusetts, the second most populous state, provided an acid test. If the Constitution had failed in Massachusetts, the entire movement might easily have bogged down. The Boston ratifying convention at first contained an antifederalist majority. It included grudging Shaysites and the aging Samuel Adams, as suspicious of government power in 1787 as he had been in 1776. The assembly buzzed with dismaying talk of summoning another constitutional convention, as though the nation had not already shot its bolt. Clearly the choice was not between this Constitution and a better one, but between this Constitution and the creaking

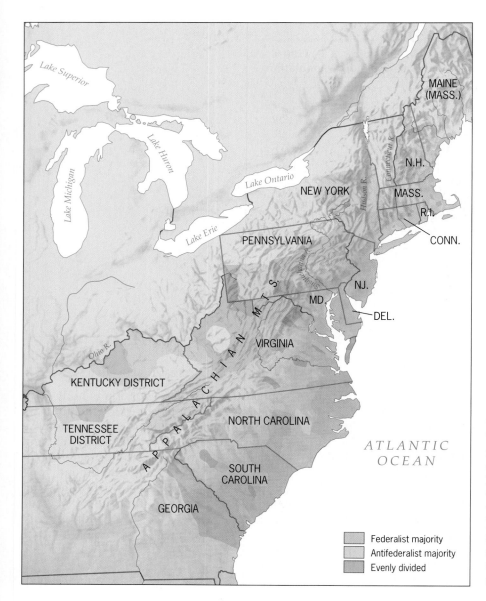

The Struggle over Ratification
This mottled map shows that federalist support tended to cluster around the coastal areas, which had enjoyed profitable commerce with the outside world, including the export of grain and tobacco. Impoverished frontiersmen, suspicious of a powerful new central government under the Constitution, were generally antifederalists.

Articles of Confederation. The absence of a bill of rights alarmed the antifederalists. But the federalists gave them solemn assurances that the first Congress would add such a safeguard by amendment, and ratification was then secured in Massachusetts by the rather narrow margin of 187 to 168.

Three more states fell into line. The last of these was New Hampshire, whose convention at first had contained a strong antifederalist majority. The federalists cleverly arranged a prompt adjournment and then won over enough waverers to secure ratification. Nine states—all but Virginia, New York, North Carolina, and Rhode Island—had now taken shelter under the "new federal roof," and the document was officially adopted on June 21, 1788. Francis Hopkinson exulted in his song "The New Roof":

Huzza! my brave boys, our work is complete;
The world shall admire Columbia's fair seat.

But such rejoicing was premature so long as the four dissenters, conspicuously New York and Virginia, dug in their heels.

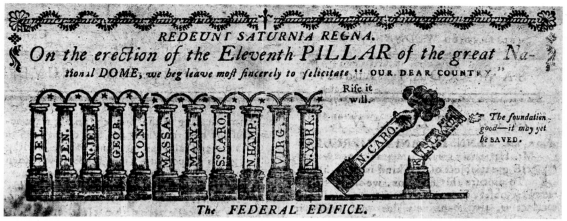

A Triumphant Cartoon It appeared in the *Massachusetts Centinel* on August 2, 1788. Note the two laggards, especially the sorry condition of Rhode Island.

The Four Laggard States

Proud Virginia, the biggest and most populous state, provided fierce antifederalist opposition. There the college-bred federalist orators, for once, encountered worthy antagonists, including the fiery Patrick Henry. He professed to see in the fearsome document the death warrant of liberty. George Washington, James Madison, and John Marshall, on the federalist side, lent influential support. With New Hampshire about to ratify, the new Union was going to be formed anyhow, and Virginia could not very well continue comfortably as an independent state. After exciting debate in the state convention, ratification carried, 89 to 79.

New York also experienced an uphill struggle, burdened as it was with its own heavily antifederalist state convention. Alexander Hamilton at heart favored a much stronger central government than that under debate, but he contributed his sparkling personality and persuasive eloquence to whipping up support for federalism as framed. He also joined John Jay and James Madison in penning a masterly series of articles for the New York newspapers. Though designed as propaganda, these essays remain the most penetrating commentary ever written on the Constitution and are still widely sold in book form as *The Federalist*. Probably the most famous of these is Madison's *Federalist* No. 10, which brilliantly refuted the conventional wisdom of the day that it was impossible to extend a republican form of government over a large territory.

Richard Henry Lee (1732–1794), a prominent antifederalist, attacked the proposed constitution in 1788:

"'Tis really astonishing that the same people, who have just emerged from a long and cruel war in defense of liberty, should now agree to fix an elective despotism upon themselves and their posterity."

The same year, prominent Patriot Patrick Henry (1736–1799) agreed that the proposed constitution endangered everything the Revolution had sought to protect:

"This constitution is said to have beautiful features; but when I come to examine these features, Sir, they appear to me horridly frightful: Among other deformities, it has an awful squinting; it squints towards monarchy: And does not this raise indignation in the breast of every American? Your President may easily become King: Your Senate is so imperfectly constructed that your dearest rights may be sacrificed by what may be a small minority; . . . Where are your checks in this Government?"

The First Coin Authorized by Congress, 1787
The Fugio cent was minted by a private company
and remained in circulation until the 1850s. The word
Fugio ("I fly") and the sundial show that time flies;
"Mind Your Business" urges diligence.

New York finally yielded. Realizing that the state
could not prosper apart from the Union, the convention
ratified the document by the close count of 30 to 27.
At the same time, it approved thirty-two proposed
amendments and—vain hope—issued a call for yet
another convention to modify the Constitution.

Last-ditch dissent developed in only two states. A
hostile convention met in North Carolina, then adjourned
without taking a vote. Rhode Island did not even summon a ratifying convention, rejecting the Constitution by
popular referendum. The two most ruggedly individualist
centers of the colonial era—homes of the "otherwise
minded"—thus ran true to form. They were to change
their course, albeit unwillingly, only after the new government had been in operation for some months.

The race for ratification, despite much apathy, was
close and quite bitter in some localities. No lives were
lost, but riotous disturbances broke out in New York and
Pennsylvania, involving bruises and bloodshed. There
was much behind-the-scenes pressure on delegates
who had promised their constituents to vote against the
Constitution. The last four states ratified, not because
they wanted to but because they had to. They could not
safely exist outside the fold.

A Conservative Triumph

The minority had triumphed—twice. A militant minority
of American radicals had engineered the military
Revolution that cast off the unwritten British constitu-

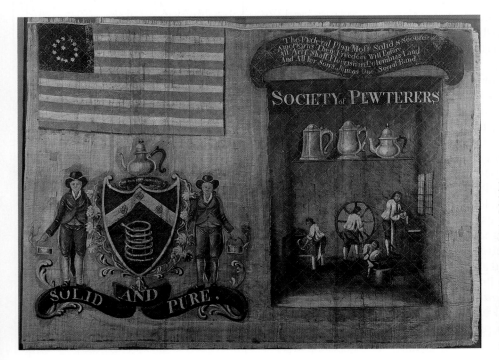

**Banner Paraded by the Society of
Pewterers in New York City, 1788**
This silk banner was carried
by members of the Society of
Pewterers in a parade in New
York City, July 23, 1788, to celebrate
the impending ratification of the
United States Constitution by
New York State. The enthusiasm
of these craftsmen for the
Constitution confirms that not
all federalists were well-to-do.

tion. A militant minority of conservatives—now embracing many of the earlier radicals—had engineered the peaceful revolution that overthrew the inadequate constitution known as the Articles of Confederation. Eleven states, in effect, had seceded from the Confederation, leaving the two still in, actually out in the cold.

A majority had not spoken. Only about one-fourth of the adult white males in the country, chiefly the propertied people, had voted for delegates to the ratifying conventions. Careful estimates indicate that if the new Constitution had been submitted to a manhood-suffrage vote, as in New York, it would have encountered much more opposition, probably defeat.

Conservatism was victorious. Safeguards had been erected against mob-rule excesses, while the republican gains of the Revolution were conserved. Radicals such as Patrick Henry, who had ousted British rule, saw themselves in turn upended by American conservatives. The federalists were convinced that by setting the drifting ship of state on a steady course, they could restore economic and political stability.

Yet if the architects of the Constitution were conservative, it is worth emphasizing that they conserved the principle of republican government through a redefinition of popular sovereignty. Unlike the antifederalists, who believed that the sovereignty of the people resided in a single branch of government—the legislature—the federalists contended that every branch—executive, judiciary, and legislature—effectively represented the people. By ingeniously embedding the doctrine of self-rule in a self-limiting system of checks and balances among these branches, the Constitution reconciled the potentially conflicting principles of liberty and order. It represented a marvelous achievement, one that elevated the ideals of the Revolution even while setting boundaries to them. One of the distinctive—and enduring—paradoxes of American history was thus revealed: in the United States, conservatives and radicals alike have championed the heritage of republican revolution.

Two Massachusetts citizens took opposite positions on the new Constitution. Jonathan Smith, a farmer unsympathetic to Shays's Rebellion of 1787, wrote,

"I am a plain man, and I get my living by the plow. I have lived in a part of the country where I have known the worth of good government by the want of it. The black cloud of Shays rebellion rose last winter in my area. It brought on a state of anarchy that led to tyranny. . . . When I saw this Constitution I found that it was a cure for these disorders. I got a copy of it and read it over and over. . . . I don't think the worse of the Constitution because lawyers, and men of learning, and moneyed men are fond of it. [They] are all embarked in the same cause with us, and we must all swim or sink together."

Amos Singletary (1721–1806), who described himself as a "poor" man, argued against the Constitution:

"We fought Great Britain—some said for a three-penny tax on tea; but it was not that. It was because they claimed a right to tax us and bind us in all cases whatever. And does not this Constitution do the same? . . . These lawyers and men of learning and money men, that talk so finely and gloss over matters so smoothly, to make us poor illiterate people swallow down the pill. . . . They expect to be the managers of the Constitution, and get all the power and money into their own hands. And then they will swallow up all us little folks, just as the whale swallowed up Jonah!"

Chronology

1774	First Continental Congress calls for abolition of slave trade
1775	Philadelphia Quakers found world's first antislavery society
1776	New Jersey constitution temporarily gives women the vote
1777	Articles of Confederation adopted by Second Continental Congress
1780	Massachusetts adopts first constitution drafted in convention and ratified by popular vote
1781	Articles of Confederation put into effect
1783	Military officers form Society of the Cincinnati
1785	Land Ordinance of 1785
1786	Virginia Statute for Religious Freedom Shays's Rebellion Meeting of five states to discuss revision of the Articles of Confederation
1787	Northwest Ordinance Constitutional Convention in Philadelphia
1788	Ratification by nine states guarantees a new government under the Constitution

VARYING VIEWPOINTS

The Constitution: Revolutionary or Counterrevolutionary?

Although the Constitution has endured over two centuries as the basis of American government, historians have differed sharply over how to interpret its origins and meaning. The so-called Nationalist School of historians, writing in the late nineteenth century, viewed the Constitution as the logical culmination of the Revolution and, more generally, as a crucial step in the God-given progress of Anglo-Saxon peoples. As described in John Fiske's *The Critical Period of American History* (1888), the young nation, buffeted by foreign threats and growing internal chaos, with only a weak central government to lean on, was saved by the adoption of a more rigorous Constitution, the ultimate fulfillment of republican ideals.

By the early twentieth century, however, the progressive historians had turned a more critical eye to the Constitution. Having observed the Supreme Court of their own day repeatedly overrule legislation designed to better social conditions for the masses, they began to view the original document as an instrument created by elite conservatives to wrest political power away from the common people. For historians like Carl Becker and Charles Beard, the Constitution was part of the Revolutionary struggle between the lower classes (small farmers, debtors, and laborers) and the upper classes (merchants, financiers, and manufacturers).

Beard's *An Economic Interpretation of the Constitution of the United States* (1913) argued that the Articles of Confederation had protected debtors and small property owners and displeased wealthy elites heavily invested in trade, the public debt, and the promotion of manufacturing. Only a stronger, more centralized government could protect their extensive property interests. Reviewing the economic holdings of the Founding Fathers, Beard determined that most of those men were indeed deeply involved in investments that would increase in value under the Constitution. In effect, Beard argued, the Constitution represented a successful attempt by conservative elites to buttress their own economic supremacy at the expense of less fortunate Americans. He further contended that the Constitution was ratified by default, because the people most disadvantaged by the new government did not possess the property qualifications needed to vote—more evidence of the class conflict underlying the struggle between the federalists and the antifederalists.

Beard's economic interpretation of the Constitution held sway through the 1940s. Historians like Merrill Jensen elaborated Beard's analysis by arguing that the 1780s were not in fact mired in chaos, but rather were hopeful times for many Americans. In the 1950s, however, this analysis fell victim to the attacks of the "consensus" historians, who sought explanations for the Constitution in factors other than class interest. Scholars such as Robert Brown and Forrest McDonald convincingly disputed Beard's evidence about delegates' property ownership and refuted his portrayal of the masses as propertyless and disfranchised. They argued that the Constitution derived from an emerging consensus that the country needed a stronger central government.

Scholars since the 1950s have searched for new ways to understand the origins of the Constitution. The most influential work has been Gordon Wood's *Creation of the American Republic* (1969). Wood reinterpreted the ratification controversy as a struggle to define the true essence of republicanism. Antifederalists so feared human inclination toward corruption that they shuddered at the prospect of putting powerful political weapons in the hands of a central government. They saw small governments susceptible to local control as the only safeguard against tyranny. The federalists, on the other hand, believed that a strong, balanced national government would rein in selfish human instincts and channel them toward the pursuit of the common good. Alarmed by the indulgences of the state governments, the federalists, James Madison in particular (especially in *Federalist* No. 10), developed the novel ideal of an "extensive republic," a polity that would achieve stability by virtue of its great size and diversity. This conception challenged the conventional wisdom that a republic could survive only if it extended over a small area with a homogeneous population. In this sense, Wood argued, the Constitution represented a bold experiment—the fulfillment, rather than the repudiation, of the most advanced ideas of the Revolutionary era—even though it emanated from traditional elites determined to curtail dangerous disruptions to the social order.

For further reading, see the Appendix. For web resources, go to **http://college.hmco.com**.

10

Launching the New Ship of State

1789–1800

I SHALL ONLY SAY THAT I HOLD WITH MONTESQUIEU,
THAT A GOVERNMENT MUST BE FITTED TO A NATION,
AS MUCH AS A COAT TO THE INDIVIDUAL; AND,
CONSEQUENTLY, THAT WHAT MAY BE GOOD AT
PHILADELPHIA MAY BE BAD AT PARIS, AND
RIDICULOUS AT PETERSBURG [RUSSIA].

ALEXANDER HAMILTON, 1799

America's new ship of state did not spread its sails to the most favorable breezes. Within twelve troubled years, the American people had risen up and thrown overboard both the British yoke and the Articles of Confederation. A decade of lawbreaking and constitution smashing was not the best training for government making. Americans had come to regard a central authority, replacing that of George III, as a necessary evil—something to be distrusted, watched, and curbed.

The finances of the infant government were likewise precarious. The revenue had declined to a trickle, whereas the public debt, with interest heavily in arrears, was mountainous. Worthless paper money, both state and national, was as plentiful as metallic money was scarce. Nonetheless, the Americans were brashly trying to erect a republic on an immense scale, something that no other people had attempted and that traditional political theory deemed impossible. The eyes of a skeptical world were on the upstart United States.

Growing Pains

When the Constitution was launched in 1789, the Republic was continuing to grow at an amazing rate. Population was doubling about every twenty-five years, and the first official census of 1790 recorded almost 4 million people. Cities had blossomed proportionately: Philadelphia numbered 42,000, New York 33,000, Boston 18,000, Charleston 16,000, and Baltimore 13,000.

America's population was still about 90 percent rural, despite the flourishing cities. All but 5 percent of the people lived east of the Appalachian Mountains. The trans-Appalachian overflow was concentrated chiefly in Kentucky, Tennessee, and Ohio, all of which were welcomed as states within fourteen years. (Vermont preceded them, becoming the fourteenth state in 1791.) Foreign visitors to America looked down their noses at the roughness and crudity resulting from ax-and-rifle pioneering life.

The French statesman Anne Robert Jacques Turgot (1727–1781) had high expectations for a united America:

"This people is the hope of the human race. . . . The Americans should be an example of political, religious, commercial and industrial liberty. . . . But to obtain these ends for us, America . . . must not become . . . a mass of divided powers, contending for territory and trade."

People of the western waters—in the stump-studded clearings of Kentucky, Tennessee, and Ohio—were particularly restive and dubiously loyal. The mouth of the Mississippi, their life-giving outlet, lay in the hands of unfriendly Spaniards. Slippery Spanish and British agents, jingling gold, moved freely among the settlers and held out seductive promises of independence. Many observers wondered whether the emerging United States would ever grow to maturity.

Washington for President

General Washington, the esteemed war hero, was unanimously drafted as president by the Electoral College in 1789—the only presidential nominee ever to be honored by unanimity. His presence was imposing: 6 feet 2 inches, 175 pounds, broad and sloping shoulders, strongly pointed chin, and pockmarks (from smallpox) on nose and cheeks. Much preferring the quiet of Mount Vernon to the turmoil of politics, he was perhaps the only president who did not in some way angle for this exalted office. Balanced rather than brilliant, he commanded his followers by strength of character rather than by the arts of the politician.

Washington's long journey from Mount Vernon to New York City, the temporary capital, was a triumphal procession. He was greeted by roaring cannon, pealing bells, flower-carpeted roads, and singing and shouting

Washington Honored This idealized portrait symbolizes the reverential awe in which Americans held "the Father of His Country."

citizens. With appropriate ceremony, he solemnly and somewhat nervously took the oath of office on April 30, 1789, on a crowded balcony overlooking Wall Street, which some have regarded as a bad omen.

Washington soon put his stamp on the new government, especially by establishing the cabinet. The Constitution does not mention a cabinet; it merely provides that the president "may require" written opinions of the heads of the executive-branch departments (see Art. II, Sec. II, para. 1 in the Appendix). But this system proved so cumbersome, and involved so much homework, that cabinet meetings gradually evolved in the Washington administration.

At first only three full-fledged department heads served under the president: Secretary of State Thomas Jefferson, Secretary of the Treasury Alexander Hamilton, and Secretary of War Henry Knox.

The Bill of Rights

The new nation faced some unfinished business. Many antifederalists had sharply criticized the Constitution drafted at Philadelphia for its failure to provide guarantees of individual rights such as freedom of religion and trial by jury. Many states had ratified the federal Constitution on the understanding that it would soon be amended to include such guarantees. Drawing up a bill of rights headed the list of imperatives facing the new government.

Amendments to the Constitution could be proposed in either of two ways—by a new constitutional convention requested by two-thirds of the states or by a two-thirds vote of both houses of Congress. Fearing that a new convention might unravel the narrow federalist victory in the ratification struggle, James Madison determined to draft the amendments himself. He then guided them through Congress, where his intellectual and political skills were quickly making him the leading figure.

Adopted by the necessary number of states in 1791, the first ten amendments to the Constitution, popularly known as the Bill of Rights, safeguard some of the most precious American principles. Among these are protections for freedom of religion, speech, and the press; the right to bear arms and to be tried by a jury; and the right to assemble and petition the government for redress of grievances. The Bill of Rights also prohibits cruel and unusual punishments and arbitrary government seizure of private property.

To guard against the danger that enumerating such rights might lead to the conclusion that they were the only ones protected, Madison inserted the crucial Ninth Amendment. It declares that specifying certain rights "shall not be construed to deny or disparage others retained by the people." In a gesture of reassurance to the states' righters, he included the equally significant Tenth Amendment, which reserves all rights not explicitly delegated or prohibited by the federal Constitution "to the States respectively, or to the people." By preserving a strong central government while specifying protections for minority and individual liberties, Madison's amendments partially swung the federalist pendulum back in an antifederalist direction. (See Amendments I–X.)

Evolution of the Cabinet

Position	Date Established	Comments
Secretary of state	1789	
Secretary of Treasury	1789	
Secretary of war	1789	Loses cabinet status, 1947
Attorney general	1789	Not head of Justice Dept. until 1870
Secretary of navy	1798	Loses cabinet status, 1947
Postmaster general	1829	Loses cabinet status, 1970
Secretary of interior	1849	
Secretary of agriculture	1889	
Secretary of commerce and labor	1903	Office divided, 1913
Secretary of commerce	1913	
Secretary of labor	1913	
Secretary of defense	1947	Subordinate to this secretary, without cabinet rank, are secretaries of army, navy, and air force
Secretary of health, education, and welfare	1953	Office divided, 1979
Secretary of housing and urban development	1965	
Secretary of transportation	1966	
Secretary of energy	1977	
Secretary of health and human services	1979	
Secretary of education	1979	
Secretary of veterans' affairs	1989	

The first Congress also nailed other newly sawed government planks into place. It created effective federal courts under the Judiciary Act of 1789. The act organized the Supreme Court, with a chief justice and five associates, as well as federal district and circuit courts, and established the office of attorney general. New Yorker John Jay, Madison's collaborator on *The Federalist* papers and one of the young Republic's most seasoned diplomats, became the first chief justice of the United States.

Hamilton Revives the Corpse of Public Credit

The key figure in the new government was still smooth-faced Treasury Secretary Alexander Hamilton, a native of the British West Indies. Hamilton's genius was unquestioned, but critics claimed he loved his adopted country more than he loved his countrymen. Doubts about his character and his loyalty to the republican experiment always swirled about his head. Hamilton regarded himself as a kind of prime minister in Washington's cabinet and on occasion thrust his hands into the affairs of other departments, including that of his archrival, Thomas Jefferson, who served as secretary of state.

A financial wizard, Hamilton set out immediately to correct the economic vexations that had crippled the Articles of Confederation. His plan was to shape the fiscal policies of the administration in such a way as to favor the wealthier groups. They, in turn, would gratefully lend the government monetary and political support. The new federal regime would thrive, the propertied classes would fatten, and prosperity would trickle down to the masses.

The youthful financier's first objective was to bolster the national credit. Without public confidence in the government, Hamilton could not secure the funds with which to float his risky schemes. He therefore boldly urged Congress to "fund" the entire national debt "at par" and to assume completely the debts incurred by the states during the recent war.

"Funding at par" meant that the federal government would pay off its debts at face value, plus accumulated interest—a then-enormous total of more than $54 million. So many people believed the infant Treasury incapable of meeting those obligations that government bonds had depreciated to ten or fifteen cents on the dollar. Yet speculators held fistfuls of them, and when Congress passed Hamilton's measure in 1790, they grabbed for more. Some of them galloped into rural areas ahead

Alexander Hamilton (1755–1804), by John Trumbull, 1792
He was one of the youngest and most brilliant of the Founding Fathers, who might have been president but for his ultraconservatism, a scandalous adultery, and a duelist's bullet. Hamilton favored a strong central government with a weak legislature to unify the infant nation and encourage industry. His chief rival, Thomas Jefferson, who extolled states' rights as a bulwark of liberty and thought the United States should remain an agricultural society, regarded Hamilton as a monarchist plotter and never forgave him for insisting that "the British Govt. was the best in the world: and that he doubted much whether any thing short of it would do in America."

of the news, buying for a song the depreciated paper holdings of farmers, war veterans, and widows.

Hamilton was willing, even eager, to have the new government shoulder additional obligations. While pushing the funding scheme, he urged Congress to assume the debts of the states, totaling some $21.5 million.

The secretary made a convincing case for "assumption." The state debts could be regarded as a proper national obligation, for they had been incurred in the

One of the most eloquent tributes to Hamilton's apparent miracle working came from Daniel Webster (1782–1852) in the Senate (1831):

"He smote the rock of the national resources, and abundant streams of revenue gushed forth. He touched the dead corpse of public credit, and it sprung upon its feet."

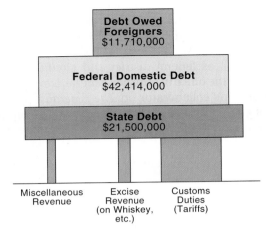

Hamilton's Financial Structure Supported by Revenues

war for independence. But foremost in Hamilton's thinking was the belief that assumption would chain the states more tightly to the "federal chariot." Thus the secretary's maneuver would shift the attachment of wealthy creditors from the states to the federal government. The support of the rich for the national administration was a crucial link in Hamilton's political strategy of strengthening the central government.

States burdened with heavy debts, like Massachusetts, were delighted by Hamilton's proposal. States with small debts, like Virginia, were less charmed. The stage was set for some old-fashioned horse trading. Virginia did not want the state debts assumed, but it did want the forthcoming federal district*—now the District of Columbia—to be located on the Potomac River. It would thus gain in commerce and prestige. Hamilton persuaded a reluctant Jefferson, who had recently come home from France, to line up enough votes in Congress for assumption. In return, Virginia would have the federal district on the Potomac. The bargain was carried through in 1790.

Customs Duties and Excise Taxes

The new ship of state thus set sail dangerously overloaded. The national debt had swelled to $75 million owing to Hamilton's insistence on honoring the outstanding federal and state obligations alike. Anyone less determined to establish such a healthy public credit could have sidestepped $13 million in back interest and could have avoided the state debts entirely.

But Hamilton, "Father of the National Debt," was not greatly worried. His objectives were as much political as economic. He believed that within limits, a national debt was a "national blessing"—a kind of union adhesive. The more creditors to whom the government owed money, the more people there would be with a personal stake in the success of his ambitious enterprise. His unique contribution was to make a debt—ordinarily a liability—an asset for vitalizing the financial system as well as the government itself.

Where was the money to come from to pay interest on this huge debt and run the government? Hamilton's first answer was customs duties, derived from a tariff. Tariff revenues, in turn, depended on a vigorous foreign trade, another crucial link in Hamilton's overall economic strategy for the new Republic.

The first tariff law, imposing a low tariff of about 8 percent on the value of dutiable imports, was speedily passed by the first Congress in 1789, even before Hamilton was sworn in. Revenue was by far the main goal, but the measure was also designed to erect a low protective wall around infant industries, which bawled noisily for more shelter than they received. Hamilton had the vision to see that the industrial revolution would soon reach America, and he argued strongly in favor of more protection for the well-to-do manufacturing groups—another vital element in his economic program. But Congress was still dominated by the agricultural and commercial interests, and it voted only two slight increases in the tariff during Washington's presidency.

Hamilton, with characteristic vigor, sought additional internal revenue and in 1791 secured from

---

*Authorized by the Constitution, Art. I, Sec. VIII, para. 17.

Selling Wallpaper—and Manufacturing, 1800
A Boston maker of wallpaper, Ebenezer Clough, incorporated on his company letterhead an endorsement of Alexander Hamilton's dream of a manufacturing nation.

Congress an excise tax on a few domestic items, notably whiskey. The new levy of seven cents a gallon was borne chiefly by the distillers who lived in the backcountry, where the wretched roads forced the farmer to reduce (and liquefy) bulky bushels of grain to horseback proportions. Whiskey flowed so freely on the frontier in the form of distilled liquor that it was used for money.

Hamilton Battles Jefferson for a Bank

As the capstone for his financial system, Hamilton proposed a bank of the United States. An enthusiastic admirer of most things English, he took as his model the Bank of England. Specifically, he proposed a powerful private institution, of which the government would be the major stockholder and in which the federal Treasury would deposit its surplus monies. The central government not only would have a convenient strongbox, but federal funds would stimulate business by remaining in circulation. The bank would also print urgently needed paper money and thus provide a sound and stable national currency, badly needed since the days when the Continental dollar was "not worth a Continental."

The proposed bank would indeed be useful. But was it constitutional?

Jefferson, whose written opinion on this question Washington requested, argued vehemently against the bank. There was, he insisted, no specific authorization in the Constitution for such a financial octopus. He was convinced that all powers not specifically granted to the central government were reserved to the states, as provided in the about-to-be-ratified Bill of Rights (see Amendment X). He therefore concluded that the states, not Congress, had the power to charter banks. Believing that the Constitution should be interpreted "literally" or "strictly," Jefferson and his states' rights disciples zealously embraced the theory of "strict construction."

Hamilton, also at Washington's request, prepared a brilliantly reasoned reply to Jefferson's arguments. Hamilton in general believed that what the Constitution did not forbid it permitted; Jefferson, in contrast, generally believed that what it did not permit it forbade. Hamilton boldly invoked the clause of the Constitution that stipulates that Congress may pass any laws "necessary and proper" to carry out the powers vested in the various government agencies (see Art. I, Sec. VIII, para. 18). The government was explicitly empowered to collect taxes and regulate trade. In carrying out these basic functions, Hamilton argued, a national bank would be not only "proper" but "necessary." By inference or implication—that is, by virtue of "implied powers"—Congress would be fully justified in establishing the Bank of the United States. In short, Hamilton contended for a "loose" or "broad" interpretation of the Constitution. He and his federalist followers thus evolved the theory of "loose construction" by invoking the "elastic clause" of the Constitution—a precedent for enormous federal powers.

Hamilton's financial views prevailed. His eloquent and realistic arguments were accepted by Washington, who reluctantly signed the bank measure into law. This explosive issue had been debated with much heat in Congress, where the old North-South cleavage still lurked ominously. The most enthusiastic support for the bank naturally came from the commercial and financial centers of the North, whereas the strongest opposition arose from the agricultural South.

The Bank of the United States, as created by Congress in 1791, was chartered for twenty years. Located in Philadelphia, it was to have a capital of $10 million, one-fifth of it owned by the federal government. Stock was thrown open to public sale. To the agreeable surprise of Hamilton, a milling crowd oversubscribed in less than two hours, pushing aside many would-be purchasers.

Mutinous Moonshiners in Pennsylvania

The Whiskey Rebellion, which flared up in southwestern Pennsylvania in 1794, sharply challenged the new national government. Hamilton's high excise tax bore harshly on these homespun pioneer folk. They regarded it not as a tax on a frivolous luxury but as a burden on an economic necessity and a medium of exchange. Even preachers of the gospel were paid in "Old Monongahela rye." Rye and corn crops distilled into alcohol were more cheaply transported to eastern markets than bales of grain. Defiant distillers finally erected whiskey poles, similar to the liberty poles of anti–stamp tax days in 1765, and raised the cry "Liberty and No Excise." Boldly tarring and feathering revenue officers, they brought collections to a halt.

President Washington, once a revolutionary, was alarmed by what he called these "self-created societies." With the hearty encouragement of Hamilton, he summoned the militia of several states. Anxious moments followed the call, for there was much doubt as to whether men in other states would muster to crush a rebellion in a fellow state. Despite some opposition, an army of about thirteen thousand rallied to the colors,

Attorney Hugh Henry Brackenridge (1748–1816) mediated between the Whiskey Rebels and the town of Pittsburgh. He later wrote of the hated excise tax,

"I saw the operation to be unequal in this country. . . . It is true that the excise paid by the country would be that only on spirits consumed in it. But even in the case of exports, the excise must be advanced in the first instance by the distiller and this would prevent effectually all the poorer part from carrying on the business. I . . . would have preferred a direct tax with a view to reach unsettled lands which all around us have been purchased by speculating men."

and two widely separated columns marched briskly forth in a gorgeous, leaf-tinted Indian summer, until knee-deep mud slowed their progress.

When the troops reached the hills of western Pennsylvania, they found no insurrection. The "Whiskey Boys" were overawed, dispersed, or captured. Washington, with an eye to healing old sores, pardoned the two small-fry convicted culprits.

The Whiskey Rebellion was minuscule—some three rebels were killed—but its consequences were mighty. George Washington's government, now substantially strengthened, commanded a new respect. Yet the foes of the administration condemned its brutal display of force—for having used a sledgehammer to crush a gnat.

The Emergence of Political Parties

Almost overnight, Hamilton's fiscal feats had established the government's sound credit rating. The Treasury could now borrow needed funds in the Netherlands on favorable terms.

But Hamilton's financial successes—funding, assumption, the excise tax, the bank, the suppression of the Whiskey Rebellion—created some political liabilities. All these schemes encroached sharply upon states' rights. Many Americans, dubious about the new Constitution in the first place, might never have approved it if they had foreseen how the states were going to be overshadowed by the federal colossus. Now, out of resentment against Hamilton's revenue-raising and centralizing policies, an organized opposition began to build. What once was a personal feud between Hamilton and Jefferson developed into a full-blown and frequently bitter political rivalry.

National political parties, in the modern sense, were unknown in America when George Washington took his inaugural oath. There had been Whigs and Tories, federalists and antifederalists, but these groups were factions rather than parties. They had sprung into existence over hotly contested special issues; they had faded away when their cause had triumphed or fizzled.

The Founders at Philadelphia had not envisioned the existence of permanent political parties. Organized opposition to the government—especially a democratic government based on popular consent—seemed tainted with disloyalty. Opposition to the government affronted the spirit of national unity that the glorious cause of the Revolution had inspired. The notion of a

Evolution of Major Parties*

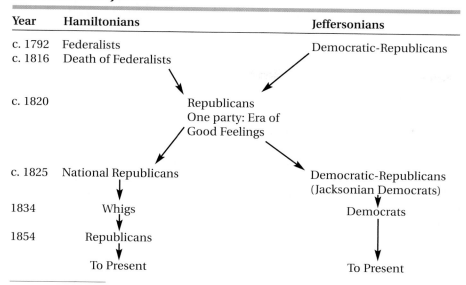

Year	Hamiltonians	Jeffersonians
c. 1792	Federalists	Democratic-Republicans
c. 1816	Death of Federalists	
c. 1820	Republicans One party: Era of Good Feelings	
c. 1825	National Republicans	Democratic-Republicans (Jacksonian Democrats)
1834	Whigs	Democrats
1854	Republicans	
	To Present	To Present

*See Appendix (Presidential Elections) for third parties.

formal party apparatus was thus a novelty in the 1790s, and when Jefferson and Madison first organized their opposition to the Hamiltonian program, they confined their activities to Congress and did not anticipate creating a long-lived and popular party. But as their antagonism to Hamilton stiffened, and as the amazingly boisterous and widely read newspapers of the day spread their political message, and Hamilton's, among the people, primitive semblances of political parties began to emerge.

The two-party system has existed in the United States since that time (see the table above). Ironically, in light of early suspicions about the very legitimacy of parties, their competition for power has actually proved to be among the indispensable ingredients of a sound democracy. The party out of power—"the loyal opposition"—traditionally plays the invaluable role of the balance wheel on the machinery of government, ensuring that politics never drifts too far out of kilter with the wishes of the people.

Republicanism Triumphant   Artists often used classical motifs to celebrate the triumph in America of republicanism—a form of government they traced back to ancient Greece and Rome.

The Impact of the French Revolution

When Washington's first administration ended in early 1793, Hamilton's domestic policies had already stimulated the formation of two political camps—Jeffersonian Democratic-Republicans and Hamiltonian Federalists. As Washington's second term began, foreign-policy issues brought the differences between them to a fever pitch.

Only a few weeks after Washington's inauguration in 1789, the curtain had risen on the first act of the French Revolution. Twenty-six years were to pass before the seething continent of Europe collapsed into a peace of exhaustion. Few non-American events have left a deeper scar on American political and social life. In a sense the French Revolution was misnamed: it was a revolution that sent tremors through much of the Western world.

In its early stages, the upheaval was surprisingly peaceful, involving as it did a successful attempt to impose constitutional shackles on Louis XVI. The American people, loving liberty and deploring despotism, cheered. They were flattered to think that the outburst in France was but the second chapter of their own glorious Revolution, as to some extent it was. Only a few ultraconservative Federalists—fearing change, reform, and "leveling" principles—were from the outset dubious or outspokenly hostile to the "despicable mobocracy." The more ardent Jeffersonians were overjoyed.

The French Revolution entered a more ominous phase in 1792, when France declared war on hostile Austria. Powerful ideals and powerful armies alike were on the march. Late in that year, the electrifying news reached America that French citizen armies had hurled

British political observer William Cobbett (1763–1835) wrote of the frenzied reaction in America to the death of Louis XVI:

"Never was the memory of a man so cruelly insulted as that of this mild and humane monarch. He was guillotined in effigy, in the capital of the Union [Philadelphia], twenty or thirty times every day, during one whole winter and part of the summer. Men, women and children flocked to the tragical exhibition, and not a single paragraph appeared in the papers to shame them from it."

back the invading foreigners and that France had proclaimed itself a republic. Americans enthusiastically sang "The Marseillaise" and other rousing French Revolutionary songs, and they renamed thoroughfares with democratic flare. King Street in New York, for example, became Liberty Street, and in Boston, Royal Exchange Alley became Equality Lane.

But centuries of pent-up poison could not be purged without baleful results. The guillotine was set up, the king was beheaded in 1793, the church was attacked, and the head-rolling Reign of Terror was begun. Back in America, God-fearing Federalist aristocrats nervously fingered their tender white necks and eyed the Jeffersonian masses apprehensively. Lukewarm Federalist

The Contrast Adaptation of a British cartoon that makes the former colonies' struggle for independence look virtuous compared to the French Revolution.

approval of the early Revolution turned, almost overnight, to heated talk of "blood-drinking cannibals."

Sober-minded Jeffersonians regretted the bloodshed. But they felt, with Jefferson, that one could not expect to be carried from "despotism to liberty in a feather bed" and that a few thousand aristocratic heads were a cheap price to pay for human freedom.

Such approbation was shortsighted, for dire peril loomed ahead. The earlier battles of the French Revolution had not hurt America directly, but now Britain was sucked into the contagious conflict. The conflagration speedily spread to the New World, where it vividly affected the expanding young American Republic. Thus was repeated the familiar story of every major European war, beginning with 1689, that involved a watery duel for control of the Atlantic Ocean. (See the table on p. 111.)

Washington's Neutrality Proclamation

Ominously, the Franco-American alliance of 1778 was still on the books. By its own terms, it was to last "forever." It bound the United States to help the French defend their West Indies against future foes, and the booming British fleets were certain to attack these strategic islands.

Many Jeffersonian Democratic-Republicans favored honoring the alliance. Aflame with the liberal ideals of the French Revolution, red-blooded Jeffersonians were eager to enter the conflict against Britain, the recent foe, at the side of France, the recent friend. America owed France its freedom, they argued, and now was the time to pay the debt of gratitude.

But President George Washington, levelheaded as usual, was not swayed by the clamor of the crowd. Backed by Hamilton, he believed that war had to be avoided at all costs. Washington was coolly playing for enormous stakes. The nation in 1793 was militarily feeble, economically wobbly, and politically disunited. But solid foundations were being laid, and American cradles were continuing to rock a bumper crop of babies. Washington wisely reasoned that if America could avoid the broils of Europe for a generation or so, it would then be populous enough and powerful enough to assert its maritime rights with strength and success. Otherwise it might invite catastrophe. The strategy of delay—of playing for time while the birthrate fought America's battles—was a cardinal policy of the Founding Fathers.

It was based on a shrewd assessment of American strengths and weaknesses at this critical moment in the young Republic's history. Hamilton and Jefferson, often poles apart on other issues, were in agreement here.

Accordingly, Washington boldly issued his Neutrality Proclamation in 1793, shortly after the outbreak of war between Britain and France. This epochal document not only proclaimed the government's official neutrality in the widening conflict but sternly warned American citizens to be impartial toward both armed camps. As America's first formal declaration of aloofness from Old World quarrels, Washington's Neutrality Proclamation proved to be a major prop of the spreading isolationist tradition. It also proved to be enormously controversial. The pro-French Jeffersonians were enraged by the Neutrality Proclamation, especially by Washington's method of announcing it unilaterally, without consulting Congress. The pro-British Federalists were heartened.

Debate soon intensified. An impetuous, thirty-year-old representative of the French Republic, Citizen Edmond Genêt, had landed at Charleston, South Carolina. With unrestrained zeal he undertook to fit out privateers and otherwise take advantage of the existing Franco-American alliance. The giddy-headed envoy—all sail and no anchor—was soon swept away by his enthusiastic reception by the Jeffersonian Republicans. He foolishly came to believe that the Neutrality Proclamation did not reflect the true wishes of the American people, and he consequently embarked upon unneutral activity not authorized by the French alliance—including the recruitment of armies to invade Spanish Florida and Louisiana, as well as British Canada. Even Madison and Jefferson were soon disillusioned by his conduct. After he threatened to appeal over the head of "Old Washington" to the sovereign voters, the president demanded Genêt's withdrawal, and the Frenchman was replaced by a less impulsive emissary.

Washington's Neutrality Proclamation clearly illustrates the truism that self-interest is the basic cement of alliances. In 1778 both France and America stood to gain; in 1793 only France. Technically, the Americans did not flout their obligation because France never officially called upon them to honor it. American neutrality in fact favored France. The French West Indies urgently needed Yankee foodstuffs. If the Americans had entered the war at France's side, the British fleets would have blockaded the American coast and cut off those essential supplies. America was thus much more useful to France as a reliable neutral provider than as a blockaded partner-in-arms.

Embroilments with Britain

President Washington's far-visioned policy of neutrality was sorely tried by the British. For ten long years, they had been retaining the chain of northern frontier posts on U.S. soil, all in defiance of the peace treaty of 1783. The London government was reluctant to abandon the lucrative fur trade in the Great Lakes region and also hoped to build up an Indian buffer state to contain the ambitious Americans. British agents openly sold firearms and firewater to the Indians of the Miami Confederacy, an alliance of eight Indian nations who terrorized Americans invading their lands. Little Turtle, war chief of the Miamis, gave notice that the confederacy regarded the Ohio River as the United States' northwestern, and their own southeastern, border. In 1790 and 1791, Little Turtle's braves defeated armies led by Generals Josiah Harmar and Arthur St. Clair, killing hundreds of soldiers and handing the United States what remains one of its worst defeats in the history of the frontier.

But in 1794, when a new army under General "Mad Anthony" Wayne routed the Miamis at the Battle of Fallen Timbers, the British refused to shelter Indians fleeing from the battle. Abandoned when it counted by their red-coated friends, the Indians soon offered Wayne the peace pipe. In the Treaty of Greenville, signed in August 1795, the confederacy gave up vast tracts of the Old Northwest, including most of present-day Indiana and Ohio. In exchange the Indians received a lump-sum payment of $20,000, an annual annuity of $9,000, the right to hunt the lands they had ceded, and, most

> *Thomas Paine (1737–1809), then in France and resenting George Washington's anti-French policies, addressed the president in an open letter (1796) that reveals his bitterness:*
>
> "And as to you, sir, treacherous in private friendship (for so you have been to me, and that in the day of danger) and a hypocrite in public life, the world will be puzzled to decide, whether you are an apostate or an imposter; whether you have abandoned good principles, or whether you ever had any."

important, what they hoped was recognition of their sovereign status. Although the treaty codified an unequal relationship, the Indians felt that it put some limits on the ability of the United States to decide the fate of Indian peoples.

On the sea frontier, the British were eager to starve out the French West Indies and naturally expected the United States to defend them under the Franco-American alliance. Hard-boiled commanders of the Royal Navy, ignoring America's rights as a neutral, struck savagely. They seized about three hundred American merchant ships in the West Indies, impressed scores of seamen into service on British vessels, and threw hundreds of others into foul dungeons.

These actions incensed patriotic Americans. A mighty outcry arose, chiefly from Jeffersonians, that America should once again fight George III in defense of its liberties. At the very least, it should cut off all supplies to its oppressor through a nationwide embargo. But the Federalists stoutly resisted all demands for drastic action. Hamilton's high hopes for economic development depended on trade with Britain. War with the world's mightiest commercial empire would pierce the heart of the Hamiltonian financial system.

Jay's Treaty and Washington's Farewell

President Washington, in a last desperate gamble to avert war, decided to send Chief Justice John Jay to

American Posts Held by the British After 1783

London in 1794. The Jeffersonians were acutely unhappy over the choice, partly because they feared that so notorious a Federalist and Anglophile would sell out his country. Arriving in London, Jay gave the Jeffersonians further cause for alarm when, at the presentation ceremony, he routinely kissed the queen's hand.

Unhappily, Jay entered the negotiations with weak cards, which were further sabotaged by Hamilton. The latter, fearful of war with Britain, secretly supplied the British with the details of America's bargaining strategy. Not surprisingly, Jay won few concessions. The British did promise to evacuate the chain of posts on U.S. soil— a pledge that inspired little confidence, since it had been made before in Paris (to the same John Jay!) in 1783. In addition, Britain consented to pay damages for the recent seizures of American ships. But the British stopped short of pledging anything about *future* maritime seizures and impressments or about supplying arms to Indians. And they forced Jay to give ground by binding the United States to pay the debts still owed to British merchants on pre-Revolutionary accounts.

Jay's unpopular pact, more than any other issue, vitalized the newborn Democratic-Republican party of Thomas Jefferson. When the Jeffersonians learned of Jay's concessions, their rage was fearful to behold. The treaty seemed like an abject surrender to Britain, as well as a betrayal of the Jeffersonian South. Southern planters would have to pay the major share of the pre-Revolutionary debts, while rich Federalist shippers were collecting damages for recent British seizures. Jeffersonian mobs hanged, burned, and guillotined in effigy that "damn'd archtraitor, Sir John Jay." Even George Washington's huge popularity was compromised by the controversy over the treaty.

Jay's Treaty had other unforeseen consequences. Fearing that the treaty foreshadowed an Anglo-American alliance, Spain moved hastily to strike a deal with the United States. Pinckney's Treaty of 1795 with Spain granted the Americans virtually everything they demanded, including free navigation of the Mississippi and the large disputed territory north of Florida. (See the map on p. 175.)

Exhausted after the diplomatic and partisan battles of his second term, President Washington decided to retire. His choice contributed powerfully to establishing a two-term tradition for American presidents.* In his Farewell Address to the nation in 1796 (never delivered orally but printed in the newspapers), Washington strongly advised the avoidance of "permanent alliances" like the still-vexatious Franco-American Treaty of 1778. Contrary to general misunderstanding, Washington did not oppose all alliances, but favored only "temporary alliances" for "extraordinary emergencies." This was admirable advice for a weak and divided nation in 1796. But what is sound counsel for a young stripling may not apply later to a mature and muscular giant.

Washington's contributions as president were enormous, even though the sparkling Hamilton at times seemed to outshine him. The central government, its fiscal feet now under it, was solidly established. The West was expanding. The merchant marine was plowing the seas. Above all, Washington had kept the nation out of both overseas entanglements and foreign wars. The experimental stage had passed, and the presidential chair could now be turned over to a less impressive figure. But republics are notoriously ungrateful. When Washington left office in 1797, he was showered with the brickbats of partisan abuse, quite in contrast with the bouquets that had greeted his arrival.

John Adams Becomes President

Who should succeed the exalted "Father of His Country"? Alexander Hamilton was the best-known member of the Federalist party, now that Washington had bowed out. But his financial policies, some of which had fattened the speculators, had made him so unpopular that he could not hope to be elected president. The Federalists were forced to turn to Washington's vice president, the experienced but ungracious John Adams, a rugged chip off old Plymouth Rock. The Democratic-Republicans naturally rallied behind their master organizer and leader, Thomas Jefferson.

Political passions ran feverishly high in the presidential campaign of 1796. The lofty presence of Washington had hitherto imposed some restraints; now the lid was off. Cultured Federalists like Fisher Ames referred to the Jeffersonians as "fire-eating salamanders, poison-sucking toads." Federalists and Democratic-Republicans even drank their ale in separate taverns. The issues of the campaign, as it turned out, focused

---

*Not broken until 1940 by Franklin D. Roosevelt and made a part of the Constitution in 1951 by the Twenty-second Amendment. (See the Appendix.)

> *Although Thomas Jefferson (1743–1826) and John Adams hardly saw eye to eye, Jefferson displayed grudging respect for Adams in a piece of private correspondence in 1787:*
>
> "He is vain, irritable, and a bad calculator of the force and probable effect of the motives which govern men. This is all the ill which can possibly be said of him. He is as disinterested as the Being who made him."

John Adams, by John Singleton Copley, 1783
When he entered Harvard College in 1751, Adams intended to prepare for the ministry, but four absorbing years of study excited him about other intellectual and career possibilities: "I was a mighty metaphysician, at least I thought myself such." Adams also tried his hand at being a mighty scientist, doctor, and orator. Upon graduation he became a schoolmaster but soon decided to take up the law.

heavily on personalities. But the Jeffersonians again assailed the too-forceful crushing of the Whiskey Rebellion and, above all, the negotiation of Jay's hated treaty.

John Adams, with most of his support in New England, squeezed through by the narrow margin of 71 votes to 68 in the Electoral College. Jefferson, as runner-up, became vice president.* One of the ablest statesmen of his day, Adams at sixty-two was a stuffy figure. Sharp-featured, bald, relatively short (five feet seven inches), and thickset ("His Rotundity"), he impressed observers as a man of stern principles who did his duty with stubborn devotion. Although learned and upright, he was a tactless and prickly intellectual aristocrat, with no appeal to the masses and with no desire to cultivate any. Many citizens regarded him with "respectful irritation."

The crusty New Englander suffered from other handicaps. He had stepped into Washington's shoes, which no successor could hope to fill. In addition, Adams was hated by Hamilton, who had resigned from the Treasury in 1795 and who now headed the war faction of the Federalist party, known as the "High Federalists." The famed financier even secretly plotted with certain members of the cabinet against the president, who had a conspiracy rather than a cabinet on his hands. Adams regarded Hamilton as "the most ruthless, impatient, artful, indefatigable and unprincipled intriguer in the United States, if not in the world." Most ominous of all, Adams inherited a violent quarrel with France—a quarrel whose gunpowder lacked only a spark.

---

*The possibility of such an inharmonious two-party combination in the future was removed by the Twelfth Amendment to the Constitution in 1804. (See the Appendix.)

Unofficial Fighting with France

The French were infuriated by Jay's Treaty. They condemned it as the initial step toward an alliance with Britain, their perpetual foe. They further assailed the pact as a flagrant violation of the Franco-American

The XYZ Affair   When President Adams's envoys to Paris were asked to pay a huge bribe as the price of doing diplomatic business, humiliated Americans rose up in wrath against France. Here an innocent young America is being plundered by Frenchmen as John Bull looks on in amusement from across the English Channel.

Treaty of 1778. French warships, in retaliation, began to seize defenseless American merchant vessels, altogether about three hundred by mid-1797. Adding insult to outrage, the Paris regime haughtily refused to receive America's newly appointed envoy and even threatened him with arrest.

President Adams kept his head, temporarily, even though the nation was mightily aroused. True to Washington's policy of steering clear of war at all costs, he tried again to reach an agreement with the French and appointed a diplomatic commission of three men, including John Marshall, the future chief justice.

Adams's envoys, reaching Paris in 1797, hoped to meet Talleyrand, the crafty French foreign minister. They were secretly approached by three go-betweens, later referred to as X, Y, and Z in the published dispatches. The French spokesmen, among other concessions, demanded an unneutral loan of 32 million florins, plus what amounted to a bribe of $250,000, for the privilege of merely talking with Talleyrand.

These terms were intolerable. The American trio knew that bribes were standard diplomatic devices in Europe, but they gagged at paying a quarter of a million dollars for mere talk, without any assurances of a settlement. Negotiations quickly broke down, and John

Marshall, on reaching New York in 1798, was hailed as a conquering hero for his steadfastness.

War hysteria swept through the United States, catching up even President Adams. The slogan of the hour became "Millions for defense, but not one cent for tribute." The Federalists were delighted at this unexpected turn of affairs, whereas all except the most rabid Jeffersonians hung their heads in shame over the misbehavior of their French friends.

War preparations in the United States were pushed along at a feverish pace, despite considerable Jeffersonian opposition in Congress. The Navy Department was created; the three-ship navy was expanded; the United States Marine Corps was reestablished (originally created in 1775, the Marine Corps had been disbanded at the end of the Revolutionary War). A new army of ten thousand men was authorized (but not fully raised).

Bloodshed was confined to the sea, and principally to the West Indies. In two and a half years of undeclared hostilities (1798–1800), American privateers and men-of-war of the new navy captured over eighty armed vessels flying the French colors, though several hundred Yankee merchant ships were lost to the enemy. Only a slight push, it seemed, might plunge both nations into a full-dress war.

Preparation for War to Defend Commerce: The Building of the Frigate *Philadelphia*. In 1803 this frigate ran onto the rocks near Tripoli harbor, and about three hundred officers and men were imprisoned by the Tripolitans. The ship was refloated for service against the Americans, but Stephen Decatur led a party of men that set it afire.

Adams Puts Patriotism Above Party

Embattled France, its hands full in Europe, wanted no war. An outwitted Talleyrand realized that to fight the United States would merely add one more foe to his enemy roster. The British, who were lending the Americans cannon and other war supplies, were actually driven closer to their wayward cousins than they were to be again for many years. Talleyrand therefore let it be known, through roundabout channels, that if the Americans would send a new minister, he would be received with proper respect.

This French furor brought to Adams a degree of personal acclaim that he had never known before—and

The firmness of President John Adams (1735–1826) was revealed in his message to Congress (June 1798):

"I will never send another minister to France without assurances that he will be received, respected, and honored as the representative of a great, free, powerful, and independent nation."

was never to know again. He doubtless perceived that a full-fledged war, crowned by the conquest of the Floridas and Louisiana, would bring new plaudits to the Federalist party—and perhaps a second term to himself. But the heady wine of popularity did not sway his final judgment. He, like other Founding Fathers, realized full well that war must be avoided while the country was relatively weak.

Adams unexpectedly exploded a bombshell when, early in 1799, he submitted to the Senate the name of a new minister to France. Hamilton and his war-hawk faction were enraged. But public opinion—Jeffersonian and reasonable Federalist alike—was favorable to one last try for peace.

America's envoys (now three) found the political skies brightening when they reached Paris early in 1800. The ambitious "Little Corporal," the Corsican Napoleon Bonaparte, had recently seized dictatorial power. He was eager to free his hands of the American squabble so that he might continue to redraw the map of Europe and perhaps create a New World empire in Louisiana. The afflictions and ambitions of the Old World were again working to America's advantage.

After a great deal of haggling, a memorable treaty known as the Convention of 1800 was signed in Paris. France agreed to annul the twenty-two-year-old marriage of (in)convenience, but as a kind of alimony the United States agreed to pay the damage claims of American shippers. So ended the nation's only peacetime military alliance for a century and a half. Its troubled history does much to explain the traditional antipathy of the American people to foreign entanglements.

John Adams, flinty to the end, deserves immense credit for his belated push for peace, even though he was moved in part by jealousy of Hamilton. Adams not only avoided the hazards of war, but also unwittingly smoothed the path for the peaceful purchase of Louisiana three years later. He should indeed rank high among the forgotten purchasers of this vast domain. If America had drifted into a full-blown war with France in 1800, Napoleon would not have sold Louisiana to Jefferson on any terms in 1803.

President Adams, the bubble of his popularity pricked by peace, was aware of his signal contribution to the nation. He later suggested as the epitaph for his tombstone (not used), "Here lies John Adams, who took upon himself the responsibility of peace with France in the year 1800."

The Federalist Witch Hunt

Exulting Federalists had meanwhile capitalized on the anti-French frenzy to drive through Congress in 1798 a sheaf of laws designed to muffle or minimize their Jeffersonian foes.

The first of these oppressive laws was aimed at supposedly pro-Jeffersonian "aliens." Most European immigrants, lacking wealth, were scorned by the aristocratic Federalist party. But they were welcomed as voters by the less prosperous and more democratic Jeffersonians. The Federalist Congress, hoping to discourage the "dregs" of Europe, erected a disheartening barrier. They raised the residence requirements for aliens who desired to become citizens from a tolerable five years to an intolerable fourteen. This drastic new law violated the traditional American policy of open-door hospitality and speedy assimilation.

Two additional Alien Laws struck heavily at undesirable immigrants. The president was empowered to deport dangerous foreigners in time of peace and to deport or imprison them in time of hostilities. Though defensible as a war measure—and an officially declared war with France seemed imminent—this was an arbitrary grant of executive power contrary to American tradition and to the spirit of the Constitution, even though the stringent Alien Laws were never enforced.

The "lockjaw" Sedition Act, the last measure of the Federalist clampdown, was a direct slap at two priceless freedoms guaranteed in the Constitution by the Bill of Rights—freedom of speech and freedom of the press (First Amendment). This law provided that anyone who impeded the policies of the government or falsely defamed its officials, including the president, would be liable to a heavy fine and imprisonment. Severe though the measure was, the Federalists believed that it was justified. The verbal violence of the day was unrestrained, and foul-penned editors, some of them exiled aliens, vilified Adams's anti-French policy in vicious terms.

Many outspoken Jeffersonian editors were indicted under the Sedition Act, and ten were brought to trial. All of them were convicted, often by packed juries swayed by prejudiced Federalist judges. Some of the victims were harmless partisans, who should have been spared the notoriety of martyrdom. Among them was Congressman Matthew Lyon (the "Spitting Lion"), who had earlier gained fame by spitting in the face of a Federalist. He was sentenced to four months in jail for writing of President Adams's "unbounded thirst for ridiculous pomp, foolish adulation, and selfish avarice." Another culprit was lucky to get off with a fine of $100 after he

> In 1800 James Callender (1758–1803) published a pamphlet that assailed the president in strong language. For blasts like the following tirade, Callender was prosecuted under the Sedition Act, fined $250, and sentenced to prison for nine months:
>
> "The reign of Mr. Adams has, hitherto, been one continued tempest of *malignant* passions. As president, he has never opened his lips, or lifted his pen, without threatening and scolding. The grand object of his administration has been to exasperate the rage of contending parties, to calumniate and destroy every man who differs from his opinions. . . . Every person holding an office must either quit it, or think and vote exactly with Mr. Adams."

Congressional Pugilists Satirical representation of Matthew Lyon's fight in Congress with the Federalist representative Roger Griswold.

had expressed the wish that the wad of a cannon fired in honor of Adams had landed in the seat of the president's breeches.

The Sedition Act seemed to be in direct conflict with the Constitution. But the Supreme Court, dominated by Federalists, was of no mind to declare this Federalist law unconstitutional. (The Federalists intentionally wrote the law to expire in 1801, so that it could not be used against them if they lost the next election.) This attempt by the Federalists to crush free speech and silence the opposition party, high-handed as it was, undoubtedly made many converts for the Jeffersonians.

Yet the Alien and Sedition Acts, despite pained outcries from the Jeffersonians they muzzled, commanded widespread popular support. Anti-French hysteria played directly into the hands of witch-hunting conservatives. In the congressional elections of 1798–1799, the Federalists, riding a wave of popularity, scored the most sweeping victory of their entire history.

The Virginia (Madison) and Kentucky (Jefferson) Resolutions

Resentful Jeffersonians naturally refused to take the Alien and Sedition Laws lying down. Jefferson himself

feared that if the Federalists managed to choke free speech and free press, they would then wipe out other precious constitutional guarantees. His own fledgling political party might even be stamped out of existence. If this had happened, the country might have slid into a dangerous one-party dictatorship.

Fearing prosecution for sedition, Jefferson secretly penned a series of resolutions, which the Kentucky legislature approved in 1798 and 1799. His friend and fellow Virginian James Madison drafted a similar but less extreme statement, which was adopted by the legislature of Virginia in 1798.

Both Jefferson and Madison stressed the compact theory—a theory popular among English political philosophers in the seventeenth and eighteenth centuries. As applied to America by the Jeffersonians, this concept meant that the thirteen sovereign states, in creating the federal government, had entered into a "compact," or contract, regarding its jurisdiction. The national government was consequently the agent or creation of the states. Since water can rise no higher than its source, the individual states were the final judges of whether their agent had broken the "compact" by overstepping the authority originally granted. Invoking this logic, Jefferson's Kentucky resolutions concluded that the federal regime *had* exceeded its constitutional powers and that with regard to the Alien and Sedition Acts, "nullification"—a refusal to accept them—was the "rightful remedy."

No other state legislatures, despite Jefferson's hopes, fell into line. Some of them flatly refused to endorse the Virginia and Kentucky resolutions. Others, chiefly in Federalist states, added ringing condemnations. Many Federalists argued that the people, not the states, had made the original compact, and that it was up to the Supreme Court—not the states—to nullify unconstitutional legislation passed by Congress. This practice, though not specifically authorized by the Constitution, was finally adopted by the Supreme Court in 1803 (see p. 219).

The Virginia and Kentucky resolutions were a brilliant formulation of the extreme states' rights view regarding the Union—indeed more sweeping in their implications than their authors had intended. They were later used by southerners to support nullification—and ultimately secession. Yet neither Jefferson nor Madison, as Founding Fathers of the Union, had any intention of breaking it up: they were groping for ways to preserve it. Their resolutions were basically campaign documents designed to crystallize opposition to the Federalist party and to unseat it in the upcoming presidential election of 1800. The only real nullification that Jefferson had in view was the nullification of Federalist abuses.

Federalists Versus Democratic-Republicans

As the presidential contest of 1800 approached, the differences between Federalists and Democratic-Republicans were sharply etched (see the table on p. 208). As might be expected, most federalists of the pre-Constitution period (1787–1789) became Federalists in the 1790s. Largely welded by Hamilton into an effective group by 1793, they openly advocated rule by the "best people." "Those who own the country," remarked Federalist John Jay, "ought to govern it." With their intellectual arrogance and Tory tastes, Hamiltonians distrusted full-blown democracy as the fountain of all mischiefs and feared the "swayability" of the untutored common folk.

Hamiltonian Federalists also advocated a strong central government with the power to crush democratic excesses like Shays's Rebellion, protect the lives and estates of the wealthy, subordinate the sovereignty-loving states, and promote foreign trade. They believed that government should support private enterprise but not interfere with it. This attitude came naturally to the merchants, manufacturers, and shippers along the Atlantic seaboard, who made up the majority of Federalist support. Farther inland, few Hamiltonians dwelled.

The hinterland was largely anti-Federalist territory. Leading the anti-Federalists, who came eventually to be known as Democratic-Republicans or sometimes simply Republicans, was Thomas Jefferson. His rivalry with Hamilton defined the archetypal conflict in American political history. The two leaders appealed to different constituencies and expressed different theories of society, politics, and diplomacy.

Lanky and relaxed in appearance, lacking personal aggressiveness, weak-voiced, and unable to deliver a rabble-rousing speech, Jefferson became a master political organizer through his ability to lead people rather than drive them. His strongest appeal was to the middle class and to the underprivileged—the "dirt" farmers, the laborers, the artisans, and the small shopkeepers.

Liberal-thinking Jefferson, with his aristocratic head set on a farmer's frame, was a bundle of inconsistencies. By one set of tests, he should have been a Federalist, for he was a Virginia aristocrat and slave-owner who lived in an imposing hilltop mansion at Monticello. A so-called traitor to his own upper class, Jefferson cherished uncommon sympathy for the common people, especially the downtrodden, the oppressed, and the persecuted. As he wrote in 1800, "I have sworn upon the altar of God eternal hostility against every form of tyranny over the mind of man."

Jeffersonian Republicans demanded a weak central regime. They believed that the best government was the one that governed least. The bulk of the power, Jefferson argued, should be retained by the states. There the people, in intimate contact with local affairs, could keep a more vigilant eye on their public servants. Otherwise a dictatorship might develop. Central authority—a kind of necessary evil—was to be kept at a minimum through a strict interpretation of the Constitution. The national debt, which he saw as a curse illegitimately bequeathed to later generations, was to be paid off.

Jeffersonian Republicans, themselves primarily agrarians, insisted that there should be no special privileges for special classes, particularly manufacturers.

The Two Political Parties, 1793–1800

Federalist Features	Democratic-Republican (Jeffersonian) Features
Rule by the "best people"	Rule by the informed masses
Hostility to extension of democracy	Friendliness toward extension of democracy
A powerful central government at the expense of states' rights	A weak central government so as to preserve states' rights
Loose interpretation of Constitution	Strict interpretation of Constitution
Government to foster business; concentration of wealth in interests of capitalistic enterprise	No special favors for business; agriculture preferred
A protective tariff	No special favors for manufacturers
Pro-British (conservative Tory tradition)	Pro-French (radical Revolutionary tradition)
National debt a blessing, if properly funded	National debt a bane; rigid economy
An expanding bureaucracy	Reduction of federal officeholders
A powerful central bank	Encouragement to state banks
Restrictions on free speech and press	Relatively free speech and press
Concentration in seacoast area	Concentration in South and Southwest; in agricultural areas and backcountry
A strong navy to protect shippers	A minimal navy for coastal defense

Agriculture, to Jefferson, was the favored branch of the economy and formed the foundation of his political thought. "Those who labor in the earth are the chosen people of God," he said. Most of his followers naturally came from the agricultural South and Southwest.

Above all, Jefferson advocated the rule of the people. But he did not propose thrusting the ballot into the hands of *every* adult white male. He favored government *for* the people, but not by *all* the people—only by those white men who were literate enough to inform themselves and wear the mantle of American citizenship worthily. Universal education would have to precede universal suffrage. The ignorant, he argued, were incapable of self-government. But he had profound faith in the reasonableness and teachableness of the masses and in their collective wisdom when taught.

Landlessness among American citizens threatened popular democracy as much as illiteracy, in Jefferson's eyes. He feared that propertyless dependents would be political pawns in the hands of their landowning superiors. How could the emergence of a landless class of voters be avoided? The answer, in part, was by slavery. A system of black slave labor in the South ensured that white yeoman farmers could remain independent landowners. Without slavery, poor whites would have to provide the cheap labor so necessary for the cultivation of tobacco and rice, and their low wages would preclude their ever owning property. Jefferson thus tortuously reconciled slaveholding—his own included—with his more democratic impulses.

Yet for his time, Jefferson's confidence that white, free men could become responsible and knowledgeable citizens was open-minded. He championed their freedom of speech, for without free speech, the misdeeds of tyranny could not be exposed. Jefferson even dared to say that given the choice of "a government without newspapers" and "newspapers without a government," he would opt for the latter. Yet no other American leader, except perhaps Abraham Lincoln, ever suffered more foul abuse from editorial pens; Jefferson might well have prayed for freedom *from* the Federalist press.

Differences over foreign policy defined another sharp distinction between Hamilton and Jefferson. Hamilton looked outward and eastward. He sought to build a strong national state that would assert and expand America's commercial interests. "No Government

Thomas Jefferson at Natural Bridge, by Caleb Boyle, c. 1801 A great statesman, he wrote his own epitaph: "Here was buried Thomas Jefferson, Author of the Declaration of Independence, of the Statute of Virginia for Religious Freedom, and Father of the University of Virginia."

Thomas Jefferson's vision of a republican America was peopled with virtuous farmers, not factory hands. As early as 1784, he wrote,

"While we have land to labor then, let us never wish to see our citizens occupied at a work-bench, or twirling a distaff. . . . For the general operations of manufacture, let our workshops remain in Europe. . . . The mobs of great cities add just so much to the support of pure government, as sores do to the strength of the human body."

could give us tranquility and happiness at home," he declared, "which did not possess sufficient stability and strength to make us respectable abroad." Foreign trade, especially with Britain, was a key cog in Hamilton's fiscal machinery, and friendship with Britain was thus indispensable. Jeffersonian Republicans, unlike the Federalist "British boot-lickers," were basically pro-French. They earnestly believed that it was to America's advantage to support the liberal ideals of the French Revolution, rather than applaud the reaction of the British Tories. Jefferson, in effect, faced inward and westward. His priorities were to protect and strengthen democracy at home, especially in the frontier regions beyond the Appalachians, rather than flex America's muscles abroad.

So as the young Republic's first full decade of nationhood came to a close, the Founders' hopes seemed already imperiled. Conflicts over domestic politics and foreign policy undermined the unity of the Revolutionary era and called into question the very viability of the American experiment in democracy. As the presidential election of 1800 approached, the danger loomed that the fragile and battered American ship of state, like many another before it and after it, would founder on the rocks of controversy. The shores of history are littered with the wreckage of nascent nations torn asunder before they could grow to a stable maturity. Why should the United States expect to enjoy a happier fate?

Chronology

1789	Constitution formally put into effect Judiciary Act of 1789 Washington elected president French Revolution begins
1790	First official census
1791	Bill of Rights adopted Vermont becomes fourteenth state Bank of the United States created Excise tax passed
1792	Washington reelected president
1792–1793	Federalist and Democratic-Republican parties formed
1793	Louis XVI beheaded; radical phase of French Revolution France declares war on Britain and Spain Washington's Neutrality Proclamation Citizen Genêt affair
1794	Whiskey Rebellion Battle of Fallen Timbers Jay's Treaty with Britain
1795	Treaty of Greenville: Indians cede Ohio Pinckney's Treaty with Spain
1796	Washington's Farewell Address
1797	Adams becomes president XYZ Affair
1798	Alien and Sedition Acts
1798–1799	Virginia and Kentucky resolutions
1798–1800	Undeclared war with France
1800	Convention of 1800: peace with France

11

The Triumphs and Travails of the Jeffersonian Republic

1800–1812

TIMID MEN . . . PREFER THE CALM OF DESPOTISM
TO THE BOISTEROUS SEA OF LIBERTY.

THOMAS JEFFERSON, 1796

In the critical presidential contest of 1800, the first in which Federalists and Democratic-Republicans functioned as two national political parties, John Adams and Thomas Jefferson again squared off against each other. The choice seemed clear and dramatic: Adams's Federalists waged a defensive struggle for strong central government and public order. Their Jeffersonian opponents presented themselves as the guardians of agrarian purity, liberty, and states' rights. The next dozen years, however, would turn what seemed like a clear-cut choice in 1800 into a messier reality, as the Jeffersonians in power were confronted with a series of opportunities and crises requiring the assertion of federal authority. As the first challengers to rout a reigning party, the Republicans were the first to learn that it is far easier to condemn from the stump than to govern consistently.

Federalist and Republican Mudslingers

In fighting for survival, the Federalists labored under heavy handicaps. Their Alien and Sedition Acts had aroused a host of enemies, although most of these critics were dyed-in-the-wool Jeffersonians anyhow. The Hamiltonian wing of the Federalist party, robbed of its glorious war with France, split openly with President Adams. Hamilton, a victim of arrogance, was so indiscreet as to attack the president in a privately printed pamphlet. Jeffersonians soon got hold of the pamphlet and gleefully published it.

The most damaging blow to the Federalists was the refusal of Adams to give them a rousing fight with

France. Their feverish war preparations had swelled the public debt and had required disagreeable new taxes, including a stamp tax. After all these unpopular measures, the war scare had petered out, and the country was left with an all-dressed-up-but-no-place-to-go feeling. The military preparations now seemed not only unnecessary but extravagant, as seamen for the "new navy" were called "John Adams's Jackasses." Adams himself was known, somewhat ironically, as "the Father of the American Navy."

Thrown on the defensive, the Federalists concentrated their fire on Jefferson himself, who became the victim of one of America's earliest "whispering campaigns." He was accused of having robbed a widow and her children of a trust fund and of having fathered numerous mulatto children by his own slave women. (Jefferson's long-rumored intimacy with one of his slaves, Sally Hemings, has been confirmed through DNA testing; see "Examining the Evidence," p. 213.) As a liberal in religion, Jefferson had earlier incurred the wrath of the orthodox clergy, largely through his successful

> *The Reverend Timothy Dwight (1752–1817), president of Yale College, predicted that in the event of Jefferson's election,*
>
> **"the Bible would be cast into a bonfire, our holy worship changed into a dance of [French] Jacobin phrensy, our wives and daughters dishonored, and our sons converted into the disciples of Voltaire and the dragoons of Marat."**

struggle to separate church and state in his native Virginia. Although Jefferson did believe in God, preachers throughout New England, stronghold of Federalism and Congregationalism, thundered against his alleged atheism. Old ladies of Federalist families, fearing Jefferson's election, even buried their Bibles or hung them in wells.

The Providential Detection (Federalist propaganda)   The American eagle snatches the Constitution from Jefferson, who is about to burn it (together with the works of Voltaire, Paine, and others) on the altar to French Revolutionary despotism.

EXAMINING THE EVIDENCE

The Thomas Jefferson–Sally Hemings Controversy Debate over whether Thomas Jefferson had sexual relations with Sally Hemings, a slave at Monticello, began as early as 1802, when James Callender published the first accusations and Federalist newspapers gleefully broadcast them throughout the country. Two years later this print, "The Philosophic Cock," attacked Jefferson by depicting him as a rooster and Hemings as a hen. The rooster, or cock, was also a symbol of revolutionary France. Jefferson's enemies sought to discredit him for personal indiscretions as well as radical sympathies. Although he resolutely denied any affair with Hemings, a charge that at first seemed only to be a politically motivated defamation refused to go away. In the 1870s two new oral sources of evidence came to light. Madison Hemings, Sally's next-to-last child, claimed that his mother had identified Jefferson as the father of all five of her children. Soon thereafter James Parton's biography of Jefferson revealed that among Jefferson's white descendants it was said that his nephew had fathered all or most of Sally's children. In the 1950s several large publishing projects on Jefferson's life and writings uncovered new evidence and inspired renewed debate. Most convincing was Dumas Malone's calculation that Jefferson had been present at Monticello nine months prior to the birth of each of Sally's children. Speculation continued throughout the rest of the century, with little new evidence, until the trustees of the Thomas Jefferson Memorial Foundation agreed to a new, more scientific method of investigation: DNA testing of the remains of Jefferson's white and possibly black descendants. Two centuries after James Callender first cast aspersions on Thomas Jefferson's morality, cutting-edge science established with little doubt that Jefferson was the father of Sally Hemings's children.

A PHILOSOPHIC COCK

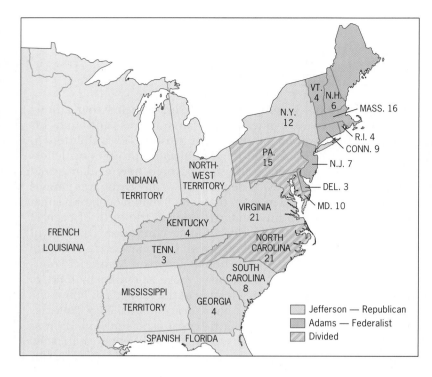

Presidential Election of 1800 (with electoral vote by state)   New York was the key state in this election, and Aaron Burr helped swing it away from the Federalists with tactics that anticipated the political "machines" of a later day. Federalists complained that Burr "travels every night from one meeting of Republicans to another, haranguing . . . them to the most zealous exertions. [He] can stoop so low as to visit every low tavern that may happen to be crowded with his dear fellow citizens." But Burr proved that the price was worth it. "We have beat you," Burr told kid-gloved Federalists after the election, "by superior *Management*."

The Jeffersonian "Revolution of 1800"

Jefferson won by a majority of 73 electoral votes to 65. In defeat, the colorless and presumably unpopular Adams polled more electoral strength than he had gained four years earlier—except for New York. The Empire State fell into the Jeffersonian basket, and with it the election, largely because Aaron Burr, a master wire-puller, turned New York to Jefferson by the narrowest of margins. The Virginian polled the bulk of his strength in the South and West, particularly in those states where universal white manhood suffrage had been adopted.

Decisive in Jefferson's victory was the three-fifths clause of the Constitution. By counting three-fifths of the slave population for the purposes of congressional and Electoral College representation, the Constitution gave white southern voters a bonus that helped Jefferson win the White House. Northern critics fumed that Jefferson was a "Negro President" and an illegitimate embodiment of the "slave power" that the southern states wielded in the nation.

Jeffersonian joy was dampened by an unexpected deadlock. Through a technicality Jefferson, the presidential candidate, and Burr, his vice-presidential running mate, received the same number of electoral votes for the presidency. Under the Constitution the tie could be broken only by the House of Representatives (see Art. II, Sec. I, para. 2). This body was controlled for several more months by the lame-duck Federalists, who preferred Burr to the hated Jefferson.* Voting in the House moved slowly to a climax, as exhausted representatives snored in their seats. The agonizing deadlock was broken at last when a few Federalists, despairing of electing Burr and hoping for moderation from Jefferson, refrained from voting. The election then went to the rightful candidate.

John Adams, as fate would have it, was the last Federalist president of the United States. His party sank slowly into the mire of political oblivion and ultimately disappeared completely in the days of Andrew Jackson.

---

*A "lame duck" has been humorously defined as a politician whose political goose has been cooked at the recent elections. The possibility of another such tie was removed by the Twelfth Amendment in 1804 (see the Appendix). Before then, each elector had two votes, with the second-place finisher becoming vice president.

Mrs. Benjamin Tallmadge and Son Henry Floyd and Daughter Maria Jones; Colonel Benjamin Tallmadge and Son William Tallmadge, by Ralph Earl, 1790 The Tallmadges were among the leading citizens of Litchfield, a Federalist stronghold in the heavily Federalist state of Connecticut. Colonel Benjamin Tallmadge served with distinction in the Revolutionary War, became a wealthy merchant and banker, and represented his state in Congress from 1801 to 1817. Mary Floyd Tallmadge, like her husband, came from a prominent Long Island family. The opulence of the Tallmadges' clothing and surroundings in these paintings abundantly testifies to the wealth, and the social pretensions, of the Federalist elite. Note the toy carriage near the feet of the Tallmadge daughter— a replica of the actual, and elegant, carriage owned by the Tallmadge family.

Jefferson later claimed that the election of 1800 was a "revolution" comparable to that of 1776. But it was no revolution in the sense of a massive popular upheaval or an upending of the political system. In truth, Jefferson had narrowly squeaked through to victory. A switch of some 250 votes in New York would have thrown the election to Adams. Jefferson meant that his election represented a return to what he considered the original spirit of the Revolution. In his eyes Hamilton and Adams had betrayed the ideals of 1776 and 1787. Jefferson's mission, as he saw it, was to restore the republican experiment, to check the growth of government power,

and to halt the decay of virtue that had set in under Federalist rule.

No less "revolutionary" was the peaceful and orderly transfer of power on the basis of an election whose results all parties accepted. This was a remarkable achievement for a raw young nation, especially after all the partisan bitterness that had agitated the country during Adams's presidency. It was particularly remarkable in that age; comparable successions would not take place in Britain for another generation. After a decade of division and doubt, Americans could take justifiable pride in the vigor of their experiment in democracy.

A Philadelphia woman wrote her sister-in-law about the pride she felt on the occasion of Thomas Jefferson's inauguration as third president of the United States in 1801:

"I have this morning witnessed one of the most interesting scenes a free people can ever witness. The changes of admin-istration, which in every government and in every age have most generally been epochs of confusion, villainy and bloodshed, in this our happy country take place without any species of distraction, or disorder."

Jefferson Inaugural Pitcher, 1801 This memento from the election of 1800 immortalized President Thomas Jefferson's words, "We are all Republicans; we are all Federalists," which turned out to be more hopeful than true. Jefferson was portrayed in the plain attire he favored, shunning the sartorial pretensions affected by many Federalists, such as the elegantly dressed Talmadges shown on p. 215.

Responsibility Breeds Moderation

"Long Tom" Jefferson was inaugurated president on March 4, 1801, in the swampy village of Washington, the crude new national capital. Tall (six feet two and a half inches), with large hands and feet, red hair ("the Red Fox"), and prominent cheekbones and chin, he was an arresting figure. Believing that the customary pomp did not befit his democratic ideals, he spurned a horse-drawn coach and strode by foot to the Capitol from his boardinghouse.

Jefferson's inaugural address, beautifully phrased, was a classic statement of democratic principles. "The will of the majority is in all cases to prevail," Jefferson declared. But, he added, "that will to be rightful must be reasonable; the minority possess their equal rights, which equal law must protect, and to violate would be oppression." Seeking to allay Federalist fears of a bull-in-the-china-closet overturn, Jefferson ingratiatingly intoned, "We are all Republicans, we are all Federalists." As for foreign affairs, he pledged "honest friendship with all nations, entangling alliances with none."

With its rustic setting, Washington lent itself admirably to the simplicity and frugality of the Jeffersonian Republicans. In this respect it contrasted sharply with the elegant atmosphere of Federalist Philadelphia, the former temporary capital. Extending democratic principles to etiquette, Jefferson established the rule of pell-mell at official dinners—that is, seating without regard to rank. The resplendent British minister, who had enjoyed precedence among the pro-British Federal-ists, was insulted.

As president, Jefferson could be shockingly uncon-ventional. He would receive callers in sloppy attire—once in a dressing gown and heel-less slippers. He started the precedent, unbroken until Woodrow Wilson's presidency 112 years later, of sending messages to Con-gress to be read by a clerk. Personal appearances, in the Federalist manner, suggested too strongly a monarchical speech from the throne. Besides, Jefferson was painfully conscious of his weak voice and unimpressive platform presence.

As if compelled by an evil twin, Jefferson was forced to reverse many of the political principles he had so vigorously championed. There were in fact two Thomas

> *The toleration of Thomas Jefferson (1743–1826) was reflected in his inaugural address:*
>
> "If there be any among us who would wish to dissolve this Union or to change its republican form, let them stand undisturbed as monuments of the safety with which error of opinion may be tolerated where reason is left free to combat it."

> *President John F. Kennedy (1917–1963) once greeted a large group of Nobel Prize winners as*
>
> "the most extraordinary collection of talent, of human knowledge, that has ever been gathered together at the White House, with the possible exception of when Thomas Jefferson dined alone."

Jeffersons. One was the scholarly private citizen, who philosophized in his study. The other was the harassed public official, who made the disturbing discovery that bookish theories worked out differently in the noisy arena of practical politics. The open-minded Virginian was therefore consistently inconsistent; it is easy to quote one Jefferson to refute the other.

The triumph of Thomas Jefferson's Democratic-Republicans and the eviction of the Federalists marked the first party overturn in American history. The vanquished naturally feared that the victors would grab all the spoils of office for themselves. But Jefferson, in keeping with his conciliatory inaugural address, showed unexpected moderation. To the dismay of his office-seeking friends, the new president dismissed few public servants for political reasons. Patronage-hungry Jeffersonians watched the Federalist appointees grow old in office and grumbled that "few die, none resign."

Jefferson quickly proved an able politician. He was especially effective in the informal atmosphere of a dinner party. There he wooed congressional representatives while personally pouring imported wines and serving the tasty dishes of his French cook. In part Jefferson had to rely on his personal charm because his party was so weak-jointed. Denied the power to dispense patronage, the Democratic-Republicans could not build a loyal political following. Opposition to the Federalists was the chief glue holding them together, and as the Federalists faded, so did Democratic-Republican unity. The era of well-developed, well-disciplined political parties still lay in the future.

Jefferson's Cabinet at Monticello Jefferson's study gave physical evidence of his fondness for ideas and inventions. He attached candles to his chair for light, read from a revolving book stand, and surrounded himself with an astronomical clock and an achromatic telescope through which he observed the eclipse of the sun in 1811. On the table is a polygraph, invented in London and promoted by Charles Willson Peale in Philadelphia. Jefferson used it to make copies of the letters he penned.

Jeffersonian Restraint

At the outset Jefferson was determined to undo the Federalist abuses begotten by the anti-French hysteria. The hated Alien and Sedition Acts had already expired. The incoming president speedily pardoned the "martyrs" who were serving sentences under the Sedition Act, and the government remitted many fines. Shortly after the Congress met, the Jeffersonians enacted the new naturalization law of 1802. This act reduced the unreasonable requirement of fourteen years of residence to the previous and more reasonable requirement of five years.

Jefferson actually kicked away only one substantial prop of the Hamiltonian system. He hated the excise tax, which bred bureaucrats and bore heavily on his farmer following, and he early persuaded Congress to repeal it. His devotion to principle thus cost the federal government about a million dollars a year in urgently needed revenue.

Swiss-born and French-accented Albert Gallatin, "Watchdog of the Treasury," proved to be as able a secretary of the Treasury as Hamilton. Gallatin agreed with Jefferson that a national debt was a bane rather than a blessing and by strict economy succeeded in reducing it substantially while balancing the budget.

Except for excising the excise tax, the Jeffersonians left the Hamiltonian framework essentially intact. They did not tamper with the Federalist programs for funding the national debt at par and assuming the Revolutionary War debts of the states. They launched no attack on the Bank of the United States, nor did they repeal the mildly protective Federalist tariff. In later years they embraced Federalism to such a degree as to recharter a bigger bank and to boost the protective tariff to higher levels.

Paradoxically, Jefferson's moderation thus further cemented the gains of the "Revolution of 1800." By shrewdly absorbing the major Federalist programs, Jefferson showed that a change of regime need not be disastrous for the defeated group. His restraint pointed the way toward the two-party system that was later to become a characteristic feature of American politics.

The "Dead Clutch" of the Judiciary

The "deathbed" Judiciary Act of 1801 was one of the last important laws passed by the expiring Federalist Congress. It created sixteen new federal judgeships and other judicial offices. President Adams remained at his desk until nine o'clock in the evening of his last day in office, supposedly signing the commissions of the Federalist "midnight judges." (Actually only three commissions were signed on his last day.)

This Federalist-sponsored Judiciary Act, though a long-overdue reform, aroused bitter resentment. "Packing" these lifetime posts with anti-Jeffersonian partisans was, in Republican eyes, a brazen attempt by the ousted party to entrench itself in one of the three powerful branches of government. Jeffersonians condemned the last-minute appointees in violent language, denouncing the trickery of the Federalists as open defiance of the people's will, expressed emphatically at the polls.

The newly elected Republican Congress bestirred itself to repeal the Judiciary Act of 1801 in the year after its passage. Jeffersonians thus swept sixteen benches from under the recently seated "midnight judges." Jeffersonians likewise had their knives sharpened for the scalp of Chief Justice John Marshall, whom Adams had appointed to the Supreme Court (as a fourth choice) in the dying days of his term. The strong-willed Marshall, with his rasping voice and steel-trap mind, was a cousin of Thomas Jefferson. Marshall's formal legal schooling had lasted only six weeks, but he dominated the Supreme Court with his powerful intellect and commanding personality. He shaped the American legal tradition more profoundly than any other single figure.

Marshall had served at Valley Forge during the Revolution. While suffering there from cold and hunger, he had been painfully impressed with the drawbacks of feeble central authority. The experience made him a lifelong Federalist, committed above all else to strengthening the power of the federal government. States' rights Jeffersonians condemned the crafty judge's "twistifications," but Marshall pushed ahead inflexibly on his Federalist course. He served for about thirty days under a Federalist administration and thirty-four years under the administrations of Jefferson and subsequent presidents. The Federalist party died out, but Marshall lived on, handing down Federalist decisions serenely for many more years. For over three decades, the ghost of Alexander Hamilton spoke through the lanky, black-robed judge.

One of the "midnight judges" of 1801 presented John Marshall with a historic opportunity. He was obscure William Marbury, whom President Adams had named a justice of the peace for the District of Columbia. When Marbury learned that his commission was being shelved by the new secretary of state, James Madison, he sued for its delivery. Chief Justice Marshall knew that his

Jeffersonian rivals, entrenched in the executive branch, would hardly spring forward to enforce a writ to deliver the commission to his fellow Federalist Marbury. He therefore dismissed Marbury's suit, avoiding a direct political showdown. But the wily Marshall snatched a victory from the jaws of this judicial defeat. In explaining his ruling, Marshall said that the part of the Judiciary Act of 1789 on which Marbury tried to base his appeal was unconstitutional. The act had attempted to assign to the Supreme Court powers that the Constitution had not foreseen.

In this self-denying opinion, Marshall greatly magnified the authority of the Court—and slapped at the Jeffersonians. Until the case of *Marbury* v. *Madison* (1803), controversy had clouded the question of who had the final authority to determine the meaning of the Constitution. Jefferson in the Kentucky resolutions (1798) had tried to allot that right to the individual states. But now his cousin on the Court had cleverly promoted the contrary principle of "judicial review"—the idea that the Supreme Court alone had the last word on the question of constitutionality. In this landmark case, Marshall inserted the keystone into the arch that supports the tremendous power of the Supreme Court in American life.*

Marshall's decision regarding Marbury spurred the Jeffersonians to seek revenge. Jefferson urged the impeachment of an arrogant and tart-tongued Supreme Court justice, Samuel Chase, who was so unpopular that Republicans named vicious dogs after him. Early in 1804 impeachment charges against Chase were voted by the House of Representatives, which then passed the question of guilt or innocence on to the Senate. The indictment by the House was based on "high crimes, and misdemeanors," as specified in the Constitution.†

Yet the evidence was plain that the intemperate judge had not been guilty of "high crimes," but only of unrestrained partisanship and a big mouth. The Senate failed to muster enough votes to convict and remove Chase. The precedent thus established was fortunate. From that day to this, no really serious attempt has been made to reshape the Supreme Court by the impeachment weapon. Jefferson's ill-advised attempt at "judge breaking" was a reassuring victory for the independence of the judiciary and for the separation of powers among the three branches of the federal government.

> *In his decision in* Marbury *v.* Madison, *Chief Justice John Marshall (1755–1835) vigorously asserted his view that the Constitution embodied a "higher" law than ordinary legislation, and that the Court must interpret the Constitution:*
>
> "The Constitution is either a superior paramount law, unchangeable by ordinary means, or it is on a level with ordinary legislative acts, and like other acts, is alterable when the legislature shall please to alter it.
>
> "If the former part of the alternative be true, then a legislative act contrary to the constitution is not law; if the latter part be true, then written constitutions are absurd attempts, on the part of the people, to limit a power in its own nature illimitable. . . .
>
> "It is emphatically the province and duty of the judicial department to say what the law is. . . .
>
> "If, then, the courts are to regard the Constitution, and the Constitution is superior to any ordinary act of the legislature, the Constitution, and not such ordinary act, must govern the case to which they are both applicable."

Jefferson, a Reluctant Warrior

One of Jefferson's first actions as president was to reduce the military establishment to a mere police force of twenty-five hundred officers and men. Critics called it penny-pinching, but Jefferson's reluctance to invest in soldiers and ships was less about money than about republican ideals. Among his fondest hopes for America was that it might transcend the bloody wars and entangling alliances of Europe. The United States would set an example for the world, forswearing military force and winning friends through "peaceful coercion." Also,

---

*The next invalidation of a federal law by the Supreme Court came fifty-four years later, with the explosive *Dred Scott* decision (see p. 417).

†For impeachment, see Art. I, Sec. II, para 5; Art. I, Sec. III, paras. 6, 7; Art. II, Sec. IV in the Appendix.

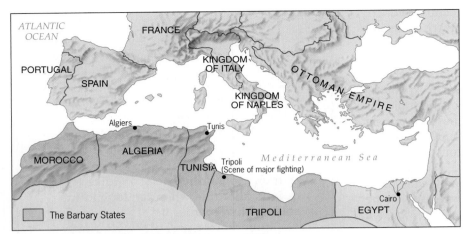

Four Barbary States of North Africa, c. 1805

the Republicans distrusted large standing armies as standing invitations to dictatorship. Navies were less to be feared, as they could not march inland and endanger liberties. Still, the farm-loving Jeffersonians saw little point in building a fleet that might only embroil the Republic in costly and corrupting wars far from America's shores.

But harsh realities forced Jefferson's principles to bend. Pirates of the North African Barbary States had long made a national industry of blackmailing and plundering merchant ships that ventured into the Mediterranean. Preceding Federalist administrations, in fact, had been forced to buy protection. At the time of the French crisis of 1798, when Americans were shouting, "Millions for defense but not one cent for tribute," twenty-six barrels of blackmail dollars were being shipped to piratical Algiers.

War across the Atlantic was not part of the Jeffersonian vision—but neither was paying tribute to a pack of pirate states. The showdown came in 1801. The pasha of Tripoli, dissatisfied with his share of protection money, informally declared war on the United States by cutting down the flagstaff of the American consulate. A gauntlet was thus thrown squarely into the face of Jefferson—the noninterventionist, the pacifist, the critic of a big-ship navy, and the political foe of Federalist shippers. He reluctantly rose to the challenge by dispatching the infant navy to the "shores of Tripoli," as related in the song of the U.S. Marine Corps. After four years of intermittent fighting, marked by spine-tingling exploits, Jefferson succeeded in extorting a treaty of peace from Tripoli in 1805. It was secured at the bargain price of only $60,000—a sum representing ransom payments for captured Americans.

Small gunboats, which the navy had used with some success in the Tripolitan War, fascinated Jefferson. Pledged to tax reduction, he advocated a large number of little coastal craft—"Jeffs" or the "mosquito fleet," as they were contemptuously called. He believed these fast but frail vessels would prove valuable in guarding American shores and need not embroil the Republic in diplomatic incidents on the high seas.

About two hundred tiny gunboats were constructed, democratically in small shipyards where votes could be made for Jefferson. Often mounting only one unwieldy gun, they were sometimes more of a menace to the crew than to the prospective enemy. During a hurricane and tidal wave at Savannah, Georgia, one of them was deposited eight miles inland in a cornfield, to the derisive glee of the Federalists. They drank toasts to American gunboats as the best in the world—on land.

The Louisiana Godsend

A secret pact, fraught with peril for America, was signed in 1800. Napoleon Bonaparte induced the king of Spain to cede to France, for attractive considerations, the immense trans-Mississippi region of Louisiana, which included the New Orleans area.

Rumors of the transfer were partially confirmed in 1802, when the Spaniards at New Orleans withdrew the right of deposit guaranteed America by the treaty of 1795. Deposit (warehouse) privileges were vital to frontier farmers who floated their produce down the Mississippi to its mouth, there to await oceangoing vessels. A roar of anger rolled up the mighty river and into its tributary valleys. American pioneers talked wildly of descending upon New Orleans, rifles in hand. Had they done so, the nation probably would have been engulfed in war with both Spain and France.

Thomas Jefferson, both pacifist and anti-entanglement, was again on the griddle. Louisiana in the senile grip of Spain posed no real threat; America could seize the territory when the time was ripe. But Louisiana in the iron fist of Napoleon, the preeminent military genius of his age, foreshadowed a dark and blood-drenched future. The United States would probably have to fight to dislodge him; and because it alone was not strong enough to defeat his armies, it would have to seek allies, contrary to the deepening anti-alliance policy.

Hoping to quiet the clamor of the West, Jefferson moved decisively. Early in 1803 he sent James Monroe to Paris to join forces with the regular minister there, Robert R. Livingston. The two envoys were instructed to buy New Orleans and as much land to its east as they could get for a maximum of $10 million. If these proposals should fail and the situation became critical, negotiations were to be opened with Britain for an alliance. "The day that France takes possession of New Orleans," Jefferson wrote, "we must marry ourselves to the British fleet and nation." That remark dramatically demonstrated Jefferson's dilemma. Though a passionate hater of war and an enemy of entangling alliances, he was proposing to make an alliance with his old foe, Britain, against his old friend, France, in order to secure New Orleans.

At this critical juncture, Napoleon suddenly decided to sell all of Louisiana and abandon his dream of a New World empire. Two developments prompted his change of mind. First, he had failed in his efforts to reconquer the sugar-rich island of Santo Domingo, for which Louisiana was to serve as a source of foodstuffs. Infuriated ex-slaves, ably led by the gifted Toussaint L'Ouverture, had put up a stubborn resistance that was ultimately broken. Then the island's second line of defense—mosquitoes carrying yellow fever—had swept away thousands of crack French troops. Santo Domingo could not be had, except perhaps at a staggering cost; hence there was no need for Louisiana's food supplies. "Damn sugar, damn coffee, damn colonies!" burst out Napoleon. Second, Bonaparte was about to end the twenty-month lull in his deadly conflict with Britain. Because the British controlled the seas, he feared that he might be forced to make them a gift of Louisiana. Rather than drive America into the arms of Britain by attempting to hold the area, he decided to sell the huge wilderness to the Americans and pocket the money for

Toussaint L'Ouverture (c. 1743–1803) A self-educated ex-slave and military genius, L'Ouverture was finally betrayed by the French, who imprisoned him in a chilly dungeon in France, where he coughed his life away. Indirectly, he did much to set up the sale of Louisiana to the United States.

his schemes nearer home. Napoleon hoped that the United States, strengthened by Louisiana, would one day be a military and naval power that would thwart the ambitions of the lordly British in the New World. The predicaments of France in Europe were again paving the way for America's diplomatic successes.

Events now unrolled dizzily. The American minister, Robert Livingston, pending the arrival of Monroe, was busily negotiating in Paris for a window on the Gulf of Mexico at New Orleans. Suddenly, out of a clear sky, the French foreign minister asked him how much he would give for all Louisiana. Scarcely able to believe his ears (he was partially deaf anyhow), Livingston nervously entered upon the negotiations. After about a week of haggling, while the fate of North America trembled in the balance, treaties were signed on April 30, 1803, ceding Louisiana to the United States for about $15 million.

When the news of the bargain reached America, Jefferson was startled. He had authorized his envoys to offer not more than $10 million for New Orleans and as much to the east in the Floridas as they could get. Instead they had signed three treaties that pledged $15 million for New Orleans, plus an immeasurable tract entirely to the west—an area that would more than double the size of the United States. They had bought a wilderness to get a city.

Once again the two Jeffersons wrestled with each other: the theorist and former strict constructionist versus the democratic visionary. Where in his beloved Constitution was the president authorized to negotiate treaties incorporating a huge new expanse into the union—an expanse containing tens of thousands of Indian, French, Spanish, and black inhabitants? There was no such clause. Yet Jefferson also perceived that the vast domain now within his reach could form a sprawling "empire of liberty" that would ensure the health and long life of America's experiment in democracy.

Conscience-stricken, Jefferson privately proposed that a constitutional amendment be passed. But his friends pointed out in alarm that in the interval Napoleon, for whom thought was action, might suddenly withdraw the offer. So Jefferson shamefacedly submitted the treaties to the Senate, while admitting to his associates that the purchase was unconstitutional.

> *In accepting the Louisiana Purchase, Jefferson thus compromised with conscience in a private letter:*
>
> "It is the case of a guardian, investing the money of his ward in purchasing an important adjacent territory; and saying to him when of age, I did this for your good; I pretend to no right to bind you; you may disavow me, and I must get out of the scrape as I can; I thought it my duty to risk myself for you."

The senators were less finicky than Jefferson. Reflecting enthusiastic public support, they registered their prompt approval of the transaction. Land-hungry Americans were not disposed to split constitutional hairs when confronted with perhaps the most magnificent real estate bargain in history—828,000 square miles at about three cents an acre.

Louisiana in the Long View

Jefferson's bargain with Napoleon was epochal. Overnight he had avoided a possible rupture with France and the consequent entangling alliance with England. By scooping up Louisiana, America secured at one bloodless stroke the western half of the richest river valley in the world and further laid the foundations of a future major power. The ideal of a great agrarian republic, as envisioned by Jefferson, could now be realized in the vast "Valley of Democracy." At the same time, the transfer established valuable precedents for future expansion: the acquisition of foreign territory and peoples by purchase and their incorporation into the Union not as vassal states but on a basis of equal membership. This was imperialism with a new and democratic face, as French Louisianans learned when the Washington government agreed to accept their legal code based on French civil law, rather than English common law. To this day Louisiana state law, uniquely in the American system, retains vestiges of its French origins. Indian peoples within the purchase area would not prove so fortunate.

The purchase also contributed to making operational the isolationist principles of Washington's Farewell Address. Avoiding entangling alliances had been only an ideal to be pursued, rather than a realistic policy, so long as America had potentially hostile and powerful neighbors. By removing virtually the last remnant of significant European power from the North American continent, the United States was now at liberty to disengage almost entirely from the ancient system of Old World rivalries.

The enormous extent of the new area was more fully unveiled by a series of explorations under Jefferson's direction. In the spring of 1804, Jefferson sent his personal secretary, Meriwether Lewis, and a young army officer named William Clark to explore the northern part of the Louisiana Purchase. Aided by the Shoshoni woman Sacajawea, Lewis and Clark ascended the "Great Muddy" (Missouri River) from St. Louis, struggled through the Rockies, and descended the Columbia River to the Pacific coast.

Meriwether Lewis   He is portrayed in this painting as he looked on his return from the great expedition through the Louisiana Purchase and the West.

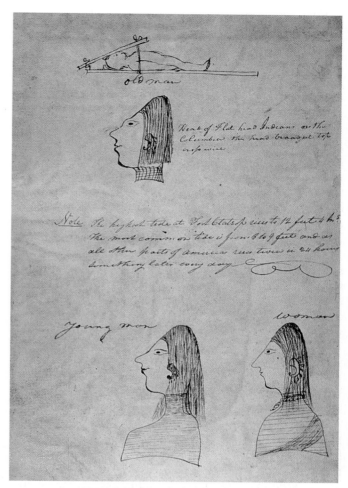

Chinook Indians, c. 1805   William Clark served as the artist and cartographer of the Lewis and Clark expedition. Here he sketched the skull-molding practice that inspired Lewis and Clark to call these Indians "Flatheads." These people were distinct from the present-day Flatheads of Montana, who got their name from the French.

Lewis and Clark's two-and-one-half-year expedition yielded a rich harvest of scientific observations, maps, knowledge of the Indians in the region, and hair-raising wilderness adventure stories. On the Great Plains, they marveled at the "immense herds of buffalo, elk, deer, and antelope feeding in one common and boundless pasture." Lewis was lucky to come back alive. When he and three other men left the expedition to explore the Marias River in present-day western Montana, a band of teenage Blackfoot Indians, armed with crude muskets by British fur-traders operating out of Canada, stole their horses. Lewis foolishly pursued the horse thieves

on foot. He shot one marauder through the belly, but the Indian returned the fire. "Being bareheaded," Lewis later wrote, "I felt the wind of his bullet very distinctly." After killing another Blackfoot and hanging one of the expedition's "peace and friendship" medals around the neck of the corpse as a warning to other Indians, Lewis and his terrified companions beat it out of the Marias country to rejoin the main party on the Missouri River.

The explorers also demonstrated the viability of an overland trail to the Pacific. Down the dusty track thousands of missionaries, fur-traders, and pioneering settlers would wend their way in the ensuing decades,

Gifts from the Great White Chief Among the objectives of the Lewis and Clark expedition was to establish good relations with the Indians in the newly acquired Louisiana Purchase. The American explorers presented all chiefs with copies of these medals, showing President Jefferson on one side and the hands of an Indian and a white man clasped in "peace and friendship" under a crossed "peace pipe" and hatchet on the other. All chiefs also received an American flag and a military uniform jacket, hat, and feather.

bolstering America's claim to the Oregon Country. Other explorers also pushed into the uncharted West. Zebulon M. Pike trekked to the headwaters of the Mississippi River in 1805–1806. The next year Pike ventured into the southern portion of the Louisiana Territory, where he sighted the Colorado peak that bears his name.

The Aaron Burr Conspiracies

In the long run, the Louisiana Purchase greatly expanded the fortunes of the United States and the power of the federal government. In the short term, the vast expanse of territory and the feeble reach of the government obliged to control it raised fears of secession and foreign intrigue.

Aaron Burr, Jefferson's first-term vice president, played no small part in provoking—and justifying—such fears. Dropped from the cabinet in Jefferson's second term, Burr joined with a group of Federalist extremists to plot the secession of New England and New York. Alexander Hamilton, though no friend of Jefferson, exposed and foiled the conspiracy. Incensed, Burr challenged Hamilton to a duel. Hamilton deplored the practice of dueling, by that date illegal in several

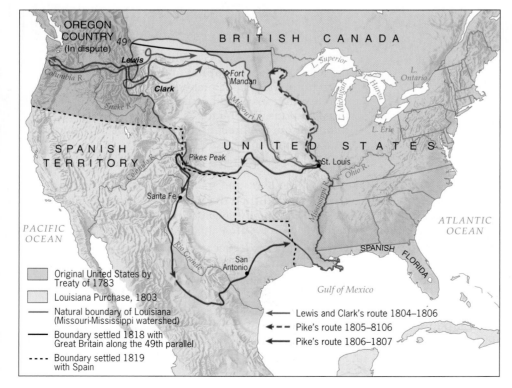

Exploring the Louisiana Purchase and the West Seeking to avert friction with France by purchasing all of Louisiana, Jefferson bought trouble because of the vagueness of the boundaries. Among the disputants were Spain in the Floridas, Spain and Mexico in the Southwest, and Great Britain in Canada.

Map legend:
- Original United States by Treaty of 1783
- Louisiana Purchase, 1803
- Natural boundary of Louisiana (Missouri-Mississippi watershed)
- Boundary settled 1818 with Great Britain along the 49th parallel
- ---- Boundary settled 1819 with Spain
- ← Lewis and Clark's route 1804–1806
- ←-- Pike's route 1805–8106
- ← Pike's route 1806–1807

states, but felt his honor was at stake. He met Burr's challenge at the appointed hour but refused to fire. Burr killed Hamilton with one shot. Burr's pistol blew the brightest brain out of the Federalist party and destroyed its one remaining hope of effective leadership.

His political career as dead as Hamilton's, Burr turned his disunionist plottings to the trans-Mississippi West. There he struck up an allegiance with General James Wilkinson, the unscrupulous military governor of the Louisiana Territory and a sometime secret agent in the pay of the Spanish crown. Burr's schemes are still shrouded in mystery, but he and Wilkinson apparently planned to separate the western part of the United States from the East and expand their new confederacy with invasions of Spanish-controlled Mexico and Florida. In the fall of 1806, Burr and sixty followers floated in flatboats down the Mississippi River to meet Wilkinson's army at Natchez. But when the general learned that Jefferson had gotten wind of the plot, he betrayed Burr and fled to New Orleans.

Burr was arrested and tried for treason. In what seemed to the Jeffersonians to be bias in favor of the accused, Chief Justice John Marshall, strictly hewing to the Constitution, insisted that a guilty verdict required proof of overt acts of treason, not merely treasonous intentions (see Art. III, Sec. III). Burr was acquitted and fled to Europe, where he urged Napoleon to make peace with Britain and launch a joint invasion of America. Burr's insurrectionary brashness demonstrated that it was one thing for the United States to purchase large expanses of western territory but quite another for it to govern them effectively.

A Precarious Neutrality

Jefferson was triumphantly reelected in 1804, with 162 electoral votes to only 14 votes for his Federalist opponent. But the laurels of Jefferson's first administration soon withered under the blasts of the new storm that broke in Europe. After unloading Louisiana in 1803, Napoleon deliberately provoked a renewal of his war with Britain—an awesome conflict that raged on for eleven long years.

For two years a maritime United States—the number one neutral carrier since 1793—enjoyed juicy commercial pickings. But a setback came in 1805. At the Battle of

Intercourse or Impartial Dealings, 1809 A cartoon by "Peter Pencil" shows Jefferson being victimized by both Britain (left) and France (right).

Trafalgar, one-eyed Horatio Lord Nelson achieved immortality by smashing the combined French and Spanish fleets off the coast of Spain, thereby ensuring Britain's supremacy on the seas. At the Battle of Austerlitz in Austria—the Battle of the Three Emperors—Napoleon crushed the combined Austrian and Russian armies, thereby ensuring his mastery of the land. Like the tiger and the shark, France and Britain now reigned supreme in their chosen elements.

Unable to hurt each other directly, the two antagonists were forced to strike indirect blows. Britain ruled the waves and waived the rules. The London government, beginning in 1806, issued a series of Orders in Council. These edicts closed the European ports under French control to foreign shipping, including American, unless the vessels first stopped at a British port. Napoleon struck back, ordering the seizure of all merchant ships, including American, that entered British ports. There was no way to trade with either nation without facing the other's guns. American vessels were, quite literally, caught between the Devil and the deep blue sea.

Even more galling to American pride than the seizure of wooden ships was the seizure of flesh-and-blood American seamen. Impressment—the forcible enlistment of sailors—was a crude form of conscription that the British, among others, had employed for over four centuries. Clubs and stretchers (for men knocked unconscious) were standard equipment of press gangs from His Majesty's man-hungry ships. Some six thousand bona fide U.S. citizens were impressed by the "piratical man-stealers" of Britain from 1808 to 1811 alone. A number of these luckless souls died or were killed in His Majesty's service, leaving their kinfolk and friends bereaved and embittered.

Britain's determination was spectacularly highlighted in 1807. A royal frigate overhauled a U.S. frigate, the *Chesapeake*, about ten miles off the coast of Virginia. The British captain bluntly demanded the surrender of four alleged deserters. London had never claimed the right to seize sailors from a foreign warship, and the American commander, though totally unprepared to fight, refused the request. The British warship thereupon fired three devastating broadsides at close range, killing three Americans and wounding eighteen. Four deserters were dragged away, and the bloody hulk called the *Chesapeake* limped back to port.

Britain was clearly in the wrong, as the London Foreign Office admitted. But London's contrition availed little; a roar of national wrath went up from infuriated Americans. Jefferson, the peace lover, could easily have had war if he had wanted it.

The Hated Embargo

National honor would not permit a slavish submission to British and French mistreatment. Yet a large-scale foreign war was contrary to the settled policy of the new Republic—and in addition it would be futile. The navy was weak, thanks largely to Jefferson's antinavalism, and the army was even weaker. A disastrous defeat would not improve America's plight.

The warring nations in Europe depended heavily upon the United States for raw materials and foodstuffs. In his eager search for an alternative to war, Jefferson seized upon this essential fact. He reasoned that if America voluntarily cut off its exports, the offending powers would be forced to bow, hat in hand, and agree to respect its rights.

Responding to the presidential lash, Congress hastily passed the Embargo Act late in 1807. This rigorous law forbade the export of all goods from the United States, whether in American or in foreign ships. More than just a compromise between submission and shooting, the embargo embodied Jefferson's idea of "peaceful coercion." If it worked, the embargo would vindicate the rights of neutral nations and point to a new way of conducting foreign affairs. If it failed, Jefferson feared the Republic would perish, subjugated to the European powers or sucked into their ferocious war.

The American economy staggered under the effect of the embargo long before Britain or France began to bend. Forests of dead masts gradually filled New England's once-bustling harbors; docks that had once rumbled were deserted (except for illegal trade); and soup kitchens cared for some of the hungry unemployed. Jeffersonian Republicans probably hurt the commerce of New England, which they avowedly were trying to protect, far more than Britain and France together were doing. Farmers of the South and West, the strongholds of Jefferson, suffered no less disastrously than New England. They were alarmed by the mounting piles of unexportable cotton, grain, and tobacco. Jefferson seemed to be waging war on his fellow citizens rather than on the offending foreign powers.

An enormous illicit trade mushroomed in 1808, especially along the Canadian border, where bands of armed Americans on loaded rafts overawed or over-powered federal agents. Irate citizens cynically transposed the letters of "Embargo" to read "O Grab Me," "Go Bar 'Em," and "Mobrage," while heartily cursing the "Dambargo."

Jefferson nonetheless induced Congress to pass iron-toothed enforcing legislation. It was so inquisitorial and tyrannical as to cause some Americans to think more kindly of George III, whom Jefferson had berated in the Declaration of Independence. One indignant New Hampshirite denounced the president with this ditty:

> *Our ships all in motion,*
> *Once whiten'd the ocean;*
> > *They sail'd and return'd with a Cargo;*
> *Now doom'd to decay*
> *They are fallen a prey,*
> > *To Jefferson, worms, and EMBARGO.*

The embargo even had the effect of reviving the moribund Federalist party. Gaining new converts, its leaders hurled their nullification of the embargo into the teeth of the "Virginia lordlings" in Washington. In 1804 the discredited Federalists had polled only 14 electoral votes out of 176; in 1808, the embargo year, the figure rose to 47 out of 175. New England seethed with talk of secession, and Jefferson later admitted that he felt the foundations of government tremble under his feet.

An alarmed Congress, yielding to the storm of public anger, finally repealed the embargo on March 1, 1809, three days before Jefferson's retirement. A half-loaf substitute was provided by the Non-Intercourse Act. This measure formally reopened trade with all the nations of the world, except the two most important,

The Embargo, 1809 This malicious cartoon accused a diminutive Madison (left) of parroting Jefferson's policy and excessively favoring the French as he says, "France wants an embargo & must have it!"

Britain and France. Though thus watered down, economic coercion continued to be the policy of the Jeffersonians from 1809 to 1812, when the nation finally plunged into war.

Launching of the Ship *Fame*, by George Ropes, Jr., 1802 Jefferson's embargo throttled thriving New England shipyards like this one, stirring bitter resentment.

A Federalist circular in Massachusetts against the embargo cried out,

"Let every man who holds the name of America dear to him, stretch forth his hands and put this accursed thing, this Embargo from him. Be resolute, act like sons of liberty, of God, and your country; nerve your arm with vengeance against the Despot [Jefferson] who would wrest the inestimable germ of your Independence from you— and you shall be *Conquerors!!!*"

Why did the embargo, Jefferson's most daring act of statesmanship, collapse after fifteen dismal months? First of all, he underestimated the bulldog determination of the British, as others have, and overestimated the dependence of both belligerents on America's trade. Bumper grain crops blessed the British Isles during these years, and the revolutionary Latin American republics unexpectedly threw open their ports for compensating commerce. With most of Europe under his control, Napoleon could afford to tighten his belt and go without American trade. The French continued to seize American ships and steal their cargoes, while their emperor mocked the United States by claiming that he was simply helping them enforce the embargo.

More critically, perhaps, Jefferson miscalculated the unpopularity of such a self-crucifying weapon and the difficulty of enforcing it. The hated embargo was not continued long enough or tightly enough to achieve the desired results—and a leaky embargo was perhaps more costly than none at all.

Curiously enough, New England plucked a new prosperity from the ugly jaws of the embargo. With shipping tied up and imported goods scarce, the resourceful Yankees reopened old factories and erected new ones. The real foundations of modern America's industrial might were laid behind the protective wall of the embargo, followed by nonintercourse and the War of 1812. Jefferson, the avowed critic of factories, may have unwittingly done more for American manufacturing than Alexander Hamilton, industry's outspoken friend.

Madison's Gamble

Following Washington's precedent, Jefferson left the presidency after two terms, happy to escape what he called the "splendid misery" of the highest office in the land. He strongly favored the nomination and election of a kindred spirit as his successor—his friend and fellow Virginian, the quiet, intellectual, and unassuming James Madison.

Madison took the presidential oath on March 4, 1809, as the awesome conflict in Europe was roaring to its climax. The scholarly Madison was small of stature, light of weight, bald of head, and weak of voice. Despite a distinguished career as a legislator, he was crippled as president by factions within his party and his cabinet. Unable to dominate Congress as Jefferson had done, Madison often found himself holding the bag for risky foreign policies not of his own making.

The Non-Intercourse Act of 1809—a watered-down version of Jefferson's embargo aimed solely at Britain and France—was due to expire in 1810. To Madison's dismay, Congress dismantled the embargo completely with a bargaining measure known as Macon's Bill No. 2. While reopening American trade with all the world, Macon's Bill dangled what Congress hoped was an attractive lure. If either Britain or France repealed its commercial restrictions, America would restore its embargo against the nonrepealing nation. To Madison the bill was a shameful capitulation. It practically admitted that the United States could not survive without one of the belligerents as a commercial ally, but it left determination of who that ally would be to the potentates of London and Paris.

Rivals for the presidency, and for the soul of the young Republic, Thomas Jefferson and John Adams died on the same day—the Fourth of July, 1826—fifty years to the day after both men had signed the Declaration of Independence. Adams's last words were,

"Thomas Jefferson still survives."

But he was wrong, for three hours earlier, Jefferson had drawn his last breath.

The crafty Napoleon saw his chance. Since 1806 Britain had justified its Orders in Council as retaliation for Napoleon's actions—implying, without promising outright, that trade restrictions would be lifted if the French decrees disappeared. Now the French held out the same half-promise. In August 1810 word came from Napoleon's foreign minister that the French decrees might be repealed if Britain also lifted its Orders in Council. The minister's message was deliberately ambiguous. Napoleon had no intention of permitting unrestricted trade between America and Britain. Rather he hoped to maneuver the United States into resuming its embargo against the British, thus creating a partial blockade against his enemy that he would not have to raise a finger to enforce.

Madison knew better than to trust Napoleon, but he gambled that the threat of seeing the United States trade exclusively with France would lead the British to repeal their restrictions—and vice versa. Closing his eyes to the emperor's obvious subterfuge, he accepted the French offer as evidence of repeal. The terms of Macon's Bill gave the British three months to live up to their implied promise by revoking the Orders in Council and reopening the Atlantic to neutral trade.

They did not. In firm control of the seas, London saw little need to bargain. As long as the war with Napoleon went on, they decided, America could trade exclusively with the British Empire—or with nobody at all. Madison's gamble failed. The president saw no choice but to reestablish the embargo against Britain alone—a decision that he knew meant the end of American neutrality and that he feared was the final step toward war.

President James Madison (1751–1836)
Although an eminent constitutionalist, legislator, and diplomat, he was not a strong chief executive. He was the only president ever to go directly to the fighting front—a foolish gesture—but he quickly rode away as the British advanced on Washington in 1814.

Tecumseh and the Prophet

Not all of Madison's party was reluctant to fight. The complexion of the Twelfth Congress, which met late in 1811, differed markedly from that of its predecessor. Recent elections had swept away many of the older "submission men" and replaced them with young hotheads, many from the South and West. Dubbed "war hawks" by their Federalist opponents, the newcomers were indeed on fire for a new war with the old enemy. The war hawks were weary of hearing how their fathers had "whipped" the British single-handedly, and they detested the manhandling of American sailors and the British Orders in Council that dammed the flow of American trade, especially western farm products headed for Europe.

Tecumseh (1768?–1813) A Shawnee Indian born in the Ohio Country, Tecumseh was a gifted organizer and leader as well as a noted warrior. He fought the tribal custom of torturing prisoners and opposed the practice of permitting any one tribe to sell land that, he believed, belonged to all Indians.

In a speech at Vincennes, Indiana Territory, Tecumseh (1768?–1813) said,

"Sell a country! Why not sell the air, the clouds, and the great sea, as well as the earth? Did not the Great Spirit make them all for the use of his children?"

Western war hawks also yearned to wipe out a renewed Indian threat to the pioneer settlers who were streaming into the trans-Allegheny wilderness. As this white flood washed through the green forests, more and more Indians were pushed toward the setting sun.

Two remarkable Shawnee brothers, Tecumseh and Tenskwatawa, known to non-Indians as "the Prophet," concluded that the time had come to stem this onrushing tide. They began to weld together a far-flung confederacy of all the tribes east of the Mississippi, inspiring a vibrant movement of Indian unity and cultural renewal. Their followers gave up textile clothing for traditional buckskin garments. Their warriors forswore alcohol, the better to fight a last-ditch battle with the "paleface" invaders. Rejecting whites' concept of "ownership," Tecumseh urged his supporters never to cede land to whites unless all Indians agreed.

Meanwhile, frontiersmen and their war-hawk spokesmen in Congress became convinced that British "scalp buyers" in Canada were nourishing the Indians'

When the war hawks won control of the House of Representatives, they elevated to the Speakership thirty-four-year-old Henry Clay of Kentucky (1777–1852), the eloquent and magnetic "Harry of the West." Clamoring for war, he thundered,

"I prefer the troubled sea of war, demanded by the honor and independence of this country, with all its calamities and desolation, to the tranquil and putrescent pool of ignominious peace."

William Henry Harrison (1773–1841), Indian fighter and later president, called Tecumseh

"one of those uncommon geniuses who spring up occasionally to produce revolutions and overturn the established order of things. If it were not for the vicinity of the United States, he would perhaps be founder of an Empire that would rival in glory that of Mexico or Peru."

growing strength. In the fall of 1811, William Henry Harrison, governor of Indiana Territory, gathered an army and advanced on Tecumseh's headquarters at the junction of the Wabash and Tippecanoe Rivers in present-day Indiana. Tecumseh was absent, recruiting supporters in the South, but the Prophet attacked Harrison's army—foolishly, in Tecumseh's eyes—with a small force of Shawnees. The Shawnees were routed and their settlement burned.

The Battle of Tippecanoe made Harrison a national hero. It also discredited the Prophet and drove Tecumseh into an alliance with the British. When America's war with Britain came, Tecumseh fought fiercely for the redcoats until his death in 1813 at the Battle of the Thames. With him perished the dream of an Indian confederacy.

Mr. Madison's War

By the spring of 1812, Madison believed war with Britain to be inevitable. The British arming of hostile Indians pushed him toward this decision, as did the whoops of the war hawks in his own party. People like Representative Felix Grundy of Tennessee, three of whose brothers had been killed in clashes with Indians, cried that there was only one way to remove the menace of the Indians: wipe out their Canadian base. "On to

Canada, on to Canada," was the war hawks' chant. Southern expansionists, less vocal, cast a covetous eye on Florida, then weakly held by Britain's ally Spain.

Above all, Madison turned to war to restore confidence in the republican experiment. For five years the Republicans had tried to steer between the warring European powers, to set a course between submission and battle. Theirs had been a noble vision, but it had brought them only international derision and internal strife. Madison and the Republicans came to believe that only a vigorous assertion of American rights could demonstrate the viability of American nationhood— and of democracy as a form of government. If America could not fight to protect itself, its experiment in republicanism would be discredited in the eyes of a scoffing world. One prominent Republican called the war a test "to determine whether the republican system adopted by the people is imbecile and transient, or whether it has force and duration worthy of the enterprise." Thus, not for the last time, did war fever and democratic idealism make common cause.

Madison asked Congress to declare war on June 1, 1812. Congress obliged him two weeks later. The vote in the House was 79 to 49 for war, in the Senate 19 to 13. The close tally revealed deep divisions over the wisdom of fighting. The split was both sectional and partisan. Support for war came from the South and West, but also from Republicans in populous middle states such as Pennsylvania and Virginia. Federalists in both North

The Present State of Our Country
Partisan disunity over the War of 1812 threatened the nation's very existence. The prowar Jeffersonian at the left is attacking the pillar of federalism; the antiwar Federalist at the right is trying to pull down democracy. The spirit of Washington warns that the country's welfare depends on all three pillars, including republicanism.

and South damned the conflict, but their stronghold was New England, which greeted the declaration of war with muffled bells, flags at half-mast, and public fasting.

Why should seafaring New England oppose the war for a free sea? The answer is that pro-British Federalists in the Northeast sympathized with Britain and resented the Republicans' sympathy with Napoleon, whom they regarded as the "Corsican butcher" and the "anti-Christ of the age." The Federalists also opposed the acquisition of Canada, which would merely add more agrarian states from the wild Northwest. This, in turn, would increase the voting strength of the Jeffersonian Republicans.

The bitterness of New England Federalists against "Mr. Madison's War" led them to treason or near-treason. They were determined, wrote one Republican versifier,

To rule the nation if they could,
But see it damned if others should.

New England gold holders probably lent more dollars to the British Exchequer than to the federal Treasury. Federalist farmers sent huge quantities of supplies and foodstuffs to Canada, enabling British armies to invade New York. New England governors stubbornly refused to permit their militia to serve outside their own states. In a sense America had to fight two enemies simultaneously: old England and New England.

Thus perilously divided, the barely United States plunged into armed conflict against Britain, then the world's most powerful empire. No sober American could have much reasonable hope of victory, but by 1812 the Jeffersonian Republicans saw no other choice.

Chronology

1800	Jefferson defeats Adams for presidency
1801	Judiciary Act of 1801
1801–1805	Naval war with Tripoli
1802	Revised naturalization law Judiciary Act of 1801 repealed
1803	*Marbury* v. *Madison* Louisiana Purchase
1804	Jefferson reelected president Impeachment of Justice Chase
1804–1806	Lewis and Clark expedition
1805	Peace treaty with Tripoli
1805–1807	Pike's explorations
1806	Burr treason trial
1807	*Chesapeake* affair Embargo Act
1808	Madison elected president
1809	Non-Intercourse Act replaces Embargo Act

1810	Macon's Bill No. 2
	Napoleon announces (falsely) repeal of
	    blockade decrees
	Madison reestablishes nonimportation
	    against Britain

1811	Battle of Tippecanoe
1812	United States declares war on Britain

For further reading, see the Appendix. For web resources, go to **http://college.hmco.com**.

12

The Second War for Independence and the Upsurge of Nationalism

~

1812–1824

THE AMERICAN CONTINENTS . . . ARE HENCEFORTH
NOT TO BE CONSIDERED AS SUBJECTS FOR FUTURE
COLONIZATION BY ANY EUROPEAN POWERS.

PRESIDENT JAMES MONROE, DECEMBER 2, 1823

The War of 1812 was an especially divisive and ill-fought war. There was no burning national anger, as there had been in 1807 following the *Chesapeake* outrage. The supreme lesson of the conflict was the folly of leading a divided and apathetic people into war. And yet, despite the unimpressive military outcome and even less decisive negotiated peace, Americans came out of the war with a renewed sense of nationhood. For the next dozen years, an awakened spirit of nationalism would inspire activities ranging from protecting manufacturing to building roads to defending the authority of the federal government over the states.

On to Canada over Land and Lakes

On the eve of the War of 1812, the regular army was ill-trained, ill-disciplined, and widely scattered. It had to be supplemented by the even more poorly trained militia, who were sometimes distinguished by their speed of foot in leaving the battlefield. Some of the ranking generals were semisenile heirlooms from the Revolutionary War, rusting on their laurels and lacking in vigor and vision.

Canada became an important battleground in the War of 1812 because British forces were weakest there. A successful American offensive might have quashed British influence among the Indians and garnered new land for settlers. But the Americans' offensive strategy was poorly conceived. Had the Americans captured Montreal, the center of population and transportation, everything to the west might have died, just as the leaves of a tree wither when the trunk is girdled. But instead of laying ax to the trunk, the Americans frittered away their strength in the three-pronged invasion of 1812. The trio of invading forces that set out from Detroit, Niagara, and Lake Champlain were all beaten back shortly after they had crossed the Canadian border.

By contrast, the British and Canadians displayed energy from the outset. Early in the war, they captured

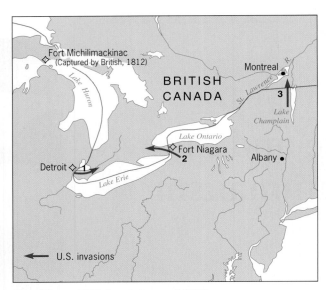

The Three U.S. Invasions of 1812

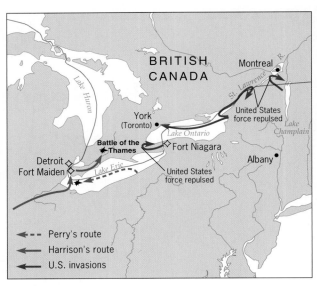

Campaigns of 1813

the American fort of Michilimackinac, which commanded the upper Great Lakes and the Indian-inhabited area to the south and west. Their brilliant defensive operations were led by the inspired British general Isaac Brock and assisted (in the American camp) by "General Mud" and "General Confusion."

When several American land invasions of Canada were again hurled back in 1813, Americans looked for success on the water. Man for man and ship for ship, the American navy did much better than the army. In comparison to British ships, American craft on the whole were more skillfully handled, had better gunners, and were manned by non-press-gang crews who were burning to avenge numerous indignities. Similarly, the American frigates, notably the *Constitution* ("Old Ironsides"), had thicker sides, heavier firepower, and larger crews, of which one sailor in six was a free black.

Control of the Great Lakes was vital, and an energetic American naval officer, Oliver Hazard Perry, managed to build a fleet of green-timbered ships on the shores of Lake Erie, manned by even greener seamen. When he captured a British fleet in a furious engagement on the lake, he reported to his superior, "We have met the enemy and they are ours." Perry's victory and his slogan infused new life into the drooping American cause. Forced to withdraw from Detroit and Fort Malden, the retreating redcoats were overtaken by General Harrison's army and beaten at the Battle of the Thames in October 1813.

Despite these successes, the Americans by late 1814, far from invading Canada, were grimly defending their own soil against the invading British. In Europe the diversionary power of Napoleon was destroyed in mid-1814, and the dangerous despot was exiled to the Mediterranean isle of Elba. The United States, which had so brashly provoked war behind the protective skirts of Napoleon, was now left to face the music alone. Thousands of victorious veteran redcoats began to pour into Canada from the Continent.

Assembling some ten thousand crack troops, the British prepared in 1814 for a crushing blow into New York along the familiar lake-river route. In the absence of roads, the invader was forced to bring supplies over the Lake Champlain waterway. A weaker American fleet, commanded by the thirty-year-old Thomas Macdonough, challenged the British. The ensuing battle was desperately fought near Plattsburgh on September 11, 1814, on floating slaughterhouses. The American flagship at one point was in grave trouble. But Macdonough, unexpectedly turning his ship about with cables, confronted the enemy with a fresh broadside and snatched victory from the fangs of defeat.

The results of this heroic naval battle were momentous. The invading British army was forced to retreat. Macdonough thus saved at least upper New York from conquest, New England from further disaffection, and the Union from possible dissolution. He also profoundly affected the concurrent negotiations of the Anglo-American peace treaty in Europe.

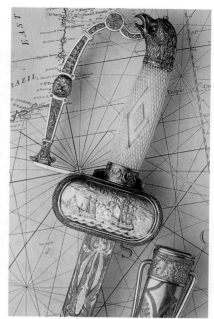

***Constitution* and *Guerrière*, 1812** The *Guerrière* was heavily outweighed and outgunned, yet its British captain eagerly—and foolishly—sought combat. His ship was destroyed. Historian Henry Adams later concluded that this duel "raised the United States in one half hour to the rank of a first-class Power in the world." The buckler on the sword from the USS *Constitution* commemorates the famous battle. Today the *Constitution*, berthed in Boston harbor, remains the oldest actively commissioned ship in the U.S. Navy.

Washington Burned and New Orleans Defended

A second formidable British force, numbering about four thousand, landed in the Chesapeake Bay area in August 1814. Advancing rapidly on Washington, it easily dispersed some six thousand panicky militia at Bladensburg ("the Bladensburg races"). The invaders then entered the capital and set fire to most of the public buildings, including the Capitol and the White House. But while Washington burned, the Americans at Baltimore held firm. The British fleet hammered Fort McHenry with their cannon but could not capture the city. Francis Scott Key, a detained American anxiously watching the bombardment from a British ship, was inspired by the doughty defenders to write the words of "The Star-Spangled Banner." Set to the tune of a saucy English tavern refrain, the song quickly attained popularity.

A third British blow of 1814, aimed at New Orleans, menaced the entire Mississippi Valley. Gaunt and hawk-faced Andrew Jackson, fresh from crushing the southwest Indians at the Battle of Horseshoe Bend, was placed in command (see the map on p. 251). His hodgepodge force consisted of seven thousand sailors,

Andrew Jackson (1767–1845) appealed to the governor of Louisiana for help recruiting free blacks to defend New Orleans in 1814:

"The free men of colour in [your] city are inured to the Southern climate and would make excellent Soldiers. . . . They must be for or against us—distrust them, and you make them your enemies, place confidence in them, and you engage them by every dear and honorable tie to the interest of the country, who extends to them equal rights and [privileges] with white men."

The Fall of Washington, or Maddy in Full Flight President Madison ("Maddy") was forced into humiliating withdrawal from the capital in 1814, when British forces put the torch to Washington, D.C.

regulars, pirates, and Frenchmen, as well as militiamen from Louisiana, Kentucky, and Tennessee. Among the defenders were two Louisiana regiments of free black volunteers, numbering about four hundred men. The Americans threw up their entrenchment, and in the words of a popular song,

> *Behind it stood our little force—*
> *None wished it to be greater;*
> *For ev'ry man was half a horse,*
> *And half an alligator.*

The overconfident British, numbering some eight thousand battle-seasoned veterans, blundered badly. They made the mistake of launching a frontal assault, on January 8, 1815, on the entrenched American riflemen and cannoneers. The attackers suffered the most devastating defeat of the entire war, losing over two thousand, killed and wounded, in half an hour, as compared with some seventy for the Americans. It was an astonishing victory for Jackson and his men.

News of the victory struck the country "like a clap of thunder," according to one contemporary. Andrew Jackson became a national hero as poets and politicians lined up to sing the praises of the defenders of New Orleans. It hardly mattered when word arrived that a peace treaty had been signed at Ghent, Belgium, ending the war two weeks before the battle. The United States had fought for honor as much as material gain. The Battle of New Orleans restored that honor, at least in American eyes, and unleashed a wave of nationalism and self-confidence.

Its wrath aroused, the Royal Navy had finally retaliated by throwing a ruinous naval blockade along America's coast and by landing raiding parties almost at will. American economic life, including fishing, was crippled. Customs revenues were choked off, and near the end of the war, the bankrupt Treasury was unable to meet its maturing obligations.

The Treaty of Ghent

Tsar Alexander I of Russia, feeling hard-pressed by Napoleon's army and not wanting his British ally to fritter away its strength in America, proposed mediation between the clashing Anglo-Saxon cousins in 1812. The tsar's feeler eventually set in motion the machinery

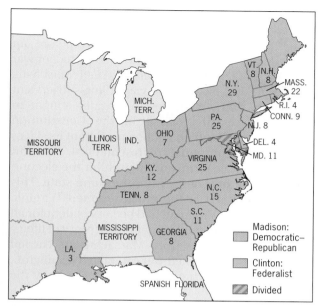

Presidential Election of 1812 (with electoral vote by state) The Federalists showed impressive strength in the North, and their presidential candidate, DeWitt Clinton, the future "Father of the Erie Canal," almost won. If the 25 electoral votes of Pennsylvania had gone to the New Yorker, he would have won, 114 to 103.

In a letter to her friend Mercy Otis Warren, Abigail Adams (1744–1818) fretted that the British were taking advantage of Americans' disagreement over the War of 1812:

"We have our firesides, our comfortable habitations, our cities, our churches and our country to defend, our rights, privileges and independence to preserve. And for these are we not justly contending? Thus it appears to me. Yet I hear from our pulpits, and read from our presses, that it is an unjust, a wicked, a ruinous, and unnecessary war. . . . A house divided upon itself—and upon that foundation do our enemies build their hopes of subduing us."

that brought five American peacemakers to the quaint Belgian city of Ghent in 1814. The bickering group was headed by early-rising, puritanical John Quincy Adams, son of John Adams, who deplored the late-hour card playing of his high-living colleague Henry Clay.

Confident after their military successes, the British envoys made sweeping demands for a neutralized Indian buffer state in the Great Lakes region, control of the Great Lakes, and a substantial part of conquered Maine. The Americans flatly rejected these terms, and the talks appeared stalemated. But news of British reverses in upper New York and at Baltimore, and increasing war-weariness in Britain, made London more willing to compromise. Preoccupied with redrafting Napoleon's map of Europe at the Congress of Vienna and eyeing still-dangerous France, the British lion resigned itself to licking its wounds.

The Treaty of Ghent, signed on Christmas Eve in 1814, was essentially an armistice. Both sides simply agreed to stop fighting and to restore conquered territory. No mention was made of those grievances for which America had ostensibly fought: the Indian menace, search and seizure, Orders in Council, impressment, and confiscations. These discreet omissions have often been cited as further evidence of the insincerity of the war hawks. Rather they are proof that the Americans had not managed to defeat the British. With neither side able to impose its will, the treaty negotiations—like the war itself—ended as a virtual draw. Relieved Americans boasted "Not One Inch of Territory Ceded or Lost"—a phrase that contrasted strangely with the "On to Canada" rallying cry of the war's outset.

Federalist Grievances and the Hartford Convention

Defiant New England remained a problem. It prospered during the conflict, owing largely to illicit trade with the enemy in Canada and to the absence of a British blockade until 1814. But the embittered opposition of the Federalists to the war continued unabated.

As the war dragged on, New England extremists became more vocal. A small minority of them proposed secession from the Union, or at least a separate peace with Britain. Ugly rumors were afloat about "Blue Light" Federalists—treacherous New Englanders who supposedly flashed lanterns on the shore so that blockading British cruisers would be alerted to the attempted escape of American ships.

The most spectacular manifestation of Federalist discontent was the ill-omened Hartford Convention. Late in 1814, when the capture of New Orleans seemed imminent, Massachusetts issued a call for a convention at Hartford, Connecticut. The states of Massachusetts, Connecticut, and Rhode Island dispatched full delegations; neighboring New Hampshire and Vermont sent partial representation. This group of prominent men, twenty-six in all, met in complete secrecy for about three weeks—December 15, 1814, to January 5, 1815—to discuss their grievances and to seek redress for their wrongs.

In truth, the Hartford Convention was actually less radical than the alarmists supposed. Though a minority of delegates gave vent to wild talk of secession, the convention's final report was quite moderate. It demanded financial assistance from Washington to compensate for lost trade and proposed constitutional amendments requiring a two-thirds vote in Congress before an embargo could be imposed, new states admitted, or war declared. Most of the demands reflected Federalist fears that a once-proud New England was falling subservient to an agrarian South and West. Delegates sought to abolish the three-fifths clause in the Constitution (which allowed the South to count a portion of its slaves in calculating proportional representation), to limit presidents to a single term, and to prohibit the election of two successive presidents from the same state. This last clause was aimed at the much-resented "Virginia Dynasty"—by 1814 a Virginian had been president for all but four years in the Republic's quarter-century of life.

Three special envoys from Massachusetts carried these demands to the burned-out capital of Washington. The trio arrived just in time to be overwhelmed by the

Massachusetts, Connecticut, and Rhode Island Contemplate Abandoning the Union, engraving by William Charles, 1814   This anti-Federalist cartoon shows Great Britain welcoming back its "Yankee boys" with open arms, promising them "plenty molasses and codfish, plenty of goods to smuggle, honours, titles, and nobility into the bargain."

glorious news from New Orleans, followed by that from Ghent. As the rest of the nation congratulated itself on a glorious victory, New England's wartime complaints seemed petty at best and treasonous at worst. Pursued by the sneers and jeers of the press, the envoys sank away in disgrace and into obscurity.

The Hartford resolutions, as it turned out, were the death dirge of the Federalist party. The Federalists were never again to mount a successful presidential campaign.

Federalist doctrines of disunity, which long survived the party, blazed a portentous trail. Until 1815 there was far more talk of nullification and secession in New England than in any other section, including the South. The outright flouting of the Jeffersonian embargo and the later crippling of the war effort were the two most damaging acts of nullification in America prior to the events leading to the Civil War.

The Second War for American Independence

The War of 1812 was a small war, involving about 6,000 Americans killed or wounded. It was but a footnote to the mighty European conflagration. In 1812, when Napoleon invaded Russia with about 500,000 men, Madison tried to invade Canada with about 5,000 men. But if the American conflict was globally unimportant, it had huge consequences for the United States.

The Republic had shown that it would resist, sword in hand, what it regarded as grievous wrongs. Other nations developed a new respect for America's fighting prowess. Naval officers like Perry and Macdonough were the most effective type of negotiators; the hot breath of their broadsides spoke the most eloquent diplomatic language. America's emissaries abroad were henceforth treated with less scorn. In a diplomatic sense, if not in a military sense, the conflict could be called the Second War for American Independence.

A new nation, moreover, was welded in the roaring furnace of armed conflict. Sectionalism, now identified with discredited New England Federalists, was dealt a black eye. The painful events of the war glaringly revealed, as perhaps nothing else could have done, the folly of sectional disunity. In a sense the most conspicuous casualty of the war was the Federalist party.

War heroes emerged, especially the two Indian-fighters Andrew Jackson and William Henry Harrison. Both of them were to become president. Left in the lurch by their British friends at Ghent, the Indians were

The War of 1812 won a new respect for America among many Britons. Michael Scott, a young lieutenant in the British navy, wrote,

"I don't like Americans; I never did, and never shall like them. . . . I have no wish to eat with them, drink with them, deal with, or consort with them in any way; but let me tell the whole truth, nor fight with them, were it not for the laurels to be acquired, by overcoming an enemy so brave, determined, and alert, and in every way so worthy of one's steel, as they have always proved."

forced to make such terms as they could. They reluctantly consented, in a series of treaties, to relinquish vast areas of forested land north of the Ohio River.

Manufacturing prospered behind the wooden wall of the British blockade. In both an economic and a diplomatic sense, the War of 1812 bred greater American independence. The industries that were thus stimulated by the fighting rendered America less dependent on Europe's workshops.

Canadian patriotism and nationalism also received a powerful stimulus from the clash. Many Canadians felt betrayed by the Treaty of Ghent. They were especially aggrieved by the failure to secure an Indian buffer state or even mastery of the Great Lakes. Canadians fully expected the frustrated Yankees to return, and for a time the Americans and British engaged in a floating arms race on the Great Lakes. But in 1817 the Rush-Bagot agreement between Britain and the United States severely limited naval armament on the lakes. Better relations brought the last border fortifications down in the 1870s, with the happy result that the United States and Canada came to share the world's longest unfortified boundary—5,527 miles long.

After Napoleon's final defeat at Waterloo in 1815, Europe slumped into a peace of exhaustion. Deposed monarchs returned to battered thrones, as the Old World took the rutted road back to conservatism, illiberalism, and reaction. But the American people were largely unaffected by these European developments. Turning their backs on the Old World, they faced resolutely toward the untamed West—and toward the task of building their democracy.

Nascent Nationalism

The most impressive by-product of the War of 1812 was a heightened nationalism—the spirit of nation-consciousness or national oneness. America may not have fought the war as one nation, but it emerged as one nation. The changed mood even manifested itself in the birth of a distinctively national literature. Washington Irving and James Fenimore Cooper attained international recognition in the 1820s, significantly as the nation's first writers of importance to use American scenes and themes. School textbooks, often British in an earlier era, were now being written by Americans for Americans. In the world of magazines, the highly intellectual *North American Review* began publication in 1815—the year of the triumph at New Orleans. Even American painters increasingly celebrated their native landscapes on their canvases.

A fresh nationalistic spirit could be recognized in many other areas as well. The rising tide of nation-consciousness even touched finance. A revived Bank of the United States was voted by Congress in 1816. A more handsome national capital began to rise from the ashes of Washington. The army was expanded to ten thousand men. The navy further covered itself with glory in 1815 when it administered a thorough beating to the piratical plunderers of North Africa. Stephen Decatur, naval hero of the War of 1812 and of the Barbary Coast expeditions, pungently captured the country's nationalist mood in a famous toast made on his return from the Mediterranean campaigns: "Our country! In her intercourse with foreign nations may she always be in the right; but our country, right or wrong!"

"The American System"

Nationalism likewise manifested itself in manufacturing. Patriotic Americans took pride in the factories that had recently mushroomed forth, largely as a result of the self-imposed embargoes and the war.

When hostilities ended in 1815, British competitors undertook to recover lost ground. They began to dump the contents of their bulging warehouses on the United

View of the Capitol, by Charles Burton, 1824 This painting of the Capitol building, much smaller than it is today, reveals the rustic conditions of the early days in the nation's capital. A series of architects worked on the Capitol, following William Thornton's original design along neoclassical, or "Greek Revival," lines. After the British burned the building in 1814, Boston's Charles Bulfinch oversaw the reconstruction of the Capitol, finally completed in 1830.

Henry Clay (1777–1852), by John Neagle, 1843
This painting hangs in the corridors of the House of Representatives, where Clay worked as a glamorous, eloquent, and ambitious congressman for many years. Best known for promoting his nationalistic "American System" of protective tariffs for eastern manufactures and federally financed canals and highways to benefit the West, Clay is surrounded here by symbols of flourishing agriculture and burgeoning industries in the new nation.

Tariff of 1816—the first tariff in American history instituted primarily for protection, not revenue. Its rates—roughly 20 to 25 percent on the value of dutiable imports—were not high enough to provide completely adequate safeguards, but the law was a bold beginning. A strongly protective trend was started that stimulated the appetites of the protected for more protection.

Nationalism was further highlighted by a grandiose plan of Henry Clay for developing a profitable home market. Still radiating the nationalism of war-hawk days, he threw himself behind an elaborate scheme known by 1824 as the American System. This system had three main parts. It began with a strong banking system, which would provide easy and abundant credit. Clay also advocated a protective tariff, behind which eastern manufacturing would flourish. Revenues gushing from the tariff would provide funds for the third component of the American System—a network of roads and canals, especially in the burgeoning Ohio Valley. Through these new arteries of transportation would flow foodstuffs and raw materials from the South and West to the North and East. In exchange, a stream of manufactured goods would flow in the return direction, knitting the country together economically and politically.

Persistent and eloquent demands by Henry Clay and others for better transportation struck a responsive chord with the public. The recent attempts to invade Canada had all failed partly because of oath-provoking roads—or no roads at all. People who have dug wagons out of hub-deep mud do not quickly forget their blisters and backaches. An outcry for better transportation, rising most noisily in the road-poor West, was one of the most striking aspects of the nationalism inspired by the War of 1812.

But attempts to secure federal funding for roads and canals stumbled on Republican constitutional scruples. Congress voted in 1817 to distribute $1.5 million to the states for internal improvements, but President Madison sternly vetoed this handout measure as unconstitutional. The individual states were thus forced to venture ahead with construction programs of their own, including the Erie Canal, triumphantly completed by New York in 1825. Jeffersonian Republicans, who had gulped down Hamiltonian loose constructionism on other important problems, choked on the idea of direct federal support of intrastate internal improvements. New England, in particular, strongly opposed federally constructed roads and canals, because such outlets would further drain away population and create competing states beyond the mountains.

States, often cutting their prices below cost in an effort to strangle the American war-baby factories in the cradle. The infant industries bawled lustily for protection. To many red-blooded Americans, it seemed as though the British, having failed to crush Yankee fighters on the battlefield, were now seeking to crush Yankee factories in the marketplace.

A nationalist Congress, out-Federalizing the old Federalists, responded by passing the path-breaking

The So-Called Era of Good Feelings

James Monroe—six feet tall, somewhat stooped, courtly, and mild-mannered—was nominated for the presidency in 1816 by the Republicans. They thus undertook to continue the so-called Virginia dynasty of Washington, Jefferson, and Madison. The fading Federalists ran a candidate for the last time in their checkered history, and he was crushed by 183 electoral votes to 34. The vanquished Federalist party was gasping its dying

> Boston's Columbian Centinel *was not the only newspaper to regard President Monroe's early months as the Era of Good Feelings.* Washington's National Intelligencer *observed in July 1817,*
>
> "Never before, perhaps, since the institution of civil government, did the same harmony, the same absence of party spirit, the same national feeling, pervade a community. The result is too consoling to dispute too nicely about the cause."

James Monroe (1758–1831), by Samuel F. B. Morse, 1819
Monroe fought in the Revolution (suffering a wound), served as minister to France, became co-purchaser of Louisiana, and rose to the presidency in 1817. An excellent administrator, he presided over the Era of Good Feelings. His inaugural address declared, "National honor is national property of the highest value." His name is imperishably attached to the Monroe Doctrine and Monrovia, the capital city of Liberia in Africa. He had strongly backed the colonization there of ex-slaves. His wife and two daughters had expensive tastes, and like plantation owner Jefferson, he died deeply in debt.

breaths, leaving the field to the triumphant Republicans and one-party rule.

In James Monroe, the man and the times auspiciously met. As the last president to wear an old-style cocked hat, he straddled two generations: the bygone age of the Founding Fathers and the emergent age of nationalism. Never brilliant, and perhaps not great, the serene Virginian with gray-blue eyes was in intellect and personal force the least distinguished of the first eight presidents. But the times called for sober administration, not dashing heroics. And Monroe was an experienced, levelheaded executive, with an ear-to-the-ground talent for interpreting popular rumblings.

Emerging nationalism was further cemented by a goodwill tour Monroe undertook early in 1817, ostensibly to inspect military defenses. He pushed northward deep into New England and then westward to Detroit, viewing en route Niagara Falls. Even in Federalist New England, "the enemy's country," he received a heart-warming welcome; a Boston newspaper was so far carried away as to announce that an "Era of Good Feelings" had been ushered in. This happy phrase has been commonly used since then to describe the administrations of Monroe.

The Era of Good Feelings, unfortunately, was something of a misnomer. Considerable tranquility and prosperity did in fact smile upon the early years of Monroe, but the period was a troubled one. The acute issues of the tariff, the bank, internal improvements, and the sale of public lands were being hotly contested. Sectionalism was crystallizing, and the conflict over slavery was beginning to raise its hideous head.

Fairview Inn or Three Mile House on Old Frederick Road, by Thomas Coke Ruckle, c. 1829
This busy scene on the Frederick Road, leading westward from Baltimore, was typical as
pioneers flooded into the newly secured West in the early 1800s.

The Panic of 1819 and the Curse of Hard Times

Much of the goodness went out of the good feelings in 1819, when a paralyzing economic panic descended. It brought deflation, depression, bankruptcies, bank failures, unemployment, soup kitchens, and over-crowded pesthouses known as debtors' prisons.

This was the first national financial panic since President Washington took office. Many factors contributed to the catastrophe of 1819, but looming large was overspeculation in frontier lands. The Bank of the United States, through its western branches, had become deeply involved in this popular type of outdoor gambling.

Financial paralysis from the panic, which lasted in some degree for several years, gave a rude setback to the nationalistic ardor. The West was especially hard hit. When the pinch came, the Bank of the United States forced the speculative ("wildcat") western banks to the wall and foreclosed mortgages on countless farms. All this was technically legal but politically unwise. In the eyes of the western debtor, the nationalist Bank of the United States soon became a kind of financial devil.

The panic of 1819 also created backwashes in the political and social world. The poorer classes—the one-suspender men and their families—were severely strapped, and in their troubles was sown the seed of Jacksonian democracy. Hard times also directed attention to the inhumanity of imprisoning debtors. In extreme cases, often overplayed, mothers were torn from their infants for owing a few dollars. Mounting agitation against imprisonment for debt bore fruit in remedial legislation in an increasing number of states.

Growing Pains of the West

The onward march of the West continued; nine frontier states had joined the original thirteen between 1791 and 1819. With an eye to preserving the North-South sectional balance, most of these commonwealths had been admitted alternately, free or slave. (See Admission of States in the Appendix.)

Why this explosive expansion? In part it was simply a continuation of the generations-old westward movement, which had been going on since early colonial days. In addition, the siren song of cheap land—"the Ohio fever"—had a special appeal to European immigrants. Eager newcomers from abroad were beginning to stream down the gangplanks in impressive numbers, especially after the war of boycotts and bullets. Land exhaustion in the older tobacco states, where the soil was "mined" rather than cultivated, likewise drove

Settlers of the Old Northwest

The Old Northwest beckoned to settlers after the War of 1812. The withdrawal of the British protector weakened the Indians' grip on the territory. Then the transportation boom of the 1820s—steamboats on the Ohio, the National Highway stretching from Pennsylvania, the Erie Canal—opened broad arteries along which the westward movement flowed.

The first wave of newcomers came mainly from Kentucky, Tennessee, and the upland regions of Virginia and the Carolinas. Most migrants were rough-hewn white farmers who had been pushed from good land to bad by an expanding plantation economy. Like Joseph Cress of North Carolina, they were relieved to relinquish "them old red filds" where you "get nothing," in return for acres of new soil that "is as black and rich you wold want it." Some settlers acquired land for the first time. John Palmer, whose family left Kentucky for Illinois in 1831, recalled his father telling him "of land so cheap that we could all be landholders, where men were all equal." Migrants from the South settled mainly in the southern portions of Ohio, Indiana, and Illinois.

As Palmer testified, the Old Northwest offered southern farmers an escape from the lowly social position they had endured as nonslaveholders in a slave society. Not that they objected to slavery or sympathized with blacks. Far from it: by enacting Black Codes in their new territories, they tried to prevent blacks from following them to paradise. They wanted their own democratic community, free of rich planters and African Americans alike.

If southern "Butternuts," as these settlers were called, dominated settlement in the 1820s, the next decade brought Yankees from the Northeast. They were as land-starved as their southern counterparts. A growing population had gobbled up most of the good land east of the Appalachians. Yankee settlers came to the Old Northwest, especially to the northern parts of Ohio, Indiana, and Illinois, eager to make the region a profitable breadbasket for the Atlantic seaboard. Unlike the Butternuts, who wanted to quit forever the imposing framework of southern society, northerners hoped to re-create the world they had left behind.

A Town Center, Marietta, Ohio
Forty-eight men from Massachusetts founded Marietta in 1788, making it the first settlement created under the provisions of the Ordinance of 1787. Within a decade the town resembled the Yankee villages they had left behind. Here and elsewhere, however, clearing the dense forests utterly transformed the landscape of the Old Northwest.

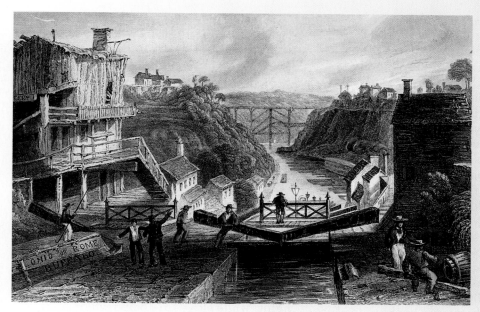

A Lock on the Erie Canal at Lockport, New York, 1838
The Erie Canal created an artificial waterway through upstate New York from the Hudson River to the Great Lakes, moving people and trade to and from the Old Northwest more quickly and cheaply.

Conflict soon emerged between Yankees and southerners. As self-sufficient farmers with little interest in producing for the market, the southerners viewed the northern newcomers as inhospitable, greedy, and excessively ambitious. "Yankee" became a term of reproach; a person who was cheated was said to have been "Yankeed." Northerners, in turn, viewed the southerners as uncivilized, a "coon dog and butcher knife tribe" with no interest in education, self-improvement, or agricultural innovation. Yankees, eager to tame both the land and its people, wanted to establish public schools and build roads, canals, and railroads—and they advocated taxes to fund such progress. Southerners opposed all these reforms, especially public schooling, which they regarded as an attempt to northernize their children.

Religion divided settlers as well. Northerners, typically Congregationalists and Presbyterians, wanted their ministers to be educated in seminaries. Southerners embraced the more revivalist Baptist and Methodist denominations. They preferred poor, humble preacher-farmers to professionally trained preachers, whom they viewed as too distant from the Lord and the people. As the Baptist preacher Alexander Campbell put it, "The scheme of a learned priesthood . . . has long since proved itself to be a grand device to keep men in ignorance and bondage."

Not everyone, of course, fitted neatly into these molds. Abraham Lincoln, with roots in Kentucky, came to adopt views more akin to those of the Yankees than the southerners, whereas his New England-born archrival, Stephen Douglas, carefully cultivated the Butternut vote for the Illinois Democratic party.

As the population swelled and the region acquired its own character, the stark contrasts between northerners and southerners started to fade. By the 1850s northerners dominated numerically, and they succeeded in establishing public schools and fashioning internal improvements. Railroads and Great Lakes shipping tied the region ever more tightly to the Northeast. Yankees and southerners sometimes allied as new kinds of cleavages emerged—between rich and poor, between city dwellers and farmers, and, once Irish and German immigrants started pouring into the region, between native Protestants and newcomer Catholics. Still, echoes of the clash between Yankees and Butternuts persisted. During the Civil War, the southern counties of Ohio, Indiana, and Illinois, where southerners had first settled, harbored sympathizers with the South and served as a key area for Confederate military infiltration into the North. Decades later these same counties became a stronghold of the Ku Klux Klan. The Old Northwest may have become firmly anchored economically to the Northeast, but vestiges of its early dual personality persisted.

people westward. Glib speculators accepted small down payments, making it easier to buy new holdings.

The western boom was stimulated by additional developments. Acute economic distress during the embargo years turned many pinched faces toward the setting sun. The crushing of the Indians in the Northwest and South by Generals Harrison and Jackson pacified the frontier and opened up vast virgin tracts of land. The building of highways improved the land routes to the Ohio Valley. Noteworthy was the Cumberland Road, begun in 1811, which ran ultimately from western Maryland to Illinois. The use of the first steamboat on western waters, also in 1811, heralded a new era of upstream navigation.

But the West, despite the inflow of settlers, was still weak in population and influence. Not potent enough politically to make its voice heard, it was forced to ally itself with other sections. Thus strengthened, it demanded cheap acreage and partially achieved its goal in the Land Act of 1820, which authorized a buyer to purchase 80 virgin acres at a minimum of $1.25 an acre in cash. The West also demanded cheap transportation and slowly got it, despite the constitutional qualms of the presidents and the hostility of easterners. Finally, the West demanded cheap money, issued by its own "wildcat" banks, and fought the powerful Bank of the United States to attain its goal (see "Makers of America: Settlers of the Old Northwest," pp. 244–245).

Antislavery Propaganda in the 1820s
These drawstring bags are made of silk and transfer-printed with "before" and "after" scenes of slavery. On the left bag, an African woman cradles her baby; on the right one, the grieving mother is childless and in chains, while slaves are being whipped in the background. These bags were purchased at an abolitionist fair, held to raise money for the antislavery movement. Purses and the like sold well at these events because women were prominent in the movement.

Slavery and the Sectional Balance

Sectional tensions, involving rivalry between the slave South and the free North over control of the beckoning West, were stunningly revealed in 1819. In that year the territory of Missouri knocked on the doors of Congress for admission as a slave state. This fertile and well-watered area contained sufficient population to warrant statehood. But the House of Representatives stymied the plans of the Missourians by passing the incendiary Tallmadge amendment. It stipulated that no more slaves should be brought into Missouri and also provided for the gradual emancipation of children born to slave parents already there. A roar of anger burst from slaveholding southerners. They were joined by many depression-cursed pioneers who favored unhampered expansion of the West and by many northerners, especially diehard Federalists, who were eager to use the issue to break the back of the "Virginia dynasty."

Southerners saw in the Tallmadge amendment, which they eventually managed to defeat in the Senate, an ominous threat to sectional balance. When the Constitution was adopted in 1788, the North and South were running neck and neck in wealth and population. But with every passing decade, the North was becoming wealthier and also more thickly settled—an advantage reflected in an increasing northern majority in the House of Representatives. Yet in the Senate, each state had two votes, regardless of size. With eleven states free and eleven slave, the southerners had maintained equality. They were therefore in a good position to thwart any northern effort to interfere with the expansion of slavery, and they did not want to lose this veto.

The future of the slave system caused southerners profound concern. Missouri was the first state entirely west of the Mississippi River to be carved out of the Louisiana Purchase, and the Missouri emancipation amendment might set a damaging precedent for all the rest of the area. Even more disquieting was another possibility. If Congress could abolish the "peculiar institution" in Missouri, might it not attempt to do likewise in the older states of the South? The wounds of the Constitutional Convention of 1787 were once more ripped open.

Burning moral questions also protruded, even though the main issue was political and economic balance. A small but growing group of antislavery agitators in the North seized the occasion to raise an outcry against the evils of slavery. They were determined that the plague of human bondage should not spread further into the untainted territories.

The Uneasy Missouri Compromise

Deadlock in Washington was at length broken in 1820 by the time-honored American solution of compromise—actually a bundle of three compromises. Courtly Henry Clay of Kentucky, gifted conciliator, played a leading role. Congress, despite abolitionist pleas, agreed to admit Missouri as a slave state. But at the same time, free-soil Maine, which until then had been a part of Massachusetts, was admitted as a separate state. The balance between North and South was thus kept at twelve states each and remained there for fifteen years. Although Missouri was permitted to retain slaves, all future bondage was prohibited in the remainder of the Louisiana Purchase north of the line of 36° 30'—the southern boundary of Missouri.

This horse-trading adjustment was politically evenhanded, though denounced by extremists on each side as a "dirty bargain." Both North and South yielded

something; both gained something. The South won the prize of Missouri as an unrestricted slave state. The North won the concession that Congress could forbid slavery in the remaining territories. More gratifying to many northerners was the fact that the immense area north of 36° 30', except Missouri, was forever closed to the blight of slavery. Yet the restriction on future slavery in the territories was not unduly offensive to the slaveowners, partly because the northern prairie land did not seem suited to slave labor. Even so, a majority of southern congressmen still voted against the compromise.

Neither North nor South was acutely displeased, although neither was completely happy. The Missouri Compromise lasted thirty-four years—a vital formative period in the life of the young Republic—and during that time it preserved the shaky compact of the states. Yet the embittered dispute over slavery heralded the future breakup of the Union. Ever after, the morality of the South's "peculiar institution" was an issue that could not be swept under the rug. The Missouri Compromise only ducked the question—it did not resolve it. Sooner or later, Thomas Jefferson predicted, it will "burst on us as a tornado."

The Missouri Compromise and the concurrent panic of 1819 should have dimmed the political star of President Monroe. Certainly both unhappy events had a dampening effect on the Era of Good Feelings. But smooth-spoken James Monroe was so popular, and the

The Missouri Compromise and Slavery, 1820–1821 Note the 36° 30' line. In the 1780s Thomas Jefferson had written of slavery in America, "Indeed I tremble for my country when I reflect that God is just; that his justice cannot sleep forever; that . . . the Almighty has no attribute which can take side with us in such a contest." Now, at the time of the Missouri Compromise, Jefferson feared that his worst forebodings were coming to pass. "I considered it at once," he said of the Missouri question, "as the knell of the Union."

While the debate over Missouri was raging, Thomas Jefferson (1743–1826) wrote to a correspondent,

"The Missouri question . . . is the most portentous one which ever yet threatened our Union. In the gloomiest moment of the revolutionary war I never had any apprehensions equal to what I feel from this source. . . . [The] question, like a firebell in the night, awakened and filled me with terror. . . . [With slavery] we have a wolf by the ears, and we can neither hold him nor safely let him go."

John Quincy Adams confided to his diary,

"I take it for granted that the present question is a mere preamble—a title-page to a great, tragic volume."

John Marshall (1755–1835) Born in a log cabin on the Virginia frontier, he attended law lectures for just a few weeks at the College of William and Mary—his only formal education. Yet Marshall would go on to prove himself a brilliant chief justice. One admiring lawyer wrote of him, "His black eyes . . . possess an irradiating spirit, which proclaims the imperial powers of the mind that sits enthroned therein."

Federalist opposition so weak, that in the presidential election of 1820, he received every electoral vote except one. Unanimity was an honor reserved for George Washington. Monroe, as it turned out, was the only president in American history to be reelected after a term in which a major financial panic began.

John Marshall and Judicial Nationalism

The upsurging nationalism of the post-Ghent years, despite the ominous setbacks concerning slavery, was further reflected and reinforced by the Supreme Court. The high tribunal continued to be dominated by the tall, thin, and aggressive Chief Justice John Marshall. One group of his decisions—perhaps the most famous—bolstered the power of the federal government at the expense of the states. A notable case in this category was *McCulloch* v. *Maryland* (1819). The suit involved an attempt by the state of Maryland to destroy a branch of the Bank of the United States by imposing a tax on its notes. John Marshall, speaking for the Court, declared the bank constitutional by invoking the Hamiltonian doctrine of implied powers (see p. 195). At the same time, he strengthened federal authority and slapped at state infringements when he denied the right of Maryland to tax the bank. With ringing emphasis, he affirmed "that the power to tax involves the power to destroy" and "that a power to create implies a power to preserve."

Marshall's ruling in this case gave the doctrine of "loose construction" its most famous formulation. The Constitution, he said, derived from the consent of the people and thus permitted the government to act for their benefit. He further argued that the Constitution was "intended to endure for ages to come and, consequently, to be adapted to the various crises of human affairs." Finally, he declared, "Let the end be legitimate, let it be within the scope of the Constitution, and all means which are appropriate, which are plainly adapted to that end, which are not prohibited, but consist with the letter and spirit of the Constitution, are constitutional."

Two years later (1821) the case of *Cohens* v. *Virginia* gave Marshall one of his greatest opportunities to defend the federal power. The Cohens, found guilty by the Virginia courts of illegally selling lottery tickets, appealed to the highest tribunal. Virginia "won," in the sense that the conviction of the Cohens was upheld. But in fact Virginia and all the individual states lost, because Marshall resoundingly asserted the right of the Supreme Court to review the decisions of the state supreme courts in all questions involving powers of the federal government. The states' rights proponents were aghast.

Hardly less significant was the celebrated "steamboat case," *Gibbons* v. *Ogden* (1824). The suit grew out of an attempt by the state of New York to grant to a private concern a monopoly of waterborne commerce between New York and New Jersey. Marshall sternly reminded the upstart state that the Constitution conferred on Congress alone the control of interstate commerce (see Art. I, Sec. VIII, para. 3). He thus struck with one hand another blow at states' rights, while upholding with the other the sovereign powers of the federal government. Interstate streams were cleared of this judicial snag; the departed spirit of Hamilton may well have applauded.

Daguerreotype of Daniel Webster (1782–1852), by Southworth and Hawes Premier orator and statesman, Webster served many years in both houses of Congress and also as secretary of state. Often regarded as presidential timber, he was somewhat handicapped by an overfondness for good food and drink and was frequently in financial difficulties. His devotion to the Union was inflexible. "One country, one constitution, and one destiny," he proclaimed in 1837.

Marshall presiding, decreed that the legislative grant was a contract (even though fraudulently secured) and that the Constitution forbids state laws "impairing" contracts (Art. I, Sec. X, para. 1). The decision was perhaps most noteworthy as further protecting property

Judicial Dikes Against Democratic Excesses

Another sheaf of Marshall's decisions bolstered judicial barriers against democratic or demagogic attacks on property rights.

The notorious case of *Fletcher* v. *Peck* (1810) arose when a Georgia legislature, swayed by bribery, granted 35 million acres in the Yazoo River country (Mississippi) to private speculators. The next legislature, yielding to an angry public outcry, canceled the crooked transaction. But the Supreme Court, with

> *When Supreme Court Chief Justice John Marshall died, a New York newspaper rejoiced:*
>
> "The chief place in the supreme tribunal of the Union will no longer be filled by a man whose political doctrines led him always . . . to strengthen government at the expense of the people."

rights against popular pressures. It was also one of the earliest clear assertions of the right of the Supreme Court to invalidate state laws conflicting with the federal Constitution.

A similar principle was upheld in the case of *Dartmouth College* v. *Woodward* (1819), perhaps the best remembered of Marshall's decisions. The college had been granted a charter by King George III in 1769, but the democratic New Hampshire state legislature had seen fit to change it. Dartmouth appealed the case, employing as counsel its most distinguished alumnus, Daniel Webster ('01). The "Godlike Daniel" reportedly pulled out all the stops of his tear-inducing eloquence when he declaimed, "It is, sir, as I have said, a small college. And yet there are those who love it."

Marshall needed no dramatics in the *Dartmouth* case. He put the states firmly in their place when he ruled that the original charter must stand. It was a contract—and the Constitution protected contracts against state encroachments. The *Dartmouth* decision had the fortunate effect of safeguarding business enterprise from domination by the state governments. But it had the unfortunate effect of creating a precedent that enabled chartered corporations, in later years, to escape the handcuffs of needed public control.

If John Marshall was a Molding Father of the Constitution, Daniel Webster was an Expounding Father. Time and again he left his seat in the Senate, stepped downstairs to the Supreme Court chamber (then located in the Capitol building), and there expounded his Federalistic and nationalistic philosophy before the supreme bench. The eminent chief justice, so Webster reported, approvingly drank in the familiar arguments as a baby sucks in its mother's milk. The two men dovetailed strikingly with each other. Webster's classic speeches in the Senate, challenging states' rights and nullification, were largely repetitious of the arguments that he had earlier presented before a sympathetic Supreme Court.

Marshall's decisions are felt even today. In this sense his nationalism was the most tenaciously enduring of the era. He buttressed the federal Union and helped to create a stable, nationally uniform environment for business. At the same time, Marshall checked the excesses of popularly elected state legislatures. In an age when white manhood suffrage was flowering and America was veering toward stronger popular control, Marshall almost single-handedly shaped the Constitution along conservative, centralizing lines that ran somewhat counter to the dominant spirit of the new country. Through him the conservative Hamiltonians partly triumphed from the tomb.

Sharing Oregon and Acquiring Florida

The robust nationalism of the years after the War of 1812 was likewise reflected in the shaping of foreign policy. To this end, the nationalistic President Monroe

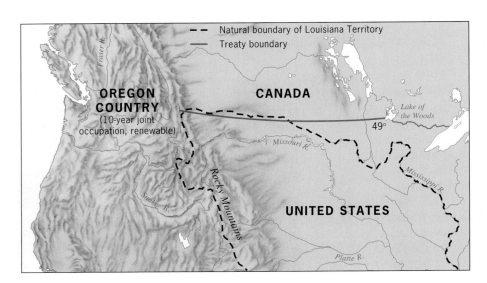

U.S.-British Boundary Settlement, 1818 Note that the United States gained considerable territory by securing a treaty boundary rather than the natural boundary of the Missouri River watershed. The line of 49° was extended westward to the Pacific Ocean under the Treaty of 1846 with Britain (see p. 380).

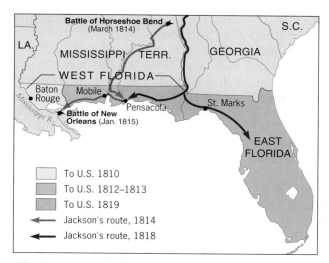

The Southeast, 1810–1819

Andrew Jackson (1767–1845), by Jean François de Vallée, 1815   This ivory miniature of Jackson as a major general in the U.S. Army was painted by a French artist living in New Orleans. It is one of the earliest surviving portraits of Jackson and depicts him at a time when he was known for his stern discipline, iron will ("Old Hickory"), and good luck.

teamed with his nationalistic secretary of state, John Quincy Adams, the cold and scholarly son of the frosty and bookish ex-president. The younger Adams, a statesman of the first rank, happily rose above the ingrown Federalist sectionalism of his native New England and proved to be one of the great secretaries of state.

To its credit, the Monroe administration negotiated the much-underrated Treaty of 1818 with Britain. This pact permitted Americans to share the coveted Newfoundland fisheries with their Canadian cousins. This multisided agreement also fixed the vague northern limits of Louisiana along the forty-ninth parallel from the Lake of the Woods (Minnesota) to the Rocky Mountains (see the map on p. 250). The treaty further provided for a ten-year joint occupation of the untamed Oregon Country, without a surrender of the rights or claims of either America or Britain.

To the south lay semitropical Spanish Florida, which many Americans believed geography and providence had destined to become part of the United States. Americans already claimed West Florida, where uninvited American settlers had torn down the hated Spanish flag in 1810. Congress ratified this grab in 1812, and during the War of 1812 against Spain's ally, Britain, a small American army seized the Mobile region. But the bulk of Florida remained, tauntingly, under Spanish rule.

An epidemic of revolutions now broke out in South America, notably in Argentina (1816), Venezuela (1817),

and Chile (1818). Americans instinctively cheered the birth of these sister republics, though the checkered histories of the Latin democracies soon provided grounds for disappointment. But the upheavals in the southern continent forced Spain to denude Florida of troops in a vain effort to squelch the rebels. General Andrew Jackson, idol of the West and scourge of the Indians, saw opportunity in the undefended swamplands. On the pretext that hostile Seminole Indians and fugitive slaves were using Florida as a refuge, Jackson secured a commission to enter Spanish territory, punish the Indians, and recapture the runaways. But he was to respect all posts under the Spanish flag.

Early in 1818 Jackson swept across the Florida border with all the fury of an avenging angel. He hanged two Indian chiefs without ceremony and, after hasty military trials, executed two British subjects for assisting the Indians. He also seized the two most important Spanish posts in the area, St. Marks and then Pensacola, where he deposed the Spanish governor, who was lucky enough to escape Jackson's jerking noose.

Jackson had clearly exceeded his instructions from Washington. Alarmed, President Monroe consulted his cabinet. Its members were for disavowing or disciplining the overzealous Jackson—all except the lone wolf John Quincy Adams, who refused to howl with the pack. An ardent patriot and nationalist, the flinty New Englander took the offensive and demanded huge concessions from Spain.

In the mislabeled Florida Purchase Treaty of 1819, Spain ceded Florida, as well as shadowy Spanish claims to Oregon, in exchange for America's abandonment of equally murky claims to Texas, soon to become part of independent Mexico. The hitherto vague western boundary of Louisiana was made to run zigzag along the Rockies to the forty-second parallel and then to turn due west to the Pacific, dividing Oregon from Spanish holdings.

The Menace of Monarchy in America

After the Napoleonic nightmare, the rethroned autocrats of Europe banded together in a kind of monarchical protective association. Determined to restore the good old days, they undertook to stamp out the democratic tendencies that had sprouted from soil they considered richly manured by the ideals of the French Revolution. The world must be made safe *from* democracy.

The crowned despots acted promptly. With complete ruthlessness they smothered the embers of rebellion in Italy (1821) and in Spain (1823). According to the European rumor factory, they were also gazing across the Atlantic. Russia, Austria, Prussia, and France, acting in partnership, would presumably send powerful fleets and armies to the revolted colonies of Spanish America and there restore the autocratic Spanish king to his ancestral domains.

Many Americans were alarmed. Naturally sympathetic to democratic revolutions, they had cheered when the Latin American republics rose from the ruins of monarchy. Americans feared that if the European powers intervened in the New World, the cause of republicanism would suffer irreparable harm. The physical security of the United States—the mother lode of democracy—would be endangered by the proximity of powerful and unfriendly forces.

The southward push of the Russian bear, from the chill region now known as Alaska, had already publicized the menace of monarchy to North America. In 1821 the tsar of Russia issued a decree extending Russian jurisdiction over one hundred miles of the open sea down to the line of 51°, an area that embraced most of the coast of present-day British Columbia. The energetic Russians had already established trading posts almost as far south as the entrance to San Francisco Bay, and the fear prevailed in the United States that they were planning to cut the Republic off from California, its prospective window on the Pacific.

Great Britain, still Ruler of the Seas, was now beginning to play a lone-hand role on the complicated international stage. In particular, it recoiled from joining hands with the continental European powers in crushing the newly won liberties of the Spanish Americans. These revolutionaries had thrown open their monopoly-bound ports to outside trade, and British shippers, as well as Americans, had found the profits sweet.

Accordingly, in August 1823 George Canning, the haughty British foreign secretary, approached the American minister in London with a startling proposition. Would the United States combine with Britain in a joint declaration renouncing any interest in acquiring Latin American territory, and specifically warning the European despots to keep their harsh hands off the Latin American republics? The American minister, lacking instructions, referred this fateful scheme to his superiors in Washington.

Monroe and His Doctrine

The tenacious nationalist, Secretary Adams, was hardheaded enough to be wary of Britons bearing gifts. Why should the lordly British, with the mightiest navy afloat, need America as an ally—an America that had neither naval nor military strength? Such a union, argued Adams, was undignified—like a tiny American "cockboat" sailing "in the wake of the British man-of-war."

Adams, ever alert, thought that he detected the joker in the Canning proposal. The British feared that the aggressive Yankees would one day seize Spanish territory in the Americas—perhaps Cuba—which would jeopardize Britain's possessions in the Caribbean. If Canning could seduce the United States into joining

Monroe first directed his verbal volley primarily at the lumbering Russian bear in the Northwest. He proclaimed, in effect, that the era of colonization in the Americas had ended and that henceforth the hunting season was permanently closed. What the great powers had they might keep, but neither they nor any other Old World governments could seize or otherwise acquire more.

At the same time, Monroe trumpeted a warning against foreign intervention. He was clearly concerned with regions to the south, where fears were felt for the fledgling Spanish American republics. Monroe bluntly directed the crowned heads of Europe to keep their hated monarchical systems out of this hemisphere. For its part the United States would not intervene in the war that the Greeks were then fighting against the Turks for their independence.

Monroe's Doctrine Appraised

The ermined monarchs of Europe were angered at Monroe's doctrine. Having resented the incendiary American experiment from the beginning, they were now deeply offended by Monroe's high-flown declaration—all the more so because of the gulf between America's pretentious pronouncements and its puny military strength. But though offended by the upstart Yankees, the European powers found their hands tied, and their frustration increased their annoyance. Even if they had worked out plans for invading the Americas, they would have been helpless before the booming broadsides of the British navy.

Monroe's solemn warning, when issued, made little splash in the newborn republics to the south. Anyone could see that Uncle Sam was only secondarily concerned about his neighbors, because he was primarily concerned about defending himself against future invasion. Only a relatively few educated Latin Americans knew of the message, and they generally recognized that the British navy—not the paper pronouncement of James Monroe—stood between them and a hostile Europe.

In truth, Monroe's message did not have much contemporary significance. Americans applauded it and then forgot it. Not until 1845 did President Polk revive it, and not until midcentury did it become an important national dogma.

Prince Klemens von Metternich (1773–1859), the Austrian statesman, regarded the United States as a renegade, revolutionary state. He reacted violently to the Monroe Doctrine:

"These United States of America . . . have astonished Europe by a new act of revolt. . . . [I]n fostering revolutions wherever they show themselves, in regretting those which have failed, in extending a helping hand to those which seem to prosper, they lend new strength to the apostles of sedition, and reanimate the courage of every conspirator. If this flood of evil doctrines and pernicious examples should extend over the whole of America, what would become of our religious and political institutions, of the moral force of our governments, and of that conservative system which has saved Europe from complete dissolution?"

---

with him in support of the territorial integrity of the New World, America's own hands would be morally tied.

A self-denying alliance with Britain would not only hamper American expansion, concluded Adams, but it was unnecessary. He suspected—correctly—that the European powers had not hatched any definite plans for invading the Americas. In any event the British navy would prevent the approach of hostile fleets because the South American markets had to be kept open at all costs for British merchants. It was presumably safe for Uncle Sam, behind the protective wooden petticoats of the British navy, to blow a defiant, nationalistic blast at all of Europe. The distresses of the Old World set the stage once again for an American diplomatic coup.

The Monroe Doctrine was born late in 1823, when the nationalistic Adams won the nationalistic Monroe over to his way of thinking. The president, in his regular annual message to Congress on December 2, 1823, incorporated a stern warning to the European powers. Its two basic features were (1) noncolonization and (2) nonintervention.

The West and Northwest, 1818–1824 The British Hudson's Bay Company moved to secure its claim to the Oregon Country in 1824, when it sent a heavily armed expedition led by Peter Skene Ogden into the Snake River country. In May 1825 Ogden's party descended the Bear River "and found it discharged into a large Lake of 100 miles in length"—one of the first documented sightings by white explorers of Great Salt Lake. (The mountain man Jim Bridger is usually credited with being the first white man to see the lake.)

Even before Monroe's stiff message, the tsar had decided to retreat. This he formally did in the Russo-American Treaty of 1824, which fixed his southernmost limits at the line of 54° 40'—the present southern tip of the Alaska panhandle.

The Monroe Doctrine might more accurately have been called the Self-Defense Doctrine. President Monroe was concerned basically with the security of his own country—not of Latin America. The United States has never willingly permitted a powerful foreign nation to secure a foothold near its strategic Caribbean vitals. Yet in the absence of the British navy or other allies, the strength of the Monroe Doctrine has never been greater than America's power to eject the trespasser. The doctrine, as often noted, was just as big as the nation's armed forces—and no bigger.

The Monroe Doctrine has had a long career of ups and downs. It was never law—domestic or international. It was not, technically speaking, a pledge or an agreement. It was merely a simple, personalized statement of the policy of President Monroe. What one president says, another may unsay. And Monroe's successors have ignored, revived, distorted, or expanded the original version, chiefly by adding interpretations. Like ivy on a tree, it has grown with America's growth.

But the Monroe Doctrine in 1823 was largely an expression of the post-1812 nationalism energizing the United States. Although directed at a specific menace in 1823, and hence a kind of period piece, the doctrine proved to be the most famous of all the long-lived offspring of that nationalism. While giving voice to a spirit of patriotism, it simultaneously deepened the illusion of isolationism. Many Americans falsely concluded, then and later, that the Republic was in fact insulated from European dangers simply because it wanted to be and because, in a nationalistic outburst, Monroe had publicly warned the Old World powers to stay away.

Chronology

1810 *Fletcher* v. *Peck* ruling asserts right of the Supreme Court to invalidate state laws deemed unconstitutional

1812 United States declares war on Britain
Madison reelected president

1812-1813 American invasions of Canada fail

1813 Battle of the Thames
Battle of Lake Erie

1814 Battle of Plattsburgh
British burn Washington
Battle of Horseshoe Bend
Treaty of Ghent signed ending War of 1812

1814-1815 Hartford Convention

1815 Battle of New Orleans

1816 Second Bank of the United States founded
Protectionist Tariff of 1816
Monroe elected president

1817 Madison vetoes Calhoun's Bonus Bill
Rush-Bagot agreement limits naval armament on Great Lakes

1818 Treaty of 1818 with Britain
Jackson invades Florida

1819 Panic of 1819
Spain cedes Florida to United States
McCulloch v. *Maryland*
Dartmouth College v. *Woodward*

1820 Missouri Compromise
Missouri and Maine admitted to Union
Land Act of 1820
Monroe reelected

1821 *Cohens* v. *Virginia*

1823 Secretary Adams proposes Monroe Doctrine

1824 Russo-American Treaty of 1824
Gibbons v. *Ogden*

1825 Erie Canal completed

For further reading, see the Appendix. For web resources, go to **http://college.hmco.com.**

13

The Rise of a Mass Democracy

1824–1840

IN THE FULL ENJOYMENT OF THE GIFTS OF HEAVEN AND THE FRUITS OF SUPERIOR INDUSTRY, ECONOMY, AND VIRTUE, EVERY MAN IS EQUALLY ENTITLED TO PROTECTION BY LAW; BUT WHEN THE LAWS UNDERTAKE TO ADD TO THOSE NATURAL AND JUST ADVANTAGES ARTIFICIAL DISTINCTIONS . . . AND EXCLUSIVE PRIVILEGES . . . THE HUMBLE MEMBERS OF SOCIETY—THE FARMERS, MECHANICS, AND LABORERS . . . HAVE A RIGHT TO COMPLAIN OF THE INJUSTICE OF THEIR GOVERNMENT.

ANDREW JACKSON, 1832

The so-called Era of Good Feelings was never entirely tranquil, but even the illusion of national consensus was shattered by the panic of 1819 and the Missouri Compromise of 1820. Economic distress and the slavery issue raised the political stakes in the 1820s and 1830s. Vigorous political conflict, once feared, came to be celebrated as necessary for the health of democracy. New political parties emerged. New styles of campaigning took hold. A new chapter opened in the history of American politics. The political landscape of 1824 was similar, in its broad outlines, to that of 1796. By 1840 it would be almost unrecognizable.

The deference, apathy, and virtually nonexistent party organizations of the Era of Good Feelings yielded to the boisterous democracy, frenzied vitality, and strong political parties of the Jacksonian era. The old suspicion of political parties as illegitimate disrupters of society's natural harmony gave way to an acceptance of the sometimes wild contentiousness of political life.

In 1828 an energetic new party, the Democrats, captured the White House. By the 1830s the Democrats faced an equally vigorous opposition party in the form of the Whigs. This two-party system institutionalized divisions that had vexed the Revolutionary generation and came to constitute an important part of the nation's checks and balances on political power.

New forms of politicking emerged in this era, as candidates used banners, badges, parades, barbecues, free drinks, and baby kissing to "get out the vote." Voter turnout rose dramatically. Only about one-quarter of eligible voters cast a ballot in the presidential election of 1824, but that proportion doubled in 1828, and in the election of 1840 it reached 78 percent. Everywhere people flexed their political muscles.

The "Corrupt Bargain" of 1824

The last of the old-style elections was marked by the controversial "corrupt bargain" of 1824. The woods were full of presidential timber as James Monroe, last of

Canvassing for a Vote, by George Caleb Bingham, 1852 This painting shows the "new politics" of the Jacksonian era. Politicians now had to take their message to the common man.

the Virginia dynasty, completed his second term. Four candidates towered above the others: John Quincy Adams of Massachusetts, highly intelligent, experienced, and aloof; Henry Clay of Kentucky, the gamy and gallant "Harry of the West"; William H. Crawford of Georgia, an able though ailing giant of a man; and Andrew Jackson of Tennessee, the gaunt and gusty hero of New Orleans.

All four rivals professed to be "Republicans." Well-organized parties had not yet emerged; their identities were so fuzzy, in fact, that John C. Calhoun appeared as the vice-presidential candidate on both the Adams and the Jackson tickets.

The results of the noisy campaign were interesting but confusing. Jackson, the war hero, clearly had the strongest personal appeal, especially in the West, where his campaign against the forces of corruption and privilege in government resonated deeply. He polled almost as many popular votes as his next two rivals combined, but he failed to win a majority of the electoral vote (see the table on p. 258). In such a deadlock, the House of Representatives, as directed by the Twelfth Amendment (see the Appendix), must choose among the top three candidates. Clay was thus eliminated, yet as Speaker of the House, he presided over the very chamber that had to pick the winner.

The influential Clay was in a position to throw the election to the candidate of his choice. He reached his decision by the process of elimination. Crawford, recently felled by a paralytic stroke, was out of the picture. Clay hated the "military chieftain" Jackson, his archrival for the allegiance of the West. Jackson, in turn, bitterly resented Clay's public denunciation of his Florida foray in 1818. The only candidate left was the puritanical Adams, with whom Clay—a free-living gambler and duelist—had never established cordial personal relations. But the two men had much in common politically: both were fervid nationalists and advocates of the American System. Shortly before the final balloting in the House, Clay met privately with Adams and assured him of his support.

Decision day came early in 1825. The House of Representatives met amid tense excitement, with sick members being carried in on stretchers. On the first ballot, thanks largely to Clay's behind-the-scenes influence, Adams was elected president. A few days later, the victor announced that Henry Clay would be the new secretary of state.

The office of secretary of state was the prize plum then, even more so than today. Three of the four preceding secretaries had reached the presidency, and

Election of 1824

Candidates	Electoral Vote	Popular Vote	Popular Percentage
Jackson	99	153,544	42.16%
Adams	84	108,740	31.89
Crawford	41	46,618	12.95
Clay	37	47,136	12.99

the high cabinet office was regarded as an almost certain pathway to the White House. According to Jackson's supporters, Adams had bribed Clay with the position, making himself, the people's second choice, the victor over Jackson, the people's first choice.

Masses of angry Jacksonians, most of them common folk, raised a roar of protest against this "corrupt bargain." The clamor continued for nearly four years. Jackson condemned Clay as the "Judas of the West," and John Randolph of Virginia publicly assailed the alliance between "the Puritan [Adams] and the black-leg [Clay]," who, he added, "shines and stinks like rotten mackerel by moonlight." Clay, outraged, challenged Randolph to a duel, though poor marksmanship and shaky nerves rendered the outcome bloodless.

No positive evidence has yet been unearthed to prove that Adams and Clay entered into a formal bargain. Clay was a natural choice for secretary of state,

and Adams was both scrupulously honest and not given to patronage. Even if a bargain had been struck, it was not necessarily corrupt. Deals of this nature have long been the stock-in-trade of politicians. But the outcry over Adams's election showed that change was in the wind. What had once been common practice was now condemned as furtive, elitist, and subversive of democracy. The next president would not be chosen behind closed doors.

A Yankee Misfit in the White House

John Quincy Adams was a chip off the old family glacier. Short, thickset, and billiard-bald, he was even more frigidly austere than his presidential father, John Adams. Shunning people, he often went for early-morning

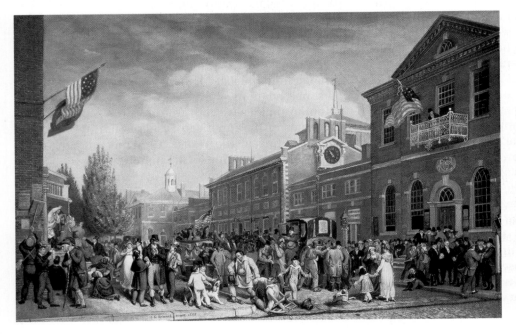

Election Day in Philadelphia, by John Lewis Krimmel, 1815 The German immigrant Krimmel recorded as early as 1815 the growing popular interest in elections that would culminate in Jacksonian democracy a decade later. Although politics was serious business, it also provided the occasion for much socializing and merriment. Even disenfranchised free blacks, women, and children turned out for the festivities on election day.

swims, sometimes stark naked, in the then-pure Potomac River. Essentially a closeted thinker rather than a politician, he was irritable, sarcastic, and tactless. Yet few individuals have ever come to the presidency with a more brilliant record in statecraft, especially in foreign affairs. He ranks as one of the most successful secretaries of state, yet one of the least successful presidents.

A man of scrupulous honor, Adams entered upon his four-year "sentence" in the White House smarting under charges of "bargain," "corruption," and "usurpation." Fewer than one-third of the voters had voted for him. As the first "minority president," he would have found it difficult to win popular support even under the most favorable conditions. He did not possess many of the usual arts of the politician and scorned those who did. He had achieved high office by commanding respect rather than by courting popularity. In an earlier era, an aloof John Adams had won the votes of propertied men by sheer ability. But with the dawning age of backslapping and baby-kissing democracy, his cold-fish son could hardly hope for success at the polls.

While Adams's enemies accused him of striking a corrupt bargain, his political allies wished that he would strike a few more. Whether through high-mindedness or political ineptitude, Adams resolutely declined to oust efficient officeholders in order to create vacancies for his supporters. During his entire administration, he removed only twelve public servants from the federal payroll. Such stubbornness caused countless Adams followers to throw up their hands in despair. If the president would not reward party workers with political plums, why should they labor to keep him in office?

Adams's nationalistic views gave him further woes. Much of the nation was turning away from post-Ghent nationalism and toward states' rights and sectionalism. But Adams swam against the tide. Confirmed nationalist that he was, Adams, in his first annual message, urged upon Congress the construction of roads and canals. He renewed George Washington's proposal for a national university and went so far as to advocate federal support for an astronomical observatory.

The public reaction to these proposals was prompt and unfavorable. To many workaday Americans grubbing out stumps, astronomical observatories seemed like a scandalous waste of public funds. The South in particular bristled. If the federal government should take on such heavy financial burdens, it would have to continue the hated tariff duties. Worse, if it could meddle in local concerns like education and roads, it might even try to lay its hand on the "peculiar institution" of black slavery.

President John Quincy Adams (1767–1848), Daguerreotype by Phillip Haas, 1843 Adams wrote in his diary in June 1819, nearly six years before becoming president, "I am a man of reserved, cold, austere, and forbidding manners: my political adversaries say, a gloomy misanthropist, and my personal enemies an unsocial savage."

Adams's land policy likewise antagonized the westerners. They clamored for wide-open expansion and resented the president's well-meaning attempts to curb feverish speculation in the public domain. The fate of the Cherokee Indians, threatened with eviction from their holdings in Georgia, brought additional bitterness. White Georgians wanted the Cherokees out. The ruggedly honest Adams attempted to deal fairly with the Indians. The Georgia governor, by threatening to resort to arms, successfully resisted the efforts of the Washington government to interpose federal authority on behalf of the Cherokees. Another fateful chapter was thus written in the nullification of the national will—and another nail was driven in Adams's political coffin.

Going "Whole Hog" for Jackson in 1828

The presidential campaign for Andrew Jackson had started early—on February 9, 1825, the day of John Quincy Adams's controversial election by the House—and it continued noisily for nearly four years.

Even before the election of 1828, the temporarily united Republicans of the Era of Good Feelings had split into two camps. One was the National Republicans, with Adams as their standard-bearer. The other was the Democratic-Republicans, with the fiery Jackson heading their ticket. Rallying cries of the Jackson zealots were "Bargain and Corruption," "Huzza for Jackson," and "All Hail Old Hickory." Jacksonites planted hickory poles for their hickory-tough hero; Adamsites adopted the oak as the symbol of their oakenly independent candidate.

Jackson's followers presented their hero as a rough-hewn frontiersman and a stalwart champion of the common man. They denounced Adams as a corrupt aristocrat and argued that the will of the people had been thwarted in 1825 by the backstairs "bargain" of Adams and Clay. The only way to right the wrong was to seat Jackson, who would then bring about "reform" by sweeping out the "dishonest" Adams gang.

Much of this talk was political hyperbole. Jackson was no frontier farmer but a wealthy planter. He had been born in a log cabin but now lived in a luxurious manor off the labor of his many slaves. And Adams, though perhaps an aristocrat, was far from corrupt. If anything, his uncompromising morals were too elevated for the job.

Mudslinging reached new lows in 1828, and the electorate developed a taste for bare-knuckle politics. Adams would not stoop to gutter tactics, but many of his backers were less squeamish. They described Jackson's mother as a prostitute and his wife as an adulteress; they printed black-bordered handbills shaped like coffins, recounting his numerous duels and brawls and trumpeting his hanging of six mutinous militiamen.

Jackson men also hit below the belt. President Adams had purchased, with his own money and for his own use, a billiard table and a set of chessmen. In the mouths of rabid Jacksonites, these items became "gaming tables" and "gambling furniture" for the "presidential palace." Criticism was also directed at the large sums Adams had received over the years in federal salaries, well earned though they had been. He was even accused of having procured a servant girl for the lust of the Russian tsar—in short, of having served as a pimp.

One anti-Jackson newspaper declared,

"General Jackson's mother was a Common Prostitute, brought to this country by the British soldiers! She afterwards married a MULATTO man with whom she had several children, of which number GENERAL JACKSON is one."

On voting day the electorate split on largely sectional lines. Jackson's strongest support came from the West and South. The middle states and the Old Northwest were divided, while Adams won the backing of his own New England and the propertied "better elements" of the Northeast. But when the popular vote was

Rachel Jackson A devoted wife who did not live to become first lady, she died a month after the election of 1828. Andrew Jackson was convinced that his enemies' vicious accusations that she was a bigamist and an adulteress had killed her. The more complicated truth was that Andrew Jackson had married Rachel Robards confident that her divorce had been granted. Two years later, when they discovered to their dismay that it had not been, they made haste to correct the marital miscue.

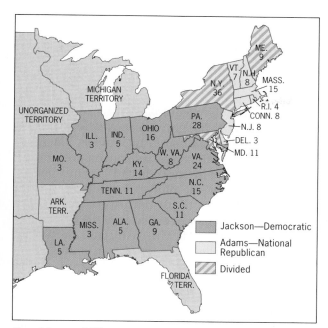

Presidential Election of 1828 (with electoral vote by state) Jackson swept the South and West, whereas Adams retained the old Federalist stronghold of the Northeast. Yet Jackson's inroads in the Northeast were decisive. He won twenty of New York's electoral votes and all twenty-eight of Pennsylvania's. If those votes had gone the other way, Adams would have been victorious—by a margin of one vote.

converted to electoral votes, General Jackson's triumph could not be denied. Old Hickory had trounced Adams by an electoral count of 178 to 83. Although a considerable part of Jackson's support was lined up by machine politicians in eastern cities, particularly in New York and Pennsylvania, the political center of gravity clearly had shifted away from the conservative eastern seaboard toward the emerging states across the mountains.

"Old Hickory" as President

The new president cut a striking figure—tall, lean, with bushy iron-gray hair brushed high above a prominent forehead, craggy eyebrows, and blue eyes. His irritability and emaciated condition resulted in part from long-term bouts with dysentery, malaria, tuberculosis, and lead poisoning from two bullets that he carried in his body from near-fatal duels. His autobiography was written in his lined face.

Jackson's upbringing had its shortcomings. Born in the Carolinas and early orphaned, "Mischievous Andy" grew up without parental restraints. As a youth he displayed much more interest in brawling and cockfighting than in his scanty opportunities for reading and spelling. Although he eventually learned to express himself in writing with vigor and clarity, his grammar was always rough-hewn and his spelling original, like that of many contemporaries. He sometimes misspelled a word two different ways in the same letter.

The youthful Carolinian shrewdly moved "up West" to Tennessee, where fighting was prized above writing. There—through native intelligence, force of personality, and powers of leadership—he became a judge and a member of Congress. Afflicted with a violent temper, he early became involved in a number of duels, stabbings, and bloody frays. His passions were so profound that on occasion he would choke into silence when he tried to speak.

The first president from the West, the first nominated at a formal party convention (in 1832), and only the second without a college education (Washington was the first), Jackson was unique. His university was adversity. He had risen from the masses, but he was not one of them, except insofar as he shared many of their prejudices. Essentially a frontier aristocrat, he owned many slaves, cultivated broad acres, and lived in one of the finest mansions in America—the Hermitage, near Nashville, Tennessee. More westerner than easterner, more country gentleman than common clay, more courtly than crude, he was hard to fit into a neat category.

Jackson's inauguration seemed to symbolize the ascendancy of the masses. "Hickoryites" poured into Washington from far away, sleeping on hotel floors and in hallways. They were curious to see their hero take

> *In 1824 Thomas Jefferson (1743–1826) said of Jackson,*
>
> "When I was President of the Senate he was a Senator; and he could never speak on account of the rashness of his feelings. I have seen him attempt it repeatedly, and as often choke with rage. His passions are no doubt cooler now . . . but he is a dangerous man."

office and perhaps hoped to pick up a well-paying office for themselves. Nobodies mingled with notables as the White House, for the first time, was thrown open to the multitude. A milling crowd of rubbernecking clerks and shopkeepers, hobnailed artisans, and grimy laborers surged in, allegedly wrecking the china and furniture and threatening the "people's champion" with cracked ribs. Jackson was hastily spirited through a side door, and the White House miraculously emptied itself when the word was passed that huge bowls of well-spiked punch had been placed on the lawns. Such was "the inaugural brawl."

To conservatives this orgy seemed like the end of the world. "King Mob" reigned triumphant as Jacksonian vulgarity replaced Jeffersonian simplicity. Fainthearted traditionalists shuddered, drew their blinds, and recalled with trepidation the opening scenes of the French Revolution.

The Spoils System

Once in power, the Democrats, famously suspicious of the federal government, demonstrated that they were not above striking some bargains of their own. Under Jackson the spoils system—that is, rewarding political supporters with public office—was introduced into the federal government on a large scale. The basic idea was as old as politics. Its name came later from Senator William Marcy's classic remark in 1832, "To the victor belong the spoils of the enemy." The system had already secured a firm hold in New York and Pennsylvania, where well-greased machines ladled out the "gravy" of office.

Jackson defended the spoils system on democratic grounds. "Every man is as good as his neighbor," he declared—perhaps "equally better." As this was believed to be so, and as the routine of office was thought to be simple enough for any upstanding American to learn quickly, why encourage the development of an aristocratic, bureaucratic, officeholding class? Better to bring in new blood, he argued; each generation deserved its turn at the public trough.

Washington was due, it is true, for a housecleaning. No party overturn had occurred since the defeat of the Federalists in 1800, and even that had not produced wholesale evictions. A few officeholders, their commissions signed by President Washington, were lingering on into their eighties, drawing breath and salary but doing little else. But the spoils system was less about finding new blood than about rewarding old cronies. "Throw their rascals out and put our rascals in," the Democrats were essentially saying. The questions asked of each appointee were not "What can he do for the country?" but "What has he done for the party?" or "Is he loyal to Jackson?"

Scandal inevitably accompanied the new system. Men who had openly bought their posts by campaign contributions were appointed to high office. Illiterates, incompetents, and plain crooks were given positions of public trust; men on the make lusted for the spoils—rather than the toils—of office. Samuel Swartwout, despite ample warnings of his untrustworthiness, was awarded the lucrative post of collector of the customs of the port of New York. Nearly nine years later, he "Swartwouted out" for England, leaving his accounts more than a million dollars short—the first person to steal a million from the Washington government.

But despite its undeniable abuse, the spoils system was an important element of the emerging two-party order, cementing as it did loyalty to party over competing claims based on economic class or geographic region. The promise of patronage provided a compelling reason for Americans to pick a party and stick with it through thick and thin.

The Tricky "Tariff of Abominations"

The touchy tariff issue had been one of John Quincy Adams's biggest headaches. Now Andrew Jackson felt his predecessor's pain. Tariffs protected American industry against competition from European manufactured goods, but they also drove up prices for all Americans and invited retaliatory tariffs on American agricultural exports abroad. The middle states had long been supporters of protectionist tariffs. In the 1820s influential New Englanders like Daniel Webster gave up their traditional defense of free trade to support higher tariffs, too. The wool and textile industries were booming, and forward-thinking Yankees came to believe that their future prosperity would flow from the factory rather than from the sea.

In 1824 Congress had increased the general tariff significantly, but wool manufacturers bleated for still-higher barriers. Ardent Jacksonites now played a cynical political game. They promoted a high-tariff bill, expecting to be defeated, which would give a black eye to President Adams. To their surprise, the tariff passed in 1828, and Andrew Jackson inherited the political hot potato.

tariff provided a convenient and plausible scapegoat. Southerners sold their cotton and other farm produce in a world market completely unprotected by tariffs but were forced to buy their manufactured goods in an American market heavily protected by tariffs. Protectionism protected Yankee and middle-state manufacturers. The farmers and planters of the Old South felt they were stuck with the bill.

But much deeper issues underlay the southern outcry—in particular, a growing anxiety about possible federal interference with the institution of slavery. The congressional debate on the Missouri Compromise had

South Carolina Belle Sewing Palmetto Cockade The "Tariff of Abominations" of 1828 drove many people in South Carolina—the "Palmetto State"—to flirt with secession. Anti-tariff protesters wore palmetto blossoms, real or sewn from fabric, to symbolize their defiance of the federal law.

Southerners, as heavy consumers of manufactured goods with little manufacturing industry of their own, were hostile to tariffs. They were particularly shocked by what they regarded as the outrageous rates of the Tariff of 1828. Hotheads branded it the "Black Tariff" or the "Tariff of Abominations." Several southern states adopted formal protests. In South Carolina flags were lowered to half-mast. "Let the *New* England beware how she imitates the *Old*," cried one eloquent South Carolinian.

Why did the South react so angrily against the tariff? Southerners believed, not illogically, that the "Yankee tariff" discriminated against them. The bustling Northeast was experiencing a boom in manufacturing, the developing West was prospering from rising property values and a multiplying population, and the energetic Southwest was expanding into virgin cotton lands. But the Old South was falling on hard times, and the

John C. Calhoun (1782–1850), attributed to Charles Bird King. c. 1818–1825 Calhoun was a South Carolinian, educated at Yale. Beginning as a strong nationalist and Unionist, he reversed himself and became the ablest of the sectionalists and disunionists in defense of the South and slavery. As a foremost nullifier, he died trying to reconcile strong states' rights with a strong Union. In his last years, he advocated a Siamese-twin presidency, probably unworkable, with one president for the North and one for the South. His former plantation home is now the site of Clemson University.

kindled those anxieties, and they were further fanned by an aborted slave rebellion in Charleston in 1822, led by a free black named Denmark Vesey. The South Carolinians, still closely tied to the British West Indies, also knew full well that their slaveowning West Indian cousins were feeling the mounting pressure of British abolitionism on the London government. Abolitionism in America might similarly use the power of the government in Washington to suppress slavery in the South. If so, now was the time, and the tariff was the issue, to take a strong stand on principle against all federal encroachments on states' rights.

South Carolinians took the lead in protesting against the "Tariff of Abominations." Their legislature went so far as to publish in 1828, though without formal endorsement, a pamphlet known as *The South Carolina Exposition.* It had been secretly written by John C. Calhoun, one of the few topflight political theorists ever produced by America. (As vice president, he was forced to conceal his authorship.) *The Exposition* denounced the recent tariff as unjust and unconstitutional. Going a stride beyond the Kentucky and Virginia resolutions of 1798, it bluntly and explicitly proposed that the states should nullify the tariff—that is, they should declare it null and void within their borders.

John C. Calhoun (1782–1850), leader of South Carolina's offensive to nullify the Tariff of 1832, saw nullification as a way of preserving the Union while preventing secession of the southern states. In his mind he was still a Unionist, even if also a southern sectionalist:

"I never use the word 'nation' in speaking of the United States. I always use the word 'union' or 'confederacy.' We are not a nation, but a union, a confederacy of equal and sovereign states."

During the crisis of 1832, some of his South Carolina compatriots had different ideas. Medals were struck off in honor of Calhoun, bearing the words, "First President of the Southern Confederacy."

"Nullies" in South Carolina

The stage was set for a showdown. Through Jackson's first term, the nullifiers—"nullies," they were called—tried strenuously to muster the necessary two-thirds vote for nullification in the South Carolina legislature. But they were blocked by a determined minority of Unionists, scorned as "submission men." Back in Washington, Congress tipped the balance by passing the new Tariff of 1832. Though it pared away the worst "abominations" of 1828, it was still frankly protective and fell far short of meeting southern demands. Worse yet, to many southerners it had a disquieting air of permanence.

South Carolina was now nerved for drastic action. Nullifiers and Unionists clashed head-on in the state election of 1832. "Nullies," defiantly wearing palmetto ribbons on their hats to mark their loyalty to the "Palmetto State," emerged with more than a two-thirds majority. The state legislature then called for a special convention. Several weeks later the delegates, meeting in Columbia, solemnly declared the existing tariff to be null and void within South Carolina. As a further act of defiance, the convention threatened to take South Carolina out of the Union if Washington attempted to collect the customs duties by force.

Such tactics might have intimidated John Quincy Adams, but Andrew Jackson was the wrong president to stare down. The cantankerous general was not a diehard supporter of the tariff, but he would not permit defiance or disunion. His military instincts rasped, Jackson privately threatened to invade the state and have the nullifiers hanged. In public he was only slightly less pugnacious. He dispatched naval and military reinforcements to the Palmetto State, while quietly preparing a sizable army. He also issued a ringing proclamation against nullification, to which the governor of South Carolina, former senator Robert Y. Hayne, responded with a counterproclamation. The lines were drawn. If civil war were to be avoided, one side would have to surrender, or both would have to compromise.

Conciliatory Henry Clay of Kentucky, now in the Senate, stepped forward. An unforgiving foe of Jackson, he had no desire to see his old enemy win new laurels by crushing the Carolinians and returning with the scalp of Calhoun dangling from his belt. Although himself a supporter of tariffs, the gallant Kentuckian therefore threw his influence behind a compromise bill that would gradually reduce the Tariff of 1832 by about 10 percent over a period of eight years. By 1842 the rates would be back at the mildly protective level of 1816.*

The compromise Tariff of 1833 finally squeezed through Congress. Debate was bitter, with most of the opposition naturally coming from protectionist New England and the middle states. Calhoun and the South favored the compromise, so it was evident that Jackson would not have to use firearms and rope. But at the same time, and partly as a face-saving device, Congress passed the Force Bill, known among Carolinians as the "Bloody Bill." It authorized the president to use the army and navy, if necessary, to collect federal tariff duties.

South Carolinians welcomed this opportunity to extricate themselves from a dangerously tight corner without loss of face. To the consternation of the Calhounites, no other southern states had sprung to their support, though Georgia and Virginia toyed with the idea. Moreover, an appreciable Unionist minority within South Carolina was gathering guns, organizing militia, and nailing Stars and Stripes to flagpoles. Faced with civil war within and invasion from without, the Columbia convention met again and repealed the ordinance of nullification. As a final but futile gesture of fist-shaking, it nullified the unnecessary Force Bill and adjourned.

Neither Jackson nor the "nullies" won a clear-cut victory in 1833. Clay was the true hero of the hour, hailed in Charleston and Boston alike for saving the country. Armed conflict had been avoided, but the fundamental issues had not been resolved. When next the "nullies" and the Union clashed, compromise would prove more elusive.

The Trail of Tears

Jackson's Democrats were committed to western expansion, but such expansion necessarily meant confrontation with the current inhabitants of the land. More than 125,000 Native Americans lived in the forests and prairies east of the Mississippi in the 1820s. Federal policy toward them varied. Beginning in the 1790s, the Washington government ostensibly recognized the tribes as separate nations and agreed to acquire land from them only through formal treaties. The Indians were shrewd and stubborn negotiators, but this availed them little when Americans routinely violated their own

covenants, erasing and redrawing treaty line after treaty line on their maps as white settlement pushed west.

Many white Americans felt respect and admiration for the Indians and believed that the Native Americans could be assimilated into white society. Much energy therefore was devoted to "civilizing" and Christianizing the Indians. The Society for Propagating the Gospel Among Indians was founded in 1787, and many denominations sent missionaries into Indian villages. In 1793 Congress appropriated $20,000 for the promotion of literacy and agricultural and vocational instruction among the Indians.

Although many tribes violently resisted white encroachment, others followed the path of accommodation. The Cherokees of Georgia made especially remarkable efforts to learn the ways of the whites. They gradually abandoned their seminomadic life and adopted a system of settled agriculture and a notion of private property. Missionaries opened schools among the Cherokees, and the Indian Sequoyah devised a Cherokee alphabet. In 1808 the Cherokee National Council legislated a written legal code, and in 1827 it adopted a written constitution that provided for executive, legislative, and judicial branches of government. Some Cherokees became prosperous cotton planters and even turned to slaveholding. Nearly thirteen hundred black slaves toiled for their Native American masters in the Cherokee nation in the 1820s. For these efforts the Cherokees—along with the Creeks, Choctaws, Chickasaws, and Seminoles—were numbered by whites among the "Five Civilized Tribes."

All this embrace of "civilization" apparently was not good enough for whites. In 1828 the Georgia legislature declared the Cherokee tribal council illegal and asserted its own jurisdiction over Indian affairs and Indian lands. The Cherokees appealed this move to the Supreme Court, which thrice upheld the rights of the Indians. But President Jackson, who clearly wanted to open Indian lands to white settlement, refused to recognize the Court's decisions. In a callous jibe at the Indians' defender, Jackson allegedly snapped, "John Marshall has made his decision; now let him enforce it."†

---

†One hundred sixty years later, in 1992, the state of Georgia formally pardoned the two white missionaries, Samuel Austin Worcester and Elihu Butler, who had figured prominently in the decision Jackson condemned. They had been convicted of living on Cherokee lands without a license from the state of Georgia. They served sixteen months at hard labor on a chain gang and later accompanied the Cherokees on the "Trail of Tears" to Oklahoma.

---

*For the history of tariff rates, see the Appendix.

Feeling some obligation to rescue "this much injured race," Jackson proposed a bodily removal of the remaining eastern tribes—chiefly Cherokees, Creeks, Choctaws, Chickasaws, and Seminoles—beyond the Mississippi. Emigration was supposed to be voluntary because it would be "cruel and unjust to compel the aborigines to abandon the graves of their fathers." Jackson evidently consoled himself with the belief that the Indians could preserve their native cultures in the wide-open West.

Jackson's policy led to the forced uprooting of more than 100,000 Indians. In 1830 Congress passed the Indian Removal Act, providing for the transplanting of all Indian tribes then resident east of the Mississippi. Ironically, the heaviest blows fell on the Five Civilized Tribes. In the ensuing decade, countless Indians died on forced marches to the newly established Indian Territory, where they were to be "permanently" free of white encroachments. The Bureau of Indian Affairs was established in 1836 to administer relations with America's original inhabitants. But as the land-hungry "palefaces"

> *Alexis de Tocqueville (1805–1859), an astute observer of the United States, criticized the misguided logic of white Americans' attitudes toward Indians in a letter to his mother:*
>
> "They [Americans] have discovered that a square mile could support ten times more civilized men than savage men, thus reason indicated that wherever civilized men could settle, it was necessary that the savages cede the place."

pushed west faster than anticipated, the government's guarantees went up in smoke. The "permanent" frontier lasted about fifteen years.

Suspicious of white intentions from the start, Sauk and Fox braves from Illinois and Wisconsin, ably led by

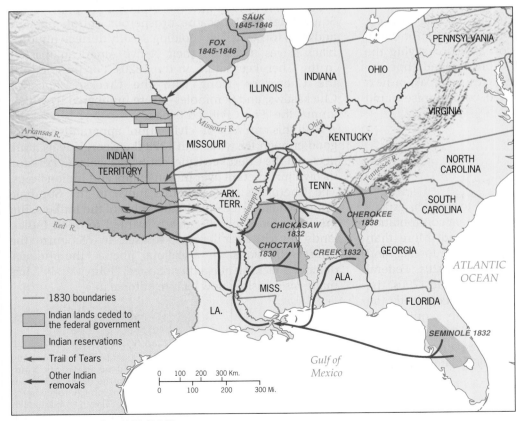

Indian Removals, 1830–1846

In 1829 Andrew Jackson (1767–1845) reflected on the condition of the Indians and on Indian-white relations:

"Our conduct toward these people is deeply interesting to our national character. . . . Our ancestors found them the uncontrolled possessors of these vast regions. By persuasion and force they have been made to retire from river to river and from mountain to mountain, until some of the tribes have become extinct and others have left but remnants to preserve for awhile their once terrible names. Surrounded by the whites with their arts of civilization, which by destroying the resources of the savage doom him to weakness and decay, the fate of the Mohegan, the Narragansett, and the Delaware is fast overtaking the Choctaw, the Cherokee, and the Creek. That this fate surely awaits them if they remain within the limits of the States does not admit of a doubt. Humanity and national honor demand that every effort should be made to avert such a calamity."

One survivor of the Indians' forced march in 1838–1839 on the "Trail of Tears" to Indian Territory, farther west, remembered,

"One each day, and all are gone. Looks like maybe all dead before we get to new Indian country, but always we keep marching on. Women cry and make sad wails. Children cry, and many men cry, and all look sad when friends die, but they say nothing and just put heads down and keep on toward west. . . . She [his mother] speak no more; we bury her and go on."

the American field commander treacherously seized their leader, Osceola, under a flag of truce. The war dragged on for five more years, but the Seminoles were doomed. Some fled deeper into the Everglades, where their descendants now live, but about four-fifths of them were moved to present-day Oklahoma, where several thousand of the tribe survive.

Black Hawk, resisted eviction. They were bloodily crushed in 1832 by regular troops, including Lieutenant Jefferson Davis of Mississippi, and by volunteers, including Captain Abraham Lincoln of Illinois.

In Florida the Seminole Indians, joined by runaway black slaves, retreated to the swampy Everglades. For seven years (1835–1842), they waged a bitter guerrilla war that took the lives of some fifteen hundred soldiers. The spirit of the Seminoles was broken in 1837, when

Black Hawk and His Son Whirling Thunder, by John Wesley Jarvis, 1833 Chief Black Hawk and his son are depicted here in captivity. After their surrender in the Black Hawk War of 1832, they were put on public display throughout the United States.

The "Trail of Tears" In the fall and winter of 1838–1839, the U.S. Army forcibly removed about 15,000 Cherokees, some of them in manacles, from their ancestral homelands in the southeastern United States and marched them to Indian Territory (present-day Oklahoma). Freezing weather and inadequate food supplies led to unspeakable suffering. The escorting troops refused to slow the forced march so that the ill could recover, and some 4,000 Cherokees died on the 116-day journey.

The Bank War

President Jackson did not hate all banks and all businesses, but he distrusted monopolistic banking and overbig businesses, as did his followers. A man of virulent dislikes, he came to share the prejudices of his own West against the "moneyed monster" known as the Bank of the United States.

What made the bank a monster in Jackson's eyes? The national government minted gold and silver coins in the mid-nineteenth century but did not issue paper money. Paper notes were printed by private banks. Their value fluctuated with the health of the bank and the amount of money printed, giving private bankers considerable power over the nation's economy.

No bank in America had more power than the Bank of the United States. In many ways the bank acted like a branch of government. It was the principal depository for the funds of the Washington government and controlled much of the nation's gold and silver. Its notes, unlike those of many smaller banks, were stable in value. A source of credit and stability, the bank was an important and useful part of the nation's expanding economy.

But the Bank of the United States was a private institution, accountable not to the people, but to its elite circle of moneyed investors. Its president, the brilliant but arrogant Nicholas Biddle, held an immense—and to many unconstitutional—amount of power over the

nation's financial affairs. Enemies of the bank dubbed him "Czar Nicolas I" and called the bank a "hydra of corruption," a serpent that grew new heads whenever old ones were cut off.

To some the bank's very existence seemed to sin against the egalitarian credo of American democracy. The conviction formed the deepest source of Jackson's opposition. The bank also won no friends in the West by foreclosing on many western farms and draining "tribute" into eastern coffers. Profit, not public service, was its first priority.

The Bank War erupted in 1832, when Daniel Webster and Henry Clay presented Congress with a bill to renew the Bank of the United States' charter. The charter was not set to expire until 1836, but Clay pushed for renewal four years early to make it an election issue in 1832. As Jackson's leading rival for the presidency, Clay, with fateful blindness, looked upon the bank issue as a surefire winner.

Clay's scheme was to ram a recharter bill through Congress and then send it on to the White House. If Jackson signed it, he would alienate his worshipful western followers. If he vetoed it, as seemed certain, he would presumably lose the presidency in the forthcoming election by alienating the wealthy and influential groups in the East. Clay seems not to have fully realized that the "best people" were now only a minority and that they generally feared Jackson anyhow.

The recharter bill slid through Congress on greased skids, as planned, but was killed by a scorching veto from Jackson. The "Old Hero" declared the monopolistic

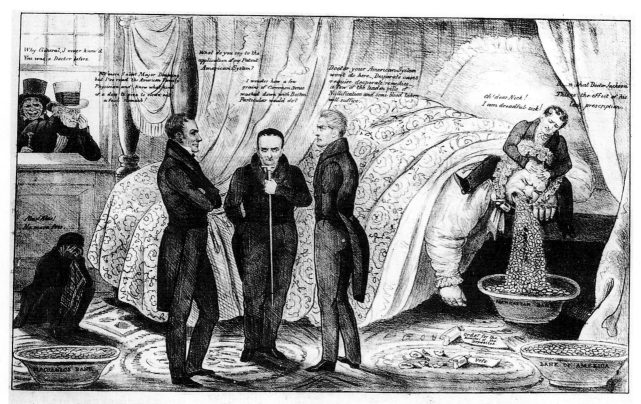

THE DOCTORS PUZZLED OR THE DESPERATE CASE OF MOTHER U.S BANK.

In Mother Bank's Sick Room Pro-bank men Henry Clay, Daniel Webster, and John Calhoun consult on the grave illness that is causing Mother Bank to cough up her deposits. While Nicholas Biddle, president of the Bank of the United States, ministers to the patient, U.S. president Andrew Jackson looks on with pleasure.

bank to be unconstitutional. Of course, the Supreme Court had earlier declared it constitutional in the case of *McCulloch* v. *Maryland* (1819), but Jackson acted as though he regarded the executive branch as superior to the judicial branch. The old general growled privately, "The Bank . . . is trying to kill me, but I will kill it."

Jackson's veto message reverberated with constitutional consequences. It not only squashed the bank bill but vastly amplified the power of the presidency. All previous vetoes had rested almost exclusively on questions of constitutionality. But though Jackson invoked the Constitution in his bank-veto message, he essentially argued that he was vetoing the bill because he personally found it harmful to the nation. In effect, he was claiming for the president alone a power equivalent to two-thirds of the votes in Congress. If the legislative and executive branches were partners in government, he implied, the president was unmistakably the senior partner.

Banker Nicholas Biddle (1786–1844) wrote to Henry Clay (August 1, 1832) expressing his satisfaction:

"I have always deplored making the Bank a party question, but since the President will have it so, he must pay the penalty of his own rashness. As to the veto message, I am delighted with it. It has all the fury of a chained panther biting the bars of his cage. It is really a manifesto of anarchy . . . and my hope is that it will contribute to relieve the country of the domination of these miserable [Jackson] people."

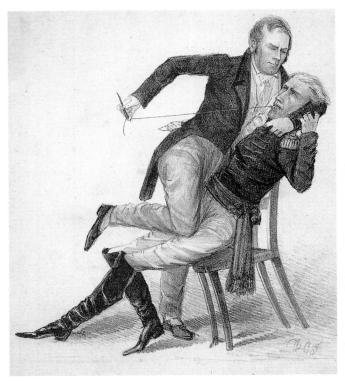

Symptoms of a Locked Jaw   An outraged and outmaneuvered Henry Clay vainly tries to "muzzle" Andrew Jackson after Jackson's stinging message vetoing the bill to recharter the Bank of the United States.

Henry Clay's political instincts continued to fail him. Delighted with the financial fallacies of Jackson's message but blind to its political appeal, he arranged to have thousands of copies printed as a campaign document. The president's sweeping accusations may indeed have seemed demagogic to the moneyed interests of the East, but they made perfect sense to the common people. The bank issue was now thrown into the noisy arena of the presidential contest of 1832.

"Old Hickory" Wallops Clay in 1832

Clay and Jackson were the chief gladiators in the looming electoral combat. The grizzled old general, who had earlier favored one term for a president and rotation in office, was easily persuaded by his cronies not to rotate himself out of office. Presidential power is a heady brew and can be habit-forming.

The ensuing campaign was raucous. The "Old Hero's" adherents again raised the hickory pole and bellowed, "Jackson Forever: Go the Whole Hog." Admirers of Clay shouted, "Freedom and Clay," while his detractors harped on his dueling, gambling, cockfighting, and fast living.

Novel features made the campaign of 1832 especially memorable. For the first time, a third party entered the field—the newborn Anti-Masonic party, which opposed the influence and fearsome secrecy of the Masonic order. Energized by the mysterious disappearance and probable murder in 1826 of a New Yorker who was threatening to expose the secret rituals of the Masons, the Anti-Masonic party quickly became a potent political force in New York and spread its influence throughout the middle Atlantic and New England states. The Anti-Masons appealed to long-standing American suspicions of secret societies, which they condemned as citadels of privilege and monopoly—a note that harmonized with the democratic chorus of the Jacksonians. But since Jackson himself was a Mason and publicly gloried in his membership, the Anti-Masonic party was also an anti-Jackson party. The Anti-Masons also attracted support from many evangelical Protestant groups seeking to use political power to effect moral and religious reforms, such as prohibiting mail delivery on Sunday and otherwise keeping the Sabbath holy. This moral busybodiness was anathema to the Jacksonians, who were generally opposed to all government meddling in social and economic life.

A further novelty of the presidential contest in 1832 was the calling of national nominating conventions (three of them) to name candidates. The Anti-Masons and a group of National Republicans added still another innovation when they adopted formal platforms, publicizing their positions on the issues.

Henry Clay and his overconfident National Republicans enjoyed impressive advantages. Ample funds flowed into their campaign chest, including $50,000 in "life insurance" from the Bank of the United States. Most of the newspaper editors, some of them "bought" with Biddle's bank loans, dipped their pens in acid when they wrote of Jackson.

Yet Jackson, idol of the masses, easily defeated the big-money Kentuckian. A Jacksonian wave again swept over the West and South, surged into Pennsylvania and New York, and even washed into rock-ribbed New England. The popular vote stood at 687,502 to 530,189 for Jackson; the electoral count was a lopsided 219 to 49.

Fistfight Between Old Hickory and Bully Nick, 1834 An aged President Andrew Jackson faces off against the bank's director, aristocratic Nicholas Biddle. Comically presented as sparring pugilists undressed in the style of the popular sport, the two are assisted by their seconds, Daniel Webster and Henry Clay for Biddle, Vice President Martin Van Buren for Jackson.

Burying Biddle's Bank

Its charter denied, the Bank of the United States was due to expire in 1836. But Jackson was not one to let the financial octopus die in peace. He was convinced that he now had a mandate from the voters for its extermination, and he feared that the slippery Biddle might try to manipulate the bank (as he did) so as to force its recharter. Jackson therefore decided in 1833 to bury the bank for good by removing federal deposits from its vaults. He proposed depositing no more funds with Biddle and gradually shrinking existing deposits by using them to defray the day-to-day expenses of the government. By slowly siphoning off the government's funds, he would bleed the bank dry and ensure its demise.

Removing the deposits involved nasty complications. Even the president's closest advisers opposed this seemingly unnecessary, possibly unconstitutional, and certainly vindictive policy. Jackson, his dander up, was forced to reshuffle his cabinet twice before he could find a secretary of the Treasury who would bend to his iron will. A desperate Biddle called in his bank's loans, evidently hoping to illustrate the bank's importance by producing a minor financial crisis. A number of wobblier banks were driven to the wall by "Biddle's Panic," but Jackson's resolution was firm. If anything, the vengeful conduct of the dying "monster" seemed to justify the earlier accusations of its adversaries.

But the death of the Bank of the United States left a financial vacuum in the American economy and kicked off a lurching cycle of booms and busts. Surplus federal funds were placed in several dozen state institutions—

the so-called "pet banks," chosen for their pro-Jackson sympathies. Without a sober central bank in control, the pet banks and smaller "wildcat" banks—fly-by-night operations that often consisted of little more than a few chairs and a suitcase full of printed notes—flooded the country with paper money.

Jackson tried to rein in the runaway economy in 1836, the year Biddle's bank breathed its last. "Wildcat" currency had become so unreliable, especially in the West, that Jackson authorized the Treasury to issue a Specie Circular—a decree that required all public lands to be purchased with "hard," or metallic, money. This drastic step slammed the brakes on the speculative boom, a neck-snapping change of direction that contributed to a financial panic and crash in 1837.

But by then Jackson had retired to his Nashville home, hailed as the hero of his age. His successor would have to deal with the damage.

The Birth of the Whigs

New political parties were gelling as the 1830s lengthened. As early as 1828, the Democratic-Republicans of Jackson had unashamedly adopted the once-tainted name "Democrats." Jackson's opponents, fuming at his ironfisted exercise of presidential power, condemned him as "King Andrew I" and began to coalesce as the Whigs—a name deliberately chosen to recollect eighteenth-century British and Revolutionary American opposition to the monarchy.

The Whig party contained so many diverse elements that it was mocked at first as "an organized incompatibility." Hatred of Jackson and his "executive usurpation" was its only apparent cement in its formative days. The Whigs first emerged as an identifiable group in the Senate, where Clay, Webster, and Calhoun joined forces in 1834 to pass a motion censuring Jackson for his single-handed removal of federal deposits from the Bank of the United States. Thereafter, the Whigs rapidly evolved into a potent national political force by attracting other groups alienated by Jackson: supporters of Clay's American System, southern states' righters offended by Jackson's stand on nullification, the larger northern industrialists and merchants, and eventually many of the evangelical Protestants associated with the Anti-Masonic party.

Whigs thought of themselves as conservatives, yet they were progressive in their support of active govern-

ment programs and reforms. Instead of boundless territorial acquisition, they called for internal improvements like canals, railroads, and telegraph lines, and they supported institutions like prisons, asylums, and public schools. The Whigs welcomed the market economy, drawing support from manufacturers in the North, planters in the South, and merchants and bankers in all sections. But they were not simply a party of wealthy fat cats, however dearly the Democrats wanted to paint them as such. By absorbing the Anti-Masonic party, the Whigs blunted much of the Democratic appeal to the common man. The egalitarian anti-Masons portrayed Jackson, and particularly his New York successor Martin Van Buren, as imperious aristocrats. This turned Jacksonian rhetoric on its head: now the Whigs claimed to be the defenders of the common man and declared the Democrats the party of cronyism and corruption.

The Election of 1836

The smooth-tongued and keen-witted vice president, Martin Van Buren of New York, was Jackson's choice for "appointment" as his successor in 1836. The hollow-cheeked Jackson, now nearing seventy, was too old and ailing to consider a third term. But he was not loath to try to serve a third term through Van Buren, something of a "yes man." Leaving nothing to chance, Jackson carefully rigged the nominating convention and rammed his favorite down the throats of the delegates. Van Buren was supported by the Jacksonites without wild enthusiasm, even though he had promised "to tread generally" in the military-booted footsteps of his predecessor.

As the election neared, the still-ramshackle organization of the Whigs showed in their inability to nominate a single presidential candidate. Their long-shot strategy was instead to run several prominent "favorite sons," each with a different regional appeal, and hope to scatter the vote so that no candidate would win a majority. The deadlock would then have to be broken by the House of Representatives, where the Whigs might have a chance. With Henry Clay rudely elbowed aside, the leading Whig "favorite son" was heavy-jawed General William Henry Harrison of Ohio, hero of the Battle of Tippecanoe (see p. 231). The fine-spun schemes of the Whigs availed nothing, however. Van Buren, the dapper "Little Magician," squirmed into office by the close popular vote of 765,483 to 739,795,

EXAMINING THE EVIDENCE

Satiric Bank Note, 1837 Political humor can take more forms than the commonly seen caustic cartoon. Occasionally historians stumble upon other examples, such as this fake bank note. A jibe at Andrew Jackson's money policies, it appeared in New York in 1837 after Jackson's insistence on shutting down the Bank of the United States resulted in the suspension of specie payments. The clever creator of this satiric bank note for six cents left little doubt about the worthlessness of the note or Jackson's responsibility for it. The six cents payable by the "Humbug Glory Bank"—whose symbols were a donkey and a "Hickory Leaf" (for Old Hickory)— were redeemable "in mint drops or Glory at cost." The bank's cashier was "Cunning Reuben," possibly an anti-Semitic allusion to usurious Jewish bankers. Can you identify other ways in which this document takes aim at Jackson's banking policies? What symbols did the note's creator assume the public would comprehend?

but by the comfortable margin of 170 to 124 votes (for all the Whigs combined) in the Electoral College.

Big Woes for the "Little Magician"

Martin Van Buren, eighth president, was the first to be born under the American flag. Short and slender, bland and bald, the adroit little New Yorker has been described as "a first-class second-rate man." An accomplished strategist and spoilsman—"the wizard of Albany"—he was also a statesman of wide experience in both legislative and administrative life. In intelligence, education, and training, he was above the average of the presidents since Jackson. The myth of his mediocrity sprouted mostly from a series of misfortunes over which he had no control.

From the outset the new president labored under severe handicaps. As a machine-made candidate, he incurred the resentment of many Democrats—those who objected to having a "bastard politician" smuggled into office beneath the tails of the old general's military coat. Jackson, the master showman, had been a dynamic type of executive whose administration had resounded with furious quarrels and cracked heads. Mild-mannered Martin Van Buren seemed to rattle about in the military boots of his testy predecessor. The people felt let down. Inheriting Andrew Jackson's mantle without his popularity, Van Buren also inherited the ex-president's numerous and vengeful enemies.

Van Buren's four years overflowed with toil and trouble. A rebellion in Canada in 1837 stirred up ugly incidents along the northern frontier and threatened to trigger war with Britain. The president's attempt to play a neutral game led to the wail, "Woe to Martin Van Buren!" The antislavery agitators in the North were in full cry. Among other grievances, they were condemning the prospective annexation of Texas (see p. 280).

Worst of all, Jackson bequeathed to Van Buren the makings of a searing depression. Much of Van Buren's energy had to be devoted to the purely negative task of battling the panic, and there were not enough rabbits in the "Little Magician's" tall silk hat. Hard times ordinarily blight the reputation of a president, and Van Buren was no exception.

Depression Doldrums and the Independent Treasury

The panic of 1837 was a symptom of the financial sickness of the times. Its basic cause was rampant speculation prompted by a mania of get-rich-quickism. Gamblers in western lands were doing a "land-office business" on borrowed capital, much of it in the shaky currency of "wildcat banks." The speculative craze spread to canals, roads, railroads, and slaves.

But speculation alone did not cause the crash. Jacksonian finance, including the Bank War and the Specie Circular, gave an additional jolt to an already teetering structure. Failures of wheat crops, ravaged by the Hessian fly, deepened the distress. Grain prices were forced so high that mobs in New York City, three weeks before Van Buren took the oath, stormed warehouses and broke open flour barrels. The panic really began before Jackson left office, but its full fury burst about Van Buren's bewildered head.

Financial stringency abroad likewise endangered America's economic house of cards. Late in 1836 the failure of two prominent British banks created tremors, and these in turn caused British investors to call in foreign loans. The resulting pinch in the United States, combined with other setbacks, heralded the beginning of the panic. Europe's economic distresses have often become America's distresses, for every major American financial panic has been affected by conditions overseas.

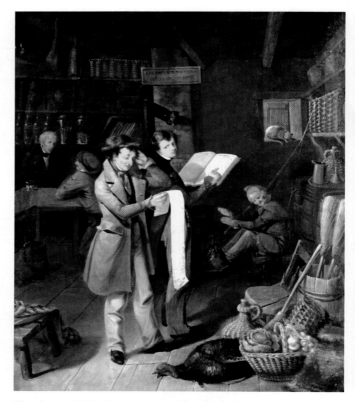

The Long Bill Americans who bought on credit, confident that they could make their payments later, were caught off guard by the Panic of 1837. Customers like the one shown here found themselves confronted with a "long bill" that they could not pay, particularly when the banks holding their savings collapsed.

Hardship was acute and widespread. American banks collapsed by the hundreds, including some "pet banks," which carried down with them several million in government funds. Commodity prices drooped, sales of public lands fell off, and customs revenues dried to a rivulet. Factories closed their doors, and unemployed workers milled in the streets.

The Whigs came forward with proposals for active government remedies for the economy's ills. They called for the expansion of bank credit, higher tariffs, and subsidies for internal improvements. But Van Buren, shackled by the Jacksonian philosophy of keeping the government's paws off the economy, spurned all such ideas.

The beleaguered Van Buren tried to apply vintage Jacksonian medicine to the ailing economy through his controversial "Divorce Bill." Convinced that some of the

Philip Hone (1780–1851), a New York businessman, described in his diary (May 10, 1837) a phase of the financial crisis:

"The savings-bank also sustained a most grievous run yesterday. They paid 375 depositors $81,000. The press was awful; the hour for closing the bank is six o'clock, but they did not get through the paying of those who were in at that time till nine o'clock. I was there with the other trustees and witnessed the madness of the people—women nearly pressed to death, and the stoutest men could scarcely sustain themselves; but they held on as with a death's grip upon the evidences of their claims, and, exhausted as they were with the pressure, they had strength to cry 'Pay! Pay!'"

financial fever was fed by the injection of federal funds into private banks, he championed the principle of "divorcing" the government from banking altogether. By establishing a so-called independent treasury, the

One foreign traveler decried the chaotic state of American currency following the demise of the Bank of the United States and the panic of 1837:

"The greatest annoyance I was subjected to in travelling was in exchanging money. It is impossible to describe the wretched state of the currency—which is all bills issued by private individuals; companies; cities and states; almost all of which are bankrupt; or what amounts to the same thing, they cannot redeem their issues. . . . And these do not pass out of the state, or frequently, out of the city in which they are issued."

government could lock its surplus money in vaults in several of the larger cities. Government funds would thus be safe, but they would also be denied to the banking system as reserves, thereby shriveling available credit resources.

Van Buren's "divorce" scheme was never highly popular. His fellow Democrats, many of whom longed for the risky but lush days of the "pet banks," supported it only lukewarmly. The Whigs condemned it, primarily because it squelched their hopes for a revived Bank of the United States. After a prolonged struggle, the Independent Treasury Bill passed Congress in 1840. Repealed the next year by the victorious Whigs, the scheme was reenacted by the triumphant Democrats in 1846 and then continued until the Republicans instituted a network of national banks during the Civil War.

Gone to Texas

Americans, greedy for land, continued to covet the vast expanse of Texas, which the United States had abandoned to Spain when acquiring Florida in 1819. The Spanish authorities wanted to populate this virtually unpeopled area, but before they could carry through their contemplated plans, the Mexicans won their independence. A new regime in Mexico City thereupon concluded arrangements in 1823 for granting a huge tract of land to Stephen Austin, with the understanding that he would bring into Texas three hundred American families. Immigrants were to be of the established Roman Catholic faith and upon settlement were to become properly Mexicanized.

These two stipulations were largely ignored. Hardy Texas pioneers remained Americans at heart, resenting the trammels imposed by a "foreign" government. They were especially annoyed by the presence of Mexican soldiers, many of whom were ragged ex-convicts.

Energetic and prolific, Texan Americans numbered about thirty thousand by 1835 (see "Makers of America: Mexican or Texican?" pp. 278–279). Most of them were law-abiding, God-fearing people, but some of them had left the "States" only one or two jumps ahead of the sheriff. "G.T.T." (Gone to Texas) became current descriptive slang. Among the adventurers were Davy Crockett, the famous rifleman, and Jim Bowie, the presumed inventor of the murderous knife that bears his name. Bowie's blade was widely known in the Southwest as the "genuine Arkansas toothpick." A

Marketing the Crockett Legend
David ("Davy") Crockett (1786–1836) was a semiliterate Tennessean who won fame as a rifleman, soldier, and three-time congressman. Rejected in politics, he left Tennessee to fight for Texas against Mexico and died at the Alamo. An accomplished storyteller and master of the frontier "tall tale," Crockett promoted his own image as a rough-hewn backwoods hero while alive. After his death a small industry developed to advertise— and embellish—his legendary exploits.

The Texas Revolution, 1836 General Houston's strategy was to retreat and use defense in depth. His line of supply from the United States was shortened as Santa Anna's lengthened. The Mexicans were forced to bring up supplies by land because the Texas navy controlled the sea. This force consisted of only four small ships, but it was big enough to do the job.

distinguished latecomer and leader was an ex-governor of Tennessee, Sam Houston. His life had been temporarily shattered in 1829 when his bride of a few weeks left him and he took up transient residence with the Arkansas Indians, who dubbed him "Big Drunk." He subsequently took the pledge of temperance.

The pioneer individualists who came to Texas were not easy to push around. Friction rapidly increased between Mexicans and Texans over issues such as slavery, immigration, and local rights. Slavery was a particularly touchy topic. Mexico emancipated its slaves in 1830 and prohibited the further importation of slaves into Texas, as well as further colonization by troublesome Americans. The Texans refused to honor these decrees. They kept their slaves in bondage, and new American settlers kept bringing more slaves into Texas. When Stephen Austin went to Mexico City in 1833 to negotiate these differences with the Mexican government, the dictator Santa Anna clapped him in jail for eight months. The explosion finally came in 1835, when Santa Anna wiped out all local rights and started to raise an army to suppress the upstart Texans.

The Lone Star Rebellion

Early in 1836 the Texans declared their independence, unfurled their Lone Star flag, and named Sam Houston

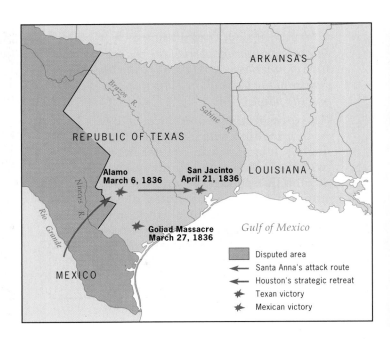

The Alamo as It Looks Today
When Moses Austin, father of famed Texas pioneer Stephen Austin, first saw this building on December 23, 1820, it was an abandoned mission, founded by Franciscan friars in 1718 as San Antonio de Valero. Renamed the Alamo, from the Spanish word for cottonwood tree, it was made into a fortress and became famous in 1836 when Santa Anna's armies wiped out its garrison of Americans.

commander in chief. Santa Anna, at the head of about six thousand men, swept ferociously into Texas. Trapping a band of nearly two hundred pugnacious Texans at the Alamo in San Antonio, he wiped them out to a man after a thirteen-day siege. Their commander, Colonel W. B. Travis, had declared, "I shall never surrender nor retreat. . . . Victory or Death." A short time later, a band of about four hundred surrounded and defeated American volunteers, having thrown down their arms at Goliad, were butchered as "pirates." All these operations further delayed the Mexican advance and galvanized American opposition.

Slain heroes like Jim Bowie and Davy Crockett, well-known in life, became legendary in death. Texan war cries—"Remember the Alamo!" "Remember Goliad!" and "Death to Santa Anna!"—swept up into the United States. Scores of vengeful Americans seized their rifles and rushed to the aid of relatives, friends, and compatriots.

Samuel ("Sam") Houston (1793–1863) After a promising career in Tennessee as a soldier, lawyer, congressman, and governor, Houston became the chief leader and hero of the Texas rebels. Elected to the U.S. Senate and the governorship of Texas, he was forced into retirement when his love for the Union caused him to spurn the Confederacy in the Civil War.

General Sam Houston's small army retreated to the east, luring Santa Anna to San Jacinto, near the site of the city that now bears Houston's name. The Mexicans

Mexican or Texican?

Moses Austin, born a Connecticut Yankee in 1761, was determined to be Spanish—if that's what it took to acquire cheap land and freedom from pesky laws. In 1798 he tramped into untracked Missouri, still part of Spanish Louisiana, and pledged his allegiance to the king of Spain. He was not pleased when the Louisiana Purchase of 1803 restored him to American citizenship. In 1820, with his old Spanish passport in his saddlebag, he rode into Spanish Texas and asked for permission to establish a colony of three hundred families.

Austin's request posed a dilemma for the Texas governor. The Spanish authorities had repeatedly stamped out the bands of American horse thieves and squatters who periodically splashed across the Red and Sabine Rivers from the United States into Spanish territory. Yet the Spanish had lured only some three thousand of their own settlers into Texas during their three centuries of rule. If the land were ever to be wrestled from the Indians and "civilized," maybe Austin's plan could do it. Hoping that this band of the "right sort" of Americans might prevent the further encroachment of the buckskinned border ruffians, the governor reluctantly agreed to Austin's proposal.

Upon Moses Austin's death in 1821, the task of realizing his dream fell to his twenty-seven-year-old son, Stephen. "I bid an everlasting farewell to my native country," Stephen Austin said, and he crossed into Texas on July 15, 1821, "determined to fulfill rigidly all the duties and obligations of a Mexican citizen" (Mexico declared its independence from Spain early in 1821 and finalized its agreement with Austin in 1823). Soon he learned fluent Spanish and was signing his name as "Don Estévan F. Austin." In his new colony between the Brazos and Colorado Rivers, he allowed "no drunkard, no gambler, no profane swearer, no idler"—and sternly enforced these rules. Not only did he banish several families as "undesirables," but he ordered the public flogging of unwanted interlopers.

José Antonio Navarro (1795–1871)   A native of San Antonio, Navarro signed the Texas declaration of independence in 1836.

Austin fell just three families short of recruiting the three hundred households that his father had contracted to bring to Texas. The original settlers were still dubbed "the Old Three Hundred," the Texas equivalent of New England's Mayflower Pilgrims or the "First Families of Virginia." Mostly Scots-Irish southerners from the trans-Appalachian frontier, the Old Three Hundred were cultured folk by frontier standards; all but four of them were literate. Other settlers followed, from Europe as well as America. Within ten years the "Anglos" (many of them French and German) outnumbered the Mexican residents, or *tejanos,* ten to one and soon evolved a distinctive "Texican" culture. The wide-ranging horse patrols organized to attack Indian camps became the

Texas Rangers; Samuel Maverick, whose unbranded calves roamed the limitless prairies, left his surname as a label for rebellious loners who refused to run with the herd; and Jared Groce, an Alabama planter whose caravan of fifty covered wagons and one hundred slaves arrived in 1822, etched the original image of the larger-than-life, big-time Texas operator.

The original Anglo-Texans brought with them the old Scots-Irish frontiersman's hostility to authority. They ignored Mexican laws and officials, including restrictions against owning or importing slaves. When the Mexican government tried to impose its will on the Anglo-Texans in the 1830s, they took up their guns. Like the American revolutionaries of the 1770s, who at first demanded only the rights of Englishmen, the Texans began by asking simply for Mexican recognition of their rights as guaranteed by the Mexican constitution of 1824. But bloodshed at the Alamo in 1836, like that at Lexington in 1775, transformed protest into rebellion.

Texas lay—and still lies—along the frontier where Hispanic and Anglo-American cultures met, mingled, and clashed. In part the Texas Revolution was a contest between those two cultures. But it was also a contest about philosophies of government, pitting liberal frontier ideals of freedom against the conservative concept of centralized control. Stephen Austin sincerely tried to "Mexicanize" himself and his followers—until the Mexican government grew too arbitrary and authoritarian. And not all the Texas revolutionaries were "Anglos." Many *tejanos* fought for Texas independence—seven perished defending the Alamo. Among the fifty-nine signers of the Texas declaration of independence were several Hispanics, including the *tejanos* José Antonio Navarro and Francisco Ruiz. Lorenzo de Zavala, an ardent Mexican liberal who had long resisted the centralizing tendencies of Mexico's dominant political party, was designated vice president of the Texas republic's interim government in 1836. Like the Austins, these *tejanos* and Mexicans had sought in Texas an escape from overbearing governmental authority. Their role in the revolution underscores the fact that the uprising was a struggle between defenders of local rights and the agents of central authority as much as it was a fight between Anglo and Mexican cultures.

West Side Main Plaza, San Antonio, Texas, by William G. M. Samuel, 1849 (detail)
Even after annexation, Texas retained a strong Spanish Mexican flavor, as the architecture and activities here illustrate.

numbered about thirteen hundred men, the Texans about nine hundred. Suddenly, on April 21, 1836, Houston turned. Taking full advantage of the Mexican siesta, the Texans wiped out the pursuing force and captured Santa Anna, who was found cowering in the tall grass near the battlefield. Confronted with thirsty bowie knives, the quaking dictator was speedily induced to sign two treaties. By their terms he agreed to withdraw Mexican troops and to recognize the Rio Grande as the extreme southwestern boundary of Texas. When released, he repudiated the agreement as illegal because it was extorted under duress.

These events put the U.S. government in a sticky situation. The Texans, though courageous, could hardly have won their independence without the help in men and supplies from their American cousins. The Washington government, as the Mexicans bitterly complained, had a solemn obligation under international law to enforce its leaky neutrality statutes. But American public opinion, overwhelmingly favorable to the Texans, openly nullified the existing legislation. The federal authorities were powerless to act, and on the day before he left office in 1837, President Jackson even extended the right hand of recognition to the Lone Star Republic, led by his old comrade-in-arms against the Indians, Sam Houston.

Many Texans wanted not just recognition of their independence but outright union with the United States. What nation in its right mind, they reasoned, would refuse so lavish a dowry? The radiant Texas bride, officially petitioning for annexation in 1837, presented herself for marriage. But the expectant groom, Uncle Sam, was jerked back by the black hand of the slavery issue. Antislavery crusaders in the North were opposing annexation with increasing vehemence. They contended that the whole scheme was merely a conspiracy cooked up by the southern "slavocracy" to bring new slave pens into the Union.

At first glance a "slavery plot" charge seemed plausible. Most of the early settlers in Texas, as well as American volunteers during the revolution, had come from the states of the South and Southwest. But scholars have concluded that the settlement of Texas was merely the normal and inexorable march of the westward movement. Most of the immigrants came from the South and Southwest simply because these states were closer. The explanation was proximity rather than conspiracy. Yet the fact remained that many Texans were slaveholders, and admitting Texas to the Union inescapably meant enlarging American slavery.

Log Cabins and Hard Cider of 1840

Martin Van Buren was renominated by the Democrats in 1840, albeit without terrific enthusiasm. The party had no acceptable alternative to what the Whigs called "Martin Van Ruin."

The Whigs, hungering for the spoils of office, scented victory in the breeze. Pangs of the panic were still being felt, and voters blamed their woes on the party in power. Learning from their mistake in 1836, the Whigs united behind one candidate, Ohio's William Henry Harrison. He was not their ablest statesman—that would have been Daniel Webster or Henry Clay—but he was believed to be their ablest vote-getter.

Campaign Flag for William Henry Harrison, 1840
As the two-party system came into its own by 1840, presidential elections became more public contests. Lively political campaigns used banners, posters, and flags to whip up voters' support. Although General Harrison was hardly a simple log cabin–living Ohioan, the Whigs disseminated this logo to persuade the voters that the Virginia-born gentleman was really a homespun Western farmer.

WM. H. HARRISON
THE OHIO FARMER

Martin Van Buren Gags on Hard Cider This 1840 "pull-card" showed Van Buren on the left as an aristocratic fop sipping champagne. When the right-hand card was pulled out, Van Buren's face soured as he discovered that his "champagne" was actually hard cider. The cartoonist clearly sympathized with Van Buren's opponent in the 1840 presidential election, William Henry Harrison, who waged the famous "log cabin and hard cider" campaign.

The aging hero, nearly sixty-eight when the campaign ended, was known for his successes against Indians and the British at the Battles of Tippecanoe (1811) and the Thames (1813). Harrison's views on current issues were only vaguely known. "Old Tippecanoe" was nominated primarily because he was issueless and enemyless—a tested recipe for electoral success that still appeals today. John Tyler of Virginia, an afterthought, was selected as his vice-presidential running mate.

The Whigs, eager to avoid offense, published no official platform, hoping to sweep their hero into office with a frothy huzza-for-Harrison campaign reminiscent of Jackson's triumph in 1828. A dull-witted Democratic editor played directly into Whig hands. Stupidly insulting the West, he lampooned Harrison as an impoverished old farmer who should be content with a pension, a log cabin, and a barrel of hard cider—the poor westerner's champagne. Whigs gleefully adopted honest hard cider and the sturdy log cabin as symbols of their campaign. Harrisonites portrayed their hero as the poor "Farmer of North Bend," who had been called from his cabin and his plow to drive corrupt Jackson spoilsmen from the "presidential palace." They denounced Van Buren as a supercilious aristocrat, a simpering dandy who wore corsets and ate French food from golden plates. As a jeering Whig campaign song proclaimed,

Old Tip, he wears a homespun shirt,
 He has no ruffled shirt, wirt, wirt.
But Matt, he has the golden plate,
 and he's a little squirt, wirt, wirt.

The Whig campaign was a masterpiece of inane hoopla. Log cabins were dished up in every conceivable form. Bawling Whigs, stimulated by fortified cider, rolled huge inflated balls from village to village and state to state—balls that represented the snowballing majority for "Tippecanoe, and Tyler too." In truth, Harrison was not lowborn, but from one of the FFVs ("First Families of Virginia"). He was not poverty-stricken. He did not live in a one-room log cabin, but rather in a sixteen-room mansion on a three-thousand-acre farm. He did not swill down gallons of hard cider (he evidently preferred whiskey). And he did not plow his fields with his own "huge paws." But such details had not mattered when General Jackson rode to victory, and they did not matter now.

The Democrats that hurrahed Jackson into the White House in 1828 now discovered to their chagrin that whooping it up for a backwoods westerner was a game two could play. Harrison won by the surprisingly close margin of 1,274,624 to 1,127,781 popular votes, but by an overwhelming electoral margin of 234 to 60. With hardly a real issue debated, though with hard

William Henry Harrison Campaign in Philadelphia, 1840 The parties of Democratic incumbent Martin Van Buren and his Whig challenger, "The Hero of Tippecanoe," took their electoral rivalry into the streets of cities like Philadelphia, launching modern-style popular politics. Harrison won, but a mere month after delivering the longest inaugural address ever (two hours), he succumbed to pneumonia and died. He served the shortest term of any president (thirty-one days). One of his forty-eight grandchildren, Benjamin Harrison, became the twenty-third president of the United States.

times blighting the incumbent's fortunes, Van Buren was washed out of Washington on a wave of apple juice. The hard-ciderites had apparently received a mandate to tear down the White House and erect a log cabin.

Although campaigners in 1840 did their best to bury substantive issues beneath the ballyhoo, voters actually faced a stark choice between two economic visions of how to cope with the nation's first major depression. Whigs sought to expand and stimulate the economy, while Democrats favored retrenchment and an end to high-flying banks and aggressive corporations.

Politics for the People

The election of 1840 conclusively demonstrated two major changes in American politics since the Era of Good Feelings. The first was the triumph of a populist democratic style. Democracy had been something of a taint in the days of the lordly Federalists. Martha Washington, the first First Lady, was shocked after a presidential reception to find a greasy smear on the wallpaper—left there, she was sure, by an uninvited "filthy democrat."

But by the 1840s, aristocracy was the taint, and democracy was respectable. Politicians were now forced to curry favor with the voting masses. Lucky indeed was the aspiring office seeker who could boast of birth in a log cabin. In 1840 Daniel Webster publicly apologized for not being able to claim so humble a birthplace, though he quickly added that his brothers could. Hopelessly handicapped was the candidate who appeared to be too clean, too well dressed, too grammatical, too highbrowishly intellectual. In truth, most high political

President Andrew Jackson advised a supporter in 1835 on how to tell the difference between Democrats and "Whigs, nullies, and blue-light federalists." In doing so, he neatly summarized the Jacksonian philosophy:

"The people ought to inquire [of political candidates]—are you opposed to a national bank; are you in favor of a strict construction of the Federal and State Constitutions; are you in favor of rotation in office; do you subscribe to the republican rule that the people are the sovereign power, the officers their agents, and that upon all national or general subjects, as well as local, they have a right to instruct their agents and representatives, and they are bound to obey or resign; in short, are they true Republicans agreeable to the true Jeffersonian creed?"

offices continued to be filled by "leading citizens." But now these wealthy and prominent men had to forsake all social pretensions and cultivate the common touch if they hoped to win elections.

Snobbish bigwigs, unhappy over the change, sneered at "coonskin congressmen" and at the newly enfranchised "bipeds of the forest." To them the tyranny of "King Numbers" was no less offensive than that of King George. But these critics protested in vain. The common man was at last moving to the center of the national political stage: the sturdy American who donned coarse trousers rather than buff breeches, who sported a coonskin cap rather than a silk top hat, and who wore no man's collar, often not even one of his own. Instead of the old divine right of kings, America was now bowing to the divine right of the people.

The Two-Party System

The second dramatic change resulting from the 1840 election was the formation of a vigorous and durable two-party system. The Jeffersonians of an earlier day had been so successful in absorbing the programs of their Federalist opponents that a full-blown two-party system had never truly emerged in the subsequent Era of Good Feelings. The idea had prevailed that parties of any sort smacked of conspiracy and "faction" and were injurious to the health of the body politic in a virtuous republic. By 1840 political parties had fully come of age, a lasting legacy of Andrew Jackson's and Martin Van Buren's tenaciousness.

Both national parties, the Democrats and the Whigs grew out of the rich soil of Jeffersonian republicanism, and each laid claim to different aspects of the republican inheritance. Jacksonian Democrats glorified the liberty of the individual and were fiercely on guard against the inroads of "privilege" into government. Whigs trumpeted the natural harmony of society and the value of community, and were willing to use government to realize their objectives. Whigs also berated those leaders—and they considered Jackson to be one—whose appeals to self-interest fostered conflict among individuals, classes, or sections.

Democrats clung to states' rights and federal restraint in social and economic affairs as their basic doctrines. Whigs tended to favor a renewed national bank, protective tariffs, internal improvements, public schools, and, increasingly, moral reforms such as the prohibition of liquor and eventually the abolition of slavery.

The two parties were thus separated by real differences of philosophy and policy. But they also had much

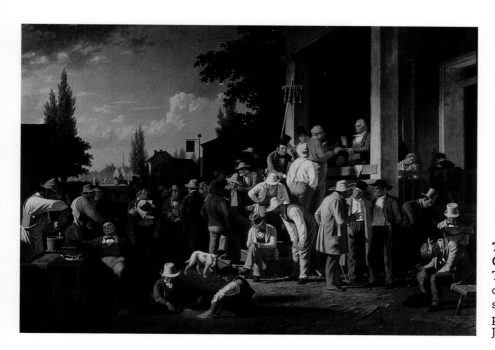

The County Election, by George Caleb Bingham, 1851–1852
The artist here gently satirizes the drinking and wheeler-dealing that sometimes marred the electoral process in the boisterous age of Jacksonian politics.

in common. Both were mass-based, "catchall" parties that tried deliberately to mobilize as many voters as possible for their cause. Although it is true that Democrats tended to be more humble folk and Whigs more prosperous, both parties nevertheless commanded the loyalties of all kinds of Americans, from all social classes and in all sections. The social diversity of the two parties had important implications. It fostered horse-trading compromises *within* each party that prevented either from assuming extreme or radical positions. By the same token, the geographical diversity of the two parties retarded the emergence of purely sectional political parties—temporarily suppressing, through compromise, the ultimately uncompromisable issue of slavery. When the two-party system began to creak in the 1850s, the Union was mortally imperiled.

Chronology

1822	Vesey slave conspiracy in Charleston, South Carolina
1823	Mexico opens Texas to American settlers
1824	Lack of electoral majority for presidency throws election into the House of Representatives
1825	House elects John Quincy Adams president
1828	Tariff of 1828 ("Tariff of Abominations") Jackson elected president The *South Carolina Exposition* published
1830	Indian Removal Act
1832	"Bank War"—Jackson vetoes bill to recharter Bank of the United States Tariff of 1832 Black Hawk War Jackson defeats Clay for presidency
1832-1833	South Carolina nullification crisis
1833	Compromise Tariff of 1833 Jackson removes federal deposits from Bank of the United States
1836	Bank of the United States expires Specie Circular issued Bureau of Indian Affairs established Battle of the Alamo Battle of San Jacinto Texas wins independence from Mexico Van Buren elected president
1837	Seminole Indians defeated and eventually removed from Florida United States recognizes Texas republic but refuses annexation Panic of 1837
1838-1839	Cherokee Indians removed on "Trail of Tears"
1840	Independent treasury established Harrison defeats Van Buren for presidency

VARYING VIEWPOINTS

What Was Jacksonian Democracy?

Aristocratic, eastern-born historians of the nineteenth century damned Jackson as a backwoods barbarian. They criticized Jacksonianism as democracy run riot—an irresponsible, ill-bred outburst that overturned the electoral system and wrecked the national financial structure.

In the late nineteenth and early twentieth centuries, however, another generation of historians came to the fore, many of whom grew up in the Midwest and rejected the elitist views of their predecessors. Frederick Jackson Turner and his disciples saw the western frontier as the fount of democratic virtue, and they hailed Jackson as a true hero sprung from the forests of the West to protect the will of the people against the moneyed interests, akin to the progressive reformers of their own day. In his famous 1893 essay, "The Significance of the Frontier in American History," Turner argued that the United States owed the survival of its democratic tradition to the rise of the West, not to its roots in the more conservative, aristocratic East.

When Arthur M. Schlesinger, Jr., published *The Age of Jackson* in 1945, however, the debate on Jacksonianism shifted dramatically. Although he shared the Turnerians' admiration for Jackson the democrat, Schlesinger cast the Jacksonian era not as a sectional conflict, but as a class conflict between poor farmers, laborers, and noncapitalists on the one hand, and the business community—epitomized by the Second Bank of the United States—on the other. In Schlesinger's eyes the Jacksonians justifiably attacked the bank as an institution dangerously independent of democratic oversight. The political mobilization of the urban working classes in support of Jackson particularly attracted Schlesinger's interest.

Soon after Schlesinger's book appeared, the discussion again shifted ground and entirely new interpretations of Jacksonianism emerged. Richard Hofstadter argued in *The American Political Tradition and the Men Who Made It* (1948) that Jacksonian democracy was not a rejection of capitalism, as Schlesinger insisted, but rather the effort of aspiring entrepreneurs to secure laissez-faire policies that would serve their own interests against their entrenched, and monopolistic, eastern competitors. In *The Jacksonian Persuasion* (1957), Marvin Meyers portrayed the Jacksonians as conservative capitalists, torn between fierce commercial ambitions and a desire to cling to the virtues of the agrarian past. In an effort to resolve this contradiction, he argued, they lashed out at scapegoats like the national bank, blaming it for the very changes their own economic energies had unleashed. Lee Benson contended in *The Concept of Jacksonian Democracy* (1961) that the political conflicts of the Jacksonian era did not correspond so much to class divisions as to different ethnic and religious splits within American society. Using new quantitative methods of analysis, Benson found no consistent demarcations—in class, occupation, or region—between the Jacksonians and their rivals. Local and cultural issues such as temperance and religion were far more influential in shaping political life than the national financial questions analyzed by previous historians.

In the 1980s Sean Wilentz and other scholars began to resurrect some of Schlesinger's argument about the importance of class to Jacksonianism. In *Chants Democratic* (1984), Wilentz maintained that Jacksonian politics could not be properly understood without reference to the changing national economy. Artisans watched in horror as new manufacturing techniques put many of them out of business and replaced their craftsmanship with the unskilled hands of wage laborers. To these anxious small producers, America's infatuation with impersonal institutions and large-scale employers threatened the very existence of a republic founded on the principle that its citizens were virtuously self-sufficient. Thus Jackson's attack on the Bank of the United States symbolized the antagonism these individuals felt toward the emergent capitalist economy and earned him their strong allegiance.

The scholarly cycle came full circle with the publication of Charles Sellers's *The Market Revolution: Jacksonian America, 1815–1846* (1991). In many ways this ambitious synthesis offered an updated version of Schlesinger's argument about class conflict. American democracy and free-market capitalism, according to

Sellers, were not twins, born from the common parentage of freedom and opportunity, reared in the wide-open young Republic, and mutually supporting each other ever since. Rather, Sellers suggested, they were really adversaries, with Jacksonians inventing mass democracy in order to hold capitalist expansion in check. Like Schlesinger's thesis, Sellers's interpretation provoked a storm of controversy. To supporters, the concept of the "market revolution" (see p. 317) provided a useful organizing tool for seeing social, cultural, political, and economic transformations as interdependent. To critics, Sellers's book suffered from a hopelessly romantic view of preindustrial society and a pronounced ideological bias. In an era of tightly contested elections, they argued, no party could expect to prevail by appealing exclusively to rich or poor along class lines. The sharpest critique of the Schlesinger-Sellers thesis can be found in William E. Gienapp, "The Myth of Class in Jacksonian Democracy." *Journal of Policy History* 6 (1994). The appearance of Melvin Stokes and Stephen Conway's *The Market Revolution in America* (1996), a collection of challenges and defenses, including a reply by Sellers, demonstrated that further research and analysis are needed to sort out the complex connections between democracy and capitalism and, more concretely, the motives of those Americans who spiritedly identified their own destinies with Andrew Jackson.

For further reading, see the Appendix. For web resources, go to **http://college.hmco.com.**

14

Forging the National Economy

1790–1860

THE PROGRESS OF INVENTION IS REALLY A
THREAT [TO MONARCHY]. WHENEVER I SEE
A RAILROAD I LOOK FOR A REPUBLIC.

RALPH WALDO EMERSON, 1866

The new nation went bounding into the nineteenth century in a burst of movement. New England Yankees, Pennsylvania farmers, and southern yeomen all pushed west in search of cheap land and prodigious opportunity, soon to be joined by vast numbers of immigrants from Europe, who also made their way to the country's fast-growing cities. But not only people were in motion. Newly invented machinery quickened the cultivation of crops and the manufacturing of goods, while workers found themselves laboring under new, more demanding expectations for their pace of work. Better roads, faster steamboats, farther-reaching canals, and tentacle-stretching railroads all helped move people, raw materials, and manufactured goods from coast to coast and Gulf to Great Lakes by the mid-nineteenth century. The momentum gave rise to a more dynamic, market-oriented, national economy.

The Westward Movement

The rise of Andrew Jackson, the first president from beyond the Appalachian Mountains, exemplified the inexorable westward march of the American people. The West, with its raw frontier, was the most typically American part of America. As Ralph Waldo Emerson wrote in 1844, "Europe stretches to the Alleghenies; America lies beyond.

"The Republic was young, and so were the people—as late as 1850, half of Americans were under the age of thirty. They were also restless and energetic, seemingly always on the move, and always westward. One "tall tale" of the frontier described chickens that voluntarily crossed their legs every spring, waiting to be tied for the

A Pioneer Homestead on the Missouri, by Karl Bodmer, 1833 The Swiss-born and Paris-trained artist Karl Bodmer painted this scene while accompanying German Prince Maximillian on his expedition across the American West. From St. Louis, the party traveled up the Missouri River by steamboat under the protection of John Jacob Astor's Fur Company. Bodmer painted scenes along the way, especially of Indians and their surroundings.

annual move west. By 1840 the "demographic center" of the American population map had crossed the Alleghenies. By the eve of the Civil War, it had marched across the Ohio River.

Legend portrays an army of muscular axmen triumphantly carving civilization out of the western woods. But in reality life was downright grim for most pioneer families. Poorly fed, ill-clad, housed in hastily erected shanties (Abraham Lincoln's family lived for a year in a three-sided lean-to made of brush and sticks), they were perpetual victims of disease, depression, and premature death. Above all, unbearable loneliness haunted them, especially the women, who were often cut off from human contact, even their neighbors, for days or even weeks, while confined to the cramped orbit of a dark cabin in a secluded clearing. Breakdowns and even madness were all too frequently the "opportunities" that the frontier offered to pioneer women.

Frontier life could be tough and crude for men as well. No-holds-barred wrestling, which permitted such niceties as the biting off of noses and the gouging out of eyes, was a popular entertainment. Pioneering

Americans, marooned by geography, were often ill-informed, superstitious, provincial, and fiercely individualistic. Ralph Waldo Emerson's popular lecture-essay "Self-Reliance" struck a deeply responsive chord. Popular literature of the period abounded with portraits of unique, isolated figures like James Fenimore Cooper's heroic Natty Bumppo and Herman Melville's restless Captain Ahab—just as Jacksonian politics aimed to emancipate the lone-wolf, enterprising businessperson. Yet even in this heyday of "rugged individualism," there were important exceptions. Pioneers, in tasks clearly beyond their own individual resources, would call upon their neighbors for logrolling and barn raising and upon their governments for help in building internal improvements.

Shaping the Western Landscape

The westward movement also molded the physical environment. Pioneers in a hurry often exhausted the land in the tobacco regions and then pushed on, leaving behind barren and rain-gutted fields. In the Kentucky bottomlands, cane as high as fifteen feet posed a seemingly insurmountable barrier to the plow. But settlers soon discovered that when the cane was burned off, European bluegrass thrived in the charred canefields. "Kentucky bluegrass," as it was somewhat inaccurately called, made ideal pasture for livestock—and lured thousands more American homesteaders into Kentucky.

The American West felt the pressure of civilization in additional ways. By the 1820s American fur-trappers were setting their traplines all over the vast Rocky Mountain region. The fur-trapping empire was based on the "rendezvous" system. Each summer, traders ventured from St. Louis to a verdant Rocky Mountain valley, made camp, and waited for the trappers and Indians to arrive with beaver pelts to swap for manufactured goods from the East. This trade thrived for some two decades; by the time beaver hats had gone out of fashion, the hapless beaver had all but disappeared from the region. Trade in buffalo robes also flourished, leading eventually to the virtually total annihilation of the massive bison herds that once blanketed the western prairies. Still farther west, on the California coast, other traders bought up prodigious quantities of sea-otter pelts, driving the once-bountiful otters to the point of near-extinction. Some historians have called this aggressive and often heedless exploitation of the West's natural bounty "ecological imperialism."

Yet Americans in this period also revered nature and admired its beauty. Indeed the spirit of nationalism fed a growing belief in the uniqueness of the American wilderness. Searching for the United States' distinctive characteristics in this nation-conscious age, many observers found the wild, unspoiled character of the land, especially in the West, to be among the young nation's defining attributes. Other countries might have impressive mountains or sparkling rivers, but none had the pristine, natural beauty of America, unspoiled by human hands and reminiscent of a time before the dawn of civilization.

Mouth of the Platte River, 900 Miles above St. Louis, by George Catlin, 1832
Catlin's West unfolded as a vast panorama of flat, open space peopled only by the Indians shown in the foreground. Catlin believed that capturing the unending prairie on canvas required a new aesthetic, the sublime horizontal, and an acceptance of a landscape bereft of man-built features, without "anything rising above the horizon, which was a perfect straight line around us, like that of the blue and boundless ocean."

Year	White	Nonwhite	Percent Nonwhite	Total Population
1790	3,172,000	757,000	19	3,929,000
1800	4,306,000	1,002,000	19	5,308,000
1810	5,862,000	1,378,000	19	7,240,000
1820	7,867,000	1,772,000	18	9,639,000
1830	10,537,000	2,329,000	18	12,866,000
1840	14,196,000	2,874,000	17	17,070,000
1850	19,553,000	3,639,000	16	23,192,000
1860	26,922,000	4,521,000	14	31,443,000

Population Increase, Including Slaves and Indians, 1790–1860 Increasing European immigration and the closing of the slave trade gradually "whitened" the population beginning in 1820. This trend continued into the early twentieth century.

This attitude toward wilderness became in time a kind of national mystique, inspiring literature and painting, and eventually kindling a powerful conservation movement.

George Catlin, a painter and student of Native American life, was among the first Americans to advocate the preservation of nature as a deliberate national policy. In 1832 he observed Sioux Indians in South Dakota recklessly slaughtering buffalo in order to trade the animals' tongues for the white man's whiskey. Appalled at this spectacle and fearing for the preservation of Indians and buffalo alike, Catlin proposed the creation of a national park. His idea later bore fruit with the creation of a national park system, beginning with Yellowstone Park in 1872.

The March of the Millions

As the American people moved west, they also multiplied at an amazing rate. By midcentury the population was still doubling approximately every twenty-five years, as in fertile colonial days.

By 1860 the original thirteen states had more than doubled in number: thirty-three stars graced the American flag. The United States was the fourth most populous nation in the western world, exceeded only by three European countries—Russia, France, and Austria.

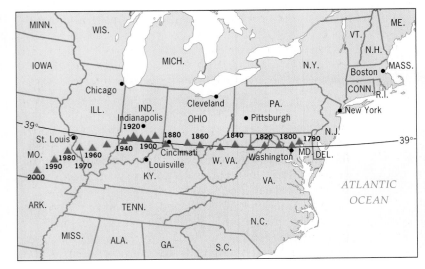

Westward Movement of Center of Population, 1790–2000 The triangles indicate the points at which a map of the United States weighted for the population of the country in a given year would balance. Note the remarkable equilibrium of the north-south pull from 1790 to about 1940, and the strong spurt west and south thereafter. The 1980 census revealed that the nation's center of population had at last moved west of the Mississippi River. The map also shows the slowing of the westward movement between 1890 and 1940—the period of heaviest immigration from Europe, which ended up mainly in East Coast cities.

Cincinnati in 1843 Famous as a processor of hogs, this "Queen City of the West" was a town of 2,540 people in 1800 and 161,044 in 1860, 45 percent of them foreign-born. Although tied to the South by downriver commerce on the Ohio and Mississippi Rivers, it remained loyal to the North during the Civil War.

Urban growth continued explosively. In 1790 there had been only two American cities that could boast populations of twenty thousand or more souls: Philadelphia and New York. By 1860 there were forty-three, and about three hundred other places claimed over five thousand inhabitants apiece. New York was the metropolis; New Orleans, the "Queen of the South"; and Chicago, the swaggering lord of the Midwest, destined to be "hog butcher for the world."

Such overrapid urbanization unfortunately brought undesirable by-products. It intensified the problems of smelly slums, feeble street lighting, inadequate policing, impure water, foul sewage, ravenous rats, and improper garbage disposal. Hogs poked their scavenging snouts about many city streets as late as the 1840s.

Irish and German Immigration by Decade, 1830–1900

Years	Irish	Germans
1831–1840	207,381	152,454
1841–1850	780,719	434,626
1851–1860	914,119	951,667
1861–1870	435,778	787,468
1871–1880	436,871	718,182
1881–1890	655,482	1,452,970
1891–1900	388,416	505,152
TOTAL	3,818,766	5,000,519

Boston in 1823 pioneered a sewer system, and New York in 1842 abandoned wells and cisterns for a piped-in water supply. The city thus unknowingly eliminated the breeding places of many disease-carrying mosquitoes.

A continuing high birthrate accounted for most of the increase in population, but by the 1840s the tides of immigration were adding hundreds of thousands more. Before this decade immigrants had been flowing in at a rate of sixty thousand a year, but suddenly the influx tripled in the 1840s and then quadrupled in the 1850s. During these two feverish decades, over a million and a half Irish, and nearly as many Germans, swarmed down the gangplanks. Why did they come?

The immigrants came partly because Europe seemed to be running out of room. The population of the Old World more than doubled in the nineteenth century, and Europe began to generate a seething pool of apparently "surplus" people. They were displaced and footloose in their homelands before they felt the tug of the American magnet. Indeed at least as many people moved about *within* Europe as crossed the Atlantic. America benefited from these people-churning changes but did not set them all in motion. Nor was the United States the sole beneficiary of the process: of the nearly 60 million people who abandoned Europe in the century after 1840, about 25 million went somewhere other than the United States.

Yet America still beckoned most strongly to the struggling masses of Europe, and the majority of migrants headed for the "land of freedom and opportunity." There was freedom from aristocratic caste and

A German immigrant living in Cincinnati wrote to his relatives in Germany in 1847:

"A lot of people come over here who were well off in Germany but were enticed to leave their fatherland by boastful and imprudent letters from their friends or children and thought they could become rich in America. This deceives a lot of people, since what can they do here? If they stay in the city they can only earn their bread at hard and unaccustomed labor. If they want to live in the country and don't have enough money to buy a piece of land that is cleared and has a house then they have to settle in the wild bush and have to work very hard to clear the trees out of the way so they can sow and plant. But people who are healthy, strong, and hard-working do pretty well."

Tens of thousands of destitute souls, fleeing the Land of Famine for the Land of Plenty, flocked to America in the "Black Forties." Ireland's great export has been population, and the Irish take their place beside the Jews and the Africans as a dispersed people (see "Makers of America: The Irish," pp. 294–295).

These uprooted newcomers—too poor to move west and buy the necessary land, livestock, and equipment—swarmed into the larger seaboard cities. Noteworthy were Boston and particularly New York, which rapidly became the largest Irish city in the world. Before many decades had passed, more people of Hibernian blood lived in America than on the "ould sod" of Erin's Isle.

The luckless Irish immigrants received no red-carpet treatment. Forced to live in squalor, they were rudely crammed into the already-vile slums. They were scorned by the older American stock, especially "proper" Protestant Bostonians, who regarded the scruffy Catholic arrivals as a social menace. Barely literate "Biddies" (Bridgets) took jobs as kitchen maids. Broad-shouldered "Paddies" (Patricks) were pushed into pick-and-shovel drudgery on canals and railroads, where thousands left their bones as victims of disease and accidental explosions. It was said that an Irishman lay buried under every railroad tie. As wage-depressing

state church; there was abundant opportunity to secure broad acres and better one's condition. Much-read letters sent home by immigrants—"America letters"—often described in glowing terms the richer life: low taxes, no compulsory military service, and "three meat meals a day." The introduction of transoceanic steamships also meant that the immigrants could come speedily, in a matter of ten or twelve days instead of ten or twelve weeks. On board, they were still jammed into unsanitary quarters, thus suffering an appalling death rate from infectious diseases, but the nightmare was more endurable because it was shorter.

The Emerald Isle Moves West

Ireland, already groaning under the heavy hand of British overlords, was prostrated in the mid-1840s. A terrible rot attacked the potato crop, on which the people had become dangerously dependent, and about one-fourth of them were swept away by disease and hunger. Starved bodies were found dead by the roadsides with grass in their mouths. All told, about 2 million perished.

Margaret McCarthy, a recent arrival in America, captured much of the complexity of the immigrant experience in a letter she wrote from New York to her family in Ireland in 1850:

"This is a good place and a good country, but there is one thing that's ruining this place. The emigrants have not money enough to take them to the interior of the country, which obliges them to remain here in New York and the like places, which causes the less demand for labor and also the great reduction in wages. For this reason I would advise no one to come to America that would not have some money after landing here that would enable them to go west in case they would get no work to do here."

> *An early-nineteenth-century French traveler recorded his impressions of America and Ireland:*
>
> "I have seen the Indian in his forests and the Negro in his chains, and thought, as I contemplated their pitiable condition, that I saw the very extreme of human wretchedness; but I did not then know the condition of unfortunate Ireland."

competitors for jobs, the Irish were hated by native workers. "No Irish Need Apply" was a sign commonly posted at factory gates and was often abbreviated to NINA. The Irish, for similar reasons, fiercely resented the blacks, with whom they shared society's basement. Race riots between black and Irish dockworkers flared up in several port cities, and the Irish were generally cool to the abolitionist cause.

The friendless "famine Irish" were forced to fend for themselves. The Ancient Order of Hibernians, a semisecret society founded in Ireland to fight rapacious landlords, served in America as a benevolent society, aiding the downtrodden. It also helped to spawn the "Molly Maguires," a shadowy Irish miners' union that rocked the Pennsylvania coal districts in the 1860s and 1870s.

The Irish tended to remain in low-skill occupations but gradually improved their lot, usually by acquiring modest amounts of property. The education of children was cut short as families struggled to save money to purchase a home. But for humble Irish peasants, cruelly cast out of their homeland, property ownership counted as a grand "success."

Politics quickly attracted these gregarious Gaelic newcomers. They soon began to gain control of powerful city machines, notably New York's Tammany Hall, and reaped the patronage rewards. Before long, beguilingly brogued Irishmen dominated police departments in many big cities, where they now drove the "Paddy wagons" that had once carted their brawling forebears to jail.

American politicians made haste to cultivate the Irish vote, especially in the politically potent state of New York. Irish hatred of the British lost nothing in the transatlantic transplanting. As the Irish-Americans increased in number—nearly 2 million arrived between 1830 and 1860—officials in Washington glimpsed political gold in those emerald green hills. Politicians often found it politically profitable to fire verbal volleys at London—a process vulgarly known as "twisting the British lion's tail."

The German Forty-Eighters

The influx of refugees from Germany between 1830 and 1860 was hardly less spectacular than that from Ireland. During these troubled years, over a million and a half Germans stepped onto American soil (see "Makers of America: The Germans," pp. 298–299). The bulk of them were uprooted farmers, displaced by crop failures and other hardships. But a strong sprinkling were liberal political refugees. Saddened by the collapse of the democratic revolutions of 1848, they had decided to leave the autocratic fatherland and flee to America—the brightest hope of democracy.

Germany's loss was America's gain. Zealous German liberals like the lanky and public-spirited Carl Schurz, a relentless foe of slavery and public corruption, contributed richly to the elevation of American political life.

Unlike the Irish, many of the Germanic newcomers possessed a modest amount of material goods. Most of them pushed out to the lush lands of the Middle West, notably Wisconsin, where they settled and established model farms. Like the Irish, they formed an influential body of voters whom American politicians shamelessly wooed. But the Germans were less potent politically because their strength was more widely scattered.

The hand of Germans in shaping American life was widely felt in still other ways. The Conestoga wagon, the Kentucky rifle, and the Christmas tree were all German contributions to American culture. Germans had fled from the militarism and wars of Europe and consequently came to be a bulwark of isolationist sentiment in the upper Mississippi Valley. Better educated on the whole than the stump-grubbing Americans, they warmly supported public schools, including their *Kindergarten* (children's garden). They likewise did much to stimulate art and music. As outspoken champions of freedom, they became relentless enemies of slavery during the fevered years before the Civil War.

Yet the Germans—often dubbed "damned Dutchmen"—were occasionally regarded with suspicion by their old-stock American neighbors. Seeking to preserve

The Irish

For a generation, from 1793 to 1815, war raged across Europe. Ruinous as it was on the Continent, the fighting brought unprecedented prosperity to the long-suffering landsmen of Ireland, groaning since the twelfth century under the yoke of English rule. For as Europe's fields lay fallow, irrigated only by the blood of its farmers, Ireland fed the hungry armies that ravened for food as well as territory. Irish farmers planted every available acre, interspersing the lowly potato amongst their fields of grain. With prices for food products ever mounting, tenant farmers reaped a temporary respite from their perpetual struggle to remain on the land. Most landlords were satisfied by the prosperity and so relaxed their pressure on tenants; others, stymied by the absence of British police forces that had been stripped of manpower to fight in Europe, had little means to enforce eviction notices.

But the peace that brought solace to battle-scarred Europe changed all this. After 1815 war-inflated wheat prices plummeted by half. Hard-pressed landlords resolved to leave vast fields unplanted. Assisted now by a strengthened British constabulary, they vowed to sweep the pesky peasants from the retired acreage. Many of those forced to leave sought work in England; some went to America. Then in 1845 a blight that ravaged the potato crop sounded the final knell for the Irish peasantry. The resultant famine spread desolation throughout the island. In five years more than a million people died. Another million sailed for America.

Of the emigrants, most were young and literate in English, the majority under thirty-five years old. Families typically pooled money to send strong young sons to the New World, where they would earn wages to pay the fares for those who waited at home. These "famine Irish" mostly remained in the port cities of the Northeast, abandoning the farmer's life for the dingy congestion of the urban metropolis.

The disembarking Irish were poorly prepared for urban life. They found progress up the economic ladder painfully slow. Their work as domestic servants or construction laborers was dull and arduous, and mortality

Outward Bound, The Quay at Dublin, 1854
Thousands fled famine in Ireland by coming to America in the 1840s and 1850s.

Saint Patrick's Day Parade in America, Union Square, c. 1870
This painting shows a Saint Patrick's Day parade in New York City. The religious festival was celebrated with greater fanfare in America than in Ireland itself, as Irish immigrants used it to boost their ethnic solidarity and assert their distinctive identity in their adopted country.

rates were astoundingly high. Escape from the potato famine hardly guaranteed a long life to an Irish American; a gray-bearded Irishman was a rare sight in nineteenth-century America. Most of the new arrivals toiled as day laborers. A fortunate few owned boardinghouses or saloons, where their dispirited countrymen sought solace in the bottle. For Irish-born women, opportunities were still scarcer; they worked mainly as domestic servants.

But it was their Roman Catholicism, more even than their penury or their perceived fondness for alcohol, that earned the Irish the distrust and resentment of their native-born, Protestant American neighbors. The cornerstone of social and religious life for Irish immigrants was the parish. Worries about safeguarding their children's faith inspired the construction of parish schools, financed by the pennies of struggling working-class Irish parents.

If Ireland's green fields scarcely equipped her sons and daughters for the scrap and scramble of economic life in America's cities, life in the Old Country nevertheless had instilled in them an aptitude for politics. Irish Catholic resistance against centuries of English Anglican domination had instructed many Old Country Irish in the ways of mass politics. That political experience readied them for the boss system of the political "machines" in America's northeastern cities. The boss's local representatives met each newcomer soon after he landed in America. Asking only for votes, the machine supplied coal in wintertime, food, and help with the law. Irish voters soon became a bulwark of the Democratic party, reliably supporting the party of Jefferson and Jackson in cities like New York and Boston. As Irish Americans like New York's "Honest John" Kelly themselves became bosses, white-collar jobs in government service opened up to the Irish. They became building inspectors, aldermen, and even policemen—an astonishing irony for a people driven from their homeland by the nightsticks and bayonets of the British police.

their language and culture, they sometimes settled in compact "colonies" and kept aloof from the surrounding community. Accustomed to the "Continental Sunday" and uncurbed by Puritan tradition, they made merry on the Sabbath and drank huge quantities of an amber beverage called *bier* (beer), which dates its real popularity in America to their coming. Their Old World drinking habits, like those of the Irish, spurred advocates of temperance in the use of alcohol to redouble their reform efforts.

Flare-ups of Antiforeignism

The invasion by this so-called immigrant "rabble" in the 1840s and 1850s inflamed the prejudices of American "nativists." They feared that these foreign hordes would outbreed, outvote, and overwhelm the old "native" stock. Not only did the newcomers take jobs from "native" Americans, but the bulk of the displaced Irish were Roman Catholics, as were a substantial minority of the Germans. The Church of Rome was still widely regarded by many old-line Americans as a "foreign" church; convents were commonly referred to as "popish brothels."

Crooked Voting A bitter "nativist" cartoon charging Irish and German immigrants with "stealing" elections.

Strong antiforeignism was reflected in the platform of the American (Know-Nothing) party in 1856:

"Americans must rule America; and to this end, native-born citizens should be selected for all state, federal, or municipal offices of government employment, in preference to naturalized citizens."

Roman Catholics were now on the move. Seeking to protect their children from Protestant indoctrination in the public schools, they began in the 1840s to construct an entirely separate Catholic educational system—an enormously expensive undertaking for a poor immigrant community, but one that revealed the strength of its religious commitment. They had formed a negligible minority during colonial days, and their numbers had increased gradually. But with the enormous influx of the Irish and Germans in the 1840s and 1850s, the Catholics became a powerful religious group. In 1840 they had ranked fifth, behind the Baptists, Methodists, Presbyterians, and Congregationalists. By 1850, with some 1.8 million communicants, they had bounded into first place—a position they have never lost.

Older-stock Americans were alarmed by these mounting figures. They professed to believe that in due time the "alien riffraff" would "establish" the Catholic Church at the expense of Protestantism and would introduce "popish idols." The noisier American "nativists" rallied for political action. In 1849 they formed the Order of the Star-Spangled Banner, which soon developed into the formidable American, or "Know-Nothing," party—a name derived from its secretiveness. "Nativists" agitated for rigid restrictions on immigration and naturalization and for laws authorizing the deportation of alien paupers. They also promoted a lurid literature of exposure, much of it pure fiction. The authors, sometimes posing as escaped nuns, described the shocking sins they imagined the cloisters concealed, including the secret burial of babies. One of these sensational books—Maria Monk's *Awful Disclosures* (1836)—sold over 300,000 copies.

Even uglier was occasional mass violence. As early as 1834, a Catholic convent near Boston was burned by a howling mob, and in ensuing years a few scattered attacks fell upon Catholic schools and churches. The most frightful flare-up occurred during 1844 in Philadelphia, where the Irish Catholics fought back against the threats of the "nativists." The City of Brotherly Love did not quiet down until two Catholic churches had been burned and some thirteen citizens had been killed and fifty wounded in several days of fighting. These outbursts of intolerance, though infrequent and generally localized in the larger cities, remain an unfortunate blot on the record of America's treatment of minority groups.

Immigrants were undeniably making America a more pluralistic society—one of the most ethnically and racially varied in the history of the world—and perhaps it was small wonder that cultural clashes would occur. Why, in fact, were such episodes not even more frequent and more violent? Part of the answer lies in the robustness of the American economy. The vigorous growth of the economy in these years both attracted immigrants in the first place and ensured that, once arrived, they could claim their share of American wealth without jeopardizing the wealth of others. Their hands and brains, in fact, helped fuel economic expansion. Immigrants and the American economy, in short, needed one another. Without the newcomers, a preponderantly agricultural United States might well have been condemned to watch in envy as the Industrial Revolution swept through nineteenth-century Europe.

Creeping Mechanization

A group of gifted British inventors, beginning about 1750, perfected a series of machines for the mass production of textiles. This harnessing of steam multiplied the power of human muscles some ten-thousandfold and ushered in the modern factory system—and with it, the so-called Industrial Revolution. It was accompanied by a no-less-spectacular transformation in agricultural production and in the methods of transportation and communication.

The factory system gradually spread from Britain—"the world's workshop"—to other lands. It took a generation or so to reach western Europe, and then the United States. Why was the youthful American Republic, eventually to become an industrial giant, so slow to embrace the machine?

For one thing, land was cheap in America. Land-starved descendants of land-starved peasants were not going to coop themselves up in smelly factories when they might till their own acres in God's fresh air and sunlight. Labor was therefore generally scarce, and enough nimble hands to operate the machines were hard to find—until immigrants began to pour ashore in the 1840s. Money for capital investment, moreover, was not plentiful in pioneering America. Raw materials lay undeveloped, undiscovered, or unsuspected. The Republic was one day to become the world's leading coal producer, but much of the coal burned in colonial times was imported all the way from Britain.

If labor was scarce, consumers were not. But the young country had difficulty producing goods of high enough quality and cheap enough cost to compete with mass-produced European products. Long-established British factories in particular provided cutthroat competition. Their superiority was attested by the fact that a few unscrupulous Yankee manufacturers, out to make a dishonest dollar, stamped their own products with fake English trademarks.

The British also enjoyed a monopoly of the textile machinery, whose secrets they were anxious to hide from foreign competitors. Parliament enacted laws, in harmony with the mercantile system, forbidding the export of the machines or the emigration of mechanics able to reproduce them.

Although a number of small manufacturing enterprises existed in the early Republic, the future industrial colossus was still snoring. Not until well past the middle of the nineteenth century did the value of the output of the factories exceed that of the farms.

Whitney Ends the Fiber Famine

Samuel Slater has been acclaimed the "Father of the Factory System" in America, and seldom can the paternity of a movement more properly be ascribed to one person. A skilled British mechanic of twenty-one, he was attracted by bounties being offered to British workers familiar with the textile machines. After memorizing the plans for the machinery, he escaped in disguise to America, where he won the backing of Moses Brown, a Quaker capitalist in Rhode Island. Laboriously reconstructing the essential apparatus with the aid of a blacksmith and a carpenter, he put into operation in 1791 the first efficient American machinery for spinning cotton thread.

The Germans

Between 1820 and 1920, a sea of Germans lapped at America's shores and seeped into its very heartland. Their numbers surpassed those of any other immigrant group, even the prolific and often-detested Irish. Yet this Germanic flood, unlike its Gaelic equivalent, stirred little panic in the hearts of native-born Americans because the Germans largely stayed to themselves, far from the madding crowds and nativist fears of northeastern cities. They prospered with astonishing ease, building towns in Wisconsin, agricultural colonies in Texas, and religious communities in Pennsylvania. They added a decidedly Germanic flavor to the heady brew of reform and community building that so animated antebellum America.

A German Homestead in Wisconsin
These settlers' Germanic heritage is evident in the architecture of the log cabin. Traditional log cabins used log walls right up to the roofline, but the Germans closed their gables with vertical board siding.

These "Germans" actually hailed from many different Old World lands, because there was no unified nation of Germany until 1871, when the ruthless and crafty Prussian Otto von Bismarck assembled the German state out of a mosaic of independent principalities, kingdoms, and duchies. Until that time, "Germans" came to America as Prussians, Bavarians, Hessians, Rhinelanders, Pomeranians, and Westphalians. They arrived at different times and for many different reasons. Some, particularly the so-called Forty-Eighters—the refugees from the abortive democratic revolutions of 1848—hungered for the democracy they had failed to win in Germany. Others, particularly Jews, Pietists, and Anabaptist groups like the Amish and the Mennonites, coveted religious freedom. And they came not only to America. Like the Italians later, many Germans sought a new life in Brazil, Argentina, and Chile. But the largest number ventured into the United States.

Typical German immigrants arrived with fatter purses than their Irish counterparts. Small landowners or independent artisans in their native countries, they did not have to settle for bottom-rung industrial employment in the grimy factories of the Northeast and instead could afford to push on to the open spaces of the American West.

In Wisconsin these immigrants found a home away from home, a place with a climate, soil, and geography much like central Europe's. Milwaukee, a crude frontier town before the Germans' arrival, became the "German Athens." It boasted a German theater, German beer gardens, a German volunteer fire company, and a German-English academy. In distant Texas, German settlements like New Braunfels and Friedrichsburg flourished. When the famous landscape architect and writer Frederick Law Olmsted stumbled upon these prairie outposts of Teutonic culture in 1857, he was shocked to be "welcomed by a figure in a blue flannel shirt and pendant beard, quoting Tacitus." These German colonies in the frontier Southwest mixed high European elegance with

"Little Germany" Cincinnati's "Over-the-Rhine" district in 1887.

Texas ruggedness. Olmsted described a visit to a German household where the settlers drank "coffee in tin cups upon Dresden saucers" and sat upon "barrels for seats, to hear a Beethoven symphony on the grand piano."

These Germanic colonizers of America's heartland also formed religious communities, none more distinctive or durable than the Amish settlements of Pennsylvania, Indiana, and Ohio. The Amish took their name from their founder and leader, the Swiss Anabaptist Jacob Amman. Like other Anabaptist groups, they shunned extravagance and reserved baptism for adults, repudiating the tradition of infant baptism practiced by most Europeans. For this they were persecuted, even imprisoned, in Europe. Seeking escape from their oppression, some five hundred Amish ventured to Pennsylvania in the 1700s, followed by three thousand in the years from 1815 to 1865.

In America they formed enduring religious communities—isolated enclaves where they could shield themselves from the corruption and the conveniences of the modern world. To this day the German-speaking Amish still travel in horse-drawn carriages and farm without heavy machinery. No electric lights brighten the darkness that nightly envelops their tidy farmhouses; no ringing telephones punctuate the reverent tranquility of their mealtime prayer; no ornaments relieve the austere simplicity of their black garments. The Amish remain a stalwart, traditional community in a rootless, turbulent society, a living testament to the religious ferment and social experiments of the antebellum era.

Amish Country, near Lancaster, Pennsylvania
For more than two centuries, the Amish people have preserved their traditional way of life.

America's First Textile Mill   When Samuel Slater first built his mill on the Blackstone River in 1791, angry neighbors tore down the dam that provided power to its water-driven machinery—an early instance of grass-roots environmental protest. This Pawtucket, Rhode Island, mill began by producing only thread, which was then distributed to home weavers who turned it into cloth. Within two years, Slater and his partners were selling their product to the far-flung markets of Salem, New York, Philadelphia, and Baltimore. By 1805, the mill featured the "mule," a new machine which made possible the spinning of finer yarns.

The ravenous mechanism was now ready, but where was the cotton fiber? Handpicking one pound of lint from three pounds of seed was a full day's work for one slave, and this process was so expensive that American-made cotton cloth was relatively rare.

Another mechanical genius, Massachusetts-born Eli Whitney, now made his mark. After graduating from Yale, he journeyed to Georgia to serve as a private tutor while preparing for the law. There he was told that the poverty of the South would be relieved if someone could only invent a workable device for separating the seed from the short-staple cotton fiber. Within ten days, in 1793, he built a crude machine called the cotton gin (short for engine) that was fifty times more effective than the handpicking process.

Few machines have ever wrought so wondrous a change. The gin affected not only the history of America but that of the world. Almost overnight the raising of cotton became highly profitable, and the South was tied

A Pioneer Woman Batting Cotton   Making cotton "batts" from the raw fiber was the first step in making "homespun" cloth. Mechanical looms and sewing machines would soon make this traditional women's work obsolete.

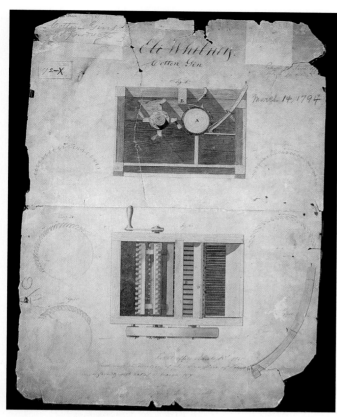

Patent for Eli Whitney's Cotton Gin
Whitney's revolutionary little machine was artfully simple. Wire hooks on a rotating cylinder pulled the cotton fibers through slots too narrow to allow seeds to pass. A set of brushes then removed the fibers. Whitney's gin made possible the mass cultivation of upland, or short-staple, cotton, which was unprofitable to raise when its seeds had to be laboriously removed by hand. Before Whitney's invention, cotton growing had been largely confined to long-staple, or Sea Island cotton, which could grow only in hot, humid coastal areas. With the advent of the cotton gin, short-staple cotton cultivation spread across the southern interior—and so did slavery.

One observer in 1836 published a newspaper account of conditions in some of the New England factories:

"The operatives work thirteen hours a day in the summer time, and from daylight to dark in the winter. At half past four in the morning the factory bell rings, and at five the girls must be in the mills. . . . So fatigued . . . are numbers of girls that they go to bed soon after receiving their evening meal, and endeavor by a comparatively long sleep to resuscitate their weakened frames for the toil of the coming day."

hand and foot to the throne of King Cotton. Human bondage had been dying out, but the insatiable demand for cotton reriveted the chains on the limbs of the downtrodden southern blacks.

South and North both prospered. Slave-driving planters cleared more acres for cotton, pushing the Cotton Kingdom westward off the depleted tidewater plains, over the Piedmont, and onto the black loam bottomlands of Alabama and Mississippi. Humming gins poured out avalanches of snowy fiber for the spindles of the Yankee machines, though for decades to come the mills of Britain bought the lion's share of southern cotton. The American phase of the Industrial Revolution, which first blossomed in cotton textiles, was well on its way.

Factories at first flourished most actively in New England, though they branched out into the more populous areas of New York, New Jersey, and Pennsylvania. The South, increasingly wedded to the production of cotton, could boast of comparatively little manufacturing. Its capital was bound up in slaves; its local consumers for the most part were desperately poor.

New England was singularly favored as an industrial center for several reasons. Its narrow belt of stony soil made farming difficult and hence made manufacturing attractive. A relatively dense population provided labor and accessible markets, shipping brought in capital, and snug seaports made easy the import of raw materials and the export of the finished products. Finally, the rapid rivers—notably the Merrimack in Massachusetts—provided abundant water power to turn the cogs of the machines. By 1860 more than 400 million pounds of southern cotton poured annually into the gaping maws of over a thousand mills, mostly in New England.

Daguerreotype of a Young Girl with Sample of Cotton Dress Fabric, c. 1850s
The growing availability of inexpensive American-made calico, or printed cotton cloth, vastly expanded women's wardrobes.

Marvels in Manufacturing

America's factories spread slowly until about 1807, when there began the fateful sequence of the embargo, nonintercourse, and the War of 1812. Stern necessity dictated the manufacture of substitutes for normal imports, while the stoppage of European commerce was temporarily ruinous to Yankee shipping. Both capital and labor were driven from the waves onto the factory floor, as New England, in the striking phrase of John Randolph, exchanged the trident for the distaff. Generous bounties were offered by local authorities for homegrown goods, "Buy American" and "Wear American" became popular slogans, and patriotism prompted the wearing of baggy homespun garments. President Madison donned some at his inauguration, where he was said to have been a walking argument for the better processing of native wool.

But the manufacturing boomlet broke abruptly with the peace of Ghent in 1815. British competitors unloaded their dammed-up surpluses at ruinously low prices, and American newspapers were so full of British advertisements for goods on credit that little space was left for news. In one Rhode Island district, all 150 mills were forced to close their doors, except the original Slater plant. Responding to pained outcries, Congress provided some relief when it passed the mildly protective Tariff of 1816—among the earliest political contests to control the shape of the economy.

Manufacturing Guns, c. 1860   A rare daguerreotype showing an operator working the Lock Frame Jigging Machine in Samuel Colt's state-of-the-art Hartford, Connecticut, gun factory.

As the factory system flourished, it embraced numerous other industries in addition to textiles. Prominent among them was the manufacturing of firearms, and here the wizardly Eli Whitney again appeared with an extraordinary contribution. Frustrated in his earlier efforts to monopolize the cotton gin, he turned to the mass production of muskets for the U.S. Army. Up to this time, each part of a firearm had been hand-tooled, and if the trigger of one broke, the trigger of another might or might not fit. About 1798 Whitney seized upon the idea of having machines make each part, so that all the triggers, for example, would be as much alike as the successive imprints of a copperplate engraving. Journeying to Washington, he reportedly dismantled ten of his new muskets in the presence of skeptical officials, scrambled the parts together, and then quickly reassembled ten different muskets.

The principle of interchangeable parts was widely adopted by 1850, and it ultimately became the basis of modern mass-production, assembly-line methods. It gave to the North the vast industrial plant that ensured military preponderance over the South. Ironically, the Yankee Eli Whitney, by perfecting the cotton gin, gave slavery a renewed lease on life, and perhaps made the Civil War more likely. At the same time, by popularizing the principle of interchangeable parts, Whitney helped factories to flourish in the North, giving the Union a decided advantage when that showdown came.

The sewing machine, invented by Elias Howe in 1846 and perfected by Isaac Singer, gave another strong boost to northern industrialization. The sewing machine became the foundation of the ready-made clothing industry, which took root about the time of the Civil War. It drove many a seamstress from the shelter of the private home to the factory, where, like a human robot, she tended the clattering mechanisms.

Each momentous new invention seemed to stimulate still more imaginative inventions. For the decade ending in 1800, only 306 patents were registered in Washington; but the decade ending in 1860 saw the amazing total of 28,000. Yet in 1838 the clerk of the Patent Office resigned in despair, complaining that all worthwhile inventions had been discovered.

Technical advances spurred equally important changes in the form and legal status of business organizations. The principle of limited liability aided the concentration of capital by permitting the individual investor, in cases of legal claims or bankruptcy, to risk no more than his own share of the corporation's stock. Fifteen Boston families formed one of the earliest investment capital companies, the Boston Associates. They eventually dominated the textile, railroad, insurance, and banking business of Massachusetts. Laws of "free incorporation," first passed in New York in 1848, meant that businessmen could create corporations without applying for individual charters from the legislature.

Samuel F. B. Morse's telegraph was among the inventions that tightened the sinews of an increasingly complex business world. A distinguished but poverty-stricken portrait painter, Morse finally secured from Congress, to the accompaniment of the usual jeers, an appropriation of $30,000 to support his experiment with "talking wires." In 1844 Morse strung a wire forty miles from Washington to Baltimore and tapped out the historic message, "What hath God wrought?" The invention brought fame and fortune to Morse, as he put distantly separated people in almost instant communication with one another. By the eve of the Civil War, a web of singing wires spanned the continent, revolutionizing news gathering, diplomacy, and finance.

Workers and "Wage Slaves"

One ugly outgrowth of the factory system was an increasingly acute labor problem. Hitherto manufacturing had been done in the home, or in the small shop, where the master craftsman and his apprentice, rubbing elbows at the same bench, could maintain an intimate and friendly relationship. The Industrial Revolution submerged this personal association in the impersonal ownership of stuffy factories in "spindle cities." Around

---

Said Abraham Lincoln (1809–1865) in a lecture in 1859,

"The patent system secured to the inventor for a limited time exclusive use of his invention, and thereby added the fuel of interest to the fire of genius in the discovery and production of new and useful things."

Ten years earlier Lincoln had received patent no. 6469 for a scheme to buoy steamboats over shoals. It was never practically applied, but he remains the only president ever to have secured a patent.

The Master Craftsman
Dignity and pride of workmanship
are evident in this tidy wheelwright's
shop. Small-scale, intimate workplaces
like this were eventually overshadowed
by the mass-production, impersonal
factory system, as in the illustrations
on pages 306 and 309.

these, like tumors, the slumlike hovels of the "wage slaves" tended to cluster.

Clearly the early factory system did not shower its benefits evenly on all. While many owners grew plump, workingpeople often wasted away at their work-benches. Hours were long, wages were low, and meals were skimpy and hastily gulped. Workers were forced to toil in unsanitary buildings that were poorly ventilated, lighted, and heated. They were forbidden by law to form labor unions to raise wages, for such cooperative activity was regarded as a criminal con-spiracy. Not surprisingly, only twenty-four recorded strikes occurred before 1835.

Especially vulnerable to exploitation were child workers. In 1820 a significant portion of the nation's industrial toilers were children under ten years of age. Victims of factory labor, many children were mentally blighted, emotionally starved, physically stunted, and even brutally whipped in special "whipping rooms." In Samuel Slater's mill of 1791, the first machine tenders were seven boys and two girls, all under twelve years of age.

By contrast, the lot of most adult wage workers improved markedly in the 1820s and 1830s. In the full flush of Jacksonian democracy, many of the states granted the laboring man the vote. Brandishing the ballot, he first strove to lighten his burden through workingmen's parties. Eventually many workers gave their loyalty to the Democratic party of Andrew Jackson, whose attack on the Bank of the United States and against all forms of "privilege" reflected their anxieties about the emerging capitalist economy. In addition to such goals as the ten-hour day, higher wages, and tolerable working conditions, they demanded public education for their children and an end to the inhuman practice of imprisonment for debt.

Employers, abhorring the rise of the "rabble" in poli-tics, fought the ten-hour day to the last ditch. They argued that reduced hours would lessen production, increase costs, and demoralize the workers. Laborers would have so much leisure time that the Devil would lead them into mischief. A red-letter gain was at length registered for labor in 1840, when President Van Buren established the ten-hour day for federal employees on public works. In ensuing years a number of states gradually fell into line by reducing the hours of workingpeople.

Day laborers at last learned that their strongest weapon was to lay down their tools, even at the risk of prosecution under the law. Dozens of strikes erupted in the 1830s and 1840s, most of them for higher wages,

EXAMINING THE EVIDENCE

The Invention of the Sewing Machine Historians of technology examine not only the documentary evidence of plans and patents left behind by inventors, but surviving machines themselves. In 1845 Elias Howe, a twenty-six-year-old apprentice to a Boston watchmaker, invented a sewing machine that could make 250 stitches a minute, five times what the swiftest hand-sewer could do. A year later Howe received a patent for his invention, but because the hand-cranked machine could only stitch straight seams for a short distance before requiring resetting, it had limited commercial appeal. Howe took his sewing machine abroad, where he worked with British manufacturers to improve it, and then returned to America and combined his patent with those of other inventors, including Isaac M. Singer.

Hundreds of thousands of sewing machines were produced beginning in the 1850s for commercial manufacturing of clothing, books, shoes, and many other products and also for home use. The sewing machine became the first widely advertised consumer product. Due to its high cost, the Singer company introduced an installment buying plan, which helped place sewing machines in most middle-class households. Why was the sewing machine able to find eager customers in commercial workshops and home sewing rooms alike? How might the sewing machine have changed other aspects of American life, such as work patterns, clothing styles, and retail selling? What other advances in technology might have been necessary for the invention of the sewing machine?

Violence broke out along the New York waterfront in 1836 when laborers striking for higher wages attacked "scabs." Philip Hone's (1780–1851) diary records:

"The Mayor, who acts with vigour and firmness, ordered out the troops, who are now on duty with loaded arms. . . . These measures have restored order for the present, but I fear the elements of disorder are at work; the bands of Irish and other foreigners, instigated by the mischievous councils of the trades-union and other combinations of discontented men, are acquiring strength and importance which will ere long be difficult to quell."

some for the ten-hour day, and a few for such unusual goals as the right to smoke on the job. The workers usually lost more strikes than they won, for the employer could resort to such tactics as the importing of strikebreakers—often derisively called "scabs" or "rats," and often fresh off the boat from the Old World. Labor long raised its voice against the unrestricted inpouring of wage-depressing and union-busting immigrant workers.

Labor's early and painful efforts at organization had netted some 300,000 trade unionists by 1830. But such encouraging gains were dashed on the rocks of hard times following the severe depression of 1837. As unemployment spread, union membership shriveled. Yet toilers won a promising legal victory in 1842. The supreme court of Massachusetts ruled in the case of *Commonwealth* v. *Hunt* that labor unions were not illegal conspiracies, provided that their methods were "honorable and peaceful." This enlightened decision

The Sewing Floor of Thompson's Skirt Factory, 1859 The burgeoning textile industry provided employment for thousands of women in antebellum America—and also produced the clothes that women wore. This view of a New York City shop in 1859 illustrates the transition from hand-sewing (on the right) to machine-stitching (on the left). It also vividly illustrates the contrast between the kinds of "sewing circles" in which women had traditionally sought companionship to the impersonal mass-production line of the modern manufacturing plant. Note especially the stark exhortation on the wall: "Strive to Excel." Contrast this impersonal scene with the workplace depicted on page 304.

> *A woman worker in the Lowell mills wrote a friend in 1844:*
>
> "You wish to know minutely of our hours of labor. We go in [to the mill] at five o'clock; at seven we come out to breakfast; at half-past seven we return to our work, and stay until half-past twelve. At one, or quarter-past one four months in the year, we return to our work, and stay until seven at night. Then the evening is all our own, which is more than some laboring girls can say, who think nothing is more tedious than a factory life."

did not legalize the strike overnight throughout the country, but it was a significant signpost of the times. Trade unions still had a rocky row to hoe, stretching ahead for about a century, before they could meet management on relatively even terms.

Women and the Economy

Women were also sucked into the clanging mechanism of factory production. Farm women and girls had an important place in the preindustrial economy, spinning yarn, weaving cloth, and making candles, soap, butter, and cheese. New factories such as the textile mills of New England undermined these activities, cranking out manufactured goods much faster than they could be made by hand at home. Yet these same factories offered employment to the very young women whose work they were displacing. Factory jobs promised greater economic independence for women, as well as the means to buy the manufactured products of the new market economy.

"Factory girls" typically toiled six days a week, earning a pittance for dreary, limb-numbing, earsplitting stints of twelve or thirteen hours—"from dark to dark." The Boston Associates, nonetheless, proudly pointed to their textile mill at Lowell, Massachusetts, as a showplace factory. The workers were virtually all New England farm girls, carefully supervised on and off the job by watchful matrons. Escorted regularly to church from their company boardinghouses and forbidden to form unions, they had few opportunities to share dissatisfactions over their grueling working conditions.

But factory jobs of any kind were still unusual for women. Opportunities for women to be economically self-supporting were scarce and consisted mainly of nursing, domestic service, and especially teaching. The dedicated Catharine Beecher, unmarried daughter of a famous preacher and sister of Harriet Beecher Stowe, tirelessly urged women to enter the teaching profession. She eventually succeeded beyond her dreams, as men left teaching for other lines of work and schoolteaching became a thoroughly "feminized" occupation. Other work "opportunities" for women beckoned in household service. Perhaps one white family in ten employed servants at midcentury, most of whom were poor white, immigrant, or black women. About 10 percent of white women were working for pay outside their own homes in 1850, and estimates are that about 20 percent of all women had been employed at some time prior to marriage.

The vast majority of workingwomen were single. Upon marriage they left their paying jobs and took up their new work (without wages) as wives and mothers. In the home they were enshrined in a "cult of domesticity," a widespread cultural creed that glorified the customary functions of the homemaker. From their pedestal, married women commanded immense moral power, and they increasingly made decisions that altered the character of the family itself.

Women's changing roles and the spreading Industrial Revolution brought some important changes in the life of the nineteenth-century home—the traditional "women's sphere." Love, not parental "arrangement," more and more frequently determined the choice of a spouse—yet parents often retained the power of veto. Families thus became more closely knit and affectionate, providing the emotional refuge that made the threatening impersonality of big-city industrialism tolerable to many people.

Most striking, families grew smaller. The average household had nearly six members at the end of the eighteenth century but fewer than five members a century later. The "fertility rate," or number of births among women age fourteen to forty-five, dropped sharply among white women in the years after the Revolution and, in the course of the nineteenth century as a whole, fell by half. Birth control was still a taboo topic for polite conversation, and contraceptive

York, Pennsylvania, Family with Negro Servant, c. 1828
This portrait of a Pennsylvania family presents a somewhat idealized picture of the home as the woman's sphere. The wife and mother sits at the center of activity; while she reads to the children, the husband and father stands by somewhat superfluously. A black servant cares for an infant in the corner, suggesting the prosperous status of this household.

technology was primitive, but clearly some form of family limitation was being practiced quietly and effectively in countless families, rural and urban alike. Women undoubtedly played a large part—perhaps the leading part—in decisions to have fewer children. This newly assertive role for women has been called "domestic feminism," because it signified the growing power and independence of women, even while they remained wrapped in the "cult of domesticity."

Smaller families, in turn, meant child-centered families, since where children are fewer, parents can lavish more care on them individually. European visitors to the United States in the nineteenth century often complained about the unruly behavior of American "brats." But though American parents may have increasingly spared the rod, they did not spoil their children. Lessons were enforced by punishments other than the hickory stick. When the daughter of novelist Harriet Beecher Stowe neglected to do her homework, her mother sent her from the dinner table and gave her "only bread and water in her own apartment." What Europeans saw as permissiveness was in reality the consequence of an emerging new idea of child-rearing, in which the child's will was not to be simply broken, but rather shaped.

In the little republic of the family, as in the Republic at large, good citizens were raised not to be meekly obedient to authority, but to be independent individuals who could make their own decisions on the basis of internalized moral standards. Thus the outlines of the "modern" family were clear by midcentury: it was small, affectionate, and child-centered, and it provided a special arena for the talents of women. Feminists of a later day might decry the stifling atmosphere of the nineteenth-century home, but to many women of the time, it seemed a big step upward from the conditions of grinding toil—often alongside men in the fields—in which their mothers had lived.

Western Farmers Reap a Revolution in the Fields

As smoke-belching factories altered the eastern skyline, flourishing farms were changing the face of the West. The trans-Allegheny region—especially the Ohio-Indiana-Illinois tier—was fast becoming the nation's breadbasket. Before long it would become a granary to the world.

Pioneer families first hacked a clearing out of the forest and then planted their painfully furrowed fields to corn. The yellow grain was amazingly versatile. It could be fed to hogs ("corn on the hoof") or distilled into liquor ("corn in the bottle"). Both these products could be transported more easily than the bulky grain itself, and they became the early western farmer's staple market items. So many hogs were butchered, traded, or shipped at Cincinnati that the city was known as the "Porkopolis" of the West.

Most western produce was at first floated down the Ohio-Mississippi River system, to feed the lusty appetite of the booming Cotton Kingdom. But western farmers were as hungry for profits as southern slaves and planters were for food. These tillers, spurred on by the easy availability of seemingly boundless acres, sought ways to bring more and more land into cultivation.

Ingenious inventors came to their aid. One of the first obstacles that frustrated the farmers was the thickly matted soil of the West, which snagged and snapped fragile wooden plows. John Deere of Illinois in 1837 finally produced a steel plow that broke the stubborn soil. Sharp and effective, it was also light enough to be pulled by horses, rather than oxen.

In the 1830s Virginia-born Cyrus McCormick contributed the most wondrous contraption of all: a mechanical mower-reaper. The clattering cogs of McCormick's horse-drawn machine were to the western farmers what the cotton gin was to the southern planters. Seated on his red-chariot reaper, a single husbandman could do the work of five men with sickles and scythes.

No other American invention cut so wide a swath. It made ambitious capitalists out of humble plowmen, who now scrambled for more acres on which to plant more fields of billowing wheat. Subsistence farming gave way to production for the market, as large-scale ("extensive"), specialized, cash-crop agriculture came to dominate the trans-Allegheny West. With it followed mounting indebtedness, as farmers bought more land and more machinery to work it. Soon hustling farmer-businesspeople were annually harvesting a larger crop than the South—which was becoming self-sufficient in food production—could devour. They began to dream of markets elsewhere—in the mushrooming factory towns of the East or across the faraway Atlantic. But they were still largely landlocked. Commerce moved north and south on the river systems. Before it could begin to move east-west in bulk, a transportation revolution would have to occur.

Highways and Steamboats

In 1789, when the Constitution was launched, primitive methods of travel were still in use. Waterborne commerce, whether along the coast or on the rivers, was slow, uncertain, and often dangerous. Stagecoaches and wagons lurched over bone-shaking roads. Passengers would be routed out to lay nearby fence rails across muddy stretches, and occasionally horses would drown in muddy pits while wagons sank slowly out of sight.

Cheap and efficient carriers were imperative if raw materials were to be transported to factories and if finished products were to be delivered to consumers. On December 3, 1803, a firm in Providence, Rhode Island, sent a shipment of yarn to a point sixty miles away, notifying the purchaser that the consignment could be expected to arrive in "the course of the winter."

McCormick Reaper Works, 1850s
Contrast this scene of "mass production" with the workplace depicted in "The Master Craftsman" on page 304.

McCormick's Miraculous Reaper   This illustration shows an early test of Cyrus McCormick's mechanical reaper near his home in Virginia in 1831. The reaper was best suited, however, to the horizonless fields of wheat on the rolling prairies of the Midwest. By the 1850s McCormick's Chicago factory was cranking out more than twenty thousand reapers a year for midwestern farmers.

A promising improvement came in the 1790s, when a private company completed the Lancaster Turnpike in Pennsylvania. It was a broad, hard-surfaced highway that thrust sixty-two miles westward from Philadelphia to Lancaster. As drivers approached the tollgate, they were confronted with a barrier of sharp pikes, which were turned aside when they paid their toll. Hence the term *turnpike*.

The Lancaster Turnpike proved to be a highly successful venture, returning as high as 15 percent annual dividends to its stockholders. It attracted a rich trade to Philadelphia and touched off a turnpike-building boom that lasted about twenty years. It also stimulated

western development. The turnpikes beckoned to the canvas-covered Conestoga wagons, whose creakings heralded a westward advance that would know no real retreat.

Western road building, always expensive, encountered many obstacles. One pesky roadblock was the noisy states' righters, who opposed federal aid to local projects. Eastern states also protested against being bled of their populations by the westward-reaching arteries.

Westerners scored a notable triumph in 1811 when the federal government began to construct the elongated National Road, or Cumberland Road. This highway ultimately stretched from Cumberland, in western Mary-

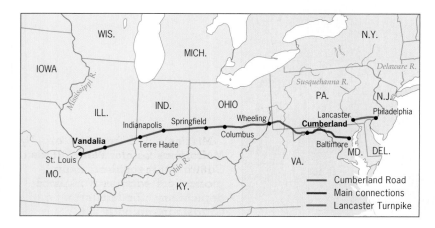

Cumberland (National) Road and Main Connections   Note also the Lancaster Turnpike.

land, to Vandalia, in Illinois, a distance of 591 miles. The War of 1812 interrupted construction, and states' rights shackles on internal improvements hampered federal grants. But the thoroughfare was belatedly brought to its destination in 1852 by a combination of aid from the states and the federal government.

The steamboat craze, which overlapped the turnpike craze, was touched off by an ambitious painter-engineer named Robert Fulton. He installed a powerful steam engine in a vessel that posterity came to know as the *Clermont* but that a dubious public dubbed "Fulton's Folly." On a historic day in 1807, the quaint little ship, belching sparks from its single smokestack, churned steadily from New York City up the Hudson River toward Albany. It made the run of 150 miles in 32 hours.

The success of the steamboat was sensational. People could now in large degree defy wind, wave, tide, and downstream current. Within a few years, Fulton had changed all of America's navigable streams into two-way arteries, thereby doubling their carrying capacity. Hitherto keelboats had been pushed up the Mississippi, with quivering poles and raucous profanity, at less than one mile an hour—a process that was prohibitively expensive. Now the steamboats could churn rapidly against the current, ultimately attaining speeds in excess of ten miles an hour. The mighty Mississippi had met its master.

By 1820 there were some sixty steamboats on the Mississippi and its tributaries; by 1860 about one thousand, some of them luxurious river palaces. Keen rivalry among the swift and gaudy steamers led to memorable races. Excited passengers would urge the captain to pile on wood at the risk of bursting the boilers, which all too often exploded, with tragic results for the floating firetraps. When the steamer *Sultana* blew up in April 1865, the explosion killed seventeen hundred passengers, including many Union prisoners of war being repatriated to the North.

Chugging steamboats played a vital role in the opening of the West and South, both of which were richly endowed with navigable rivers. Like bunches of grapes on a vine, population clustered along the banks of the broad-flowing streams. Cotton growers and other farmers made haste to take up and turn over the now-profitable soil. Not only could they float their produce out to market, but, hardly less important, they could ship in at low cost their shoes, hardware, and other manufactured necessities.

"Clinton's Big Ditch" in New York

A canal-cutting craze paralleled the boom in turnpikes and steamboats. A few canals had been built around

Mississippi in Time of Peace, by Mrs. Frances Flora Bond Palmer, 1865 By the mid-nineteenth century, steamboats had made the Mississippi a bustling river highway—as it remains today.

falls and elsewhere in colonial days, but ambitious projects lay in the future. Resourceful New Yorkers, cut off from federal aid by states' righters, themselves dug the Erie Canal, linking the Great Lakes with the Hudson River. They were blessed with the driving leadership of Governor DeWitt Clinton, whose grandiose project was scoffingly called "Clinton's Big Ditch" or "the Governor's Gutter."

Begun in 1817, the canal eventually ribboned 363 miles. On its completion in 1825, a garlanded canal boat glided from Buffalo, on Lake Erie, to the Hudson River and on to New York harbor. There, with colorful ceremony, Governor Clinton emptied a cask of water from the lake to symbolize "the marriage of the waters."

The water from Clinton's keg baptized the Empire State. Mule-drawn passengers and bulky freight could now be handled with thrift and dispatch, at the dizzy speed of five miles an hour. The cost of shipping a ton of grain from Buffalo to New York City fell from $100 to $5, and the time of transit from about twenty days to six.

Ever-widening economic ripples followed the completion of the Erie Canal. The value of land along the route skyrocketed, and new cities—such as Rochester and Syracuse—blossomed. Industry in the state boomed. The new profitability of farming in the Old Northwest—notably in Ohio, Michigan, Indiana, and Illinois—attracted thousands of European immigrants to the unaxed and untaxed lands now available.

Flotillas of steamships soon plied the Great Lakes, connecting with canal barges at Buffalo. Interior waterside villages like Cleveland, Detroit, and Chicago exploded into mighty cities.

Other profound economic and political changes followed the canal's completion. The price of potatoes in New York City was cut in half, and many dispirited New England farmers, no longer able to face the ruinous competition, abandoned their rocky holdings and went elsewhere. Some became mill hands, thus speeding the industrialization of America. Others, finding it easy to go west over the Erie Canal, took up new farmland south of the Great Lakes, where they were joined by thousands of New Yorkers and other northerners. Still others shifted to fruit, vegetable, and dairy farming. The transformations in the Northeast—canal consequences—showed how long-established local market structures could be swamped by the emerging behemoth of a continental economy.

The Iron Horse

The most significant contribution to the development of such an economy proved to be the railroad. It was fast, reliable, cheaper than canals to construct, and not frozen over in winter. Able to go almost anywhere, even

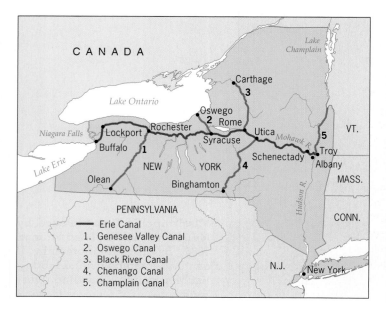

Erie Canal and Main Branches The Erie Canal system, and others like it, tapped the fabulous agricultural potential of the Midwest, while canal construction and maintenance provided employment for displaced eastern farmers squeezed off the land by competition from their more productive midwestern cousins. The transportation revolution thus simultaneously expanded the nation's acreage under cultivation and speeded the shift of the work force from agricultural to manufacturing and "service" occupations. In 1820 more than three-quarters of American workers labored on farms; by 1850 only a little more than half of them were so employed. (Also see the map on the top of page 313.)

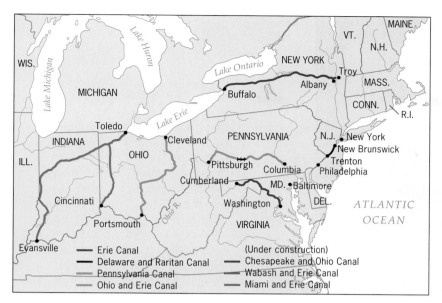

Principal Canals in 1840 Note that the canals mainly facilitated east-west traffic, especially along the great Lake Erie artery. No comparable network of canals existed in the South—a disparity that helps to explain northern superiority in the Civil War that came two decades later.

through the Allegheny barrier, it defied terrain and weather. The first railroad appeared in the United States in 1828. By 1860, only thirty-two years later, the United States boasted thirty thousand miles of railroad track, three-fourths of it in the rapidly industrializing North.

At first the railroad faced strong opposition from vested interests, especially canal backers. Anxious to protect its investment in the Erie Canal, the New York legislature in 1833 prohibited the railroads from carrying freight—at least temporarily. Early railroads were also considered a dangerous public menace, for flying sparks could set fire to nearby haystacks and houses, and appalling railway accidents could turn the wooden "miniature hells" into flaming funeral pyres for their riders.

Railroad pioneers had to overcome other obstacles as well. Brakes were so feeble that the engineer might miss the station twice, both arriving and backing up. Arrivals and departures were conjectural, and numerous differences in gauge (the distance between the rails) meant frequent changes of trains for passengers. In 1840 there were seven transfers between Philadelphia and Charleston. But gauges gradually became standardized, better brakes did brake, safety devices were adopted, and the Pullman "sleeping palace" was introduced in 1859. America at long last was being bound together with braces of iron, later to be made of steel.

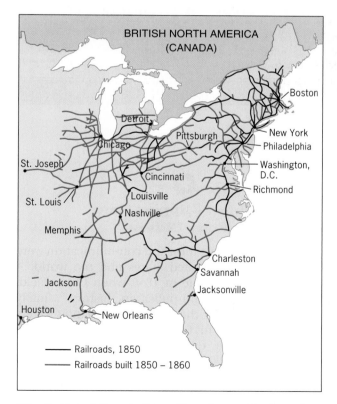

The Railroad Revolution Note the explosion of new railroad construction in the 1850s and its heavy concentration in the North.

Poster-Timetable for Baltimore & Susquehanna Railroad, 1840 Advertising the Baltimore & Susquehanna's train schedule alone was not sufficient to get passengers to their destinations. A typical trip often entailed coordinating legs on other railroad lines, stagecoaches, and canal boats.

Cables, Clippers, and Pony Riders

Other forms of transportation and communication were binding together the United States and the world. A crucial development came in 1858 when Cyrus Field, called "the greatest wire-puller in history," finally stretched a cable under the deep North Atlantic waters from Newfoundland to Ireland. Although this initial cable went dead after three weeks of public rejoicing, a heavier cable laid in 1866 permanently linked the American and European continents.

The United States merchant marine encountered rough sailing during much of the early nineteenth century. American vessels had been repeatedly laid up by the embargo, the War of 1812, and the panics of 1819

and 1837. American naval designers made few contributions to maritime progress. A pioneer American steamer, the Savannah, had crept across the Atlantic in 1819, but it used sail most of the time and was pursued for a day by a British captain who thought it afire.

In the 1840s and 1850s, a golden age dawned for American shipping. Yankee naval yards, notably Donald McKay's at Boston, began to send down the ways sleek new craft called clipper ships. Long, narrow, and majestic, they glided across the sea under towering masts and clouds of canvas. In a fair breeze, they could outrun any steamer.

The stately clippers sacrificed cargo space for speed, and their captains made killings by hauling high-value cargoes in record times. They wrested much of the tea-carrying trade between the Far East and Britain from their slower-sailing British competitors, and they sped

Chariot of Fame Clipper Ship, by Duncan McFarlane, 1854

thousands of impatient adventurers to the goldfields of California and Australia.

But the hour of glory for the clipper was relatively brief. On the eve of the Civil War, the British had clearly won the world race for maritime ascendancy with their iron tramp steamers ("teakettles"). Although slower and less romantic than the clipper, these vessels were steadier, roomier, more reliable, and hence more profitable.

As late as 1877, stagecoach passengers were advised in print,

"Never shoot on the road as the noise might frighten the horses. . . . Don't point out where murders have been committed, especially if there are women passengers. . . . Expect annoyances, discomfort, and some hardships."

No story of rapid American communication would be complete without including the Far West. By 1858 horse-drawn overland stagecoaches, immortalized by Mark Twain's *Roughing It,* were a familiar sight. Their dusty tracks stretched from the bank of the muddy Missouri River clear to California.

Even more dramatic was the Pony Express, established in 1860 to carry mail speedily the two thousand lonely miles from St. Joseph, Missouri, to Sacramento, California. Daring, lightweight riders, leaping onto wiry ponies saddled at stations approximately ten miles apart, could make the trip in an amazing ten days. These unarmed horsemen galloped on, summer or winter, day or night, through dust or snow, past Indians and bandits. The speeding postmen missed only one trip, though the whole enterprise lost money heavily and folded after only eighteen legend-leaving months.

Just as the clippers had succumbed to steam, so were the express riders unhorsed by Samuel Morse's clacking keys, which began tapping messages to California in 1861. The swift ships and the fleet ponies ushered out a dying technology of wind and muscle. In the future, machines would be in the saddle.

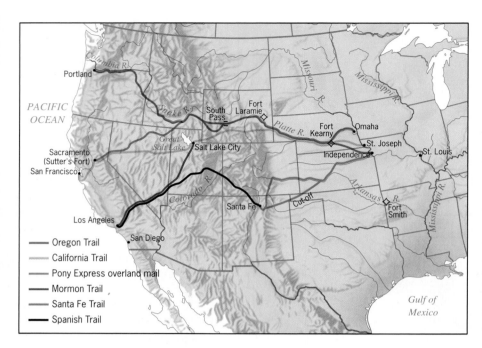

Main Routes West Before the Civil War Mark Twain described his stagecoach trip to California in the 1860s in *Roughing It*: "We began to get into country, now, threaded here and there with little streams. These had high, steep banks on each side, and every time we flew down one bank and scrambled up the other, our party inside got mixed somewhat. First we would all be down in a pile at the forward end of the stage, . . . and in a second we would shoot to the other end, and stand on our heads. And . . . as the dust rose from the tumult, we would all sneeze in chorus, and the majority of us would grumble, and probably say some hasty thing, like: 'Take your elbow out of my ribs!—can't you quit crowding?'"

The Transport Web Binds the Union

More than anything else, the desire of the East to tap the West stimulated the "transportation revolution." Until about 1830 the produce of the western region drained southward to the cotton belt or to the heaped-up wharves of New Orleans. The steamboat vastly aided the reverse flow of finished goods up the watery western arteries and helped bind West and South together. But the truly revolutionary changes in commerce and communication came in the three decades before the Civil War, as canals and railroad tracks radiated out from the East, across the Alleghenies and into the blossoming heartland. The ditch-diggers and tie-layers were attempting nothing less than a conquest of nature itself. They would offset the "natural" flow of trade on the interior rivers by laying down an impressive grid of "internal improvements."

The builders succeeded beyond their wildest dreams. The Mississippi was increasingly robbed of its traffic, as goods moved eastward on chugging trains, puffing lake boats, and mule-tugged canal barges. Governor Clinton had in effect picked up the mighty Father of Waters and flung it over the Alleghenies, forcing it to empty into the sea at New York City. By the 1840s the city of Buffalo handled more western pro-

duce than New Orleans. Between 1836 and 1860, grain shipments through Buffalo increased a staggering sixtyfold. New York City became the seaboard queen of the nation, a gigantic port through which a vast hinterland poured its wealth and to which it daily paid economic tribute.

By the eve of the Civil War, a truly continental economy had emerged. The principle of division of labor, which spelled productivity and profits in the factory, applied on a national scale as well. Each region now specialized in a particular type of economic activity. The South raised cotton for export to New England and Britain; the West grew grain and livestock to feed factory workers in the East and in Europe; the East made machines and textiles for the South and the West.

The economic pattern thus woven had fateful political and military implications. Many southerners regarded the Mississippi as a silver chain that naturally linked together the upper valley states and the Cotton Kingdom. They would become convinced, as secession approached in the 1850s, that some or all of these states would have to secede with them or be strangled. But they would overlook the man-made links that increasingly bound the upper Mississippi Valley to the East in intimate commercial union. Southern rebels would have to fight not only Northern armies but the tight bonds of an interdependent continental economy. Economically, the two northerly sections were Siamese twins.

The Market Revolution

No less revolutionary than the political upheavals of the antebellum era was the "market revolution" that transformed a subsistence economy of scattered farms and tiny workshops into a national network of industry and commerce. Greater mechanization and a more robust market-oriented economy raised new legal questions about winners and losers. How tightly should patents protect inventions? Should the government regulate monopolies? Who should own the technologies and networks that made America hum in the 1840s and 1850s?

Under Chief Justice John Marshall, the U.S. Supreme Court vigilantly protected contract rights by requiring state governments to grant irrevocable charters. Monopolies easily developed, as new companies found it difficult to break into markets. After Marshall died in 1835, the climate began to change and the winds of economic opportunity blew more freely. When the proprietors of Boston's Charles River Bridge (which included Harvard College) sued the owners of the new Warren Bridge for unconstitutionally violating their original contract, the new chief justice, Roger B. Taney, sided with the newcomers and argued that "the rights of the community" outweighed any exclusive corporate rights. Taney's decision opened new entrepreneurial channels and encouraged greater competition. So did the passage of more liberal state incorporation laws beginning in the 1830s, granting investors the benefit of "limited liability" if their companies were sued or went bankrupt.

As more and more Americans—mill workers as well as farmhands, women as well as men—linked their economic fate to the burgeoning market economy, the self-sufficient households of colonial days were transformed. Most families had once raised all their own food, spun their own wool, and bartered with their neighbors for the few necessities they could not make themselves. In growing numbers they now scattered to work for wages in the mills, or they planted just a few crops for sale at market and used the money to buy goods made by strangers in far-off factories. As store-bought fabric, candles, and soap replaced homemade products, a quiet revolution occurred in the household division of labor and status. Traditional women's work was rendered superfluous and devalued. The home itself, once a center of economic production in which all family members cooperated, grew into a place of refuge from the world of work, a refuge that became increasingly the special and separate sphere of women.

The Levee at New Orleans, 1854
With the expansion of cotton growing into the new states of the trans-Appalachian Southwest and the coming of the steamboat, the entire Cotton Kingdom paid economic tribute to New Orleans, Queen City of the South. With a banner slung from the flagstaff, the captain of the dangerously overloaded "Henry Frank" boasted of the number of bales his boat carried.

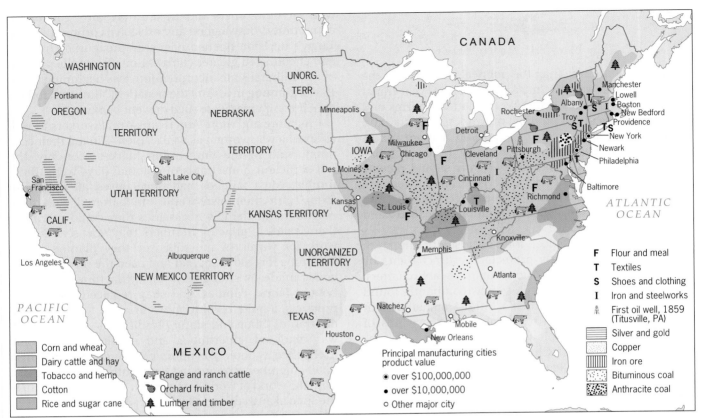

Industry and Agriculture, 1860   Still a nation of farmers on the eve of the Civil War, Americans had nevertheless made an impressive start on their own Industrial Revolution, especially in the Northeast.

Revolutionary advances in manufacturing and transportation brought increased prosperity to all Americans, but they also widened the gulf between the rich and the poor. Millionaires had been rare in the early days of the Republic, but by the eve of the Civil War, several specimens of colossal financial success were strutting across the national stage. Spectacular was the case of fur-trader and real estate speculator John Jacob Astor, who left an estate of $30 million on his death in 1848.

Cities bred the greatest extremes of economic inequality. Unskilled workers, then as always, fared worst. Many of them came to make up a floating mass of "drifters," buffeted from town to town by the shifting prospects for menial jobs. These wandering workers accounted at various times for up to half the population of the brawling industrial centers. Although their numbers were large, they left little behind them but the homely fruits of their transient labor. Largely unstoried and unsung, they are among the forgotten men and women of American history.

Many myths about "social mobility" grew up over the buried memories of these unfortunate day laborers. Mobility did exist in industrializing America—but not in the proportions that legend often portrays. Rags-to-riches success stories were relatively few.

Yet America, with its dynamic society and wide-open spaces, undoubtedly provided more "opportunity" than did the contemporary countries of the Old World—which is why millions of immigrants packed their bags and headed for New World shores. Moreover, a rising tide lifts all boats, and the improvement in overall standards of living was real. Wages for unskilled workers in a labor-hungry America rose about 1 percent a year from 1820 to 1860. This general prosperity helped defuse the potential class conflict that might otherwise have exploded—and that did explode in many European countries.

Chronology

c. 1750	Industrial Revolution begins in Britain
1791	Samuel Slater builds first U.S. textile factory
1793	Eli Whitney invents cotton gin
1798	Whitney develops interchangeable parts for muskets
1807	Robert Fulton's first steamboat Embargo spurs American manufacturing
1811	Cumberland Road construction begins
1817	Erie Canal construction begins
1825	Erie Canal completed
1828	First railroad in United States
1830s	Cyrus McCormick invents mechanical mower-reaper
1834	Anti-Catholic riot in Boston
1837	John Deere develops steel plow
1840	President Van Buren establishes ten-hour day for federal employees
1842	Massachusetts declares labor unions legal in *Commonwealth* v. *Hunt*
c. 1843–1868	Era of clipper ships
1844	Samuel Morse invents telegraph Anti-Catholic riot in Philadelphia
1845–1849	Potato famine in Ireland
1846	Elias Howe invents sewing machine
1848	First general incorporation laws in New York Democratic revolutions collapse in Germany
1849	American, or Know-Nothing, party formed
1852	Cumberland Road completed
1858	Cyrus Field lays first transatlantic cable
1860	Pony Express established
1861	First transcontinental telegraph
1866	Permanent transatlantic cable established

15

The Ferment of Reform and Culture

1790–1860

WE [AMERICANS] WILL WALK ON OUR OWN FEET;
WE WILL WORK WITH OUR OWN HANDS; WE WILL
SPEAK OUR OWN MINDS.

RALPH WALDO EMERSON, "THE AMERICAN SCHOLAR," 1837

A third revolution accompanied the reformation of American politics and the transformation of the American economy in the mid-nineteenth century. This was a diffuse yet deeply felt commitment to improve the character of ordinary Americans, to make them more upstanding, God-fearing, and literate. Some high-minded souls were disillusioned by the rough-and-tumble realities of democratic politics. Others, notably women, were excluded from the political game altogether. As the young Republic grew, increasing numbers of Americans poured their considerable energies into religious revivals and reform movements.

Reform campaigns of all types flourished in sometimes bewildering abundance. There was not "a reading man" who was without some scheme for a new utopia in his "waistcoat pocket," claimed Ralph Waldo Emerson. Reformers promoted better public schools and rights for women, as well as miracle medicines, polygamy, celibacy, rule by prophets, and guidance by spirits. Societies were formed against alcohol, tobacco, profanity, and the transit of mail on the Sabbath. Eventually overshadowing all other reforms was the great crusade against slavery (see pp. 362–368).

Many reformers drew their crusading zeal from religion. Beginning in the late 1790s and boiling over into the early nineteenth century, the Second Great Awakening swept through America's Protestant churches, transforming the place of religion in American life and sending a generation of believers out on their missions to perfect the world.

Reviving Religion

Church attendance was still a regular ritual for about three-fourths of the 23 million Americans in 1850. Alexis de Tocqueville declared that there was "no country in the world where the Christian religion retains a greater influence over the souls of men than in America." Yet the religion of these years was not the old-time religion of colonial days. The austere Calvinist rigor had long been seeping out of the American churches. The rationalist ideas of the French Revolutionary era had done much to soften the older orthodoxy. Thomas Paine's widely circulated book *The Age of Reason* (1794) had shockingly declared that all churches were "set up to terrify and enslave mankind, and monopolize power and profit." American anticlericalism was seldom that virulent, but many of the Founding Fathers, including

Jefferson and Franklin, embraced the liberal doctrines of Deism that Paine promoted. Deists relied on reason rather than revelation, on science rather than the Bible. They rejected the concept of original sin and denied Christ's divinity. Yet Deists believed in a Supreme Being who had created a knowable universe and endowed human beings with a capacity for moral behavior.

Deism helped to inspire an important spinoff from the severe Puritanism of the past—the Unitarian faith, which began to gather momentum in New England at the end of the eighteenth century. Unitarians held that God existed in only *one* person (hence *uni*tarian), and not in the orthodox Trinity (God the Father, God the Son, and God the Holy Spirit). Although denying the deity of Jesus, Unitarians stressed the essential goodness of human nature rather than its vileness; they proclaimed their belief in free will and the possibility of salvation through good works; they pictured God not as a stern Creator but as a loving Father. Embraced by many leading thinkers (including Ralph Waldo Emerson), the Unitarian movement appealed mostly to intellectuals whose rationalism and optimism contrasted sharply with the hellfire doctrines of Calvinism, especially predestination and human depravity.

A boiling reaction against the growing liberalism in religion set in about 1800. A fresh wave of roaring revivals, beginning on the southern frontier but soon rolling even into the cities of the Northeast, sent the Second Great Awakening surging across the land.

Sweeping up even more people than the First Great Awakening (see p. 96) almost a century earlier, the Second Awakening was one of the most momentous episodes in the history of American religion. This tidal wave of spiritual fervor left in its wake countless converted souls, many shattered and reorganized churches, and numerous new sects. It also encouraged an effervescent evangelicalism that bubbled up into innumerable areas of American life—including prison reform, the temperance cause, the women's movement, and the crusade to abolish slavery.

The Second Great Awakening was spread to the masses on the frontier by huge "camp meetings." As many as twenty-five thousand people would gather for an encampment of several days to drink the hellfire gospel as served up by an itinerant preacher. Thousands of spiritually starved souls "got religion" at these gatherings and in their ecstasy engaged in frenzies of rolling, dancing, barking, and jerking. Many of the "saved" soon backslid into their former sinful ways, but the revivals boosted church membership and stimulated a variety of humanitarian reforms. Responsive easterners were moved to do missionary work in the West with Indians, in Hawaii, and in Asia.

Methodists and Baptists reaped the most abundant harvest of souls from the fields fertilized by revivalism. Both sects stressed personal conversion (contrary to predestination), a relatively democratic control of church affairs, and a rousing emotionalism. As a frontier jingle ran,

Religious Camp Meeting by J. Maze Burbank, 1839 At huge, daylong encampments, repentant sinners dedicated themselves to lives of personal rectitude and social reform. Fire-and-brimstone preachers like the one depicted here inspired convulsions, speaking in tongues, and ecstatic singing and dancing among the converted. Out of this religious upheaval grew many of the movements for social improvement in the pre–Civil War decades, including the abolitionist crusade.

The devil hates the Methodists
Because they sing and shout the best.

Powerful Peter Cartwright (1785–1872) was the best known of the Methodist "circuit riders," or traveling frontier preachers. This ill-educated but sinewy servant of the Lord ranged for a half-century from Tennessee to Illinois, calling upon sinners to repent. With bellowing voice and flailing arms, he converted thousands of souls to the Lord. Not only did he lash the Devil with his tongue, but with his fists he knocked out rowdies who tried to break up his meetings. His Christianity was definitely muscular.

Charles Grandison Finney (1792–1875), 1834
The charismatic Finney appears here at age forty-two, at the height of his career as an evangelist. A mesmerizer of audiences, he was said to have converted over a half million people. In 1834, Finney had just led a series of enormously successful revivals in cities along the Erie Canal. The next year he would establish a theology department at the newly founded Oberlin College in Ohio, where he helped train a generation of ministers and served as president from 1851 to 1866.

Bell-voiced Charles Grandison Finney was the greatest of the revival preachers. Trained as a lawyer, Finney abandoned the bar to become an evangelist after a deeply moving conversion experience as a young man. Tall and athletically built, Finney held huge crowds spellbound with the power of his oratory and the pungency of his message. He led massive revivals in Rochester and New York City in 1830 and 1831. Finney preached a version of the old-time religion, but he was also an innovator. He devised the "anxious bench," where repentant sinners could sit in full view of the congregation, and he encouraged women to pray aloud in public. Holding out the promise of a perfect Christian kingdom on earth, Finney denounced both alcohol and slavery. He eventually served as president of Oberlin College in Ohio, which he helped to make a hotbed of revivalist activity and abolitionism.

A key feature of the Second Great Awakening was the feminization of religion, in terms of both church membership and theology. Middle-class women, the wives and daughters of businessmen, were the first and most fervent enthusiasts of religious revivalism. They made up the majority of new church members, and they were most likely to stay within the fold when the tents were packed up and the traveling evangelists left town.

In his lecture "Hindrances to Revivals," delivered in the 1830s, Charles Grandison Finney (1792–1875) proposed the excommunication of drinkers and slaveholders:

"Let the churches of all denominations speak out on the subject of temperance, let them close their doors against all who have anything to do with the death-dealing abomination, and the cause of temperance is triumphant. A few years would annihilate the traffic. Just so with slavery. . . . It is a great national sin. It is a sin of the church. The churches by their silence, and by permitting slaveholders to belong to their communion, have been consenting to it. . . . The church cannot turn away from this question. It is a question for the church and for the nation to decide, and God will push it to a decision."

Perhaps women's greater ambivalence than men about the changes wrought by the expanding market economy made them such eager converts to piety. It helped as well that evangelicals preached a gospel of female spiritual worth and offered women an active role in bringing their husbands and families back to God. That accomplished, many women turned to saving the rest of society. They formed a host of benevolent and charitable organizations and spearheaded crusades for most, if not all, of the era's ambitious reforms.

Denominational Diversity

Revivals also furthered the fragmentation of religious faiths. Western New York, where many descendants of New England Puritans had settled, was so blistered by sermonizers preaching "hellfire and damnation" that it came to be known as the "Burned-Over District."

Millerites, or Adventists, who mustered several hundred thousand adherents, rose from the superheated soil of the Burned-Over District in the 1830s. Named after the eloquent and commanding William Miller, they interpreted the Bible to mean that Christ would return to earth on October 22, 1844. Donning their go-to-meeting clothes, they gathered in prayerful assemblies to greet their Redeemer. The failure of Jesus to descend on schedule dampened but did not destroy the movement.

Like the First Great Awakening, the Second Great Awakening tended to widen the lines between classes and regions. The more prosperous and conservative denominations in the East were little touched by revivalism, and Episcopalians, Presbyterians, Congregationalists, and Unitarians continued to rise mostly from the wealthier, better-educated levels of society. Methodists, Baptists, and the members of the other new sects spawned by the swelling evangelistic fervor tended to come from less prosperous, less "learned" communities in the rural South and West.

Religious diversity further reflected social cleavages when the churches faced up to the slavery issue. By 1844–1845 both the southern Baptists and the southern Methodists had split with their northern brethren over human bondage. The Methodists came to grief over the case of a slaveowning bishop in Georgia, whose second wife added several household slaves to his estate. In 1857 the Presbyterians, North and South, parted company. The secession of the southern churches foreshadowed the secession of the southern states. First the churches split, then the political parties split, and then the Union split.

A Desert Zion in Utah

The smoldering spiritual embers of the Burned-Over District kindled one especially ardent flame in 1830. In that year Joseph Smith—a rugged visionary, proud of his prowess at wrestling—reported that he had received some golden plates from an angel. When deciphered, they constituted the Book of Mormon, and the Church of Jesus Christ of Latter-Day Saints (Mormons) was launched. It was a native American product, a new religion, destined to spread its influence worldwide.

After establishing a religious oligarchy, Smith ran into serious opposition from his non-Mormon neighbors, first in Ohio and then in Missouri and Illinois. His cooperative sect antagonized rank-and-file Americans, who were individualistic and dedicated to free enterprise. The Mormons aroused further anger by voting as a unit and by openly but understandably drilling their militia for defensive purposes. Accusations of polygamy likewise arose and increased in intensity, for Joseph Smith was reputed to have several wives.

Continuing hostility finally drove the Mormons to desperate measures. In 1844 Joseph Smith and his brother were murdered and mangled by a mob in Carthage, Illinois, and the movement seemed near collapse. The falling torch was seized by a remarkable Mormon Moses named Brigham Young. Stern and austere in contrast to Smith's charm and affability, the barrel-chested Brigham Young had received only eleven days of formal schooling. But he quickly proved to be an aggressive leader, an eloquent preacher, and a gifted administrator. Determined to escape further persecution, Young in 1846–1847 led his oppressed and despoiled Latter-Day Saints over vast rolling plains to Utah as they sang "Come, Come, Ye Saints."

Overcoming pioneer hardships, the Mormons soon made the desert bloom like a new Eden by means of ingenious and cooperative methods of irrigation. The crops of 1848, threatened by hordes of crickets, were saved when flocks of gulls appeared, as if by a miracle, to gulp down the invaders. (A monument to the seagulls stands in Salt Lake City today.)

Semiarid Utah grew remarkably. By the end of 1848, some five thousand settlers had arrived, and other large bands were to follow them. Many dedicated Mormons in the 1850s actually made the thirteen-hundred-mile trek across the plains pulling two-wheeled carts.

Under the rigidly disciplined management of Brigham Young, the community became a prosperous

> *Polygamy was an issue of such consequence that it was bracketed with slavery in the Republican national platform of 1856:*
>
> "It is both the right and the imperative duty of Congress to prohibit in the Territories those twin relics of barbarism—Polygamy and Slavery."

Free Schools for a Free People

Tax-supported primary schools were scarce in the early years of the Republic. They had the odor of pauperism about them, since they existed chiefly to educate the children of the poor—the so-called ragged schools. Advocates of "free" public education met stiff opposition. A midwestern legislator cried that he wanted only this simple epitaph when he died: "Here lies an enemy of public education."

Well-to-do, conservative Americans gradually saw the light. If they did not pay to educate "other folkses brats," the "brats" might grow up into a dangerous, ignorant rabble—armed with the vote. Taxation for education was an insurance premium that the wealthy paid for stability and democracy.

Tax-supported public education, though miserably lagging in the slavery-cursed South, triumphed between 1825 and 1850. Hard-toiling laborers wielded increased influence and demanded instruction for their children. Most important was the gaining of manhood suffrage for whites in Jackson's day. A free vote cried aloud for free education. A civilized nation that was both ignorant and free, declared Thomas Jefferson, "never was and never will be."

The famed little red schoolhouse—with one room, one stove, one teacher, and often eight grades—became the shrine of American democracy. Regrettably, it was an

frontier theocracy and a cooperative commonwealth. Young married as many as twenty-seven women—some of them wives in name only—and begot fifty-six children. The population was further swelled by thousands of immigrants from Europe, where the Mormons had established a flourishing missionary movement.

A crisis developed when the Washington government was unable to control the hierarchy of Brigham Young, who had been made territorial governor in 1850. A federal army marched in 1857 against the Mormons, who harassed its lines of supply and rallied to die in their last dusty ditch. Fortunately the quarrel was finally adjusted without serious bloodshed. The Mormons later ran afoul of the antipolygamy laws passed by Congress in 1862 and 1882, and their unique marital customs delayed statehood for Utah until 1896.

Joseph Smith Preaching to the Indians, by Carl Christian Anton Christensen This painting was one of a series of twenty-two recording the beginnings of the Mormon Church, created by a Danish convert who migrated to the Great Salt Lake valley in 1857. The artist stitched the paintings together into a huge scroll and carried it with him as he lectured throughout the West. Mormon founder Smith and his followers felt a special duty to carry their faith to the Indians, whom they considered one of the lost tribes of Israel. That did not stop the Mormons, however, from driving Indians from the Utah Territory to free up land for their own settlement.

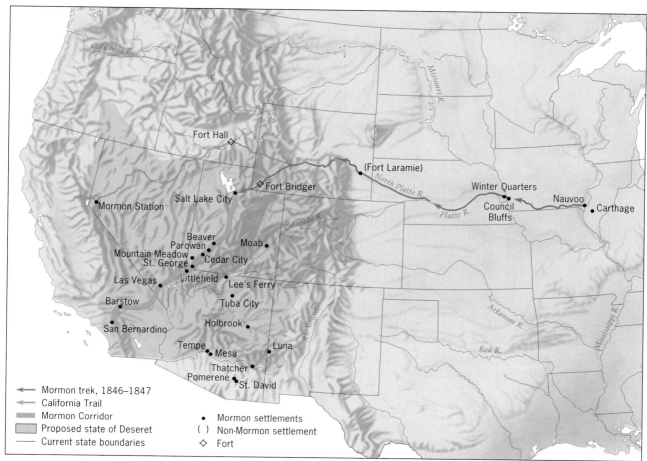

The Mormon World After Joseph Smith's murder at Carthage in 1844, the Mormons abandoned their thriving settlement at Nauvoo, Illinois (which had about twenty thousand inhabitants in 1845) and set out for the valley of the Great Salt Lake, then still part of Mexico. When the Treaty of Guadalupe Hidalgo (see p. 384) in 1848 brought the vast Utah Territory into the United States, the Mormons rapidly expanded their desert colony, which they called Deseret, especially along the "Mormon Corridor" that stretched from Salt Lake to southern California.

imperfect shrine. Early free schools stayed open only a few months of the year. Schoolteachers, most of them men in this era, were too often ill-trained, ill-tempered, and ill-paid. They frequently put more stress on "lickin'" (with a hickory stick) than on "larnin'." These knights of the blackboard often "boarded around" in the community, and some knew scarcely more than their older pupils. They usually taught only the "three Rs"—"readin', 'ritin', and 'rithmetic." To many rugged Americans, suspicious of "book larnin'," this was enough.

Reform was urgently needed. Into the breach stepped Horace Mann (1796–1859), a brilliant and idealistic graduate of Brown University. As secretary of the Massachusetts Board of Education, he campaigned effectively for more and better schoolhouses, longer school terms, higher pay for teachers, and an expanded curriculum. His influence radiated out to other states, and impressive improvements were chalked up. Yet education remained an expensive luxury for many communities. As late as 1860, the nation counted only about a hundred public secondary schools—and nearly a million white adult illiterates. Black slaves in the South were legally forbidden to receive instruction in reading or writing, and even free blacks, in the North as well as the South, were usually excluded from the schools.

Educational advances were aided by improved textbooks, notably those of Noah Webster (1758–1843), a Yale-educated Connecticut Yankee who was known

The Country School, by Winslow Homer, 1871   Stark and simple by latter-day standards, the one-room schoolhouse nevertheless contributed richly to the development of the young Republic.

as the "Schoolmaster of the Republic." His "reading lessons," used by millions of children in the nineteenth century, were partly designed to promote patriotism.

> *Abraham Lincoln (1809–1865) wrote of his education (1859),*
>
> "There were some schools so-called [in Indiana], but no qualification was ever required of a teacher beyond 'readin', writin' and cipherin' to the rule of three. . . . There was absolutely nothing to excite ambition for education. Of course, when I came of age I did not know much. Still, somehow, I could read, write and cipher to the rule of three, but that was all. I have not been to school since. The little advance I now have upon this store of education, I have picked up from time to time under the pressure of necessity. I was raised to work, which I continued till I was twenty-two."

Webster devoted twenty years to his famous dictionary, published in 1828, which helped to standardize the American language.

Equally influential was Ohioan William H. McGuffey (1800–1873), a teacher-preacher of rare power. His grade-school readers, first published in the 1830s, sold 122 million copies in the following decades. *McGuffey's Readers* hammered home lasting lessons in morality, patriotism, and idealism.

Higher Goals for Higher Learning

Higher education was likewise stirring. The religious zeal of the Second Great Awakening led to the planting of many small, denominational, liberal arts colleges, chiefly in the South and West. Too often they were academically anemic, established more to satisfy local pride than genuinely to advance the cause of learning. Like their more venerable, ivy-draped brethren, the new colleges offered a narrow, tradition-bound curriculum of Latin, Greek, mathematics, and moral philosophy. On new and old campuses alike, there was little intellectual vitality and much boredom.

The first state-supported universities sprang up in the South, beginning with North Carolina in 1795. Federal land grants nourished the growth of state institutions of higher learning. Conspicuous among the early group was the University of Virginia, founded in 1819. It was largely the brainchild of Thomas Jefferson, who designed its beautiful architecture and who at times watched its construction through a telescope from his hilltop home. He dedicated the university to freedom from religious or political shackles, and modern languages and the sciences received unusual emphasis.

Women's higher education was frowned upon in the early decades of the nineteenth century. A woman's place was believed to be in the home, and training in needlecraft seemed more important than training in algebra. In an era when the clinging-vine bride was the ideal, coeducation was regarded as frivolous. Prejudices also prevailed that too much learning injured the feminine brain, undermined health, and rendered a young lady unfit for marriage. The teachers of Susan B. Anthony, the future feminist, refused to instruct her in long division.

Women's schools at the secondary level began to attain some respectability in the 1820s, thanks in part to the dedicated work of Emma Willard (1787–1870). In 1821 she established the Troy (New York) Female Seminary. Oberlin College, in Ohio, jolted traditionalists in 1837 when it opened its doors to women as well as men. (Oberlin had already created shock waves by admitting black students.) In the same year, Mary Lyon established an outstanding women's school, Mount Holyoke Seminary (later College), in South Hadley, Massachusetts. Mossback critics scoffed that "they'll be educatin' cows next."

Adults who craved more learning satisfied their thirst for knowledge at private subscription libraries or, increasingly, at tax-supported libraries. House-to-house peddlers also did a lush business in feeding the public appetite for culture. Traveling lecturers helped to carry

The Women Graduates of the Oberlin College Class of 1855 Oberlin was the first coeducational institution of higher education in the United States, accepting women in 1837, two years after it had welcomed African Americans. Feminists continued to pressure for coeducation, and by 1872 ninety-seven American universities accepted women. At some of these institutions, however, such as Radcliffe College of Harvard University and Barnard College of Columbia University, women were educated in associated schools, not alongside male students.

An editorial in the popular women's magazine Godey's Lady's Book in 1845, probably written by editor Sarah Josepha Hale (1788–1879), argued for better education for women as a benefit to all of society:

"The mass of mankind are very ignorant and wicked. Wherefore is this? Because the mother, whom God constituted the first teacher of every human being, has been degraded by men from her high office; or, what is the same thing, been denied those privileges of education which only can enable her to discharge her duty to her children with discretion and effect. . . . If half the effort and expense had been directed to enlighten and improve the minds of females which have been lavished on the other sex, we should now have a very different state of society."

learning to the masses through the lyceum lecture associations, which numbered about three thousand by 1835. The lyceums provided platforms for speakers in such areas as science, literature, and moral philosophy. Talented talkers like Ralph Waldo Emerson journeyed thousands of miles on the lyceum circuits, casting their pearls of civilization before appreciative audiences.

Magazines flourished in the pre–Civil War years, but most of them withered after a short life. The *North American Review*, founded in 1815, was the long-lived leader of the intellectuals. *Godey's Lady's Book*, founded in 1830, survived until 1898 and attained the enormous circulation (for those days) of 150,000. It was devoured devotedly by millions of women, many of whom read the dog-eared copies of their relatives and friends.

An Age of Reform

As the young Republic grew, reform campaigns of all types flourished in sometimes bewildering abundance. Some reformers were simply crackbrained cranks. But most were intelligent, inspired idealists,

usually touched by the fire of evangelical religion then licking through the pews and pulpits of American churches. The optimistic promises of the Second Great Awakening inspired countless souls to do battle against earthly evils. These modern idealists dreamed anew the old Puritan vision of a perfected society: free from cruelty, war, intoxicating drink, discrimination, and—ultimately—slavery. Women were particularly prominent in these reform crusades, especially in their own struggle for suffrage. For many middle-class women, the reform campaigns provided a unique opportunity to escape the confines of the home and enter the arena of public affairs.

In part the practical, activist Christianity of these reformers resulted from their desire to reaffirm traditional values as they plunged ever further into a world disrupted and transformed by the turbulent forces of a market economy. Mainly middle-class descendants of pioneer farmers, they were often blissfully unaware that they were witnessing the dawn of the industrial era, which posed unprecedented problems and called for novel ideas. They either ignored the factory workers, for example, or blamed their problems on bad habits. With naive single-mindedness, reformers sometimes applied conventional virtue to refurbishing an older order—while events hurtled them headlong into the new.

Imprisonment for debt continued to be a nightmare, though its extent has been exaggerated. As late as 1830, hundreds of penniless people were languishing in filthy holes, sometimes for owing less than one dollar. The poorer working classes were especially hard hit by this merciless practice. But as the embattled laborer won the ballot and asserted himself, state legislatures gradually abolished debtors' prisons.

Criminal codes in the states were likewise being softened, in accord with more enlightened European practices. The number of capital offenses was being reduced, and brutal punishments, such as whipping and branding, were being slowly eliminated. A refreshing idea was taking hold that prisons should reform as well as punish—hence "reformatories," "houses of correction," and "penitentiaries" (for penance).

Sufferers from so-called insanity were still being treated with incredible cruelty. The medieval concept had been that the mentally deranged were cursed with unclean spirits; the nineteenth-century idea was that they were willfully perverse and depraved—to be treated only as beasts. Many crazed persons were chained in jails or poor-houses with sane people.

Into this dismal picture stepped a formidable New England teacher-author, Dorothea Dix (1802–1887). A

Dorothea Dix (1802–1887) A tireless reformer, she worked mightily to improve the treatment of the mentally ill. At the outbreak of the Civil War, she was appointed superintendent of women nurses for the Union forces.

physically frail woman afflicted with persistent lung trouble, she possessed infinite compassion and willpower. She traveled some sixty thousand miles in eight years and assembled her damning reports on insanity and asylums from firsthand observations. Though she never raised her voice, Dix's message was loud and clear. Her classic petition of 1843 to the Massachusetts legislature, describing cells so foul that visitors were driven back by the stench, turned legislative stomachs and hearts. Her persistent prodding resulted in improved conditions and in a gain for the concept that the demented were not willfully perverse but mentally ill.

Agitation for peace also gained momentum in the pre–Civil War years. In 1828 the American Peace Society was formed, with a ringing declaration of war on war. A leading spirit was William Ladd, who orated when his legs were so badly ulcerated that he had to sit on a stool. His ideas were finally to bear some fruit in the international organizations for collective security of the twentieth century. The American peace crusade, linked with a European counterpart, was making promising progress by midcentury, but it was set back by the bloodshed of the Crimean War in Europe and the Civil War in America.

Demon Rum—The "Old Deluder"

The ever-present drink problem attracted dedicated reformers. Custom, combined with a hard and monotonous life, led to the excessive drinking of hard liquor, even among women, clergymen, and members of Congress. Weddings and funerals all too often became disgraceful brawls, and occasionally a drunken mourner would fall into the open grave with the corpse. Heavy drinking decreased the efficiency of labor, and poorly safeguarded machinery operated under the influence of alcohol increased the danger of accidents occurring at work. Drunkenness also fouled the sanctity of the family, threatening the spiritual welfare—and physical safety—of women and children.

After earlier and feebler efforts, the American Temperance Society was formed at Boston in 1826.

In presenting her case to the Massachusetts legislature for more humane treatment for the mentally ill, Dorothea Dix (1802–1887) quoted from the notebook she carried with her as she traveled around the state:

"Lincoln. A woman in a cage. *Medford.* One idiotic subject chained, and one in a close stall for seventeen years. *Pepperell.* One often doubly chained, hand and foot; another violent; several peaceable now. . . . *Dedham.* The insane disadvantageously placed in the jail. In the almshouse, two females in stalls . . . ; lie in wooden bunks filled with straw; always shut up. One of these subjects is supposed curable. The overseers of the poor have declined giving her a trial at the hospital, as I was informed, on account of expense."

Temperance Banner Lithograph, by Kellogg and Comstock, c. 1848–1850 Among the many evils of alcohol, reformers fulminated especially against its corrupting effects on family life. Here a young man is torn between a drink-bearing temptress and a maiden who exemplifies the virtues of womanly purity.

Within a few years, about a thousand local groups sprang into existence. They implored drinkers to sign the temperance pledge and organized children's clubs, known as the "Cold Water Army." Temperance crusaders also made effective use of pictures, pamphlets, and lurid lecturers, some of whom were reformed drunkards. A popular temperance song ran,

> We've done with our days of carousing,
> Our nights, too, of frolicsome glee;
> For now with our sober minds choosing,
> We've pledged ourselves never to spree.

The most popular anti-alcohol tract of the era was T. S. Arthur's melodramatic novel, *Ten Nights in a Barroom and What I Saw There* (1854). It described in shocking detail how a once-happy village was ruined by Sam Slade's tavern. The book was second only to Stowe's *Uncle Tom's Cabin* as a best seller in the 1850s, and it enjoyed a highly successful run on the stage. Its touching theme song began with the words of a little girl:

> Father, dear father, come home with me now,
> The clock in the belfry strikes one.

Early foes of Demon Drink adopted two major lines of attack. One was to stiffen the individual's will to resist the wiles of the little brown jug. The moderate reformers thus stressed "temperance" rather than "teetotalism," or the total elimination of intoxicants. But less patient zealots came to believe that temptation should be removed by legislation. Prominent among this group was Neal S. Dow of Maine, a blue-nosed reformer who, as a mayor of Portland and an employer of labor, had often witnessed the debauching effect of alcohol—to say nothing of the cost to his pocketbook of work time lost because of drunken employees.

Dow—the "Father of Prohibition"—sponsored the so-called Maine Law of 1851. This drastic new statute, hailed as "the law of Heaven Americanized," prohibited the manufacture and sale of intoxicating liquor. Other states in the North followed Maine's example, and by 1857 about a dozen had passed various prohibitory laws. But these figures are deceptive, for within a decade some of the statutes were repealed or declared unconstitutional, if not openly flouted.

It was clearly impossible to legislate thirst for alcohol out of existence, especially in localities where public sentiment was hostile. Yet on the eve of the Civil War, the prohibitionists had registered inspiring gains. There was much less drinking among women than earlier in the century and probably much less per capita consumption of hard liquor.

Women in Revolt

When the nineteenth century opened, it was still a man's world, both in America and in Europe. A wife was supposed to immerse herself in her home and subordinate herself to her lord and master (her husband). Like black slaves, she could not vote; like black slaves, she could be legally beaten by her overlord "with a reasonable instrument." When she married, she could not retain title to her property; it passed to her husband.

Yet American women, though legally regarded as perpetual minors, fared better than their European cousins. French visitor Alexis de Tocqueville noted that in his native France, rape was punished only lightly, whereas in America it was one of the few crimes punishable by death.

Despite these relative advantages, women were still "the submerged sex" in America in the early part of the century. But as the decades unfolded, women increasingly surfaced to breathe the air of freedom and self-determination. In contrast to women in colonial times, many women now avoided marriage altogether—about 10 percent of adult women remained "spinsters" at the time of the Civil War.

Gender differences were strongly emphasized in nineteenth-century America—largely because the burgeoning market economy was increasingly separating women and men into sharply distinct economic roles. Women were thought to be physically and emotionally weak, but also artistic and refined. Endowed with finely tuned moral sensibilities, they were the keepers of society's conscience, with special responsibility to teach the young how to be good and productive citizens of the Republic. Men were considered strong but crude, always in danger of slipping into some savage or beastly way of life if not guided by the gentle hands of their loving ladies.

The home was a woman's special sphere, the centerpiece of the "cult of domesticity." Even reformers like Catharine Beecher, who urged her sisters to seek employment as teachers, endlessly celebrated the role of the good homemaker. But some women increasingly felt that the glorified sanctuary of the home was in fact a gilded cage. They yearned to tear down the bars that separated the private world of women from the public world of men.

Clamorous female reformers—most of them white and well-to-do—began to gather strength as the century neared its halfway point. Most were broad-gauge battlers; while demanding rights for women, they joined in the general reform movement of the age, fighting for temperance and the abolition of slavery. Like men, they had been touched by the evangelical spirit that offered the promise of earthly reward for human endeavor. Neither foul eggs nor foul words, when hurled by disapproving men, could halt women heartened by these doctrines.

The women's rights movement was mothered by some arresting characters. Prominent among them was Lucretia Mott, a sprightly Quaker whose ire had been aroused when she and her fellow female delegates to the London antislavery convention of 1840 were not recognized. Elizabeth Cady Stanton, a mother of seven who had insisted on leaving "obey" out of her marriage ceremony, shocked fellow feminists by going so far as to advocate suffrage for women. Quaker-reared Susan B. Anthony, a

militant lecturer for women's rights, fearlessly exposed herself to rotten garbage and vulgar epithets. She became such a conspicuous advocate of female rights that progressive women everywhere were called "Suzy Bs."

Other feminists challenged the man's world. Dr. Elizabeth Blackwell, a pioneer in a previously forbidden profession for women, was the first female graduate of a medical college. Precocious Margaret Fuller edited a transcendentalist journal, *The Dial,* and took part in the struggle to bring unity and republican government to Italy. She died in a shipwreck off New York's Fire Island while returning to the United States in 1850. The talented Grimké sisters, Sarah and Angelina, championed antislavery. Lucy Stone retained her maiden name after marriage—hence the latter-day "Lucy Stoners," who follow her example. Amelia Bloomer revolted against the current "street sweeping" female attire by donning a short skirt with Turkish trousers—"bloomers," they were called—amid

Stellar Suffragists Elizabeth Cady Stanton (left) and Susan B. Anthony (right) were two of the most persistent battlers for women's rights. Their National Woman Suffrage Association fought for women's equality in courts and workplaces as well as at the polls.

much bawdy ridicule about "Bloomerism" and "loose habits." A jeering male rhyme of the times jabbed,

Gibbey, gibbey gab
The women had a confab
And demanded the rights
To wear the tights
Gibbey, gibbey gab.

Unflinching feminists met at Seneca Falls, New York, in a memorable Woman's Rights Convention (1848). The defiant Stanton read a "Declaration of Sentiments," which in the spirit of the Declaration of Independence declared that "all men and women are created equal." One resolution formally demanded the ballot for females. Amid scorn and denunciation from press and pulpit, the Seneca Falls meeting launched the modern women's rights movement.

The crusade for women's rights was eclipsed by the campaign against slavery in the decade before the Civil War. Still, any white male, even an idiot, over the age of twenty-one could vote, while no woman could. Yet women were gradually being admitted to colleges, and some states, beginning with Mississippi in 1839, were even permitting wives to own property after marriage.

Wilderness Utopias

Bolstered by the utopian spirit of the age, various reformers, ranging from the high-minded to the "lunatic fringe," set up more than forty communities of a cooperative, communistic, or "communitarian" nature. Seeking human betterment, a wealthy and idealistic Scottish textile manufacturer, Robert Owen, founded in 1825 a communal society of about a thousand people at New Harmony, Indiana. Little harmony prevailed in the colony, which, in addition to hard-working visionaries, attracted a sprinkling of radicals, work-shy theorists, and outright scoundrels. The colony sank in a morass of contradiction and confusion.

> *When early feminist Lucy Stone (1818–1893) married fellow abolitionist Henry B. Blackwell (1825–1909) in West Brookfield, Massachusetts, in 1855, they added the following vow to their nuptial ceremony:*
>
> "While acknowledging our mutual affection by publicly assuming the relation of husband and wife, yet in justice to ourselves and a great principle, we deem it a duty to declare that this act on our part implies no . . . promise of voluntary obedience to such of the present laws of marriage, as refuse to recognize the wife as an independent, rational being, while they confer upon the husband an injurious and unnatural superiority."

What It Would Be If Some Ladies Had Their Own Way The men in the antifeminist cartoon are sewing, tending the baby, and washing clothes. This scene seemed absurd then, but not a century later.

EXAMINING THE EVIDENCE

Dress as Reform Among the many social movements that swept nineteenth-century America, dress reform emerged in the 1840s as a critique of materialism and the constraints that fashion imposed on women. Medical professionals, social reformers, and transcendentalist intellectuals all argued that corsets constricting vital organs and voluminous skirts dragging along garbage-strewn streets unfairly restricted women's mobility, prevented women from bearing healthy children, and even induced serious sickness and death. The "Bloomer costume" depicted in this illustration from *Harper's New Monthly Magazine* in 1851 included Turkish-style trousers, a jacket, and a short overskirt that came to the knees. Named after reformer Amelia Bloomer (1818–1894), who publicized the new style in her magazine, *The Lily,* the bloomer dress was first adopted by utopian communities such as the Owenites in New Harmony, Indiana, and the Oneidans in New York. Radical social critic Henry David Thoreau also advocated rational dress as a way of rejecting the artificial desires created by industrialization. But while applauded by reformers, new-style dress was viciously ridiculed by mainstream society, as this print demonstrates. Critics claimed that women blurred gender distinctions by adopting "male" attire, endangering the family and even American civilization. After only a decade, practitioners gave up wearing bloomers in public, adopting plain and simplified clothing instead. But Owenites, some Mormons, women's rights advocates, farmers, and travelers on the overland trail continued to wear bloomers in private. How did dress reform intersect with other religious and social movements of the era? Why did bloomers upset so many antebellum Americans? Have there been other historical eras when new styles of dress came to symbolize broader social change?

Brook Farm in Massachusetts, comprising two hundred acres of grudging soil, was started in 1841 with the brotherly and sisterly cooperation of about twenty intellectuals committed to the philosophy of transcendentalism (see p. 340). They prospered reasonably well until 1846, when they lost by fire a large new communal building shortly before its completion. The whole venture in "plain living and high thinking" then collapsed in debt. The Brook Farm experiment inspired Nathaniel Hawthorne's classic novel *The Blithedale Romance* (1852), whose main character was modeled on the feminist writer Margaret Fuller.

A more radical experiment was the Oneida Community, founded in New York in 1848. It practiced free love ("complex marriage"), birth control (through "male continence," or *coitus reservatus*), and the eugenic selection of parents to produce superior offspring. This curious enterprise flourished for more than thirty years, largely because its artisans made superior steel traps and Oneida Community (silver) Plate (see "Makers of America: The Oneida Community," pp. 336–337).

Various communistic experiments, mostly small in scale, have been attempted since Jamestown. But in competition with democratic free enterprise and free land, virtually all of them sooner or later failed or changed their methods. Among the longest-lived sects were the Shakers. Led by Mother Ann Lee, they began in the 1770s to set up the first of a score or so of religious communities. The Shakers attained a membership of about six thousand in 1840, but since their monastic customs prohibited both marriage and sexual relations, they were virtually extinct by 1940.

The Dawn of Scientific Achievement

Early Americans, confronted with pioneering problems, were more interested in practical gadgets than in pure science. Jefferson, for example, was a gifted amateur inventor who won a gold medal for a new type of plow. Noteworthy also were the writings of the mathematician Nathaniel Bowditch (1733–1838) on practical navigation and of the oceanographer Matthew F. Maury (1806–1873) on ocean winds and currents. These writers promoted safety, speed, and economy. But as far as basic science was concerned, Americans were best known for borrowing and adapting the findings of Europeans.

Yet the Republic was not without scientific talent. The most influential American scientist of the first half of the nineteenth century was Professor Benjamin Silliman (1779–1864), a pioneer chemist and geologist who taught and wrote brilliantly at Yale College for more than fifty years. Professor Louis Agassiz (1807–1873), a distinguished French Swiss immigrant, served for a quarter of a century at Harvard College. A path-breaking student of biology who sometimes carried snakes in his pockets, he insisted on original research and deplored the reigning overemphasis on memory work. Professor Asa Gray (1810–1888) of Harvard College, the Columbus of American botany,

Women Planting Corn, by Olof Krans, 1894–1896 The Shakers' emphasis on simplicity and ingenuity, and their segregation of the sexes, were captured in this painting of the Bishop Hill community in Illinois. The prongs on the poles measured the distance between rows, and the knots on the rope showed the women how far apart to plant the corn.

(left) Passenger Pigeons, by John Audubon; (right) John J. Audubon (1785–1851)
An astute naturalist and a gifted artist, Audubon drew the birds of America in
loving detail. Ironically, he had to go to Britain in the 1820s to find a publisher for
his pioneering depictions of the unique beauty of American wildlife. Born in Haiti
and educated in France, he achieved fame as America's greatest ornithologist.

published over 350 books, monographs, and papers. His
textbooks set new standards for clarity and interest.

Lovers of American bird lore owed much to
the French-descended naturalist John J. Audubon
(1785–1851), who painted wildfowl in their natural habi-
tat. His magnificently illustrated *Birds of America*
attained considerable popularity. The Audubon Society
for the protection of birds was named after him, although
as a young man he shot much feathered game for sport.

Medicine in America, despite a steady growth of
medical schools, was still primitive by modern standards.
Bleeding remained a common cure and a curse as well.
Smallpox plagues were still dreaded, and the yellow
fever epidemic of 1793 in Philadelphia took several
thousand lives. "Bring out your dead!" was the daily cry
of the corpse-wagon drivers.

People everywhere complained of ill health—
malaria, the "rheumatics," the "miseries," and the chills.
Illness often resulted from improper diet, hurried eat-

ing, perspiring and cooling off too rapidly, and ignorance of germs and sanitation. "We was sick every fall,
regular," wrote the mother of future president James
Garfield. Life expectancy was still dismayingly short—
about forty years for a white person born in 1850, and
less for blacks. The suffering from decayed or ulcerated
teeth was enormous; tooth extraction was often practiced by the muscular village blacksmith.

Self-prescribed patent medicines were common
(one dose for people, two for horses) and included
Robertson's Infallible Worm Destroying Lozenges. Fad
diets proved popular, including the whole-wheat bread
and crackers regimen of Sylvester Graham. Among
home remedies was the rubbing of tumors with dead
toads. The use of medicine by the regular doctors was
often harmful, and Dr. Oliver Wendell Holmes declared
in 1860 that if the medicines, as then employed, were
thrown into the sea, humans would be better off and the
fish worse off.

The Oneida Community

John Humphrey Noyes (1811–1886), the founder of the Oneida Community, repudiated the old Puritan doctrines that God was vengeful and that sinful mankind was doomed to dwell in a vale of tears. Noyes believed in a benign deity, in the sweetness of human nature, and in the possibility of a perfect Christian community on earth. "The more we get acquainted with God," he declared, "the more we shall find it our special duty to be happy."

That sunny thought was shared by many early-nineteenth-century American utopians (a word derived from Greek that slyly combines the meanings of "a good place" and "no such place"). But Noyes added some wrinkles of his own. The key to happiness, he taught, was the suppression of selfishness. True Christians should possess no private property—nor should they indulge in exclusive emotional relationships, which bred jealousy, quarreling, and covetousness. Material things and sexual partners alike, Noyes preached, should be shared. Marriage should not be monogamous. Instead all members of the community should be free to love one another in "complex marriage." Noyes called his system "Bible Communism."

Tall and slender, with piercing blue eyes and reddish hair, the charismatic Noyes began voicing these ideas in his hometown of Putney, Vermont, in the 1830s. He soon attracted a group of followers who called themselves the Putney Association, a kind of extended family whose members farmed five hundred acres by day and sang and prayed together in the evenings. They sustained their spiritual intensity by submitting to "Mutual Criticism," in which the person being criticized would sit in silence while other members frankly discussed his or her faults and merits. "I was, metaphorically, stood upon my head and allowed to drain till all the self-righteousness had dripped out of me," one man wrote of his experience with Mutual Criticism.

The Putney Association also indulged in sexual practices that outraged the surrounding community's sense of moral propriety. Indicted for adultery in 1847, Noyes led his followers to Oneida, in the supposedly more tolerant region of New York's Burned-Over District, the following year. Several affiliated communities were also established, the most important of which was at Wallingford, Connecticut.

The Oneidans struggled in New York until they were joined in the 1850s by Sewell Newhouse, a clever inventor of steel animal traps. The manufacture of Newhouse's traps, and other products such as sewing silk and various types of bags, put the Oneida Community on a sound financial footing. By the 1860s Oneida was a flourishing commonwealth of some three hundred people. Men and women shared equally in all the community's tasks, from field to factory to kitchen. The members lived under one roof in Mansion House, a sprawling building that boasted central heating, a well-stocked library, and a common dining hall, as well as the "Big Hall" where members gathered nightly for prayer and entertainment. Children at the age of three were removed from direct parental care and raised communally in the Children's House until the age of thirteen or fourteen, when they took up jobs in the community's industries. They imbibed their religious doctrines with their school lessons:

> I-spirit
> With me never shall stay,
> We-spirit
> Makes us happy and gay.

Oneida's apparent success fed the utopian dreams of others, and for a time it became a great tourist attraction. Visitors from as far away as Europe came to picnic on the shady lawns, speculating on the sexual secrets that Mansion House guarded, while their hosts fed them strawberries and cream and entertained them with music.

But eventually the same problems that had driven Noyes and his band from Vermont began to shadow their lives at Oneida. Their New York neighbors grew increasingly horrified at the Oneidans' licentious sexual practices, including the selective breeding program by which the community matched mates and gave permission—or orders—to procreate, without regard to the niceties of matrimony. "It was somewhat startling to me," one straight-laced visitor commented, "to hear *Miss* _____ speak about her baby."

Yielding to their neighbors' criticisms, the Oneidans gave up complex marriage in 1879. Soon other "communistic" practices withered away as well. The communal dining hall became a restaurant, where meals were bought with money, something many Oneidans had never used before. In 1880 the Oneidans abandoned communism altogether and became a joint-stock company specializing in the manufacture of silver tableware. Led by Noyes's son Pierrepont, Oneida Community, Ltd., grew into the world's leading manufacturer of stainless steel knives, forks, and spoons, with annual sales by the 1990s of some half a billion dollars.

As for Mansion House, it still stands in central New York, but it now serves as a museum and private residence. The "Big Hall" is the site of Oneida, Ltd.'s annual shareholders' meetings. Ironically, what grew from Noyes's religious vision was not utopia but a mighty capitalist corporation.

Mansion House A sprawling, resplendent building, it formed the center of the Oneida Community's life and was a stunning specimen of mid-nineteenth-century architectural and engineering achievement.

A Bag Bee on the Lawn of Mansion House The fledgling community supported itself in part by bag manufacturing. Men and women shared equally in the bag-making process.

The Founding Father
John Humphrey Noyes (1811–1886).

An outbreak of cholera occurred in New York City in 1832, and a wealthy businessman, Philip Hone (1780–1851), wrote in his diary for the Fourth of July,

"The alarm about the cholera has prevented all the usual jollification under the public authority. . . . The Board of Health reports to-day twenty new cases and eleven deaths since noon yesterday. The disease is here in all its violence and will increase. God grant that its ravages may be confined, and its visit short."

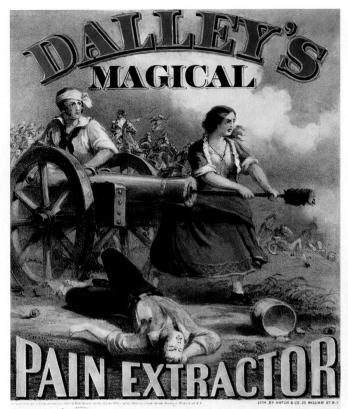

Victims of surgical operations were ordinarily tied down, often after a stiff drink of whiskey. The surgeon then sawed or cut with breakneck speed, undeterred by the piercing shrieks of the patient. A priceless boon for medical progress came in the early 1840s, when several American doctors and dentists, working independently, successfully employed laughing gas and ether as anesthetics.

Artistic Achievements

Architecturally, America contributed little of note in the first half of the century. The rustic Republic, still under pressure to erect shelters in haste, was continuing to imitate European models. Public buildings and other important structures followed Greek and Roman lines, which seemed curiously out of place in a wilderness setting. A remarkable Greek revival came between 1820 and 1850, partly stimulated by the heroic efforts of the Greeks in the 1820s to wrest independence from the "terrible Turk." About midcentury strong interest developed in a revival of Gothic forms, with their emphasis on pointed arches and large windows.

Talented Thomas Jefferson, architect of revolution, was probably the ablest American architect of his generation. He brought a classical design to his Virginia hilltop home, Monticello—perhaps the most stately mansion in the nation. The quadrangle of the University of Virginia at Charlottesville, another of Jefferson's creations, remains one of the finest examples of classical architecture in America.

Early Advertising Hawkers of patent medicines pioneered the techniques of modern advertising. Here a painkiller is promoted by invoking the totally irrelevant image of Molly Pitcher. The legendary subject of a poem by John Greenleaf Whittier, Pitcher reputedly took her fallen husband's place at a cannon during the Revolutionary War Battle of Monmouth in 1778. What this exploit had to do with anesthetics is by no means clear, but it supposedly sold the product.

The art of painting continued to be handicapped. It suffered from the dollar-grabbing of a raw civilization; from the hustle, bustle, and absence of leisure; from the lack of a wealthy class to sit for portraits—and then pay for them. Some of the earliest painters were forced to go to England, where they found both training and patrons. America exported artists and imported art.

Painting, like the theater, also suffered from the Puritan prejudice that art was a sinful waste of time—and often obscene. John Adams boasted that "he would not give a sixpence for a bust of Phidias or a painting by

The Oxbow, by Thomas Cole, 1836   This rendering of the oxbow of the Connecticut River near Northampton, Massachusetts, after a thunderstorm is considered one of Cole's (1801–1848) masterpieces. A leader of the so-called Hudson River school, Cole wandered on foot over the mountains and rivers of New York State and New England, making pencil studies from which he painted in his studio during the winter. He and other members of this group transformed their realistic sketches into lyrical, romantic celebrations of the beauty of the American wilderness.

Raphael." When Edward Everett, the eminent Boston scholar and orator, placed a statue of Apollo in his home, he had its naked limbs draped.

Competent painters nevertheless emerged. Gilbert Stuart (1755–1828), a spendthrift Rhode Islander and one of the most gifted of the early group, wielded his brush in Britain in competition with the best artists. He produced several portraits of Washington, all of them somewhat idealized and dehumanized. Truth to tell, by the time he posed for Stuart, the famous general had lost his natural teeth and some of the original shape of his face. Charles Willson Peale (1741–1827), a Marylander, painted some sixty portraits of Washington, who patiently sat for about fourteen of them. John Trumbull (1756–1843), who had fought in the Revolutionary War, recaptured its scenes and spirit on scores of striking canvases.

During the nationalistic upsurge after the War of 1812, American painters of portraits turned increasingly from human landscapes to romantic mirrorings of local landscapes. The Hudson River school excelled in this type of art. At the same time, portrait painters gradually encoun-

tered some unwelcome competition from the invention of a crude photograph known as the daguerreotype, perfected about 1839 by a Frenchman, Louis Daguerre.

Music was slowly shaking off the restraints of colonial days, when the prim Puritans had frowned upon nonreligious singing. Rhythmic and nostalgic "darky" tunes, popularized by whites, were becoming immense hits by midcentury. Special favorites were the uniquely American minstrel shows, featuring white actors with blackened faces. "Dixie," later adopted by the Confederates as their battle hymn, was written in 1859, ironically in New York City by an Ohioan. The most famous black songs, also ironically, came from a white Pennsylvanian, Stephen C. Foster (1826–1864). His one excursion into the South occurred in 1852, after he had published "Old Folks at Home." Foster made a valuable contribution to American folk music by capturing the plaintive spirit of the slaves. An odd and pathetic figure, he finally lost both his art and his popularity and died in a charity ward after drowning his sorrows in drink.

The Blossoming of a National Literature

"Who reads an American book?" sneered a British critic of 1820. The painful truth was that the nation's rough-hewn, pioneering civilization gave little encouragement to "polite" literature. Much of the reading matter was imported or plagiarized from Britain.

Busy conquering a continent, the Americans poured most of their creative efforts into practical outlets. Praiseworthy were political essays, like *The Federalist* of Hamilton, Jay, and Madison; pamphlets, like Tom Paine's *Common Sense;* and political orations, like the masterpieces of Daniel Webster. In the category of nonreligious books published before 1820, Benjamin Franklin's *Autobiography* (1818) is one of the few that achieved genuine distinction. His narrative is a classic in its simplicity, clarity, and inspirational quality. Even so, it records only a fragment of "Old Ben's" long, fruitful, and amorous life.

A genuinely American literature received a strong boost from the wave of nationalism that followed the War of Independence and especially the War of 1812. By 1820 the older seaboard areas were sufficiently removed from the survival mentality of tree-chopping and butter-churning so that literature could be supported as a profession. The Knickerbocker Group in New York blazed brilliantly across the literary heavens, thus enabling America for the first time to boast of a literature to match its magnificent landscapes.

Washington Irving (1783–1859), born in New York City, was the first American to win international recognition as a literary figure. Steeped in the traditions of New Netherland, he published in 1809 his *Knickerbocker's History of New York,* with its amusing caricatures of the Dutch. When the family business failed, Irving was forced to turn to the goose-feather pen. In 1819–1820 he published *The Sketch Book,* which brought him immediate fame at home and abroad. Combining a pleasing style with delicate charm and quiet humor, he used English as well as American themes and included such immortal Dutch American tales as "Rip Van Winkle" and "The Legend of Sleepy Hollow." Europe was amazed to find at last an American with a feather in his hand, not in his hair. Later turning to Spanish locales and biography, Irving did much to interpret America to Europe and Europe to America. He was, said the Englishman William Thackeray, "the first ambassador whom the New World of letters sent to the Old."

James Fenimore Cooper (1789–1851) was the first American novelist, as Washington Irving was the first general writer, to gain world fame and to make New World themes respectable. Marrying into a wealthy family, he settled down on the frontier of New York. Reading one day to his wife from an insipid English novel, Cooper remarked in disgust that he could write a better book himself. His wife challenged him to do so—and he did.

After an initial failure, Cooper launched out upon an illustrious career in 1821 with his second novel, *The Spy*—an absorbing tale of the American Revolution. His stories of the sea were meritorious and popular, but his fame rests most enduringly on the *Leatherstocking Tales.* A dead-eye rifleman named Natty Bumppo, one of nature's noblemen, meets with Indians in stirring adventures like *The Last of the Mohicans.* James Fenimore Cooper's novels had a wide sale among Europeans, some of whom came to think of all American people as born with tomahawk in hand. Actually Cooper was exploring the viability and destiny of America's republican experiment, by contrasting the undefiled values of "natural men," children of the wooded wilderness, with the artificiality of modern civilization.

A third member of the Knickerbocker group in New York was the belated Puritan William Cullen Bryant (1794–1878), transplanted from Massachusetts. At age sixteen he wrote the meditative and melancholy "Thanatopsis" (published in 1817), which was one of the first high-quality poems produced in the United States. Critics could hardly believe that it had been written on "this side of the water." Although Bryant continued with poetry, he was forced to make his living by editing the influential *New York Evening Post.* For over fifty years, he set a model for journalism that was dignified, liberal, and conscientious.

Trumpeters of Transcendentalism

A golden age in American literature dawned in the second quarter of the nineteenth century, when an amazing outburst shook New England. One of the mainsprings of this literary flowering was transcendentalism, especially around Boston, which preened itself as "the Athens of America."

The transcendentalist movement of the 1830s resulted in part from a liberalizing of the straightjacket Puritan theology. It also owed much to foreign influences, including the German romantic philosophers and the religions of Asia. The transcendentalists rejected the prevailing theory, derived from John Locke, that all knowledge comes to the mind through the senses. Truth, rather, "transcends" the senses: it cannot be found by observation alone. Every person possesses an inner light that can illuminate the highest truth and put him or her in direct touch with God, or the "Oversoul."

These mystical doctrines of transcendentalism defied precise definition, but they underlay concrete beliefs. Foremost was a stiff-backed individualism in matters religious as well as social. Closely associated was a commitment to self-reliance, self-culture, and self-discipline. These traits naturally bred hostility to authority and to formal institutions of any kind, as well as to all conventional wisdom. Finally came exaltation of the dignity of the individual, whether black or white—the mainspring of a whole array of humanitarian reforms.

Best known of the transcendentalists was Boston-born Ralph Waldo Emerson (1803–1882). Tall, slender, and intensely blue-eyed, he mirrored serenity in his noble features. Trained as a Unitarian minister, he early forsook his pulpit and ultimately reached a wider audience by pen and platform. He was a never-failing favorite as a lyceum lecturer and for twenty years took a western tour every winter. Perhaps his most thrilling public effort was a Phi Beta Kappa address, "The American Scholar," delivered at Harvard College in 1837. This brilliant appeal was an intellectual declaration of independence, for it urged American writers to throw off European traditions and delve into the riches of their own backyards.

Hailed as both a poet and a philosopher, Emerson was not of the highest rank as either. He was more influential as a practical philosopher and through his fresh and vibrant essays enriched countless thousands of humdrum lives. Catching the individualistic mood of the Republic, he stressed self-reliance, self-improvement, self-confidence, optimism, and freedom. The secret of Emerson's popularity lay largely in the fact that his ideals reflected those of an expanding America. By the 1850s he was an outspoken critic of slavery, and he ardently supported the Union cause in the Civil War.

Henry David Thoreau (1817–1862) was Emerson's close associate—a poet, a mystic, a transcendentalist, and a nonconformist. Condemning a government that supported slavery, he refused to pay his Massachusetts poll tax and was jailed for a night.* A gifted prose writer, he is well known for *Walden: Or Life in the Woods* (1854).

> *In 1849 Henry David Thoreau (1817–1862) published "Resistance to Civil Government," (later renamed "Civil Disobedience"), asserting:*
>
> "All men recognize the right of revolution; the right to refuse allegiance to and to resist the government, when its tyranny or its inefficiency are great and endurable. But almost all say that such is not the case now. . . . I say, when a sixth of the population of a nation which has undertaken to be the refuge of liberty are slaves, and a whole country is unjustly overrun and conquered by a foreign army, and subjected to military law, I think that it is not too soon for honest men to rebel and revolutionize. What makes this duty more urgent is the fact, that the country so overrun is not our own, but ours is the invading army."

The book is a record of Thoreau's two years of simple existence in a hut that he built on the edge of Walden Pond, near Concord, Massachusetts. A stiff-necked individualist, he believed that he should reduce his bodily wants so as to gain time for a pursuit of truth through study and meditation. Thoreau's *Walden* and his essay *On the Duty of Civil Disobedience* exercised a strong influence in furthering idealistic thought, both in America and abroad. His writings later encouraged Mahatma Gandhi to resist British rule in India and, still later, inspired the development of American civil rights leader Martin Luther King, Jr.'s thinking about nonviolence.

Bold, brassy, and swaggering was the open-collared figure of Brooklyn's Walt Whitman (1819–1892). In his famous collection of poems *Leaves of Grass* (1855), he gave free rein to his gushing genius with what he called a "barbaric yawp." Highly romantic, emotional, and unconventional, he dispensed with titles, stanzas, rhymes, and at times even regular meter. He handled sex with shocking frankness, although he laundered

---

*The story (probably apocryphal) is that Emerson visited Thoreau at the jail and asked, "Why are you here?" The reply came, "Why are you *not* here?"

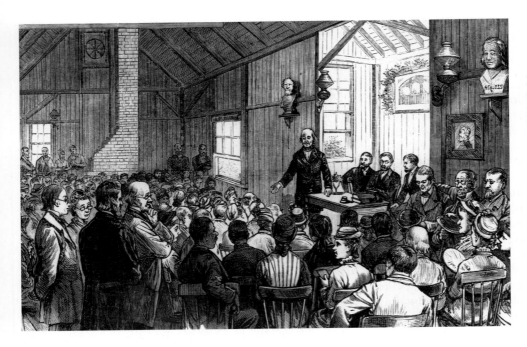

Ralph Waldo Emerson (1803–1882) Public lecturing provided a way for Emerson to put his ideas before a larger audience than his readers and to support his family. His philosophical observations included such statements as "The less government we have, the better—the fewer laws, and the less confided power"; "To be great is to be misunderstood"; "Every hero becomes a bore at last"; "Shallow men believe in luck"; and "When you strike a king, you must kill him."

his verses in later editions, and his book was banned in Boston.

Whitman's *Leaves of Grass* was at first a financial failure. The only three enthusiastic reviews that it received were written by the author himself—anonymously. But in time the once-withered *Leaves of Grass*, revived and honored, won for Whitman an enormous following in both America and Europe. His fame increased immensely among "Whitmaniacs" after his death.

Leaves of Grass gained for Whitman the informal title "Poet Laureate of Democracy." Singing with transcendental abandon of his love for the masses, he caught the exuberant enthusiasm of an expanding America that had turned its back on the Old World:

> *All the Past we leave behind;*
> *We debouch upon a newer, mightier world,*
> *varied world;*
> *Fresh and strong the world we seize—world*
> *of labor and the march—*
> *Pioneers! O Pioneers!*

Here at last was the native art for which critics had been crying.

Glowing Literary Lights

Certain other literary giants were not actively associated with the transcendentalist movement, though not completely immune to its influences. Professor Henry Wadsworth Longfellow (1807–1882), who for many years taught modern languages at Harvard College, was one of the most popular poets ever produced in America. Handsome and urbane, he lived a generally serene life, except for the tragic deaths of two wives, the second of whom perished before his eyes when her dress caught fire. Writing for the genteel classes, he was adopted by the less cultured masses. His wide knowledge of European literature supplied him with many themes, but some of his most admired poems—"Evangeline," "The Song of Hiawatha," and "The Courtship of Miles Standish"—were based on American traditions. Immensely popular in Europe, Longfellow was the only American ever to be honored with a bust in the Poets' Corner of Westminster Abbey.

A fighting Quaker, John Greenleaf Whittier (1807–1892), with piercing dark eyes and swarthy complexion, was the uncrowned poet laureate of the antislavery crusade. Less talented as a writer than Longfellow, he was vastly more important in influencing social action. His poems cried aloud against inhumanity, injustice, and intolerance, against

> *The outworn rite, the old abuse,*
> *The pious fraud transparent grown.*

Undeterred by insults and the stoning of mobs, Whittier helped arouse a callous America on the slavery issue. A supreme conscience rather than a sterling poet or intellect, Whittier was one of the moving forces of his generation, whether moral, humanitarian, or spiritual.

Gentle and lovable, he was preeminently the poet of human freedom.

Many-sided professor James Russell Lowell (1819–1891), who succeeded Professor Longfellow at Harvard, ranks as one of America's better poets. He was also a distinguished essayist, literary critic, editor, and diplomat—a diffusion of talents that hampered his poetical output. Lowell is remembered as a political satirist in his *Biglow Papers*, especially those of 1846 dealing with the Mexican War. Written partly as poetry in the Yankee dialect, the *Papers* condemned in blistering terms the alleged slavery-expansion designs of the Polk administration.

The scholarly Dr. Oliver Wendell Holmes (1809–1894), who taught anatomy with a sparkle at Harvard Medical School, was a prominent poet, essayist, novelist, lecturer, and wit. A nonconformist and a fascinating conversationalist, he shone among a group of literary lights who regarded Boston as "the hub of the universe." His poem "The Last Leaf," in honor of the last "white Indian" of the Boston Tea Party, came to apply to himself. Dying at the age of eighty-five, he was the "last leaf" among his distinguished contemporaries.*

Two women writers whose work remains enormously popular today were also tied to this New England literary world. Louisa May Alcott (1832–1888) grew up in Concord, Massachusetts, in the bosom of transcendentalism, alongside neighbors Emerson, Thoreau, and Fuller. Her philosopher father Bronson Alcott occupied himself more devotedly to ideas than earning a living, leaving his daughter to write *Little Women* (1868) and

Walt Whitman This portrait of the young poet appeared in the first edition of *Leaves of Grass* (1855).

In 1876 the London Saturday Review *referred to Walt Whitman (1819–1892) as the author of a volume of*

"so-called poems which were chiefly remarkable for their absurd extravagances and shameless obscenity, and who has since, we are glad to say, been little heard of among decent people."

In 1888 Whitman wrote,

"I had my choice when I commenced. I bid neither for soft eulogies, big money returns, nor the approbation of existing schools and conventions. . . . I have had my say entirely my own way, and put it unerringly on record—the value thereof to be decided by time."

other books to support her mother and sisters. Not far away in Amherst, Massachusetts, poet Emily Dickinson (1830–1886) lived as a recluse but created her own original world through precious gems of poetry. In deceptively spare language and simple rhyme schemes, she explored universal themes of nature, love, death, and immortality. Although she refused during her lifetime to publish any of her poems, when she died, nearly two thousand of them were found among her papers and eventually made their way into print.

The most noteworthy literary figure produced by the South before the Civil War, unless Edgar Allan Poe is regarded as a southerner, was novelist William Gilmore Simms (1806–1870). Quantitatively, at least, he was

---

*Oliver Wendell Holmes had a son with the same name who became a distinguished justice of the Supreme Court (1902–1932) and who lived to be ninety-four, less two days.

great: eighty-two books flowed from his ever-moist pen, winning for him the title "the Cooper of the South." His themes dealt with the southern frontier in colonial days and with the South during the Revolutionary War. But he was neglected by his own section, even though he married into the socially elite and became a slaveowner. The high-toned planter aristocracy would never accept the son of a poor Charleston storekeeper.

Literary Individualists and Dissenters

Not all writers in these years believed so keenly in human goodness and social progress. Edgar Allan Poe (1809–1849), who spent much of his youth in Virginia, was an eccentric genius. Orphaned at an early age, cursed with ill health, and married to a child-wife of thirteen who fell fatally ill of tuberculosis, he suffered hunger, cold, poverty, and debt. Failing at suicide, he took refuge in the bottle and dissipated his talent early. Poe was a gifted lyric poet, as "The Raven" attests. A master stylist, he also excelled in the short story, especially of the horror type, in which he shared his alcoholic nightmares with fascinated readers. If he did not invent the modern detective novel, he at least set new high standards in tales like "The Gold Bug."

Poe was fascinated by the ghostly and ghastly, as in "The Fall of the House of Usher" and other stories. He reflected a morbid sensibility distinctly at odds with the usually optimistic tone of American culture. Partly for this reason, Poe has perhaps been even more prized by Europeans than by Americans. His brilliant career was cut short when he was found drunk in a Baltimore gutter and shortly thereafter died.

Two other writers reflected the continuing Calvinist obsession with original sin and with the never-ending struggle between good and evil. In somber Salem, Massachusetts, writer Nathaniel Hawthorne (1804–1864) grew up in an atmosphere heavy with the memories of his Puritan forebears and the tragedy of his father's premature death on an ocean voyage. His masterpiece was *The Scarlet Letter* (1850), which describes the Puritan practice of forcing an adulteress to wear a scarlet "A" on her clothing. The tragic tale chronicles the psychological effects of sin on the guilty heroine and her secret lover (the father of her baby), a minister of the gospel in Puritan Boston. In *The Marble Faun* (1860), Hawthorne dealt with a group of young American artists who witness a mysterious murder in Rome. The book explores the

Louisa May Alcott (1832–1888) In search of independence for herself and financial security for her family, Alcott worked as a seamstress, governess, teacher, and housemaid until her writing finally brought her success. Her much-loved, largely autobiographical novel, *Little Women*, has remained in print continuously from 1868 until our own day.

concepts of the omnipresence of evil and the dead hand of the past weighing upon the present.

Herman Melville (1819–1891), an orphaned and ill-educated New Yorker, went to sea as a youth and served eighteen adventuresome months on a whaler. "A whale ship was my Yale College and my Harvard," he wrote. Jumping ship in the South Seas, he lived among cannibals, from whom he providently escaped uneaten. His fresh and charming tales of the South Seas were immediately popular, but his masterpiece, *Moby Dick* (1851), was not. This epic novel is a complex allegory of good and evil, told in terms of the conflict between a whaling captain, Ahab, and a giant white whale, Moby Dick. Captain Ahab, having lost a leg to the marine monster, lives only for revenge. His pursuit finally ends when Moby Dick rams and sinks Ahab's ship, leaving only one survivor. The whale's exact identity and Ahab's motives remain obscure. In the end the

Capturing a Sperm Whale, painted by William Page from a sketch by C. B. Hulsart, 1835 This painting and Melville's *Moby Dick* vividly portray the hazards of whaling. Despite the dangers, it proved to be an important industry from colonial times to the end of the nineteenth century

sea, like the terrifyingly impersonal and unknowable universe of Melville's imagination, simply rolls on.

Moby Dick was widely ignored at the time of its publication; people were accustomed to more straightforward and upbeat prose. A disheartened Melville continued to write unprofitably for some years, part of the time eking out a living as a customs inspector, and then died in relative obscurity and poverty. Ironically, his brooding masterpiece about the mysterious white whale had to wait until the more jaded twentieth century for readers and for proper recognition.

Portrayers of the Past

A distinguished group of American historians was emerging at the same time that other writers were winning distinction. Energetic George Bancroft (1800–1891), who as secretary of the navy helped found the Naval Academy at Annapolis in 1845, has deservedly received the title "Father of American History." He published a spirited, superpatriotic history of the United States to 1789 in six (originally ten) volumes (1834–1876), a work that grew out of his vast researches in dusty archives in Europe and America.

Two other historians are read with greater pleasure and profit today. William H. Prescott (1796–1859), who accidentally lost the sight of an eye while in college, conserved his remaining weak vision and published classic accounts of the conquest of Mexico (1843) and Peru (1847). Francis Parkman (1823–1893), whose eyes were so defective that he wrote in darkness with the aid of a guiding machine, penned a brilliant series of volumes beginning in 1851. In epic style he chronicled the struggle between France and Britain in colonial times for the mastery of North America.

Early American historians of prominence were almost without exception New Englanders, largely because the Boston area provided well-stocked libraries and a stimulating literary tradition. These writers numbered abolitionists among their relatives and friends and hence were disposed to view unsympathetically the slavery-cursed South. This "made in New England" interpretation dominated the writing of American history until the close of the nineteenth century, when pressure for national reconciliation overcame regional bias. "The history of the United States has been written by Boston," one pro-southern historian bitterly complained, "and largely written wrong."

Chronology

1700s	First Shaker communities formed	**1835**	Lyceum movement flourishes
1794	Thomas Paine publishes *The Age of Reason*	**1837**	Oberlin College admits female students Mary Lyon establishes Mount Holyoke Seminary Emerson delivers "The American Scholar" address
1795	University of North Carolina founded		
1800	Second Great Awakening begins		
1819	Jefferson founds University of Virginia	**1841**	Brook Farm commune established
1821	Cooper publishes *The Spy,* his first successful novel Emma Willard establishes Troy (New York) Female Seminary	**1843**	Dorothea Dix petitions Massachusetts legislature on behalf of the insane
		1846–1847	Mormon migration to Utah
1825	New Harmony commune established	**1848**	Seneca Falls Woman's Rights Convention held Oneida Community established
1826	American Temperance Society founded		
1828	Noah Webster publishes dictionary American Peace Society founded	**1850**	Hawthorne publishes *The Scarlet Letter*
1830	Joseph Smith founds Mormon Church *Godey's Lady's Book* first published	**1851**	Melville publishes *Moby Dick* Maine passes first law prohibiting liquor
1830–1831	Finney conducts revivals in eastern cities	**1855**	Whitman publishes *Leaves of Grass*

VARYING VIEWPOINTS

Reform: Who? What? How? and Why?

Early chronicles of the antebellum period universally lauded the era's reformers, portraying them as idealistic, altruistic crusaders intent on improving American society.

After World War II, however, some historians began to detect selfish and even conservative motives underlying the apparent benevolence of the reformers. This view described the advocates of reform as anxious, upper-class men and women threatened by the ferment of life in antebellum America. The pursuit of reforms like temperance, asylums, prisons, and mandatory public education represented a means of asserting "social control." In this vein, one

historian described a reform movement as "the anguished protest of an aggrieved class against a world they never made." In Michael Katz's treatment of early educational reform, proponents were community leaders who sought a school system that would ease the traumas of America's industrialization by inculcating business-oriented values and discipline in the working classes.

The wave of reform activity in the 1960s prompted a reevaluation of the reputations of the antebellum reformers. These more recent interpretations found much to admire in the authentic religious commitments of reformers and especially in the participation of women, who sought various social improvements as an extension of their function as protectors of the home and family.

The scholarly treatment of abolitionism is a telling example of how reformers and their campaigns have risen and fallen in the estimation of historians. To northern historians writing in the late nineteenth century, abolitionists were courageous men and women so devoted to uprooting the evil of slavery that they were willing to dedicate their lives to a cause that often ostracized them from their communities. By the mid-twentieth century, an interpretation more favorable to the South prevailed, one that blamed the fanaticism of the abolitionists for the Civil War. But as the racial climate in the United States began to change during the 1960s, historians once again showed sympathy for the abolitionist struggle, and by the end of the twentieth century abolitionist men and women were revered as ideologically committed individuals dedicated not just to freeing the enslaved but to saving the moral soul of America.

Scholars animated by the modern feminist movement have inspired a reconsideration of women's reform activity. It had long been known, of course, that women were active participants in charitable organizations. But not until Nancy Cott, Kathryn Sklar, Mary Ryan, and other historians began to look more closely at what Cott has called "the bonds of womanhood" did the links between women's domestic lives and their public benevolent behavior fully emerge. Carroll Smith-Rosenberg showed in her study of the New York Female Moral Reform Society, for example, that members who set out at first to convert prostitutes to evangelical Protestantism and to close down the city's many brothels soon developed an ideology of female autonomy that rejected male dominance. When men behaved in immoral or illegal ways, women reformers claimed that they had the right—even the duty—to leave the confines of their homes and actively work to purify society. More recently, historians Nancy Hewitt and Lori Ginzberg have challenged the assumption that all women reformers embraced a single definition of female identity. Instead they have emphasized the importance of class differences in shaping women's reform work, which led inevitably to tensions within female ranks. Giving more attention to the historical evolution of female reform ideology, Ginzberg has also detected a shift from an early focus on moral uplift to a more class-based appeal for social control.

Historians of the suffrage movement have emphasized another kind of exclusivity among women reformers—the boundaries of race. Ellen DuBois has shown that after a brief alliance with the abolitionist movement, many female suffrage reformers abandoned the cause of black liberation in an effort to achieve their own goal with less controversy. Whatever historians may conclude about the liberating or leashing character of early reform, it is clear by now that they have to contend with the ways in which class, gender, and race divided reformers, making the plural—*reform movements*—the more accurate depiction of the impulse to "improve" that pervaded American society in the early nineteenth century.

For further reading, see the Appendix. For web resources, go to **http://college.hmco.com**.

PART THREE

TESTING THE NEW NATION

⟞⟝

1820–1877

The Civil War of 1861 to 1865 was the awesome trial by fire of American nationhood, and of the American soul. All Americans knew, said Abraham Lincoln, that slavery "was somehow the cause of this war." The war tested, in Lincoln's ringing phrase at Gettysburg, whether any nation "dedicated to the proposition that all men are created equal . . . can long endure." How did this great and bloody conflict come about? And what were its results?

American slavery was by any measure a "peculiar institution." Slavery was rooted in both racism and economic exploitation, and depended for its survival on brutal repression. Yet the American slave population was the only enslaved population in history that grew by means of its own biological reproduction—a fact that suggests to many historians that conditions under slavery in the United States were somehow less punitive than those in other slave societies. Indeed a distinctive and durable African American culture managed to flourish under slavery, further suggesting that the slave regime provided some "space" for African American cultural development. But however benignly it might be painted, slavery still remained a cancer in the heart of American democracy, a moral outrage that mocked the nation's claim to be a model of social and political enlightenment. As time went on, more and more voices called more and more stridently for its abolition.

Returning from the Cotton Fields in South Carolina
African American slaves planted and picked virtually all the cotton that formed the foundation of the nineteenth-century southern economy. The white South ferociously defended its "peculiar institution" of slavery, which ended at last only in the fires of the Civil War.

The nation lived uneasily with slavery from the outset. Thomas Jefferson was only one among many in the founding generation who felt acutely the conflict between the high principle of equality and the ugly reality of slavery. The federal government in the early Republic took several steps to check the growth of slavery. It banned slavery in the Old Northwest in 1787, prohibited the further importation of slaves after 1808, and declared in the Missouri Compromise of 1820 that the vast western territories secured in the Louisiana Purchase were forever closed to slavery north of the state of Missouri. Antislavery sentiment even abounded in the South in the immediate post-Revolutionary years. But as time progressed, and especially after Eli Whitney's invention of the cotton gin in the 1790s, the southern planter class became increasingly dependent on slave labor to wring profits from the sprawling plantations that carpeted the South. As cotton cultivation spread westward, the South's stake in slavery grew deeper, and the abolitionist outcry grew louder.

The controversy over slavery significantly intensified following the war with Mexico in the 1840s. "Mexico will poison us," predicted the philosopher Ralph Waldo Emerson, and he proved to be distressingly prophetic. The lands acquired from Mexico—most of the present-day American Southwest, from Texas to California—reopened the question of extending slavery into the western territories. The decade and a

half that followed the Mexican War—from 1846 to 1861—witnessed a series of ultimately ineffective efforts to come to grips with that question, including the ill-starred Compromise of 1850, the conflict-breeding Kansas-Nebraska Act of 1854, and the Supreme Court's inflammatory decision in the *Dred Scott* case of 1857. Ultimately, the slavery question was settled by force of arms, in the Civil War itself.

The Civil War, as Lincoln observed, was assuredly about slavery. But as Lincoln also repeatedly insisted, the war was about the viability of the Union as well and about the strength of democracy itself. Could a democratic government, built on the principle of popular consent, rightfully deny some of its citizens the same right to independence that the American revolutionaries had exercised in seceding from the British Empire in 1776? Southern rebels, calling the conflict "The War for Southern Independence," asked that question forcefully, but ultimately it, too, was answered not in the law courts or in the legislative halls but on the battlefield.

The Civil War unarguably established the supremacy of the Union, and it ended slavery as well. But as the victorious Union set about the task of "reconstruction" after the war's end in 1865, a combination of weak northern will and residual southern power frustrated the goal of making the emancipated blacks full-fledged American citizens. The Civil War in the end brought nothing but freedom—but over time, freedom proved a powerful tool indeed.

The 1st Virginia Regiment
These Virginia militiamen were photographed in 1859 while attending the trial of the abolitionist John Brown for treason against the State of Virginia. Two years later, their regiment formed part of the Confederate army that struck for southern independence.

16

The South and the Slavery Controversy

1793–1860

IF YOU PUT A CHAIN AROUND THE NECK OF A SLAVE,
THE OTHER END FASTENS ITSELF AROUND YOUR OWN.

RALPH WALDO EMERSON, 1841

At the dawn of the Republic, slavery faced an uncertain future. Touched by Revolutionary idealism, some southern leaders, including Thomas Jefferson, were talking openly of freeing their slaves. Others predicted that the iron logic of economics would eventually expose slavery's unprofitability, speeding its demise.

But the introduction of Eli Whitney's cotton gin in 1793 scrambled all those predictions. Whitney's invention made possible the wide-scale cultivation of short-staple cotton. The white fiber rapidly became the dominant southern crop, eclipsing tobacco, rice, and sugar. The explosion of cotton cultivation created an insatiable demand for labor, chaining the slave to the gin and the planter to the slave. As the nineteenth century opened, the reinvigoration of southern slavery carried fateful implications for blacks and whites alike—and threatened the survival of the nation itself.

"Cotton Is King!"

As time passed, the Cotton Kingdom developed into a huge agricultural factory, pouring out avalanches of the fluffy fiber. Quick profits drew planters to the loamy bottomlands of the Gulf states. As long as the soil was still vigorous, the yield was bountiful and the rewards were high. Caught up in an economic spiral, the planters bought more slaves and land to grow more cotton, so as to buy still more slaves and land.

Northern shippers reaped a large part of the profits from the cotton trade. They would load bulging bales of cotton at southern ports, transport them to England, sell their fleecy cargo for pounds sterling, and buy needed manufactured goods for sale in the United States. To a large degree, the prosperity of both North and South rested on the bent backs of southern slaves.

Cotton accounted for half the value of all American exports after 1840. The South produced more than half of the entire world's supply of cotton—a fact that held foreign nations in partial bondage. Britain was then the leading industrial power. Its most important single manufacture in the 1850s was cotton cloth, from which about one-fifth of its population, directly or indirectly, drew its livelihood. About 75 percent of this precious supply of fiber came from the white-carpeted acres of the South.

Southern leaders were fully aware that Britain was tied to them by cotton threads, and this dependence

Cotton as King In this Northern Civil War cartoon, the Confederacy appears as a lighted bomb.

by the few, in this case heavily influenced by a planter aristocracy. In 1850 only 1,733 families owned more than 100 slaves each, and this select group provided the cream of the political and social leadership of the section and nation. Here was the mint-julep South of the tall-columned and white-painted plantation mansion—the "big house," where dwelt the "cottonocracy."

The planter aristocrats, with their blooded horses and Chippendale chairs, enjoyed a lion's share of southern wealth. They could educate their children in the finest schools, often in the North or abroad. Their money provided the leisure for study, reflection, and statecraft, as was notably true of men like John C. Calhoun (a Yale graduate) and Jefferson Davis (a West Point graduate). They felt a keen sense of obligation to serve the public. It was no accident that Virginia and the other southern states produced a higher proportion of front-rank statesmen before 1860 than the "dollar-grubbing" North.

But even in its best light, dominance by a favored aristocracy was basically undemocratic. It widened the gap between rich and poor. It hampered tax-supported public education, because the rich planters could and did send their children to private institutions.

A favorite author of elite southerners was Sir Walter Scott, whose manors and castles, graced by brave Ivanhoes and fair Rowenas, helped them idealize a feudal society, even when many of their economic activities were undeniably capitalistic. Southern aristocrats, who

gave them a heady sense of power. In their eyes "Cotton was King," the gin was his throne, and the black bondsmen were his henchmen. If war should ever break out between North and South, northern warships would presumably cut off the outflow of cotton. Fiber-famished British factories would then close their gates, starving mobs would force the London government to break the blockade, and the South would triumph. Cotton was a powerful monarch indeed.

The Planter "Aristocracy"

Before the Civil War, the South was in some respects not so much a democracy as an oligarchy—or a government

Thomas Jefferson (1743–1826) wrote in 1786,

"What a stupendous, what an incomprehensible machine is man! Who can endure toil, famine, stripes, imprisonment & death itself in vindication of his own liberty, and the next moment . . . inflict on his fellow men a bondage, one hour of which is fraught with more misery than ages of that which he rose in rebellion to oppose."

Unlike George Washington, Jefferson freed only a couple of his slaves in his will; the rest were sold to pay off his large debts.

Harvesting Cotton
This Currier & Ives print shows slaves of both sexes harvesting cotton, which was then "ginned," baled, carted to the riverbank, and taken by paddle wheeler downriver to New Orleans.

sometimes staged jousting tournaments, strove to perpetuate a type of medievalism that had died out in Europe—or was rapidly dying out.* Mark Twain later accused Sir Walter Scott of having had a hand in starting the Civil War. The British novelist, Twain said, aroused the southerners to fight for a decaying social structure— "a sham civilization."

The plantation system also shaped the lives of southern women. The mistress of a great plantation commanded a sizable household staff of mostly female slaves. She gave daily orders to cooks, maids, seamstresses, laundresses, and body servants. Relationships between mistresses and slaves ranged from affectionate to atrocious. Some mistresses showed tender regard for their bondswomen, and some slave women took pride in their status as "members" of the household. But slavery strained even the bonds of womanhood. Virtually no slaveholding women believed in abolition, and relatively few protested when the husbands and children of their slaves were sold. One plantation mistress harbored a special affection for her slave Annica but noted in her diary that "I whipt Annica" for insolence.

Slaves of the Slave System

Unhappily, the moonlight-and-magnolia tradition concealed much that was worrisome, distasteful, and sordid. Plantation agriculture was wasteful, largely because King Cotton and his money-hungry subjects despoiled the good earth. Quick profits led to excessive cultivation, or "land butchery," which in turn caused a heavy leakage of population to the West and Northwest.

The economic structure of the South became increasingly monopolistic. As the land wore thin, many small farmers sold their holdings to more prosperous neighbors and went north or west. The big got bigger and the small smaller. When the Civil War finally erupted, a large percentage of southern farms had passed from the hands of the families that had originally cleared them.

Another cancer in the bosom of the South was the financial instability of the plantation system. The temptation to overspeculate in land and slaves caused many planters, including Andrew Jackson in his later years, to plunge in beyond their depth. Although the black slaves might in extreme cases be fed for as little as ten cents a day, there were other expenses. The slaves represented a heavy investment of capital, perhaps $1,200 each in the case of prime field hands, and they might deliberately injure themselves or run away. An entire slave quarter might be wiped out by disease or even by lightning, as happened in one instance to twenty ill-fated blacks.

---

*Oddly enough, by legislative enactment, jousting became the official state sport of Maryland in 1962.

Basil Hall (1788–1844), an Englishman, visited part of the cotton belt on a river steamer (1827–1828). Noting the preoccupation with cotton, he wrote,

"All day and almost all night long, the captain, pilot, crew, and passengers were talking of nothing else; and sometimes our ears were so wearied with the sound of cotton! cotton! cotton! that we gladly hailed a fresh inundation of company in hopes of some change— but alas! . . . 'What's cotton at?' was the first eager inquiry. 'Ten cents [a pound],' 'Oh, that will never do!'"

The Cotton Kingdom also repelled large-scale European immigration, which added so richly to the manpower and wealth of the North. In 1860 only 4.4 percent of the southern population were foreign-born, as compared with 18.7 percent for the North. German and Irish immigration to the South was generally discouraged by the competition of slave labor, by the high cost of fertile land, and by European ignorance of cotton growing. The diverting of non-British immigration to the North caused the white South to become the most Anglo-Saxon section of the nation.

The White Majority

Only a handful of southern whites lived in Grecian-pillared mansions. Below those 1,733 families in 1850 who owned a hundred or more slaves were the less wealthy slaveowners. They totaled in 1850 some 345,000 families, representing about 1,725,000 white persons. Over two-thirds of these families—255,268 in all— owned fewer than ten slaves each. All told, only about one-fourth of white southerners owned slaves or belonged to a slaveowning family.

The smaller slaveowners did not own a majority of the slaves, but they made up a majority of the masters. These lesser masters were typically small farmers. With the striking exception that their households contained a slave or two, or perhaps an entire slave family, the style of their lives probably resembled that of small farmers in the North more than it did that of the southern planter aristocracy. They lived in modest farmhouses and sweated beside their bondsmen in the cotton fields, laboring callus for callus just as hard as their slaves.

Beneath the slaveowners on the population pyramid was the great body of whites who owned no slaves

Dominance by King Cotton likewise led to a dangerous dependence on a one-crop economy, whose price level was at the mercy of world conditions. The whole system discouraged a healthy diversification of agriculture and particularly of manufacturing.

Southern planters resented watching the North grow fat at their expense. They were pained by the heavy outward flow of commissions and interest to northern middlemen, bankers, agents, and shippers. True souls of the South, especially by the 1850s, deplored the fact that when born, they were wrapped in Yankee-made swaddling clothes and that they spent the rest of their lives in servitude to Yankee manufacturing. When they died, they were laid in coffins held together with Yankee nails and were buried in graves dug with Yankee shovels. The South furnished the corpse and the hole in the ground.

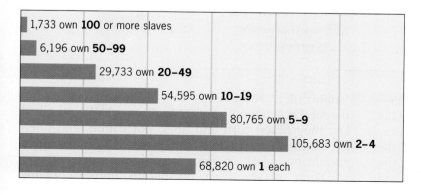

Slaveowning Families, 1850 More than half of all slaveholding families owned fewer than four slaves. In contrast, 2 percent of slaveowners owned more than fifty slaves each. A tiny slaveholding elite held a majority of slave property in the South. The great majority of white southerners owned no slaves at all.

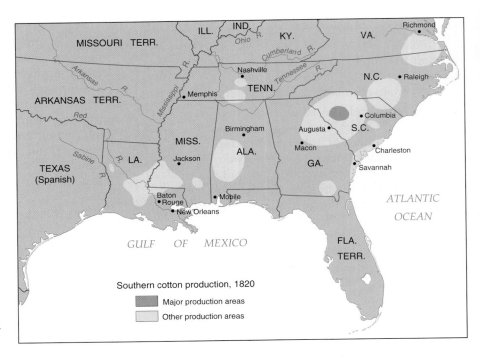

Southern Cotton Production, 1820

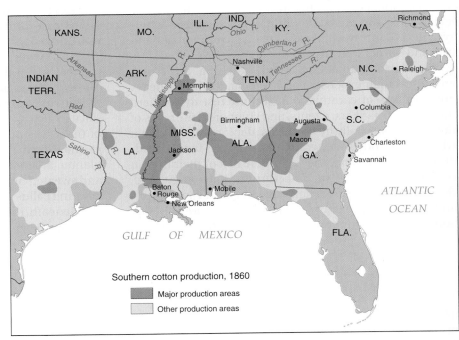

Southern Cotton Production, 1860

at all. By 1860 their numbers had swelled to 6,120,825—three-quarters of all southern whites. Shouldered off the richest bottomlands by the mighty planters, they scratched a simple living from the thinner soils of the backcountry and the mountain valleys. To them the riches of the Cotton Kingdom were a distant dream, and they often sneered at the lordly pretensions of the cotton "snobocracy." These red-necked farmers participated in the market economy scarcely at all. As subsistence farmers, they raised corn and hogs, not cotton, and often lived isolated lives, punctuated periodically by extended socializing and sermonizing at religious camp meetings.

Some of the least prosperous nonslaveholding whites were scorned even by slaves as "poor white

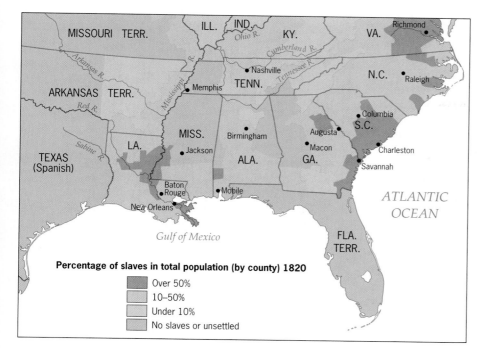

Distribution of Slaves, 1820

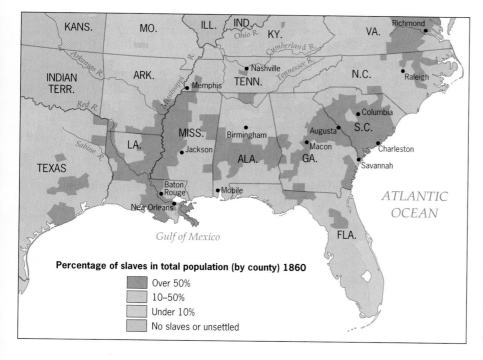

Distribution of Slaves, 1860
The philosopher Ralph Waldo Emerson, a New Englander, declared in 1856, "I do not see how a barbarous community and a civilized community can constitute a state. I think we must get rid of slavery or we must get rid of freedom."

trash." Known also as "hillbillies," "crackers," or "clay eaters," they were often described as listless, shiftless, and misshapen. Later investigations have revealed that many of them were not simply lazy but sick, suffering from malnutrition and parasites, especially hookworm.

All these whites without slaves had no direct stake in the preservation of slavery, yet they were among the stoutest defenders of the slave system. Why? The answer is not far to seek.

The carrot on the stick ever dangling before their eyes was the hope of buying a slave or two and of parlaying their paltry holdings into riches—all in accord with the "American dream" of upward social mobility. They also took fierce pride in their presumed racial superiority, which would be watered down if the slaves were freed. Many of the poorer whites were hardly better off economically than the slaves; some, indeed, were not so well-off. But even the most wretched whites could take perverse comfort from the knowledge that they outranked someone in status: the still more wretched African American slave. Thus did the logic of economics join with the illogic of racism in buttressing the slave system.

In a special category among white southerners were the mountain whites, more or less marooned in the valleys of the Appalachian range that stretched from western Virginia to northern Georgia and Alabama. Civilization had largely passed them by, and they still lived under spartan frontier conditions. They were a kind of living ancestry, for some of them retained Elizabethan speech forms and habits that had long since died out in Britain.

As independent small farmers, hundreds of miles distant from the heart of the Cotton Kingdom and rarely if ever in sight of a slave, these mountain whites had little in common with the whites of the flatlands. Many of them, including future president Andrew Johnson of Tennessee, hated both the haughty planters and their gangs of blacks. They looked upon the impending strife between North and South as "a rich man's war but a poor man's fight."

When the war came, the tough-fibered mountain whites constituted a vitally important peninsula of Unionism jutting down into the secessionist Southern sea. They ultimately played a significant role in crippling the Confederacy. Their attachment to the Union party of Abraham Lincoln was such that for generations after the Civil War, the only concentrated Republican strength in the solid South was to be found in the southern highlands.

Free Blacks: Slaves Without Masters

Precarious in the extreme was the standing of the South's free blacks, who numbered about 250,000 by 1860. In the upper South, the free black population traced its origins to a wavelet of emancipation inspired by the idealism of Revolutionary days. In the deeper South, many free blacks were mulattoes, usually the emancipated children of a white planter and his black mistress. Throughout the South were some free blacks who had purchased their freedom with earnings from labor after hours. Many free blacks

> *"Arthur Lee, Freeman," petitioned the General Assembly of Virginia in 1835 for permission to remain in the state despite a law against the residency of free blacks. After asserting his upstanding moral character, he implored,*
>
> "He therefore most respectfully and earnestly prays that you will pass a law permitting him on the score of long and meritorious service to remain in the State, together with his wife and four children, and not force him in his old age to seek a livelihood in a new Country."

owned property, especially in New Orleans, where a sizable mulatto community prospered. Some, such as William T. Johnson, the "barber of Natchez," even owned slaves. He was the master of fifteen bondsmen; his diary records that in June 1848 he flogged two slaves and a mule.

The free blacks in the South were a kind of "third race." These people were prohibited from working in certain occupations and forbidden from testifying against whites in court. They were always vulnerable to being hijacked back into slavery by unscrupulous slave traders. As free men and women, they were walking examples of what might be achieved by emancipation and hence were resented and detested by defenders of the slave system.

Free blacks were also unpopular in the North, where about another 250,000 of them lived. Several states forbade their entrance, most denied them the right to vote, and some barred blacks from public schools. In 1835 New Hampshire farmers hitched their oxen to a small schoolhouse that had dared to enroll fourteen black children and dragged it into a swamp. Northern blacks were especially hated by the pick-and-shovel Irish immigrants, with whom they competed for menial jobs. Much of the agitation in the North against the spread of slavery into the new territories in the 1840s and 1850s grew out of race prejudice, not humanitarianism.

Antiblack feeling was in fact frequently stronger in the North than in the South. The gifted and eloquent former slave Frederick Douglass, an abolitionist and self-educated orator of rare power, was several times mobbed and beaten by northern rowdies. It was sometimes observed that white southerners, who were often suckled and reared by black nurses, liked the black as an individual but despised the race. The white northerner, on the other hand, often professed to like the race but disliked individual blacks.

Plantation Slavery

In society's basement in the South of 1860 were nearly 4 million black human chattels. Their numbers had quadrupled since the dawn of the century, as the booming cotton economy created a seemingly unquenchable demand for slave labor. Legal importation of African slaves into America ended in 1808, when Congress outlawed slave imports. But the price of "black ivory" was so high in the years before the Civil War that uncounted thousands of blacks were smuggled into the South, despite the death penalty for slavers. Although several were captured, southern juries repeatedly acquitted them. Only one slave trader was ever executed, N. P. Gordon, and this took place in New York in 1862, the second year of the Civil War. Yet the huge bulk of the increase in the slave population came not from imports but instead from natural reproduction—a fact that distinguished slavery in America from that in other New World societies and that implied much about the tenor of the slave regime and the conditions of family life under slavery.

A Market in People (left) Held captive in a net, a slave sits on the Congo shore, waiting to be sold and shipped. (right) Once in the United States, slaves continued to be treated like commodities. This woman suffers the humiliation of an inventory number pinned to her dress, most likely for her sale at a slave auction or transport to a new owner.

The Cruelty of Slavery Slaveowners used devices like this collar with bells to discipline and patrol their slaves. This female slave toiling in New Orleans had a collar riveted around her neck, designed to prevent her from hiding from her master or escaping.

Above all, the planters regarded the slaves as investments, into which they had sunk nearly $2 billion of their capital by 1860. Slaves were the primary form of wealth in the South, and as such they were cared for as any asset is cared for by a prudent capitalist. Accordingly, they were sometimes, though by no means always, spared dangerous work, like putting a roof on a house. If a neck was going to be broken, the master preferred it to be that of a wage-earning Irish laborer rather than that of a prime field hand, worth $1,800 by 1860 (a price that had quintupled since 1800). Tunnel blasting and swamp draining were often consigned to itinerant gangs of expendable Irishmen because those perilous tasks were "death on niggers and mules."

Slavery was profitable for the great planters, though it hobbled the economic development of the region as a whole. The profits from the cotton boom sucked ever more slaves from the upper to the lower South, so that by 1860 the Deep South states of South Carolina, Florida, Mississippi, Alabama, and Louisiana each had a majority or near-majority of blacks and accounted for about half of all slaves in the South.

Breeding slaves in the way that cattle are bred was not openly encouraged. But thousands of blacks from the soil-exhausted slave states of the Old South, especially tobacco-depleted Virginia, were "sold down the river" to toil as field-gang laborers on the cotton frontier of the lower Mississippi Valley. Women who bore thirteen or fourteen babies were prized as "rattlin' good breeders," and some of these fecund females were promised their freedom when they had produced ten. White masters all too frequently would force their attentions on female slaves, fathering a sizable mulatto population, most of which remained enchained.

A Slave Auction   Abraham Lincoln said in 1865, "Whenever I hear anyone arguing for slavery, I feel a strong impulse to see it tried on him personally."

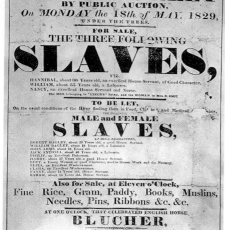

Slave auctions were brutal sights. The open selling of human flesh under the hammer, sometimes with cattle and horses, was among the most revolting aspects of slavery. On the auction block, families were separated with distressing frequency, usually for economic reasons such as bankruptcy or the division of "property" among heirs. The sundering of families in this fashion was perhaps slavery's greatest psychological horror. Abolitionists decried the practice, and Harriet Beecher Stowe seized on the emotional power of this theme by putting it at the heart of the plot of *Uncle Tom's Cabin.*

★

Life Under the Lash

White southerners often romanticized about the happy life of their singing, dancing, banjo-strumming, joyful "darkies." But how did the slaves actually live? There is no simple answer to this question. Conditions varied greatly from region to region, from large plantation to small farm, and from master to master. Everywhere, of course, slavery meant hard work, ignorance, and oppression. The slaves—both men and women—usually toiled from dawn to dusk in the fields, under the watchful eyes and ready whip-hand of a white overseer or black "driver." They had no civil or political rights, other than minimal protection from arbitrary murder or unusually cruel punishment. Some states offered further protections, such as banning the sale of a child under the age of ten away from his or her mother. But all such laws were difficult to enforce, since slaves were forbidden to testify in court or even to have their marriages legally recognized.

> *In 1852 Maria Perkins, a woman enslaved in Virginia, wrote plaintively to her husband about the disruption that the commercial traffic in slaves was visiting upon their family:*
>
> "I write you a letter to let you know of my distress my master has sold albert to a trader on Monday court day and myself and other child is for sale also and I want you to let hear from you very soon before next cort if you can I dont know when I dont want you to wait till Christmas I want you to tell Dr Hamelton and your master if either will buy me they can attend to it know and then I can go after-wards I dont want a trader to get me they asked me if I had got any person to buy me and I told them no they took me to the court houste too they never put me up a man buy the name of brady bought albert and is gone I dont know whare they say he lives in Scottesville my things is in several places some is in staunton and if I should be sold I dont know what will become of them I dont expect to meet with the luck to get that way till I am quite heart sick nothing more I am and ever will be your kind wife Maria Perkins."

monsters in any population, and the planter class contained its share. But the typical planter had too much of his own prosperity riding on the backs of his slaves to beat them bloody on a regular basis.

By 1860 most slaves were concentrated in the "black belt" of the Deep South that stretched from South Carolina and Georgia into the new southwest states of Alabama, Mississippi, and Louisiana. This was the region of the southern frontier, into which the explosively growing Cotton Kingdom had burst in a few short decades. As on all frontiers, life was often rough and raw, and in general the lot of the slave was harder here than in the more settled areas of the Old South.

A majority of blacks lived on larger plantations that harbored communities of twenty or more slaves. In some counties of the Deep South, especially along the

Slave Nurse and Young White Master Southern whites would not allow slaves to own property or exercise civil rights, but, paradoxically, they often entrusted them with the raising of their own precious children. Many a slave "mammy" served as a surrogate mother for the offspring of the planter class.

Floggings were common, for the whip was the substitute for the wage-incentive system and the most visible symbol of the planter's mastery. Strong-willed slaves were sometimes sent to "breakers," whose technique consisted mostly in lavish laying on of the lash. As an abolitionist song of the 1850s lamented,

> *To-night the bond man, Lord*
> *Is bleeding in his chains;*
> *And loud the falling lash is heard*
> *On Carolina's plains!*

But savage beatings made sullen laborers, and lash marks hurt resale values. There are, to be sure, sadistic

Arise! Arise! and weep no more
dry up your tears, we shall part
no more. Come rose we go to
Tennessee,
that happy Shore to old virginia
never — never — return.

Slaves Being Marched from Staunton, Virginia, to Tennessee, by Lewis Miller, 1853 In this folk painting of slaves in transit from the upper South to the new cotton lands of the lower South, couples travel together and children accompany parents. In reality the forced movement of slaves often involved the painful separation of family members.

Tags Identifying Slaves and Free Blacks in Charleston All slaves in Charleston, South Carolina, were reminded of their status as property by the tags they were forced to wear, marked with their skills—such as porter or mechanic or carpenter—and the year the tag was issued. After 1848 even free blacks had to wear tags, ensuring that no African American could be anonymous in the city.

lower Mississippi River, blacks accounted for more than 75 percent of the population. There the family life of slaves tended to be relatively stable, and a distinctive African American slave culture developed. Forced separations of spouses, parents, and children were evidently more common on smaller plantations and in the upper South. Slave marriage vows sometimes proclaimed, "Until death or *distance* do you part."

With impressive resilience, blacks managed to sustain family life in slavery, and most slaves were raised in stable two-parent households. Continuity of family identity across generations was evidenced in the widespread practice of naming children for grandparents or adopting the surname not of a current master, but of a forebear's master. African Americans also displayed their African cultural roots when they avoided marriage between first cousins, in contrast to the frequent intermarriage of close relatives among the ingrown planter aristocracy.

African roots were also visible in the slaves' religious practices. Though heavily Christianized by the itinerant evangelists of the Second Great Awakening, blacks in slavery molded their own distinctive religious forms from a mixture of Christian and African elements. They emphasized those aspects of the Christian heritage that seemed most pertinent to their own situation—especially the captivity of the Israelites in Egypt. One of their most haunting spirituals implored,

> *Tell old Pharaoh*
> *"Let my people go."*

And another lamented,

> *Nobody knows de trouble I've had*
> *Nobody knows but Jesus*

African practices also persisted in the "responsorial" style of preaching, in which the congregation frequently punctuated the minister's remarks with assents and amens—an adaptation of the give-and-take between caller and dancers in the African ringshout dance.

The Burdens of Bondage

Slavery was intolerably degrading to the victims. They were deprived of the dignity and sense of responsibility that come from independence and the right to make choices. They were denied an education, because reading brought ideas, and ideas brought discontent. Many states passed laws forbidding their instruction, and perhaps nine-tenths of adult slaves at the beginning of the Civil War were totally illiterate. For all slaves—indeed for virtually all blacks, slave or free—the "American dream" of bettering one's lot through study and hard work was a cruel and empty mockery.

Not surprisingly, victims of the "peculiar institution" devised countless ways to throw sand in its gears. When workers are not voluntarily hired and adequately compensated, they can hardly be expected to work with alacrity. Accordingly, slaves often slowed the pace of their labor to the barest minimum that would spare them the lash, thus fostering the myth of black "laziness" in the minds of whites. They filched food from the "big house" and pilfered other goods that had been produced or purchased by their labor. They sabotaged expensive equipment, stopping the work routine altogether until repairs were accomplished. Occasionally they even poisoned their masters' food.

The slaves also universally pined for freedom. Many took to their heels as runaways, frequently in search of a separated family member. A black girl, asked if her mother was dead, replied, "Yassah, massah, she is daid, but she's free." Others rebelled, though never successfully. In 1800 an armed insurrection led by a slave named Gabriel in Richmond, Virginia, was foiled by informers, and its leaders were hanged. Denmark Vesey, a free black, led another ill-fated rebellion in Charleston, South Carolina, in 1822. Also betrayed by informers, Vesey and more than thirty followers were publicly strung from the gallows. In 1831 the semiliterate Nat Turner, a visionary black preacher, led an uprising that slaughtered about sixty Virginians, mostly women and children. Reprisals were swift and bloody.

The dark taint of slavery also left its mark on whites. It fostered the brutality of the whip, the bloodhound, and the branding iron. White southerners increasingly lived in a state of imagined siege, surrounded by potentially rebellious blacks inflamed by abolitionist propaganda from the North. Their fears bolstered an intoxicating theory of biological racial superiority and turned the South into a reactionary backwater in an era

of progress—one of the last bastions of slavery in the Western world. The defenders of slavery were forced to degrade themselves, along with their victims. As Booker T. Washington, a distinguished black leader and former slave, later observed, whites could not hold blacks in a ditch without getting down there with them.

Early Abolitionism

The inhumanity of the "peculiar institution" gradually caused antislavery societies to sprout forth. Abolitionist sentiment first stirred at the time of the Revolution, especially among Quakers. Because of the widespread loathing of blacks, some of the earliest abolitionist efforts focused on transporting blacks bodily back to Africa. The American Colonization Society was founded for this purpose in 1817, and in 1822 the Republic of Liberia, on the fever-stricken West African coast, was established for former slaves. Its capital, Monrovia, was

"Am I Not a Man and a Brother? Am I Not a Woman and a Sister?"   A popular appeal.

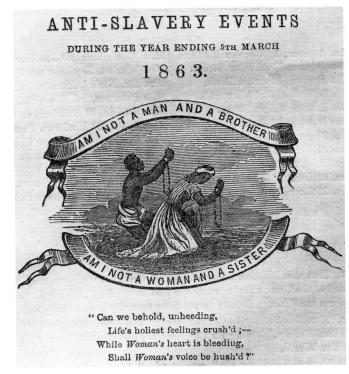

ANTI-SLAVERY EVENTS

DURING THE YEAR ENDING 5TH MARCH

1863.

AM I NOT A MAN AND A BROTHER

AM I NOT A WOMAN AND A SISTER

" Can we behold, unheeding,
   Life's holiest feelings crush'd ;—
While *Woman's* heart is bleeding,
   Shall *Woman's* voice be hush'd ?"

EXAMINING THE EVIDENCE

Bellegrove Plantation, Donaldsville, Louisiana, Built 1857 The sugar-growing Bellegrove Plantation—on the banks of the Mississippi River ninety-five miles north of New Orleans—was laid out on a grander scale than many southern plantations. In this rendering from an advertisement for Bellegrove's sale in 1867, the planter John Orr's home was identified as a "mansion," and quarters for his field hands proved extensive: twenty double cabins built for slaves (now for "Negroes") and a dormitory, described in the ad but not pictured here, housing 150 laborers. Because of the unhealthy work involved in cultivating sugar cane, such as constant digging of drainage canals to keep the cane from rotting in standing water, many planters hired immigrant (usually Irish) labor to keep their valuable slaves out of physical danger. The presence of a hospital between the slave cabins and the mansion indicates the very real threat to health. The layout of Bellegrove reflects the organization of production as well as the social relations on a sugar plantation. The storehouse where preserved sugar awaited shipping stood closest to the Mississippi River, the principal transportation route, whereas the sugar house, the most important building on the plantation, with its mill, boilers, and cooking vats for converting syrup into sugar, dominated the canefields. Although the "big house" and slave quarters stood in close proximity, hedges surrounding the planter's home shut out views of both sugar production and labor. Within the slave quarters, the overseer's larger house signified his superior status, while the arrangement of cabins ensured his supervision of domestic as well as work life. What else does the physical layout of the plantation reveal about settlement patterns, sugar cultivation, and social relationships along the Mississippi?

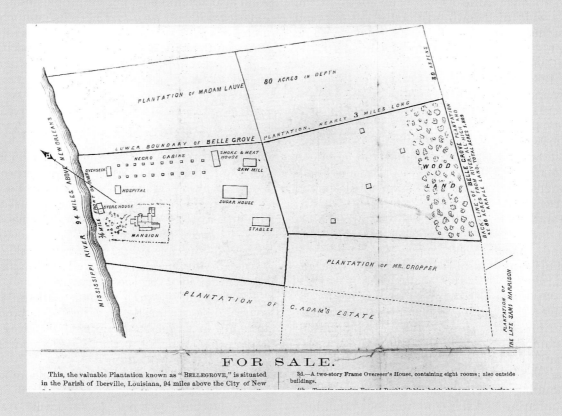

FOR SALE.

This, the valuable Plantation known as "BELLEGROVE," is situated in the Parish of Iberville, Louisiana, 94 miles above the City of New

3d.—A two-story Frame Overseer's House, containing eight rooms; also outside buildings.

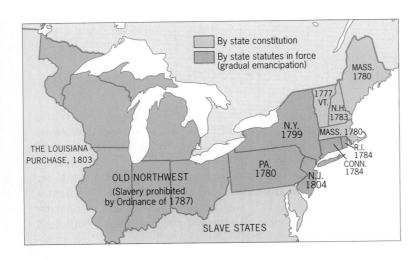

Early Emancipation in the North

named after President Monroe. Some fifteen thousand freed blacks were transported there over the next four decades. But most blacks had no wish to be transplanted into a strange civilization after having become partially Americanized. By 1860 virtually all southern slaves were no longer Africans, but native-born African Americans, with their own distinctive history and culture. Yet the colonization idea appealed to some antislaveryites, including Abraham Lincoln, until the time of the Civil War.

In the 1830s the abolitionist movement took on new energy and momentum, mounting to the proportions of a crusade. American abolitionists took heart in 1833 when their British counterparts unchained the slaves in the West Indies. Most important, the religious spirit of the Second Great Awakening now inflamed the hearts of many abolitionists against the sin of slavery. Prominent among them was lanky, tousle-haired Theodore Dwight Weld, who had been evangelized by Charles Grandison Finney in New York's Burned-Over District in the 1820s. Self-educated and simple in manner and speech, Weld appealed with special power and directness to his rural audiences of untutored farmers.

Spiritually inspired by Finney, Weld was materially aided by two wealthy and devout New York merchants, the brothers Arthur and Lewis Tappan. In 1832 they paid his way to Lane Theological Seminary in Cincinnati, Ohio, which was presided over by the formidable Lyman Beecher, father of a remarkable brood, including novelist Harriet Beecher Stowe, reformer Catharine Beecher, and preacher-abolitionist Henry Ward Beecher. Expelled along with several other students in 1834 for organizing an eighteen-day debate on slavery, Weld and his fellow "Lane Rebels"—full of the energy and idealism of youth—fanned out across the Old Northwest preaching the antislavery gospel. Humorless and deadly earnest, Weld also assembled a potent propaganda pamphlet, *American Slavery as It Is* (1839). Its compelling arguments made it among the most effective abolitionist tracts and greatly influenced Harriet Beecher Stowe's *Uncle Tom's Cabin*.

Radical Abolitionism

On New Year's Day, 1831, a shattering abolitionist blast came from the bugle of William Lloyd Garrison, a mild-looking reformer of twenty-six. The emotionally high-strung son of a drunken father and a spiritual child of the Second Great Awakening, Garrison published in Boston the first issue of his militantly antislavery newspaper, *The Liberator*. With this mighty paper broadside, Garrison triggered a thirty-year war of words and in a sense fired one of the opening barrages of the Civil War.

Stern and uncompromising, Garrison nailed his colors to the masthead of his weekly. He proclaimed in strident tones that under no circumstances would he tolerate the poisonous weed of slavery, but would stamp it out at once, root and branch:

> I will be as harsh as truth and as uncompromising as justice. . . . I am in earnest—I will not equivocate—I will not excuse—I will not retreat a single inch—and I WILL BE HEARD!

William Lloyd Garrison (1805–1879) The most conspicuous and most vilified of the abolitionists, Garrison was a nonresistant pacifist and a poor organizer. He favored northern secession from the South and antagonized both sections with his intemperate language.

Sojourner Truth Also known simply as "Isabella," she held audiences spellbound with her deep, resonant voice and the religious passion with which she condemned the sin of slavery. This photo was taken about 1870.

Other dedicated abolitionists rallied to Garrison's standard, and in 1833 they founded the American Anti-Slavery Society. Prominent among them was Wendell Phillips, a Boston patrician known as "abolition's golden trumpet." A man of strict principle, he would eat no cane sugar and wear no cotton cloth, since both were produced by southern slaves.

Black abolitionists distinguished themselves as living monuments to the cause of African American freedom. Their ranks included David Walker, whose incendiary *Appeal to the Colored Citizens of the World* (1829) advocated a bloody end to white supremacy. Also noteworthy were Sojourner Truth, a freed black woman in New York who fought tirelessly for black emancipation and women's rights, and Martin Delaney, one of the few black leaders to take seriously the notion of mass recolonization of Africa. In 1859 he visited West Africa's Niger Valley seeking a suitable site for relocation.

The greatest of the black abolitionists was Frederick Douglass. Escaping from bondage in 1838 at the age of twenty-one, he was "discovered" by the abolitionists in 1841 when he gave a stunning impromptu speech at an antislavery meeting in Massachusetts. Thereafter he lectured widely for the cause, despite frequent beatings and threats against his life. In 1845 he published his classic autobiography, *Narrative of the Life of Frederick Douglass*. It depicted his remarkable origins as the son of a black slave woman and a white father, his struggle to learn to read and write, and his eventual escape to the North.

Douglass was as flexibly practical as Garrison was stubbornly principled. Garrison often appeared to be more interested in his own righteousness than in the substance of the slavery evil itself. He repeatedly demanded that the "virtuous" North secede from the "wicked" South. Yet he did not explain how the creation

Frederick Douglass (1817?–1895), the remarkable ex-slave, told of Mr. Covey, a white owner who bought a single female slave "as a breeder." She gave birth to twins at the end of the year:

"At this addition to the human stock Covey and his wife were ecstatic with joy. No one dreamed of reproaching the woman or finding fault with the hired man, Bill Smith, the father of the children, for Mr. Covey himself had locked the two up together every night, thus inviting the result."

probing the moral wound in America's underbelly but offering no acceptable balm to ease the pain.

Douglass, on the other hand, along with other abolitionists, increasingly looked to politics to end the blight of slavery. These political abolitionists backed the Liberty party in 1840, the Free Soil party in 1848, and eventually the Republican party in the 1850s. In the end, most abolitionists, including even the pacifistic Garrison himself, followed the logic of their beliefs and supported a frightfully costly fratricidal war as the price of emancipation.

High-minded and courageous, the abolitionists were men and women of goodwill and various colors who faced the cruel choice that people in many ages have had thrust upon them: when is evil so enormous that it must be denounced, even at the risk of precipitating bloodshed and butchery?

of an independent slave republic would bring an end to the "damning crime" of slavery. Renouncing politics, on the Fourth of July, 1854, he publicly burned a copy of the Constitution as "a covenant with death and an agreement with hell" (a phrase he borrowed from a Shaker condemnation of marriage). Critics, including some of his former supporters, charged that Garrison was cruelly

Frederick Douglass (1817?–1895)   Born a slave in Maryland, Douglass escaped to the North and became the most prominent of the black abolitionists. Gifted as an orator, writer, and editor, he continued to battle for the civil rights of his people after emancipation. Near the end of a distinguished career, he served as U.S. minister to Haiti.

After hearing Frederick Douglass speak in Bristol, England, in 1846, Mary A. Estlin wrote to an American abolitionist,

"[T]here is but one opinion of him. Wherever he goes he arouses sympathy in your cause and love for himself. . . . Our expectations were highly roused by his narrative, his printed speeches, and the eulogisms of the friends with whom he has been staying: but he far exceeds the picture we had formed both in outward graces, intellectual power and culture, and eloquence."*

*From Clare Taylor, ed., *British and American Abolitionists, An Episode in Transatlantic Understanding* (Edinburgh University Press, 1974), p. 282.

The South Lashes Back

Antislavery sentiment was not unknown in the South, and in the 1820s antislavery societies were more numerous south of the Mason-Dixon line* than north of it. But after about 1830, the voice of white southern abolitionism was silenced. In a last gasp of southern questioning of slavery, the Virginia legislature debated and eventually defeated various emancipation proposals in 1831–1832. That debate marked a turning point. Thereafter all the slave states tightened their slave codes and moved to prohibit emancipation of any kind, voluntary or compensated. Nat Turner's rebellion in 1831 sent a wave of hysteria sweeping over the snowy cotton fields, and planters in growing numbers slept with pistols by their pillows. Although Garrison had no demonstrable connection with the Turner conspiracy, his *Liberator* appeared at about the same time, and he was bitterly condemned as a terrorist and an inciter of murder. The state of Georgia offered $5,000 for his arrest and conviction.

The nullification crisis of 1832 further implanted haunting fears in white southern minds, conjuring up nightmares of black incendiaries and abolitionist devils. Jailings, whippings, and lynchings now greeted rational efforts to discuss the slavery problem in the South.

Proslavery whites responded by launching a massive defense of slavery as a positive good. In doing so, they forgot their own section's previous doubts about the morality of the "peculiar institution." Slavery, they claimed, was supported by the authority of the Bible and the wisdom of Aristotle. It was good for the Africans, who were lifted from the barbarism of the jungle and clothed with the blessings of Christian civilization. Slavemasters strongly encouraged religion in the slave quarters. A catechism for blacks contained such passages as,

> *Q. Who gave you a master and a mistress?*
> *A. God gave them to me.*
> *Q. Who says that you must obey them?*
> *A. God says that I must.*

White apologists also pointed out that master-slave relationships really resembled those of a family. On many plantations, especially those of the Old South of Virginia and Maryland, this argument had a certain

---

*Originally the southern boundary of colonial Pennsylvania.

plausibility. A slave's tombstone bore this touching inscription:

> *JOHN:*
> *A faithful servant:*
> *and true friend:*
> *Kindly, and considerate:*
> *Loyal, and affectionate:*
> *The family he served*
> *Honours him in death:*
> *But, in life they gave him love:*
> *For he was one of them*

Southern whites were quick to contrast the "happy" lot of their "servants" with that of the overworked northern wage slaves, including sweated women and stunted children. The blacks mostly toiled in the fresh air and sunlight, not in dark and stuffy factories. They did not have to worry about slack times or unemployment, as did the "hired hands" of the North. Provided with a jail-like form of Social Security, they were cared for in sickness and old age, unlike northern workers, who were set adrift when they had outlived their usefulness.

These curious proslavery arguments only widened the chasm between a backward-looking South and a forward-looking North—and indeed much of the rest of the Western world. The southerners reacted defensively to the pressure of their own fears and bristled before the merciless nagging of the northern abolitionists. Increasingly the white South turned in upon itself and grew hotly intolerant of any embarrassing questions about the status of slavery.

Regrettably, also, the controversy over free people endangered free speech in the entire country. Piles of petitions poured in upon Congress from the antislavery reformers, and in 1836 sensitive southerners drove through the House the so-called Gag Resolution. It required all such antislavery appeals to be tabled without debate. This attack on the right of petition aroused the sleeping lion in the aged ex-president, Representative John Quincy Adams, and he waged a successful eight-year fight for its repeal.

Southern whites likewise resented the flooding of their mails with incendiary abolitionist literature. Even if blacks could not read, they could interpret the inflammatory drawings, such as those that showed masters knocking out slaves' teeth with clubs. In 1835 a mob in Charleston, South Carolina, looted the post office and burned a pile of abolitionist propaganda. Capitulating to southern pressures, the Washington government in 1835 ordered southern postmasters to destroy abolitionist

A Two-Way Proslavery Cartoon
Published in New York, the cartoon
shows a chilled and rejected free
black in the North (left) disconsolately
passing a grogshop, while (right) a
happy southern slave enjoys life
with a fishing rod in the company
of a white youth.

material and called on southern state officials to arrest federal postmasters who did not comply. Such was "freedom of the press" as guaranteed by the Constitution.

The Abolitionist Impact in the North

Abolitionists—especially the extreme Garrisonians—were for a long time unpopular in many parts of the North. Northerners had been brought up to revere the Constitution and to regard the clauses on slavery as a lasting bargain. The ideal of Union, hammered home by the thundering eloquence of Daniel Webster and others, had taken deep root, and Garrison's wild talk of secession grated harshly on northern ears.

The North also had a heavy economic stake in Dixieland. By the late 1850s, southern planters owed northern bankers and other creditors about $300 million, and much of this immense sum would be lost—as, in fact, it later was—should the Union dissolve. New England textile mills were fed with cotton raised by the slaves, and a disrupted labor system might cut off this vital supply and bring unemployment. The Union during these critical years was partly bound together with cotton threads, tied by lords of the loom in collaboration with the so-called lords of the lash. It was

not surprising that strong hostility developed in the North against the boat-rocking tactics of the radical antislaveryites.

Repeated tongue-lashings by the extreme abolitionists provoked many mob outbursts in the North, some led by respectable gentlemen. A gang of young toughs broke into Lewis Tappan's New York house in 1834 and demolished its interior, while a crowd in the street cheered. In 1835 Garrison, with a rope tied around him, was dragged through the streets of Boston by the so-called Broadcloth Mob but escaped almost miraculously. Reverend Elijah P. Lovejoy of Alton, Illinois, not content to assail slavery, impugned the chastity of Catholic women. His printing press was destroyed four times, and in 1837 he was killed by a mob and became "the martyr abolitionist." So unpopular were the antislavery zealots that ambitious politicians, like Lincoln, usually avoided the taint of Garrisonian abolition like the plague.

Yet by the 1850s the abolitionist outcry had made a deep dent in the northern mind. Many citizens had come to see the South as the land of the unfree and the home of a hateful institution. Few northerners were prepared to abolish slavery outright, but a growing number, including Lincoln, opposed extending it to the western territories. People of this stamp, commonly called "free-soilers," swelled their ranks as the Civil War approached.

Chronology

1793	Whitney's cotton gin transforms southern economy
1800	Gabriel slave rebellion in Virginia
1808	Congress outlaws slave trade
1817	American Colonization Society formed
1820	Missouri Compromise
1822	Vesey slave rebellion in Charleston, South Carolina Republic of Liberia established in Africa
1829	Walker publishes *Appeal to the Colored Citizens of the World*
1831	Nat Turner slave rebellion in Virginia Garrison begins publishing *The Liberator*
1831-1832	Virginia legislature debates slavery and emancipation
1833	British abolish slavery in West Indies American Anti-Slavery Society founded
1834	Abolitionist students expelled from Lane Theological Seminary
1835	U.S. Post Office orders destruction of abolitionist mail "Broadcloth Mob" attacks Garrison
1836	House of Representatives passes "Gag Resolution"
1837	Mob kills abolitionist Lovejoy in Alton, Illinois
1839	Weld publishes *American Slavery as It Is*
1845	Douglass publishes *Narrative of the Life of Frederick Douglass*
1848	Free Soil party organized

VARYING VIEWPOINTS

What Was the True Nature of Slavery?

By the early twentieth century, the predictable accounts of slavery written by partisans of the North or South had receded in favor of a romantic vision of the Old South conveyed through popular literature, myth, and, increasingly, scholarship. That vision was persuasively validated by the publication of Ulrich Bonnell Phillips's landmark study, *American Negro Slavery* (1918). Phillips made three key arguments. First, he claimed that slavery was a dying economic institution, unprofitable to the slaveowner and an obstacle to the economic development of the South as a whole. Second, he contended that slavery was a rather benign institution and that the planters, contrary to abolitionist charges of ruthless exploitation, treated their chattels with kindly paternalism. Third, he reflected the dominant racial attitudes of his time in his belief that blacks were inferior and

submissive by nature and did not abhor the institution that enslaved them.

For nearly a century, historians have debated these assertions, sometimes heatedly. More sophisticated economic analysis has refuted Phillips's claim that slavery would have withered away without a war. Economic historians have demonstrated that slavery was a viable, profitable, expanding economic system and that slaves constituted a worthwhile investment for their owners. The price of a prime field hand rose dramatically, even in the 1850s.

No such definitive conclusion has yet been reached in the disputes over slave treatment. Beginning in the late 1950s, historians came increasingly to emphasize the harshness of the slave system. One study, Stanley Elkins's *Slavery* (1959), went so far as to compare the "peculiar institution" to the Nazi concentration camps of World War II. Both were "total institutions," Elkins contended, which "infantilized" their victims.

More recently, scholars such as Eugene Genovese have moved beyond debating whether slavery was kind or cruel. Without diminishing the deprivations and pains of slavery, Genovese has conceded that slavery embraced a strange form of paternalism, a system that reflected not the benevolence of southern slaveholders, but their need to control and coax work out of their reluctant and often recalcitrant "investments." Furthermore, within this paternalist system, black slaves were able to make reciprocal demands of their white owners and to protect a "cultural space" of their own in which family and religion particularly could flourish. The crowning paradox of slaveholder paternalism was that in treating their property more humanely, slaveowners implicitly recognized the humanity of their slaves and thereby subverted the racist underpinnings upon which their slave society existed.

The revised conceptions of the master-slave relationship also spilled over into the debate about slave personality. Elkins accepted Phillips's portrait of the slave as a childlike "Sambo" but saw it as a consequence of slavery rather than a congenital attribute of African Americans. Kenneth Stampp, rejecting the Sambo stereotype, stressed the frequency and variety of slave resistance, both mild and militant. A third view, imaginatively documented in the work of Lawrence Levine, argues that the Sambo character was an act, an image that slaves used to confound their masters without incurring punishment. Levine's *Black Culture and Black Consciousness* (1977) shares with books by John Blassingame and Herbert Gutman an emphasis on the tenacity with which slaves maintained their own culture and kin relations, despite the hardships of bondage. Most recently, historians have attempted to avoid the polarity of repression versus autonomy. They assert the debasing oppression of slavery, while also acknowledging slaves' ability to resist the dehumanizing effects of enslavement. The challenge before historians today is to capture the vibrancy of slave culture and its legacy for African American society after emancipation, without diminishing the brutality of life under the southern slave regime.

A new sensitivity to gender, spurred by the growing field of women's history, has also expanded the horizons of slavery studies. Historians such as Elizabeth Fox-Genovese, Jacqueline Jones, and Catherine Clinton have focused on the ways in which slavery differed for men and women, both slaves and slaveholders. Enslaved black women, for example, had the unique task of negotiating an identity out of their dual responsibilities as plantation laborer, even sometimes caretaker of white women and children, and anchor of the black family. By tracing the interconnectedness of race and gender in the American South, these historians have also shown how slavery shaped conceptions of masculinity and femininity within southern society, further distinguishing its culture from that of the North.

Scholarship on slavery continues to grow. The newest work by Philip D. Morgan and Ira Berlin has drawn attention to how both the institution of slavery and the experience of the enslaved changed over time. They contend that slavery was far from monolithic. Rather it adapted to particular geographic and environmental factors, which influenced the diet and work routines of slaves and shaped the degree of autonomy in family life and culture that slaves were able to carve out. Slavery also changed from one generation to the next. As southern slaveholders responded to new social and economic conditions, they gradually altered the legal status of slaves, making slavery a hereditary condition, outlawing manumission in many places, rendering freedom for the enslaved increasingly difficult to attain, and placing onerous restrictions on the work opportunities and mobility of free African Americans.

For further reading, see the Appendix. For web resources, go to **http://college.hmco.com**.

Manifest Destiny and Its Legacy

1841–1848

> OUR MANIFEST DESTINY [IS] TO OVERSPREAD THE CONTINENT ALLOTTED BY PROVIDENCE FOR THE FREE DEVELOPMENT OF OUR YEARLY MULTIPLYING MILLIONS.
>
> JOHN L. O'SULLIVAN, 1845*

Territorial expansion dominated American diplomacy and politics in the 1840s. Settlers swarming into the still-disputed Oregon Country aggravated relations with Britain, which had staked its own claims in the Pacific Northwest. The clamor to annex Texas to the Union provoked bitter tension with Mexico, which continued to regard Texas as a Mexican province in revolt. And when Americans began casting covetous eyes on Mexico's northernmost province, the great prize of California, open warfare erupted between the United States and its southern neighbor. Victory over Mexico added vast new domains to the United States, but it also raised thorny questions about the status of slavery in the newly acquired territories—questions that would be answered in blood in the Civil War of the 1860s.

The Accession of "Tyler Too"

A horde of hard-ciderites descended upon Washington early in 1841, clamoring for the spoils of office. Newly elected President Harrison, bewildered by the uproar, was almost hounded to death by Whig spoilsmen.

The real leaders of the Whig party regarded "Old Tippecanoe" as little more than an impressive figurehead. Daniel Webster, as secretary of state, and Henry Clay, the uncrowned king of the Whigs and their ablest spokesman in the Senate, would grasp the helm. The aging general was finally forced to rebuke the overzealous Clay and pointedly remind him that he, William Henry Harrison, was president of the United States.

Unluckily for Clay and Webster, their schemes soon hit a fatal snag. Before the new term had fairly started, Harrison contracted pneumonia. Wearied by official functions and plagued by office seekers, the enfeebled old warrior died after only four weeks in the White House—by far the shortest administration in American history, following by far the longest inaugural address.

The "Tyler too" part of the Whig ticket, hitherto only a rhyme, now claimed the spotlight. What manner of man did the nation now find in the presidential chair? Six feet tall, slender, blue-eyed, and fair-haired, with classical features and a high forehead, John Tyler was a Virginia gentleman of the old school—gracious and kindly, yet stubbornly attached to principle. He had earlier resigned from the Senate, quite unnecessarily, rather than accept distasteful instructions from the Virginia legislature. Still a lone wolf, he had forsaken the

---

*Earliest known use of the term *Manifest Destiny,* sometimes called "Manifest Desire."

Jacksonian Democratic fold for that of the Whigs, largely because he could not stomach the dictatorial tactics of Jackson.

Tyler's enemies accused him of being a Democrat in Whig clothing, but this charge was only partially true. The Whig party, like the Democratic party, was something of a catchall, and the accidental president belonged to the minority wing, which embraced a number of Jeffersonian states' righters. Tyler had in fact been put on the ticket partly to attract the vote of this fringe group, many of whom were influential southern gentry.

Yet Tyler, high-minded as he was, should never have consented to run on the ticket. Although the dominant Clay-Webster group had published no platform, every alert politician knew what the unpublished platform contained. And on virtually every major issue, the obstinate Virginian was at odds with the majority of his adoptive Whig party, which was pro-bank, pro–protective tariff, and pro–internal improvements. "Tyler too" rhymed with "Tippecanoe," but there the harmony ended. As events turned out, President Harrison, the Whig, served for only 4 weeks, whereas Tyler, the ex-Democrat who was still largely a Democrat at heart, served for 204 weeks.

John Tyler: A President Without a Party

After their hard-won, hard-cider victory, the Whigs brought their not-so-secret platform out of Clay's waist-coat pocket. To the surprise of no one, it outlined a strongly nationalistic program.

Financial reform came first. The Whig Congress hastened to pass a law ending the independent treasury system, and President Tyler, disarmingly agreeable, signed it. Clay next drove through Congress a bill for a "Fiscal Bank," which would establish a new Bank of the United States.

Tyler's hostility to a centralized bank was notorious, and Clay—the "Great Compromiser"—would have done well to conciliate him. But the Kentuckian, robbed repeatedly of the presidency by lesser men, was in an imperious mood and riding for a fall. When the bank bill reached the presidential desk, Tyler flatly vetoed it on both practical and constitutional grounds. A drunken mob gathered late at night near the White House and shouted insultingly, "Huzza for Clay!" "A Bank! A Bank!" "Down with the Veto!"

The stunned Whig leaders tried once again. Striving to pacify Tyler's objections to a "Fiscal Bank," they passed another bill providing for a "Fiscal Corporation." But the president, still unbending, vetoed the offensive substitute. The Democrats were jubilant: they had been saved from another financial "monster" only by the pneumonia that had felled Harrison.

Whig extremists, seething with indignation, condemned Tyler as "His Accidency" and as an "Executive Ass." Widely burned in effigy, he received numerous letters threatening him with death. A wave of influenza then sweeping the country was called the "Tyler grippe." To the delight of Democrats, the stiff-necked Virginian was formally expelled from his party by a caucus of Whig congressmen, and a serious attempt to impeach him was broached in the House of Representatives. His entire cabinet resigned in a body, except Secretary of State Webster, who was then in the midst of delicate negotiations with England.

The proposed Whig tariff also felt the prick of the president's well-inked pen. Tyler appreciated the necessity of bringing additional revenue to the Treasury. But old Democrat that he was, he looked with a frosty eye on the major tariff scheme of the Whigs because it provided, among other features, for a distribution

Manifest Destiny: A Caricature The spirit of Manifest Destiny swept the nation in the 1840s, and threatened to sweep it to extremes. This cartoon from 1848 lampoons proslavery Democratic presidential candidate Lewis Cass as a veritable war machine, bent on the conquest of territory ranging from New Mexico to Cuba and even Peru.

Life in an American Hotel, 1856
A British caricature of American rudeness and readiness with the pistol. Frances Trollope, a British visitor to the United States in the 1820s, wrote in her scathing book, *Domestic Manners of the Americans* (1831), that in America, "the gentlemen spit, talk of elections. . . . The ladies look at each other's dresses till they know every pin by heart."

among the states of revenue from the sale of public lands in the West. Tyler could see no point in squandering federal money when the federal Treasury was not overflowing, and he again wielded an emphatic veto.

Chastened Clayites redrafted their tariff bill. They chopped out the offensive dollar-distribution scheme and pushed down the rates to about the moderately protective level of 1832, roughly 32 percent on dutiable goods. Tyler had no fondness for a protective tariff, but realizing the need for additional revenue, he reluctantly signed the law of 1842. In subsequent months the pressure for higher customs duties slackened as the country gradually edged its way out of the depression. The Whig slogan, "Harrison, Two Dollars a Day and Roast Beef," was reduced by unhappy Democrats to, "Ten Cents a Day and Bean Soup."

A War of Words with Britain

Hatred of Britain during the nineteenth century came to a head periodically and had to be lanced by treaty settlement or by war. The poison had festered ominously by 1842.

Anti-British passions were composed of many ingredients. At bottom lay the bitter, red-coated memories of the two Anglo-American wars. In addition, the genteel pro-British Federalists had died out, eventually yielding to the boisterous Jacksonian Democrats. British travelers, sniffing with aristocratic noses at the crude scene, wrote acidly of American tobacco spitting, slave auctioneering, lynching, eye gouging, and other unsavory features of the rustic Republic. Travel books penned by these critics, whose views were avidly read on both sides of the Atlantic, stirred up angry outbursts in America.

But the literary fireworks did not end here. British magazines added fuel to the flames when, enlarging on the travel books, they launched sneering attacks on Yankee shortcomings. American journals struck back with "you're another" arguments, thus touching off the "Third War with England." Fortunately, this British-American war was fought with paper broadsides, and only ink was spilled. British authors, including Charles Dickens, entered the fray with gall-dipped pens, for they were being denied rich royalties by the absence of an American copyright law.*

Sprawling America, with expensive canals to dig and railroads to build, was a borrowing nation in the nineteenth century. Imperial Britain, with its overflowing

---

*Not until 1891 did Congress extend copyright privileges to foreign authors.

coffers, was a lending nation. The well-heeled creditor is never popular with the down-at-the-heels debtor, and the phrase "bloated British bond-holder" rolled bitterly from many an American tongue. When the panic of 1837 broke and several states defaulted on their bonds or repudiated them openly, honest Englishmen assailed Yankee trickery. One of them offered a new stanza for an old song:

> Yankee Doodle borrows cash,
> Yankee Doodle spends it,
>   And then he snaps his fingers at
> The jolly flat [simpleton] who lends it.

Troubles of a more dangerous sort came closer to home in 1837 when a short-lived insurrection erupted in Canada. It was supported by such a small minority of Canadians that it never had a real chance of success. Yet hundreds of hot-blooded Americans, hoping to strike a blow for freedom against the hereditary enemy, furnished military supplies or volunteered for armed service. The Washington regime tried arduously, though futilely, to uphold its weak neutrality regulations. But again, as in the case of Texas, it simply could not enforce unpopular laws in the face of popular opposition.

A provocative incident on the Canadian frontier brought passions to a boil in 1837. An American steamer, the *Caroline,* was carrying supplies to the insurgents across the swift Niagara River. It was finally attacked on the New York shore by a determined British force, which set the vessel on fire. Lurid American illustrators showed the flaming ship, laden with shrieking souls, plummeting over Niagara Falls. The craft in fact sank short of the plunge, and only one American was killed.

This unlawful invasion of American soil—a counter-violation of neutrality—had alarming aftermaths. Washington officials lodged vigorous but ineffective protests. Three years later, in 1840, the incident was dramatically revived in the state of New York. A Canadian named McLeod, after allegedly boasting in a tavern of his part in the *Caroline* raid, was arrested and indicted for murder. The London Foreign Office, which regarded the *Caroline* raiders as members of a sanctioned armed force and not as criminals, made clear that his execution would mean war. Fortunately, McLeod was freed after establishing an alibi. It must have been airtight, for it was good enough to convince a New York jury. The tension forthwith eased, but it snapped taut again in 1841, when British officials in the Bahamas offered asylum to 130 Virginia slaves who had rebelled and captured the American ship *Creole.* Britain had abolished slavery within its empire in 1834, raising southern fears that its Caribbean possessions would become Canada-like havens for escaped slaves.

Manipulating the Maine Maps

An explosive controversy of the early 1840s involved the Maine boundary dispute. The St. Lawrence River is icebound several months of the year, as the British, remembering the War of 1812, well knew. They were determined, as a defensive precaution against the Yankees, to build a road westward from the seaport of Halifax to Quebec. But the proposed route ran through disputed territory—claimed also by Maine under the misleading peace treaty of 1783. Tough-knuckled lumberjacks from both Maine and Canada entered the disputed no-man's-land of the tall-timbered Aroostook River valley. Ugly fights flared up, and both sides summoned the local militia. The small-scale lumberjack clash, which was dubbed the "Aroostook War," threatened to widen into a full-dress shooting war.

As the crisis deepened in 1842, the London Foreign Office took an unusual step. It sent to Washington a nonprofessional diplomat, the conciliatory financier Lord Ashburton, who had married a wealthy American woman. He speedily established cordial relations with Secretary Webster, who had recently been lionized during a visit to Britain.

The two statesmen, their nerves frayed by protracted negotiations in the heat of a Washington summer, finally agreed to compromise on the Maine boundary. On the basis of a rough, split-the-difference arrangement, the Americans were to retain some 7,000 square miles of the 12,000 square miles of wilderness in dispute. The British got less land but won the desired Halifax-Quebec route. During the negotiations the *Caroline* affair,

Maine Boundary Settlement, 1842

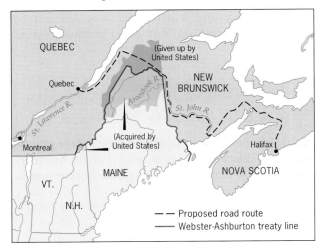

> *Thomas J. Green (1801–1863), who served as a brigadier general in the Texas Revolution, published a pamphlet in 1845 to make the case for American support of an independent Texas:*
>
> "Both the government of the United States and Texas are founded upon the same political code. They have the same common origin—the same language, laws, and religion—the same pursuits and interests; and though they may remain independent of each other as to government, they are identified in weal and wo'—they will flourish side by side and the blight which affects the one will surely reach the other."

malingering since 1837, was patched up by an exchange of diplomatic notes.

An overlooked bonus sneaked by in the small print of the same treaty: the British, in adjusting the U.S.-Canadian boundary farther west, surrendered 6,500 square miles. The area was later found to contain the priceless Mesabi iron ore of Minnesota.

The Lone Star of Texas Shines Alone

During the uncertain eight years since 1836, Texas had led a precarious existence. Mexico, refusing to recognize Texas's independence, regarded the Lone Star Republic as a province in revolt, to be reconquered in the future. Mexican officials loudly threatened war if the American eagle should ever gather the fledgling republic under its protective wings.

The Texans were forced to maintain a costly military establishment. Vastly outnumbered by their Mexican foe, they could not tell when he would strike again. Mexico actually did make two halfhearted raids that, though ineffectual, foreshadowed more fearsome efforts. Confronted with such perils, Texas was driven to open negotiations with Britain and France, in the hope of

securing the defensive shield of a protectorate. In 1839 and 1840, the Texans concluded treaties with France, Holland, and Belgium.

Britain was intensely interested in an independent Texas. Such a republic would check the southward surge of the American colossus, whose bulging biceps posed a constant threat to nearby British possessions in the New World. A puppet Texas, dancing to strings pulled by Britain, could be turned upon the Yankees. Subsequent clashes would create a smoke-screen diversion, behind which foreign powers could move into the Americas and challenge the insolent Monroe Doctrine. French schemers were likewise attracted by the hoary game of divide and conquer. These actions would result, they hoped, in the fragmentation and militarization of America.

Dangers threatened from other foreign quarters. British abolitionists were busily intriguing for a foothold in Texas. If successful in freeing the few blacks there, they presumably would inflame the nearby slaves of the South. In addition, British merchants regarded Texas as a potentially important free-trade area—an offset to the tariff-walled United States. British manufacturers likewise perceived that those vast Texas plains constituted one of the great cotton-producing areas of the future. An independent Texas would relieve British looms of their chronic dependence on American fiber—a supply that might be cut off in time of crisis by embargo or war.

The Belated Texas Nuptials

Partly because of the fears aroused by British schemers, Texas became a leading issue in the presidential campaign of 1844. The foes of expansion assailed annexation, while southern hotheads cried, "Texas or Disunion." The proexpansion Democrats under James K. Polk finally triumphed over the Whigs under Henry Clay, the hardy perennial candidate. Lame duck president Tyler thereupon interpreted the narrow Democratic victory, with dubious accuracy, as a "mandate" to acquire Texas.

Eager to crown his troubled administration with this splendid prize, Tyler deserves much of the credit for shepherding Texas into the fold. Many "conscience Whigs" feared that Texas in the Union would be red meat to nourish the lusty "slave power." Aware of their opposition, Tyler despaired of securing the needed two-thirds vote for a treaty in the Senate. He therefore arranged for annexation by a joint resolution. This solution required only a simple majority in both houses of Congress. After a spirited debate, the resolution passed early in 1845, and Texas was formally invited to become the twenty-eighth star on the American flag.

Mexico angrily charged that the Americans had despoiled it of Texas. This was to some extent true in 1836, but hardly true in 1845, for the area was no longer Mexico's to be despoiled of. As the years stretched out, realistic observers could see that the Mexicans would not be able to reconquer their lost province. Yet Mexico left the Texans dangling by denying their right to dispose of themselves as they chose.

By 1845 the Lone Star Republic had become a danger spot, inviting foreign intrigue that menaced the American people. The continued existence of Texas as an independent nation threatened to involve the United States in a series of ruinous wars, both in America and in Europe. Americans were in a "lick all creation" mood when they sang "Uncle Sam's Song to Miss Texas":

> *If Mexy back'd by secret foes,*
> *Still talks of getting you, gal;*
> *Why we can lick 'em all you know*
> *And then annex 'em too, gal.*

What other power would have spurned the imperial domain of Texas? The bride was so near, so rich, so fair, so willing. Whatever the peculiar circumstances of the Texas Revolution, the United States can hardly be accused of unseemly haste in achieving annexation. Nine long years were surely a decent wait between the beginning of the courtship and the consummation of the marriage.

Oregon Fever Populates Oregon

The so-called Oregon Country was an enormous wilderness. It sprawled magnificently west of the Rockies to the Pacific Ocean, and north of California to the line of 54° 40'—the present southern tip of the Alaska panhandle. All or substantial parts of this immense area were claimed at one time or another by four nations: Spain, Russia, Britain, and the United States.

Two claimants dropped out of the scramble. Spain, though the first to raise its banner in Oregon, bartered away its claims to the United States in the so-called Florida Treaty of 1819. Russia retreated to the line of 54° 40' by the treaties of 1824 and 1825 with America and Britain. These two remaining rivals now had the field to themselves.

British claims to Oregon were strong—at least to that portion north of the Columbia River. They were

St. Louis in 1846, by Henry Lewis   Thousands of pioneers like these pulling away from St. Louis said farewell to civilization as they left the Mississippi River and headed across the untracked plains to Oregon in the 1840s.

The National Wagon Road Guide, 1858 By the 1850s official guidebooks, like the one shown here, helped travelers make their way along the Overland Trail to the West.

based squarely on prior discovery and exploration, on treaty rights, and on actual occupation. The most important colonizing agency was the far-flung Hudson's Bay Company, which was trading profitably with the Indians of the Pacific Northwest for furs.

Americans, for their part, could also point pridefully to exploration and occupation. Captain Robert Gray in 1792 had stumbled upon the majestic Columbia River, which he named after his ship; and the famed Lewis and Clark expedition of 1804–1806 had ranged overland through the Oregon Country to the Pacific. This shaky American toehold was ultimately strengthened by the presence of missionaries and other settlers, a sprinkling of whom reached the grassy Willamette River valley, south of the Columbia, in the 1830s. These men and women of God, in saving the soul of the Indian, were instrumental in saving the soil of Oregon for the United States. They stimulated interest in a faraway domain that countless Americans had earlier assumed would not be settled for centuries.

Scattered American and British pioneers in Oregon continued to live peacefully side by side. At the time of negotiating the Treaty of 1818 (see pp. 250–251), the United States had sought to divide the vast domain at the forty-ninth parallel. But the British, who regarded the Columbia River as the St. Lawrence of the West, were unwilling to yield this vital artery. A scheme for peaceful "joint occupation" was thereupon adopted, pending future settlement.

The handful of Americans in the Willamette Valley was suddenly multiplied in the early 1840s, when "Oregon fever" seized hundreds of restless pioneers. In increasing numbers, their creaking covered wagons jolted over the two-thousand-mile Oregon Trail as the human rivulet widened into a stream.* By 1846 about five thousand Americans had settled south of the Columbia River, some of them tough "border ruffians," expert with bowie knife and "revolving pistol."

The British, in the face of this rising torrent of humanity, could muster only seven hundred or so subjects north of the Columbia. Losing out lopsidedly

---

*The average rate of progress in covered wagons was one to two miles an hour. This amounted to about one hundred miles a week, or about five months for the entire journey. Thousands of humans, in addition to horses and oxen, died en route. One estimate is seventeen deaths a mile for men, women, and children.

in the population race, they were beginning to see the wisdom of arriving at a peaceful settlement before being engulfed by their neighbors.

A curious fact is that only a relatively small segment of the Oregon Country was in actual controversy by 1845. The area in dispute consisted of the rough quadrangle between the Columbia River on the south and east, the forty-ninth parallel on the north, and the Pacific Ocean on the west (see the map on p. 381). Britain had repeatedly offered the line of the Columbia; America had repeatedly offered the forty-ninth parallel. The whole fateful issue was now tossed into the presidential election of 1844, where it was largely overshadowed by the question of annexing Texas.

A Mandate (?) for Manifest Destiny

The two major parties nominated their presidential standard-bearers in May 1844. Ambitious but often frustrated Henry Clay, easily the most popular man in the country, was enthusiastically chosen by the Whigs at Baltimore. The Democrats, meeting there later, seemed hopelessly deadlocked. Van Buren's opposition to annexing Texas ensured his defeat, given domination of the party by southern expansionists. Finally party delegates trotted out and nominated James K. Polk of Tennessee, America's first "dark-horse" or "surprise" presidential candidate.

Polk may have been a dark horse, but he was hardly an unknown or decrepit nag. Speaker of the House of Representatives for four years and governor of Tennessee for two terms, he was a determined, industrious, ruthless, and intelligent public servant. Sponsored by Andrew Jackson, his friend and neighbor, he was rather implausibly touted by Democrats as yet another "Young Hickory." Whigs attempted to jeer him into oblivion with the taunt, "Who is James K. Polk?" They soon found out.

The campaign of 1844 was in part an expression of the mighty emotional upsurge known as Manifest Destiny. Countless citizens in the 1840s and 1850s, feeling a sense of mission, believed that Almighty God had "manifestly" destined the American people for a hemispheric career. They would irresistibly spread their uplifting and ennobling democratic institutions over at least the entire continent, and possibly over South America as well. Land greed and ideals—"empire" and "liberty"—were thus conveniently conjoined.

Expansionist Democrats were strongly swayed by the intoxicating spell of Manifest Destiny. They came out flat-footedly in their platform for the "Reannexation of Texas"* and the "Reoccupation of Oregon," all the way to 54° 40'. Outbellowing the Whig log-cabinites in the game of slogans, they shouted "All of Oregon or None." They also condemned Clay as a "corrupt bargainer," a dissolute character, and a slaveowner. (Their own candidate, Polk, also owned slaves—a classic case of the pot calling the kettle black.)

The Whigs, as noisemakers, took no backseat. They countered with such slogans as "Hooray for Clay" and "Polk, Slavery, and Texas, or Clay, Union, and Liberty." They also spread the lie that a gang of Tennessee slaves had been seen on their way to a southern market branded with the initials J. K. P. (James K. Polk).

On the crucial issue of Texas, the acrobatic Clay tried to ride two horses at once. The "Great Compromiser" appears to have compromised away the presidency when he wrote a series of confusing letters. They seemed to say that while he personally favored annexing slaveholding Texas (an appeal to the South), he also favored postponement (an appeal to the North). He might have lost more ground if he had not "straddled," but he certainly alienated the more ardent antislaveryites.

In the stretch drive, "Dark Horse" Polk nipped Henry Clay at the wire, 170 to 105 votes in the Electoral College and 1,338,464 to 1,300,097 in the popular column. Clay would have won if he had not lost New York State by a scant 5,000 votes. There the tiny antislavery Liberty party absorbed nearly 16,000 votes, many of which would otherwise have gone to the unlucky Kentuckian. Ironically, the anti-Texas Liberty party, by spoiling Clay's chances and helping to ensure the election of pro-Texas Polk, hastened the annexation of Texas.

Land-hungry Democrats, flushed with victory, proclaimed that they had received a mandate from the voters to take Texas. But a presidential election is seldom, if ever, a clear-cut mandate on anything. The only way to secure a true reflection of the voters' will is to hold a special election on a given issue. The picture that emerged in 1844 was one not of mandate but of muddle. What else could there have been when the results were so close, the personalities so colorful, and the issues so numerous—including Oregon, Texas, the tariff, slavery, the bank, and internal improvements? Yet this unclear "mandate" was interpreted by President Tyler as a crystal-clear charge to annex Texas—and he

---

*The United States had given up its claims to Texas in the so-called Florida Purchase Treaty with Spain in 1819 (see p. 252). The slogan "Fifty-four forty or fight" was evidently not coined until two years later, in 1846.

Westward the Course of Empire Takes Its Way This romantic tribute to the spirit of Manifest Destiny was commissioned by Congress in 1860 and may still be seen in the Capitol.

signed the joint resolution three days before leaving the White House.

Polk the Purposeful

"Young Hickory" Polk, unlike "Old Hickory" Jackson, was not an impressive figure. Of middle height (five feet eight inches), lean, white-haired (worn long), gray-eyed, and stern-faced, he took life seriously and drove himself mercilessly into a premature grave. His burdens were increased by an unwillingness to delegate authority. Methodical and hard-working but not brilliant, he was shrewd, narrow-minded, conscientious, and persistent. "What he went for he fetched," wrote a contemporary. Purposeful in the highest degree, he developed a positive four-point program and with remarkable success achieved it completely in less than four years.

One of Polk's goals was a lowered tariff. His secretary of the Treasury, wispy Robert J. Walker, devised a tariff-for-revenue bill that reduced the average rates of the Tariff of 1842 from about 32 percent to 25 percent. With the strong support of low-tariff southerners, Walker lobbied the measure through Congress, though not without loud complaints from the Clayites, especially in New England and the middle states, that American

manufacturing would be ruined. But these prophets of doom missed the mark. The Walker Tariff of 1846 proved to be an excellent revenue producer, largely because it was followed by boom times and heavy imports.

A second objective of Polk was the restoration of the independent treasury, unceremoniously dropped by the Whigs in 1841. Pro-bank Whigs in Congress raised a storm of opposition, but victory at last rewarded the president's efforts in 1846.

The third and fourth points on Polk's "must list" were the acquisition of California and the settlement of the Oregon dispute.

"Reoccupation" of the "whole" of Oregon had been promised northern Democrats in the campaign of 1844. But southern Democrats, once they had annexed Texas, rapidly cooled off. Polk, himself a southerner, had no intention of insisting on the 54° 40' pledge of his own platform. But feeling bound by the three offers of his predecessors to London, he again proposed the compromise line of 49°. The British minister in Washington, on his own initiative, brusquely spurned this olive branch.

The next move on the Oregon chessboard was up to Britain. Fortunately for peace, the ministry began to experience a change of heart. British anti-expansionists ("Little Englanders") were now persuaded that the Columbia River was not after all the St. Lawrence of the West and that the turbulent American hordes might one

Fort Vancouver, Oregon Country, c. 1846 Fort Vancouver, on the Columbia River near its confluence with the Willamette River (see the map on p. 381), was the economic hub of the Oregon Country during the early years of settlement. Founded as a Hudson's Bay Company fur-trading outpost, the fort was handed over to the Americans when Britain ceded the Oregon Country to the United States in 1846.

day seize the Oregon Country. Why fight a hazardous war over this wilderness on behalf of an unpopular monopoly, the Hudson's Bay Company, which had already "furred out" much of the area anyhow?

Early in 1846 the British, hat in hand, came around and themselves proposed the line of 49°. President Polk, irked by the previous rebuff, threw the decision squarely into the lap of the Senate. The senators speedily accepted the offer and approved the subsequent treaty, despite a few diehard shouts of "Fifty-four forty forever!" and "Every foot or not an inch!" The fact that the United States was then a month deep in a war with Mexico doubtless influenced the Senate's final vote.

Satisfaction with the Oregon settlement among Americans was not unanimous. The northwestern states, hotbed of Manifest Destiny and "fifty-four fortyism," joined the antislavery forces in condemning what they regarded as a base betrayal by the South. Why *all* of Texas

but not *all* of Oregon? Because, retorted the expansionist Senator Benton of Missouri, "Great Britain is powerful and Mexico is weak."

So Polk, despite all the campaign bluster, got neither "fifty-four forty" nor a fight. But he did get something that in the long run was better: a reasonable compromise without a rifle being raised.

House Vote on Tariff of 1846

Region	For	Against
New England	9	19
Middle states	18	44
West and Northwest	29	10
South and Southwest	58	20
TOTAL	114	93

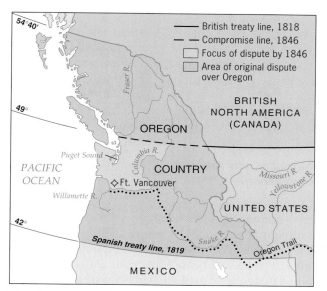

The Oregon Controversy, 1846

recalled its minister from Washington following annexation. Diplomatic relations were completely severed.

Deadlock with Mexico over Texas was further tightened by a question of boundaries. During the long era of Spanish Mexican occupation, the southwestern boundary of Texas had been the Nueces River. But the expansive Texans, on rather far-fetched grounds, were claiming the more southerly Rio Grande instead. Polk, for his part, felt a strong moral obligation to defend Texas in its claim, once it was annexed.

The Mexicans were far less concerned about this boundary quibble than was the United States. In their eyes all of Texas was still theirs, although temporarily in revolt, and a dispute over the two rivers seemed pointless. Yet Polk was careful to keep American troops out of virtually all of the explosive no-man's-land between the Nueces and the Rio Grande, as long as there was any real prospect of peaceful adjustment.

The golden prize of California continued to cause Polk much anxiety. Disquieting rumors (now known to have been ill-founded) were circulating that Britain was

Misunderstandings with Mexico

Faraway California was another worry of Polk's. He and other disciples of Manifest Destiny had long coveted its verdant valleys, and especially the spacious bay of San Francisco. This splendid harbor was widely regarded as America's future gateway to the Pacific Ocean.

The population of California in 1845 was curiously mixed. It consisted of perhaps thirteen thousand sun-blessed Spanish Mexicans and as many as seventy-five thousand dispirited Indians. There were fewer than a thousand "foreigners," mostly Americans, some of whom had "left their consciences" behind them as they rounded Cape Horn. Given time, these transplanted Yankees might yet bring California into the Union by "playing the Texas game."

Polk was eager to buy California from Mexico, but relations with Mexico City were dangerously embittered. Among other friction points, the United States had claims against the Mexicans for some $3 million in damages to American citizens and their property. The revolution-riddled regime in Mexico had formally agreed to assume most of this debt but had been forced to default on its payments.

A more serious bone of contention was Texas. The Mexican government, after threatening war if the United States should acquire the Lone Star Republic, had

El Patrón, by James Walker, c. 1840 The California ranchero's way of life was soon to be extinguished when California became part of the United States in 1848 and thousands of American gold-seekers rushed into the state the following year.

about to buy or seize California—a grab that Americans could not tolerate under the Monroe Doctrine. In a last desperate throw of the dice, Polk dispatched John Slidell to Mexico City as minister late in 1845. The new envoy, among other alternatives, was instructed to offer a maximum of $25 million for California and territory to the east. But the proud Mexican people would not even permit Slidell to present his "insulting" proposition.

American Blood on American (?) Soil

A frustrated Polk was now prepared to force a showdown. On January 13, 1846, he ordered four thousand men, under General Zachary Taylor, to march from the Nueces River to the Rio Grande, provocatively near Mexican forces. Polk's presidential diary reveals that he expected at any moment to hear of a clash. When none occurred after an anxious wait, he informed his cabinet on May 9, 1846, that he proposed to ask Congress to declare war on the basis of (1) unpaid claims and (2) Slidell's rejection. These, at best, were rather flimsy pretexts. Two cabinet members spoke up and said that they would feel better satisfied if Mexican troops should fire first.

That very evening, as fate would have it, news of bloodshed arrived. On April 25, 1846, Mexican troops had crossed the Rio Grande and attacked General Taylor's command, with a loss of sixteen Americans killed or wounded.

Polk, further aroused, sent a vigorous war message to Congress. He declared that despite "all our efforts"

> On June 1, 1860, less than a year before he became president, Abraham Lincoln (1809–1865) wrote,
>
> "The act of sending an armed force among the Mexicans was unnecessary, inasmuch as Mexico was in no way molesting or menacing the United States or the people thereof; and . . . it was unconstitutional, because the power of levying war is vested in Congress, and not in the President."

to avoid a clash, hostilities had been forced upon the country by the shedding of "American blood upon the American soil." A patriotic Congress overwhelmingly voted for war, and enthusiastic volunteers cried, "Ho for the Halls of the Montezumas!" and "Mexico or Death!" Inflamed by the war fever, even antislavery Whig bastions melted and joined with the rest of the nation, though they later condemned "Jimmy Polk's war." As James Russell Lowell of Massachusetts lamented,

> Massachusetts, God forgive her,
> She's akneelin' with the rest.

In his message to Congress, Polk was making history—not writing it. Like many presidents with ambitious foreign-policy goals, he felt justified in bending the truth if that was what it took to bend a reluctant public toward war. If he had been a historian, Polk would have explained that American blood had been shed on soil that the Mexicans had good reason to regard as their own. A gangling, rough-featured Whig congressman from Illinois, one Abraham Lincoln, introduced certain resolutions that requested information as to the precise "spot" on American soil where American blood had been shed. He pushed his "spot" resolutions with such persistence that he came to be known as the "spotty Lincoln," who could die of "spotted fever." The more extreme antislavery agitators of the North, many of them Whigs, branded the president a liar—"Polk the Mendacious."

Did Polk provoke war? California was an imperative point in his program, and Mexico would not sell it at any price. The only way to get it was to use force or wait for an internal American revolt. Yet delay seemed dangerous, for the claws of the British lion might snatch the ripening California fruit from the talons of the American eagle. Grievances against Mexico were annoying yet tolerable; in later years America endured even worse ones. But in 1846 patience had ceased to be a virtue, as far as Polk was concerned. Bent on grasping California by fair means or foul, he pushed the quarrel to a bloody showdown.

Both sides, in fact, were spoiling for a fight. Feisty Americans, especially southwestern expansionists, were eager to teach the Mexicans a lesson. The Mexicans, in turn, were burning to humiliate the "Bullies of the North." Possessing a considerable standing army, heavily overstaffed with generals, they boasted of invading the United States, freeing the black slaves, and lassoing whole regiments of Americans. They were hoping that the quarrel with Britain over Oregon would blossom into a full-dress war, as it came near doing, and further pin down the hated *yanquis*. A conquest of Mexico's vast and arid expanses seemed fantastic, especially in view of the bungling American invasion of Canada in 1812.

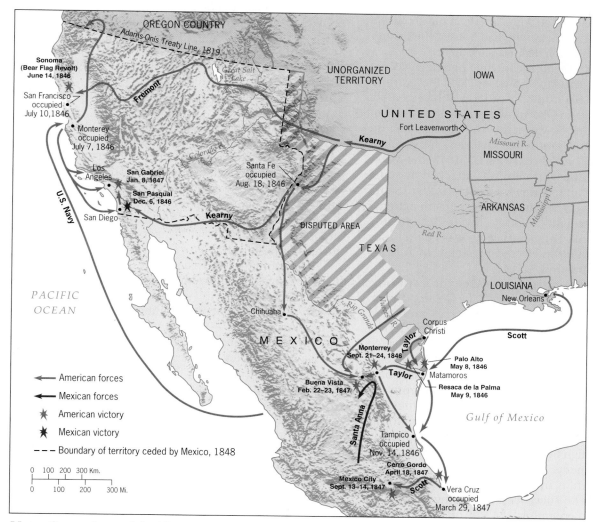

Major Campaigns of the Mexican War

Both sides were fired by moral indignation. The Mexican people could fight with the flaming sword of righteousness, for had not the "insolent" Yankee picked a fight by polluting their soil? Many earnest Americans, on the other hand, sincerely believed that Mexico was the aggressor.

The Mastering of Mexico

Polk wanted California—not war. But when war came, he hoped to fight it on a limited scale and then pull out when he had captured the prize. The dethroned Mexican dictator Santa Anna, then exiled with his teenage bride in Cuba, let it be known that if the American blockading squadron would permit him to slip into Mexico, he would sell out his country. Incredibly, Polk agreed to this discreditable intrigue. But the double-crossing Santa Anna, once he returned to Mexico, proceeded to rally his countrymen to a desperate defense of their soil.

American operations in the Southwest and in California were completely successful. In 1846 General Stephen W. Kearny led a detachment of seventeen hundred troops over the famous Santa Fe Trail from Fort Leavenworth to Santa Fe. This sun-baked outpost, with its drowsy plazas, was easily captured. But before Kearny could reach California, the fertile province was won. When war broke out, Captain John C. Frémont, the dashing explorer, just "happened" to be there with several dozen well-armed men. In helping to overthrow Mexican rule in 1846, he collaborated with American naval officers and with the local Americans, who had hoisted the banner of the short-lived California Bear Flag Republic.

General Zachary Taylor meanwhile had been spearheading the main thrust. Known as "Old Rough and Ready" because of his iron constitution and incredibly unsoldierly appearance—he sometimes wore a Mexican straw hat—he fought his way across the Rio Grande into Mexico. After several gratifying victories, he reached Buena Vista. There, on February 22–23, 1847, his weakened force of five thousand men was attacked by some twenty thousand march-weary troops under Santa Anna. The Mexicans were finally repulsed with extreme difficulty, and overnight Zachary Taylor became the "Hero of Buena Vista." One Kentuckian was heard to say that "Old Zack" would be elected president in 1848 by "spontaneous combustion."

Sound American strategy now called for a crushing blow at the enemy's vitals—Mexico City. General Taylor, though a good leader of modest-sized forces, could not win decisively in the semideserts of northern Mexico. The command of the main expedition, which pushed inland from the coastal city of Vera Cruz early in 1847, was entrusted to General Winfield Scott. A handsome giant of a man, Scott had emerged as a hero from the War of 1812 and had later earned the nickname "Old Fuss and Feathers" because of his resplendent uniforms and strict discipline. He was severely handicapped in the Mexican campaign by inadequate numbers of troops, by expiring enlistments, by a more numerous enemy, by mountainous terrain, by disease, and by political backbiting at home. Yet he succeeded in battling his way up to Mexico City by September 1847 in one of the most brilliant campaigns in American military annals. He proved to be the most distinguished general produced by his country between 1783 and 1861.

Fighting Mexico for Peace

Polk was anxious to end the shooting as soon as he could secure his territorial goals. Accordingly, he sent along with Scott's invading army the chief clerk of the State Department, Nicholas P. Trist, who among other weaknesses was afflicted with an overfluid pen. Trist and Scott arranged for an armistice with Santa Anna, at a cost of $10,000. The wily dictator pocketed the bribe and then used the time to bolster his defenses.

Negotiating a treaty with a sword in one hand and a pen in the other was ticklish business. Polk,

disgusted with his blundering envoy, abruptly recalled Trist. The wordy diplomat then dashed off a sixty-five-page letter explaining why he was not coming home. The president was furious. But Trist, grasping a fleeting opportunity to negotiate, signed the Treaty of Guadalupe Hidalgo on February 2, 1848, and forwarded it to Washington.

The terms of the treaty were breathtaking. They confirmed the American title to Texas and yielded the enormous area stretching westward to Oregon and the ocean and embracing coveted California. This total expanse, including Texas, was about one-half of Mexico. The United States agreed to pay $15 million for the land and to assume the claims of its citizens against Mexico in the amount of $3,250,000 (see "Makers of America: The Californios," pp. 386–387).

Polk submitted the treaty to the Senate. Although Trist had proved highly annoying, he had generally followed his original instructions. And speed was imperative. The antislavery Whigs in Congress—dubbed "Mexican Whigs" or "Conscience Whigs"—were denouncing this "damnable war" with increasing heat. Having secured control of the House in 1847, they were even threatening to vote down supplies for the armies in the field. If they had done so, Scott probably would have been forced to retreat, and the fruits of victory might have been tossed away.

Another peril impended. A swelling group of expansionists, intoxicated by Manifest Destiny, was clamoring for all of Mexico. If America had seized it, the nation would have been saddled with an expensive and

Early in 1848 the New York Evening Post *demanded,*

"Now we ask, whether any man can coolly contemplate the idea of recalling our troops from the [Mexican] territory we at present occupy . . . and . . . resign this beautiful country to the custody of the ignorant cowards and profligate ruffians who have ruled it for the last twenty-five years? Why, humanity cries out against it. Civilization and Christianity protest against this reflux of the tide of barbarism and anarchy."

Such was one phase of Manifest Destiny.

War News from Mexico, by Richard Caton Woodville The newfangled telegraph kept the nation closely informed of events in far-off Mexico.

vexatious policing problem. Farseeing southerners like Calhoun, alarmed by the mounting anger of antislavery agitators, realized that the South would do well not to be too greedy. The treaty was finally approved by the Senate, 38 to 14. Oddly enough, it was condemned both by those opponents who wanted all of Mexico and by opponents who wanted none of it.

Victors rarely pay an indemnity, especially after a costly conflict has been "forced" on them. Yet Polk, who had planned to offer $25 million before fighting the war, arranged to pay $18,250,000 after winning it. Cynics have charged that the Americans were pricked by guilty consciences; apologists have pointed proudly to the "Anglo-Saxon spirit of fair play." A decisive factor was the need for haste, while there was still a responsible Mexican government to carry out the treaty and before political foes in the United States, notably the antislavery zealots, sabotaged Polk's expansionist program.

Profit and Loss in Mexico

As wars go, the Mexican War was a small one. It cost some thirteen thousand American lives, most of them taken by disease. But the fruits of the fighting were enormous.

America's total expanse, already vast, was increased by about one-third (counting Texas)—an addition even greater than that of the Louisiana Purchase. A sharp stimulus was given to the spirit of Manifest Destiny, for as the proverb has it, the appetite comes with eating.

The Mexican War proved to be the blood-spattered schoolroom of the Civil War. The campaigns provided priceless field experience for most of the officers destined to become leading generals in the forthcoming conflict, including Captain Robert E. Lee and Lieutenant Ulysses S. Grant. The Military Academy at West Point, founded in 1802, fully justified its existence through the

The Californios

In 1848 the United States, swollen with the spoils of war, reckoned the costs and benefits of the conflict with Mexico. Thousands of Americans had fallen in battle, and millions of dollars had been invested in a war machine. For this expenditure of blood and money, the nation was repaid with ample land—and with people, the former citizens of Mexico who now became, whether willingly or not, Americans. The largest single addition to American territory in history, the Mexican Cession stretched the United States from sea to shining sea. It secured Texas, brought in vast tracts of the desert Southwest, and included the great prize—the fruited valleys and port cities of California. There, at the conclusion of the Mexican War, dwelled some thirteen thousand Californios—descendants of the Spanish and Mexican conquerors who had once ruled California.

The Spanish had first arrived in California in 1769, extending their New World empire and outracing Russian traders to bountiful San Francisco Bay. Father Junipero Serra, an enterprising Franciscan friar, soon established twenty-one missions along the coast. Indians in the iron grip of the missions were encouraged to adopt Christianity and were often forced to toil endlessly as farmers and herders, in the process suffering disease and degradation. These frequently maltreated mission Indians occupied the lowest rungs on the ladder of Spanish colonial society.

Upon the loftiest rungs perched the Californios. Pioneers from the Mexican heartland of New Spain, they had trailed Serra to California, claiming land and civil offices in their new home. Yet even the proud Californios had deferred to the all-powerful Franciscan missionaries until Mexico threw off the Spanish colonial yoke in 1821, whereupon the infant Mexican government turned an anxious eye toward its frontier outpost.

Mexico now emptied its jails to send settlers to the sparsely populated north, built and garrisoned fortresses, and, most important, transferred authority from the missions to secular (that is, governmental) authorities. This "secularization" program attacked and eroded the immense power of the missions and of their Franciscan masters—with their bawling herds of cattle, debased Indian workers, millions of acres of land, and

Mission San Gabriel, Founded in 1771

California Indians Dancing at the Mission
in San José, by Sykes, 1806

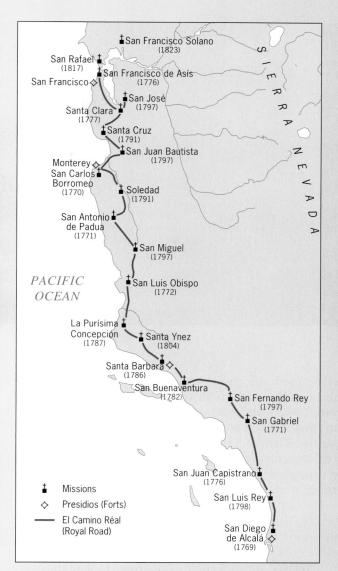

San Francisco Solano
(1823)

San Rafael
(1817)

San Francisco de Asís
(1776)

San Francisco ◇

San José
(1797)

Santa Clara
(1777)

Santa Cruz
(1791)

San Juan Bautista
(1797)

Monterey ◇
San Carlos
Borromeo
(1770)

Soledad
(1791)

San Antonio
de Padua
(1771)

San Miguel
(1797)

PACIFIC
OCEAN

San Luis Obispo
(1772)

La Purísima
Concepción
(1787)

Santa Ynez
(1804)

Santa Barbara
(1786)

San Buenaventura
(1782)

San Fernando Rey
(1797)

San Gabriel
(1771)

San Juan Capistrano
(1776)

San Luis Rey
(1798)

San Diego
de Alcalá
(1769)

SIERRA NEVADA

✝ Missions
◇ Presidios (Forts)
— El Camino Réal
   (Royal Road)

Spanish Missions and Presidios

lucrative foreign trade. The frocked friars had commanded their fiefdoms so self-confidently that earlier reform efforts had dared to go no further than levying a paltry tax on the missions and politely requesting that the missionaries limit their floggings of Indians to fifteen lashes per week. But during the 1830s, the power of the missions weakened, and much of their land and their assets were confiscated by the Californios. Vast *ranchos* (ranches) formed, and from those citadels the Californios ruled in their turn until the Mexican War.

The Californios' glory faded in the wake of the American victory, even though in some isolated places they clung to their political offices for a decade or two. Overwhelmed by the inrush of Anglo gold-diggers—some eighty-seven thousand after the discovery at Sutter's Mill in 1848—and undone by the waning of the pastoral economy, the Californios saw their recently acquired lands and their recently established political power slip through their fingers. When the Civil War broke out in 1861, so harshly did the word *Yankee* ring in their ears that many Californios supported the South.

By 1870 the Californios' brief ascendancy had utterly vanished—a short and sad tale of riches to rags

in the face of the Anglo onslaught. Half a century later, beginning in 1910, hundreds of thousands of young Mexicans would flock into California and the Southwest. They would enter a region liberally endowed with Spanish architecture and artifacts, bearing the names of Spanish missions and Californio *ranchos*. But they would find it a land dominated by Anglos, a place far different from that which their Californio ancestors had settled so hopefully in earlier days.

Storming the Fortress of Chapultepec, Mexico, 1847 The American success at Chapultepec contributed heavily to the final victory over Mexico. One American commander lined up several Irish American deserters on a gallows facing the castle and melodramatically dropped the trapdoors beneath them just as the United States flag was raised over the captured battlement. According to legend, the flag was raised by First Lieutenant George Pickett, later immortalized as the leader of "Pickett's Charge" in the Civil War Battle of Gettysburg, 1863.

well-trained officers. Useful also was the navy, which did valuable work in throwing a crippling blockade around Mexican ports. A new academy at Annapolis had just been established by Navy Secretary and historian George Bancroft in 1846. The Marine Corps, in existence since 1798, won new laurels and to this day sings in its stirring hymn about the Halls of Montezuma.

The army waged war without defeat and without a major blunder, despite formidable obstacles and a half-dozen or so achingly long marches. Chagrined British critics, as well as other foreign skeptics, reluctantly revised upward their estimate of Yankee military prowess. Opposing armies, moreover, emerged with increased respect for each other. The Mexicans, though poorly led, fought heroically. At Chapultepec, near Mexico City, the teenage lads of the military academy there (*los niños*) perished to a boy.

Long-memoried Mexicans have never forgotten that their northern enemy tore away about half of their country. The argument that they were lucky not to lose all of it, and that they had been paid something for their land, has scarcely lessened their bitterness. The war also marked an ugly turning point in the relations between the United States and Latin America as a whole. Hitherto, Uncle Sam had been regarded with some complacency, even friendliness. Henceforth, he was increasingly feared as the "Colossus of the North." Suspicious neigh-

bors to the south condemned him as a greedy and untrustworthy bully, who might next despoil them of their soil.

Most ominous of all, the war rearoused the snarling dog of the slavery issue, and the beast did not stop yelping until drowned in the blood of the Civil War. Abolitionists assailed the Mexican conflict as one provoked by the southern "slavocracy" for its own evil purposes. As James Russell Lowell had Hosea Biglow drawl in his Yankee dialect,

> They jest want this Californy
>   So's to lug new slave-states in
> To abuse ye, an' to scorn ye,
>   An' to plunder ye like sin.

In line with Lowell's charge, the bulk of the American volunteers were admittedly from the South and Southwest. But, as in the case of the Texas Revolution, the basic explanation was proximity rather than conspiracy.

Quarreling over slavery extension also erupted on the floors of Congress. In 1846, shortly after the shooting started, Polk had requested an appropriation of $2 million with which to buy a peace. Representative David Wilmot of Pennsylvania, fearful of the southern "slavocracy," introduced a fateful amendment. It stipulated that slavery should never exist in any of the territory to be wrested from Mexico.

The disruptive Wilmot amendment twice passed the House, but not the Senate. Southern members, unwilling to be robbed of prospective slave states, fought the restriction tooth and nail. Antislavery men, in Congress and out, battled no less bitterly for the exclusion of slaves. The "Wilmot Proviso" never became federal law, but it was eventually endorsed by the legislatures of all but one of the free states, and it came to symbolize the burning issue of slavery in the territories.

In a broad sense, the opening shots of the Mexican War were the opening shots of the Civil War. President Polk left the nation the splendid physical heritage of California and the Southwest but also the ugly moral heritage of an embittered slavery dispute. "Mexico will poison us," said the philosopher Ralph Waldo Emerson. Even the great champion of the South, John C. Calhoun, had prophetically warned that "Mexico is to us the forbidden fruit . . . the penalty of eating it would be to subject our institutions to political death." Mexicans could later take some satisfaction in knowing that the territory wrenched from them had proved to be a venomous apple of discord that could well be called Santa Anna's revenge.

Chronology

1837	Canadian rebellion and *Caroline* incident
1840	Antislavery Liberty party organized
1841	Harrison dies after four weeks in office Tyler assumes presidency
1842	Aroostook War over Maine boundary Webster-Ashburton treaty
1844	Polk defeats Clay in "Manifest Destiny" election
1845	United States annexes Texas
1846	Walker Tariff Independent treasury restored United States settles Oregon dispute with Britain
1846	United States and Mexico clash over Texas boundary Kearny takes Santa Fe Frémont conquers California Wilmot Proviso passes House of Representatives
1846–1848	Mexican War
1847	Battle of Buena Vista Scott takes Mexico City
1848	Treaty of Guadalupe Hidalgo

For further reading, see the Appendix. For web resources, go to **http://college.hmco.com**.

18

Renewing the Sectional Struggle

1848–1854

SECESSION! PEACEABLE SECESSION!
SIR, YOUR EYES AND MINE ARE NEVER
DESTINED TO SEE THAT MIRACLE.

DANIEL WEBSTER,
SEVENTH OF MARCH SPEECH, 1850

The year 1848, highlighted by a rash of revolutions in Europe, was filled with unrest in America. The Treaty of Guadalupe Hidalgo had officially ended the war with Mexico, but it had initiated a new and perilous round of political warfare in the United States. The vanquished Mexicans had been forced to relinquish an enormous tract of real estate, including Texas, California, and all the area between. The acquisition of this huge domain raised anew the burning issue of extending slavery into the territories. Northern antislaveryites had rallied behind the Wilmot Proviso, which flatly prohibited slavery in any territory acquired in the Mexican War. Southern senators had blocked the passage of the proviso, but the issue would not die. Ominously, debate over slavery in the area of the Mexican Cession threatened to disrupt the ranks of both Whigs and Democrats and split national politics along North-South sectional lines.

The Popular Sovereignty Panacea

Each of the two great political parties was a vital bond of national unity, for each enjoyed powerful support in both North and South. If they should be replaced by two purely sectional groupings, the Union would be in peril. To politicians, the wisest strategy seemed to be to sit on the lid of the slavery issue and ignore the boiling beneath. Even so, the cover bobbed up and down ominously in response to the agitation of zealous northern abolitionists and impassioned southern "fire-eaters."

Anxious Democrats were forced to seek a new standard-bearer in 1848. President Polk, broken in health by overwork and chronic diarrhea, had pledged himself to a single term. The Democratic National Convention at Baltimore turned to an aging leader,

General Lewis Cass, a veteran of the War of 1812. Although a senator and diplomat of wide experience and considerable ability, he was sour-visaged and somewhat pompous. His enemies dubbed him General "Gass" and quickly noted that *Cass* rhymed with *jackass*. The Democratic platform, in line with the lid-sitting strategy, was silent on the burning issue of slavery in the territories.

But Cass himself had not been silent. His views on the extension of slavery were well known because he was the reputed father of "popular sovereignty." This was the doctrine that stated that the sovereign people of a territory, under the general principles of the Constitution, should themselves determine the status of slavery.

Popular sovereignty had a persuasive appeal. The public liked it because it accorded with the democratic tradition of self-determination. Politicians liked it because it seemed a comfortable compromise between the free-soilers' bid for a ban on slavery in the territories and southern demands that Congress protect slavery in the territories. Popular sovereignty tossed the slavery problem into the laps of the people in the various territories. Advocates of the principle thus hoped to dissolve the most stubborn national issue of the day into a series of local issues. Yet popular sovereignty had one fatal defect: it might serve to spread the blight of slavery.

Political Triumphs for General Taylor

The Whigs, meeting in Philadelphia, cashed in on the "Taylor fever." They nominated frank and honest Zachary Taylor, the "Hero of Buena Vista," who had never held civil office or even voted for president. Henry Clay, the living embodiment of Whiggism, should logically have been nominated. But Clay had made too many speeches—and too many enemies.

As usual, the Whigs pussyfooted in their platform. Eager to win at any cost, they dodged all troublesome issues and merely extolled the homespun virtues of their candidate. The self-reliant old frontier fighter had not committed himself on the issue of slavery extension. But as a wealthy resident of Louisiana, living on a sugar plantation, he owned scores of slaves.

Ardent antislavery men in the North, distrusting both Cass and Taylor, organized the Free Soil party. Aroused by the conspiracy of silence in the Democratic and Whig platforms, the Free-Soilers made no bones about their own stand. They came out foursquare for

General Zachary Taylor (1784–1850)
This Democratic campaign cartoon of 1848 charges that Taylor's reputation rested on Mexican skulls.

the Wilmot Proviso and against slavery in the territories. Going beyond other antislavery groups, they broadened their appeal by advocating federal aid for internal improvements and by urging free government homesteads for settlers.

The new party assembled a strange assortment of new fellows in the same political bed. It attracted industrialists miffed at Polk's reduction of protective tariffs. It appealed to Democrats resentful of Polk's settling for part of Oregon while insisting on all of Texas—a disparity that suggested a menacing southern dominance in the Democratic party. It harbored many northerners whose hatred was directed not so much at slavery as at blacks and who gagged at the prospect of sharing the newly acquired western territories with African

Americans. It also contained a large element of "conscience Whigs," heavily influenced by the abolitionist crusade, who condemned slavery on moral grounds. The Free-Soilers trotted out wizened former president Van Buren and marched into the fray, shouting, "Free soil, free speech, free labor, and free men." These freedoms provided the bedrock on which the Free-Soilers built their party. Free-Soilers condemned slavery not so much for enslaving blacks but for destroying the chances of free white workers to rise up from wage-earning dependence to the esteemed status of self-employment. Free-Soilers argued that only with free soil in the West could a traditional American commitment to upward mobility continue to flourish. If forced to compete with slave labor, more costly wage labor would inevitably wither away, and with it the chance for the American worker to own property. As the first widely inclusive party organized around the issue of slavery and confined to a single section, the Free Soil party foreshadowed the emergence of the Republican party six years later.

With the slavery issue officially shoved under the rug by the two major parties, the politicians on both sides opened fire on personalities. The amateurish Taylor had to be carefully watched, lest his indiscreet pen puncture the reputation won by his sword. His admirers puffed him up as a gallant knight and a Napoleon, and sloganized his remark, allegedly uttered during the Battle of Buena Vista, "General Taylor never surrenders." Taylor's wartime popularity pulled him through. He harvested 1,360,967 popular and 163 electoral votes, as compared with Cass's 1,222,342 popular and 127 electoral votes. Free-Soiler Van Buren, although winning no state, polled 291,263 ballots and apparently diverted enough Democratic strength from Cass in the crucial state of New York to throw the election to Taylor.

"Californy Gold"

Tobacco-chewing President Taylor—with his stumpy legs, rough features, heavy jaw, black hair, ruddy complexion, and squinty gray eyes—was a military square peg in a political round hole. He would have been spared much turmoil if he could have continued to sit on the slavery lid. But the discovery of gold on the American River near Sutter's Mill, California, early in 1848, blew the cover off.

A horde of adventurers poured into the valleys of California. Singing "O Susannah!" and shouting "Gold! Gold! Gold!" they began tearing frantically at the yellow-graveled streams and hills. A fortunate few of the bearded miners "struck it rich" at the "diggings." But the

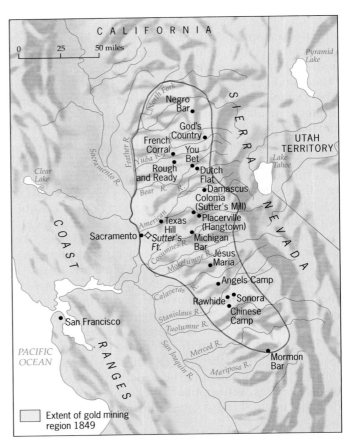

California Gold Rush Country   Miners from all over the world swarmed over the rivers that drained the western slope of California's Sierra Nevada. Their nationalities and religions, their languages and their ways of life, are recorded in the colorful place names they left behind.

luckless many, who netted blisters instead of nuggets, probably would have been money well ahead if they had stayed at home unaffected by "gold fever," which was often followed by more deadly fevers. The most reliable profits were made by those who mined the miners, notably by charging outrageous rates for laundry and other personal services. Some soiled clothing was even sent as far away as the Hawaiian Islands for washing.

The overnight inpouring of tens of thousands of people into the future Golden State completely overwhelmed the one-horse government of California. A distressingly high proportion of the newcomers were lawless men, accompanied or followed by virtueless women. A contemporary song ran,

Oh what was your name in the States?
Was it Thompson or Johnson or Bates?

Placer Miners in California
Cheap but effective, placer mining consisted of literally "washing" the gold out of surface deposits. No deep excavation was required. This crew of male and female miners in California in 1852 was using a "long tom" sluice that washed relatively large quantities of ore.

Did you murder your wife,
And fly for your life?
Say, what was your name in the States?

An outburst of crime inevitably resulted from the presence of so many miscreants and outcasts. Robbery, claim jumping, and murder were commonplace, and such violence was only partly discouraged by rough vigilante justice. In San Francisco, from 1848 to 1856, there were scores of lawless killings but only three semilegal hangings.

A majority of Californians, as decent and law-abiding citizens needing protection, grappled earnestly with the problem of erecting an adequate state government. Privately encouraged by President Taylor, they drafted a constitution in 1849 that excluded slavery and then boldly applied to Congress for admission. California would thus bypass the usual territorial stage, thwarting southern congressmen seeking to block free soil. Southern politicians, alarmed by the Californians' "impertinent" stroke for freedom, arose in violent opposition. Would California prove to be the golden straw that broke the back of the Union?

Sectional Balance and the Underground Railroad

The South of 1850 was relatively well-off. It then enjoyed, as it had from the beginning, more than its share of the nation's leadership. It had seated in the White House the war hero Zachary Taylor, a Virginia-

A married woman wrote from the California goldfields to her sister in New England in 1853,

"i tell you the woman are in great demand in this country no matter whether they are married or not   you need not think strange if you see me coming home with some good looking man some of these times with a pocket full of rocks. . . . it is all the go here for Ladys to leave there Husbands   two out of three do it   there is a first rate Chance for a single woman   she can have her choice of thousands   i wish mother was here she could marry a rich man and not have to lift her hand to do her work. "

The idea that many ne'er-do-wells went west is found in the Journals (January 1849) of Ralph Waldo Emerson (1803–1882):

"If a man is going to California, he announces it with some hesitation; because it is a confession that he has failed at home."

born, slaveowning planter from Louisiana. It boasted a majority in the cabinet and on the Supreme Court. If outnumbered in the House, the South had equality in the Senate, where it could at least neutralize northern maneuvers. Its cotton fields were expanding, and cotton prices were profitably high. Few sane people, North or South, believed that slavery was seriously threatened where it already existed below the Mason-Dixon line. The fifteen slave states could easily veto any proposed constitutional amendment.

Yet the South was deeply worried, as it had been for several decades, by the ever-tipping political balance. There were then fifteen slave states and fifteen free states. The admission of California would destroy the delicate equilibrium in the Senate, perhaps forever. Potential slave territory under the American flag was running short, if it had not in fact disappeared. Agitation had already developed in the territories of New Mexico and Utah for admission as nonslave states. The fate of California might well establish a precedent for the rest of the Mexican Cession territory—an area purchased largely with southern blood.

A Stop on the Underground Railroad   Sliding shelves in the wall of the Reverend Alexander Dobbin's home in Gettysburg, Pennsylvania, concealed a crawl space large enough to hide several escaping slaves.

Texas and the Disputed Area Before the Compromise of 1850

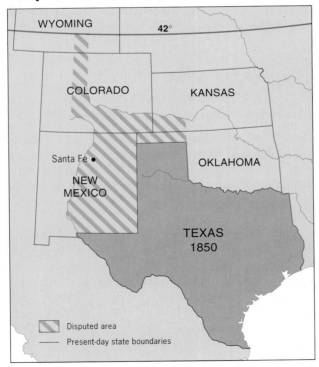

Texas nursed an additional grievance of its own. It claimed a huge area east of the Rio Grande and north to the forty-second parallel, embracing in part about half the territory of present-day New Mexico. The federal government was proposing to detach this prize, while hot-blooded Texans were threatening to descend upon Santa Fe and seize what they regarded as rightfully theirs. The explosive quarrel foreshadowed shooting.

Many southerners were also angered by the nagging agitation in the North for the abolition of slavery in the District of Columbia. They looked with alarm on the prospect of a ten-mile-square oasis of free soil thrust between slaveholding Maryland and slaveholding Virginia.

Even more disagreeable to the South was the loss of runaway slaves, many of whom were assisted north by the Underground Railroad. This virtual freedom train consisted of an informal chain of "stations" (antislavery homes), through which scores of "passengers" (runaway slaves) were spirited by "conductors" (usually white and black abolitionists) from the slave states to the free-soil sanctuary of Canada.

The most amazing of these "conductors" was an illiterate runaway slave from Maryland, fearless Harriet Tubman. During nineteen forays into the South, she rescued more than three hundred slaves, including her aged parents, and deservedly earned the title "Moses." Lively imaginations later exaggerated the reach of the Underground Railroad and its "stationmasters," but its importance was undisputed.

By 1850 southerners were demanding a new and more stringent fugitive-slave law. The old one, passed by Congress in 1793, had proved inadequate to cope with runaways, especially since unfriendly state authorities failed to provide needed cooperation. Unlike cattle thieves, the abolitionists who ran the Underground Railroad did not gain personally from their lawlessness. But to the slaveowners, the loss was infuriating, whatever the motives. The moral judgments of the abolitionists seemed, in some ways, more galling than outright theft. They reflected not only a holier-than-thou attitude but a refusal to obey the laws solemnly passed by Congress.

Estimates indicate that the South in 1850 was losing perhaps 1,000 runaways a year out of its total of some 4 million slaves. In fact, more blacks probably gained their freedom by self-purchase or voluntary emancipation than ever escaped. But the principle weighed heavily with the slavemasters. They rested their argument on the Constitution, which protected slavery, and on the laws of Congress, which provided for slave-catching. "Although the loss of property is felt," said a southern senator, "the loss of honor is felt still more."

Harriet Tubman, Premier Assistant of Runaway Slaves
John Brown called her "General Tubman" for her effective work in helping slaves escape to Canada on the Underground Railroad. During the Civil War, she served as a Union spy behind Confederate lines. Herself illiterate, she worked after the war to bring education to the freed slaves in North Carolina.

Twilight of the Senatorial Giants

Southern fears were such that Congress was confronted with catastrophe in 1850. Free-soil California was banging on the door for admission. "Fire-eaters" in the South were voicing ominous threats of secession. In October 1849 southerners had announced their intention to convene the following year in Nashville, Tennessee, to consider withdrawing from the Union. The failure of Congress to act could easily mean the failure of the United States as a country. The crisis brought into the congressional forum the most distinguished assemblage of statesmen since the Constitutional Convention of 1787—the Old Guard of the dying generation and the young gladiators of the new. That "immortal trio"—Clay, Calhoun, and Webster—appeared together for the last time on the public stage.

Henry Clay, now seventy-three years of age, played a crucial role. The "Great Compromiser" had come to the Senate from Kentucky to reprise the role he had played twice before, in the Missouri and nullification crises. The once-glamorous statesman—though disillusioned, enfeebled, and racked by a cruel cough—was still eloquent, conciliatory, and captivating. He proposed and skillfully defended a series of compromises. He was ably seconded by thirty-seven-year-old Senator Stephen A. Douglas of Illinois, the "Little Giant" (five feet four inches), whose role was less spectacular but even more important. Clay urged with all his persuasiveness that the North and South both make concessions and that the North partially yield by enacting a more feasible fugitive-slave law.

Senator John C. Calhoun, the "Great Nullifier," then sixty-eight and dying of tuberculosis, championed the South in his last formal speech. Too weak to deliver it himself, he sat bundled up in the Senate chamber, his eyes glowing within a stern face, while a younger colleague read his fateful words. "I have, Senators, believed from the first that the agitation on the subject of slavery would, if not prevented by some timely and effective measure, end in disunion." Although approving the purpose of Clay's proposed concessions, Calhoun rejected them as not providing adequate safeguards for southern rights. His impassioned plea was to leave slavery alone, return runaway slaves, give the South its rights as a minority, and restore the political balance. He had in view, as was later revealed, an utterly unworkable scheme of electing two presidents, one from the North and one from the South, each wielding a veto.

Calhoun died in 1850, before the debate was over, murmuring the sad words, "The South! The South! God knows what will become of her!" Appreciative fellow citizens in Charleston erected to his memory an imposing monument, which bore the inscription "Truth, Justice, and the Constitution." Calhoun had labored to preserve the Union and had taken his stand on the Constitution, but his proposals in their behalf almost undid both.

Daniel Webster next took the Senate spotlight to uphold Clay's compromise measures in his last great speech, a three-hour effort. Now sixty-eight years old and suffering from a liver complaint aggravated by high living, he had lost some of the fire in his magnificent voice. Speaking deliberately and before overflowing galleries, he urged all reasonable concessions to the South, including a new fugitive-slave law with teeth.

As for slavery in the territories, asked Webster, why legislate on the subject? To do so was an act of sacrilege, for Almighty God had already passed the Wilmot Proviso. The good Lord had decreed—through climate, topography, and geography—that a plantation economy, and hence a slave economy, could not profitably exist in the Mexican Cession territory.* Webster sanely concluded that compromise, concession, and sweet reasonableness would provide the only solutions. "Let us not be pygmies," he pleaded, "in a case that calls for men."

If measured by its immediate effects, Webster's famed Seventh of March speech, 1850, was his finest. It helped turn the tide in the North toward compromise. The clamor for printed copies became so great that Webster mailed out more than 100,000, remarking that 200,000 would not satisfy the demand. His tremendous effort visibly strengthened Union sentiment. It was especially pleasing to the banking and commercial centers of the North, which stood to lose millions of dollars by secession. One prominent Washington banker canceled two notes of Webster's, totaling $5,000, and sent him a personal check for $1,000 and a message of congratulations.

Ralph Waldo Emerson, the philosopher and moderate abolitionist, was outraged by Webster's support of concessions to the South in the Fugitive Slave Act. In February 1851 he wrote in his Journal,

"I opened a paper to-day in which he [Webster] pounds on the old strings [of liberty] in a letter to the Washington Birthday feasters at New York. 'Liberty! liberty!' Pho! Let Mr. Webster, for decency's sake, shut his lips once and forever on this word. The word *liberty* in the mouth of Mr. Webster sounds like the word *love* in the mouth of a courtesan."

---

*Webster was wrong here; within one hundred years, California had become one of the great cotton-producing states of the Union.

Compromise of 1850

Concessions to the North	Concessions to the South
California admitted as a free state	The remainder of the Mexican Cession area to be formed into the territories of New Mexico and Utah, without restriction on slavery, hence open to popular sovereignty
Territory disputed by Texas and New Mexico to be surrendered to New Mexico	Texas to receive $10 million from the federal government as compensation
Abolition of the slave trade (but not slavery) in the District of Columbia	A more stringent fugitive-slave law, going beyond that of 1793

But the Free-Soilers and abolitionists, who had assumed Webster was one of them, upbraided him as a traitor, worthy of bracketing with Benedict Arnold. The poet Whittier lamented,

> *So fallen! so lost! the light withdrawn*
> *Which once he wore!*
> *The glory from his gray hairs gone*
> *For evermore!*

These reproaches were most unfair. Webster had long regarded slavery as evil but disunion as worse.

Deadlock and Danger on Capitol Hill

The stormy congressional debate of 1850 was not finished, for the Young Guard from the North were yet to have their say. This was the group of newer leaders who, unlike the aging Old Guard, had not grown up with the Union. They were more interested in purging and purifying it than in patching and preserving it.

William H. Seward, the wiry and husky-throated freshman senator from New York, was the able spokesman for many of the younger northern radicals. A strong antislaveryite, he came out unequivocally against concession. He seemed not to realize that compromise had brought the Union together and that when the sections could no longer compromise, they would have to part company.

Seward argued earnestly that Christian legislators must obey God's moral law as well as man's mundane law. He therefore appealed, with reference to excluding slavery in the territories, to an even "higher law" than the Constitution. This alarming phrase, wrenched from

its context, may have cost him the presidential nomination and the presidency in 1860.

As the great debate in Congress ran its heated course, deadlock seemed certain. Blunt old President Taylor, who had allegedly fallen under the influence of men like "Higher Law" Seward, seemed bent on vetoing any compromise passed by Congress. His military ire was aroused by the threats of Texas to seize Santa Fe. He appeared to be doggedly determined to "Jacksonize" the dissenters, if need be, by leading an army against the Texans in person and hanging all "damned traitors." If troops had begun to march, the South probably would have rallied to the defense of Texas, and the Civil War might have erupted in 1850.

Breaking the Congressional Logjam

At the height of the controversy in 1850, President Taylor unknowingly helped the cause of concession by dying suddenly, probably of an acute intestinal disorder. Portly, round-faced Vice President Millard Fillmore, a colorless and conciliatory New York lawyer-politician, took over the reins. As presiding officer of the Senate, he had been impressed with the arguments for conciliation, and he gladly signed the series of compromise measures that passed Congress after seven long months of stormy debate. The balancing of interests in the Compromise of 1850 was delicate in the extreme.

The struggle to get these measures accepted by the country was hardly less heated than in Congress. In the northern states, "Union savers" like Senators Clay, Webster, and Douglas orated on behalf of the compromise. The ailing Clay himself delivered more than seventy speeches, as a powerful sentiment for acceptance

Henry Clay Proposing the Compromise of 1850
This engraving captures one of the most dramatic moments in the history of the United States Senate. Vice President Millard Fillmore presides, while on the floor sit several of the "Senatorial Giants" of the era, including Daniel Webster, Stephen A. Douglas, and John C. Calhoun.

gradually crystallized in the North. It was strengthened by a growing spirit of goodwill, which sprang partly from a feeling of relief and partly from an upsurge of prosperity enriched by California gold.

But the "fire-eaters" of the South were still violently opposed to concessions. One extreme South Carolina newspaper avowed that it loathed the Union and hated the North as much as it did Hell itself. A movement in the South to boycott northern goods gained some headway, but in the end the southern Unionists, assisted by the warm glow of prosperity, prevailed.

In June 1850 the assemblage of southern extremists met in Nashville, ironically near the burial place of Andrew Jackson. The delegates not only took a strong position in favor of slavery but condemned the compromise measures then being hammered out in Congress. Meeting again in November after the bills had passed, the convention proved to be a dud. By that time southern opinion had reluctantly accepted the verdict of Congress.

Like the calm after a storm, a second Era of Good Feelings dawned. Disquieting talk of secession subsided. Peace-loving people, both North and South, were determined that the compromises should be a "finality" and that the explosive issue of slavery should be buried. But this placid period proved all too brief.

Balancing the Compromise Scales

Who got the better deal in the Compromise of 1850? The answer is clearly the North. California, as a free state, tipped the Senate balance permanently against the South. The territories of New Mexico and Utah were open to slavery on the basis of popular sovereignty. But the iron law of nature—the "highest law" of all—had loaded the dice in favor of free soil. Southerners urgently needed more slave territory to restore the "sacred balance." If they could not carve new states out of the recent conquests from Mexico, where else might they get them? The Caribbean was one answer.

Even the apparent gains of the South rang hollow. Disgruntled Texas was to be paid $10 million toward discharging its indebtedness, but in the long run this was a modest sum. The immense area in dispute had been torn from the side of slaveholding Texas and was almost certain to be free. The South had halted the drive toward abolition in the District of Columbia, at least temporarily, by permitting the outlawing of the slave *trade* in the federal district. But even this move was an entering wedge toward complete emancipation in the nation's capital.

Free
Slave
Decision left to territory

Slavery After the Compromise of 1850 Regarding the Fugitive Slave Act provisions of the Compromise of 1850, Ralph Waldo Emerson declared (May 1851) at Concord, Massachusetts, "The act of Congress . . . is a law which every one of you will break on the earliest occasion—a law which no man can obey, or abet the obeying, without loss of self-respect and forfeiture of the name of gentleman." Privately he wrote in his *Journal*, "This filthy enactment was made in the nineteenth century, by people who could read and write. I will not obey it, by God."

Most alarming of all, the drastic new Fugitive Slave Law of 1850—"the Bloodhound Bill"—stirred up a storm of opposition in the North. The fleeing slaves could not testify in their own behalf, and they were denied a jury trial. These harsh practices, some citizens feared, threatened to create dangerous precedents for white Americans. The federal commissioner who handled the case of a fugitive would receive five dollars if the runaway were freed and ten dollars if not—an arrangement that strongly resembled a bribe. Freedom-loving northerners who aided the slave to escape were liable to heavy fines and jail sentences. They might even be ordered to join the slave-catchers, and this possibility rubbed salt into old sores.

So abhorrent was this "Man-Stealing Law" that it touched off an explosive chain reaction in the North.

A Ride for Liberty, by Eastman Johnson In this famous painting, Johnson, a New England artist, brilliantly evokes the anxiety of fleeing slaves.

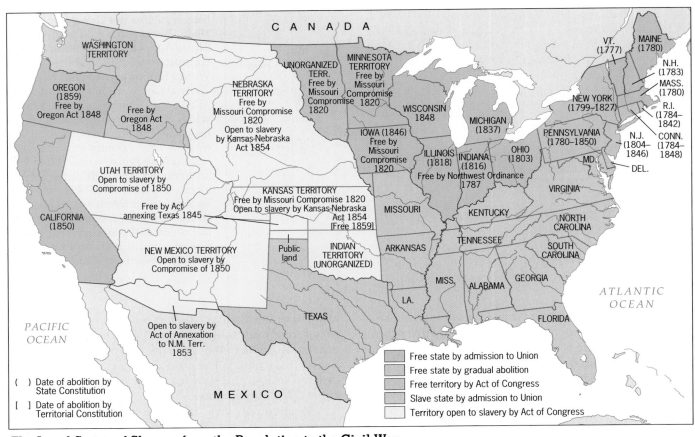

The Legal Status of Slavery, from the Revolution to the Civil War

Many shocked moderates, hitherto passive, were driven into the swelling ranks of the antislaveryites. When a runaway slave from Virginia was captured in Boston in 1854, he had to be removed from the city under heavy federal guard through streets lined with sullen Yankees and shadowed by black-draped buildings festooned with flags flying upside down. One prominent Bostonian who witnessed this grim spectacle wrote that "we went to bed one night old-fashioned, conservative, Compromise Union Whigs and waked up stark mad Abolitionists."

The Underground Railroad stepped up its timetable, and infuriated northern mobs rescued slaves from their pursuers. Massachusetts, in a move toward nullification suggestive of South Carolina in 1832, made it a penal offense for any state official to enforce the new federal statute. Other states passed "personal liberty laws," which denied local jails to federal officials and otherwise hampered enforcement. The abolitionists rent the heavens with their protests against the man-stealing statute. A meeting presided over by William Lloyd Garrison in

1851 declared, "We execrate it, we spit upon it, we trample it under our feet."

Beyond question, the Fugitive Slave Law was an appalling blunder on the part of the South. No single irritant of the 1850s was more persistently galling to both sides, and none did more to awaken in the North a spirit of antagonism against the South. The southerners in turn were embittered because the northerners would not in good faith execute the law—the one real and immediate southern "gain" from the Great Compromise. Slavecatchers, with some success, redoubled their efforts.

Should the shooting showdown have come in 1850? From the standpoint of the secessionists, yes; from the standpoint of the Unionists, no. Time was fighting for the North. With every passing decade, this huge section was forging further ahead in population and wealth—in crops, factories, foundries, ships, and railroads.

Delay also added immensely to the moral strength of the North—to its will to fight for the Union. In 1850 countless thousands of northern moderates were unwilling to pin the South to the rest of the nation with bayonets. But the inflammatory events of the 1850s did much to bolster the Yankee will to resist secession, whatever the cost. This one feverish decade gave the North time to accumulate the material and moral strength that provided the margin of victory. Thus the Compromise of 1850, from one point of view, won the Civil War for the Union.

Defeat and Doom for the Whigs

Meeting in Baltimore, the Democratic nominating convention of 1852 startled the nation. Hopelessly deadlocked, it finally stampeded to the second "dark-horse" candidate in American history, an unrenowned lawyer-politician, Franklin Pierce, from the hills of New Hampshire. The Whigs tried to jeer him back into obscurity with the cry, "Who is Frank Pierce?" Democrats replied, "The Young Hickory of the Granite Hills."

Pierce was a weak and indecisive figure. Youngish, handsome, militarily erect, smiling, and convivial, he had served without real distinction in the Mexican War. As a result of a painful groin injury that caused him to fall off a horse, he was known as the "Fainting General," though scandalmongers pointed to a fondness for alcohol. But he was enemyless because he had been inconspicuous, and as a prosouthern northerner, he was acceptable to the slavery wing of the Democratic party. His platform revived the Democrats' commitment to territorial expansion as pursued by President Polk and emphatically endorsed the Compromise of 1850, Fugitive Slave Law and all.

The Whigs, also convening in Baltimore, missed a splendid opportunity to capitalize on their record in statecraft. Able to boast of a praiseworthy achievement in the Compromise of 1850, they might logically have nominated President Fillmore or Senator Webster, both of whom were associated with it. But having won in the past only with military heroes, they turned to another, "Old Fuss and Feathers" Winfield Scott, perhaps the ablest American general of his generation. Although he was a huge and impressive figure, his manner bordered on haughtiness. His personality not only repelled the masses but eclipsed his genuinely statesmanlike achievements. The Whig platform praised the Compromise of 1850 as a lasting arrangement, though less enthusiastically than the Democrats.

With slavery and sectionalism to some extent soft-pedaled, the campaign again degenerated into a dull and childish attack on personalities. Democrats ridiculed Scott's pomposity; Whigs charged that Pierce was the hero of "many a well-fought *bottle*." Democrats cried exultantly, "We Polked 'em in '44; we'll Pierce 'em in '52."

Luckily for the Democrats, the Whig party was hopelessly split. Antislavery Whigs of the North swallowed Scott as their nominee but deplored his platform, which endorsed the hated Fugitive Slave Law. The current phrase ran, "We accept the candidate but spit on the platform." Southern Whigs, who doubted Scott's loyalty to the Compromise of 1850 and especially the Fugitive Slave Law, accepted the platform but spat on the candidate. More than five thousand Georgia Whigs—"finality men"—voted in vain for Webster, although he had died nearly two weeks before the election.

General Scott, victorious on the battlefield, met defeat at the ballot box. His friends remarked whimsically that he was not used to "running." Actually, he was stabbed in the back by his fellow Whigs, notably in the South. In addition, Free Soil party candidate John P. Hale, senator from New Hampshire, siphoned off northern Whig votes that might have gone to Scott. Hale walked away with a respectable 5 percent of the popular vote. The pliant Pierce won in a landslide, 254 electoral votes to 42, although the popular count was closer, 1,601,117 to 1,385,453.

The election of 1852 was fraught with frightening significance, though it may have seemed tame at the time. It marked the effective end of the disorganized Whig party and, within a few years, its complete death. The Whigs' demise augured the eclipse of *national* parties and the worrisome rise of purely *sectional* political alignments. The Whigs were governed at times by the crassest opportunism, and they won only two presidential elections (1840, 1848) in their colorful career, both with war heroes. They finally choked to death trying to swallow the distasteful Fugitive Slave Law. But their great contribution—and a noteworthy one indeed—was to help uphold the ideal of the Union through their electoral strength in the South and through the eloquence of leaders like Henry Clay and Daniel Webster. Both of these statesmen, by unhappy coincidence, died during the 1852 campaign. But the good they had done lived after them and contributed powerfully to the eventual preservation of a *united* United States.

Expansionist Stirrings South of the Border

The intoxicating victory in the Mexican War, coupled with the discovery of gold in California just nine days before the war's end, reinvigorated the spirit of Manifest Destiny. The rush to the Sierra Nevada goldfields aroused particular concerns about the fate of Central America. Since the days of Balboa, this narrow neck of land had stimulated dreams of a continuous Atlantic-to-Pacific transportation route that would effectively sever the two American continents. Whoever controlled that route would hold imperial sway over all maritime nations, especially the United States.

Increasing British encroachment into the area—including the British seizure of the port of San Juan (renamed Greytown) on Nicaragua's "Mosquito Coast"—drove the governments of both the United States and New Granada (later Colombia) to conclude an important treaty in 1848. It guaranteed the American right of transit across the isthmus in return for Washington's pledge to maintain the "perfect neutrality" of the route so that the "free transit of traffic might not be interrupted." The agreement later provided a fig leaf of legal cover for Theodore Roosevelt's assertion of American control of the Panama Canal Zone in 1903. It also led to the construction of the first "transcontinental" railroad. Completed in 1855 at a cost of thousands of lives lost to pestilence and accident, it ran forty-eight miles from coast to coast through the green hell of the Panamanian jungle. A full-blown confrontation with Britain was avoided by the Clayton-Bulwer Treaty in 1850, which stipulated that neither America nor Britain would fortify or seek exclusive control over any future isthmian waterway (later rescinded by the Hay-Pauncefote Treaty of 1901; see p. 648).

Southern "slavocrats" cast especially covetous eyes southward in the 1850s. They lusted for new slave territory after the Compromise of 1850 seemingly closed most of the Mexican Cession to the "peculiar institution." In 1856 a Texan proposed a toast that was drunk with gusto: "To the Southern republic bounded on the north by the Mason and Dixon line and on the South by the Isthmus of Tehuantepec [southern Mexico], including Cuba and all other lands on our Southern shore." Nicaragua beckoned beguilingly. A brazen American adventurer, William Walker, tried repeatedly to grab control of this Central American country. (He had earlier tried and failed to seize Baja California from Mexico and turn it into a slave state.) Backed by an armed force recruited largely in the South, he installed himself as president in July 1856 and promptly legalized slavery. One southern newspaper proclaimed to the planter aristocracy that Walker—the "gray-eyed man of destiny"—"now offers Nicaragua to you and your slaves, at a time when you have not a friend on the face of the earth." But a coalition of Central American nations formed an alliance to overthrow him. President Pierce withdrew

Central America, c. 1850, Showing British Possessions and Proposed Canal Routes Until President Theodore Roosevelt swung into action with his big stick in 1903, a Nicaraguan canal, closer to the United States, was generally judged more desirable than a canal across Panama.

diplomatic recognition, and the gray-eyed man's destiny was to crumple before a Honduran firing squad in 1860.

Sugar-rich Cuba, lying just off the nation's southern doorstep, was also an enticing prospect for annexation. This remnant of Spain's once-mighty New World empire already held a large population of enslaved blacks, and it might be carved into several states, restoring the political balance in the Senate. President Polk had considered offering Spain $100 million for Cuba, but the proud Spaniards replied that they would sooner see the island sunk into the sea than in the hands of the hated Yankees.

Rebuffed as buyers, some southern adventurers now undertook to shake the tree of Manifest Destiny. During 1850–1851 two "filibustering" expeditions (from the Spanish *filibustero*, meaning "freebooter" or "pirate"), each numbering several hundred armed men, descended upon Cuba. Both feeble efforts were repelled, and the last one ended in tragedy when the leader and fifty followers—some of them from the "best families" of the South—were summarily shot or strangled. So outraged were the southerners that an angry mob sacked Spain's consulate in New Orleans.

Spanish officials in Cuba rashly forced a showdown in 1854, when they seized an American steamer, *Black Warrior,* on a technicality. Now was the time for President Pierce, dominated as he was by the South, to provoke a war with Spain and seize Cuba. The major powers of Europe—England, France, and Russia—were about to become bogged down in the Crimean War and hence were unable to aid Spain.

An incredible cloak-and-dagger episode followed. The secretary of state instructed the American ministers in Spain, England, and France to prepare confidential recommendations for the acquisition of Cuba. Meeting initially at Ostend, Belgium, the three envoys drew up a top-secret dispatch, soon known as the Ostend Manifesto. This startling document urged that the administration offer $120 million for Cuba. If Spain refused, and if its continued ownership endangered American interests, the United States would "be justified in wresting" the island from the Spanish.

The secret Ostend Manifesto quickly leaked out. Northern free-soilers, already angered by the Fugitive Slave Law and other gains for slavery, rose up in wrath against the "manifesto of brigands." The shackled black hands of Harriet Beecher Stowe's Uncle Tom, whose plight had already stung the conscience of the North, now held the South back. The red-faced Pierce administration hurriedly dropped its reckless schemes for Cuba. The slavery issue thus checked territorial expansion in the 1850s.

> *The first platform of the newly born (antislavery) Republican party in 1856 lashed out at the Ostend Manifesto, with its transparent suggestion that Cuba be seized. The plank read,*
>
> "Resolved, That the highwayman's plea, that 'might makes right,' embodied in the Ostend Circular, was in every respect unworthy of American diplomacy, and would bring shame and dishonor upon any Government or people that gave it their sanction."

The Allure of Asia

The acquisition of California and Oregon had made the United States a Pacific power—or would-be power. How could Americans now tap more deeply the supposedly rich markets of Asia? Rivalry with the British lion once again played a role. Britain had recently humbled China in the Opium War, fought to secure the right of British traders to peddle opium in the Celestial Kingdom. At the war's conclusion in 1842, Britain gained free access to five so-called treaty ports, as well as outright control of the island of Hong Kong (where it remained for another century and a half). Prodded by Boston merchants fearful of seeing Britain horn in on their lucrative trade with China, President Tyler thereupon dispatched Caleb Cushing, a dashing Massachusetts lawyer-scholar, to secure comparable concessions for the United States. Cushing's four warships arrived at Macao, in southern China, in early 1844, bearing gifts that included a weathervane and a pair of six-shooters.

Impressed by Cushing's charm and largesse—and also eager for a counterweight to the meddlesome British—silk-gowned Chinese diplomats signed the Treaty of Wanghia, the first formal diplomatic agreement between the United States and China, on July 3, 1844. Cushing was interested in commerce, not colonies, and he secured some vital rights and privileges from the Chinese. "Most favored nation" status afforded the United States any and all trading terms accorded to other powers. "Extraterritoriality" provided for trying Americans accused of crimes in China before American officials, not in Chinese courts. (Cushing was prompted to seek this particular immunity by the memory of a seaman on a U.S. vessel who was strangled to death by Chinese authorities for what was apparently the accidental drowning of a Chinese woman.) American trade with China flourished thanks to Cushing's treaty, though it never reached the proportions his backers had dreamed of. More immediately important was the opportunity it opened for American missionaries, thousands of whom soon flooded prayerfully through the treaty ports to convert the "heathen Chinese." Fatefully, America had now aligned itself with the Western powers that chronically menaced China's cultural integrity. All of them would one day reap a bitter harvest of resentment.

Success in China soon inspired a still more consequential mission to pry open the bamboo gates of Japan. After some disagreeable experiences with the European world, Japan, at about the same time Jamestown was settled, withdrew into an almost airtight cocoon of isolationism and remained there for more than two centuries. The long-ruling warrior dynasty known as the Tokugawa Shogunate was so protective of Japan's insularity that it prohibited shipwrecked foreign sailors from leaving and refused to readmit Japanese sailors who had been washed up on foreign shores. Meanwhile, industrial and democratic revolutions were convulsing the Western world, while Japan remained placidly secluded. By 1853 Japan was ready to emerge from its self-imposed quarantine.

In 1852 President Millard Fillmore dispatched to Japan a fleet of warships commanded by Commodore Matthew C. Perry. The brother of the hero of the Battle of Lake Erie in 1813, Perry had prepared diligently for his mission, voraciously reading about Japan, querying whalers about Pacific Ocean currents, and collecting specimens of American technology with which to impress the Japanese. His four awesome, smoke-belching "black ships" steamed into Edo (later Tokyo) Bay on July 8, 1853, inciting near-panic among the shocked Japanese. After tense negotiations, during which Perry threatened to blast his way ashore if necessary, Perry stepped onto the beach, preceded by two conspicuously tall African American flag bearers. From elaborately carved gold-trimmed boxes, Perry produced silk-bound letters requesting free trade and friendly relations. He handed them to the wary Japanese delegation and then tactfully withdrew, promising to return the following year to receive the Japanese reply.

True to his word, Perry returned in February 1854 with an even larger force of seven men-of-war. Once again he combined bluster and grace, plying the Japa-

Commodore Perry and Flag Bearer, by an Anonymous Japanese Artist, c. 1853 (detail) Painted at the time of the opening of Japan, this scene shows Perry and his steward from the point of view of a Japanese artist.

nese with gifts, including a miniature steam locomotive and 350 feet of track. With this display of pomp and bravado, he persuaded the Japanese to sign the landmark Treaty of Kanagawa on March 31, 1854. It provided for proper treatment of shipwrecked sailors, American coaling rights in Japan, and the establishment of consular relations. Perry had inserted only a commercial toe in the door, but he had cracked Japan's two-century shell of isolation wide open. Within little more than a decade, the "Meiji Restoration" would end the era of the Shogunate and propel the Land of the Rising Sun headlong into the modern world—and an eventual epochal military clash with the United States.

Pacific Railroad Promoters and the Gadsden Purchase

Acute transportation problems were another legacy of the Mexican War. The newly acquired prizes of California and Oregon might just as well have been islands some eight thousand miles west of the nation's capital. The sea routes to and from the Isthmus of Panama, to say nothing of those around South America, were too long. Covered-wagon travel past bleaching animal bones was possible, but slow and dangerous. A popular song recalled,

> *They swam the wide rivers and crossed the tall peaks,*
> *And camped on the prairie for weeks upon weeks.*
> *Starvation and cholera and hard work and slaughter,*
> *They reached California spite of hell and high water.*

Feasible land transportation was imperative—or the newly won possessions on the Pacific Coast might break away. Camels were even proposed as the answer. Several score of these temperamental beasts—"ships of the desert"—were imported from the Near East, but mule-driving Americans did not adjust to them. A transcontinental railroad was clearly the only real solution to the problem.

Railroad promoters, both North and South, had projected many drawing-board routes to the Pacific Coast. But the estimated cost in all cases was so great that for many years there could obviously be only one line. Should its terminus be in the North or in the South? The favored section would reap rich rewards in wealth, population, and influence. The South, losing the economic race with the North, was eager to extend a railroad through adjacent southwestern territory all the way to California.

Another chunk of Mexico now seemed desirable, because the campaigns of the recent war had shown that the best railway route ran slightly south of the Mexican border. Secretary of War Jefferson Davis, a Mississippian, arranged to have James Gadsden, a prominent South Carolina railroad man, appointed minister to Mexico. Finding Santa Anna in power for the sixth and last time, and as usual in need of money, Gadsden made gratifying headway. He negotiated a treaty in 1853, which ceded to the United States the Gadsden Purchase area for $10 million. The transaction aroused much criticism among northerners, who objected to paying a huge sum for a cactus-strewn desert nearly the size of Gadsden's South Carolina. Undeterred, the Senate approved the pact, in the process shortsightedly eliminating a window on the Sea of Cortez.

No doubt the Gadsden Purchase enabled the South to claim the coveted railroad with even greater insistence. A southern track would be easier to build because the mountains were less high and because the route, unlike the proposed northern lines, would not pass through unorganized territory. Texas was already a state at this point, and New Mexico (with the Gadsden Purchase added) was a formally organized territory, with federal troops available to provide protection against marauding tribes of Indians. Any northern or central railroad line would have to be thrust through the unorganized territory of Nebraska, where the buffalo and Indians roamed.

Northern railroad boosters quickly replied that if organized territory were the test, then Nebraska should be organized. Such a move was not premature, because thousands of land-hungry pioneers were already poised

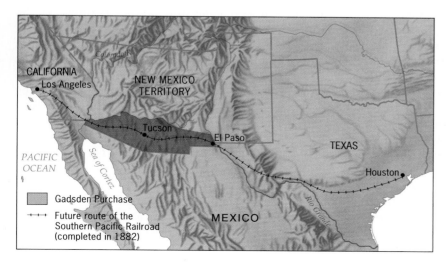

The Gadsden Purchase, 1853

on the Nebraska border. But all schemes proposed in Congress for organizing the territory were greeted with apathy or hostility by many southerners. Why should the South help create new free-soil states and thus cut its own throat by facilitating a northern railroad?

Douglas's Kansas-Nebraska Scheme

At this point in 1854, Senator Stephen A. Douglas of Illinois delivered a counterstroke to offset the Gadsden thrust for southern expansion westward. A squat, bull-necked, and heavy-chested figure, the "Little Giant" radiated the energy and breezy optimism of the self-made man. An ardent booster for the West, he longed to break the North-South deadlock over westward expansion and stretch a line of settlements across the continent. He had also invested heavily in Chicago real estate and in railway stock and was eager to have the Windy City become the eastern terminus of the proposed Pacific railroad. He would thus endear himself to the voters of Illinois, benefit his section, and enrich his own purse.

A veritable "steam engine in breeches," Douglas threw himself behind a legislative scheme that would enlist the support of a reluctant South. The proposed Territory of Nebraska would be sliced into two territories, Kansas and Nebraska. Their status regarding slavery would be settled by popular sovereignty—a democratic concept to which Douglas and his western constituents were deeply attached. Kansas, which lay due west of slaveholding Missouri, would presumably choose to become a slave state. But Nebraska, lying west of free-soil Iowa, would presumably become a free state.

Douglas's Kansas-Nebraska scheme flatly contradicted the Missouri Compromise of 1820, which had forbidden slavery in the proposed Nebraska Territory north of the sacred 36° 30' line. The only way to open the region to popular sovereignty was to repeal the ancient compact outright. This bold step Douglas was now prepared to take, even at the risk of shattering the uneasy truce patched together by the Compromise of 1850.

Many southerners, who had not conceived of Kansas as slave soil, rose to the bait. Here was a chance to gain one more slave state. The pliable President Pierce, under the thumb of southern advisers, threw his full weight behind the Kansas-Nebraska Bill.

But the Missouri Compromise, then thirty-four years old, could not be brushed aside lightly. Whatever Congress passes it can repeal, but by this time the North had come to regard the sectional pact as almost as

Douglas Hatches a Slavery Problem   Note the already hatched Missouri Compromise, Squatter Sovereignty, and Filibuster (in Cuba), and the about-to-hatch Free Kansas and Dred Scott decision. So bitter was the outcry against Douglas at the time of the Kansas-Nebraska controversy that he claimed with exaggeration that he could have traveled from Boston to Chicago at night by the light from his burning effigies.

sacred as the Constitution itself. Free-soil members of Congress struck back with a vengeance. They met their match in the violently gesticulating Douglas, who was the ablest rough-and-tumble debater of his generation. Employing twisted logic and oratorical fireworks, he rammed the bill through Congress, with strong support from many southerners. So heated were political passions that bloodshed was barely averted. Some members carried a concealed revolver or a bowie knife—or both.

Douglas's motives in prodding anew the snarling dog of slavery have long puzzled historians. His personal interests have already been mentioned. In addition, his foes accused him of angling for the presidency in 1856. Yet his admirers have argued plausibly in his defense that if he had not championed the ill-omened bill, someone else would have.

The truth seems to be that Douglas acted somewhat impulsively and recklessly. His heart did not bleed over the issue of slavery, and he declared repeatedly that he did not care whether it was voted up or down in the

> *Massachusetts senator Charles Sumner (1811–1874) described the Kansas-Nebraska Bill as "at once the worst and the best Bill on which Congress ever acted." It was the worst because it represented a victory for the slave power in the short run. But it was the best, he said prophetically, because it*
>
> "annuls all past compromises with slavery, and makes all future compromises impossible. Thus it puts freedom and slavery face to face, and bids them grapple. Who can doubt the result?"

predicted a "hell of a storm," but he grossly underestimated its proportions. His critics in the North, branding him a "Judas" and a "traitor," greeted his name with frenzied boos, hisses, and "three groans for Doug." But he still enjoyed a high degree of popularity among his following in the Democratic party, especially in Illinois, a stronghold of popular sovereignty.

Congress Legislates a Civil War

The Kansas-Nebraska Act—a curtain-raiser to a terrible drama—was one of the most momentous measures ever to pass Congress. By one way of reckoning, it greased the slippery slope to Civil War.

Antislavery northerners were angered by what they condemned as an act of bad faith by the "Nebrascals" and their "Nebrascality." All future compromise with the South would be immeasurably more difficult, and without compromise there was bound to be conflict.

Henceforth the Fugitive Slave Law of 1850, previously enforced in the North only halfheartedly, was a dead letter. The Kansas-Nebraska Act wrecked two compromises: that of 1820, which it repealed specifically, and that of 1850, which northern opinion repealed indirectly. Emerson wrote, "The Fugitive [Slave] Law did much to unglue the eyes of men, and now the Nebraska

territories. What he failed to perceive was that hundreds of thousands of his fellow citizens in the North *did* feel deeply on this moral issue. They regarded the repeal of the Missouri Compromise as an intolerable breach of faith, and they would henceforth resist to the last trench all future southern demands for slave territory. As Abraham Lincoln said, the North wanted to give to pioneers in the West "a clean bed, with no snakes in it."

Genuine leaders, like skillful chess players, must foresee the possible effects of their moves. Douglas

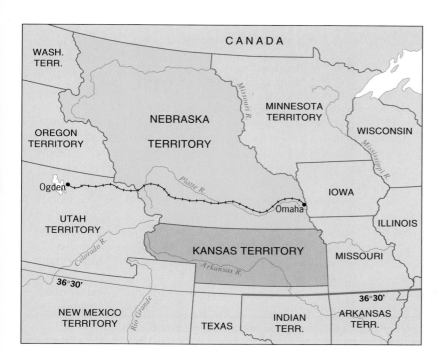

Kansas and Nebraska, 1854
The future Union Pacific Railroad (completed in 1869) is shown. Note the Missouri Compromise line of 36° 30' (1820).

Bill leaves us staring." Northern abolitionists and southern "fire-eaters" alike saw less and less they could live with. The growing legion of antislaveryites gained numerous recruits, who resented the grasping move by the "slavocracy" for Kansas. The southerners, in turn, became inflamed when the free-soilers tried to control Kansas, contrary to the presumed "deal."

The proud Democrats—a party now over half a century old—were shattered by the Kansas-Nebraska Act. They did elect a president in 1856, but he was the last one they were to boost into the White House for twenty-eight long years.

Undoubtedly the most durable offspring of the Kansas-Nebraska blunder was the new Republican party. It sprang up spontaneously in the Middle West, notably in Wisconsin and Michigan, as a mighty moral protest against the gains of slavery. Gathering together dissatisfied elements, it soon included disgruntled Whigs (among them Abraham Lincoln), Democrats, Free-Soilers, Know-Nothings, and other foes of the Kansas-Nebraska Act. The hodgepodge party spread eastward with the swiftness of a prairie fire and with the zeal of a religious crusade. Unheard-of and unheralded at the beginning of 1854, when the nativist Know-Nothings instead seemed to be the rising party of the North, it elected a Republican Speaker of the House of Representatives within two years. Never really a third-party movement, its wide wingspan gave it flight overnight as the second major political party—and a purely sectional one at that.

At long last the dreaded sectional rift had appeared. The new Republican party would not be allowed south of the Mason-Dixon line. Countless southerners subscribed wholeheartedly to the sentiment that it was "a nigger stealing, stinking, putrid, abolition party." The Union was in dire peril.

Chronology

1844	Caleb Cushing signs Treaty of Wanghia with China
1848	Treaty of Guadalupe Hidalgo ends Mexican War Taylor defeats Cass and Van Buren for presidency
1849	California gold rush
1850	Fillmore assumes presidency after Taylor's death Compromise of 1850, including Fugitive Slave Law Clayton-Bulwer Treaty with Britain
1852	Pierce defeats Scott for presidency
1853	Gadsden Purchase from Mexico
1854	Commodore Perry opens Japan Ostend Manifesto proposes seizure of Cuba Kansas-Nebraska Act Republican party organized
1856	William Walker becomes president of Nicaragua and legalizes slavery

For further reading, see the Appendix. For web resources, go to **http://college.hmco.com**.

19

Drifting Toward Disunion

◈

1854–1861

A HOUSE DIVIDED AGAINST ITSELF CANNOT STAND.
I BELIEVE THIS GOVERNMENT CANNOT ENDURE
PERMANENTLY HALF SLAVE AND HALF FREE.

ABRAHAM LINCOLN, 1858

The slavery question continued to churn the cauldron of controversy throughout the 1850s. As moral temperatures rose, prospects for a peaceful political solution to the slavery issue simply evaporated. Kansas Territory erupted in violence between proslavery and antislavery factions in 1855. Two years later the Supreme Court's *Dred Scott* decision invalidated the Missouri Compromise of 1820, which had imposed a shaky lid on the slavery problem for more than a generation. Attitudes on both sides progressively hardened. When in 1860 the newly formed Republican party nominated for president Abraham Lincoln, an outspoken opponent of the further expansion of slavery, the stage was set for all-out civil war.

Stowe and Helper: Literary Incendiaries

Sectional tensions were further strained in 1852, and later, by an inky phenomenon. Harriet Beecher Stowe, a wisp of a woman and the mother of a half-dozen children, published her heartrending novel *Uncle Tom's Cabin*. Dismayed by the passage of the Fugitive Slave Law, she was determined to awaken the North to the wickedness of slavery by laying bare its terrible inhumanity, especially the cruel splitting of families. Her wildly popular book relied on powerful imagery and touching pathos. "God wrote it," she explained in

Harriet Beecher Stowe (1811–1896), Daguerreotype by Southworth and Hawes   Stowe was a remarkable woman whose pen helped to change the course of history.

"The Book That Made This Great War"
Lincoln's celebrated remark to author Harriet Beecher Stowe reflected the enormous emotional impact of her impassioned novel.

later years—a reminder that the deeper sources of her antislavery sentiments lay in the evangelical religious crusades of the Second Great Awakening.

The success of the novel at home and abroad was sensational. Several hundred thousand copies were published in the first year, and the totals soon ran into the millions as the tale was translated into more than a score of languages. It was also put on the stage in "Tom shows" for lengthy runs. No other novel in American history—perhaps in all history—can be compared with it as a political force. To millions of people, it made slavery appear almost as evil as it really was.

When Mrs. Stowe was introduced to President Lincoln in 1862, he reportedly remarked with twinkling eyes, "So you're the little woman who wrote the book that made this great war." The truth is that *Uncle Tom's Cabin* did help start the Civil War—and win it. The South condemned that "vile wretch in petticoats" when it learned that hundreds of thousands of fellow Americans

were reading and believing her "unfair" indictment. Mrs. Stowe had never witnessed slavery at first hand in the Deep South, but she had seen it briefly during a visit to Kentucky, and she had lived for many years in Ohio, a center of Underground Railroad activity.

Uncle Tom, endearing and enduring, left a profound impression on the North. Uncounted thousands of readers swore that henceforth they would have nothing to do with the enforcement of the Fugitive Slave Law. The tale was devoured by millions of impressionable youths in the 1850s—some of whom later became the Boys in Blue who volunteered to fight the Civil War through to its grim finale. The memory of a beaten and dying Uncle Tom helped sustain them in their determination to wipe out the plague of slavery.

The novel was immensely popular abroad, especially in Britain and France. Countless readers wept over the kindly Tom and the angelic Eva, while deploring the brutal Simon Legree. When the guns in America finally

EXAMINING THE EVIDENCE

Harriet Beecher Stowe, *Uncle Tom's Cabin* As works of fiction, novels pose tricky problems to historians, whose principal objective is to get the factual record straight. Works of the imagination are notoriously unreliable as descriptions of reality, and only rarely is it known with any degree of certainty what a reader might have felt when confronting a particular fictional passage or theme. Yet a novel like Harriet Beecher Stowe's *Uncle Tom's Cabin* had such an unarguably large impact on the American (and worldwide) debate over slavery that historians have inevitably looked to it for evidence of the mid-nineteenth-century ideas and attitudes to which Stowe appealed. The passage quoted here is especially rich in such evidence—and even offers an explanation for the logic of the novel's title. Stowe cleverly aimed to mobilize not simply her readers' sense of injustice, but also their sentiments, on behalf of the antislavery cause. Why is the *cabin* described here so central to Stowe's novel? What sentimental values does the cabin represent? What is the nature of the threat to those values? What does it say about nineteenth-century American culture that Stowe's appeal to sentiment succeeded so much more dramatically in exciting antislavery passions than did the factual and moral arguments of many other (mostly male) abolitionists?

> THE February morning looked gray and drizzling through the window of Uncle Tom's cabin. It looked on downcast faces, the images of mournful hearts. The little table stood out before the fire, covered with an ironing-cloth; a coarse but clean shirt or two, fresh from the iron, hung on the back of a chair by the fire, and Aunt Chloe had another spread out before her on the table. Carefully she rubbed and ironed every fold and every hem, with the most scrupulous exactness, every now and then raising her hand to her face to wipe off the tears that were coursing down her cheeks.
>
> Tom sat by, with his Testament open on his knee, and his head leaning upon his hand; — but neither spoke. It was yet early, and the children lay all asleep together in their little rude trundle-bed.
>
> Tom, who had, to the full, the gentle, domestic heart, which, woe for them! has been a peculiar characteristic of his unhappy race, got up and walked silently to look at his children.
>
> "It's the last time," he said.

began to boom, the common people of England sensed that the triumph of the North would spell the end of the black curse. The governments in London and Paris seriously considered intervening in behalf of the South, but they were sobered by the realization that many of their own people, aroused by the "Tom-mania," might not support them.

Another trouble-brewing book appeared in 1857, five years after the debut of Uncle Tom. Titled *The Impending Crisis of the South,* it was written by Hinton R. Helper, a nonaristocratic white from North Carolina. Hating both slavery and blacks, he attempted to prove by an array of statistics that indirectly the nonslaveholding whites were the ones who suffered most from the millstone of slavery. Unable to secure a publisher in the South, he finally managed to find one in the North.

Helper's influence was negligible among the poorer whites to whom he addressed his message. Yet the South's planter elite certainly took note of Helper's audacity, which fueled their fears that the nonslaveholding majority might abandon them. *The Impending Crisis of the South,* with its "dirty allusions," was banned in the South and fed to the flames at book-burning parties. In the North untold thousands of copies, many

In the closing scenes of Harriet Beecher Stowe's novel, Uncle Tom's brutal master, Simon Legree, orders the $1,200 slave savagely beaten (to death) by two fellow slaves. Through tears and blood, Tom exclaims,

"No! no! no! my soul an't yours, Mas'r! You haven't bought it,—ye can't buy it! It's been bought and paid for, by one that is able to keep it,—no matter, no matter, you can't harm me!" "I can't," said Legree, with a sneer; "we'll see,— we'll see! Here, Sambo, Quimbo, give this dog such a breakin' in as he won't get over, this month!"

in condensed form, were distributed as campaign literature by the Republicans. Southerners were further embittered when they learned that their northern brethren were spreading these wicked "lies." Thus did southerners, reacting much as they did to *Uncle Tom's Cabin*, become increasingly unwilling to sleep under the same federal roof with their hostile Yankee bedfellows.

The North-South Contest for Kansas

The rolling plains of Kansas had meanwhile been providing an example of the worst possible workings of popular sovereignty, although admittedly under abnormal conditions.

Newcomers who ventured into Kansas were a motley lot. Most of the northerners were just ordinary westward-moving pioneers in search of richer lands beyond the sunset. But a small part of the inflow was financed by groups of northern abolitionists or free-soilers. The most famous of these antislavery organizations was the New England Emigrant Aid Company, which sent about two thousand people to the troubled area to forestall the South—and also to make a profit. Shouting "Ho for Kansas," many of them carried the deadly new breech-loading Sharps rifles, nicknamed "Beecher's Bibles" after the Reverend Henry Ward Beecher (Harriet Beecher Stowe's brother), who had helped raise money for their purchase. Many of the Kansas-bound pioneers sang Whittier's marching song (1854):

> *We cross the prairie as of old*
> *The pilgrims crossed the sea,*
> *To make the West, as they the East,*
> *The homestead of the free!*

Southern spokesmen, now more than ordinarily touchy, raised furious cries of betrayal. They had supported the Kansas-Nebraska scheme of Douglas with the unspoken understanding that Kansas would become slave and Nebraska free. The northern "Nebrascals," allegedly by foul means, were now apparently out to "abolitionize" *both* Kansas and Nebraska.

A few southern hotheads, quick to respond in kind, attempted to "assist" small groups of well-armed slaveowners to Kansas. Some carried banners proclaiming,

> *Let Yankees tremble, abolitionists fall,*
> *Our motto is, "Give Southern Rights to All."*

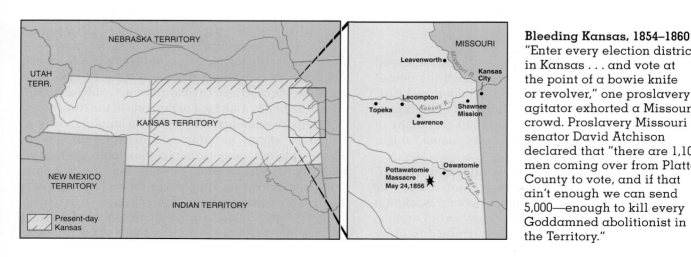

Bleeding Kansas, 1854–1860 "Enter every election district in Kansas . . . and vote at the point of a bowie knife or revolver," one proslavery agitator exhorted a Missouri crowd. Proslavery Missouri senator David Atchison declared that "there are 1,100 men coming over from Platte County to vote, and if that ain't enough we can send 5,000—enough to kill every Goddamned abolitionist in the Territory."

But planting blacks on Kansas soil was a losing game. Slaves were valuable and volatile property, and foolish indeed were owners who would take them where bullets were flying and where the soil might be voted free under popular sovereignty. The census of 1860 found only 2 slaves among 107,000 souls in all Kansas Territory and only 15 in Nebraska. There was much truth in the charge that the whole quarrel over slavery in the territories revolved around "an imaginary Negro in an impossible place."

Crisis conditions in Kansas rapidly worsened. When the day came in 1855 to elect members of the first territorial legislature, proslavery "border ruffians" poured in from Missouri to vote early and often. The slavery supporters triumphed and then set up their own puppet government at Shawnee Mission. The free-soilers, unable to stomach this fraudulent conspiracy, established an extralegal regime of their own in Topeka. The confused Kansans thus had their choice between two governments—one based on fraud, the other on illegality.

Tension mounted as settlers also feuded over conflicting land claims. The breaking point came in 1856 when a gang of proslavery raiders, alleging provocation, shot up and burned a part of the free-soil town of Lawrence. This outrage was but the prelude to a bloodier tragedy.

Kansas in Convulsion

The fanatical figure of John Brown now stalked upon the Kansas battlefield. Spare, gray-bearded, and iron-willed, he was obsessively dedicated to the abolitionist cause. The power of his glittering gray eyes was such, so he claimed, that his stare could force a dog or cat to slink out of a room. Becoming involved in dubious dealings, including horse stealing, he moved to Kansas from Ohio with a part of his large family. Brooding over the recent attack on Lawrence, "Old Brown" of Osawatomie led a band of his followers to Pottawatomie Creek in May 1856. There they literally hacked to pieces five surprised men, presumed to be proslaveryites. This fiendish butchery besmirched the free-soil cause and brought vicious retaliation from the proslavery forces.

Civil war in Kansas thus erupted in 1856 and continued intermittently until it merged with the large-scale Civil War of 1861–1865. Altogether, the Kansas conflict destroyed millions of dollars' worth of property, paralyzed agriculture in certain areas, and cost scores of lives.

John Brown (1800–1859) This daguerreotype of the militant abolitionist Brown tells a tale of two men, the sitter and the photographer. It was taken in 1847 when Brown was running a wool-brokerage house in Springfield, Massachusetts, and working closely with other New England abolitionists, including Frederick Douglass. Brown made his way to the Hartford studio of free black photographer Augustus Washington, who was the son of an Asian woman and a former black slave and well known in abolitionist circles. Six years later, Washington would close his successful studio and take his family to Liberia, convinced that American blacks would do better in their own country in Africa than as free men in the United States (see pp. 362–364).

Yet by 1857 Kansas had enough people, chiefly free-soilers, to apply for statehood on a popular-sovereignty basis. The proslavery forces, then in the saddle, devised a tricky document known as the Lecompton Constitution. The people were not allowed to vote for or against the constitution as a whole, but for the constitution either "with slavery" or "with no slavery." If they voted against

SOUTHERN CHIVALRY — ARGUMENT VERSUS CLUB'S.

Preston Brooks Caning Charles Sumner, 1856 Cartoonist John Magee of Philadelphia depicted Brooks's beating of Sumner in the Senate as a display of southern ruthlessness in defending slavery, ironically captioned "southern chivalry."

slavery, one of the remaining provisions of the constitution would protect the owners of slaves already in Kansas. So whatever the outcome, there would still be black bondage in Kansas. Many free-soilers, infuriated by this ploy, boycotted the polls. Left to themselves, the proslaveryites approved the constitution with slavery late in 1857.

The scene next shifted to Washington. President Pierce had been succeeded by the no-less-pliable James Buchanan, who was also strongly under southern influence. Blind to sharp divisions within his own Democratic party, Buchanan threw the weight of his administration behind the notorious Lecompton Constitution. But Senator Douglas, who had championed true popular sovereignty, would have none of this semipopular fraudulency. Deliberately tossing away his strong support in the South for the presidency, he fought courageously for fair play and democratic principles. The outcome was a compromise that, in effect, submitted the entire Lecompton Constitution to a popular vote. The free-soil voters thereupon thronged to the polls and snowed it under. Kansas remained a territory until 1861, when the southern secessionists left Congress.

President Buchanan, by antagonizing the numerous Douglas Democrats in the North, hopelessly divided the once-powerful Democratic party. Until then, it had been the only remaining *national* party, for the Whigs were dead and the Republicans were sectional. With the

disruption of the Democrats came the snapping of one of the last important strands in the rope that was barely binding the Union together.

"Bully" Brooks and His Bludgeon

"Bleeding Kansas" also spattered blood on the floor of the Senate in 1856. Senator Charles Sumner of Massachusetts, a tall and imposing figure, was a leading abolitionist—one of the few prominent in political life. Highly educated but cold, humorless, intolerant, and egotistical, he had made himself one of the most disliked men in the Senate. Brooding over the turbulent miscarriage of popular sovereignty, he delivered a blistering speech titled "The Crime Against Kansas." Sparing few epithets, he condemned the proslavery men as "hirelings picked from the drunken spew and vomit of an uneasy civilization." He also referred insultingly to South Carolina and to its white-haired senator Andrew Butler, one of the best-liked members of the Senate.

Hot-tempered Congressman Preston S. Brooks of South Carolina now took vengeance into his own hands. Ordinarily gracious and gallant, he resented the insults to his state and to its senator, a distant cousin. His code of honor called for a duel, but in the South one fought only with one's social equals. And had not the coarse

> *Regarding the Brooks assault on Sumner, one of the more moderate antislavery journals* (Illinois State Journal) *declared,*
>
> "Brooks and his Southern allies have deliberately adopted the monstrous creed that any man who dares to utter sentiments which they deem wrong or unjust, shall be brutally assailed."
>
> *One of the milder southern responses came from the* Petersburg (Virginia) Intelligencer:
>
> "Although Mr. Brooks ought to have selected some other spot for the altercation than the Senate chamber, if he had broken every bone in Sumner's carcass it would have been a just retribution upon this slanderer of the South and her individual citizens."

language of the Yankee, who probably would reject a challenge, dropped him to a lower order? To Brooks, the only alternative was to chastise the senator as one would beat an unruly dog. On May 22, 1856, he approached Sumner, then sitting at his Senate desk, and pounded the orator with an eleven-ounce cane until it broke. The victim fell bleeding and unconscious to the floor, while several nearby senators refrained from interfering.

Sumner had been provocatively insulting, but this counteroutrage put Brooks in the wrong. The House of Representatives could not muster enough votes to expel the South Carolinian, but he resigned and was triumphantly reelected. Southern admirers deluged Brooks with canes, some of them gold-headed, to replace the one that had been broken. The injuries to Sumner's head and nervous system were serious. He was forced to leave his seat for three and a half years and go to Europe for treatment that was both painful and costly. Meanwhile, Massachusetts defiantly reelected him, leaving his seat eloquently empty. Bleeding Sumner was thus joined with bleeding Kansas as a political issue.

The free-soil North was mightily aroused against the "uncouth" and "cowardly" "Bully" Brooks. Copies of Sumner's abusive speech, otherwise doomed to obscurity, were sold by the tens of thousands. Every blow that struck the senator doubtless made thousands of Republican votes. The South, although not unanimous in approving Brooks, was angered not only because Sumner had made such an intemperate speech but because it had been so extravagantly applauded in the North.

The Sumner-Brooks clash and the ensuing reactions revealed how dangerously inflamed passions were becoming, North and South. It was ominous that the cultured Sumner should have used the language of a barroom bully and that the gentlemanly Brooks should have employed the tactics and tools of a thug. Emotion was displacing thought. The blows rained on Sumner's head were, broadly speaking, among the first blows of the Civil War.

"Old Buck" Versus "The Pathfinder"

With bullets whining in Kansas, the Democrats met in Cincinnati to nominate their presidential standard-bearer of 1856. They shied away from both the weak-kneed President Pierce and the dynamic Douglas. Each was too indelibly tainted by the Kansas-Nebraska Act. The delegates finally chose James Buchanan (pronounced by many Buck-anan), who was muscular, white-haired, and tall (six feet), with a short neck and a protruding chin. Because of an eye defect, he carried his head cocked to one side. A well-to-do Pennsylvania lawyer, he had been serving as minister to London during the recent Kansas-Nebraska uproar. He was therefore "Kansas-less," and hence relatively enemyless. But in a crisis that called for giants, "Old Buck" Buchanan was mediocre, irresolute, and confused.

Delegates of the fast-growing Republican party met in Philadelphia with bubbling enthusiasm. "Higher Law" Seward was their most conspicuous leader, and he probably would have arranged to win the nomination had he been confident that this was a "Republican year." The final choice was Captain John C. Frémont, the so-called Pathfinder of the West—a dashing but erratic explorer-soldier-surveyor who was supposed to find the path to the White House. The black-bearded and flashy young adventurer was virtually without political experience, but like Buchanan he was not tarred with the Kansas brush. The Republican platform came out vigorously against the extension of slavery into the territories, while the Democrats declared no less emphatically for popular sovereignty.

An ugly dose of antiforeignism was injected into the campaign, even though slavery extension loomed

> *Spiritual overtones developed in the Frémont campaign, especially over slavery. The* Independent, *a prominent religious journal, saw in Frémont's nomination "the good hand of God." As election day neared, it declared,*
>
> "Fellow-Christians! Remember it is for Christ, for the nation, and for the world that you vote at this election! Vote as you pray! Pray as you vote!"

largest. The recent influx of immigrants from Ireland and Germany had alarmed "nativists," as many old-stock Protestants were called. They organized the American party, also known as the Know-Nothing party because of its secretiveness, and in 1856 nominated the lackluster ex-president Millard Fillmore. Antiforeign and anti-Catholic, these superpatriots adopted the slogan "Americans Must Rule America." Remnants of

the dying Whig party likewise endorsed Fillmore, and they and the Know-Nothings threatened to cut into Republican strength.

Republicans fell in behind Frémont with the zeal of crusaders. Shouting "We Follow the Pathfinder" and "We Are Buck Hunting," they organized glee clubs, which sang (to the tune of "The Marseillaise"),

> *Arise, arise ye brave!*
> *And let our war-cry be,*
> *Free speech, free press, free soil, free men,*
> *Fré-mont and victory!*

"And free love," sneered the Buchanan supporters ("Buchaneers").

Mudslinging bespattered both candidates. "Old Fogy" Buchanan was assailed because he was a bachelor: the fiancée of his youth had died after a lovers' quarrel. Frémont was reviled because of his illegitimate birth, for his young mother had left her elderly husband, a Virginia planter, to run away with a French adventurer. In due season she gave birth to John in Savannah, Georgia—further to shame the South. More harmful to Frémont was the allegation, which alienated many bigoted Know-Nothings and other "nativists," that he was a Roman Catholic.

A Know-Nothing Party Mob, Baltimore, c. 1856–1860 These armed ruffians were campaigning in Baltimore for their ultranationalistic, anti-immigrant, anti-Catholic candidate.

society." Republican defiance of the exalted tribunal was intensified by an awareness that a majority of its members were southerners and by the conviction that it had debased itself—"sullied the ermine"—by wallowing in the gutter of politics.

Southerners in turn were inflamed by all this defiance. They began to wonder anew how much longer they could remain joined to a section that refused to honor the Supreme Court, to say nothing of the constitutional compact that had established it.

The Financial Crash of 1857

Bitterness caused by the *Dred Scott* decision was deepened by hard times, which dampened a period of feverish prosperity. Late in 1857 a panic burst about Buchanan's harassed head. The storm was not so bad economically as the panic of 1837, but psychologically it was probably the worst of the nineteenth century.

What caused the crash? Inpouring California gold played its part by helping to inflate the currency. The demands of the Crimean War had overstimulated the growing of grain, while frenzied speculation in land and railroads had further ripped the economic fabric. When the collapse came, over five thousand businesses failed within a year. Unemployment, accompanied by hunger meetings in urban areas, was widespread. "Bread or Death" stated one desperate slogan.

The North, including its grain growers, was hardest hit. The South, enjoying favorable cotton prices abroad, rode out the storm with flying colors. Panic conditions seemed further proof that cotton was king and that its economic kingdom was stronger than that of the North. This fatal delusion helped drive the overconfident southerners closer to a shooting showdown.

Financial distress in the North, especially in agriculture, gave a new vigor to the demand for free farms of 160 acres from the public domain. For several decades interested groups had been urging the federal government to abandon its ancient policy of selling the land for revenue. Instead, the argument ran, acreage should be given outright to the sturdy pioneers as a reward for risking health and life to develop it.

A scheme to make outright gifts of homesteads encountered two-pronged opposition. Eastern industrialists had long been unfriendly to free land; some of them feared that their underpaid workers would be drained off to the West. The South was even more bitterly opposed, partly because gang-labor slavery

Wall Street, Half Past Two O'clock, October 13, 1857, by James H. Cafferty and Charles G. Rosenberg The panic of 1857 further burdened President Buchanan, already reeling from the armed clashes in Kansas and the controversy over the *Dred Scott* decision.

could not flourish on a mere 160 acres. Free farms would merely fill up the territories more rapidly with free-soilers and further tip the political balance against the South. In 1860, after years of debate, Congress finally passed a homestead act—one that made public lands available at a nominal sum of twenty-five cents an acre. But the homestead act was stabbed to death by the veto pen of President Buchanan, near whose elbow sat leading southern sympathizers.

The panic of 1857 also created a clamor for higher tariff rates. Several months before the crash, Congress, embarrassed by a large Treasury surplus, had enacted the Tariff of 1857. The new law, responding to pressures from the South, reduced duties to about 20 percent on dutiable goods—the lowest point since the War of 1812. Hardly had the revised rates been placed on the books when financial misery descended like a black pall. Northern manufacturers, many of them Republicans, noisily blamed their misfortunes on the low tariff. As the surplus melted away in the Treasury, industrialists in the North pointed to the need for higher duties. But what really concerned them was their desire for increased protection. Thus the panic

Abraham Lincoln, a Most Uncommon Common Man
This daguerreotype of Lincoln was done by Mathew B. Brady, a distinguished photographer of the era.

he attended a frontier school for not more than a year; being an avid reader, he was mainly self-educated. All his life he said, "git," "thar," and "heered." Although narrow-chested and somewhat stoop-shouldered, he shone in his frontier community as a wrestler and weight lifter, and spent some time, among other pioneering pursuits, as a splitter of logs for fence rails. A superb teller of earthy and amusing stories, he would oddly enough plunge into protracted periods of melancholy.

Lincoln's private and professional lives were not especially noteworthy. He married "above himself" socially, into the influential Todd family of Kentucky, and the temperamental outbursts of his high-strung wife, known by her enemies as the "she wolf," helped to school him in patience and forbearance. After reading a little law, he gradually emerged as one of the dozen or so better-known trial lawyers in Illinois, although still accustomed to carrying important papers in his stovepipe hat. He was widely referred to as "Honest Abe," partly because he would refuse cases that he had to suspend his conscience to defend.

The rise of Lincoln as a political figure was less than rocketlike. After making his mark in the Illinois legislature as a Whig politician of the logrolling variety, he served one undistinguished term in Congress, 1847–1849. Until 1854, when he was forty-five years of age, he had done nothing to establish a claim to statesmanship. But the passage of the Kansas-Nebraska Act

of 1857 gave the Republicans two surefire economic issues for the election of 1860: protection for the unprotected and farms for the farmless.

An Illinois Rail-Splitter Emerges

The Illinois senatorial election of 1858 now claimed the national spotlight. Senator Douglas's term was about to expire, and the Republicans decided to run against him a rustic Springfield lawyer, one Abraham Lincoln. The Republican candidate—6 feet 4 inches in height and 180 pounds in weight—presented an awkward but arresting figure. Lincoln's legs, arms, and neck were abnormally long; his head was crowned by coarse, black, and unruly hair; and his face was sad, sunken, and weather-beaten.

Lincoln was no silver-spoon child of the elite. Born in 1809 in a Kentucky log cabin to impoverished parents,

In 1832, when Abraham Lincoln (1809–1865) became a candidate for the Illinois legislature, he delivered a speech at a political gathering:

"I presume you all know who I am. I am humble Abraham Lincoln. I have been solicited by many friends to become a candidate for the Legislature. My [Whiggish] politics are short and sweet, like the old woman's dance. I am in favor of a national bank. I am in favor of the internal-improvement system, and a high protective tariff. These are my sentiments and political principles. If elected, I shall be thankful; if not, it will be all the same."

He was elected two years later.

in that year lighted within him unexpected fires. After mounting the Republican bandwagon, he emerged as one of the foremost politicians and orators of the Northwest. At the Philadelphia convention of 1856, where John Frémont was nominated, Lincoln actually received 110 votes for the vice-presidential nomination.

The Great Debate: Lincoln Versus Douglas

Lincoln, as Republican nominee for the Senate seat, boldly challenged Douglas to a series of joint debates. This was a rash act, because the stumpy senator was probably the nation's most devastating debater. Douglas promptly accepted Lincoln's challenge, and seven meetings were arranged from August to October 1858.

At first glance the two contestants seemed ill-matched. The well-groomed and polished Douglas, with bearlike figure and bullhorn voice, presented a striking contrast to the lanky Lincoln, with his baggy clothes and unshined shoes. Moreover, "Old Abe," as he was called in both affection and derision, had a piercing, high-pitched voice and was often ill at ease

Lincoln expressed his views on the relation of the black and white races in 1858, in his first debate with Stephen A. Douglas:

"I, as well as Judge Douglas, am in favor of the race to which I belong, having the superior position. I have never said anything to the contrary, but I hold that notwithstanding all this, there is no reason in the world why the negro is not entitled to all the natural rights enumerated in the Declaration of Independence, the right to life, liberty, and the pursuit of happiness. I hold that he is as much entitled to those rights as the white man. I agree with Judge Douglas he is not my equal in many respects—certainly not in color, perhaps not in moral or intellectual endowment. But in the right to eat the bread, without leave of anybody else, which his own hand earns, he is my equal and the equal of Judge Douglas, and the equal of every living man."

Lincoln and Douglas Debate, 1858 Thousands attended each of the seven Lincoln-Douglas debates. Douglas is shown here sitting to Lincoln's right in the debate at Charleston, Illinois, in September. On one occasion Lincoln quipped that Douglas's logic would prove that a horse chestnut was a chestnut horse.

when he began to speak. But as he threw himself into an argument, he seemed to grow in height, while his glowing eyes lighted up a rugged face. He relied on logic rather than on table-thumping.

The most famous debate came at Freeport, Illinois, where Lincoln nearly impaled his opponent on the horns of a dilemma. Suppose, he queried, the people of a territory should vote slavery down? The Supreme Court in the *Dred Scott* decision had decreed that they could not. Who would prevail, the Court or the people?

Legend to the contrary, Douglas and some southerners had already publicly answered the Freeport question. The "Little Giant" therefore did not hesitate to meet the issue head-on, honestly and consistently. His reply to Lincoln became known as the "Freeport Doctrine." No matter how the Supreme Court ruled, Douglas argued, slavery would stay down if the people voted it down. Laws to protect slavery would have to be passed by the territorial legislatures. These would not be forthcoming in the absence of popular approval, and black bondage would soon disappear. Douglas, in truth, had American history on his side. Where public opinion does not support the federal government, as in the case of Jefferson's embargo, the law is almost impossible to enforce.

The upshot was that Douglas defeated Lincoln for the Senate seat. The "Little Giant's" loyalty to popular sovereignty, which still had a powerful appeal in Illinois, probably was decisive. Senators were then chosen by state legislatures; and in the general election that followed the debates, more pro-Douglas members were elected than pro-Lincoln members. Yet thanks to inequitable apportionment, the districts carried by Douglas supporters represented a smaller population than those carried by Lincoln supporters. "Honest Abe" thus won a clear moral victory.

Lincoln possibly was playing for larger stakes than just the senatorship. Although defeated, he had shambled into the national limelight in company with the most prominent northern politicians. Newspapers in the East published detailed accounts of the debates, and Lincoln began to emerge as a potential Republican nominee for president. But Douglas, in winning Illinois, hurt his own chances of winning the presidency, while further splitting his splintering party. After his opposition to the Lecompton Constitution for Kansas and his further defiance of the Supreme Court at Freeport, southern Democrats were determined to break up the party (and the Union) rather than accept him. The Lincoln-Douglas debate platform thus proved to be one of the preliminary battlefields of the Civil War.

John Brown: Murderer or Martyr?

The gaunt, grim figure of John Brown of bleeding Kansas infamy now appeared again in an even more terrible way. His fantastical scheme was to invade the South secretly with a handful of followers, call upon the slaves to rise, furnish them with arms, and establish a kind of black free state as a sanctuary. Brown secured several thousand dollars for firearms from northern abolitionists and finally arrived in hilly western Virginia with some twenty men, including several blacks. At scenic Harpers Ferry, he seized the federal arsenal in October 1859, incidentally killing seven innocent people, including a free black, and injuring ten or so more. But the slaves, largely ignorant of Brown's strike, failed to rise, and the wounded Brown and the remnants of his tiny band were quickly captured by U.S. Marines under the command

Upon hearing of John Brown's execution, escaped slave and abolitionist Harriet Tubman (c. 1820–1913) paid him the highest tribute for his self-sacrifice:

"I've been studying, and studying upon it, and its clar to me, it wasn't John Brown that died on that gallows. When I think how he gave up his life for our people, and how he never flinched, but was so brave to the end; its clar to me it wasn't mortal man, it was God in him."

Not all opponents of slavery, however, shared Tubman's reverence for Brown. Republican presidential candidate Abraham Lincoln dismissed Brown as deluded:

"[The Brown] affair, in its philosophy, corresponds with the many attempts, related in history, at the assassination of kings and emperors. An enthusiast broods over the oppression of a people till he fancies himself commissioned by Heaven to liberate them. He ventures the attempt, which ends in little else than his own execution."

Last Moments of John Brown, by Thomas Hovenden Sentenced to be hanged, John Brown wrote to his brother, "I am quite cheerful in view of my approaching end, being fully persuaded that I am worth inconceivably more to hang than for any other purpose. . . . I count it all joy. 'I have fought the good fight,' and have, as I trust, 'finished my course.' " This painting of Brown going to his execution may have been inspired by the journalist Horace Greeley, who was not present but wrote that "a black woman with a little child stood by the door. He stopped for a moment, and stooping, kissed the child." That scene never took place, as Brown was escorted from the jail only by a detachment of soldiers. But this painting has become famous as a kind of allegorical expression of the pathos of Brown's martyrdom for the abolitionist cause.

of Lieutenant Colonel Robert E. Lee. Ironically, within two years Lee became the preeminent general in the Confederate army.

"Old Brown" was convicted of murder and treason after a hasty but legal trial. His presumed insanity was supported by affidavits from seventeen friends and relatives, who were trying to save his neck. Actually thirteen of his near relations were regarded as insane, including his mother and grandmother. Governor Wise of Virginia would have been wiser, so his critics say, if he had only clapped the culprit into a lunatic asylum.

But Brown—"God's angry man"—was given every opportunity to pose and to enjoy martyrdom. Though perhaps of unsound mind, he was clever enough to see that he was worth much more to the abolitionist cause dangling from a rope than in any other way. His demeanor during the trial was dignified and courageous, his last words ("this *is* a beautiful country") were to become legendary, and he marched up the scaffold steps without flinching. His conduct was so exemplary, his devotion to freedom so inflexible, that he took on

an exalted character, however deplorable his previous record may have been. So the hangman's trap was sprung, and Brown plunged not into oblivion but into world fame. A memorable marching song of the impending Civil War ran,

> *John Brown's body lies a-mould'ring in the grave,*
> *His soul is marching on.*

The effects of Harpers Ferry were calamitous. In the eyes of the South, already embittered, "Osawatomie Brown" was a wholesale murderer and an apostle of treason. Many southerners asked how they could possibly remain in the Union while a "murderous gang of abolitionists" was financing armed bands to "Brown" them. Moderate northerners, including Republican leaders, openly deplored this mad exploit. But the South naturally concluded that the violent abolitionist view was shared by the entire North, dominated by "Brown-loving" Republicans.

Abolitionists and other ardent free-soilers were infuriated by Brown's execution. Many of them were

THE NATIONAL GAME. THREE "OUTS" AND ONE "RUN".
ABRAHAM WINNING THE BALL.

Lincoln Hits a Home Run in 1860 Currier & Ives, the producer of popular, inexpensive colored prints, portrayed Lincoln's victory over (from left to right) John Bell, Stephen Douglas, and John C. Breckinridge, as a baseball game. Baseball developed in New York in the 1840s, and by 1860, the National Association of Baseball Players boasted fifty clubs, several playing regular schedules and charging admission. This cartoon is thought to be the first time baseball was used as a metaphor for politics. Note that Lincoln is beardless. By February, 1861, when he left Springfield, Illinois, by train for the White House, he was fully bearded, having followed the advice of an eleven-year-old girl from Westfield, New York, who urged him to grow whiskers because "you would look a great deal better for your face is so thin."

ignorant of his bloody past and his even more bloody purposes, and they were outraged because the Virginians had hanged so earnest a reformer who was working for so righteous a cause. On the day of his execution, free-soil centers in the North tolled bells, fired guns, lowered flags, and held rallies. Some spoke of "Saint John" Brown, and the serene Ralph Waldo Emerson compared the new martyr-hero with Jesus. The gallows became a cross. E. C. Stedman wrote,

And Old Brown,
Osawatomie Brown,
May trouble you more than ever,
*   when you've nailed his coffin down!*

Election of 1860

Candidate	Popular Vote	Percentage of Popular Vote	Electoral Vote
Lincoln	1,865,593	39.79%	180 (every vote of the free states except for 3 of New Jersey's 7 votes)
Douglas	1,382,713	29.40	12 (only Missouri and 3 of New Jersey's 7 votes)
Breckinridge	848,356	18.20	72 (all the cotton states)
Bell	592,906	12.61	39 (Virginia, Kentucky, Tennessee)

The ghost of the martyred Brown would not be laid to rest.

The Disruption of the Democrats

Beyond question the presidential election of 1860 was the most fateful in American history. On it hung the issue of peace or civil war.

Deeply divided, the Democrats met in Charleston, South Carolina, with Douglas the leading candidate of the northern wing of the party. But the southern "fire-eaters" regarded him as a traitor, as a result of his unpopular stand on the Lecompton Constitution and the Freeport Doctrine. After a bitter wrangle over the platform, the delegates from most of the cotton states walked out. When the remainder could not scrape together the necessary two-thirds vote for Douglas, the entire body dissolved. The first tragic secession was the secession of southerners from the Democratic National Convention. Departure became habit-forming.

The Democrats tried again in Baltimore. This time the Douglas Democrats, chiefly from the North, were firmly in the saddle. Many of the cotton-state delegates again took a walk, and the rest of the convention enthusiastically nominated their hero. The platform came out squarely for popular sovereignty and, as a sop to the South, against obstruction of the Fugitive Slave Law by the states.

Angered southern Democrats promptly organized a rival convention in Baltimore, in which many of the northern states were unrepresented. They selected as their leader the stern-jawed vice president, John C. Breckinridge, a man of moderate views from the border

state of Kentucky. The platform favored the extension of slavery into the territories and the annexation of slave-populated Cuba.

A middle-of-the-road group, fearing for the Union, hastily organized the Constitutional Union party, sneered at as the "Do Nothing" or "Old Gentleman's" party. It consisted mainly of former Whigs and Know-Nothings, a veritable "gathering of graybeards." Desperately anxious to elect a compromise candidate, they met in Baltimore and nominated for the presidency John Bell of Tennessee. They went into battle ringing hand bells for Bell and waving handbills for "The Union, the Constitution, and the Enforcement of the Laws."

A Rail-Splitter Splits the Union

Elated Republicans, scenting victory in the breeze as their opponents split hopelessly, gathered in Chicago in a huge, boxlike wooden structure called the Wigwam. William H. Seward was by far the best known of the contenders. But his radical utterances, including his "irrepressible conflict" speech at Rochester in 1858, had ruined his prospects.* His numerous enemies coined the slogan "Success Rather Than Seward." Lincoln, the favorite son of Illinois, was definitely a "Mr. Second Best," but he was a stronger candidate because he had made fewer enemies. Overtaking Seward on the third ballot, he was nominated amid scenes of the wildest excitement.

---

*Seward had referred to an "irrepressible conflict" between slavery and freedom, though not necessarily a bloody one.

The Republican platform had a seductive appeal for just about every important nonsouthern group: for the free-soilers, nonextension of slavery; for the northern manufacturers, a protective tariff; for the immigrants, no abridgment of rights; for the Northwest, a Pacific railroad; for the West, internal improvements at federal expense; and for the farmers, free homesteads from the public domain. Alluring slogans included "Vote Yourselves a Farm" and "Land for the Landless."

Southern secessionists promptly served notice that the election of the "baboon" Lincoln—the "abolitionist" rail-splitter—would split the Union. In fact, "Honest Abe," though hating slavery, was no outright abolitionist. As late as February 1865, he was inclined to favor cash compensation to the owners of freed slaves. But for the time being, he saw fit, perhaps mistakenly, to issue no statements to quiet southern fears. He had already put himself on record, and fresh statements might stir up fresh antagonisms.

As the election campaign ground noisily forward, Lincoln enthusiasts staged roaring rallies and parades, complete with pitch-dripping torches and oilskin capes. They extolled "High Old Abe," the "Woodchopper of the West," and the "Little Giant Killer," while groaning dismally for "Poor Little Doug." Enthusiastic "Little Giants" and "Little Dougs" retorted with "We want a statesman, not a rail-splitter, as President." Douglas himself waged a vigorous speaking campaign, even in the South, and threatened to put the noose with his own hands around the neck of the first secessionist.

The returns, breathlessly awaited, proclaimed a sweeping victory for Lincoln (see the table on p. 425).

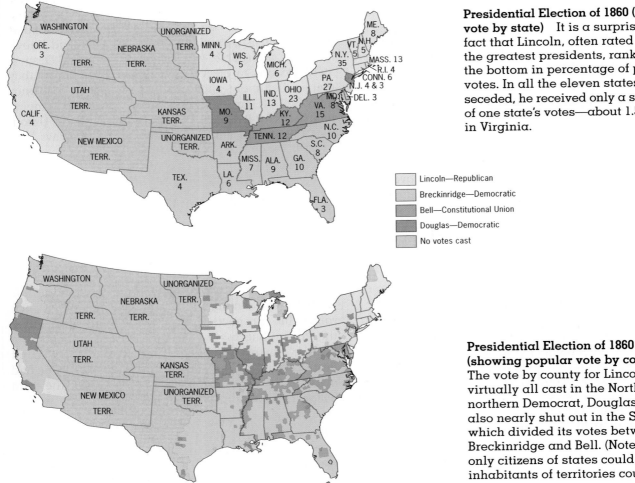

Presidential Election of 1860 (electoral vote by state) It is a surprising fact that Lincoln, often rated among the greatest presidents, ranks near the bottom in percentage of popular votes. In all the eleven states that seceded, he received only a scattering of one state's votes—about 1.5 percent in Virginia.

Lincoln—Republican
Breckinridge—Democratic
Bell—Constitutional Union
Douglas—Democratic
No votes cast

Presidential Election of 1860 (showing popular vote by county) The vote by county for Lincoln was virtually all cast in the North. The northern Democrat, Douglas, was also nearly shut out in the South, which divided its votes between Breckinridge and Bell. (Note that only citizens of states could vote; inhabitants of territories could not.)

The Electoral Upheaval of 1860

Awkward "Abe" Lincoln had run a curious race. To a greater degree than any other holder of the nation's highest office (except John Quincy Adams), he was a minority president. Sixty percent of the voters preferred some other candidate. He was also a sectional president, for in ten southern states, where he was not allowed on the ballot, he polled no popular votes. The election of 1860 was virtually two elections: one in the North, the other in the South. South Carolinians rejoiced over Lincoln's victory; they now had their excuse to secede. In winning the North, the "rail-splitter" had split off the South.

Douglas, though scraping together only twelve electoral votes, made an impressive showing. Boldly breaking with tradition, he campaigned energetically for himself. (Presidential candidates customarily maintained a dignified silence.) He drew important strength from all sections and ranked a fairly close second in the popular-vote column. In fact, the Douglas Democrats and the Breckinridge Democrats together amassed 365,476 more votes than did Lincoln.

A myth persists that if the Democrats had only united behind Douglas, they would have triumphed. Yet the cold figures tell a different story. Even if the "Little Giant" had received all the electoral votes cast for all three of Lincoln's opponents, the "rail-splitter" would have won, 169 to 134 instead of 180 to 123. Lincoln still would have carried the populous states of the North and the Northwest. On the other hand, if the Democrats had not broken up, they could have entered the campaign with higher enthusiasm and better organization and might have won.

Significantly, the verdict of the ballot box did not indicate a strong sentiment for secession. Breckinridge, while favoring the extension of slavery, was no disunionist. Although the candidate of the "fire-eaters," he polled fewer votes in the slave states than the combined strength of his opponents, Douglas and Bell. He even failed to carry his own Kentucky.

Yet the South, despite its electoral defeat, was not badly off. It still had a five-to-four majority on the Supreme Court. Although the Republicans had elected Lincoln, they controlled neither the Senate nor the House of Representatives. The federal government could not touch slavery in those states where it existed except by a constitutional amendment, and such an amendment could be defeated by one-fourth of the states. The fifteen slave states numbered nearly one-half of the total—a fact not fully appreciated by southern firebrands.

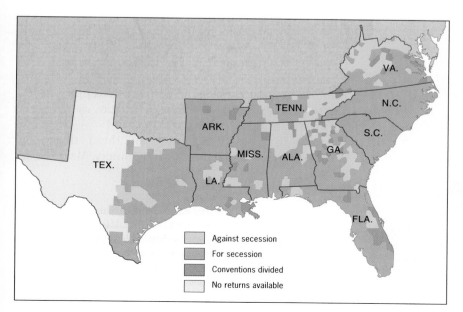

Southern Opposition to Secession, 1860–1861 (showing vote by county) This county vote shows the opposition of the antiplanter, antislavery mountain whites in the Appalachian region. There was also considerable resistance to secession in Texas, where Governor Sam Houston, who led the Unionists, was deposed by secessionists.

The state of South Carolina, leader of the secessionist movement, justified its retreat from the Union in its declaration of independence of December 1860:

"We affirm that the ends for which this [Federal] government was instituted have been defeated, and the government itself has been made destructive of them by the action of the non-slaveholding states. . . . For twenty five years this agitation has been steadily increasing, until it has now secured to its aid the power of the common government. Observing the forms of the constitution, a sectional party has found within that article establishing the executive department the means of subverting the constitution itself."

Three days after Lincoln's election, Horace Greeley's influential New York Tribune *(November 9, 1860) declared,*

"If the cotton States shall decide that they can do better out of the Union than in it, we insist on letting them go in peace. The right to secede may be a revolutionary one, but it exists nevertheless. . . . Whenever a considerable section of our Union shall deliberately resolve to go out, we shall resist all coercive measures designed to keep it in. We hope never to live in a republic, whereof one section is pinned to the residue by bayonets."

After the secession movement got well under way, Greeley's Tribune *changed its tune.*

The Secessionist Exodus

But a tragic chain reaction of secession now began to erupt. South Carolina, which had threatened to go out if the "sectional" Lincoln came in, was as good as its word. Four days after the election of the "Illinois baboon" by "insulting" majorities, its legislature voted unanimously to call a special convention. Meeting at Charleston in December 1860, the convention unanimously voted to secede. During the next six weeks, six other states of the lower South, though somewhat less united, followed the leader over the precipice: Alabama, Mississippi, Florida, Georgia, Louisiana, and Texas. Four more were to join them later, bringing the total to eleven.

With the eyes of destiny upon them, the seven seceders, formally meeting at Montgomery, Alabama, in

Jefferson Davis (1808–1889), President of the Confederacy   Faced with grave difficulties, he was probably as able a man for the position as the Confederacy could have chosen. Ironically, Davis and Lincoln had both sprung from the same Kentucky soil. The Davis family had moved south from Kentucky, the Lincoln family north.

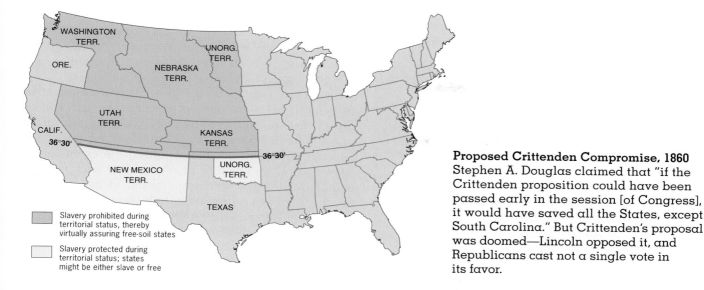

Proposed Crittenden Compromise, 1860
Stephen A. Douglas claimed that "if the Crittenden proposition could have been passed early in the session [of Congress], it would have saved all the States, except South Carolina." But Crittenden's proposal was doomed—Lincoln opposed it, and Republicans cast not a single vote in its favor.

February 1861, created a government known as the Confederate States of America. As their president they chose Jefferson Davis, a dignified and austere recent member of the U.S. Senate from Mississippi. He was a West Pointer and a former cabinet member with wide military and administrative experience; but he suffered from chronic ill health, as well as from a frustrated ambition to be a Napoleonic strategist.

The crisis, already critical enough, was deepened by the "lame duck"* interlude. Lincoln, although elected president in November 1860, could not take office until four months later, March 4, 1861. During this period of protracted uncertainty, when he was still a private citizen in Illinois, seven of the eleven deserting states pulled out of the Union.

President Buchanan, the aging incumbent, has been blamed for not holding the seceders in the Union by sheer force—for wringing his hands instead of secessionist necks. Never a vigorous man and habitually conservative, he was now nearly seventy, and although devoted to the Union, he was surrounded by prosouthern advisers. As an able lawyer wedded to the Constitution, he did not believe that the southern states could legally secede. Yet he could find no authority in the Constitution for stopping them with guns.

"Oh for one hour of Jackson!" cried the advocates of strong-arm tactics. But "Old Buck" Buchanan was not

"Old Hickory," and he was faced with a far more complex and serious problem. One important reason why he did not resort to force was that the tiny standing army of some fifteen thousand men, then widely scattered, was urgently needed to control the Indians in the West. Public opinion in the North, at that time, was far from willing to unsheathe the sword. Fighting would merely shatter all prospects of adjustment, and until the guns began to boom, there was still a flickering hope of reconciliation rather than a contested divorce. The weakness lay not so much in Buchanan as in the Constitution and in the Union itself. Ironically, when Lincoln became president in March, he essentially continued Buchanan's wait-and-see policy.

The Collapse of Compromise

Impending bloodshed spurred final and frantic attempts at compromise—in the American tradition. The most promising of these efforts was sponsored by Senator James Henry Crittenden of Kentucky, on whose shoulders had fallen the mantle of a fellow Kentuckian, Henry Clay.

The proposed Crittenden amendments to the Constitution were designed to appease the South. Slavery in the territories was to be prohibited north of 36° 30', but south of that line it was to be given federal protection in all territories existing or "hereafter to be

---

*The "lame duck" period was shortened to ten weeks in 1933 by the Twentieth Amendment (see the Appendix).

> One reason why the Crittenden Compromise failed in December 1860 was the prevalence of an attitude reflected in a private letter of Senator James Henry Hammond (1807–1864) of South Carolina on April 19:
>
> "I firmly believe that the slave-holding South is now the controlling power of the world—that no other power would face us in hostility. Cotton, rice, tobacco, and naval stores command the world; and we have sense to know it, and are sufficiently Teutonic to carry it out successfully. The North without us would be a motherless calf, bleating about, and die of mange and starvation."

acquired" (such as Cuba). Future states, north or south of 36° 30', could come into the Union with or without slavery, as they should choose. In short, the slavery supporters were to be guaranteed full rights in the southern territories, as long as they were territories, regardless of the wishes of the majority under popular sovereignty. Federal protection in a territory south of 36° 30' might conceivably, though improbably, turn the entire area permanently to slavery.

Lincoln flatly rejected the Crittenden scheme, which offered some slight prospect of success, and all hope of compromise evaporated. For this refusal he must bear a heavy responsibility. Yet he had been elected on a platform that opposed the extension of slavery, and he felt that as a matter of principle, he could not afford to yield, even though gains for slavery in the territories might be only temporary. Larger gains might come later in Cuba and Mexico. Crittenden's proposal, said Lincoln, "would amount to a perpetual covenant of war against every people, tribe, and state owning a foot of land between here and Tierra del Fuego."

As for the supposedly spineless "Old Fogy" Buchanan, how could he have prevented the Civil War by starting a civil war? No one has yet come up with a satisfactory answer. If he had used force on South Carolina in December 1860, the fighting almost certainly would have erupted three months sooner than it did, and under less favorable circumstances for the Union. The North would have appeared as the heavy-handed aggressor. And the crucial Border States, so vital to the Union, probably would have been driven into the arms of their "wayward sisters."

Farewell to Union

Secessionists who parted company with their sister states left for a number of avowed reasons, mostly relating in some way to slavery. They were alarmed by the inexorable tipping of the political balance against them—"the despotic majority of numbers." The "crime"

Jeff Davis on His Own Platform, or The Last "Act of Secession," c. 1861
This northern cartoon expressed the sentiment of many people north of the Mason-Dixon line that secession was a self-defeating move, doomed to failure.

> *Regarding the Civil War, the London* Times *(November 7, 1861) editorialized,*
>
> "The contest is really for empire on the side of the North, and for independence on that of the South, and in this respect we recognize an exact analogy between the North and the Government of George III, and the South and the Thirteen Revolted Provinces."

of the North, observed James Russell Lowell, was the census returns. Southerners were also dismayed by the triumph of the new sectional Republican party, which seemed to threaten their rights as a slaveholding minority. They were weary of free-soil criticism, abolitionist nagging, and northern interference, ranging from the Underground Railroad to John Brown's raid. "All we ask is to be let alone," declared Confederate president Jefferson Davis in an early message to his congress.

Many southerners supported secession because they felt sure that their departure would be unopposed, despite "Yankee yawp" to the contrary. They were confident that the clodhopping and codfishing Yankee would not or could not fight. They believed that northern manufacturers and bankers, so heavily dependent on southern cotton and markets, would not dare to cut their own economic throats with their own unionist swords. But should war come, the immense debt owed to northern creditors by the South—happy thought—could be promptly repudiated, as it later was.

Southern leaders regarded secession as a golden opportunity to cast aside their generations of "vassalage" to the North. An independent Dixieland could develop its own banking and shipping and trade directly with Europe. The low Tariff of 1857, passed largely by southern votes, was not in itself menacing. But who could tell when the "greedy" Republicans would win control of Congress and drive through their own oppressive protective tariff? For decades this fundamental friction had pitted the North, with its manufacturing plants, against the South, with its agricultural exports.

Worldwide impulses of nationalism—then stirring in Italy, Germany, Poland, and elsewhere—were fermenting in the South. This huge area, with its distinctive culture, was not so much a section as a subnation. It could not view with complacency the possibility of being lorded over, then or later, by what it regarded as a hostile nation of northerners.

The principles of self-determination—of the Declaration of Independence—seemed to many southerners to apply perfectly to them. Few, if any, of the seceders felt that they were doing anything wrong or immoral. The thirteen original states had voluntarily entered the Union, and now seven—ultimately eleven—southern states were voluntarily withdrawing from it.

Historical parallels ran even deeper. In 1776 thirteen American colonies, led by the rebel George Washington, had seceded from the British Empire by throwing off the yoke of King George III. In 1860–1861, eleven American states, led by the rebel Jefferson Davis, were seceding from the Union by throwing off the yoke of "King" Abraham Lincoln. With that burden gone, the South was confident that it could work out its own peculiar destiny more quietly, happily, and prosperously.

> *James Russell Lowell (1819–1891), the northern poet and essayist, wrote in the* Atlantic Monthly *shortly after the secessionist movement began,*
>
> "The fault of the free States in the eyes of the South is not one that can be atoned for by any yielding of special points here and there. Their offense is that they are free, and that their habits and prepossessions are those of freedom. Their crime is the census of 1860. Their increase in numbers, wealth, and power is a standing aggression. It would not be enough to please the Southern States that we should stop asking them to abolish slavery: what they demand of us is nothing less than that we should abolish the spirit of the age. Our very thoughts are a menace."

Chronology

1852   Harriet Beecher Stowe publishes *Uncle Tom's Cabin*

1854   Kansas-Nebraska Act
Republican party forms

1856   Buchanan defeats Frémont and Fillmore for presidency
Sumner beaten by Brooks in Senate chamber
Brown's Pottawatomie Massacre

1856–1860   Civil war in "bleeding Kansas"

1857   *Dred Scott* decision
Lecompton Constitution rejected

1857   Panic of 1857
Tariff of 1857
Hinton R. Helper publishes *The Impending Crisis of the South*

1858   Lincoln-Douglas debates

1859   Brown raids Harpers Ferry

1860   Lincoln wins four-way race for presidency
South Carolina secedes from the Union
Crittenden Compromise fails

1861   Seven seceding states form Confederate States of America

VARYING VIEWPOINTS

The Civil War: Repressible or Irrepressible?

Few topics have generated as much controversy among American historians as the causes of the Civil War. The very names employed to describe the conflict—notably "Civil War" or "War Between the States" or even "War for Southern Independence"—reveal much about the various authors' points of view. Interpretations of the great conflict have naturally differed according to section and have been charged with both emotional and moral fervor. Yet despite long and keen interest in the origins of the conflict, the causes of the Civil War remain as passionately debated today as they were a century ago.

The so-called Nationalist School of the late nineteenth century, typified in the work of historian James Ford Rhodes, claimed that slavery caused the Civil War. Defending the necessity and inevitability of the war, these northern-oriented historians credited the conflict with ending slavery and preserving the Union. But in the early twentieth century, progressive historians, led by Charles and Mary Beard, presented a more skeptical interpretation. The Beards argued that the war was not fought over slavery per se, but rather was a deeply rooted economic struggle between an industrial North and an agricultural South. Anointing the Civil War the "Second American Revolution," the Beards claimed that the war precipitated vast changes in American class relations and shifted the political balance of power by magnifying the influence of business magnates and industrialists while destroying the plantation aristocracy of the South.

Shaken by the disappointing results of World War I, a new wave of historians argued that the Civil War, too, had actually been a big mistake. Rejecting the nationalist interpretation that the clash was inevitable, James G. Randall and Avery Craven asserted that the war had been a "repressible conflict." Neither slavery nor the economic differences between North and South were sufficient causes for war. Instead Craven and others attributed the bloody confrontation to the breakdown of political institutions, the passion of overzealous reformers, and the ineptitude of a blundering generation of political leaders.

Following the Second World War, however, a neonationalist view regained authority, echoing the earlier views of Rhodes in depicting the Civil War as an unavoidable conflict between two societies, one slave and one free. For Allan Nevins and David M. Potter, irreconcilable differences in morality, politics, culture, social values, and economies increasingly eroded the ties between the sections and inexorably set the United States on the road to Civil War.

Eric Foner and Eugene Genovese have emphasized each section's nearly paranoid fear that the survival of its distinctive way of life was threatened by the expansion of the other section. In *Free Soil, Free Labor, Free Men* (1970), Foner emphasized that most northerners detested slavery not because it enslaved blacks, but because its existence—and particularly its rapid extension—threatened the position of free white laborers. This "free labor ideology" increasingly became the foundation stone upon which the North claimed its superiority over the South. Eugene Genovese has argued that the South felt similarly endangered. Convinced that the southern labor system was more humane than the northern factory system, southerners saw northern designs to destroy their way of life lurking at every turn—and every territorial battle.

Some historians have placed party politics at the center of their explanations for the war. For them, no event was more consequential than the breakdown of the Jacksonian party system. When the slavery issue tore apart both the Democratic and the Whig parties, the last ligaments binding the nation together were snapped, and the war inevitably came.

More recently, historians of the "Ethnocultural School," especially Michael Holt, have acknowledged the significance of the collapse of the established parties, but have offered a different analysis of how that breakdown led to war. They note that the two great national parties before the 1850s focused attention on issues such as the tariff, banking, and internal improvements, thereby muting sectional differences over slavery. According to this argument, the erosion of the traditional party system is blamed not on growing differences over slavery, but on a temporary *consensus* between the two parties in the 1850s on almost all national issues *other than* slavery. In this peculiar political atmosphere, the slavery issue rose to the fore, encouraging the emergence of Republicans in the North and secessionists in the South. In the absence of regular, national, two-party conflict over economic issues, purely regional parties (like the Republicans) coalesced. They identified their opponents not simply as competitors for power but as threats to their way of life, even to the life of the Republic itself.

For further reading, see the Appendix. For web resources, go to **http://college.hmco.com**.

20

Girding for War: The North and the South

1861–1865

I CONSIDER THE CENTRAL IDEA PERVADING THIS STRUGGLE IS THE NECESSITY THAT IS UPON US, OF PROVING THAT POPULAR GOVERNMENT IS NOT AN ABSURDITY. WE MUST SETTLE THIS QUESTION NOW, WHETHER IN A FREE GOVERNMENT THE MINORITY HAVE THE RIGHT TO BREAK UP THE GOVERNMENT WHENEVER THEY CHOOSE. IF WE FAIL IT WILL GO FAR TO PROVE THE INCAPABILITY OF THE PEOPLE TO GOVERN THEMSELVES.

ABRAHAM LINCOLN, MAY 7, 1861

Abraham Lincoln solemnly took the presidential oath of office on March 4, 1861, after having slipped into Washington at night, partially disguised to thwart assassins. He thus became president not of the *United* States of America, but of the dis-United States of America. Seven had already departed; eight more teetered on the edge. The girders of the unfinished Capitol dome loomed nakedly in the background, as if to symbolize the imperfect state of the Union. Before the nation was restored—and the slaves freed at last—the American people would endure four years of anguish and bloodshed, and Lincoln would face tortuous trials of leadership such as have been visited upon few presidents.

The Menace of Secession

Lincoln's inaugural address was firm yet conciliatory: there would be no conflict unless the South provoked it. Secession, the president declared, was wholly impractical, because "physically speaking, we cannot separate."

Here Lincoln put his finger on a profound geographical truth. The North and South were Siamese twins, bound inseparably together. If they had been divided by the Pyrenees Mountains or the Danube River, a sectional divorce might have been more feasible. But the Appalachian Mountains and the mighty Mississippi River both ran the wrong way.

Uncontested secession would create new controversies. What share of the national debt should the South be forced to take with it? What portion of the jointly held federal territories, if any, should the Confederate states be allotted—areas so largely won with Southern blood? How would the fugitive-slave issue be resolved? The Underground Railroad would certainly redouble its activity, and it would have to transport its passengers only across the Ohio River, not all the way to Canada. Was it conceivable that all such problems could have been solved without ugly armed clashes?

A *united* United States had hitherto been the paramount republic in the Western Hemisphere. If this powerful democracy should break into two hostile parts, the European nations would be delighted. They could gleefully transplant to America their ancient concept of the balance of power. Playing the no-less-ancient game of divide and conquer, they could incite one snarling fragment of the dis-United States against the other. The colonies of the European powers in the New World, notably those of Britain, would thus be made safer against the rapacious Yankees. And European imperialists, with no unified republic to stand across their path, could more easily defy the Monroe Doctrine and seize territory in the Americas.

South Carolina Assails Fort Sumter

The issue of the divided Union came to a head over the matter of federal forts in the South. As the seceding states left, they had seized the United States' arsenals, mints, and other public property within their borders. When Lincoln took office, only two significant forts in the South still flew the Stars and Stripes. The more important of the pair was square-walled Fort Sumter, in Charleston harbor, with fewer than a hundred men.

Ominously, the choices presented to Lincoln by Fort Sumter were all bad. This stronghold had provisions that would last only a few weeks—until the middle of April 1861. If no supplies were forthcoming, its commander would have to surrender without firing a shot. Lincoln, quite understandably, did not feel that such a weak-kneed course squared with his obligation to protect federal property. But if he sent reinforcements, the South Carolinians would undoubtedly fight back; they could not tolerate a federal fort blocking the mouth of their most important Atlantic seaport.

After agonizing indecision, Lincoln adopted a middle-of-the-road solution. He notified the South Carolinians

Secretary of State William H. Seward (1801–1872) entertained the dangerous idea that if the North picked a fight with one or more European nations, the South would once more rally around the flag. On April Fools' Day, 1861, he submitted to Lincoln a memorandum:

"I would demand explanations from Spain and France, categorically, at once. I would seek explanations from Great Britain and Russia. . . . And, if satisfactory explanations are not received from Spain and France . . . would convene Congress and declare war against them."

Lincoln quietly but firmly quashed Seward's scheme.

that an expedition would be sent to *provision* the garrison, though not to *reinforce* it. He promised "no effort to throw in men, arms, and ammunition." But to Southern eyes "provision" still spelled "reinforcement."

A Union naval force was next started on its way to Fort Sumter—a move that the South regarded as an act of aggression. On April 12, 1861, the cannon of the Carolinians opened fire on the fort, while crowds in Charleston applauded and waved handkerchiefs. After a thirty-four-hour bombardment, which took no lives, the dazed garrison surrendered.

The shelling of the fort electrified the North, which at once responded with cries of "Remember Fort Sumter" and "Save the Union." Hitherto countless Northerners had been saying that if the Southern states wanted to go, they should not be pinned to the rest of the nation with bayonets. "Wayward sisters, depart in peace" was a common sentiment, expressed even by the commander of the army, war hero General Winfield Scott, now so feeble at seventy-five that he had to be boosted onto his horse.

But the assault on Fort Sumter provoked the North to a fighting pitch: the fort was lost, but the Union was saved. Lincoln had turned a tactical defeat into a calculated victory. Southerners had wantonly fired upon the glorious Stars and Stripes, and honor demanded an

Fort Sumter, South Carolina, April, 1861 The interior of Fort Sumter in Charleston Harbor shortly after the Union's beleaguered force surrendered and fled. Confederate soldiers posed in front of the fort's bombarded walls while their flag flew victoriously above them

armed response. Lincoln promptly (April 15) issued a call to the states for seventy-five thousand militiamen, and volunteers sprang to the colors in such enthusiastic numbers that many were turned away—a mistake that was not often repeated. On April 19 and 27, the president proclaimed a leaky blockade of Southern seaports.

The call for troops, in turn, aroused the South much as the attack on Fort Sumter had aroused the North. Lincoln was now waging war—from the Southern view an aggressive war—on the Confederacy. Virginia, Arkansas, and Tennessee, all of which had earlier voted down secession, reluctantly joined their embattled sister states, as did North Carolina. Thus the seven states became eleven as the "submissionists" and "Union shriekers" were overcome. Richmond, Virginia, replaced Montgomery, Alabama, as the Confederate capital—too near Washington for strategic comfort on either side.

Brothers' Blood and Border Blood

The only slave states left were the crucial Border States. This group consisted of Missouri, Kentucky, Maryland, Delaware, and later West Virginia—the "mountain white" area that somewhat illegally tore itself from the side of Virginia in mid-1861. If the North had fired the first shot, some or all of these doubtful states probably would have seceded, and the South might well have

succeeded. The border group actually contained a white population more than half that of the entire Confederacy. Maryland, Kentucky, and Missouri would almost double the manufacturing capacity of the South and increase by nearly half its supply of horses and mules. The strategic prize of the Ohio River flowed along the northern border of Kentucky and West Virginia. Two of its navigable tributaries, the Cumberland and Tennessee Rivers, penetrated deep into the heart of Dixie, where much of the Confederacy's grain, gunpowder,

Abraham Lincoln (1809–1865), Kentucky-born like Jefferson Davis, was aware of Kentucky's crucial importance. In September 1861 he remarked,

"I think to lose Kentucky is nearly the same as to lose the whole game. Kentucky gone, we cannot hold Missouri, nor, I think, Maryland. These all against us, and the job on our hands is too large for us. We would as well consent to separation at once, including the surrender of this capital [Washington]."

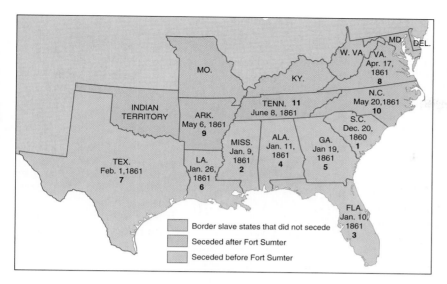

Seceding States (with dates and order of secession)   Note the long interval—nearly six months—between the secession of South Carolina, the first state to go, and that of Tennessee, the last state to leave the Union. These six months were a time of terrible trial for moderate Southerners. When a Georgia statesman pleaded for restraint and negotiations with Washington, he was rebuffed with the cry, "Throw the bloody spear into this den of incendiaries!"

and iron was produced. Small wonder that Lincoln reportedly said he *hoped* to have God on his side, but he *had* to have Kentucky.

In dealing with the Border States, President Lincoln did not rely solely on moral suasion but successfully used methods of dubious legality. In Maryland he declared martial law where needed and sent in troops, because this state threatened to cut off Washington from the North. Lincoln also deployed Union soldiers in western Virginia and notably in Missouri, where they fought beside Unionists in a local civil war within the larger Civil War.

Any official statement of the North's war aims was profoundly influenced by the teetering Border States. At the very outset, Lincoln was obliged to declare publicly that he was not fighting to free the blacks. An antislavery declaration would no doubt have driven the Border States into the welcoming arms of the South. An antislavery war was also extremely unpopular in the so-called Butternut region of southern Ohio, Indiana, and Illinois. That area had been settled largely by Southerners who had carried their racial prejudices with them when they crossed the Ohio River (see "Makers of America: Settlers of the Old Northwest," pp. 244–245). It was to be a hotbed of pro-Southern sentiment throughout the war. Sensitive to this delicate political calculus, Lincoln insisted repeatedly—even though undercutting his moral high ground—that his paramount purpose was to save the Union at all costs. Thus the war began not as one between slave soil and free soil, but one for the Union—with slave-

holders on both sides and many proslavery sympathizers in the North.

Slavery also colored the character of the war in the West. In Indian Territory (present-day Oklahoma), most of the Five Civilized Tribes—the Cherokees, Creeks, Choctaws, Chickasaws, and Seminoles—sided with the Confederacy. Some of these Indians, notably the Cherokees, owned slaves and thus felt themselves to be making common cause with the slaveowning South. To secure their loyalty, the Confederate government agreed to take over federal payments to the tribes and invited the Native Americans to send delegates to the Confederate congress. In return the tribes supplied troops to the Confederate army. Meanwhile, a rival faction of Cherokees and most of the Plains Indians sided with the

Lincoln wrote to the antislavery editor Horace Greeley in August 1862, even as he was about to announce the Emancipation Proclamation,

"If I could save the Union without freeing any slave, I would do it; and if I could save it by freeing all the slaves, I would do it; and if I could do it by freeing some and leaving others alone, I would also do that."

Union, only to be rewarded after the war with a relentless military campaign to herd them onto reservations or into oblivion.

Unhappily, the conflict between "Billy Yank" and "Johnny Reb" was a brothers' war (see "Makers of America: Billy Yank and Johnny Reb," pp. 240–241). There were many Northern volunteers from the Southern states and many Southern volunteers from the Northern states. The "mountain whites" of the South sent north some 50,000 men, and the loyal slave states contributed some 300,000 soldiers to the Union. In many a family of the Border States, one brother rode north to fight with the Blue, another south to fight with the Gray. Senator Crittenden of Kentucky, who fathered the abortive Crittenden Compromise, fathered two sons: one became a general in the Union army, the other a general in the Confederate army. Lincoln's own Kentucky-born wife had four brothers who fought for the Confederacy.

The Balance of Forces

When war broke out, the South seemed to have great advantages. The Confederacy could fight defensively behind interior lines. The North had to invade the vast territory of the Confederacy, conquer it, and drag it bodily back into the Union. In fact, the South did not have to win the war in order to win its independence. If it merely fought the invaders to a draw and stood firm, Confederate independence would be won. Fighting on their own soil for self-determination and preservation of their way of life, Southerners at first enjoyed an advantage in morale as well.

Militarily, the South from the opening volleys of the war had the most talented officers. Most conspicuous among a dozen or so first-rate commanders was gray-haired General Robert E. Lee, whose knightly bearing and chivalric sense of honor embodied the Southern ideal. Lincoln had unofficially offered him command of the Northern armies, but when Virginia seceded, Lee felt honor-bound to go with his native state. Lee's chief lieutenant for much of the war was black-bearded Thomas J. ("Stonewall") Jackson, a gifted tactical theorist and a master of speed and deception.

Besides their brilliant leaders, ordinary Southerners were also bred to fight. Accustomed to managing horses and bearing arms from boyhood, they made excellent cavalrymen and foot soldiers. Their high-pitched "rebel yell" ("yeeeahhh") was designed to strike terror into the hearts of fuzz-chinned Yankee recruits. "There is nothing

Friendly Enemies   The man on the right is George Armstrong Custer. The youngest general in the Union army, this brilliant young officer survived the Civil War only to lose his life and that of every soldier under his command to Sioux warriors at the Battle of the Little Bighorn in 1876—"Custer's Last Stand." The man on the left is a Southern soldier and prisoner of war. He and Custer had been classmates at West Point.

like it on this side of the infernal region," one Northern soldier declared. "The peculiar corkscrew sensation that it sends down your backbone can never be told. You have to feel it."

As one immense farm, the South seemed to be handicapped by the scarcity of factories. Yet by seizing federal weapons, running Union blockades, and developing their own ironworks, Southerners managed to obtain sufficient weaponry. "Yankee ingenuity" was not confined to Yankees.

Nevertheless, as the war dragged on, grave shortages of shoes, uniforms, and blankets disabled the South. Even with immense stores of food on Southern farms, civilians and soldiers often went hungry because of supply problems. "Forward, men! They have cheese in their haversacks," cried one Southern officer as he

The Technology of War   One of the new machines of destruction that made the Civil War the first mechanized war, this eight-and-a-half ton federal mortar sat on a railroad flatcar in Petersburg, Virginia, ready to hurl two-hundred-pound missiles as far as two and a half miles. This powerful artillery piece rode on the tracks of a captured Southern railroad—itself another artifact of modern technology that figured heavily in the war. Of the 31,256 miles of railroad track in the United States in 1861, less than 30 percent, or 9,283 miles, were in the Confederate states, soon reduced by Union capture and destruction to 6,000 miles. The Confederate government's failure to understand the military importance of railroads contributed substantially to its defeat.

attacked the Yankees. Much of the hunger was caused by a breakdown of the South's rickety transportation system, especially where the railroad tracks were cut or destroyed by the Yankee invaders.

The economy was the greatest Southern weakness; it was the North's greatest strength. The North was not only a huge farm but a sprawling factory as well.

Yankees boasted about three-fourths of the nation's wealth, including three-fourths of the thirty thousand miles of railroads.

The North also controlled the sea. With its vastly superior navy, it established a blockade that, though a sieve at first, soon choked off Southern supplies and eventually shattered Southern morale. Its sea power

Billy Yank and Johnny Reb

Prussian general Helmuth von Moltke (1800–1891) allegedly remarked that the American Civil War was merely a contest waged by "armed mobs." Whether he meant it or not, the Prussian's famous insult actually contains an important insight. Unlike the professional standing armies of nineteenth-century Europe, Civil War armies were overwhelmingly amateur and volunteer. Taken from all walks of life, citizen-soldiers gave the Civil War drama its uniquely plebeian cast.

With 2 million men in Union blue and 1 million men in Confederate gray, Civil War soldiers represented a vast cross section of American society. (At nearly 10 percent of the 1860 population, the same rate of mobilization would amount to more than 27 million troops today.) Most soldiers had been farmers or farm laborers. Poor unskilled workers, despite vehement antidraft rhetoric to the contrary, were actually underrepresented. Most troops were native-born, but immigrants did serve in rough proportion to their presence in the general population. Black fighting men accounted for about 10 percent of Union enlistments by war's end (see

A Union Private

"Blacks Battle Bondage," pp. 462–463). Perhaps one-third of the soldiers were married. Nearly 40 percent were under twenty-two years of age at the time of enlistment.

Inheritors of the values of Jacksonian mass democracy and Victorian sentiments, Civil War citizen-soldiers brought strong ideological commitments to the struggle. Neither army regulars nor reluctant conscripts, these men fought in the name of country, duty, honor, manhood, and righteousness. Though enemies, Union and Confederate soldiers shared a common commitment to the patriotic "spirit of '76" and the cause of liberty, independence, and republican government. A man's moral obligation to defend his country and preserve his personal reputation provided added motivation. Many interpreted the war as a religious crusade. In short, convictions, not coercion, created Civil War armies.

Despite their similarities, "Billy Yank" (the ordinary Union soldier) and "Johnny Reb" (the typical Confederate) were not necessarily cut from the same cloth. Both armies reflected the societies from which they came. Billy Yank tended to be more literate, intellectual, practical, and efficient, while Johnny Reb was often more jocular, emotional, religious, and personally concerned about the war. Defense of home and hearth meant more to Confederate troops, for the simple reason that most of the fighting

Members of the Third New Hampshire Regiment's Band in Quarters, Hilton Head, South Carolina, March–April 1865 Band members played, lived, and ate together. Although companies ordinarily had assigned cooks, sometimes other soldiers had to fill in. One band member wrote home, "Wish you could have seen our supper last night," but then added wistfully, "though I believe I should rather have been where I could [have] seen or rather have partaken of yours."

occurred on Southern soil. Above all else, the men in gray maintained a distinctive rural individualism and homegrown disrespect for authority. Their counterparts in blue, often familiar with the strict regimen of Northern cities and factories, adapted more quickly to army discipline.

One aspect of soldiering Johnny Reb and Billy Yank shared was the dull routine of camp life. For all its promises of adventure, the life of a Civil War soldier could be downright boring and unpleasant. Men spent fifty days in camp for every one in battle. Reveille, roll call, and drill were daily chores. A soldier's first concern was usually his stomach, even when pork ("sowbelly"), beef ("salt horse"), coffee, and bread (or its

A Confederate Soldier

unwelcome substitute, "hardtack") were in abundance. Food shortages plagued both armies, especially the Confederates as the war progressed. Uniforms deteriorated from "finery" to "tatters," as did moral standards. Gambling, drinking, stealing, swearing, and Sabbath-breaking proliferated; even widespread religious revivals could not keep up.

The gravest hardship of all, however, was disease. Germs—especially camp and campaign maladies like dysentery, diarrhea, typhoid, and malaria—took twice as many lives as bullets. By modern standards, the mortality rates of wounded soldiers were appallingly high. (World War II marked the first time in American warfare when more soldiers died from combat wounds than from sickness and disease.) Without proper medical understanding of sterilization or sanitation, the risk of sepsis (bacterial infection) accompanied every wound. Head, chest, and stomach wounds were usually considered fatal; arm and leg injuries often resulted in amputation. Only the presence of nurses made life in field hospitals tolerable. Overcoming the vocal hostility of male army doctors and the filth, stench, and agony of these hospitals, some twenty thousand women volunteered as nurses during the war. Working with the maimed and the dying was never pleasant, but female nurses earned the respect of countless wounded soldiers for their dedicated service.

Yet for all its brutality, not even the field hospital could match the traumatic experience of combat. Tension mounted in the final moments before battle, as officers strove to maintain close-order ranks in the face of harrowing enemy gunfire. Artillery shells blanketed the battlefield with a smoky haze. Bullets zinged through the air like a driving rain. Once soldiers joined the action, a rush of adrenaline could transform frightened civilians into frenzied and ferocious fighters. First-timers likened the experience to "seeing the elephant" (an antebellum expression of awe). One sight of mangled limbs or one whiff of decaying flesh was often enough to push men over the edge. "Even when I sleep," a Massachusetts soldier moaned, "I hear the whistling of the shells and the shouts and groans, and to sum it up in two [sic] words it is *horrible*." Given the extraordinary stress of battle, many men avoided combat as much as they could.

Shell-shocked and weary, most soldiers returned home from the war utterly transformed. For nearly a decade and a half, silence reigned, as veterans and civilians entered into a tacit agreement to put the ordeal behind them. By 1880 interest revived in the war, and a new battle over its proper meaning commenced. Ignoring the conflict's original significance as a moral victory for slave emancipation, many Americans embraced a new reconciliationist and white supremacist script. In the interest of sectional harmony and national prosperity, Northerners abandoned earlier commitments to black rights. A reunion of sections spelled a division of races. Casting aside their original ideological convictions, many Americans came to regard the conflict as a tragic brothers' war meaningful only for its show of martial valor. Principles that had compelled 3 million men to enlist and caused 620,000 to die were largely forgotten. Instead a sentimental, sanitized, and whitened version of the Civil War became commonplace by the late nineteenth century. Von Moltke's "armed mobs" came to be remembered as the noblest of knights.

Leg Amputation on the Battlefields of Virginia A surgeon wearing hat and sword amputates the leg of a wounded soldier, while an anesthetist (facing the camera) holds a sponge dipped in chloroform over the patient's nose. A surgical assistant ties a tourniquet to stem the flows of blood. Other soldiers, dressed in Zouave uniforms from North Africa popular among some Northern and Southern regiments, watch closely, likely aware of the dangers accompanying such crude surgery. An estimated 30 percent of amputees died from postoperative complications, most often infection.

Manufacturing by Sections, 1860

Section	Number of Establishments	Capital Invested	Average Number of Laborers	Annual Value of Products	Percentage of Total Value
New England	20,671	$ 257,477,783	391,836	$ 468,599,287	24.8%
Middle states	53,387	435,061,964	546,243	802,338,392	42.5
Western states	36,785	194,212,543	209,909	384,606,530	20.4
Southern states	20,631	95,975,185	110,721	155,531,281	8.3
Pacific states	8,777	23,380,334	50,204	71,229,989	3.8
Territories	282	3,747,906	2,333	3,556,197	0.2
TOTAL	140,533	$1,009,855,715	1,311,246	$1,885,861,676	

Recruiting Immigrants for the Union Army
This poster in several languages appeals to immigrants to enlist. Immigrant manpower provided the Union with both industrial and military muscle.

also enabled the North to exchange huge quantities of grain for munitions and supplies from Europe, thus adding the output from the factories of Europe to its own.

The Union also enjoyed a much larger reserve of manpower. The loyal states had a population of some 22 million; the seceding states had 9 million people, including about 3.5 million slaves. Adding to the North's overwhelming supply of soldiery were ever-more immigrants from Europe, who continued to pour into the North even during the war (see the table on p. 443). Over 800,000 newcomers arrived between 1861 and 1865, most of them British, Irish, and German. Large numbers of them were induced to enlist in the Union army. Altogether about one-fifth of the Union forces were foreign-born, and in some units military commands were given in four different languages.

Whether immigrant or native, ordinary Northern boys were much less prepared than their Southern counterparts for military life. Yet the Northern "clodhoppers" and "shopkeepers" eventually adjusted themselves to soldiering and became known for their discipline and determination.

The American minister to Britain wrote,
"The great body of the aristocracy and the commercial classes are anxious to see the United States go to pieces [but] the middle and lower class sympathise with us [because they] see in the convulsion in America an era in the history of the world, out of which must come in the end a general recognition of the right of mankind to the produce of their labor and the pursuit of happiness."

Immigration to United States, 1860–1866

Year	Total	Britain	Ireland	Germany	All Others
1860	153,640	29,737	48,637	54,491	20,775
1861	91,918	19,675	23,797	31,661	16,785
1862	91,985	24,639	23,351	27,529	16,466
1863	176,282	66,882	55,916	33,162	20,322
1864	193,418	53,428	63,523	57,276	19,191
1865*	248,120	82,465	29,772	83,424	52,459
1866	318,568	94,924	36,690	115,892	71,062

*Only the first three months of 1865 were war months.

The North was much less fortunate in its higher commanders. Lincoln was forced to use a costly trial-and-error method to sort out effective leaders from the many incompetent political officers, until he finally uncovered a general, Ulysses Simpson Grant, who was determined to slog his way to victory at whatever cost in life and limb.

In the long run, as the Northern strengths were brought to bear, they outweighed those of the South. But when the war began, the chances for Southern independence were unusually favorable—certainly better than the prospects for success of the thirteen colonies in 1776. The turn of a few events could easily have produced a different outcome.

The might-have-beens are fascinating. *If* the Border States had seceded, *if* the uncertain states of the upper Mississippi Valley had turned against the Union, *if* a wave of Northern defeatism had demanded an armistice, and *if* Britain and/or France had broken the Union's naval blockade of Southern ports, the South might well have won. All of these possibilities almost became realities, but none of them actually occurred, and lacking their impetus, the South could not hope to win.

Dethroning King Cotton

Successful revolutions, including the American Revolution of 1776, have generally succeeded because of foreign intervention. The South counted on it, did not get it, and lost. Of all the Confederacy's potential assets, none counted more weightily than the prospect of foreign intervention. Europe's ruling classes were openly sympathetic to the Confederate cause. They had long abhorred the incendiary example of the American democratic experiment, and they cherished a kind of fellow-feeling for the South's semifeudal, aristocratic social order.

In contrast, the masses of workingpeople in Britain, and to some extent in France, were pulling and praying for the North. Many of them had read *Uncle Tom's Cabin,* and they sensed that the war—though at the outset officially fought only over the question of union—might extinguish slavery if the North emerged victorious. The common folk of Britain could not yet cast the ballot, but they could cast the brick. Their certain hostility to any official intervention on behalf of the South evidently had a sobering effect on the British government. Thus the dead hands of Uncle Tom helped Uncle Sam by restraining the British and French ironclads from piercing the Union blockade. Yet the fact remained that British textile mills depended on the American South for 75 percent of their cotton supplies. Wouldn't silent looms force London to speak? Humanitarian sympathies aside, Southerners counted on hard economic need to bring Britain to their aid. Why did King Cotton fail them?

He failed in part because he had been so lavishly productive in the immediate prewar years of 1857–1860. Enormous exports of cotton in those years had piled up surpluses in British warehouses. When the shooting started in 1861, British manufacturers had on hand a hefty oversupply of fiber. The real pinch did not come until about a year and a half later, when thousands of hungry operatives were thrown out of work. But by this time Lincoln had announced his slave-emancipation policy, and the "wage slaves" of Britain were not going to demand a war to defend the slaveowners of the South.

The Confederacy Gets No Help from Europe Despite repeated pleas from Confederate diplomats for recognition and aid, both France and England refrained from intervening in the American conflict—not least because of the Union's demonstrated strength on the battlefield and its economic importance to European importers.

The direst effects of the "cotton famine" in Britain were relieved in several ways. Hunger among unemployed workers was partially eased when certain kind-hearted Americans sent over several cargoes of foodstuffs. As Union armies penetrated the South, they captured or bought considerable supplies of cotton and shipped them to Britain; the Confederates also ran a limited quantity through the blockade. In addition, the cotton growers of Egypt and India, responding to high prices, increased their output. Finally, booming war industries in England, which supplied both the North and the South, relieved unemployment.

King Wheat and King Corn—the monarchs of Northern agriculture—proved to be more potent potentates than King Cotton. During these war years, the North, blessed with ideal weather, produced bountiful crops of grain and harvested them with McCormick's mechanical reaper. In the same period, the British suffered a series of bad harvests. They were forced to import huge quantities of grain from America, which happened to have the cheapest and most abundant supply. If the British had broken the blockade to gain cotton, they would have provoked the North to war and would have lost this precious granary. Unemployment for some seemed better than hunger for all. Hence one Yankee journal could exult,

> Wave the stars and stripes high o'er us,
> Let every freeman sing . . .
> Old King Cotton's dead and buried;
>   brave young Corn is King.

As the Civil War neared the end of its third year, the London Times *(January 7, 1864) could boast,*

"We are as busy, as rich, and as fortunate in our trade as if the American war had never broken out, and our trade with the States had never been disturbed. Cotton was no King, notwithstanding the prerogatives which had been loudly claimed for him."

The Decisiveness of Diplomacy

America's diplomatic front has seldom been so critical as during the Civil War. The South never wholly abandoned its dream of foreign intervention, and Europe's rulers schemed to take advantage of America's distress.

The first major crisis with Britain came over the *Trent* affair, late in 1861. A Union warship cruising on the high seas north of Cuba stopped a British mail steamer, the *Trent*, and forcibly removed two Confederate diplomats bound for Europe.

Britons were outraged: upstart Yankees could not so boldly offend the Mistress of the Seas. War preparations buzzed, and red-coated troops embarked for Canada, with bands blaring "I Wish I Was in Dixie." The London Foreign Office prepared an ultimatum demanding surrender of the prisoners and an apology. But luckily, slow communications gave passions on both sides a chance to cool. Lincoln came to see the *Trent* prisoners as "white elephants" and reluctantly released them. "One war at a time," he reportedly said.

Another major crisis in Anglo-American relations arose over the unneutral building in Britain of Confederate commerce-raiders, notably the *Alabama*. These vessels were not warships within the meaning of loopholed British law because they left their shipyards unarmed and picked up their guns elsewhere. The *Alabama* escaped in 1862 to the Portuguese Azores, and there took on weapons and a crew from two British ships that followed it. Although flying the Confederate flag and officered by Confederates, it was manned by Britons and never entered a Confederate port. Britain was thus the chief naval base of the Confederacy.

The *Alabama* lighted the skies from Europe to the Far East with the burning hulks of Yankee merchantmen. All told, this "British pirate" captured over sixty vessels. Competing British shippers were delighted, while an angered North had to divert naval strength from its blockade for wild-goose chases. The barnacled *Alabama* finally accepted a challenge from a stronger

Union cruiser off the coast of France in 1864 and was quickly destroyed.

The *Alabama* was beneath the waves, but the issue of British-built Confederate raiders stayed afloat. Under prodding by the American minister, Charles Francis Adams, the British gradually perceived that allowing such ships to be built was a dangerous precedent that might someday be used against them. In 1863 London openly violated its own leaky laws and seized another raider being built for the South. But despite greater official efforts by Britain to remain truly neutral, Confederate commerce-destroyers, chiefly British-built, captured more than 250 Yankee ships, severely crippling the American merchant marine, which never fully recovered. Glowering Northerners looked farther north and talked openly of securing revenge by grabbing Canada when the war was over.

Foreign Flare-ups

A final Anglo-American crisis was touched off in 1863 by the Laird rams—two Confederate warships being constructed in the shipyard of John Laird and Sons in Great Britain. Designed to destroy the wooden ships of the Union navy with their iron rams and large-caliber guns, they were far more dangerous than the swift but lightly armed *Alabama*. If delivered to the South, they

On the Deck of the *Alabama* Captain Raphael Semmes leans jauntily against a deck gun aboard his fearful Confederate raider. The *Alabama* sank sixty-four Union ships before it was sunk by the USS *Kearsarge* off the coast of Cherbourg, France, in June 1864.

probably would have sunk the blockading squadrons and then brought Northern cities under their fire. In retaliation the North doubtless would have invaded Canada, and a full-dress war with Britain would have erupted. But Minister Adams took a hard line, warning that "this is war" if the rams were released. At the last minute, the London government relented and bought the two ships for the Royal Navy. Everyone seemed satisfied—except the disappointed Confederates. Britain also eventually repented its sorry role in the *Alabama* business. It agreed in 1871 to submit the *Alabama* dispute to arbitration, and in 1872 paid American claimants $15.5 million for damages caused by wartime commerce-raiders.

American rancor was also directed at Canada, where despite the vigilance of British authorities, Southern agents plotted to burn Northern cities. One Confederate raid into Vermont left three banks plundered and one American citizen dead. Hatred of England burned especially fiercely among Irish Americans, and they unleashed their fury on Canada. They raised several tiny "armies" of a few hundred green-shirted men and launched invasions of Canada, notably in 1866 and 1870. The Canadians condemned the Washington government for permitting such violations of neutrality, but the administration was hampered by the presence of so many Irish American voters.

As fate would have it, two great nations emerged from the fiery furnace of the American Civil War. One was a reunited United States, and the other was a united Canada. The British Parliament established the Dominion of Canada in 1867. It was partly designed to bolster the Canadians, both politically and spiritually, against the possible vengeance of the United States.

Emperor Napoleon III of France, taking advantage of America's preoccupation with its own internal problems, dispatched a French army to occupy Mexico City in 1863. The following year he installed on the ruins of the crushed republic his puppet, Austrian archduke Maximilian, as emperor of Mexico. Both sending the army and enthroning Maximilian were flagrant violations of the Monroe Doctrine. Napoleon was gambling that the Union would collapse and thus America would be too weak to enforce its "hands-off" policy in the Western Hemisphere.

The North, as long as it was convulsed by war, pursued a walk-on-eggs policy toward France. But when the shooting stopped in 1865, Secretary of State Seward, speaking with the authority of nearly a million war-tempered bayonets, prepared to march south. Napoleon realized that his costly gamble was doomed. He reluc-

tantly took "French leave" of his ill-starred puppet in 1867, and Maximilian soon crumpled ingloriously before a Mexican firing squad.

President Davis Versus President Lincoln

The Confederate government, like King Cotton, harbored fatal weaknesses. Its constitution, borrowing liberally from that of the Union, contained one deadly defect. Created by secession, it could not logically deny future secession to its constituent states. Jefferson Davis, while making his bow to states' rights, had in view a well-knit central government. But determined states' rights supporters fought him bitterly to the end. The Richmond regime encountered difficulty even in persuading certain state troops to serve outside their own borders. The governor of Georgia, a belligerent states' righter, at times seemed ready to secede from the secession and fight both sides. States' rights were no less damaging to the Confederacy than Yankee firepower.

Sharp-featured President Davis—tense, humorless, legalistic, and stubborn—was repeatedly in hot water. Although an eloquent orator and an able administrator, he at no time enjoyed real personal popularity and was often at loggerheads with his congress. At times there was serious talk of impeachment. Unlike Lincoln, Davis was somewhat imperious and inclined to defy rather than lead public opinion. Suffering acutely from neuralgia and other nervous disorders (including a tic), he overworked himself with the details of both civil government and military operations. No one could doubt his courage, sincerity, integrity, and devotion to the South, but the task proved beyond his powers. It was probably beyond the powers of any mere mortal.

Lincoln also had his troubles, but on the whole they were less prostrating. The North enjoyed the prestige of a long-established government, financially stable and fully recognized both at home and abroad. Lincoln, the inexperienced prairie politician, proved superior to the more experienced but less flexible Davis. Able to relax with droll stories at critical times, "Old Abe" grew as the war dragged on. Tactful, quiet, patient, yet firm, he developed a genius for interpreting and leading a fickle public opinion. Holding aloft the banner of Union with inspiring utterances, he demonstrated charitableness toward the South and forbearance toward backbiting colleagues. "Did [Secretary of War Edwin] Stanton say I was a damned fool?" he reportedly replied to a tale-

Lincoln at Sharpsburg, October 1962 Deeply committed to his responsibilities as commander-in-chief, President Lincoln visited Union forces on the battlefield several times during the war. With him here at Antietam are the detective Allan Pinkerton, who provided intelligence to the Union army, and General John McClernand, who often accompanied the President on his travels (see pp. 459–460).

bearer. "Then I dare say I must be one, for Stanton is generally right and he always says what he means."

Limitations on Wartime Liberties

"Honest Abe" Lincoln, when inaugurated, laid his hand on the Bible and swore a solemn oath to uphold the Constitution. Then, feeling driven by necessity, he proceeded to tear a few holes in that hallowed document. He understandably concluded that if he did not do so, and patch the parchment later, there might not be a Constitution of a *united* United States to mend. The "rail-splitter" was no hairsplitter.

But such infractions were not, in general, sweeping. Congress, as is often true in times of crisis, generally accepted or confirmed the president's questionable acts. Lincoln, though accused of being a "Simple Susan Tyrant," did not believe that his ironhanded authority would continue once the Union was preserved. As he pointedly remarked in 1863, a man suffering from "temporary illness" would not persist in feeding on bitter medicines for "the remainder of his healthful life."

Congress was not in session when war erupted, so Lincoln gathered the reins into his own hands. Brushing aside legal objections, he boldly proclaimed a blockade. (His action was later upheld by the Supreme Court.) He arbitrarily increased the size of the Federal army—something that only Congress can do under the Constitution (see Art. I, Sec. VIII, para. 12). (Congress later approved.) He directed the secretary of the Treasury to advance $2 million without appropriation or security to three private citizens for military purposes—a grave irregularity contrary to the Constitution (see Art. I, Sec. IX, para. 7). He suspended the precious privilege of the writ of habeas corpus, so that anti-Unionists might be summarily arrested. In taking this step, he defied a dubious ruling by the chief justice that the safeguards of habeas corpus could be set aside only by the authorization of Congress (see Art. I, Sec. IX, para. 2).

Lincoln's regime was guilty of many other high-handed acts. For example, it arranged for "supervised" voting in the Border States. There the intimidated citizen, holding a colored ballot indicating his party preference, had to march between two lines of armed troops. The federal officials also ordered the suspension of certain newspapers and the arrest of their editors on grounds of obstructing the war.

Jefferson Davis was less able than Lincoln to exercise arbitrary power, mainly because of confirmed states' righters who fanned an intense spirit of localism. To the very end of the conflict, the owners of horse-drawn vans in Petersburg, Virginia, prevented the sensible joining of the incoming and outgoing tracks of a militarily vital railroad. The South seemed willing to lose the war before it would surrender local rights—and it did.

Volunteers and Draftees: North and South

Ravenous, the gods of war demanded men—lots of men. Northern armies were at first manned solely by volunteers, with each state assigned a quota based on

The New York City Draft Riots, 1863   Mostly Irish American mobs convulsed the city for days and were in the end put down only by a merciless application of Federal firepower.

population. But in 1863, after volunteering had slackened, Congress passed a federal conscription law for the first time on a nationwide scale in the United States. The provisions were grossly unfair to the poor. Rich boys, including young John D. Rockefeller, could hire substitutes to go in their places or purchase exemption outright by paying $300. "Three-hundred-dollar men" was the scornful epithet applied to these slackers. Draftees who did not have the necessary cash complained that their banditlike government demanded "three hundred dollars or your life."

The draft was especially damned in the Democratic strongholds of the North, notably in New York City. A frightful riot broke out in 1863, touched off largely by underprivileged and antiblack Irish Americans, who shouted, "Down with Lincoln!" and "Down with the draft!" For several days the city was at the mercy of a rampaging, pillaging mob. Scores of lives were lost, and the victims included many lynched blacks. Elsewhere in the North, conscription met with resentment and an occasional minor riot.

More than 90 percent of the Union troops were volunteers, since social and patriotic pressures to enlist were strong. As able-bodied men became scarcer, generous bounties for enlistment were offered by federal, state, and local authorities. An enterprising and money-wise volunteer might legitimately pocket more than $1,000.

With money flowing so freely, an unsavory crew of "bounty brokers" and "substitute brokers" sprang up, at home and abroad. They combed the poorhouses of the British Isles and western Europe, and many an Irishman or German was befuddled with whiskey and induced to enlist. A number of the slippery "bounty boys" deserted, volunteered elsewhere, and netted another handsome haul. The records reveal that one "bounty jumper" repeated his profitable operation thirty-two times. But desertion was by no means confined to "bounty jumpers." The rolls of the Union army recorded about 200,000 deserters of all classes, and the Confederate authorities were plagued with a runaway problem of similar dimensions.

Like the North, the South at first relied mainly on volunteers. But since the Confederacy was much less

Number of Men in Uniform at Date Given

Date	Union	Confederate
July 1861	186,751	112,040
January 1862	575,917	351,418
March 1862	637,126	401,395
January 1863	918,121	446,622
January 1864	860,737	481,180
January 1865	959,460	445,203

populous, it scraped the bottom of its manpower barrel much more quickly. Quipsters observed that any man who could see lightning and hear thunder was judged fit for service. The Richmond regime, robbing both "cradle and grave" (ages seventeen to fifty), was forced to resort to conscription as early as April 1862, nearly a year earlier than the Union.

Confederate draft regulations also worked serious injustices. As in the North, a rich man could hire a substitute or purchase exemption. Slaveowners or overseers with twenty slaves might also claim exemption. These special privileges, later modified, made for bad feelings among the less prosperous, many of whom complained that this was "a rich man's war but a poor man's fight." Why sacrifice one's life to save an affluent neighbor's slaves? No large-scale draft riots broke out in the South, as in New York City. But the Confederate conscription agents often found it prudent to avoid those areas inhabited by sharpshooting mountain whites, who were branded "Tories," "traitors," and "Yankee-lovers."

The Economic Stresses of War

Blessed with a lion's share of the wealth, the North rode through the financial breakers much more smoothly than the South. Excise taxes on tobacco and alcohol were substantially increased by Congress. An income tax was levied for the first time in the nation's experience, and although the rates were painlessly low by later standards, they netted millions of dollars.

Customs receipts likewise proved to be important revenue-raisers. Early in 1861, after enough antiprotection Southern members had seceded, Congress passed the Morrill Tariff Act, superseding the low Tariff of 1857. It increased the existing duties some 5 to 10 percent, boosting them to about the moderate level of the Walker Tariff of 1846. But these modest rates were soon pushed sharply upward by the necessities of war. The increases were designed partly to raise additional revenue and partly to provide more protection for the prosperous manufacturers who were being plucked by the new internal taxes. A protective tariff thus became identified with the Republican party, as American industrialists, mostly Republicans, waxed fat on these welcome benefits.

The Washington Treasury also issued greenbacked paper money, totaling nearly $450 million, at face value. This printing-press currency was inadequately supported by gold, and hence its value was determined by the nation's credit. Greenbacks thus fluctuated with the

fortunes of Union arms and at one low point were worth only 39 cents on the gold dollar. The holders of the notes, victims of creeping inflation, were indirectly taxed as the value of the currency slowly withered in their hands.

Yet borrowing far outstripped both greenbacks and taxes as a money-raiser. The federal Treasury netted $2,621,916,786 through the sale of bonds, which bore interest and which were payable at a later date. The modern technique of selling these issues to the people directly through "drives" and payroll deductions had not yet been devised. Accordingly, the Treasury was forced to market its bonds through the private banking house of Jay Cooke and Company, which received a commission of three-eighths of 1 percent on all sales. With both profits and patriotism at stake, the bankers succeeded in making effective appeals to citizen purchasers.

A financial landmark of the war was the National Banking System, authorized by Congress in 1863. Launched partly as a stimulant to the sale of government bonds, it was also designed to establish a standard bank-note currency. (The country was then flooded with depreciated "rag money" issued by unreliable bankers.) Banks that joined the National Banking System could buy government bonds and issue sound paper money backed by them. The war-born National Banking Act thus turned out to be the first significant step taken toward a unified banking network since 1836, when the "monster" Bank of the United States was killed by Andrew Jackson. Spawned by the war, this new system continued to function for fifty years, until replaced by the Federal Reserve System in 1913.

An impoverished South was beset by different financial woes. Customs duties were choked off as the coils of the Union blockade tightened. Large issues of Confederate bonds were sold at home and abroad, amounting to nearly $400 million. The Richmond regime also increased taxes sharply and imposed a 10 percent levy on farm produce. But in general the states' rights Southerners were immovably opposed to heavy direct taxation by the central authority: only about 1 percent of the total income was raised in this way.

As revenue began to dry up, the Confederate government was forced to print blue-backed paper money with complete abandon. "Runaway inflation" occurred as Southern presses continued to grind out the poorly backed treasury notes, totaling in all more than $1 billion. The Confederate paper dollar finally sank to the point where it was worth only 1.6 cents when Lee surrendered. Overall, the war inflicted a 9,000 percent inflation rate on the Confederacy, contrasted with 80 percent for the Union.

A contemporary (October 22, 1863) Richmond diary portrays the ruinous effects of inflation:

"A poor woman yesterday applied to a merchant in Carey Street to purchase a barrel of flour. The price he demanded was $70. 'My God!' exclaimed she, 'how can I pay such prices? I have seven children; what shall I do?' 'I don't know, madam,' said he coolly, 'unless you eat your children.'"

The North's Economic Boom

Wartime prosperity in the North was little short of miraculous. The marvel is that a divided nation could fight a costly conflict for four long years and then emerge seemingly more prosperous than ever before.

New factories, sheltered by the friendly umbrella of the new protective tariffs, mushroomed forth. Soaring prices, resulting from inflation, unfortunately pinched the day laborer and the white-collar worker to some extent. But the manufacturers and businesspeople raked in "the fortunes of war."

The Civil War bred a millionaire class for the first time in American history, though a few individuals of extreme wealth could have been found earlier. Many of these newly rich were noisy, gaudy, brassy, and given to extravagant living. Their emergence merely illustrates the truth that some gluttony and greed always mar the devotion and self-sacrifice called forth by war. The story of speculators and peculators was roughly the same in both camps. But graft was more flagrant in the North than in the South, partly because there was more to steal.

Yankee "sharpness" appeared at its worst. Dishonest agents, putting profits above patriotism, palmed off aged and blind horses on government purchasers. Unscrupulous Northern manufacturers supplied shoes with cardboard soles and fast-disintegrating uniforms of reprocessed or "shoddy" wool rather than virgin wool. Hence the reproachful term "shoddy millionaires" was doubly fair. One profiteer reluctantly admitted that his profits were "painfully large."

Newly invented laborsaving machinery enabled the North to expand economically, even though the cream of its manpower was being drained off to the fighting front. The sewing machine wrought wonders in fabricating uniforms and military footwear.

The marriage of military need and innovative machinery largely ended the production of custom-tailored clothing. Graduated standard measurements were introduced, creating "sizes" that were widely used in the civilian garment industry forever after.

Clattering mechanical reapers, which numbered about 250,000 by 1865, proved hardly less potent than thundering guns. They not only released tens of thousands of farm boys for the army but fed them their field rations. They produced vast surpluses of grain that, when sent abroad, helped dethrone King Cotton. They provided profits with which the North was able to buy munitions and supplies from abroad. They contributed to the feverish prosperity of the North—a prosperity that enabled the Union to weather the war with flying colors.

Other industries were humming. The discovery of petroleum gushers in 1859 had led to a rush of "Fifty-Niners" to Pennsylvania. The result was the birth of a new industry, with its "petroleum plutocracy" and "coal oil Johnnies." Pioneers continued to push westward during the war, altogether an estimated 300,000 people. Major magnets were free gold nuggets and free land under the Homestead Act of 1862. Strong propellants were the federal draft agents. The only major Northern industry to suffer a crippling setback was the ocean-carrying trade, which fell prey to the *Alabama* and other raiders.

The Civil War was a women's war, too. The protracted conflict opened new opportunities for women. When men departed in uniform, women often took their jobs. In Washington, D.C., five hundred women clerks ("government girls") became government workers, with over one hundred in the Treasury Department alone. The booming military demand for shoes and clothing, combined with technological marvels like the sewing machine, likewise drew countless women into industrial employment. Before the war one industrial worker in four had been female; during the war the ratio rose to one in three.

Other women, on both sides, stepped up to the fighting front—or close behind it. More than four hundred women accompanied husbands and sweethearts into battle by posing as male soldiers. Other women took on dangerous spy missions. One woman was executed for smuggling gold to the Confederacy. Dr. Elizabeth Blackwell, America's first female physician, helped organize the U.S. Sanitary Commission to assist the Union armies

Booth at the Sanitary Fair in Chicago, 1863 The Chicago Sanitary Fair was the first of many such fairs throughout the nation to raise funds for soldier relief efforts. Mainly organized by women, the fair sold captured Confederate flags, battle relics, handicrafts like these potholders (right), and donated items, including President Lincoln's original draft of the Emancipation Proclamation (which garnered $3,000 in auction). When the fair closed, the Chicago headquarters of the U.S. Sanitary Commission had raised $100,000, and its female managers had gained organizational experience that many would put to work in the postwar movement for women's rights.

in the field. The commission trained nurses, collected medical supplies, and equipped hospitals. Commission work helped many women to acquire the organizational skills and the self-confidence that would propel the women's movement forward after the war. Heroically energetic Clara Barton and dedicated Dorothea Dix, superintendent of nurses for the Union army, helped transform nursing from a lowly service into a respected profession—and in the process opened up another major sphere of employment for women in the postwar era. Equally renowned in the South was Sally Tompkins, who ran a Richmond infirmary for wounded Confederate soldiers and was awarded the rank of captain by Confederate president Jefferson Davis. Still other women, North as well as South, organized bazaars and fairs that raised millions of dollars for the relief of widows, orphans, and disabled soldiers.

A Crushed Cotton Kingdom

The South fought to the point of exhaustion. The suffocation caused by the blockade, together with the destruction wrought by invaders, took a terrible toll. Possessing 30 percent of the national wealth in 1860, the South claimed only 12 percent in 1870. Before the war the average per capita income of Southerners (including slaves) was about two-thirds that of Northerners. The Civil War squeezed the average southern income to two-fifths of the Northern level, where it remained for the rest of the century. The South's bid for independence exacted a cruel and devastating cost.

Transportation collapsed. The South was even driven to the economic cannibalism of pulling up rails from the less-used lines to repair the main ones.

Window weights were melted down into bullets; gourds replaced dishes; pins became so scarce that they were loaned with reluctance.

To the brutal end, the South mustered remarkable resourcefulness and spirit. Women buoyed up their menfolk, many of whom had seen enough of war at first hand to be heartily sick of it. A proposal was made by a number of women that they cut off their long hair and sell it abroad. But the project was not adopted, partly because of the blockade. The self-sacrificing women took pride in denying themselves the silks and satins of their Northern sisters. The chorus of a song, "The Southern Girl," touched a cheerful note:

> So hurrah! hurrah! For Southern Rights, hurrah!
> Hurrah! for the homespun dress the Southern ladies wear.

At war's end the Northern Captains of Industry had conquered the Southern Lords of the Manor. A crippled South left the capitalistic North free to work its own way, with high tariffs and other benefits. The manufacturing moguls of the North, ushering in the full-fledged Industrial Revolution, were headed for increased dominance over American economic and political life. Hitherto the agrarian "slavocracy" of the South had partially checked the ambitions of the rising plutocracy of the North. Now cotton capitalism had lost out to industrial capitalism. The South of 1865 was to be rich in little but amputees, war heroes, ruins, and memories.

Chronology

1861	Confederate government formed
	Lincoln takes office (March 4)
	Fort Sumter fired upon (April 12)
	Four upper South states secede (April–June)
	Morrill Tariff Act passed
	Trent affair
	Lincoln suspends writ of habeas corpus
1862	Confederacy enacts conscription
	Homestead Act
1862-1864	*Alabama* raids Northern shipping
1863	Union enacts conscription
	New York City draft riots
	National Banking System established
1863-1864	Napoleon III installs Archduke Maximilian as emperor of Mexico
1864	*Alabama* sunk by Union warship

21

The Furnace of Civil War

1861–1865

MY PARAMOUNT OBJECT IN THIS STRUGGLE IS TO SAVE THE UNION, AND IS NOT EITHER TO SAVE OR TO DESTROY SLAVERY.

ABRAHAM LINCOLN, 1862

When President Lincoln issued his call to the states for seventy-five thousand militiamen on April 15, 1861, he envisioned them serving for only ninety days. Reaffirming his limited war aims, he declared that he had "no purpose, directly or indirectly, to interfere with slavery in the States where it exists." With a swift flourish of federal force, he hoped to show the folly of secession and rapidly return the rebellious states to the Union. But the war was to be neither brief nor limited. When the guns fell silent four years later, hundreds of thousands of soldiers on both sides lay dead, slavery was ended forever, and the nation faced the challenge of reintegrating the defeated but still recalcitrant South into the Union.

Bull Run Ends the "Ninety-Day War"

Northern newspapers, at first sharing Lincoln's expectation of a quick victory, raised the cry, "On to Richmond!" In this yeasty atmosphere, a Union army of some thirty thousand men drilled near Washington in the summer of 1861. It was ill-prepared for battle, but the press and the public clamored for action. Lincoln eventually concluded that an attack on a smaller Confederate force at Bull Run (Manassas Junction), some thirty miles southwest of Washington, might be worth a try. If successful, it would demonstrate the superiority of Union arms. It might even lead to the capture of the Confederate capital at Richmond, one hundred miles to the south. If Richmond fell, secession would be thoroughly discredited, and the Union could be restored without damage to the economic and social system of the South.

Raw Yankee recruits swaggered out of Washington toward Bull Run on July 21, 1861, as if they were headed for a sporting event. Congressmen and spectators trailed along with their lunch baskets to witness the fun. At first the battle went well for the Yankees. But "Stonewall" Jackson's gray-clad warriors stood like a stone wall (here he won his nickname), and Confederate reinforcements arrived unexpectedly. Panic seized the green Union troops, many of whom fled in shameful confusion. The Confederates, themselves too exhausted or disorganized to pursue, feasted on captured lunches.

Preparing for Battle These troops of the 69th New York State Militia, a largely Irish regiment, were photographed attending Sunday morning Mass in May 1861, just weeks before the Battle of Bull Run. Because the regiment was camped near Washington, D.C., women were able to visit.

An observer behind the Union lines described the Federal troops' pell-mell retreat from the battlefield at Bull Run:

"We called to them, tried to tell them there was no danger, called them to stop, implored them to stand. We called them cowards, denounced them in the most offensive terms, put out our heavy revolvers, and threatened to shoot them, but all in vain; a cruel, crazy, mad, hopeless panic possessed them, and communicated to everybody about in front and rear. The heat was awful, although now about six; the men were exhausted—their mouths gaped, their lips cracked and blackened with powder of the cartridges they had bitten off in battle, their eyes staring in frenzy; no mortal ever saw such a mass of ghastly wretches."

The "military picnic" at Bull Run, though not decisive militarily, bore significant psychological and political consequences, many of them paradoxical. Victory was worse than defeat for the South, because it inflated an already dangerous overconfidence. Many of the Southern soldiers promptly deserted, some boastfully to display their trophies, others feeling that the war was now surely over. Southern enlistments fell off sharply, and preparations for a protracted conflict slackened. Defeat was better than victory for the Union, because it dispelled all illusions of a one-punch war and caused the Northerners to buckle down to the staggering task at hand. It also set the stage for a war that would be waged not merely for the cause of Union but also, eventually, for the abolitionist ideal of emancipation.

"Tardy George" McClellan and the Peninsula Campaign

Northern hopes brightened later in 1861, when General George B. McClellan was given command of the Army of the Potomac, as the major Union force near Washington was now called. Red-haired and red-mustached, strong and stocky, McClellan was a brilliant, thirty-four-year-old West Pointer. As a serious student of warfare who was dubbed "Young Napoleon," he had seen plenty of fighting, first in the Mexican War and then as an observer of the Crimean War in Russia.

Cocky George McClellan embodied a curious mixture of virtues and defects. He was a superb organizer and drillmaster, and he injected splendid morale into the Army of the Potomac. Hating to sacrifice his troops, he was idolized by his men, who affectionately called him "Little Mac." But he was a perfectionist who seems not to have realized that an army is never ready to the last button and that wars cannot be won without running some risks. He consistently but erroneously believed that the enemy outnumbered him, partly because his intelligence reports from the head of Pinkerton's Detective Agency

The Army of the Potomac Marching up Pennsylvania Avenue, Washington, D.C., 1861 In this painting Union troops parade before the Battle of Bull Run. Colorfully uniformed, they are a regiment of Zouaves, who adopted the name and style of military dress from a legendarily dashing French infantry unit. But bright uniforms were not enough to win battles, and these troops were soon to be routed by the Confederates.

were unreliable. He was overcautious—Lincoln once accused him of having "the slows"—and he addressed the president in an arrogant tone that a less forgiving person would never have tolerated. Privately the general referred to his chief as a "baboon."

As McClellan doggedly continued to drill his army without moving it toward Richmond, the derisive Northern watchword became "All Quiet Along the Potomac." The song of the hour was "Tardy George" (McClellan). After threatening to "borrow" the army if it was not going to be used, Lincoln finally issued firm orders to advance.

A reluctant McClellan at last decided upon a waterborne approach to Richmond, which lies at the western base of a narrow peninsula formed by the James and York Rivers—hence the name given to this historic

Masterly Inactivity, or Six Months on the Potomac, 1862 McClellan and his Confederate foe view each other cautiously while their troops engage in visits, weddings, and sports.

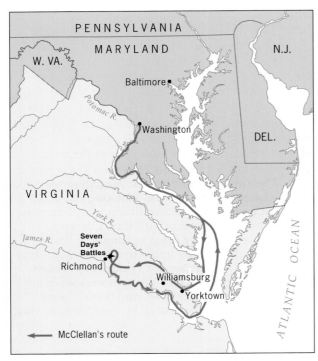

Peninsula Campaign, 1862

McClellan's route

encounter: the Peninsula Campaign. McClellan warily inched toward the Confederate capital in the spring of 1862 with about 100,000 men. After taking a month to capture historic Yorktown, which bristled with imitation wooden cannon, he finally came within sight of the spires of Richmond. At this crucial juncture, Lincoln diverted McClellan's anticipated reinforcements to chase "Stonewall" Jackson, whose lightning feints in the Shenandoah Valley seemed to put Washington, D.C., in jeopardy. Stalled in front of Richmond, McClellan was further frustrated when "Jeb" Stuart's Confederate cavalry rode completely around his army on reconnaissance. Then General Robert E. Lee launched a devastating counterattack—the Seven Days' Battles—June 26–July 2, 1862. The Confederates slowly drove McClellan back to

Civil War Scene (detail)
A Federal brigade repulses a Confederate assault at Williamsburg, Virginia, in 1862, as the Peninsula Campaign presses toward Richmond. General Winfield Scott Hancock commanded the troops. For his success in this action, Hancock earned the nickname "The Superb."

A *Confederate soldier assigned to burial detail after the Seven Days' Battles (1862) wrote,*

"The sights and smells that assailed us were simply indescribable . . . corpses swollen to twice their original size, some of them actually burst asunder with the pressure of foul gasses. . . . The odors were so nauseating and so deadly that in a short time we all sickened and were lying with our mouths close to the ground, most of us vomiting profusely."

McClellan had succeeded in taking Richmond and ending the war in mid-1862, the Union would probably have been restored with minimal disruption to the "peculiar institution." Slavery would have survived, at least for a time. By his successful defense of Richmond and defeat of McClellan, Lee had in effect ensured that the war would endure until slavery was uprooted and the Old South thoroughly destroyed. Lincoln himself, who had earlier professed his unwillingness to tamper with slavery where it already existed, now declared that the rebels "cannot experiment for ten years trying to destroy the government and if they fail still come back into the Union unhurt." He began to draft an emancipation proclamation.

Union strategy now turned toward total war. As finally developed, the Northern military plan had six components: first, slowly suffocate the South by blockading its coasts; second, liberate the slaves and hence undermine the very economic foundations of the Old South; third, cut the Confederacy in half by seizing control of the Mississippi River backbone; fourth, chop the Confederacy to pieces by sending troops through Georgia and the Carolinas; fifth, decapitate it by capturing its capital at Richmond; and sixth (this was Ulysses Grant's idea especially), try everywhere to engage the enemy's main strength and to grind it into submission.

the sea. The Union forces abandoned the Peninsula Campaign as a costly failure, and Lincoln temporarily abandoned McClellan as commander of the Army of the Potomac—though Lee's army had suffered some twenty thousand casualties to McClellan's ten thousand.

Lee had achieved a brilliant, if bloody, triumph. Yet the ironies of his accomplishment are striking. If

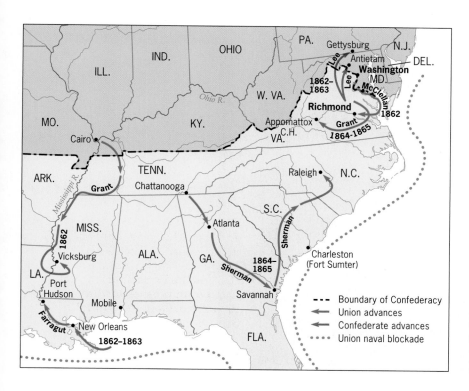

Main Thrusts, 1861–1865
Northern strategists at first believed that the rebellion could be snuffed out quickly by a swift, crushing blow. But the stiffness of Southern resistance to the Union's early probes, and the North's inability to strike with sufficient speed and severity, revealed that the conflict would be a war of attrition, long and bloody.

The War at Sea

The blockade started leakily: it was not clamped down all at once but was extended by degrees. A watertight patrol of some thirty-five hundred miles of coast was impossible for the hastily improvised Northern navy, which counted converted yachts and ferryboats in its fleet. But blockading was simplified by concentrating on the principal ports and inlets where dock facilities were available for loading bulky bales of cotton.

How was the blockade regarded by the naval powers of the world? Ordinarily, they probably would have defied it, for it was never completely effective and was especially sievelike at the outset. But Britain, the greatest maritime nation, recognized it as binding and warned its shippers that they ignored it at their peril. Britain plainly did not want to tie its hands in a future war by insisting that Lincoln maintain impossibly high blockading standards.

Blockade-running was risky but profitable, as the growing scarcity of Southern goods drove prices skyward. The most successful blockade runners were swift, gray-painted steamers, scores of which were specially built in Scotland. A leading rendezvous was the West Indies port of Nassau, in the British Bahamas, where at one time thirty-five of the speedy ships rode at anchor.

When news reached Washington that the Merrimack *had sunk two wooden Yankee warships with ridiculous ease, President Lincoln, much "excited," summoned his advisers. Secretary of the Navy Gideon Welles (1802–1878) recorded,*

"The most frightened man on that gloomy day . . . was the Secretary of War [Stanton]. He was at times almost frantic. . . . The Merrimack, he said, would destroy every vessel in the service, could lay every city on the coast under contribution, could take Fortress Monroe. . . . Likely the first movement of the Merrimack would be to come up the Potomac and disperse Congress, destroy the Capitol and public buildings."

The low-lying craft would take on cargoes of arms brought in by tramp steamers from Britain, leave with fraudulent papers for "Halifax" (Canada), and then return a few days later with a cargo of cotton. The risks

Battle of the *Merrimack* **and the** *Monitor,* **March 9, 1862**

were great, but the profits would mount to 700 percent and more for lucky gamblers. Two successful voyages might well pay for capture on a third. The lush days of blockade-running finally passed as Union squadrons gradually pinched off the leading Southern ports, from New Orleans to Charleston.

The Northern navy enforced the blockade with high-handed practices. Yankee captains, for example, would seize British freighters on the high seas, if laden with war supplies for the tiny port of Nassau and other halfway stations. The justification was that obviously these shipments were "ultimately" destined, by devious routes, for the Confederacy.

London, although not happy, acquiesced in this disagreeable doctrine of "ultimate destination" or "continuous voyage." British blockaders might need to take advantage of the same far-fetched interpretation in a future war—as in fact they did in the world war of 1914–1918.

The most alarming Confederate threat to the blockade came in 1862. Resourceful Southerners raised and reconditioned a former wooden U.S. warship, the *Merrimack*, and plated its sides with old iron railroad rails. Renamed the *Virginia*, this clumsy but powerful monster easily destroyed two wooden ships of the Union navy in the Virginia waters of Chesapeake Bay; it also threatened catastrophe to the entire Yankee blockading fleet. (Actually the homemade ironclad was not a seaworthy craft.)

A tiny Union ironclad, the *Monitor*, built in about one hundred days, arrived on the scene in the nick of time. For four hours, on March 9, 1862, the little "Yankee cheesebox on a raft" fought the wheezy *Merrimack* to a standstill. Britain and France had already built several powerful ironclads, but the first battle-testing of these new craft heralded the doom of wooden warships. A few months after the historic battle, the Confederates destroyed the *Merrimack* to keep it from the grasp of advancing Union troops.

The Pivotal Point: Antietam

Robert E. Lee, having broken the back of McClellan's assault on Richmond, next moved northward. At the Second Battle of Bull Run (August 29–30, 1862), he encountered a Federal force under General John Pope. A handsome, dashing, soldierly figure, Pope boasted that in the western theater of war, from which he had recently come, he had seen only the backs of the enemy.

Lee quickly gave him a front view, furiously attacking Pope's troops and inflicting a crushing defeat.

Emboldened by this success, Lee daringly thrust into Maryland. He hoped to strike a blow that would not only encourage foreign intervention but also seduce the still-wavering Border State and its sisters from the Union. The Confederate troops sang lustily:

> *Thou wilt not cower in the dust,*
> *Maryland! my Maryland!*
> *Thy gleaming sword shall never rust,*
> *Maryland! my Maryland!*

But the Marylanders did not respond to the siren song. The presence among the invaders of so many blanketless, hatless, and shoeless soldiers dampened the state's ardor.

Events finally converged toward a critical battle at Antietam Creek, Maryland. Lincoln, yielding to popular pressure, hastily restored "Little Mac" to active command of the main Northern army. His soldiers tossed their caps skyward and hugged his horse as they hailed his return. Fortune shone upon McClellan when two Union soldiers found a copy of Lee's battle plans wrapped around a packet of three cigars dropped by a careless Confederate officer. With this crucial piece of intelligence in hand, McClellan succeeded in halting Lee at Antietam on September 17, 1862, in one of the bitterest and bloodiest days of the war.

Antietam was more or less a draw militarily. But Lee, finding his thrust parried, retired across the Potomac. McClellan, from whom much more had been hoped, was removed from his field command for the second and final time. His numerous critics, condemning him for not having boldly pursued the ever-dangerous Lee, finally got his scalp.

The landmark Battle of Antietam was one of the decisive engagements of world history—probably the most decisive of the Civil War. Jefferson Davis was perhaps never again so near victory as on that fateful summer day. The British and French governments were on the verge of diplomatic mediation, a form of interference sure to be angrily resented by the North. An almost certain rebuff by Washington might well have spurred Paris and London into armed collusion with Richmond. But both capitals cooled off when the Union displayed unexpected power at Antietam, and their chill deepened with the passing months.

Bloody Antietam was also the long-awaited "victory" that Lincoln needed for launching his Emancipation Proclamation. The abolitionists had long been clamoring for action: Wendell Phillips was denouncing the president

The Killing Fields of Antietam
These Confederate corpses testified to the awful slaughter of the battle. The twelve-hour fight at Antietam Creek ranks as the bloodiest single day of the war, with more than ten thousand Confederate casualties and even more on the Union side. "At last the battle ended," one historian wrote, "smoke heavy in the air, the twilight quivering with the anguished cries of thousands of wounded men."

as a "first-rate second-rate man." By midsummer of 1862, with the Border States safely in the fold, Lincoln was ready to move. But he believed that to issue such an edict on the heels of a series of military disasters would be folly. It would seem like a confession that the North, unable to conquer the South, was forced to call upon the slaves to murder their masters. Lincoln therefore decided to wait for the outcome of Lee's invasion.

Antietam served as the needed emancipation springboard. The halting of Lee's offensive was just enough of a victory to justify Lincoln's issuing, on September 23, 1862, the preliminary Emancipation Proclamation. This hope-giving document announced that on January 1, 1863, the president would issue a final proclamation.

On the scheduled date, he fully redeemed his promise, and the Civil War became more of a moral crusade as the fate of slavery and the South it had sustained was sealed. The war now became more of what Lincoln called a "remorseless revolutionary struggle." After January 1, 1863, Lincoln said, "The character of the war will be changed. It will be one of subjugation. . . . The [old] South is to be destroyed and replaced by new propositions and ideas."

A Proclamation Without Emancipation

Lincoln's Emancipation Proclamation of 1863 declared "forever free" the slaves in those Confederate states still in rebellion. Bondsmen in the loyal Border States were not affected, nor were those in specific conquered areas in the South—all told, about 800,000. The tone of the document was dull and legalistic (one historian has said that it had all the moral grandeur of a bill of lading). But if Lincoln stopped short of a clarion call for a holy war to achieve freedom, he pointedly concluded his historic document by declaring that the Proclamation was "an act of justice" and calling for "the considerate judgment of mankind and the gracious favor of Almighty God."

The presidential pen did not formally strike the shackles from a single slave. Where Lincoln could presumably free the slaves—that is, in the loyal Border States—he refused to do so, lest he spur disunion. Where he could not—that is, in the Confederate states—he tried to. In short, where he *could* he would not, and where he *would* he could not. Thus the Emancipation Proclamation was stronger on proclamation than emancipation.

Yet much unofficial do-it-yourself liberation did take place. Thousands of jubilant slaves, learning of the proclamation, flocked to the invading Union armies, stripping already run-down plantations of their work force. In this sense the Emancipation Proclamation was heralded by the drumbeat of running feet. But many fugitives would have come anyhow, as they had from the war's outset. One in seven Southern slaves ran away to Union camps. Their presence in the camps and their perseverance against all odds convinced many Northern soldiers of slavery's evils and helped put emancipation atop Lincoln's agenda. By issuing the proclamation,

> *Not everyone in the North welcomed Lincoln's Emancipation Proclamation, as this condemnation from* the Cincinnati Enquirer *reveals:*
>
> "The hundreds of thousands, if not millions of slaves [the act] will emancipate will come North and West and will either be competitors with our white mechanics and laborers, degrading them by competition, or they will have to be supported as paupers and criminals at the public expense."

Public reactions to the long-awaited proclamation of 1863 were varied. "God bless Abraham Lincoln," exulted the antislavery editor Horace Greeley in his *New York Tribune*. But many ardent abolitionists complained that Lincoln had not gone far enough. On the other hand, formidable numbers of Northerners, especially in the "Butternut" regions of the Old Northwest and the Border States, felt that he had gone too far. A cynical Democratic rhymester quipped,

> *Honest old Abe, when the war first began,*
> *Denied abolition was part of his plan;*
> *Honest old Abe has since made a decree,*
> *The war must go on till the slaves are all free.*
> *As both can't be honest, will some one tell how,*
> *If honest Abe then, he is honest Abe now?*

Opposition mounted in the North against supporting an "abolition war"; ex-president Pierce and others felt that emancipation should not be "inflicted" on the slaves. Many Boys in Blue, especially from the Border States, had volunteered to fight for the Union, not against slavery. Desertions increased sharply. The crucial congressional elections in the autumn of 1862 went heavily against the administration, particularly in New York, Pennsylvania, and Ohio. Democrats even carried Lincoln's Illinois, although they did not secure control of Congress.

The Emancipation Proclamation caused an outcry to rise from the South that "Lincoln the fiend" was trying to stir up the "hellish passions" of a slave insurrection. Aristocrats of Europe, noting that the proclamation

Lincoln addressed the refugees' plight and strengthened the moral cause of the Union at home and abroad. At the same time, Lincoln's proclamation clearly foreshadowed the ultimate doom of slavery. This was legally achieved by action of the individual states and by their ratification of the Thirteenth Amendment (see the Appendix) in 1865, eight months after the Civil War had ended. The Emancipation Proclamation also fundamentally changed the nature of the war because it effectively removed any chance of a negotiated settlement. Both sides now knew that the war would be a fight to the finish.

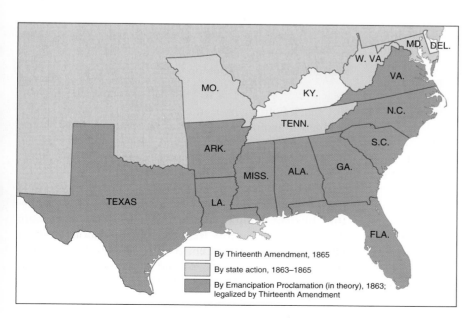

Legend:
- By Thirteenth Amendment, 1865
- By state action, 1863–1865
- By Emancipation Proclamation (in theory), 1863; legalized by Thirteenth Amendment

Emancipation in the South
President Lincoln believed that emancipation of the slaves, accompanied by compensation to their owners, would be fairest to the South. He formally proposed such an amendment to the Constitution in December 1862. What finally emerged was the Thirteenth Amendment of 1865, which freed all slaves *without* compensation.

Abraham Lincoln defended his policies toward blacks in an open letter to Democrats on August 26, 1863:

"You say you will not fight to free negroes. Some of them seem willing to fight for you; but, no matter. Fight you, then, exclusively to save the Union. I issued the proclamation on purpose to aid you in saving the Union."

applied only to rebel slaveholders, were inclined to sympathize with Southern protests. But the Old World working classes, especially in Britain, reacted otherwise. They sensed that the proclamation spelled the ultimate doom of slavery, and many laborers were more determined than ever to oppose intervention. Gradually the diplomatic position of the Union improved.

The North now had much the stronger moral cause. In addition to preserving the Union, it had committed itself to freeing the slaves. The moral position of the South was correspondingly diminished.

Blacks Battle Bondage

As Lincoln moved to emancipate the slaves, he also took steps to enlist blacks in the armed forces. Although some African Americans had served in the Revolution and the War of 1812, the regular army contained no blacks at the war's outset, and the War Department refused to accept those free Northern blacks who tried to volunteer. (The Union navy, however, enrolled many blacks, mainly as cooks, stewards, and firemen.)

But as manpower ran low and emancipation was proclaimed, black enlistees were accepted, sometimes over ferocious protests from Northern as well as Southern whites. By war's end some 180,000 blacks served in the Union army, most of them from the slave states, but many from the free-soil North. Blacks accounted for about 10 percent of the total enlistments in the Union forces on land and sea and included two Massachusetts regiments raised largely through the efforts of the ex-slave Frederick Douglass.

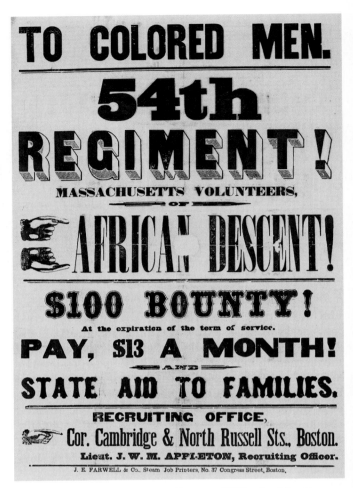

Recruiting Black Troops in Boston, 1863 Led by the white Boston Brahmin Robert Gould Shaw, the 54th Massachusetts Regiment lost nearly half its men, including Shaw, in a futile attack on South Carolina's Fort Wagner in July 1863. A memorial to the regiment stands today on the Boston Common.

Black fighting men unquestionably had their hearts in the war against slavery that the Civil War had become after Lincoln proclaimed emancipation. Service also offered them a chance to prove their manhood and to strengthen their claim to full citizenship at war's end. Participating in about five hundred engagements, they received twenty-two Congressional Medals of Honor—the highest military award. Their casualties were extremely heavy; more than thirty-eight thousand died, whether from battle, sickness, or reprisals from vengeful masters. Many, when captured, were put to death as slaves in revolt, for not until 1864 did the South recognize them as prisoners of war. In one notorious case,

A Bit of War History: Contraband, Recruit, Veteran, by Thomas Waterman Wood, 1865–1866 This painting dramatically commemorates the contributions and sacrifices of the 180,000 African Americans who served in the Union army during the Civil War.

several black soldiers were massacred after they had formally surrendered at Fort Pillow, Tennessee. Thereafter vengeful black units cried "Remember Fort Pillow" as they swung into battle and vowed to take no prisoners.

For reasons of pride, prejudice, and principle, the Confederacy could not bring itself to enlist slaves until a

An affidavit by a Union sergeant described the fate of one group of black Union troops captured by the Confederates:

"All the negroes found in blue uniform or with any outward marks of a Union soldier upon him was killed—I saw some taken into the woods and hung—Others I saw stripped of all their clothing and they stood upon the bank of the river with their faces riverwards and then they were shot—Still others were killed by having their brains beaten out by the butt end of the muskets in the hands of the Rebels."

month before the war ended, and then it was too late. Meanwhile, tens of thousands were forced into labor battalions, the building of fortifications, the supplying of armies, and other war-connected activities. Slaves, moreover, were "the stomach of the Confederacy," for they kept the farms going while the white men fought.

Involuntary labor did not imply slave support for the Confederacy. In many ways the actions of Southern slaves hamstrung the Confederate war effort and subverted the institution of slavery. Fear of slave insurrection necessitated Confederate "home guards," keeping many eligible young white men from the front. Everyday forms of slave resistance, such as slowdowns, strikes, and open defiance, diminished productivity and undermined discipline. When Union troops neared, slave assertiveness increased. As "intelligent contraband," slaves served as Union spies, guides, and scouts or provided shelter to escaped Northern prisoners of war. By war's end nearly half a million slaves took the ultimate risk of revolting "with their feet," abandoning their plantations. Many who remained, especially in the urban South, negotiated new working conditions in factories and on farms. Although they stopped short of violent uprising, slaves contributed powerfully to the collapse of slavery and the disintegration of the antebellum Southern way of life.

> *In August 1863 Lincoln wrote to Grant that enlisting black soldiers*
>
> "works doubly, weakening the enemy and strengthening us."
>
> *In December 1863 he announced,*
>
> "It is difficult to say they are not as good soldiers as any."
>
> *In August 1864 he said,*
>
> "Abandon all the posts now garrisoned by black men, take 150,000 [black] men from our side and put them in the battlefield or cornfield against us, and we would be compelled to abandon the war in three weeks."

Lee's Last Lunge at Gettysburg

After Antietam, Lincoln replaced McClellan as commander of the Army of the Potomac with General A. E. Burnside, whose ornate side-whiskers came to be known as "burnsides" or "sideburns." Protesting his unfitness for this responsibility, Burnside proved it when he launched a rash frontal attack on Lee's strong position at Fredericksburg, Virginia, on December 13, 1862. A chicken could not have lived in the line of fire, remarked one Confederate officer. More than ten thousand Northern soldiers were killed or wounded in "Burnside's Slaughter Pen."

A new slaughter pen was prepared when General Burnside yielded his command to "Fighting Joe" Hooker, an aggressive officer but a headstrong subordinate. At Chancellorsville, Virginia, on May 2–4, 1863, Lee daringly divided his numerically inferior force and sent "Stonewall" Jackson to attack the Union flank. The strategy worked. Hooker, temporarily dazed by a near hit from a cannonball, was badly beaten but not crushed. This victory was probably Lee's most brilliant, but it was dearly bought. Jackson was mistakenly shot by his own men in the gathering dusk and died a few days later. "I have lost my right arm," lamented Lee. Southern folklore relates how Jackson outflanked the angels while galloping into heaven.

Lee now prepared to follow up his stunning victory by invading the North again, this time through Pennsylvania. A decisive blow would add strength to the noisy peace prodders in the North and would also encourage foreign intervention—still a Southern hope. Three days before the battle was joined, Union general George G. Meade—scholarly, unspectacular, abrupt—was aroused from his sleep at 2 A.M. with the unwelcome news that he would replace Hooker.

Quite by accident, Meade took his stand atop a low ridge flanking a shallow valley near quiet little Gettysburg, Pennsylvania. There his 92,000 men in blue locked in furious combat with Lee's 76,000 gray-clad warriors. The battle seesawed across the rolling green slopes for three agonizing days, July 1–3, 1863, and the outcome was in doubt until the very end. The failure of General George Pickett's magnificent but futile charge finally broke the back of the Confederate attack—and broke the heart of the Confederate cause.

Pickett's charge has been called the "high tide of the Confederacy." It defined both the northernmost point reached by any significant Southern force and the last real chance for the Confederates to win the war. As the Battle of Gettysburg raged, a Confederate peace delegation was moving under a flag of truce toward the Union lines near Norfolk, Virginia. Jefferson Davis hoped his negotiators would arrive in Washington from the south

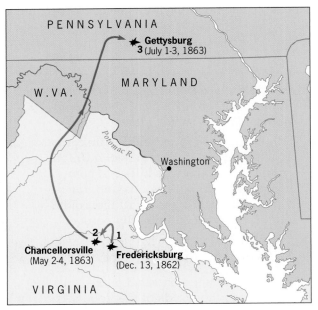

The Road to Gettysburg, December 1862–July 1863

EXAMINING THE EVIDENCE

Abraham Lincoln's Gettysburg Address

Political speeches are unfortunately all too often composed of claptrap, platitudes, and just plain bunk—and they are frequently written by someone other than the person delivering them. But Abraham Lincoln's address at the dedication of the cemetery at Gettysburg battlefield on November 19, 1863, has long been recognized as a masterpiece of political oratory and as a foundational document of the American political system, as weighty a statement of the national purpose as the Declaration of Independence (which it deliberately echoes in its statement that all men are created equal) or even the Constitution itself. In just 272 simple but eloquent words that Lincoln himself indisputably wrote, he summarized the case for American nationhood. What were his principal arguments? What values did he invoke? What did he think was at stake in the Civil War? (Conspicuously, he made no direct mention of slavery in this address.) Another speech that Lincoln gave in 1861 offers some clues. He said, "I have often inquired of myself what great principle or idea it was that kept this [nation] together. It was not the mere separation of the colonies from the motherland, but that sentiment in the Declaration of Independence which gave liberty not alone to the people of this country, but hope to the world, for all future time."

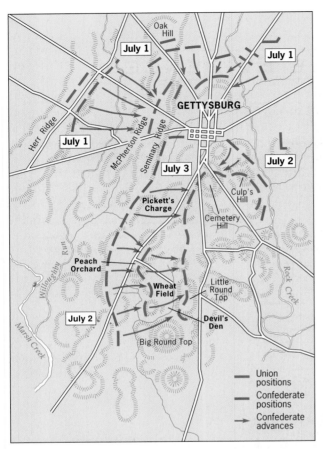

The Battle of Gettysburg, 1863 With the failure of Pickett's Charge, the fate of the Confederacy was sealed—though the Civil War dragged on for almost two more bloody years.

just as Lee's triumphant army marched on it from Gettysburg to the north. But the victory at Gettysburg belonged to Lincoln, who refused to allow the Confederate peace mission to pass through Union lines. From now on, the Southern cause was doomed. Yet the men of Dixie fought on for nearly two years longer, through sweat, blood, and weariness of spirit.

Later in that dreary autumn of 1863, with the graves still fresh, Lincoln journeyed to Gettysburg to dedicate the cemetery. He read a two-minute address, following a two-hour speech by the orator of the day, a former president of Harvard. Lincoln's noble remarks were branded by the London *Times* as "ludicrous" and by Democratic editors as "dishwatery" and "silly." The address attracted relatively little attention at the time, but the president was speaking for the ages.

The War in the West

Events in the western theater of the war at last provided Lincoln with an able general who did not have to be shelved after every reverse. Ulysses S. Grant had been a mediocre student at West Point, distinguishing himself only in horsemanship, although he did fairly well at mathematics. After fighting creditably in the Mexican War, he was stationed at isolated frontier posts, where boredom and loneliness drove him to drink. Resigning from the army to avoid a court-martial for drunkenness, he failed at various business ventures, and when war came, he was working in his father's leather store in Illinois for $50 a month.

Grant did not cut much of a figure. The shy and silent shopkeeper was short, stooped, awkward, stubble-bearded, and sloppy in dress. He managed with some difficulty to secure a colonelcy in the volunteers. From then on, his military experience—combined with his boldness, resourcefulness, and tenacity—catapulted him on a meteoric rise.

Grant's first signal success came in the northern Tennessee theater. After heavy fighting, he captured Fort Henry and Fort Donelson on the Tennessee and Cumberland Rivers in February 1862. When the Confederate commander at Fort Donelson asked for terms, Grant bluntly demanded "an unconditional and immediate surrender."

Grant's triumph in Tennessee was crucial. It not only riveted Kentucky more securely to the Union but also opened the gateway to the strategically important region of Tennessee, as well as to Georgia and the heart of Dixie. Grant next attempted to exploit his victory by capturing the junction of the main Confederate north-south and east-west railroads in the Mississippi Valley at Corinth, Mississippi. But a Confederate force foiled his plans in a gory battle at Shiloh, just over the Tennessee border from Corinth, on April 6–7, 1862. Though Grant successfully counterattacked, the impressive Confederate showing at Shiloh confirmed that there would be no quick end to the war in the West.

Lincoln resisted all demands for the removal of "Unconditional Surrender" Grant, insisting, "I can't spare this man; he fights." When talebearers later told Lincoln that Grant drank too much, the president allegedly replied, "Find me the brand, and I'll send a barrel to each of my other generals." There is no evidence that Grant's drinking habits seriously impaired his military performance.

Other Union thrusts in the West were in the making. In the spring of 1862, a flotilla commanded by David G. Farragut joined with a Northern army to strike the South a blow by seizing New Orleans. With Union gunboats both ascending and descending the Mississippi, the eastern part of the Confederacy was left with a jeopardized back door. Through this narrowing entrance, between Vicksburg, Mississippi, and Port Hudson, Louisiana, flowed herds of vitally needed cattle and other provisions from Louisiana and Texas. The fortress of Vicksburg, located on a hairpin turn of the Mississippi, was the South's sentinel protecting the lifeline to the western sources of supply.

General Grant was now given command of the Union forces attacking Vicksburg and in the teeth of grave difficulties displayed rare skill and daring. The siege of Vicksburg was his best-fought campaign of the war. The beleaguered city at length surrendered, on July 4, 1863, with the garrison reduced to eating mules and rats. Five days later came the fall of Port Hudson, the last Southern bastion on the Mississippi. The spinal cord of the Confederacy was now severed, and, in Lincoln's quaint phrase, the Father of Waters at last flowed "unvexed to the sea."

The Union victory at Vicksburg (July 4, 1863) came the day after the Confederate defeat at Gettysburg. The political significance of these back-to-back military successes was monumental. Reopening the Mississippi helped to quell the Northern peace agitation in the "Butternut" area of the Ohio River valley. Confederate control of the Mississippi had cut off that region's usual trade routes down the Ohio-Mississippi River system to New Orleans, thus adding economic pain to that border section's already shaky support for the "abolition war." The twin victories also conclusively tipped the diplomatic scales in favor of the North, as Britain stopped delivery of the Laird rams to the Confederates and as France killed a deal for the sale of six naval vessels to the Richmond government. By the end of 1863, all Confederate hopes for foreign help were irretrievably lost.

Sherman Scorches Georgia

General Grant, the victor of Vicksburg, was now transferred to the east Tennessee theater, where Confederates had driven Union forces from the battlefield at

General Ulysses S. Grant and General Robert E. Lee
Trained at West Point, Grant (left) proved to be a better general than a president. Oddly, he hated the sight of blood and recoiled from rare beef. Lee (right), a gentlemanly general in an ungentlemanly business, remarked when the Union troops were bloodily repulsed at Fredericksburg, "It is well that war is so terrible, or we should get too fond of it."

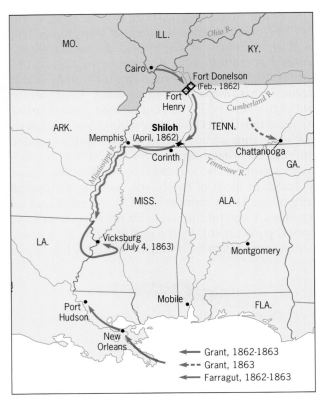

The Mississippi River and Tennessee, 1862–1863

Chickamauga into the city of Chattanooga, to which they then laid siege. Grant won a series of desperate engagements in November 1863 in the vicinity of besieged Chattanooga, including Missionary Ridge and Lookout Mountain ("the Battle Above the Clouds"). Chattanooga was liberated, the state was cleared of Confederates, and the way was thus opened for an invasion of Georgia. Grant was rewarded by being made general in chief.

Georgia's conquest was entrusted to General William Tecumseh Sherman. Red-haired and red-bearded, grim-faced and ruthless, he captured Atlanta in September 1864 and burned the city in November of that year. He then daringly left his supply base, lived off the country for some 250 miles, and weeks later emerged at Savannah on the sea. A rousing Northern song ("Marching Through Georgia") put it,

"Sherman's dashing Yankee boys will never reach the coast!"
So the saucy rebels said—and 't was a handsome boast.

But Sherman's hated "Blue Bellies," sixty thousand strong, cut a sixty-mile swath of destruction through

Georgia. They burned buildings, leaving only the blackened chimneys ("Sherman's Sentinels"). They tore up railroad rails, heated them red-hot, and twisted them into "iron doughnuts" and "Sherman's hairpins." They bayoneted family portraits and ran off with valuable "souvenirs." "War . . . is all hell," admitted Sherman later, and he proved it by his efforts to "make Georgia howl." One of his major purposes was to destroy supplies destined for the Confederate army and to weaken the morale of the men at the front by waging war on their homes.

Sherman was a pioneer practitioner of "total war." His success in "Shermanizing" the South was attested by increasing numbers of Confederate desertions. Although his methods were brutal, he probably shortened the struggle and hence saved lives. But there can be no doubt that the discipline of his army at times broke down, as roving riffraff (Sherman's "bummers") engaged in an orgy of pillaging. "Sherman the Brute" was universally damned in the South.

After seizing Savannah as a Christmas present for Lincoln, Sherman's army veered north into South Car-

A Study in Black and White
Soldiers of the 7th Tennessee Cavalry posed with their slaves—whose bondage the Confederacy fought to perpetuate.

olina, where the destruction was even more vicious. Many Union soldiers believed that this state, the "hell-hole of secession," had wantonly provoked the war. The capital city, Columbia, burst into flames, in all probability the handiwork of the Yankee invader. Crunching northward, Sherman's conquering army had rolled deep into North Carolina by the time the war ended.

The Politics of War

Presidential elections come by the calendar and not by the crisis. As fate would have it, the election of 1864 fell most inopportunely in the midst of war.

Political infighting in the North added greatly to Lincoln's cup of woe. Factions within his own party, distrusting his ability or doubting his commitment to abolition, sought to tie his hands or even remove him from office. Conspicuous among his critics was a group led by the overambitious secretary of the Treasury, Salmon Chase. Especially burdensome to Lincoln was the creation of the Congressional Committee on the Conduct of the War, formed in late 1861. It was dominated by "radical" Republicans who resented the expansion of presidential power in wartime and who pressed Lincoln zealously on emancipation.

Most dangerous of all to the Union cause were the Northern Democrats. Deprived of the talent that had

departed with the Southern wing of the party, those Democrats remaining in the North were left with the taint of association with the seceders. Tragedy befell the Democrats—and the Union—when their gifted leader, Stephen A. Douglas, died of typhoid fever seven weeks after the war began. Unshakably devoted to the Union,

Sherman's March, 1864–1865

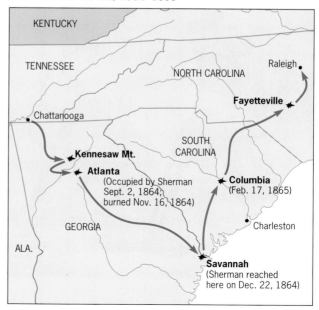

A letter picked up on a dead Confederate in North Carolina and addressed to his "deer sister" concluded that

it was "dam fulishness" trying to "lick shurmin." He had been getting "nuthin but hell & lots uv it" ever since he saw the "dam yanks," and he was "tirde uv it." He would head for home now, but his old horse was "plaid out." If the "dam yankees" had not got there yet, it would be a "dam wunder." They were thicker than "lise on a hen and a dam site ornerier."

he probably could have kept much of his following on the path of loyalty.

Democracy Versus Rebellion   The two American combatants exchange blows while Britain and France look on. Note the copperhead snake that threatens to distract the Union. "Copperhead" was the name given to those Northern Democrats who were willing to settle for a negotiated peace with the Confederacy.

Lacking a leader, the Democrats divided. A large group of "War Democrats" patriotically supported the Lincoln administration, but tens of thousands of "Peace Democrats" did not. At the extreme were the so-called Copperheads, named for the poisonous snake, which strikes without a warning rattle. Copperheads openly obstructed the war through attacks against the draft, against Lincoln, and especially, after 1863, against emancipation. They denounced the president as the "Illinois Ape" and condemned the "Nigger War." They commanded considerable political strength in the southern parts of Ohio, Indiana, and Illinois.

Notorious among the Copperheads was a sometime congressman from Ohio, Clement L. Vallandigham. This tempestuous character possessed brilliant oratorical gifts and unusual talents for stirring up trouble. A Southern partisan, he publicly demanded an end to the "wicked and cruel" war. The civil courts in Ohio were open, and he should have been tried in them for sedition. But he was convicted by a military tribunal in 1863 for treasonable utterances and was then sentenced to prison. Lincoln decided that if Vallandigham liked the Confederates so much, he ought to be banished to their lines. This was done.

Vallandigham was not so easily silenced. Working his way to Canada, he ran for the governorship of Ohio on foreign soil and polled a substantial but insufficient vote. He returned to his own state before the war ended, and although he defied "King Lincoln" and spat upon a military decree, he was not further prosecuted. The strange case of Vallandigham inspired Edward Everett Hale to write his moving but fictional story of Philip Nolan, *The Man Without a Country* (1863), which was immensely popular in the North and which helped stimulate devotion to the Union. Nolan was a young army officer found guilty of participation in the Aaron Burr plot of 1806 (see p. 224). He had cried out in court, "Damn the United States! I wish I may never hear of the United States again!" For this outburst he was condemned to a life of eternal exile on American warships.

The Election of 1864

As the election of 1864 approached, Lincoln's precarious authority depended on his retaining Republican support while spiking the threat from the Peace Democrats and Copperheads.

Union Party, 1864 The blue area represents the Union party.

Fearing defeat, the Republican party executed a clever maneuver. Joining with the War Democrats, it proclaimed itself to be the Union party. Thus the Republican party passed temporarily out of existence.

Lincoln's renomination at first encountered surprisingly strong opposition. Hostile factions whipped up considerable agitation to shelve homely "Old Abe" in favor of his handsome nemesis, Secretary of the Treasury Chase. Lincoln was accused of lacking force, of being overready to compromise, of not having won the war, and of having shocked many sensitive souls by his ill-timed and earthy jokes. ("Prince of Jesters," one journal called him.) But the "ditch Lincoln" move collapsed, and he was nominated by the Union party without serious dissent.

Lincoln's running mate was ex-tailor Andrew Johnson, a loyal War Democrat from Tennessee who had been a small slaveowner when the conflict began. He was placed on the Union party ticket to "sew up" the election by attracting War Democrats and the voters in the Border States, and, sadly, with no proper regard for the possibility that Lincoln might die in office. Southerners and Copperheads alike condemned both candidates as birds of a feather: two ignorant, third-rate, boorish, backwoods politicians born in log cabins.

Embattled Democrats—regular and Copperhead—nominated the deposed and overcautious war hero General McClellan. The Copperheads managed to force into the Democratic platform a plank denouncing the prosecution of the war as a failure. But McClellan, who could not otherwise have faced his old comrades-in-arms, repudiated this defeatist declaration.

The campaign was noisy and nasty. The Democrats cried, "Old Abe removed McClellan. We'll now remove

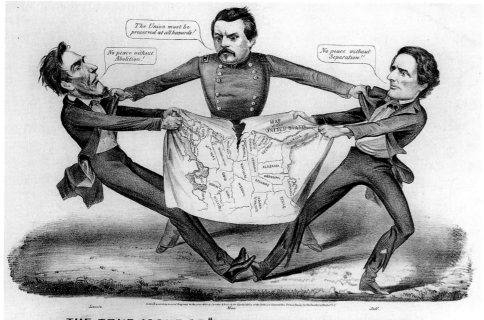

THE TRUE ISSUE OR "THATS WHATS THE MATTER".

McClellan as Mediator, 1865 This 1864 poster shows Presidents Lincoln and Davis trying to tear the country in half, while former general George McClellan, the candidate of the Democratic party, attempts to mediate.

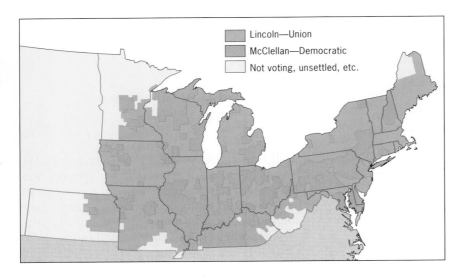

Presidential Election of 1864 (showing popular vote by county) Lincoln also carried California, Oregon, and Nevada, but there was a considerable McClellan vote in each. Note McClellan's strength in the Border States and in the southern tier of Ohio, Indiana, and Illinois—the so-called "Butternut" region.

Old Abe." They also sang, "Mac Will Win the Union Back." The Union party supporters shouted for "Uncle Abe and Andy" and urged, "Vote as you shot." Their most effective slogan, growing out of a remark by Lincoln, was "Don't swap horses in the middle of the river."

Lincoln's reelection was at first gravely in doubt. The war was going badly, and Lincoln himself gave way to despondency, fearing that political defeat was imminent. The anti-Lincoln Republicans, taking heart, started a new movement to "dump" Lincoln in favor of someone else.

But the atmosphere of gloom was changed electrically, as balloting day neared, by a succession of Northern victories. Admiral Farragut captured Mobile, Alabama, after defiantly shouting the now famous order, "Damn the torpedoes! Go ahead." General Sherman seized Atlanta. General ("Little Phil") Sheridan laid waste the verdant Shenandoah Valley of Virginia so thoroughly that in his words "a crow could not fly over it without carrying his rations with him."

The president pulled through, but nothing more than necessary was left to chance. At election time

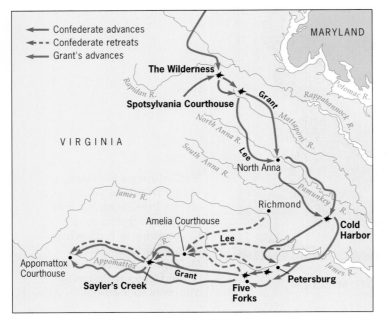

Grant's Virginia Campaign, 1864–1865 The Wilderness Campaign pitted soldier against desperate soldier in some of the most brutal and terrifying fighting of the Civil War. "No one could see the fight fifty feet from him," a Union private recalled of his month spent fighting in Virginia. "The lines were very near each other, and from the dense underbrush and the tops of trees came puffs of smoke, the 'ping' of the bullets and the yell of the enemy. It was a blind and bloody hunt to the death, in bewildering thickets, rather than a battle."

many Northern soldiers were furloughed home to support Lincoln at the polls. One Pennsylvania veteran voted forty-nine times—once for himself and once for each absent member of his company. Other Northern soldiers were permitted to cast their ballots at the front.

Lincoln, bolstered by the "bayonet vote," vanquished McClellan by 212 electoral votes to 21, losing only Kentucky, Delaware, and New Jersey. But "Little Mac" ran a closer race than the electoral count indicates. He netted a healthy 45 percent of the popular vote, 1,803,787 to Lincoln's 2,206,938, piling up much support in the Southerner-infiltrated states of the Old Northwest, in New York, and also in his native state of Pennsylvania (see the top map on p. 472).

One of the most crushing losses suffered by the South was the defeat of the Northern Democrats in 1864. The removal of Lincoln was the last ghost of a hope for a Confederate victory, and the Southern soldiers would wishfully shout, "Hurrah for McClellan!" When Lincoln triumphed, desertions from the sinking Southern ship increased sharply.

Grant Outlasts Lee

After Gettysburg, Grant was brought in from the West over Meade, who was blamed for failing to pursue the defeated but always dangerous Lee. Lincoln needed a general who, employing the superior resources of the North, would have the intestinal stamina to drive ever forward, regardless of casualties. A soldier of bulldog tenacity, Grant was the man for this meat-grinder type of warfare. His overall basic strategy was to assail the enemy's armies simultaneously, so that they could not assist one another and hence could be destroyed piecemeal. His personal motto was "When in doubt, fight." A grimly determined Grant, with more than 100,000 men, struck toward Richmond. He engaged Lee in a series of furious battles in the Wilderness of Virginia, during May and June of 1864, notably in the leaden hurricane of the "Bloody Angle" and "Hell's Half Acre." In this Wilderness Campaign, Grant suffered about 50,000 casualties, or nearly as many men as Lee commanded at the start. But Lee lost about as heavily in proportion.

The Burning of Richmond, April 1865 The proud Confederate capital, after holding out against repeated Union assaults, was evacuated and burned in the final days of the war.

In a ghastly gamble, on June 3, 1864, Grant ordered a frontal assault on the impregnable position of Cold Harbor. The Union soldiers advanced to almost certain death with papers pinned on their backs bearing their names and addresses. In a few minutes, about seven thousand men were killed or wounded.

Public opinion in the North was appalled by this "blood and guts" type of fighting. Critics cried that "Grant the Butcher" had gone insane. But Grant's reputation was undeserved, while Lee's was overrated. Lee's rate of loss (at one casualty for every five soldiers) was the highest of any general in the war. By contrast, Grant lost one of ten. Grant had intended to fight battles out in the open, a tactic he had perfected in the West. It was Lee, not Grant, who turned the eastern campaign into a war of attrition fought in the trenches. With fewer men, Lee could no longer seize the offensive, as he had at Chancellorsville or Gettysburg. Lee's new defensive posture in turn forced Grant into some brutal arithmetic. Grant could trade two men for one and still beat the enemy to his knees. "I propose to fight it out on this line," he wrote, "if it takes all summer." It did—and it also took all autumn, all winter, and a part of the spring.

In February 1865 the Confederates, tasting the bitter dregs of defeat, tried desperately to negotiate for peace between the "two countries." Lincoln himself met with Confederate representatives aboard a Union ship moored at Hampton Roads, Virginia, to discuss peace terms. But Lincoln could accept nothing short of Union and emancipation, and the Southerners could accept nothing short of independence. So the tribulation wore on—amid smoke and agony—to its terrible climax.

The end came with dramatic suddenness. Rapidly advancing Northern troops captured Richmond and cornered Lee at Appomattox Courthouse in Virginia, in April 1865. Grant—stubble-bearded and informally dressed—met with Lee on the ninth, Palm Sunday, and granted generous terms of surrender. Among other concessions, the hungry Confederates were allowed to keep their horses for spring plowing.

Tattered Southern veterans—"Lee's Ragamuffins"— wept as they took leave of their beloved commander. The elated Union soldiers cheered, but they were silenced by Grant's stern admonition, "The war is over; the rebels are our countrymen again."

Lincoln traveled to conquered Richmond and sat in Jefferson Davis's evacuated office just forty hours after the Confederate president had left it. "Thank God I have lived to see this," he said. With a small escort of sailors, he walked the blasted streets of the city. Freed slaves began to recognize him, and crowds gathered to see and touch "Father Abraham." One black man fell to his knees before the Emancipator, who said to him, "Don't kneel to me. This is not right. You must kneel to God only, and thank Him for the liberty you will enjoy hereafter." Sadly, as many freed slaves were to discover, the hereafter of their full liberty was a long time coming.

The Martyrdom of Lincoln

On the night of April 14, 1865 (Good Friday), only five days after Lee's surrender, Ford's Theater in Washington witnessed its most sensational drama. A half-crazed, fanatically pro-Southern actor, John Wilkes Booth, slipped behind Lincoln as he sat in his box and shot him in the head. After lying unconscious all night, the Great Emancipator died the following morning. "Now he belongs to the ages," remarked the once-critical Secretary Stanton— probably the finest words he ever spoke.

Lincoln expired in the arms of victory, at the very pinnacle of his fame. From the standpoint of his reputation, his death could not have been better timed if he had hired the assassin. A large number of his countrymen had not suspected his greatness, and many others had even doubted his ability. But his dramatic death helped to erase the memory of his shortcomings and caused his nobler qualities to stand out in clearer relief.

The full impact of Lincoln's death was not at once apparent to the South. Hundreds of bedraggled

---

The New York Herald *editorialized on April 16, 1865, that the South had the most to lose from Lincoln's assassination:*

"In the death of President Lincoln we feel the pressure of a heavy national calamity; but the great and irrevocable decree of the loyal States that Union must and shall be preserved will lose nothing of its force, but will be immensely if not terribly strengthened. In striking Abraham Lincoln and his kindly disposed Secretary of State the assassins struck at the best friends in the government to the prostrate rebels of the South."

The Funeral of President Lincoln, New-York, April 25th, 1865.

New York Mourns Lincoln's Death, April 25, 1865 Lincoln's body traveled by train to lie in state in fourteen cities before arriving at his final resting place of Springfield, Illinois. In New York City, 160,000 mourners accompanied the hearse as the funeral procession slowly made its way down Broadway. Scalpers sold choice window seats for four dollars and up. Blacks were barred from participating, until the mayor changed his mind at the last minute—but only if they marched at the rear. This souvenir stereo view, bringing the scene to three-dimensional life when seen through the popular device of a hand-held stereopticon, allowed many more Americans to observe the funeral than could be there in person

ex-Confederate soldiers cheered, as did some Southern civilians and Northern Copperheads, when they learned of the assassination. This reaction was only natural, because Lincoln had kept the war grinding on to the bitter end. If he had only been willing to stop the shooting, the South would have won.

As time wore on, increasing numbers of Southerners perceived that Lincoln's death was a calamity for them. Belatedly they recognized that his kindliness and moderation would have been the most effective shields between them and vindictive treatment by the victors. The assassination unfortunately increased the bitterness in the North, partly because of the fantastic rumor that Jefferson Davis had plotted it.

A few historians have argued that Andrew Johnson, now president-by-bullet, was crucified in Lincoln's stead. The implication is that if the "rail-splitter" had lived, he would have suffered Johnson's fate of being impeached by the embittered members of his own party, who demanded harshness, not forbearance, toward the South.

The crucifixion thesis does not stand up under scrutiny. Lincoln no doubt would have clashed with Congress; in fact, he had already found himself in some hot water. The legislative branch normally struggles to win back the power that has been wrested from it by the executive in time of crisis. But the sure-footed and experienced Lincoln could hardly have blundered into the same quicksands that engulfed Johnson. Lincoln was a victorious president, and there is no arguing with victory. In addition to his powers of leadership refined in the war crucible, Lincoln possessed in full measure tact, sweet reasonableness, and an uncommon amount of common sense. Andrew Johnson, hot-tempered and impetuous, lacked all of these priceless qualities.

Ford's Theater, with its tragic murder of Lincoln, set the stage for the wrenching ordeal of Reconstruction.

The Aftermath of the Nightmare

The Civil War took a grisly toll in gore, about as much as all of America's subsequent wars combined. Over 600,000 men died in action or of disease, and in all over a million were killed or seriously wounded. To its lasting hurt, the nation lost the cream of its young manhood and potential leadership. In addition, tens of thousands of babies went unborn because potential fathers were at the front.

Direct monetary costs of the conflict totaled about $15 billion. But this colossal figure does not include continuing expenses, such as pensions and interest on the national debt. The intangible costs—dislocations, disunities, wasted energies, lowered ethics, blasted lives, bitter memories, and burning hates—cannot be calculated.

The greatest constitutional decision of the century, in a sense, was written in blood and handed down at Appomattox Courthouse, near which Lee surrendered. The extreme states' righters were crushed. The national government, tested in the fiery furnace of war, emerged unbroken. Nullification and secession, those twin nightmares of previous decades, were laid to rest.

Beyond doubt the Civil War—the nightmare of the Republic—was the supreme test of American democracy. It finally answered the question, in the words of

Nora August: The Fruits of Emancipation
An unidentified Union soldier carved this ivory bust of the freedwoman Nora August during the Civil War. Note the elaborately braided hair—a direct adaptation of a West African style. The anonymous sculptor etched the following legend into the base of the statue: "Carved from life. Retreat Plantation. Presented to the Nurses of Darien GA in the year of Our Lord 1865. Nora August (slave). Age 23 years. Purchased from the Market, St. Augustine, Florida, April 17th 1860. Now a Free Woman."

Prisoners from the Front, by Winslow Homer, 1866
This celebrated painting reflects the artist's firsthand observations of the war. Homer brilliantly captured the enduring depths of sectional animosity. The Union officer somewhat disdainfully asserts his command of the situation; the beaten and disarmed Confederates exhibit an out-at-the-elbows pride and defiance.

Lincoln at Gettysburg, whether a nation dedicated to such principles "can long endure." The preservation of democratic ideals, though not an officially announced war aim, was subconsciously one of the major objectives of the North.

Victory for Union arms also provided inspiration to the champions of democracy and liberalism the world over. The great English Reform Bill of 1867, under which Britain became a true political democracy, was passed two years after the Civil War ended. American democracy had proved itself, and its success was an additional argument used by the disfranchised British masses in securing similar blessings for themselves.

The "Lost Cause" of the South was lost, but few Americans today would argue that the result was not for the best. The shameful cancer of slavery was sliced away by the sword, and African Americans were at last in a position to claim their rights to life, liberty, and the pursuit of happiness. The nation was again united politically, though for many generations still divided spiritually by the passions of the war. Grave dangers were averted by a Union victory, including the indefinite prolongation of the "peculiar institution," the unleashing of the slave power on weak Caribbean neighbors, and the transformation of the area from Panama to Hudson Bay into an armed camp, with several heavily armed and hostile states constantly snarling and sniping at one another. America still had a long way to go to make the promises of freedom a reality for all its citizens, black and white. But emancipation laid the necessary groundwork, and a united and democratic United States was free to fulfill its destiny as the dominant republic of the hemisphere—and eventually of the world.

Chronology

1861 First Battle of Bull Run

1862 Grant takes Fort Henry and Fort Donelson
Battle of Shiloh
McClellan's Peninsula Campaign
Seven Days' Battles
Second Battle of Bull Run
Naval battle of the *Merrimack* (the *Virginia*) and the *Monitor*
Battle of Antietam
Preliminary Emancipation Proclamation
Battle of Fredericksburg
Northern army seizes New Orleans

1863 Final Emancipation Proclamation

1863 Battle of Chancellorsville
Battle of Gettysburg
Fall of Vicksburg
Fall of Port Hudson

1864 Sherman's march through Georgia
Grant's Wilderness Campaign
Battle of Cold Harbor
Lincoln defeats McClellan for presidency

1865 Hampton Roads Conference
Lee surrenders to Grant at Appomattox
Lincoln assassinated
Thirteenth Amendment ratified

VARYING VIEWPOINTS

What Were the Consequences of the Civil War?

With the end of the Civil War in 1865, the United States was permanently altered, despite the reunification of the Union and the Confederacy. Slavery was officially banned, secession was a dead issue, and industrial growth surged forward. For the first time, the United States could securely consider itself as a singular nation rather than a union of states. Though sectional differences remained, there would be no return to the unstable days of precarious balancing between Northern and Southern interests. With the Union's victory, power rested firmly with the North, and it would orchestrate the future development of the country. According to historian Eric Foner, the war redrew the economic and political map of the country.

The constitutional impact of the terms of the Union victory created some of the most far-reaching transformations. The first twelve amendments to the Constitution, ratified before the war, had all served to limit government power. In contrast, the Thirteenth Amendment, which abolished slavery, and the revolutionary Fourteenth Amendment, which conferred citizenship and guaranteed civil rights to all those born in the United States, marked unprecedented expansions of federal power.

Historian James McPherson has noted still other ways in which the Civil War extended the authority of the central government. It expanded federal powers of taxation. It encouraged the government to develop the National Banking System, print currency, and conscript an army. It made the federal courts more influential. And through the Freedmen's Bureau, which aided former slaves in the South, it instituted the first federal social welfare agency. With each of these actions, the nation moved toward a more powerful federal government, invested with the authority to protect civil rights, aid its citizens, and enforce laws in an aggressive manner that superseded state powers. Some scholars have disputed whether the Civil War marked an absolute watershed in American history. They correctly note that racial inequality scandalously persisted after the Civil War, despite the abolition of slavery and the supposed protections extended by federal civil rights legislation. Others have argued that the industrial growth of the post–Civil War era had its real roots in the Jacksonian era, and thus cannot be ascribed solely to war. Thomas Cochran has even argued that the Civil War may have retarded overall industrialization rather than advancing it. Regional differences between North and South endured, moreover, even down to the present day.

Yet the argument that the Civil War launched a modern America remains convincing. The lives of Americans, white and black, North and South, were transformed by the war experience. Industry entered a period of unprecedented growth, having been stoked by the transportation and military needs of the Union army. The emergence of new, national legal and governmental institutions marked the birth of the modern American state. All considered, it is hard to deny that the end of the Civil War brought one chapter of the nation's history to a close, while opening another.

For further reading, see the Appendix. For web resources, go to **http://college.hmco.com**.

22

The Ordeal of Reconstruction

1865–1877

WITH MALICE TOWARD NONE, WITH CHARITY FOR ALL,
WITH FIRMNESS IN THE RIGHT AS GOD GIVES US TO SEE
THE RIGHT, LET US STRIVE ON TO FINISH THE WORK WE
ARE IN, TO BIND UP THE NATION'S WOUNDS, TO CARE FOR
HIM WHO SHALL HAVE BORNE THE BATTLE AND FOR HIS
WIDOW AND ORPHAN, TO DO ALL WHICH MAY ACHIEVE AND
CHERISH A JUST AND LASTING PEACE AMONG OURSELVES
AND WITH ALL NATIONS.

ABRAHAM LINCOLN, SECOND INAUGURAL, MARCH 4, 1865

The battle was done, the buglers silent. Bone-weary and bloodied, the American people, North and South, now faced the staggering challenges of peace. Four questions loomed large. How would the South, physically devastated by war and socially revolutionized by emancipation, be rebuilt? How would liberated blacks fare as free men and women? How would the Southern states be reintegrated into the Union? And who would direct the process of Reconstruction—the Southern states themselves, the president, or Congress?

The Problems of Peace

Other questions also clamored for answers. What should be done with the captured Confederate ringleaders, all of whom were liable to charges of treason? During the war a popular Northern song had been "Hang Jeff Davis to a Sour Apple Tree," and even innocent children had lisped it. Davis was temporarily clapped into irons during the early days of his two-year imprisonment. But he and his fellow "conspirators" were finally released, partly because the odds were that no Virginia jury would convict them. All rebel leaders were finally pardoned by President Johnson as sort of a Christmas present in 1868. But Congress did not remove all remaining civil disabilities until thirty years later and only posthumously restored Davis's citizenship more than a century later.

Dismal indeed was the picture presented by the war-racked South when the rattle of musketry faded. Not only had an age perished, but a civilization had collapsed, in both its economic and its social structure. The moonlight-and-magnolia Old South, largely imaginary in any case, had forever gone with the wind.

Richmond Devastated Charleston, Atlanta, and other Southern cities looked much the same, resembling bombed-out Berlin and Dresden in 1945.

Handsome cities of yesteryear, such as Charleston and Richmond, were rubble-strewn and weed-choked. An Atlantan returned to his once-fair hometown and remarked, "Hell has laid her egg, and right here it hatched."

Economic life had creaked to a halt. Banks and businesses had locked their doors, ruined by runaway inflation. Factories were smokeless, silent, dismantled. The transportation system had broken down completely. Before the war five different railroad lines had converged on Columbia, South Carolina; now the nearest connected track was twenty-nine miles away. Efforts to untwist the rails corkscrewed by Sherman's soldiers proved bumpily unsatisfactory.

Agriculture—the economic lifeblood of the South— was almost hopelessly crippled. Once-white cotton fields now yielded a lush harvest of nothing but green weeds. The slave-labor system had collapsed, seed was scarce, and livestock had been driven off by plundering Yankees. Pathetic instances were reported of men hitching themselves to plows, while women and children gripped the handles. Not until 1870 did the seceded states produce as large a cotton crop as that of the fateful year 1860, and much of that yield came from new acreage in the Southwest.

The princely planter aristocrats were humbled by the war—at least temporarily. Reduced to proud poverty, they faced charred and gutted mansions, lost investments, and almost worthless land. Their investments of more than $2 billion in slaves, their primary form of wealth, had evaporated with emancipation.

Beaten but unbent, many high-spirited white Southerners remained dangerously defiant. They cursed the "damnyankees" and spoke of "your government" in Washington, instead of "our government." One Southern bishop refused to pray for President Andrew Johnson, though Johnson proved to be in sore need of divine guidance. Conscious of no crime, these former Confederates continued to believe that their view of secession was correct and that the "lost cause" was still a just war. One popular anti-Union song ran,

I'm glad I fought agin her, I only wish we'd won,
And I ain't axed any pardon for anything I've done.

Such attitudes boded ill for the prospects of painlessly binding up the Republic's wounds.

Freedmen Define Freedom

Confusion abounded in the still-smoldering South about the precise meaning of "freedom" for blacks. Emancipation took effect haltingly and unevenly in different parts of the conquered Confederacy. As Union armies marched in and out of various localities, many blacks found themselves emancipated and then re-enslaved. A North Carolina slave estimated that he had celebrated freedom about twelve times. Blacks from one Texas county fleeing to the free soil of the liberated county next door were attacked by slaveowners as they swam across the river that marked the county line. The next day, trees along the riverbank were bent with swinging corpses—a grisly warning to others dreaming of liberty. Other planters resisted emancipation more legalistically, stubbornly protesting that slavery was lawful until state legislatures or the Supreme Court declared otherwise. For many slaves the shackles of bondage were not struck off in a single mighty blow; long-suffering blacks often had to wrench free of their chains link by link.

The variety of responses to emancipation, by whites as well as blacks, illustrated the sometimes startling complexity of the master-slave relationship. Loyalty to the plantation master prompted some slaves to resist the liberating Union armies, while other slaves' pent-up bitterness burst forth violently on the day of liberation. Many newly emancipated slaves, for example, joined Union troops in pillaging their masters' possessions. In one instance a group of Virginia slaves laid twenty lashes on the back of their former master—a painful dose of his own favorite medicine.

Prodded by the bayonets of Yankee armies of occupation, all masters were eventually forced to recognize their slaves' permanent freedom. The once-commanding planter would assemble his former human chattels in front of the porch of the "big house" and announce their liberty. Though some blacks initially responded to news of their emancipation with suspicion and uncertainty, they soon celebrated their newfound freedom. Many took new names in place of the ones given by their masters and demanded that whites formally address them as "Mr." or "Mrs." Others abandoned the coarse cottons that had been their only clothing as slaves and sought silks, satins, and other finery. Though many whites perceived such behavior as insubordinate, they were forced to recognize the realities of emancipation. "Never before had I a word of impudence from any of our black folk," wrote one white Southerner, "but they are not ours any longer."

Tens of thousands of emancipated blacks took to the roads, some to test their freedom, others to search for long-lost spouses, parents, and children. Emancipation thus strengthened the black family, and many newly

Commemorating Emancipation Day
These African Americans in Richmond, Virginia, commemorated the twenty-fifth anniversary of the Emancipation Proclamation in 1888 by paying their respects to the "Great Emancipator," Abraham Lincoln.

Houston H. Holloway, age twenty at the time of his emancipation, recalled his feelings upon hearing of his freedom:

"I felt like a bird out of a cage. Amen. Amen. Amen. I could hardly ask to feel any better than I did that day. . . . The week passed off in a blaze of glory."

The reunion of long-lost relatives also inspired joy; one Union officer wrote home,

"Men are taking their wives and children, families which had been for a long time broken up are united and oh! such happiness. I am glad I am here."

former masters to work in towns and cities, where existing black communities provided protection and mutual assistance. Whole communities sometimes moved together in search of opportunity. From 1878 to 1880, some twenty-five thousand blacks from Louisiana, Texas, and Mississippi surged in a mass exodus to Kansas. The westward flood of these "Exodusters" was stemmed only when steamboat captains refused to transport more black migrants across the Mississippi River.

The church became the focus of black community life in the years following emancipation. As slaves, blacks had worshiped alongside whites, but now they formed their own churches pastored by their own ministers. Black churches grew robustly. The 150,000-member black Baptist Church of 1850 reached 500,000 by 1870, while the African Methodist Episcopal Church quadrupled in size from 100,000 to 400,000 in the first decade after emancipation. These churches formed the bedrock of black community life, and they soon gave rise to other benevolent, fraternal, and mutual aid societies. All these organizations helped blacks protect their newly won freedom.

freed men and women formalized "slave marriages" for personal and pragmatic reasons, including the desire to make their children legal heirs. Other blacks left their

Educating Young Feedmen and Women, 1870s Freed slaves in the South regarded schooling as the key to improving their children's lives and the fulfillment of a long-sought right that had been denied blacks in slavery. These well-dressed school children are lined up outside their rural, one-room schoolhouse alongside their teachers, both black and white.

EXAMINING THE EVIDENCE

Letter from a Freedman to His Old Master, 1865 What was it like to experience the transition from slavery to freedom? Four million southern blacks faced this exhilarating and formidable prospect with the end of the war. For historians, recovering the African American perspective on emancipation is challenging. Unlike their white masters, freed blacks left few written records. But one former slave captured in a letter to his "Old Master" (whose surname he bore) the heroic determination of many blacks to build new independent and dignified lives for themselves and their families.

During the war Jourdon Anderson escaped slavery in Tennessee with his wife and two daughters. After relocating to the relative safety of Ohio, he received a communication from his former owner asking him to return. In his bold reply, reportedly "dictated by the old servant" himself, Anderson expressed his family's new expectations for life as free people and an uneasiness about his former master's intentions. He made reference to his "comfortable home," his daughters' schooling, the church that he and his wife were free to attend regularly, and the peace of mind that came with knowing that "my girls [would not be] brought to shame by the violence and wickedness of their young masters." To test the white man's sincerity, Anderson and his wife asked for the astronomical figure of $11,680 in back wages from decades as slaves. He closed by reiterating that "the great desire of my life is to give my children an education and have them form virtuous habits." This rare letter demonstrates that many black correspondents may have been illiterate, but they were hardly inarticulate. And they asserted themselves as parents, workers, and citizens not only from the distance of a former free state like Ohio but also deep within the former slave states of the South. Was the tone of Anderson's letter (and postscript) serious or tongue-in-cheek? What did "freedom" mean for Anderson and other blacks in the months following emancipation? How did the eventual accomplishments of Reconstruction correspond with the initial expectations of people like Anderson and his former owner?

Letter from a Freedman to his Old Master.

The following is a genuine document. It was *dictated* by the old servant, and contains his ideas and forms of expression.   [Cincinnati Commercial.

DAYTON, Ohio, August 7, 1865.
To my Old Master, Col. P. H. ANDERSON, Big Spring, Tennessee.

SIR: I got your letter and was glad to find that you had not forgotten Jordan, and that you wanted me to come back and live with you again, promising to do better for me than anybody else can. I have often felt uneasy about you. I thought the Yankees would have hung you long before this for harboring Rebs. they found at your house. I suppose they never heard about your going to Col. Martin's to kill the Union soldier that was left by his company in their stable. Although you shot at me twice before I left you, I did not want to hear of your being hurt, and am glad you are still living. It would do me good to go back to the dear old home again and see Miss Mary and Miss Martha and Allen, Esther, Green and Lee. Give my love to them all, and tell them I hope we will meet in the better world, if not in this. I would have gone back to see you all when I was working in the Nashville Hospital, but one of the neighbors told me Henry intended to shoot me if he ever got a chance.

I want to know particularly what the good chance is you propose to give me. I am doing tolerably well here; I get $25 a month, with victuals and clothing; have a comfortable home for Mandy (the folks here call her Mrs. Anderson), and the children, Milly Jane and Grundy, go to school and are learning well; the teacher says Grundy has a head for a preacher. They go to Sunday-School, and Mandy and me attend church

As to my freedom, which you say I can have, there is nothing to be gained on that score, as I got my free-papers in 1864 from the Provost-Marshal-General of the Department at Nashville. Mandy says she would be afraid to go back without some proof that you are sincerely disposed to treat us justly and kindly—and we have concluded to test your sincerity by asking you to send us our wages for the time we served you. This will make us forget and forgive old sores, and rely on your justice and friendship in the future. I served you faithfully for thirty-two years, and Mandy twenty years, at $25 a month for me, and $2 a week for Mandy. Our earnings would amount to $11,680. Add to this the interest for the time our wages has been kept back and deduct what you paid for our clothing and three doctor's visits to me, and pulling a tooth for Mandy, and the balance will show what we are in justice entitled to. Please send the money by Adams Express, in care of V. Winters, esq., Dayton, Ohio. If you fail to pay us for faithful labors in the past we can have little faith in your promises in the future.

P. S.—Say howdy to George Carter, and thank him for taking the pistol from you when you were shooting at me.

Emancipation also meant education for many blacks. Learning to read and write had been a privilege generally denied to them under slavery. Freedmen wasted no time establishing societies for self-improvement, which undertook to raise funds to purchase land, build schoolhouses, and hire teachers. One member of a North Carolina education society asserted that "a schoolhouse would be the first proof of their *independence*." Southern blacks soon found, however, that the demand outstripped the supply of qualified black teachers. They accepted the aid of Northern white women sent by the American Missionary Association, who volunteered their services as teachers. They also turned to the federal government for help. The freed blacks were going to need all the friends—and power—they could muster in Washington.

The Freedmen's Bureau

Abolitionists had long preached that slavery was a degrading institution. Now the emancipators were faced with the brutal reality that the freedmen were overwhelmingly unskilled, unlettered, without property or money, and with scant knowledge of how to survive as free people. To cope with this problem throughout the conquered South, Congress created the Freedmen's Bureau on March 3, 1865.

On paper at least, the bureau was intended to be a kind of primitive welfare agency. It was to provide food, clothing, medical care, and education both to freedmen and to white refugees. Heading the bureau was a warmly sympathetic friend of blacks, Union general Oliver O. Howard, who later founded and served as president of Howard University in Washington, D.C.

> *Women from the North enthusiastically embraced the opportunity to go south and teach in Freedmen's Bureau schools for emancipated blacks. One volunteer explained her motives:*
>
> "I thought I must do something, not having money at my command, what could I do but give myself to the work. . . . I would go to them, and give them my life if necessary."

The bureau achieved its greatest successes in education. It taught an estimated 200,000 blacks how to read. Many former slaves had a passion for learning, partly because they wanted to close the gap between themselves and whites and partly because they longed to read the Word of God. In one elementary class in North Carolina sat four generations of the same family, ranging from a six-year-old child to a seventy-five-year-old grandmother.

But in other areas, the bureau's accomplishments were meager—or even mischievous. Although the bureau was authorized to settle former slaves on forty-acre tracts confiscated from the Confederates, little land actually made it into blacks' hands. Instead local administrators often collaborated with planters in expelling blacks from towns and cajoling them into signing labor contracts to work for their former masters. Still, the white South resented the bureau as a meddlesome federal interloper that threatened to upset white racial dominance. President Andrew Johnson, who shared the white supremacist views of most white Southerners, repeatedly tried to kill it, and it expired in 1872.

Johnson: The Tailor President

Few presidents have ever been faced with a more perplexing sea of troubles than that confronting Andrew Johnson. What manner of man was this medium-built, dark-eyed, black-haired Tennessean, now chief executive by virtue of the bullet that killed Lincoln?

No citizen, not even Lincoln, has ever reached the White House from humbler beginnings. Born to impoverished parents in North Carolina and orphaned early, Johnson never attended school but was apprenticed to a tailor at age ten. Ambitious to get ahead, he taught himself to read, and later his wife taught him to write and do simple arithmetic. Like many another self-made man, he was inclined to overpraise his maker.

Johnson early became active in politics in Tennessee, where he had moved when seventeen years old. He shone as an impassioned champion of poor whites against the planter aristocrats, although he himself ultimately owned a few slaves. He excelled as a two-fisted stump speaker before angry and heckling crowds, who on occasion greeted his political oratory with cocked pistols, not just cocked ears. Elected to Congress, he attracted much favorable attention in the North (but not the South) when he refused to secede with his own state.

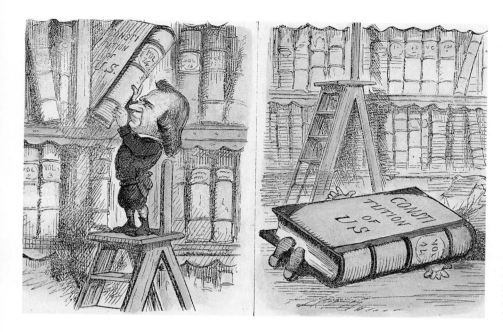

Crushed by the Constitution
President Andrew Johnson revered the U.S. Constitution but eventually felt its awesome weight in his impeachment trial.

After Tennessee was partially "redeemed" by Union armies, he was appointed war governor and served courageously in an atmosphere of danger.

Political exigency next thrust Johnson into the vice presidency. Lincoln's Union party in 1864 needed to attract support from the War Democrats and other pro-Southern elements, and Johnson, a Democrat, seemed to be the ideal man. Unfortunately, he appeared at the vice-presidential inaugural ceremonies the following March in a scandalous condition. He had recently been afflicted with typhoid fever, and although not known as a heavy drinker, he was urged by his friends to take a stiff bracer of whiskey. This he did—with unfortunate results.

"Old Andy" Johnson was no doubt a man of parts—unpolished parts. He was intelligent, able, forceful, and gifted with homespun honesty. Steadfastly devoted to duty and to the people, he was a dogmatic champion of states' rights and the Constitution. He would often present a copy of the document to visitors, and he was buried with one as a pillow.

Yet the man who had raised himself from the tailor's bench to the president's chair was a misfit. A Southerner who did not understand the North, a Tennessean who had earned the distrust of the South, a Democrat who had never been accepted by the Republicans, a president who had never been elected to the office, he was not at home in a Republican White House. Hotheaded, contentious, and stubborn, he was the wrong man in the wrong place at the wrong time. A Reconstruction policy devised by angels might well have failed in his tactless hands.

Presidential Reconstruction

Even before the shooting war had ended, the political war over Reconstruction had begun. Abraham Lincoln believed that the Southern states had never legally withdrawn from the Union. Their formal restoration to the Union would therefore be relatively simple. Accordingly, Lincoln in 1863 proclaimed his "10 percent" Reconstruction plan. It decreed that a state could be reintegrated into the Union when 10 percent of its voters in the presidential election of 1860 had taken an oath of allegiance to the United States and pledged to abide by emancipation. The next step would be formal erection of a state government. Lincoln would then recognize the purified regime.

Lincoln's proclamation provoked a sharp reaction in Congress, where Republicans feared the restoration of the planter aristocracy to power and the possible re-enslavement of blacks. Republicans therefore rammed through Congress in 1864 the Wade-Davis Bill.

> *Before President Andrew Johnson (1808–1875) softened his Southern policy, his views were radical. Speaking on April 21, 1865, he declared,*
>
> "It is not promulgating anything that I have not heretofore said to say that traitors must be made odious, that treason must be made odious, that traitors must be punished and impoverished. They must not only be punished, but their social power must be destroyed. If not, they will still maintain an ascendancy, and may again become numerous and powerful; for, in the words of a former Senator of the United States, 'When traitors become numerous enough, treason becomes respectable.'"

The bill required that 50 percent of a state's voters take the oath of allegiance and demanded stronger safeguards for emancipation than Lincoln's as the price of readmission to the Union. Lincoln "pocket-vetoed" this bill by refusing to sign it after Congress had adjourned. Republicans were outraged. They refused to seat delegates from Louisiana after that state had reorganized its government in accordance with Lincoln's 10 percent plan in 1864.

The controversy surrounding the Wade-Davis Bill had revealed deep differences between the president and Congress. Unlike Lincoln, many in Congress insisted that the seceders had indeed left the Union—had "committed suicide" as republican states—and had therefore forfeited all their rights. They could be readmitted only as "conquered provinces" on such conditions as Congress should decree.

This episode further revealed differences among Republicans. Two factions were emerging. The majority moderate group tended to agree with Lincoln that the seceded states should be restored to the Union as simply and swiftly as reasonable—though on Congress's terms, not the president's. The minority radical group believed that the South should atone more painfully for its sins. Before the South should be restored, the radicals wanted its social structure uprooted, the haughty planters punished, and the newly emancipated blacks protected by federal power.

Some of the radicals were secretly pleased when the assassin's bullet felled Lincoln, for the martyred president had shown tenderness toward the South. Spiteful "Andy" Johnson, who shared their hatred for the planter aristocrats, would presumably also share their desire to reconstruct the South with a rod of iron.

Johnson soon disillusioned them. He agreed with Lincoln that the seceded states had never legally been outside the Union. Thus he quickly recognized several of Lincoln's 10 percent governments, and on May 29, 1865, he issued his own Reconstruction proclamation. It disfranchised certain leading Confederates, including those with taxable property worth more than $20,000, though they might petition him for personal pardons. It called for special state conventions, which were required to repeal the ordinances of secession, repudiate all Confederate debts, and ratify the slave-freeing Thirteenth Amendment. States that complied with these conditions, Johnson declared, would be swiftly readmitted to the Union.

Johnson, savoring his dominance over the high-toned aristocrats who now begged his favor, granted pardons in

> *Early in 1866 one congressman quoted a Georgian:*
>
> "The blacks eat, sleep, move, live, only by the tolerance of the whites, who hate them. The blacks own absolutely nothing but their bodies; their former masters own everything, and will sell them nothing. If a black man draws even a bucket of water from a well, he must first get the permission of a white man, his enemy. . . . If he asks for work to earn his living, he must ask it of a white man; and the whites are determined to give him no work, except on such terms as will make him a serf and impair his liberty."

abundance. Bolstered by the political resurrection of the planter elite, the recently rebellious states moved rapidly in the second half of 1865 to organize governments. But as the pattern of the new governments became clear, Republicans of all stripes grew furious.

The Baleful Black Codes

Among the first acts of the new Southern regimes sanctioned by Johnson was the passage of the iron-toothed Black Codes. These laws were designed to regulate the affairs of the emancipated blacks, much as the slave statutes had done in pre–Civil War days. Mississippi passed the first such law in November 1865, and other Southern states soon followed suit. The Black Codes

Sharecroppers Picking Cotton Although many freed slaves found themselves picking cotton on their former masters' plantation, they took comfort that they were at least paid wages and could work as a family unit. In time, however, they became ensnared in the web of debt that their planter-bosses spun to keep a free labor force tightly bound to them.

varied in severity from state to state (Mississippi's was the harshest and Georgia's the most lenient), but they had much in common. The Black Codes aimed, first of all, to ensure a stable and subservient labor force. The crushed Cotton Kingdom could not rise from its weeds until the fields were once again put under hoe and plow—and many whites wanted to make sure that they retained the tight control they had exercised over black field hands and plow drivers in the days of slavery.

Dire penalties were therefore imposed by the codes on blacks who "jumped" their labor contracts, which usually committed them to work for the same employer for one year, and generally at pittance wages. Violators could be made to forfeit back wages or could be forcibly dragged back to work by a paid "Negro-catcher." In Mississippi the captured freedmen could be fined and then hired out to pay their fines—an arrangement that closely resembled slavery itself.

The codes also sought to restore as nearly as possible the pre-emancipation system of race relations. Freedom was legally recognized, as were some other privileges, such as the right to marry. But all the codes forbade a black to serve on a jury; some even barred blacks from renting or leasing land. A black could be punished for "idleness" by being sentenced to work on a chain gang. Nowhere were blacks allowed to vote.

These oppressive laws mocked the ideal of freedom, so recently purchased by buckets of blood. The Black Codes imposed terrible burdens on the unfettered blacks, struggling against mistreatment and poverty to make their way as free people. The worst features of the Black Codes would eventually be repealed, but their revocation could not by itself lift the liberated blacks into economic independence. Lacking capital, and with little to offer but their labor, thousands of impoverished former slaves slipped into the status of sharecropper farmers, as did many landless whites. Luckless sharecroppers gradually sank into a morass of virtual peonage and remained there for generations. Formerly slaves to masters, countless blacks as well as poorer whites in effect became slaves to the soil and to their creditors. Yet the dethroned planter aristocracy resented even this pitiful concession to freedom. Sharecropping was the "wrong policy," said one planter. "It makes the laborer too independent; he becomes a partner, and has a right to be consulted."

The Black Codes made an ugly impression in the North. If the former slaves were being re-enslaved, people asked one another, had not the Boys in Blue spilled their blood in vain? Had the North really won the war?

Congressional Reconstruction

These questions grew more insistent when the congressional delegations from the newly reconstituted Southern states presented themselves in the Capitol in December 1865. To the shock and disgust of the Republicans, many former Confederate leaders were on hand to claim their seats.

The appearance of these ex-rebels was a natural but costly blunder. Voters of the South, seeking able representatives, had turned instinctively to their experienced statesmen. But most of the Southern leaders were tainted by active association with the "lost cause." Among them were four former Confederate generals, five colonels, and various members of the Richmond cabinet and Congress. Worst of all, there was the shrimpy but brainy Alexander Stephens, ex–vice president of the Confederacy, still under indictment for treason.

The presence of these "whitewashed rebels" infuriated the Republicans in Congress. The war had been fought to restore the Union, but not on these kinds of terms. The Republicans were in no hurry to embrace their former enemies—virtually all of them Democrats—in the chambers of the Capitol. While the South had been "out" from 1861 to 1865, the Republicans in Congress had enjoyed a relatively free hand. They had passed much legislation that favored the North, such as the Morrill Tariff, the Pacific Railroad Act, and the Homestead Act. Now many Republicans balked at giving up this political advantage. On the first day of the congressional session, December 4, 1865, they banged shut the door in the face of the newly elected Southern delegations.

Looking to the future, the Republicans were alarmed to realize that a restored South would be stronger than ever in national politics. Before the war a black slave had counted as three-fifths of a person in apportioning congressional representation. Now the slave was five-fifths of a person. Eleven Southern states had seceded and been subdued by force of arms. But now, owing to full counting of free blacks, the rebel states were entitled to twelve more votes in Congress, and twelve more presidential electoral votes, than they had previously enjoyed. Again, angry voices in the North raised the cry, Who won the war?

Republicans had good reason to fear that ultimately they might be elbowed aside. Southerners might join hands with Democrats in the North and win control of

An Inflexible President, 1866   This Republican cartoon shows Johnson knocking blacks out of the Freedmen's Bureau by his veto (see p. 489).

Congress or maybe even the White House. If this happened, they could perpetuate the Black Codes, virtually re-enslaving the blacks. They could dismantle the economic program of the Republican party by lowering tariffs, rerouting the transcontinental railroad, repealing the free-farm Homestead Act, possibly even repudiating the national debt. President Johnson thus deeply disturbed the congressional Republicans when he announced on December 6, 1865, that the recently rebellious states had satisfied his conditions and that in his view the Union was now restored.

Johnson Clashes with Congress

A clash between president and Congress was now inevitable. It exploded into the open in February 1866, when the president vetoed a bill (later repassed) extending the life of the controversial Freedmen's Bureau.

Aroused, the Republicans swiftly struck back. In March 1866 they passed the Civil Rights Bill, which conferred on blacks the privilege of American citizenship and struck at the Black Codes. President Johnson resolutely vetoed this forward-looking measure on constitutional grounds, but in April congressmen steamrollered it over his veto—something they repeatedly did henceforth. The hapless president, dubbed "Sir Veto" and "Andy Veto," had his presidential wings clipped, as Congress increasingly assumed the dominant role in running the government. One critic called Johnson "the dead dog of the White House."

The Republicans now undertook to rivet the principles of the Civil Rights Bill into the Constitution as the Fourteenth Amendment. They feared that the Southerners might one day win control of Congress and repeal the hated law. The proposed amendment, as approved by Congress and sent to the states in June 1866, was sweeping. It (1) conferred civil rights, including citizenship but excluding the franchise, on the freedmen; (2) reduced proportionately the representation of a state in Congress and in the Electoral College if it denied blacks the ballot; (3) disqualified from federal and state office former Confederates who as federal officeholders had once sworn "to support the Constitution of the United States"; and (4) guaranteed the federal debt, while repudiating all Confederate debts. (See the text of the Fourteenth Amendment in the Appendix.)

The radical faction was disappointed that the Fourteenth Amendment did not grant the right to vote, but all Republicans were agreed that no state should be welcomed back into the Union fold without first ratifying the Fourteenth Amendment. Yet President Johnson advised the Southern states to reject it, and all of the "sinful eleven," except Tennessee, defiantly spurned the amendment. Their spirit was reflected in a Southern song:

And I don't want no pardon for what I was or am,
I won't be reconstructed and I don't give a damn.

Swinging 'Round the Circle with Johnson

As 1866 lengthened, the battle grew between the Congress and the president. The root of the controversy was Johnson's "10 percent" governments that had passed the most stringent Black Codes. Congress had tried to temper the worst features of the codes by extending the life of the embattled Freedmen's Bureau and passing the Civil Rights Bill. Both measures Johnson had vetoed. Now the issue was whether Reconstruction was to be carried on with or without the Fourteenth Amendment. The Republicans would settle for nothing less.

The crucial congressional elections of 1866—more crucial than some presidential elections—were fast approaching. Johnson was naturally eager to escape from the clutch of Congress by securing a majority favorable to his soft-on-the-South policy. Invited to dedicate a Chicago monument to Stephen A. Douglas, he undertook to speak at various cities en route in support of his views.

Johnson's famous "swing 'round the circle," beginning in the late summer of 1866, was a seriocomedy of errors. The president delivered a series of "give 'em hell" speeches, in which he accused the radicals in Congress of having planned large-scale antiblack riots and murder in the South. As he spoke, hecklers hurled insults

Principal Reconstruction Proposals and Plans

Year	Proposal or Plan
1864–1865	Lincoln's 10 percent proposal
1865–1866	Johnson's version of Lincoln's proposal
1866–1867	Congressional plan: 10 percent plan with Fourteenth Amendment
1867–1877	Congressional plan of military Reconstruction: Fourteenth Amendment plus black suffrage, later established nationwide by Fifteenth Amendment

Representative Thaddeus Stevens (1792–1868), in a congressional speech on January 3, 1867, urged the ballot for blacks out of concern for them and out of bitterness against Southern whites:

"I am for Negro suffrage in every rebel state. If it be just, it should not be denied; if it be necessary, it should be adopted; if it be a punishment to traitors, they deserve it."

runaway slaves in court without fee and, before dying, insisted on burial in a black cemetery. His affectionate devotion to blacks was matched by his vitriolic hatred of rebellious white Southerners. A masterly parliamentarian with a razor-sharp mind and withering wit, Stevens was a leading figure on the Joint (House-Senate) Committee on Reconstruction.

Still opposed to rapid restoration of the Southern states, the radicals wanted to keep them out as long as possible and apply federal power to bring about a drastic social and economic transformation in the South. But moderate Republicans, more attuned to time-honored principles of states' rights and self-government, recoiled from the full implications of the radical program. They preferred policies that restrained the states from abridging citizens' rights, rather than

at him. Reverting to his stump-speaking days in Tennessee, he shouted back angry retorts, amid cries of "You be damned" and "Don't get mad, Andy." The dignity of his high office sank to a new low, as the old charges of drunkenness were revived.

As a vote-getter, Johnson was highly successful—for the opposition. His inept speechmaking heightened the cry "Stand by Congress" against the "Tailor of the Potomac." When the ballots were counted, the Republicans had rolled up more than a two-thirds majority in both houses of Congress.

Republican Principles and Programs

The Republicans now had a veto-proof Congress and virtually unlimited control of Reconstruction policy. But moderates and radicals still disagreed over the best course to pursue in the South.

The radicals in the Senate were led by the courtly and principled idealist Charles Sumner, long since recovered from his prewar caning on the Senate floor, who tirelessly labored not only for black freedom but for racial equality. In the House the most powerful radical was Thaddeus Stevens, crusty and vindictive congressman from Pennsylvania. Seventy-four years old in 1866, he was a curious figure, with a protruding lower lip, a heavy black wig covering his bald head, and a deformed foot. An unswerving friend of blacks, he had defended

Thaddeus Stevens (1792–1868) Stevens, who regarded the seceded states as "conquered provinces," promoted much of the major Reconstruction legislation, including the Fourteenth (civil rights) Amendment. Reconstruction, he said, must "revolutionize Southern institutions, habits, and manners. . . . The foundation of their institutions . . . must be broken up and relaid, or all our blood and treasure have been spent in vain."

Eng^d by G.E. Perine & Co N.York

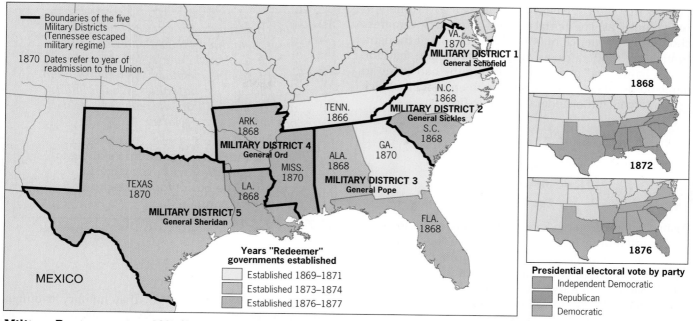

Military Reconstruction, 1867 (five districts and commanding generals)
For many white Southerners, military Reconstruction amounted to turning the knife in the wound of defeat. An often-repeated story of later years had a Southerner remark, "I was sixteen years old before I discovered that damnyankee was two words."

Southern Reconstruction by State

State	Readmitted to Representation in Congress	Home Rule (Democratic or "Redeemer" Regime) Reestablished	Comments
Tennessee	July 24, 1866		Ratified Fourteenth Amendment in 1866 and hence avoided military Reconstruction*
Arkansas	June 22, 1868	1874	
North Carolina	June 25, 1868	1870	
Alabama	June 25, 1868	1874	
Florida	June 25, 1868	1877	Federal troops restationed in 1877, as result of Hayes-Tilden electoral bargain
Louisiana	June 25, 1868	1877	Same as Florida
South Carolina	June 25, 1868	1877	Same as Florida
Virginia	January 26, 1870	1869	
Mississippi	February 23, 1870	1876	
Texas	March 30, 1870	1874	
Georgia	[June 25, 1868] July 15, 1870	1872	Readmitted June 25, 1868, but returned to military control after expulsion of blacks from legislature

*For many years Tennessee was the only state of the secession to observe Lincoln's birthday as a legal holiday. Many southern states still observe the birthdays of Jefferson Davis and Robert E. Lee.

policies that directly involved the federal government in individual lives. The actual policies adopted by Congress showed the influence of both these schools of thought, though the moderates, as the majority faction, had the upper hand. And one thing both groups had come to agree on by 1867 was the necessity to enfranchise black voters, even if it took federal troops to do it.

Reconstruction by the Sword

Against a backdrop of vicious and bloody race riots that had erupted in several Southern cities, Congress passed the Reconstruction Act on March 2, 1867. Supplemented by later measures, this drastic legislation divided the South into five military districts, each commanded by a Union general and policed by blue-clad soldiers, about twenty thousand all told. The act also temporarily disfranchised tens of thousands of former Confederates.

Congress additionally laid down stringent conditions for the readmission of the seceded states. The wayward states were required to ratify the Fourteenth Amendment, giving the former slaves their rights as citizens. The bitterest pill of all to white Southerners was the stipulation that they guarantee in their state constitutions full suffrage for their former adult male slaves. Yet the act, reflecting moderate sentiment, stopped short of giving the freedmen land or education at federal expense. The overriding purpose of the moderates was to create an electorate in Southern states that would vote those states back into the Union on acceptable terms and thus free the federal government from direct responsibility for the protection of black rights. As later events would demonstrate, this approach proved woefully inadequate to the cause of justice for blacks.

The radical Republicans were still worried. The danger loomed that once the unrepentant states were readmitted, they would amend their constitutions so as to withdraw the ballot from blacks. The only ironclad safeguard was to incorporate black suffrage in the federal Constitution. This goal was finally achieved by the Fifteenth Amendment, passed by Congress in 1869 and ratified by the required number of states in 1870 (see the Appendix).

Military Reconstruction of the South not only usurped certain functions of the president as commander in chief but set up a martial regime of dubious legality. The Supreme Court had already ruled, in the case *Ex parte Milligan* (1866), that military tribunals could not try civilians, even during wartime, in areas where the civil courts were open. Peacetime military rule seemed starkly contrary to the spirit of the Constitution. But the circumstances were extraordinary in the Republic's history, and for the time being the Supreme Court avoided offending the Republican Congress.

Prodded into line by federal bayonets, the Southern states got on with the task of constitution making. By 1870 all of them had reorganized their governments and had been accorded full rights. The hated "bluebellies" remained until the new Republican regimes—usually called "radical" regimes—appeared to be firmly entrenched. Yet when the federal troops finally left a state, its government swiftly passed back into the hands of white "Redeemers," or "Home Rule" regimes, which were inevitably Democratic. Finally, in 1877, the last federal muskets were removed from state politics, and the "solid" Democratic South congealed.

The prominent suffragist and abolitionist Susan B. Anthony (1820–1906) was outraged over the proposed exclusion of women from the Fourteenth Amendment. In a conversation with her former male allies Wendell Phillips and Theodore Tilton, she reportedly held out her arm and declared,

"Look at this, all of you. And hear me swear that I will cut off this right arm of mine before I will ever work for or demand the ballot for the negro and not the woman."

No Women Voters

The passage of the three Reconstruction-era Amendments—the Thirteenth, Fourteenth, and Fifteenth—delighted former abolitionists but deeply disappointed advocates of women's rights. Women had played a prominent part in the prewar abolitionist movement and had often pointed out that both women and blacks lacked basic civil rights, especially the crucial right to vote. The struggle for black freedom and the crusade for women's rights, therefore, were one and the same in the eyes of many women. Yet during the war, feminist leaders such as Elizabeth Cady Stanton and Susan B. Anthony had temporarily suspended their own demands and worked wholeheartedly for the cause of black emancipation. The Woman's Loyal League had gathered nearly 400,000 signatures on petitions asking Congress to pass a constitutional amendment prohibiting slavery.

Now, with the war ended and the Thirteenth Amendment passed, feminist leaders believed that their time had come. They reeled with shock, however, when the wording of the Fourteenth Amendment, which defined equal national citizenship, for the first time inserted the word *male* into the Constitution in referring to a citizen's right to vote. Both Stanton and Anthony campaigned actively against the Fourteenth Amendment despite the pleas of Frederick Douglass, who had long supported woman suffrage but believed that this was "the Negro's hour." When the Fifteenth Amendment proposed to prohibit denial of the vote on the basis of "race, color, or previous condition of servitude," Stanton and Anthony wanted the word *sex* added to the list. They lost this battle, too. Fifty years would pass before the Constitution granted women the right to vote.

> *At a constitutional convention in Alabama, freed people affirmed their rights in the following declaration:*
>
> "We claim exactly the same rights, privileges and immunities as are enjoyed by white men—we ask nothing more and will be content with nothing less. . . . The law no longer knows white nor black, but simply men, and consequently we are entitled to ride in public conveyances, hold office, sit on juries and do everything else which we have in the past been prevented from doing solely on the ground of color."

The Realities of Radical Reconstruction in the South

Blacks now had freedom, of a sort. Their friends in Congress had only haltingly and somewhat belatedly

Freedmen Voting, Richmond, Virginia, 1871 The exercise of democratic rights by former slaves constituted a political and social revolution in the South and was bitterly resented by whites.

secured the franchise for them. Both Presidents Lincoln and Johnson had proposed to give the ballot gradually to selected blacks who qualified for it through education, property ownership, or military service. Moderate Republicans and even many radicals at first hesitated to bestow suffrage on the freedmen. The Fourteenth Amendment, in many ways the heart of the Republican program for Reconstruction, had fallen short of guaranteeing the right to vote. (It envisioned for blacks the same status as that of women—citizenship without voting rights.) But by 1867 hesitation had given way to a hard determination to enfranchise the former slaves wholesale and immediately, while thousands of white Southerners were being denied the vote. By glaring contrast, most of the Northern states, before ratification of the Fifteenth Amendment in 1870, withheld the ballot from their tiny black minorities. White Southerners naturally concluded that the Republicans were hypocritical in insisting that blacks in the South be allowed to vote.

Having gained their right to suffrage, Southern black men seized the initiative and began to organize politically. Their primary vehicle became the Union League, originally a pro-Union organization based in the North. Assisted by Northern blacks, freedmen turned the League into a network of political clubs that educated members in their civic duties and campaigned for Republican candidates. The league's mission soon expanded to include building black churches and schools, representing black grievances before local employers and government, and recruiting militias to protect black communities from white retaliation.

Though African American women did not obtain the right to vote, they too assumed new political roles. Black women faithfully attended the parades and rallies common in black communities during the early years of Reconstruction and helped assemble mass meetings in the newly constructed black churches. They even showed up at the constitutional conventions held throughout the South in 1867, monitoring the proceedings and participating in informal votes outside the convention halls.

But black men elected as delegates to the state constitutional conventions held the greater political authority. They formed the backbone of the black political community. At the conventions, they sat down with whites to hammer out new state constitutions, which most importantly provided for universal male suffrage. Though the subsequent elections produced no black governors or majorities in state senates, black political participation expanded exponentially during Reconstruction. Between 1868 and 1876, fourteen black congressmen and two black senators, Hiram Revels

Black Reconstruction
A composite portrait of the first black senators and representatives in the Forty-first and Forty-second Congresses. Senator Hiram Revels, on the left, was elected in 1870 to the seat that had been occupied by Jefferson Davis when the South seceded.

The following excerpt is part of a heartrending appeal to Congress in 1871 by a group of Kentucky blacks:

"We believe you are not familiar with the description of the Ku Klux Klans riding nightly over the country, going from county to county, and in the county towns, spreading terror wherever they go by robbing, whipping, ravishing, and killing our people without provocation, compelling colored people to break the ice and bathe in the chilly waters of the Kentucky River.

"The [state] legislature has adjourned. They refused to enact any laws to suppress Ku-Klux disorder. We regard them [the Ku-Kluxers] as now being licensed to continue their dark and bloody deeds under cover of the dark night. They refuse to allow us to testify in the state courts where a white man is concerned. We find their deeds are perpetrated only upon colored men and white Republicans. We also find that for our services to the government and our race we have become the special object of hatred and persecution at the hands of the Democratic Party. Our people are driven from their homes in great numbers, having no redress only [except] the United States court, which is in many cases unable to reach them."

them "scalawags" and "carpetbaggers." The so-called scalawags were Southerners, often former Unionists and Whigs. The former Confederates accused them, often with wild exaggeration, of plundering the treasuries of the Southern states through their political influence in the radical governments. The carpetbaggers, on the other hand, were supposedly sleazy Northerners who had packed all their worldly goods into a carpetbag suitcase at war's end and had come South to seek personal power and profit. In fact, most were former Union soldiers and Northern businessmen and professionals who wanted to play a role in modernizing the "New South."

How well did the radical regimes rule? The radical legislatures passed much desirable legislation and introduced many badly needed reforms. For the first time in Southern history, steps were taken toward establishing adequate public schools. Tax systems were streamlined; public works were launched; and property rights were guaranteed to women. Many welcome reforms were retained by the all-white "Redeemer" governments that later returned to power.

Despite these achievements, graft ran rampant in many "radical" governments. This was especially true in South Carolina and Louisiana, where conscienceless promoters and other pocket-padders used politically inexperienced blacks as pawns. The worst "black-and-white" legislatures purchased, as "legislative supplies," such "stationery" as hams, perfumes, suspenders, bonnets, corsets, champagne, and a coffin. One "thrifty" carpetbag governor in a single year "saved" $100,000 from a salary of $8,000. Yet this sort of corruption was by no means confined to the South in these postwar years. The crimes of the Reconstruction governments were no more outrageous than the scams and felonies being perpetrated in the North at the same time, especially in Boss Tweed's New York.

The Ku Klux Klan

and Blanche K. Bruce, both of Mississippi, served in Washington, D.C. Blacks also served in state governments as lieutenant governors and representatives, and in local governments as mayors, magistrates, sheriffs, and justices of the peace.

The sight of former slaves holding office deeply offended their onetime masters, who lashed out with particular fury at the freedmen's white allies, labeling

Deeply embittered, some Southern whites resorted to savage measures against "radical" rule. Many whites resented the success and ability of black legislators as much as they resented alleged "corruption." A number of secret organizations mushroomed forth, the most notorious of which was the "Invisible Empire of the South," or Ku Klux Klan, founded in Tennessee in 1866. Besheeted nightriders, their horses' hooves muffled, would

The Ku Klux Klan, Tennessee, 1868 This night-riding terrorist has even masked the identity of his horse.

approach the cabin of an "upstart" black and hammer on the door. In ghoulish tones one thirsty horseman would demand a bucket of water. Then, under pretense of drinking, he would pour it into a rubber attachment con-

A black leader protested to whites in 1868,

"It is extraordinary that a race such as yours, professing gallantry, chivalry, education, and superiority, living in a land where ringing chimes call child and sire to the Gospel of God—that with all these advantages on your side, you can make war upon the poor defenseless black man."

cealed beneath his mask and gown, smack his lips, and declare that this was the first water he had tasted since he was killed at the Battle of Shiloh. If fright did not produce the desired effect, force was employed.

Such tomfoolery and terror proved partially effective. Many ex-bondsmen and white "carpetbaggers," quick to take a hint, shunned the polls. Those stubborn souls who persisted in their "upstart" ways were flogged, mutilated, or even murdered. In one Louisiana parish in 1868, whites in two days killed or wounded two hundred victims; a pile of twenty-five bodies was found half-buried in the woods. By such atrocious practices were blacks "kept in their place"—that is, down. The Klan became a refuge for numerous bandits and cutthroats. Any scoundrel could don a sheet.

Congress, outraged by this night-riding lawlessness, passed the harsh Force Acts of 1870 and 1871. Federal troops were able to stamp out much of the "lash law," but by this time the Invisible Empire had already done its work of intimidation. Many of the outlawed groups continued their tactics in the guise of "dancing clubs," "missionary societies," and "rifle clubs."

White resistance undermined attempts to empower blacks politically. The white South, for many decades, openly flouted the Fourteenth and Fifteenth Amendments. Wholesale disfranchisement of blacks, starting conspicuously about 1890, was achieved by intimidation, fraud, and trickery. Among various underhanded schemes were literacy tests, unfairly administered by whites to the advantage of illiterate whites. In the eyes of white Southerners, the goal of white supremacy fully justified these dishonorable devices.

Johnson Walks the Impeachment Plank

Radicals meanwhile had been sharpening their hatchets for President Johnson. Annoyed by the obstruction of the "drunken tailor" in the White House, they falsely accused him of maintaining there a harem of "dissolute women." Not content with curbing his authority, they decided to remove him altogether by constitutional processes.*

As an initial step, Congress in 1867 passed the Tenure of Office Act—as usual, over Johnson's veto.

---

*For impeachment, see Art. I, Sec. II, para. 5; Art. I, Sec. III, paras. 6, 7; Art. II, Sec. IV, in the Appendix.

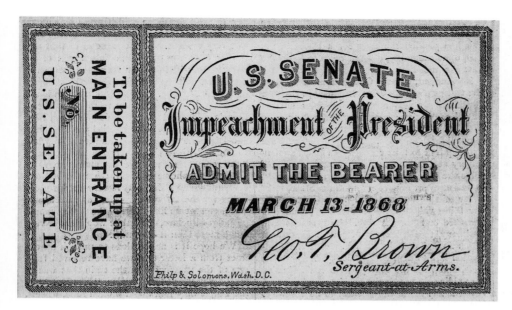

Contrary to precedent, the new law required the president to secure the consent of the Senate before he could remove his appointees once they had been approved by that body. One purpose was to freeze into the cabinet the secretary of war, Edwin M. Stanton, a holdover from the Lincoln administration. Although outwardly loyal to Johnson, he was secretly serving as a spy and informer for the radicals.

Johnson provided the radicals with a pretext to begin impeachment proceedings when he abruptly dismissed Stanton early in 1868. The House of Representatives immediately voted 126 to 47 to impeach Johnson for "high crimes and misdemeanors," as required by the Constitution, charging him with various violations of the Tenure of Office Act. Two additional articles related to Johnson's verbal assaults on the Congress, involving "disgrace, ridicule, hatred, contempt, and reproach."

A Not-Guilty Verdict for Johnson

With evident zeal the radical-led Senate now sat as a court to try Johnson on the dubious impeachment charges. The House conducted the prosecution. The trial aroused intense public interest and, with one thousand tickets printed, proved to be the biggest show

of 1868. Johnson kept his dignity and sobriety and maintained a discreet silence. His battery of attorneys argued that the president, convinced that the Tenure of Office Act was unconstitutional, had fired Stanton merely to put a test case before the Supreme Court. (That slow-moving tribunal finally ruled indirectly in Johnson's favor fifty-eight years later.) House prosecutors, including oily-tongued Benjamin F. Butler and embittered Thaddeus Stevens, had a harder time building a compelling case for impeachment.

On May 16, 1868, the day for the first voting in the Senate, the tension was electric, and heavy breathing could be heard in the galleries. By a margin of only one vote, the radicals failed to muster the two-thirds majority for Johnson's removal. Seven independent-minded Republican senators, courageously putting country above party, voted "not guilty."

Several factors shaped the outcome. Fears of creating a destabilizing precedent played a role, as did principled opposition to abusing the constitutional mechanism of checks and balances. Political considerations also figured conspicuously. As the vice presidency remained vacant under Johnson, his successor would have been radical Republican Ben Wade, the president pro tempore of the Senate. Wade was disliked by many members of the business community for his high-tariff, soft-money, prolabor views, and was distrusted by moderate Republicans. Meanwhile,

Alaska and the Lower Forty-eight States (a size comparison)

Johnson indicated through his attorney that he would stop obstructing Republican policies in return for remaining in office.

Diehard radicals were infuriated by their failure to muster a two-thirds majority for Johnson's removal. "The Country is going to the Devil!" cried the crippled Stevens as he was carried from the hall. But the nation, though violently aroused, accepted the verdict with a good temper that did credit to its political maturity. In a less stable republic, an armed uprising might have erupted against the president.

The nation thus narrowly avoided a dangerous precedent that would have gravely weakened one of the three branches of the federal government. Johnson was clearly guilty of bad speeches, bad judgment, and bad temper, but not of "high crimes and misdemeanors." From the standpoint of the radicals, his greatest crime had been to stand inflexibly in their path.

The Purchase of Alaska

Johnson's administration, though largely reduced to a figurehead, achieved its most enduring success in the field of foreign relations.

The Russians by 1867 were in a mood to sell the vast and chilly expanse of land now known as Alaska. They had already overextended themselves in North America, and they saw that in the likely event of another war with Britain, they probably would lose their defenseless northern province to the sea-dominant British. Alaska, moreover, had been ruthlessly "furred out" and was a growing economic liability. The Russians were therefore quite eager to unload their "frozen asset" on the Americans, and they put out seductive feelers in Washington. They preferred the United States to any other purchaser, primarily because they wanted to strengthen further the Republic as a barrier against their ancient enemy, Britain.

In 1867 Secretary of State William Seward, an ardent expansionist, signed a treaty with Russia that transferred Alaska to the United States for the bargain price of $7.2 million. But Seward's enthusiasm for these frigid wastes was not shared by his ignorant or uninformed countrymen, who jeered at "Seward's Folly," "Seward's Icebox," "Frigidia," and "Walrussia." The American people, still preoccupied with Reconstruction and other internal vexations, were economy-minded and anti-expansionist.

Then why did Congress and the American public sanction the purchase? For one thing Russia, alone among the powers, had been conspicuously friendly to the North during the recent Civil War. Americans did not feel that they could offend their great and good friend, the tsar, by hurling his walrus-covered icebergs back into his face. Besides, the territory was rumored to be teeming with furs, fish, and gold, and it might yet "pan out" profitably—as it later did with natural resources, including oil and gas. So Congress and the country accepted "Seward's Polar Bear Garden," somewhat derisively but nevertheless hopefully.

The Heritage of Reconstruction

Many white Southerners regarded Reconstruction as a more grievous wound than the war itself. It left a festering scar that would take generations to heal. They resented the upending of their social and racial system, political empowerment of blacks, and the insult of federal intervention in their local affairs. Yet few rebellions have ended with the victors sitting down to a love feast with the vanquished. Given the explosiveness of the issues that had caused the war, and the bitterness of the fighting, the wonder is that Reconstruction was not far harsher than it was. The fact is that Lincoln, Johnson, and most Republicans had no clear picture at war's end of what federal policy toward the South should be. Policymakers groped for the right policies, influenced as much by Southern responses to defeat and emancipation as by any plans of their own to impose a specific program on the South.

The Republicans acted from a mixture of idealism and political expediency. They wanted both to protect the freed slaves and to promote the fortunes of the Republican party. In the end their efforts backfired badly. Reconstruction conferred only fleeting benefits on blacks and virtually extinguished the Republican party in the South for nearly one hundred years.

Is This a Republican Form of Government?, by Thomas Nast, *Harpers' Weekly,* **1876**   The nation's most prominent political cartoonist expressed his despair at the tragic way that Reconstruction had ended—with few real gains for the former slaves.

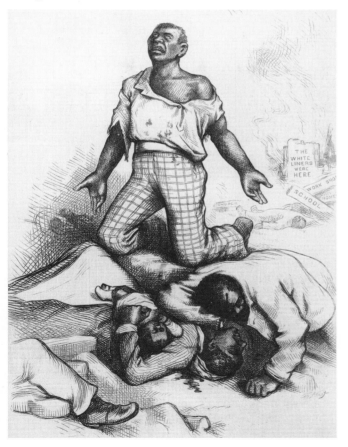

The remarkable (1817?–1895) wro⌐

"Though slavery w⌐ wrongs of my peo⌐ Though they were n⌐ were not yet quite free⌐ truly free whose liberty⌐ upon the thought, feeling,⌐ of others, and who has him⌐ means in his own hands for g⌐ protecting, defending, and ma⌐ that liberty. Yet the Negro after h⌐ emancipation was precisely in thi⌐ state of destitution. . . . He was free from the individual master, but the slave of society. He had neither money, property, nor friends. He was free from the old plantation, but he had nothing but the dusty road under his feet. He was free from the old quarter that once gave him shelter, but a slave to the rains of summer and the frosts of winter. He was, in a word, literally turned loose, naked, hungry, and destitute, to the open sky."

Moderate Republicans never fully appreciated the extensive effort necessary to make the freed slaves completely independent citizens, nor the lengths to which Southern whites would go to preserve their system of racial dominance. Had Thaddeus Stevens's radical program of drastic economic reforms and heftier protection of political rights been enacted, things might well have been different. But deep-seated racism, ingrained American resistance to tampering with property rights, and rigid loyalty to the principle of local self-government, combined with spreading indifference in the North to the plight of blacks, formed too formidable an obstacle. Despite good intentions by Republicans, the Old South was in many ways more resurrected than reconstructed.

Chronology

...oln announces "10 percent" ...econstruction plan	
...ncoln vetoes Wade-Davis Bill	
Lincoln assassinated	
Johnson issues Reconstruction proclamation	
Congress refuses to seat Southern congressmen	
Freedmen's Bureau established	
Southern states pass Black Codes	
66 Congress passes Civil Rights Bill over Johnson's veto	
Congress passes Fourteenth Amendment	
Johnson-backed candidates lose congressional election	
Ex parte Milligan case	
Ku Klux Klan founded	

1867	Reconstruction Act
	Tenure of Office Act
	United States purchases Alaska from Russia
1868	Johnson impeached and acquitted
	Johnson pardons Confederate leaders
1870	Fifteenth Amendment ratified
1870–1871	Force Acts
1872	Freedmen's Bureau ended
1877	Reconstruction ends

VARYING VIEWPOINTS

How Radical Was Reconstruction?

Few topics have triggered as much intellectual warfare as the "dark and bloody ground" of Reconstruction. The period provoked questions—sectional, racial, and constitutional—about which people felt deeply and remain deeply divided even today. Scholarly argument goes back conspicuously to a Columbia University historian, William A. Dunning, whose students, in the early 1900s, published a series of histories of the Reconstruction South. Dunning and his disciples were influenced by the turn-of-the-century spirit of sectional conciliation as well as by current theories about black racial inferiority. Sympathizing with the white South, they wrote about the Reconstruction period as a kind of national disgrace, foisted upon a prostrate region by vindictive and self-seeking radical Republican politicians. If the South had wronged the North by seceding, the North had wronged the South by reconstructing.

A second cycle of scholarship in the 1920s was impelled by a widespread suspicion that the Civil War itself had been a tragic and unnecessary blunder. Attention now shifted to Northern politicians. Scholars like Howard Beale further questioned the motives of the radical Republicans. To Beale and others, the radicals had masked a ruthless desire to exploit Southern labor and resources behind a false front of "concern" for the freed slaves. Moreover, Northern advocacy of black voting rights was merely a calculated attempt to ensure a Republican political presence in the defeated South. The unfortunate Andrew Johnson, in this view, had valiantly tried to uphold constitutional principles in the face of this cynical Northern onslaught.

Although ignored by his contemporaries, scholar, black nationalist, and founder of the National Association for the Advancement of Colored People W. E. B. Du Bois wrote a sympathetic history of Reconstruction in 1935 that became the basis for historians' interpretations ever since. Following World War II, Kenneth Stampp and others, influenced by the modern civil rights movement, built on Du Bois's argument and claimed that Reconstruction had been a noble though ultimately failed attempt to extend American principles of equity and justice. The radical Republicans and the carpetbaggers were now heroes, whereas Andrew Johnson was castigated for his obstinate racism. By the early 1970s, this view had become orthodoxy, and it generally holds sway today. Yet some scholars, such as Michael Benedict and Leon Litwack, disillusioned with the inability to achieve full racial justice in the 1960s and 1970s, began once more to scrutinize the motives of Northern politicians immediately after the Civil War. They claimed to discover that Reconstruction had never been very radical and that the Freedmen's Bureau and other agencies had merely allowed white planters to maintain their dominance over local politics as well as over the local economy.

More recently, Eric Foner has powerfully reasserted the argument that Reconstruction was a truly radical and noble attempt to establish an interracial democracy. Drawing upon the work of Du Bois, Foner has emphasized the comparative approach to American Reconstruction. Clearly, Foner admits, Reconstruction did not create full equality, but it did allow blacks to form political organizations and churches, to vote, and to establish some measure of economic independence. In South Africa, the Caribbean, and other areas once marked by slavery, the freed slaves never received these opportunities. Many of the benefits of Reconstruction were erased by white southerners during the Gilded Age, but in the twentieth century, the constitutional principles and organizations developed during Reconstruction provided the focus and foundation for the modern civil rights movement—which some have called the second Reconstruction. Steven Hahn's *A Nation Under Our Feet: Black Political Struggles in the Rural South from Slavery to the Great Migration* (2003) is the latest contribution to the literature on Reconstruction. Hahn emphasizes the assertiveness and ingenuity of African Americans in creating new political opportunities for themselves after emancipation.

For further reading, see the Appendix. For web resources, go to **http://college.hmco.com**.

APPENDIX

SUGGESTED READINGS

CHAPTER 1

PRIMARY SOURCE DOCUMENTS

Various English editions of Hernán Cortés's correspondence from Mexico are available, including *Five Letters, 1519–1526* (1929), trans. by J. Bayard Morris.* An important source from a *conquistador*'s perspective is Bernal Diaz del Castillo, *Historia Verdadera de la Conquista de la Nueva España*, selections of which have been recently translated into English in *The Discovery and Conquest of Mexico, 1517–1521*, edited by Genaro Garcia (1996). Bartolomé de Las Casas, *Thirty Very Judicial Propositions** (1552), and Juan Ginés de Sepúlveda, *The Second Democrates** (1547), reflect the Spanish *conquistadores'* efforts to understand the native peoples of the New World. See also Las Casas's *The Destruction of the Indies* (1542). *The Broken Spears: The Aztec Account of the Conquest of Mexico,** edited by Miguel León-Portilla (1962), is an anthology of texts compiled from indigenous sources. Olaudah Equiano, *Equiano's Travels** (1789), is a fascinating account by an African in the New World in the eighteenth century.

SECONDARY SOURCES

Brian M. Fagan reviews the evidence concerning the earliest humans to arrive in the Americas in *The Great Journey: The Peopling of Ancient America* (1987). Archaeologist Tom Dillehay revises estimates of settlement of the New World in *The Settlement of the Americas: A New Prehistory* (2000), which presents exciting new archaeological evidence. Alice Beck Keyhoe gives an engaging account of American Indian nations during the fifteen thousand years before Columbus in *America Before the European Invasions* (2002). For more on the pre-Columbian history of the Americas, see Norman Hammond, *Ancient Maya Civilization* (1982); Brian M. Fagan, *Kingdoms of Gold, Kingdoms of Jade: The Americas Before Columbus* (1991); and Stuart J. Fiedel, *Prehistory of the Americas* (1992). For a terrific study in cross-cultural perceptions between Columbus and Indians, see Tzvetan Todorov, *The Conquest of America* (1984). Immanuel Wallerstein, *The Modern World System: Capitalist Agriculture and the Origins of the European World in the Sixteenth Century* (1974), provides a theoretical overview of European colonization's international economic background. Early African history is sketched in J. D. Fage, *A History of West Africa* (1969), and John Thornton discusses Africa's role in the world economy in *Africa and Africans in the Making of the Atlantic World, 1400–1800* (1992). A fascinating brief synthesis of early European contact with the Americas is J. H. Elliott, *The Old World and the New,*

1492–1650 (1970). For a comparative study, see Anthony Pagen, *Lords of All Worlds: Ideologies of Empire in Spain, Britain, and France* (1995). Alfred W. Crosby, Jr., discusses *The Columbian Exchange: Biological and Cultural Consequences of 1492* (1972). See the same author's *Ecological Imperialism: The Biological Expansion of Europe, 900–1900* (1986). A marvelously illustrated volume portraying the impact of America on the European imagination is Hugh Honour, *The New Golden Land* (1975). See also Kirkpatrick Sale, *The Conquest of Paradise: Christopher Columbus and the Columbian Legacy* (1990), and Herman J. Viola and Carolyn Margolis, *Seeds of Change: Five Hundred Years Since Columbus* (1991). D. W. Meinig presents a geographical overview of immigration in *The Shaping of America: A Geographical Perspective on 500 Years of History: Atlantic America, 1492–1800* (1986). Patricia Seed compares different forms of European conquest in *Ceremonies of Possession* (1995). For an engaging and comprehensive study of New World Iberian colonies from the preconquest period to the early nineteenth century, see Mark A. Burkholder and Lyman L. Johnson, *Colonial Latin America* (2000). Various aspects of the Spanish and Portuguese conquests of America are described in Charles Gibson, *Spain in America* (1966), and L. McAlister, *Spain and Portugal in the New World, 1492–1700* (1984). William H. Prescott, *History of the Conquest of Mexico* (1843) and *History of the Conquest of Peru* (1847), are two fascinating narrative histories of the nineteenth century. Nathan Wachtel presents the Indians' view of the Spanish conquest in *The Vision of the Vanquished* (1977). The spread of Spanish America northward is traced in Edward H. Spicer, *Cycles of Conquest: The Impact of Spain, Mexico, and the United States on the Indians of the Southwest, 1533–1960* (1962); Andrew L. Knaut, *The Pueblo Revolt of 1680: Conquest and Resistance in Seventeenth-Century New Mexico* (1997); Ramon A. Gutierrez, *When Jesus Came, the Corn Mothers Went Away* (1991); and David J. Weber's masterful synthesis, *The Spanish Frontier in North America* (1992).

CHAPTER 2

PRIMARY SOURCE DOCUMENTS

Richard Hakluyt, *Divers Voyages Touching the Discovery of America and the Islands Adjacent*, edited by J. W. Jones (1850), supplied the rationale for the establishment of English colonies in North America. John Smith, "Generall Historie of Virginia," in *Travels and Works of Captain John Smith,** edited by Edward Arber (1910), is an account by the amazing, vain man who steered Jamestown through its precarious first few years.

SECONDARY SOURCES

England's involvement in overseas settlement in the sixteenth century is described in David B. Quinn, *England and the Discovery of America, 1481–1620* (1974). In *The Elizabethans and the Irish* (1966), Quinn details the role of Ireland in the origins of Elizabethan colo-

---

*An asterisk indicates that the document, or an excerpt from it, can be found in David M. Kennedy and Thomas A. Bailey, eds., *The American Spirit: United States History as Seen by Contemporaries*, 11th ed. (Boston: Houghton Mifflin, 2006)

nization. The international economic background to colonization is sketched in Ralph Davis, *The Rise of the Atlantic Economies* (1973), and in Kenneth R. Andrews, *Trade, Plunder, and Settlement: Maritime Enterprise and the Genesis of the British Empire, 1480–1630* (1984). The immediate English backdrop is colorfully presented in Peter Laslett, *The World We Have Lost* (1965), and in Carl Bridenbaugh, *Vexed and Troubled Englishmen, 1590–1642* (1968). James Lang, *Conquest and Commerce: Spain and England in the Americas* (1975), is a comparative chronicle of colonial rivalries; Jack P. Greene, *Pursuits of Happiness: The Social Development of Early Modern British Colonies and the Formation of American Culture* (1988), compares the process of English colonization in different regions of North America and the Caribbean. Contact between Indian and European cultures is handled in Colin G. Calloway, *New Worlds for All: Indians, Europeans, and the Remaking of America* (1997), and James Axtell, *The Invasion Within: The Contest of Cultures in Colonial America* (1985). James Merrell, *The Indians' New World* (1989), which describes the wrenching experiences of the Catawba Indians, is the best ethnohistorical account of a single tribe for the early period. See also Daniel K. Richter, *The Ordeal of the Longhouse: The Peoples of the Iroquois League in the Era of European Colonization* (1992), and Richard White, *The Middle Ground: Indians, Empires, and Republics in the Great Lakes Region, 1650–1815* (1991). The Chesapeake region has continued to receive attention, especially in Paul G. E. Clemens, *The Atlantic Economy and Colonial Maryland's Eastern Shore* (1980); Lois Green Carr et al., eds., *Colonial Chesapeake Society* (1988); Lois Green Carr et al., Robert Cole's *World: Agriculture and Society in Early Maryland* (1991); Philip D. Morgan, *Slave Counterpoint: Black Culture in the Eighteenth-Century Chesapeake and Lowcountry* (1998); and James Horn, *Adapting to a New World: English Society in the Seventeenth-Century Chesapeake* (1994). Richard Dunn, *Sugar and Slaves: The Rise of the Planter Class in the English West Indies, 1624–1713* (1972), describes South Carolina society's West Indian roots. The most comprehensive account of the various colonial economies is contained in John J. McCusker and Russell R. Menard, *The Economy of British North America, 1607–1789* (1985). The role of slavery in early colonial society is examined perceptively in Edmund S. Morgan, *American Slavery, American Freedom* (1975). For a unique and important study of the role gender played in shaping racial ideologies in colonial Virginia, see Kathleen Brown, *Good Wives, Nasty Wenches, and Anxious Patriarchs* (1996). See also Peter Wood's account of South Carolina, *Black Majority* (1974), and Ira Berlin's overview, *Many Thousands Gone: The First Two Centuries of Slavery in North America* (1998). Gary Nash analyzes relations among Indians, European colonists, and blacks in *Red, White, and Black: The Peoples of Early America* (1974), as do Daniel H. Usner, Jr., in *Indians, Settlers, and Slaves in a Frontier Exchange Economy: The Lower Mississippi Valley Before 1783* (1992), and Timothy Silver in *A New Face on the Countryside: Indians, Colonists, and Slaves in South Atlantic Forests, 1500–1800* (1990). Daniel K. Richter examines European colonists through the eyes of Native Americans in *Facing East from Indian Country: A Native History of Early America* (2003).

CHAPTER 3

PRIMARY SOURCE DOCUMENTS

John Winthrop, "A Model of Christian Charity" (1630), in *The American Primer,* edited by Daniel Boorstin, outlines the goals of the Puritan errand into the wilderness. Winthrop's "Speech on Liberty"* (1645), in his *History of New England* (1853), established the colony's

fundamental political principles. William Bradford, *Of Plymouth Plantation,** edited by Samuel E. Morison (1952), is a rich contemporary account.

SECONDARY SOURCES

New England has received more scholarly attention than any other colonial region. Harry Stout, *The New England Soul: Preaching and Culture in Colonial New England* (1986), is a comprehensive account. A brilliant and complex intellectual history is Perry Miller, *The New England Mind* (2 vols., 1939, 1953), a work that has long been a landmark for other scholars. Sacvan Bercovitch traces the heritage of the New England temperament in *The Puritan Origins of the American Self* (1975). Also see David Jaffe, *People of the Wachusett: Greater New England in History and Memory* (1999). Other interpretations of Puritanism include Charles Hambrick-Stowe, *The Practice of Piety* (1982), and Andrew Delbanco, *The Puritan Ordeal* (1989). David Hall, *Worlds of Wonder, Days of Judgment: Popular Religious Belief in Early New England* (1989), describes the relation between high Puritan doctrine and lay belief and practice. Jon Butler, *Awash in a Sea of Faith: Christianizing the American People* (1990), is comprehensive. John T. Ellis pays special attention to religious issues in *Catholics in Colonial America* (1965), as does Edmund S. Morgan in *Roger Williams: The Church and State* (1967). On other religious minorities, see Carla Gardina Pestana, *Quakers and Baptists in Colonial Massachusetts* (1991). For analyses of Puritan-Indian relations, see Francis Jennings, *The Invasion of America* (1975), and Neal Salisbury, *Manitou and Providence* (1982). For a fascinating account of some settlers' assimilation into Indian society, see John Demos, *The Unredeemed Captive: A Family Story from Early America* (1994). David S. Lovejoy discusses the impact of England's Glorious Revolution on the colonies in *The Glorious Revolution in America* (1975). Areas outside New England are dealt with in Gary Nash, *Quakers and Politics: Pennsylvania, 1681–1726* (1971); Patricia Bonomi, *A Factious People: Politics and Society in Colonial New York* (1971); Richard and Mary Dunn, eds., *The World of William Penn* (1986); Oliver A. Rink, *Holland on the Hudson: An Economic and Social History of Dutch New York* (1986); and Joyce D. Goodfriend, *Before the Melting Pot: Society and Culture in Colonial New York City, 1664–1730* (1992). The essays in Michael Zuckerman, ed., *Friends and Neighbors: Group Life in America's First Plural Society* (1982), argue that the middle colonies provide the best early model for America as a whole. Timothy H. Breen, *Puritans and Adventurers* (1980), draws contrasts between Virginia and New England.

CHAPTER 4

PRIMARY SOURCE DOCUMENTS

The first slave laws of Virginia are collected in Warren M. Billings, ed., *The Old Dominion in the Seventeenth Century** (1975), as are first-hand accounts of Bacon's Rebellion. See also George L. Burr, ed., *Narratives of the Witchcraft Cases, 1648–1706** (1914).

SECONDARY SOURCES

On life and labor in the Chesapeake, consult Thad W. Tate and David L. Ammerman, eds., *The Chesapeake in the Seventeenth Century* (1979). Further probing economic conflicts and their role in the introduction of slavery is Timothy H. Breen and Stephen Innes, *Myne Owne Ground: Race and Freedom on Virginia's Eastern Shore, 1640–1676* (1980). Gloria Main chronicles *The Tobacco Colony: Life in Early Maryland, 1650–1719* (1982). Darrett B. Rutman and Anita H. Rutman examine Virginia in *A Place in Time: Middlesex County, Virginia 1650–1750* (1984). Daniel Blake Smith looks *Inside the Great House: Planter Family Life in Eighteenth-Century Chesapeake Society* (1980). Kenneth A. Lockridge analyzes the life of one of Virginia's most celebrated residents in *The Diary and Life of William Byrd II of Virginia, 1674–1744* (1987). Winthrop Jordan's fascinating *White over Black: American Attitudes Toward the Negro, 1550–1812* (1968) discusses the evolution of racial thought. Rhys Isaac's masterful *The Transformation of Virginia 1740–1790* (1999) explores the tumultuous role of religious and political conflicts in shaping colonial Virginia. Life in New England's towns and homes is scrutinized in John Demos, *A Little Commonwealth: Family Life in Plymouth Colony* (1970); Philip Greven, *Four Generations: Population, Land, and Family in Colonial Andover, Massachusetts* (1970); Kenneth Lockridge, *New England Town: Dedham* (1970); Christine Heyrman, *Commerce and Culture: The Maritime Communities of Colonial Massachusetts, 1690–1750* (1984); and Daniel Vickers, *Farmers and Fishermen: Two Centuries of Work in Essex County, Massachusetts, 1630–1850* (1994). For a less idealized portrait of early New England, see John F. Martin, *Profits in the Wilderness: Entrepreneurship and the Founding of New England Towns in the Seventeenth Century* (1991); Margret Ellen Newell, *From Dependency to Independence: Economic Revolution in Colonial New England* (1998); and Stephen Innes, *Creating the Commonwealth: The Economic Culture of Puritan New England* (1995). For more on the role of gender in seventeenth-century society, see Laurel T. Ulrich, *Good Wives: Image and Reality in the Lives of Women in Northern New England, 1650–1750* (1982); Marylynn Salmon, *Women and the Law of Property in Early America* (1986); Mary Beth Norton, *Founding Mothers and Fathers* (1996); Cornelia Hughes Dayton, *Women Before the Bar: Gender, Law, and Society in Connecticut, 1639–1789* (1995); Lisa Wilson, *Ye Heart of a Man: The Domestic Life of Men in Colonial New England* (1999); and Philip Greven, *The Protestant Temperament* (1977), which analyzes child-rearing practices. Edmund S. Morgan describes the crisis that beset the original Puritans when their children displayed a lesser degree of religiosity in *Visible Saints* (1963). David Grayson Allen emphasizes the persistence of English customs in *In English Ways: The Movement of Societies and the Transferral of English Local Law and Custom to Massachusetts Bay in the Seventeenth Century* (1981). See also David Cressy, *Coming Over: Migration and Communication Between England and New England in the Seventeenth Century* (1987), and David Hackett Fischer, *Albion's Seed: Four British Folkways in America* (1989). Witchcraft is the subject of Paul Boyer and Stephen Nissenbaum's *Salem Possessed* (1974), John Demos's *Entertaining Satan* (1982), and Carol F. Karlsen's *The Devil in the Shape of a Woman: Witchcraft in Colonial New England* (1987). Mary Beth Norton's recent reinterpretation of the Salem witchcraft trials, *In the Devil's Snare: The Salem Witchcraft Crisis of 1692* (2002), emphasizes New England's experience of frontier conflict in King William's War. See also Richard Godbeer, *The Devil's Dominion: Magic and Religion in Early New England* (1992), and Peter Charles Hoffer, *The Devil's Disciples: Makers of the Salem Witchcraft Trials* (1996). A sweeping survey that emphasizes the diversity of cultures already present in seventeenth-century America is E. Brooks Holifield, *Era of Persuasion: American Thought and Culture, 1521–1680* (1989). The relationship of Indians and New England whites to their envi-ronment is the subject of William Cronon's intriguing *Changes in the Land* (1983). David Konig, *Law and Society in Puritan Massachusetts: Essex County, 1629–1692* (1979), considers the role of law in mitigating social tensions.

CHAPTER 5

PRIMARY SOURCE DOCUMENTS

Noting the ethnic diversity of colonial American society, Michel-Guillaume Jean de Crèvecoeur, *Letters from an American Farmer** (1904), and Benjamin Franklin, "Observations on the Increase of Mankind,"* in Jared Sparks, ed., *The Works of Benjamin Franklin* (1840), respectively celebrate and express unease at that diversity. Franklin's entertaining *Autobiography** (1868) is an indispensable guide to the values and preoccupations of his time. It includes an account of George Whitefield's visit to Philadelphia during the Great Awakening.

SECONDARY SOURCES

Social history is painted with broad strokes in James Henretta, *The Evolution of American Society, 1700–1815* (1973), and Jack Greene, *Pursuits of Happiness* (1988). Population trends are detailed in Robert V. Wells, *The Population of the British Colonies in America before 1776* (1975). Philip D. Curtin studies black slaves and white indentured servants in *The African Slave Trade: A Census* (1969). Russell Menard's pioneering work in historical demography, *Migrants, Servants and Slaves: Unfree Labor in Colonial British America* (2001), and Sharon V. Salinger, *"To Serve Well and Faithfully": Labor and Indentured Servants in Pennsylvania, 1682–1800* (1987). Bernard Bailyn captures the human face of migration and settlement on the eve of the Revolution in his masterful *Voyagers to the West* (1986). Several works detail the experiences of the very diverse groups who came to America during this period. The lives of convicts relocated to the United States are explored in A. Roger Ekirch, *Bound for America: The Transportation of British Convicts to the Colonies, 1718–1775* (1987); British immigrants in Bernard Bailyn, *The Peopling of British North America* (1986); Scottish immigrants in Alan L. Karras, *Sojourners in the Sun: Scottish Migrants in Jamaica and the Chesapeake, 1740–1800* (1992); German immigrants in Marianne S. Wokek, *Trade in Strangers: The Beginnings of Mass Migration to North America* (1999); and colonial immigration in general in Ida Altman and James Horn, eds., *"To Make America": European Emigration in the Early Modern Period* (1991). Large-scale economic patterns are traced in John J. McCusker and Russell R. Menard, *The Economy of British America, 1607–1789* (1991), and Alice H. Jones, *The Wealth of a Nation to Be: The American Colonies on the Eve of the Revolution* (1980). The complex interactions between whites and blacks are documented in Mechal Sobel, *The World They Made Together: Black and White Values in Eighteenth-Century Virginia* (1987), and William D. Piersen, *Black Yankees: The Development of an Afro-American Subculture in Eighteenth-Century New England* (1988). The toiling classes are probed in Gerald W. Mullin, *Flight and Rebellion: Slave Resistance in Eighteenth-Century Virginia* (1972); Gary B. Nash, *The Urban Crucible: Social Change, Political Consciousness and the Origins of the American Revolution* (1979); Allen Kulikoff, *Tobacco and Slaves: The Development of Southern Cultures in the Chesapeake, 1680–1800* (1986); Robert Orwell, *Masters, Slaves, and Subjects: The*

Culture of Power in the South Carolina Low Country (1998); and Marcus Rediker, *Between the Devil and the Deep Blue Sea: Merchant Seamen, Pirates, and the Anglo-American Maritime World, 1700–1750* (1987). Nash links social conflict to the Great Awakening, as does Richard L. Bushman, *From Puritan to Yankee: Character and Social Order in Connecticut, 1690–1765* (1967). Patricia Bonomi also emphasizes religious conflict as a promoter of Revolutionary ideology in *Under the Cope of Heaven: Religion, Society, and Politics in Colonial America* (1986), as do the essayists in Ronald Hoffman and Peter J. Albert, eds., *Religion in a Revolutionary Age* (1994). Alan Heimert first explored the significance of the Great Awakening in *Religion and the American Mind* (1966); his interpretation has been revised by Jon Butler in *Awash in a Sea of Faith* (1992). John Butler has also written a cultural history on the development of American identity in the late eighteenth century in *Becoming America: The Revolution Before 1776* (2000). Other important works on religion include David S. Lovejoy, *Religious Enthusiasm in the New World: Heresy to Revolution* (1985), and Susan Juster, *Disorderly Women: Sexual Politics and Evangelicalism in Revolutionary New England* (1994). Cultural history is imaginatively presented in Howard M. Jones, *O Strange New World: American Culture in the Formative Years* (1964). Henry May's *The Enlightenment in America* is comprehensive (1976). The sometimes heroic dedication to education is portrayed by Lawrence Cremin, *American Education: The Colonial Experience, 1607–1783* (1970), and the general social implications of the early educational system are studied in James Axtell, *School upon a Hill* (1974). Colonial politics are interpreted in a most suggestive way in Bernard Bailyn, *The Origins of American Politics* (1965). More fine-grained local studies are John Gilman Kolp, *Gentlemen and Freeholders: Electoral Politics in Colonial Virginia* (1998); Richard L. Bushman, *King and People in Provincial Massachusetts* (1985); Robert Zemsky, *Merchants, Farmers and River Gods: An Essay on Eighteenth-Century American Politics* (1971); Jackson Turner Main, *Society and Economy in Colonial Connecticut* (1985); Patricia Bonomi, *A Factious People: Politics and Society in Colonial New York* (1971); James T. Lemon, *The Best Poor Man's Country* (1972), which deals with Pennsylvania; and Daniel Blake Smith, *Inside the Great House: Planter Family Life in Eighteenth-Century Chesapeake Society* (1980). Timothy Breen examines the ways in which the increasing indebtedness of the Virginia planters changed their behavior in *Tobacco Culture: The Mentality of the Great Tidewater Planters on the Eve of Revolution* (1985).

CHAPTER 6

PRIMARY SOURCE DOCUMENTS

"The Albany Plan of the Union" was the first great statement of colonial unity; "The Proclamation of 1763" forbade settlement west of the Appalachians. Both are collected in Henry Steele Commager, *Documents of American History*. Adolph B. Benson, ed., *The America of 1750; Petar Kalm's Travels in North America* (1937),* records the observations of a visiting Swedish naturalist with a keen eye for the behavior of humans.

SECONDARY SOURCES

A cutting-edge study of the major themes in Atlantic history is presented in David Armitage, ed., *The British Atlantic World, 1500–1800* (2002). For an analysis of Britain's concept of empire, also see

Armitage's *Ideological Origins of the British Empire* (2000) and David Hancock, *Citizens of the World: London Merchants and the Integration of the British Atlantic Community* (1995). Further efforts to analyze the colonial empire are James Henretta, "*Salutary Neglect*": *Colonial Administration under the Duke of Newcastle* (1972); Michael Kammen's especially interesting *Empire and Interest* (1970); and John Brewer, *The Sinews of Power: War, Money and the English State, 1688–1783* (1989). The empire as seen through British eyes is captured in Paul David Nelson, *William Tryon and the Course of Empire: A Life in British Imperial Service* (1990). The French colonial effort is described in George M. Wrong, *The Rise and Fall of New France* (2 vols., 1928). William John Eccles presents a vivid study of French exploration and settlement in North America and the West Indies in *The French in North America, 1500–1783* (1998). Calvin Martin, *Keepers of the Game* (1978), offers a provocative interpretation of the fur trade and its impact on Indian societies. Other works on the role of Indians in larger imperial struggles include Armstrong Starkey, *European and Native American Warfare, 1615–1815* (1998); Francis Jennings, *Empire of Fortune: Crowns, Colonies and Tribes in the Seven Years War in America* (1988); Gregory Evans Dowd, *A Spirited Resistance: The North American Indian Struggle for Unity, 1745–1815* (1992); and Richard White, *The Middle Ground: Indians, Empires, and Republics in the Great Lakes Region, 1650–1815* (1991). The wars for empire in the eighteenth century are vividly narrated by Fred Anderson in *Crucible of War: The Seven Years' War and the Fate of Empire in British North America, 1754–1766* (2001). Anderson's *A People's Army: Massachusetts Soldiers and Society in the Seven Years' War* (1984) discusses the experience of colonial soldiers in forging resistance to Britain. Alan Rogers, *Empire and Liberty: American Resistance to the British Authority, 1755–1763* (1974), investigates American participation in the Seven Years' War, as does Douglas E. Leach, *Roots of Conflict: British Armed Forces and Colonial Americans, 1677–1763* (1986). Classic accounts are Francis Parkman's several volumes, condensed in *The Battle for North America*, edited by John Tebbel (1948), and *The Parkman Reader*, edited by Samuel E. Morison (1955).

CHAPTER 7

PRIMARY SOURCE DOCUMENTS

Adam Smith, *An Inquiry into the Nature and Causes of the Wealth of Nations** (1776), is a penetrating analysis of British mercantilism. An intriguing Loyalist account of the Revolution, since reprinted, is Peter Oliver, *Origin and Progress of the American Rebellion* (1781). Patrick Henry, "Speech Before the Virginia House of Burgesses Against the Stamp Act"* (1765), was an influential statement of colonial opposition to British policy, as was John Dickinson's response to the Townshend Acts, *Letters from a Farmer in Pennsylvania* (1768). Revolutionary writings may also be found in Bernard Bailyn, ed., *Pamphlets of the American Revolution, 1750–1776* (1965). For contemporary accounts of the beginning of hostilities, see Peter Force, ed., *American Archives*, 4th series, vol. 2* (1839). For visual sources from the period, consult the edition compiled by Donald H. Cresswell, *The American Revolution in Drawings and Prints* (1975).

SECONDARY SOURCES

The Revolution is interpreted as a divinely ordained event in George Bancroft's *History of the United States of America* (1852). Edmund S.

Morgan, *The Birth of the Republic, 1763–1789* (1959), is a brief account of the Revolutionary era. It stresses the happy coincidence of the revolutionaries' principles and their interests, as do Daniel Boorstin, *The Genius of American Politics* (1953), and Robert E. Brown, *Middle-Class Democracy and the Revolution in Massachusetts, 1691–1780* (1955). Lawrence Gipson, *The Coming of the Revolution, 1763–1775* (1954), summarizes his fifteen-volume masterwork. A more recent effort at a general synthesis is Robert Middlekauff, *The Glorious Cause: The American Revolution, 1763–1789* (1982). Robert R. Palmer, *The Age of the Democratic Revolution: A Political History of Europe and America, 1760–1800* (2 vols., 1959, 1964), places American events in the larger context of Western history. Two enlightening collections of essays are Jack P. Greene, ed., *The Reinterpretation of the American Revolution, 1763–1789* (1968), and Alfred F. Young, ed., *The American Revolution* (1976), which generally represents a "New Left" revisionist view, a perspective also found in Edward A. Countryman, *The American Revolution* (1987). For an examination of ordinary people's experience in the Revolution, see Ray Raphael, *A People's History of the American Revolution* (2001). An interesting effort to blend British and American perspectives is Ian R. Christie and Benjamin W. Labaree, *Empire or Independence, 1760–1776* (1976). The sources of American dissatisfaction with the British imperial system can be traced in Carl Ubbelohde, *The American Colonies in the British Empire, 1607–1763* (1968), and Thomas C. Barrow, *Trade and Empire: The British Customs Service in Colonial America* (1967). Oliver M. Dickerson, *The Navigation Acts and the American Revolution* (1951), concludes that the navigation system did not put undue burdens on the colonies. Bernhard Knollenberg examines the effects of the British tightening of the imperial system in the 1760s in *Origin of the American Revolution, 1759–1766* (1960), as does Michael Kammen in *Empire and Interest* (1970). John Shy imaginatively explores an important aspect of the imperial system's effect on America in *Toward Lexington: The Role of the British Army in the Coming of the American Revolution* (1965). A perceptive short account of the American reaction to British initiatives is Edmund S. Morgan and Helen M. Morgan, *The Stamp Act Crisis* (1953). Benjamin W. Labaree discusses another instance of American reaction in *The Boston Tea Party* (1964). Pauline Maier focuses on the crucial role of the "mob" in *From Resistance to Revolution: Colonial Radicals and the Development of American Opposition to Britain, 1765–1776* (1972). The British side is told in Peter D. G. Thomas, *British Politics and the Stamp Act Crisis* (1975), *The Townshend Duties Crisis* (1987), and *Tea Party to Independence* (1991). Bernard Bailyn's seminal *Ideological Origins of the American Revolution* (1967) stresses the importance of ideas in pushing the Revolution forward, as well as the colonists' fears of a conspiracy against their liberties. John Philip Reid emphasizes legal ideas in *Constitutional History of the American Revolution: The Authority of Rights* (1987), as does Jerrilyn Greene Marston in *King and Congress: The Transfer of Political Legitimacy, 1774–1776* (1987). Useful local studies of American resistance are Richard D. Brown, *Revolutionary Politics in Massachusetts* (1970); Woody Holton, *Forced Founders: Indians, Debtors, Slaves, and the Making of the American Revolution in Virginia* (1999). Richard Ryerson, *The Revolution Is Now Begun: The Radical Committees of Philadelphia, 1765–1776* (1978); Joseph S. Tiedmann, *Reluctant Revolutionaries: New York City and the Road to Independence, 1763–1776* (1997); and David Hackett Fischer, *Paul Revere's Ride* (1994). On the meaning of the Revolution for African Americans, see Sylvia R. Frey, *Water from the Rock: Black Resistance in a Revolutionary Age* (1991). Ordinary artisans' involvement in

Revolutionary events is the subject of Alfred F. Young's *The Shoemaker and the Tea Party* (1999). Helpful biographies of key Revolutionary figures include Richard Beeman, *Patrick Henry* (1974); Merrill D. Peterson, *Thomas Jefferson and the New Nation* (1970); Dumas Malone, *Jefferson and His Time* (5 vols., 1948–1974); C. Bradley Thompson, *John Adams and the Spirit of Liberty* (1998); and Pauline Maier, *The Old Revolutionaries: Political Lives in the Age of Samuel Adams* (1980). Imaginative cultural history is found in Robert A. Gross, *The Minutemen and Their World* (1976). Edward A. Countryman emphasizes class conflict in *A People in Revolution: The American Revolution and Political Society in New York, 1760–1790* (1981). A psychological approach to the problem of the Revolutionary generation's assault on established authority is taken in Jay Fliegelman, *Prodigals and Pilgrims: The American Revolution Against Patriarchal Authority, 1750–1800* (1982).

CHAPTER 8

PRIMARY SOURCE DOCUMENTS

Thomas Paine's fiery *Common Sense** (1776) is the manifesto of the Revolution. "The Declaration of Independence"* (1776) is one of the foundations of American political theory. For eyewitness accounts of the war, see John C. Dann, *The Revolution Remembered* (1980). See also the "Treaty of Peace with Great Britain" (1783), in Henry Steele Commager, *Documents of American History*.

SECONDARY SOURCES

The war is sketched in Don Higginbotham's excellent military history, *The War of American Independence: Military Attitudes, Policies, and Practice, 1763–1789* (1971). On the implications of the Revolutionary conflict, see John Shy, *A People Numerous and Armed: Reflections on the Military Struggle for American Independence* (1976); E. Wayne Carp, *To Starve the Army at Pleasure: Continental Army Administration and American Political Culture, 1775–1783* (1984); Charles Royster, *A Revolutionary People at War: The Continental Army and the American Character* (1980); Mark V. Kwasny, *Washington's Partisan War, 1775–1783* (1996); and Ronald Hoffman et al., eds., *An Uncivil War: The Southern Backcountry During the American Revolution* (1985). The conflict is considered in its European setting in Piers Mackesy, *The War for America, 1775–1783* (1964). Carl Becker's classic *The Declaration of Independence* (1922) is masterful; on the same subject, see also Garry Wills, *Inventing America: Jefferson's Declaration of Independence* (1980), and Pauline Maier, *American Scripture: The Making of the Declaration of Independence* (1997). The role of the Loyalists is treated in Robert M. Calhoon, *The Loyalists in Revolutionary America* (1973); Mary Beth Norton, *The British-Americans: The Loyalist Exiles in England* (1972); John E. Ferling, *The Loyalist Mind: Joseph Galloway and the American Revolution* (1977); Robert M. Calhoon, *Loyalists and Community in North America* (1994); Janice Potter-MacKinnon, *While the Women Only Wept: Loyalist Refugee Women* (1993); and Bernard Bailyn's unusually sensitive biography of the governor of colonial Massachusetts, *The Ordeal of Thomas Hutchinson* (1974). General treatments of an often-neglected subject are Benjamin Quarles, *The Negro in the American Revolution* (1961); Ronald Hoffman and Ira Berlin, eds., *Slavery and Freedom in the Age of the American Revolution* (1983); and Sylvia R. Frey, *Water from the Rock: Black Resistance in a*

Revolutionary Age (1991). See also Duncan J. MacLeod, *Slavery, Race and the American Revolution* (1974), and David B. Davis, *The Problem of Slavery in the Age of Revolution, 1770–1823* (1975), an able, gracefully written book. International implications are developed in James H. Hutson, *John Adams and the Diplomacy of the American Revolution* (1980), and Jonathan R. Dull, *A Diplomatic History of the American Revolution* (1985). Attention to the social history of the Revolution has been largely inspired by John F. Jameson's seminal *The American Revolution Considered as a Social Movement* (1926). Jackson T. Main, *The Social Structure of Revolutionary America* (1969), takes the exploration further along the same lines, with conclusions somewhat at variance with Jameson's. Local studies of this issue include Alan Taylor, *Liberty Men and Great Proprietors: The Revolutionary Settlement on the Maine Frontier, 1760–1820* (1990); Steven Rosswurm, *Arms, Country, and Class: The Philadelphia Militia and the "Lower Sort" During the American Revolution* (1987); and Billy G. Smith, *The "Lower Sort": Philadelphia's Laboring People, 1750–1800* (1990). For information on the role of Indians in the Revolution, see Barbara Graymont, *The Iroquois in the American Revolution* (1972); Isabel T. Kelsay, *Joseph Brant, 1743–1807: Man of Two Worlds* (1984); and Colin G. Calloway, *The American Revolution in Indian Country* (1995). Thomas Doerflinger describes economic change during the Revolution in *A Vigorous Spirit of Enterprise: Merchants and Economic Development in Revolutionary Philadelphia* (1986). Interesting biographies are Samuel E. Morison's swashbuckling *John Paul Jones* (1959); Eric Foner, *Tom Paine and Revolutionary America* (1976); and James T. Flexner, *George Washington in the American Revolution, 1775–1783* (1968). British troubles are laid bare in William B. Willcox, *Portrait of a General: Sir Henry Clinton in the War of Independence* (1964). Women are the subject of Linda K. Kerber, *Women of the Republic: Intellect and Ideology in Revolutionary America* (1980); Mary Beth Norton, *Liberty's Daughters: The Revolutionary Experience of American Women* (1980); and Joy Day Buel and Richard Buel, Jr., *The Way of Duty: A Woman and Her Family in Revolutionary America* (1984). Michael Kammen brilliantly evokes the ways that the Revolution has been enshrined in the national memory in *A Season of Youth: The American Revolution and the Historical Imagination* (1978).

CHAPTER 9

PRIMARY SOURCE DOCUMENTS

A comparison of the text of the Articles of Confederation (1781), in Henry Steele Commager, *Documents of American History*, with the Constitution* makes an intriguing study. See also Madison, Hamilton, and Jay's explanations of the Constitution in *The Federalist* papers, especially *Federalist* No. 10.* Additional primary sources may be found in Bernard Bailyn, ed., *The Debate on the Constitution: Federalist and Antifederalist Speeches, Articles, and Letters During the Struggle over Ratification* (1993). For visual sources from the period, consult *The American Revolution in Drawings and Prints* (1975), a volume compiled by Donald H. Cresswell.

SECONDARY SOURCES

John Fiske, in *The Critical Period of American History* (1888), portrayed America under the Articles of Confederation as a crisis-ridden country. His view is sharply qualified by Merrill Jensen in *The New Nation* (1950). Jack N. Rakove's *The Beginnings of National Politics* (1979) offers a history of the Continental Congress that substantially revises Jensen's work. Especially informative is Gordon S. Wood's massive and brilliant study of the entire period, *The Creation of the American Republic, 1776–1787* (1969), and his equally compelling work, *The Radicalism of the American Revolution* (1991), which documents the relative egalitarianism that swept revolutionary society during and after the war. For a similar argument that relies on the material culture of the era, see Richard Bushman, *The Refinement of America: Persons, Houses, Cities* (1992). See also Richard B. Morris, *The Forging of the Union, 1781–1787* (1987). For the intellectual foundations of the political economy, see Cathy Matson and Peter Onuf, *A Union of Interests: Political and Economic Thought in Revolutionary America* (1990). An influential transatlantic perspective on the roots of American republicanism is J. G. A. Pocock, *The Machiavellian Moment: Florentine Political Thought and the Atlantic Republican Tradition* (1975). Edmund S. Morgan also looks at both Britain and America in *Inventing the People: The Rise of Popular Sovereignty in England and America* (1988). On the state constitutions, see Jackson T. Main, *The Sovereign States, 1775–1783* (1973), and Willi P. Adams, *The First American Constitutions* (1980). Peter S. Onuf carefully examines the Northwest Ordinance in *Statehood and Union: A History of the Northwest Ordinance* (1987). On the Constitutional Convention, see Richard Bernstein's superb synthesis of current scholarship, *Are We to Be a Nation? The Making of the Constitution* (1987). Bernstein's work was one of a host of useful studies inspired by the bicentennial of the drafting of the Constitution. Others include Ruth Bloch, *Visionary Republic: Millennial Themes in American Thought, 1756–1800* (1986); Richard Beeman et al., eds., *Beyond Confederation: Origins of the Constitution and American National Identity* (1987); Leonard Levy, *Original Intent and the Framers' Constitution* (1988); and Jack N. Rakove, *Original Meanings: Politics and Ideas in the Making of the Constitution* (1996). For a more general interpretation of the Constitution's role in American society, see Michael G. Kammen, *A Machine That Would Go of Itself* (1986). Thornton Anderson, *Creating the Constitution* (1993), and Robert A. Rutland, *The Ordeal of the Constitution* (1966), describe the ratification struggle. Charles A. Beard caused a stir with the class-based analysis he offered in *An Economic Interpretation of the Constitution of the United States* (1913). It is seriously weakened by two blistering attacks: Robert E. Brown, *Charles Beard and the Constitution* (1956), and Forrest McDonald, *We the People: The Economic Origins of the Constitution* (1958). See also McDonald's *E Pluribus Unum: The Formation of the American Republic, 1776–1790* (1965). Jackson T. Main, *The Anti-Federalists* (1961), partially rehabilitates Beard. Gary Nash's *Race and Revolution* (1990) offers a perceptive study of controversies over race and slavery in the making of the Constitution, as do the contributors to John P. Kaminski, ed., *A Necessary Evil? Slavery and the Debate over the Constitution* (1995). David Szatmary is perceptive on *Shays' Rebellion* (1980), as are the contributors to Robert Gross, ed., *In Debt to Shays* (1993). On similar episodes of agrarian radicalism, see Alan Taylor, *Liberty Men and Great Proprietors: The Revolutionary Settlement on the Maine Frontier, 1760–1820* (1990). Charles R. Kesler has edited a collection of essays on *The Federalist* papers entitled *Saving the Revolution: The Federalist Papers and the American Founding* (1987). Also see Morton White, *Philosophy, The Federalist, and the Constitution* (1987). A concise summary of the original federalist-antifederalist debate is Herbert J. Storing, *What the Anti-Federalists Were For* (1981). Relevant biographical studies of merit are Richard Brookhiser, *Alexander Hamilton, American* (1999), and Jack Rakove, *James Madison and the Creation of the American Republic* (2002). For an engaging study of the political negotiations and infighting among several members of the founding generations, see Joseph Ellis, *Founding Brothers: the Revolutionary Generation* (2001).

CHAPTER 10

PRIMARY SOURCE DOCUMENTS

"The Report on Manufactures" (in Daniel Boorstin, ed., *American Primer*), the last of Alexander Hamilton's messages to Congress, presented the case for the development of American industry. Thomas Jefferson expounded his views in *Notes on the State of Virginia* (1784). For further study of the Hamiltonian-Jeffersonian debate, see Harold C. Syrett, ed. *The Papers of Alexander Hamilton* (27 vols., 1961–1987), and Julian Boyd et al., eds., *The Papers of Thomas Jefferson* (30 vols., 1950–2003). Important salvos in the battle between national power and state sovereignty, and between Federalists and Jeffersonians, were the Virginia* and Kentucky resolutions (1798) and the reply of Rhode Island* (1799). Washington's Farewell Address* (1796) established the foundation for American attitudes about party politics and foreign policy. See also Benjamin Franklin Bache's stinging editorial on Washington's retirement, *Philadelphia Aurora** (1797).

SECONDARY SOURCES

Perceptive introductions are provided in James Roger Sharp's succinct *American Politics in the Early Republic: The New Nation in Crisis* (1993) and Stanley Elkins and Eric McKitrick's comprehensive work, *The Age of Federalism: The Early American Republic, 1788–1800* (1993). On administration, see Ronald Hoffman, *Launching the "Extended Republic": The Federalist Era* (1996). On the economy, see Paul Gilje, *Wages of Independence: Capitalism in the Early American Republic* (1997). Innovative work on political culture in the early national period can be found in James Sharp, *American Politics in the Early Republic* (1993), and Joanne Freeman, *Affairs of Honor* (2001). On the Bill of Rights, see Bernard Schwartz, *The Great Rights of Mankind: A History of the American Bill of Rights* (1991), and Patrick L. Conley and John P. Kaminski, eds., *The Bill of Rights and the States: The Colonial and Revolutionary Origins of American Liberties* (1992). On the use of party politics, see Richard Hofstadter's thoughtful *The Idea of a Party System* (1969); Richard Buel, Jr., *Securing the Revolution: Ideology in American Politics, 1789–1815* (1972); John Zvesper, *Political Philosophy and Rhetoric: A Study of the Origins of American Party Politics* (1977); John F. Hoadley, *Origins of American Political Parties, 1789–1803* (1986); and Lance Banning, ed., *After the Constitution: Party Conflict in the New Republic* (1989). Other interpretations of that subject, stressing the ideology of republicanism, are Drew McCoy, *The Elusive Republic: Political Economy in Jeffersonian America* (1980), and Lance Banning, *The Jeffersonian Persuasion* (1978). Charles G. Steffens examines the political beliefs of workers in *The Mechanics of Baltimore: Workers and Politics in the Age of Revolution, 1763–1812* (1984), as do Michael Merrill and Sean Wilentz in their introduction to the edited volume *The Key of Liberty: The Life and Democratic Writings of William Manning, "A Laborer," 1747–1814* (1992). For a trenchant analysis of Jeffersonianism, see Joyce Appleby, *Capitalism and a New Social Order: The Republican Vision* (1984), whose analysis emphasizes the role of liberalism in American political thought, a point previously made by Louis Hartz in *The Liberal Tradition in America* (1955). Also

illuminating is Gerald Stourzh, *Alexander Hamilton and the Idea of Republican Government* (1970). Thomas P. Slaughter focuses on *The Whiskey Rebellion: Frontier Epilogue to the American Revolution* (1986). A comprehensive biography is James T. Flexner, *George Washington and the New Nation, 1783–1793* (1969). Consult also Forrest McDonald, *The Presidency of George Washington* (1974), and Garry Wills, *Cincinnatus: George Washington and the Enlightenment* (1984). Of special interest is Richard H. Kohn, *Eagle and Sword: The Federalists and the Creation of the Military Establishment in America, 1783–1802* (1975). On aspects of foreign policy, see Alexander De Conde, *Entangling Alliance* (1958); Gilbert Lycan, *Alexander Hamilton and American Foreign Policy* (1970); Jerald Combs, *The Jay Treaty* (1970); Lawrence S. Kaplan, *Colonies into Nation: American Diplomacy, 1763–1801* (1972); and Daniel G. Lang, *Foreign Policy in the Early Republic: The Law of Nations and the Balance of Power* (1985). For the view from across the Atlantic, see Charles R. Ritcheson, *Aftermath of Revolution: British Policy Toward the United States, 1783–1795* (1969). On Adams, consult Page Smith, *John Adams* (2 vols., 1962), and Stephen G. Kurtz, *The Presidency of John Adams* (1957). James M. Smith, *Freedom's Fetters* (1956), treats the Alien and Sedition Acts, as does Leonard Levy in *Legacy of Suppression* (1960).

CHAPTER 11

PRIMARY SOURCE DOCUMENTS

Thomas Jefferson's "First Inaugural Address" (1801), in Henry Steele Commager, *Documents of American History*, echoed the themes of Washington's Farewell Address and set the tone for his presidency. Reuben G. Thwaites, ed., *Original Journals of the Lewis and Clark Expedition** (1904), chronicles the explorers' adventures. For the political flavor of the age, see the debate over the Embargo Act* (1807); for constitutional history, read the decision of John Marshall in *Marbury* v. *Madison** (1803). See James Madison, "War Message"* (1812), in James D. Richardson, ed., *Messages and Papers of the Presidents*, vol. 1 (1896), and the protest of thirty-four Federalist congressmen, *Annals of Congress,** 12th Cong., 1st sess., 2219–2221 (1812). John Marshall's decision in *McCulloch* v. *Maryland,** 4 Wheaton 316 (1819), is a leading statement of the era's surging nationalism.

SECONDARY SOURCES

A monument of American historical writing is Henry Adams, *History of the United States During the Administrations of Jefferson and Madison* (9 vols., 1889–1891), available in a one-volume abridgement edited by Ernest Samuels. Especially fascinating are Adams's prologue and epilogue on the United States in 1800 and 1817. A brief introduction is given in Marshall Smelser, *The Democratic Republic, 1801–1815* (1968). For a succinct study of Marshall's life and legal thought, see Jean Edward Smith, *John Marshall: Definer of a Nation* (1996). A helpful analysis of challenges faced by the judiciary is Richard E. Ellis, *The Jeffersonian Crisis: Courts and Politics in the New Republic* (1971). For a broad understanding of legal developments in this period, see Lawrence Friedman, *A History of American Law* (1973); Morton J. Horwitz, *The Transformation of American Law, 1780–1860* (1977); and Alfred H. Kelly, Winfred A. Harbison, and Herman Belz, *The American Constitution: Its Origins and Development* (6th ed., 1983). On the Supreme Court, see R. Kent

Newmyer, *The Supreme Court Under Marshall and Taney* (1986), and G. Edward White, *The Marshall Court and Cultural Change, 1815–1835* (1988). Politics are treated in a broad, imaginative context in James S. Young, *The Washington Community, 1800–1829* (1966). For the important role women played in early America's political society, see Catherine Allgor, *Parlor Politics* (2000). See also Robert M. Johnstone, Jr., *Jefferson and the Presidency* (1979), and the Joyce Appleby, Lance Banning, and Drew McCoy volumes cited in Chapter 10. Other works include Joseph Ellis, *American Sphinx: The Character of Thomas Jefferson* (1997), and Robert B. Tucker and David Hendrickson, *Empire of Liberty: The Statecraft of Thomas Jefferson* (1990). Noble E. Cunningham, Jr., *In Pursuit of Reason: The Life of Thomas Jefferson* (1987), is a short biography. The standard scholarly biography is Merrill D. Peterson, *Thomas Jefferson and the New Nation* (1970). Peterson has also scrutinized *The Jefferson Image in the American Mind* (1960). Forrest McDonald is highly critical of his subject in *The Presidency of Thomas Jefferson* (1976). Leonard Levy debunks Jefferson's liberalism in *Jefferson and Civil Liberties* (1963); Anthony Wallace examines Jefferson's racial ideas and his policies toward Native Americans in *Jefferson and the Indians* (1999); and Gary Wills does the same for black slaves in *Negro President: Thomas Jefferson and the Slave Power* (2003). See also Reginald Horsman, *Expansion and American Indian Policy, 1783–1812* (1967), and Gregory Evans Dowd, *A Spirited Resistance: The North American Indian Struggle for Unity, 1745–1815* (1992). Donald Jackson, *Thomas Jefferson and the Stony Mountain: Exploring the West from Monticello* (1981), captures Jefferson's fascination with the West. See also Stephen E. Ambrose's spirited biography of Meriwether Lewis, *Undaunted Courage* (1996). An engaging and recent study of the origins and diplomacy of the Louisiana Purchase is Jon Kukla's *A Wilderness so Immense* (2003). The embargo is treated in Burton Spivak, *Jefferson's English Crisis: Commerce, Embargo and the Republican Revolution* (1979). See also Doron S. Ben-Atar, *The Origins of Jeffersonian Commercial Policy and Diplomacy* (1993). Daniel Boorstin vividly evokes the intellectual climate of the age in *The Lost World of Thomas Jefferson* (1948). Irving Brant looks at *James Madison, Secretary of State* (1953), and F. E. Ewing examines Jefferson's powerful Treasury secretary in *America's Forgotten Statesman: Albert Gallatin* (1959). An important work that sets the War of 1812 in a broad context of early American history is J. C. A. Stagg, *Mr. Madison's War: Politics, Diplomacy and Warfare in the Early American Republic* (1983). Also see Steven Watts, *The Republic Reborn: War and the Making of Liberal America, 1790–1820* (1987), and Donald R. Hickey, *The War of 1812: A Forgotten Conflict* (1989). On the causes of the war, Julius W. Pratt, *Expansionists of 1812* (1925), stresses western pressures; Bradford Perkins, *Prologue to War: England and the United States, 1805–1812* (1961), and Reginald Horsman, *The Causes of the War of 1812* (1962), discuss free seas; and Roger H. Brown, *The Republic in Peril, 1812* (1964), emphasizes the need for saving the republican form of government.

CHAPTER 12

PRIMARY SOURCE DOCUMENTS

Timothy Dwight offers a participant's view of the opposition to the War of 1812 in *The History of the Hartford Convention** (1833). Charles F. Adams, ed., *Memoirs of John Quincy Adams** (1875), offers a behind-the-scenes portrait of the creation of the Monroe Doctrine. See also the text of Monroe's public statement in James D. Richardson, ed., *Messages and Papers of the Presidents,** vol. 2 (1896).

"The Missouri Compromise" (1819–1820), in Henry Steele Commager, *Documents of American History*, reveals the dangerous sectional animosities underlying such national pride.

SECONDARY SOURCES

On the War of 1812, see the books by J. C. A. Stagg, Steven Watts, and Donald R. Hickey cited in Chapter 11. Lester D. Langley, *The Americans in the Age of Revolution, 1750–1850* (1996), takes a comparative approach to the history of the Western Hemisphere. On Indian affairs and westward expansion, see Dorothy Jones, *License for Empire: Colonialism by Treaty in Early America* (1982), and the works of R. David Edmunds, *The Shawnee Prophet* (1983) and *Tecumseh and the Quest for Indian Leadership* (1984). The relevant volumes of Henry Adams's nine-volume *History of the United States* (1889–1891) still contain magnificent reading, both on the war and on the peace. Federalist reaction to Republican foreign policy is vividly etched in David H. Fisher, *The Revolution of American Conservatism* (1965), and James M. Banner, *To the Hartford Convention: The Federalists and the Origins of Party Politics in Massachusetts* (1970). Consult also James H. Broussard, *The Southern Federalists, 1800–1816* (1979). Irving Brant argues that James Madison was a strong president in *James Madison: Commander in Chief, 1812–1836* (1961). More recent treatments of Madison include Robert A. Rutland, *James Madison: The Founding Father* (1987); Drew R. McCoy, *The Last of the Fathers: James Madison and the Republican Legacy* (1989); and Jack N. Rakove, *James Madison and the Creation of the American Republic* (1990). Other useful biographical studies are Robert Remini, *Henry Clay: Statesman for the Union* (1991), and David Heidler, *Old Hickory's War: Andrew Jackson and the Quest for Empire* (2003). An excellent introduction to nationalism is George Dangerfield, *The Awakening of American Nationalism, 1815–1828* (1965). See also Robert H. Wiebe's ambitious *Opening of American Society: From the Adoption of the Constitution to the Eve of Disunion* (1984). Arand Otto Mayr and Robert C. Post, eds., detail *Yankee Enterprise: The Rise of the American System of Manufactures* (1981). Glover Moore, *The Missouri Controversy, 1819–1821* (1953), and Charles S. Sydnor, *The Development of Southern Sectionalism, 1819–1848* (1948), place the Missouri Compromise in a broader context. On the Monroe Doctrine, the classic text is Dexter Perkins, *A History of the Monroe Doctrine* (1955). James E. Lewis, *The American Union and the Problem of Neighborhood* (1998), places the Monroe Doctrine in a new interpretive context. Ernest R. May ties the doctrine to domestic politics, especially the impending election of 1824, in *The Making of the Monroe Doctrine* (1975). See also Harry Ammon, *James Monroe: The Quest for National Identity* (1971), as well as James Lewis, *John Quincy Adams: Policymaker for the Union* (2001).

CHAPTER 13

PRIMARY SOURCE DOCUMENTS

Davy Crockett, *Exploits and Adventures in Texas** (1836), is a lively description of the democratic political order of Jacksonian America. James Fenimore Cooper's *The American Democrat** (1838) offers an incisive commentary on the era's politics, while C. W. Janson, *The Stranger in America, 1793–1806** (1807), exposes the seamier aspects of American egalitarianism. A still-powerful classic treatise on the Jacksonian period is Alexis de Tocqueville, *Democracy in America* (1835, 1840). On the Bank War, see Andrew Jackson, "Veto Message"*

(July 10, 1832), in James D. Richardson, ed., *Messages and Papers of the Presidents,* vol. 2 (1896); *The Nullification Era: A Documentary Record,* edited by William W. Freehling; and Daniel Webster's "Speech on Jackson's Veto of the U.S. Bank Bill" (1832), in Richard Hofstadter, ed., *Great Issues in American History.* On the "Tariff of Abominations" and its implications, see the "Webster-Hayne Debate"* (1830). *The Diary of Philip Hone, 1828–1851* (1927) presents the everyday reflections of a Whig mayor of New York.

SECONDARY SOURCES

Overviews of Jacksonian politics include Arthur M. Schlesinger, Jr., *The Age of Jackson* (1945); Harry L. Watson, *Liberty and Power: The Politics of Jacksonian America* (1990); and Charles Sellers, *The Market Revolution: Jacksonian America, 1815–1846* (1991). For a more temporally focused approach that still uses a broad lens, see Louis P. Masur, *1831: Year of Eclipse.* Edward Pessen, *Jacksonian America: Society, Personality, and Politics* (rev. ed., 1978), is a good general introduction that sharply disputes Tocqueville's findings. See also Frederick Jackson Turner, *The Frontier in American History* (1920), which casts Jackson as an exemplar of the democratic spirit of the frontier. Marvin Meyers, *The Jacksonian Persuasion* (1957), and John William Ward, *Andrew Jackson: Symbol for an Age* (1955), examine the broader cultural significance of "Old Hickory" and his supporters. Lee Benson, *The Concept of Jacksonian Democracy: New York as a Test Case* (1961), attacks Schlesinger's emphasis on eastern labor's support for Jackson. For a general overview of political participation, see Glenn C. Altschuler and Stuart M. Blumin, *Rude Republic: Americans and Their Politics in the Nineteenth Century* (2001). On the evolution of mass-based political parties, see Lawrence Kohl, *The Politics of Individualism: Parties and the American Character in the Jacksonian Era* (1989); Richard P. McCormick, *The Second American Party System* (1966); and two books by Ronald P. Formisano, *The Birth of Mass Political Parties: Michigan, 1827–1861* (1971) and *The Transformation of Political Culture: Massachusetts Parties, 1790s–1840s* (1983). See also Amy Bridges, *A City in the Republic: Antebellum New York and the Origins of Machine Politics* (1984), and Richard L. McCormick's general survey of party politics from Jackson into the twentieth century, *The Party Period and Public Policy: American Politics from the Age of Jackson to the Progressive Era* (1986). Four works that consider Jacksonian politics in the South are William J. Cooper, *The South and the Politics of Slavery, 1828–1856* (1978); J. Mills Thornton III, *Politics and Power in a Slave Society: Alabama, 1800–1860* (1978); William W. Freehling, *The Road to Disunion: Secessionists at Bay, 1776–1854* (1990); and Harry L. Watson, *Jacksonian Politics and Community Conflict: The Emergence of the Second American Party System in Cumberland County, North Carolina* (1981), which discusses the opponents of Jackson. Robert V. Remini has a three-volume biography of Jackson; *Andrew Jackson and the Course of American Freedom* (1981) and *Andrew Jackson and the Course of American Democracy* (1984) cover the presidential years. Remini also has a fine biography of Clay, *Henry Clay: Statesman for the Union* (1991). A masterful analysis of the period's most celebrated statesmen is Merrill D. Peterson, *The Great Triumvirate: Webster, Clay, and Calhoun* (1987). On Van Buren, see John Niven, *Martin Van Buren: The Romantic Age of American Politics* (1983). Incisive analysis can be found in Richard Hofstadter's essay on Jackson in *The American Political Tradition and the Men Who Made It* (1948). See also Daniel Feller, *The Jacksonian Promise 1815–1840* (1995). On nullification, see Richard E. Ellis, *The Union at Risk: Jacksonian Democracy, States' Rights and the Nullification Crisis* (1987). An impressive study of the nullification crisis with a regionally specific focus is William W. Freehling's *Prelude to Civil War: The Nullification Controversy in South Carolina, 1816–1836* (1966). On Calhoun, see Gerald M. Capers, *John C. Calhoun, Opportunist* (1960), and John Niven, *John C. Calhoun and the Price of Union* (1988). Jacksonians are charged with ignorance and hypocrisy in Bray Hammond, *Banks and Politics in America from the Revolution to the Civil War* (1957). John McFaul looks at the broader picture in *The Politics of Jacksonian Finance* (1972), and Robert V. Remini focuses on political questions in *Andrew Jackson and the Bank War* (1967). For an insightful and imaginative personal biography of Jackson, see Andrew Burstein, *The Passions of Andrew Jackson* (2003). Jackson's Indian policies are scrutinized in Ronald N. Satz, *American Indian Policy in the Jacksonian Era* (1975). See also Michael D. Green, *The Politics of Indian Removal* (1982), and Anthony Wallace, *The Long, Bitter Trail: Andrew Jackson and the Indians* (1993). For studies of the so-called "Five Civilized Tribes," see Charles Hudson, *The Southeastern Indians* (1976), and William G. McLaughlin, *Cherokee Renascence in the New Republic* (1986). Daniel W. Howe provides a stimulating analysis of Jackson's opponents in *The Political Culture of the American Whigs* (1980). For an illuminating and comprehensive study of the Whig party, see Michael F. Holt, *The Rise and Fall of the American Whig Party* (1999). Attempts to connect politics with the economic changes of the era include Charles Sellers's provocative synthesis, *The Market Revolution: Jacksonian America, 1815–1846* (1991), and Melvyn Stokes and Stephen Conway, eds., *The Market Revolution in America* (1996).

CHAPTER 14

PRIMARY SOURCE DOCUMENTS

Seth Luther, *An Address to the Working-Men of New England** (1833), is the eloquent appeal of an uneducated working-class labor reformer. On the transportation revolution, see John H. B. Latrobe, *The First Steamboat Voyage on the Western Waters** (1871), and Mark Twain's classic *Life on the Mississippi** (1883). Lemuel Shaw's decision of 1842 in *Commonwealth v. Hunt,* 4 Metc. III (in Henry Steele Commager, *Documents of American History*) is regarded as the "Magna Carta of American labor organization." Ralph Waldo Emerson's address "The Young American," printed in *The Dial* (April 1844), expresses his enthusiasm for a new era of technological advancement. Thomas Dublin has edited *Farm to Factory: Women's Letters, 1830–1860* (rev. ed., 1993), and Charles Dickens's *American Notes* (1842) offers a European perspective on American urbanization and growth.

SECONDARY SOURCES

On immigration, see Maldwyn Jones, *American Immigration* (1960); John Bodnar, *The Transplanted: A History of Immigrants in Urban America* (1985); Hasia Diner, *Erin's Daughters in America* (1983); and Kerby A. Miller, *Emigrants and Exiles: Ireland and the Irish Exodus to North America* (1985). Bruce Levine, *The Spirit of 1848: German Immigrants, Labor Conflict, and the Coming of the Civil War* (1992), discusses German refugees and their new place in America. Solid introductions are George R. Taylor, *The Transportation Revolution, 1815–1860* (1951); Clarence H. Danhoff, *Change in Agriculture: The Northern United States, 1820–1870* (1969); and Douglas C. North, *Economic Growth in the United States, 1790–1860* (1961). See also

North's *Growth and Welfare in the American Past* (rev. ed., 1974). The events of the period are placed in a larger context of economic history in Stuart Bruchey, *The Roots of American Economic Growth, 1607–1861* (1965), and Albert W. Niemi, *U.S. Economic History: A Survey of the Major Issues* (1975). On government and private sponsorship of new technologies and infrastructure, see John Lauritz Larson, *Internal Improvement: National Public Works and the Promise of Popular Government in the Early United States* (2001). Thomas C. Cochran, *Frontiers of Change: Early Industrialism in America* (1981), treats industrialization as culturally inspired change. Two fascinating case studies of the coming of industrialism are Alan Dawley, *Class and Community: The Industrial Revolution in Lynn* (1977), and Anthony F. C. Wallace, *Rockdale: The Growth of an American Village in the Early Industrial Revolution* (1978). The laboring classes are chronicled in Bruce Laurie, *Artisans into Workers: Labor in Nineteenth-Century America* (1989). Consult also Herbert Gutman's path-breaking *Work, Culture, and Society in Industrializing America* (1976); Sean Wilentz's insightful *Chants Democratic: New York City and the Rise of the American Working Class, 1788–1850* (1984); David A. Zonderman's *Aspirations and Anxieties: New England Workers and the Mechanized Factory System, 1815–1850* (1992); and David R. Roediger's *The Wages of Whiteness: Race and the Making of the American Working Class* (1991). The experiences of women workers are the focus of Thomas Dublin, *Women at Work: The Transformation of Work and Community in Lowell, Massachusetts, 1826–1860* (1979), and Christine Stansell, *City of Women: Sex and Class in New York, 1780–1860* (1986). Mary Blewett puts the gender identities of both men and women at the center of *Men, Women, and Work: Class, Gender, and Protest in the New England Shoe Industry, 1780–1910* (1988). On the introduction of technology, see David H. Hounshell, *From the American System to Mass Production, 1800–1932: The Development of Manufacturing Technology in the United States* (1984), and David F. Hawke, *Nuts and Bolts of the Past: A History of American Technology, 1776–1860* (1988). Ideological aspects of this process are described in John F. Kasson, *Civilizing the Machine: Technology and Republican Values in America, 1776–1900* (1976), and David Nye, *Consuming Power: A Social History of American Energies* (1998). For a fascinating study of how industrialization shaped daily routine and time, see Michael O'Malley, *Keeping Watch: A History of American Time* (1996). The canal era is comprehensively described in Carter Goodrich, *Government Promotion of American Canals and Railroads, 1800–1890* (1960), and Ronald E. Shaw, *Canals for a Nation: The Canal Era in the United States, 1790–1860* (1990). On the Erie Canal, see Carol Sheriff, *The Artificial River* (1996). On railroads, consult Robert Fogel, *Railroads and American Economic Growth* (1964), which presents the startling thesis that the iron horse in fact did little to promote growth. For a different view, see Albert Fishlow, *American Railroads and the Transformation of the Ante-Bellum Economy* (1965), and James A. Ward, *Railroads and the Character of America, 1820–1887* (1986). The organization and management of railroad corporations is treated in Alfred D. Chandler, Jr., *The Visible Hand: The Managerial Revolution in American Business* (1977). The legal foundation of the market revolution is discussed in Morton Horwitz, *The Transformation of American Law, 1780–1860* (1977). Steven Hahn and Jonathan Prude, eds., *The Countryside in the Age of Capitalist Transformation: Essays in the Social History of Rural America* (1985), is a provocative look at the impact of the transportation and industrial revolutions on the countryside. See also Christopher Clark, *The Roots of Rural Capitalism: Western Massachusetts, 1780–1860* (1990), and Alan Kulikoff, *The Agrarian*

Origins of American Capitalism (1992). On urbanization, see Allan R. Pred, *Urban Growth and the Circulation of Information: The United States System of Cities, 1790–1840* (1973), and Elizabeth Blackmar, *Manhattan for Rent, 1785–1850* (1989).

CHAPTER 15

Primary Source Documents

Alexis de Tocqueville, *Democracy in America** (1835, 1840), has stood for over a century and a half as the classic analysis of the American character. Joseph Smith, *The Pearl of Great Price** (1929), contains an account of the Mormon leader's religious visions, which capture the religious restiveness of the age. William H. McGuffey, *Fifth Eclectic Reader* (1879), was a popular school text. On the women's movement, see the "Seneca Falls Manifesto"* (1848), which laid the foundations of the feminist movement. Catharine Beecher and Harriet Beecher Stowe, *The American Woman's Home** (1869), discusses the role of women. Stowe's classic novel, *Uncle Tom's Cabin* (1852), offers an emotional appeal against slavery and a fascinating portrait of slavery, religion, and family life in antebellum America.

Secondary Sources

A magisterial synthesis is Daniel Boorstin, *The Americans: The National Experience* (1965). Satisfying detail is found in two Russell B. Nye books: *The Cultural Life of the New Nation, 1776–1830* (1960) and *Society and Culture in America, 1830–1860* (1974). Alexis de Tocqueville's classic account of life in the young Republic is brilliantly analyzed by James R. Schlieffer in *The Making of Tocqueville's "Democracy in America"* (1980). On the rise of the middle class, see Karen Halttunen, *Confidence Men and Painted Women* (1982); Richard L. Bushman, *The Refinement of America: Persons, Houses, Cities* (1992); and Stuart M. Blumin, *The Emergence of the Middle Class* (1989). Sydney E. Ahlstrom, *Religious History of the American People* (1972), is sweeping. On revivalism, see Nathan O. Hatch, *The Democratization of American Christianity* (1989), and Paul Johnson, *A Shopkeeper's Millennium: Society and Revivals in Rochester, New York, 1815–1837* (1978), which links revivals to economic change. Bushman describes the origins of Mormonism in *Joseph Smith and the Beginnings of Mormonism* (1984), and Leonard J. Arrington analyzes the most celebrated Mormon leader in *Brigham Young: American Moses* (1984). On the Shakers, see Stephen J. Stein, *The Shaker Experience in America* (1992). On reform broadly, see Ronald Walters, *American Reformers, 1815–1860* (1978), and Robert Abzug, *Cosmos Crumbling: American Reform and the Religious Imagination* (1994). For particular movements, consult David Rothman, *The Discovery of the Asylum* (1971); Gerald Grob, *Mental Institutions in America: Social Policy to 1875* (1973); and David Gallagher, *Voice for the Mad: The Life of Dorothea Dix* (1995). On the development of hospitals, see Charles Rosenberg, *The Care of Strangers: The Rise of America's Hospital System* (1987). On juvenile delinquency, see Joseph Hawes, *Children in Urban Society* (1971). On prohibition, see Ian Tyrrell, *Sobering Up: From Temperance to Prohibition in Antebellum America* (1979), and William Rorabaugh, *The Alcoholic Republic* (1979). On education, see Lawrence A. Cremin, *American Education: The National Experience, 1789–1860* (1980), and Carl F. Kaestle and Maris A. Vinovskis, *Education and Social Change in Nineteenth-Century Massachusetts* (1980). An alternative interpretation of the rise of public education can be found in Michael Katz, *The*

Irony of Early School Reform (1968), and Samuel Bowles and Herbert Gintis, *Schooling in Capitalist America* (1976). Vinovskis offers a critique of these authors in *The Origins of Public High Schools: A Reexamination of the Beverly High School Controversy* (1985). A recent study of one Utopian community is Spencer Klaw, *Without Sin: The Life and Death of the Oneida Community* (1993). Women's history for this period is explored in a number of studies, including Carroll Smith-Rosenberg, *Religion and the Rise of the American City* (1971); Nancy Cott, *The Bonds of Womanhood: "Woman's Sphere" in New England; 1780–1835* (1977); Ellen Carol DuBois, *Feminism and Suffrage* (1978); Ruth Bordin, *Women and Temperance* (1981); Estelle B. Freedman, *Their Sisters' Keepers: Women's Prison Reform in America, 1830–1930* (1981); Barbara Epstein, *The Politics of Domesticity* (1981); Nancy Hewitt, *Women's Activism and Social Change: Rochester, New York, 1822–1872* (1984); Lori D. Ginzberg, *Women and the Work of Benevolence* (1990); and Ann Douglas, T*he Feminization of American Culture* (1977). Family history is covered in Steven Mintz and Susan Kellogg, *Domestic Revolutions: A Social History of American Family Life* (1988); Jeanne Boydston, *Home and Work: Housework, Wages, and the Ideology of Labor in the Early Republic* (1990); Joseph F. Kett, *Rites of Passage: Adolescence in America* (1976); Lewis Perry, *Childhood, Marriage, and Reform: Henry Clarke Wright, 1797–1870* (1980); Carl N. Degler, *At Odds: Women and the Family in America from the Revolution to the Present* (1980); and Mary P. Ryan, *Cradle of the Middle Class: The Family in Oneida County, New York* (1981). See also Kathryn Kish Sklar, *Catharine Beecher: A Study in Domesticity* (1973). Suzanne Lebsock, *The Free Women of Petersburg* (1984), discusses these issues in a southern context. For the relationship of nature to the emerging American culture, see Henry Nash Smith, *Virgin Land: The American West as Symbol and Myth* (1950); Leo Marx, *The Machine in the Garden: Technology and the Pastoral Ideal in America* (1964); and Barbara Novak, *Nature and Culture: American Landscape and Painting, 1825–1875* (1980). Studies with a cultural focus include Joseph Ellis, *After the Revolution: Profiles of Early American Culture* (1979), and Anne Rose, *Voices of the Marketplace: American Thought and Culture, 1830–1860* (1995). See also Lawrence Buell, *New England Literary Culture: From Revolution Through Renaissance* (1986), and Kenneth Cmiel, *Democratic Eloquence: The Fight over Popular Speech in Nineteenth-Century America* (1990). Edward L. Widmer, *Young America: The Flowering of Democracy in New York City* (1999), explores the literary-political nexus at the heart of Gotham culture in the 1840s. On three critically important transcendentalist figures, see Charles Capper, *Margaret Fuller: An American Romantic Life* (1992), and Robert D. Richardson's excellent volumes, *Emerson: The Mind on Fire* (1995) and *Thoreau: A Life of the Mind* (1986). Perry Miller, *The Raven and the Whale: The War of Words and Wits in the Era of Poe and Melville* (1956), remains a classic account of the New York literati in the age of the "American Renaissance."

CHAPTER 16

PRIMARY SOURCE DOCUMENTS

Two influential abolitionist documents are Theodore Dwight Weld, *American Slavery As It Is** (1839), and the inaugural editorial of William Lloyd Garrison in *The Liberator** (1831). Roy P. Basler, ed., *The Collected Works of Abraham Lincoln* (1933), contains the Great Emancipator's assessment of abolitionism in 1854. For southern perspectives, see James Henry Hammond's famous "Cotton Is King" speech, *Congressional Globe*, 36th Cong., 1st sess., 961 (March 3,

1858).* Frederick Law Olmsted, *The Cotton Kingdom* (1861), chronicles the future landscape architect's observations while traveling through the South in the 1850s. Famous firsthand accounts of slavery include Frederick Douglass, *Narrative of the Life of Frederick Douglass* (1845), and Harriet Jacobs, *Incidents in the Life of a Slave Girl* (1861). John W. Blassingame, ed., *Slave Testimony* (1977), also offers a rich collection of slave narratives.

SECONDARY SOURCES

A good introduction to southern history is Clement Eaton, *A History of the Old South: The Emergence of a Reluctant Nation* (1975). For a discussion of the intellectual's place in a southern agrarian society, see Drew Gilpin Faust, *A Sacred Circle: The Dilemma of the Intellectual in the Old South, 1840–1860* (1977). Always incisive is C. Vann Woodward, *The Burden of Southern History* (1960). On white politics and society, see Bruce Collins, *White Society in the Antebellum South* (1985); Bertram Wyatt-Brown, *Honor and Violence in the Old South* (1986); and Drew Gilpin Faust's perceptive biography, *James Henry Hammond and the Old South: A Design for Mastery* (1982). Nonslaveholding whites are documented in Frank L. Owsley, *Plain Folk of the Old South* (1949), and Stephanie McCurry, *Masters of Small Worlds: Yeoman Households, Gender Relations, and the Political Culture of the Antebellum South Carolina Low Country* (1995). Important interpretations of the "peculiar institution" include Eugene Genovese, *Roll, Jordan, Roll: The World the Slaves Made* (1974); Barbara Jeanne Fields, *Slavery and Freedom on the Middle Ground: Maryland During the Nineteenth Century* (1985); Gavin Wright, *The Political Economy of the Cotton South* (1978); and Eugene Genovese and Elizabeth Fox-Genovese, *Fruits of Merchant Capital* (1983). James Oakes has questioned many of Genovese's interpretations in *The Ruling Race: A History of American Slaveholders* (1982) and *Slavery and Freedom: An Interpretation of the Old South* (1990). Catherine Clinton examines *The Plantation Mistress* (1982); Elizabeth Fox-Genovese discusses southern women more generally in *Within the Plantation Household: Black and White Women of the Old South* (1988). See also Deborah Gray White, *Ar'n't I a Woman? Female Slaves in the Plantation South* (1985); Melton Alonza McLaurin, *Celia, a Slave* (1991); and Brenda E. Stevenson, *Life in Black and White: Family and Community in the Slave South* (1996). There is a rich and varied literature on slavery and African Americans; a good place to start is John Hope Franklin, *From Slavery to Freedom* (8th ed., 2000), and Peter J. Parish, *Slavery: History and Historians* (1989). The modern debate on slavery began with Ulrich B. Phillips's apologia *American Negro Slavery* (1918); a darker view of the same subject is found in Kenneth M. Stampp, *The Peculiar Institution* (1956). Consult also Stanley Elkins's controversial essay, *Slavery* (2nd ed., 1968), which also has interesting observations on the abolitionists. Considerable furor surrounded the publication of Robert Fogel and Stanley Engerman's *Time on the Cross: The Economics of American Slavery* (2 vols., 1974). For contrasting views and rebuttals, see John W. Blassingame, *The Slave Community* (rev. ed., 1979); Herbert Gutman, *The Black Family in Slavery and Freedom, 1750–1925* (1976); Paul David, *Reckoning with Slavery* (1976); Lawrence Levine, *Black Culture and Black Consciousness: Afro-American Folk Thought from Slavery to Freedom* (1977); Albert J. Raboteau, *Slave Religion: The "Invisible Institution" in the Antebellum South* (1978); and Sterling Stuckey, *Slave Culture: Nationalist Theory and the Foundations of Black America* (1987). Vincent Harding, *There Is a River: The Black Struggle for Freedom in America* (1981), discusses slave resistance and revolt, a subject handled rather differently in Peter Kolchin's fascinating comparative study, *Unfree Labor: American Slavery and Russian Serfdom* (1987). John Hope Franklin, *Runaway Slaves: Rebels on the Plantation* (1999), analyzes the motivations and consequences of slaves who escaped from their owners' farms and plantations. Manisha Sinha, *The Counterrevolution of Slavery: Politics and Ideology in Antebellum South Carolina* (2000), is an important new study that links political radicalism with the practice of slavery. Another political history of the South is Lacy K. Ford, Jr., *The Origins of Southern Radicalism: The South Carolina Upcountry, 1800–1860* (1988), which tells the story of this Unionist stronghold. A study that compares the development of race relations in South Africa and the United States is George M. Frederickson, *White Supremacy: A Comparative Study in American and South African History* (1981). Ira Berlin examines how the institution of slavery developed in discrete chronological stages in *Many Thousands Gone: The First Two Centuries of Slavery in North America* (1998) and tells the story of free blacks in *Slaves Without Masters* (1975), which should be supplemented by Michael P. Johnson and James L. Roark, *Black Masters: A Free Family of Color in the Old South* (1984). See also Harry Reed, *Platform for Change: The Foundation of the Northern Free Black Community, 1775–1865* (1994), for the situation of blacks outside the South. For an important study of interracial families in the antebellum South, see Joshua Rothman, *Notorious in the Neighborhood: Sex and Families Across the Color Line in Virginia, 1787–1861* (2003). On the experience of the antebellum slave trade, see Walter Johnson, *Soul by Soul: Life Inside the Antebellum Slave Market* (2001). Valuable community studies include Charles Joyner, *Down by the Riverside: A South Carolina Slave Community* (1984); Suzanne Lebsock, *The Free Women of Petersburg: Status and Culture in a Southern Town, 1784–1860* (1984); and Orville Vernon Burton, *In My Father's House Are Many Mansions: Family and Community in Edgefield, South Carolina* (1985). David B. Davis provides indispensable background to the history of abolitionism in *The Problem of Slavery in Western Culture* (1966) and *The Problem of Slavery in the Age of Revolution* (1975), as does Thomas Bender, ed., in *The Antislavery Debate* (1992). The best brief history of the abolitionists is James B. Stewart, *Holy Warriors* (1976). Ronald E. Walters emphasizes the constraints that American culture placed on abolitionists in *The Antislavery Appeal: American Abolitionism After 1830* (1976). Aileen Kraditor is favorably disposed toward William Lloyd Garrison in *Means and Ends in American Abolitionism: Garrison and His Critics* (1967). See also Julie Roy Jeffrey, *The Great Silent Army of Abolitionism: Ordinary Women in the Antislavery Movement* (1998). For provocative appraisals, see Lewis Perry and Michael Fellman, eds., *Antislavery Reconsidered: New Perspectives on the Abolitionists* (1979). Benjamin Quarles examines *Black Abolitionists* (1969), as do Jane H. Pease and William H. Pease in *They Who Would Be Free: Blacks Search for Freedom, 1830–1861* (1974), and Shirley J. Yee in *Black Women Abolitionists: A Study in Activism, 1828–1860* (1992). Sojourner Truth is the subject of Nell Irvin Painter, *Sojourner Truth: A Life, a Symbol* (1996). The most prominent black abolitionist is portrayed in Waldo E. Martin, Jr., *The Mind of Frederick Douglass* (1984), and William S. McFeely, *Frederick Douglass* (1990).

CHAPTER 17

PRIMARY SOURCE DOCUMENTS

Trader Josiah Gregg describes the Santa Fe trade in his 1845 book, *Commerce of the Prairies,* edited by Max L. Moorehead (1954), and historian Francis Parkman's classic *The California and Oregon Trail*

(1849) draws a fascinating picture of the Pacific Coast. Colorful reminiscences of the pioneers are collected in Dale Morgan, ed., *Overland in 1846: Diaries and Letters of the California-Oregon Trail** (1963), and Sandra Myres, *Ho for California! Women's Overland Diaries from the Huntington Library* (1980). Stella M. Drumm, ed., *Down the Santa Fe Trail and into Mexico, 1846–1847,* is a fascinating firsthand account of New Mexico during the Mexican War written by the daughter of a prominent trader (1975). The outbreak and conduct of the war also come alive in Allan Nevins, ed., *Polk: The Diary of a President, 1845–1849* (1929).

SECONDARY SOURCES

Frederick Merk, *Manifest Destiny and Mission in American History* (1963), is a good introduction. For more recent explanations of American motivations during the imperialistic decade of the 1840s, see Thomas R. Hietala, *Manifest Design: Anxious Aggrandizement in Late Jacksonian America* (1985); Robert E. May, *Manifest Destiny's Underworld: Filibustering in Antebellum America* (2002); and Sam W. Haynes and Christopher Morris, eds., *Manifest Destiny and Empire: American Antebellum Expansionism* (1997). For explorations of the role racial thought played in Manifest Destiny, see Reginald Horsman, *Race and Manifest Destiny: The Origins of American Racial Anglo-Saxonism* (1981); the early chapters of Richard D. White, *"It's Your Misfortune and None of My Own": A History of the American West* (1992); and Michael A. Morrison, *Slavery and the American West: The Eclipse of Manifest Destiny* (1997). Norman A. Graebner, *Empire on the Pacific* (1955), discusses Polk's drive to acquire California, and Theodore J. Karamanski, *Fur Trade and Exploration: Opening the Far Northwest, 1821–1852* (1983), gives a vivid depiction of the Pacific region (1983). The definitive account of the American Southwest before U.S. invasion is David Weber's *The Mexican Frontier, 1821–1846* (1982), which traces the gradual drift of the region away from Mexican control. David M. Pletcher's *The Diplomacy of the Annexation of Texas, Oregon, and the Mexican War* (1973) is a thorough, balanced account of annexation and the coming of the war. On the conflict with Mexico, see Richard Bruce Winders, *Crisis in the Southwest: The United States, Mexico, and the Struggle over Texas* (2002); James McCaffrey, *Army of Manifest Destiny: The American Soldier in the Mexican War* (1992); and Paul Foos, *A Short, Offhand Killing Affair: Soldiers and Social Conflict During the U.S.-Mexican War* (2002). The perspectives of Mexicans are analyzed in Josefina Zoraida Vázquez, *The United States and Mexico* (1985); Gene M. Brack, *Mexico Views Manifest Destiny, 1821–1846* (1976); and Iris Engstrand et al., *Culture y Cultura: Consequences of the U.S.-Mexican War, 1846–1848* (1998). John H. Schroeder analyzes an important aspect of the conflict in *Mr. Polk's War: American Opposition and Dissent, 1846–1848* (1973). Richard Francaviglia et al., eds., *Dueling Eagles: Reinterpreting the U.S.-Mexican War 1846–1848* (2000), compiles the most recent scholarly perspectives. The second volume of Charles Sellers's excellent three-volume biography of James K. Polk focuses on the years 1843 to 1846 (1966); Paul H. Bergeron scrutinizes Polk's administration in *The Presidency of James K. Polk* (1987); and William Dusinberre explores the influence of Polk's life as a slaveowner on his public policies in *Slavemaster President: The Double Career of James K. Polk* (2003). Robert W. Johannsen uses the war to investigate American culture in *To the Halls of the Montezumas: The Mexican War in the American Imagination* (1985). John Mack Faragher provides an in-depth look at the westward migration of one community in *Sugar Creek: Life on the Illinois Prairie* (1986). Linda S. Hudson, *Mistress of Manifest Destiny: A*

Biography of Jane McManus Storm Cazneau, 1807–1878 (2001), chronicles the life of a woman who propagandized for westward expansion. Gregg Cantrell, *Stephen F. Austin, Empresario of Texas* (1999), is a biography of the key figure in Anglo-American colonization in Texas. For an insightful look at the cultural exchange brought about by the gold rush, see Susan Lee Johnson, *Roaring Camp: The Social World of the California Gold Rush* (2001). Three works that explore the experiences of women in the West are Julie Roy Jeffrey, *Frontier Women* (1979); Glenda Riley, *The Female Frontier* (1988); and Susan Armitage and Elizabeth Jameson, eds., *The Women's West* (1987).

CHAPTER 18

PRIMARY SOURCE DOCUMENTS

The *Congressional Globe* for 1850 contains the dramatic orations of a dying generation of American statesmen on the Compromise of 1850. See the speeches by Webster,* Calhoun,* and Clay in Richard Hofstadter, ed., *Great Issues in American History*. The debate on the Kansas-Nebraska Bill can be found in the 1854 volume of the same source, which includes addresses by Stephen A. Douglas* and his opponent, Salmon P. Chase.*

SECONDARY SOURCES

Earlier interpretations of the sectional crisis include Charles A. and Mary R. Beard, *The Rise of American Civilization* (1927); Avery Craven, *The Repressible Conflict, 1830–1861* (1939); and Allan Nevins, *The Ordeal of the Union* (1947). A compelling account of the events of the 1850s is David M. Potter's masterful *The Impending Crisis, 1848–1861* (1976). A concise summary of the events leading to the war is also available in the opening chapters of James M. McPherson, *Battle Cry of Freedom: The Civil War Era* (1988). Comprehensive treatments may be found in David H. Donald, Jean H. Baker, and Michael F. Holt, *The Civil War and Reconstruction* (rev. ed., 2001); William J. Cooper, *The South and the Politics of Slavery* (1978); Kenneth Stampp, ed., *The Imperiled Union: Essays on the Background of the Civil War* (1980); Richard H. Sewell, *A House Divided: Sectionalism and Civil War, 1848–1860* (1988); and William Freehling, *Road to Disunion: Secessionists at Bay, 1776–1854* (1990). The standard work is Holman Hamilton, *Prologue to Conflict: The Crisis and Compromise of 1850* (1964). See also Mark J. Stegmaier, *Texas, New Mexico, and the Compromise of 1850: Boundary Dispute and Sectional Crisis* (1996). On the southern view of events, see Kenneth S. Greenberg, *Masters and Statesmen: The Political Culture of American Slavery* (1985), and Eugene Genovese, *The World the Slaveholders Made* (1969). The emergence of the Republican party after 1854 can be studied in Eric Foner's brilliant discussion of ideology, *Free Soil, Free Labor, Free Men* (1970), and William Gienapp, *The Origins of the Republican Party, 1852–1856* (1987). Also see Michael Holt, *Forging a Majority: The Formation of the Republican Party in Pittsburgh* (1969); Paul Kleppner, *The Third Electoral System, 1853–1892: Parties, Voters, and Political Cultures* (1979); Bruce Levine, *Half Slave and Half Free: The Roots of the Civil War* (1992); and Frederick J. Blue, *The Free Soilers: Third Party Politics, 1848–1854* (1973). On the Know-Nothing party, see Tyler Anbinder, *Nativism and Slavery: The Northern Know-Nothings and the Politics of the 1850s* (1992). Holt has developed his views in *The Political Crisis of the 1850s* (1978), an unusually provocative book. Party politics are treated in two books by Joel H. Silbey, *The Shrine of Party:*

Congressional Voting Behavior, 1841–1852 (1967) and his unorthodox *Partisan Imperative: The Dynamics of American Politics Before the Civil War* (1985). Richard H. Sewell, *Ballots for Freedom: Antislavery Politics in the United States, 1837–1860* (1976), is a standard work. A biographical approach is taken in Merrill Peterson, *The Great Triumvirate: Webster, Clay, and Calhoun* (1987). Robert Trennert examines the impact of westward migration and the gold rush on U.S. Indian policy in *Alternative to Extinction: Federal Indian Policy and the Beginnings of the Reservation System, 1846–1851* (1975).

CHAPTER 19

PRIMARY SOURCE DOCUMENTS

Harriet Beecher Stowe, *Uncle Tom's Cabin** (1852), and Hinton R. Helper, *The Impending Crisis of the South** (1857), are vivid and important. The Lincoln-Douglas debates* (1858) frame the issues of the 1850s and remain classics of American oratory. William W. Freehling and Craig M. Simpson, eds., *Secession Debated: Georgia's Showdown in 1860* (1992), features a dramatic debate between Unionist Alexander Stephens and secessionist Robert Toombs.

SECONDARY SOURCES

For comprehensive treatments of events leading up to the Civil War, refer to Chapter 18 for the titles by David M. Potter, James M. McPherson, William J. Cooper, Kenneth Stampp, Richard H. Sewell, Allan Nevins, and David H. Donald, Jean H. Baker, and Michael F. Holt. Gabor S. Boritt, ed., *Why the Civil War Came* (1996), is an informative compilation of articles on the causes of the war. Leonard L. Richards, *The Slave Power: The Free North and Southern Domination, 1780–1860* (2000), and Ward M. McAfee, ed., *The Slaveholding Republic* (2001), give interpretations on the coming of the war. David H. Donald, *Charles Sumner and the Coming of the Civil War* (1960), is an outstanding biography. A more recent biography is Frederick J. Blue, *Charles Sumner and the Conscience of the North* (1994). On the literary attack on slavery, see Thomas F. Gossett, *Uncle Tom's Cabin and American Culture* (1985). Nicole Etcheson, *Bleeding Kansas: Contested Liberty in the Civil War Era* (2004), tells the story of the first frontier war over slavery expansion. On the Buchanan administration, see Kenneth M. Stampp, *America in 1857: A Nation on the Brink* (1990), and Michael J. Birkner, ed., *James Buchanan and the Political Crisis of the 1850s* (1996). On the Lincoln-Douglas debates, see Harry V. Jaffa, *Crisis of the House Divided* (1959). Don E. Fehrenbacher brilliantly and thoroughly dissects *The Dred Scott Case* (1978). The final moments before fighting began are scrutinized in David M. Potter, *Lincoln and His Party in the Secession Crisis* (1942). The Southern side of the question appears in Steven A. Channing, *Crisis of Fear: Secession of South Carolina* (1970), and William L. Barney, *The Secessionist Impulse: Alabama and Mississippi* (1974). On Southern Unionists' role in beginning the war, see Daniel W. Crofts, *Reluctant Confederates: Upper South Unionists in the Secession Crisis* (1989). Jean H. Baker, *Affairs of Party: The Political Culture of Northern Democrats in the Mid-Nineteenth Century* (1983), and Robert W. Johannsen, *Stephen A. Douglas* (1973), present matters from the Democratic perspective. See also J. Mills Thornton III, *Power and Politics in a Slave Society: Alabama 1820–1860* (1978), and Marc W. Kruman, *Parties and Politics in North Carolina, 1836–1865* (1983). Stephen B. Oates paints a vivid portrait of John Brown in *To Purge This Land with Blood*

(1970), as Joan Hedrick does of Harriet Beecher Stowe in *Harriet Beecher Stowe: A Life* (1994). For a broader view, see Paul Finkelman, *And His Soul Goes Marching On: Responses to John Brown and the Harpers Ferry Raid* (1995).

CHAPTER 20

PRIMARY SOURCE DOCUMENTS

The Constitution of the Confederacy (1861) makes an interesting contrast to the U.S. Constitution. Two diaries that describe life behind Confederate lines are those of John B. Jones, published as Earl S. Miers, ed., *A Rebel War Clerk's Diary** (1958), and C. Vann Woodward, ed., *Mary Chesnut's Civil War* (1981). A comprehensive collection of primary sources about every aspect of the war can be found in William Gienapp, ed., *The Civil War and Reconstruction: A Documentary Collection* (2001). It contains Lincoln's Gettysburg Address* (1863), which poetically proclaims the president's highest war aims.

SECONDARY SOURCES

Two extensive biographies of Abraham Lincoln are Stephen B. Oates, *With Malice Toward None: The Life of Abraham Lincoln* (1977), and William Gienapp, *Abraham Lincoln and Civil War America* (2002). See also Garry Wills, *Lincoln at Gettysburg: The Words That Remade America* (1992), and David H. Donald, *Lincoln* (1995). On Mary Todd Lincoln, see Jean H. Baker, *Mary Todd Lincoln: A Biography* (1987). In *Jefferson Davis, American* (2000), William J. Cooper provides a counterpoint to the rich literature on the life of Lincoln. Home-front politics are treated in James A. Rawley, *The Politics of Union* (1974), and Joel Silbey, *A Respectable Minority: The Democratic Party in the Civil War Era* (1977). See also Eric Foner, *Politics and Ideology in the Age of the Civil War* (1980). Mark Neely has written several books on Civil War politics, including *Southern Rights: Political Prisoners and the Myth of Confederate Constitutionalism* (1999) and *The Union Divided: Party Conflict in the Civil War North* (2002). George C. Rable's *The Confederate Republic* (1994) is a comprehensive study of politics in the Confederacy. Lincoln's problems are analyzed in LaWanda Cox, *Lincoln and Black Freedom* (1981). See also Hans L. Trefousse, *The Radical Republicans: Lincoln's Vanguard for Racial Justice* (1969). Eugene C. Murdoch analyzes the military draft in the North in *One Million Men* (1971). Iver Bernstein treats *The New York City Draft Riots* (1990). Gerald F. Linderman examines the motivations of soldiers in *Embattled Courage: The Experience of Combat in the Civil War* (1987). Mary E. Massey presents the interesting story of women in the Civil War in *Bonnet Brigades* (1966). That topic also figures in Elizabeth D. Leonard, *Yankee Women: Gender Battles in the Civil War* (1994). See also the essays in Catherine Clinton and Nina Silber, eds., *Divided Houses: Gender and the Civil War* (1992), and Drew Gilpin Faust, *Mothers of Invention: Women of the Slaveholding South in the American Civil War* (1996). William Freehling, *The South vs. The South: How Anti-Confederate Southerners Shaped the Course of the Civil War* (2001), argues that Southern social divisions contributed to the Union victory. For more on the Confederacy, see Emory M. Thomas, *The Confederate Nation, 1861–1865* (1979), and Drew Gilpin Faust, *The Creation of Confederate Nationalism* (1988). Economic matters are handled in Ralph L. Andreano, ed., *The Economic Impact of the American Civil War* (1962); David T. Gilchrist and W. David Lewis, eds., *Economic Change in the Civil War Era*

(1965); and Heather Cox Richardson, *The Greatest Nation of the Earth: Republican Economic Policies During the Civil War* (1997). Two useful anthologies are David H. Donald, ed., *Why the North Won the Civil War* (1960), and Robert P. Swierenga, ed., *Beyond the Civil War Synthesis: Political Essays on the Civil War Era* (1975). Richard E. Beringer et al. present a different viewpoint in *Why the South Lost the Civil War* (1986). The war's literary legacy is keenly analyzed in Edmund Wilson's classic *Patriotic Gore* (1962) and in Daniel Aaron's *The Unwritten War: American Writers and the Civil War* (1973). On the religious impact of the war, see Randall M. Miller et al., *Religion and the American Civil War* (1998). David W. Blight, *Race and Reunion: The Civil War in American Memory* (2001), is a study of how Americans have remembered their bloodiest conflict.

CHAPTER 21

PRIMARY SOURCE DOCUMENTS

Abraham Lincoln's 1862 reply to Horace Greeley's "Prayer of Twenty Millions"* (*Collected Works of Abraham Lincoln*, edited by Roy P. Basler, 1953) is an early statement of the president's war aims. See also, in the same collection, the Emancipation Proclamation (1863). Reminiscences of the military struggle include Eliza Andrews, *The War-Time Journal of a Georgia Girl** (1908) and *Memoirs of General William T. Sherman** (1887). Also of interest is Stephen Crane's classic war novel, *The Red Badge of Courage* (1895).

SECONDARY SOURCES

A compelling single-volume account of the war is James M. McPherson, *Battle Cry of Freedom: The Civil War Era* (1988). Geoffrey C. Ward's *The Civil War* (1990) is beautifully illustrated, and James G. Randall, *Lincoln the President* (4 vols., 1945–1955), provides a wealth of rich detail. Other capable one-volume studies include Peter J. Parish, *The American Civil War* (1975), and Phillip S. Paludan, *"A People's Contest": The Union and the Civil War, 1861–1865* (1988). See also the multivolume study by Shelby Foote, *The Civil War* (3 vols., 1958–1974), and Allan Nevins's monumental *Ordeal of the Union* (8 vols., 1947–1971). Bruce Catton has a series of a dozen or so readable books on aspects of the Civil War, including *A Stillness at Appomattox* (1953) and *This Hallowed Ground* (1956). Herman Hattaway and Archer Jones discuss *How the North Won* (1983). On the home front, see Reid Mitchell, *The Vacant Chair: The Northern Soldier Leaves Home* (1993); William Blair, *Virginia's Private War: Feeding Body and Soul in the Confederacy, 1861–1865* (1998); and David Williams, *Rich Man's War: Class, Caste, and Confederate Defeat in the Lower Chattahoochee Valley* (1998). On the "modern" character of the war, see Charles B. Royster, *The Destructive War: William Tecumseh Sherman, Stonewall Jackson, and the Americans* (1991). David P. Crook, *The North, the South, and the Powers* (1974), discusses the relationship of the combatants to England. James M. McPherson, *Abraham Lincoln and the Second American Revolution* (1991), posits a fateful clash between competing ways of life in North and South. Bell I. Wiley's descriptions of common soldiers, *The Life of Johnny Reb* (1943) and *The Life of Billy Yank* (1952), are classics. See also Benjamin Quarles, *The Negro in the Civil War* (1953), and James M. McPherson's collection of documents, *The Negro's Civil War* (1965). More recent accounts of the black experience include Ira Berlin et al., *Freedom: A Documentary History of Emancipation, 1861–1867*, Series 2: *The Black Military Experience* (1982), and Joseph Glatthaar, *Forged in Battle: The Civil War Alliance of*

Black Soldiers and White Officers (1990). Emancipation is treated in Louis Gerteis, *From Contraband to Freedmen; Federal Policy Toward Southern Blacks, 1861–1865* (1973); Herman Belz, *Emancipation and Equal Rights: Politics and Constitutionalism During the Civil War Reconstruction* (1978); Willie Lee Rose, *Rehearsal for Reconstruction: The Port Royal Experiment* (1964); LaWanda Cox, *Lincoln and Black Freedom* (1981); and Leon Litwack's powerful *Been in the Storm So Long* (1979). On the abolitionists' role in securing emancipation, see James M. McPherson, *The Struggle for Equality* (1964), and David W. Blight, *Federick Douglass' Civil War: Keeping Faith in Jubilee* (1989). The Southern response is discussed in Robert Durden, *The Gray and the Black: The Confederate Debate on Emancipation* (1973). The two leading Civil War generals are masterfully treated in Douglas S. Freeman, *R. E. Lee* (4 vols., 1934–1935), and William S. McFeely, *Grant* (1981). On the legal end to slavery in America, consult Michael Vorenberg, *Final Freedom: The Civil War, the Abolition of Slavery, and the Thirteenth Amendment* (2001).

CHAPTER 22

PRIMARY SOURCE DOCUMENTS

Booker T. Washington's classic autobiography, *Up from Slavery** (1901), records one freedman's experiences. Contemporary comments on Reconstruction include the laments of editor Edwin L. Godkin, *The Nation** (December 7, 1871), and Frederick Douglass, *Life and Times of Frederick Douglass** (1882), as well as the debates in the *Congressional Globe** (1867–1868) between radicals such as Thaddeus Stevens and moderates such as Lyman Trumbull.

SECONDARY SOURCES

Eric Foner, *Reconstruction: America's Unfinished Revolution, 1863–1877* (1988), is a superb synthesis of current scholarship. Overall accounts may be found in David H. Donald, Jean H. Baker, and Michael F. Holt, *The Civil War and Reconstruction* (rev. ed., 2001), and James M. McPherson, *Ordeal by Fire: The Civil War and Reconstruction* (1981), perhaps the best brief introduction. Lincoln's early efforts at Reconstruction are handled in Peyton McCrary, *Abraham Lincoln and Reconstruction* (1978), and Herman Belz, *Emancipation and Equal Rights* (1978). Willie Lee Rose engagingly describes *Rehearsal for Reconstruction: The Port Royal Experiment* (1964). Dan Carter, *When the War Was Over: The Failure of Self-Reconstruction in the South, 1865–1867* (1985), and Eric L. McKitrick, *Andrew Johnson and Reconstruction: Principle and Prejudice, 1865–1866* (1963), chart the first years of the period. Sympathetic to the radical Republicans are James M. McPherson, *The Struggle for Equality* (1964), and Hans L. Trefousse, *The Radical Republicans* (1969). See also David Montgomery, *Beyond Equality: Labor and the Radical Republicans, 1862–1872* (1967). Siding with the radicals in the impeachment fight are Michael L. Benedict, *The Impeachment and Trial of Andrew Johnson* (1973), and Hans L. Trefousse, *Impeachment of a President* (1975). Steven Hahn exhaustively examines the post–Civil War genesis of African American political traditions in *A Nation Under Our Feet* (2003). Conditions in the South are analyzed in W. E. B. Du Bois's controversial classic *Black Reconstruction* (1935) and Leon F. Litwack's brilliantly evocative *Been in*

the Storm So Long (1979), a revealing study of the initial responses, by both blacks and whites, to emancipation. An excellent account of the southern economy after the war is Gavin Wright, *Old South, New South: Revolutions in the Southern Economy Since the Civil War* (1986). It can be usefully supplemented by Roger Ransom and Richard L. Sutch, *One Kind of Freedom: The Economic Consequences of Emancipation* (1977). Julie Saville, *The Work of Reconstruction* (1994), highlights the efforts of newly freed slaves to shape the economic arrangements of the postwar South. See also James Roark, *Masters Without Slaves: Southern Planters in the Civil War and Reconstruction* (1977), and Lawrence Powell, *New Masters: Northern Planters During the Civil War and Reconstruction* (1980). Barbara Fields looks at the border state of Maryland in *Slavery and Freedom on the Middle Ground* (1985). William McFeely offers an excellent biography of *Frederick Douglass* (1991). Dewey W. Grantham, *Life and Death of the Solid South* (1988); Edward L. Ayers, *The Promise of the New South: Life After Reconstruction* (1992); Dwight Billings, *Planters and the Making of a "New South": Class, Politics and Development in North Carolina, 1865–1900* (1979); and Jonathan M. Wiener, *Social Origins of the New South: Alabama, 1860–1885* (1978), elucidate the political economy of the postbellum South. Joel Williamson offers a psychological portrait of race relations in *The Crucible of Race: Black-White Relations in the American South Since Emancipation* (1984). Consult also Thomas Holt, *Black over White: Negro Political Leadership in South Carolina During Reconstruction* (1977), and Martha Hodes, *White Women, Black Men: Illicit Sex in the Nineteenth-Century South* (1997). C. Vann Woodward, *The Strange Career of Jim Crow* (rev. ed., 1974), is a classic study of the origins of segregation. His views have drawn criticism in Harold O. Rabinowitz, *Race Relations in the Urban South, 1865–1890* (rev. ed., 1996). See also Rabinowitz's *Southern Black Leaders of the Reconstruction Era* (1982). The Freedmen's Bureau has been the subject of several studies, including Claude Oubré, *Forty Acres and a Mule: The Freedmen's Bureau and Black Land Ownership* (1978), and Donald Nieman, *To Set the Law in Motion: The Freedmen's Bureau and the Legal Rights of Blacks, 1865–1868* (1979). Nell Irvin Painter follows African Americans who chose to leave the South altogether in *Exodusters: Black Migration to Kansas After Reconstruction* (1976). Special studies of value are William P. Vaughn, *Schools for All* (1974); William C. Gillette, *The Right to Vote: Politics and the Passage of the 15th Amendment* (1965); Stanley I. Kutler, *Judicial Power and Reconstruction Politics* (1968); and Harold M. Hyman, *A More Perfect Union: The Impact of the Civil War and Reconstruction on the Constitution* (1973). Richard N. Current rehabilitates the maligned carpetbaggers in *Those Terrible Carpetbaggers* (1988). Provocative scholarship is presented in Kenneth M. Stampp and Leon Litwack, eds., *Reconstruction: An Anthology of Revisionist Writings* (1969), and Robert P. Swierenga, ed., *Beyond the Civil War Synthesis* (1975). J. Morgan Kousser and James M. McPherson, eds., *Region, Race, and Reconstruction: Essays in Honor of C. Vann Woodward* (1982), contains some intriguing essays. Eric Foner looks at emancipation in a comparative perspective in *Nothing but Freedom* (1983). A comprehensive study of the climax of this troubled period is William Gillette, *Retreat from Reconstruction, 1869–1879* (1979). Also see Michael Perman, *The Road to Redemption: Southern Politics, 1869–1879* (1984). David W. Blight's highly acclaimed *Race and Reunion: The Civil War in American Memory* (2001) details the postbellum battle to determine the way Americans remembered the war

DOCUMENTS

Declaration of Independence

In Congress, July 4, 1776

The Unanimous Declaration of the Thirteen United States of America

[Bracketed material in color has been inserted by the authors. For adoption background see pp. 145–146.]

When, in the course of human events, it becomes necessary for one people to dissolve the political bonds which have connected them with another, and to assume, among the powers of the earth, the separate and equal station to which the laws of nature and of nature's God entitle them, a decent respect to the opinions of mankind requires that they should declare the causes which impel them to the separation.

We hold these truths to be self-evident: That all men are created equal; that they are endowed by their Creator with certain unalienable rights; that among these are life, liberty, and the pursuit of happiness; that, to secure these rights, governments are instituted among men, deriving their just powers from the consent of the governed; that whenever any form of government becomes destructive of these ends, it is the right of the people to alter or to abolish it, and to institute new government, laying its foundation on such principles, and organizing its powers in such form, as to them shall seem most likely to effect their safety and happiness. Prudence, indeed, will dictate that governments long established should not be changed for light and transient causes; and accordingly all experience hath shown that mankind are more disposed to suffer, while evils are sufferable, than to right themselves by abolishing the forms to which they are accustomed. But when a long train of abuses and usurpations, pursuing invariably the same object, evinces a design to reduce them under absolute despotism, it is their right, it is their duty, to throw off such government, and to provide new guards for their future security. Such has been the patient sufferance of these colonies; and such is now the necessity which constrains them to alter their former systems of government. The history of the present King of Great Britain is a history of repeated injuries and usurpations, all having in direct object the establishment of an absolute tyranny over these states. To prove this, let facts be submitted to a candid world.

He has refused his assent to laws, the most wholesome and necessary for the public good. [See royal veto, p. 124.]

He has forbidden his governors to pass laws of immediate and pressing importance, unless suspended in their operation till his assent should be obtained; and, when so suspended, he has utterly neglected to attend to them.

He has refused to pass other laws for the accommodation of large districts of people [by establishing new countries], unless those people would relinquish the right of representation in the legislature, a right inestimable to them, and formidable to tyrants only.

He has called together legislative bodies at places unusual, uncomfortable, and distant from the depository of their public records, for the sole purpose of fatiguing them into compliance with his measures. [e.g., removal of Massachusetts Assembly to Salem, 1774.]

He has dissolved representative houses repeatedly, for opposing, with manly firmness, his invasions on the rights of the people. [e.g., Virginia Assembly, 1765.]

He has refused for a long time, after such dissolutions, to cause others to be elected; whereby the legislative powers, incapable of annihilation, have returned to the people at large for their exercise; the state remaining, in the mean time, exposed to all the dangers of invasions from without and convulsions within.

He has endeavored to prevent the population [populating] of these states; for that purpose obstructing the laws for naturalization of foreigners; refusing to pass others to encourage their migration hither, and raising the conditions of new appropriations of lands. [e.g., Proclamation of 1763, p. 121.]

He has obstructed the administration of justice, by refusing his assent to laws for establishing judiciary powers.

He has made judges dependent on his will alone, for the tenure of their offices, and the amount and payment of their salaries. [See Townshend Acts, p. 129.]

He has erected a multitude of new offices, and sent hither swarms of officers to harass our people and eat out their substance. [See enforcement of Navigation Laws, p. 131.]

He has kept among us, in times of peace, standing armies, without the consent of our legislatures. [See pp. 126, 130.]

He has affected to render the military independent of, and superior to, the civil power.

He has combined with others to subject us to a jurisdiction foreign to our constitution, and unacknowledged by our laws, giving his assent to their acts of pretended legislation:

> For quartering large bodies of armed troops among us [See Boston Massacre, p. 129];
>
> For protecting them, by a mock trial, from punishment for any murders which they should commit on the inhabitants of these states [See 1774 Acts, pp. 132–133];
>
> For cutting off our trade with all parts of the world [See Boston Port Act, p. 132];
>
> For imposing taxes on us without our consent [See Stamp Act, pp. 125–126];
>
> For depriving us, in many cases, of the benefits of trial by jury;
>
> For transporting us beyond seas, to be tried for pretended offenses;
>
> For abolishing the free system of English laws in a neighboring province [Quebec], establishing therein an arbitrary government, and enlarging its boundaries, so as to render it at once an example and fit instrument for introducing the same absolute rule into these colonies [Quebec Act, p. 133];
>
> For taking away our charters, abolishing our most valuable laws, and altering fundamentally the forms of our governments [e.g., in Massachusetts, p. 133];
>
> For suspending our own legislatures, and declaring themselves invested with power to legislate for us in all cases whatsoever [See Stamp Act repeal, p. 127.]

He has abdicated government here, by declaring us out of his protection and waging war against us. [Proclamation, pp. 141–142.]

He has plundered our seas, ravaged our coasts, burned our towns, and destroyed the lives of our people. [e.g., the burning of Falmouth (Portland), p. 142.]

He is at this time transporting large armies of foreign mercenaries [Hessians, p. 142] to complete the works of death, desolation, and tyranny already begun with circumstances of cruelty and perfidy scarcely paralleled in the most barbarous ages, and totally unworthy the head of a civilized nation.

He has constrained our fellow-citizens, taken captive on the high seas [by impressment], to bear arms against their country, to become the executioners of their friends and brethren, or to fall themselves by their hands.

He has excited domestic insurrection among us [i.e., among slaves], and has endeavored to bring on the inhabitants of our frontiers the merciless Indian savages, whose known rule of warfare is an undistinguished destruction of all ages, sexes, and conditions.

In every stage of these oppressions we have petitioned for redress in the most humble terms; our repeated petitions have been answered only by repeated injury. [e.g., pp. 140–143.] A prince, whose character is thus marked by every act which may define a tyrant, is unfit to be the ruler of a free people.

Nor have we been wanting in our attentions to our British brethren. We have warned them, from time to time, of attempts by their legislature to extend an unwarrantable jurisdiction over us. We have reminded them of the circumstances of our emigration and settlement here. We have appealed to their native justice and magnanimity; and we have conjured them, by the ties of our common kindred, to disavow these usurpations, which would inevitably interrupt our connections and correspondence. They, too, have been deaf to the voice of justice and of consanguinity [blood relationship]. We must, therefore, acquiesce in the necessity which denounces [announces] our separation, and hold them, as we hold the rest of mankind, enemies in war, in peace friends.

We, therefore, the representatives of the United States of America, in General Congress assembled, appealing to the Supreme Judge of the world for the rectitude of our intentions, do, in the name and by the authority of the good people of these colonies, solemnly publish and declare, That these United Colonies are, and of right ought to be, FREE AND INDEPENDENT STATES; that they are absolved from all allegiance to the British crown, and that all political connection between them and the state of Great Britain is, and ought to be, totally dissolved; and that, as free and independent states, they have full power to levy war, conclude peace, contract alliances, establish commerce, and do all other acts and things which independent states may of right do. And for the support of this declaration, with a firm reliance on the protection of Divine Providence, we mutually pledge to each other our lives, our fortunes, and our sacred honor.

[Signed by]

JOHN HANCOCK [President]
[and fifty-five others]

Constitution of the United States of America

[Boldface headings and bracketed explanatory matter and marginal comments (both in color) have been inserted for the reader's convenience. Passages that are no longer operative are printed in italic type.]

PREAMBLE

We the people of the United States, in order to form a more perfect union, establish justice, insure domestic tranquility, provide for the common defense, promote the general welfare, and secure the blessings of liberty to ourselves and our posterity, do ordain and establish this CONSTITUTION for the United States of America.

Article I. *Legislative Department*

SECTION I. Congress

Legislative power vested in a two-house Congress. All legislative powers herein granted shall be vested in a Congress of the United States, which shall consist of a Senate and a House of Representatives.

SECTION II. House of Representatives

1. The people elect representatives biennially. The House of Representatives shall be composed of members chosen every second year by the people of the several States, and the electors [voters] in each State shall have the qualifications requisite for electors of the most numerous branch of the State Legislature.

2. Who may be representatives. No person shall be a Representative who shall not have attained the age of twenty-five years, and been seven years a citizen of the United States, and who shall not, when elected, be an inhabitant of that State in which he shall be chosen.

See 1787 compromise, p. 179.

See 1787 compromise, p. 180.

3. Representation in the House based on population; census. Representatives and direct taxes[1] shall be apportioned among the several States which may be included within this Union, according to their respective numbers, *which shall be determined by adding to the whole number of free persons, including those bound to service for a term of years* [apprentices and indentured servants], *and excluding Indians not taxed, three-fifths of all other persons* [slaves].[2] The actual enumeration [census] shall be made within three years after the first meeting of the Congress of the United States, and within every subsequent term of ten years, in such manner as they shall by law direct. The number of Representatives shall not exceed one for every thirty thousand, but each State shall have at least one Representative; *and until such enumeration shall be made, the State of New Hampshire shall be entitled to choose three, Massachusetts eight, Rhode Island and Providence Plantations one, Connecticut five, New York six, New Jersey four, Pennsylvania eight, Delaware one, Maryland six, Virginia ten, North Carolina five, South Carolina five, and Georgia three.*

---

[1]Modified in 1913 by the Sixteenth Amendment re income taxes (see p. 683).

[2]The word *slave* appears nowhere in the original, unamended Constitution. The three-fifths rule ceased to be in force when the Thirteenth Amendment was adopted in 1865 (see p. 72 and amendments below).

4. Vacancies in the House are filled by election. When vacancies happen in the representation from any State, the Executive authority [governor] therefore shall issue writs of election [call a special election] to fill such vacancies.

5. The House selects its Speaker; has sole power to vote impeachment charges (i.e., indictments). The House of Representatives shall choose their Speaker and other officers; and shall have the sole power of impeachment.

See Chase and Johnson trials, pp. 219, 496–497; Nixon trial preliminaries, pp. 949–950; and discussion of Clinton's impeachment, pp. 996–997.

SECTION III.

Senate

1. Senators represent the states. The Senate of the United States shall be composed of two Senators from each State, *chosen by the legislature thereof,*[1] for six Years; and each Senator shall have one vote.

2. One-third of senators chosen every two years; vacancies. *Immediately after they shall be assembled in consequence of the first election, they shall be divided as equally as may be into three classes. The seats of the Senators of the first class shall be vacated at the expiration of the second year, of the second class at the expiration of the fourth year, and of the third class at the expiration of the sixth year,* so that one-third may be chosen every second year; *and if vacancies happen by resignation or otherwise, during the recess of the legislature of any State, the Executive* [governor] *thereof may make temporary appointments until the next meeting of the legislature, which shall then fill such vacancies.*[2]

3. Who may be senators. No person shall be a Senator who shall not have attained to the age of thirty years, and been nine years a citizen of the United States, and who shall not, when elected, be an inhabitant of that State for which he shall be chosen.

4. The vice president presides over the Senate. The Vice President of the United States shall be President of the Senate, but shall have no vote, unless they be equally divided [tied].

5. The Senate chooses its other officers. The Senate shall choose their other officers, and also a President *pro tempore,* in the absence of the Vice President, or when he shall exercise the office of the President of the United States.

See Chase and Johnson trials, pp. 219, 496–497; and discussion of Clinton's impeachment, pp. 996–997.

6. The Senate has sole power to try impeachments. The Senate shall have the sole power to try all impeachments. When sitting for that purpose, they shall be on oath or affirmation. When the President of the United States is tried, the Chief Justice shall preside[3]: and no person shall be convicted without the concurrence of two-thirds of the members present.

7. Penalties for impeachment conviction. Judgment in cases of impeachment shall not extend further than to removal from office, and disqualification to hold and enjoy any office of honor, trust or profit under the United States: but the party convicted shall nevertheless be liable and subject to indictment, trial, judgment and punishment, according to law.

SECTION IV.

Election and Meetings of Congress

1. Regulation of elections. The times, places and manner of holding elections for Senators and Representatives shall be prescribed in each State by the legislature thereof; but the Congress may at any time by law make or alter such regulations, except as to the places of choosing Senators.

2. Congress must meet once a year. The Congress shall assemble at least once in every year, and such meeting *shall be on the first Monday in December, unless they shall by law appoint a different day.*[4]

---

[1]Repealed in favor of popular election in 1913 by the Seventeenth Amendment.
[2]Changed in 1913 by the Seventeenth Amendment.
[3]The vice president, as next in line, would be an interested party.
[4]Changed in 1933 to January 3 by the Twentieth Amendment (see p. 792 and below).

SECTION V.   Organization and Rules of the Houses

1. Each house may reject members; quorums. Each house shall be the judge of the elections, returns and qualifications of its own members, and a majority of each shall constitute a quorum to do business; but a smaller number may adjourn from day to day, and may be authorized to compel the attendance of absent members, in such manner, and under such penalties, as each house may provide.

See "Bully" Brooks case, pp. 414–415.

2. Each house makes its own rules. Each house may determine the rules of its proceedings, punish its members for disorderly behavior, and with the concurrence of two-thirds, expel a member.

3. Each house must keep and publish a record of its proceedings. Each house shall keep a journal of its proceedings, and from time to time publish the same, excepting such parts as may in their judgment require secrecy; and the yeas and nays of the members of either house on any question shall, at the desire of one-fifth of those present, be entered on the journal.

4. Both houses must agree on adjournment. Neither house, during the session of Congress, shall, without the consent of the other, adjourn for more than three days, nor to any other place than that in which the two houses shall be sitting.

SECTION VI.   Privileges of and Prohibitions upon Congressmen

1. Congressional salaries; immunities. The Senators and Representatives shall receive a compensation for their services, to be ascertained by law and paid out of the treasury of the United States. They shall in all cases except treason, felony and breach of the peace, be privileged from arrest during their attendance at the session of their respective houses, and in going to and returning from the same; and for any speech or debate in either house, they shall not be questioned in any other place [i.e., they shall be immune from libel suits].

2. A congressman may not hold any other federal civil office. No Senator or Representative shall, during the time for which he was elected, be appointed to any civil office under the authority of the United States, which shall have been created, or the emoluments whereof shall have been increased, during such time; and no person holding any office under the United States shall be a member of either house during his continuance in office.

SECTION VII.   Method of Making Laws

See 1787 compromise, p. 179.

1. Money bills must originate in the House. All bills for raising revenue shall originate in the House of Representatives; but the Senate may propose or concur with amendments as on other bills.

Nixon, more than any predecessors, "impounded" billions of dollars voted by Congress for specific purposes, because he disapproved of them. The courts generally failed to sustain him, and his impeachment foes regarded wholesale impoundment as a violation of his oath to "faithfully execute" the laws.

2. The president's veto power; Congress may override. Every bill which shall have passed the House of Representatives and the Senate, shall, before it become a law, be presented to the President of the United States; if he approve he shall sign it, but if not he shall return it with his objections to that house in which it shall have originated, who shall enter the objections at large on their journal, and proceed to reconsider it. If after such reconsideration two-thirds of that house shall agree to pass the bill, it shall be sent, together with the objections, to the other house, by which it shall likewise be reconsidered, and, if approved by two-thirds of that house, it shall become a law. But in all such cases the votes of both houses shall be determined by yeas and nays, and the names of the persons voting for and against the bill shall be entered on the journal of each house respectively. If any bill shall not be returned by the President within ten days (Sundays excepted) after it shall have been presented to him, the same shall be a law, in like manner as if he had signed it, unless the Congress by their adjournment prevent its return, in which case it shall not be a law [this is the so-called pocket veto].

3. All measures requiring the agreement of both houses go to president for approval. Every order, resolution, or vote to which the concurrence of the Senate and House of Representatives may be necessary (except on a question of adjournment) shall be presented to the President of the United States; and before the same shall take effect, shall be approved by him, or being disapproved by him, shall be repassed by two-thirds of the Senate and House of Representatives, according to the rules and limitations prescribed in the case of a bill.

SECTION VIII. **Powers Granted to Congress**

Congress has certain enumerated powers:

1. It may lay and collect taxes. The Congress shall have power to lay and collect taxes, duties, imposts, and excises, to pay the debts and provide for the common defense and general welfare of the United States; but all duties, imposts and excises shall be uniform throughout the United States;

2. It may borrow money. To borrow money on the credit of the United States;

3. It may regulate foreign and interstate trade. To regulate commerce with foreign nations, and among the several States, and with the Indian tribes;

For 1798 naturalization see p. 205.

4. It may pass naturalization and bankruptcy laws. To establish an uniform rule of naturalization, and uniform laws on the subject of bankruptcies throughout the United States;

5. It may coin money. To coin money, regulate the value thereof, and of foreign coin, and fix the standard of weights and measures;

6. It may punish counterfeiters. To provide for the punishment of counterfeiting the securities and current coin of the United States;

7. It may establish a postal service. To establish post offices and post roads;

8. It may issue patents and copyrights. To promote the progress of science and useful arts by securing for limited times to authors and inventors the exclusive right to their respective writings and discoveries;

9. It may establish inferior courts. To constitute tribunals inferior to the Supreme Court;

See Judiciary Act of 1789, p. 193.

10. It may punish crimes committed on the high seas. To define and punish piracies and felonies committed on the high seas [i.e., outside the three-mile limit] and offenses against the law of nations [international law];

11. It may declare war; authorize privateers. To declare war,[1] grant letters of marque and reprisal,[2] and make rules concerning captures on land and water;

12. It may maintain an army. To raise and support armies, but no appropriation of money to that use shall be for a longer term than two years;[3]

13. It may maintain a navy. To provide and maintain a navy;

14. It may regulate the army and navy. To make rules for the government and regulation of the land and naval forces;

15. It may call out the state militia. To provide for calling forth the militia to execute the laws of the Union, suppress insurrections, and repel invasions;

See Whiskey Rebellion, p. 196.

16. It shares with the states control of militia. To provide for organizing, arming, and disciplining the militia, and for governing such part of them as may be employed in the service of the United States, reserving to the States respectively the appointment of the officers, and the authority of training the militia according to the discipline prescribed by Congress;

---

[1] Note that presidents, though they can provoke war (see the case of Polk, p. 382) or wage it after it is declared, cannot declare it.

[2] Papers issued private citizens in wartime authorizing them to capture enemy ships.

[3] A reflection of fear of standing armies earlier expressed in the Declaration of Independence.

17. It makes laws for the District of Columbia and other federal areas. To exercise exclusive legislation in all cases whatsoever, over such district (not exceeding ten miles square) as may, by cession of particular States, and the acceptance of Congress, become the seat of government of the United States,[1] and to exercise like authority over all places purchased by the consent of the legislature of the State, in which the same shall be, for the erection of forts, magazines, arsenals, dock-yards, and other needful buildings;—and

Congress has certain implied powers:

This is the famous "elastic clause"; See p. 195.

18. It may make laws necessary for carrying out the enumerated powers. To make all laws which shall be necessary and proper for carrying into execution the foregoing powers, and all other powers vested by this Constitution in the government of the United States, or in any departure or officer thereof.

SECTION IX.   **Powers Denied to the Federal Government**

See 1787 slave compromise, p. 181.

1. Congressional control of slave trade postponed until 1808. *The migration or importation of such persons as any of the States now existing shall think proper to admit shall not be prohibited by the Congress prior to the year 1808; but a tax or duty may be imposed on such importation, not exceeding $10 for each person.*

See Lincoln's unlawful suspension, p. 447.

2. The writ of habeas corpus[2] may be suspended only in cases of rebellion or invasion. The privilege of the writ of habeas corpus shall not be suspended, unless when in cases of rebellion or invasion the public safety may require it.

3. Attainders[3] and ex post facto laws[4] forbidden. No bill of attainder or ex post facto law shall be passed.

4. Direct taxes must be apportioned according to population. No capitation [head or poll tax] or other direct, tax shall be laid, unless in proportion to the census or enumeration herein before directed to be taken.[5]

5. Export taxes forbidden. No tax or duty shall be laid on articles exported from any State.

6. Congress must not discriminate among states in regulating commerce. No preference shall be given by any regulation of commerce or revenue to the ports of one State over those of another; nor shall vessels bound to, or from, one State, be obliged to enter, clear, or pay duties in another.

See Lincoln's unlawful infraction, p. 447.

7. Public money may not be spent without congressional appropriation; accounting. No money shall be drawn from the treasury, but in consequence of appropriations made by law; and a regular statement and account of the receipts and expenditures of all public money shall be published from time to time.

8. Titles of nobility prohibited; foreign gifts. No title of nobility shall be granted by the United States; and no person holding office of profit or trust under them, shall, without the consent of Congress, accept of any present, emolument, office, or title, of any kind whatever, from any king, prince, or foreign state.

---

[1]The District of Columbia, ten miles square, was established in 1791 with a cession from Virginia (see p. 194).

[2]A writ of habeas corpus is a document that enables a person under arrest to obtain an immediate examination in court to ascertain whether he or she is being legally held.

[3]A bill of attainder is a special legislative act condemning and punishing an individual without a judicial trial.

[4]An ex post facto law is one that fixes punishments for acts committed before the law was passed.

[5]Modified in 1913 by the Sixteenth Amendment (see p. 691 and amendments below).

SECTION X.   Powers Denied to the States

Absolute prohibitions on the states:

On contracts see Fletcher *v.* Peck, *p. 249.*

1. The states are forbidden to do certain things. No State shall enter into any treaty, alliance, or confederation; grant letters of marque and reprisal [i.e., authorize privateers]; coin money; emit bills of credit [issue paper money]; make anything but gold and silver coin a [legal] tender in payment of debts; pass any bill of attainder,[1] ex post facto,[1] or law impairing the obligation of contracts, or grant any title of nobility.

Conditional prohibitions on the states:

Cf. Confederation chaos, pp. 172–173.

2. The states may not levy duties without the consent of Congress. No State shall, without the consent of Congress, lay any imposts or duties on imports or exports, except what may be absolutely necessary for executing its inspection laws: and the net produce of all duties and imposts, laid by any State on imports or exports, shall be for the use of the treasury of the United States; and all such laws shall be subject to the revision and control of the Congress.

3. Certain other federal powers are forbidden the states except with the consent of Congress. No State shall, without the consent of Congress, lay any duty of tonnage [i.e., duty on ship tonnage], keep [nonmilitia] troops or ships of war in time of peace, enter into any agreement or compact with another State, or with a foreign power, or engage in war, unless actually invaded, or in such imminent danger as will not admit of delay.

Article II.   *Executive Department*

SECTION I.   President and Vice President

1. The president is the chief executive; term of office. The executive power shall be vested in a President of the United States of America. He shall hold his office during the term of four years,[2] and, together with the Vice President, chosen for the same term, be elected as follows:

See 1787 compromise, pp. 180–181.

See 1876 Oregon case, p. 510.

2. The president is chosen by electors. Each State shall appoint, in such manner as the legislature thereof may direct, a number of electors, equal to the whole number of Senators and Representatives to which the State may be entitled in the Congress; but no Senator or Representative, or person holding an office of trust or profit under the United States, shall be appointed an elector.

A majority of the electoral votes needed to elect a president. *The electors shall meet in their respective States, and vote by ballot for two persons, of whom one at least shall not be an inhabitant of the same State with themselves. And they shall make a list of all the persons voted for, and of the number of votes for each; which list they shall sign and certify, and transmit sealed to the seat of government of the United States, directed to the President of the Senate. The President of the Senate shall, in the presence of the Senate and House of Representatives, open all the certificates, and the votes shall be counted. The person having the greatest number of votes shall be the President, if such number be a majority of the*

See Burr-Jefferson disputed election of 1800, p. 214.

whole number of electors appointed; and if there be more than one who have such majority, and have an equal number of votes, then the House of Representatives shall immediately choose by ballot one of them for President; and if no person have a majority, then from the five highest on the list the said house shall in like manner choose the President. But in choosing the President the votes shall be taken by States, the representation from each State

---

[1]For definitions see footnotes 3 and 4 on preceding page.

[2]No reference to reelection; for anti–third term Twenty-second Amendment, see below.

having one vote; a quorum for this purpose shall consist of a member or members from two-thirds of the States, and a majority of all the States shall be necessary to a choice. In every case, after the choice of the President, the person having the greatest number of votes of the electors shall be the Vice President. But if there should remain two or more who have equal votes, the Senate shall choose from them by ballot the Vice President.[1]

See Jefferson as vice president in 1796, p. 202.

3. Congress decides time of meeting of Electoral College. The Congress may determine the time of choosing the electors and the day on which they shall give their votes; which day shall be the same throughout the United States.

To provide for foreign-born people, like Alexander Hamilton, born in the British West Indies.

4. Who may be president. No person except a natural-born citizen, *or a citizen of the United States at the time of the adoption of this Constitution,* shall be eligible to the office of President; neither shall any person be eligible to that office who shall not have attained to the age of thirty-five years, and been fourteen years a resident within the United States [i.e., a legal resident].

Modified by Twentieth and Twenty-fifth Amendments below.

5. Replacements for president. In case of the removal of the President from office or of his death, resignation, or inability to discharge the powers and duties of said office, the same shall devolve on the Vice President, and the Congress may by law provide for the case of removal, death, resignation, or inability, both of the President and Vice President, declaring what officer shall then act as President, and such officer shall act accordingly, until the disability be removed, or a President shall be elected.

6. The president's salary. The President shall, at stated times, receive for his services a compensation, which shall neither be increased or diminished during the period for which he shall have been elected, and he shall not receive within that period any other emolument from the United States, or any of them.

7. The president's oath of office. Before he enter on the execution of his office, he shall take the following oath or affirmation:—"I do solemnly swear (or affirm) that I will faithfully execute the office of the President of the United States, and will to the best of my ability preserve, protect and defend the Constitution of the United States."

SECTION II.   **Powers of the President**

See cabinet evolution, p. 192.

1. The president has important military and civil powers. The President shall be commander in chief of the army and navy of the United States, and of the militia of the several States, when called into the actual service of the United States; he may require the opinion, in writing, of the principal officer in each of the executive departments, upon any subject relating to the duties of their respective offices, and he shall have power to grant reprieves and pardons for offenses against the United States, except in cases of impeachment.[2]

For president's removal power, see p. 496.

2. The president may negotiate treaties and nominate federal officials. He shall have power, by and with the advice and consent of the Senate, to make treaties, provided two-thirds of the Senators present concur; and he shall nominate, and by and with the advice and consent of the Senate, shall appoint ambassadors, other public ministers and consuls, judges of the Supreme Court, and all other officers of the United States, whose appointments are not herein otherwise provided for, and which shall be established by law: but the Congress may by law vest the appointment of such inferior officers, as they think proper, in the President alone, in the courts of law, or in the heads of departments.

3. The president may fill vacancies during Senate recess. The President shall have power to fill up all vacancies that may happen during the recess of the Senate, by granting commissions which shall expire at the end of their next session.

---

[1]Repealed in 1804 by the Twelfth Amendment (for text see below).

[2]To prevent the president's pardoning himself or his close associates, as was feared in the case of Richard Nixon. See p. 952.

SECTION III. **Other Powers and Duties of the President**

For president's personal appearances, see p. 683.

Messages; extra sessions; receiving ambassadors; execution of the laws. He shall from time to time give to the Congress information of the state of the Union, and recommend to their consideration such measures as he shall judge necessary and expedient; he may, on extraordinary occasions, convene both houses, or either of them, and in case of disagreement between them, with respect to the time of adjournment, he may adjourn them to such time as he shall think proper; he shall receive ambassadors and other public ministers; he shall take care that the laws be faithfully executed, and shall commission all the officers of the United States.

SECTION IV. **Impeachment**

See discussion of Presidents Johnson, pp. 496–497; Nixon, pp. 949–950; and Clinton, pp. 996–997.

Civil officers may be removed by impeachment. The President, Vice President and all civil officers[1] of the United States shall be removed from office on impeachment for, and on conviction of, treason, bribery, and other high crimes and misdemeanors.

Article III. *Judicial Department*

SECTION I. **The Federal Courts**

See Judiciary Act of 1789, p. 193.

The judicial power belongs to the federal courts. The judicial power of the United States shall be vested in one Supreme Court, and in such inferior courts as the Congress may from time to time ordain and establish. The judges, both of the Supreme and inferior courts, shall hold their offices during good behavior, and shall, at stated times, receive for their services a compensation which shall not be diminished[2] during their continuance in office.

SECTION II. **Jurisdiction of Federal Courts**

1. Kinds of cases that may be heard. The judicial power shall extend to all cases, in law and equity, arising under this Constitution, the laws of the United States, and treaties made, or which shall be made, under their authority;—to all cases affecting ambassadors, other public ministers and consuls;—to all cases of admiralty and maritime jurisdiction;—to controversies to which the United States shall be a party;—to controversies between two or more States;—*between a State and citizens of another State*[3];—between citizens of different States;—between citizens of the same State claiming lands under grants of different States, and between a State, or the citizens thereof, and foreign states, citizens or subjects.

2. Jurisdiction of the Supreme Court. In all cases affecting ambassadors, other public ministers and consuls, and those in which a State shall be a party, the Supreme Court shall have original jurisdiction.[4] In all the other cases before mentioned, the Supreme Court shall have appellate jurisdiction,[5] both as to law and fact, with such exceptions, and under such regulations, as the Congress shall make.

3. Trial for federal crime is by jury. The trial of all crimes, except in cases of impeachment, shall be by jury; and such trial shall be held in the State where the said crimes shall have been committed; but when not committed within any State, the trial shall be at such place or places as the Congress may by law have directed.

---

[1] i.e., all federal executive and judicial officers, but not members of Congress or military personnel.

[2] In 1978, in a case involving federal judges, the Supreme Court ruled that diminution of salaries by inflation was irrelevant.

[3] The Eleventh Amendment (see below) restricts this to suits by a state against citizens of another state.

[4] i.e., such cases must originate in the Supreme Court.

[5] i.e., it hears other cases only when they are appealed to it from a lower federal court or a state court.

SECTION III.   **Treason**

See Burr trial, p. 225.

1. Treason defined. Treason against the United States shall consist only in levying war against them, or in adhering to their enemies, giving them aid and comfort. No person shall be convicted of treason unless on the testimony of two witnesses to the same overt act, or on confession in open court.

2. Congress fixes punishment for treason. The Congress shall have power to declare the punishment of treason, but no attainder of treason shall work corruption of blood, or forfeiture except during the life of the person attained.[1]

Article IV.   *Relations of the States to One Another*

SECTION I.   **Credit to Acts, Records, and Court Proceedings**

Each state must respect the public acts of the others. Full faith and credit shall be given in each State to the public acts, records, and judicial proceedings of every other State.[2] And the Congress may by general laws prescribe the manner in which such acts, records, and proceedings shall be proved [attested], and the effect thereof.

SECTION II.   **Duties of States to States**

1. Citizenship in one state is valid in all. The citizens of each State shall be entitled to all privileges and immunities of citizens in the several States.

This stipulation is sometimes openly flouted. In 1978 Governor Jerry Brown of California, acting on humanitarian grounds, refused to surrender to South Dakota an American Indian, Dennis Banks, who was charged with murder in an armed uprising.

Basis of fugitive-slave laws; see pp. 399–400.

2. Fugitives from justice must be surrendered by the state to which they have fled. A person charged in any State with treason, felony, or other crime, who shall flee from justice, and be found in another State, shall on demand of the executive authority [governor] of the State from which he fled, be delivered up, to be removed to the State having jurisdiction of the crime.

3. Slaves and apprentices must be returned. *No person held to service or labor in one State, under the laws thereof, escaping into another, shall, in consequence of any law or regulation therein, be discharged from such service or labor, but shall be delivered up on claim of the party to whom such service or labor may be due.*[3]

SECTION III.   **New States and Territories**

e.g., Maine (1820); see p. 247.

1. Congress may admit new states. New States may be admitted by the Congress into this Union; but no new State shall be formed or erected within the jurisdiction of any other State; nor any State be formed by the junction of two or more States, or parts of States, without the consent of the legislatures of the States concerned as well as of the Congress.[4]

2. Congress regulates federal territory and property. The Congress shall have power to dispose of and make all needful rules and regulations respecting the territory or other property belonging to the United States; and nothing in this Constitution shall be so construed as to prejudice any claims of the United States, or of any particular State.

SECTION IV.   **Protection to the States**

See Cleveland and the Pullman strike, p. 617.

United States guarantees to states representative government and protection against invasion and rebellion. The United States shall guarantee to every State in this Union a

---

[1] i.e., punishment only for the offender; none for his or her heirs.

[2] e.g., a marriage in one is valid in all.

[3] Invalidated in 1865 by the Thirteenth Amendment (for text see below).

[4] Loyal West Virginia was formed by Lincoln in 1862 from seceded Virginia. This act was of dubious constitutionality and was justified in part by the wartime powers of the president. See pp. 436–437.

republican form of government, and shall protect each of them against invasion; and on application of the legislature, or of the executive [governor] (when the legislature cannot be convened), against domestic violence.

Article V.   *The Process of Amendment*

The Constitution may be amended in four ways. The Congress, whenever two-thirds of both houses shall deem it necessary, shall propose amendments to this Constitution, or, on the application of the legislature of two-thirds of the several States, shall call a convention for proposing amendments, which, in either case, shall be valid to all intents and purposes, as part of this Constitution, when ratified by the legislatures of three-fourths of the several States, or by conventions in three-fourths thereof, as the one or the other mode of ratification may be proposed by the Congress; provided *that no amendments which may be made prior to the year one thousand eight hundred and eight shall in any manner affect the first and fourth clauses in the ninth section of the first article;*[1] and that no State, without its consent, shall be deprived of its equal suffrage in the Senate.

Article VI.   *General Provisions*

This pledge honored by Hamilton, pp. 193–194.

1. The debts of the Confederation are taken over. All debts contracted and engagements entered into, before the adoption of this Constitution, shall be as valid against the United States under this Constitution, as under the Confederation.

2. The Constitution, federal laws, and treaties are the supreme law of the land. This Constitution, and the laws of the United States which shall be made in pursuance thereof; and all treaties made, or which shall be made, under the authority of the United States, shall be the supreme law of the land; and the judges in every State shall be bound thereby, anything in the Constitution or laws of any State to the contrary notwithstanding.

3. Federal and state officers bound by oath to support the Constitution. The Senators and Representatives before mentioned, and the members of the several State legislatures, and all executive and judicial officers, both of the United States and of the several States, shall be bound by oath or affirmation to support this Constitution; but no religious test shall ever be required as a qualification to any office or public trust under the United States.

Article VII.   *Ratification of the Constitution*

See 1787 irregularity, pp. 181–183.

The Constitution effective when ratified by conventions in nine states. The ratification of the conventions of nine States shall be sufficient for the establishment of this Constitution between the States so ratifying the same.

Done in Convention by the unanimous consent of the States present, the seventeenth day of September in the year of our Lord one thousand seven hundred and eighty-seven and of the Independence of the United States of America the twelfth. In witness whereof we have hereunto subscribed our names.

[Signed by]

G° WASHINGTON

Presidt and Deputy from Virginia
[and thirty-eight others]

---

[1]This clause, regarding slave trade and direct taxes, became inoperative in 1808

AMENDMENTS TO THE CONSTITUTION

Amendment I.   *Religious and Political Freedom*

For background of Bill of Rights, see pp. 192–193.

Congress must not interfere with freedom of religion, speech or press, assembly, and petition. Congress shall make no law respecting an establishment of religion,[1] or prohibiting the free exercise thereof; or abridging the freedom of speech, or of the press; or the right of the people peaceably to assemble, and to petition the government for a redress of grievances.

Amendment II.   *Right to Bear Arms*

The people may bear arms. A well-regulated militia being necessary to the security of a free State, the right of the people to keep and bear arms [i.e., for military purposes] shall not be infringed.[2]

Amendment III.   *Quartering of Troops*

See Declaration of Independence and British quartering above.

Soldiers may not be arbitrarily quartered on the people. No soldier shall, in time of peace, be quartered in any house without the consent of the owner, nor in time of war, but in a manner to be prescribed by law.

Amendment IV.   *Searches and Seizures*

A reflection of colonial grievances against the crown.

Unreasonable searches are forbidden. The right of the people to be secure in their persons, houses, papers, and effects, against unreasonable searches and seizures, shall not be violated, and no [search] warrants shall issue but upon probable cause, supported by oath or affirmation, and particularly describing the place to be searched, and the persons or things to be seized.

Amendment V.   *Right to Life, Liberty, and Property*

When witnesses refuse to answer questions in court, they routinely "take the Fifth Amendment."

The individual is guaranteed certain rights when on trial and the right to life, liberty, and property. No person shall be held to answer for a capital, or otherwise infamous crime, unless on a presentment [formal charge] or indictment of a grand jury, except in cases arising in the naval forces, or in the militia, when in actual service in time of war or public danger; nor shall any person be subject for the same offense to be twice put in jeopardy of life or limb; nor shall be compelled in any criminal case to be a witness against himself, nor be deprived of life, liberty, or property, without due process of law; nor shall private property be taken for public use [i.e., by eminent domain] without just compensation.

Amendment VI.   *Protection in Criminal Trials*

See Declaration of Independence above.

An accused person has important rights. In all criminal prosecutions, the accused shall enjoy the right to a speedy and public trial, by an impartial jury of the State and district

---

[1] In 1787 "an establishment of religion" referred to an "established church," or one supported by all taxpayers, whether members or not. But the courts have often acted under this article to keep religion, including prayers, out of the public schools.

[2] The courts, with "militia" in mind, have consistently held that the "right" to bear arms is a limited one.

wherein the crime shall have been committed, which district shall have been previously ascertained by law, and to be informed of the nature and cause of the accusation; to be confronted with the witnesses against him; to have compulsory process [subpoena] for obtaining witnesses in his favor, and to have the assistance of counsel for his defense.

Amendment VII. *Suits at Common Law*

The rules of common law are recognized. In suits at common law, where the value in controversy shall exceed twenty dollars, the right of trial by jury shall be preserved, and no fact tried by a jury shall be otherwise re-examined in any court of the United States, than according to the rules of the common law.

Amendment VIII. *Bail and Punishments*

Excessive fines and unusual punishments are forbidden. Excessive bail shall not be required, nor excessive fines imposed, nor cruel and unusual punishment inflicted.

Amendment IX. *Concerning Rights Not Enumerated*

The Ninth and Tenth Amendments were bulwarks of southern states' rights before the Civil War.

The people retain rights not here enumerated. The enumeration in the Constitution, of certain rights, shall not be construed to deny or disparage others retained by the people.

Amendment X. *Powers Reserved to the States and to the People*

A concession to states' rights, p. 194.

Powers not delegated to the federal government are reserved to the states and the people. The powers not delegated to the United States by the Constitution, nor prohibited by it to the States, are reserved to the States respectively, or to the people.

Amendment XI. *Suits Against a State*

The federal courts have no authority in suits by citizens against a state. The judicial power of the United States shall not be construed to extend to any suit in law or equity, commenced or prosecuted against one of the United States by citizens of another State, or by citizens or subjects of any foreign state. [Adopted 1798.]

Amendment XII. *Election of President and Vice President*

Forestalls repetition of 1800 electoral dispute, p. 214.

See 1876 disputed election. pp. 510–511.

See 1824 election, pp. 256–258.

1. Changes in manner of electing president and vice president; procedure when no presidential candidate receives electoral majority. The electors shall meet in their respective States, and vote by ballot for President and Vice President, one of whom, at least, shall not be an inhabitant of the same state with themselves; they shall name in their ballots the person voted for as President, and in distinct ballots the person voted for as Vice President, and they shall make distinct lists of all persons voted for as President, and of all persons voted for as Vice President, and of the number of votes for each, which lists they shall sign and certify, and transmit sealed to the seat of government of the United States, directed to the President of the Senate;—the President of the Senate shall, in the presence of the Senate and House of Representatives, open all the certificates and the votes shall be counted;—the person having the greatest number of votes for President shall be the President, if such number be a majority of the whole number of electors appointed; and if no person have such majority, then from the persons having the highest numbers not exceeding three on the list of those voted for as President, the House of Representatives shall choose immediately, by ballot, the President. But in choosing the President, the votes shall be taken by States, the representation from each State having one vote; a quorum for this purpose shall consist of a member or members from two-thirds of the States, and a majority of all the States shall be necessary to a choice. And if the House of Representatives shall not choose a President whenever the right of choice shall devolve upon them, before *the fourth day of March*[1] next following, then the Vice President shall act as President, as in the case of the death or other constitutional disability of the President.

2. Procedure when no vice presidential candidate receives electoral majority. The person having the greatest number of votes as Vice President, shall be the Vice President, if such number be a majority of the whole number of electors appointed; and if no person have a majority, then from the two highest numbers on the list the Senate shall choose the Vice President; a quorum for the purpose shall consist of two-thirds of the whole number of Senators, and a majority of the whole number shall be necessary to a choice. But no person constitutionally ineligible to the office of President shall be eligible to that of Vice President of the United States. [Adopted 1804.]

Amendment XIII. *Slavery Prohibited*

For background see pp. 460–462.

Slavery forbidden. 1. Neither slavery[2] nor involuntary servitude, except as a punishment for crime whereof the party shall have been duly convicted, shall exist within the United States, or any place subject to their jurisdiction.

2. Congress shall have power to enforce this article by appropriate legislation. [Adopted 1865.]

Amendment XIV. *Civil Rights for Ex-slaves,[3] etc.*

For background see pp. 488–489.

For corporations as "persons," see pp. 543–544.

Abolishes three-fifths rule for slaves, Art. I., Sec. II, para. 3.

1. Ex-slaves made citizens; U.S. citizenship primary. All persons born or naturalized in the United States, and subject to the jurisdiction thereof, are citizens of the United States and of the State wherein they reside. No State shall make or enforce any law which shall abridge the privileges or immunities of citizens of the United States; nor shall any State deprive any person of life, liberty, or property, without due process of law; nor deny to any person within its jurisdiction the equal protection of the laws.

2. When a state denies citizens the vote, its representation shall be reduced. Representatives shall be apportioned among the several States according to their respective numbers, counting the whole number of persons in each State, excluding Indians not taxed. But when the right to vote at any election for the choice of Electors for President and Vice President of the United States, Representatives in Congress, the executive and judicial officers of a State, or the members of the legislature thereof, is denied to any of the male inhabitants of such State, being twenty-one years of age and citizens of the United States, or in any way abridged, except for participation in rebellion, or other crime, the basis of representation therein shall be reduced in the proportion which the number of such make citizens shall bear to the whole number of male citizens twenty-one years of age in such State.[4]

Leading ex-Confederates denied office. See p. 489.

3. Certain persons who have been in rebellion are ineligible for federal and state office. No person shall be a Senator or Representative in Congress, or Elector of President and Vice President, or hold any office, civil or military, under the United States, or under any State, who, having previously taken an oath, as a member of Congress, or as an officer

---

[1]Changed to January 20 by the Twentieth Amendment (for text see below).

[2]The only explicit mention of slavery in the Constitution.

[3]Occasionally an offender is prosecuted under the Thirteenth Amendment for keeping an employee or other person under conditions approximating slavery.

[4]The provisions concerning "male" inhabitants were modified by the Nineteenth Amendment, which enfranchised women. The legal voting age was changed from twenty-one to eighteen by the Twenty-sixth Amendment.

of the United States, or as a member of any State legislature, or as an executive or judicial officer of any State, to support the Constitution of the United States, shall have engaged in insurrection or rebellion against the same, or given aid or comfort to the enemies thereof. But Congress may, by a vote of two-thirds of each house, remove such disability.

The ex-Confederates were thus forced to repudiate their debts and pay pensions to their own veterans, plus taxes for the pensions of Union veterans, their conquerors.

4. Debts incurred in aid of rebellion are void. The validity of the public debt of the United States, authorizing by law, including debts incurred for payment of pensions and bounties for services in suppressing insurrection or rebellion, shall not be questioned. But neither the United States nor any State shall assume or pay any debt or obligation incurred in aid of insurrection or rebellion against the United States, or any claim for the loss or emancipation of any slave; but all such debts, obligations, and claims shall be held illegal and void.

5. Enforcement. The Congress shall have power to enforce, by appropriate legislation, the provisions of this article. [Adopted 1868.]

Amendment XV.   *Suffrage for Blacks*

For background see p. 492.

Black males are made voters. 1. The right of the citizens of the United States to vote shall not be denied or abridged by the United States or by any State on account of race, color, or previous condition of servitude.

2. The Congress shall have power to enforce this article by appropriate legislation. [Adopted 1870.]

Amendment XVI.   *Income Taxes*

For background see p. 683.

Congress has power to lay and collect income taxes. The Congress shall have power to lay and collect taxes on incomes, from whatever source derived, without apportionment among the several States, and without regard to any census or enumeration. [Adopted 1913.]

Amendment XVII.   *Direct Election of Senators*

Senators shall be elected by popular vote. 1. The Senate of the United States shall be composed of two Senators from each State, elected by the people thereof, for six years; and each Senator shall have one vote. The electors in each State shall have the qualifications requisite for electors of [voters for] the most numerous branch of the State legislatures.

2. When vacancies happen in the representation of any State in the Senate, the executive authority of such State shall issue writs of election to fill such vacancies: Provided, that the Legislature of any State may empower the executive thereof to make temporary appointments until the people fill the vacancies by election as the Legislature may direct.

3. This amendment shall not be so construed as to affect the election or term of any Senator chosen before it becomes valid as part of the Constitution. [Adopted 1913.]

Amendment XVIII.   *National Prohibition*

For background see p. 725.

The sale or manufacture of intoxicating liquors is forbidden. 1. *After one year from the ratification of this article the manufacture, sale, or transportation of intoxicating liquors within, the importation thereof into, or the exportation thereof from the United States and all territory subject to the jurisdiction thereof, for beverage purposes, is hereby prohibited.*

2. *The Congress and the several States shall have concurrent power to enforce this article by appropriate legislation.*

3. *This article shall be inoperative unless it shall have been ratified as an amendment to the Constitution by the legislatures of the several States, as provided by the Constitution,* *within seven years from the date of the submission thereof to the States by the Congress.* [Adopted 1919; repealed 1933 by Twenty-first Amendment.]

Amendment XIX.   *Woman Suffrage*

For background see pp. 702–703.

Women guaranteed the right to vote. 1. The right of citizens of the United States to vote shall not be denied or abridged by the United States or by any State on account of sex.

2. Congress shall have power to enforce this article by appropriate legislation. [Adopted 1920.]

Amendment XX.   *Presidential and Congressional Terms*

Shortens lame duck periods by modifying Art. I, Sec. IV, para. 2.

1. Presidential, vice presidential, and congressional terms of office begin in January. The terms of the President and Vice President shall end at noon on the 20th day of January, and the terms of Senators and Representatives at noon on the 3d day of January, of the years in which such terms would have ended if this article had not been ratified; and the terms of their successors shall then begin.

2. New meeting date for Congress. The Congress shall assemble at least once in every year, and such meeting shall begin at noon on the 3d day of January, unless they shall by law appoint a different day.

3. Emergency presidential and vice presidential succession. If, at the time fixed for the beginning of the term of the President, the President-elect shall have died, the Vice President–elect shall become President. If a President shall not have been chosen before the time fixed for the beginning of his term, or if the President-elect shall have failed to qualify, then the Vice President–elect shall act as President until a President shall have qualified; and the Congress may by law provide for the case wherein neither a President-elect nor a Vice President–elect shall have qualified, declaring who shall then act as President, or the manner in which one who is to act shall be selected, and such persons shall act accordingly until a President or Vice President shall have qualified.

4. The Congress may by law provide for the case of the death of any of the persons from whom the House of Representatives may choose a President whenever the right of choice shall have devolved upon them, and for the case of the death of any of the persons from whom the Senate may choose a Vice President whenever the right of choice shall have devolved upon them.

5. Sections 1 and 2 shall take effect on the 15th day of October following the ratification of this article.

6. This article shall be inoperative unless it shall have been ratified as an amendment to the Constitution by the Legislatures of three-fourths of the several States within seven years from the date of its submission. [Adopted 1993.]

Amendment XXI.   *Prohibition Repealed*

For background see pp. 782–783.

1. Eighteenth Amendment repealed. The eighteenth article of amendment to the Constitution of the United States is hereby repealed.

2. Local laws honored. The transportation or importation into any State, Territory, or Possession of the United States for delivery or use therein of intoxicating liquors, in violation of the laws thereof, is hereby prohibited.

3. This article shall be inoperative unless it shall have been ratified as an amendment to the Constitution by conventions in the several States, as provided in the Constitution, within seven years from the date of the submission thereof to the States by the Congress. [Adopted 1933.]

Amendment XXII.

Sometimes referred to as the anti–Franklin Roosevelt amendment.

Anti–Third Term Amendment

1. Presidential term is limited. No person shall be elected to the office of President more than twice, and no person who has held the office of President, or acted as President, for more than two years of a term to which some other person was elected President shall be elected to the office of President more than once. But this article shall not apply to any person holding the office of President when this article was proposed by the Congress [i.e., Truman], and shall not prevent any person who may be holding the office of President, during the term within which this article becomes operative [i.e., Truman] from holding the office of President or acting as President during the remainder of such term.

2. This article shall be inoperative unless it shall have been ratified as an amendment to the Constitution by the legislatures of three-fourths of the several States within seven years from the date of its submission to the States by the Congress. [Adopted 1951.]

Amendment XXIII.

Designed to give the District of Columbia three electoral votes and to quiet the century-old cry of "No taxation without representation." Yet the District of Columbia still has only one nonvoting member of Congress.

District of Columbia Vote

1. Presidential electors for the District of Columbia. The District, constituting the seat of government of the United States, shall appoint in such manner as the Congress shall direct:

A number of electors of President and Vice President equal to the whole number of Senators and Representatives in Congress to which the District would be entitled if it were a State, but in no event more than the least populous State; they shall be in addition to those appointed by the States, but they shall be considered for the purposes of the election of President and Vice President, to be electors appointed by a State; and they shall meet in the District and perform such duties as provided by the twelfth article of amendment.

2. Enforcement. The Congress shall have the power to enforce this article by appropriate legislation. [Adopted 1961.]

Amendment XXIV.

Designed to end discrimination against poor people, including southern blacks who were often denied the vote through inability to pay poll taxes. See p. 924.

Poll Tax

1. Payment of poll tax or other taxes not to be prerequisite for voting in federal elections. The right of citizens of the United States to vote in any primary or other election for President or Vice President, for electors for President or Vice President, or for Senator or Representative in Congress, shall not be denied or abridged by the United States or any State by reason of failure to pay any poll tax or other tax.

2. Enforcement. The Congress shall have the power to enforce this article by appropriate legislation. [Adopted 1964.]

Amendment XXV.

Gerald Ford was the first "appointed president." See pp. 949, 952.

Presidential Succession and Disability

1. Vice president to become president. In case of the removal of the President from office or of his death or resignation, the Vice President shall become President.[1]

2. Successor to vice president provided. Whenever there is a vacancy in the office of the Vice President, the President shall nominate a Vice President who shall take office upon confirmation by a majority vote of both Houses of Congress.

---

[1]The original Constitution (Art. II, Sec. I, para. 5) was vague on this point, stipulating that "the powers and duties" of the president, but not necessarily the title, should "devolve" on the vice president. President Tyler, the first "accidental president," assumed not only the powers and duties but the title as well.

3. Vice president to serve for disabled president. Whenever the President transmits to the President pro tempore of the Senate and the Speaker of the House of Representatives his written declaration that he is unable to discharge the powers and duties of his office, and until he transmits to them a written declaration to the contrary, such powers and duties shall be discharged by the Vice President as Acting President.

4. Procedure for disqualifying or requalifying president. Whenever the Vice President and a majority of either the principal officers of the executive departments or of such other body as Congress may by law provide, transmit to the President pro tempore of the Senate and the Speaker of the House of Representatives their written declaration that the President is unable to discharge the powers and duties of his office, the Vice President shall immediately assume the powers and duties of the office as Acting President.

Thereafter, when the President transmits to the President pro tempore of the Senate and the Speaker of the House of Representatives his written declaration that no inability exists, he shall resume the powers and duties of his office unless the Vice President and a majority of either the principal officers of the executive department[s] or of such other body as Congress may by law provide, transmit within four days to the President pro tempore of the Senate and the Speaker of the House of Representatives their written declaration that the President is unable to discharge the powers and duties of his office. Thereupon Congress shall decide the issue, assembling within forty-eight hours for that purpose if not in session. If the Congress, within twenty-one days after receipt of the latter written declaration, or, if Congress is not in session, within twenty-one days after Congress is required to assemble, determines by two-thirds vote of both Houses that the President is unable to discharge the powers and duties of his office, the Vice President shall continue to discharge the same as Acting President; otherwise, the President shall resume the powers and duties of his office. [Adopted 1967.]

Amendment XXVI.   *Lowering Voting Age*

A response to the current revolt of youth. See p. 942.

1. Ballot for eighteen-year-olds. The right of citizens of the United States, who are eighteen years of age or older, to vote shall not be denied or abridged by the United States or any state on account of age.

2. Enforcement. The Congress shall have the power to enforce this article by appropriate legislation. [Adopted 1971.]

Amendment XXVII.   *Restricting Congressional Pay Raises*

Reflects anti-incumbent sentiment of early 1990s. First proposed by James Madison in 1789; took 203 years to be ratified.

Congress not allowed to increase its current pay. No law varying the compensation for the services of the Senators and Representatives shall take effect, until an election of Representatives shall have intervened. [Adopted 1992.]

An American Profile:
The United States
and Its People

Population, Percentage Change, and Racial Composition for the United States, 1790–2002

| Census | Population of United States | Increase over Preceding Census | | Racial Composition, Percent Distribution* | | | |
		Number	Percentage	White	Black	Latino	Asian
1790	3,929,214			80.7	19.3	NA	NA
1800	5,308,483	1,379,269	35.1	81.1	18.9	NA	NA
1810	7,239,881	1,931,398	36.4	81.0	19.0	NA	NA
1820	9,638,453	2,398,572	33.1	81.6	18.4	NA	NA
1830	12,866,020	3,227,567	33.5	81.9	18.1	NA	NA
1840	17,069,453	4,203,433	32.7	83.2	16.8	NA	NA
1850	23,191,876	6,122,423	35.9	84.3	15.7	NA	NA
1860	31,433,321	8,251,445	35.6	85.6	14.1	NA	NA
1870	39,818,449	8,375,128	26.6	86.2	13.5	NA	NA
1880	50,155,783	10,337,334	26.0	86.5	13.1	NA	NA
1890	62,947,714	12,791,931	25.5	87.5	11.9	NA	NA
1900	75,994,575	13,046,861	20.7	87.9	11.6	NA	0.3
1910	91,972,266	15,997,691	21.0	88.9	10.7	NA	0.3
1920	105,710,620	13,738,354	14.9	89.7	9.9	NA	0.3
1930	122,775,046	17,064,426	16.1	89.8	9.7	NA	0.4
1940	131,669,275	8,894,229	7.2	89.8	9.8	NA	0.4
1950	150,697,361	19,028,086	14.5	89.5	10.0	NA	0.4
1960†	179,323,175	28,625,814	19.0	88.6	10.5	NA	0.5
1970	203,235,298	23,912,123	13.3	87.6	11.1	NA	0.7
1980	226,504,825	23,269,527	11.4	85.9	11.8	6.4	1.5
1990	248,709,873	22,205,048	9.8	83.9	12.3	9.0	2.9
2000	282,177,754	33,467,881	12.0	81.0	12.7	12.5	3.8
2002	287,973,924	5,796,170	2.0	80.1	12.7	13.4	4.0

*Not every racial group included (e.g., no Native Americans). Persons of Latino origin may be of any race. Data for 1980, 1990, 2000, 2002 add up to more than 100% because those who identify themselves as "Latino" could still be counted as "White."
†First year for which figures include Alaska and Hawaii.
(Sources: Census Bureau, *Historical Statistics of the United States*, updated by relevant *Statistical Abstract of the United States*.)

Population Density and Distribution, 1790–2000

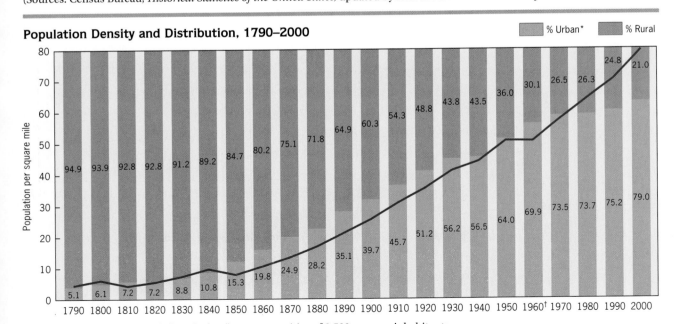

*The Bureau of the Census defines "urban" as communities of 2,500 or more inhabitants.
†First year for which figures include Alaska and Hawaii.
(Sources: Census Bureau, *Historical Statistics of the United States*, updated by relevant *Statistical Abstract of the United States*.)

Changing Characteristics of the U.S. Population

Birthrates per thousand women ages 15–44

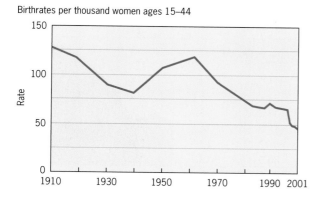

Life expectancy at birth

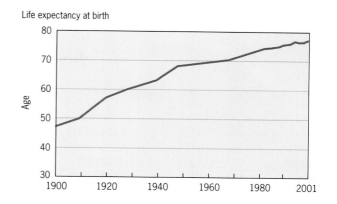

Median age of population (years)

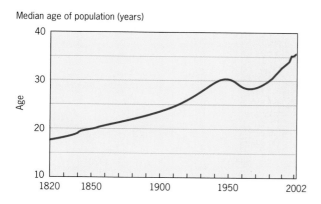

Infant mortality

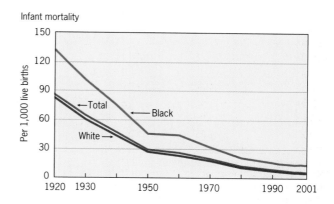

Household size

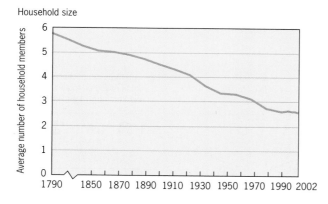

Median age at first marriage

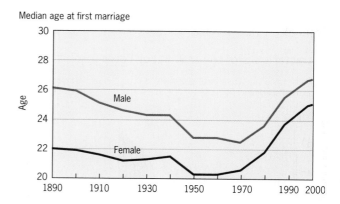

(Sources: *Historical Statistics of the United States* and *Statistical Abstract of the United States,* relevant years.)

Changing Lifestyles in Modern America

Households with all
plumbing facilities, 1940–2000

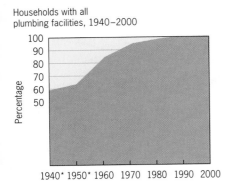

Occupied households with
electric service, 1900–2000

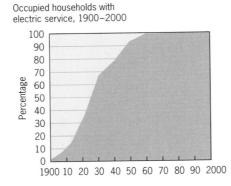

Occupied households with
telephones, 1920–2001

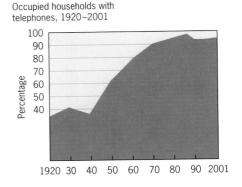

Motor-vehicle registrations,
1900–2001

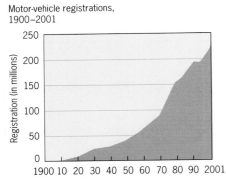

Households with television sets,
1946–2001

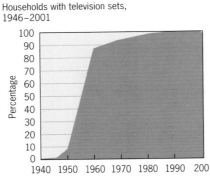

Households with videocassette
recorders (VCRs), 1970–2001

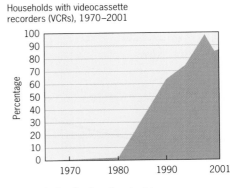

*Except for 1940 and 1950, figures for "all plumbing facilities" (not detailed in source). For 1940, figure is for flush toilet, inside structure, private use (64.7 percent had flush toilet and private and/or shared inside structure, and 60.9 percent had installed bath or shower). For 1950, figure designates units with private toilet and bath and hot running water (flush toilet, private or shared inside structure is 74.3 percent; installed bathtub or shower, 72.9 percent).
(Sources: *Historical Statistics of the United States* and *Statistical Abstract of the United States*, relevant years.)

Characteristics of the U.S. Labor Force

Total labor force (age 16 or over, employed and
unemployed seeking work)

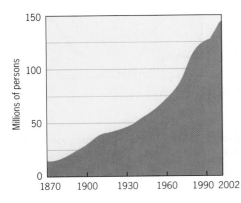

Gender composition of labor force, 1900–2002
(percentage of men and women in civilian labor force)

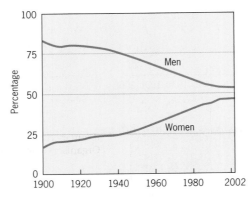

Top three occupational categories
(rank based on total numbers) for
workers age 14 and older

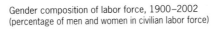

	farm	manual*	white collar†	service
Rank	1	2	3	
1900	farm	manual	white collar	
1920	manual	farm	white collar	
1940	manual	white collar	farm	
1960	white collar	manual	service	
1980	white collar	manual	service	
2002	white collar	manual	service	

*Manual workers = operators, fabricators, and laborers plus precision production, craft, and repair.
†White-collar workers = managerial and professional plus technical, sales, and administrative support.
(Sources: *Historical Statistics of the United States* and *Statistical Abstract of the United States*, relevant years, and Department of Labor, Bureau of Labor Statistics, *Handbook of Labor Statistics*, relevant years.)

Leading Economic Sectors (various years)

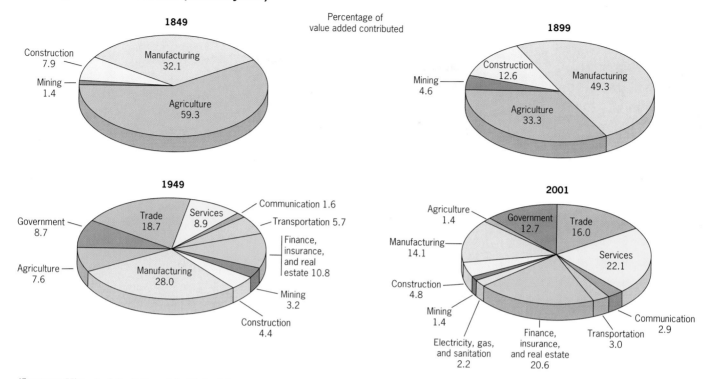

Percentage of value added contributed

1849

Construction 7.9
Mining 1.4
Manufacturing 32.1
Agriculture 59.3

1899

Construction 12.6
Mining 4.6
Manufacturing 49.3
Agriculture 33.3

1949

Government 8.7
Agriculture 7.6
Trade 18.7
Services 8.9
Communication 1.6
Transportation 5.7
Finance, insurance, and real estate 10.8
Manufacturing 28.0
Mining 3.2
Construction 4.4

2001

Agriculture 1.4
Manufacturing 14.1
Construction 4.8
Mining 1.4
Government 12.7
Trade 16.0
Services 22.1
Communication 2.9
Transportation 3.0
Finance, insurance, and real estate 20.6
Electricity, gas, and sanitation 2.2

(Sources: *Historical Statistics of the United States, Statistical Abstract of the United States,* relevant years, and Bureau of Economic Analysis.)

Per Capita Disposable Personal Income in Constant (1987) Dollars, 1940–2002

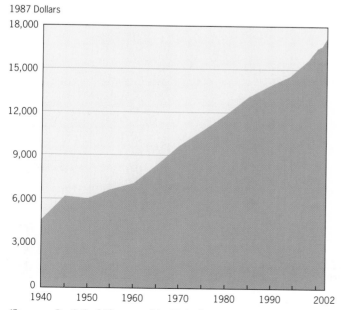

(Sources: *Statistical Abstract of the United States,* relevant years, and John J. McCusker, "Comparing the Purchasing Power of Money in the U.S.," [2004], Economic History Services http://www.eh.net/hmit/ppowerusd/)

Comparative Tax Burdens (percentage of gross domestic product paid as taxes in major industrial countries, 2000)

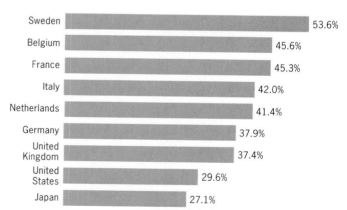

Sweden 53.6%
Belgium 45.6%
France 45.3%
Italy 42.0%
Netherlands 41.4%
Germany 37.9%
United Kingdom 37.4%
United States 29.6%
Japan 27.1%

(Sources: *Statistical Abstract of the United States,* relevant years, and Organisation for Economic Co-operation and Development.)

The Federal Budget Dollar and How It Is Spent, by Major Category

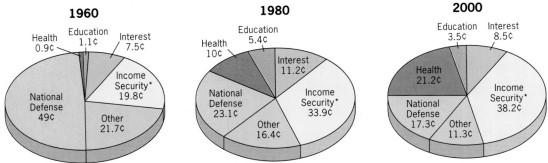

*Includes Social Security payments to the elderly and disabled, unemployment compensation, and welfare. Note the shifting emphasis in the budget from defense spending to health and income security, and to interest payments on the national debt.

(Source: *Statistical Abstract of the United States,* relevant years.)

The U.S. Balance of Trade, 1900–2002

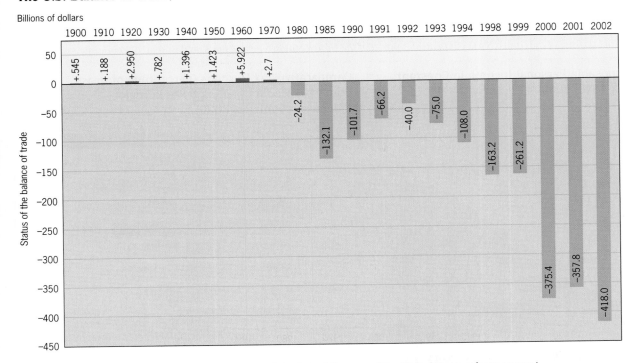

(Sources: *Historical Statistics of the United States* and *Statistical Abstract of the United States,* relevant years.)

Tariff Levies on Dutiable Imports, 1821–2003 (ratio of duties to value of dutiable imports)

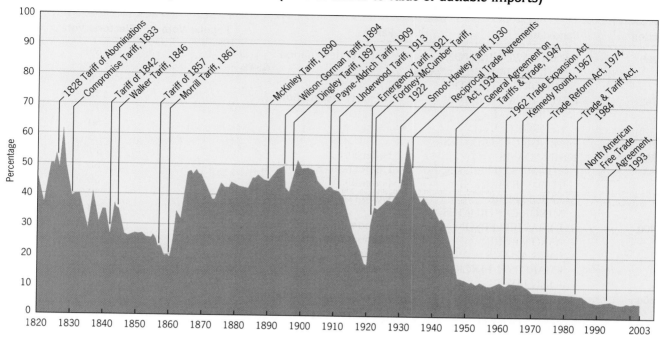

(Sources: *Historical Statistics of the United States, Statistical Abstract of the United States,* relevant years, and United States International Trade Commission.)

Gross Domestic Product in Current and Constant 1995 Dollars*

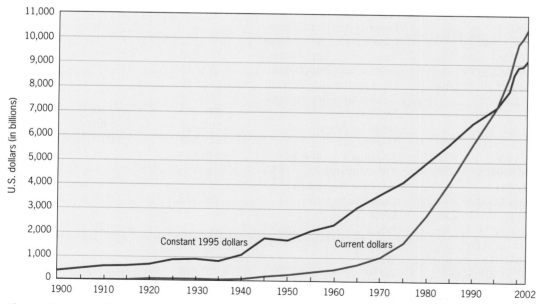

(Source: *Statistical Abstract of the United States,* relevant years.)

*Gross *national* product before 1960. Gross national product includes income from overseas investment and excludes profits generated in the United States but accruing to foreign accounts. Gross *domestic* product excludes overseas profits owed to American accounts but includes the value of all items originating in the United States, regardless of the ultimate destination of the profits. Until recent years, those factors made for negligible differences in the calculation of *national* and *domestic* product, but most economists now prefer the latter methodology.

Presidential Elections*

Election	Candidates	Parties	Popular Vote	Electoral Vote
1789	GEORGE WASHINGTON	No party designation		69
	JOHN ADAMS			34
	MINOR CANDIDATES			35
1792	GEORGE WASHINGTON	No party designation		132
	JOHN ADAMS			77
	GEORGE CLINTON			50
	MINOR CANDIDATES			5
1796	JOHN ADAMS	Federalist		71
	THOMAS JEFFERSON	Democratic-Republican		68
	THOMAS PINCKNEY	Federalist		59
	AARON BURR	Democratic-Republican		30
	MINOR CANDIDATES			48
1800	THOMAS JEFFERSON	Democratic-Republican		73
	AARON BURR	Democratic-Republican		73
	JOHN ADAMS	Federalist		65
	CHARLES C. PINCKNEY	Federalist		64
	JOHN JAY	Federalist		1
1804	THOMAS JEFFERSON	Democratic-Republican		162
	CHARLES C. PINCKNEY	Federalist		14
1808	JAMES MADISON	Democratic-Republican		122
	CHARLES C. PINCKNEY	Federalist		47
	GEORGE CLINTON	Democratic-Republican		6
1812	JAMES MADISON	Democratic-Republican		128
	DEWITT CLINTON	Federalist		89
1816	JAMES MONROE	Democratic-Republican		183
	RUFUS KING	Federalist		34
1820	JAMES MONROE	Democratic-Republican		231
	JOHN Q. ADAMS	Independent Republican		1
1824	JOHN Q. ADAMS (Min.)†	Democratic-Republican	108,740	84
	ANDREW JACKSON	Democratic-Republican	153,544	99
	WILLIAM H. CRAWFORD	Democratic-Republican	46,618	41
	HENRY CLAY	Democratic-Republican	47,136	37
1828	ANDREW JACKSON	Democratic	647,286	178
	JOHN Q. ADAMS	National Republican	508,064	83
1832	ANDREW JACKSON	Democratic	687,502	219
	HENRY CLAY	National Republican	530,189	49
	WILLIAM WIRT	Anti-Masonic	33,108	7
	JOHN FLOYD	National Republican		11
1836	MARTIN VAN BUREN	Democratic	765,483	170
	WILLIAM H. HARRISON	Whig		73
	HUGH L. WHITE	Whig	739,795	26
	DANIEL WEBSTER	Whig		14
	W. P. MANGUM	Whig		11
1840	WILLIAM H. HARRISON	Whig	1,274,624	234
	MARTIN VAN BUREN	Democratic	1,127,781	60
1844	JAMES K. POLK (Min.)†	Democratic	1,338,464	170
	HENRY CLAY	Whig	1,300,097	105
	JAMES G. BIRNEY	Liberty	62,300	

* Candidates receiving less than 1 percent of the popular vote are omitted. Before the Twelfth Amendment (1804), the Electoral College voted for two presidential candidates, and the runner-up became vice president. Basic figures are taken primarily from *Historical Statistics of the United States, Colonial Times to 1970* (1975), pp. 1073–1074, and *Statistical Abstract of the United States,* relevant years.

† "Min." indicates minority president—one receiving less than 50 percent of all popular votes.

Presidential Elections (continued)

Election	Candidates	Parties	Popular Vote	Electoral Vote
1848	ZACHARY TAYLOR	Whig	1,360,967	163
	LEWIS CASS	Democratic	1,222,342	127
	MARTIN VAN BUREN	Free Soil	291,263	
1852	FRANKLIN PIERCE	Democratic	1,601,117	254
	WINFIELD SCOTT	Whig	1,385,453	42
	JOHN P. HALE	Free Soil	155,825	
1856	JAMES BUCHANAN (Min.)*	Democratic	1,832,955	174
	JOHN C. FRÉMONT	Republican	1,339,932	114
	MILLARD FILLMORE	American	871,731	8
1860	ABRAHAM LINCOLN (Min.)*	Republican	1,865,593	180
	STEPHEN A. DOUGLAS	Democratic	1,382,713	12
	JOHN C. BRECKINRIDGE	Democratic	848,356	72
	JOHN BELL	Constitutional Union	592,906	39
1864	ABRAHAM LINCOLN	Union	2,206,938	212
	GEORGE B. MC CLELLAN	Democratic	1,803,787	21
1868	ULYSSES S. GRANT	Republican	3,013,421	214
	HORATIO SEYMOUR	Democratic	2,706,829	80
1872	ULYSSES S. GRANT	Republican	3,596,745	286
	HORACE GREELEY	Democratic Liberal Republican	2,843,446	66
1876	RUTHERFORD B. HAYES (Min.)*	Republican	4,036,572	185
	SAMUEL J. TILDEN	Democratic	4,284,020	184
1880	JAMES A. GARFIELD (Min.)*	Republican	4,453,295	214
	WINFIELD S. HANCOCK	Democratic	4,414,082	155
	JAMES B. WEAVER	Greenback-Labor	308,578	
1884	GROVER CLEVELAND (Min.)*	Democratic	4,879,507	219
	JAMES G. BLAINE	Republican	4,850,293	182
	BENJAMIN F. BUTLER	Greenback-Labor	175,370	
	JOHN P. ST. JOHN	Prohibition	150,369	
1888	BENJAMIN HARRISON (Min.)*	Republican	5,447,129	233
	GROVER CLEVELAND	Democratic	5,537,857	168
	CLINTON B. FISK	Prohibition	249,506	
	ANSON J. STREETER	Union Labor	146,935	
1892	GROVER CLEVELAND (Min.)*	Democratic	5,555,426	277
	BENJAMIN HARRISON	Republican	5,182,690	145
	JAMES B. WEAVER	People's	1,029,846	22
	JOHN BIDWELL	Prohibition	264,133	
1896	WILLIAM MC KINLEY	Republican	7,102,246	271
	WILLIAM J. BRYAN	Democratic	6,492,559	176
1900	WILLIAM MC KINLEY	Republican	7,218,491	292
	WILLIAM J. BRYAN	Democratic; Populist	6,356,734	155
	JOHN C. WOOLLEY	Prohibition	208,914	
1904	THEODORE ROOSEVELT	Republican	7,628,461	336
	ALTON B. PARKER	Democratic	5,084,223	140
	EUGENE V. DEBS	Socialist	402,283	
	SILAS C. SWALLOW	Prohibition	258,536	
1908	WILLIAM H. TAFT	Republican	7,675,320	321
	WILLIAM J. BRYAN	Democratic	6,412,294	162
	EUGENE V. DEBS	Socialist	420,793	
	EUGENE W. CHAFIN	Prohibition	253,840	

* "Min." indicates minority president—one receiving less than 50 percent of all popular votes.

Presidential Elections (continued)

Election	Candidates	Parties	Popular Vote	Electoral Vote
1912	WOODROW WILSON (Min.)*	Democratic	6,296,547	435
	THEODORE ROOSEVELT	Progressive	4,118,571	88
	WILLIAM H. TAFT	Republican	3,486,720	8
	EUGENE V. DEBS	Socialist	900,672	
	EUGENE W. CHAFIN	Prohibition	206,275	
1916	WOODROW WILSON (Min.)*	Democratic	9,127,695	277
	CHARLES E. HUGHES	Republican	8,533,507	254
	A. L. BENSON	Socialist	585,113	
	J. F. HANLY	Prohibition	220,506	
1920	WARREN G. HARDING	Republican	16,143,407	404
	JAMES M. COX	Democratic	9,130,328	127
	EUGENE V. DEBS	Socialist	919,799	
	P. P. CHRISTENSEN	Farmer-Labor	265,411	
1924	CALVIN COOLIDGE	Republican	15,718,211	382
	JOHN W. DAVIS	Democratic	8,385,283	136
	ROBERT M. LA FOLLETTE	Progressive	4,831,289	13
1928	HERBERT C. HOOVER	Republican	21,391,993	444
	ALFRED E. SMITH	Democratic	15,016,169	87
1932	FRANKLIN D. ROOSEVELT	Democratic	22,809,638	472
	HERBERT C. HOOVER	Republican	15,758,901	59
	NORMAN THOMAS	Socialist	881,951	
1936	FRANKLIN D. ROOSEVELT	Democratic	27,752,869	523
	ALFRED M. LANDON	Republican	16,674,665	8
	WILLIAM LEMKE	Union	882,479	
1940	FRANKLIN D. ROOSEVELT	Democratic	27,307,819	449
	WENDELL L. WILLKIE	Republican	22,321,018	82
1944	FRANKLIN D. ROOSEVELT	Democratic	25,606,585	432
	THOMAS E. DEWEY	Republican	22,014,745	99
1948	HARRY S TRUMAN (Min.)*	Democratic	24,179,345	303
	THOMAS E. DEWEY	Republican	21,991,291	189
	J. STROM THURMOND	States' Rights Democratic	1,176,125	39
	HENRY A. WALLACE	Progressive	1,157,326	
1952	DWIGHT D. EISENHOWER	Republican	33,936,234	442
	ADLAI E. STEVENSON	Democratic	27,314,992	89
1956	DWIGHT D. EISENHOWER	Republican	35,590,472	457
	ADLAI E. STEVENSON	Democratic	26,022,752	73
1960	JOHN F. KENNEDY (Min.)*†	Democratic	34,226,731	303
	RICHARD M. NIXON	Republican	34,108,157	219
1964	LYNDON B. JOHNSON	Democratic	43,129,566	486
	BARRY M. GOLDWATER	Republican	27,178,188	52
1968	RICHARD M. NIXON (Min.)*	Republican	31,785,480	301
	HUBERT H. HUMPHREY, JR.	Democratic	31,275,166	191
	GEORGE C. WALLACE	American Independent	9,906,473	46
1972	RICHARD M. NIXON	Republican	47,169,911	520
	GEORGE S. MC GOVERN	Democratic	29,170,383	17
1976	JIMMY CARTER	Democratic	40,828,657	297
	GERALD R. FORD	Republican	39,145,520	240

* "Min." indicates minority president—one receiving less than 50 percent of all popular votes.
†Six Democratic electors in Alabama, all eight unpledged Democratic electors in Mississippi, and one Republican elector in Oklahoma voted for Senator Harry F. Byrd.

Presidential Elections (continued)

Election	Candidates	Parties	Popular Vote	Electoral Vote
1980	RONALD W. REAGAN	Republican	43,899,248	489
	JIMMY CARTER	Democratic	35,481,435	49
	JOHN B. ANDERSON	Independent	5,719,437	0
1984	RONALD W. REAGAN	Republican	52,609,797	525
	WALTER MONDALE	Democratic	36,450,613	13
1988	GEORGE BUSH	Republican	47,946,422	426
	MICHAEL DUKAKIS	Democratic	41,016,429	111
1992	WILLIAM CLINTON (Min.)*	Democratic	44,909,889	370
	GEORGE BUSH	Republican	39,104,545	168
	H. ROSS PEROT	Independent	19,742,267	
1996	WILLIAM CLINTON (Min.)*	Democratic	47,401,898	379
	ROBERT DOLE	Republican	39,198,482	159
	H. ROSS PEROT	Reform	7,874,283	
2000	GEORGE W. BUSH (Min.)*	Republican	50,456,002	271
	ALBERT GORE, JR.	Democratic	50,999,897	266
	RALPH NADER	Green	2,783,728	0
2004	GEORGE W. BUSH	Republican	60,693,281	286
	JOHN KERRY	Democratic	57,355,978	252
	RALPH NADER	Green	405,623	0

* "Min." indicates minority president—one receiving less than 50 percent of all popular votes.

Presidents and Vice Presidents

Term	President	Vice President
1789–1793	George Washington	John Adams
1793–1797	George Washington	John Adams
1797–1801	John Adams	Thomas Jefferson
1801–1805	Thomas Jefferson	Aaron Burr
1805–1809	Thomas Jefferson	George Clinton
1809–1813	James Madison	George Clinton (d. 1812)
1813–1817	James Madison	Elbridge Gerry (d. 1814)
1817–1821	James Monroe	Daniel D. Tompkins
1821–1825	James Monroe	Daniel D. Tompkins
1825–1829	John Quincy Adams	John C. Calhoun
1829–1833	Andrew Jackson	John C. Calhoun (resigned 1832)
1833–1837	Andrew Jackson	Martin Van Buren
1837–1841	Martin Van Buren	Richard M. Johnson
1841–1845	William H. Harrison (d. 1841)	John Tyler
	John Tyler	
1845–1849	James K. Polk	George M. Dallas
1849–1853	Zachary Taylor (d. 1850)	Millard Fillmore
	Millard Fillmore	
1853–1857	Franklin Pierce	William R. D. King (d. 1853)
1857–1861	James Buchanan	John C. Breckinridge

Presidents and Vice Presidents (continued)

Term	President	Vice President
1861–1865	Abraham Lincoln	Hannibal Hamlin
1865–1869	Abraham Lincoln (d. 1865)	Andrew Johnson
	Andrew Johnson	
1869–1873	Ulysses S. Grant	Schuyler Colfax
1873–1877	Ulysses S. Grant	Henry Wilson (d. 1875)
1877–1881	Rutherford B. Hayes	William A. Wheeler
1881–1885	James A. Garfield (d. 1881)	Chester A. Arthur
	Chester A. Arthur	
1885–1889	Grover Cleveland	Thomas A. Hendricks (d. 1885)
1889–1893	Benjamin Harrison	Levi P. Morton
1893–1897	Grover Cleveland	Adlai E. Stevenson
1897–1901	William McKinley	Garret A. Hobart (d. 1899)
1901–1905	William McKinley (d. 1901)	Theodore Roosevelt
	Theodore Roosevelt	
1905–1909	Theodore Roosevelt	Charles W. Fairbanks
1909–1913	William H. Taft	James S. Sherman (d. 1912)
1913–1917	Woodrow Wilson	Thomas R. Marshall
1917–1921	Woodrow Wilson	Thomas R. Marshall
1921–1925	Warren G. Harding (d. 1923)	Calvin Coolidge
	Calvin Coolidge	
1925–1929	Calvin Coolidge	Charles G. Dawes
1929–1933	Herbert Hoover	Charles Curtis
1933–1937	Franklin D. Roosevelt	John N. Garner
1937–1941	Franklin D. Roosevelt	John N. Garner
1941–1945	Franklin D. Roosevelt	Henry A. Wallace
1945–1949	Franklin D. Roosevelt (d. 1945)	Harry S Truman
	Harry S Truman	
1949–1953	Harry S Truman	Alben W. Barkley
1953–1957	Dwight D. Eisenhower	Richard M. Nixon
1957–1961	Dwight D. Eisenhower	Richard M. Nixon
1961–1965	John F. Kennedy (d. 1963)	Lyndon B. Johnson
	Lyndon B. Johnson	
1965–1969	Lyndon B. Johnson	Hubert H. Humphrey, Jr.
1969–1974	Richard M. Nixon	Spiro T. Agnew (resigned 1973); Gerald R. Ford
1974–1977	Gerald R. Ford	Nelson A. Rockefeller
1977–1981	Jimmy Carter	Walter F. Mondale
1981–1985	Ronald Reagan	George Bush
1985–1989	Ronald Reagan	George Bush
1989–1993	George Bush	J. Danforth Quayle III
1993–2001	William Clinton	Albert Gore, Jr.
2001–2004–	George W. Bush	Richard Cheney
2004–	George W. Bush	Richard Cheney

Admission of States

(See p. 183 for order in which the original thirteen entered the Union.)

Order of Admission	State	Date of Admission	Order of Admission	State	Date of Admission
14	Vermont	Mar. 4, 1791	33	Oregon	Feb. 14, 1859
15	Kentucky	June 1, 1792	34	Kansas	Jan. 29, 1861
16	Tennessee	June 1, 1796	35	W. Virginia	June 20, 1863
17	Ohio	Mar. 1, 1803	36	Nevada	Oct. 31, 1864
18	Louisiana	April 30, 1812	37	Nebraska	Mar. 1, 1867
19	Indiana	Dec. 11, 1816	38	Colorado	Aug. 1, 1876
20	Mississippi	Dec. 10, 1817	39	N. Dakota	Nov. 2, 1889
21	Illinois	Dec. 3, 1818	40	S. Dakota	Nov. 2, 1889
22	Alabama	Dec. 14, 1819	41	Montana	Nov. 8, 1889
23	Maine	Mar. 15, 1820	42	Washington	Nov. 11, 1889
24	Missouri	Aug. 10, 1821	43	Idaho	July 3, 1890
25	Arkansas	June 15, 1836	44	Wyoming	July 10, 1890
26	Michigan	Jan. 26, 1837	45	Utah	Jan. 4, 1896
27	Florida	Mar. 3, 1845	46	Oklahoma	Nov. 16, 1907
28	Texas	Dec. 29, 1845	47	New Mexico	Jan. 6, 1912
29	Iowa	Dec. 28, 1846	48	Arizona	Feb. 14, 1912
30	Wisconsin	May 29, 1848	49	Alaska	Jan. 3, 1959
31	California	Sept. 9, 1850	50	Hawaii	Aug. 21, 1959
32	Minnesota	May 11, 1858			

Estimates of Total Costs and Number of Battle Deaths of Major U.S. Wars*

War	Total Costs[†] (millions of dollars)	Original Costs	Number of Battle Deaths
Vietnam Conflict	$352,000	$140,600	47,355[‡]
Korean Conflict	164,000	54,000	33,629
World War II	664,000	288,000	291,557
World War I	112,000	26,000	53,402
Spanish-American War	6,460	400	385
Civil War { Union only	12,952	3,200	140,414
Civil War { Confederacy (est.)	N.A.	1,000	94,000
Mexican War	147	73	1,733
War of 1812	158	93	2,260
American Revolution	190	100	6,824

* Deaths from disease and other causes are not shown. In earlier wars especially, owing to poor medical and sanitary practices, nonbattle deaths substantially exceeded combat casualties.
[†] The difference between total costs and original costs is attributable to continuing postwar payments for items such as veterans' benefits, interest on war debts, and so on.
[‡] 1957–1990
(Sources: *Historical Statistics of the United States, Statistical Abstract of the United States,* relevant years, and *The World Almanac and Book of Facts, 1986.*)

PHOTOGRAPH CREDITS

Historical Society of Pennsylvania; p. 176 "The Looking Glass 1787," by Amos Doolittle (detail) Library of Congress; p. 178 Independence National Historic Park; p. 180 Fraunces Tavern Museum; p. 186 (top) The Bank of New York; p. 186 (bottom) New-York Historical Society.

Chapter 10
p. 191 The Metropolitan Museum of Art. Gift of Edgar William and Bernice Garbisch; p. 193 Credit Swiss First Boston Collection of Americana, NYC; p. 195 Courtesy, American Antiquarian Society; p. 197 Henry Francis du Pont Winterthur Museum; p. 198 Boston Public Library; p. 202 Harvard University Art Museums, Bequest of Ward Nicholas Boylston to Harvard College; p. 203 The Lilly Library, Indiana University, Bloomington; p. 204 New York Public Library; p. 206 Granger Collection; p. 209 Kirby Collection of Historic Paintings, Lafayette College, Easton, PA.

Chapter 11
p. 212 Massachusetts Historical Society; p. 213 American Antiquarian Society; p. 215 (left) Litchfield Historical Society. Photo © 1993 Robert Houser; p. 215 (right) Litchfield Historical Society. Photo © 1993 Robert Houser; p. 216 Collection of Janice L. and David J. Frent; p. 217 Robert C. Lautman/Thomas Jefferson Memorial Foundation, Inc.; p. 221 Library of Congress; p. 223 (right) Missouri Historical Society; p. 223 (left) New-York Historical Society; p. 224 American Numismatic Society; p. 225 Houghton Library, Harvard University; p. 227 (top) The Free Library of Philadelphia; p. 227 (bottom) Peabody Essex Museum, Salem, MA; p. 229 White House Historical Association; p. 230 Field Museum of Natural History, Chicago; p. 231 New York Public Library, Prints Division, Astor, Lenox and Tilden Foundation.

Chapter 12
p. 235 (left) Corbis-Bettmann; p. 235 (right) Steve Dunwell/Image Bank; p. 236 (top) Anne S. K. Brown Military Collection, Brown University Library; p. 238 Huntington Library, San Marino, CA; p. 240 Metropolitan Museum of Art; p. 241 Architect of the Capitol; p. 242 White House Historical Association. Gift of Michael Straight; p. 243 Maryland Historical Society; p. 244 The Granger Collection; p. 245 The Granger Collection; p. 246 The Daughters of the American Revolution; p. 248 Collection of the Supreme Court of the United States; p. 249 Metropolitan Museum of Art. Gift of I. N. Phelps Stokes, Edward S. Hawes, Alice Mary Hawes, Marion Augusta Hawes, 1937; p. 251 Historic Hudson Valley, Tarrytown, New York.

Chapter 13
p. 257 Nelson-Atkins Museum of Art, Kansas City, MO. Purchase: Nelson Trust; p. 258 Courtesy, The Henry Francis du Pont Winterthur Museum; p. 259 Metropolitan Museum of Art. Gift of I. N. Phelps Stokes, Edward S. Hawes, Alice Mary Hawes; p. 260 The Granger Collection; p. 263 (top) The Granger Collection; p. 263 (bottom) National Portrait Gallery, Art Resource; p. 267 Thomas Gilcrease Institute of American History and Art, Tulsa, Oklahoma; p. 268 The Granger Collection; p. 269 Brown Brothers; p. 270 Tennessee Historical Society; p. 271 Library Company of Philadelphia; p. 273 New-York Historical Society; p. 274 Cincinnati Art Museum, acc#1924.185; p. 276 The Granger Collection; p. 277 (bottom) Museum of Fine Arts, Houston; p. 277 (top) Phyl Picardi/Stock Boston; p. 278 Texas State Library, Archives Division, Austin; p. 279 Witte Museum, San Antonio, TX; p. 280 New-York Historical Society; p. 281 Smithsonian Institution; p. 282 (bottom) Library of Congress; p. 282 Franklin Delano Library, Hyde Park, NY; p. 283 Boatmen's National Bank of St. Louis.

Chapter 14
p. 288 Courtesy of Arthur J. Phelan—The Phelan Collection; p. 289 Smithsonian American Art Museum, Gift of Mrs. Joseph Harrison, Jr./Art Resource, NY; p. 291 Public Library of Cincinnati; p. 294 New-York Historical Society; p. 295 Museum of the City of New York; p. 296 The Granger Collection; p. 298 State Historical Society of Wisconsin; p. 299 (top) Cincinnati Historical Society; p. 299 (bottom) Bob Sacha; p. 300 (left) Smithsonian Institution, Washington DC/The Bridgeman Art Library; p. 300 (right) Slater Mill Historic Site; p. 300 (bottom) University of Texas; p. 301 Jonathan Wallen/National Archives; p. 302 (top) Collection of Matthew Isenburg; p. 302 (bottom) Courtesy of the Museum of Connecticut History p. 304 E.R. Fisher; p. 305 Jonathan Wallen/National Archives; p. 305 National Museum of American History, Smithsonian Institution; p. 306 The Granger Collection; p. 308 St. Louis Art Museum. Bequest of Edgar William and Bernice Chrysler Garbisch; p. 309 State Historical Society of Wisconsin; p. 310 Chicago Historical Society; p. 311 M. and M. Karolik Collection, Museum of Fine Arts, Boston; p. 314 Old Print Shop, New York; p. 315 Peabody and Essex Museum, Salem, MA; p. 317 Library of Congress.

Chapter 15
p. 321 New Bedford Whaling Museum; p. 322 Oberlin College Archives, Oberlin, Ohio; p. 324 Brigham Young University Art Museum; p. 326 St. Louis Art Museum; p. 327 Oberlin College Archives, Oberlin, Ohio; p. 329 Houghton Library, Harvard University; p. 330 Connecticut Historical Society; p. 331 Corbis-Bettmann; p. 332 Stock Montage, Inc.; p. 333 Corbis-Bettmann; p. 334 Bishop Hill State Historic Site, Bishop Hill, Illinois; p. 335 (left) New-York Historical Society; p. 335 (right) American Museum of Natural History; p. 338 The Granger Collection; p. 337 (right) The Granger Collection; p. 337 (bottom) Oneida Community Mansion House; p. 337 (top) Oneida Community Mansion House; p. 339 Metropolitan Museum of Art; p. 342 Corbis-Bettmann; p. 343 New York Public Library; p. 344 Corbis-Bettmann; p. 345 Peabody and Essex Museum, Salem, MA.

Part Three
p. 348 New-York Historical Society; p. 349 Cook Collection, Valentine Museum, Richmond, VA.

Chapter 16
p. 352 The Granger Collection; p. 357 (left) Musée de l'Homme, Paris; p. 357 (right) © The Burns Archive; p. 358 (left) Historic New Orleans College; p. 358 (upper right) The Granger Collection; p. 359 (bottom) The Granger Collection; p. 359 (top) Chicago Historical Society; p. 360 Missouri Historical Society; p. 361 (top) Abby Aldrich Rockefeller Collection, Colonial Williamsburg; p. 361 (bottom) Charleston Museum; p. 363 Historic New Orleans Collection; p. 365 (left) Corbis-Bettmann; p. 365 (right) Art Resource; p. 366 Onondaga Historical Association.

Chapter 17
p. 372 Library of Congress; p. 376 St. Louis Art Museum; p. 377 Denver Public Library; p. 379 Art Resource; p. 380 Yale Collection of Western Americana, Beinecke Rare Book and Manuscript Library; p. 381 Bancroft Library, University of California; p. 385 Masco Corporation; p. 386 Culver Pictures; p. 387 Bancroft Library; p. 388 West Point Museum.

Chapter 18
p. 391 New-York Historical Society; p. 393 California State Library; p. 394 (top) Louis Psihoyos; p. 394 (bottom) Louis Psihoyos; p. 395 The Granger Collection; p. 398 Chicago Historical Society; p. 399 Brooklyn Museum. Gift of Miss Gwendolyn O. L. Conkling; p. 404 The Chrysler Museum, Norfolk, VA, Norfolk Newspaper's Art Trust.

INDEX